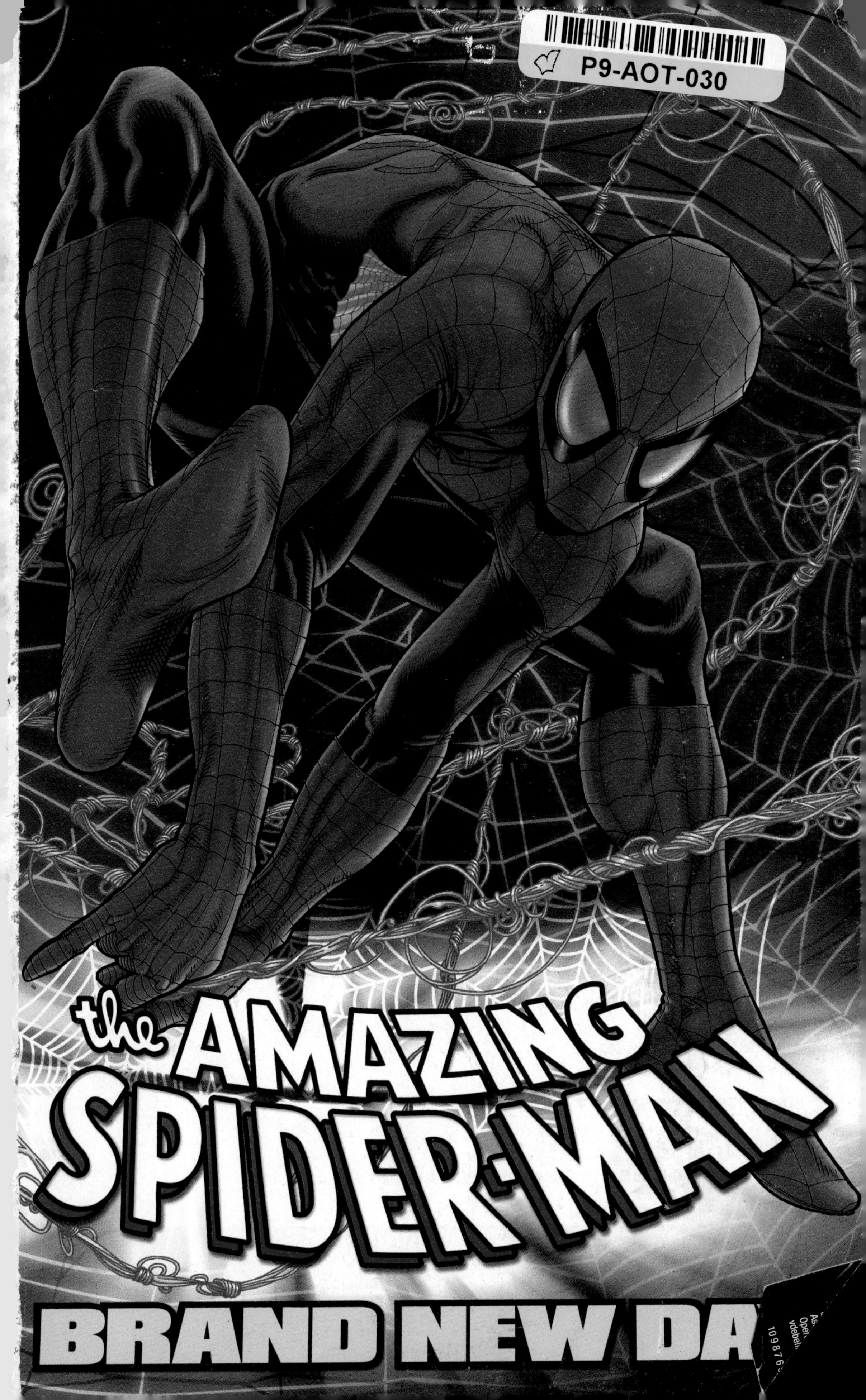
the AMAZING
SPIDER-MAN
BRAND NEW DA

the AMAZING SPIDER-MAN
BRAND NEW DAY

SPIDER-MAN: SWING SHIFT

Writer: **DAN SLOTT**
Penciler: **PHIL JIMENEZ**
Inkers: **ANDY LANNING** with **JOHN DELL**
Colorist: **JEROMY COX**

AMAZING SPIDER-MAN #546-548

Writer: **DAN SLOTT**
Penciler: **STEVE MCNIVEN**
Inker: **DEXTER VINES**
Colorists: **MORRY HOLLOWELL** (#546-547) & **DAVE STEWART** (#548)

"PARK AVENUE INTERLUDE"

Writer: **MARC GUGGENHEIM**
Penciler: **GREG LAND**
Inker: **JAY LEISTEN**
Colorist: **JUSTIN PONSOR**

"THE ASTONISHING AUNT MAY"

Writer: **BOB GALE**
Artist: **PHIL WINSLADE**
Colorist: **CHRIS CHUCKRY**

"HARRY AND THE HOLLISTERS"

Writer: **ZEB WELLS**
Artist: **MIKE DEODATO**
Colorist: **RAIN BEREDO**

AMAZING SPIDER-MAN #549-551

Writer: **MARC GUGGENHEIM**
Artist: **SALVADOR LARROCA**
Colorists: **JASON KEITH** (#549) & **STEPHANE PERU** (#550-551)

SPIDER-MAN: BRAND NEW DAY — THE COMPLETE COLLECTION VOL. 1. Contains material originally published in magazine form as FREE COMIC BOOK DAY 2007 (SPIDER-MAN), AMAZING SPIDER-MAN #546-564 and SPIDER-MAN: SWING SHIFT DIRECTOR'S CUT. First printing 2016. ISBN# 978-0-7851-9561-0. Published by MARVEL WORLDWIDE, INC., a subsidiary of MARVEL ENTERTAINMENT, LLC. OFFICE OF PUBLICATION: 135 West 50th Street, New York, NY 10020. Copyright © 2016 MARVEL No similarity between any of the names, characters, persons, and/or institutions in this magazine with those of any living or dead person or institution is intended, and any such similarity which may exist is purely coincidental. **Printed in the U.S.A.** ALAN FINE, President, Marvel Entertainment; DAN BUCKLEY, President, TV, Publishing & Brand Management; JOE QUESADA, Chief Creative Officer; TOM BREVOORT, SVP of Publishing; DAVID BOGART, SVP of Business Affairs & Operations, Publishing & Partnership; C.B. CEBULSKI, VP of Brand Management & Development, ia; DAVID GABRIEL, SVP of Sales & Marketing, Publishing; JEFF YOUNGQUIST, VP of Production & Special Projects; DAN CARR, Executive Director of Publishing Technology; ALEX MORALES, Director of Publishing ations; SUSAN CRESPI, Production Manager; STAN LEE, Chairman Emeritus. For information regarding advertising in Marvel Comics or on Marvel.com, please contact Vit DeBellis, Integrated Sales Manager, at ic@marvel.com For Marvel subscription inquiries, please call 888-511-5480. **Manufactured between 3/4/2016 and 4/11/2016 by R.R. DONNELLEY INC., SALEM, VA, USA.**

AMAZING SPIDER-MAN #552-554

Writer: **BOB GALE**
Penciler: **PHIL JIMENEZ**
Inkers: **ANDY LANNING**
with **DANNY MIKI** (#554) & **PHIL JIMENEZ** (#554)
Colorist: **JEROMY COX**

AMAZING SPIDER-MAN #555-557

Writer: **ZEB WELLS**
Penciler: **CHRIS BACHALO**
Inkers: **TIM TOWNSEND**
with **MARK IRWIN** (#557), **WAYNE FAUCHER** (#557),
JAIME MENDOZA (#557) & **AL VEY** (#557)
Colorists: **CHRIS BACHALO** & **STUDIO F'S ANTONIO FABELA**

AMAZING SPIDER-MAN #558

Writer: **BOB GALE**
Penciler: **BARRY KITSON**
Inker: **MARK FARMER**
Colorists: **AVALON'S IAN HANNIN** & **MATT MILLA**
Special thanks to James Hodgkins

AMAZING SPIDER-MAN #559-561

Writer: **DAN SLOTT**
Artist: **MARCOS MARTIN**
Colorist: **JAVIER RODRIGUEZ**

AMAZING SPIDER-MAN #562-563

Writer: **BOB GALE**
Penciler: **MIKE MCKONE**
Inkers: **ANDY LANNING** (#562) & **MARLO ALQUIZA** (#563)
Colorists: **JEROMY COX** (#562-563) & **ANTONIO FABELA** (#563)

AMAZING SPIDER-MAN #564

Writers: **MARC GUGGENHEIM, BOB GALE** & **DAN SLOTT**
Penciler: **PAULO SIQUEIRA**
Inkers: **AMILTON SANTOS** & **PAULO SIQUEIRA**
Colorist: **ANTONIO FABELA**

Spider-Man created by **STAN LEE** & **STEVE DITKO**

Letterers: **VC'S CORY PETIT**
with **CHRIS ELIOPOULOS** (SWING SHIFT) & **JOE CARAMAGNA** (#553)
Spidey's Braintrust: **BOB GALE, MARC GUGGENHEIM, DAN SLOTT** & **ZEB WELLS**

Assistant Editor: **TOM BRENNAN**
Editor: **STEPHEN WACKER**
Executive Editor: **TOM BREVOORT**

Collection Editor: **JENNIFER GRÜNWALD**
Assistant Editor: **SARAH BRUNSTAD**
Associate Managing Editor: **ALEX STARBUCK**
Editor, Special Projects: **MARK D. BEAZLEY**
Senior Editor, Special Projects: **JEFF YOUNGQUIST**
SVP Print, Sales & Marketing: **DAVID GABRIEL**

Editor in Chief: **AXEL ALONSO**
Chief Creative Officer: **JOE QUESADA**
Publisher: **DAN BUCKLEY**
Executive Producer: **ALAN FINE**

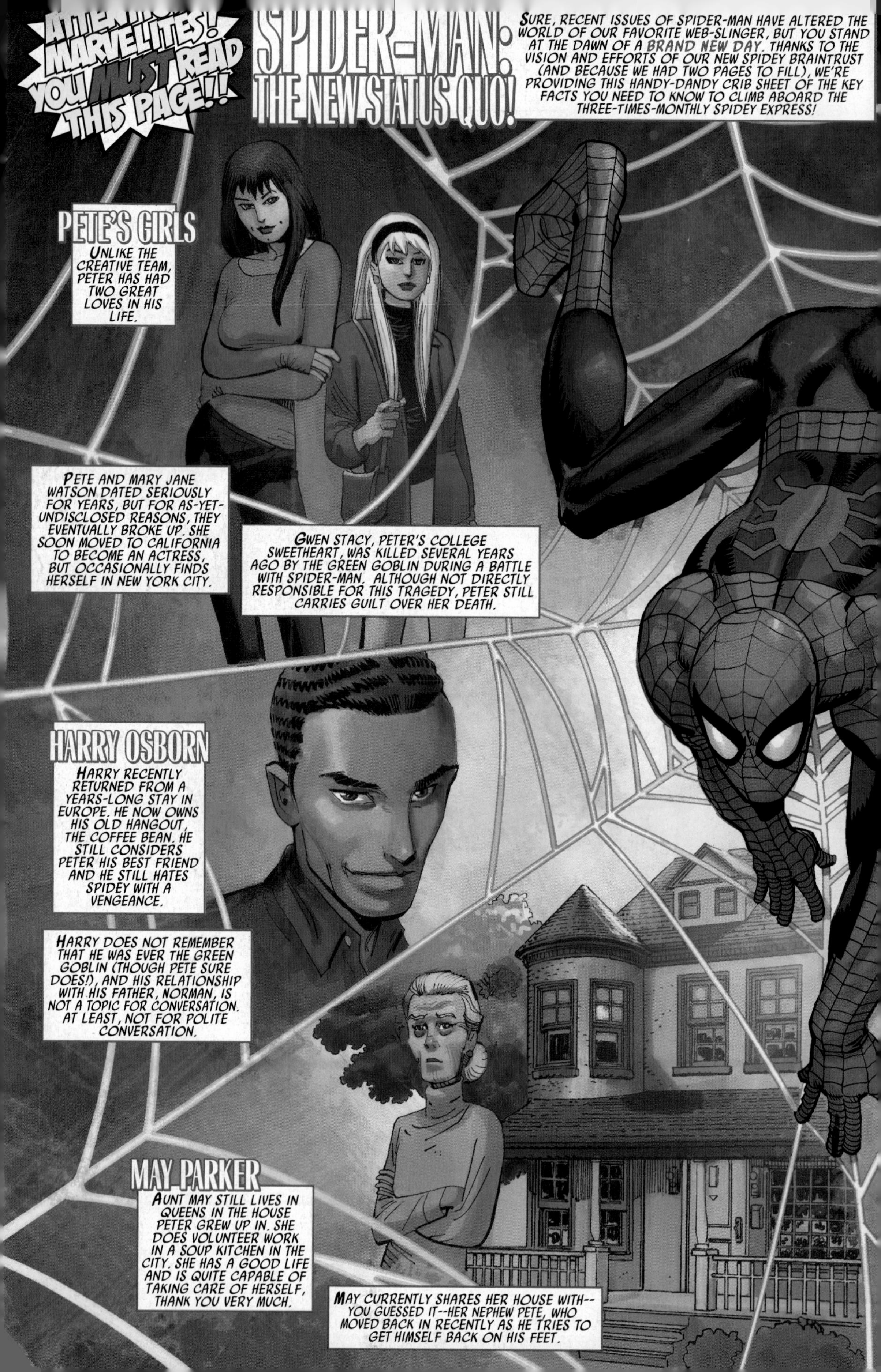

ATTENTION MARVELITES! YOU MUST READ THIS PAGE!!
SPIDER-MAN: THE NEW STATUS QUO!
SURE, RECENT ISSUES OF SPIDER-MAN HAVE ALTERED THE WORLD OF OUR FAVORITE WEB-SLINGER, BUT YOU STAND AT THE DAWN OF A BRAND NEW DAY. THANKS TO THE VISION AND EFFORTS OF OUR NEW SPIDEY BRAINTRUST (AND BECAUSE WE HAD TWO PAGES TO FILL), WE'RE PROVIDING THIS HANDY-DANDY CRIB SHEET OF THE KEY FACTS YOU NEED TO KNOW TO CLIMB ABOARD THE THREE-TIMES-MONTHLY SPIDEY EXPRESS!
PETE'S GIRLS
UNLIKE THE CREATIVE TEAM, PETER HAS HAD TWO GREAT LOVES IN HIS LIFE.
PETE AND MARY JANE WATSON DATED SERIOUSLY FOR YEARS, BUT FOR AS-YET-UNDISCLOSED REASONS, THEY EVENTUALLY BROKE UP. SHE SOON MOVED TO CALIFORNIA TO BECOME AN ACTRESS, BUT OCCASIONALLY FINDS HERSELF IN NEW YORK CITY.
GWEN STACY, PETER'S COLLEGE SWEETHEART, WAS KILLED SEVERAL YEARS AGO BY THE GREEN GOBLIN DURING A BATTLE WITH SPIDER-MAN. ALTHOUGH NOT DIRECTLY RESPONSIBLE FOR THIS TRAGEDY, PETER STILL CARRIES GUILT OVER HER DEATH.
HARRY OSBORN
HARRY RECENTLY RETURNED FROM A YEARS-LONG STAY IN EUROPE. HE NOW OWNS HIS OLD HANGOUT, THE COFFEE BEAN. HE STILL CONSIDERS PETER HIS BEST FRIEND AND HE STILL HATES SPIDEY WITH A VENGEANCE.
HARRY DOES NOT REMEMBER THAT HE WAS EVER THE GREEN GOBLIN (THOUGH PETE SURE DOES!), AND HIS RELATIONSHIP WITH HIS FATHER, NORMAN, IS NOT A TOPIC FOR CONVERSATION. AT LEAST, NOT FOR POLITE CONVERSATION.
MAY PARKER
AUNT MAY STILL LIVES IN QUEENS IN THE HOUSE PETER GREW UP IN. SHE DOES VOLUNTEER WORK IN A SOUP KITCHEN IN THE CITY. SHE HAS A GOOD LIFE AND IS QUITE CAPABLE OF TAKING CARE OF HERSELF, THANK YOU VERY MUCH.
MAY CURRENTLY SHARES HER HOUSE WITH--YOU GUESSED IT--HER NEPHEW PETE, WHO MOVED BACK IN RECENTLY AS HE TRIES TO GET HIMSELF BACK ON HIS FEET.

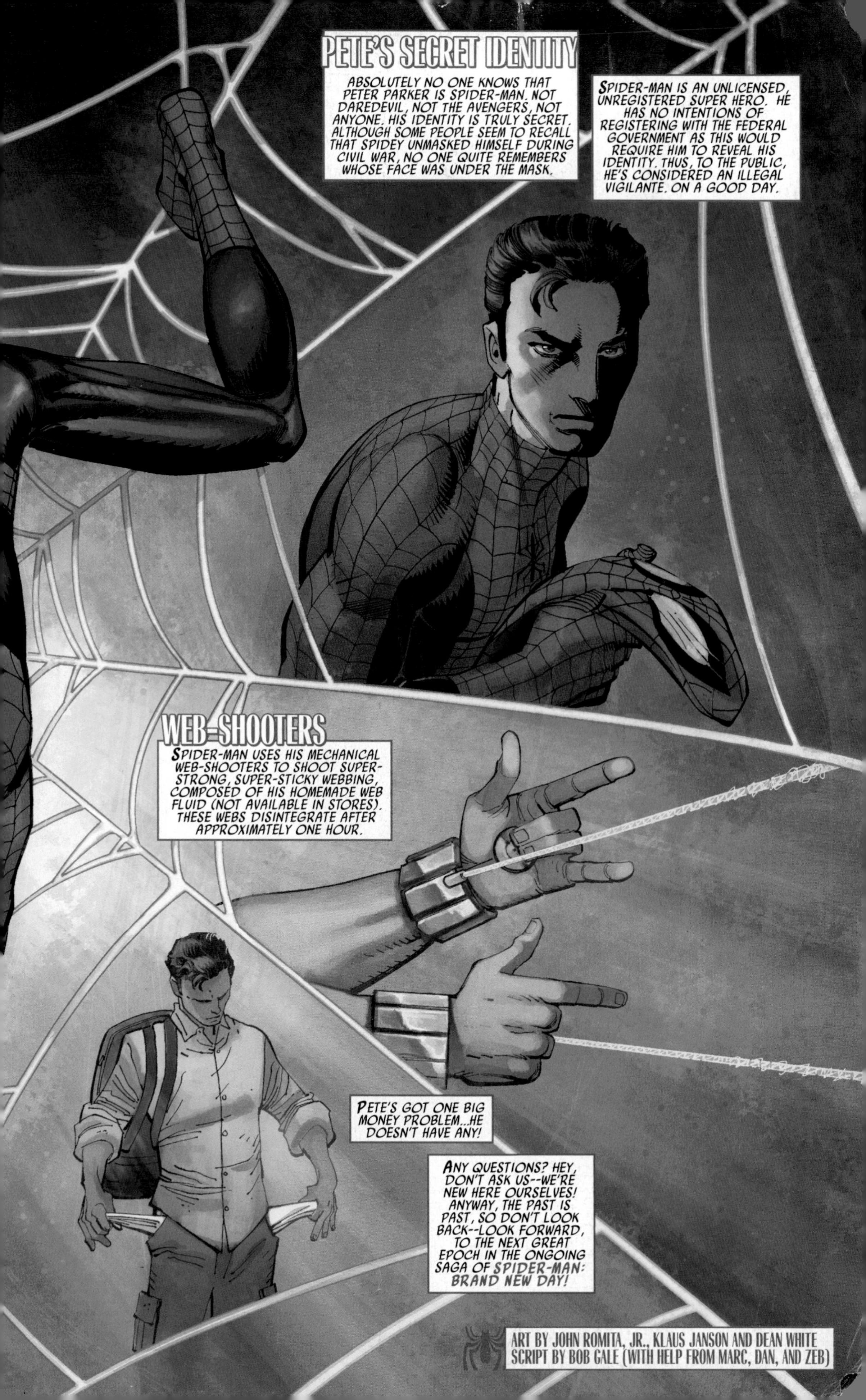
PETE'S SECRET IDENTITY
ABSOLUTELY NO ONE KNOWS THAT PETER PARKER IS SPIDER-MAN. NOT DAREDEVIL, NOT THE AVENGERS, NOT ANYONE. HIS IDENTITY IS TRULY SECRET. ALTHOUGH SOME PEOPLE SEEM TO RECALL THAT SPIDEY UNMASKED HIMSELF DURING CIVIL WAR, NO ONE QUITE REMEMBERS WHOSE FACE WAS UNDER THE MASK.
SPIDER-MAN IS AN UNLICENSED, UNREGISTERED SUPER HERO. HE HAS NO INTENTIONS OF REGISTERING WITH THE FEDERAL GOVERNMENT AS THIS WOULD REQUIRE HIM TO REVEAL HIS IDENTITY. THUS, TO THE PUBLIC, HE'S CONSIDERED AN ILLEGAL VIGILANTE. ON A GOOD DAY.
WEB-SHOOTERS
SPIDER-MAN USES HIS MECHANICAL WEB-SHOOTERS TO SHOOT SUPER-STRONG, SUPER-STICKY WEBBING, COMPOSED OF HIS HOMEMADE WEB FLUID (NOT AVAILABLE IN STORES). THESE WEBS DISINTEGRATE AFTER APPROXIMATELY ONE HOUR.
PETE'S GOT ONE BIG MONEY PROBLEM...HE DOESN'T HAVE ANY!
ANY QUESTIONS? HEY, DON'T ASK US--WE'RE NEW HERE OURSELVES! ANYWAY, THE PAST IS PAST, SO DON'T LOOK BACK--LOOK FORWARD, TO THE NEXT GREAT EPOCH IN THE ONGOING SAGA OF SPIDER-MAN: BRAND NEW DAY!
ART BY JOHN ROMITA, JR., KLAUS JANSON AND DEAN WHITE
SCRIPT BY BOB GALE (WITH HELP FROM MARC, DAN, AND ZEB)

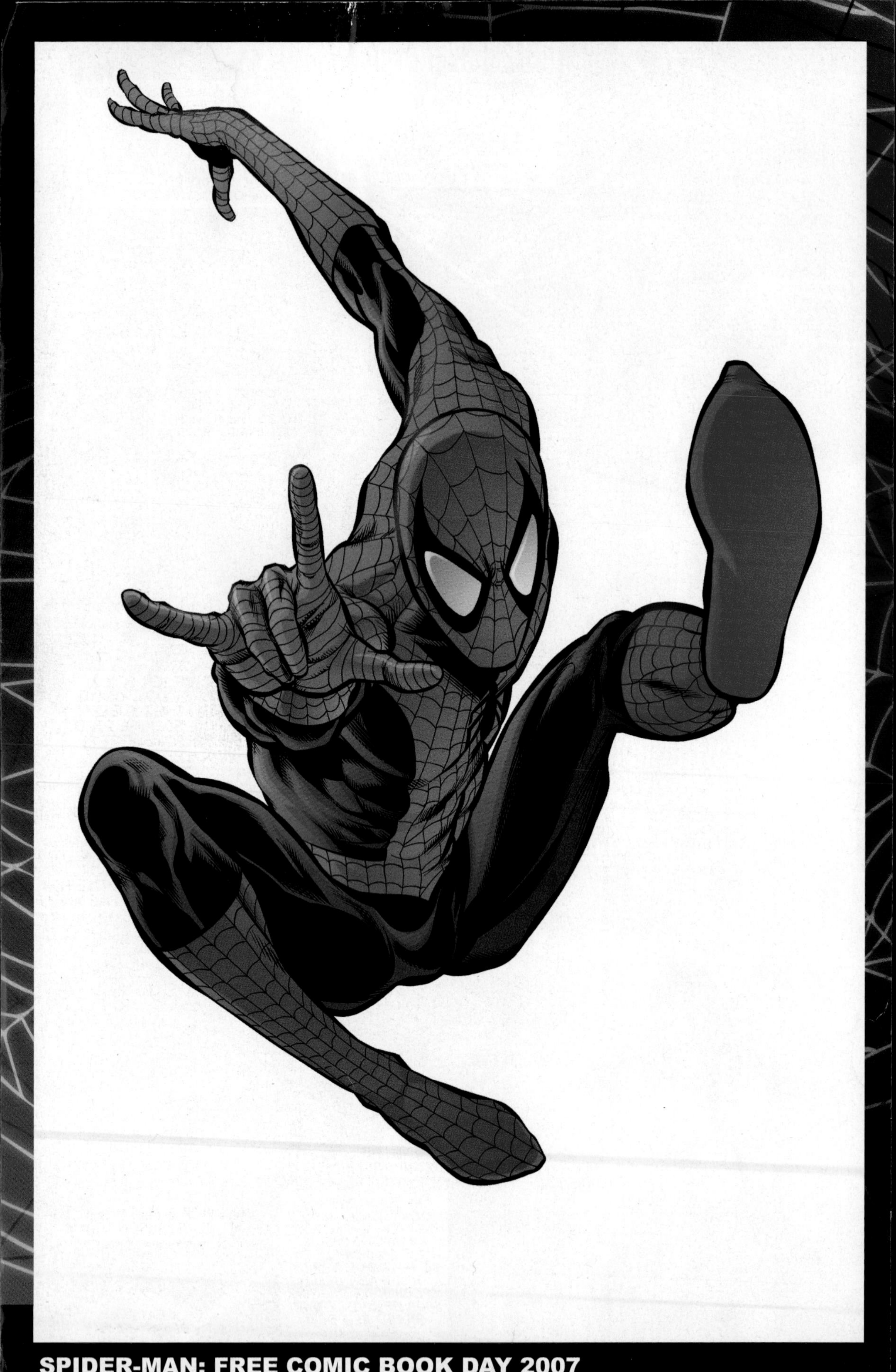

SPIDER-MAN: FREE COMIC BOOK DAY 2007
COVER BY **PHIL JIMENEZ & JEROMY COX**

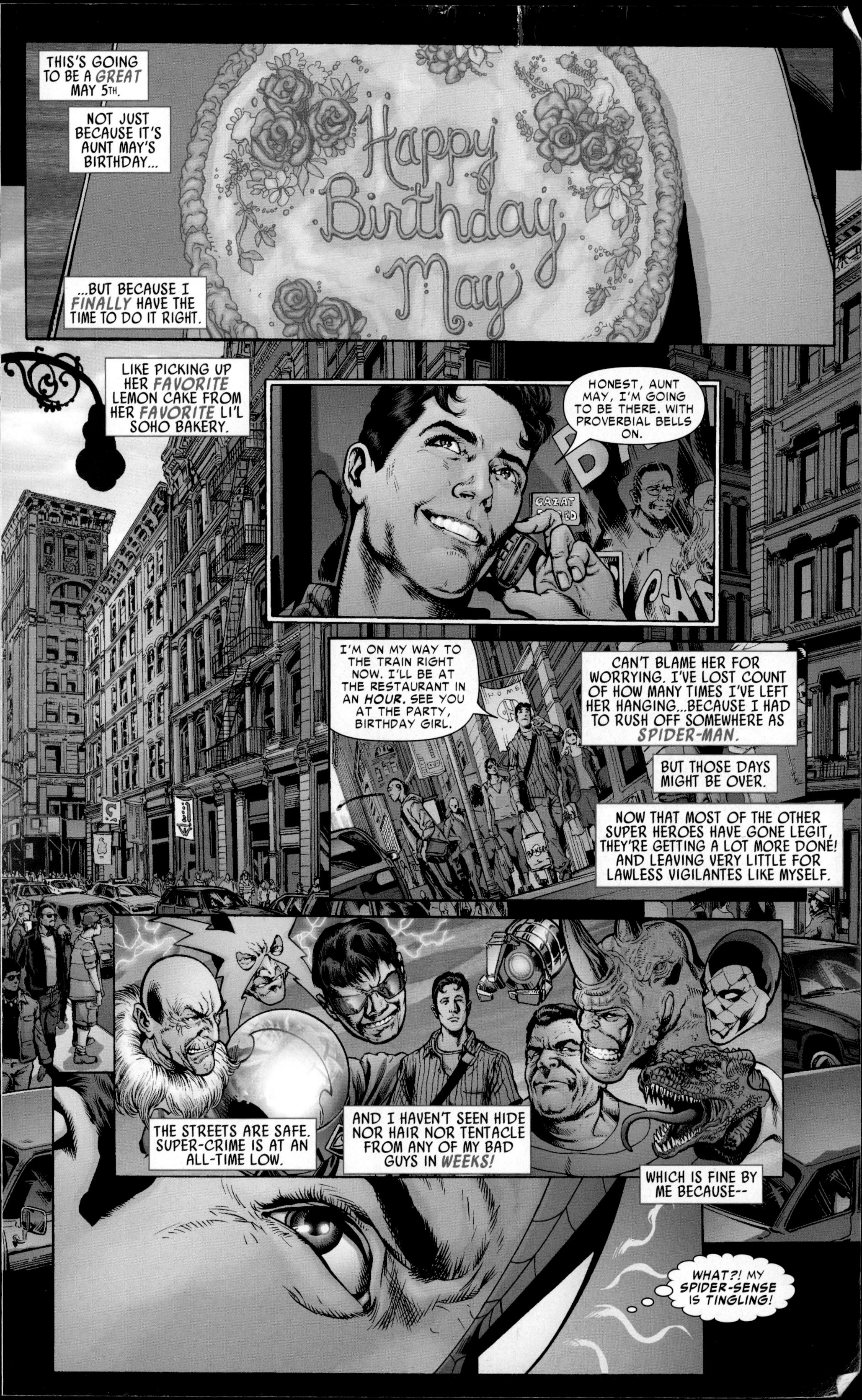
THIS'S GOING TO BE A GREAT MAY 5TH.
NOT JUST BECAUSE IT'S AUNT MAY'S BIRTHDAY...
Happy Birthday May
...BUT BECAUSE I FINALLY HAVE THE TIME TO DO IT RIGHT.
LIKE PICKING UP HER FAVORITE LEMON CAKE FROM HER FAVORITE LI'L SOHO BAKERY.
HONEST, AUNT MAY, I'M GOING TO BE THERE. WITH PROVERBIAL BELLS ON.
I'M ON MY WAY TO THE TRAIN RIGHT NOW. I'LL BE AT THE RESTAURANT IN AN HOUR. SEE YOU AT THE PARTY, BIRTHDAY GIRL.
CAN'T BLAME HER FOR WORRYING. I'VE LOST COUNT OF HOW MANY TIMES I'VE LEFT HER HANGING...BECAUSE I HAD TO RUSH OFF SOMEWHERE AS SPIDER-MAN.
BUT THOSE DAYS MIGHT BE OVER.
NOW THAT MOST OF THE OTHER SUPER HEROES HAVE GONE LEGIT, THEY'RE GETTING A LOT MORE DONE! AND LEAVING VERY LITTLE FOR LAWLESS VIGILANTES LIKE MYSELF.
THE STREETS ARE SAFE. SUPER-CRIME IS AT AN ALL-TIME LOW.
AND I HAVEN'T SEEN HIDE NOR HAIR NOR TENTACLE FROM ANY OF MY BAD GUYS IN WEEKS!
WHICH IS FINE BY ME BECAUSE--
WHAT?! MY SPIDER-SENSE IS TINGLING!

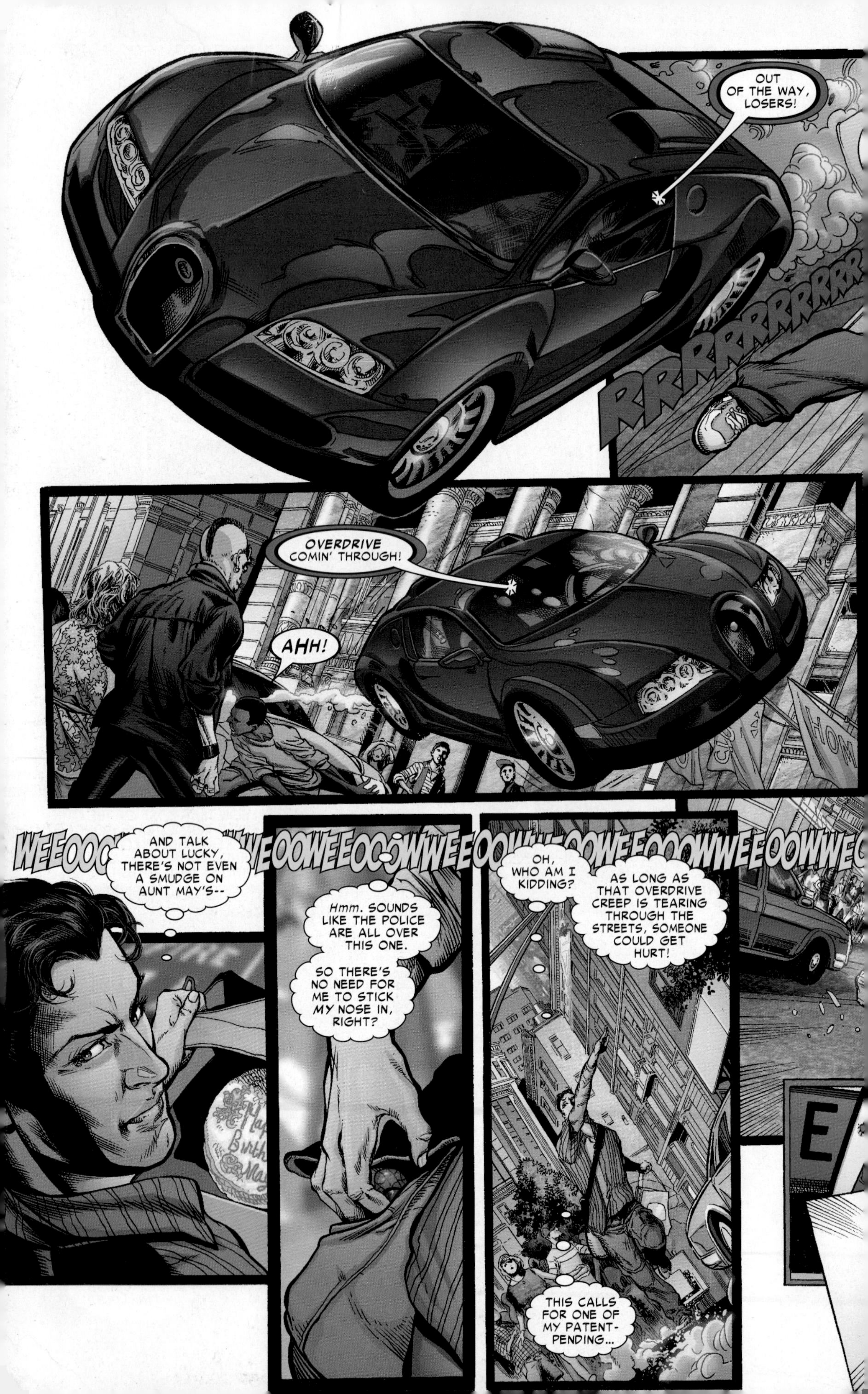
OUT OF THE WAY, LOSERS!
RRRRRRRRRRR
OVERDRIVE COMIN' THROUGH!
AHH!
WEEOOOWEEOOWEEOOWWEEOOWWEEOOWEEOOOWWEEOOWWE
AND TALK ABOUT LUCKY, THERE'S NOT EVEN A SMUDGE ON AUNT MAY'S--
Hmm. SOUNDS LIKE THE POLICE ARE ALL OVER THIS ONE.
SO THERE'S NO NEED FOR ME TO STICK MY NOSE IN, RIGHT?
OH, WHO AM I KIDDING?
AS LONG AS THAT OVERDRIVE CREEP IS TEARING THROUGH THE STREETS, SOMEONE COULD GET HURT!
THIS CALLS FOR ONE OF MY PATENT-PENDING...

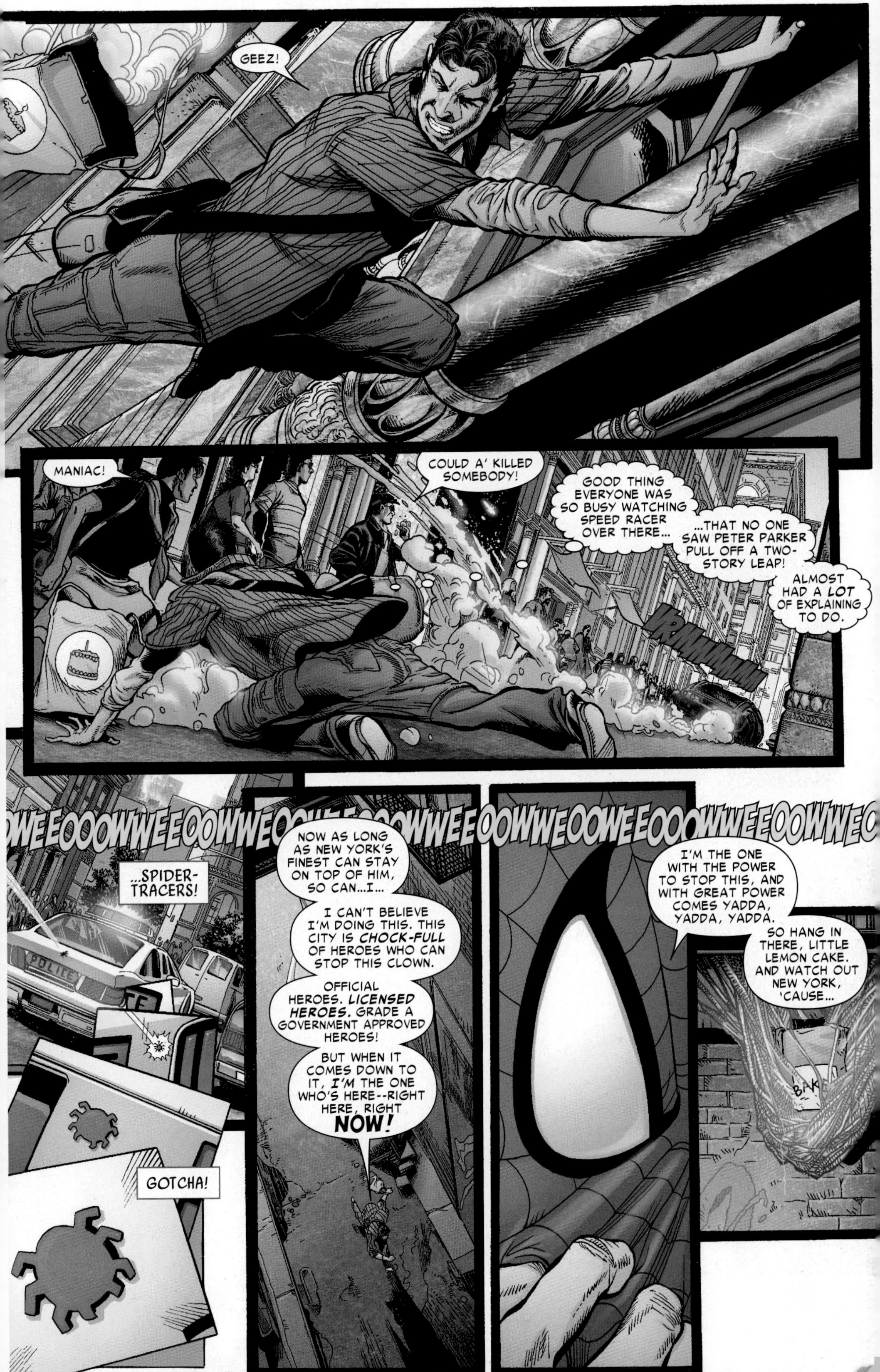
GEEZ!
MANIAC!
COULD A' KILLED SOMEBODY!
GOOD THING EVERYONE WAS SO BUSY WATCHING SPEED RACER OVER THERE...
...THAT NO ONE SAW PETER PARKER PULL OFF A TWO-STORY LEAP!
ALMOST HAD A *LOT* OF EXPLAINING TO DO.
VRMMMMM
OWEEOOOWWEEOOWWEOOWEEOOWWEEOOWWEOOWEEOOOWWEEOOWWEO
...SPIDER-TRACERS!
POLICE
GOTCHA!
NOW AS LONG AS NEW YORK'S FINEST CAN STAY ON TOP OF HIM, SO CAN...I...
I CAN'T BELIEVE I'M DOING THIS. THIS CITY IS *CHOCK-FULL* OF HEROES WHO CAN STOP THIS CLOWN.
OFFICIAL HEROES. ***LICENSED HEROES.*** GRADE A GOVERNMENT APPROVED HEROES!
BUT WHEN IT COMES DOWN TO IT, *I'M* THE ONE WHO'S HERE--RIGHT HERE, RIGHT **NOW!**
I'M THE ONE WITH THE POWER TO STOP THIS, AND WITH GREAT POWER COMES YADDA, YADDA, YADDA.
SO HANG IN THERE, LITTLE LEMON CAKE. AND WATCH OUT NEW YORK, 'CAUSE...

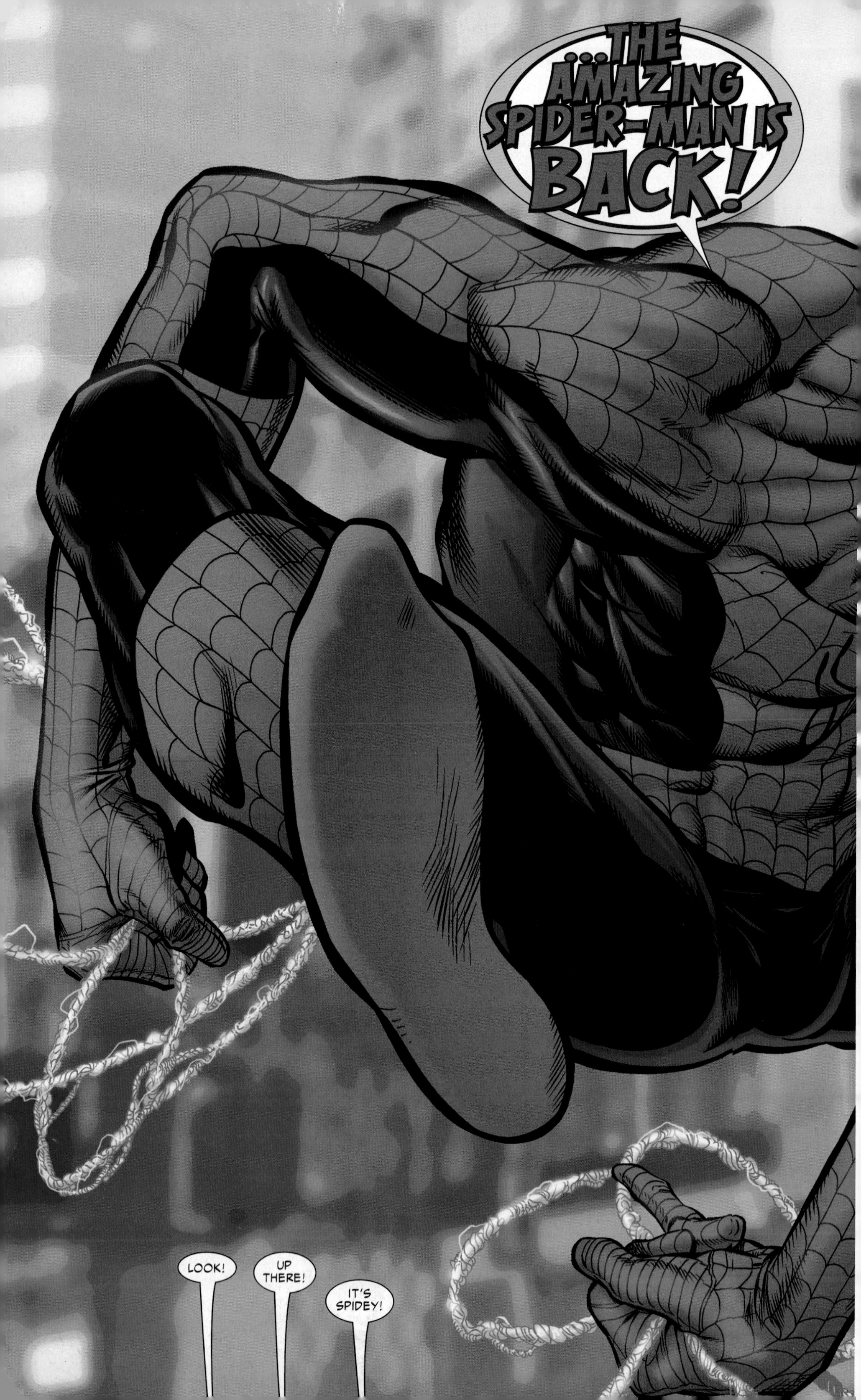
...THE AMAZING SPIDER-MAN IS BACK!
LOOK!
UP THERE!
IT'S SPIDEY!

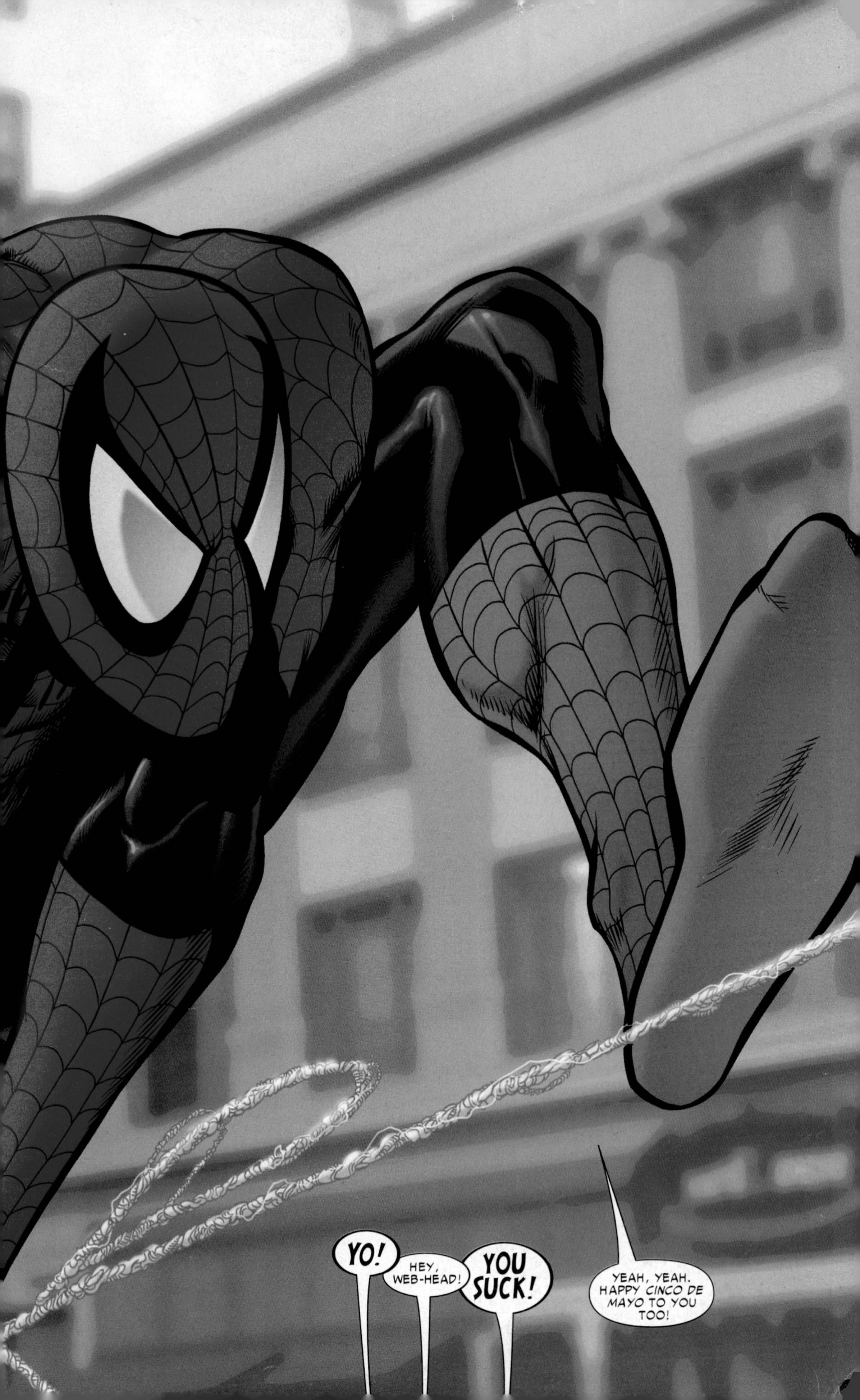
YO!
HEY, WEB-HEAD!
YOU SUCK!
YEAH, YEAH. HAPPY CINCO DE MAYO TO YOU TOO!

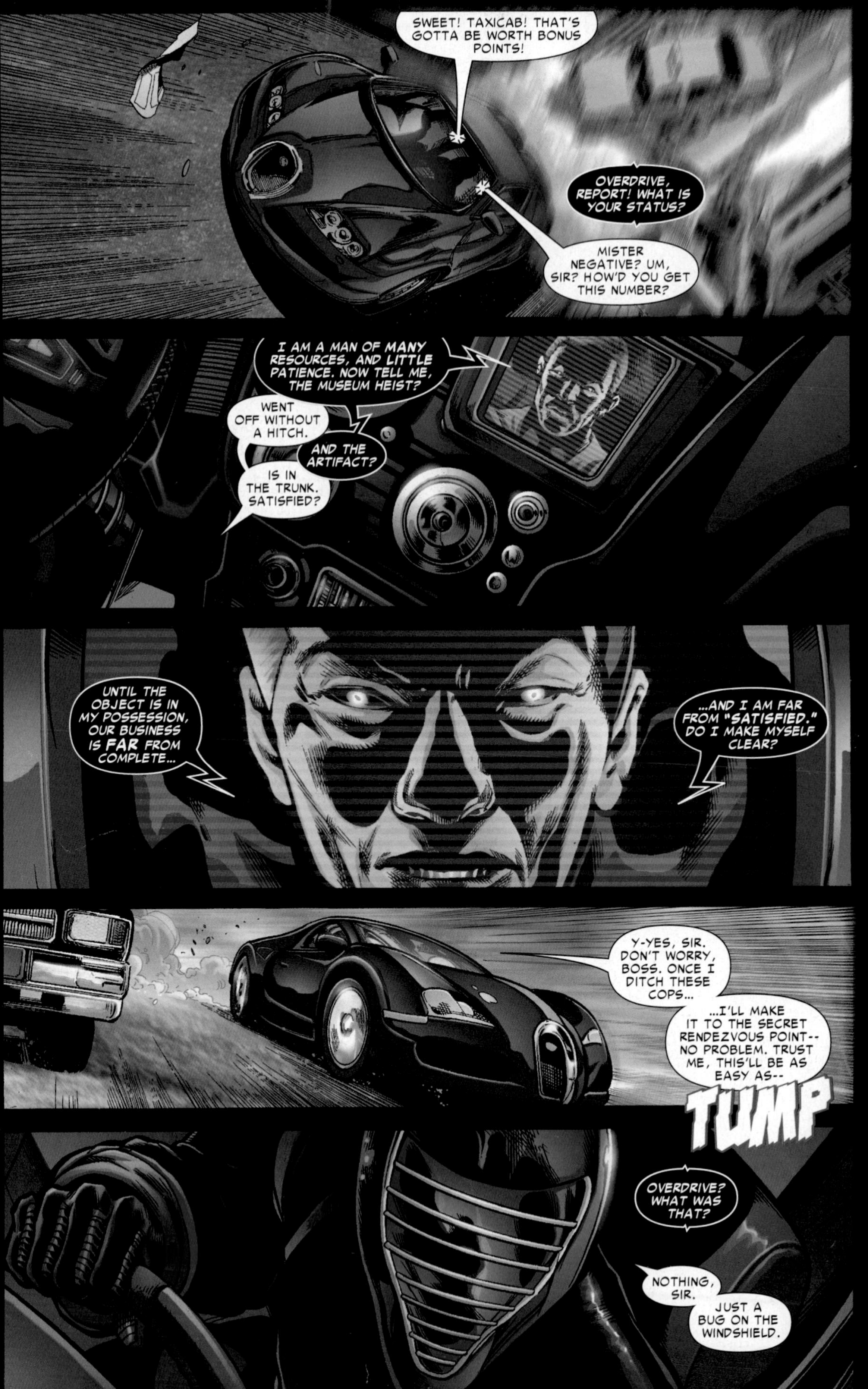
SWEET! TAXICAB! THAT'S GOTTA BE WORTH BONUS POINTS!
OVERDRIVE, REPORT! WHAT IS YOUR STATUS?
MISTER NEGATIVE? UM, SIR? HOW'D YOU GET THIS NUMBER?
I AM A MAN OF MANY RESOURCES, AND LITTLE PATIENCE. NOW TELL ME, THE MUSEUM HEIST?
WENT OFF WITHOUT A HITCH.
AND THE ARTIFACT?
IS IN THE TRUNK. SATISFIED?
UNTIL THE OBJECT IS IN MY POSSESSION, OUR BUSINESS IS FAR FROM COMPLETE...
...AND I AM FAR FROM "SATISFIED." DO I MAKE MYSELF CLEAR?
Y-YES, SIR. DON'T WORRY, BOSS. ONCE I DITCH THESE COPS...
...I'LL MAKE IT TO THE SECRET RENDEZVOUS POINT-- NO PROBLEM. TRUST ME, THIS'LL BE AS EASY AS--
TUMP
OVERDRIVE? WHAT WAS THAT?
NOTHING, SIR.
JUST A BUG ON THE WINDSHIELD.

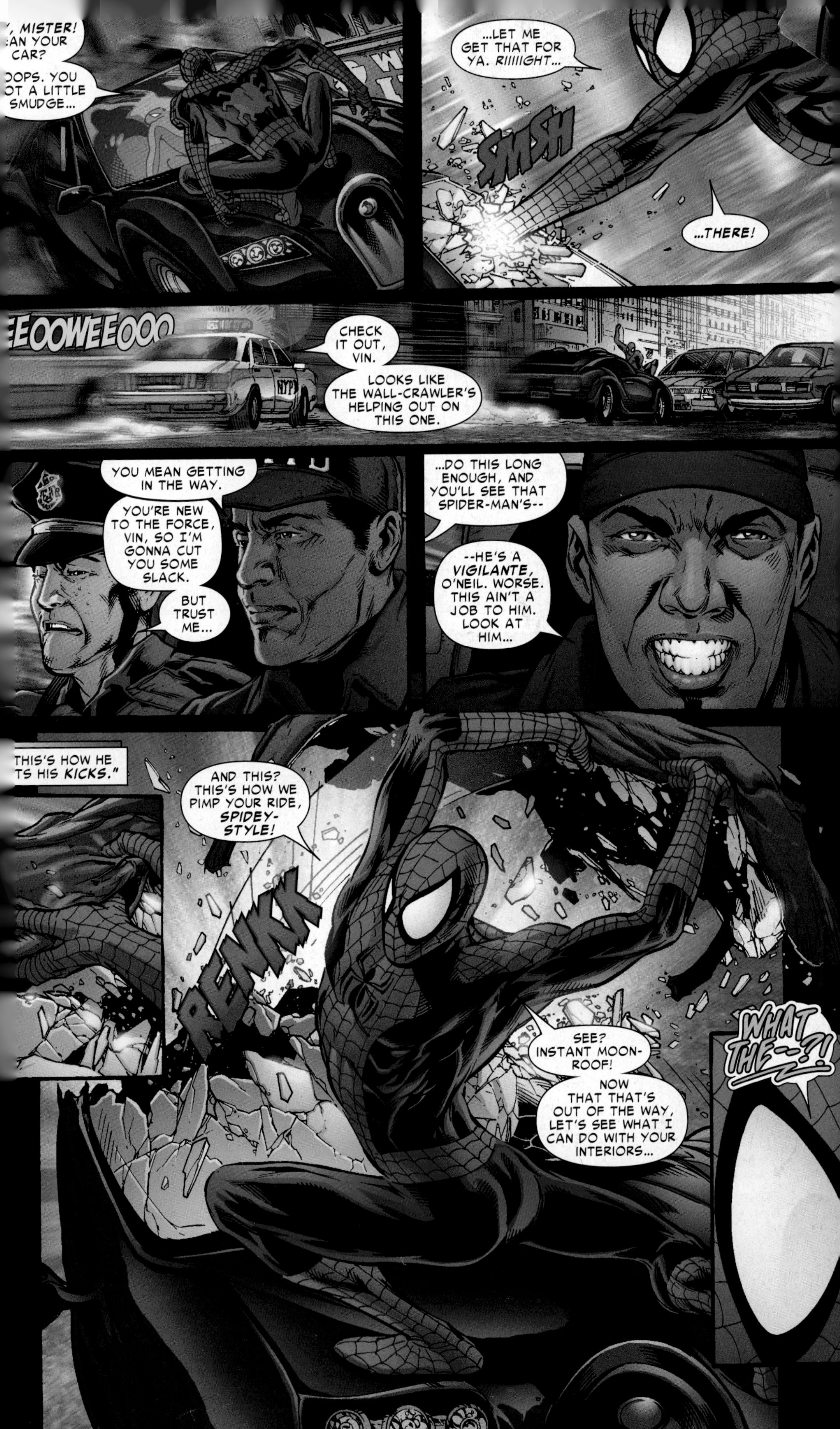

, MISTER! EAN YOUR CAR?
OOPS. YOU OT A LITTLE SMUDGE...
...LET ME GET THAT FOR YA. RIIIIIGHT...
SMSH
...THERE!
EEOOWEEOOO
CHECK IT OUT, VIN.
LOOKS LIKE THE WALL-CRAWLER'S HELPING OUT ON THIS ONE.
YOU MEAN GETTING IN THE WAY.
YOU'RE NEW TO THE FORCE, VIN, SO I'M GONNA CUT YOU SOME SLACK.
BUT TRUST ME...
...DO THIS LONG ENOUGH, AND YOU'LL SEE THAT SPIDER-MAN'S--
--HE'S A VIGILANTE, O'NEIL. WORSE. THIS AIN'T A JOB TO HIM. LOOK AT HIM...
THIS'S HOW HE TS HIS KICKS."
AND THIS? THIS'S HOW WE PIMP YOUR RIDE, SPIDEY-STYLE!
RENKK
SEE? INSTANT MOON-ROOF!
NOW THAT THAT'S OUT OF THE WAY, LET'S SEE WHAT I CAN DO WITH YOUR INTERIORS...
WHAT THE--?!

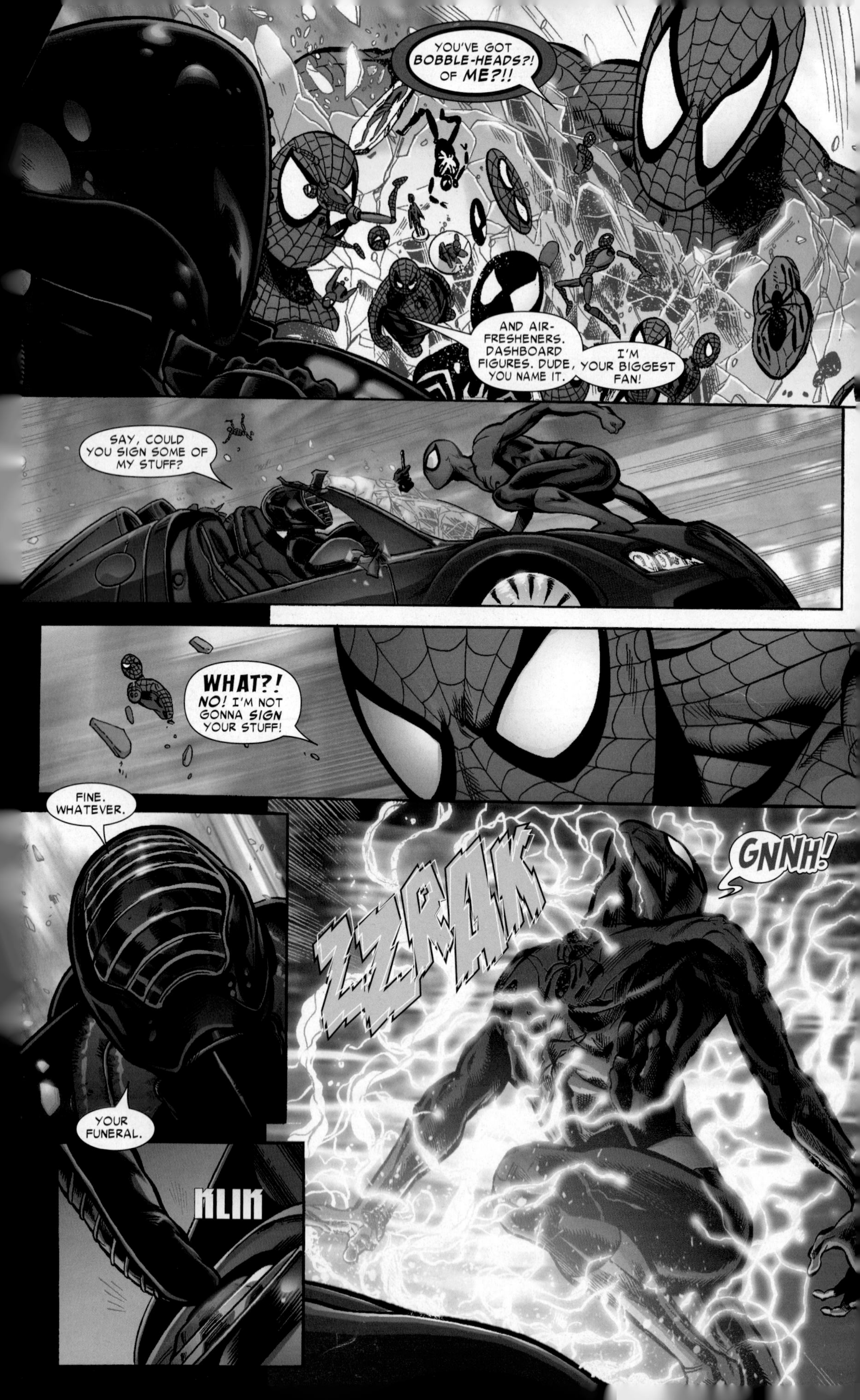
YOU'VE GOT BOBBLE-HEADS?! OF ME?!!
AND AIR-FRESHENERS. DASHBOARD FIGURES. DUDE, YOU NAME IT.
I'M YOUR BIGGEST FAN!
SAY, COULD YOU SIGN SOME OF MY STUFF?
WHAT?! NO! I'M NOT GONNA SIGN YOUR STUFF!
FINE. WHATEVER.
YOUR FUNERAL.
KLIK
ZZRAK
GNNH!

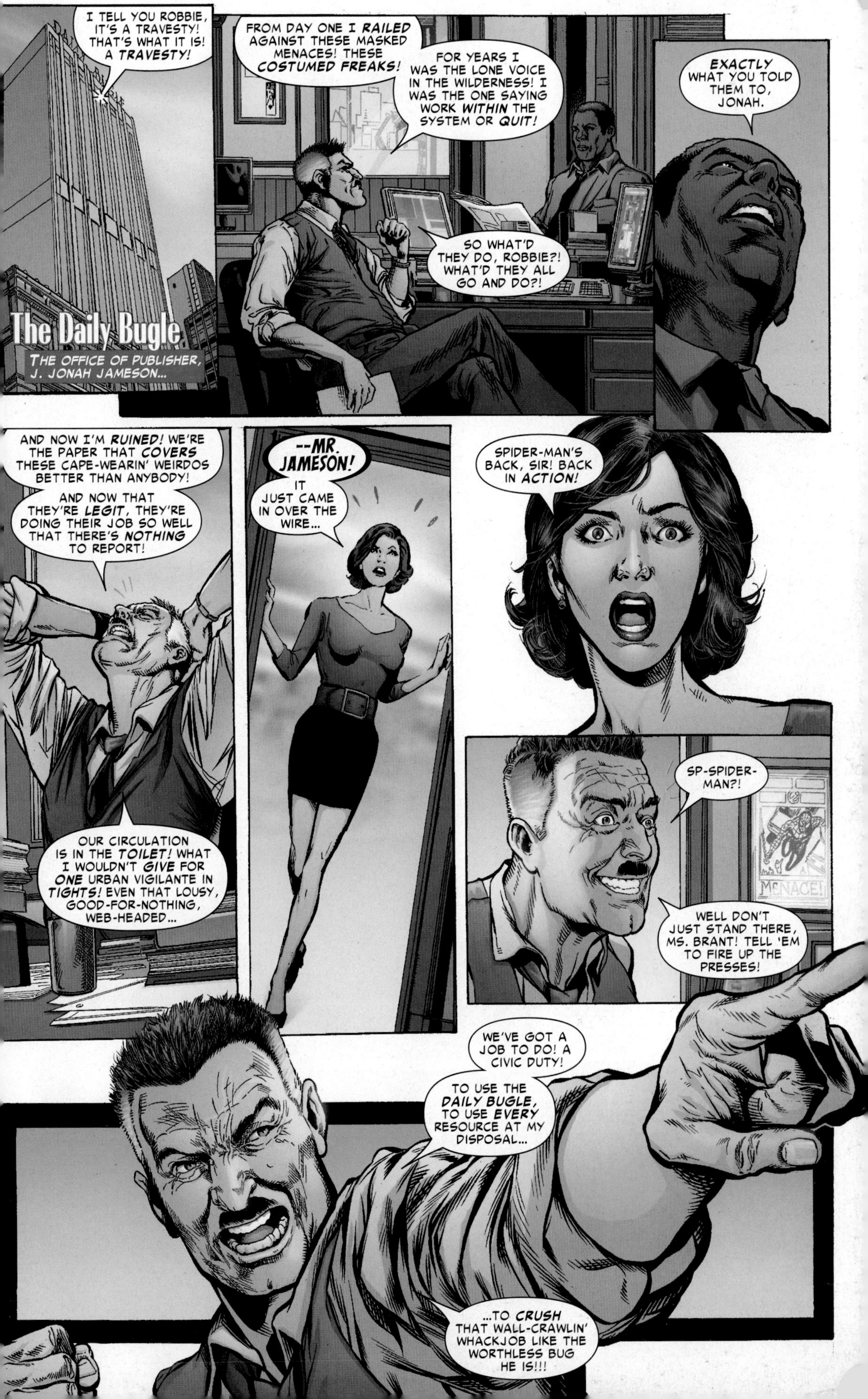

I TELL YOU ROBBIE, IT'S A TRAVESTY! THAT'S WHAT IT IS! A TRAVESTY!
The Daily Bugle
THE OFFICE OF PUBLISHER, J. JONAH JAMESON...
FROM DAY ONE I RAILED AGAINST THESE MASKED MENACES! THESE COSTUMED FREAKS!
FOR YEARS I WAS THE LONE VOICE IN THE WILDERNESS! I WAS THE ONE SAYING WORK WITHIN THE SYSTEM OR QUIT!
SO WHAT'D THEY DO, ROBBIE?! WHAT'D THEY ALL GO AND DO?!
EXACTLY WHAT YOU TOLD THEM TO, JONAH.
AND NOW I'M RUINED! WE'RE THE PAPER THAT COVERS THESE CAPE-WEARIN' WEIRDOS BETTER THAN ANYBODY!
AND NOW THAT THEY'RE LEGIT, THEY'RE DOING THEIR JOB SO WELL THAT THERE'S NOTHING TO REPORT!
OUR CIRCULATION IS IN THE TOILET! WHAT I WOULDN'T GIVE FOR ONE URBAN VIGILANTE IN TIGHTS! EVEN THAT LOUSY, GOOD-FOR-NOTHING, WEB-HEADED...
--MR. JAMESON!
IT JUST CAME IN OVER THE WIRE...
SPIDER-MAN'S BACK, SIR! BACK IN ACTION!
SP-SPIDER-MAN?!
MENACE!
WELL DON'T JUST STAND THERE, MS. BRANT! TELL 'EM TO FIRE UP THE PRESSES!
WE'VE GOT A JOB TO DO! A CIVIC DUTY!
TO USE THE DAILY BUGLE, TO USE EVERY RESOURCE AT MY DISPOSAL...
...TO CRUSH THAT WALL-CRAWLIN' WHACKJOB LIKE THE WORTHLESS BUG HE IS!!!

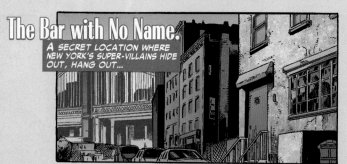

The Bar with No Name.

A SECRET LOCATION WHERE NEW YORK'S SUPER-VILLAINS HIDE OUT, HANG OUT...

...AND SHOOT SOME POOL.

WE ARE RECEIVING REPORTS THAT THE POLICE ARE IN THE MIDDLE OF A HIGH-SPEED CHASE ACROSS MIDTOWN MANHATTAN...

...WITH A NEW UNREGISTERED SUPERHUMAN, OVERDRIVE...

...AND THE VIGILANTE KNOWN AS SPIDER-MAN!

THIS JUST IN-- SPIDER-MAN HAS JUST BEEN THROWN FROM THE FIRST VEHICLE!

C'MON. A NEW GUY? WHAT'S THE POINT? HE ALWAYS BEATS THE NEW GUYS.

YOU NEVER KNOW. HE'S GOTTA LOSE SOMETIME, RIGHT?

COOL CAR.

A CAR? HA! I'M STRONGER THAN A CAR!

I'LL GIVE HIM 5-TO-1 ODDS.

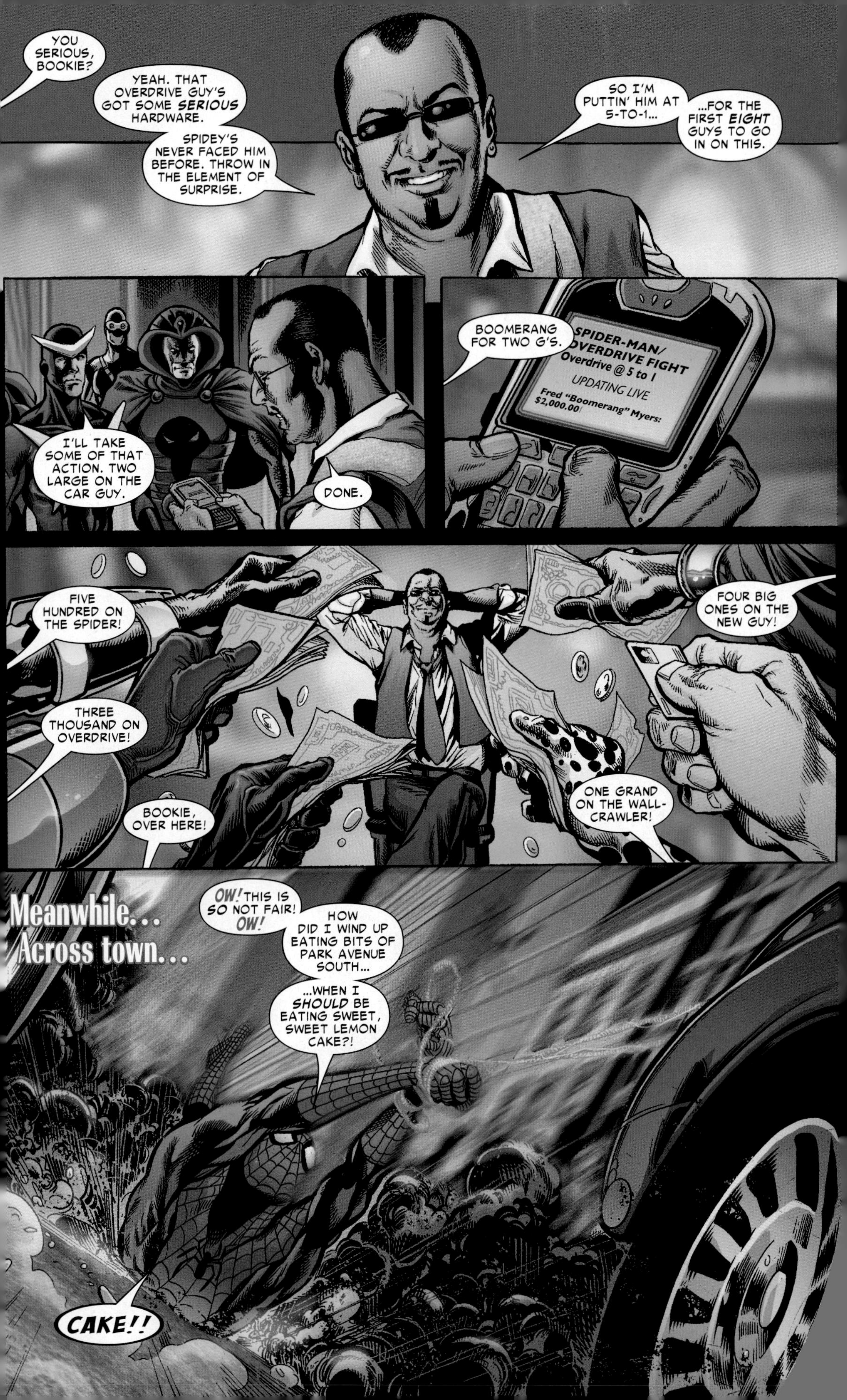
YOU SERIOUS, BOOKIE?
YEAH. THAT OVERDRIVE GUY'S GOT SOME SERIOUS HARDWARE.
SPIDEY'S NEVER FACED HIM BEFORE. THROW IN THE ELEMENT OF SURPRISE.
SO I'M PUTTIN' HIM AT 5-TO-1...
...FOR THE FIRST EIGHT GUYS TO GO IN ON THIS.
I'LL TAKE SOME OF THAT ACTION. TWO LARGE ON THE CAR GUY.
DONE.
BOOMERANG FOR TWO G'S.
SPIDER-MAN/ OVERDRIVE FIGHT
Overdrive @ 5 to 1
UPDATING LIVE
Fred "Boomerang" Myers: $2,000.00
FIVE HUNDRED ON THE SPIDER!
FOUR BIG ONES ON THE NEW GUY!
THREE THOUSAND ON OVERDRIVE!
BOOKIE, OVER HERE!
ONE GRAND ON THE WALL-CRAWLER!
Meanwhile... Across town...
OW! THIS IS SO NOT FAIR! OW!
HOW DID I WIND UP EATING BITS OF PARK AVENUE SOUTH...
...WHEN I SHOULD BE EATING SWEET, SWEET LEMON CAKE?!
CAKE!!

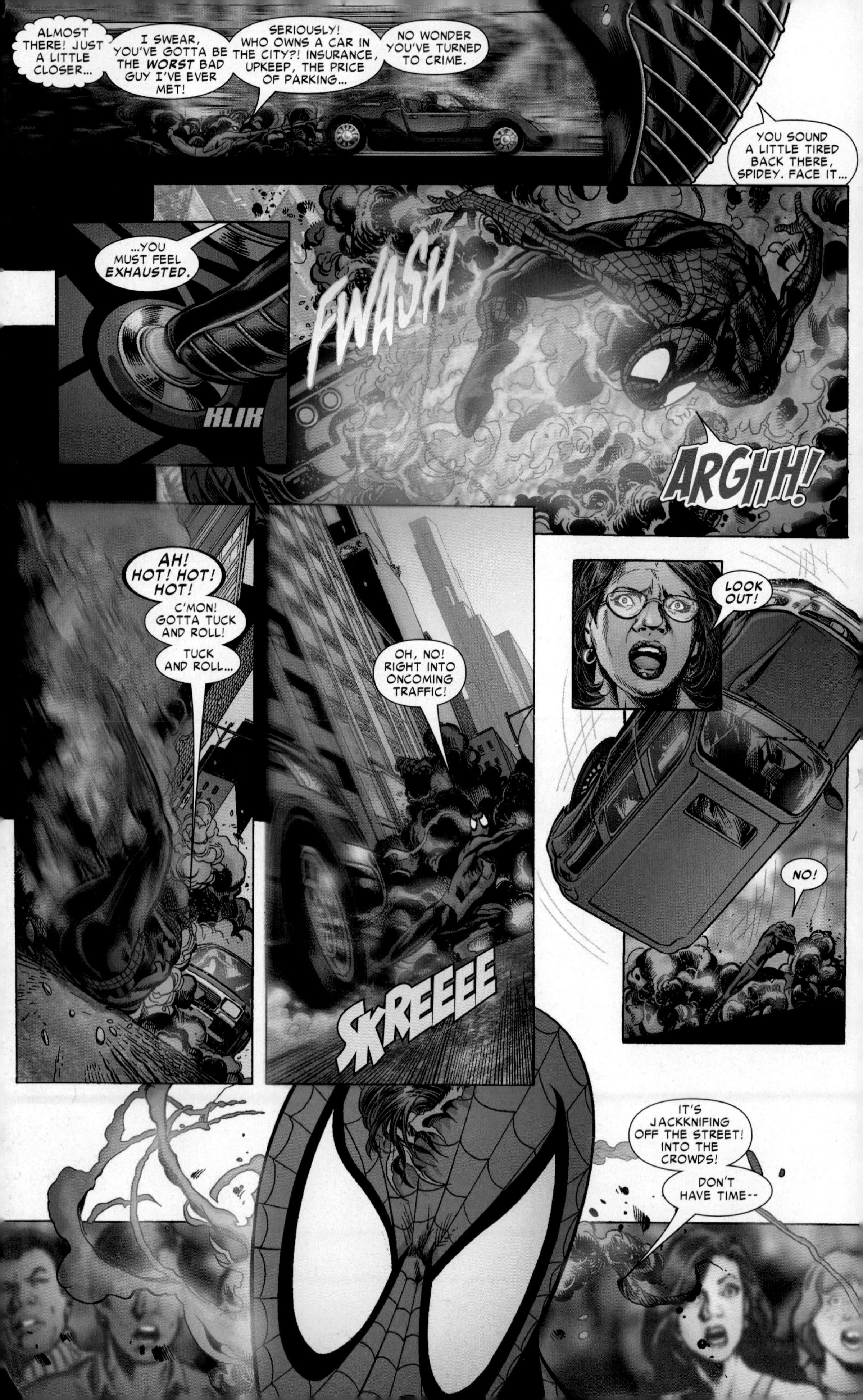
ALMOST THERE! JUST A LITTLE CLOSER...
I SWEAR, YOU'VE GOTTA BE THE WORST BAD GUY I'VE EVER MET!
SERIOUSLY! WHO OWNS A CAR IN THE CITY?! INSURANCE, UPKEEP, THE PRICE OF PARKING...
NO WONDER YOU'VE TURNED TO CRIME.
YOU SOUND A LITTLE TIRED BACK THERE, SPIDEY. FACE IT...
...YOU MUST FEEL EXHAUSTED.
KLIK
FWASH
ARGHH!
AH! HOT! HOT! HOT!
C'MON! GOTTA TUCK AND ROLL!
TUCK AND ROLL...
OH, NO! RIGHT INTO ONCOMING TRAFFIC!
SKREEEE
LOOK OUT!
NO!
IT'S JACKKNIFING OFF THE STREET! INTO THE CROWDS!
DON'T HAVE TIME--

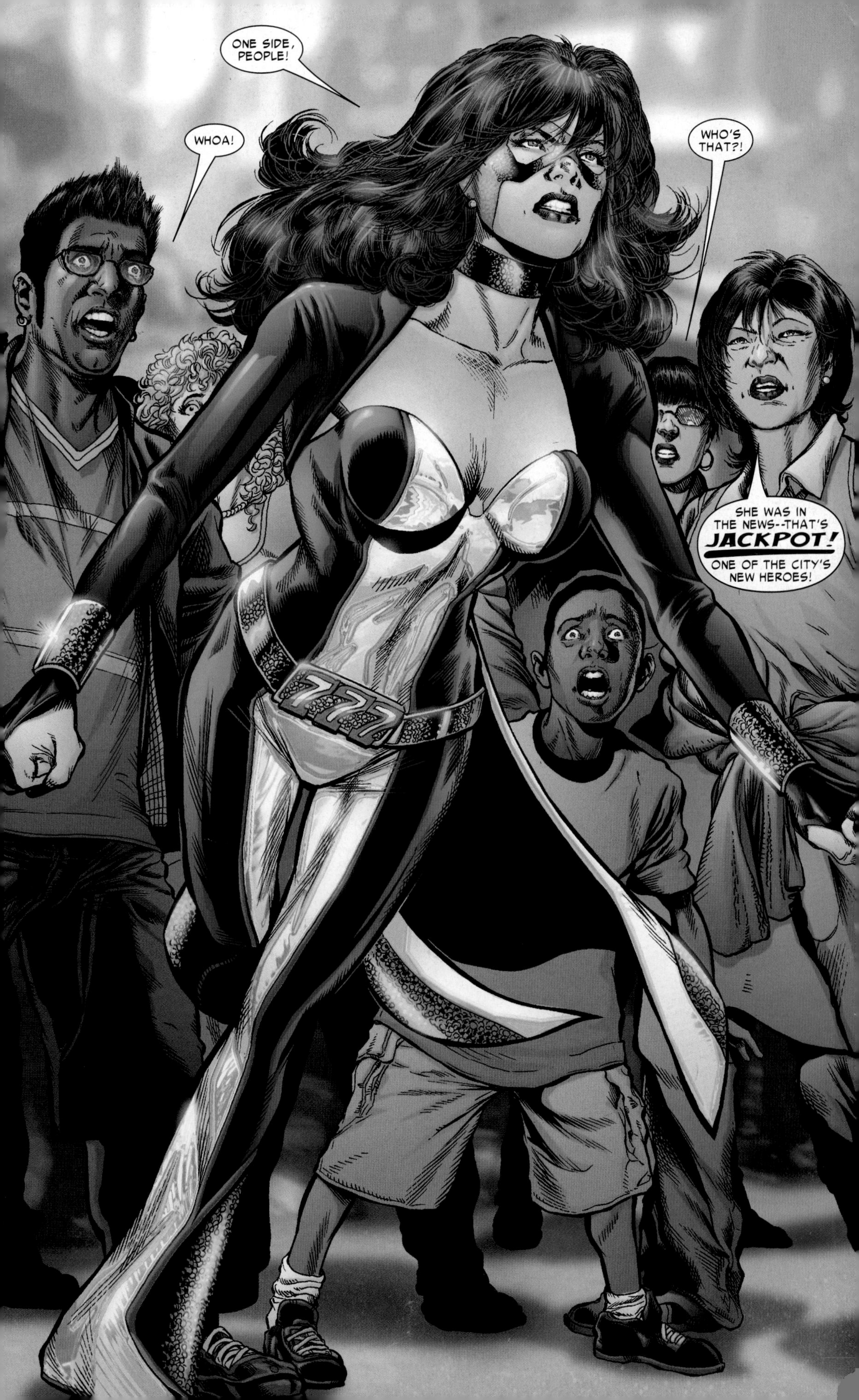
ONE SIDE, PEOPLE!
WHOA!
WHO'S THAT?!
SHE WAS IN THE NEWS--THAT'S JACKPOT! ONE OF THE CITY'S NEW HEROES!

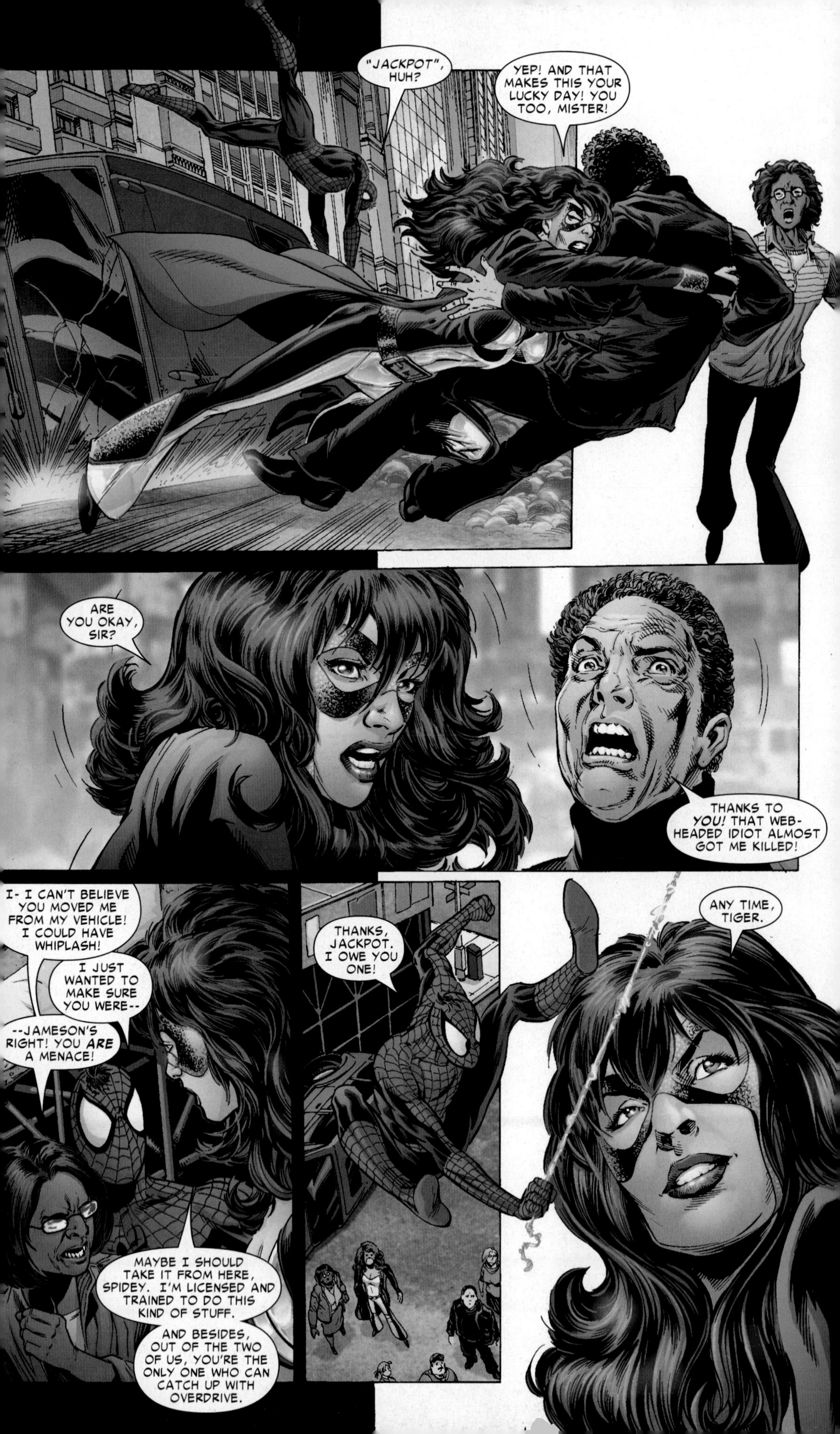
"JACKPOT", HUH?
YEP! AND THAT MAKES THIS YOUR LUCKY DAY! YOU TOO, MISTER!
ARE YOU OKAY, SIR?
THANKS TO *YOU!* THAT WEB-HEADED IDIOT ALMOST GOT ME KILLED!
I- I CAN'T BELIEVE YOU MOVED ME FROM MY VEHICLE! I COULD HAVE WHIPLASH!
I JUST WANTED TO MAKE SURE YOU WERE--
--JAMESON'S RIGHT! YOU *ARE* A MENACE!
MAYBE I SHOULD TAKE IT FROM HERE, SPIDEY. I'M LICENSED AND TRAINED TO DO THIS KIND OF STUFF.
AND BESIDES, OUT OF THE TWO OF US, YOU'RE THE ONLY ONE WHO CAN CATCH UP WITH OVERDRIVE.
THANKS, JACKPOT. I OWE YOU ONE!
ANY TIME, TIGER.

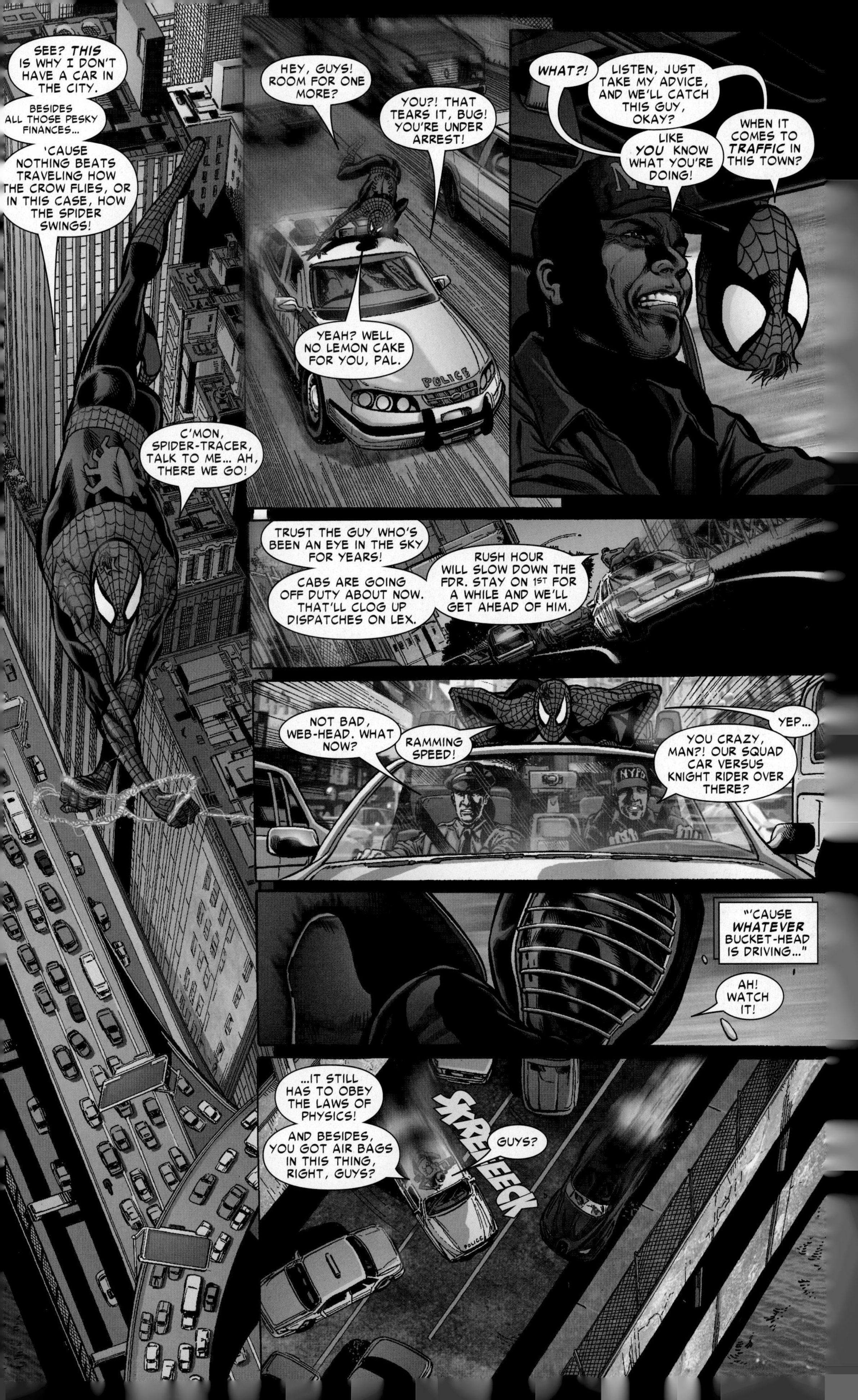
SEE? THIS IS WHY I DON'T HAVE A CAR IN THE CITY.
BESIDES ALL THOSE PESKY FINANCES...
'CAUSE NOTHING BEATS TRAVELING HOW THE CROW FLIES, OR IN THIS CASE, HOW THE SPIDER SWINGS!
C'MON, SPIDER-TRACER, TALK TO ME... AH, THERE WE GO!
HEY, GUYS! ROOM FOR ONE MORE?
YOU?! THAT TEARS IT, BUG! YOU'RE UNDER ARREST!
YEAH? WELL NO LEMON CAKE FOR YOU, PAL.
POLICE
WHAT?!
LISTEN, JUST TAKE MY ADVICE, AND WE'LL CATCH THIS GUY, OKAY?
LIKE YOU KNOW WHAT YOU'RE DOING!
WHEN IT COMES TO TRAFFIC IN THIS TOWN?
TRUST THE GUY WHO'S BEEN AN EYE IN THE SKY FOR YEARS!
CABS ARE GOING OFF DUTY ABOUT NOW. THAT'LL CLOG UP DISPATCHES ON LEX.
RUSH HOUR WILL SLOW DOWN THE FDR. STAY ON 1ST FOR A WHILE AND WE'LL GET AHEAD OF HIM.
NOT BAD, WEB-HEAD. WHAT NOW?
RAMMING SPEED!
YEP...
YOU CRAZY, MAN?! OUR SQUAD CAR VERSUS KNIGHT RIDER OVER THERE?
NYPD
"'CAUSE WHATEVER BUCKET-HEAD IS DRIVING..."
AH! WATCH IT!
...IT STILL HAS TO OBEY THE LAWS OF PHYSICS!
AND BESIDES, YOU GOT AIR BAGS IN THIS THING, RIGHT, GUYS?
SKREEEECK
GUYS?

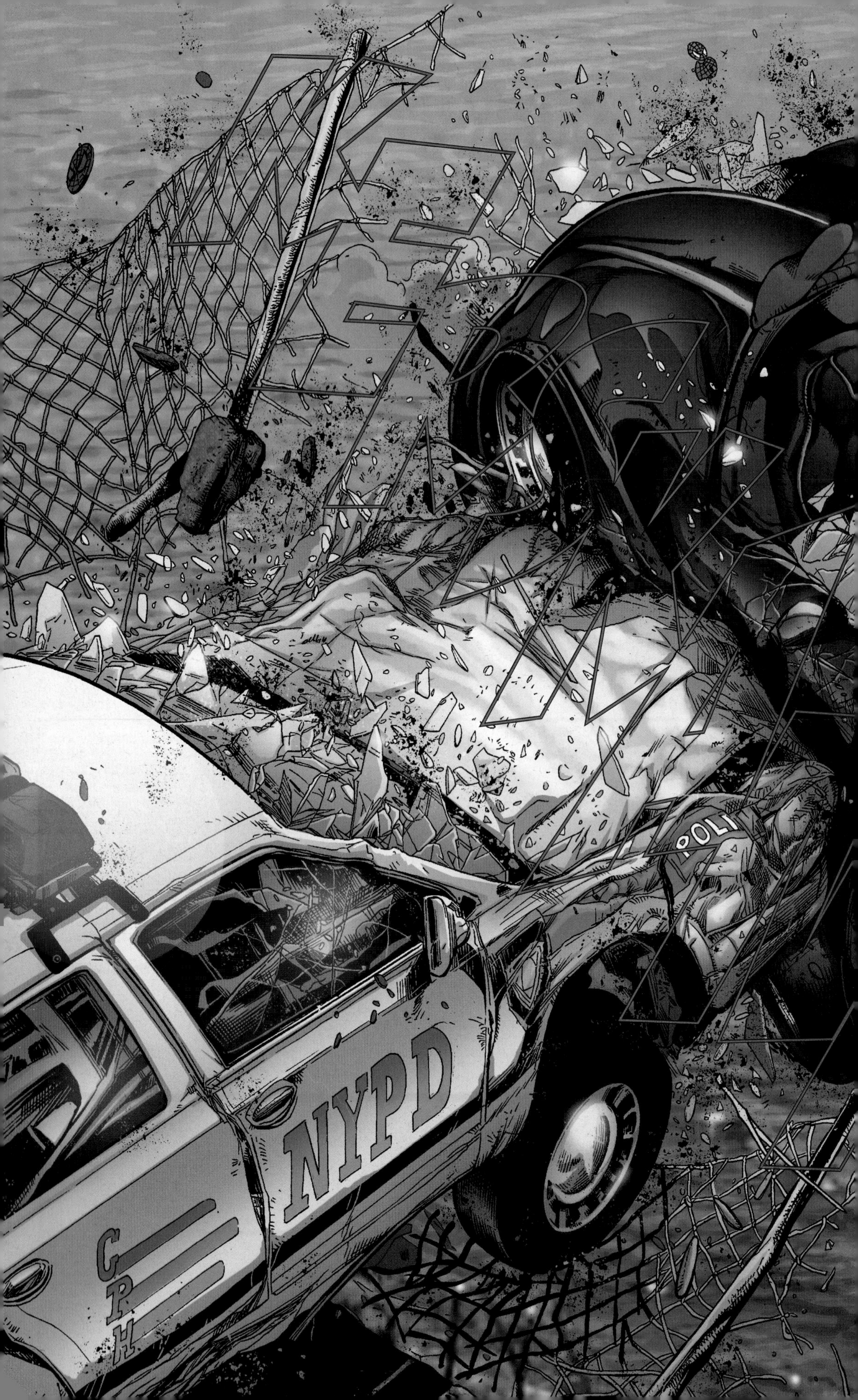
NYPD
POLI
CPH

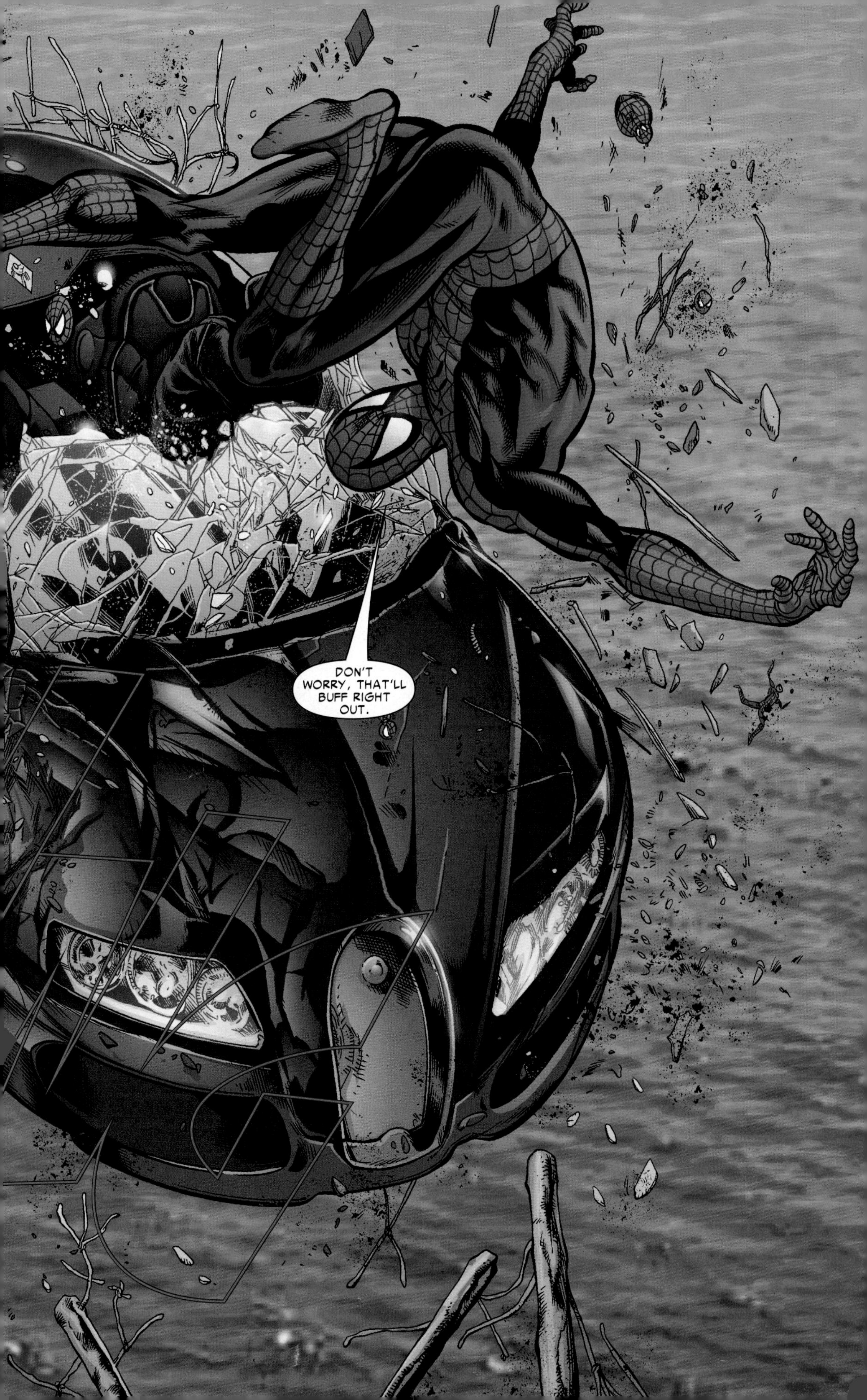
DON'T WORRY, THAT'LL BUFF RIGHT OUT.

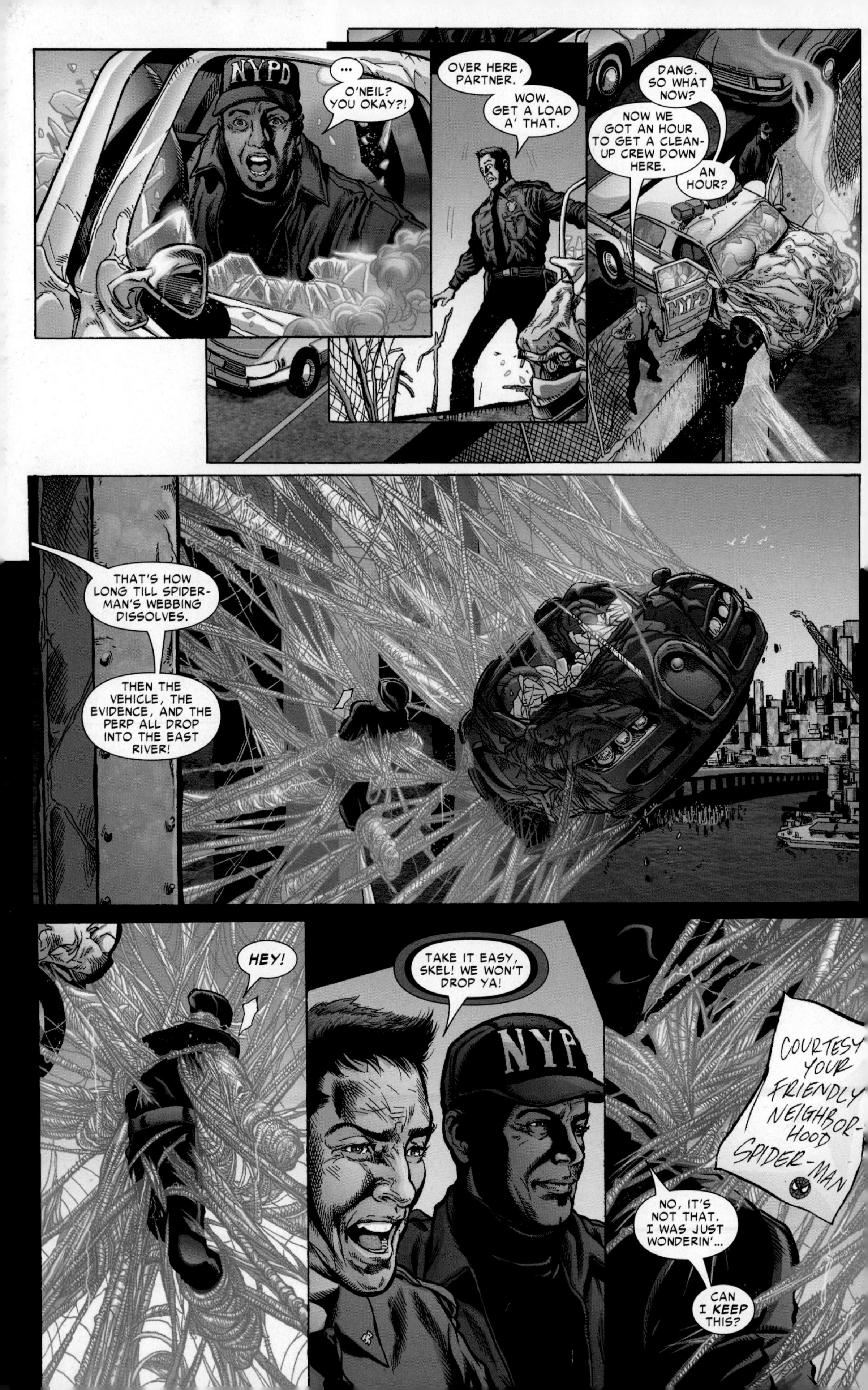
...
O'NEIL? YOU OKAY?!
OVER HERE, PARTNER.
WOW. GET A LOAD A' THAT.
DANG. SO WHAT NOW?
NOW WE GOT AN HOUR TO GET A CLEAN-UP CREW DOWN HERE.
AN HOUR?
THAT'S HOW LONG TILL SPIDER-MAN'S WEBBING DISSOLVES.
THEN THE VEHICLE, THE EVIDENCE, AND THE PERP ALL DROP INTO THE EAST RIVER!
HEY!
TAKE IT EASY, SKEL! WE WON'T DROP YA!
COURTESY YOUR FRIENDLY NEIGHBOR-HOOD SPIDER-MAN
NO, IT'S NOT THAT. I WAS JUST WONDERIN'...
CAN I KEEP THIS?

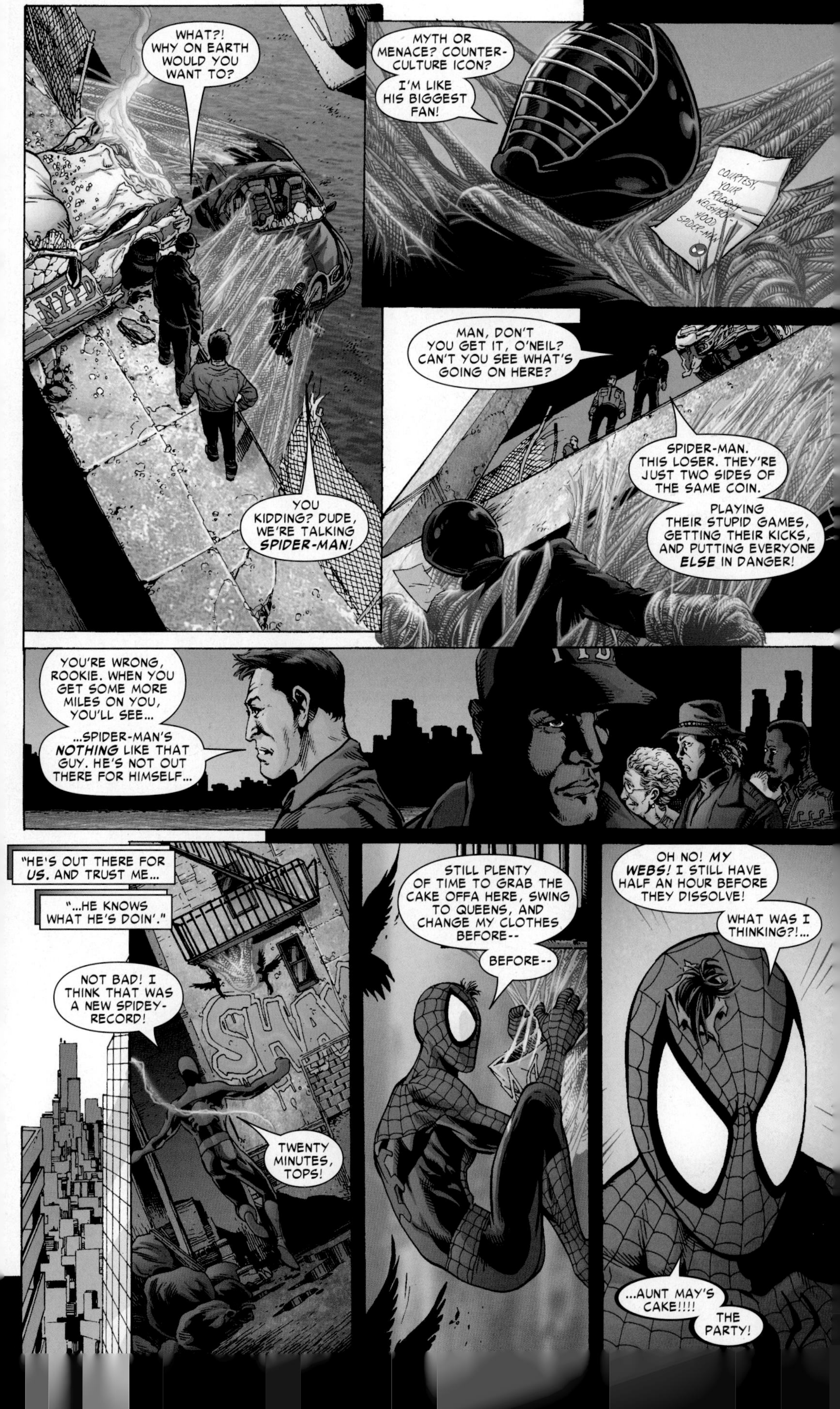
WHAT?! WHY ON EARTH WOULD YOU WANT TO?
MYTH OR MENACE? COUNTER-CULTURE ICON?
I'M LIKE HIS BIGGEST FAN!
COURTESY, YOUR FRIENDLY NEIGHBOR-HOOD SPIDER-MAN
YOU KIDDING? DUDE, WE'RE TALKING SPIDER-MAN!
MAN, DON'T YOU GET IT, O'NEIL? CAN'T YOU SEE WHAT'S GOING ON HERE?
SPIDER-MAN. THIS LOSER. THEY'RE JUST TWO SIDES OF THE SAME COIN.
PLAYING THEIR STUPID GAMES, GETTING THEIR KICKS, AND PUTTING EVERYONE ELSE IN DANGER!
YOU'RE WRONG, ROOKIE. WHEN YOU GET SOME MORE MILES ON YOU, YOU'LL SEE...
...SPIDER-MAN'S NOTHING LIKE THAT GUY. HE'S NOT OUT THERE FOR HIMSELF...
"HE'S OUT THERE FOR US. AND TRUST ME...
"...HE KNOWS WHAT HE'S DOIN'."
NOT BAD! I THINK THAT WAS A NEW SPIDEY-RECORD!
TWENTY MINUTES, TOPS!
STILL PLENTY OF TIME TO GRAB THE CAKE OFFA HERE, SWING TO QUEENS, AND CHANGE MY CLOTHES BEFORE--
BEFORE--
OH NO! MY WEBS! I STILL HAVE HALF AN HOUR BEFORE THEY DISSOLVE!
WHAT WAS I THINKING?!...
...AUNT MAY'S CAKE!!!!
THE PARTY!

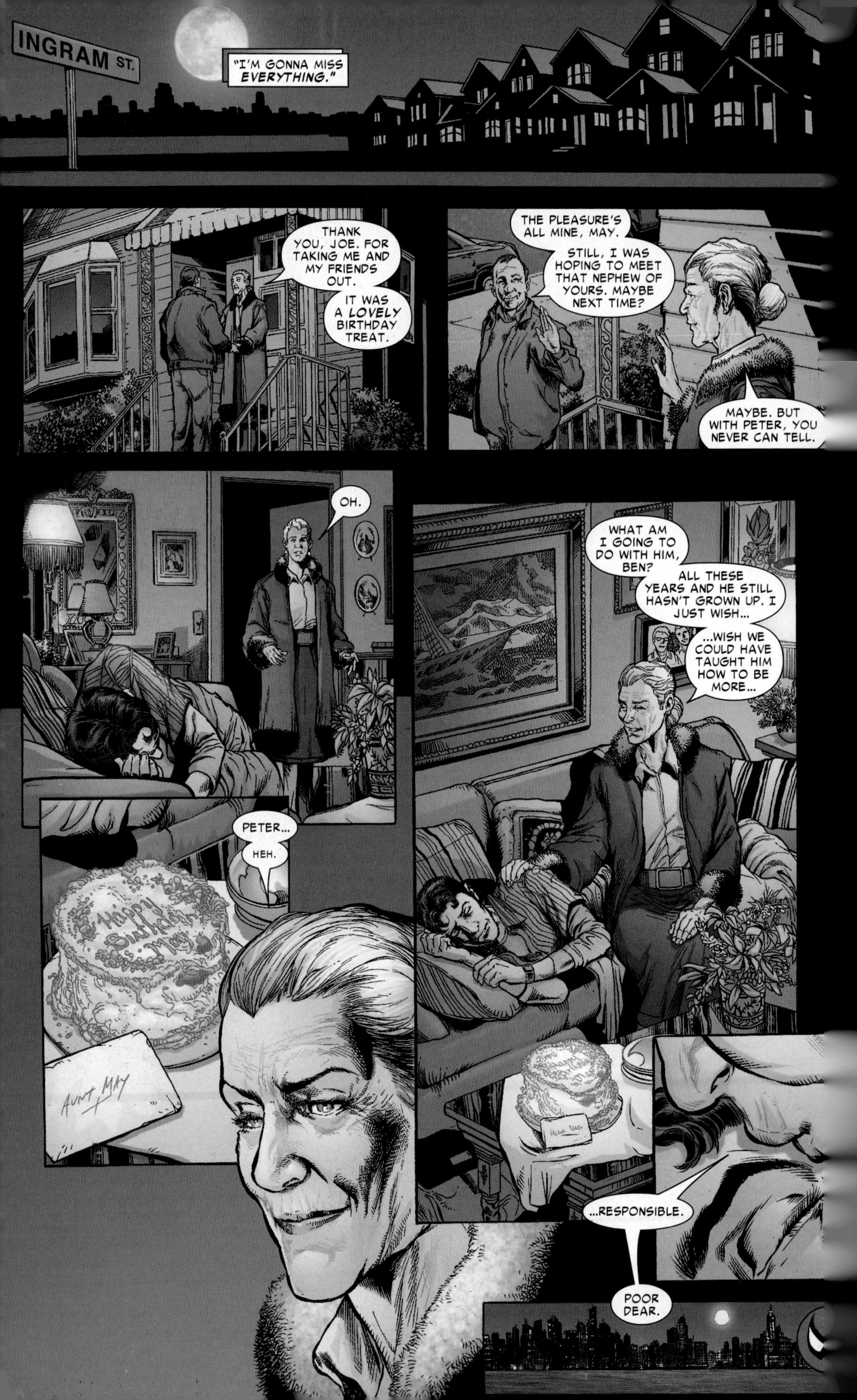

INGRAM ST.
"I'M GONNA MISS EVERYTHING."
THANK YOU, JOE. FOR TAKING ME AND MY FRIENDS OUT.
IT WAS A LOVELY BIRTHDAY TREAT.
THE PLEASURE'S ALL MINE, MAY.
STILL, I WAS HOPING TO MEET THAT NEPHEW OF YOURS. MAYBE NEXT TIME?
MAYBE. BUT WITH PETER, YOU NEVER CAN TELL.
OH.
WHAT AM I GOING TO DO WITH HIM, BEN?
ALL THESE YEARS AND HE STILL HASN'T GROWN UP. I JUST WISH...
...WISH WE COULD HAVE TAUGHT HIM HOW TO BE MORE...
PETER...
HEH.
Happy Birthday May
AUNT MAY
...RESPONSIBLE.
POOR DEAR.

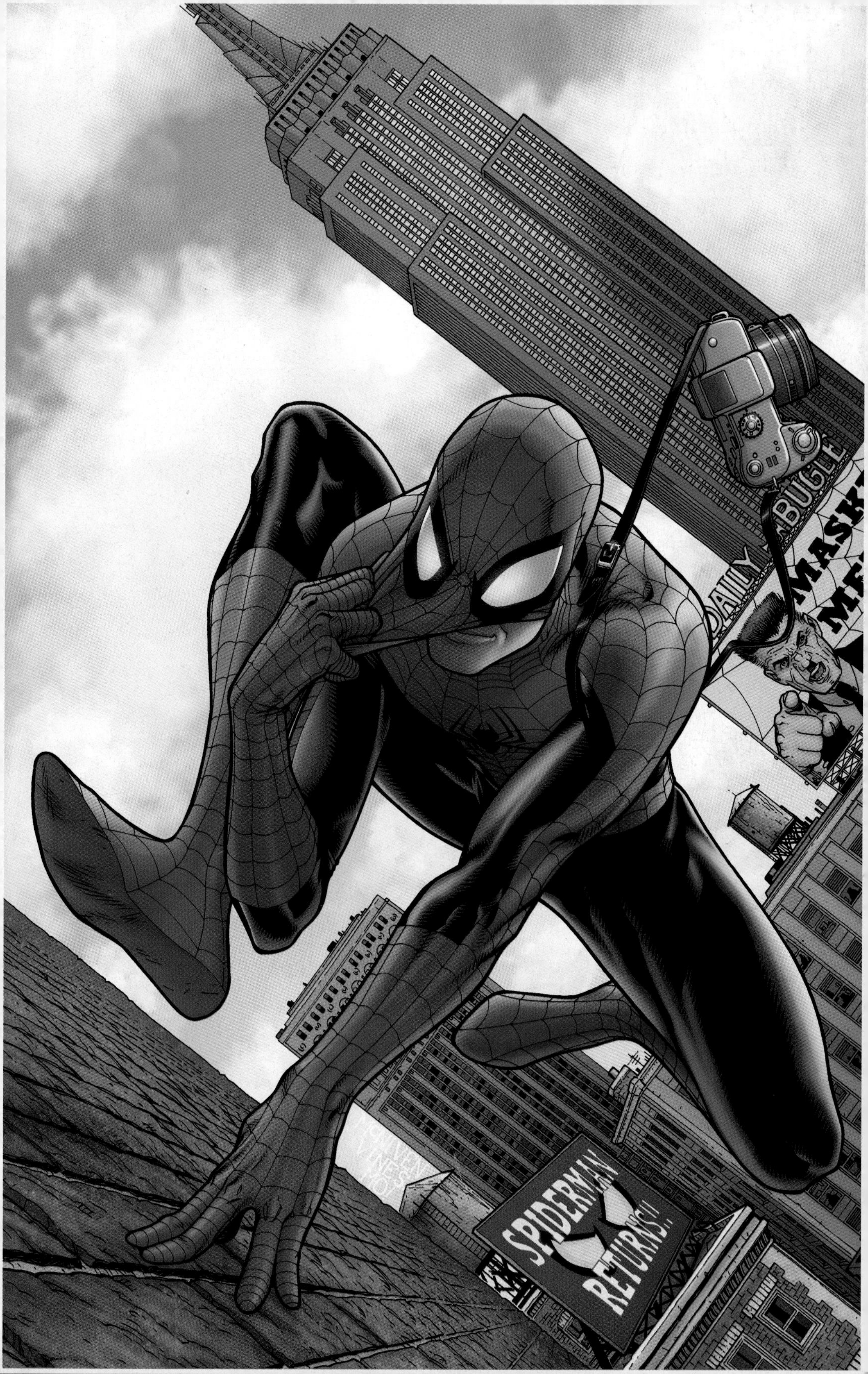
DAILY BUGLE
SPIDERMAN RETURNS!!

AMAZING SPIDER-MAN #546

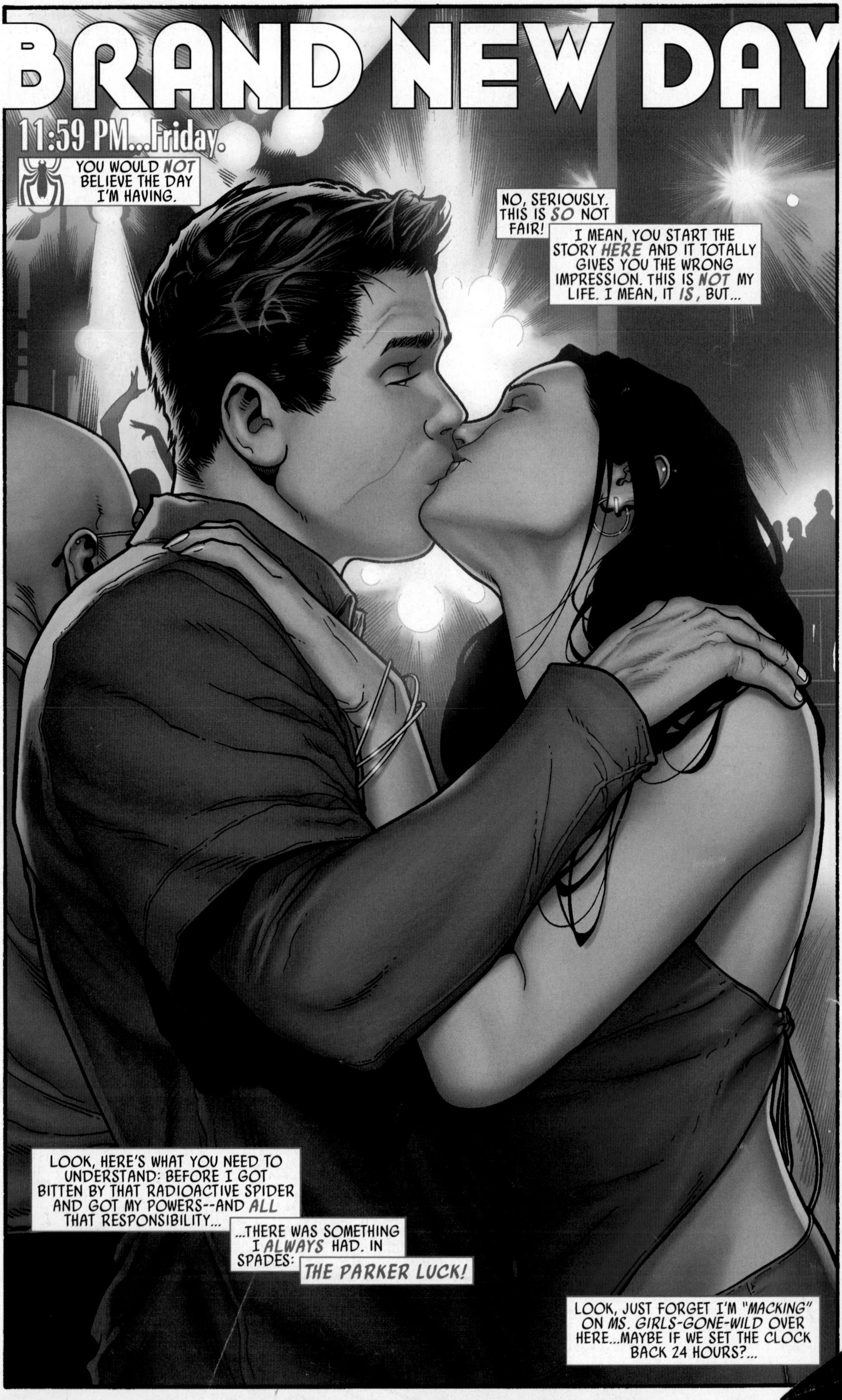
BRAND NEW DAY
11:59 PM...Friday.
YOU WOULD NOT BELIEVE THE DAY I'M HAVING.
NO, SERIOUSLY. THIS IS SO NOT FAIR!
I MEAN, YOU START THE STORY HERE AND IT TOTALLY GIVES YOU THE WRONG IMPRESSION. THIS IS NOT MY LIFE. I MEAN, IT IS, BUT...
LOOK, HERE'S WHAT YOU NEED TO UNDERSTAND: BEFORE I GOT BITTEN BY THAT RADIOACTIVE SPIDER AND GOT MY POWERS--AND ALL THAT RESPONSIBILITY...
...THERE WAS SOMETHING I ALWAYS HAD. IN SPADES:
THE PARKER LUCK!
LOOK, JUST FORGET I'M "MACKING" ON MS. GIRLS-GONE-WILD OVER HERE...MAYBE IF WE SET THE CLOCK BACK 24 HOURS?...

WHILE ATTENDING A DEMONSTRATION IN RADIOLOGY, HIGH SCHOOL STUDENT **PETER PARKER** WAS BITTEN BY A SPIDER WHICH HAD ACCIDENTALLY BEEN EXPOSED TO **RADIOACTIVE RAYS.** THROUGH A MIRACLE OF SCIENCE, PETER SOON FOUND THAT HE HAD **GAINED** THE SPIDER'S POWERS...AND HAD, IN EFFECT, BECOME A HUMAN SPIDER! FROM THAT DAY ON HE WAS...

THE AMAZING SPIDER-MAN™

DAN SLOTT WRITER | STEVE McNIVEN PENCILER | DEXTER VINES INKER | MORRY HOLLOWELL COLORS | VC'S CORY PETIT LETTERS | GALE, GUGGENHEIM, SLOTT, WELLS SPIDEY'S BRAINTRUST

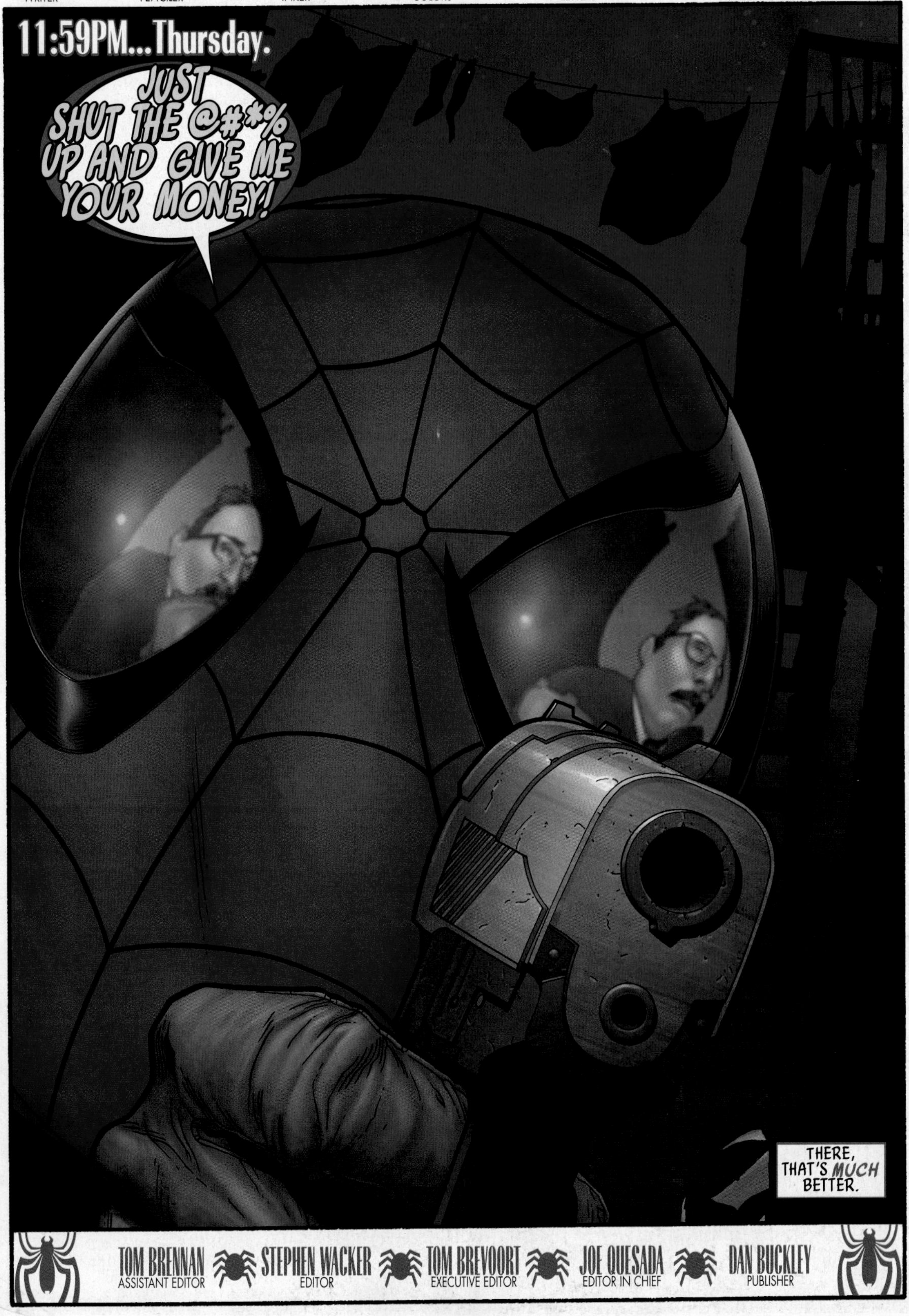
11:59PM...Thursday.
JUST SHUT THE @#*% UP AND GIVE ME YOUR MONEY!
THERE, THAT'S *MUCH* BETTER.

TOM BRENNAN ASSISTANT EDITOR | STEPHEN WACKER EDITOR | TOM BREVOORT EXECUTIVE EDITOR | JOE QUESADA EDITOR IN CHIEF | DAN BUCKLEY PUBLISHER

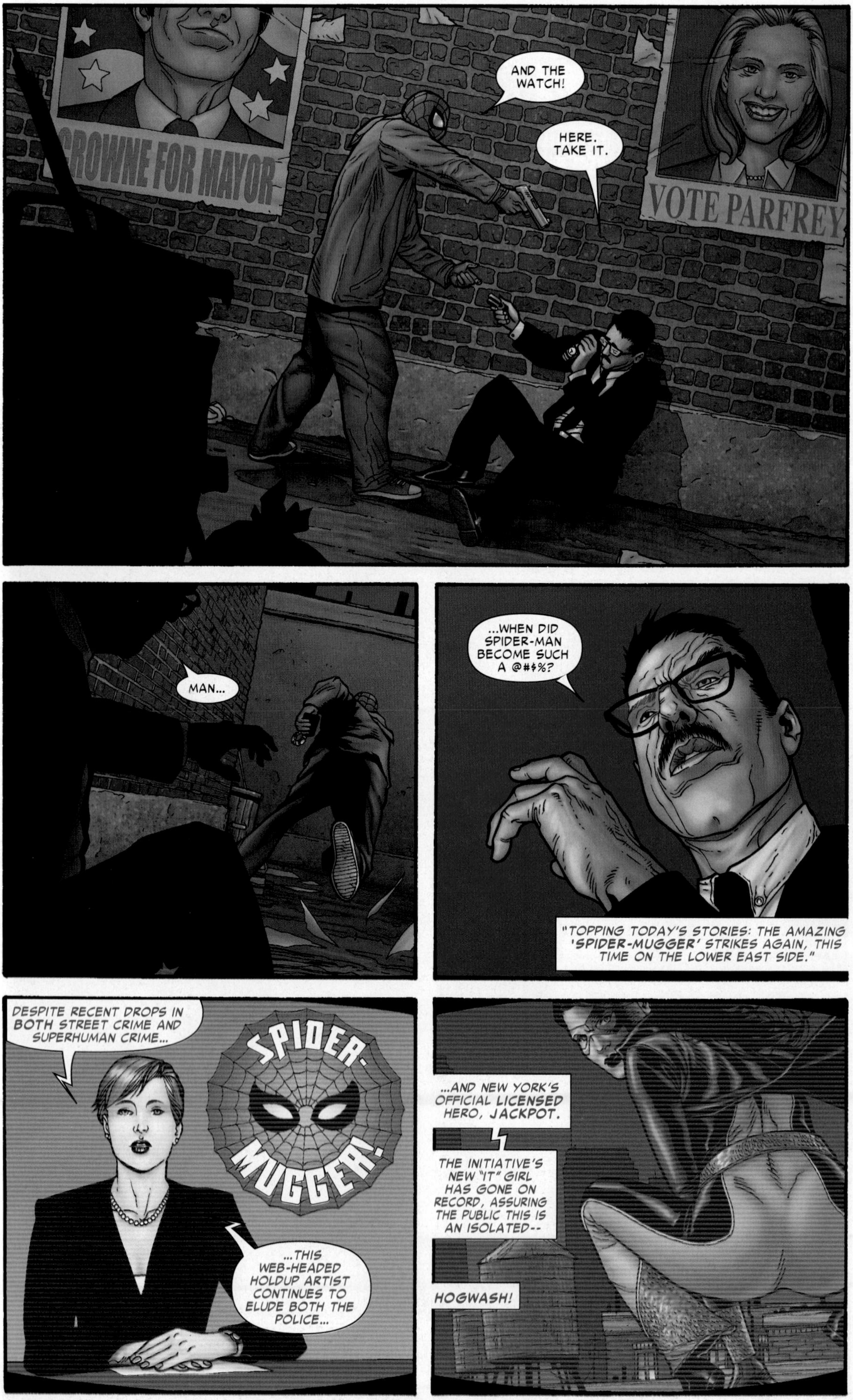
CROWNE FOR MAYOR
VOTE PARFREY
AND THE WATCH!
HERE. TAKE IT.
MAN...
...WHEN DID SPIDER-MAN BECOME SUCH A @#$%?
"TOPPING TODAY'S STORIES: THE AMAZING 'SPIDER-MUGGER' STRIKES AGAIN, THIS TIME ON THE LOWER EAST SIDE."
DESPITE RECENT DROPS IN BOTH STREET CRIME AND SUPERHUMAN CRIME...
SPIDER-MUGGER!
...THIS WEB-HEADED HOLDUP ARTIST CONTINUES TO ELUDE BOTH THE POLICE...
...AND NEW YORK'S OFFICIAL LICENSED HERO, JACKPOT.
THE INITIATIVE'S NEW "IT" GIRL HAS GONE ON RECORD, ASSURING THE PUBLIC THIS IS AN ISOLATED--
HOGWASH!

"ISOLATED," MY EYE! THIS DIRTBAG'S JUST *ANOTHER* LOWLIFE WHO'S BEEN *INSPIRED* BY THAT NO-GOOD, WALL-CRAWLING CRIMINAL, SPIDER-MAN!

J. JONAH JAMESON

INSPIRED? BUT MR. JAMESON, OUTSIDE OF ONE BRIEF SIGHTING...

...SPIDER-MAN HASN'T BEEN SEEN OR HEARD FROM IN MONTHS.

THEN YOU'RE *NOT* LOOKING CLOSE ENOUGH. HE'S *EVERYWHERE.* THAT MASK?

THIS HALLOWEEN IT OUTSOLD THE MASKS OF THE LAST TWO PRESIDENTS AND ALL THOSE MOVIE SLASHER GUYS *COMBINED!*

FOR *YEARS* I WARNED THE PUBLIC THAT SPIDER-MAN WAS A *MENACE!* WELL, GUESS WHAT? HE'S *WORSE!*

HE'S A *MOVEMENT!* HE'S *MERCHANDISE!*

WELL, PROFITABLE FOR *SOME,* AT LEAST.

hannel News 8 Channel

MR. JAMESON, YOUR PAPER USED TO BE NEW YORK'S NUMBER ONE SOURCE FOR SPIDER-MAN COVERAGE.

NOW, WITHOUT ANY SPIDEY STORIES TO RUN, YOUR CIRCULATION IS RUMORED TO BE AT AN *ALL-TIME LOW.* WOULD YOU CARE TO--

NO COMMENT.

BUT SURELY--

NO COMMENT!!

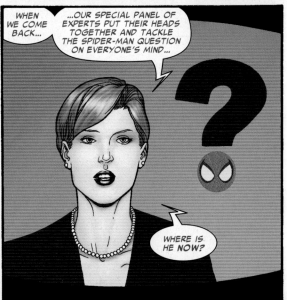

WHEN WE COME BACK...

...OUR SPECIAL PANEL OF EXPERTS PUT THEIR HEADS TOGETHER AND TACKLE THE SPIDER-MAN QUESTION ON EVERYONE'S MIND...

WHERE IS HE NOW?

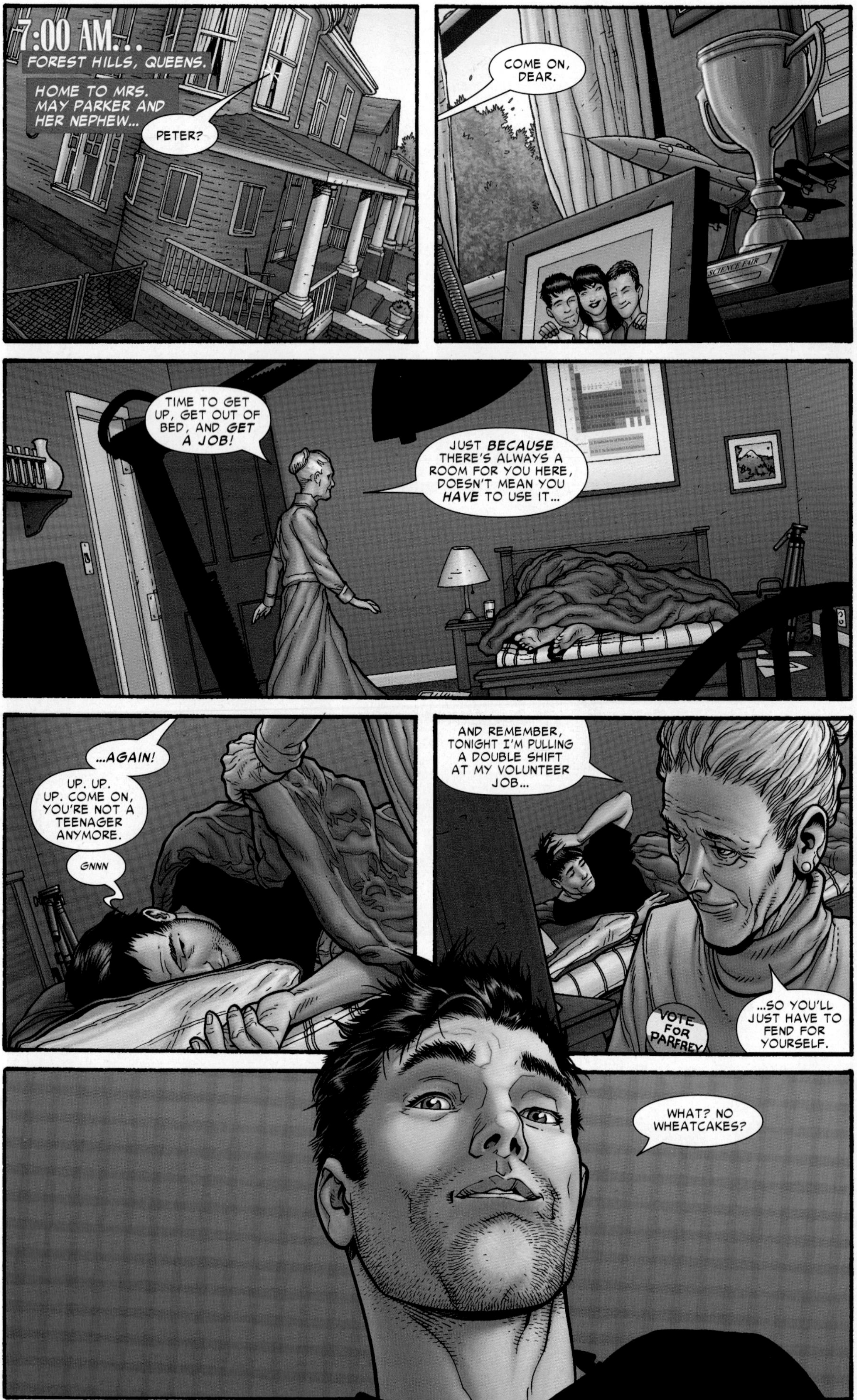
7:00 AM...
FOREST HILLS, QUEENS.
HOME TO MRS. MAY PARKER AND HER NEPHEW...
PETER?
COME ON, DEAR.
SCIENCE FAIR
TIME TO GET UP, GET OUT OF BED, AND GET A JOB!
JUST BECAUSE THERE'S ALWAYS A ROOM FOR YOU HERE, DOESN'T MEAN YOU HAVE TO USE IT...
...AGAIN!
UP. UP. UP. COME ON, YOU'RE NOT A TEENAGER ANYMORE.
GNNN
AND REMEMBER, TONIGHT I'M PULLING A DOUBLE SHIFT AT MY VOLUNTEER JOB...
VOTE FOR PARFREY
...SO YOU'LL JUST HAVE TO FEND FOR YOURSELF.
WHAT? NO WHEATCAKES?

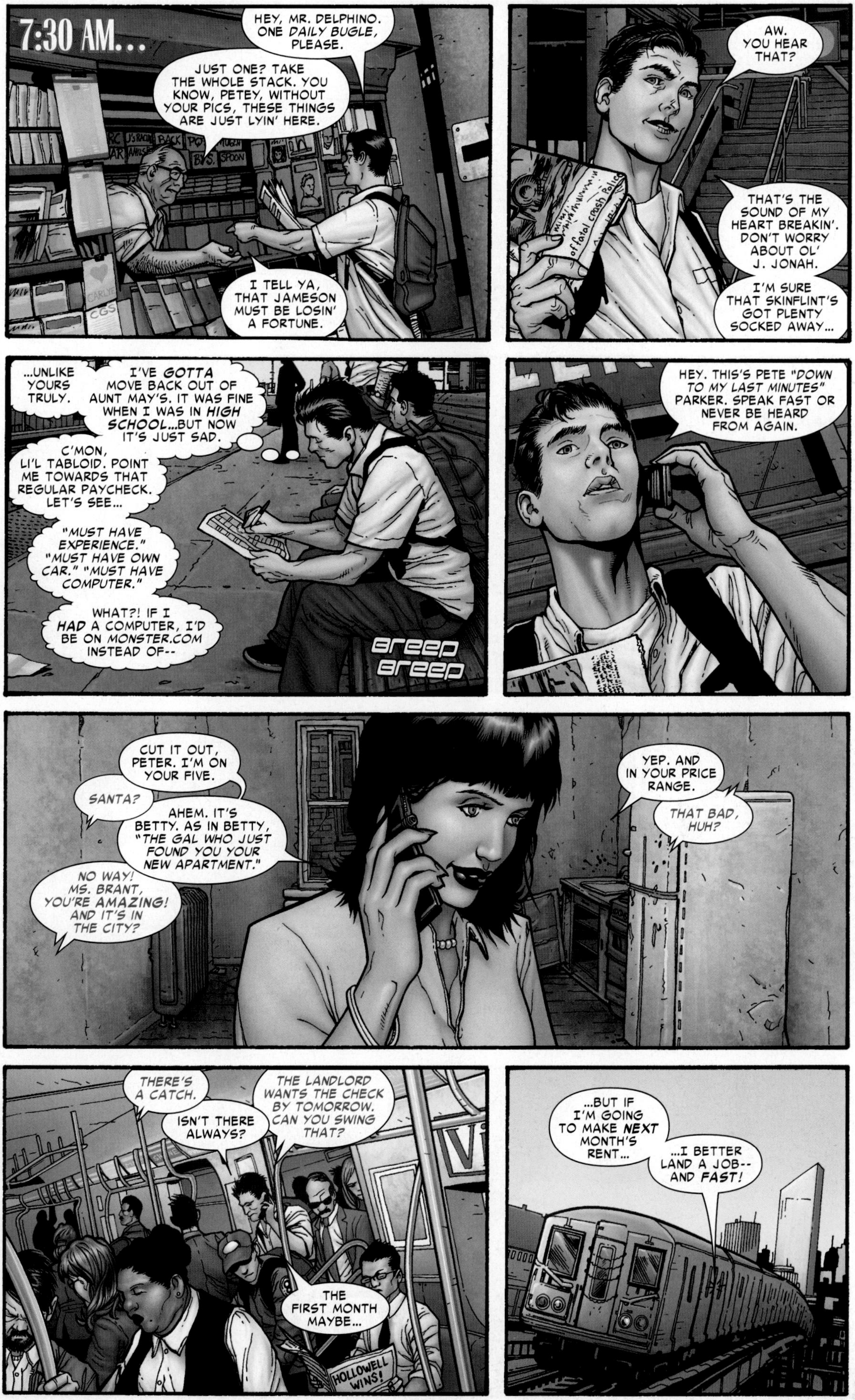

7:30 AM...
HEY, MR. DELPHINO. ONE DAILY BUGLE, PLEASE.
JUST ONE? TAKE THE WHOLE STACK. YOU KNOW, PETEY, WITHOUT YOUR PICS, THESE THINGS ARE JUST LYIN' HERE.
I TELL YA, THAT JAMESON MUST BE LOSIN' A FORTUNE.
AW. YOU HEAR THAT?
THAT'S THE SOUND OF MY HEART BREAKIN'. DON'T WORRY ABOUT OL' J. JONAH.
I'M SURE THAT SKINFLINT'S GOT PLENTY SOCKED AWAY...
...UNLIKE YOURS TRULY.
I'VE GOTTA MOVE BACK OUT OF AUNT MAY'S. IT WAS FINE WHEN I WAS IN HIGH SCHOOL...BUT NOW IT'S JUST SAD.
C'MON, LI'L TABLOID. POINT ME TOWARDS THAT REGULAR PAYCHECK. LET'S SEE...
"MUST HAVE EXPERIENCE." "MUST HAVE OWN CAR." "MUST HAVE COMPUTER."
WHAT?! IF I HAD A COMPUTER, I'D BE ON MONSTER.COM INSTEAD OF--
BREEP BREEP
HEY. THIS'S PETE "DOWN TO MY LAST MINUTES" PARKER. SPEAK FAST OR NEVER BE HEARD FROM AGAIN.
CUT IT OUT, PETER. I'M ON YOUR FIVE.
SANTA?
AHEM. IT'S BETTY. AS IN BETTY, "THE GAL WHO JUST FOUND YOU YOUR NEW APARTMENT."
NO WAY! MS. BRANT, YOU'RE AMAZING! AND IT'S IN THE CITY?
YEP. AND IN YOUR PRICE RANGE.
THAT BAD, HUH?
THERE'S A CATCH.
ISN'T THERE ALWAYS?
THE LANDLORD WANTS THE CHECK BY TOMORROW. CAN YOU SWING THAT?
THE FIRST MONTH MAYBE...
HOLLOWELL WINS!
...BUT IF I'M GOING TO MAKE NEXT MONTH'S RENT...
...I BETTER LAND A JOB-- AND FAST!

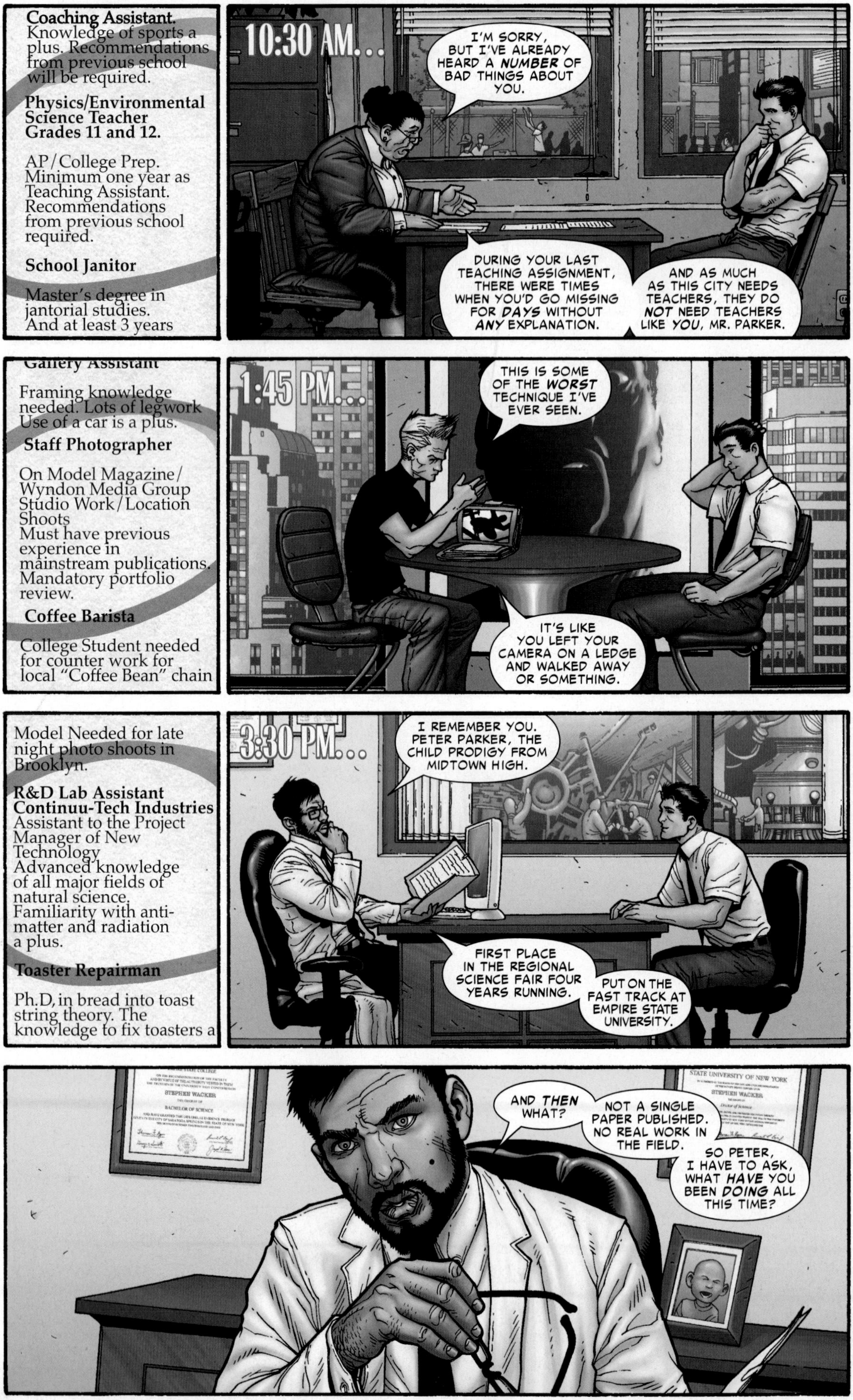
Coaching Assistant.
Knowledge of sports a plus. Recommendations from previous school will be required.
Physics/Environmental Science Teacher Grades 11 and 12.
AP/College Prep. Minimum one year as Teaching Assistant. Recommendations from previous school required.
School Janitor
Master's degree in jantorial studies. And at least 3 years
10:30 AM...
I'M SORRY, BUT I'VE ALREADY HEARD A NUMBER OF BAD THINGS ABOUT YOU.
DURING YOUR LAST TEACHING ASSIGNMENT, THERE WERE TIMES WHEN YOU'D GO MISSING FOR DAYS WITHOUT ANY EXPLANATION.
AND AS MUCH AS THIS CITY NEEDS TEACHERS, THEY DO NOT NEED TEACHERS LIKE YOU, MR. PARKER.
Gallery Assistant
Framing knowledge needed. Lots of legwork Use of a car is a plus.
Staff Photographer
On Model Magazine/ Wyndon Media Group Studio Work/Location Shoots
Must have previous experience in mainstream publications. Mandatory portfolio review.
Coffee Barista
College Student needed for counter work for local "Coffee Bean" chain
1:45 PM...
THIS IS SOME OF THE WORST TECHNIQUE I'VE EVER SEEN.
IT'S LIKE YOU LEFT YOUR CAMERA ON A LEDGE AND WALKED AWAY OR SOMETHING.
Model Needed for late night photo shoots in Brooklyn.
R&D Lab Assistant Continuu-Tech Industries
Assistant to the Project Manager of New Technology
Advanced knowledge of all major fields of natural science. Familiarity with anti-matter and radiation a plus.
Toaster Repairman
Ph.D, in bread into toast string theory. The knowledge to fix toasters a
3:30 PM...
I REMEMBER YOU. PETER PARKER, THE CHILD PRODIGY FROM MIDTOWN HIGH.
FIRST PLACE IN THE REGIONAL SCIENCE FAIR FOUR YEARS RUNNING.
PUT ON THE FAST TRACK AT EMPIRE STATE UNIVERSITY.
STEPHEN WACKER
BACHELOR OF SCIENCE
STATE UNIVERSITY OF NEW YORK
STEPHEN WACKER
AND THEN WHAT?
NOT A SINGLE PAPER PUBLISHED. NO REAL WORK IN THE FIELD.
SO PETER, I HAVE TO ASK, WHAT HAVE YOU BEEN DOING ALL THIS TIME?

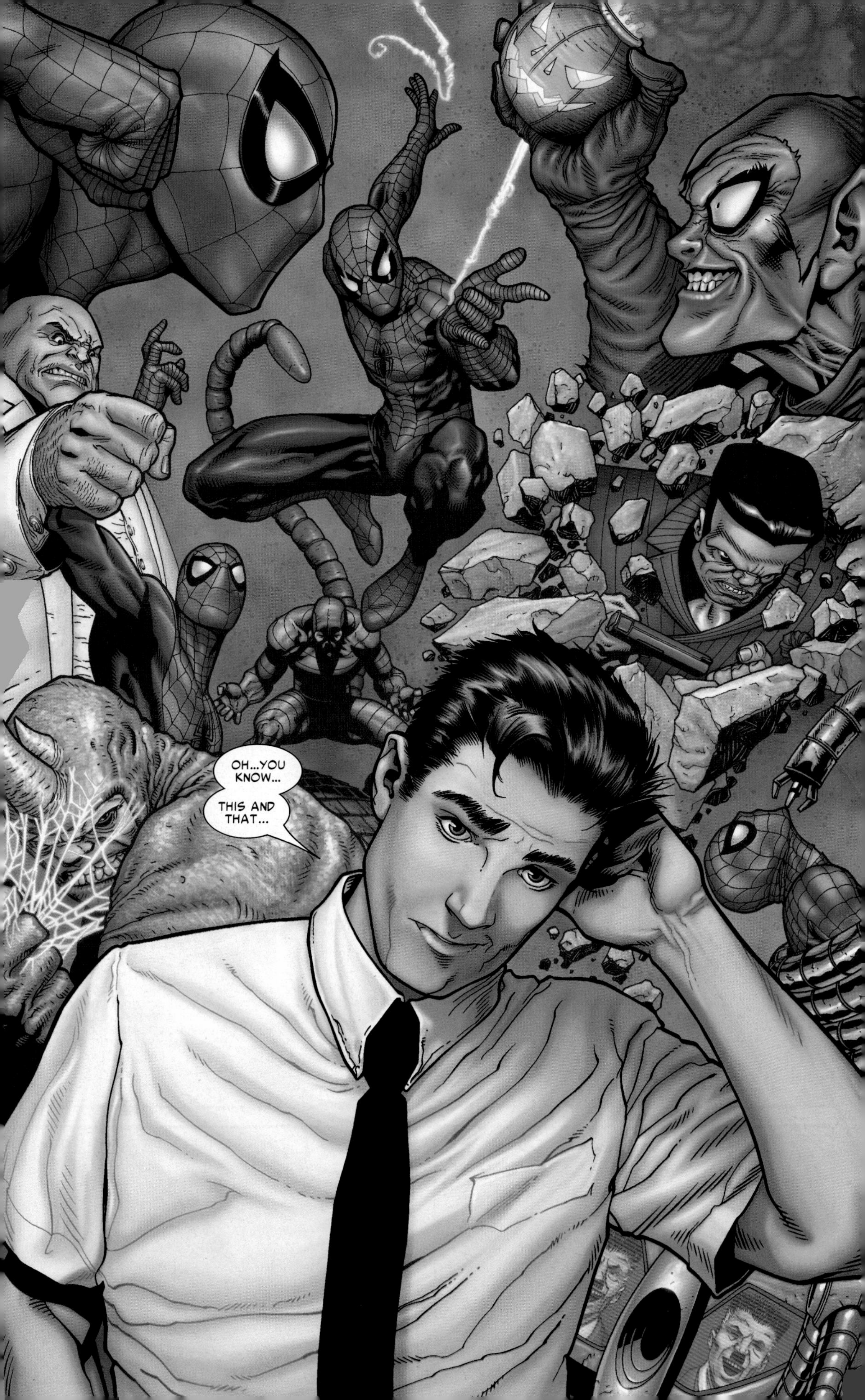
OH...YOU KNOW...
THIS AND THAT...

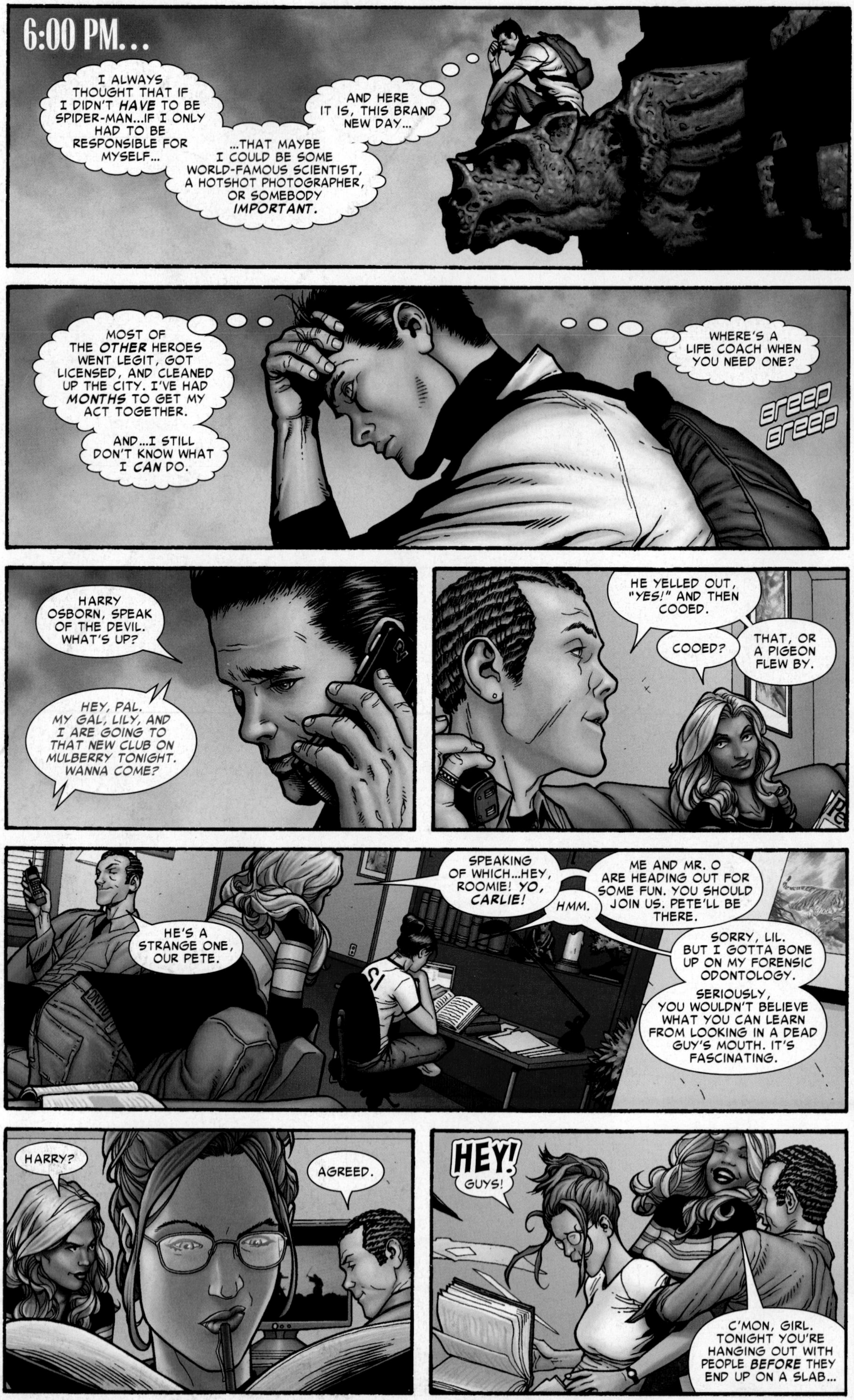
6:00 PM...
I ALWAYS THOUGHT THAT IF I DIDN'T HAVE TO BE SPIDER-MAN...IF I ONLY HAD TO BE RESPONSIBLE FOR MYSELF...
...THAT MAYBE I COULD BE SOME WORLD-FAMOUS SCIENTIST, A HOTSHOT PHOTOGRAPHER, OR SOMEBODY IMPORTANT.
AND HERE IT IS, THIS BRAND NEW DAY...
MOST OF THE OTHER HEROES WENT LEGIT, GOT LICENSED, AND CLEANED UP THE CITY. I'VE HAD MONTHS TO GET MY ACT TOGETHER.
AND...I STILL DON'T KNOW WHAT I CAN DO.
WHERE'S A LIFE COACH WHEN YOU NEED ONE?
BREEP BREEP
HARRY OSBORN, SPEAK OF THE DEVIL. WHAT'S UP?
HEY, PAL. MY GAL, LILY, AND I ARE GOING TO THAT NEW CLUB ON MULBERRY TONIGHT. WANNA COME?
HE YELLED OUT, "YES!" AND THEN COOED.
COOED?
THAT, OR A PIGEON FLEW BY.
HE'S A STRANGE ONE, OUR PETE.
SPEAKING OF WHICH...HEY, ROOMIE! YO, CARLIE!
ME AND MR. O ARE HEADING OUT FOR SOME FUN. YOU SHOULD JOIN US. PETE'LL BE THERE.
HMM.
SORRY, LIL. BUT I GOTTA BONE UP ON MY FORENSIC ODONTOLOGY.
SERIOUSLY, YOU WOULDN'T BELIEVE WHAT YOU CAN LEARN FROM LOOKING IN A DEAD GUY'S MOUTH. IT'S FASCINATING.
HARRY?
AGREED.
HEY! GUYS!
C'MON, GIRL. TONIGHT YOU'RE HANGING OUT WITH PEOPLE BEFORE THEY END UP ON A SLAB...

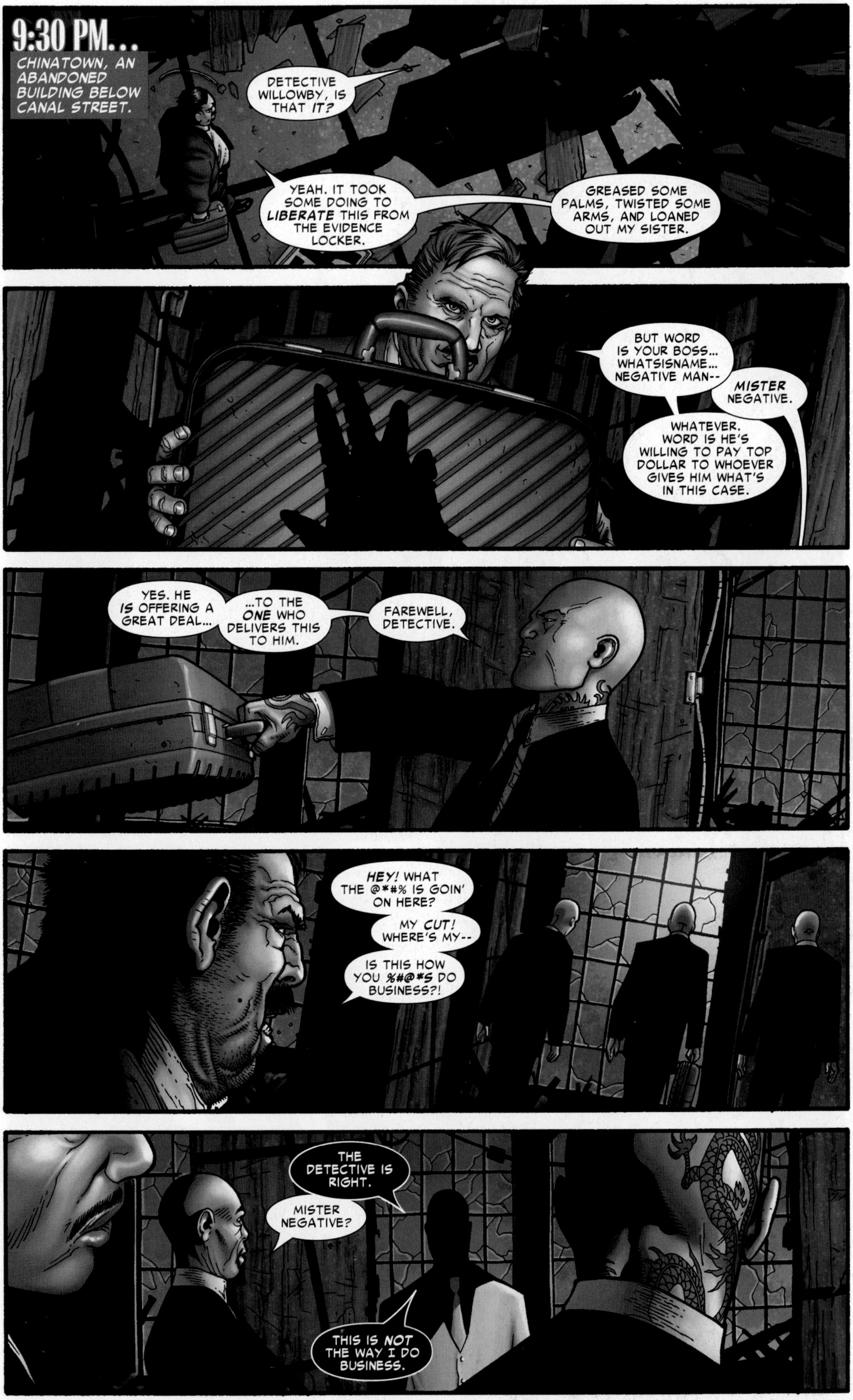
9:30 PM...
CHINATOWN, AN ABANDONED BUILDING BELOW CANAL STREET.
DETECTIVE WILLOWBY, IS THAT IT?
YEAH. IT TOOK SOME DOING TO LIBERATE THIS FROM THE EVIDENCE LOCKER.
GREASED SOME PALMS, TWISTED SOME ARMS, AND LOANED OUT MY SISTER.
BUT WORD IS YOUR BOSS... WHATSISNAME... NEGATIVE MAN--
MISTER NEGATIVE.
WHATEVER. WORD IS HE'S WILLING TO PAY TOP DOLLAR TO WHOEVER GIVES HIM WHAT'S IN THIS CASE.
YES. HE IS OFFERING A GREAT DEAL...
...TO THE ONE WHO DELIVERS THIS TO HIM.
FAREWELL, DETECTIVE.
HEY! WHAT THE @*#% IS GOIN' ON HERE?
MY CUT! WHERE'S MY--
IS THIS HOW YOU %#@*S DO BUSINESS?!
THE DETECTIVE IS RIGHT.
MISTER NEGATIVE?
THIS IS NOT THE WAY I DO BUSINESS.

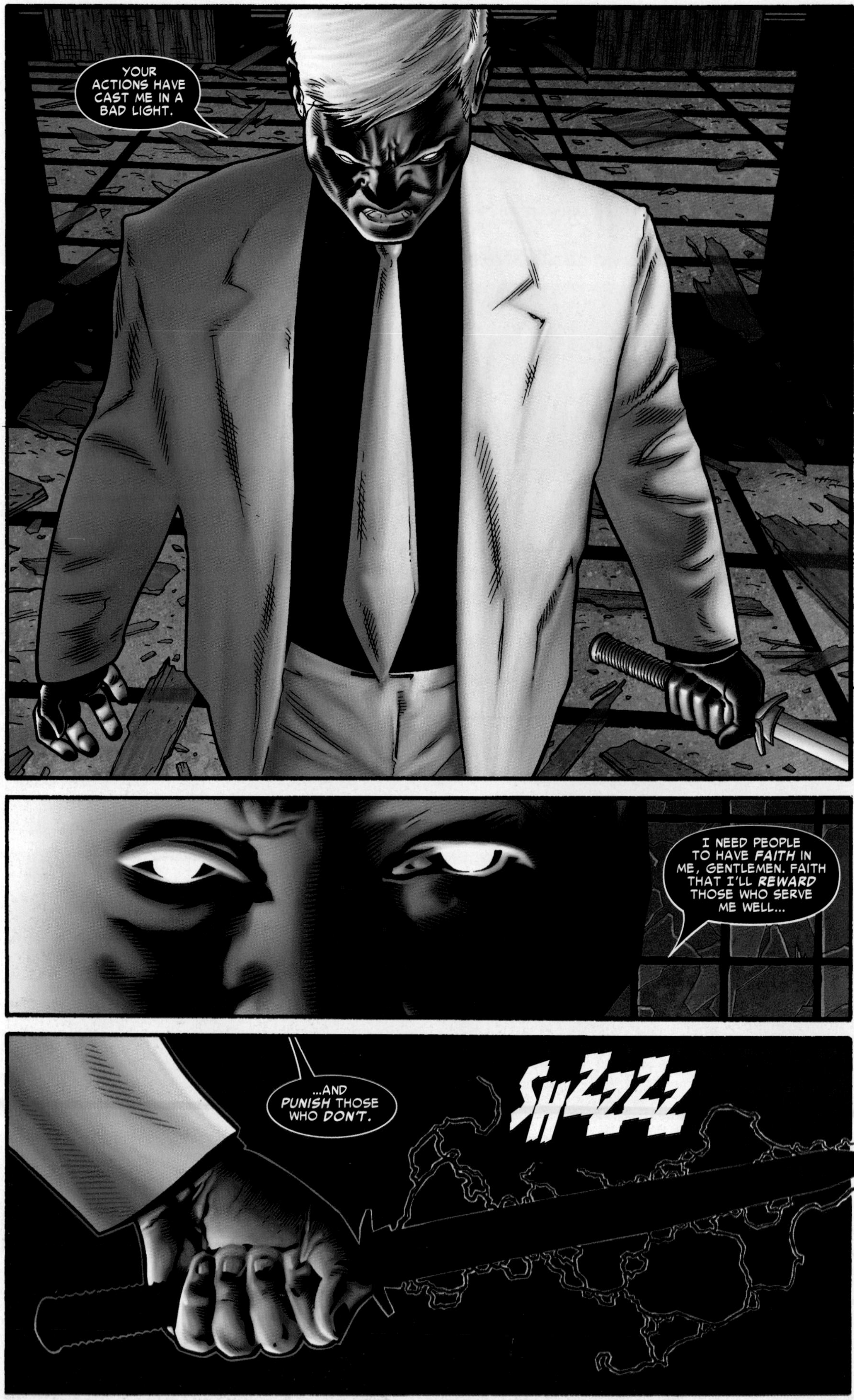
YOUR ACTIONS HAVE CAST ME IN A BAD LIGHT.
I NEED PEOPLE TO HAVE *FAITH* IN ME, GENTLEMEN. FAITH THAT I'LL *REWARD* THOSE WHO SERVE ME WELL...
...AND *PUNISH* THOSE WHO *DON'T*.
SHZZZZ

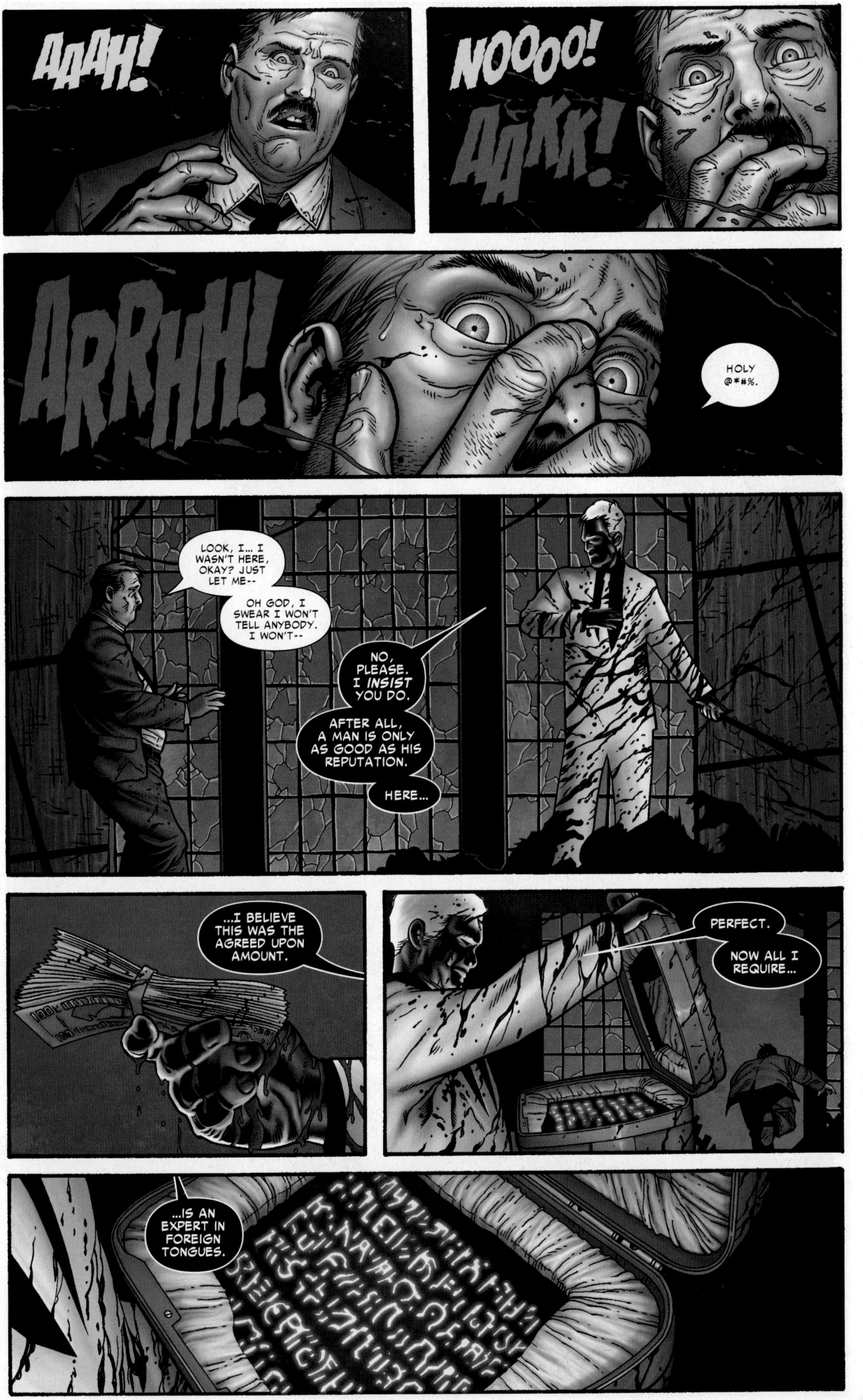
AAAH!
NOOOO!
AAKK!
ARRHH!
HOLY @*#%.
LOOK, I... I WASN'T HERE, OKAY? JUST LET ME--
OH GOD, I SWEAR I WON'T TELL ANYBODY. I WON'T--
NO, PLEASE. I INSIST YOU DO.
AFTER ALL, A MAN IS ONLY AS GOOD AS HIS REPUTATION.
HERE...
...I BELIEVE THIS WAS THE AGREED UPON AMOUNT.
PERFECT.
NOW ALL I REQUIRE...
...IS AN EXPERT IN FOREIGN TONGUES.

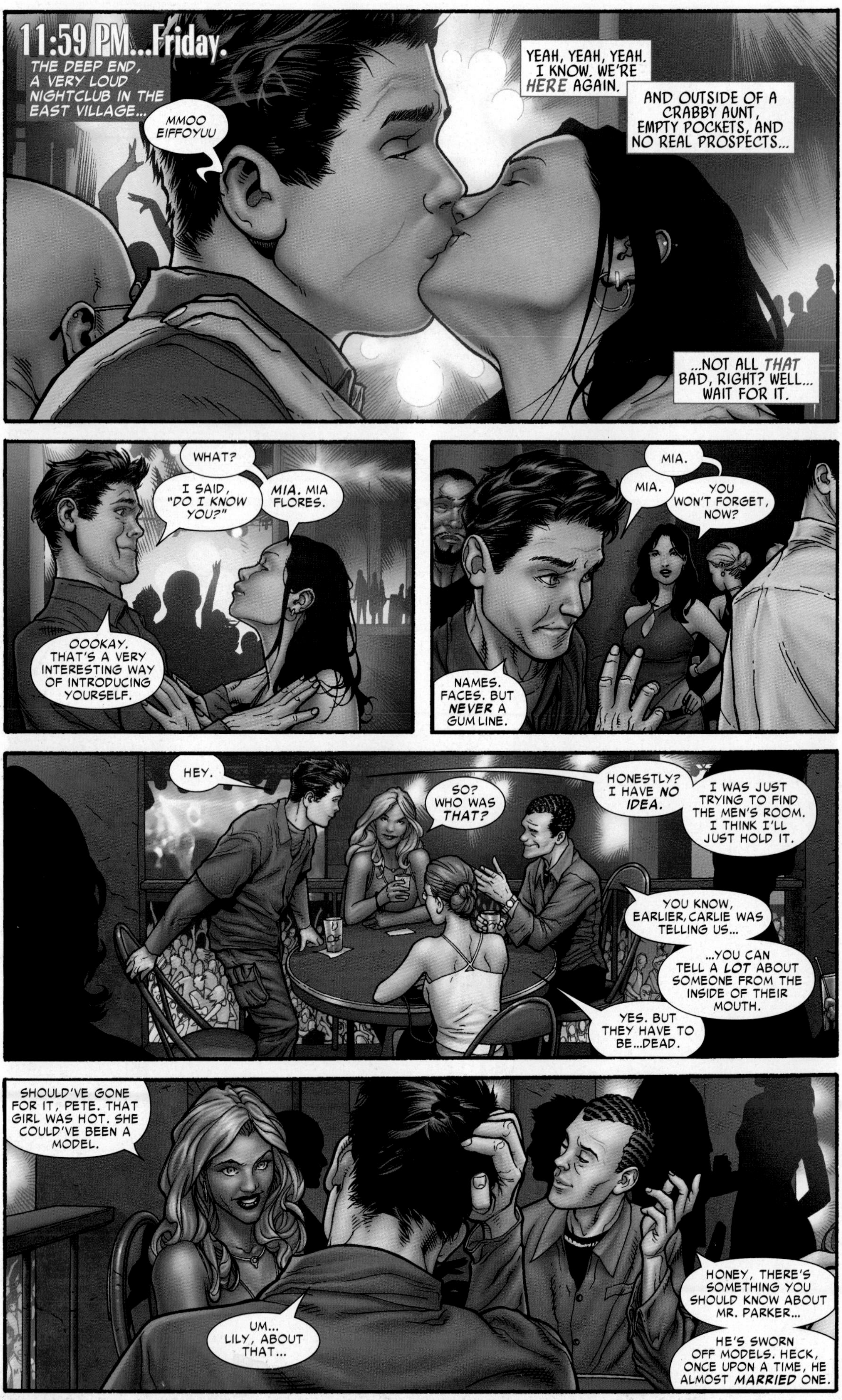
11:59 PM...Friday.
THE DEEP END, A VERY LOUD NIGHTCLUB IN THE EAST VILLAGE...
MMOO EIFFOYUU
YEAH, YEAH, YEAH. I KNOW. WE'RE HERE AGAIN.
AND OUTSIDE OF A CRABBY AUNT, EMPTY POCKETS, AND NO REAL PROSPECTS...
...NOT ALL THAT BAD, RIGHT? WELL... WAIT FOR IT.
WHAT?
I SAID, "DO I KNOW YOU?"
MIA. MIA FLORES.
OOOKAY. THAT'S A VERY INTERESTING WAY OF INTRODUCING YOURSELF.
MIA.
MIA.
YOU WON'T FORGET, NOW?
NAMES. FACES. BUT NEVER A GUM LINE.
HEY.
SO? WHO WAS THAT?
HONESTLY? I HAVE NO IDEA.
I WAS JUST TRYING TO FIND THE MEN'S ROOM. I THINK I'LL JUST HOLD IT.
YOU KNOW, EARLIER, CARLIE WAS TELLING US...
...YOU CAN TELL A LOT ABOUT SOMEONE FROM THE INSIDE OF THEIR MOUTH.
YES. BUT THEY HAVE TO BE...DEAD.
SHOULD'VE GONE FOR IT, PETE. THAT GIRL WAS HOT. SHE COULD'VE BEEN A MODEL.
UM... LILY, ABOUT THAT...
HONEY, THERE'S SOMETHING YOU SHOULD KNOW ABOUT MR. PARKER...
HE'S SWORN OFF MODELS. HECK, ONCE UPON A TIME, HE ALMOST MARRIED ONE.

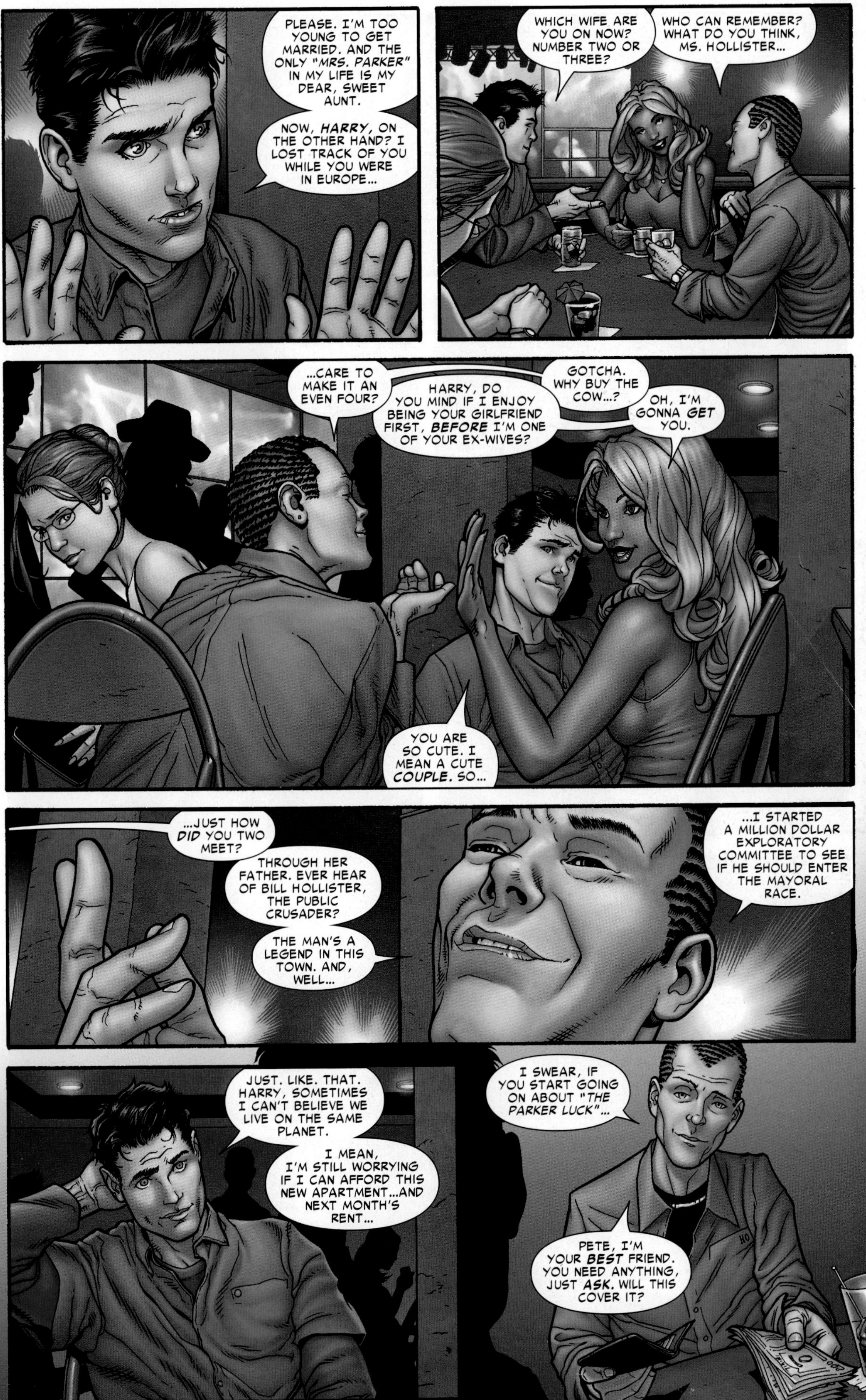
PLEASE. I'M TOO YOUNG TO GET MARRIED. AND THE ONLY "MRS. PARKER" IN MY LIFE IS MY DEAR, SWEET AUNT.
NOW, HARRY, ON THE OTHER HAND? I LOST TRACK OF YOU WHILE YOU WERE IN EUROPE...
WHICH WIFE ARE YOU ON NOW? NUMBER TWO OR THREE?
WHO CAN REMEMBER? WHAT DO YOU THINK, MS. HOLLISTER...
...CARE TO MAKE IT AN EVEN FOUR?
HARRY, DO YOU MIND IF I ENJOY BEING YOUR GIRLFRIEND FIRST, BEFORE I'M ONE OF YOUR EX-WIVES?
GOTCHA. WHY BUY THE COW...?
OH, I'M GONNA GET YOU.
YOU ARE SO CUTE. I MEAN A CUTE COUPLE. SO...
...JUST HOW DID YOU TWO MEET?
THROUGH HER FATHER. EVER HEAR OF BILL HOLLISTER, THE PUBLIC CRUSADER?
THE MAN'S A LEGEND IN THIS TOWN. AND, WELL...
...I STARTED A MILLION DOLLAR EXPLORATORY COMMITTEE TO SEE IF HE SHOULD ENTER THE MAYORAL RACE.
JUST. LIKE. THAT. HARRY, SOMETIMES I CAN'T BELIEVE WE LIVE ON THE SAME PLANET.
I MEAN, I'M STILL WORRYING IF I CAN AFFORD THIS NEW APARTMENT...AND NEXT MONTH'S RENT...
I SWEAR, IF YOU START GOING ON ABOUT "THE PARKER LUCK"...
PETE, I'M YOUR BEST FRIEND. YOU NEED ANYTHING, JUST ASK. WILL THIS COVER IT?

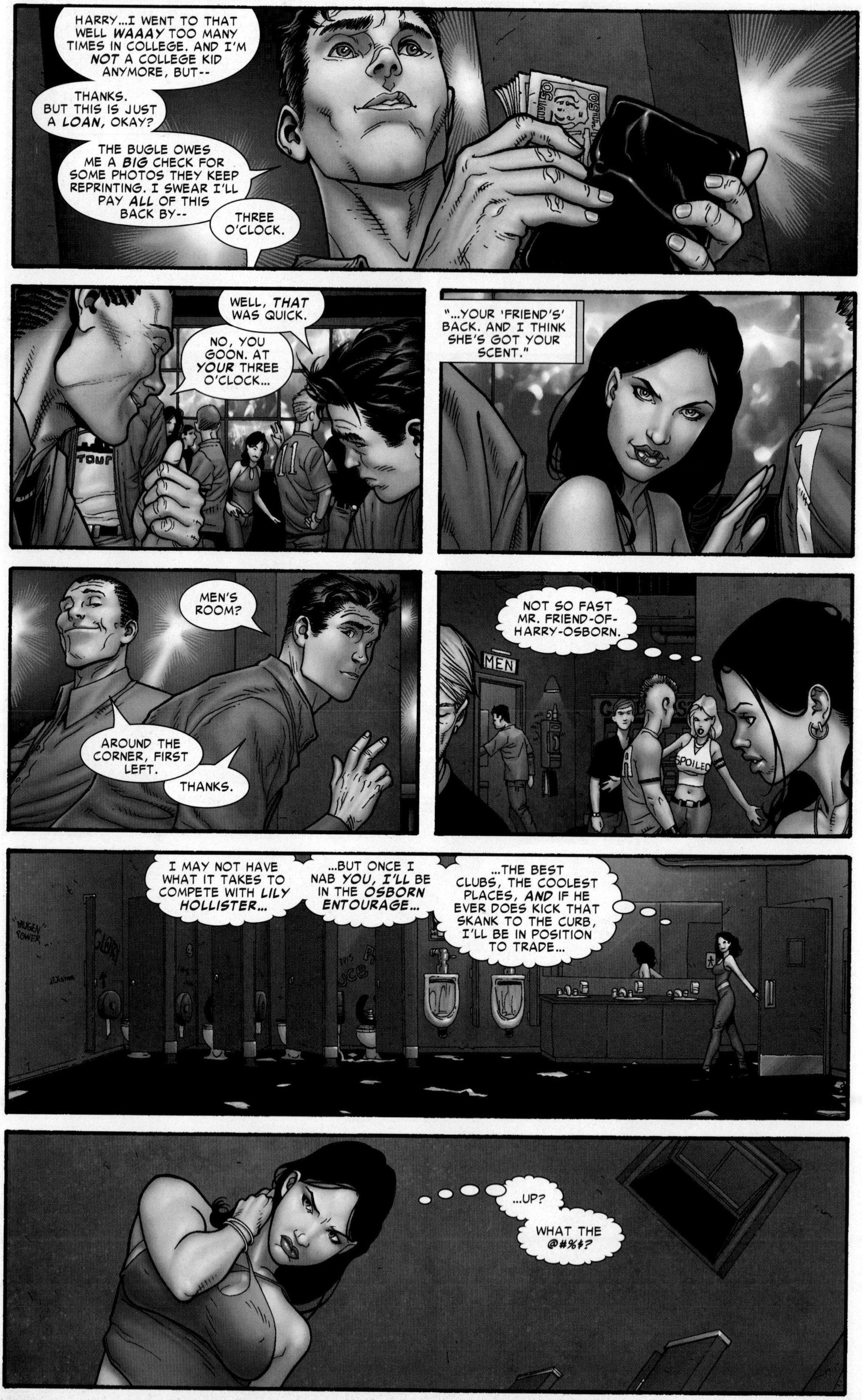

HARRY...I WENT TO THAT WELL WAAAY TOO MANY TIMES IN COLLEGE. AND I'M NOT A COLLEGE KID ANYMORE, BUT--
THANKS. BUT THIS IS JUST A LOAN, OKAY?
THE BUGLE OWES ME A BIG CHECK FOR SOME PHOTOS THEY KEEP REPRINTING. I SWEAR I'LL PAY ALL OF THIS BACK BY--
THREE O'CLOCK.
WELL, THAT WAS QUICK.
NO, YOU GOON. AT YOUR THREE O'CLOCK...
"...YOUR 'FRIEND'S' BACK. AND I THINK SHE'S GOT YOUR SCENT."
MEN'S ROOM?
AROUND THE CORNER, FIRST LEFT.
THANKS.
NOT SO FAST MR. FRIEND-OF-HARRY-OSBORN.
MEN
SPOILED
I MAY NOT HAVE WHAT IT TAKES TO COMPETE WITH LILY HOLLISTER...
...BUT ONCE I NAB YOU, I'LL BE IN THE OSBORN ENTOURAGE...
...THE BEST CLUBS, THE COOLEST PLACES, AND IF HE EVER DOES KICK THAT SKANK TO THE CURB, I'LL BE IN POSITION TO TRADE...
...UP?
WHAT THE @#%$?

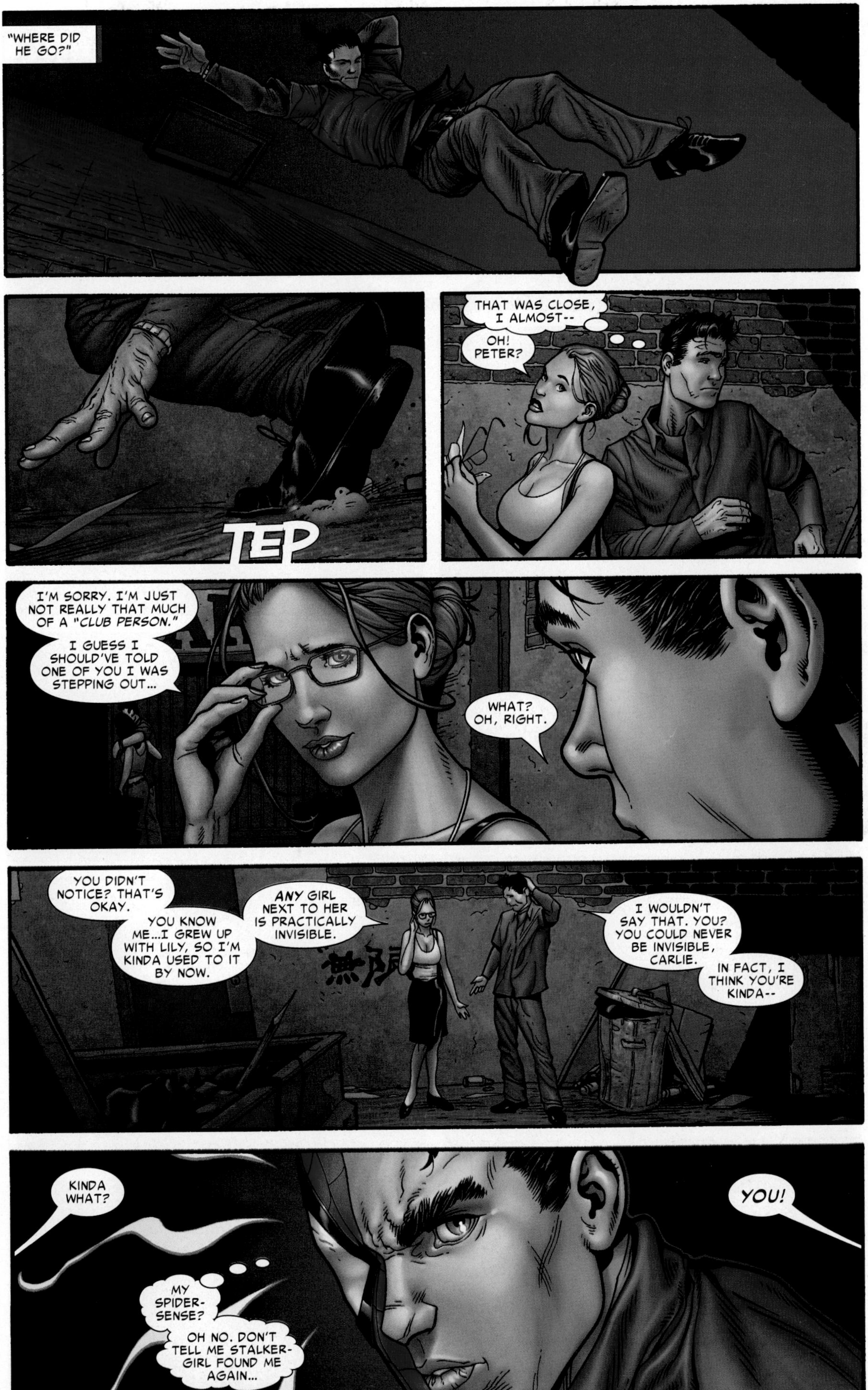
"WHERE DID HE GO?"
TEP
THAT WAS CLOSE, I ALMOST--
OH! PETER?
I'M SORRY. I'M JUST NOT REALLY THAT MUCH OF A "CLUB PERSON."
I GUESS I SHOULD'VE TOLD ONE OF YOU I WAS STEPPING OUT...
WHAT? OH, RIGHT.
YOU DIDN'T NOTICE? THAT'S OKAY.
YOU KNOW ME...I GREW UP WITH LILY, SO I'M KINDA USED TO IT BY NOW.
ANY GIRL NEXT TO HER IS PRACTICALLY INVISIBLE.
I WOULDN'T SAY THAT. YOU? YOU COULD NEVER BE INVISIBLE, CARLIE.
IN FACT, I THINK YOU'RE KINDA--
KINDA WHAT?
YOU!
MY SPIDER-SENSE?
OH NO. DON'T TELL ME STALKER-GIRL FOUND ME AGAIN...

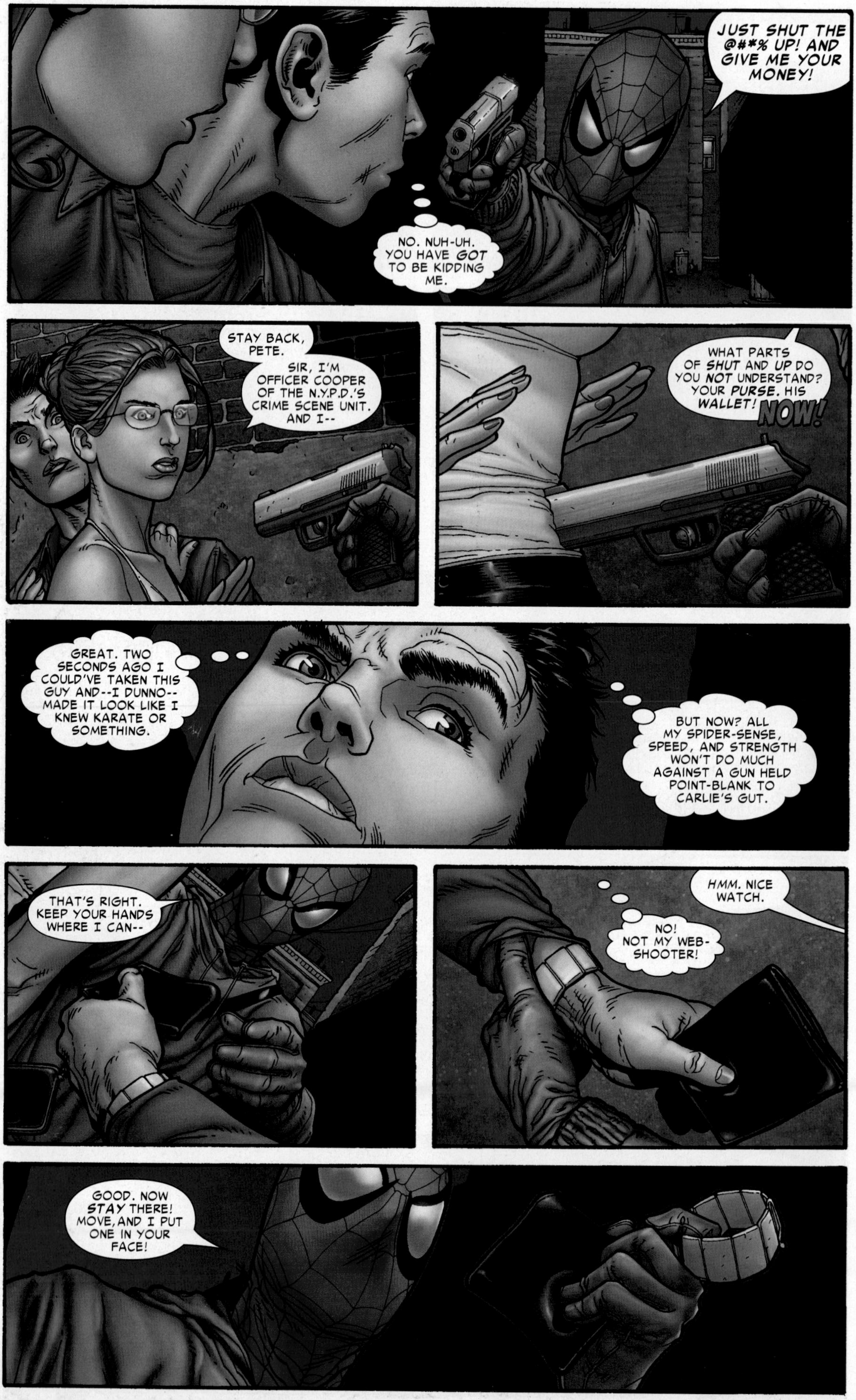
JUST SHUT THE @#*% UP! AND GIVE ME YOUR MONEY!
NO. NUH-UH. YOU HAVE GOT TO BE KIDDING ME.
STAY BACK, PETE.
SIR, I'M OFFICER COOPER OF THE N.Y.P.D.'S CRIME SCENE UNIT. AND I--
WHAT PARTS OF SHUT AND UP DO YOU NOT UNDERSTAND? YOUR PURSE. HIS WALLET! NOW!
GREAT. TWO SECONDS AGO I COULD'VE TAKEN THIS GUY AND--I DUNNO--MADE IT LOOK LIKE I KNEW KARATE OR SOMETHING.
BUT NOW? ALL MY SPIDER-SENSE, SPEED, AND STRENGTH WON'T DO MUCH AGAINST A GUN HELD POINT-BLANK TO CARLIE'S GUT.
THAT'S RIGHT. KEEP YOUR HANDS WHERE I CAN--
HMM. NICE WATCH.
NO! NOT MY WEB-SHOOTER!
GOOD. NOW STAY THERE! MOVE, AND I PUT ONE IN YOUR FACE!

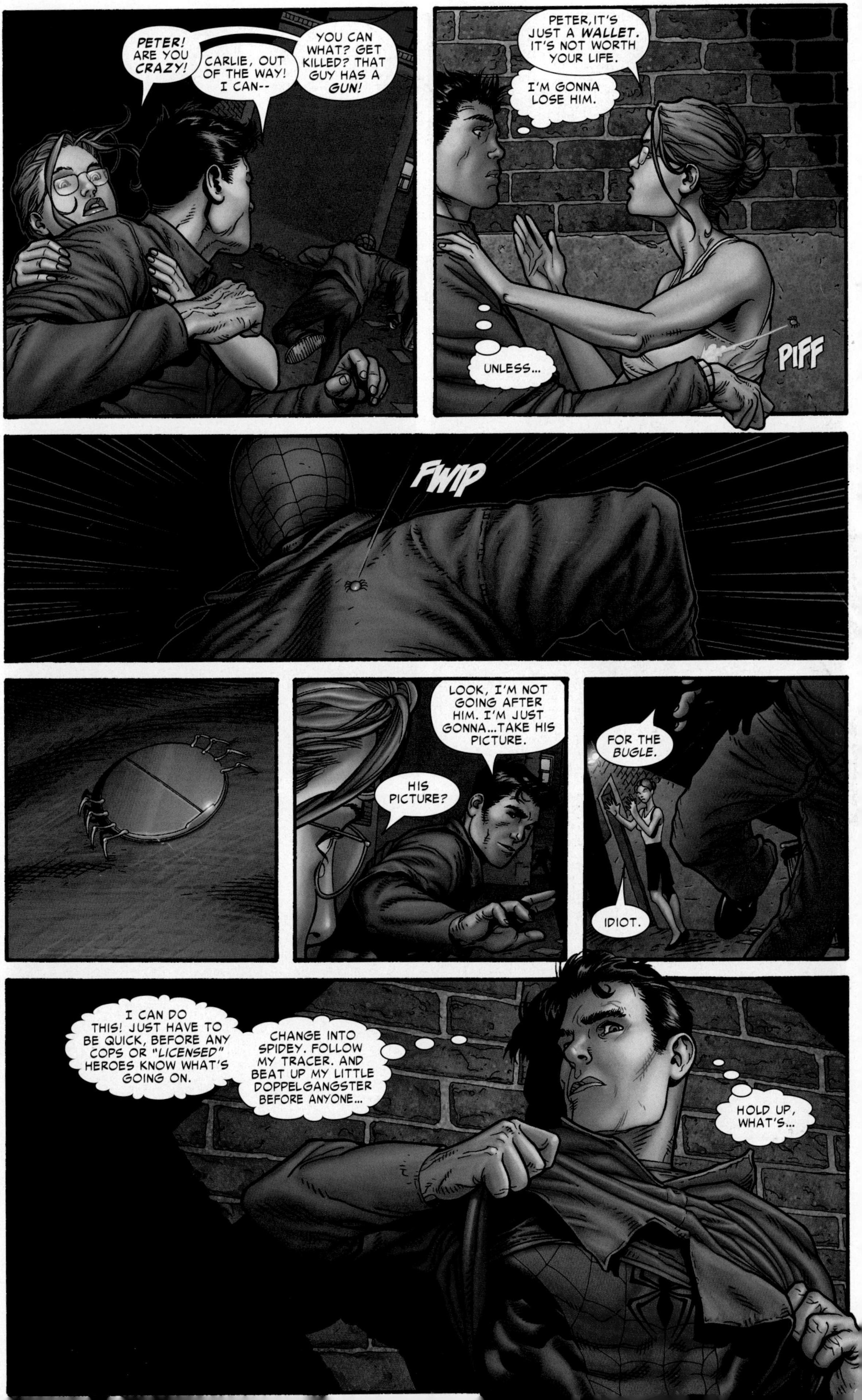
PETER! ARE YOU CRAZY!
CARLIE, OUT OF THE WAY! I CAN--
YOU CAN WHAT? GET KILLED? THAT GUY HAS A GUN!
PETER, IT'S JUST A WALLET. IT'S NOT WORTH YOUR LIFE.
I'M GONNA LOSE HIM.
UNLESS...
PIFF
FWIP
LOOK, I'M NOT GOING AFTER HIM. I'M JUST GONNA...TAKE HIS PICTURE.
HIS PICTURE?
FOR THE BUGLE.
IDIOT.
I CAN DO THIS! JUST HAVE TO BE QUICK, BEFORE ANY COPS OR "LICENSED" HEROES KNOW WHAT'S GOING ON.
CHANGE INTO SPIDEY. FOLLOW MY TRACER. AND BEAT UP MY LITTLE DOPPELGANGSTER BEFORE ANYONE...
HOLD UP, WHAT'S...

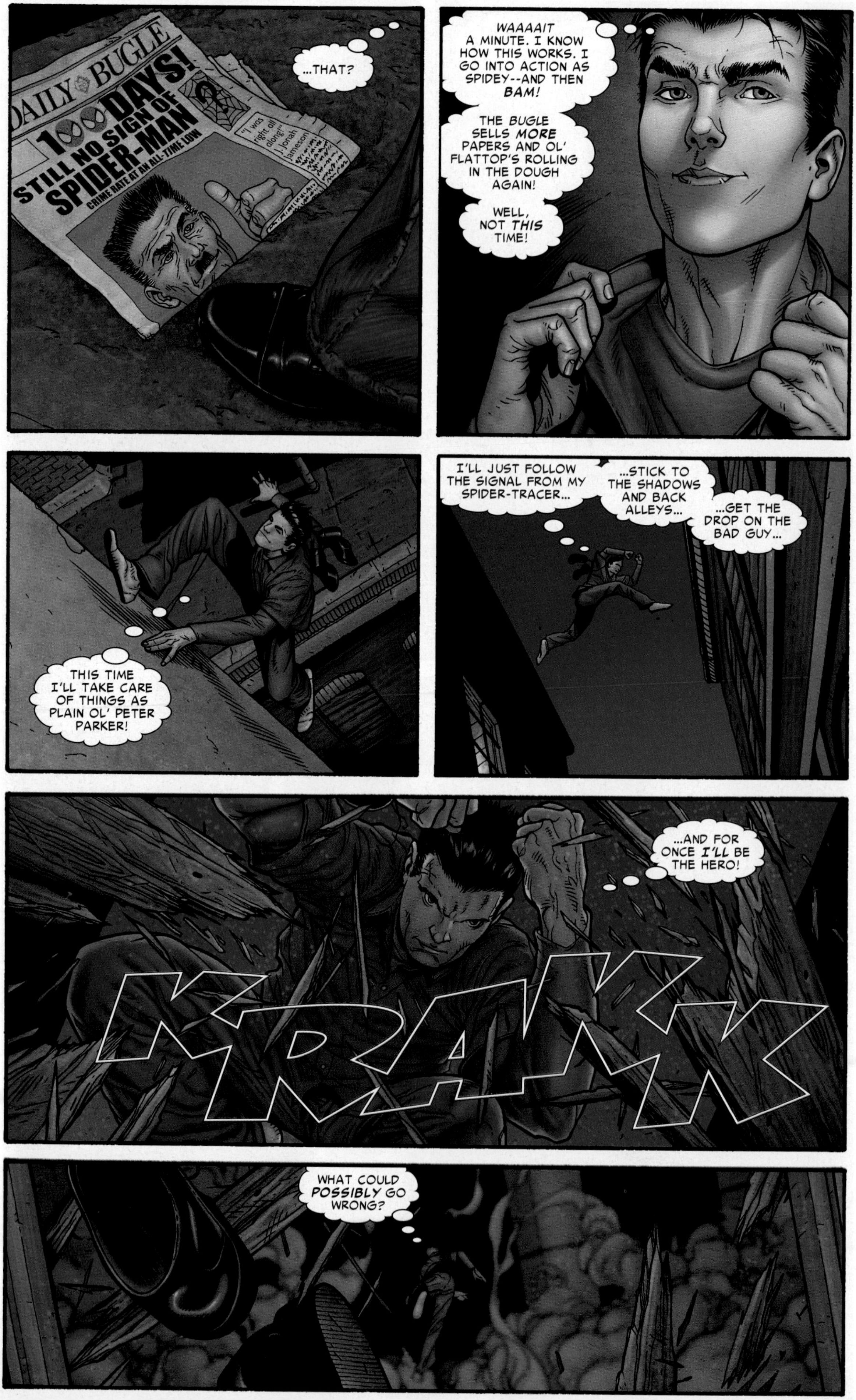
DAILY BUGLE
100 DAYS!
STILL NO SIGN OF SPIDER-MAN
CRIME RATE AT AN ALL-TIME LOW
"I was right all along!" J. Jonah Jameson
...THAT?
WAAAAIT A MINUTE. I KNOW HOW THIS WORKS. I GO INTO ACTION AS SPIDEY--AND THEN BAM!
THE BUGLE SELLS MORE PAPERS AND OL' FLATTOP'S ROLLING IN THE DOUGH AGAIN!
WELL, NOT THIS TIME!
THIS TIME I'LL TAKE CARE OF THINGS AS PLAIN OL' PETER PARKER!
I'LL JUST FOLLOW THE SIGNAL FROM MY SPIDER-TRACER...
...STICK TO THE SHADOWS AND BACK ALLEYS...
...GET THE DROP ON THE BAD GUY...
...AND FOR ONCE I'LL BE THE HERO!
KRAKK
WHAT COULD POSSIBLY GO WRONG?

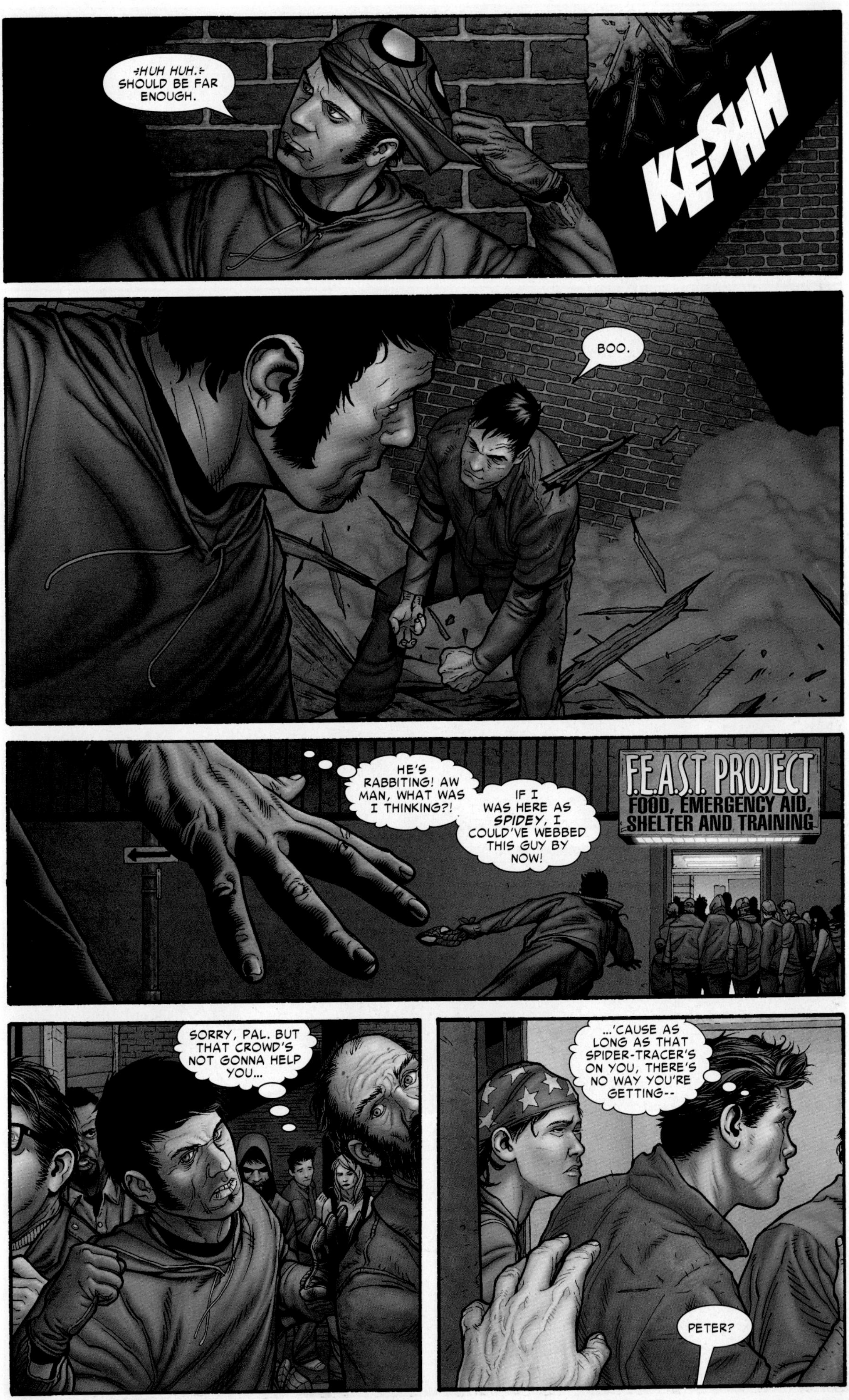
HUH HUH. SHOULD BE FAR ENOUGH.
KESHH
BOO.
HE'S RABBITING! AW MAN, WHAT WAS I THINKING?!
IF I WAS HERE AS SPIDEY, I COULD'VE WEBBED THIS GUY BY NOW!
F.E.A.S.T. PROJECT
FOOD, EMERGENCY AID, SHELTER AND TRAINING
SORRY, PAL. BUT THAT CROWD'S NOT GONNA HELP YOU...
...'CAUSE AS LONG AS THAT SPIDER-TRACER'S ON YOU, THERE'S NO WAY YOU'RE GETTING--
PETER?

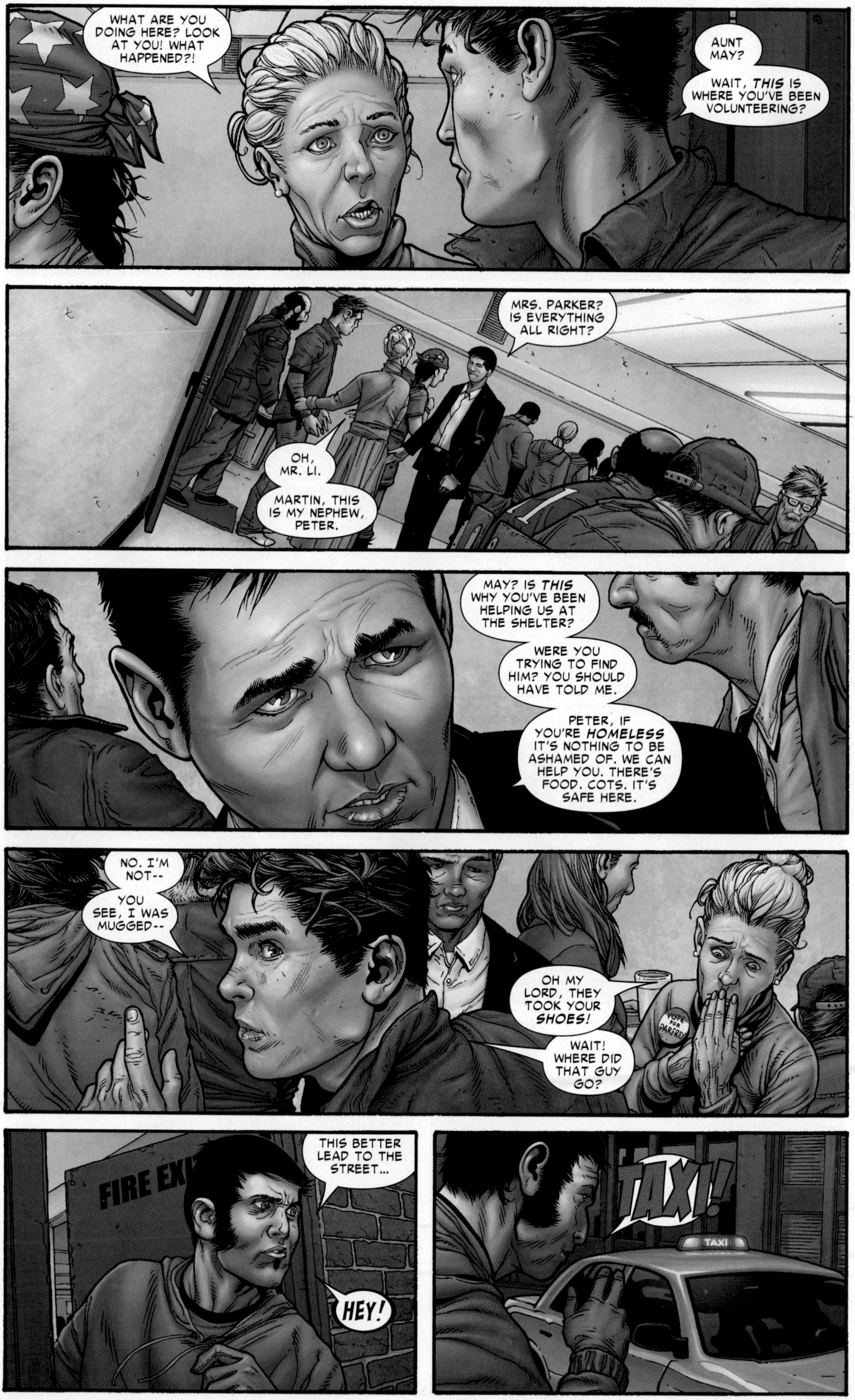
WHAT ARE YOU DOING HERE? LOOK AT YOU! WHAT HAPPENED?!
AUNT MAY?
WAIT, THIS IS WHERE YOU'VE BEEN VOLUNTEERING?
MRS. PARKER? IS EVERYTHING ALL RIGHT?
OH, MR. LI.
MARTIN, THIS IS MY NEPHEW, PETER.
MAY? IS THIS WHY YOU'VE BEEN HELPING US AT THE SHELTER?
WERE YOU TRYING TO FIND HIM? YOU SHOULD HAVE TOLD ME.
PETER, IF YOU'RE HOMELESS IT'S NOTHING TO BE ASHAMED OF. WE CAN HELP YOU. THERE'S FOOD. COTS. IT'S SAFE HERE.
NO. I'M NOT--
YOU SEE, I WAS MUGGED--
OH MY LORD, THEY TOOK YOUR SHOES!
WAIT! WHERE DID THAT GUY GO?
FIRE EX
THIS BETTER LEAD TO THE STREET...
HEY!
TAXI!
TAXI

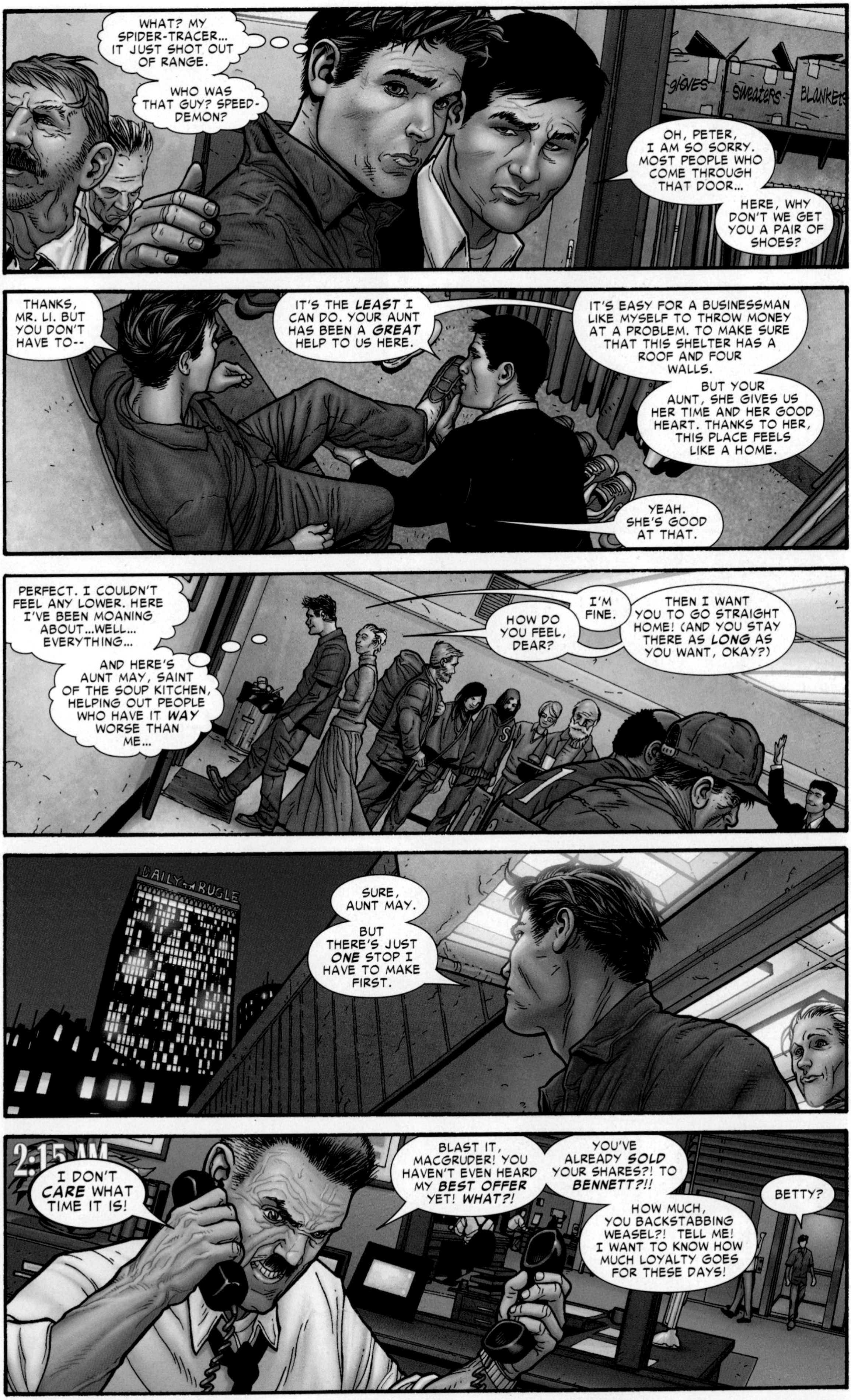
WHAT? MY SPIDER-TRACER... IT JUST SHOT OUT OF RANGE.
WHO WAS THAT GUY? SPEED-DEMON?
OH, PETER, I AM SO SORRY. MOST PEOPLE WHO COME THROUGH THAT DOOR...
HERE, WHY DON'T WE GET YOU A PAIR OF SHOES?
GLOVES
SWEATERS
BLANKETS
THANKS, MR. LI. BUT YOU DON'T HAVE TO--
IT'S THE LEAST I CAN DO. YOUR AUNT HAS BEEN A GREAT HELP TO US HERE.
IT'S EASY FOR A BUSINESSMAN LIKE MYSELF TO THROW MONEY AT A PROBLEM. TO MAKE SURE THAT THIS SHELTER HAS A ROOF AND FOUR WALLS.
BUT YOUR AUNT, SHE GIVES US HER TIME AND HER GOOD HEART. THANKS TO HER, THIS PLACE FEELS LIKE A HOME.
YEAH. SHE'S GOOD AT THAT.
PERFECT. I COULDN'T FEEL ANY LOWER. HERE I'VE BEEN MOANING ABOUT...WELL... EVERYTHING...
AND HERE'S AUNT MAY, SAINT OF THE SOUP KITCHEN, HELPING OUT PEOPLE WHO HAVE IT WAY WORSE THAN ME...
HOW DO YOU FEEL, DEAR?
I'M FINE.
THEN I WANT YOU TO GO STRAIGHT HOME! (AND YOU STAY THERE AS LONG AS YOU WANT, OKAY?)
DAILY BUGLE
SURE, AUNT MAY.
BUT THERE'S JUST ONE STOP I HAVE TO MAKE FIRST.
2:15 AM
I DON'T CARE WHAT TIME IT IS!
BLAST IT, MACGRUDER! YOU HAVEN'T EVEN HEARD MY BEST OFFER YET! WHAT?!
YOU'VE ALREADY SOLD YOUR SHARES?! TO BENNETT?!!
HOW MUCH, YOU BACKSTABBING WEASEL?! TELL ME! I WANT TO KNOW HOW MUCH LOYALTY GOES FOR THESE DAYS!
BETTY?

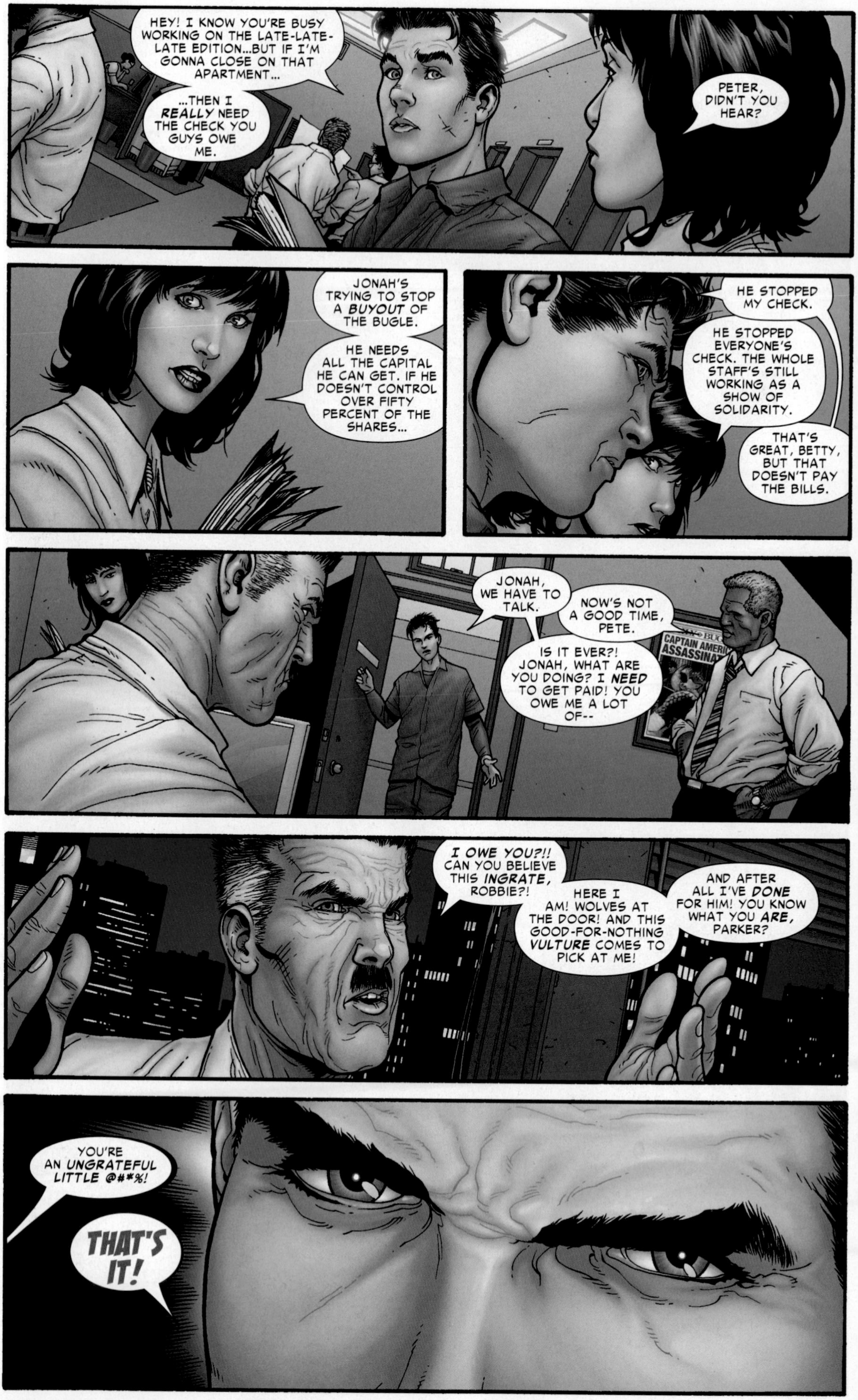
HEY! I KNOW YOU'RE BUSY WORKING ON THE LATE-LATE-LATE EDITION...BUT IF I'M GONNA CLOSE ON THAT APARTMENT...
...THEN I REALLY NEED THE CHECK YOU GUYS OWE ME.
PETER, DIDN'T YOU HEAR?
JONAH'S TRYING TO STOP A BUYOUT OF THE BUGLE.
HE NEEDS ALL THE CAPITAL HE CAN GET. IF HE DOESN'T CONTROL OVER FIFTY PERCENT OF THE SHARES...
HE STOPPED MY CHECK.
HE STOPPED EVERYONE'S CHECK. THE WHOLE STAFF'S STILL WORKING AS A SHOW OF SOLIDARITY.
THAT'S GREAT, BETTY, BUT THAT DOESN'T PAY THE BILLS.
JONAH, WE HAVE TO TALK.
NOW'S NOT A GOOD TIME, PETE.
IS IT EVER?! JONAH, WHAT ARE YOU DOING? I NEED TO GET PAID! YOU OWE ME A LOT OF--
CAPTAIN AMERIC
ASSASSINAT
I OWE YOU?!! CAN YOU BELIEVE THIS INGRATE, ROBBIE?!
HERE I AM! WOLVES AT THE DOOR! AND THIS GOOD-FOR-NOTHING VULTURE COMES TO PICK AT ME!
AND AFTER ALL I'VE DONE FOR HIM! YOU KNOW WHAT YOU ARE, PARKER?
YOU'RE AN UNGRATEFUL LITTLE @#*%!
THAT'S IT!

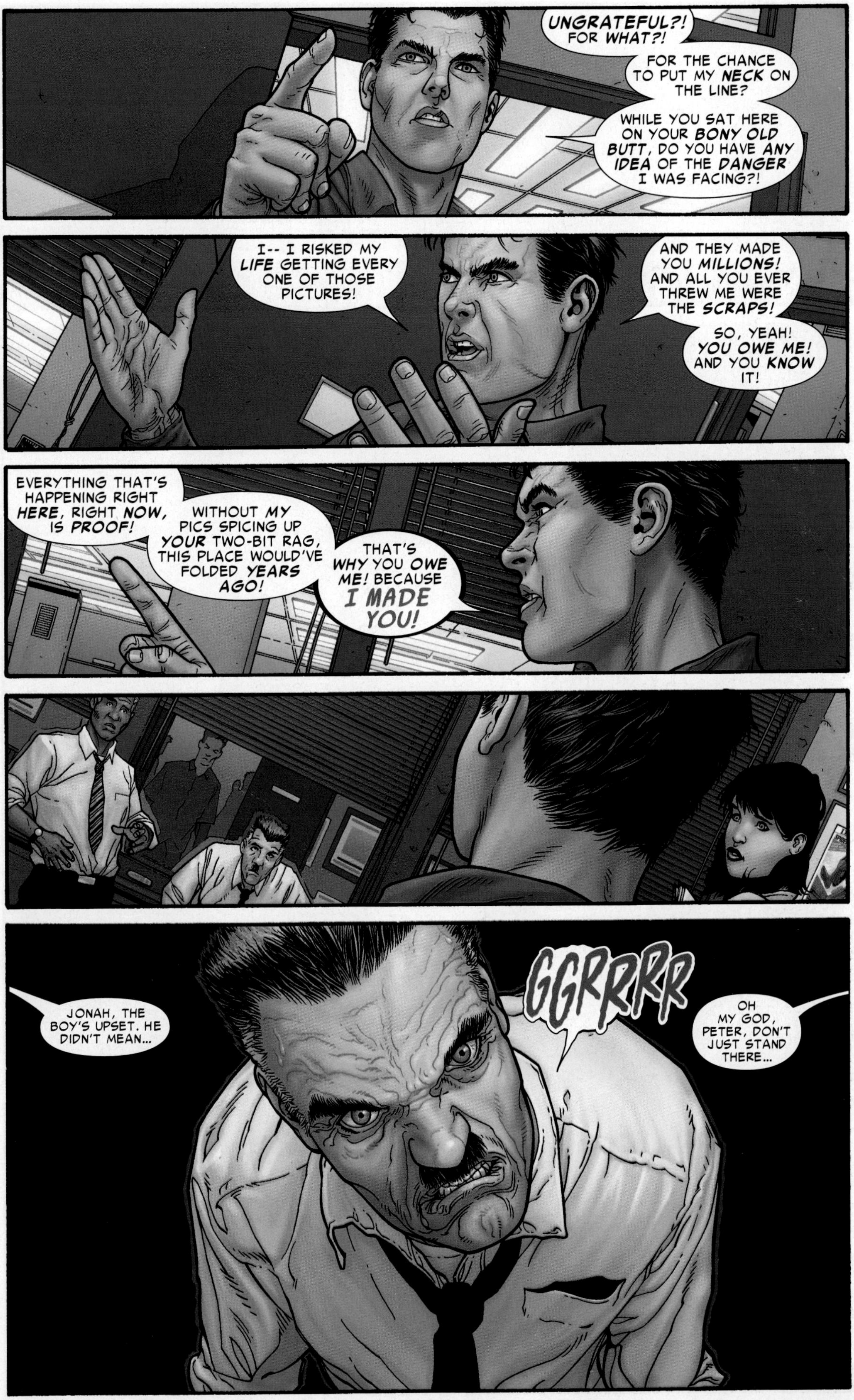
UNGRATEFUL?! FOR WHAT?!
FOR THE CHANCE TO PUT MY NECK ON THE LINE?
WHILE YOU SAT HERE ON YOUR BONY OLD BUTT, DO YOU HAVE ANY IDEA OF THE DANGER I WAS FACING?!
I-- I RISKED MY LIFE GETTING EVERY ONE OF THOSE PICTURES!
AND THEY MADE YOU MILLIONS! AND ALL YOU EVER THREW ME WERE THE SCRAPS!
SO, YEAH! YOU OWE ME! AND YOU KNOW IT!
EVERYTHING THAT'S HAPPENING RIGHT HERE, RIGHT NOW, IS PROOF!
WITHOUT MY PICS SPICING UP YOUR TWO-BIT RAG, THIS PLACE WOULD'VE FOLDED YEARS AGO!
THAT'S WHY YOU OWE ME! BECAUSE I MADE YOU!
JONAH, THE BOY'S UPSET. HE DIDN'T MEAN...
GGRRRR
OH MY GOD, PETER, DON'T JUST STAND THERE...

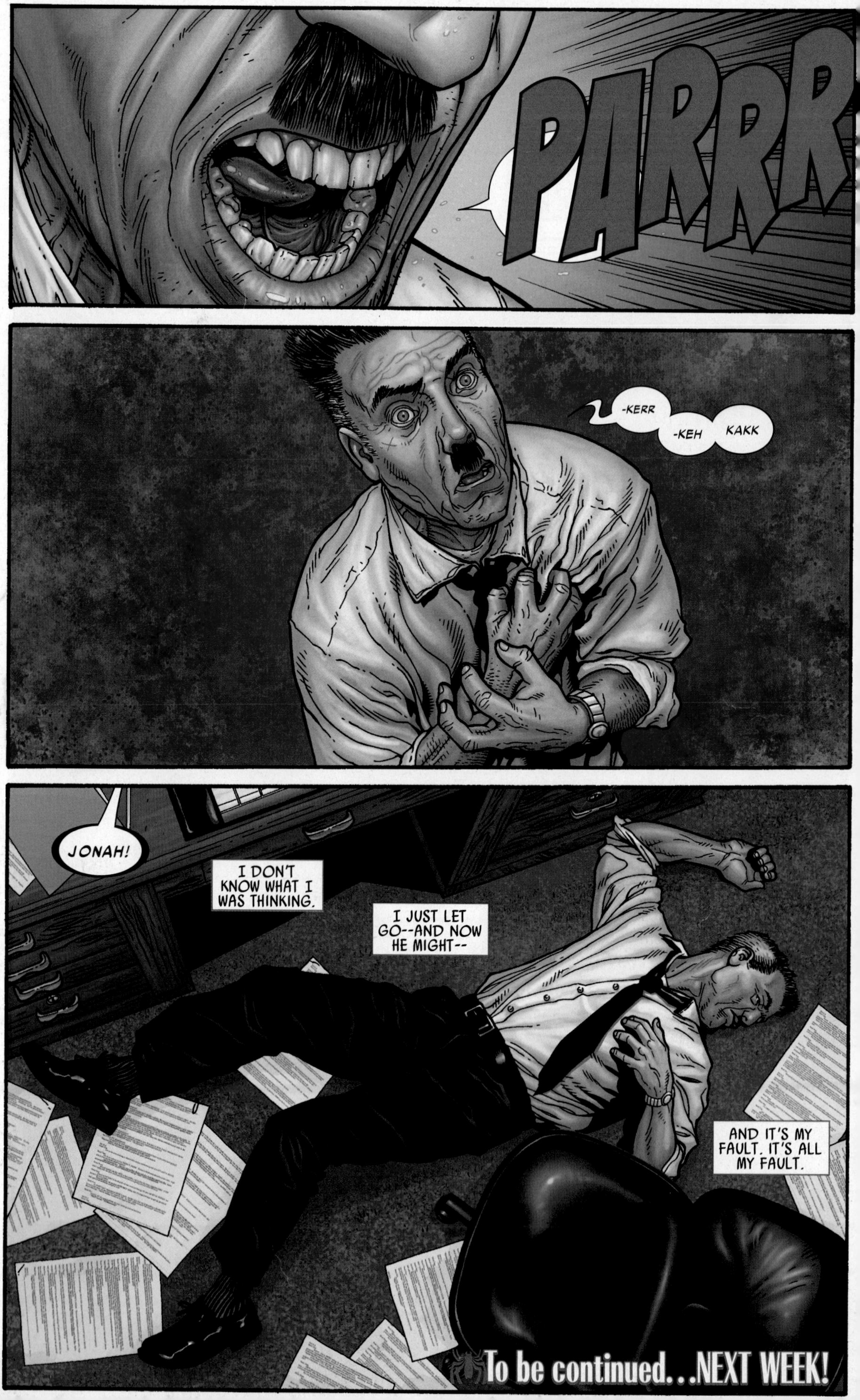
PARRR
-KERR
-KEH
KAKK
JONAH!
I DON'T KNOW WHAT I WAS THINKING.
I JUST LET GO--AND NOW HE MIGHT--
AND IT'S MY FAULT. IT'S ALL MY FAULT.
To be continued. . .NEXT WEEK!

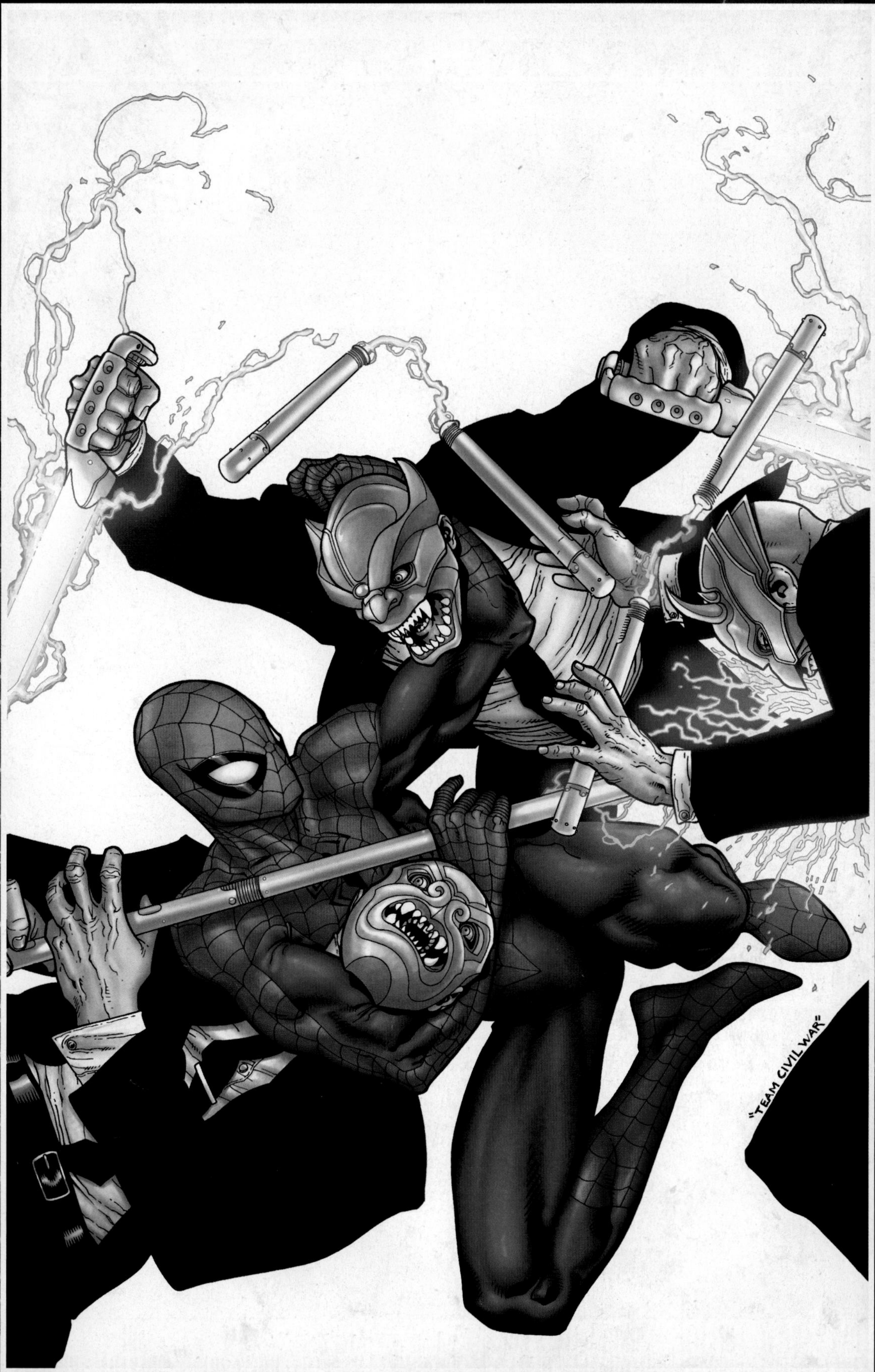
"TEAM CIVIL WAR"

AMAZING SPIDER-MAN #547
COVER BY **STEVE MCNIVEN, DEXTER VINES & MORRY HOLLOWELL**

WHILE ATTENDING A DEMONSTRATION IN RADIOLOGY, HIGH SCHOOL STUDENT **PETER PARKER** WAS BITTEN BY A SPIDER WHICH HAD ACCIDENTALLY BEEN EXPOSED TO **RADIOACTIVE RAYS.** THROUGH A MIRACLE OF SCIENCE, PETER SOON FOUND THAT HE HAD **GAINED** THE SPIDER'S POWERS…AND HAD, IN EFFECT, BECOME A HUMAN SPIDER! FROM THAT DAY ON HE WAS…

THE AMAZING SPIDER-MAN™

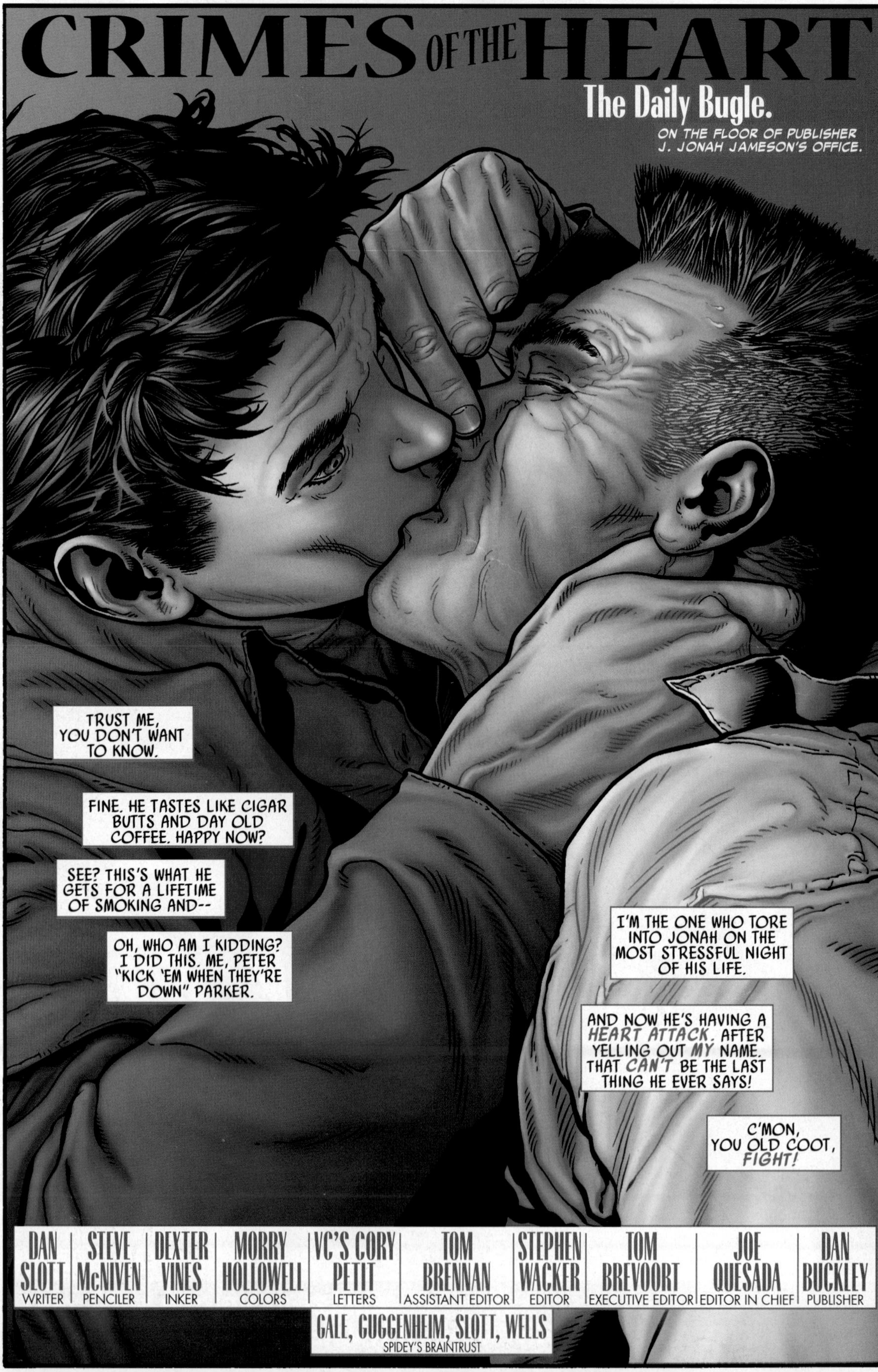

CRIMES OF THE HEART
The Daily Bugle.
ON THE FLOOR OF PUBLISHER J. JONAH JAMESON'S OFFICE.
TRUST ME, YOU DON'T WANT TO KNOW.
FINE. HE TASTES LIKE CIGAR BUTTS AND DAY OLD COFFEE. HAPPY NOW?
SEE? THIS'S WHAT HE GETS FOR A LIFETIME OF SMOKING AND--
OH, WHO AM I KIDDING? I DID THIS. ME, PETER "KICK 'EM WHEN THEY'RE DOWN" PARKER.
I'M THE ONE WHO TORE INTO JONAH ON THE MOST STRESSFUL NIGHT OF HIS LIFE.
AND NOW HE'S HAVING A HEART ATTACK, AFTER YELLING OUT MY NAME. THAT CAN'T BE THE LAST THING HE EVER SAYS!
C'MON, YOU OLD COOT, FIGHT!
DAN SLOTT WRITER
STEVE McNIVEN PENCILER
DEXTER VINES INKER
MORRY HOLLOWELL COLORS
VC'S CORY PETIT LETTERS
TOM BRENNAN ASSISTANT EDITOR
STEPHEN WACKER EDITOR
TOM BREVOORT EXECUTIVE EDITOR
JOE QUESADA EDITOR IN CHIEF
DAN BUCKLEY PUBLISHER
GALE, GUGGENHEIM, SLOTT, WELLS SPIDEY'S BRAINTRUST

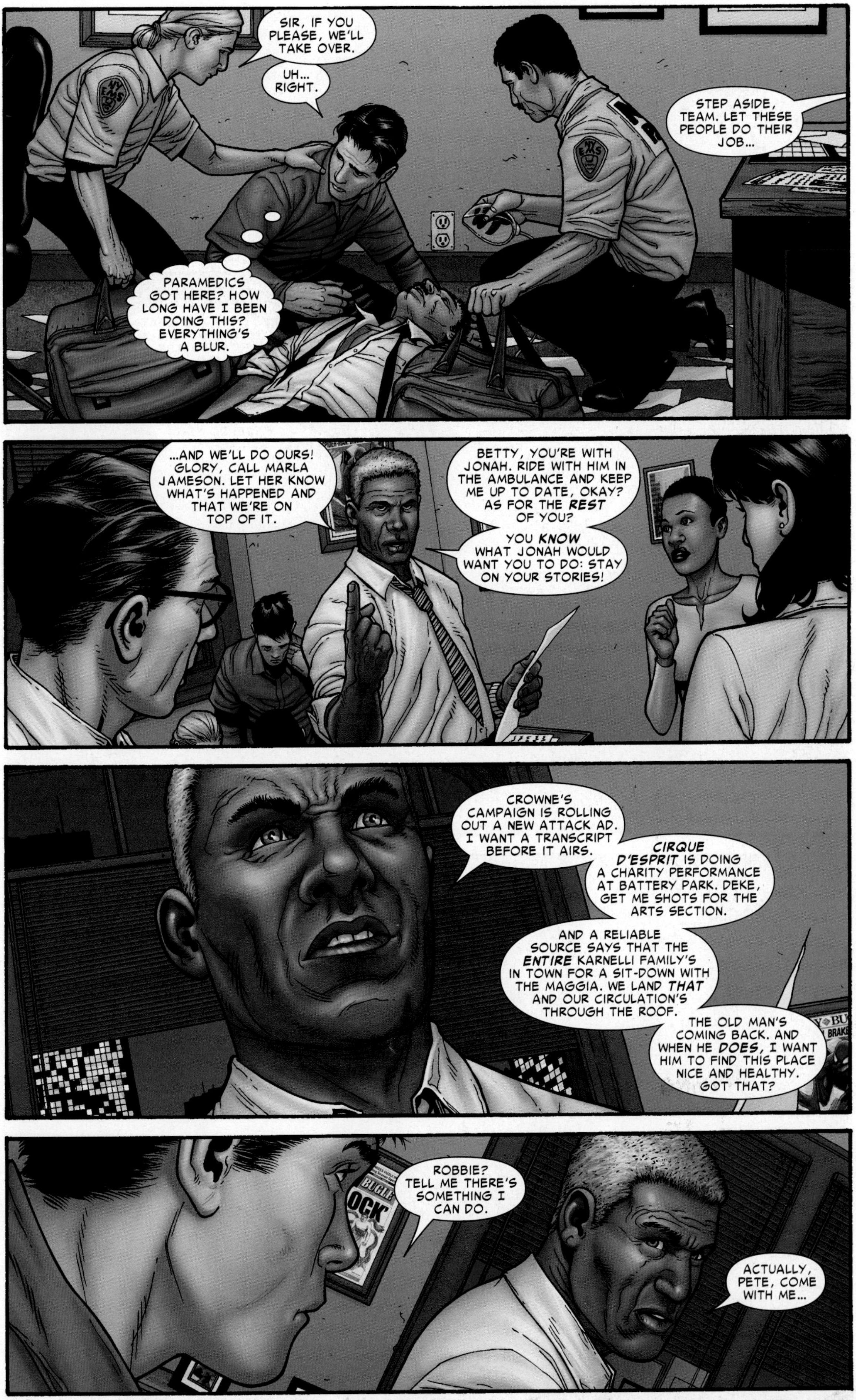
SIR, IF YOU PLEASE, WE'LL TAKE OVER.
UH... RIGHT.
STEP ASIDE, TEAM. LET THESE PEOPLE DO THEIR JOB...
PARAMEDICS GOT HERE? HOW LONG HAVE I BEEN DOING THIS? EVERYTHING'S A BLUR.
...AND WE'LL DO OURS! GLORY, CALL MARLA JAMESON. LET HER KNOW WHAT'S HAPPENED AND THAT WE'RE ON TOP OF IT.
BETTY, YOU'RE WITH JONAH. RIDE WITH HIM IN THE AMBULANCE AND KEEP ME UP TO DATE, OKAY? AS FOR THE REST OF YOU?
YOU KNOW WHAT JONAH WOULD WANT YOU TO DO: STAY ON YOUR STORIES!
CROWNE'S CAMPAIGN IS ROLLING OUT A NEW ATTACK AD. I WANT A TRANSCRIPT BEFORE IT AIRS.
CIRQUE D'ESPRIT IS DOING A CHARITY PERFORMANCE AT BATTERY PARK. DEKE, GET ME SHOTS FOR THE ARTS SECTION.
AND A RELIABLE SOURCE SAYS THAT THE ENTIRE KARNELLI FAMILY'S IN TOWN FOR A SIT-DOWN WITH THE MAGGIA. WE LAND THAT AND OUR CIRCULATION'S THROUGH THE ROOF.
THE OLD MAN'S COMING BACK. AND WHEN HE DOES, I WANT HIM TO FIND THIS PLACE NICE AND HEALTHY. GOT THAT?
ROBBIE? TELL ME THERE'S SOMETHING I CAN DO.
ACTUALLY, PETE, COME WITH ME...

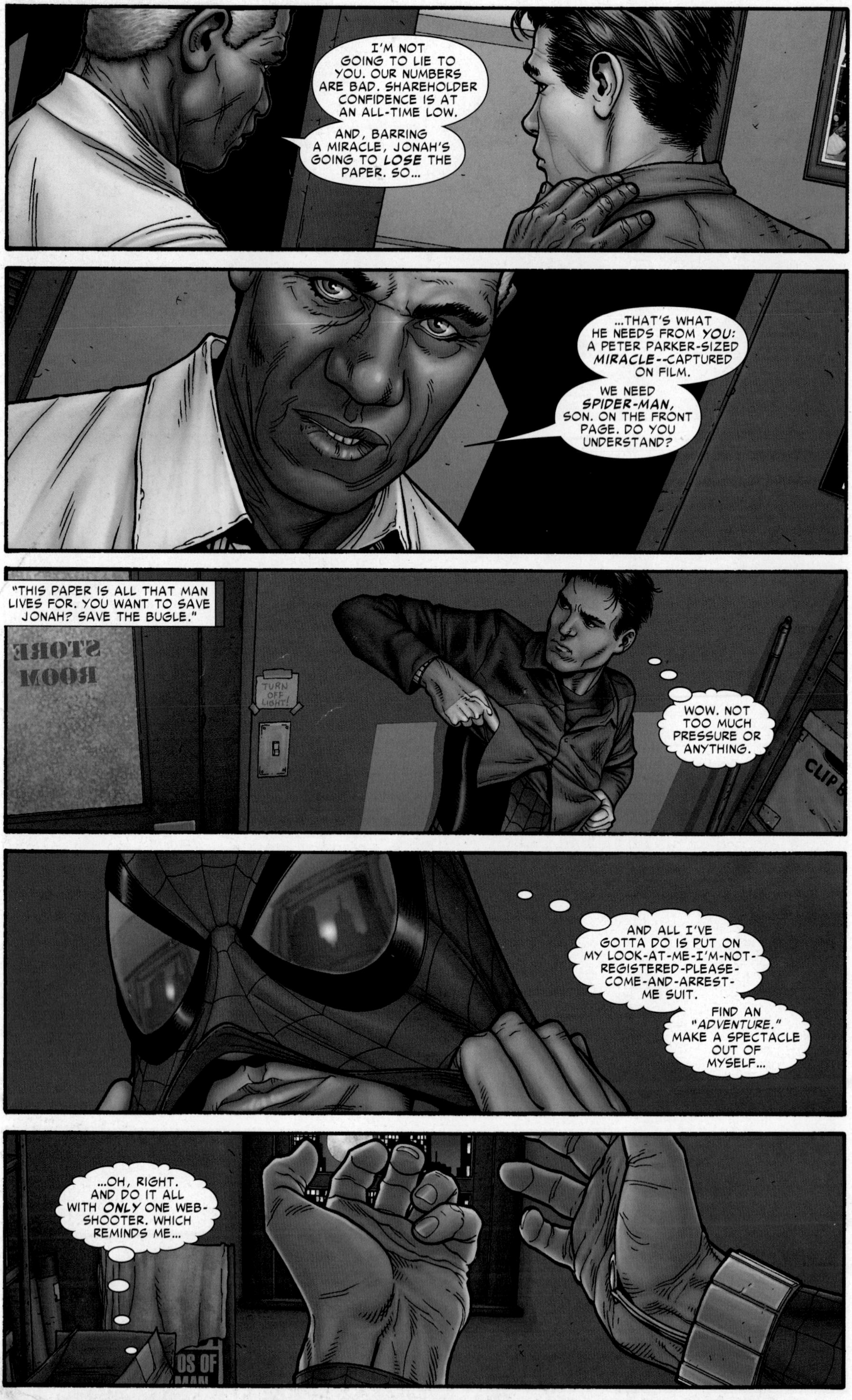
I'M NOT GOING TO LIE TO YOU. OUR NUMBERS ARE BAD. SHAREHOLDER CONFIDENCE IS AT AN ALL-TIME LOW.
AND, BARRING A MIRACLE, JONAH'S GOING TO *LOSE* THE PAPER. SO...
...THAT'S WHAT HE NEEDS FROM *YOU*: A PETER PARKER-SIZED *MIRACLE*--CAPTURED ON FILM.
WE NEED *SPIDER-MAN*, SON. ON THE FRONT PAGE. DO YOU UNDERSTAND?
"THIS PAPER IS ALL THAT MAN LIVES FOR. YOU WANT TO SAVE JONAH? SAVE THE BUGLE."
STORE ROOM
TURN OFF LIGHT!
WOW. NOT TOO MUCH PRESSURE OR ANYTHING.
AND ALL I'VE GOTTA DO IS PUT ON MY LOOK-AT-ME-I'M-NOT-REGISTERED-PLEASE-COME-AND-ARREST-ME SUIT.
FIND AN "*ADVENTURE*." MAKE A SPECTACLE OUT OF MYSELF...
...OH, RIGHT. AND DO IT ALL WITH *ONLY* ONE WEB-SHOOTER. WHICH REMINDS ME...

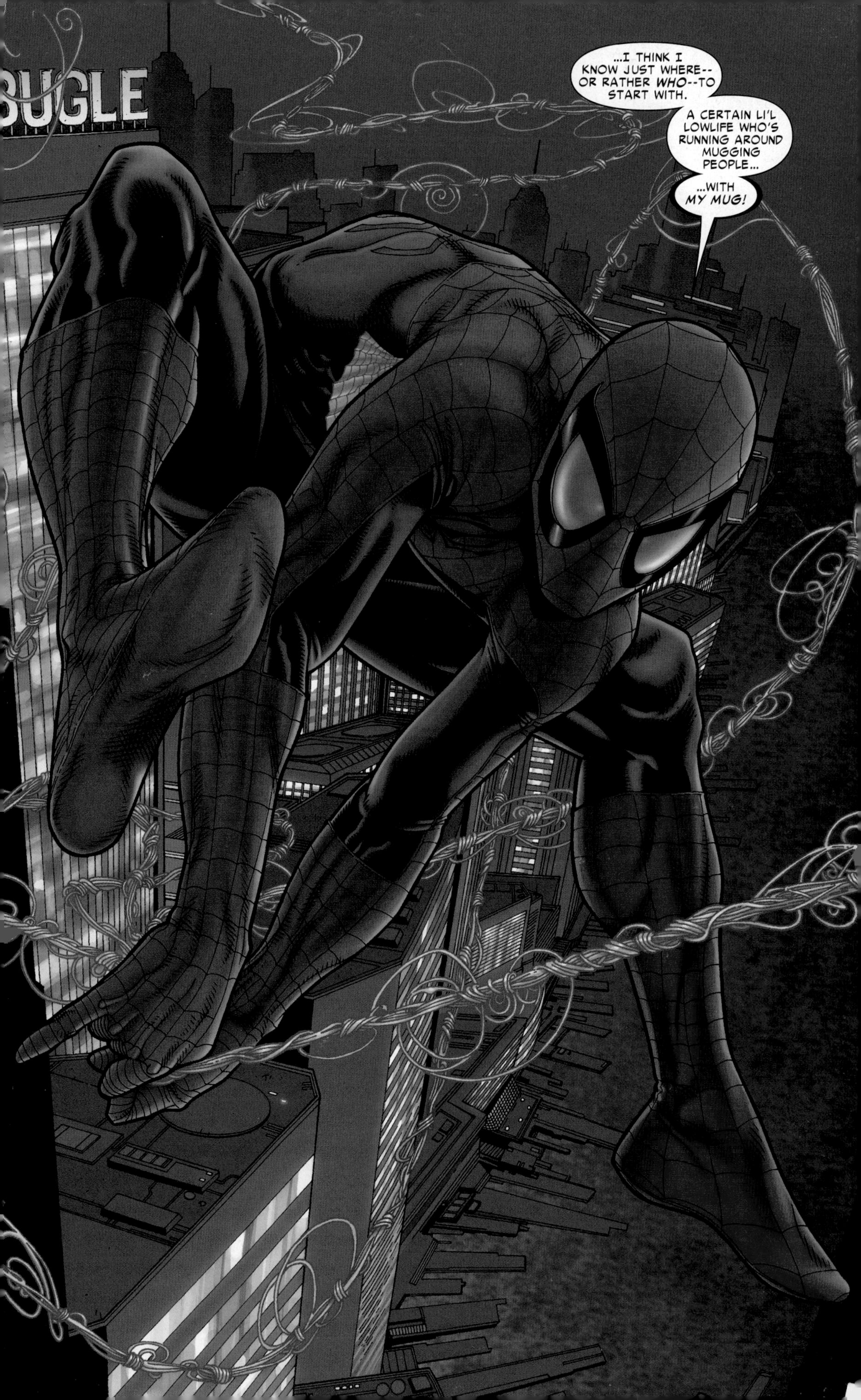

BUGLE
...I THINK I KNOW JUST WHERE-- OR RATHER WHO--TO START WITH.
A CERTAIN LI'L LOWLIFE WHO'S RUNNING AROUND MUGGING PEOPLE...
...WITH MY MUG!

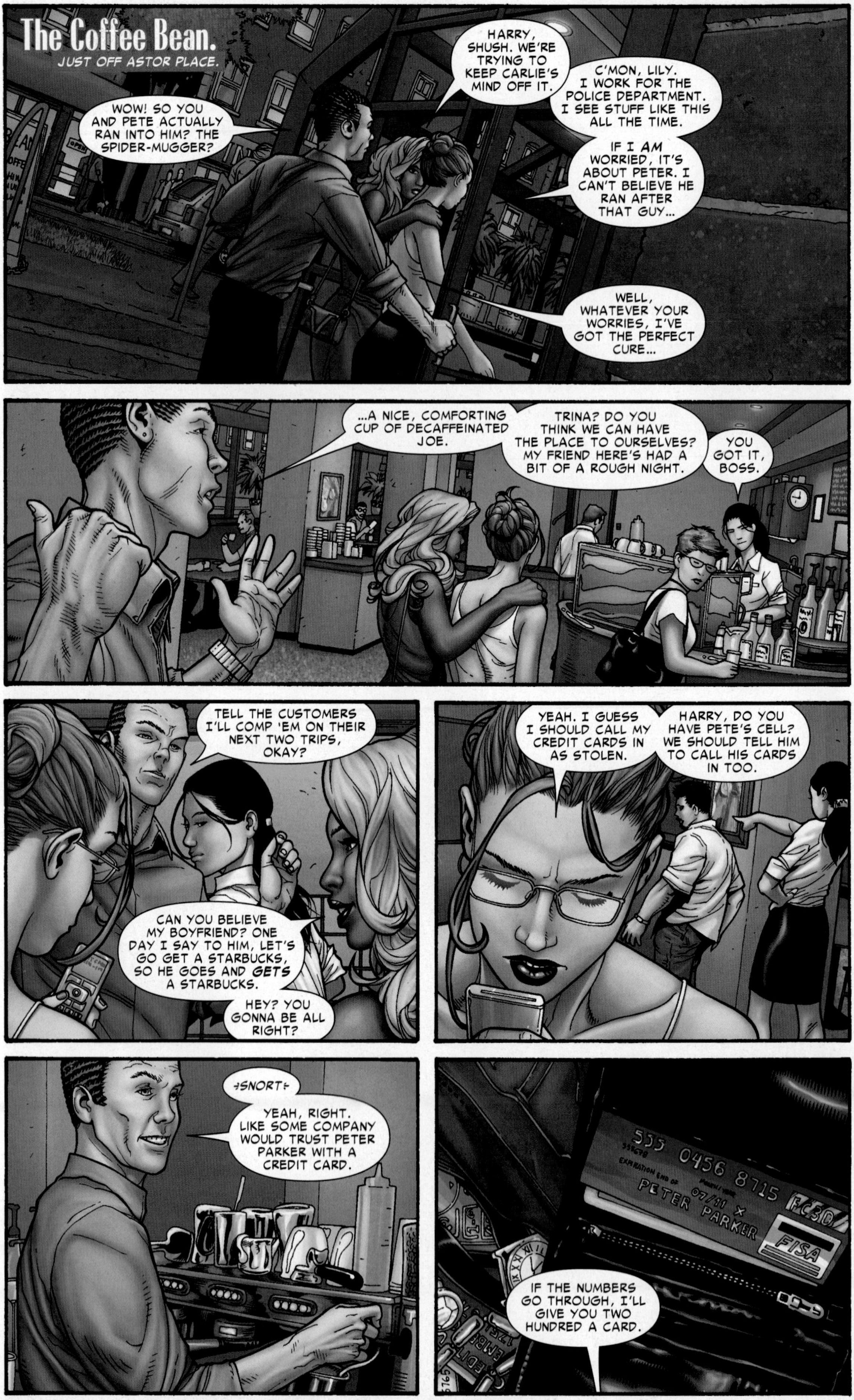
The Coffee Bean.
JUST OFF ASTOR PLACE.
WOW! SO YOU AND PETE ACTUALLY RAN INTO HIM? THE SPIDER-MUGGER?
HARRY, SHUSH. WE'RE TRYING TO KEEP CARLIE'S MIND OFF IT.
C'MON, LILY. I WORK FOR THE POLICE DEPARTMENT. I SEE STUFF LIKE THIS ALL THE TIME.
IF I *AM* WORRIED, IT'S ABOUT PETER. I CAN'T BELIEVE HE RAN AFTER THAT GUY...
WELL, WHATEVER YOUR WORRIES, I'VE GOT THE PERFECT CURE...
...A NICE, COMFORTING CUP OF DECAFFEINATED JOE.
TRINA? DO YOU THINK WE CAN HAVE THE PLACE TO OURSELVES? MY FRIEND HERE'S HAD A BIT OF A ROUGH NIGHT.
YOU GOT IT, BOSS.
TELL THE CUSTOMERS I'LL COMP 'EM ON THEIR NEXT TWO TRIPS, OKAY?
CAN YOU BELIEVE MY BOYFRIEND? ONE DAY I SAY TO HIM, LET'S GO GET A STARBUCKS, SO HE GOES AND **GETS** A STARBUCKS.
HEY? YOU GONNA BE ALL RIGHT?
YEAH. I GUESS I SHOULD CALL MY CREDIT CARDS IN AS STOLEN.
HARRY, DO YOU HAVE PETE'S CELL? WE SHOULD TELL HIM TO CALL HIS CARDS IN TOO.
SNORT
YEAH, RIGHT. LIKE SOME COMPANY WOULD TRUST PETER PARKER WITH A CREDIT CARD.
555 0456 8715
PETER PARKER
FISA
IF THE NUMBERS GO THROUGH, I'LL GIVE YOU TWO HUNDRED A CARD.

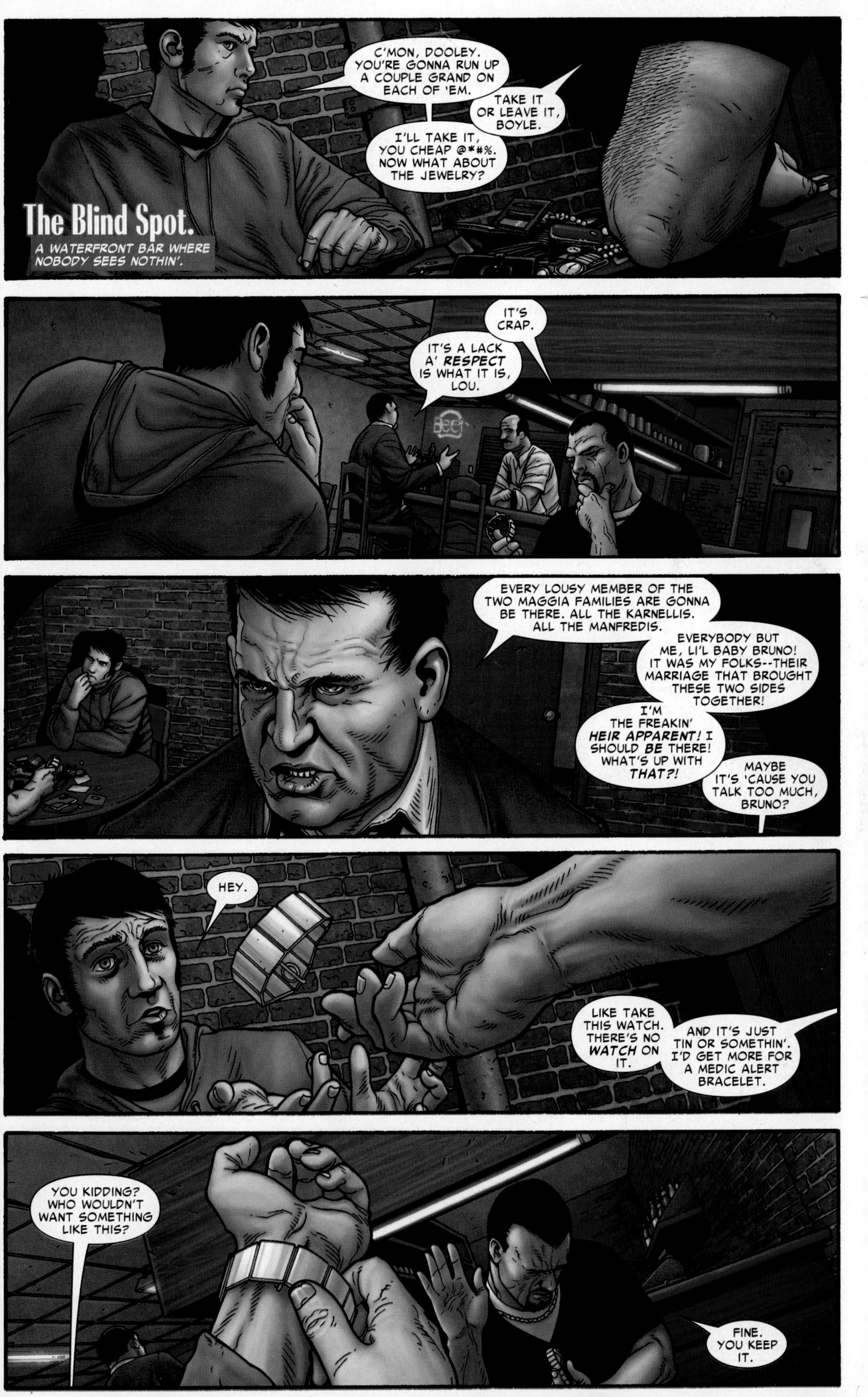
C'MON, DOOLEY. YOU'RE GONNA RUN UP A COUPLE GRAND ON EACH OF 'EM.
TAKE IT OR LEAVE IT, BOYLE.
I'LL TAKE IT, YOU CHEAP @*#%. NOW WHAT ABOUT THE JEWELRY?
The Blind Spot.
A WATERFRONT BAR WHERE NOBODY SEES NOTHIN'.
IT'S CRAP.
IT'S A LACK A' RESPECT IS WHAT IT IS, LOU.
EVERY LOUSY MEMBER OF THE TWO MAGGIA FAMILIES ARE GONNA BE THERE. ALL THE KARNELLIS. ALL THE MANFREDIS.
EVERYBODY BUT ME, LI'L BABY BRUNO! IT WAS MY FOLKS--THEIR MARRIAGE THAT BROUGHT THESE TWO SIDES TOGETHER!
I'M THE FREAKIN' HEIR APPARENT! I SHOULD BE THERE! WHAT'S UP WITH THAT?!
MAYBE IT'S 'CAUSE YOU TALK TOO MUCH, BRUNO?
HEY.
LIKE TAKE THIS WATCH. THERE'S NO WATCH ON IT.
AND IT'S JUST TIN OR SOMETHIN'. I'D GET MORE FOR A MEDIC ALERT BRACELET.
YOU KIDDING? WHO WOULDN'T WANT SOMETHING LIKE THIS?
FINE. YOU KEEP IT.

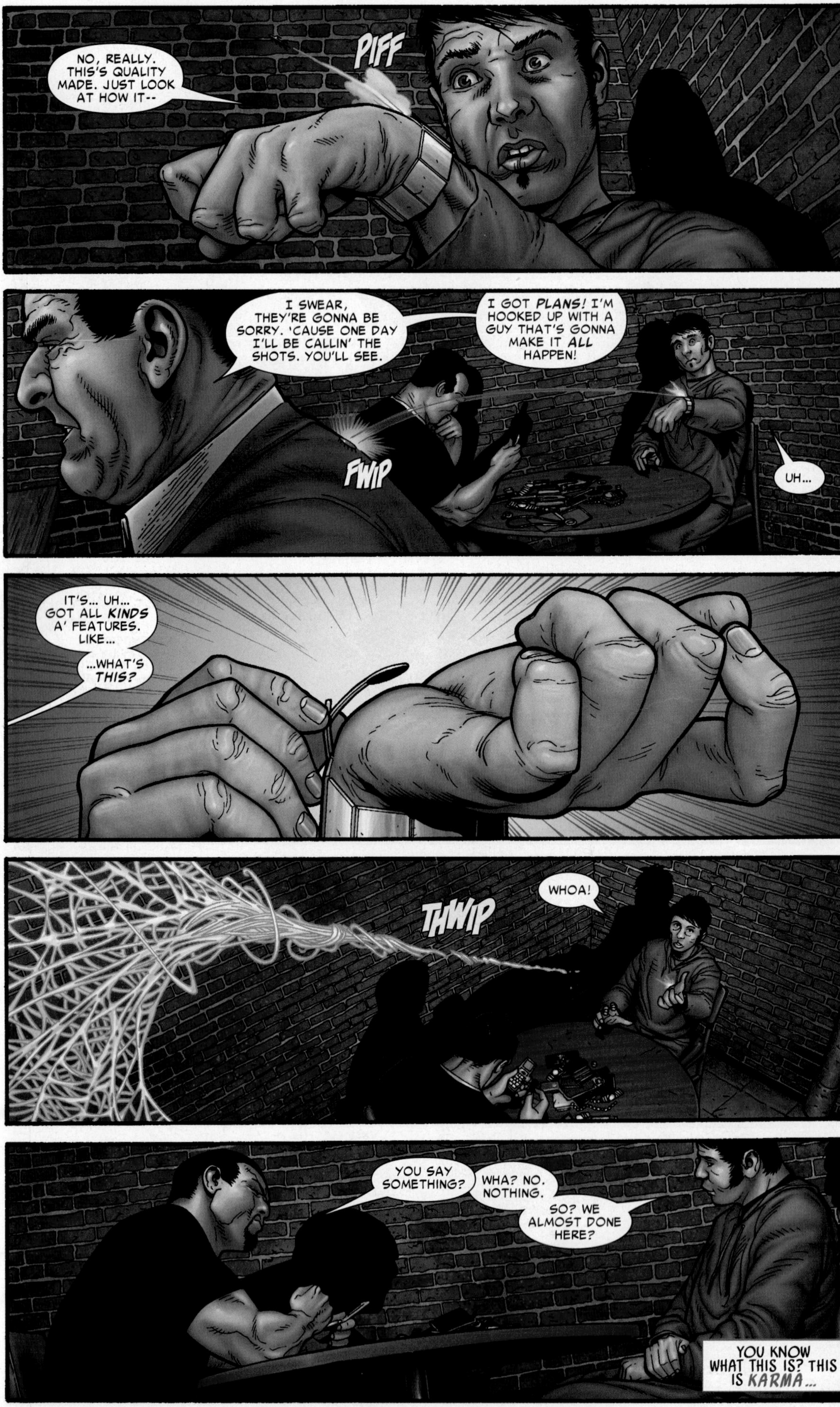
NO, REALLY. THIS'S QUALITY MADE. JUST LOOK AT HOW IT--
PIFF
I SWEAR, THEY'RE GONNA BE SORRY. 'CAUSE ONE DAY I'LL BE CALLIN' THE SHOTS. YOU'LL SEE.
I GOT PLANS! I'M HOOKED UP WITH A GUY THAT'S GONNA MAKE IT ALL HAPPEN!
FWIP
UH...
IT'S... UH... GOT ALL KINDS A' FEATURES. LIKE...
...WHAT'S THIS?
THWIP
WHOA!
YOU SAY SOMETHING?
WHA? NO. NOTHING.
SO? WE ALMOST DONE HERE?
YOU KNOW WHAT THIS IS? THIS IS KARMA...

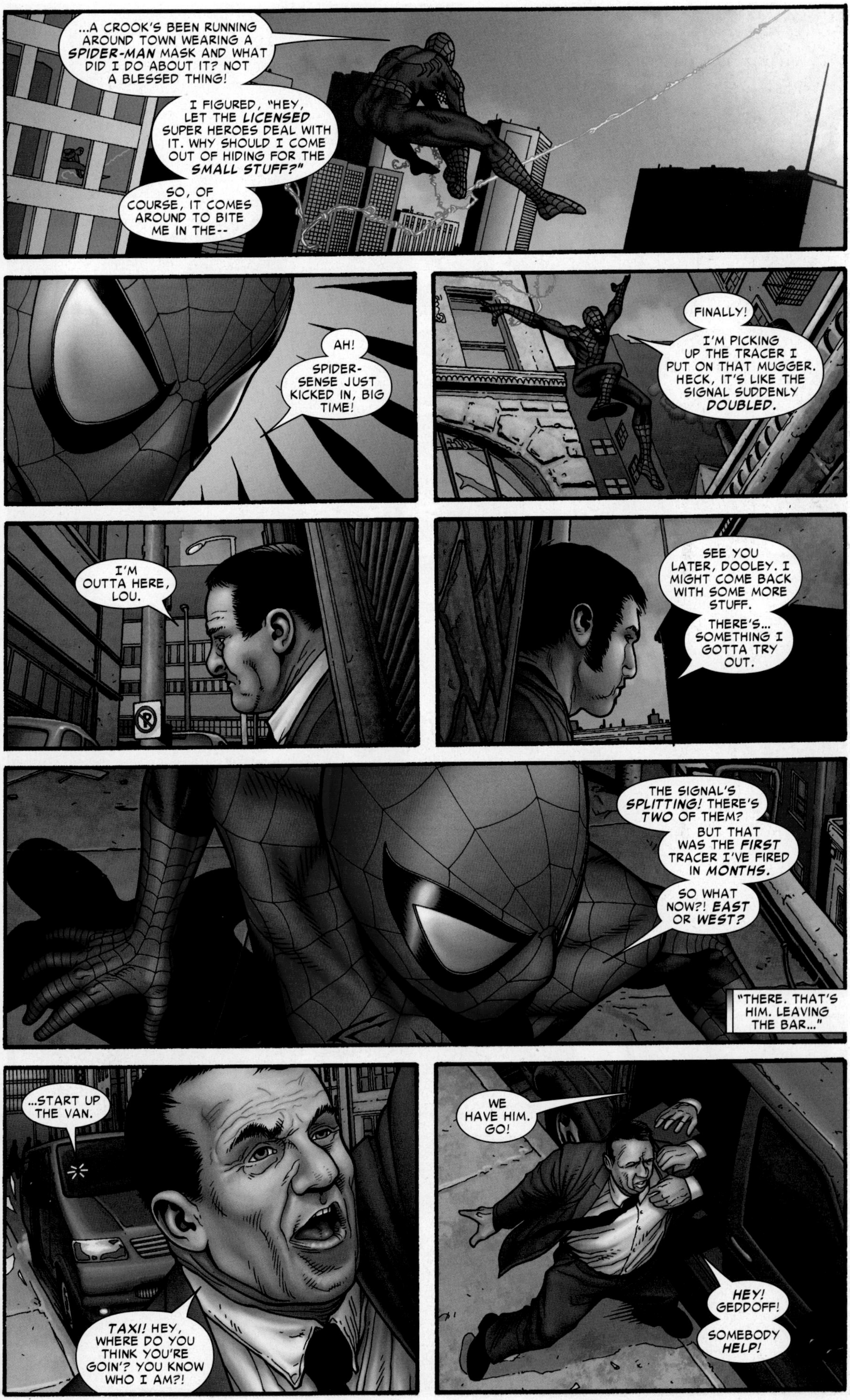
...A CROOK'S BEEN RUNNING AROUND TOWN WEARING A SPIDER-MAN MASK AND WHAT DID I DO ABOUT IT? NOT A BLESSED THING!
I FIGURED, "HEY, LET THE LICENSED SUPER HEROES DEAL WITH IT. WHY SHOULD I COME OUT OF HIDING FOR THE SMALL STUFF?"
SO, OF COURSE, IT COMES AROUND TO BITE ME IN THE--
AH!
SPIDER-SENSE JUST KICKED IN, BIG TIME!
FINALLY!
I'M PICKING UP THE TRACER I PUT ON THAT MUGGER. HECK, IT'S LIKE THE SIGNAL SUDDENLY DOUBLED.
I'M OUTTA HERE, LOU.
SEE YOU LATER, DOOLEY. I MIGHT COME BACK WITH SOME MORE STUFF.
THERE'S... SOMETHING I GOTTA TRY OUT.
THE SIGNAL'S SPLITTING! THERE'S TWO OF THEM?
BUT THAT WAS THE FIRST TRACER I'VE FIRED IN MONTHS.
SO WHAT NOW?! EAST OR WEST?
"THERE. THAT'S HIM. LEAVING THE BAR..."
...START UP THE VAN.
TAXI! HEY, WHERE DO YOU THINK YOU'RE GOIN'? YOU KNOW WHO I AM?!
WE HAVE HIM. GO!
HEY! GEDDOFF!
SOMEBODY HELP!

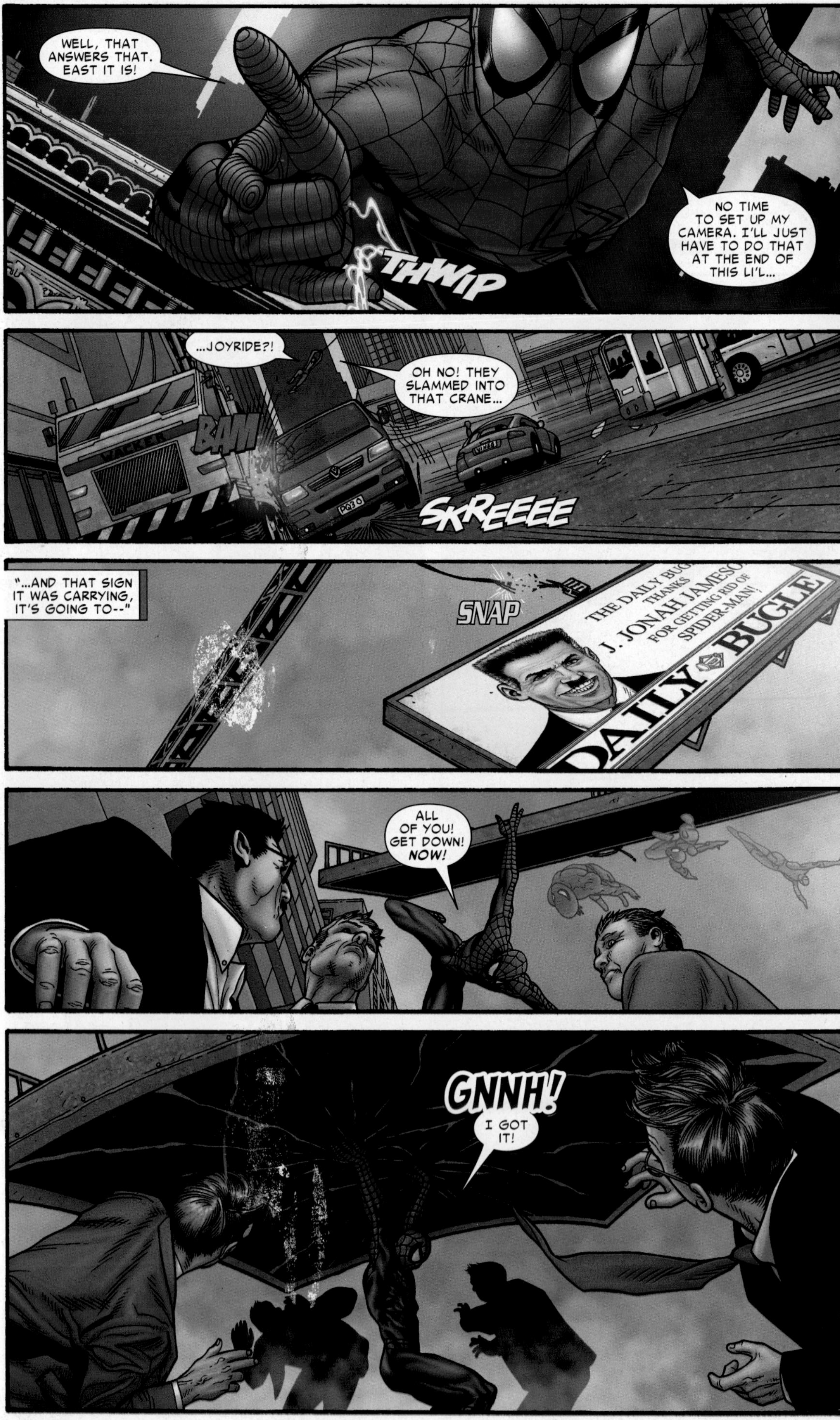

WELL, THAT ANSWERS THAT. EAST IT IS!
THWIP
NO TIME TO SET UP MY CAMERA. I'LL JUST HAVE TO DO THAT AT THE END OF THIS LI'L...
...JOYRIDE?!
OH NO! THEY SLAMMED INTO THAT CRANE...
BAM
SKREEEEE
"...AND THAT SIGN IT WAS CARRYING, IT'S GOING TO--"
SNAP
THE DAILY BUGLE THANKS J. JONAH JAMESON FOR GETTING RID OF SPIDER-MAN!
DAILY BUGLE
ALL OF YOU! GET DOWN! NOW!
GNNH!
I GOT IT!

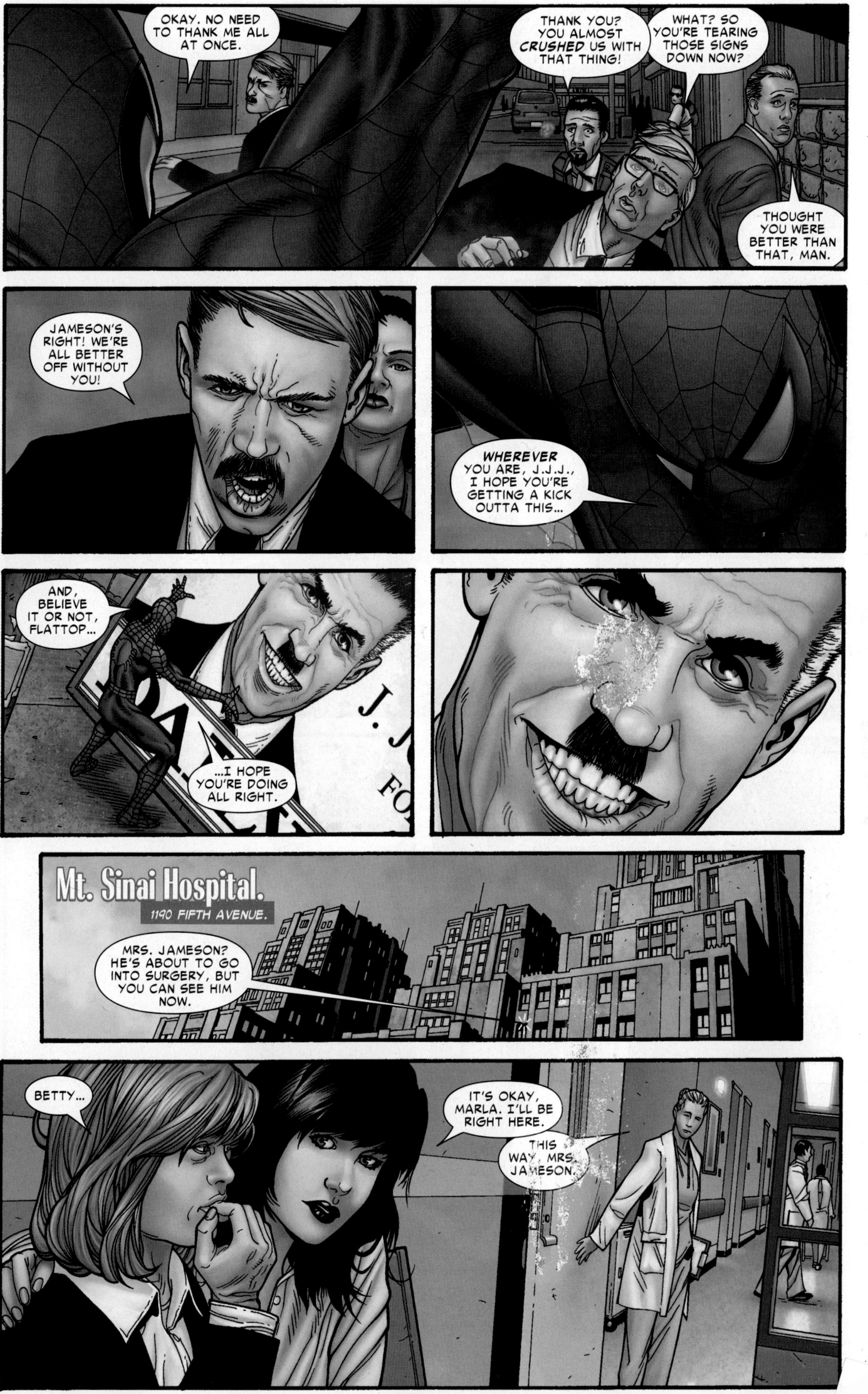
OKAY. NO NEED TO THANK ME ALL AT ONCE.
THANK YOU? YOU ALMOST CRUSHED US WITH THAT THING!
WHAT? SO YOU'RE TEARING THOSE SIGNS DOWN NOW?
THOUGHT YOU WERE BETTER THAN THAT, MAN.
JAMESON'S RIGHT! WE'RE ALL BETTER OFF WITHOUT YOU!
WHEREVER YOU ARE, J.J.J., I HOPE YOU'RE GETTING A KICK OUTTA THIS...
AND, BELIEVE IT OR NOT, FLATTOP...
...I HOPE YOU'RE DOING ALL RIGHT.
Mt. Sinai Hospital.
1190 FIFTH AVENUE.
MRS. JAMESON? HE'S ABOUT TO GO INTO SURGERY, BUT YOU CAN SEE HIM NOW.
BETTY...
IT'S OKAY, MARLA. I'LL BE RIGHT HERE.
THIS WAY, MRS. JAMESON.

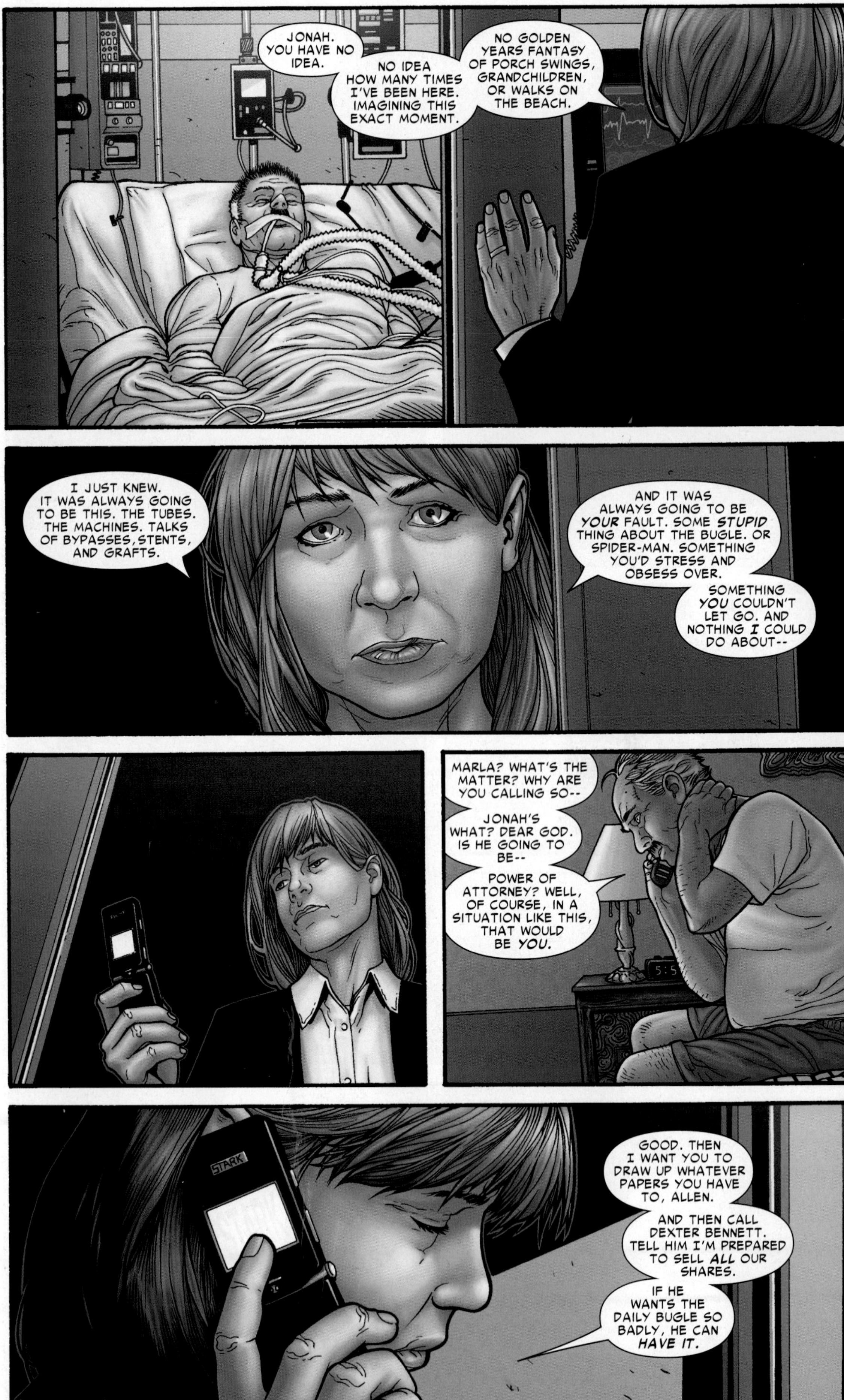
JONAH. YOU HAVE NO IDEA.
NO IDEA HOW MANY TIMES I'VE BEEN HERE. IMAGINING THIS EXACT MOMENT.
NO GOLDEN YEARS FANTASY OF PORCH SWINGS, GRANDCHILDREN, OR WALKS ON THE BEACH.
I JUST KNEW. IT WAS ALWAYS GOING TO BE THIS. THE TUBES. THE MACHINES. TALKS OF BYPASSES, STENTS, AND GRAFTS.
AND IT WAS ALWAYS GOING TO BE YOUR FAULT. SOME STUPID THING ABOUT THE BUGLE. OR SPIDER-MAN. SOMETHING YOU'D STRESS AND OBSESS OVER.
SOMETHING YOU COULDN'T LET GO. AND NOTHING I COULD DO ABOUT--
MARLA? WHAT'S THE MATTER? WHY ARE YOU CALLING SO--
JONAH'S WHAT? DEAR GOD. IS HE GOING TO BE--
POWER OF ATTORNEY? WELL, OF COURSE, IN A SITUATION LIKE THIS, THAT WOULD BE YOU.
STARK
GOOD. THEN I WANT YOU TO DRAW UP WHATEVER PAPERS YOU HAVE TO, ALLEN.
AND THEN CALL DEXTER BENNETT. TELL HIM I'M PREPARED TO SELL ALL OUR SHARES.
IF HE WANTS THE DAILY BUGLE SO BADLY, HE CAN HAVE IT.

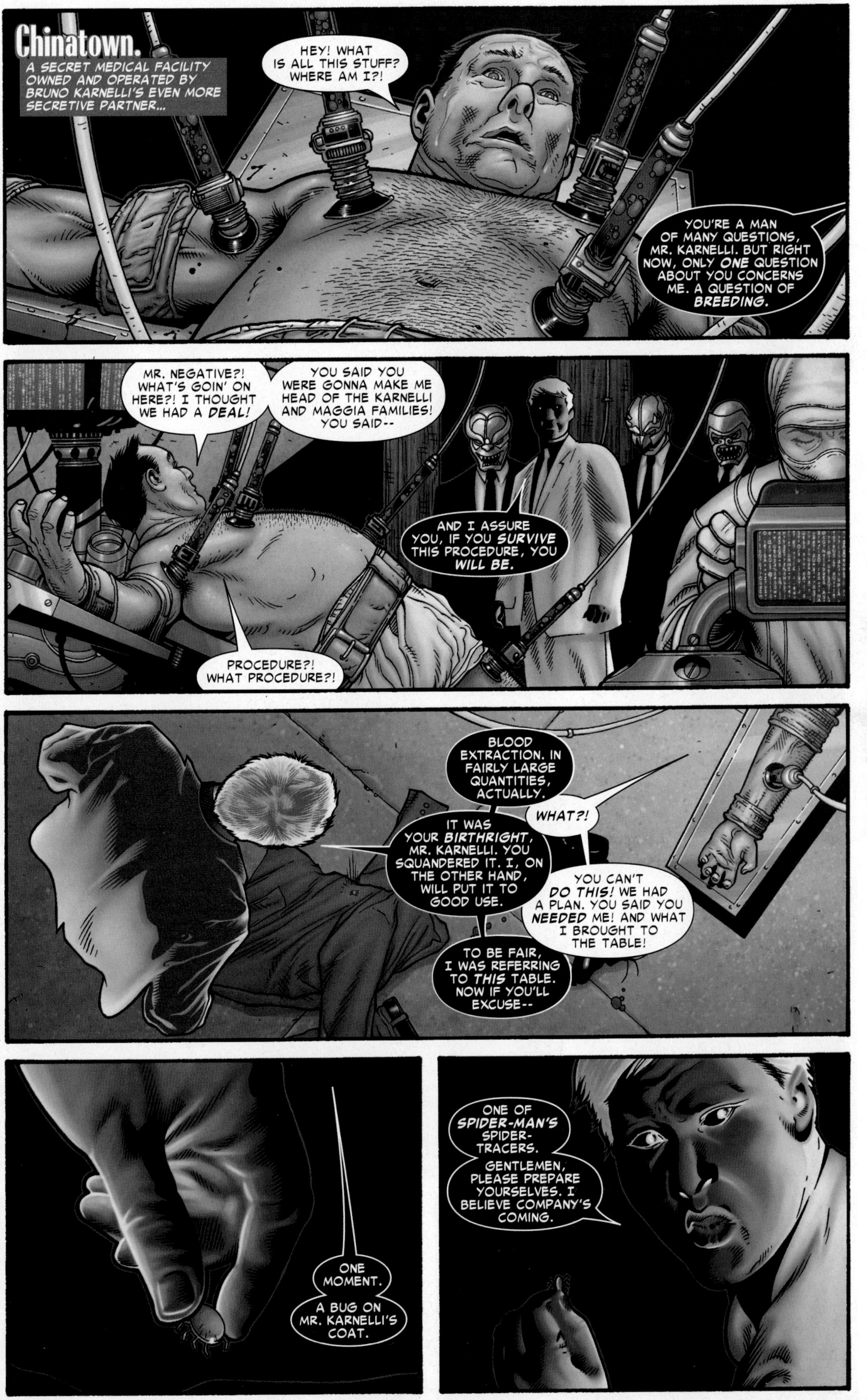
Chinatown.
A SECRET MEDICAL FACILITY OWNED AND OPERATED BY BRUNO KARNELLI'S EVEN MORE SECRETIVE PARTNER...
HEY! WHAT IS ALL THIS STUFF? WHERE AM I?!
YOU'RE A MAN OF MANY QUESTIONS, MR. KARNELLI. BUT RIGHT NOW, ONLY ONE QUESTION ABOUT YOU CONCERNS ME. A QUESTION OF BREEDING.
MR. NEGATIVE?! WHAT'S GOIN' ON HERE?! I THOUGHT WE HAD A DEAL!
YOU SAID YOU WERE GONNA MAKE ME HEAD OF THE KARNELLI AND MAGGIA FAMILIES! YOU SAID--
AND I ASSURE YOU, IF YOU SURVIVE THIS PROCEDURE, YOU WILL BE.
PROCEDURE?! WHAT PROCEDURE?!
BLOOD EXTRACTION. IN FAIRLY LARGE QUANTITIES, ACTUALLY.
WHAT?!
IT WAS YOUR BIRTHRIGHT, MR. KARNELLI. YOU SQUANDERED IT. I, ON THE OTHER HAND, WILL PUT IT TO GOOD USE.
YOU CAN'T DO THIS! WE HAD A PLAN. YOU SAID YOU NEEDED ME! AND WHAT I BROUGHT TO THE TABLE!
TO BE FAIR, I WAS REFERRING TO THIS TABLE. NOW IF YOU'LL EXCUSE--
ONE MOMENT.
A BUG ON MR. KARNELLI'S COAT.
ONE OF SPIDER-MAN'S SPIDER-TRACERS.
GENTLEMEN, PLEASE PREPARE YOURSELVES. I BELIEVE COMPANY'S COMING.

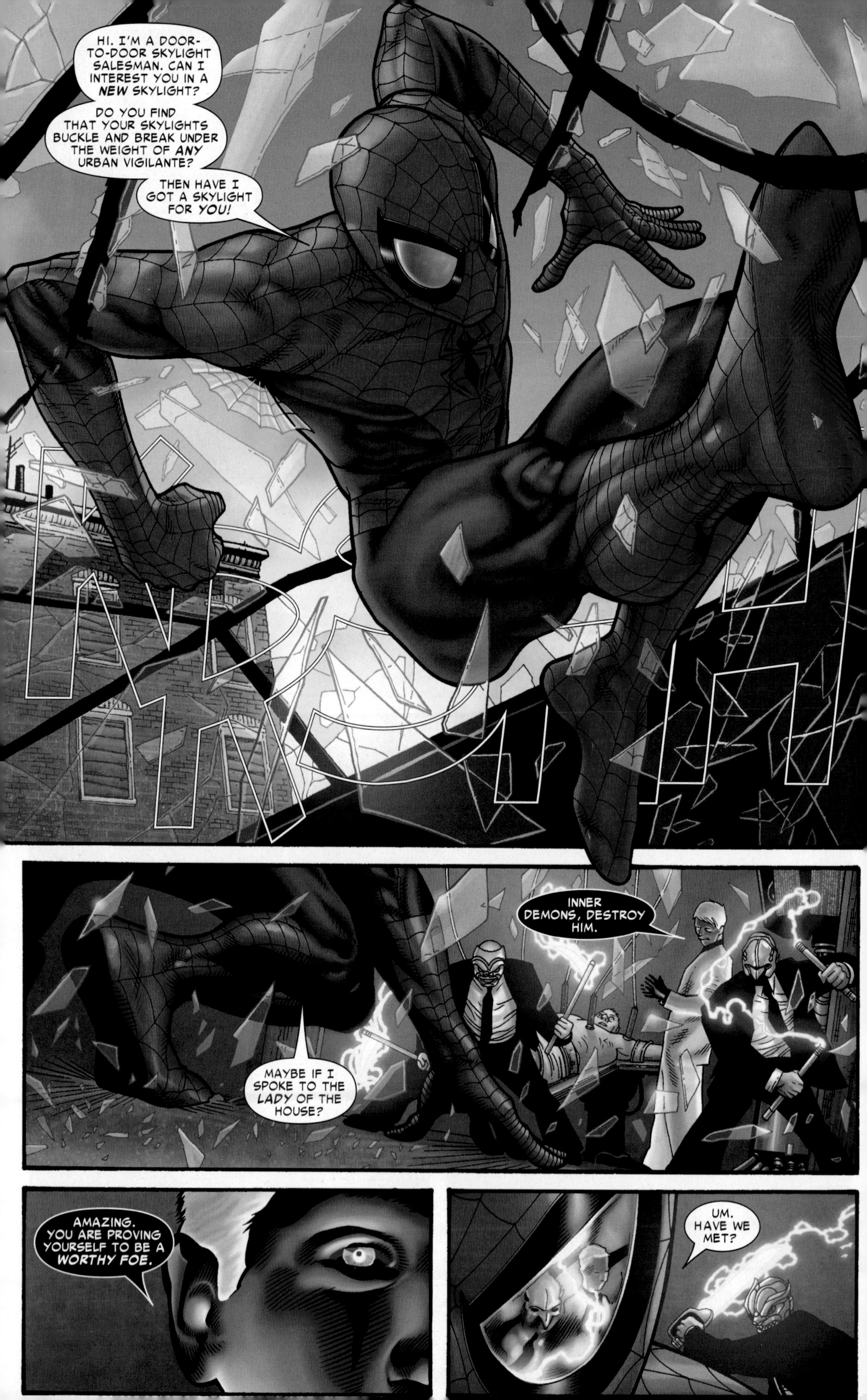
HI. I'M A DOOR-TO-DOOR SKYLIGHT SALESMAN. CAN I INTEREST YOU IN A NEW SKYLIGHT?
DO YOU FIND THAT YOUR SKYLIGHTS BUCKLE AND BREAK UNDER THE WEIGHT OF ANY URBAN VIGILANTE?
THEN HAVE I GOT A SKYLIGHT FOR YOU!
MAYBE IF I SPOKE TO THE LADY OF THE HOUSE?
INNER DEMONS, DESTROY HIM.
AMAZING. YOU ARE PROVING YOURSELF TO BE A WORTHY FOE.
UM. HAVE WE MET?

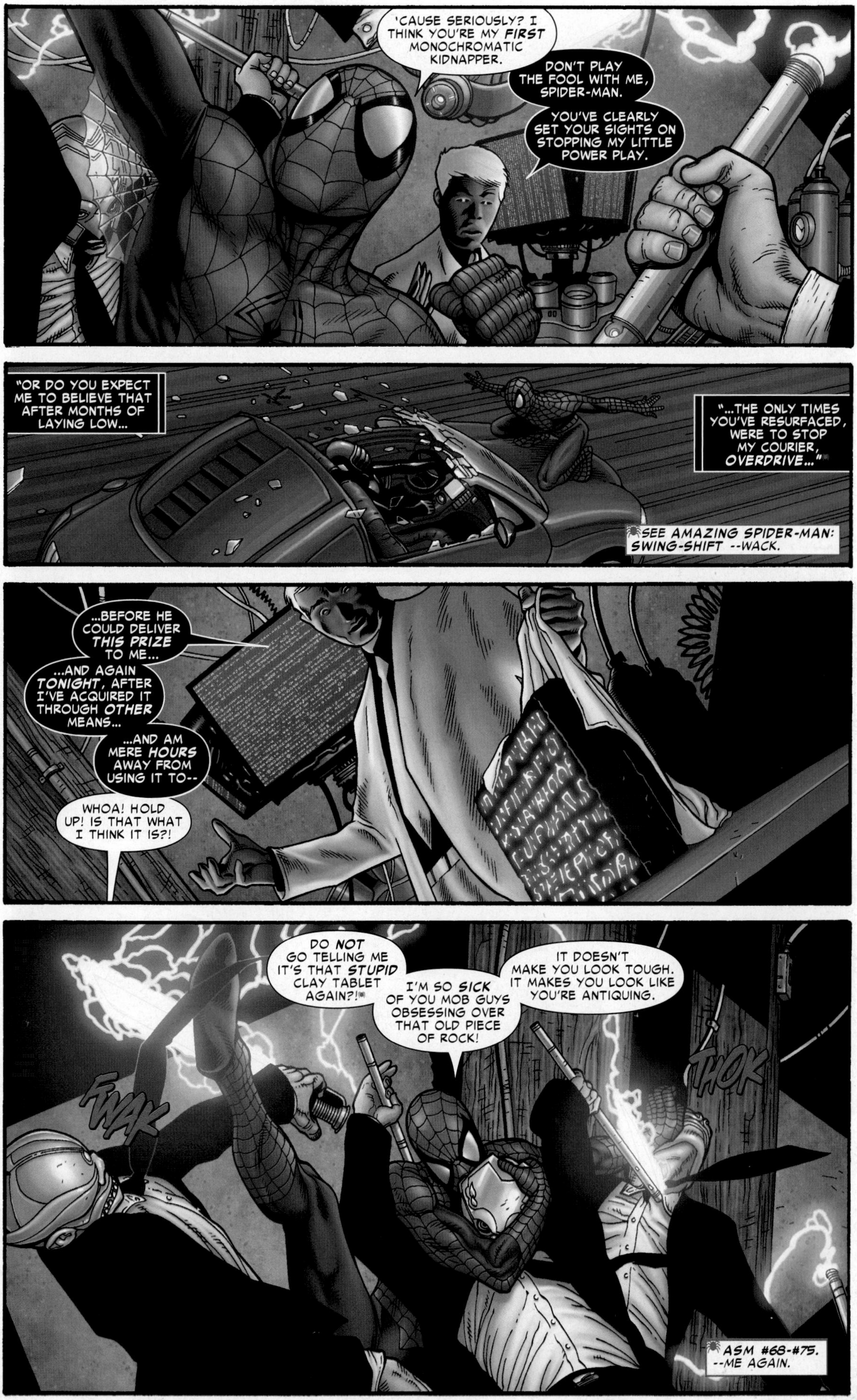
'CAUSE SERIOUSLY? I THINK YOU'RE MY *FIRST* MONOCHROMATIC KIDNAPPER.
DON'T PLAY THE FOOL WITH ME, SPIDER-MAN.
YOU'VE CLEARLY SET YOUR SIGHTS ON STOPPING MY LITTLE POWER PLAY.
"OR DO YOU EXPECT ME TO BELIEVE THAT AFTER MONTHS OF LAYING LOW...
"...THE ONLY TIMES YOU'VE RESURFACED, WERE TO STOP MY COURIER, *OVERDRIVE*..."
SEE *AMAZING SPIDER-MAN: SWING-SHIFT* --WACK.
...BEFORE HE COULD DELIVER *THIS PRIZE* TO ME...
...AND AGAIN *TONIGHT*, AFTER I'VE ACQUIRED IT THROUGH *OTHER* MEANS...
...AND AM MERE *HOURS* AWAY FROM USING IT TO--
WHOA! HOLD UP! IS THAT WHAT I THINK IT IS?!
DO *NOT* GO TELLING ME IT'S THAT *STUPID* CLAY TABLET AGAIN?!
I'M SO *SICK* OF YOU MOB GUYS OBSESSING OVER THAT OLD PIECE OF ROCK!
IT DOESN'T MAKE YOU LOOK TOUGH. IT MAKES YOU LOOK LIKE YOU'RE ANTIQUING.
FWAK
THOK
ASM #68-#75. --ME AGAIN.

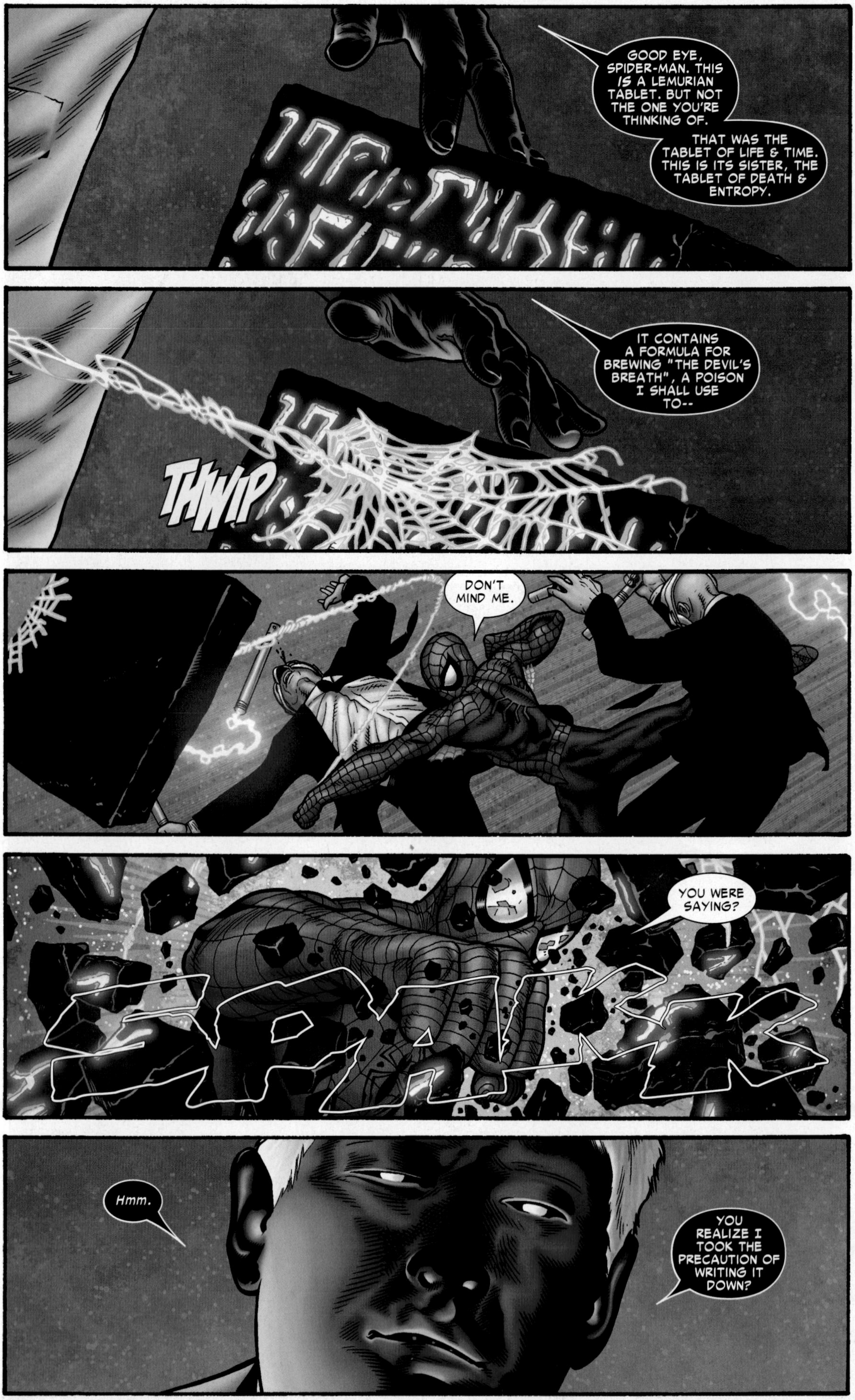
GOOD EYE, SPIDER-MAN. THIS IS A LEMURIAN TABLET. BUT NOT THE ONE YOU'RE THINKING OF.
THAT WAS THE TABLET OF LIFE & TIME. THIS IS ITS SISTER, THE TABLET OF DEATH & ENTROPY.
IT CONTAINS A FORMULA FOR BREWING "THE DEVIL'S BREATH", A POISON I SHALL USE TO--
THWIP
DON'T MIND ME.
YOU WERE SAYING?
SPAKK
Hmm.
YOU REALIZE I TOOK THE PRECAUTION OF WRITING IT DOWN?

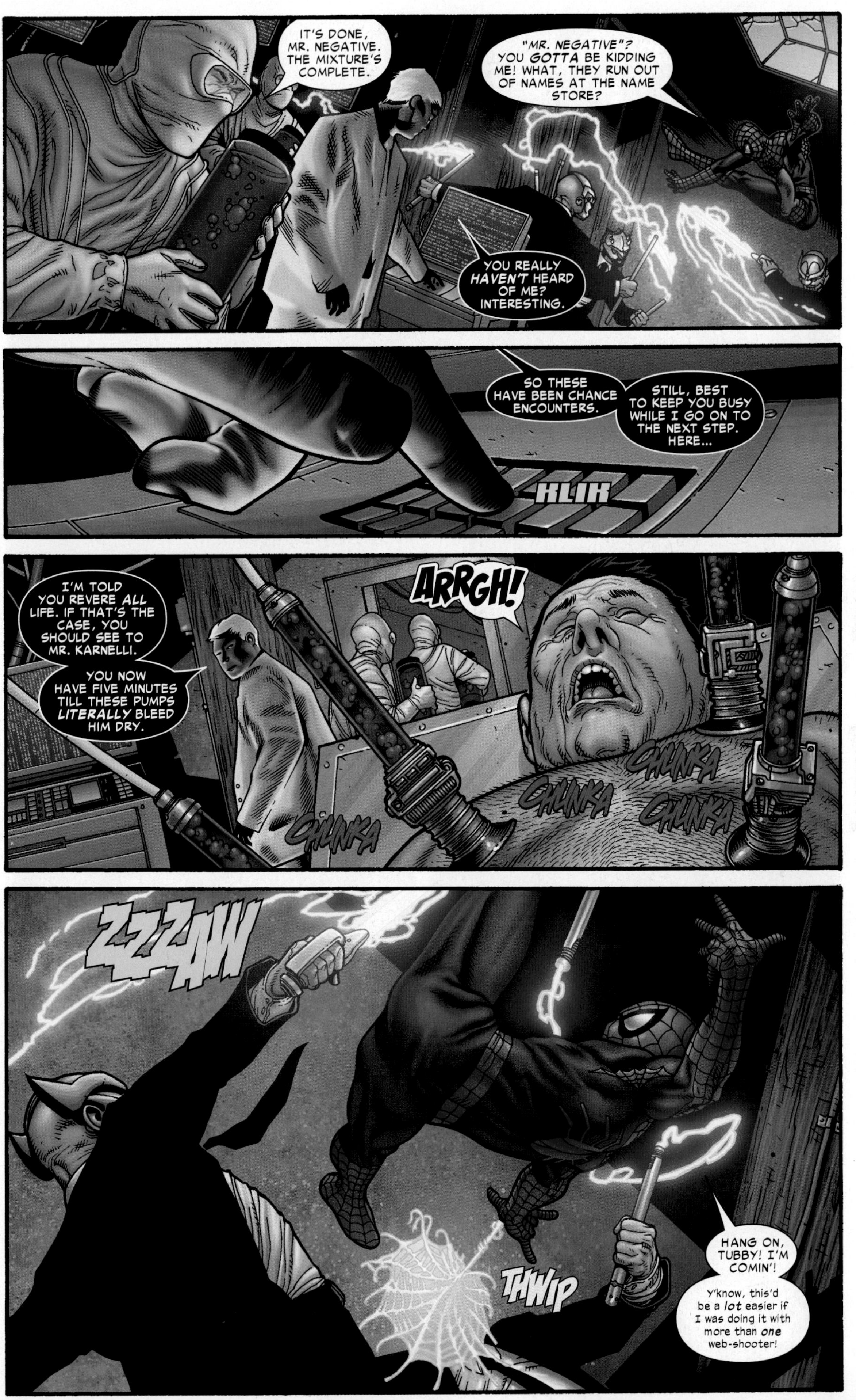
IT'S DONE, MR. NEGATIVE. THE MIXTURE'S COMPLETE.
"MR. NEGATIVE"? YOU GOTTA BE KIDDING ME! WHAT, THEY RUN OUT OF NAMES AT THE NAME STORE?
YOU REALLY HAVEN'T HEARD OF ME? INTERESTING.
SO THESE HAVE BEEN CHANCE ENCOUNTERS.
STILL, BEST TO KEEP YOU BUSY WHILE I GO ON TO THE NEXT STEP. HERE...
KLIK
I'M TOLD YOU REVERE ALL LIFE. IF THAT'S THE CASE, YOU SHOULD SEE TO MR. KARNELLI.
YOU NOW HAVE FIVE MINUTES TILL THESE PUMPS LITERALLY BLEED HIM DRY.
ARRGH!
CHUNKA
CHUNKA
CHUNKA
CHUNKA
ZZZAW
THWIP
HANG ON, TUBBY! I'M COMIN'!
Y'know, this'd be a lot easier if I was doing it with more than one web-shooter!

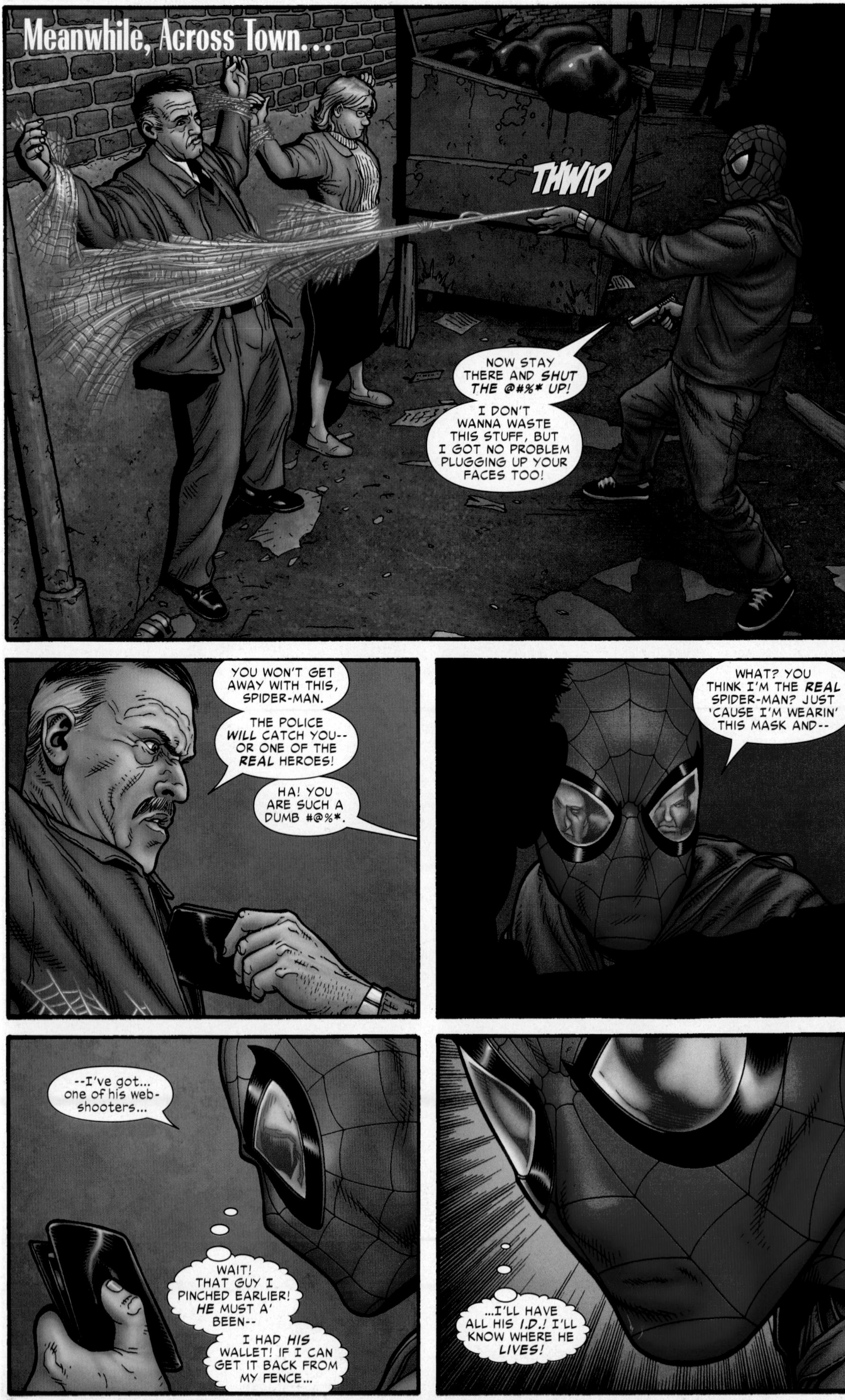
Meanwhile, Across Town...
THWIP
NOW STAY THERE AND SHUT THE @#%* UP!
I DON'T WANNA WASTE THIS STUFF, BUT I GOT NO PROBLEM PLUGGING UP YOUR FACES TOO!
YOU WON'T GET AWAY WITH THIS, SPIDER-MAN.
THE POLICE WILL CATCH YOU--OR ONE OF THE REAL HEROES!
HA! YOU ARE SUCH A DUMB #@%*.
WHAT? YOU THINK I'M THE REAL SPIDER-MAN? JUST 'CAUSE I'M WEARIN' THIS MASK AND--
--I've got... one of his web-shooters...
WAIT! THAT GUY I PINCHED EARLIER! HE MUST A' BEEN--
I HAD HIS WALLET! IF I CAN GET IT BACK FROM MY FENCE...
...I'LL HAVE ALL HIS I.D.! I'LL KNOW WHERE HE LIVES!

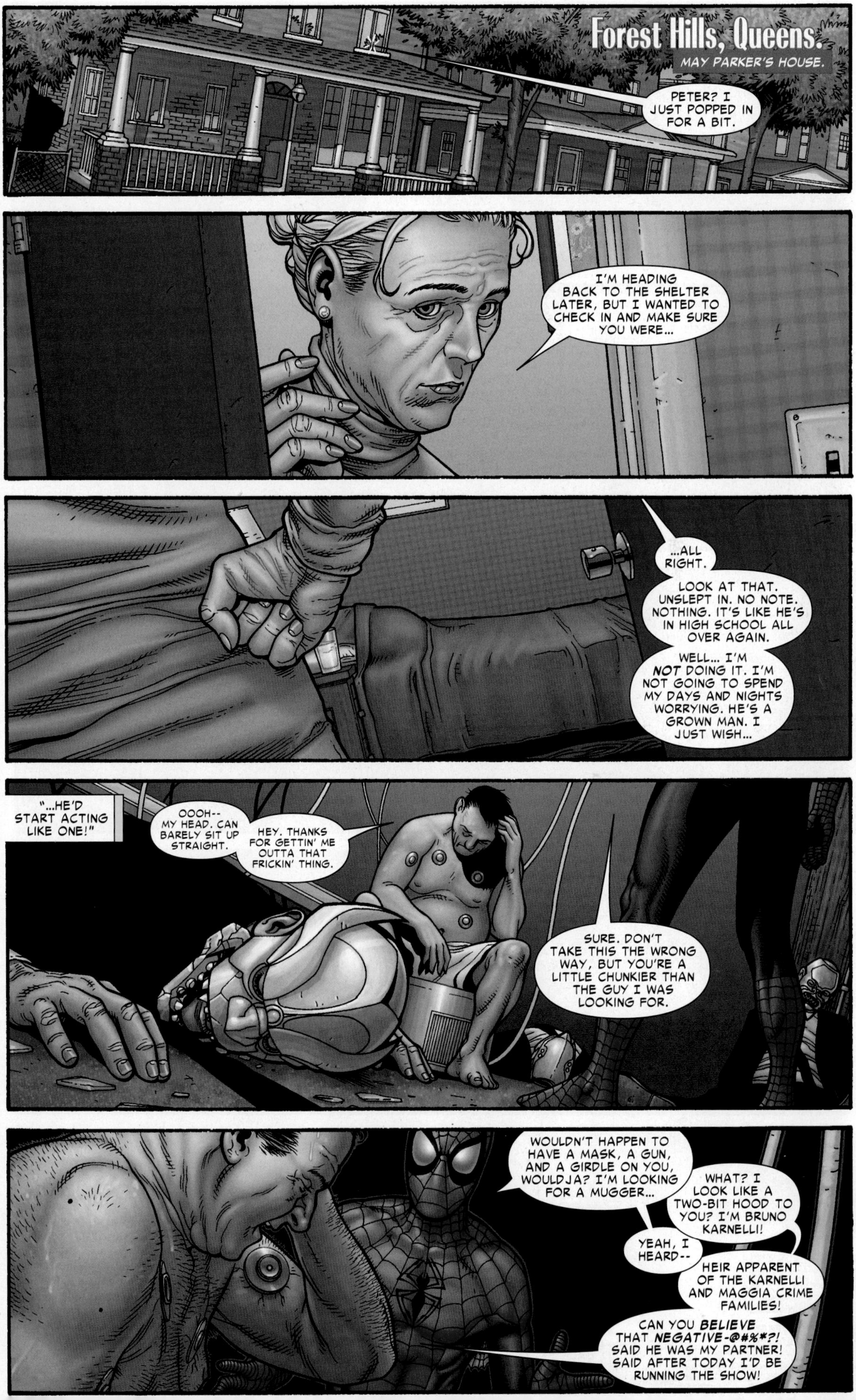
Forest Hills, Queens.
MAY PARKER'S HOUSE.
PETER? I JUST POPPED IN FOR A BIT.
I'M HEADING BACK TO THE SHELTER LATER, BUT I WANTED TO CHECK IN AND MAKE SURE YOU WERE...
...ALL RIGHT.
LOOK AT THAT. UNSLEPT IN. NO NOTE. NOTHING. IT'S LIKE HE'S IN HIGH SCHOOL ALL OVER AGAIN.
WELL... I'M *NOT* DOING IT. I'M NOT GOING TO SPEND MY DAYS AND NIGHTS WORRYING. HE'S A GROWN MAN. I JUST WISH...
"...HE'D START ACTING LIKE ONE!"
OOOH-- MY HEAD. CAN BARELY SIT UP STRAIGHT.
HEY. THANKS FOR GETTIN' ME OUTTA THAT FRICKIN' THING.
SURE. DON'T TAKE THIS THE WRONG WAY, BUT YOU'RE A LITTLE CHUNKIER THAN THE GUY I WAS LOOKING FOR.
WOULDN'T HAPPEN TO HAVE A MASK, A GUN, AND A GIRDLE ON YOU, WOULDJA? I'M LOOKING FOR A MUGGER...
WHAT? I LOOK LIKE A TWO-BIT HOOD TO YOU? I'M BRUNO KARNELLI!
YEAH, I HEARD--
HEIR APPARENT OF THE KARNELLI AND MAGGIA CRIME FAMILIES!
CAN YOU *BELIEVE* THAT *NEGATIVE*-@#%*?! SAID HE WAS MY PARTNER! SAID AFTER TODAY I'D BE RUNNING THE SHOW!

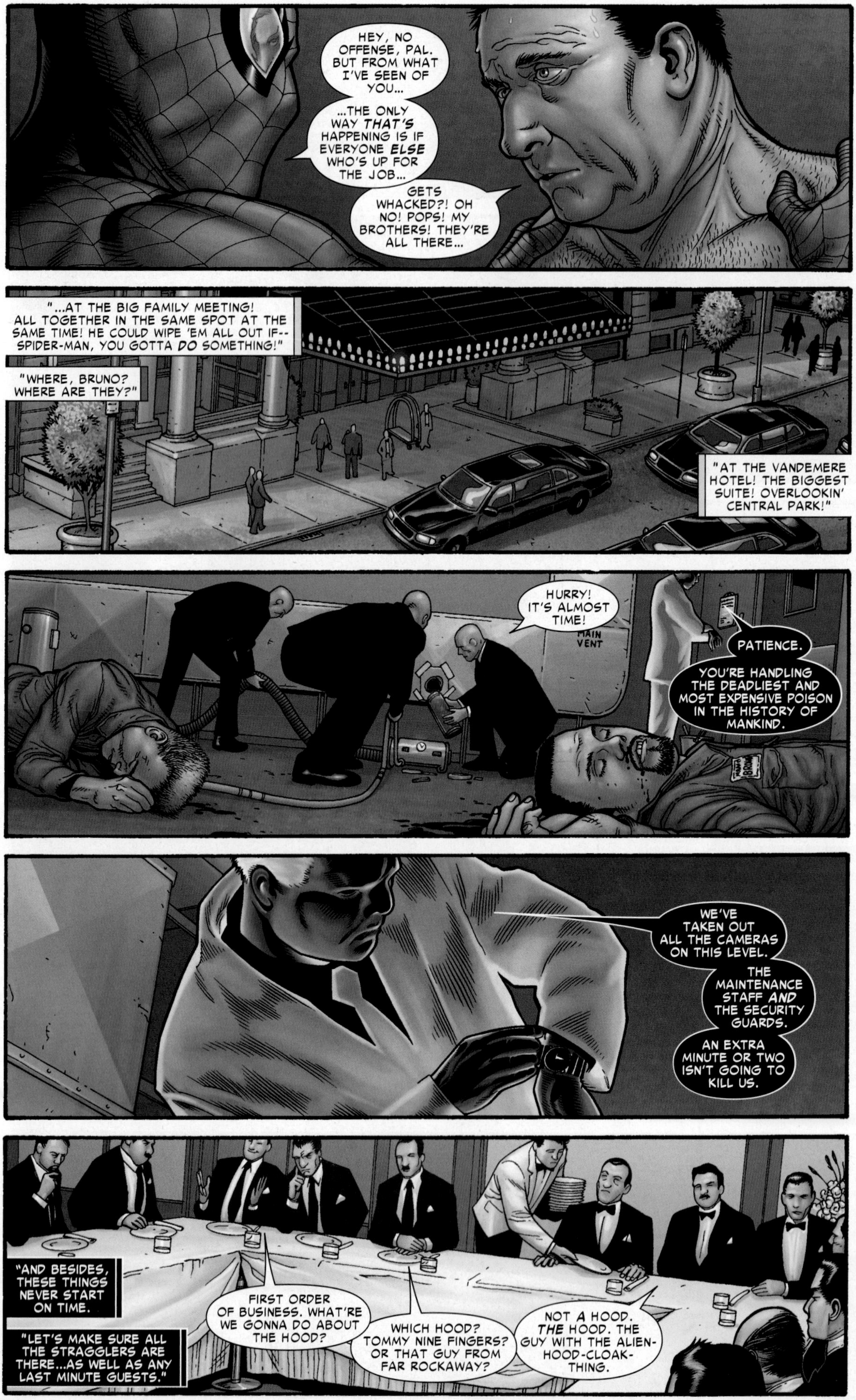
HEY, NO OFFENSE, PAL. BUT FROM WHAT I'VE SEEN OF YOU...
...THE ONLY WAY THAT'S HAPPENING IS IF EVERYONE ELSE WHO'S UP FOR THE JOB...
GETS WHACKED?! OH NO! POPS! MY BROTHERS! THEY'RE ALL THERE...
"...AT THE BIG FAMILY MEETING! ALL TOGETHER IN THE SAME SPOT AT THE SAME TIME! HE COULD WIPE 'EM ALL OUT IF-- SPIDER-MAN, YOU GOTTA DO SOMETHING!"
"WHERE, BRUNO? WHERE ARE THEY?"
"AT THE VANDEMERE HOTEL! THE BIGGEST SUITE! OVERLOOKIN' CENTRAL PARK!"
HURRY! IT'S ALMOST TIME!
MAIN VENT
PATIENCE.
YOU'RE HANDLING THE DEADLIEST AND MOST EXPENSIVE POISON IN THE HISTORY OF MANKIND.
WE'VE TAKEN OUT ALL THE CAMERAS ON THIS LEVEL.
THE MAINTENANCE STAFF AND THE SECURITY GUARDS.
AN EXTRA MINUTE OR TWO ISN'T GOING TO KILL US.
"AND BESIDES, THESE THINGS NEVER START ON TIME.
"LET'S MAKE SURE ALL THE STRAGGLERS ARE THERE...AS WELL AS ANY LAST MINUTE GUESTS."
FIRST ORDER OF BUSINESS. WHAT'RE WE GONNA DO ABOUT THE HOOD?
WHICH HOOD? TOMMY NINE FINGERS? OR THAT GUY FROM FAR ROCKAWAY?
NOT A HOOD. THE HOOD. THE GUY WITH THE ALIEN-HOOD-CLOAK-THING.

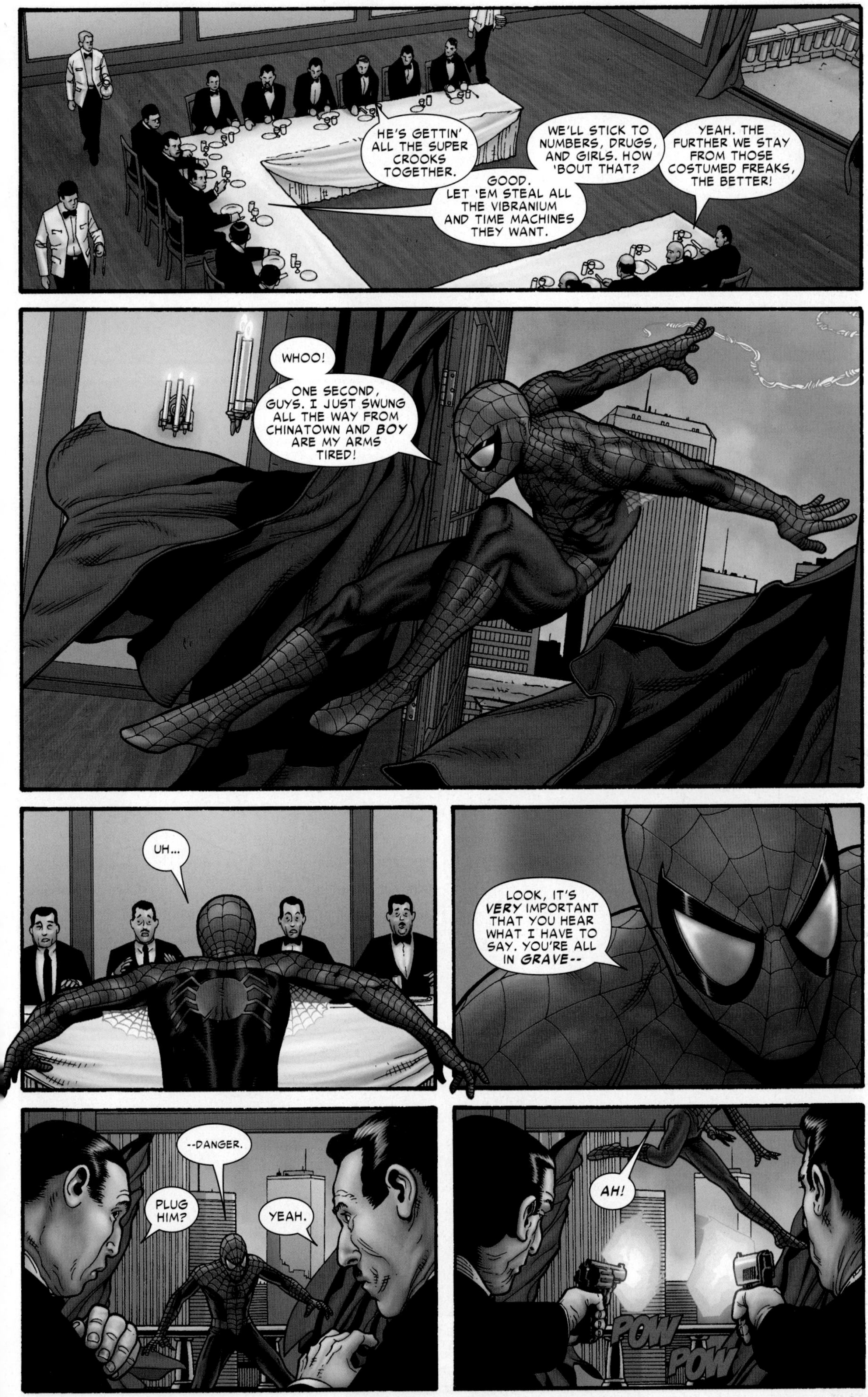
HE'S GETTIN' ALL THE SUPER CROOKS TOGETHER.
GOOD. LET 'EM STEAL ALL THE VIBRANIUM AND TIME MACHINES THEY WANT.
WE'LL STICK TO NUMBERS, DRUGS, AND GIRLS. HOW 'BOUT THAT?
YEAH. THE FURTHER WE STAY FROM THOSE COSTUMED FREAKS, THE BETTER!
WHOO!
ONE SECOND, GUYS. I JUST SWUNG ALL THE WAY FROM CHINATOWN AND BOY ARE MY ARMS TIRED!
UH...
LOOK, IT'S VERY IMPORTANT THAT YOU HEAR WHAT I HAVE TO SAY. YOU'RE ALL IN GRAVE--
--DANGER.
PLUG HIM?
YEAH.
AH!
POW
POW

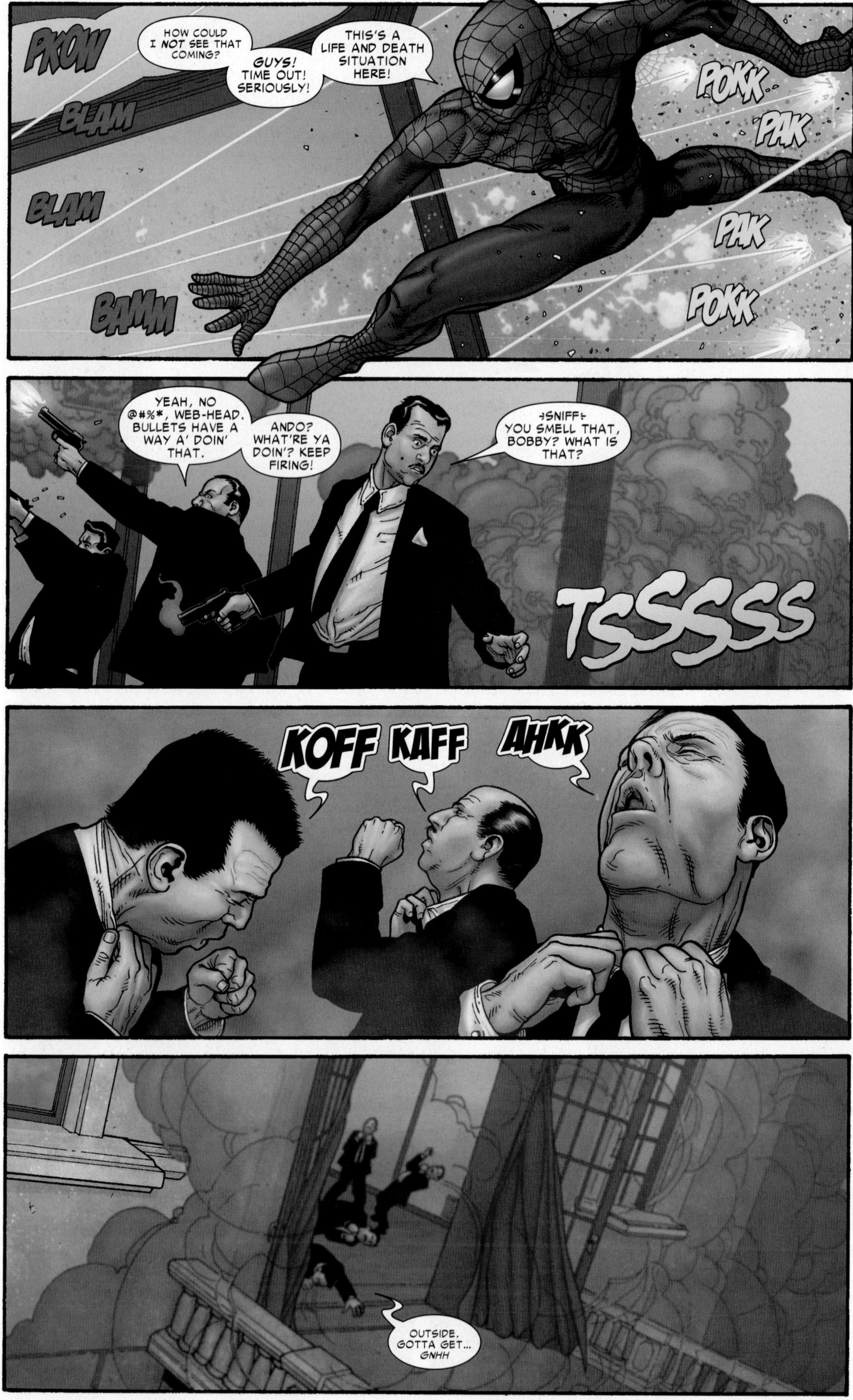
PKOW
BLAM
BLAM
BAMM
HOW COULD I NOT SEE THAT COMING?
GUYS! TIME OUT! SERIOUSLY!
THIS'S A LIFE AND DEATH SITUATION HERE!
POKK
PAK
PAK
POKK
YEAH, NO @#%*, WEB-HEAD. BULLETS HAVE A WAY A' DOIN' THAT.
ANDO? WHAT'RE YA DOIN'? KEEP FIRING!
SNIFF YOU SMELL THAT, BOBBY? WHAT IS THAT?
TSSSSS
KOFF
KAFF
AHKK
OUTSIDE. GOTTA GET... GNHH

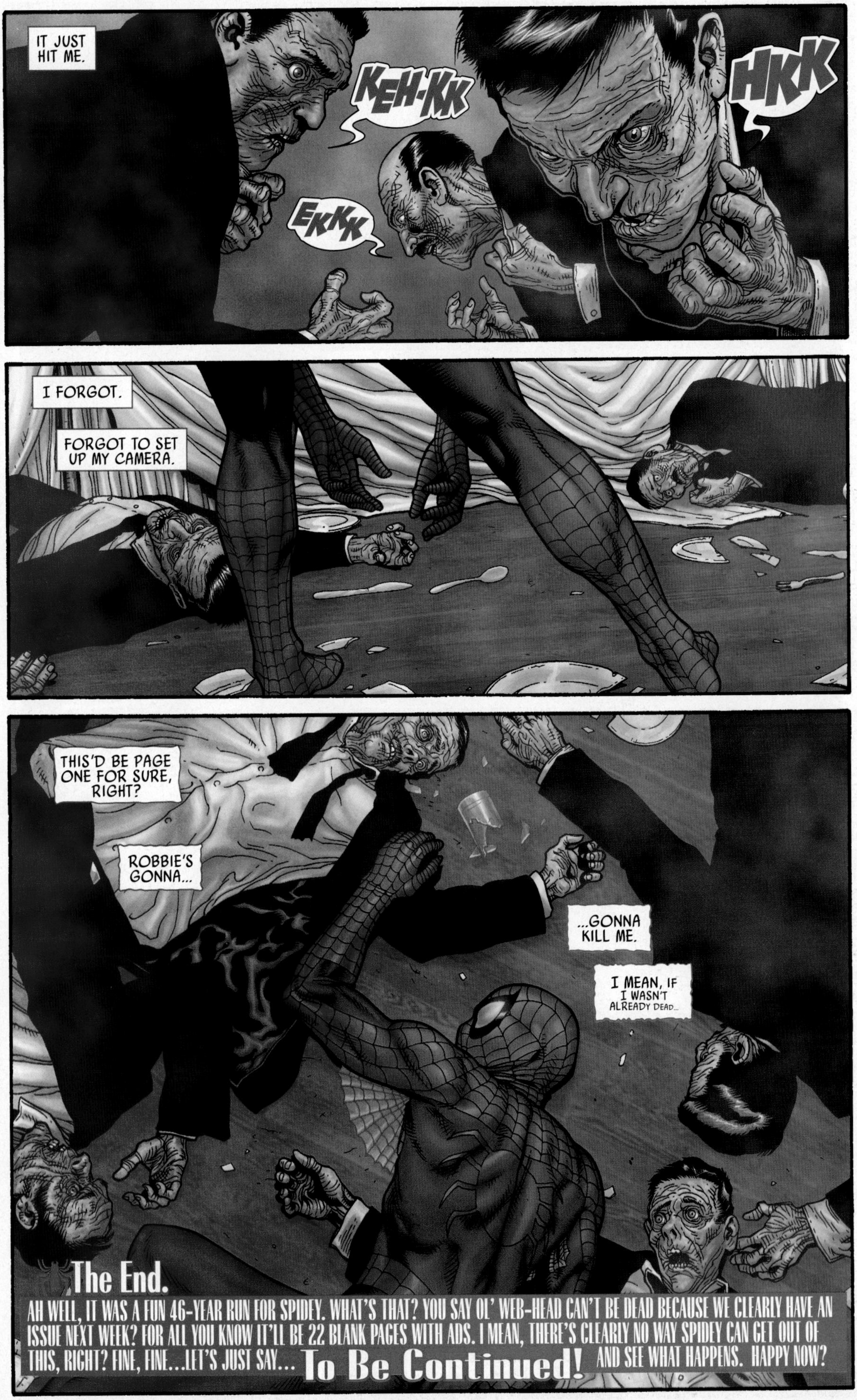
IT JUST HIT ME.
KEH-KK
HKK
EKKK
I FORGOT.
FORGOT TO SET UP MY CAMERA.
THIS'D BE PAGE ONE FOR SURE, RIGHT?
ROBBIE'S GONNA...
...GONNA KILL ME.
I MEAN, IF I WASN'T ALREADY DEAD...
The End.
AH WELL, IT WAS A FUN 46-YEAR RUN FOR SPIDEY. WHAT'S THAT? YOU SAY OL' WEB-HEAD CAN'T BE DEAD BECAUSE WE CLEARLY HAVE AN ISSUE NEXT WEEK? FOR ALL YOU KNOW IT'LL BE 22 BLANK PAGES WITH ADS. I MEAN, THERE'S CLEARLY NO WAY SPIDEY CAN GET OUT OF THIS, RIGHT? FINE, FINE...LET'S JUST SAY... To Be Continued! AND SEE WHAT HAPPENS. HAPPY NOW?

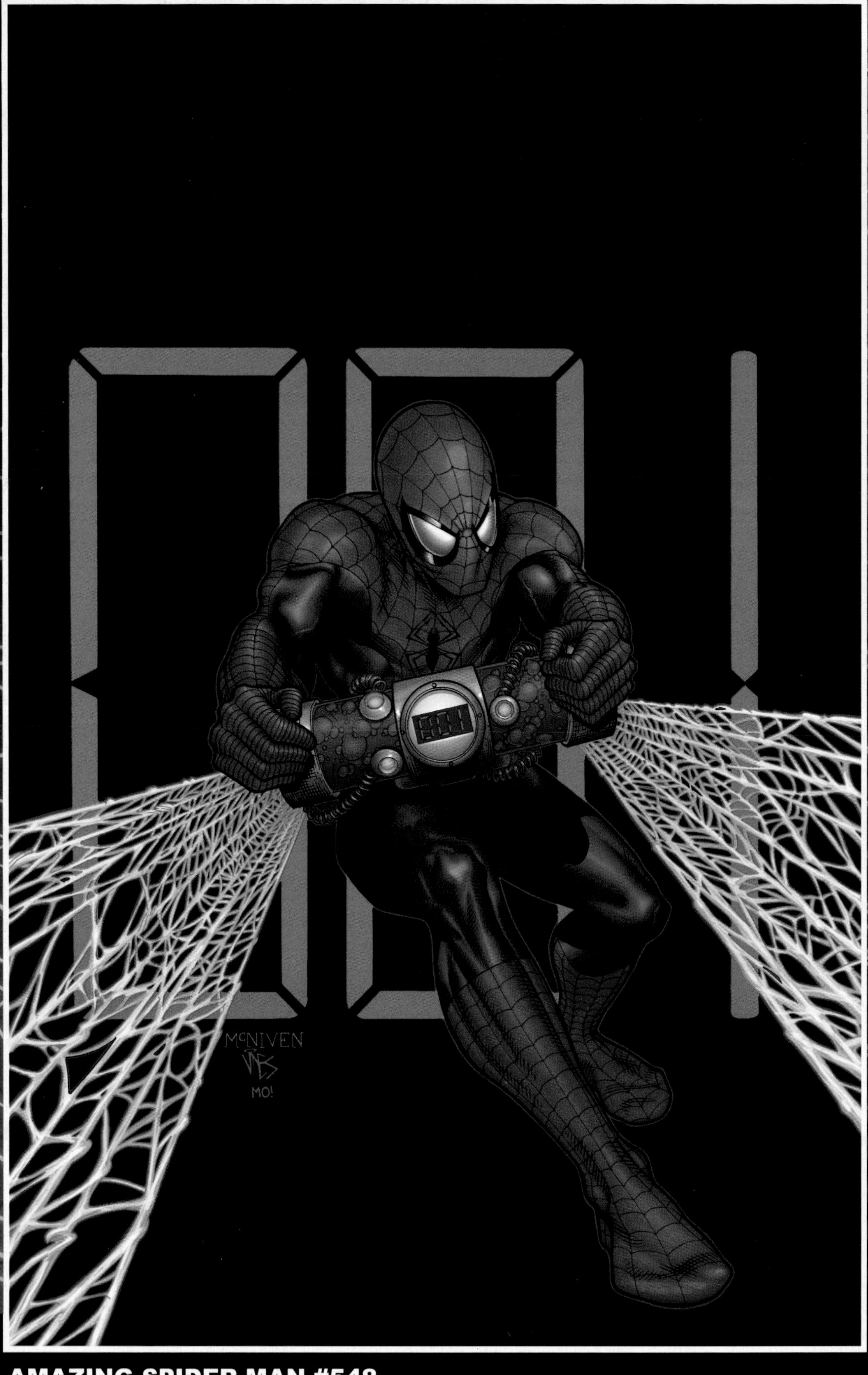
McNIVEN
MO!

AMAZING SPIDER-MAN #548
COVER BY **STEVE MCNIVEN, DEXTER VINES & MORRY HOLLOWELL**

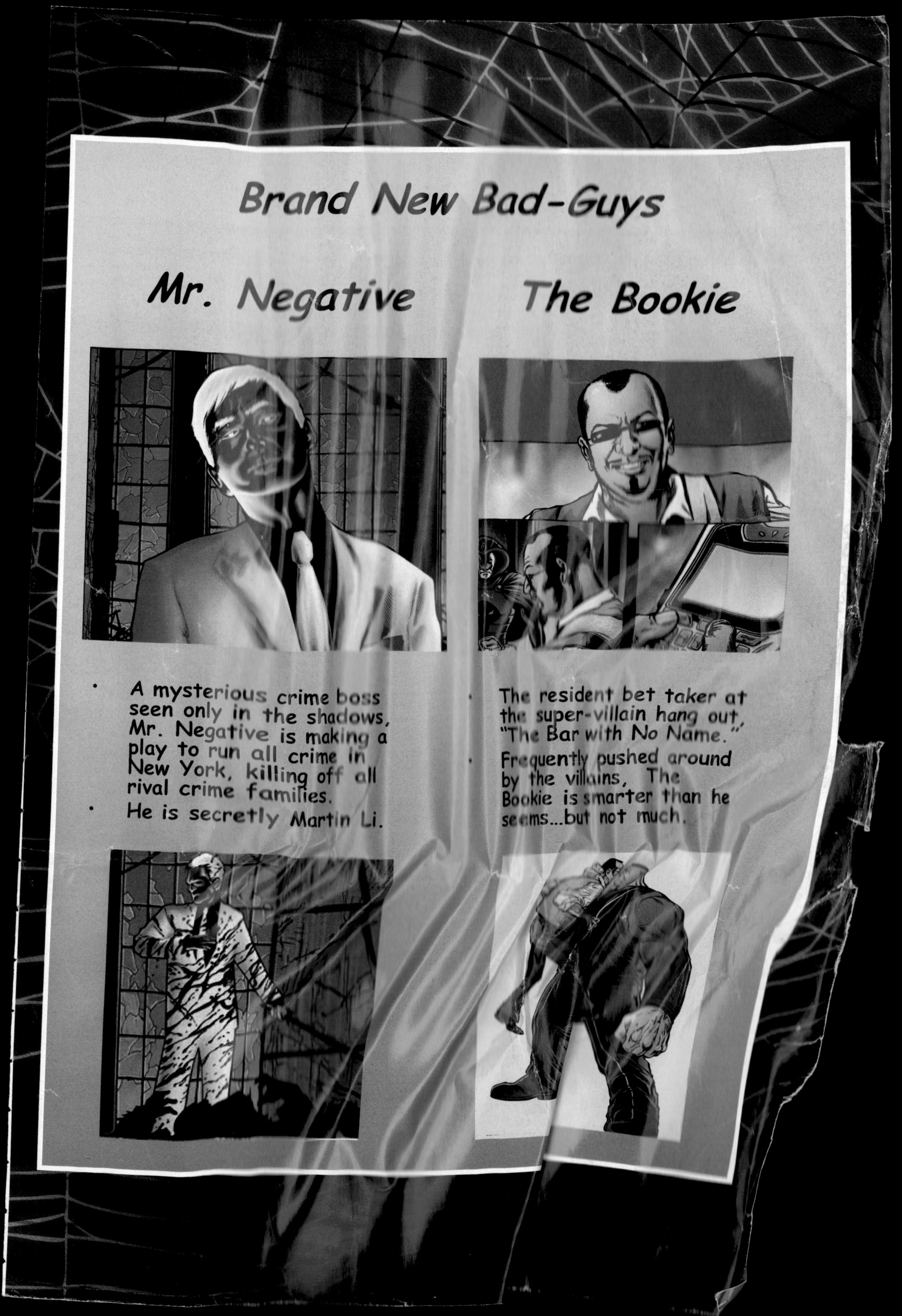
Brand New Bad-Guys
Mr. Negative
The Bookie
A mysterious crime boss seen only in the shadows, Mr. Negative is making a play to run all crime in New York, killing off all rival crime families.
He is secretly Martin Li.
The resident bet taker at the super-villain hang out, "The Bar with No Name."
Frequently pushed around by the villains, The Bookie is smarter than he seems...but not much.

Screwball

- More a public exhibitionist than villain, Screwball stages crimes to lure superheroes out for fights that she records and broadcasts on her website.

Overdrive

- A tech-powered villain who's wired into any kind of automobile, Overdrive is one of Mr. Negative's lackeys...and a Spider-Man fanboy.

Paper Doll

- A super-powered celebrity stalker, Paper Doll is paper-thin - a flat, malleable body. Her killing blow is her ability to encompass your entire body and crush the life out of you.

WHILE ATTENDING A DEMONSTRATION IN RADIOLOGY, HIGH SCHOOL STUDENT **PETER PARKER** WAS BITTEN BY A SPIDER WHICH HAD ACCIDENTALLY BEEN EXPOSED TO **RADIOACTIVE RAYS.** THROUGH A MIRACLE OF SCIENCE, PETER SOON FOUND THAT HE HAD **GAINED** THE SPIDER'S POWERS...AND HAD, IN EFFECT, BECOME A HUMAN SPIDER! FROM THAT DAY ON HE WAS...

THE AMAZING SPIDER-MAN™

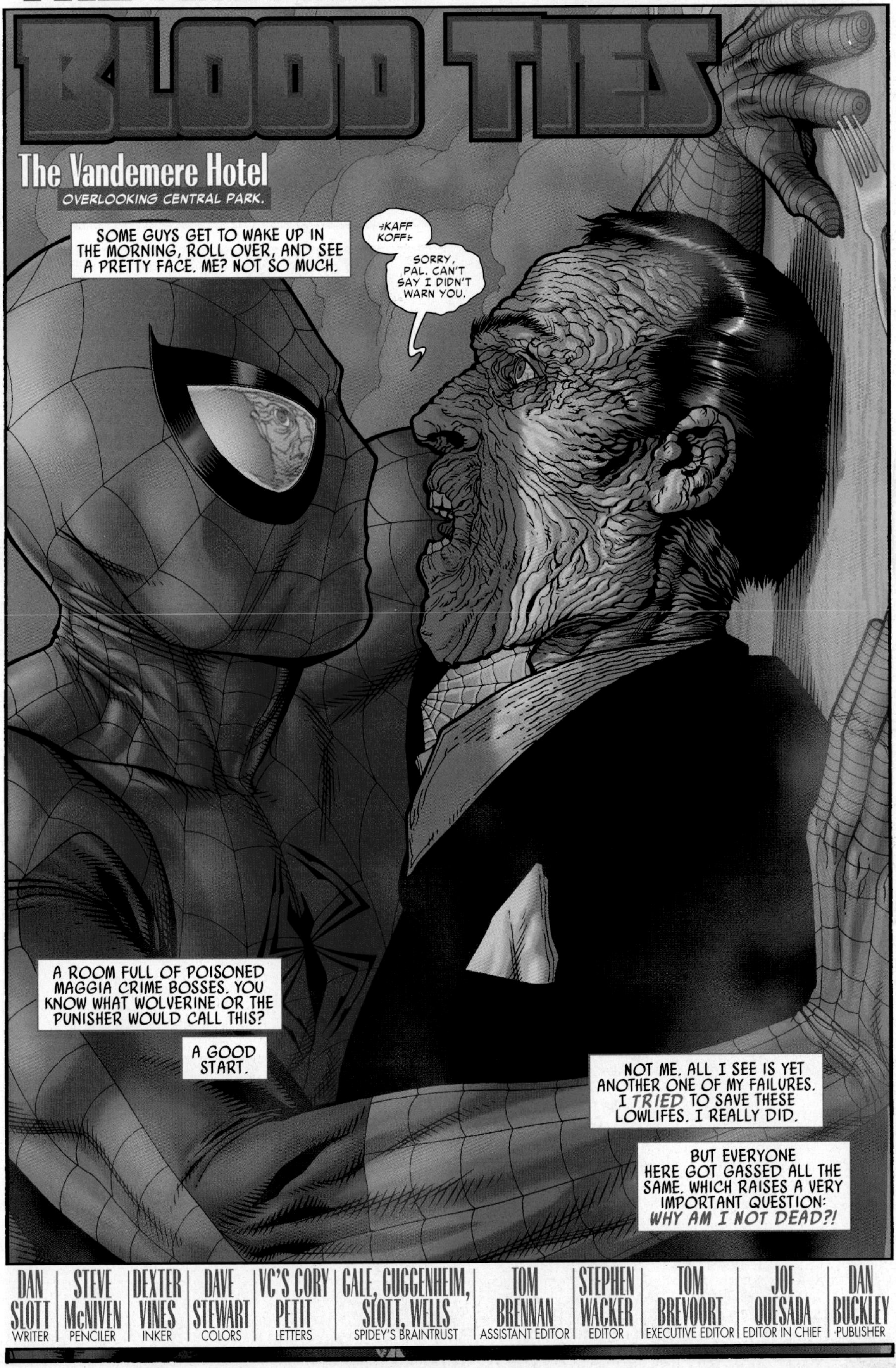
BLOOD TIES
The Vandemere Hotel
OVERLOOKING CENTRAL PARK.
SOME GUYS GET TO WAKE UP IN THE MORNING, ROLL OVER, AND SEE A PRETTY FACE. ME? NOT SO MUCH.
KAFF KOFF
SORRY, PAL. CAN'T SAY I DIDN'T WARN YOU.
A ROOM FULL OF POISONED MAGGIA CRIME BOSSES. YOU KNOW WHAT WOLVERINE OR THE PUNISHER WOULD CALL THIS?
A GOOD START.
NOT ME. ALL I SEE IS YET ANOTHER ONE OF MY FAILURES. I TRIED TO SAVE THESE LOWLIFES. I REALLY DID.
BUT EVERYONE HERE GOT GASSED ALL THE SAME. WHICH RAISES A VERY IMPORTANT QUESTION: WHY AM I NOT DEAD?!

DAN SLOTT WRITER | STEVE McNIVEN PENCILER | DEXTER VINES INKER | DAVE STEWART COLORS | VC'S CORY PETIT LETTERS | GALE, GUGGENHEIM, SLOTT, WELLS SPIDEY'S BRAINTRUST | TOM BRENNAN ASSISTANT EDITOR | STEPHEN WACKER EDITOR | TOM BREVOORT EXECUTIVE EDITOR | JOE QUESADA EDITOR IN CHIEF | DAN BUCKLEY PUBLISHER

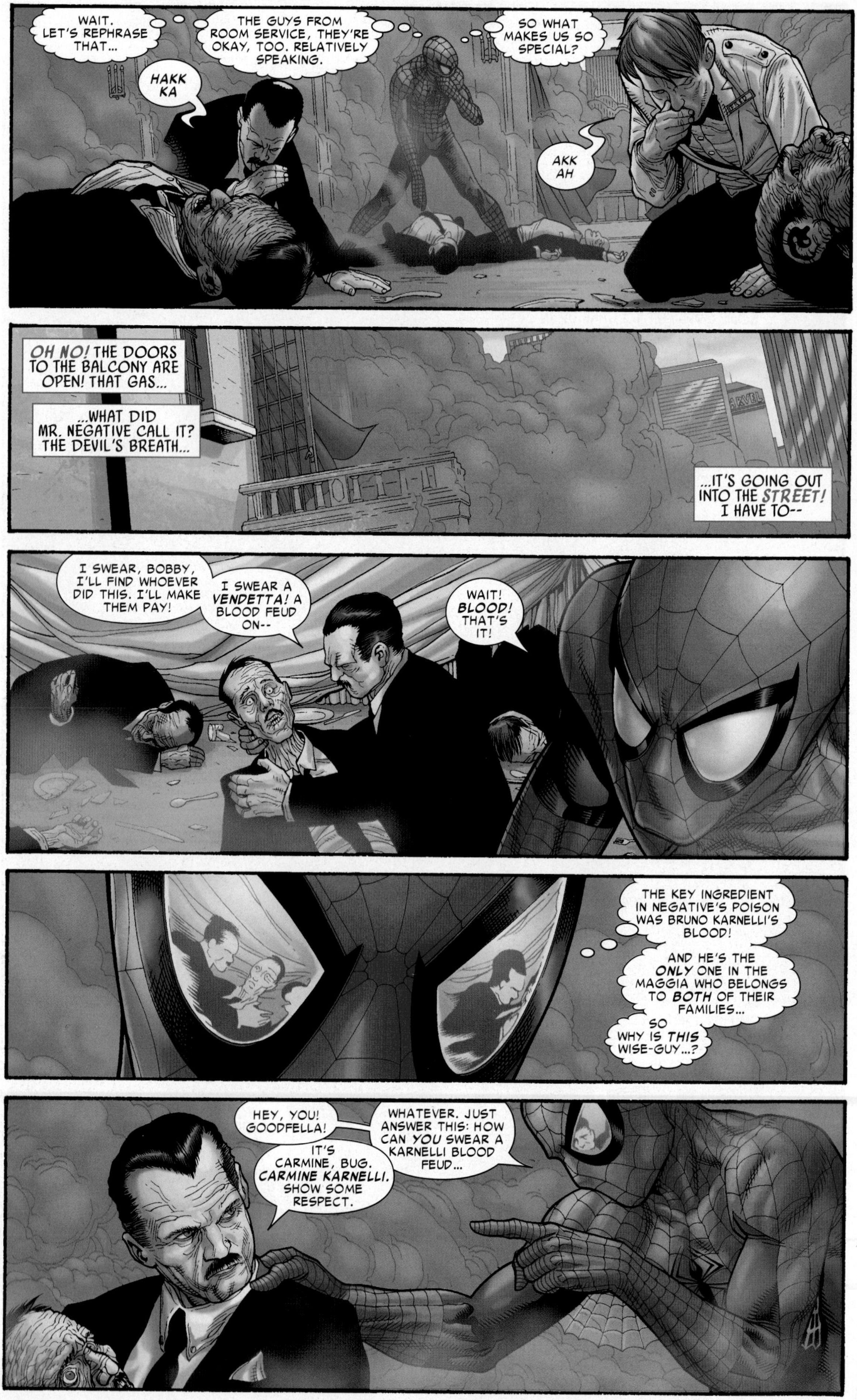
WAIT. LET'S REPHRASE THAT...
THE GUYS FROM ROOM SERVICE, THEY'RE OKAY, TOO. RELATIVELY SPEAKING.
SO WHAT MAKES US SO SPECIAL?
HAKK KA
AKK AH
OH NO! THE DOORS TO THE BALCONY ARE OPEN! THAT GAS...
...WHAT DID MR. NEGATIVE CALL IT? THE DEVIL'S BREATH...
...IT'S GOING OUT INTO THE STREET! I HAVE TO--
I SWEAR, BOBBY, I'LL FIND WHOEVER DID THIS. I'LL MAKE THEM PAY!
I SWEAR A VENDETTA! A BLOOD FEUD ON--
WAIT! BLOOD! THAT'S IT!
THE KEY INGREDIENT IN NEGATIVE'S POISON WAS BRUNO KARNELLI'S BLOOD!
AND HE'S THE ONLY ONE IN THE MAGGIA WHO BELONGS TO BOTH OF THEIR FAMILIES...
SO WHY IS THIS WISE-GUY...?
HEY, YOU! GOODFELLA!
IT'S CARMINE, BUG. CARMINE KARNELLI. SHOW SOME RESPECT.
WHATEVER. JUST ANSWER THIS: HOW CAN YOU SWEAR A KARNELLI BLOOD FEUD...

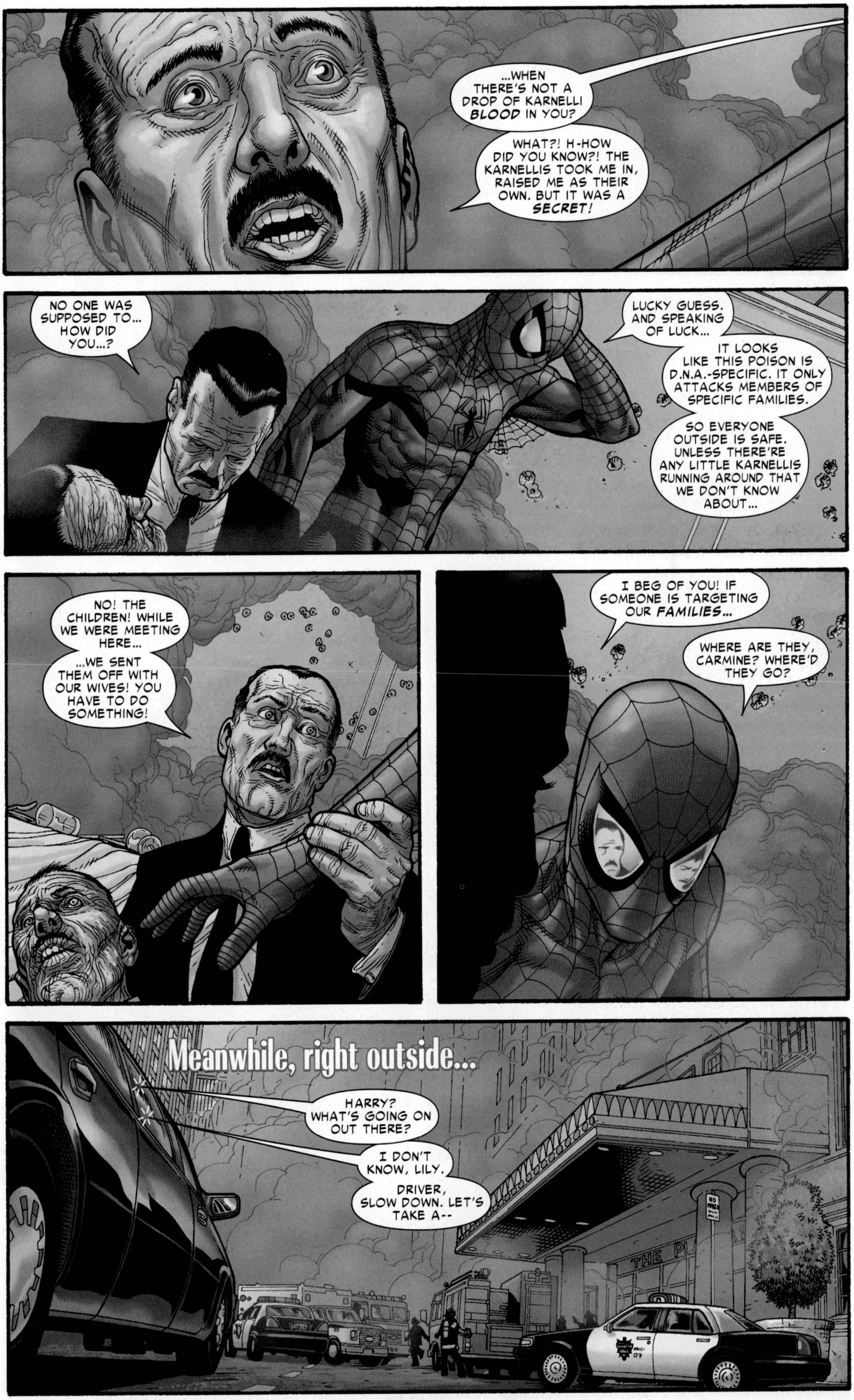
...WHEN THERE'S NOT A DROP OF KARNELLI *BLOOD* IN YOU?
WHAT?! H-HOW DID YOU KNOW?! THE KARNELLIS TOOK ME IN, RAISED ME AS THEIR OWN. BUT IT WAS A ***SECRET!***
NO ONE WAS SUPPOSED TO... HOW DID YOU...?
LUCKY GUESS. AND SPEAKING OF LUCK...
IT LOOKS LIKE THIS POISON IS D.N.A.-SPECIFIC. IT ONLY ATTACKS MEMBERS OF SPECIFIC FAMILIES.
SO EVERYONE OUTSIDE IS SAFE. UNLESS THERE'RE ANY LITTLE KARNELLIS RUNNING AROUND THAT WE DON'T KNOW ABOUT...
NO! THE CHILDREN! WHILE WE WERE MEETING HERE...
...WE SENT THEM OFF WITH OUR WIVES! YOU HAVE TO DO SOMETHING!
I BEG OF YOU! IF SOMEONE IS TARGETING OUR *FAMILIES*...
WHERE ARE THEY, CARMINE? WHERE'D THEY GO?
Meanwhile, right outside...
HARRY? WHAT'S GOING ON OUT THERE?
I DON'T KNOW, LILY.
DRIVER, SLOW DOWN. LET'S TAKE A--

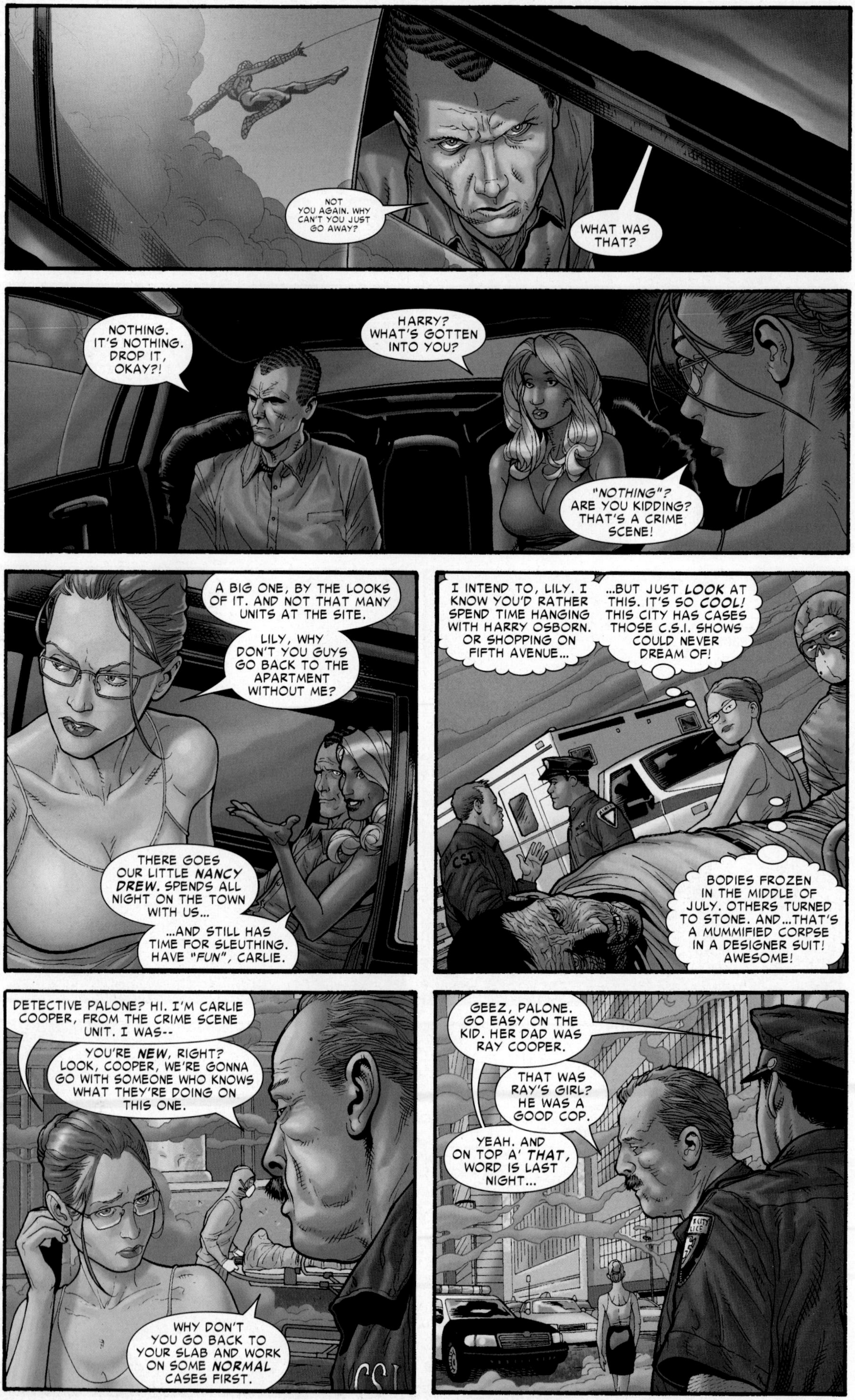
NOT YOU AGAIN. WHY CAN'T YOU JUST GO AWAY?
WHAT WAS THAT?
NOTHING. IT'S NOTHING. DROP IT, OKAY?!
HARRY? WHAT'S GOTTEN INTO YOU?
"NOTHING"? ARE YOU KIDDING? THAT'S A CRIME SCENE!
A BIG ONE, BY THE LOOKS OF IT. AND NOT THAT MANY UNITS AT THE SITE.
LILY, WHY DON'T YOU GUYS GO BACK TO THE APARTMENT WITHOUT ME?
THERE GOES OUR LITTLE NANCY DREW. SPENDS ALL NIGHT ON THE TOWN WITH US...
...AND STILL HAS TIME FOR SLEUTHING. HAVE "FUN", CARLIE.
I INTEND TO, LILY. I KNOW YOU'D RATHER SPEND TIME HANGING WITH HARRY OSBORN. OR SHOPPING ON FIFTH AVENUE...
...BUT JUST LOOK AT THIS. IT'S SO COOL! THIS CITY HAS CASES THOSE C.S.I. SHOWS COULD NEVER DREAM OF!
BODIES FROZEN IN THE MIDDLE OF JULY. OTHERS TURNED TO STONE. AND...THAT'S A MUMMIFIED CORPSE IN A DESIGNER SUIT! AWESOME!
DETECTIVE PALONE? HI. I'M CARLIE COOPER, FROM THE CRIME SCENE UNIT. I WAS--
YOU'RE NEW, RIGHT? LOOK, COOPER, WE'RE GONNA GO WITH SOMEONE WHO KNOWS WHAT THEY'RE DOING ON THIS ONE.
WHY DON'T YOU GO BACK TO YOUR SLAB AND WORK ON SOME NORMAL CASES FIRST.
GEEZ, PALONE. GO EASY ON THE KID. HER DAD WAS RAY COOPER.
THAT WAS RAY'S GIRL? HE WAS A GOOD COP.
YEAH. AND ON TOP A' THAT, WORD IS LAST NIGHT...

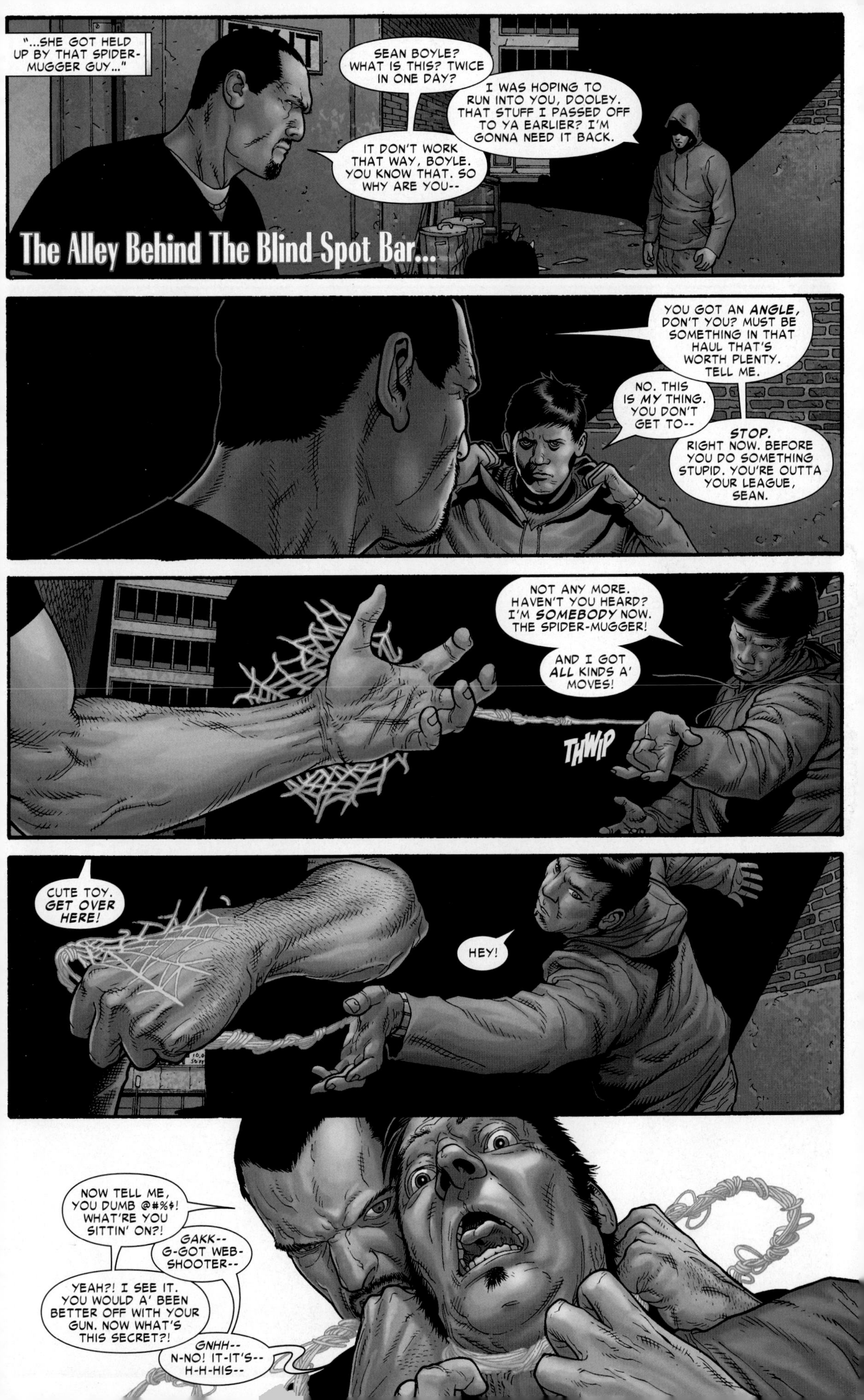
"...SHE GOT HELD UP BY THAT SPIDER-MUGGER GUY..."
SEAN BOYLE? WHAT IS THIS? TWICE IN ONE DAY?
I WAS HOPING TO RUN INTO YOU, DOOLEY. THAT STUFF I PASSED OFF TO YA EARLIER? I'M GONNA NEED IT BACK.
IT DON'T WORK THAT WAY, BOYLE. YOU KNOW THAT. SO WHY ARE YOU--
The Alley Behind The Blind Spot Bar...
YOU GOT AN ANGLE, DON'T YOU? MUST BE SOMETHING IN THAT HAUL THAT'S WORTH PLENTY. TELL ME.
NO. THIS IS MY THING. YOU DON'T GET TO--
STOP. RIGHT NOW. BEFORE YOU DO SOMETHING STUPID. YOU'RE OUTTA YOUR LEAGUE, SEAN.
NOT ANY MORE. HAVEN'T YOU HEARD? I'M SOMEBODY NOW. THE SPIDER-MUGGER!
AND I GOT ALL KINDS A' MOVES!
THWIP
CUTE TOY. GET OVER HERE!
HEY!
NOW TELL ME, YOU DUMB @#%$! WHAT'RE YOU SITTIN' ON?!
GAKK-- G-GOT WEB-SHOOTER--
YEAH?! I SEE IT. YOU WOULD A' BEEN BETTER OFF WITH YOUR GUN. NOW WHAT'S THIS SECRET?!
GNHH-- N-NO! IT-IT'S-- H-H-HIS--

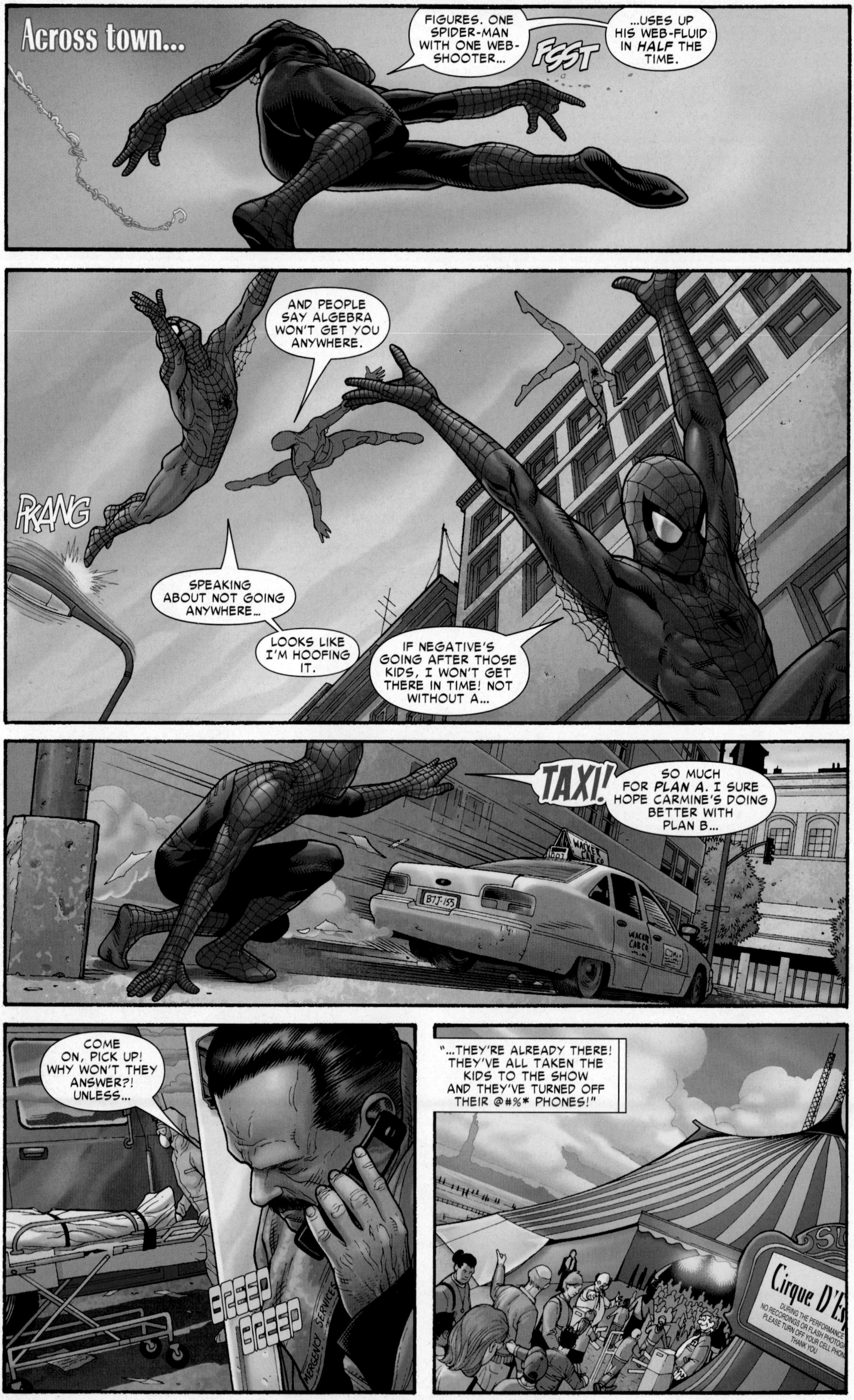
Across town...
FIGURES. ONE SPIDER-MAN WITH ONE WEB-SHOOTER...
FSST
...USES UP HIS WEB-FLUID IN HALF THE TIME.
AND PEOPLE SAY ALGEBRA WON'T GET YOU ANYWHERE.
PKANG
SPEAKING ABOUT NOT GOING ANYWHERE...
LOOKS LIKE I'M HOOFING IT.
IF NEGATIVE'S GOING AFTER THOSE KIDS, I WON'T GET THERE IN TIME! NOT WITHOUT A...
TAXI!
SO MUCH FOR PLAN A. I SURE HOPE CARMINE'S DOING BETTER WITH PLAN B...
COME ON, PICK UP! WHY WON'T THEY ANSWER?! UNLESS...
BEEP BEEP
"...THEY'RE ALREADY THERE! THEY'VE ALL TAKEN THE KIDS TO THE SHOW AND THEY'VE TURNED OFF THEIR @#%* PHONES!"
DURING THE PERFORMANCE
THANK YOU

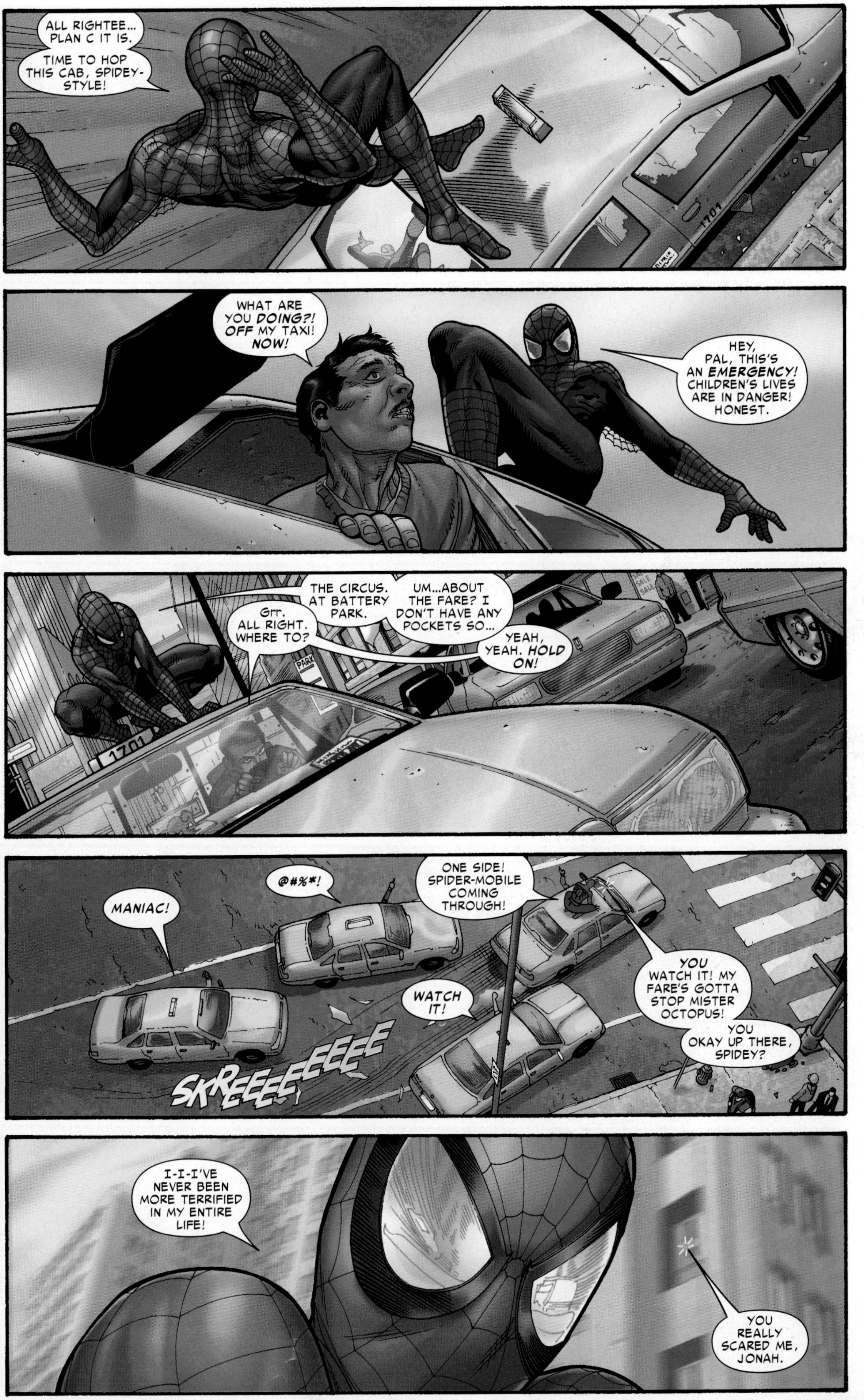
ALL RIGHTEE... PLAN C IT IS.
TIME TO HOP THIS CAB, SPIDEY-STYLE!
1701
WHAT ARE YOU DOING?! OFF MY TAXI! NOW!
HEY, PAL, THIS'S AN EMERGENCY! CHILDREN'S LIVES ARE IN DANGER! HONEST.
Grr. ALL RIGHT. WHERE TO?
THE CIRCUS. AT BATTERY PARK.
UM...ABOUT THE FARE? I DON'T HAVE ANY POCKETS SO...
YEAH, YEAH. HOLD ON!
PARK
1701
MANIAC!
@#%*!
ONE SIDE! SPIDER-MOBILE COMING THROUGH!
WATCH IT!
YOU WATCH IT! MY FARE'S GOTTA STOP MISTER OCTOPUS!
YOU OKAY UP THERE, SPIDEY?
SKREEEEEEEEEE
I-I-I'VE NEVER BEEN MORE TERRIFIED IN MY ENTIRE LIFE!
YOU REALLY SCARED ME, JONAH.

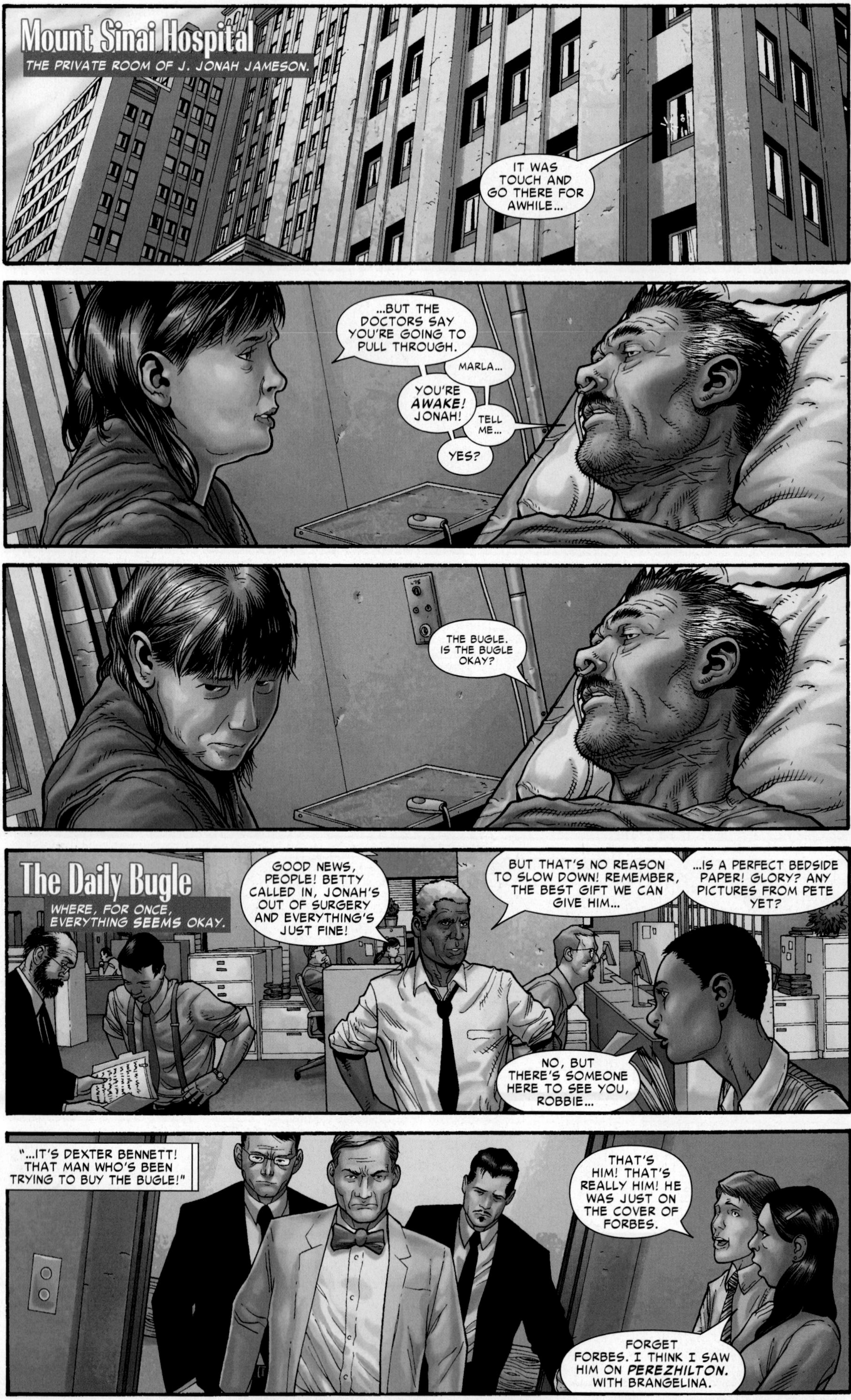

Mount Sinai Hospital
THE PRIVATE ROOM OF J. JONAH JAMESON.
IT WAS TOUCH AND GO THERE FOR AWHILE...
...BUT THE DOCTORS SAY YOU'RE GOING TO PULL THROUGH.
MARLA...
YOU'RE AWAKE! JONAH!
TELL ME...
YES?
THE BUGLE. IS THE BUGLE OKAY?
The Daily Bugle
WHERE, FOR ONCE, EVERYTHING SEEMS OKAY.
GOOD NEWS, PEOPLE! BETTY CALLED IN, JONAH'S OUT OF SURGERY AND EVERYTHING'S JUST FINE!
BUT THAT'S NO REASON TO SLOW DOWN! REMEMBER, THE BEST GIFT WE CAN GIVE HIM...
...IS A PERFECT BEDSIDE PAPER! GLORY? ANY PICTURES FROM PETE YET?
NO, BUT THERE'S SOMEONE HERE TO SEE YOU, ROBBIE...
"...IT'S DEXTER BENNETT! THAT MAN WHO'S BEEN TRYING TO BUY THE BUGLE!"
THAT'S HIM! THAT'S REALLY HIM! HE WAS JUST ON THE COVER OF FORBES.
FORGET FORBES. I THINK I SAW HIM ON PEREZHILTON. WITH BRANGELINA.

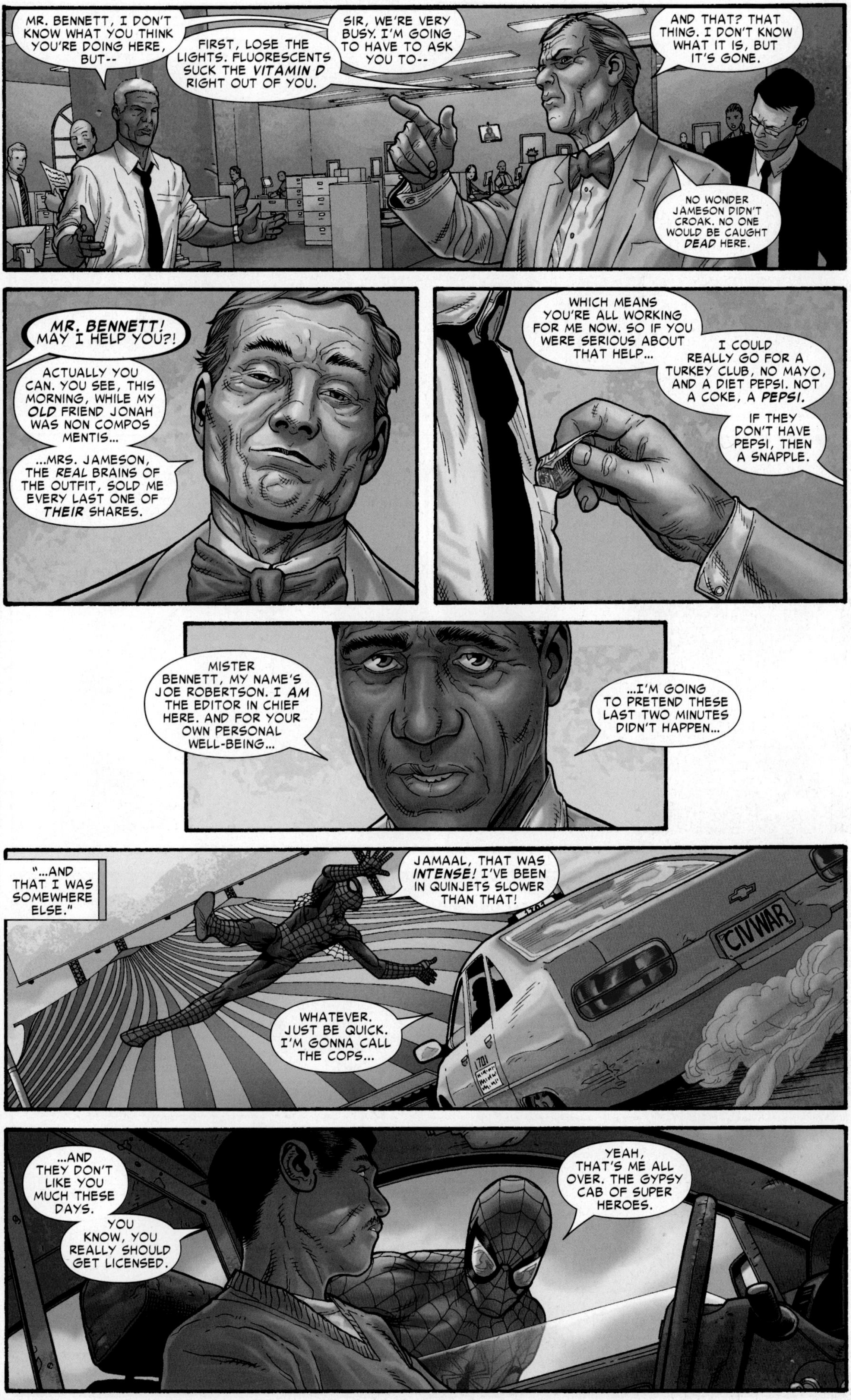
MR. BENNETT, I DON'T KNOW WHAT YOU THINK YOU'RE DOING HERE, BUT--
FIRST, LOSE THE LIGHTS. FLUORESCENTS SUCK THE VITAMIN D RIGHT OUT OF YOU.
SIR, WE'RE VERY BUSY. I'M GOING TO HAVE TO ASK YOU TO--
AND THAT? THAT THING. I DON'T KNOW WHAT IT IS, BUT IT'S GONE.
NO WONDER JAMESON DIDN'T CROAK. NO ONE WOULD BE CAUGHT DEAD HERE.
MR. BENNETT! MAY I HELP YOU?!
ACTUALLY YOU CAN. YOU SEE, THIS MORNING, WHILE MY OLD FRIEND JONAH WAS NON COMPOS MENTIS...
...MRS. JAMESON, THE REAL BRAINS OF THE OUTFIT, SOLD ME EVERY LAST ONE OF THEIR SHARES.
WHICH MEANS YOU'RE ALL WORKING FOR ME NOW. SO IF YOU WERE SERIOUS ABOUT THAT HELP...
I COULD REALLY GO FOR A TURKEY CLUB, NO MAYO, AND A DIET PEPSI. NOT A COKE, A PEPSI.
IF THEY DON'T HAVE PEPSI, THEN A SNAPPLE.
MISTER BENNETT, MY NAME'S JOE ROBERTSON. I AM THE EDITOR IN CHIEF HERE. AND FOR YOUR OWN PERSONAL WELL-BEING...
...I'M GOING TO PRETEND THESE LAST TWO MINUTES DIDN'T HAPPEN...
"...AND THAT I WAS SOMEWHERE ELSE."
JAMAAL, THAT WAS INTENSE! I'VE BEEN IN QUINJETS SLOWER THAN THAT!
CIVWAR
WHATEVER. JUST BE QUICK. I'M GONNA CALL THE COPS...
...AND THEY DON'T LIKE YOU MUCH THESE DAYS.
YOU KNOW, YOU REALLY SHOULD GET LICENSED.
YEAH, THAT'S ME ALL OVER. THE GYPSY CAB OF SUPER HEROES.

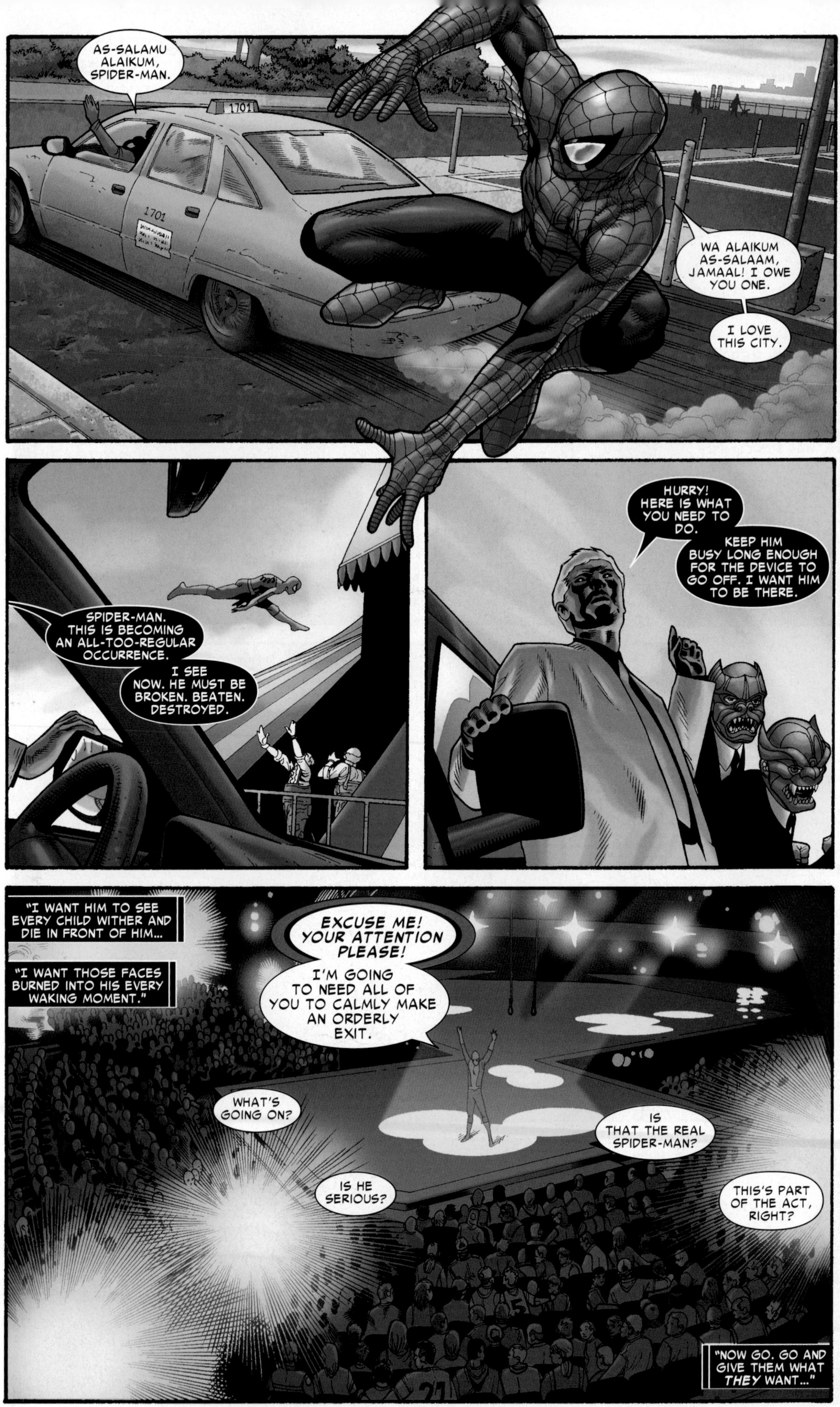

AS-SALAMU ALAIKUM, SPIDER-MAN.
1701
WA ALAIKUM AS-SALAAM, JAMAAL! I OWE YOU ONE.
I LOVE THIS CITY.
SPIDER-MAN. THIS IS BECOMING AN ALL-TOO-REGULAR OCCURRENCE.
I SEE NOW. HE MUST BE BROKEN. BEATEN. DESTROYED.
HURRY! HERE IS WHAT YOU NEED TO DO.
KEEP HIM BUSY LONG ENOUGH FOR THE DEVICE TO GO OFF. I WANT HIM TO BE THERE.
"I WANT HIM TO SEE EVERY CHILD WITHER AND DIE IN FRONT OF HIM...
"I WANT THOSE FACES BURNED INTO HIS EVERY WAKING MOMENT."
EXCUSE ME! YOUR ATTENTION PLEASE!
I'M GOING TO NEED ALL OF YOU TO CALMLY MAKE AN ORDERLY EXIT.
WHAT'S GOING ON?
IS THAT THE REAL SPIDER-MAN?
IS HE SERIOUS?
THIS'S PART OF THE ACT, RIGHT?
"NOW GO. GO AND GIVE THEM WHAT *THEY* WANT..."

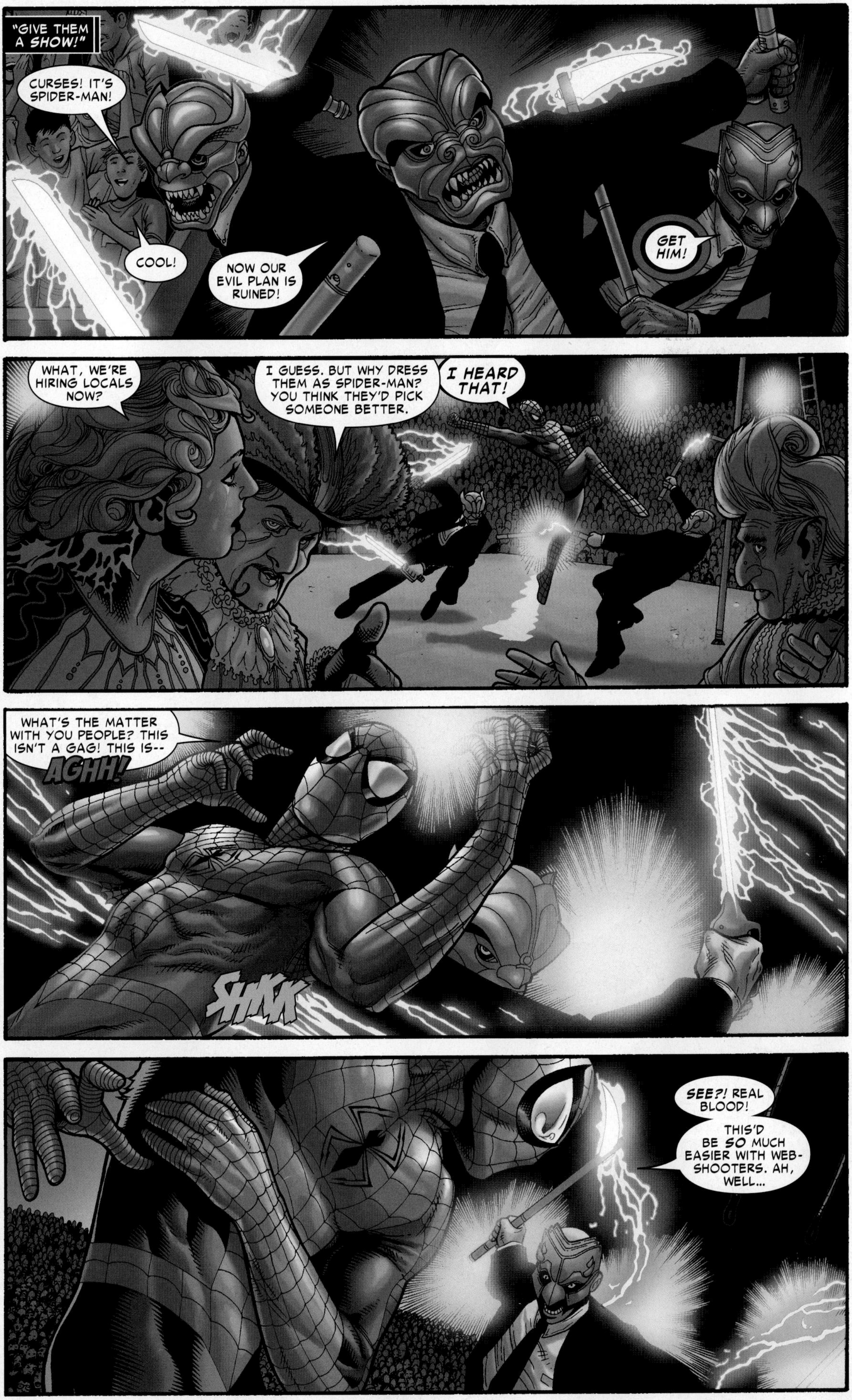
"GIVE THEM A *SHOW!*"
CURSES! IT'S SPIDER-MAN!
COOL!
NOW OUR EVIL PLAN IS RUINED!
GET HIM!
WHAT, WE'RE HIRING LOCALS NOW?
I GUESS. BUT WHY DRESS THEM AS SPIDER-MAN? YOU THINK THEY'D PICK SOMEONE BETTER.
I HEARD THAT!
WHAT'S THE MATTER WITH YOU PEOPLE? THIS ISN'T A GAG! THIS IS--
AGHH!
SHKK
SEE?! REAL BLOOD!
THIS'D BE *SO* MUCH EASIER WITH WEB-SHOOTERS. AH, WELL...

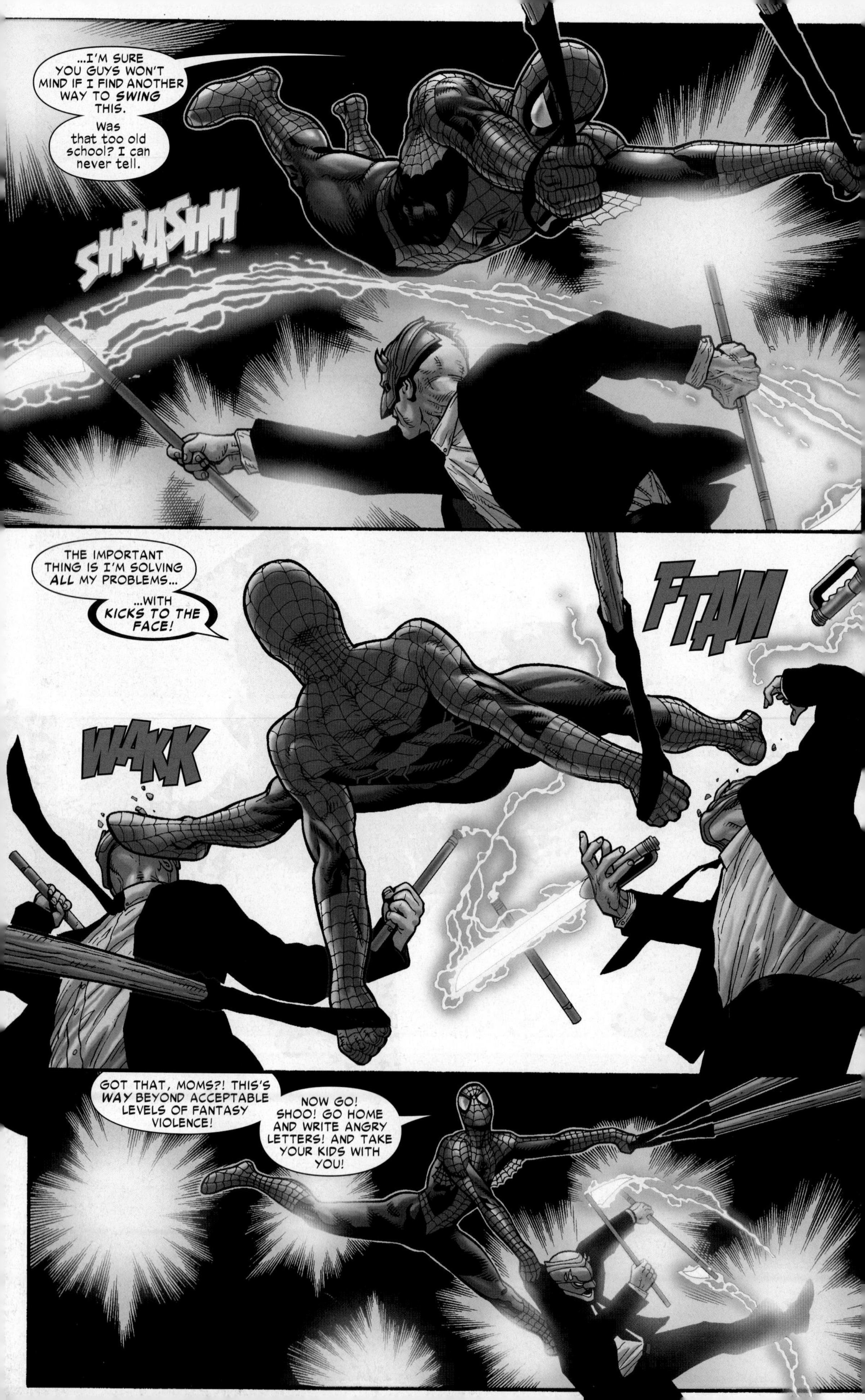
...I'M SURE YOU GUYS WON'T MIND IF I FIND ANOTHER WAY TO SWING THIS.
Was that too old school? I can never tell.
SHRASHH
THE IMPORTANT THING IS I'M SOLVING ALL MY PROBLEMS...
...WITH KICKS TO THE FACE!
FTAM
WAKK
GOT THAT, MOMS?! THIS'S WAY BEYOND ACCEPTABLE LEVELS OF FANTASY VIOLENCE!
NOW GO! SHOO! GO HOME AND WRITE ANGRY LETTERS! AND TAKE YOUR KIDS WITH YOU!

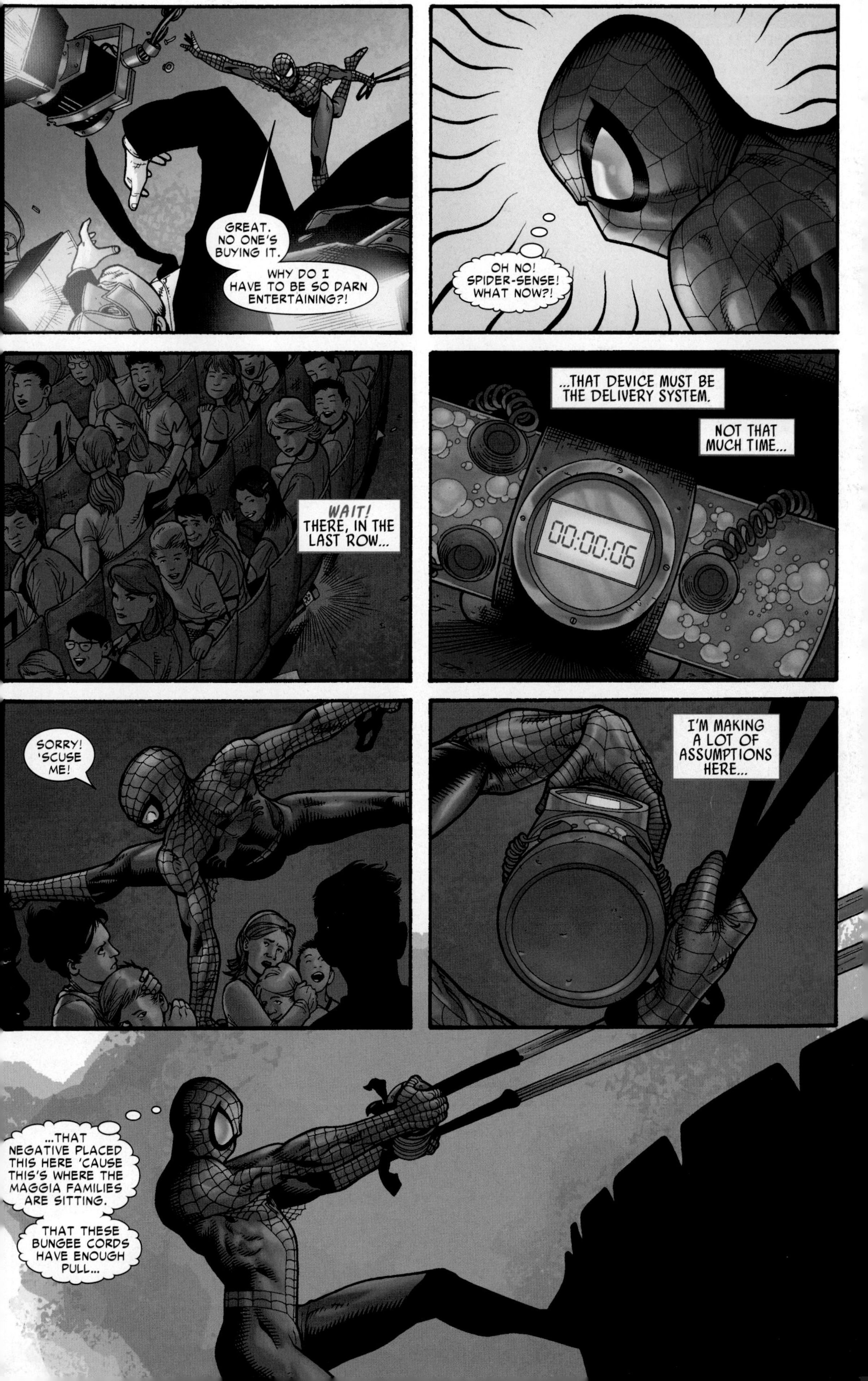
GREAT. NO ONE'S BUYING IT.
WHY DO I HAVE TO BE SO DARN ENTERTAINING?!
OH NO! SPIDER-SENSE! WHAT NOW?!
WAIT! THERE, IN THE LAST ROW...
...THAT DEVICE MUST BE THE DELIVERY SYSTEM.
NOT THAT MUCH TIME...
00:00:06
SORRY! 'SCUSE ME!
I'M MAKING A LOT OF ASSUMPTIONS HERE...
...THAT NEGATIVE PLACED THIS HERE 'CAUSE THIS'S WHERE THE MAGGIA FAMILIES ARE SITTING.
THAT THESE BUNGEE CORDS HAVE ENOUGH PULL...

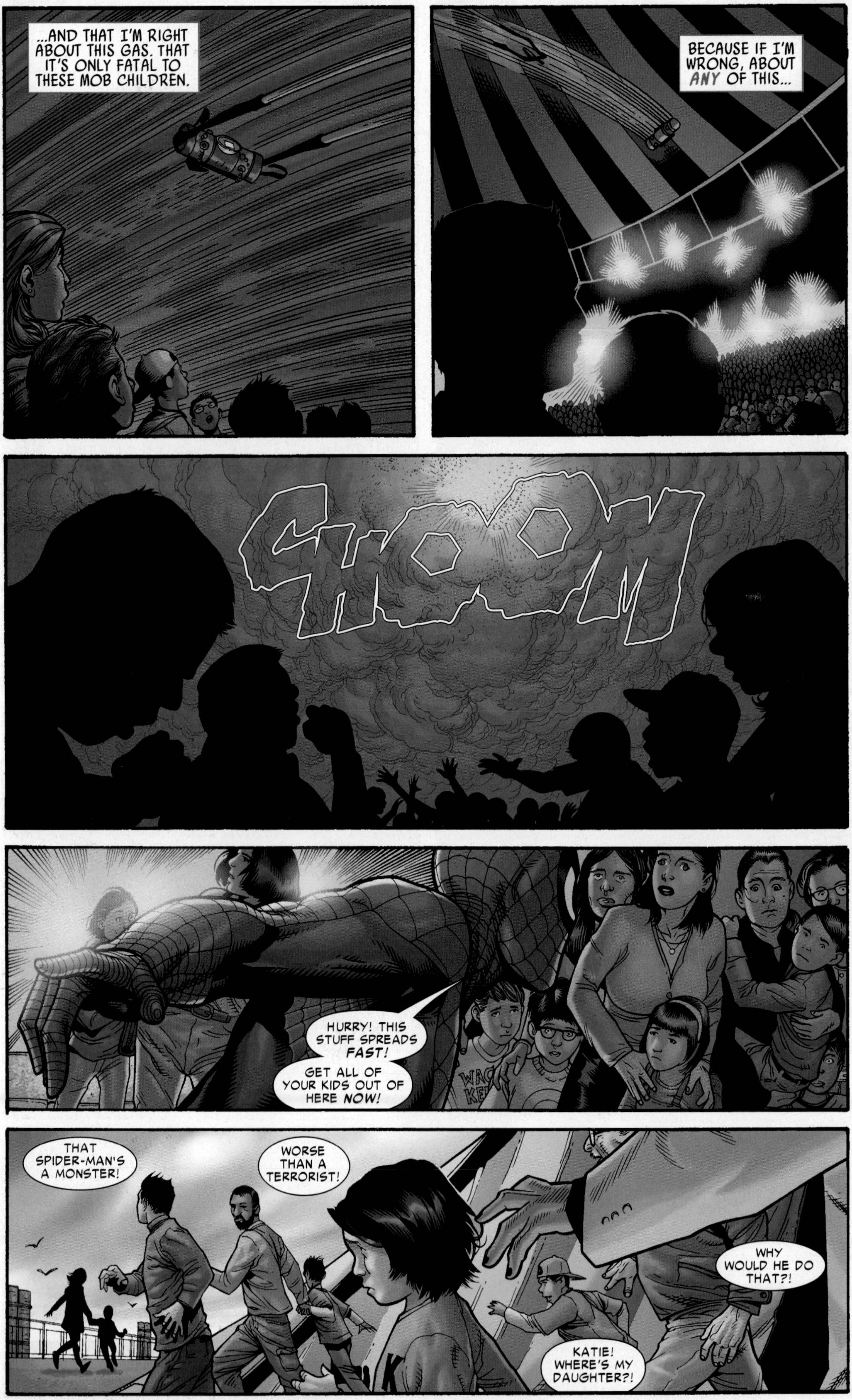
...AND THAT I'M RIGHT ABOUT THIS GAS. THAT IT'S ONLY FATAL TO THESE MOB CHILDREN.
BECAUSE IF I'M WRONG, ABOUT ANY OF THIS...
SHOOM
HURRY! THIS STUFF SPREADS FAST!
GET ALL OF YOUR KIDS OUT OF HERE NOW!
THAT SPIDER-MAN'S A MONSTER!
WORSE THAN A TERRORIST!
WHY WOULD HE DO THAT?!
KATIE! WHERE'S MY DAUGHTER?!

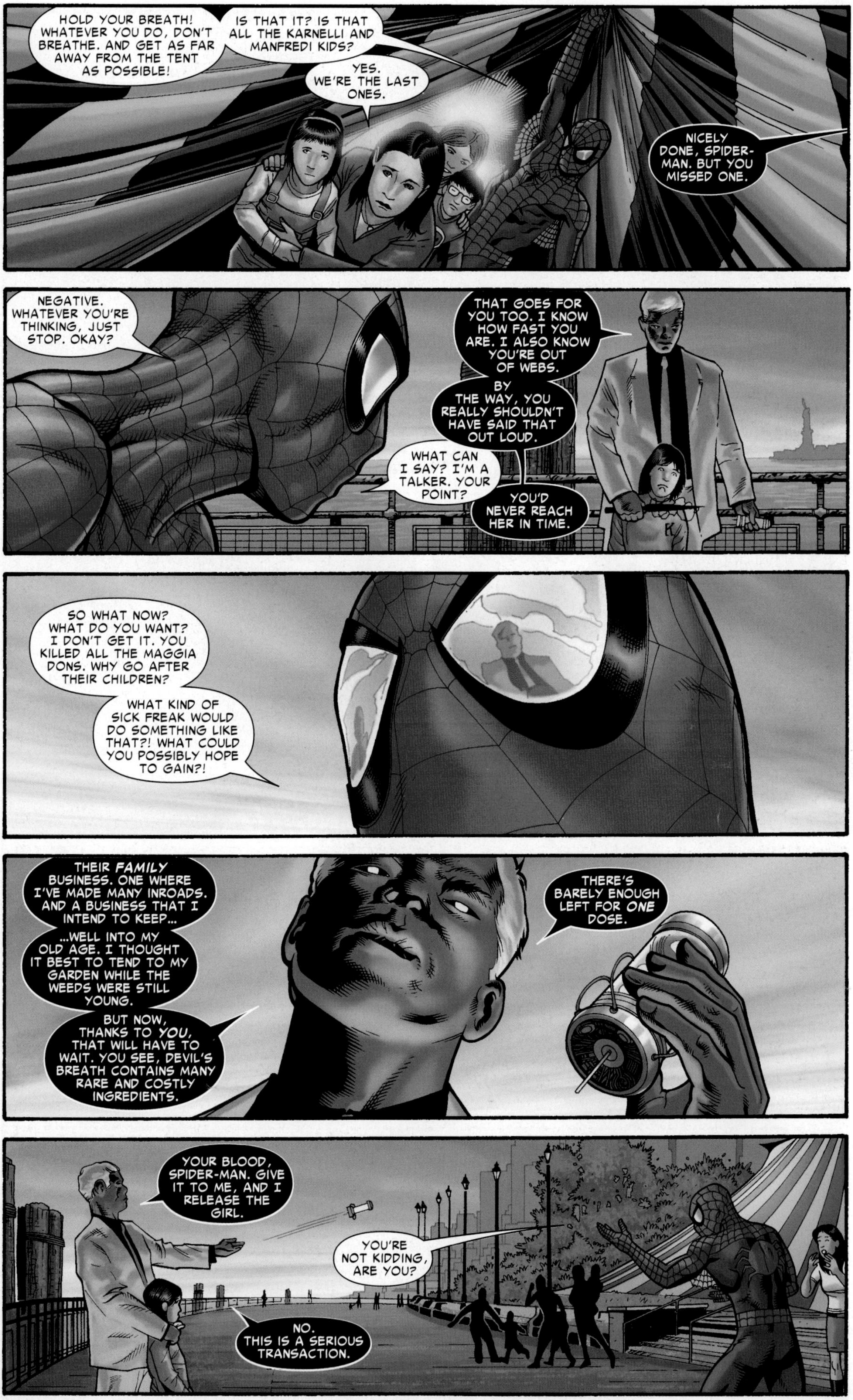
HOLD YOUR BREATH! WHATEVER YOU DO, DON'T BREATHE. AND GET AS FAR AWAY FROM THE TENT AS POSSIBLE!
IS THAT IT? IS THAT ALL THE KARNELLI AND MANFREDI KIDS?
YES. WE'RE THE LAST ONES.
NICELY DONE, SPIDER-MAN. BUT YOU MISSED ONE.
NEGATIVE. WHATEVER YOU'RE THINKING, JUST STOP. OKAY?
THAT GOES FOR YOU TOO. I KNOW HOW FAST YOU ARE. I ALSO KNOW YOU'RE OUT OF WEBS.
BY THE WAY, YOU REALLY SHOULDN'T HAVE SAID THAT OUT LOUD.
WHAT CAN I SAY? I'M A TALKER. YOUR POINT?
YOU'D NEVER REACH HER IN TIME.
SO WHAT NOW? WHAT DO YOU WANT? I DON'T GET IT. YOU KILLED ALL THE MAGGIA DONS. WHY GO AFTER THEIR CHILDREN?
WHAT KIND OF SICK FREAK WOULD DO SOMETHING LIKE THAT?! WHAT COULD YOU POSSIBLY HOPE TO GAIN?!
THEIR *FAMILY* BUSINESS. ONE WHERE I'VE MADE MANY INROADS. AND A BUSINESS THAT I INTEND TO KEEP...
...WELL INTO MY OLD AGE. I THOUGHT IT BEST TO TEND TO MY GARDEN WHILE THE WEEDS WERE STILL YOUNG.
BUT NOW, THANKS TO *YOU*, THAT WILL HAVE TO WAIT. YOU SEE, DEVIL'S BREATH CONTAINS MANY RARE AND COSTLY INGREDIENTS.
THERE'S BARELY ENOUGH LEFT FOR *ONE* DOSE.
YOUR BLOOD, SPIDER-MAN. GIVE IT TO ME, AND I RELEASE THE GIRL.
YOU'RE NOT KIDDING, ARE YOU?
NO. THIS IS A SERIOUS TRANSACTION.

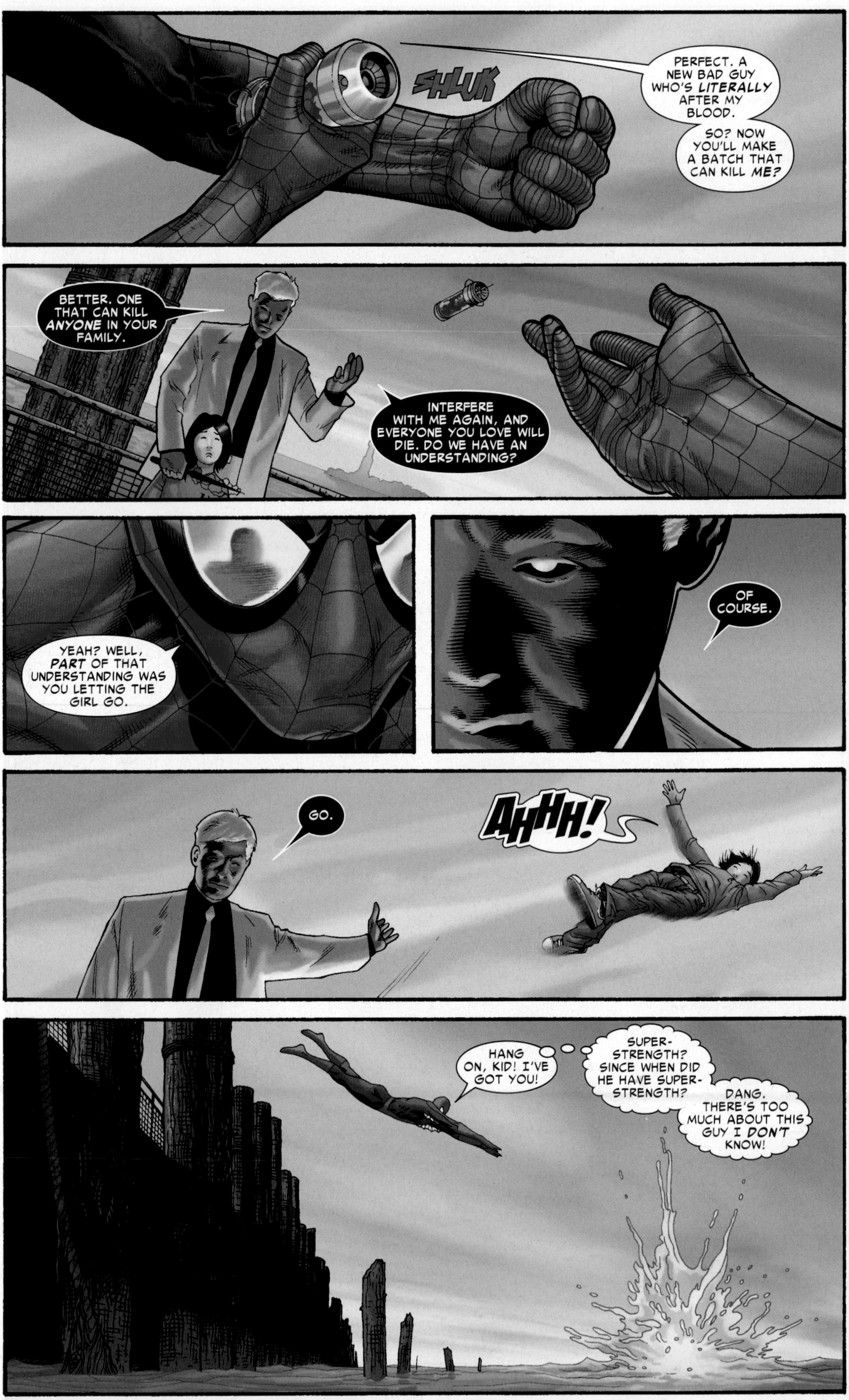
SHLUK
PERFECT. A NEW BAD GUY WHO'S *LITERALLY* AFTER MY BLOOD.
SO? NOW YOU'LL MAKE A BATCH THAT CAN KILL *ME?*
BETTER. ONE THAT CAN KILL *ANYONE* IN YOUR FAMILY.
INTERFERE WITH ME AGAIN, AND EVERYONE YOU LOVE WILL DIE. DO WE HAVE AN UNDERSTANDING?
YEAH? WELL, *PART* OF THAT UNDERSTANDING WAS YOU LETTING THE GIRL GO.
OF COURSE.
GO.
AHHH!
HANG ON, KID! I'VE GOT YOU!
SUPER-STRENGTH? SINCE WHEN DID HE HAVE SUPER-STRENGTH?
DANG. THERE'S TOO MUCH ABOUT THIS GUY I *DON'T* KNOW!

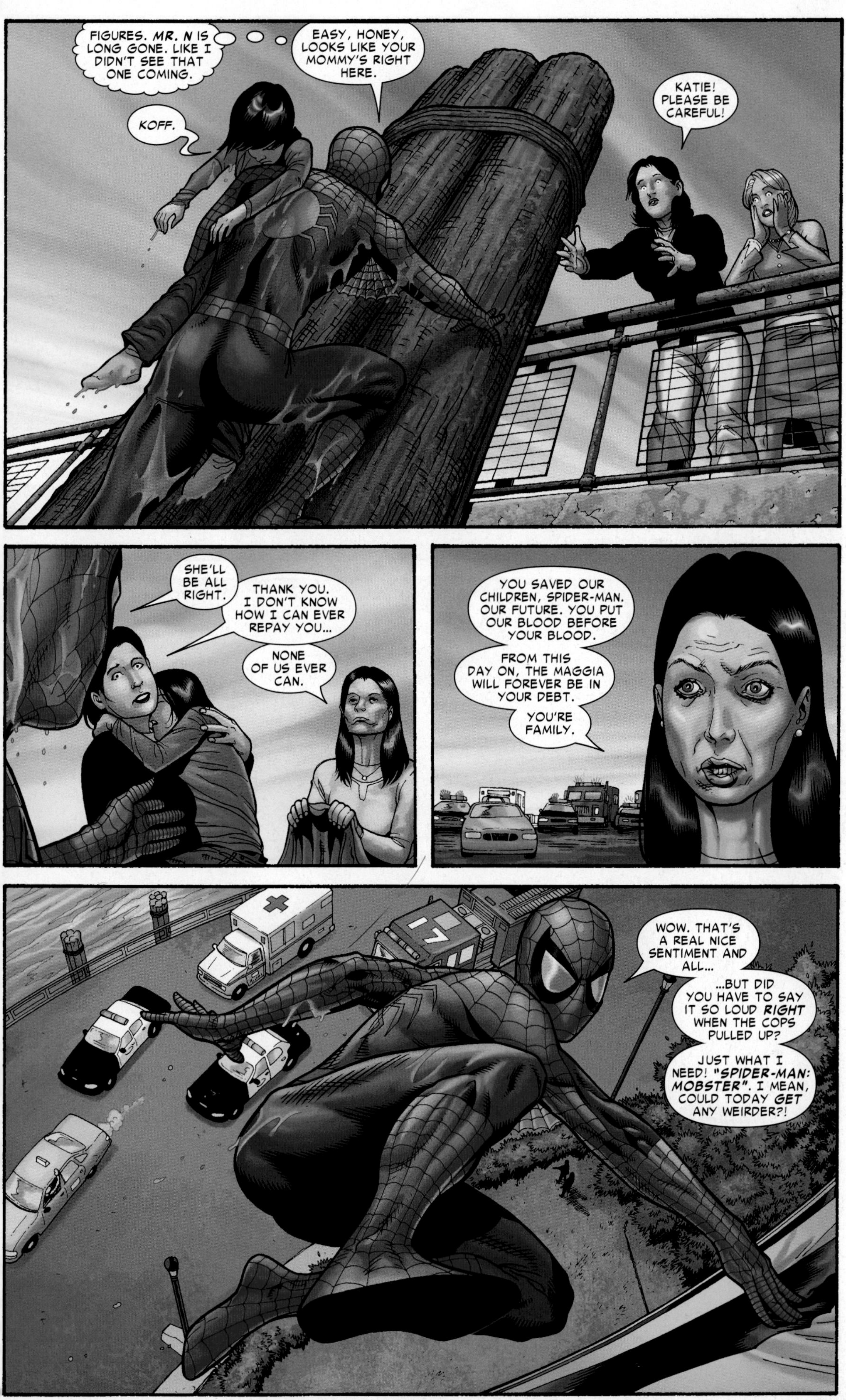
FIGURES. MR. N IS LONG GONE. LIKE I DIDN'T SEE THAT ONE COMING.
EASY, HONEY, LOOKS LIKE YOUR MOMMY'S RIGHT HERE.
KOFF.
KATIE! PLEASE BE CAREFUL!
SHE'LL BE ALL RIGHT.
THANK YOU. I DON'T KNOW HOW I CAN EVER REPAY YOU...
NONE OF US EVER CAN.
YOU SAVED OUR CHILDREN, SPIDER-MAN. OUR FUTURE. YOU PUT OUR BLOOD BEFORE YOUR BLOOD.
FROM THIS DAY ON, THE MAGGIA WILL FOREVER BE IN YOUR DEBT.
YOU'RE FAMILY.
WOW. THAT'S A REAL NICE SENTIMENT AND ALL...
...BUT DID YOU HAVE TO SAY IT SO LOUD RIGHT WHEN THE COPS PULLED UP?
JUST WHAT I NEED! "SPIDER-MAN: MOBSTER". I MEAN, COULD TODAY GET ANY WEIRDER?!

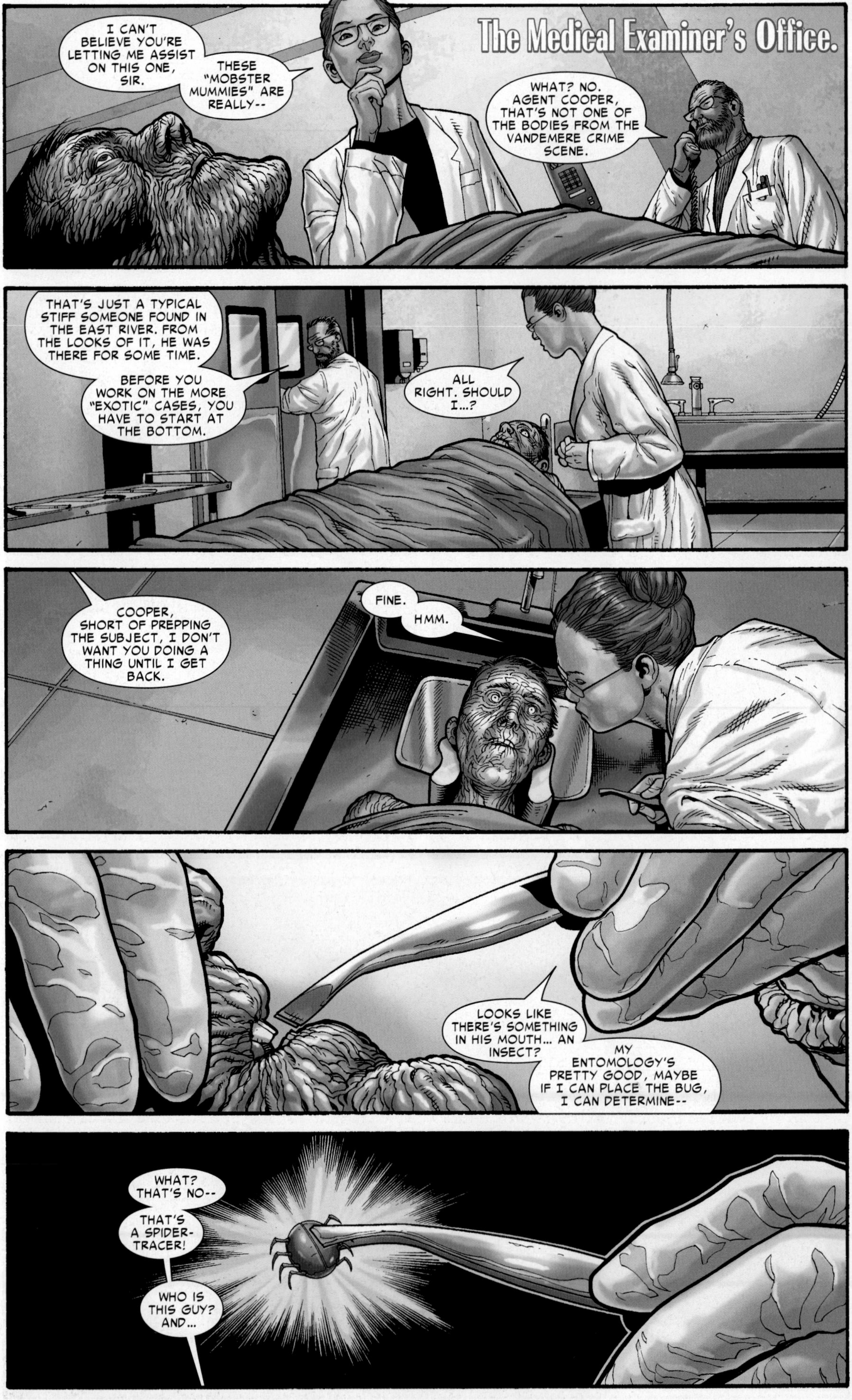
The Medical Examiner's Office.
I CAN'T BELIEVE YOU'RE LETTING ME ASSIST ON THIS ONE, SIR.
THESE "MOBSTER MUMMIES" ARE REALLY--
WHAT? NO. AGENT COOPER, THAT'S NOT ONE OF THE BODIES FROM THE VANDEMERE CRIME SCENE.
THAT'S JUST A TYPICAL STIFF SOMEONE FOUND IN THE EAST RIVER. FROM THE LOOKS OF IT, HE WAS THERE FOR SOME TIME.
BEFORE YOU WORK ON THE MORE "EXOTIC" CASES, YOU HAVE TO START AT THE BOTTOM.
ALL RIGHT. SHOULD I...?
COOPER, SHORT OF PREPPING THE SUBJECT, I DON'T WANT YOU DOING A THING UNTIL I GET BACK.
FINE.
HMM.
LOOKS LIKE THERE'S SOMETHING IN HIS MOUTH... AN INSECT?
MY ENTOMOLOGY'S PRETTY GOOD, MAYBE IF I CAN PLACE THE BUG, I CAN DETERMINE--
WHAT? THAT'S NO--
THAT'S A SPIDER-TRACER!
WHO IS THIS GUY? AND...

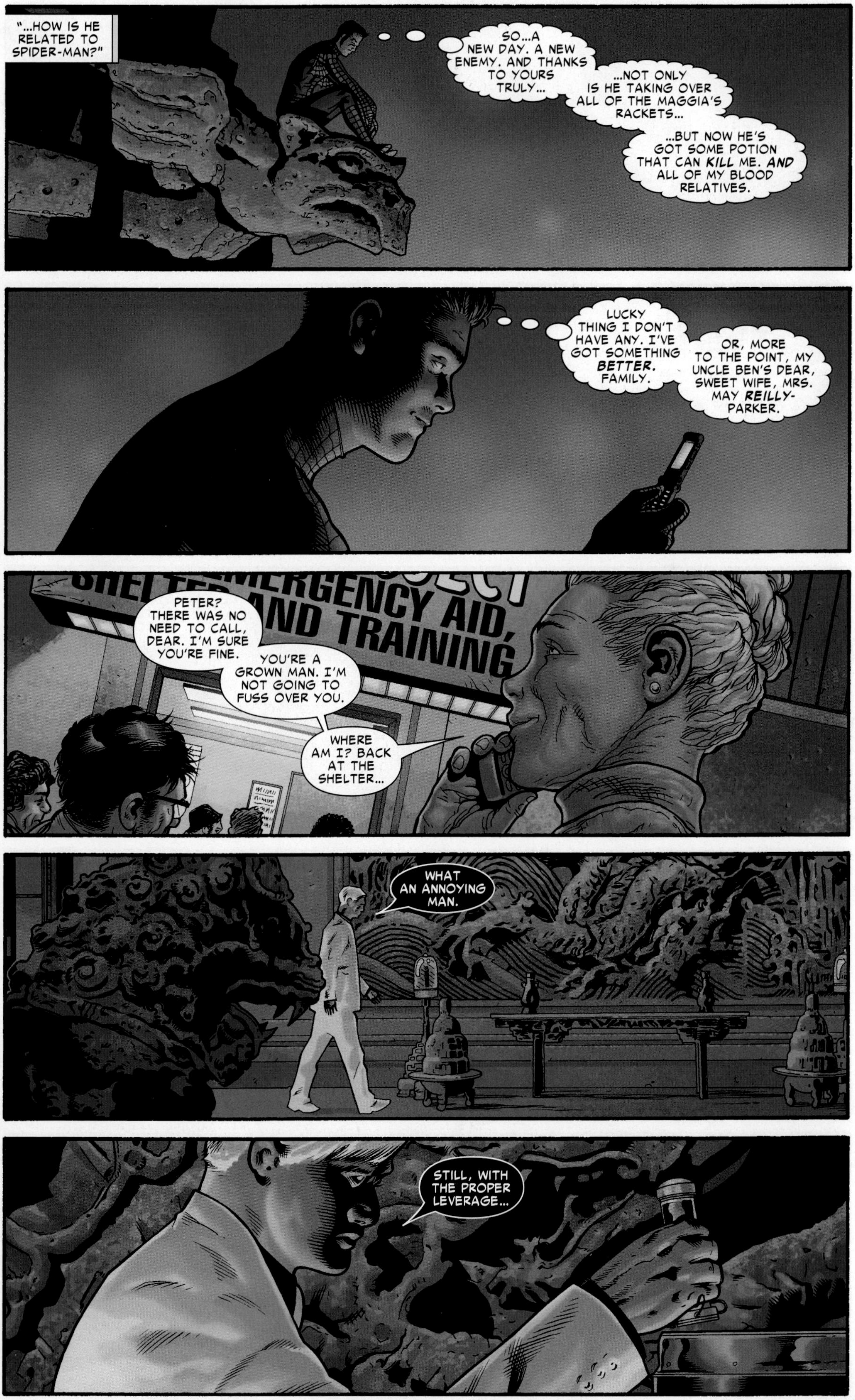
"...HOW IS HE RELATED TO SPIDER-MAN?"
SO...A NEW DAY. A NEW ENEMY. AND THANKS TO YOURS TRULY...
...NOT ONLY IS HE TAKING OVER ALL OF THE MAGGIA'S RACKETS...
...BUT NOW HE'S GOT SOME POTION THAT CAN KILL ME. AND ALL OF MY BLOOD RELATIVES.
LUCKY THING I DON'T HAVE ANY. I'VE GOT SOMETHING BETTER. FAMILY.
OR, MORE TO THE POINT, MY UNCLE BEN'S DEAR, SWEET WIFE, MRS. MAY REILLY-PARKER.
EMERGENCY AID, SHELTER AND TRAINING
PETER? THERE WAS NO NEED TO CALL, DEAR. I'M SURE YOU'RE FINE.
YOU'RE A GROWN MAN. I'M NOT GOING TO FUSS OVER YOU.
WHERE AM I? BACK AT THE SHELTER...
WHAT AN ANNOYING MAN.
STILL, WITH THE PROPER LEVERAGE...

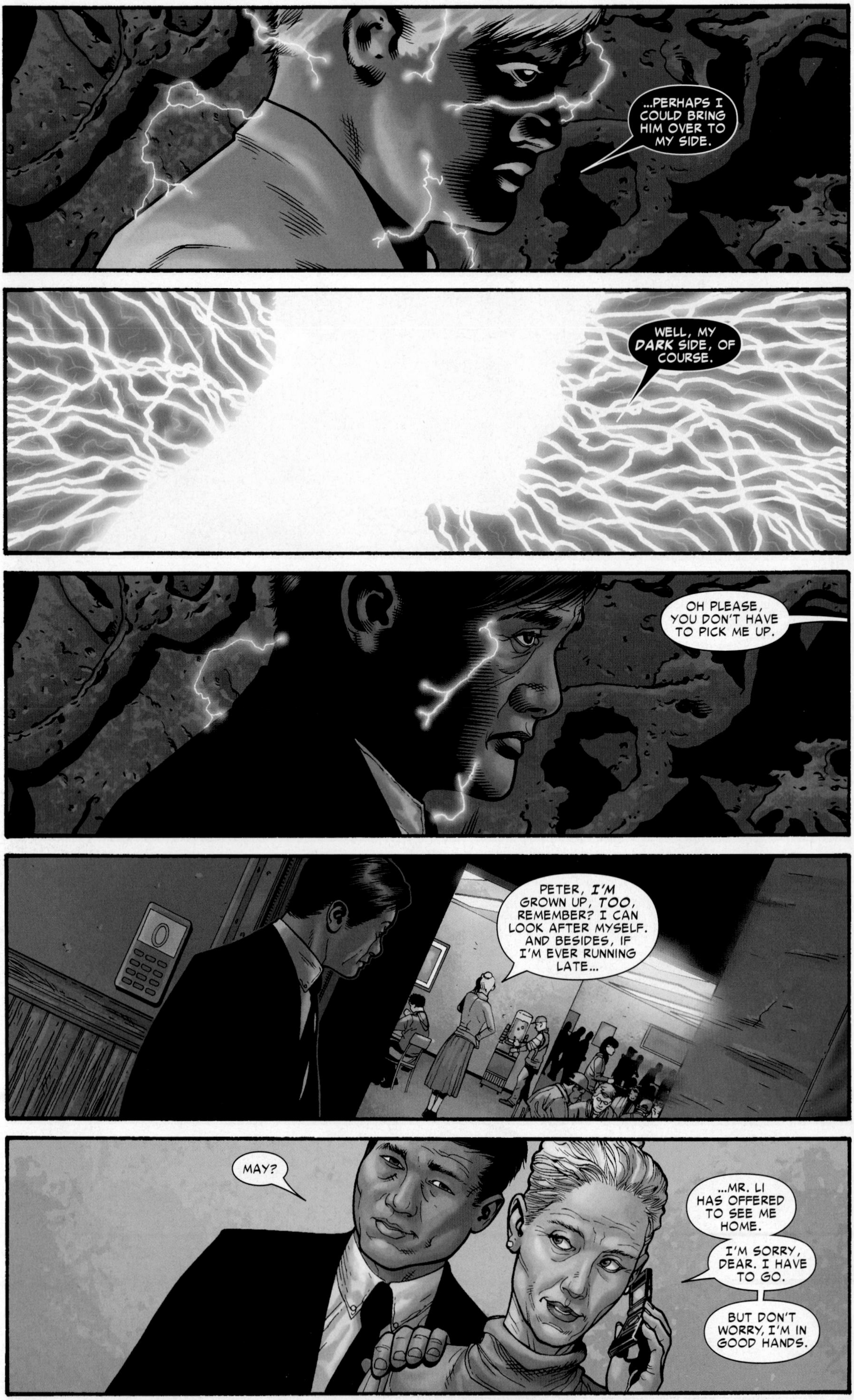
...PERHAPS I COULD BRING HIM OVER TO MY SIDE.
WELL, MY DARK SIDE, OF COURSE.
OH PLEASE, YOU DON'T HAVE TO PICK ME UP.
PETER, I'M GROWN UP, TOO, REMEMBER? I CAN LOOK AFTER MYSELF. AND BESIDES, IF I'M EVER RUNNING LATE...
MAY?
...MR. LI HAS OFFERED TO SEE ME HOME.
I'M SORRY, DEAR. I HAVE TO GO.
BUT DON'T WORRY, I'M IN GOOD HANDS.

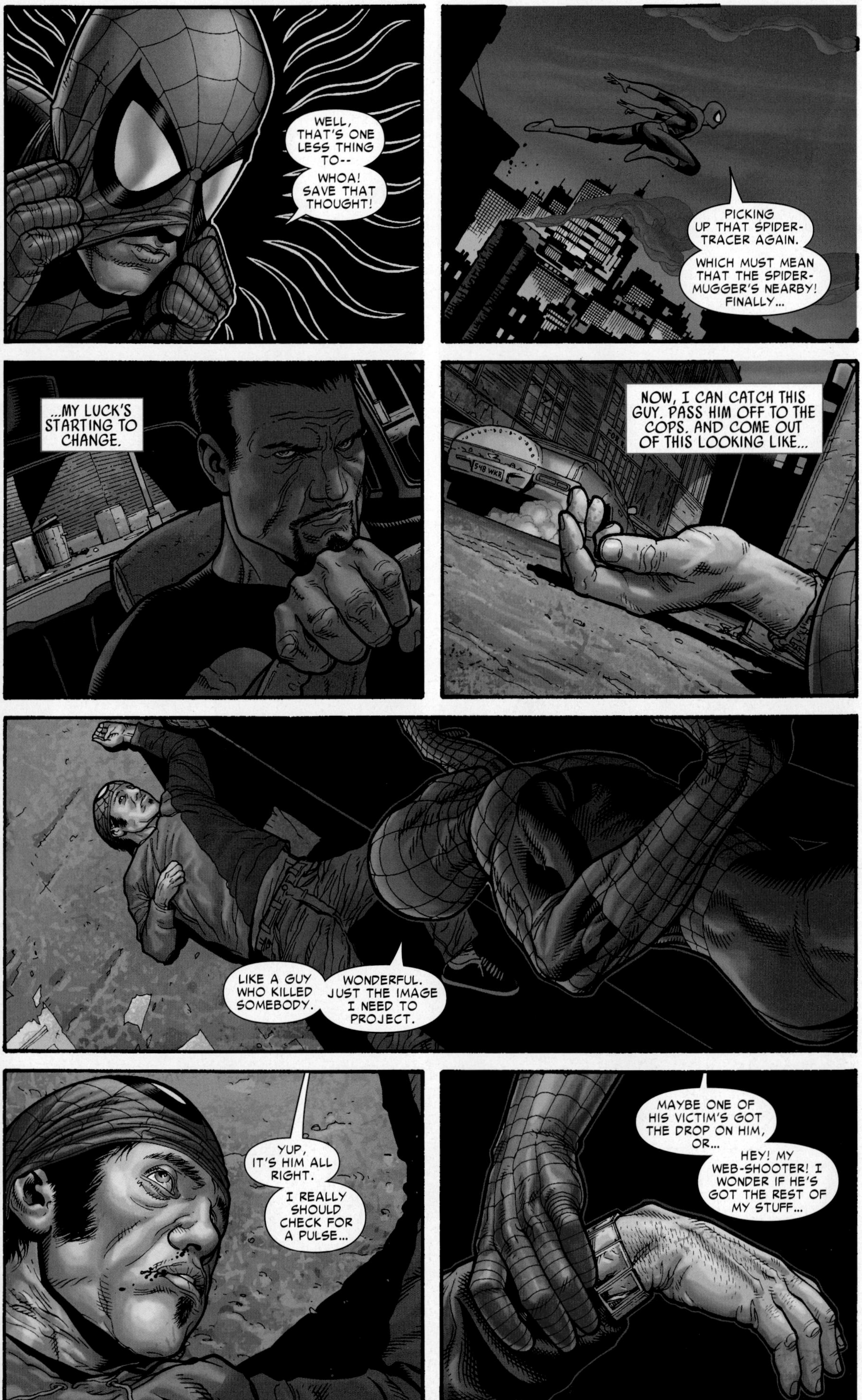
WELL, THAT'S ONE LESS THING TO-- WHOA! SAVE THAT THOUGHT!
PICKING UP THAT SPIDER-TRACER AGAIN.
WHICH MUST MEAN THAT THE SPIDER-MUGGER'S NEARBY! FINALLY...
...MY LUCK'S STARTING TO CHANGE.
NOW, I CAN CATCH THIS GUY. PASS HIM OFF TO THE COPS. AND COME OUT OF THIS LOOKING LIKE...
LIKE A GUY WHO KILLED SOMEBODY.
WONDERFUL. JUST THE IMAGE I NEED TO PROJECT.
YUP, IT'S HIM ALL RIGHT.
I REALLY SHOULD CHECK FOR A PULSE...
MAYBE ONE OF HIS VICTIM'S GOT THE DROP ON HIM, OR...
HEY! MY WEB-SHOOTER! I WONDER IF HE'S GOT THE REST OF MY STUFF...

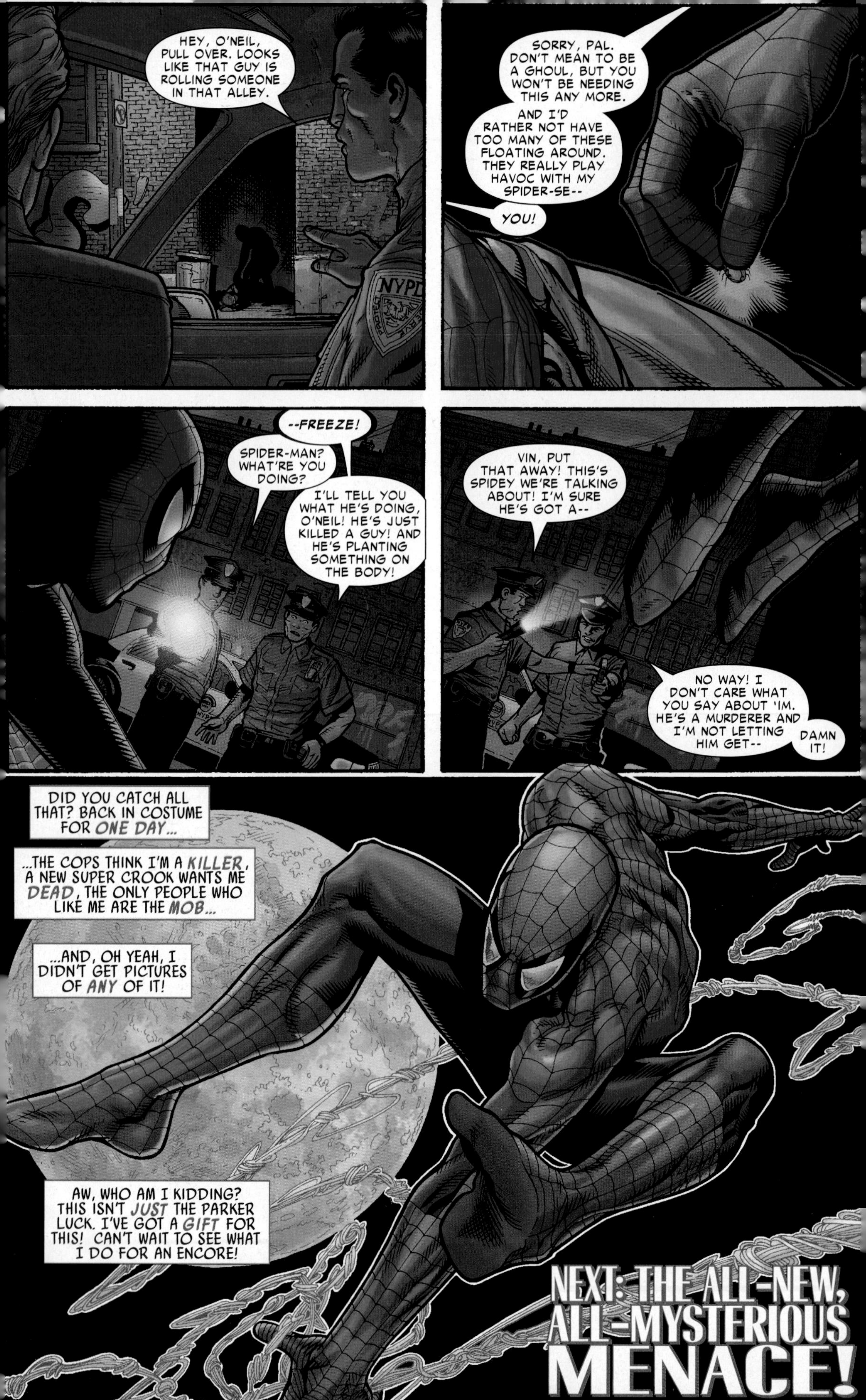
HEY, O'NEIL, PULL OVER. LOOKS LIKE THAT GUY IS ROLLING SOMEONE IN THAT ALLEY.
SORRY, PAL. DON'T MEAN TO BE A GHOUL, BUT YOU WON'T BE NEEDING THIS ANY MORE.
AND I'D RATHER NOT HAVE TOO MANY OF THESE FLOATING AROUND. THEY REALLY PLAY HAVOC WITH MY SPIDER-SE--
YOU!
--FREEZE!
SPIDER-MAN? WHAT'RE YOU DOING?
I'LL TELL YOU WHAT HE'S DOING, O'NEIL! HE'S JUST KILLED A GUY! AND HE'S PLANTING SOMETHING ON THE BODY!
VIN, PUT THAT AWAY! THIS'S SPIDEY WE'RE TALKING ABOUT! I'M SURE HE'S GOT A--
NO WAY! I DON'T CARE WHAT YOU SAY ABOUT 'IM. HE'S A MURDERER AND I'M NOT LETTING HIM GET--
DAMN IT!
DID YOU CATCH ALL THAT? BACK IN COSTUME FOR ONE DAY...
...THE COPS THINK I'M A KILLER, A NEW SUPER CROOK WANTS ME DEAD, THE ONLY PEOPLE WHO LIKE ME ARE THE MOB...
...AND, OH YEAH, I DIDN'T GET PICTURES OF ANY OF IT!
AW, WHO AM I KIDDING? THIS ISN'T JUST THE PARKER LUCK. I'VE GOT A GIFT FOR THIS! CAN'T WAIT TO SEE WHAT I DO FOR AN ENCORE!
NEXT: THE ALL-NEW, ALL-MYSTERIOUS MENACE!

PARK AVENUE INTERLUDE

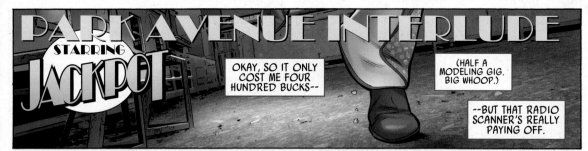

STARRING **JACKPOT**

OKAY, SO IT ONLY COST ME FOUR HUNDRED BUCKS--

(HALF A MODELING GIG. BIG WHOOP.)

--BUT THAT RADIO SCANNER'S REALLY PAYING OFF.

JUST MY SECOND NIGHT OUT ON PATROL--

("ON PATROL." I'LL JUST NEVER GET OVER SAYING THAT. SO COOL.)

--AND I'VE ALREADY CAUGHT ONE.

SOME LOONY-TUNEY IN A DEMON MASK HIJACKED AN *ARMORED TRUCK* FULL OF *EXPLOSIVES* AND...

AH, THERE WE GO!

OKAY, SO I JUST JUMPED OFF A TEN-STORY *BUILDING* TOWARDS A SPEEDING VEHICLE.

C'MON C'MON C'MON C'MON C'MON C'MON...

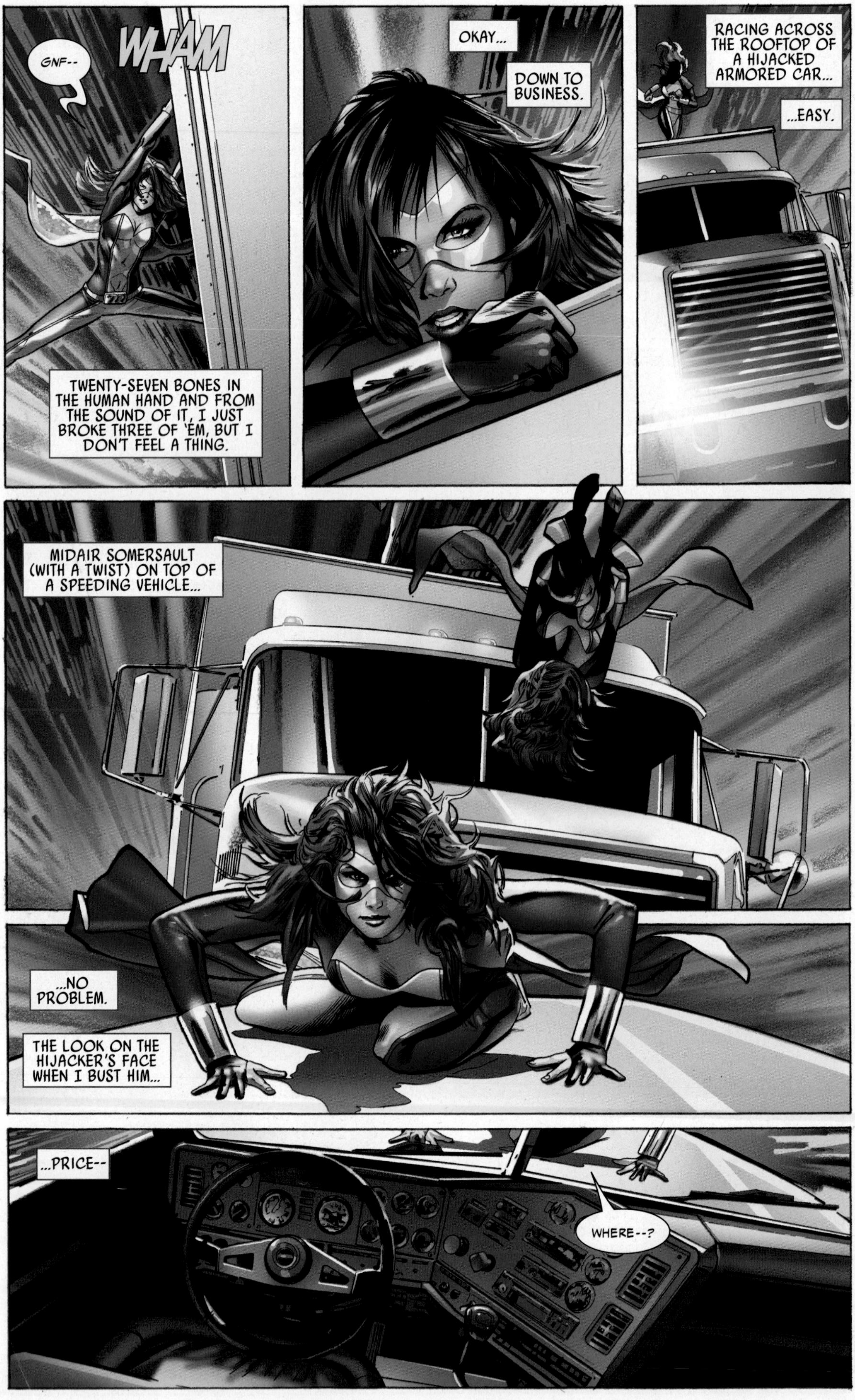
WHAM
GNF--
TWENTY-SEVEN BONES IN THE HUMAN HAND AND FROM THE SOUND OF IT, I JUST BROKE THREE OF 'EM, BUT I DON'T FEEL A THING.
OKAY...
DOWN TO BUSINESS.
RACING ACROSS THE ROOFTOP OF A HIJACKED ARMORED CAR...
...EASY.
MIDAIR SOMERSAULT (WITH A TWIST) ON TOP OF A SPEEDING VEHICLE...
...NO PROBLEM.
THE LOOK ON THE HIJACKER'S FACE WHEN I BUST HIM...
...PRICE--
WHERE--?

OKAY, SO MAYBE THIS IS A FEW DIFFERENT KINDS OF BAD.

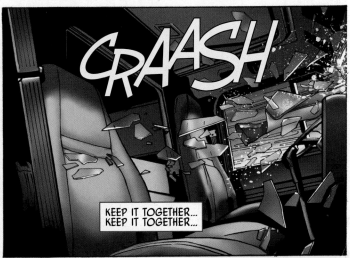

CRAASH

KEEP IT TOGETHER... KEEP IT TOGETHER...

BRAKE PEDAL... BRAKE PEDAL...

CLANG

HA! HA! HA! HA! HA!

SHHEEOOOO

SKREEEEECH

THIS GUY'S A $%^#ING MENACE...

WELL, I'M GONNA GET YOU, TIGER. COUNT ON IT...

UNFORTUNATELY, TRUE BELIEVER, YOU'LL HAVE TO WAIT 'TIL NEXT MONTH TO SEE HER TRY!

MARC GUGGENHEIM
WRITER

GREG LAND
PENCILER

JAY LEISTEN
INKER

JUSTIN PONSOR
COLORS

VC'S CORY PETIT
LETTERS

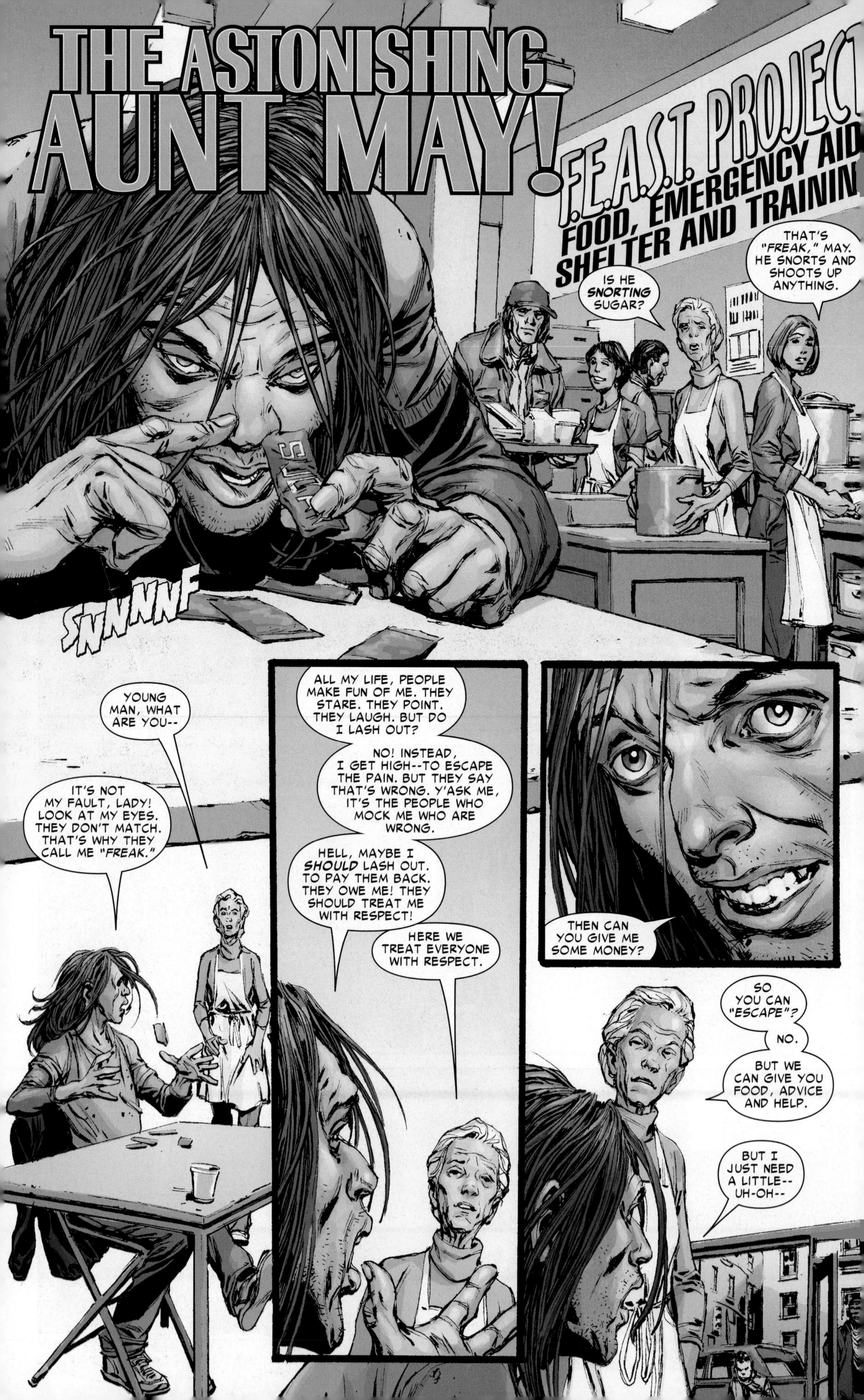

THE ASTONISHING AUNT MAY!
F.E.A.S.T. PROJECT
FOOD, EMERGENCY AID SHELTER AND TRAININ
IS HE SNORTING SUGAR?
THAT'S "FREAK," MAY. HE SNORTS AND SHOOTS UP ANYTHING.
SNNNNF
YOUNG MAN, WHAT ARE YOU--
IT'S NOT MY FAULT, LADY! LOOK AT MY EYES. THEY DON'T MATCH. THAT'S WHY THEY CALL ME "FREAK."
ALL MY LIFE, PEOPLE MAKE FUN OF ME. THEY STARE. THEY POINT. THEY LAUGH. BUT DO I LASH OUT?
NO! INSTEAD, I GET HIGH--TO ESCAPE THE PAIN. BUT THEY SAY THAT'S WRONG. Y'ASK ME, IT'S THE PEOPLE WHO MOCK ME WHO ARE WRONG.
HELL, MAYBE I SHOULD LASH OUT. TO PAY THEM BACK. THEY OWE ME! THEY SHOULD TREAT ME WITH RESPECT!
HERE WE TREAT EVERYONE WITH RESPECT.
THEN CAN YOU GIVE ME SOME MONEY?
SO YOU CAN "ESCAPE"?
NO.
BUT WE CAN GIVE YOU FOOD, ADVICE AND HELP.
BUT I JUST NEED A LITTLE-- UH-OH--

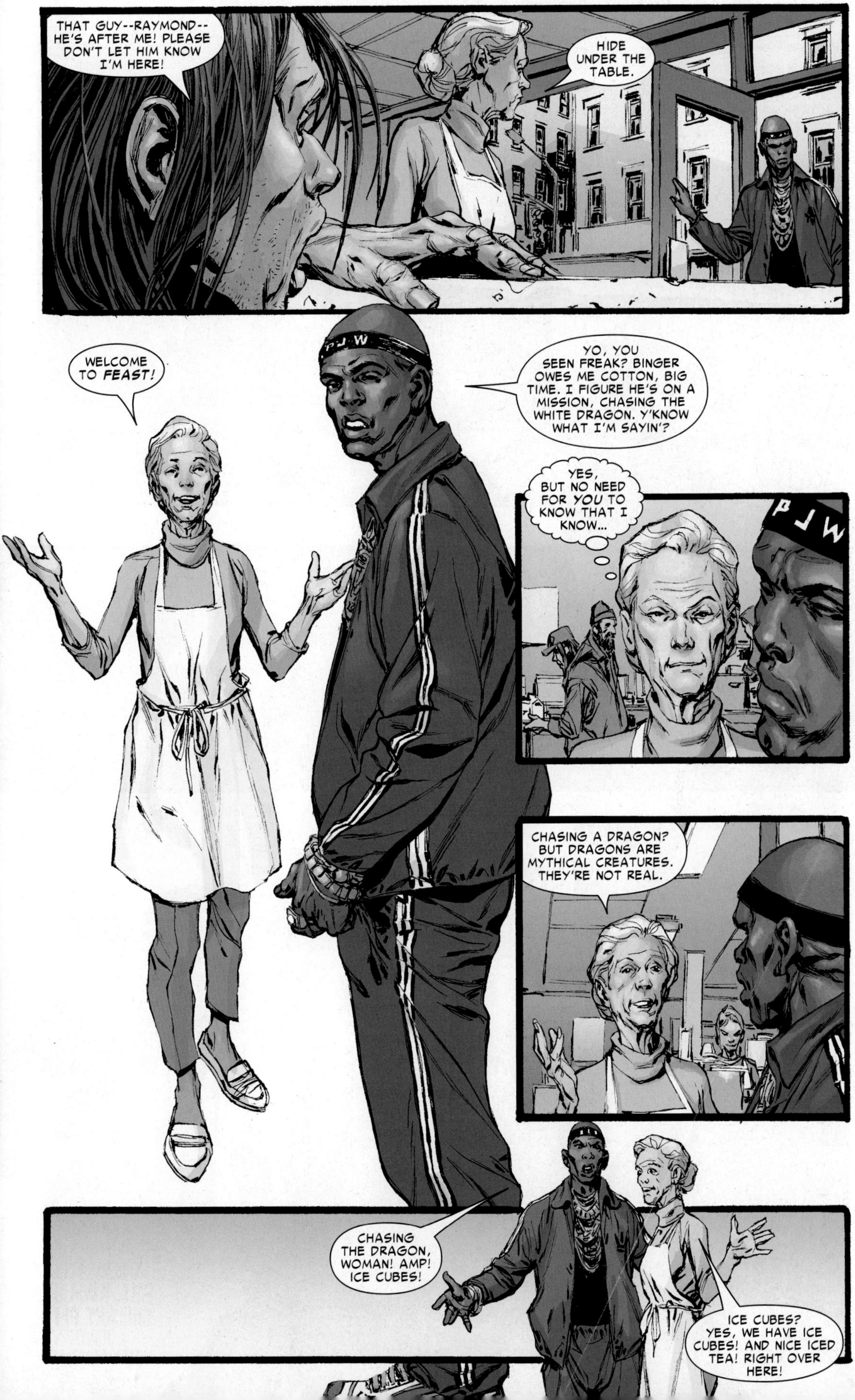
THAT GUY--RAYMOND--HE'S AFTER ME! PLEASE DON'T LET HIM KNOW I'M HERE!
HIDE UNDER THE TABLE.
WELCOME TO FEAST!
YO, YOU SEEN FREAK? BINGER OWES ME COTTON, BIG TIME. I FIGURE HE'S ON A MISSION, CHASING THE WHITE DRAGON. Y'KNOW WHAT I'M SAYIN'?
YES, BUT NO NEED FOR YOU TO KNOW THAT I KNOW...
CHASING A DRAGON? BUT DRAGONS ARE MYTHICAL CREATURES. THEY'RE NOT REAL.
CHASING THE DRAGON, WOMAN! AMP! ICE CUBES!
ICE CUBES? YES, WE HAVE ICE CUBES! AND NICE ICED TEA! RIGHT OVER HERE!

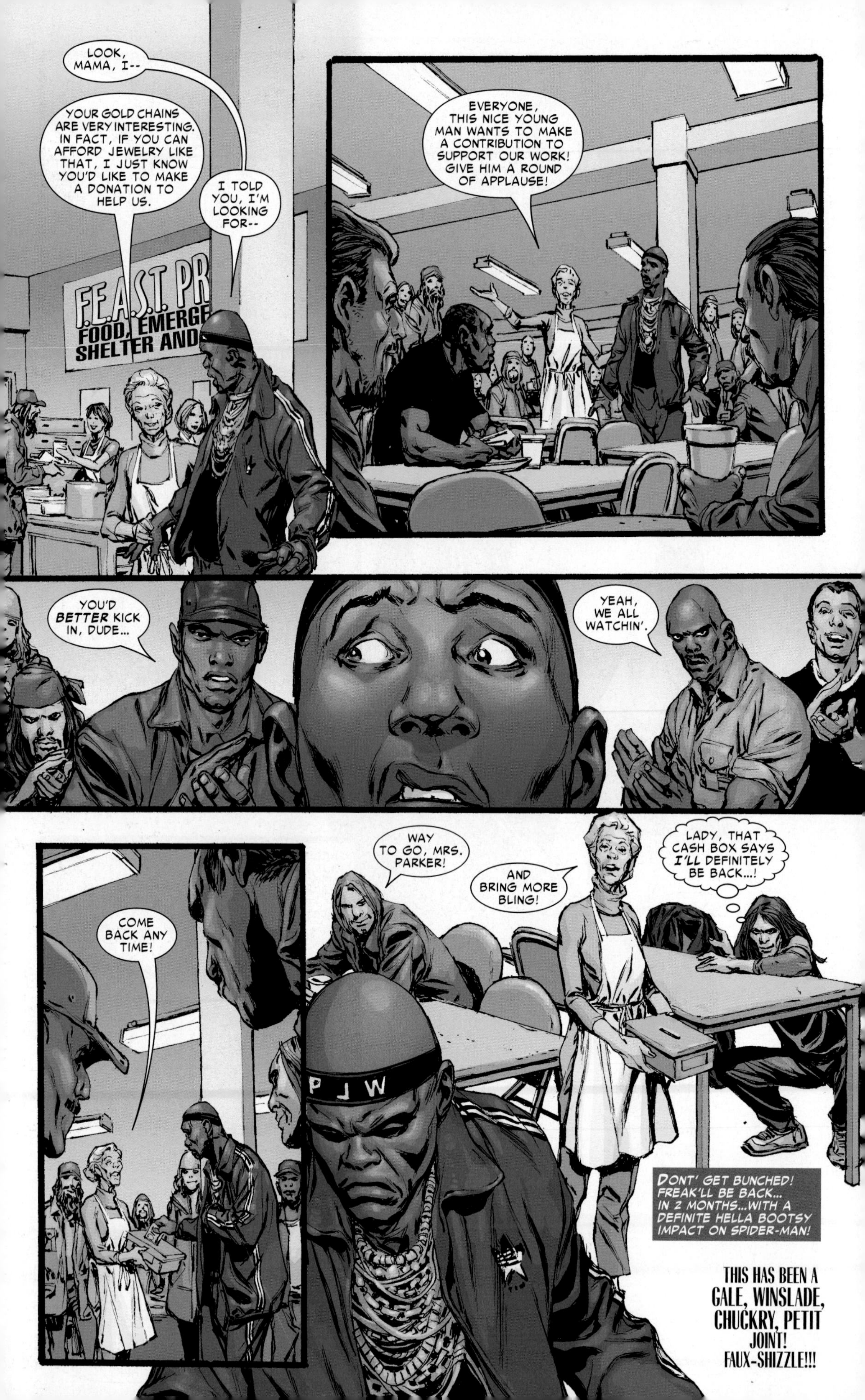
LOOK, MAMA, I--
YOUR GOLD CHAINS ARE VERY INTERESTING. IN FACT, IF YOU CAN AFFORD JEWELRY LIKE THAT, I JUST KNOW YOU'D LIKE TO MAKE A DONATION TO HELP US.
I TOLD YOU, I'M LOOKING FOR--
F.E.A.S.T. PR
FOOD, EMERGE
SHELTER AND
EVERYONE, THIS NICE YOUNG MAN WANTS TO MAKE A CONTRIBUTION TO SUPPORT OUR WORK! GIVE HIM A ROUND OF APPLAUSE!
YOU'D *BETTER* KICK IN, DUDE...
YEAH, WE ALL WATCHIN'.
COME BACK ANY TIME!
WAY TO GO, MRS. PARKER!
AND BRING MORE BLING!
LADY, THAT CASH BOX SAYS *I'LL* DEFINITELY BE BACK...!
PJW
DONT' GET BUNCHED! FREAK'LL BE BACK... IN 2 MONTHS...WITH A DEFINITE HELLA BOOTSY IMPACT ON SPIDER-MAN!
THIS HAS BEEN A GALE, WINSLADE, CHUCKRY, PETIT JOINT! FAUX-SHIZZLE!!!

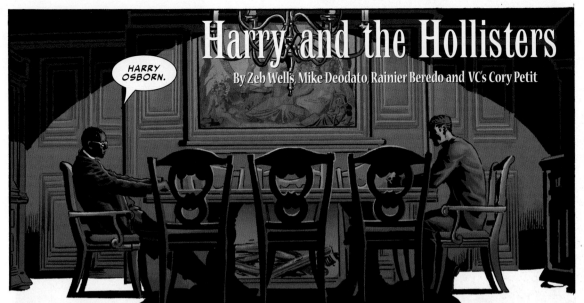

Harry and the Hollisters

By Zeb Wells, Mike Deodato, Rainier Beredo and VC's Cory Petit

HARRY OSBORN.

SIR.

MY DAUGHTER'S DATING *HARRY OSBORN.*

Tah-dah...

HAVEN'T HEARD THE NAME OSBORN IN A WHILE.

WELL, THAT'S A GOOD THING COMING FROM NEW YORK'S TOUGHEST D.A., RIGHT?

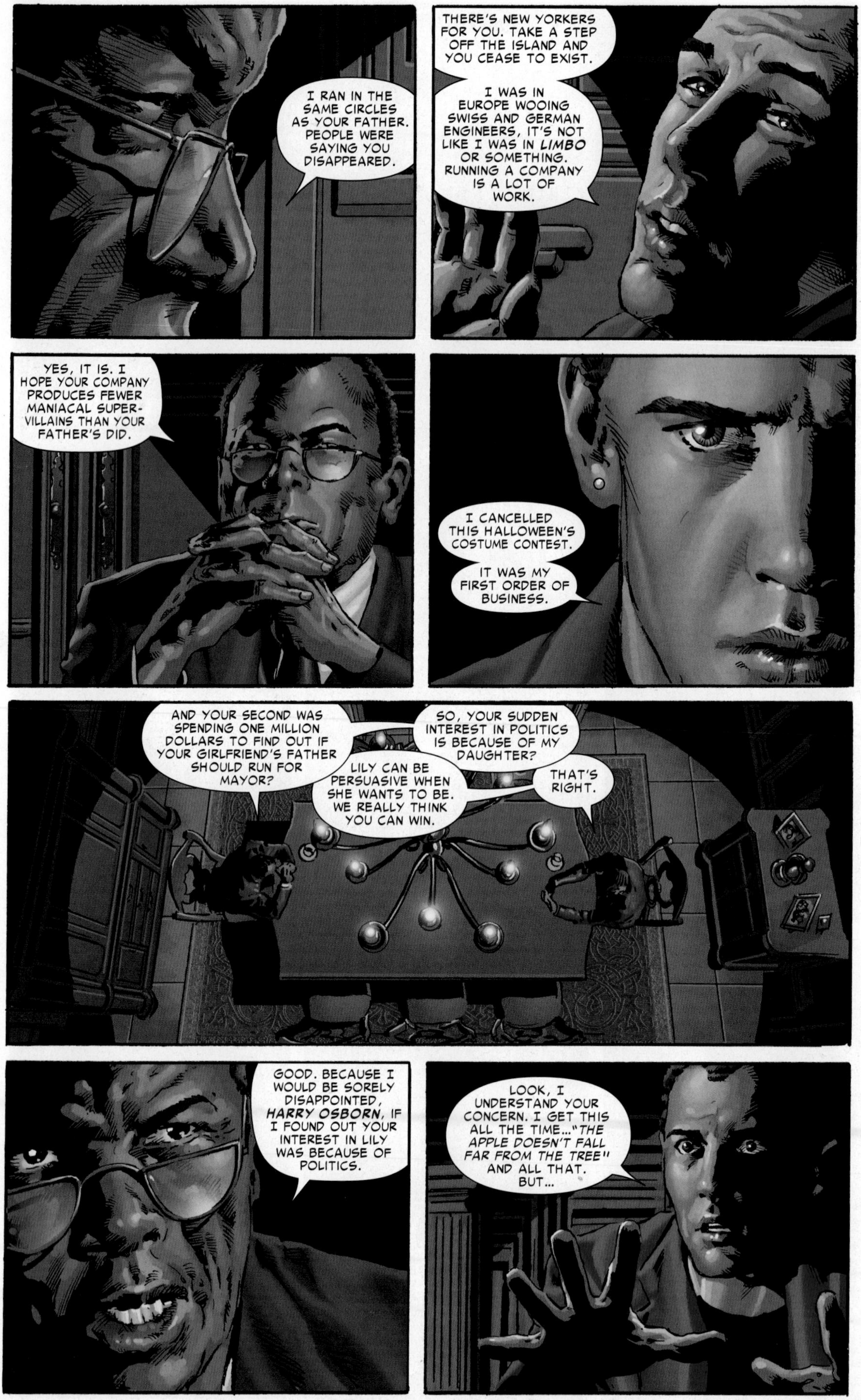
I RAN IN THE SAME CIRCLES AS YOUR FATHER. PEOPLE WERE SAYING YOU DISAPPEARED.
THERE'S NEW YORKERS FOR YOU. TAKE A STEP OFF THE ISLAND AND YOU CEASE TO EXIST.
I WAS IN EUROPE WOOING SWISS AND GERMAN ENGINEERS, IT'S NOT LIKE I WAS IN *LIMBO* OR SOMETHING. RUNNING A COMPANY IS A LOT OF WORK.
YES, IT IS. I HOPE YOUR COMPANY PRODUCES FEWER MANIACAL SUPER-VILLAINS THAN YOUR FATHER'S DID.
I CANCELLED THIS HALLOWEEN'S COSTUME CONTEST.
IT WAS MY FIRST ORDER OF BUSINESS.
AND YOUR SECOND WAS SPENDING ONE MILLION DOLLARS TO FIND OUT IF YOUR GIRLFRIEND'S FATHER SHOULD RUN FOR MAYOR?
SO, YOUR SUDDEN INTEREST IN POLITICS IS BECAUSE OF MY DAUGHTER?
LILY CAN BE PERSUASIVE WHEN SHE WANTS TO BE. WE REALLY THINK YOU CAN WIN.
THAT'S RIGHT.
GOOD. BECAUSE I WOULD BE SORELY DISAPPOINTED, **HARRY OSBORN**, IF I FOUND OUT YOUR INTEREST IN LILY WAS BECAUSE OF POLITICS.
LOOK, I UNDERSTAND YOUR CONCERN. I GET THIS ALL THE TIME..."*THE APPLE DOESN'T FALL FAR FROM THE TREE*" AND ALL THAT. BUT...

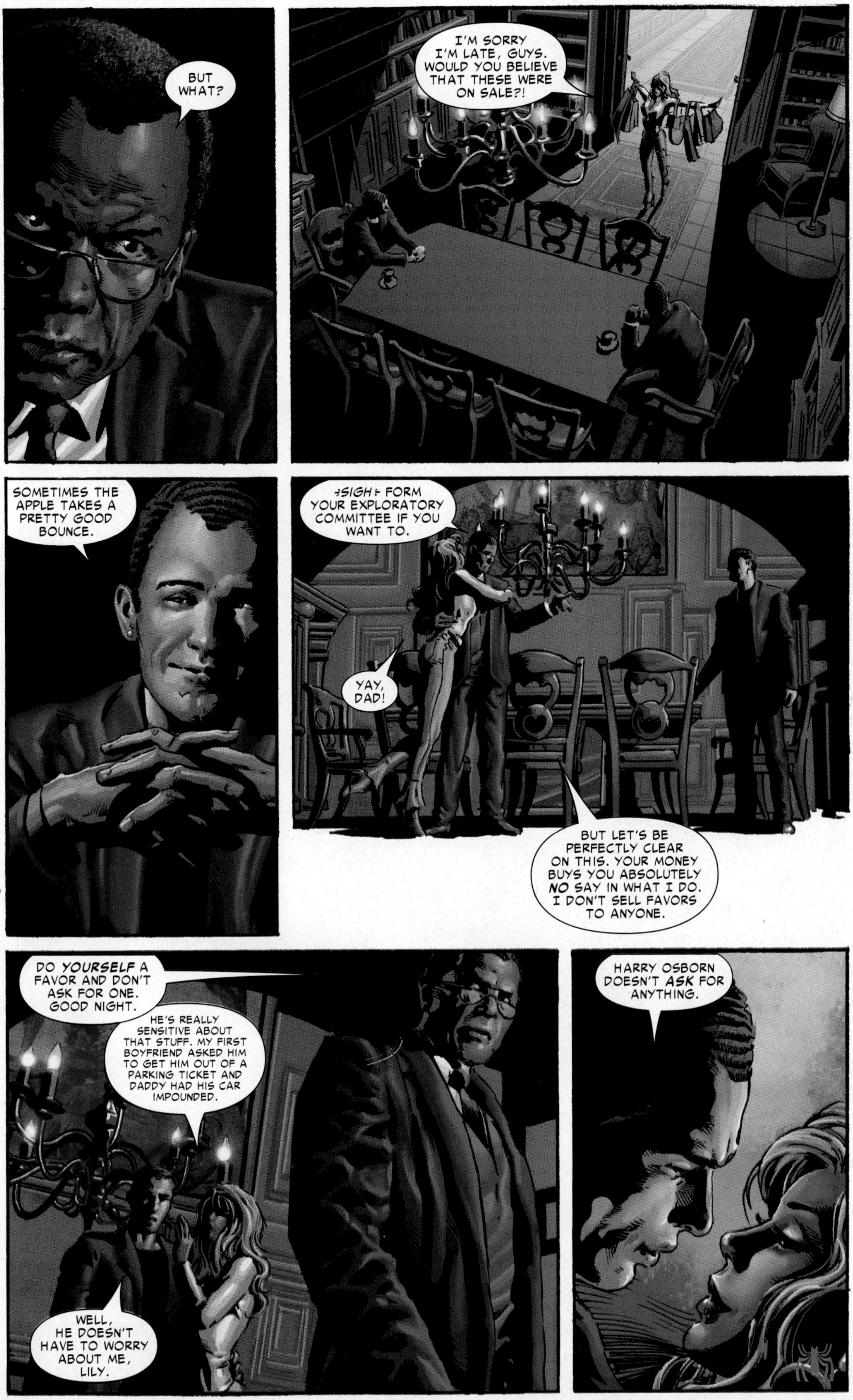
BUT WHAT?
I'M SORRY I'M LATE, GUYS. WOULD YOU BELIEVE THAT THESE WERE ON SALE?!
SOMETIMES THE APPLE TAKES A PRETTY GOOD BOUNCE.
=SIGH= FORM YOUR EXPLORATORY COMMITTEE IF YOU WANT TO.
YAY, DAD!
BUT LET'S BE PERFECTLY CLEAR ON THIS. YOUR MONEY BUYS YOU ABSOLUTELY NO SAY IN WHAT I DO. I DON'T SELL FAVORS TO ANYONE.
DO YOURSELF A FAVOR AND DON'T ASK FOR ONE. GOOD NIGHT.
HE'S REALLY SENSITIVE ABOUT THAT STUFF. MY FIRST BOYFRIEND ASKED HIM TO GET HIM OUT OF A PARKING TICKET AND DADDY HAD HIS CAR IMPOUNDED.
WELL, HE DOESN'T HAVE TO WORRY ABOUT ME, LILY.
HARRY OSBORN DOESN'T ASK FOR ANYTHING.

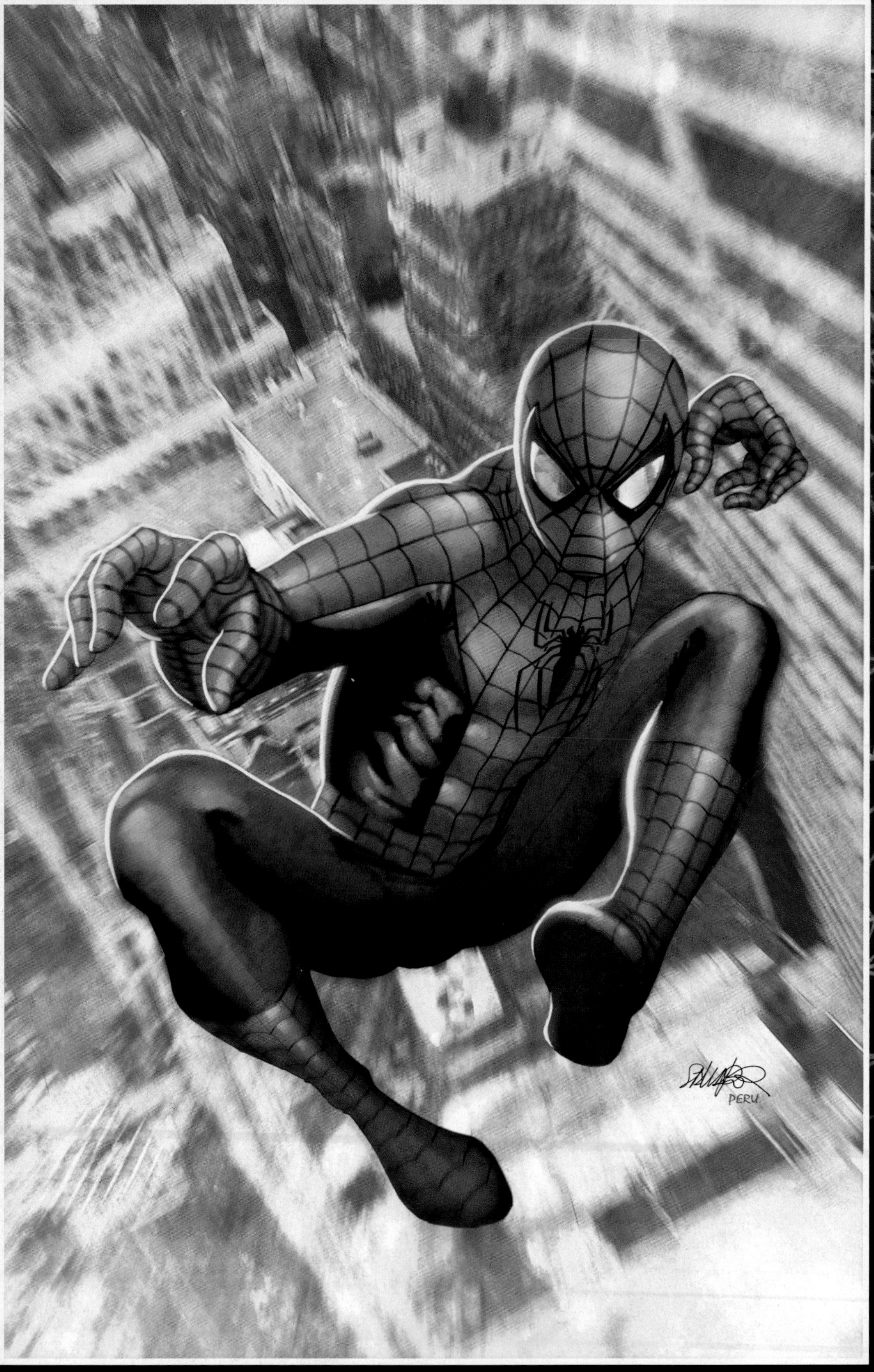
PERU

AMAZING SPIDER-MAN #549
COVER BY **SALVADOR LARROCA & STEPHANE PERU**

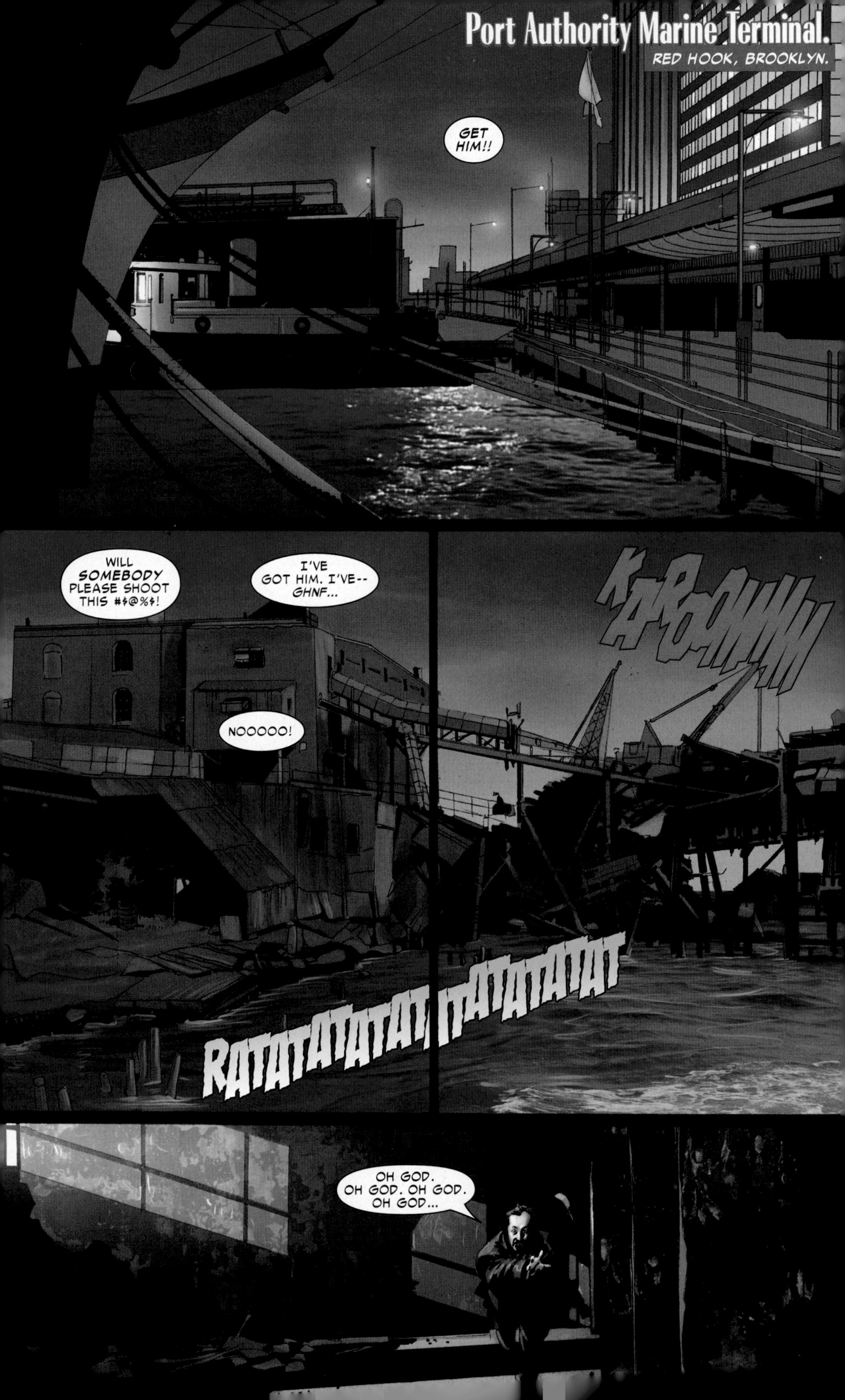
Port Authority Marine Terminal.
RED HOOK, BROOKLYN.
GET HIM!!
WILL SOMEBODY PLEASE SHOOT THIS #$@%$!
I'VE GOT HIM. I'VE-- GHNF...
NOOOOO!
KA-BOOMMM
RATATATATATAT
TATATATATAT
OH GOD. OH GOD. OH GOD. OH GOD...

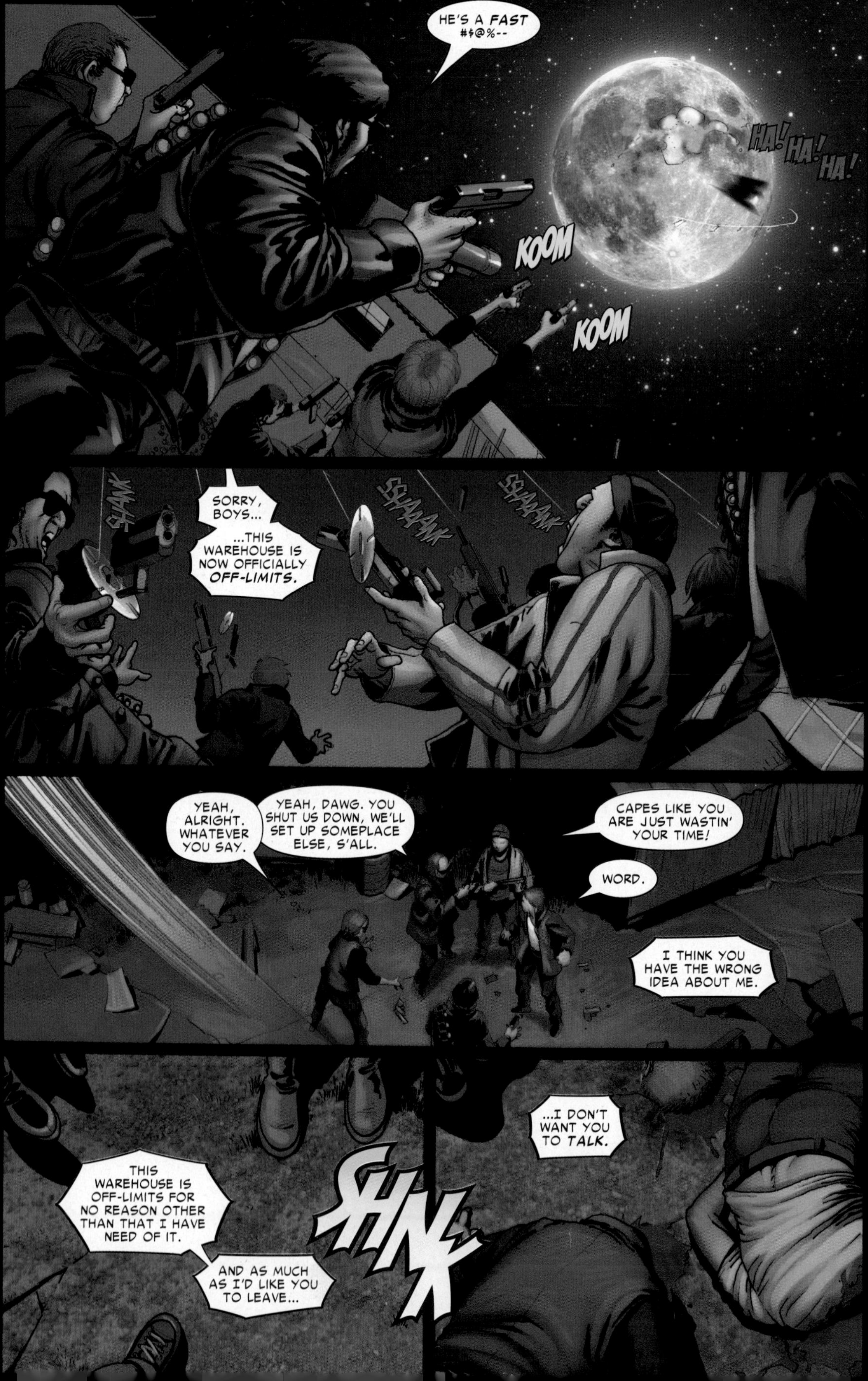
HE'S A FAST #$@%--
HA! HA! HA!
KOOM
KOOM
SHAAANK
SORRY, BOYS...
...THIS WAREHOUSE IS NOW OFFICIALLY OFF-LIMITS.
SHAAANK
SHAAANK
YEAH, ALRIGHT. WHATEVER YOU SAY.
YEAH, DAWG. YOU SHUT US DOWN, WE'LL SET UP SOMEPLACE ELSE, S'ALL.
CAPES LIKE YOU ARE JUST WASTIN' YOUR TIME!
WORD.
I THINK YOU HAVE THE WRONG IDEA ABOUT ME.
THIS WAREHOUSE IS OFF-LIMITS FOR NO REASON OTHER THAN THAT I HAVE NEED OF IT.
AND AS MUCH AS I'D LIKE YOU TO LEAVE...
SHNK
...I DON'T WANT YOU TO TALK.

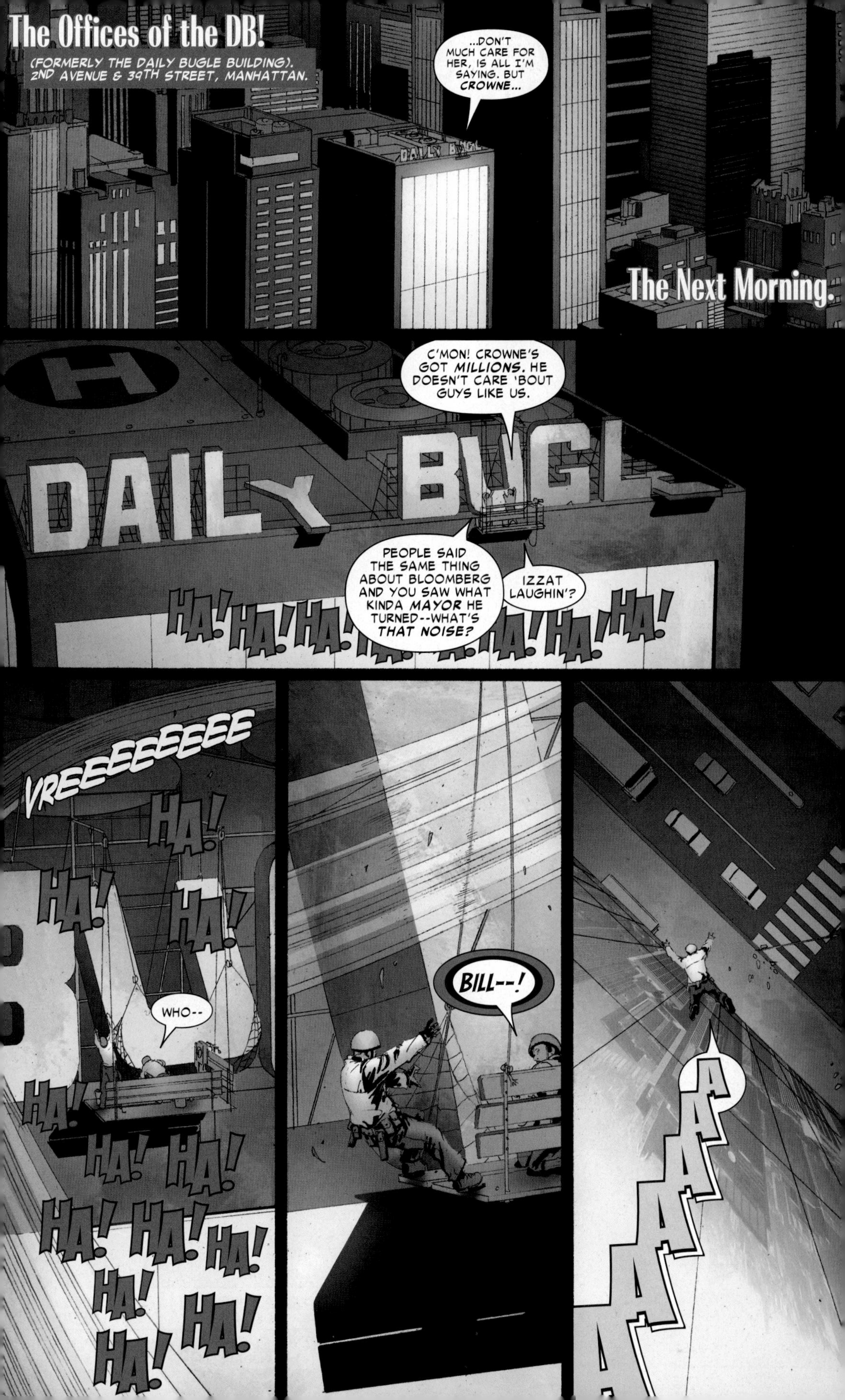
The Offices of the DB!
(FORMERLY THE DAILY BUGLE BUILDING).
2ND AVENUE & 39TH STREET, MANHATTAN.
...DON'T MUCH CARE FOR HER, IS ALL I'M SAYING. BUT CROWNE...
The Next Morning.
C'MON! CROWNE'S GOT MILLIONS. HE DOESN'T CARE 'BOUT GUYS LIKE US.
DAILY BUGL
PEOPLE SAID THE SAME THING ABOUT BLOOMBERG AND YOU SAW WHAT KINDA MAYOR HE TURNED--WHAT'S THAT NOISE?
IZZAT LAUGHIN'?
HA! HA! HA! HA! HA! HA!
VREEEEEEEEEE
HA! HA! HA!
WHO--
HA! HA! HA! HA! HA! HA! HA! HA! HA!
BILL--!
AAAAAAAA

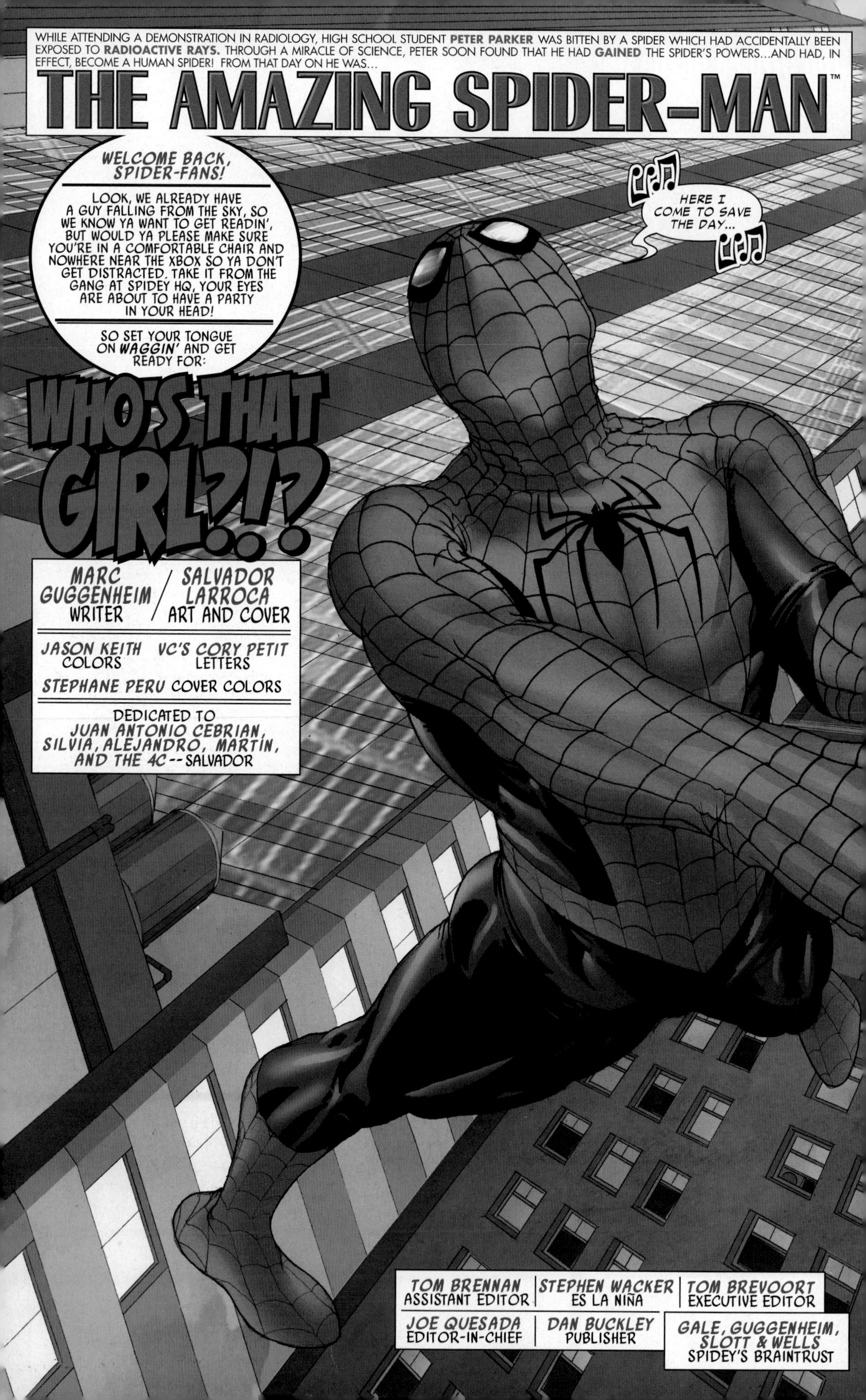
WHILE ATTENDING A DEMONSTRATION IN RADIOLOGY, HIGH SCHOOL STUDENT PETER PARKER WAS BITTEN BY A SPIDER WHICH HAD ACCIDENTALLY BEEN EXPOSED TO RADIOACTIVE RAYS. THROUGH A MIRACLE OF SCIENCE, PETER SOON FOUND THAT HE HAD GAINED THE SPIDER'S POWERS...AND HAD, IN EFFECT, BECOME A HUMAN SPIDER! FROM THAT DAY ON HE WAS...
THE AMAZING SPIDER-MAN™
WELCOME BACK, SPIDER-FANS!
LOOK, WE ALREADY HAVE A GUY FALLING FROM THE SKY, SO WE KNOW YA WANT TO GET READIN', BUT WOULD YA PLEASE MAKE SURE YOU'RE IN A COMFORTABLE CHAIR AND NOWHERE NEAR THE XBOX SO YA DON'T GET DISTRACTED. TAKE IT FROM THE GANG AT SPIDEY HQ, YOUR EYES ARE ABOUT TO HAVE A PARTY IN YOUR HEAD!
SO SET YOUR TONGUE ON WAGGIN' AND GET READY FOR:
HERE I COME TO SAVE THE DAY...
WHO'S THAT GIRL?!?
MARC GUGGENHEIM WRITER / SALVADOR LARROCA ART AND COVER
JASON KEITH COLORS
VC'S CORY PETIT LETTERS
STEPHANE PERU COVER COLORS
DEDICATED TO JUAN ANTONIO CEBRIAN, SILVIA, ALEJANDRO, MARTÍN, AND THE 4C -- SALVADOR
TOM BRENNAN ASSISTANT EDITOR
STEPHEN WACKER ES LA NIÑA
TOM BREVOORT EXECUTIVE EDITOR
JOE QUESADA EDITOR-IN-CHIEF
DAN BUCKLEY PUBLISHER
GALE, GUGGENHEIM, SLOTT & WELLS SPIDEY'S BRAINTRUST

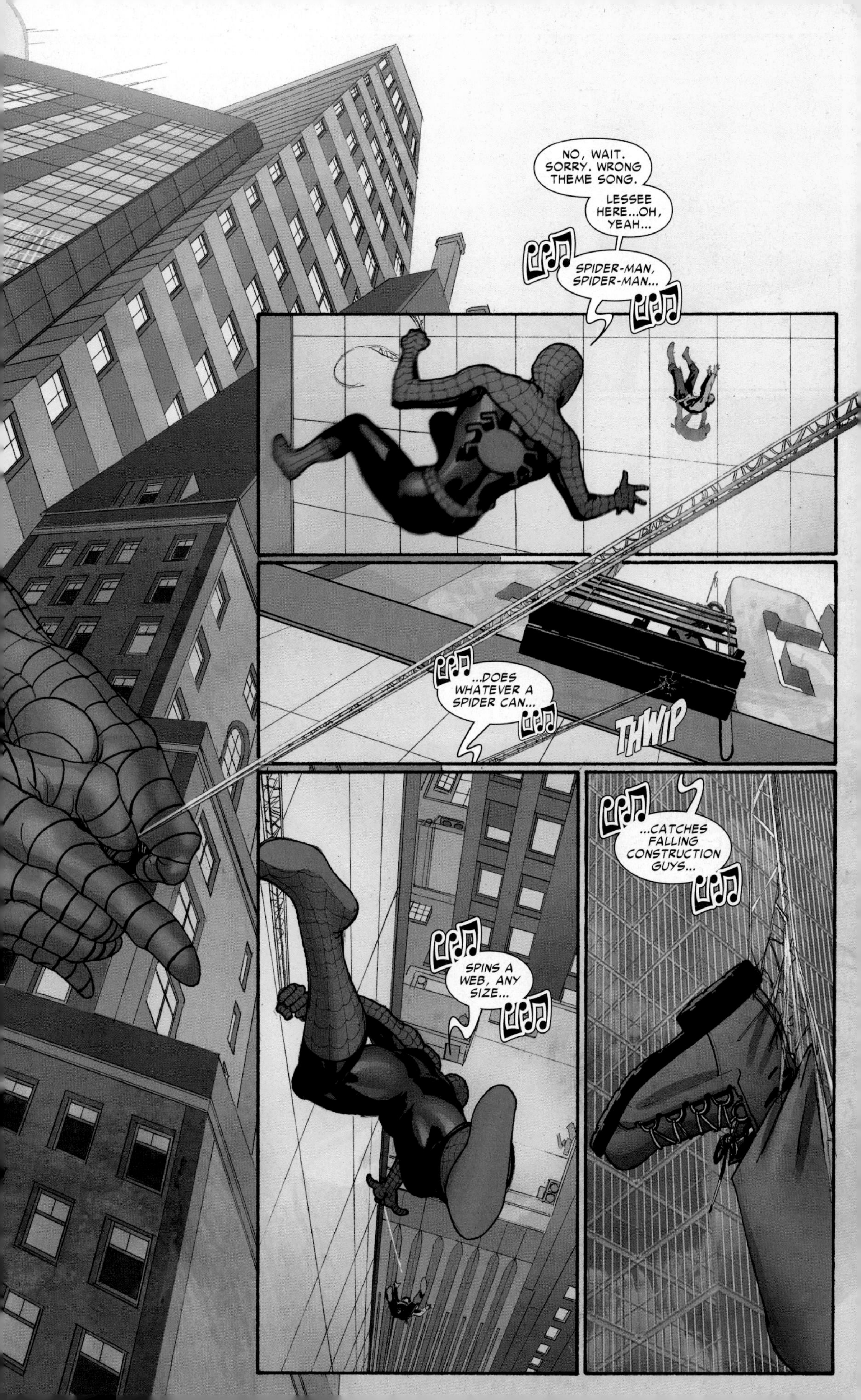
NO, WAIT. SORRY. WRONG THEME SONG.
LESSEE HERE...OH, YEAH...
SPIDER-MAN, SPIDER-MAN...
...DOES WHATEVER A SPIDER CAN...
THWIP
SPINS A WEB, ANY SIZE...
...CATCHES FALLING CONSTRUCTION GUYS...

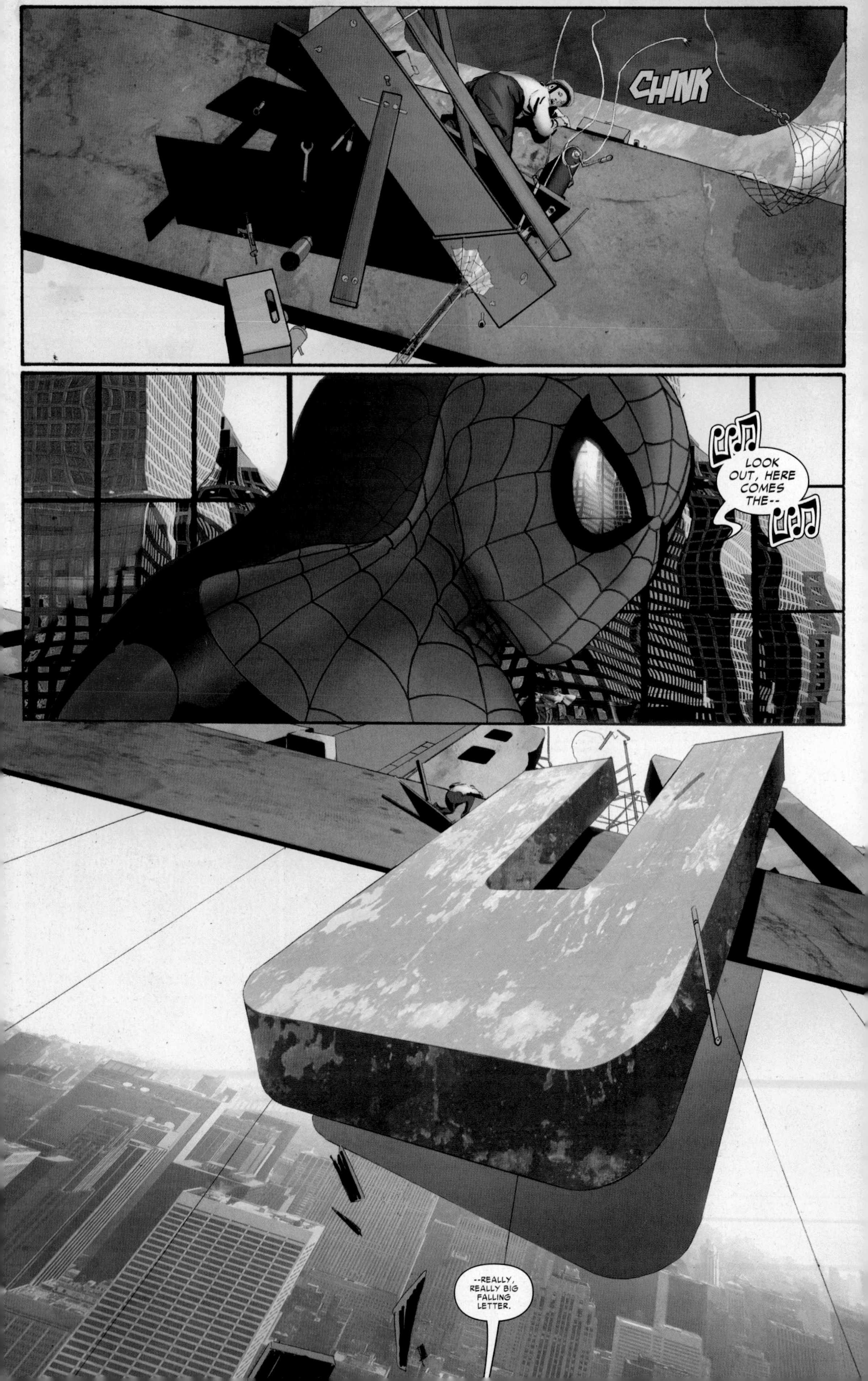
CHINK
LOOK OUT, HERE COMES THE--
--REALLY, REALLY BIG FALLING LETTER.

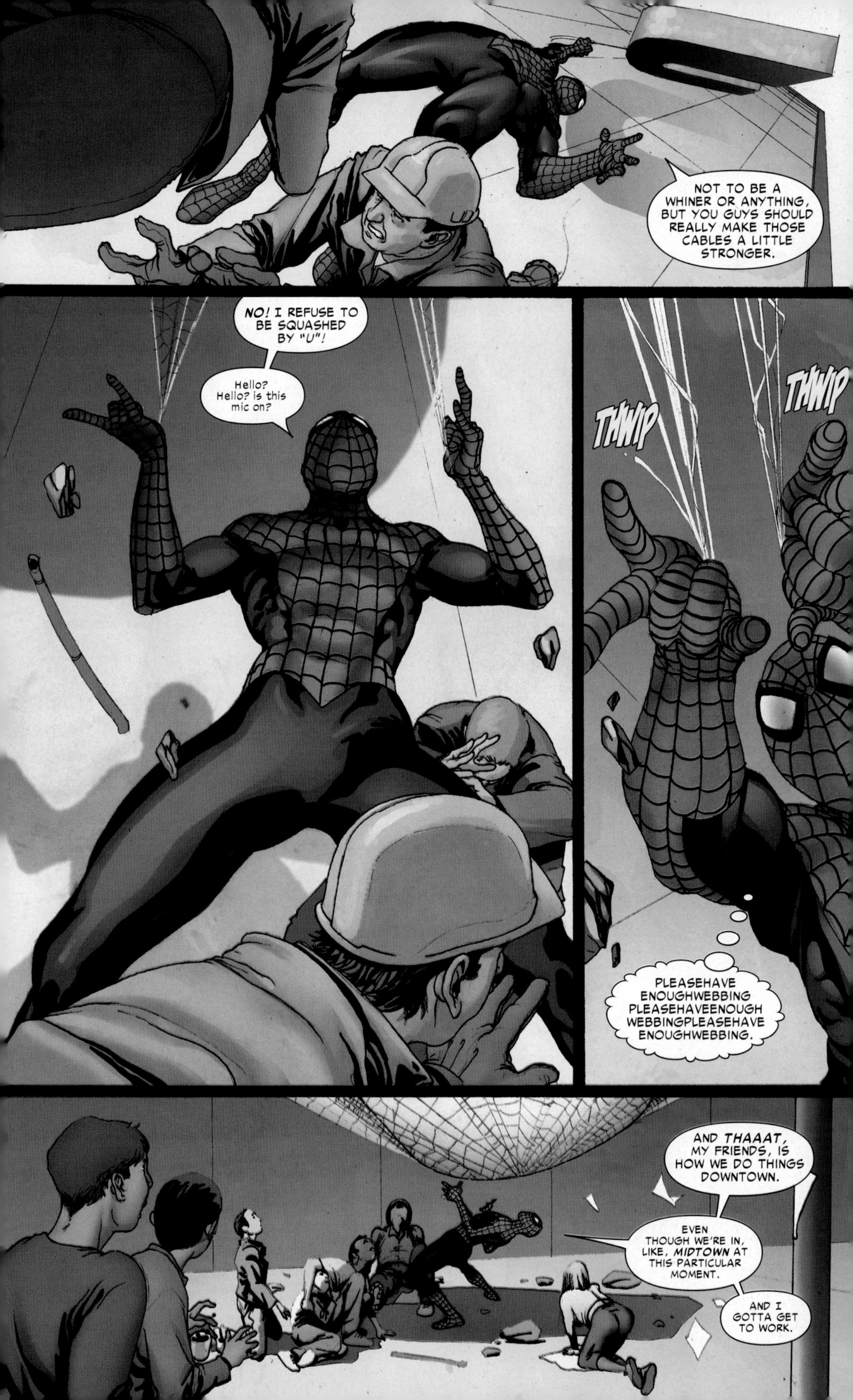

NOT TO BE A WHINER OR ANYTHING, BUT YOU GUYS SHOULD REALLY MAKE THOSE CABLES A LITTLE STRONGER.
NO! I REFUSE TO BE SQUASHED BY "U"!
Hello? Hello? is this mic on?
THWIP
THWIP
PLEASEHAVE ENOUGHWEBBING PLEASEHAVEENOUGH WEBBINGPLEASEHAVE ENOUGHWEBBING.
AND THAAAT, MY FRIENDS, IS HOW WE DO THINGS DOWNTOWN.
EVEN THOUGH WE'RE IN, LIKE, MIDTOWN AT THIS PARTICULAR MOMENT.
AND I GOTTA GET TO WORK.

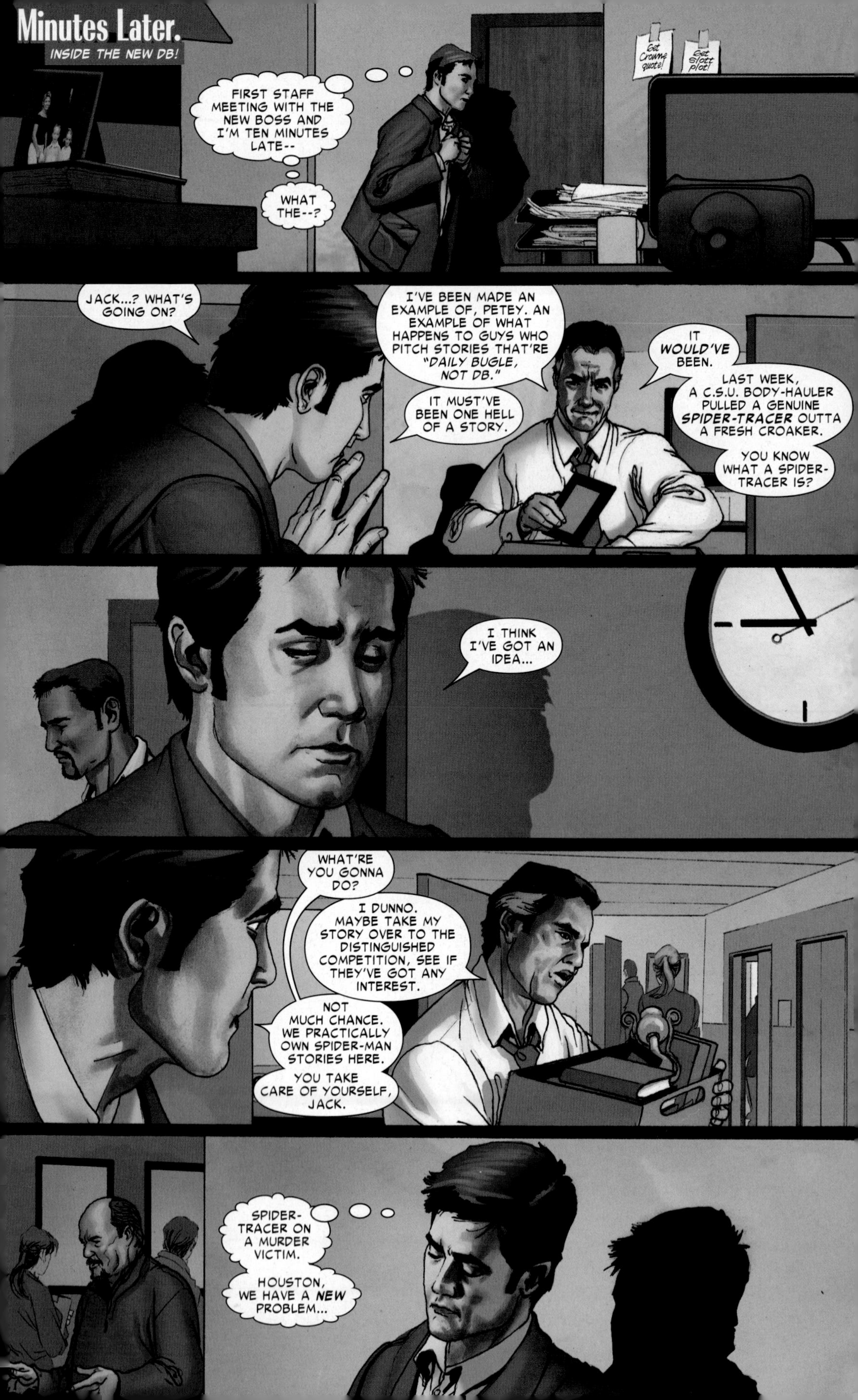
Minutes Later.
INSIDE THE NEW DB!
Get Crowne quote!
Get Slott plot!
FIRST STAFF MEETING WITH THE NEW BOSS AND I'M TEN MINUTES LATE--
WHAT THE--?
JACK...? WHAT'S GOING ON?
I'VE BEEN MADE AN EXAMPLE OF, PETEY. AN EXAMPLE OF WHAT HAPPENS TO GUYS WHO PITCH STORIES THAT'RE "DAILY BUGLE, NOT DB."
IT MUST'VE BEEN ONE HELL OF A STORY.
IT WOULD'VE BEEN.
LAST WEEK, A C.S.U. BODY-HAULER PULLED A GENUINE SPIDER-TRACER OUTTA A FRESH CROAKER.
YOU KNOW WHAT A SPIDER-TRACER IS?
I THINK I'VE GOT AN IDEA...
WHAT'RE YOU GONNA DO?
I DUNNO. MAYBE TAKE MY STORY OVER TO THE DISTINGUISHED COMPETITION, SEE IF THEY'VE GOT ANY INTEREST.
NOT MUCH CHANCE. WE PRACTICALLY OWN SPIDER-MAN STORIES HERE.
YOU TAKE CARE OF YOURSELF, JACK.
SPIDER-TRACER ON A MURDER VICTIM.
HOUSTON, WE HAVE A NEW PROBLEM...

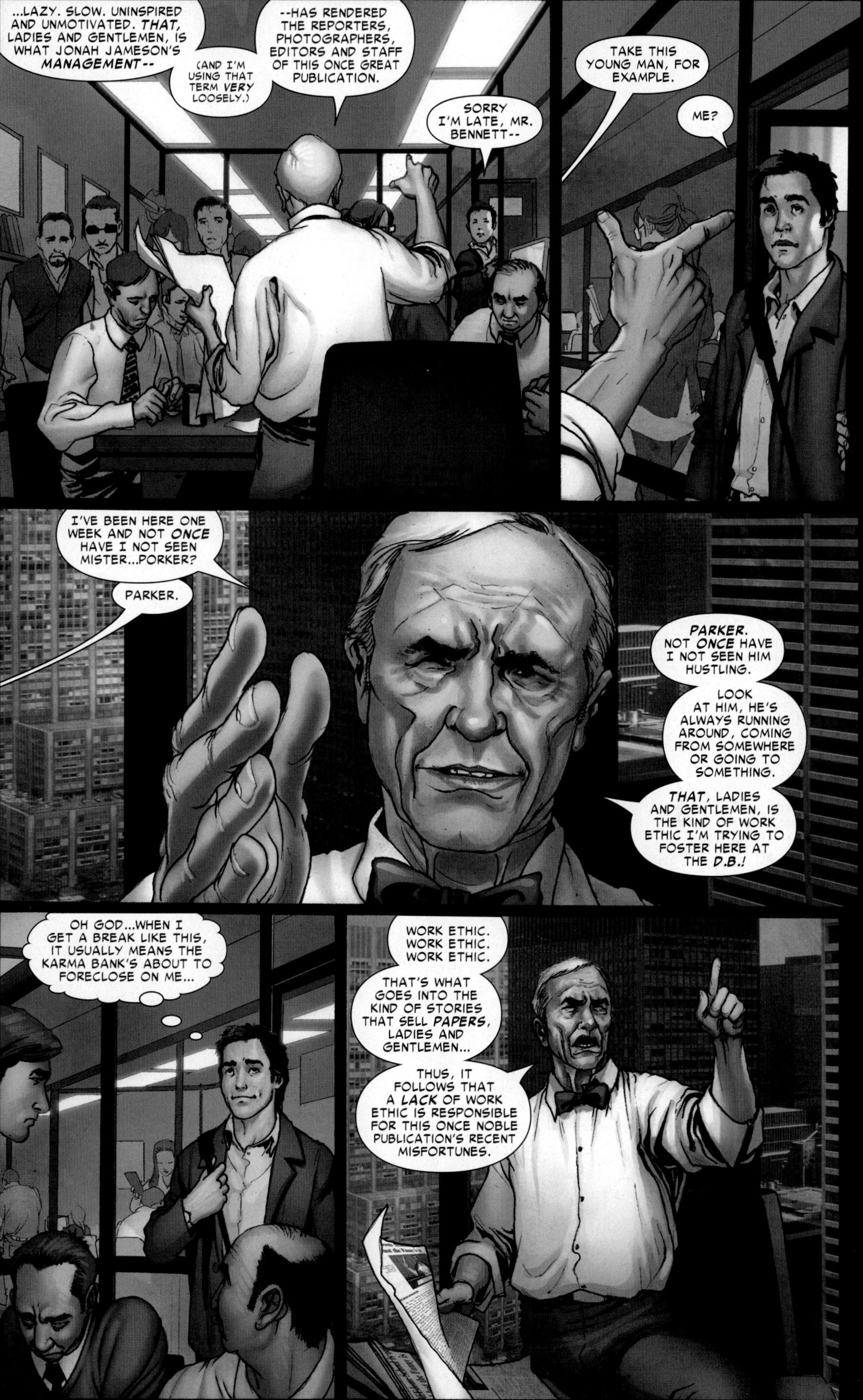
...LAZY. SLOW. UNINSPIRED AND UNMOTIVATED. THAT, LADIES AND GENTLEMEN, IS WHAT JONAH JAMESON'S MANAGEMENT--
(AND I'M USING THAT TERM VERY LOOSELY.)
--HAS RENDERED THE REPORTERS, PHOTOGRAPHERS, EDITORS AND STAFF OF THIS ONCE GREAT PUBLICATION.
SORRY I'M LATE, MR. BENNETT--
TAKE THIS YOUNG MAN, FOR EXAMPLE.
ME?
I'VE BEEN HERE ONE WEEK AND NOT ONCE HAVE I NOT SEEN MISTER...PORKER?
PARKER.
PARKER. NOT ONCE HAVE I NOT SEEN HIM HUSTLING.
LOOK AT HIM, HE'S ALWAYS RUNNING AROUND, COMING FROM SOMEWHERE OR GOING TO SOMETHING.
THAT, LADIES AND GENTLEMEN, IS THE KIND OF WORK ETHIC I'M TRYING TO FOSTER HERE AT THE D.B.!
OH GOD...WHEN I GET A BREAK LIKE THIS, IT USUALLY MEANS THE KARMA BANK'S ABOUT TO FORECLOSE ON ME...
WORK ETHIC. WORK ETHIC. WORK ETHIC.
THAT'S WHAT GOES INTO THE KIND OF STORIES THAT SELL PAPERS, LADIES AND GENTLEMEN...
THUS, IT FOLLOWS THAT A LACK OF WORK ETHIC IS RESPONSIBLE FOR THIS ONCE NOBLE PUBLICATION'S RECENT MISFORTUNES.

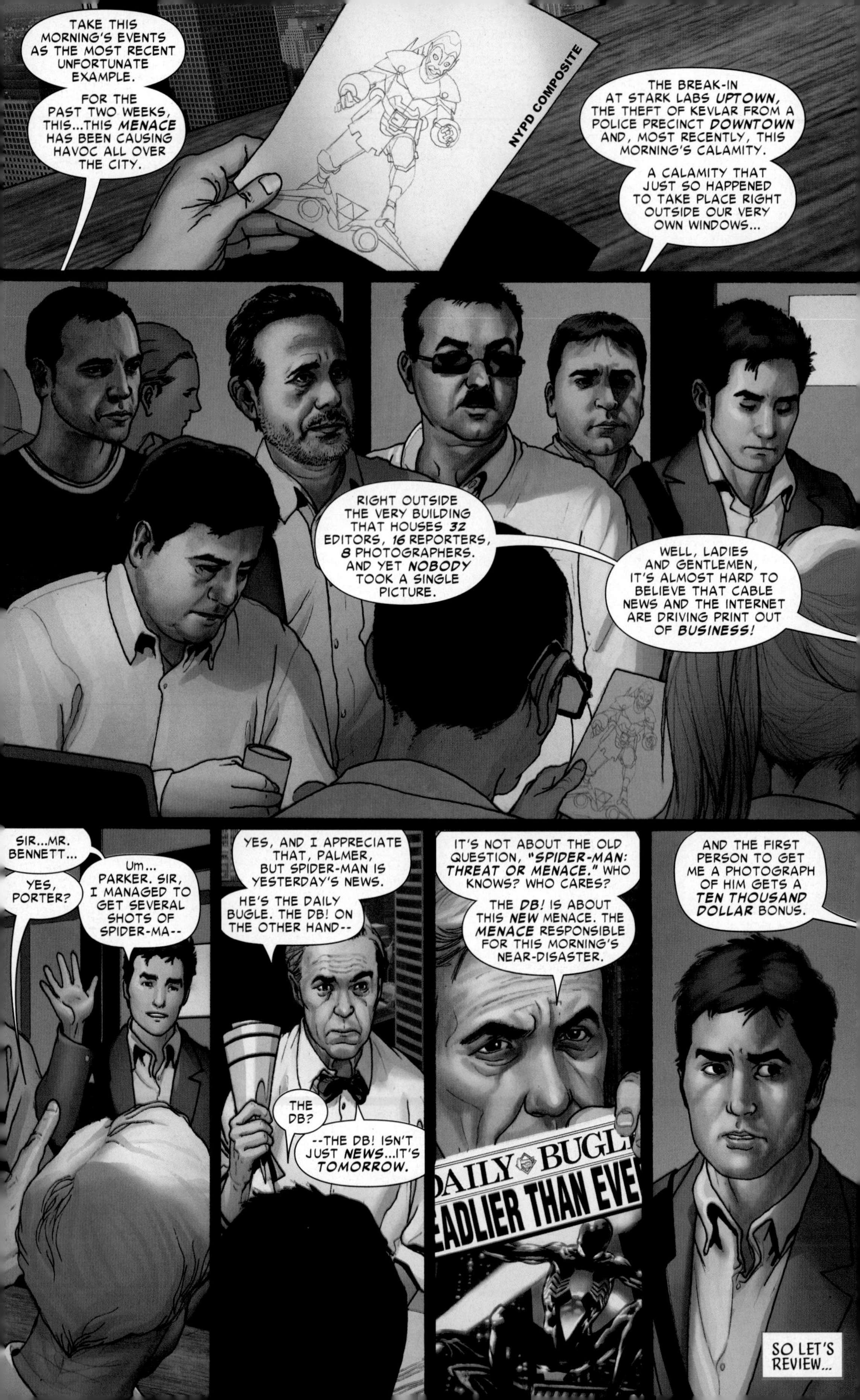
TAKE THIS MORNING'S EVENTS AS THE MOST RECENT UNFORTUNATE EXAMPLE.
FOR THE PAST TWO WEEKS, THIS...THIS MENACE HAS BEEN CAUSING HAVOC ALL OVER THE CITY.
NYPD COMPOSITE
THE BREAK-IN AT STARK LABS UPTOWN, THE THEFT OF KEVLAR FROM A POLICE PRECINCT DOWNTOWN AND, MOST RECENTLY, THIS MORNING'S CALAMITY.
A CALAMITY THAT JUST SO HAPPENED TO TAKE PLACE RIGHT OUTSIDE OUR VERY OWN WINDOWS...
RIGHT OUTSIDE THE VERY BUILDING THAT HOUSES 32 EDITORS, 16 REPORTERS, 8 PHOTOGRAPHERS. AND YET NOBODY TOOK A SINGLE PICTURE.
WELL, LADIES AND GENTLEMEN, IT'S ALMOST HARD TO BELIEVE THAT CABLE NEWS AND THE INTERNET ARE DRIVING PRINT OUT OF BUSINESS!
SIR...MR. BENNETT...
YES, PORTER?
Um... PARKER. SIR, I MANAGED TO GET SEVERAL SHOTS OF SPIDER-MA--
YES, AND I APPRECIATE THAT, PALMER, BUT SPIDER-MAN IS YESTERDAY'S NEWS.
HE'S THE DAILY BUGLE. THE DB! ON THE OTHER HAND--
THE DB?
--THE DB! ISN'T JUST NEWS...IT'S TOMORROW.
IT'S NOT ABOUT THE OLD QUESTION, "SPIDER-MAN: THREAT OR MENACE." WHO KNOWS? WHO CARES?
THE DB! IS ABOUT THIS NEW MENACE. THE MENACE RESPONSIBLE FOR THIS MORNING'S NEAR-DISASTER.
DAILY BUGL
EADLIER THAN EVE
AND THE FIRST PERSON TO GET ME A PHOTOGRAPH OF HIM GETS A TEN THOUSAND DOLLAR BONUS.
SO LET'S REVIEW...

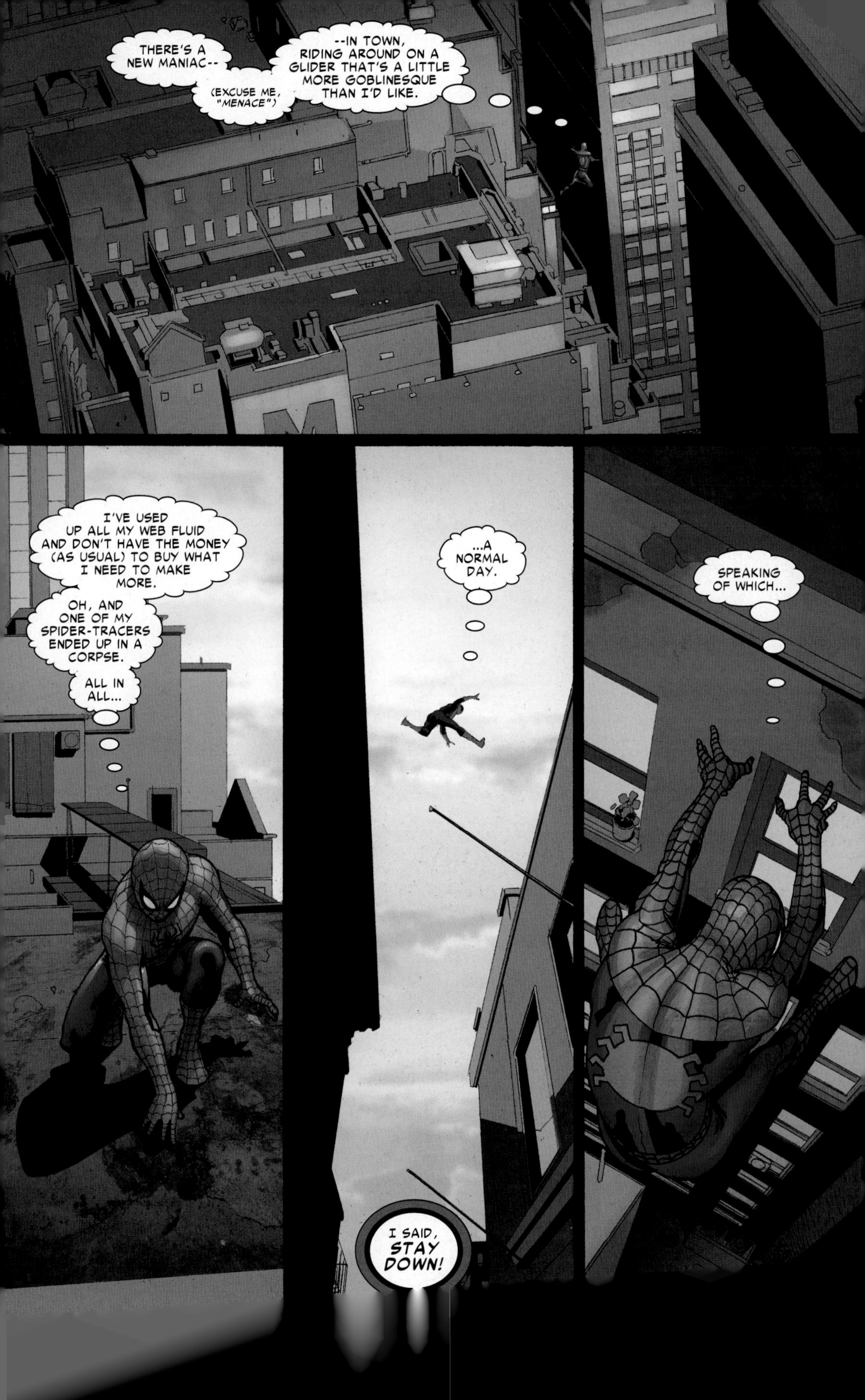
THERE'S A NEW MANIAC--
--IN TOWN, RIDING AROUND ON A GLIDER THAT'S A LITTLE MORE GOBLINESQUE THAN I'D LIKE.
(EXCUSE ME, "MENACE")
I'VE USED UP ALL MY WEB FLUID AND DON'T HAVE THE MONEY (AS USUAL) TO BUY WHAT I NEED TO MAKE MORE.
OH, AND ONE OF MY SPIDER-TRACERS ENDED UP IN A CORPSE.
ALL IN ALL...
...A NORMAL DAY.
SPEAKING OF WHICH...
I SAID, STAY DOWN!

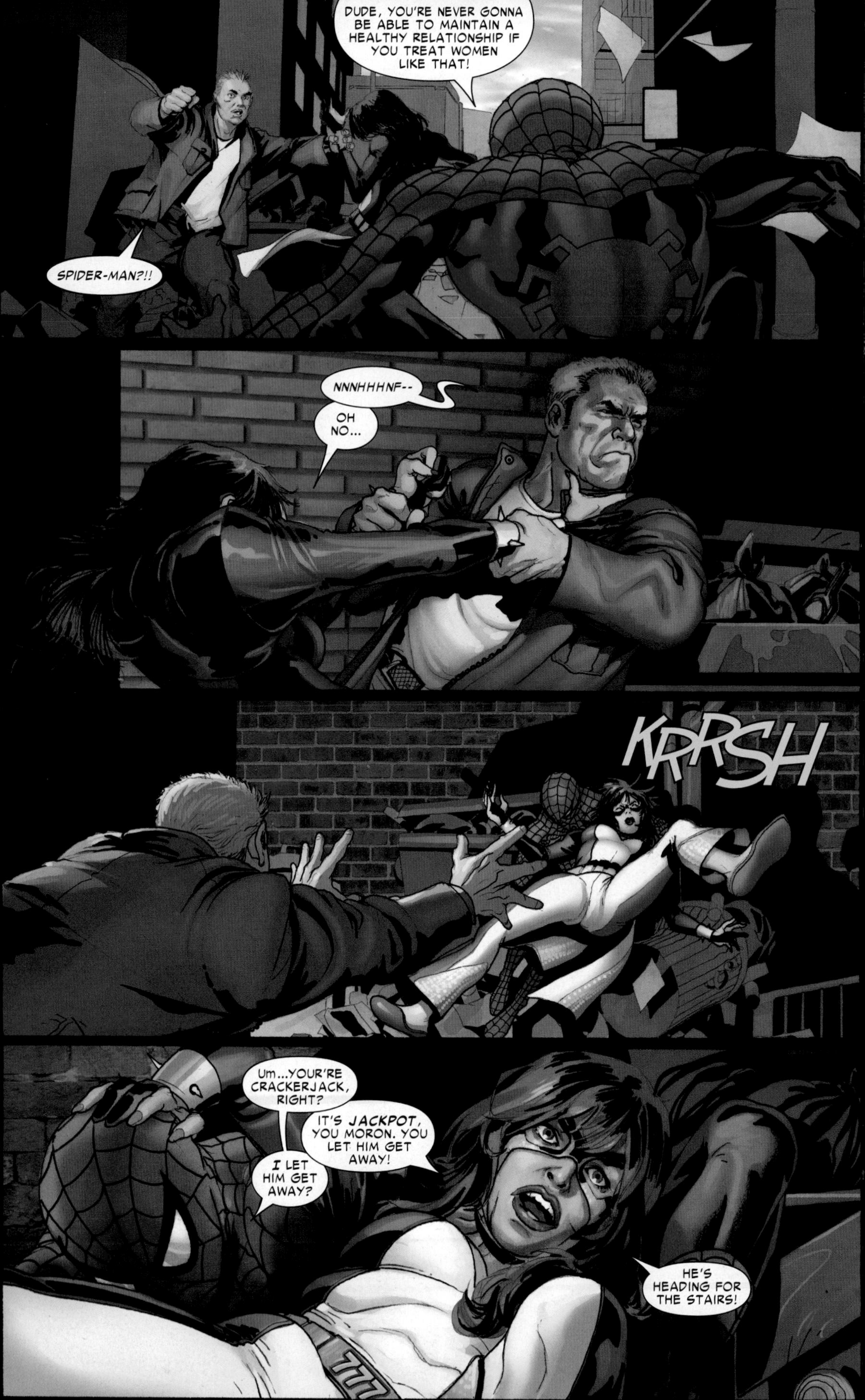

DUDE, YOU'RE NEVER GONNA BE ABLE TO MAINTAIN A HEALTHY RELATIONSHIP IF YOU TREAT WOMEN LIKE THAT!
SPIDER-MAN?!!
NNNHHHNF--
OH NO...
KRRSH
Um...YOUR'RE CRACKERJACK, RIGHT?
IT'S JACKPOT, YOU MORON. YOU LET HIM GET AWAY!
I LET HIM GET AWAY?
HE'S HEADING FOR THE STAIRS!

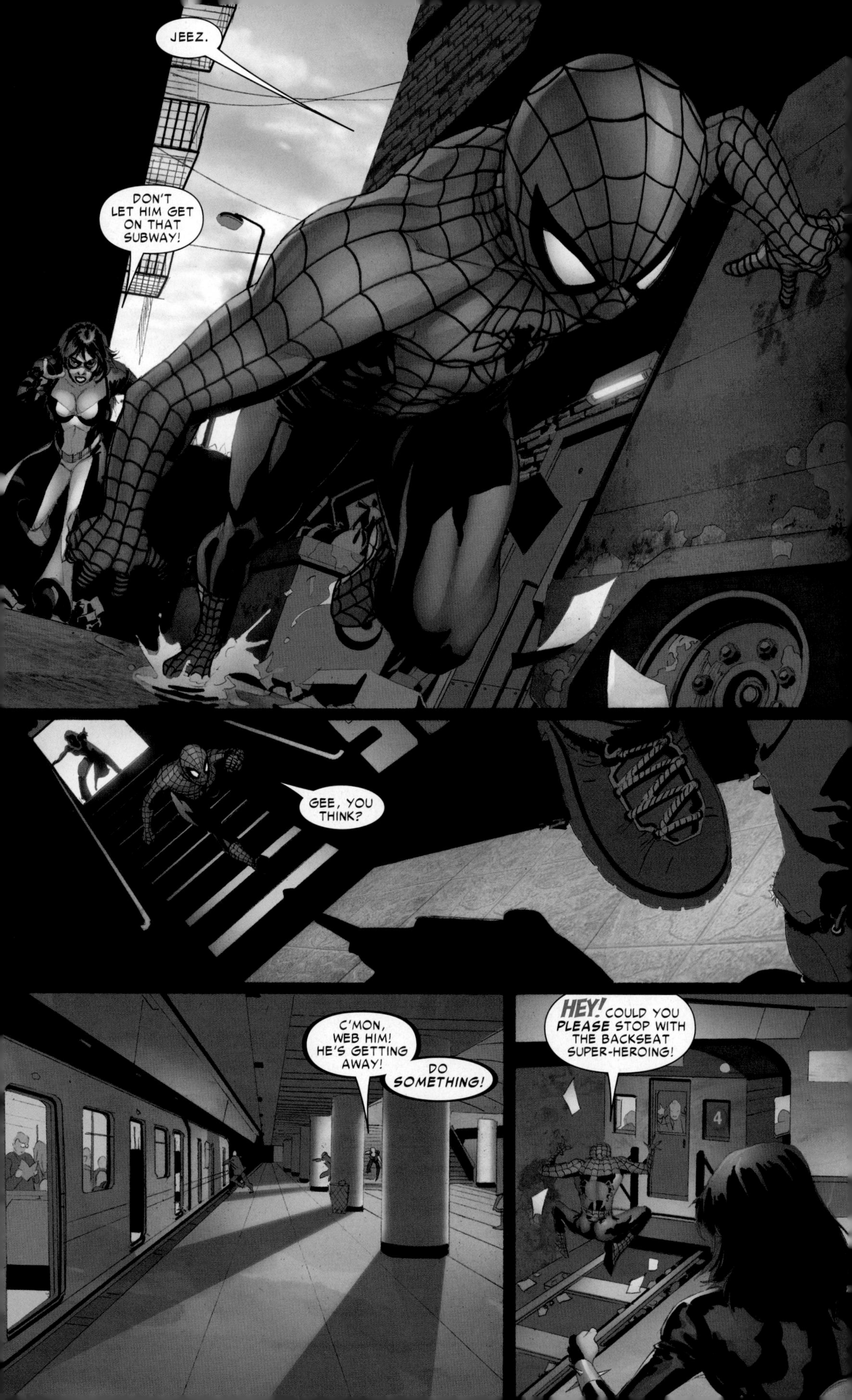
JEEZ.
DON'T LET HIM GET ON THAT SUBWAY!
GEE, YOU THINK?
C'MON, WEB HIM! HE'S GETTING AWAY!
DO SOMETHING!
HEY! COULD YOU PLEASE STOP WITH THE BACKSEAT SUPER-HEROING!
4

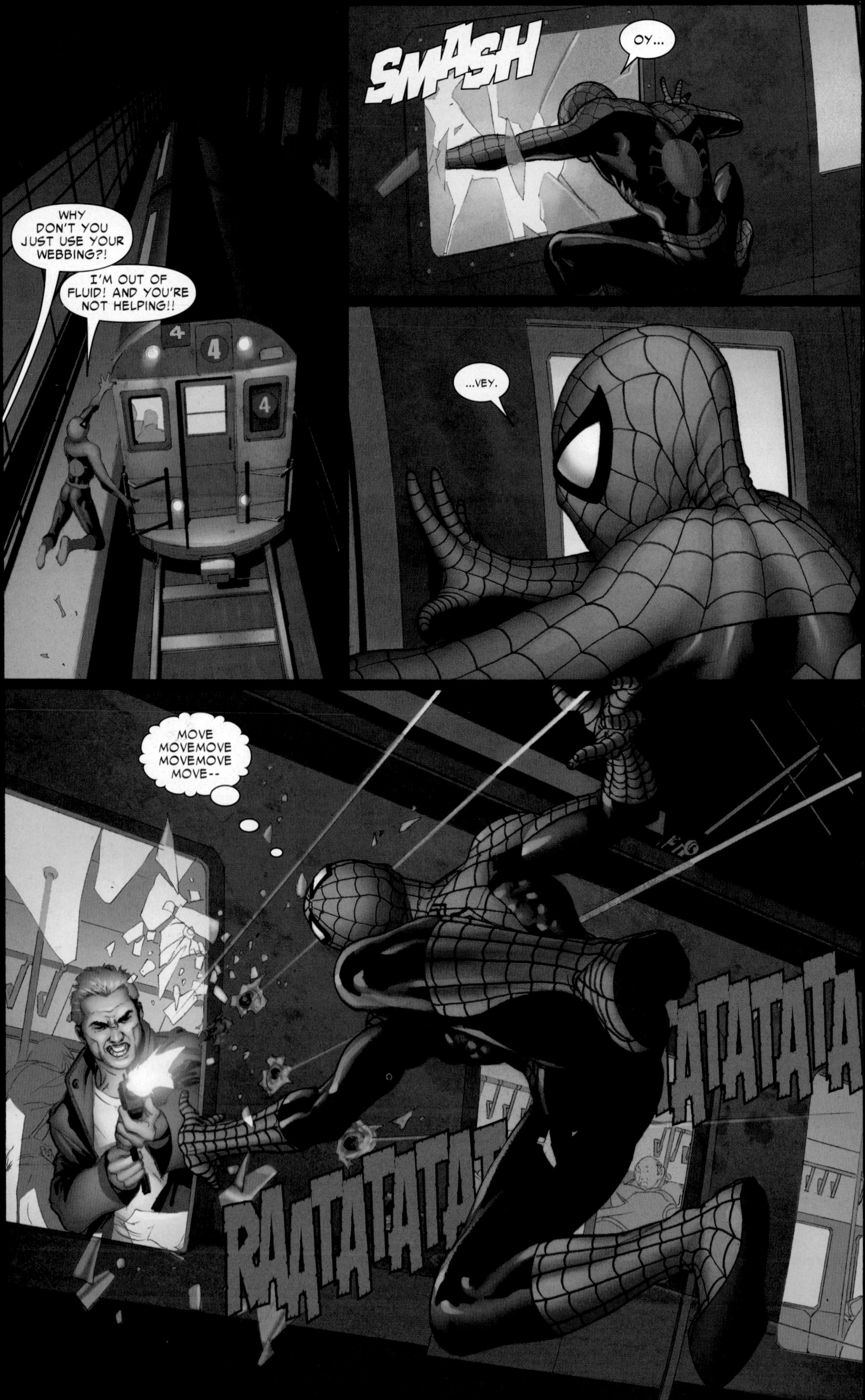
SMASH
OY...
WHY DON'T YOU JUST USE YOUR WEBBING?!
I'M OUT OF FLUID! AND YOU'RE NOT HELPING!!
...VEY.
MOVE MOVEMOVE MOVEMOVE MOVE--
RAATATATAT
TATATATA

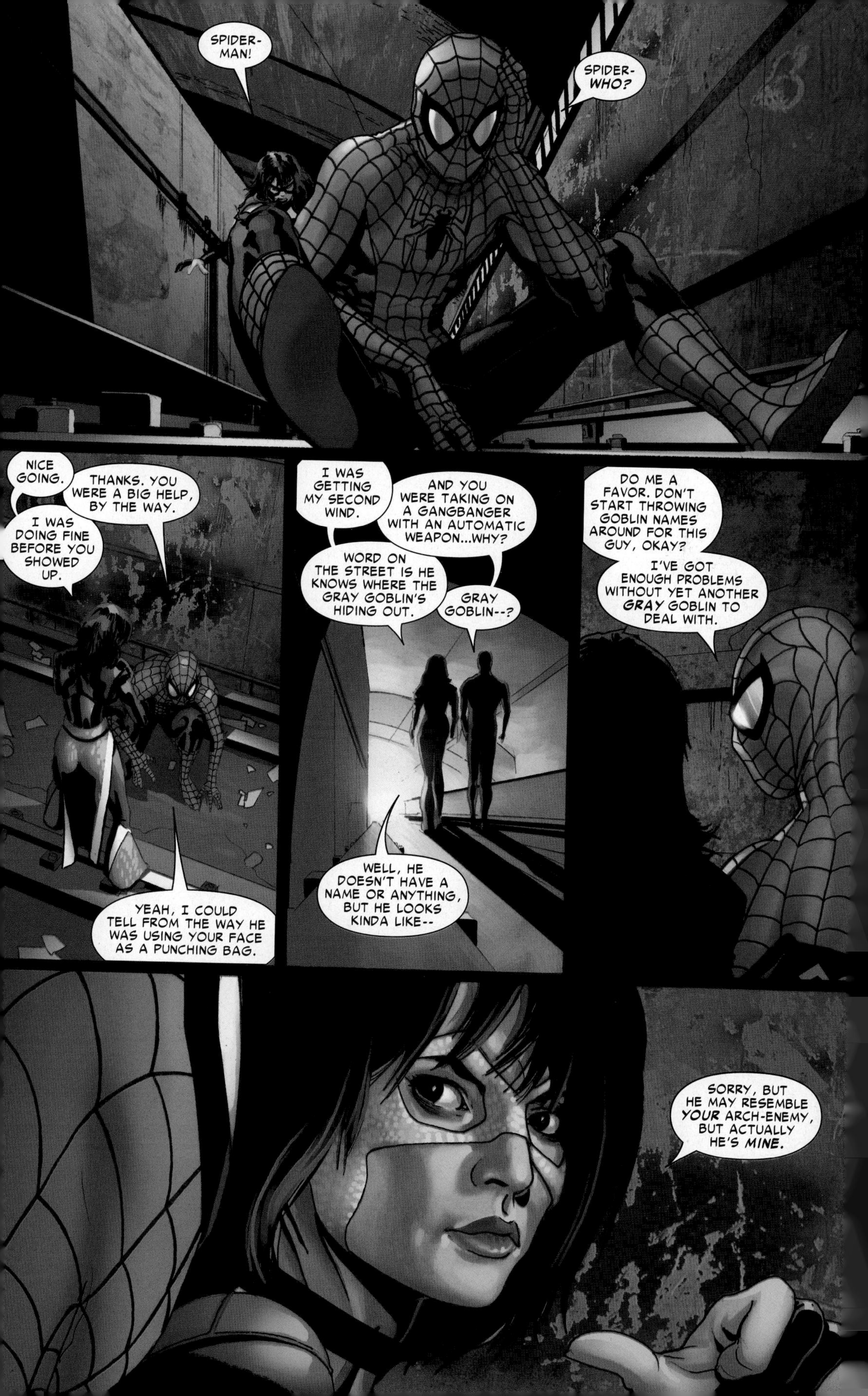
SPIDER-MAN!
SPIDER-WHO?
NICE GOING.
THANKS. YOU WERE A BIG HELP, BY THE WAY.
I WAS DOING FINE BEFORE YOU SHOWED UP.
YEAH, I COULD TELL FROM THE WAY HE WAS USING YOUR FACE AS A PUNCHING BAG.
I WAS GETTING MY SECOND WIND.
AND YOU WERE TAKING ON A GANGBANGER WITH AN AUTOMATIC WEAPON...WHY?
WORD ON THE STREET IS HE KNOWS WHERE THE GRAY GOBLIN'S HIDING OUT.
GRAY GOBLIN--?
WELL, HE DOESN'T HAVE A NAME OR ANYTHING, BUT HE LOOKS KINDA LIKE--
DO ME A FAVOR. DON'T START THROWING GOBLIN NAMES AROUND FOR THIS GUY, OKAY?
I'VE GOT ENOUGH PROBLEMS WITHOUT YET ANOTHER GRAY GOBLIN TO DEAL WITH.
SORRY, BUT HE MAY RESEMBLE YOUR ARCH-ENEMY, BUT ACTUALLY HE'S MINE.

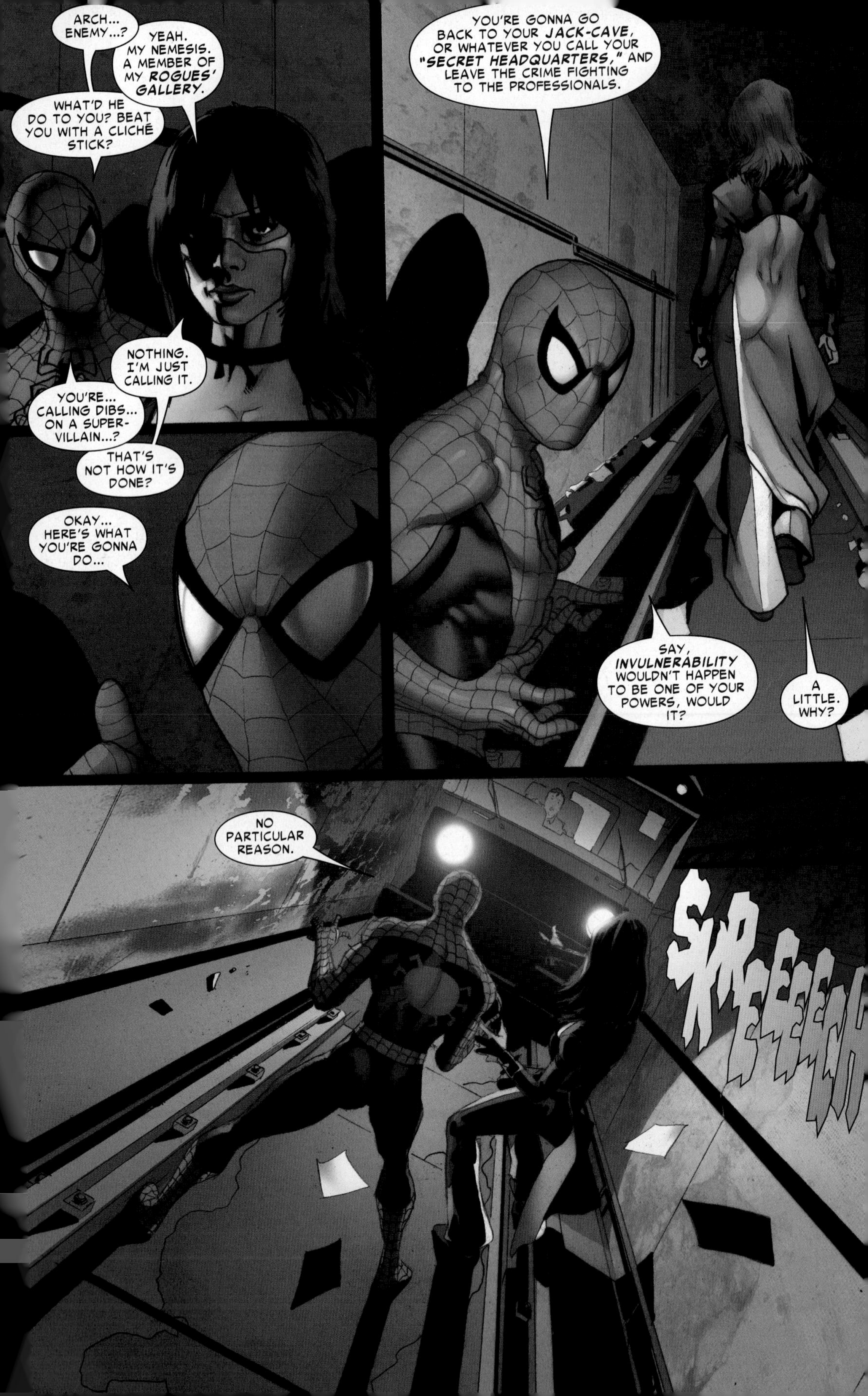
ARCH... ENEMY...?
YEAH. MY NEMESIS. A MEMBER OF MY ROGUES' GALLERY.
WHAT'D HE DO TO YOU? BEAT YOU WITH A CLICHÉ STICK?
NOTHING. I'M JUST CALLING IT.
YOU'RE... CALLING DIBS... ON A SUPER-VILLAIN...?
THAT'S NOT HOW IT'S DONE?
OKAY... HERE'S WHAT YOU'RE GONNA DO...
YOU'RE GONNA GO BACK TO YOUR JACK-CAVE, OR WHATEVER YOU CALL YOUR "SECRET HEADQUARTERS," AND LEAVE THE CRIME FIGHTING TO THE PROFESSIONALS.
SAY, INVULNERABILITY WOULDN'T HAPPEN TO BE ONE OF YOUR POWERS, WOULD IT?
A LITTLE. WHY?
NO PARTICULAR REASON.
SKREEEECH

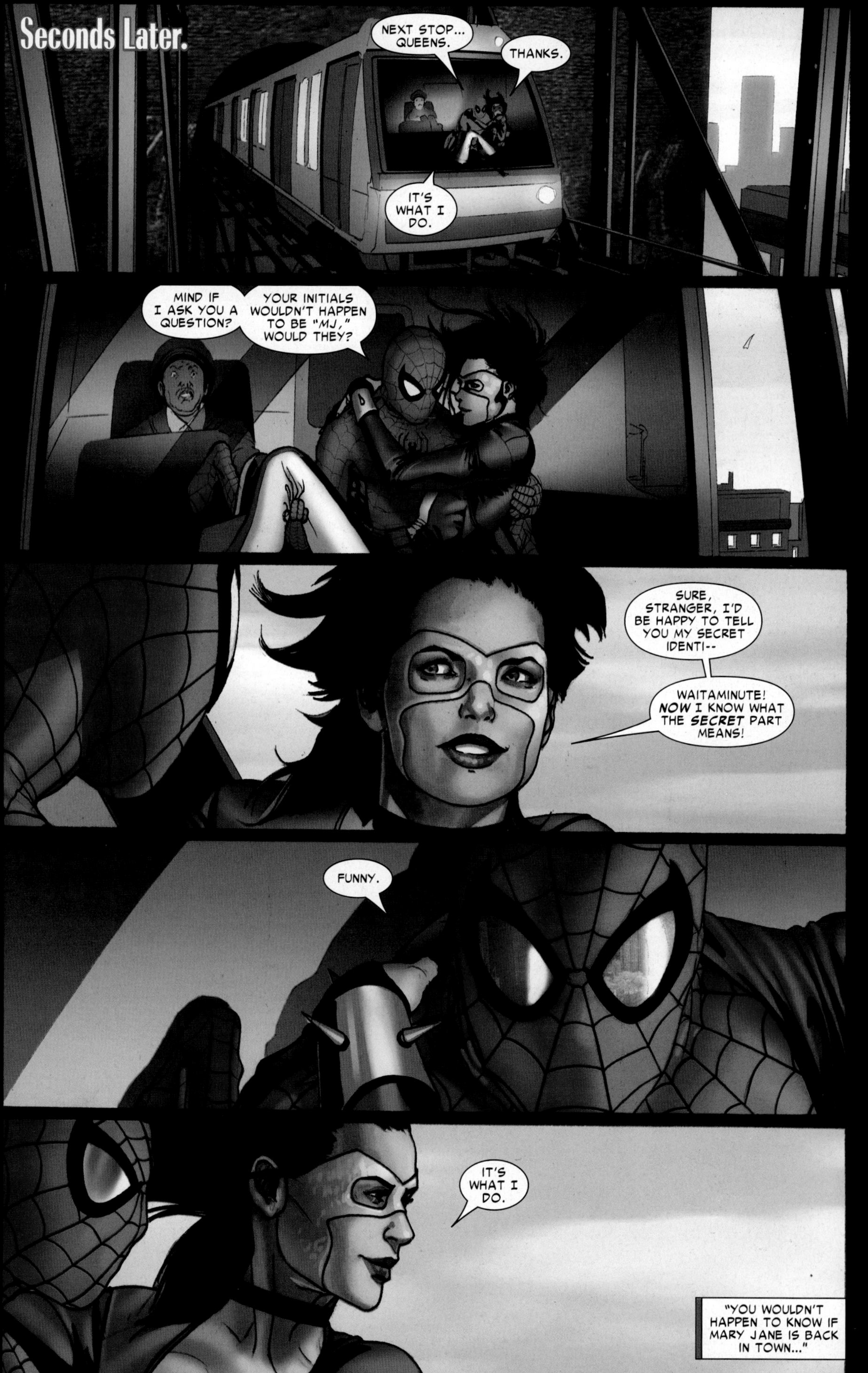

Seconds Later.
NEXT STOP... QUEENS.
THANKS.
IT'S WHAT I DO.
MIND IF I ASK YOU A QUESTION?
YOUR INITIALS WOULDN'T HAPPEN TO BE "MJ," WOULD THEY?
SURE, STRANGER, I'D BE HAPPY TO TELL YOU MY SECRET IDENTI--
WAITAMINUTE! NOW I KNOW WHAT THE SECRET PART MEANS!
FUNNY.
IT'S WHAT I DO.
"YOU WOULDN'T HAPPEN TO KNOW IF MARY JANE IS BACK IN TOWN..."

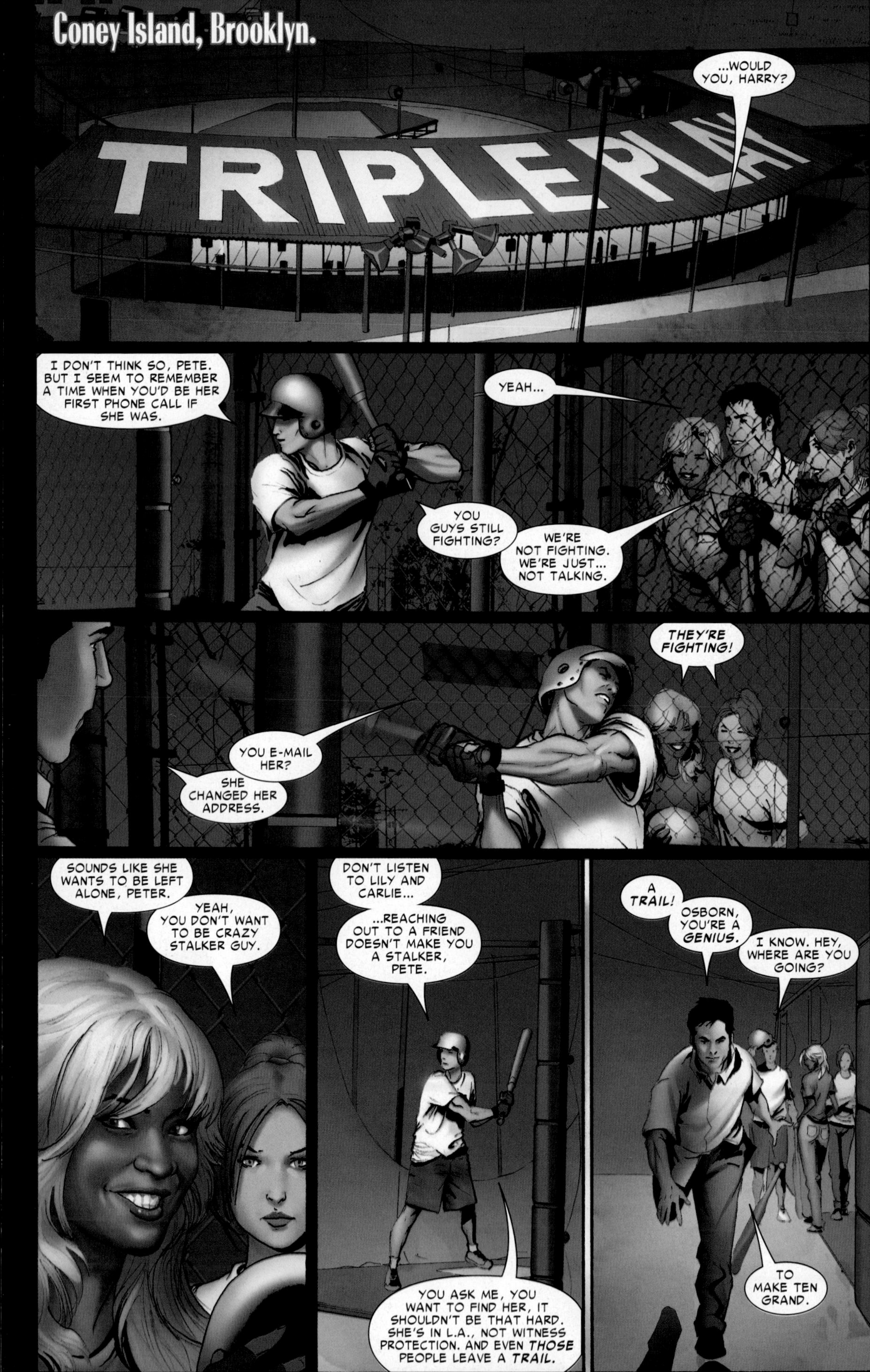
Coney Island, Brooklyn.
...WOULD YOU, HARRY?
TRIPLE PLAY
I DON'T THINK SO, PETE. BUT I SEEM TO REMEMBER A TIME WHEN YOU'D BE HER FIRST PHONE CALL IF SHE WAS.
YEAH...
YOU GUYS STILL FIGHTING?
WE'RE NOT FIGHTING. WE'RE JUST... NOT TALKING.
THEY'RE FIGHTING!
YOU E-MAIL HER?
SHE CHANGED HER ADDRESS.
SOUNDS LIKE SHE WANTS TO BE LEFT ALONE, PETER.
YEAH, YOU DON'T WANT TO BE CRAZY STALKER GUY.
DON'T LISTEN TO LILY AND CARLIE...
...REACHING OUT TO A FRIEND DOESN'T MAKE YOU A STALKER, PETE.
YOU ASK ME, YOU WANT TO FIND HER, IT SHOULDN'T BE THAT HARD. SHE'S IN L.A., NOT WITNESS PROTECTION. AND EVEN *THOSE* PEOPLE LEAVE A *TRAIL*.
A *TRAIL*!
OSBORN, YOU'RE A *GENIUS*.
I KNOW. HEY, WHERE ARE YOU GOING?
TO MAKE TEN GRAND.

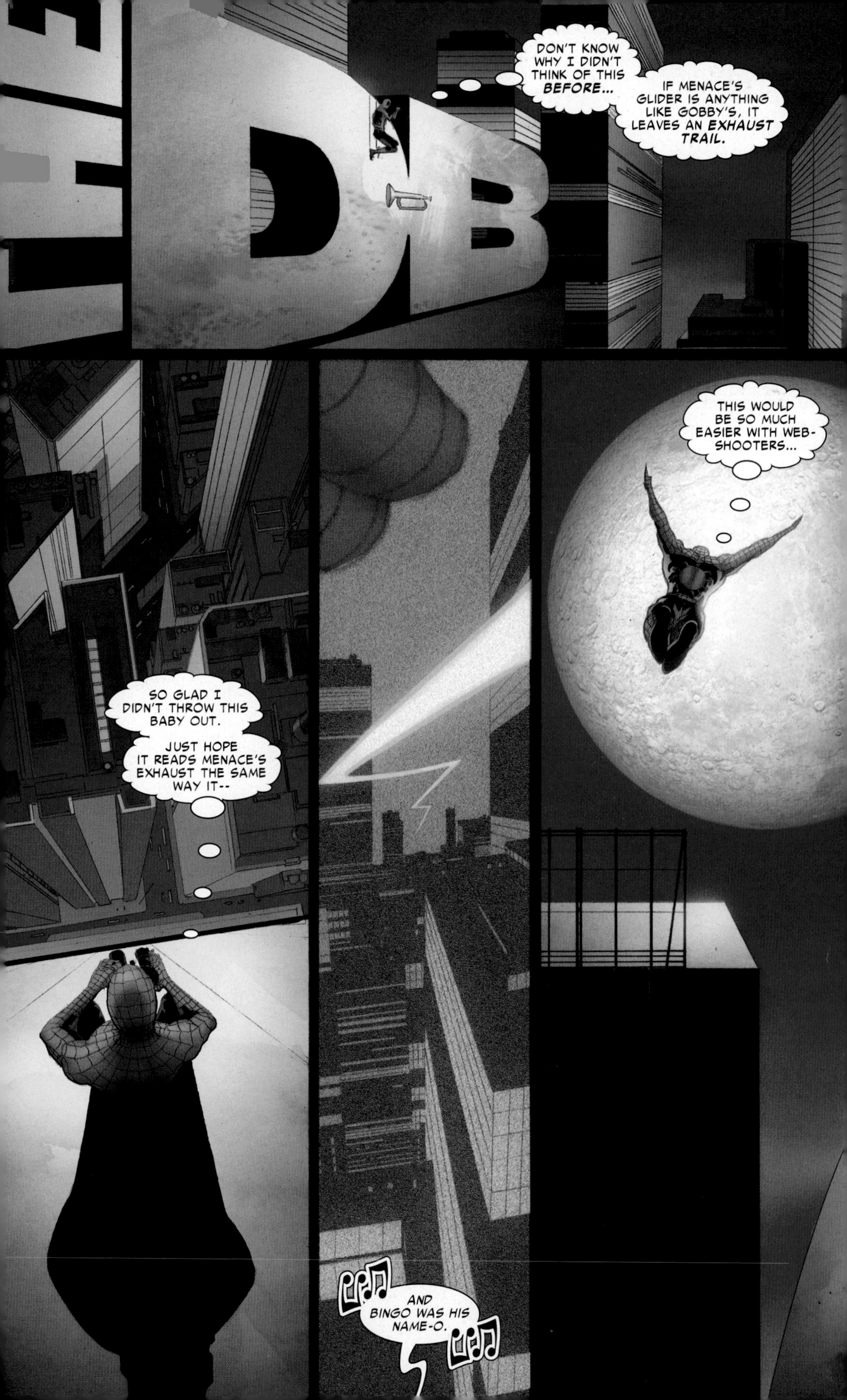
THE DB
DON'T KNOW WHY I DIDN'T THINK OF THIS *BEFORE...*
IF MENACE'S GLIDER IS ANYTHING LIKE GOBBY'S, IT LEAVES AN *EXHAUST TRAIL.*
SO GLAD I DIDN'T THROW THIS BABY OUT.
JUST HOPE IT READS MENACE'S EXHAUST THE SAME WAY IT--
THIS WOULD BE SO MUCH EASIER WITH WEB-SHOOTERS...
AND BINGO WAS HIS NAME-O.

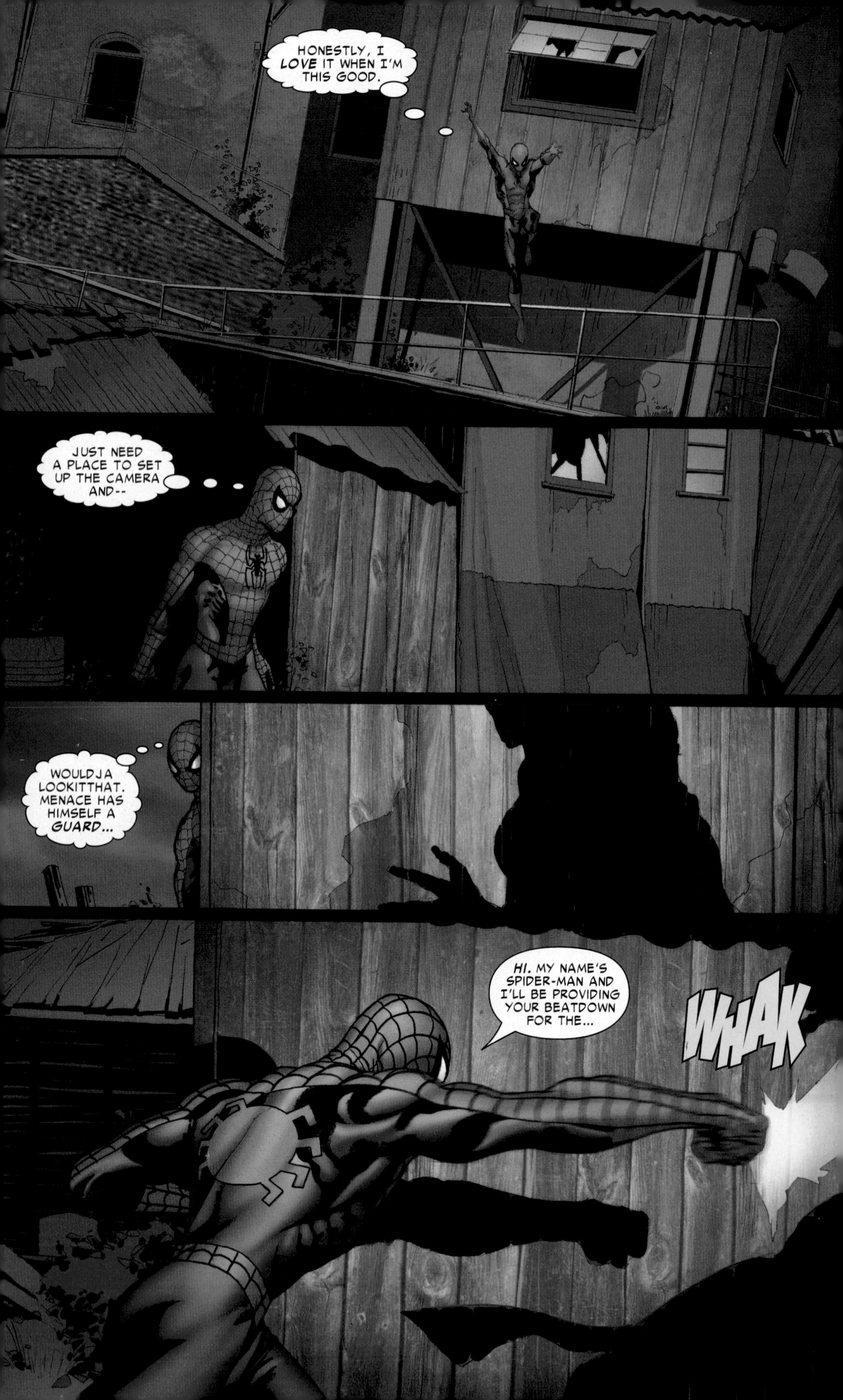
HONESTLY, I LOVE IT WHEN I'M THIS GOOD.
JUST NEED A PLACE TO SET UP THE CAMERA AND--
WOULDJA LOOKITTHAT. MENACE HAS HIMSELF A GUARD...
HI. MY NAME'S SPIDER-MAN AND I'LL BE PROVIDING YOUR BEATDOWN FOR THE...
WHAK

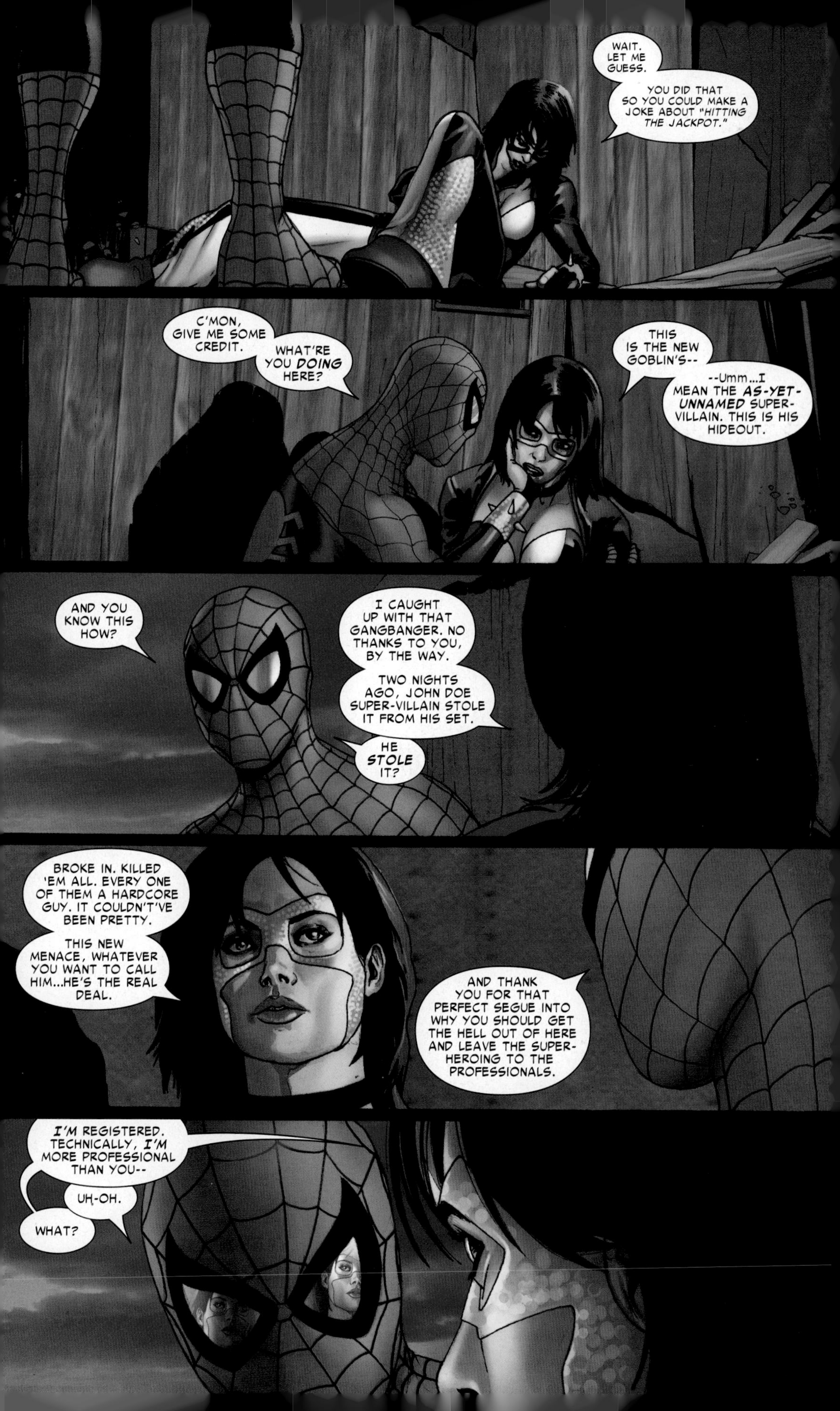
WAIT. LET ME GUESS.
YOU DID THAT SO YOU COULD MAKE A JOKE ABOUT "HITTING THE JACKPOT."
C'MON, GIVE ME SOME CREDIT.
WHAT'RE YOU DOING HERE?
THIS IS THE NEW GOBLIN'S--
--Umm...I MEAN THE AS-YET-UNNAMED SUPER-VILLAIN. THIS IS HIS HIDEOUT.
AND YOU KNOW THIS HOW?
I CAUGHT UP WITH THAT GANGBANGER. NO THANKS TO YOU, BY THE WAY.
TWO NIGHTS AGO, JOHN DOE SUPER-VILLAIN STOLE IT FROM HIS SET.
HE STOLE IT?
BROKE IN. KILLED 'EM ALL. EVERY ONE OF THEM A HARDCORE GUY. IT COULDN'T'VE BEEN PRETTY.
THIS NEW MENACE, WHATEVER YOU WANT TO CALL HIM...HE'S THE REAL DEAL.
AND THANK YOU FOR THAT PERFECT SEGUE INTO WHY YOU SHOULD GET THE HELL OUT OF HERE AND LEAVE THE SUPER-HEROING TO THE PROFESSIONALS.
I'M REGISTERED. TECHNICALLY, I'M MORE PROFESSIONAL THAN YOU--
UH-OH.
WHAT?

YOU ARE ENGAGED IN CONDUCT FALLING UNDER THE JURISDICTION OF THE SUPERHUMAN REGISTRATION ACT!
IDENTIFY YOURSELF OR FACE IMMEDIATE ARREST AND INCARCERATION.
WE'VE GOT COMPANY.
FACE IT, TIGER. YOU'RE UNDER ARREST!
NEXT ISSUE:
THE MENACE OF...
MENACE!

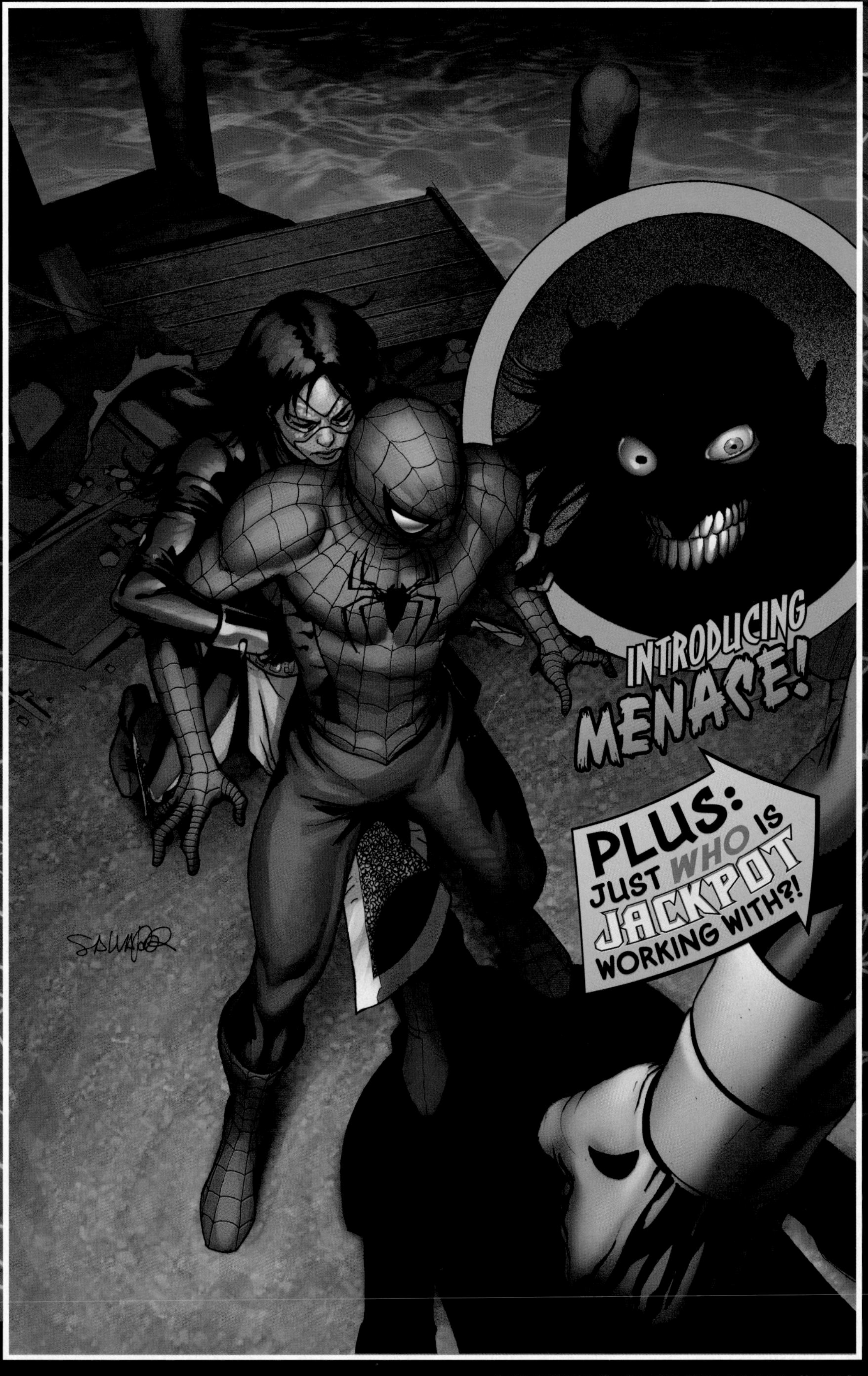
INTRODUCING MENACE!
PLUS: JUST WHO IS JACKPOT WORKING WITH?!

AMAZING SPIDER-MAN #550

WHILE ATTENDING A DEMONSTRATION IN RADIOLOGY, HIGH SCHOOL STUDENT **PETER PARKER** WAS BITTEN BY A SPIDER WHICH HAD ACCIDENTALLY BEEN EXPOSED TO **RADIOACTIVE RAYS.** THROUGH A MIRACLE OF SCIENCE, PETER SOON FOUND THAT HE HAD **GAINED** THE SPIDER'S POWERS...AND HAD, IN EFFECT, BECOME A HUMAN SPIDER! FROM THAT DAY ON HE WAS...

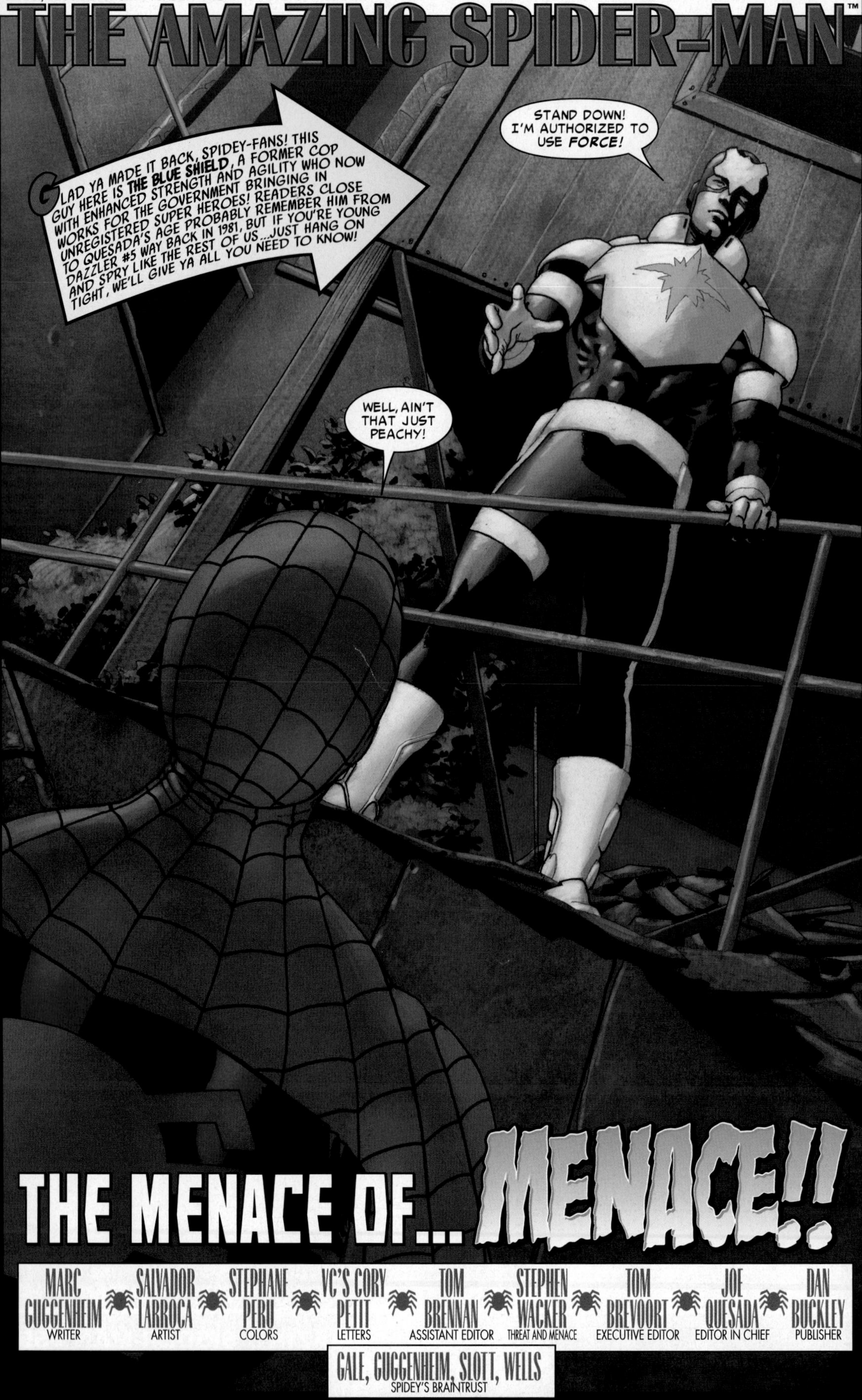

THE AMAZING SPIDER-MAN™
GLAD YA MADE IT BACK, SPIDEY-FANS! THIS GUY HERE IS THE BLUE SHIELD, A FORMER COP WITH ENHANCED STRENGTH AND AGILITY WHO NOW WORKS FOR THE GOVERNMENT BRINGING IN UNREGISTERED SUPER HEROES! READERS CLOSE TO QUESADA'S AGE PROBABLY REMEMBER HIM FROM DAZZLER #5 WAY BACK IN 1981, BUT IF YOU'RE YOUNG AND SPRY LIKE THE REST OF US...JUST HANG ON TIGHT, WE'LL GIVE YA ALL YOU NEED TO KNOW!
STAND DOWN! I'M AUTHORIZED TO USE FORCE!
WELL, AIN'T THAT JUST PEACHY!
THE MENACE OF... MENACE!!
MARC GUGGENHEIM WRITER
SALVADOR LARROCA ARTIST
STEPHANE PERU COLORS
VC'S CORY PETIT LETTERS
TOM BRENNAN ASSISTANT EDITOR
STEPHEN WACKER THREAT AND MENACE
TOM BREVOORT EXECUTIVE EDITOR
JOE QUESADA EDITOR IN CHIEF
DAN BUCKLEY PUBLISHER
GALE, GUGGENHEIM, SLOTT, WELLS SPIDEY'S BRAINTRUST

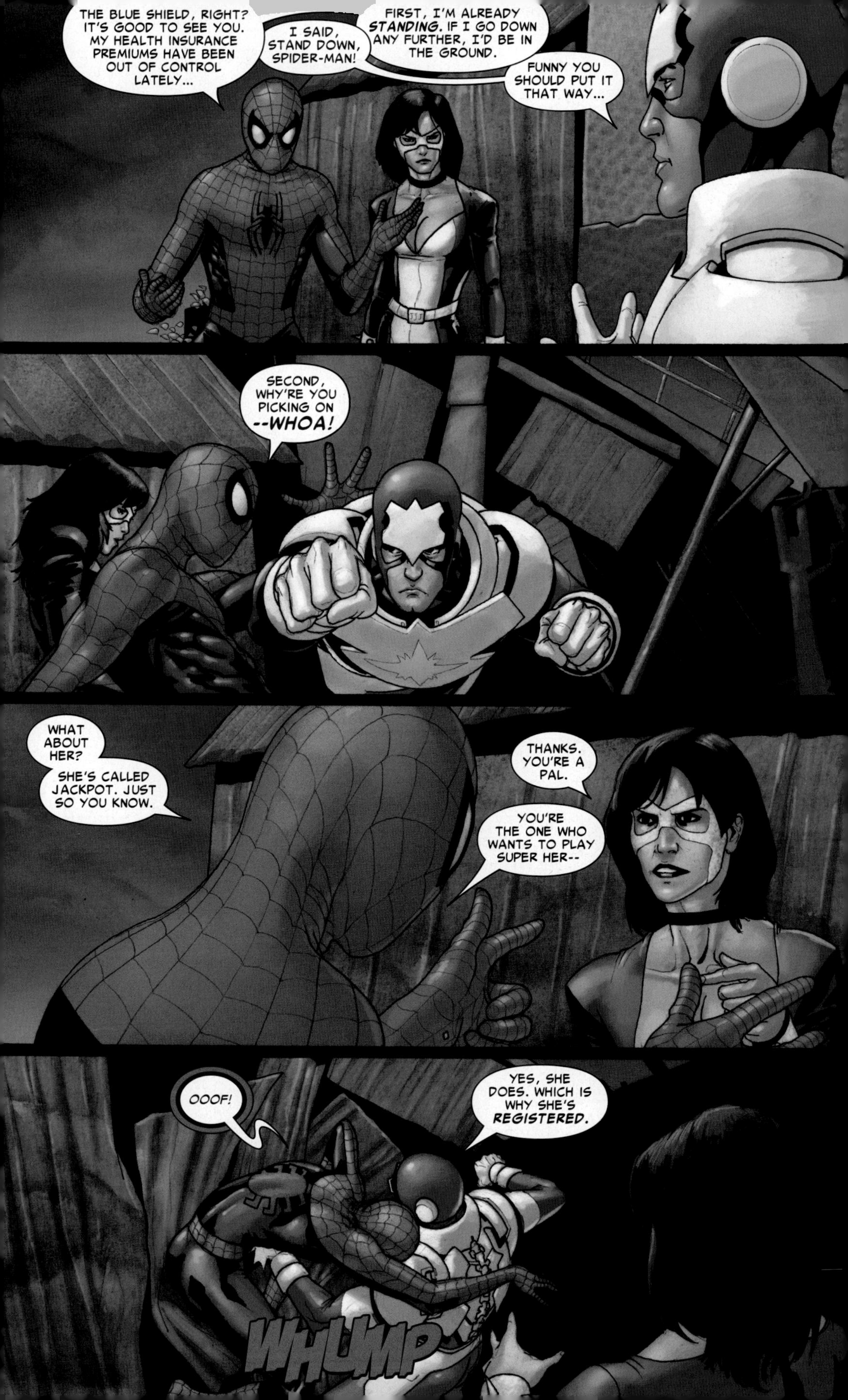
THE BLUE SHIELD, RIGHT? IT'S GOOD TO SEE YOU. MY HEALTH INSURANCE PREMIUMS HAVE BEEN OUT OF CONTROL LATELY...
I SAID, STAND DOWN, SPIDER-MAN!
FIRST, I'M ALREADY STANDING. IF I GO DOWN ANY FURTHER, I'D BE IN THE GROUND.
FUNNY YOU SHOULD PUT IT THAT WAY...
SECOND, WHY'RE YOU PICKING ON --WHOA!
WHAT ABOUT HER?
SHE'S CALLED JACKPOT. JUST SO YOU KNOW.
THANKS. YOU'RE A PAL.
YOU'RE THE ONE WHO WANTS TO PLAY SUPER HER--
OOOF!
YES, SHE DOES. WHICH IS WHY SHE'S REGISTERED.
WHUMP

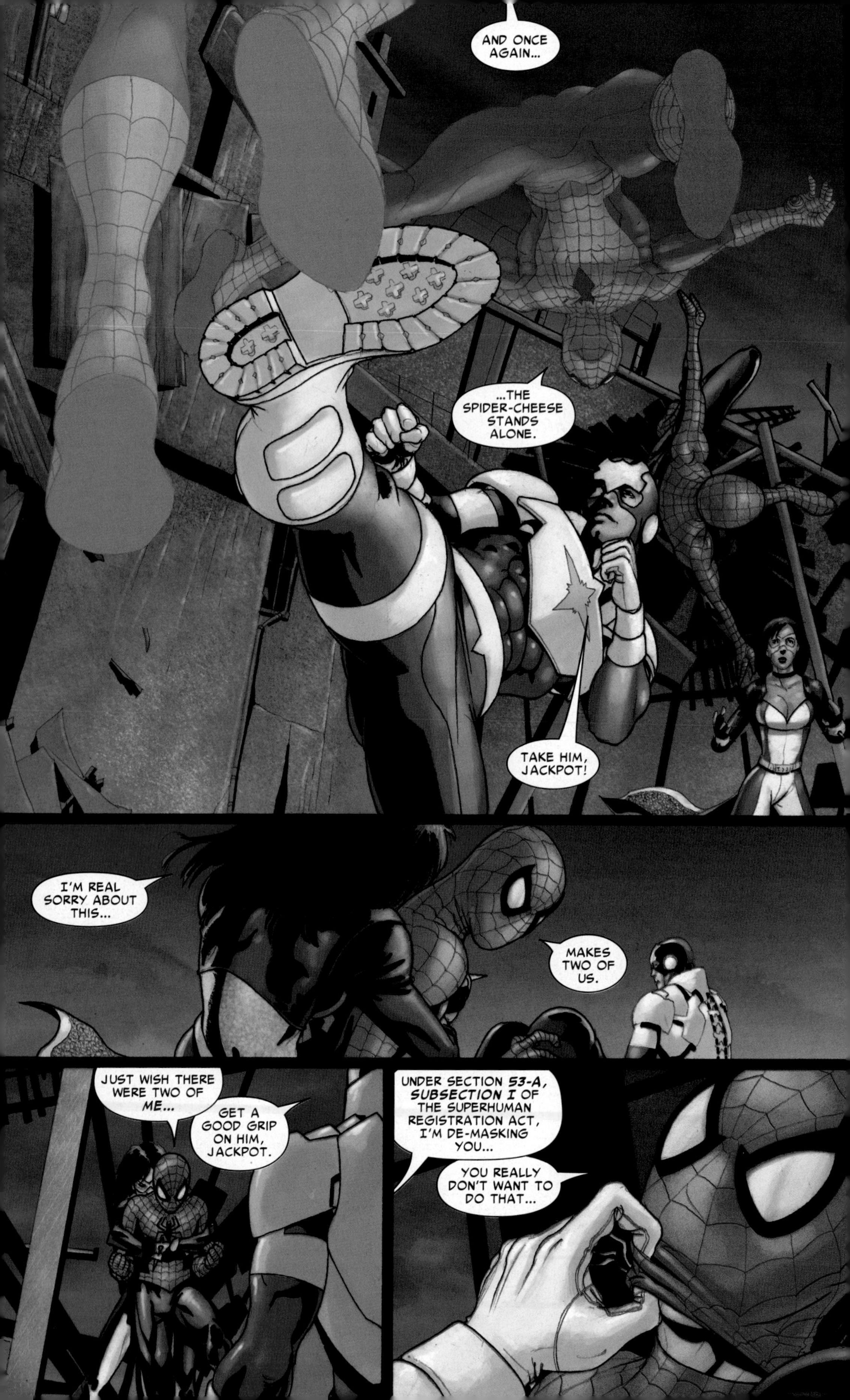
AND ONCE AGAIN...
...THE SPIDER-CHEESE STANDS ALONE.
TAKE HIM, JACKPOT!
I'M REAL SORRY ABOUT THIS...
MAKES TWO OF US.
JUST WISH THERE WERE TWO OF *ME*...
GET A GOOD GRIP ON HIM, JACKPOT.
UNDER SECTION *53-A, SUBSECTION I* OF THE SUPERHUMAN REGISTRATION ACT, I'M DE-MASKING YOU...
YOU REALLY DON'T WANT TO DO THAT...

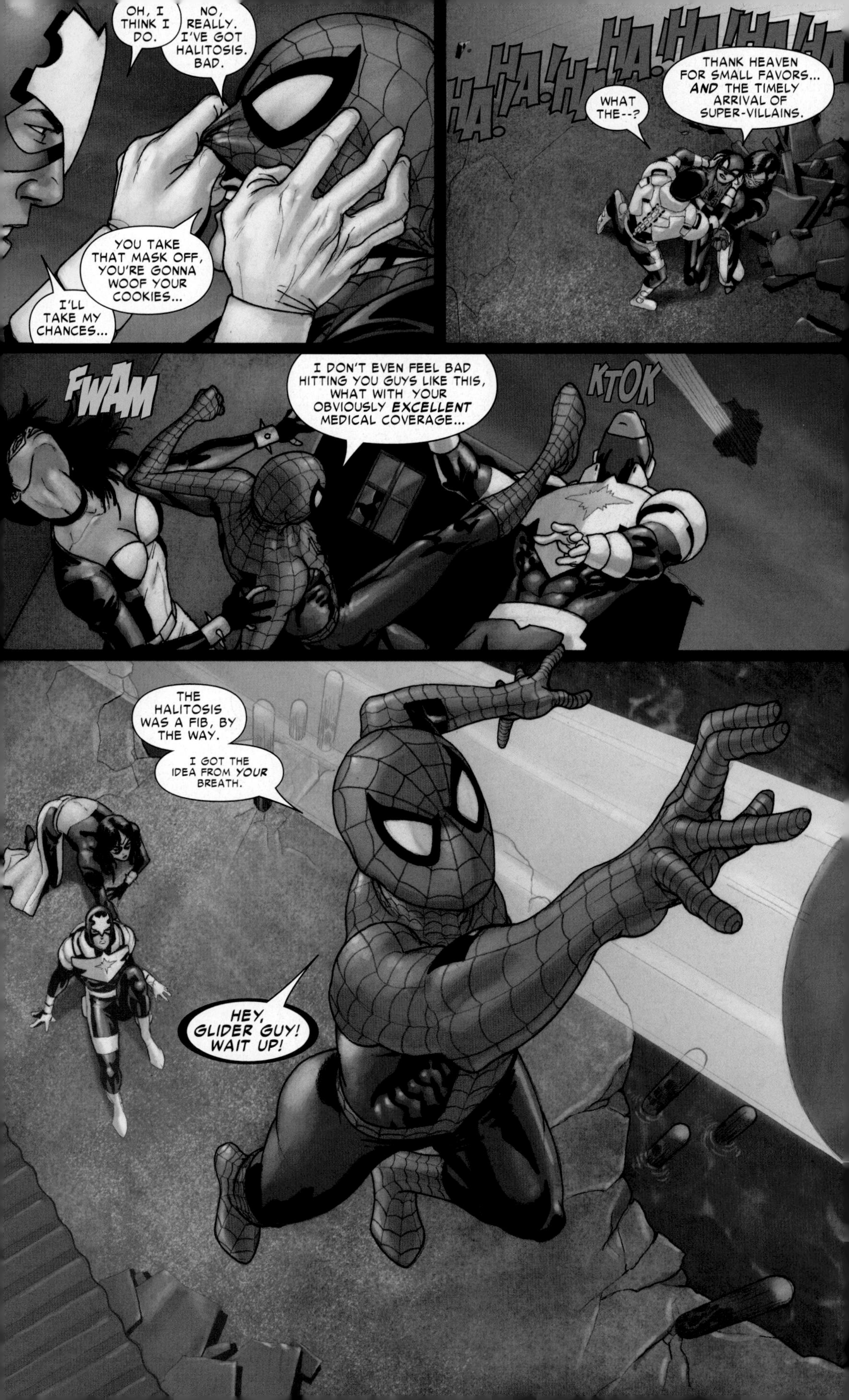
OH, I THINK I DO.
NO, REALLY. I'VE GOT HALITOSIS. BAD.
YOU TAKE THAT MASK OFF, YOU'RE GONNA WOOF YOUR COOKIES...
I'LL TAKE MY CHANCES...
HA! HA! HA! HA! HA! HA! HA!
WHAT THE--?
THANK HEAVEN FOR SMALL FAVORS... AND THE TIMELY ARRIVAL OF SUPER-VILLAINS.
FWAM
I DON'T EVEN FEEL BAD HITTING YOU GUYS LIKE THIS, WHAT WITH YOUR OBVIOUSLY EXCELLENT MEDICAL COVERAGE...
KTOK
THE HALITOSIS WAS A FIB, BY THE WAY.
I GOT THE IDEA FROM YOUR BREATH.
HEY, GLIDER GUY! WAIT UP!

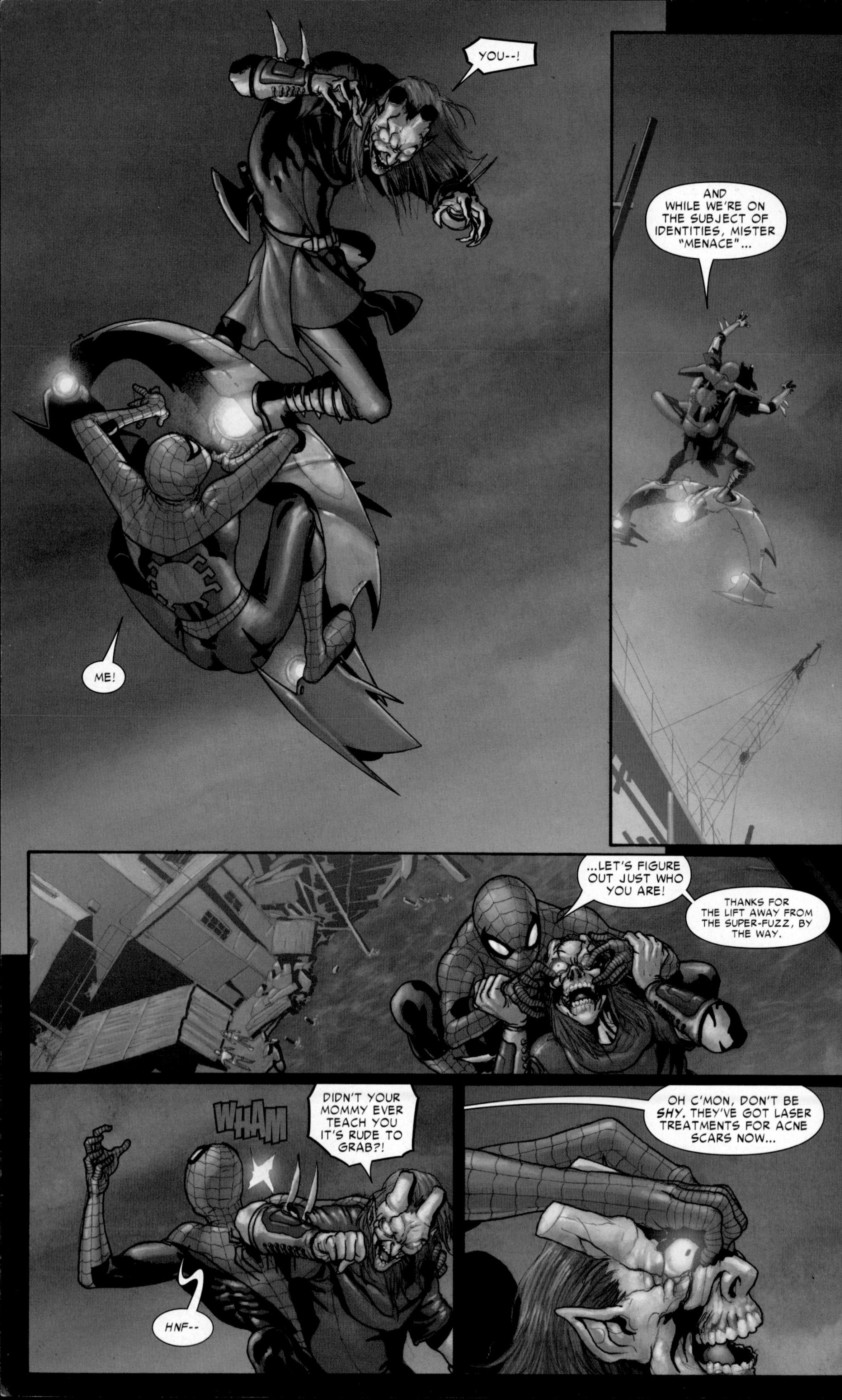
YOU--!
ME!
AND WHILE WE'RE ON THE SUBJECT OF IDENTITIES, MISTER "MENACE"...
...LET'S FIGURE OUT JUST WHO YOU ARE!
THANKS FOR THE LIFT AWAY FROM THE SUPER-FUZZ, BY THE WAY.
WHAM
DIDN'T YOUR MOMMY EVER TEACH YOU IT'S RUDE TO GRAB?!
HNF--
OH C'MON, DON'T BE SHY. THEY'VE GOT LASER TREATMENTS FOR ACNE SCARS NOW...

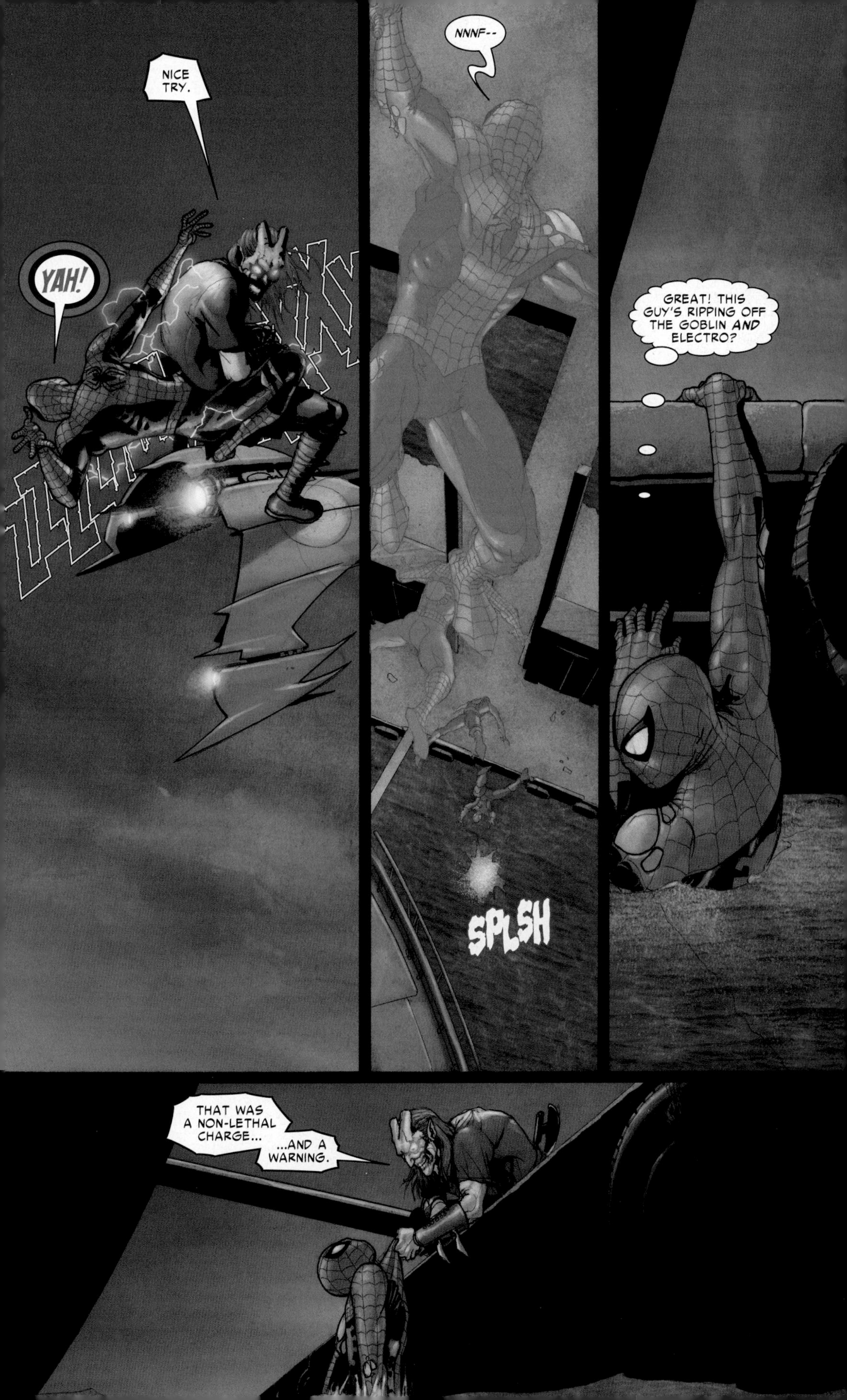
NICE TRY.
YAH!
NNNF--
SPLSH
GREAT! THIS GUY'S RIPPING OFF THE GOBLIN AND ELECTRO?
THAT WAS A NON-LETHAL CHARGE...
...AND A WARNING.

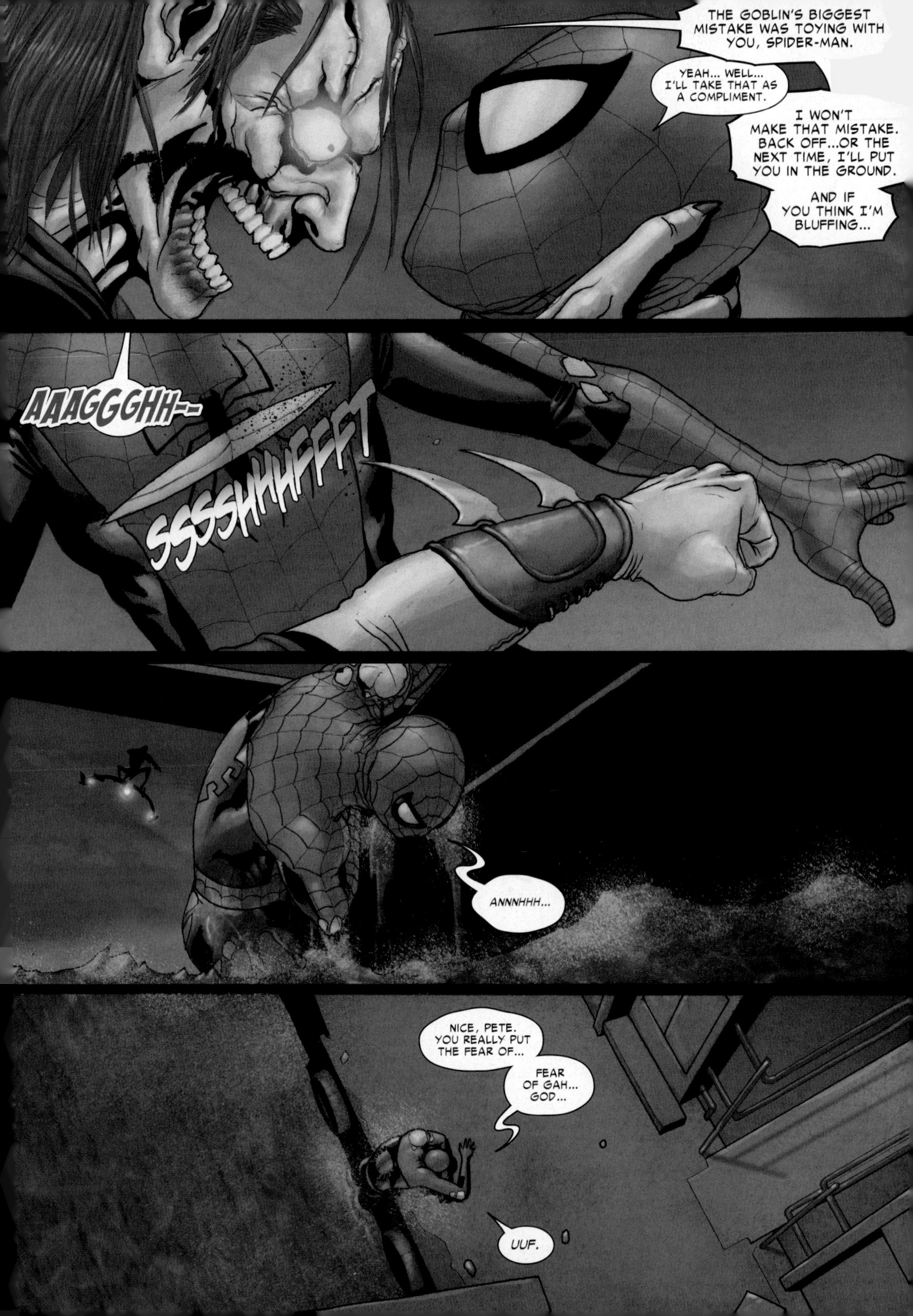
THE GOBLIN'S BIGGEST MISTAKE WAS TOYING WITH YOU, SPIDER-MAN.
YEAH... WELL... I'LL TAKE THAT AS A COMPLIMENT.
I WON'T MAKE THAT MISTAKE. BACK OFF...OR THE NEXT TIME, I'LL PUT YOU IN THE GROUND.
AND IF YOU THINK I'M BLUFFING...
AAAGGGHH--
SSSSHHHFFFT
ANNNHHH...
NICE, PETE. YOU REALLY PUT THE FEAR OF...
FEAR OF GAH... GOD...
UUF.

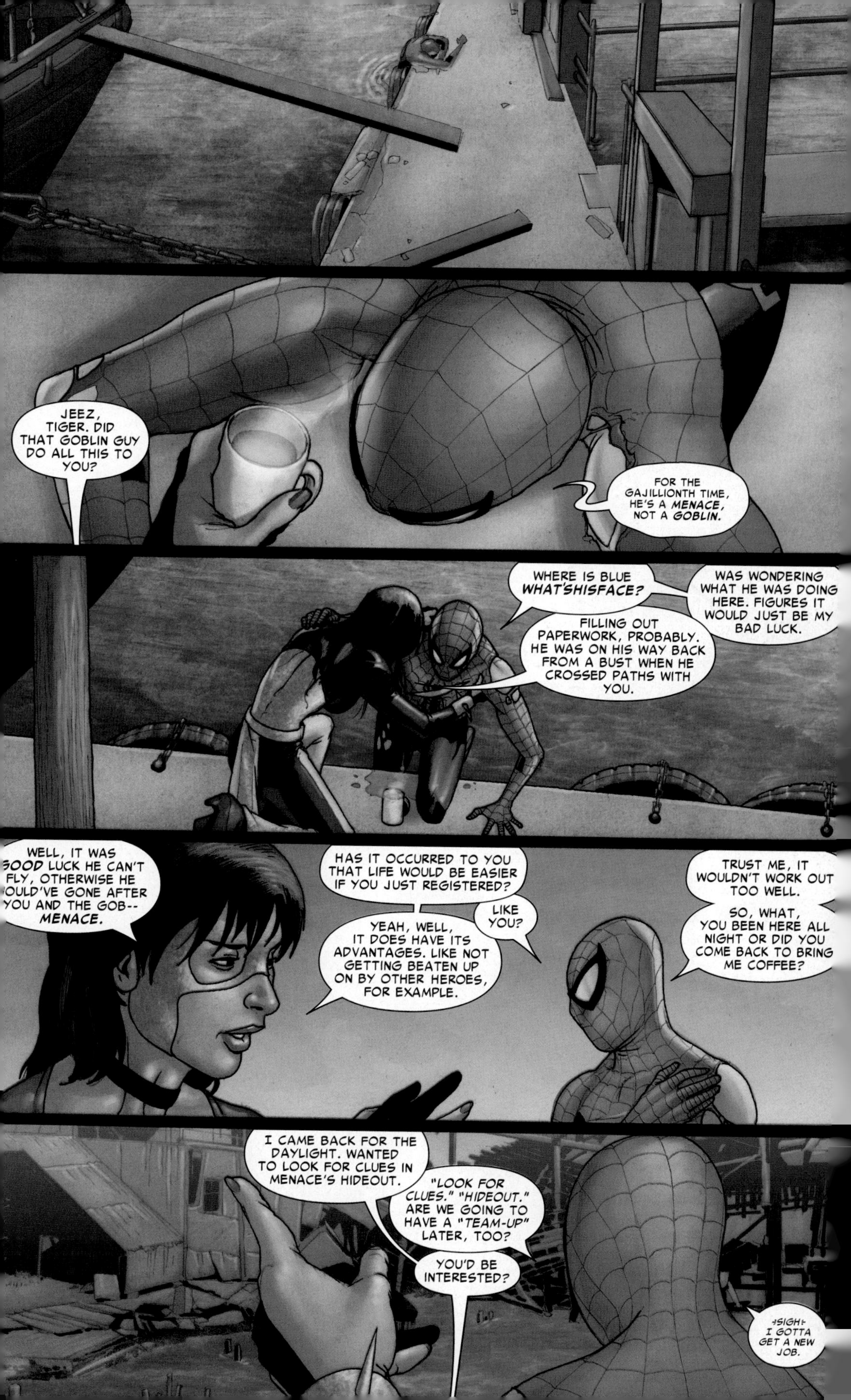
JEEZ, TIGER. DID THAT GOBLIN GUY DO ALL THIS TO YOU?
FOR THE GAJILLIONTH TIME, HE'S A *MENACE*, NOT A *GOBLIN*.
WHERE IS BLUE ***WHAT'SHISFACE?***
FILLING OUT PAPERWORK, PROBABLY. HE WAS ON HIS WAY BACK FROM A BUST WHEN HE CROSSED PATHS WITH YOU.
WAS WONDERING WHAT HE WAS DOING HERE. FIGURES IT WOULD JUST BE MY BAD LUCK.
WELL, IT WAS ***GOOD*** LUCK HE CAN'T FLY, OTHERWISE HE WOULD'VE GONE AFTER YOU AND THE GOB-- ***MENACE.***
HAS IT OCCURRED TO YOU THAT LIFE WOULD BE EASIER IF YOU JUST REGISTERED?
LIKE YOU?
YEAH, WELL, IT DOES HAVE ITS ADVANTAGES. LIKE NOT GETTING BEATEN UP ON BY OTHER HEROES, FOR EXAMPLE.
TRUST ME, IT WOULDN'T WORK OUT TOO WELL.
SO, WHAT, YOU BEEN HERE ALL NIGHT OR DID YOU COME BACK TO BRING ME COFFEE?
I CAME BACK FOR THE DAYLIGHT. WANTED TO LOOK FOR CLUES IN MENACE'S HIDEOUT.
"LOOK FOR CLUES." "HIDEOUT." ARE WE GOING TO HAVE A "TEAM-UP" LATER, TOO?
YOU'D BE INTERESTED?
SIGH I GOTTA GET A NEW JOB.

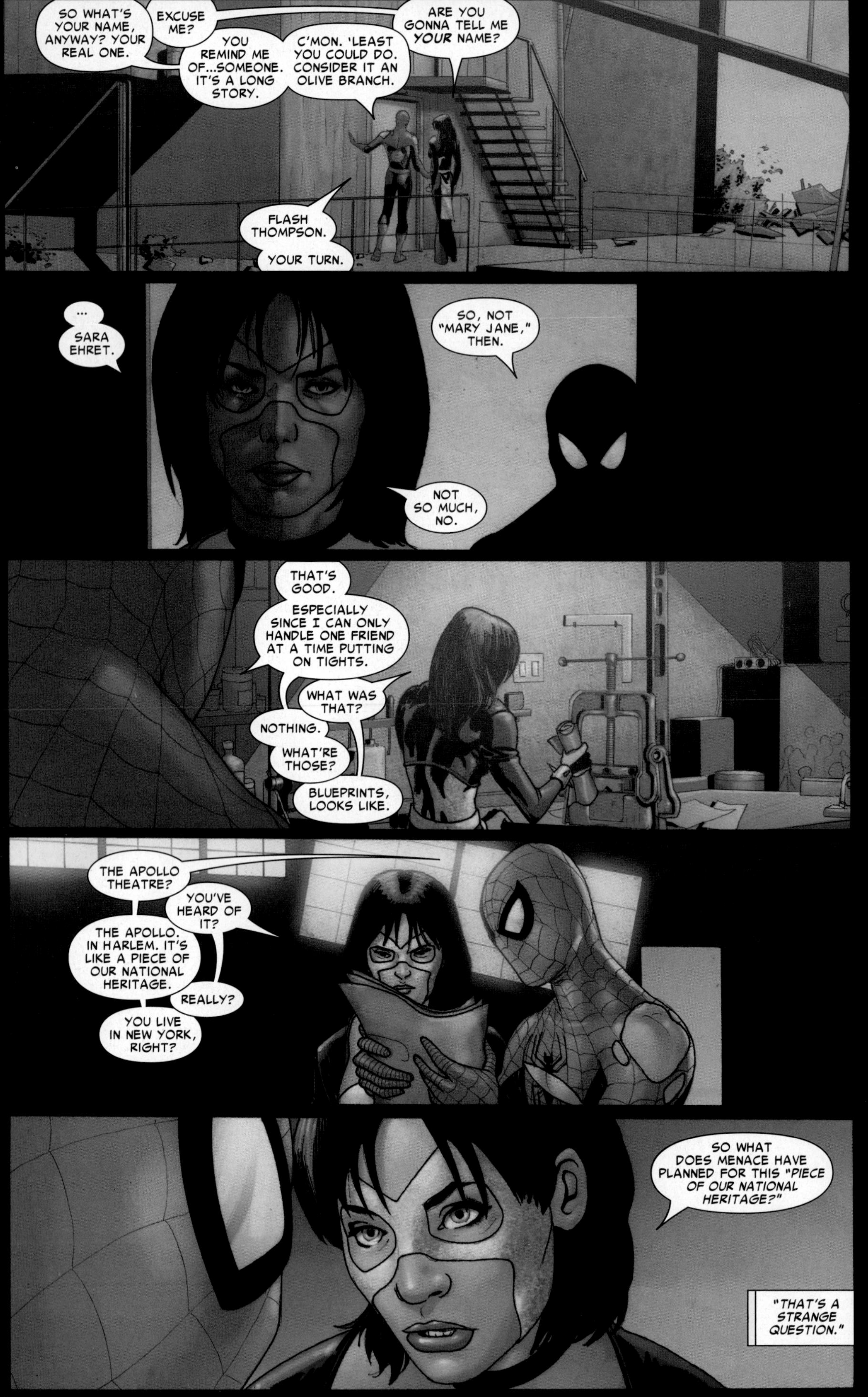
SO WHAT'S YOUR NAME, ANYWAY? YOUR REAL ONE.
EXCUSE ME?
YOU REMIND ME OF...SOMEONE. IT'S A LONG STORY.
ARE YOU GONNA TELL ME *YOUR* NAME?
C'MON. 'LEAST YOU COULD DO. CONSIDER IT AN OLIVE BRANCH.
FLASH THOMPSON.
YOUR TURN.
... SARA EHRET.
SO, NOT "MARY JANE," THEN.
NOT SO MUCH, NO.
THAT'S GOOD.
ESPECIALLY SINCE I CAN ONLY HANDLE ONE FRIEND AT A TIME PUTTING ON TIGHTS.
WHAT WAS THAT?
NOTHING.
WHAT'RE THOSE?
BLUEPRINTS, LOOKS LIKE.
THE APOLLO THEATRE?
YOU'VE HEARD OF IT?
THE APOLLO. IN HARLEM. IT'S LIKE A PIECE OF OUR NATIONAL HERITAGE.
REALLY?
YOU LIVE IN NEW YORK, RIGHT?
SO WHAT DOES MENACE HAVE PLANNED FOR THIS *"PIECE OF OUR NATIONAL HERITAGE?"*
"THAT'S A STRANGE QUESTION."

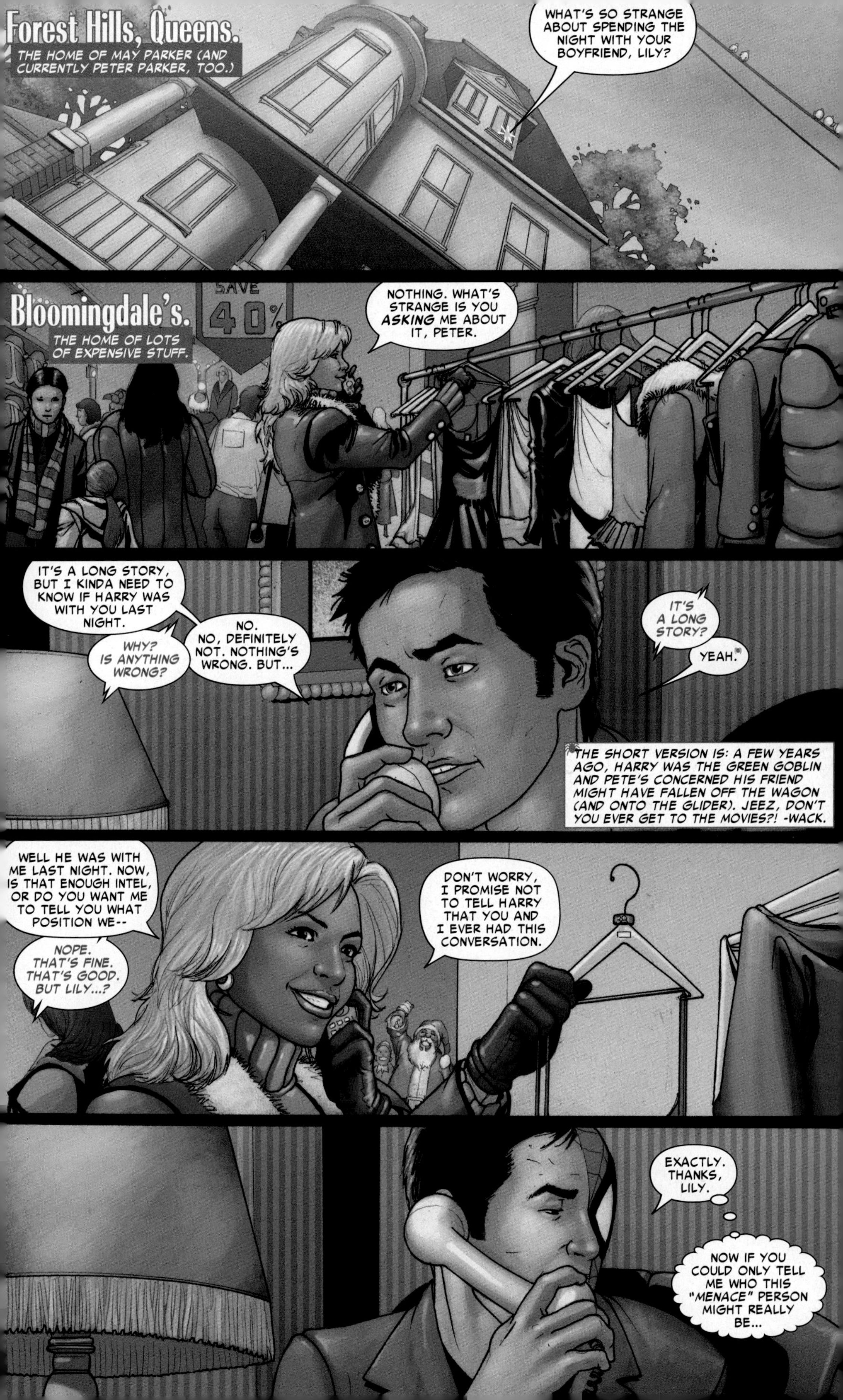
Forest Hills, Queens.
THE HOME OF MAY PARKER (AND CURRENTLY PETER PARKER, TOO.)
WHAT'S SO STRANGE ABOUT SPENDING THE NIGHT WITH YOUR BOYFRIEND, LILY?
Bloomingdale's.
THE HOME OF LOTS OF EXPENSIVE STUFF.
SAVE 40%
NOTHING. WHAT'S STRANGE IS YOU ASKING ME ABOUT IT, PETER.
IT'S A LONG STORY, BUT I KINDA NEED TO KNOW IF HARRY WAS WITH YOU LAST NIGHT.
WHY? IS ANYTHING WRONG?
NO. NO, DEFINITELY NOT. NOTHING'S WRONG. BUT...
IT'S A LONG STORY?
YEAH.
THE SHORT VERSION IS: A FEW YEARS AGO, HARRY WAS THE GREEN GOBLIN AND PETE'S CONCERNED HIS FRIEND MIGHT HAVE FALLEN OFF THE WAGON (AND ONTO THE GLIDER). JEEZ, DON'T YOU EVER GET TO THE MOVIES?! -WACK.
WELL HE WAS WITH ME LAST NIGHT. NOW, IS THAT ENOUGH INTEL, OR DO YOU WANT ME TO TELL YOU WHAT POSITION WE--
NOPE. THAT'S FINE. THAT'S GOOD. BUT LILY...?
DON'T WORRY, I PROMISE NOT TO TELL HARRY THAT YOU AND I EVER HAD THIS CONVERSATION.
EXACTLY. THANKS, LILY.
NOW IF YOU COULD ONLY TELL ME WHO THIS "MENACE" PERSON MIGHT REALLY BE...

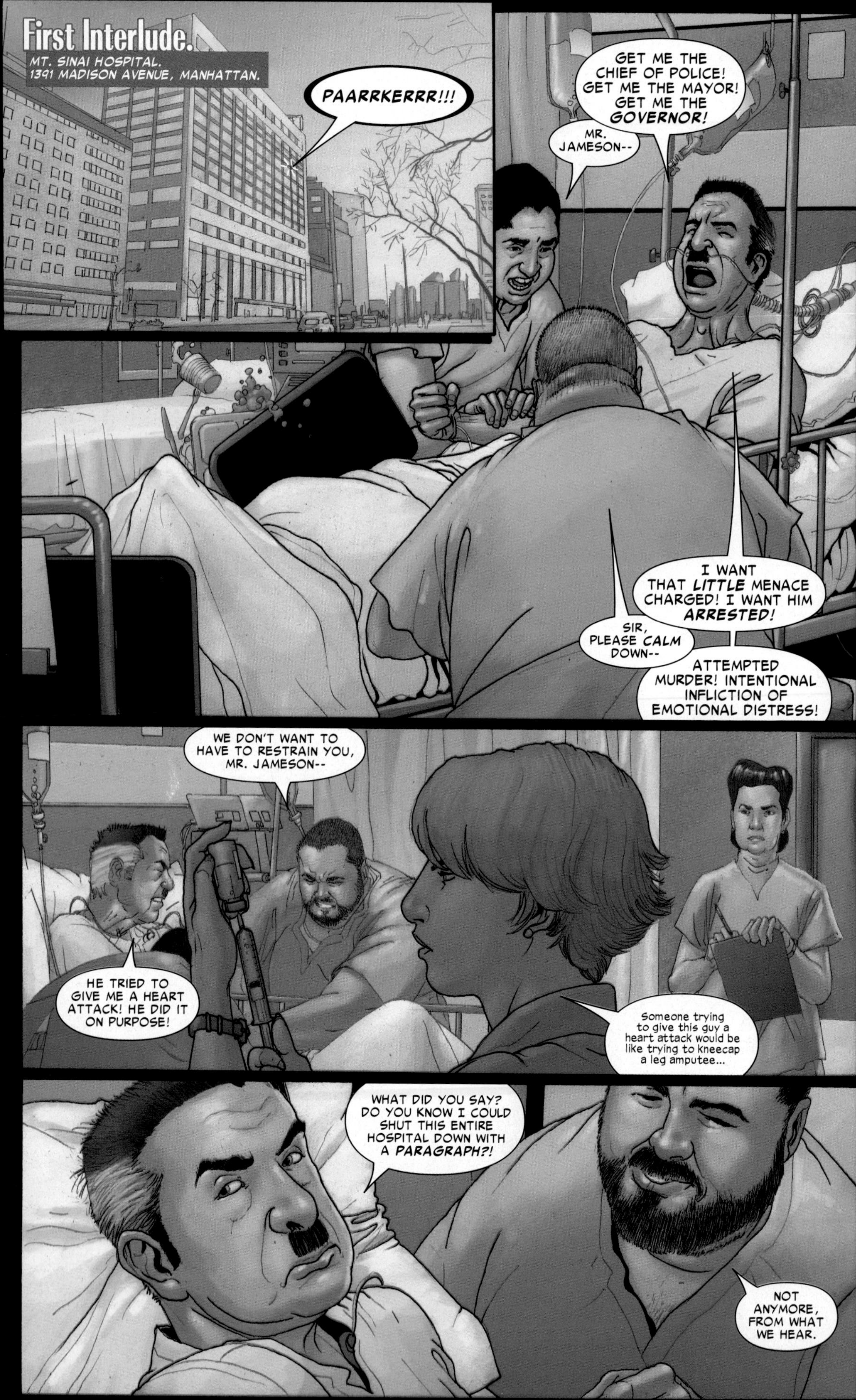
First Interlude.
MT. SINAI HOSPITAL.
1391 MADISON AVENUE, MANHATTAN.
PAARRKERRR!!!
GET ME THE CHIEF OF POLICE! GET ME THE MAYOR! GET ME THE GOVERNOR!
MR. JAMESON--
I WANT THAT LITTLE MENACE CHARGED! I WANT HIM ARRESTED!
SIR, PLEASE CALM DOWN--
ATTEMPTED MURDER! INTENTIONAL INFLICTION OF EMOTIONAL DISTRESS!
WE DON'T WANT TO HAVE TO RESTRAIN YOU, MR. JAMESON--
HE TRIED TO GIVE ME A HEART ATTACK! HE DID IT ON PURPOSE!
Someone trying to give this guy a heart attack would be like trying to kneecap a leg amputee...
WHAT DID YOU SAY? DO YOU KNOW I COULD SHUT THIS ENTIRE HOSPITAL DOWN WITH A PARAGRAPH?!
NOT ANYMORE, FROM WHAT WE HEAR.

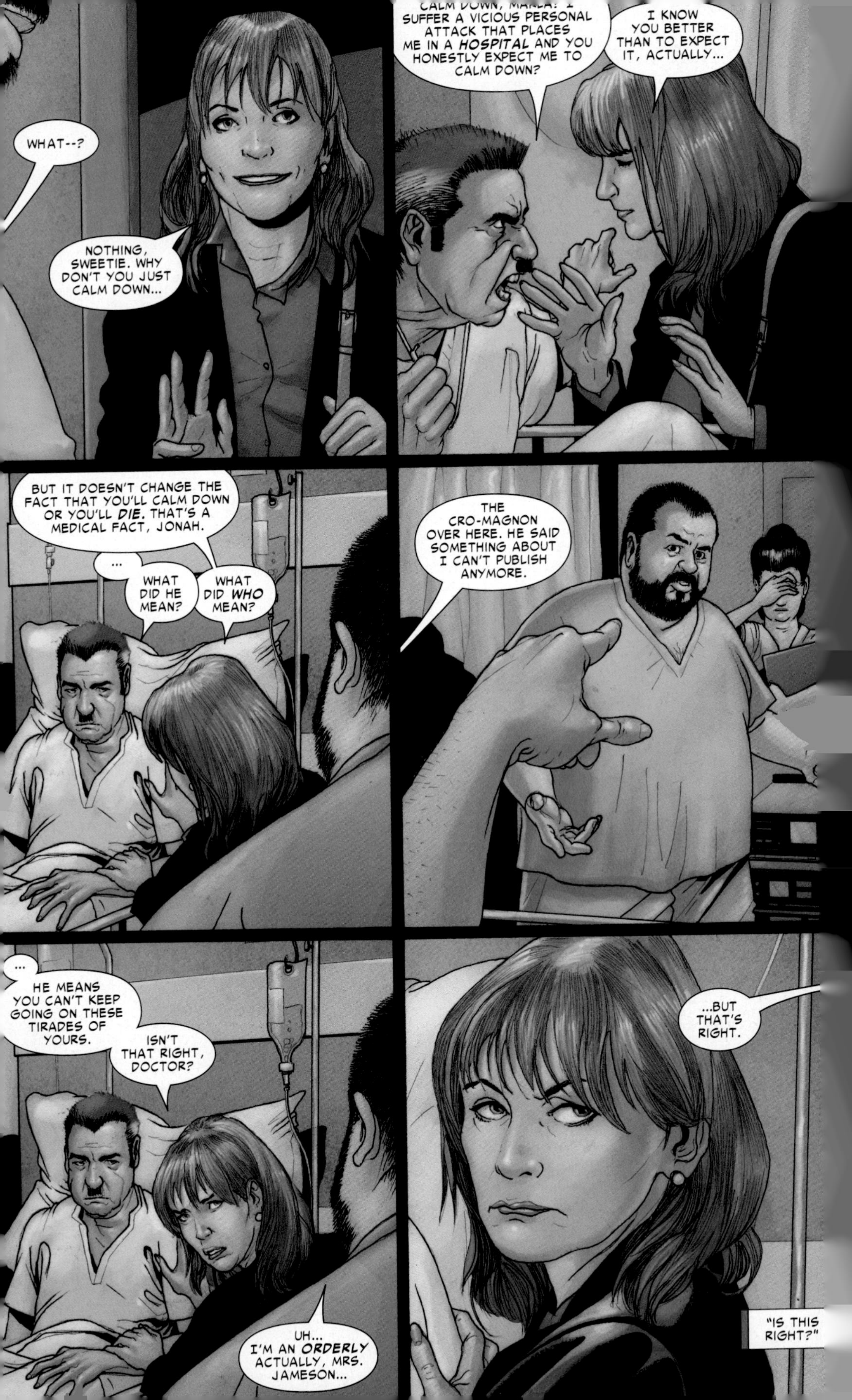
WHAT--?
NOTHING, SWEETIE. WHY DON'T YOU JUST CALM DOWN...
CALM DOWN, MARLA? I SUFFER A VICIOUS PERSONAL ATTACK THAT PLACES ME IN A *HOSPITAL* AND YOU HONESTLY EXPECT ME TO CALM DOWN?
I KNOW YOU BETTER THAN TO EXPECT IT, ACTUALLY...
BUT IT DOESN'T CHANGE THE FACT THAT YOU'LL CALM DOWN OR YOU'LL *DIE*. THAT'S A MEDICAL FACT, JONAH.
...
WHAT DID HE MEAN?
WHAT DID *WHO* MEAN?
THE CRO-MAGNON OVER HERE. HE SAID SOMETHING ABOUT I CAN'T PUBLISH ANYMORE.
...
HE MEANS YOU CAN'T KEEP GOING ON THESE TIRADES OF YOURS.
ISN'T THAT RIGHT, DOCTOR?
UH... I'M AN *ORDERLY* ACTUALLY, MRS. JAMESON...
...BUT THAT'S RIGHT.
"IS THIS RIGHT?"

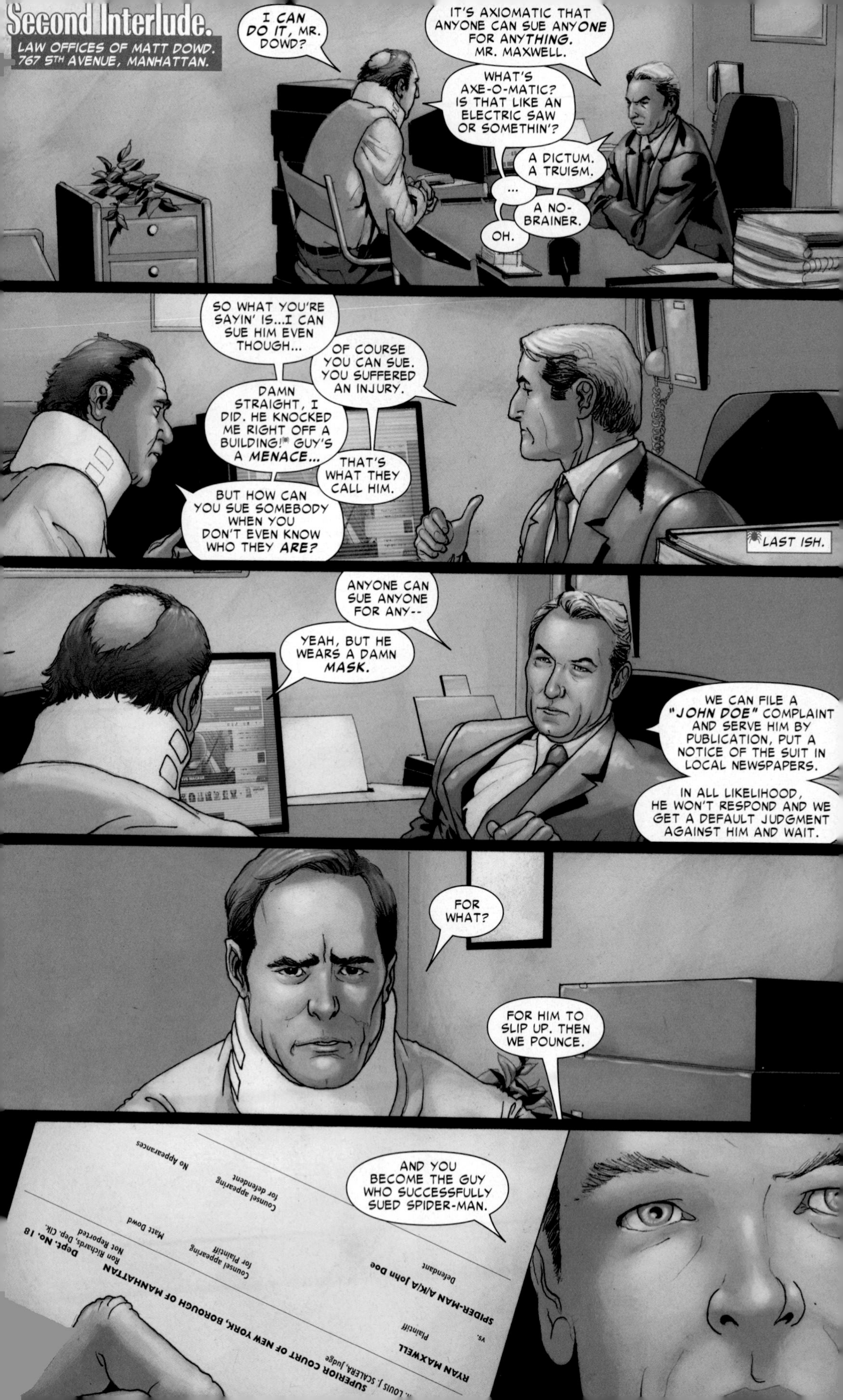
Second Interlude.
LAW OFFICES OF MATT DOWD. 767 5TH AVENUE, MANHATTAN.
I CAN DO IT, MR. DOWD?
IT'S AXIOMATIC THAT ANYONE CAN SUE ANYONE FOR ANYTHING. MR. MAXWELL.
WHAT'S AXE-O-MATIC? IS THAT LIKE AN ELECTRIC SAW OR SOMETHIN'?
A DICTUM. A TRUISM.
...
A NO-BRAINER.
OH.
SO WHAT YOU'RE SAYIN' IS...I CAN SUE HIM EVEN THOUGH...
OF COURSE YOU CAN SUE. YOU SUFFERED AN INJURY.
DAMN STRAIGHT, I DID. HE KNOCKED ME RIGHT OFF A BUILDING!* GUY'S A MENACE...
THAT'S WHAT THEY CALL HIM.
BUT HOW CAN YOU SUE SOMEBODY WHEN YOU DON'T EVEN KNOW WHO THEY ARE?
*LAST ISH.
ANYONE CAN SUE ANYONE FOR ANY--
YEAH, BUT HE WEARS A DAMN MASK.
WE CAN FILE A "JOHN DOE" COMPLAINT AND SERVE HIM BY PUBLICATION, PUT A NOTICE OF THE SUIT IN LOCAL NEWSPAPERS.
IN ALL LIKELIHOOD, HE WON'T RESPOND AND WE GET A DEFAULT JUDGMENT AGAINST HIM AND WAIT.
FOR WHAT?
FOR HIM TO SLIP UP. THEN WE POUNCE.
AND YOU BECOME THE GUY WHO SUCCESSFULLY SUED SPIDER-MAN.
SUPERIOR COURT OF NEW YORK, BOROUGH OF MANHATTAN
Dept. No. 18
Ron Richards, Dep. Clk.
Not Reported
RYAN MAXWELL
Plaintiff
vs.
SPIDER-MAN A/K/A John Doe
Defendant
Counsel appearing for Plaintiff
Matt Dowd
Counsel appearing for defendant
No Appearances

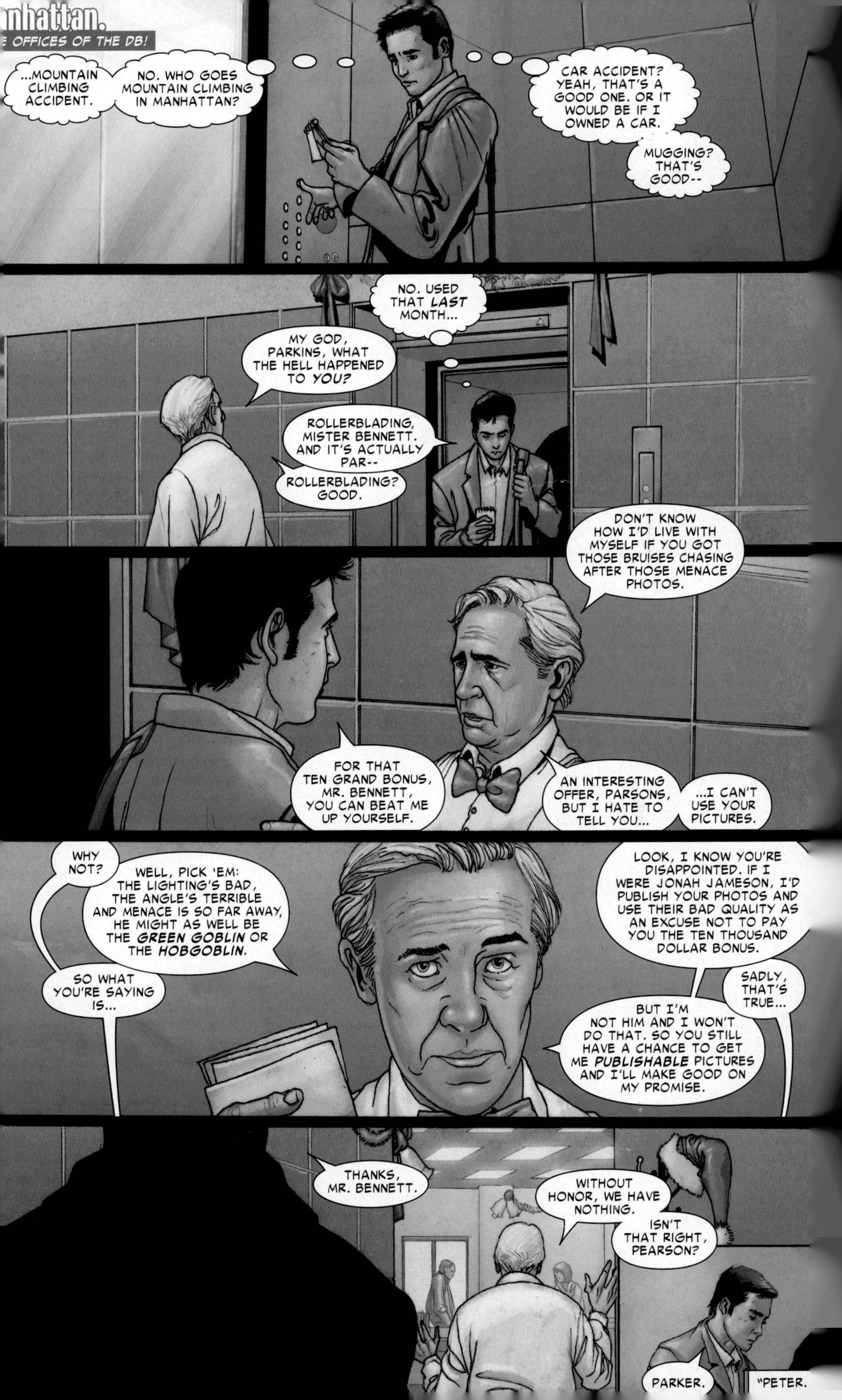

NHATTAN.
E OFFICES OF THE DB!
...MOUNTAIN CLIMBING ACCIDENT.
NO. WHO GOES MOUNTAIN CLIMBING IN MANHATTAN?
CAR ACCIDENT? YEAH, THAT'S A GOOD ONE. OR IT WOULD BE IF I OWNED A CAR.
MUGGING? THAT'S GOOD--
NO. USED THAT LAST MONTH...
MY GOD, PARKINS, WHAT THE HELL HAPPENED TO YOU?
ROLLERBLADING, MISTER BENNETT. AND IT'S ACTUALLY PAR--
ROLLERBLADING? GOOD.
DON'T KNOW HOW I'D LIVE WITH MYSELF IF YOU GOT THOSE BRUISES CHASING AFTER THOSE MENACE PHOTOS.
FOR THAT TEN GRAND BONUS, MR. BENNETT, YOU CAN BEAT ME UP YOURSELF.
AN INTERESTING OFFER, PARSONS, BUT I HATE TO TELL YOU...
...I CAN'T USE YOUR PICTURES.
WHY NOT?
WELL, PICK 'EM: THE LIGHTING'S BAD, THE ANGLE'S TERRIBLE AND MENACE IS SO FAR AWAY, HE MIGHT AS WELL BE THE GREEN GOBLIN OR THE HOBGOBLIN.
SO WHAT YOU'RE SAYING IS...
LOOK, I KNOW YOU'RE DISAPPOINTED. IF I WERE JONAH JAMESON, I'D PUBLISH YOUR PHOTOS AND USE THEIR BAD QUALITY AS AN EXCUSE NOT TO PAY YOU THE TEN THOUSAND DOLLAR BONUS.
SADLY, THAT'S TRUE...
BUT I'M NOT HIM AND I WON'T DO THAT. SO YOU STILL HAVE A CHANCE TO GET ME PUBLISHABLE PICTURES AND I'LL MAKE GOOD ON MY PROMISE.
THANKS, MR. BENNETT.
WITHOUT HONOR, WE HAVE NOTHING.
ISN'T THAT RIGHT, PEARSON?
PARKER.
"PETER.

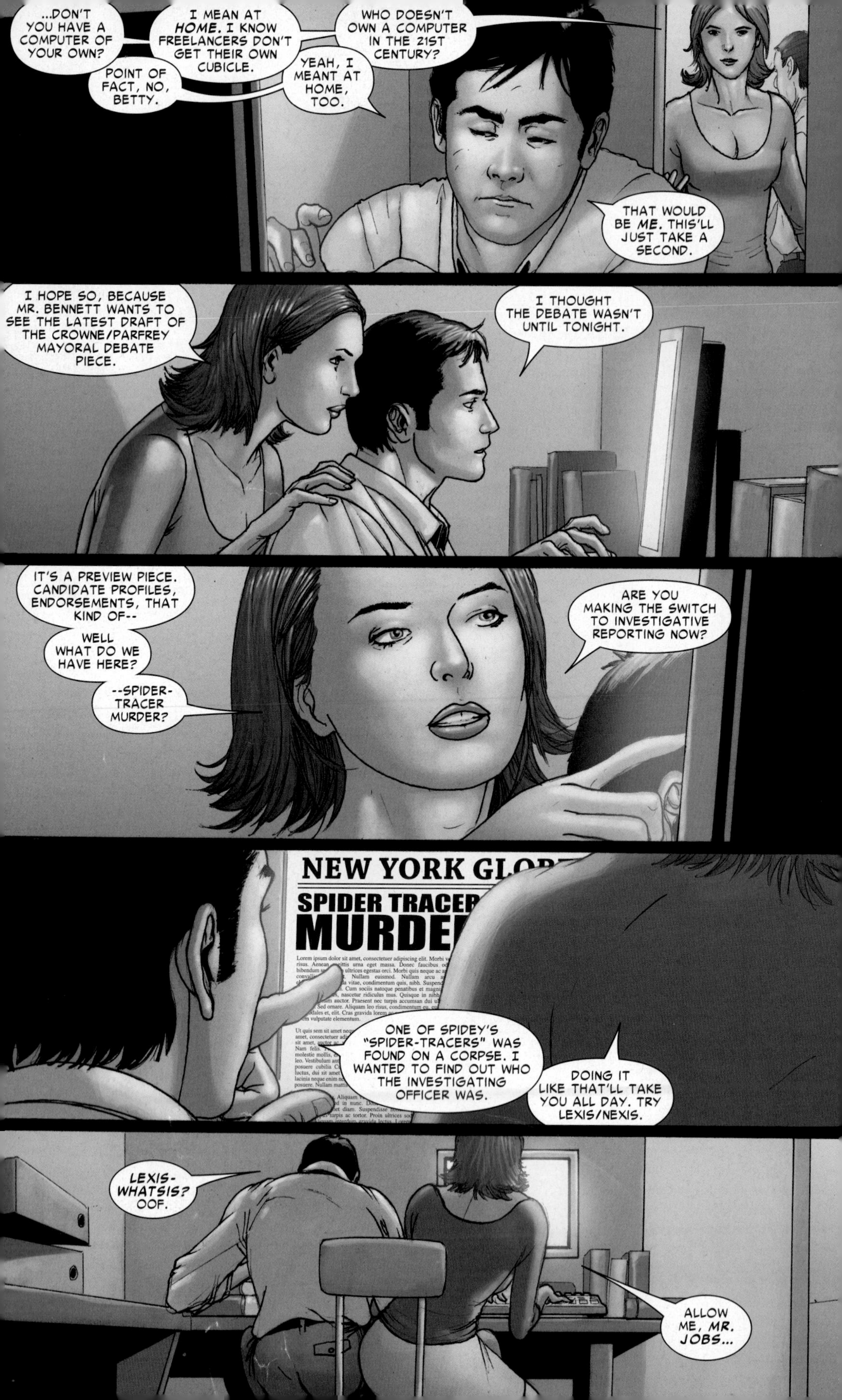

...DON'T YOU HAVE A COMPUTER OF YOUR OWN?
I MEAN AT *HOME*. I KNOW FREELANCERS DON'T GET THEIR OWN CUBICLE.
WHO DOESN'T OWN A COMPUTER IN THE 21ST CENTURY?
POINT OF FACT, NO, BETTY.
YEAH, I MEANT AT HOME, TOO.
THAT WOULD BE *ME*. THIS'LL JUST TAKE A SECOND.
I HOPE SO, BECAUSE MR. BENNETT WANTS TO SEE THE LATEST DRAFT OF THE CROWNE/PARFREY MAYORAL DEBATE PIECE.
I THOUGHT THE DEBATE WASN'T UNTIL TONIGHT.
IT'S A PREVIEW PIECE. CANDIDATE PROFILES, ENDORSEMENTS, THAT KIND OF--
WELL WHAT DO WE HAVE HERE?
--SPIDER-TRACER MURDER?
ARE YOU MAKING THE SWITCH TO INVESTIGATIVE REPORTING NOW?
NEW YORK GLOB
SPIDER TRACER
MURDE
ONE OF SPIDEY'S "SPIDER-TRACERS" WAS FOUND ON A CORPSE. I WANTED TO FIND OUT WHO THE INVESTIGATING OFFICER WAS.
DOING IT LIKE THAT'LL TAKE YOU ALL DAY. TRY LEXIS/NEXIS.
LEXIS-WHATSIS? OOF.
ALLOW ME, *MR. JOBS...*

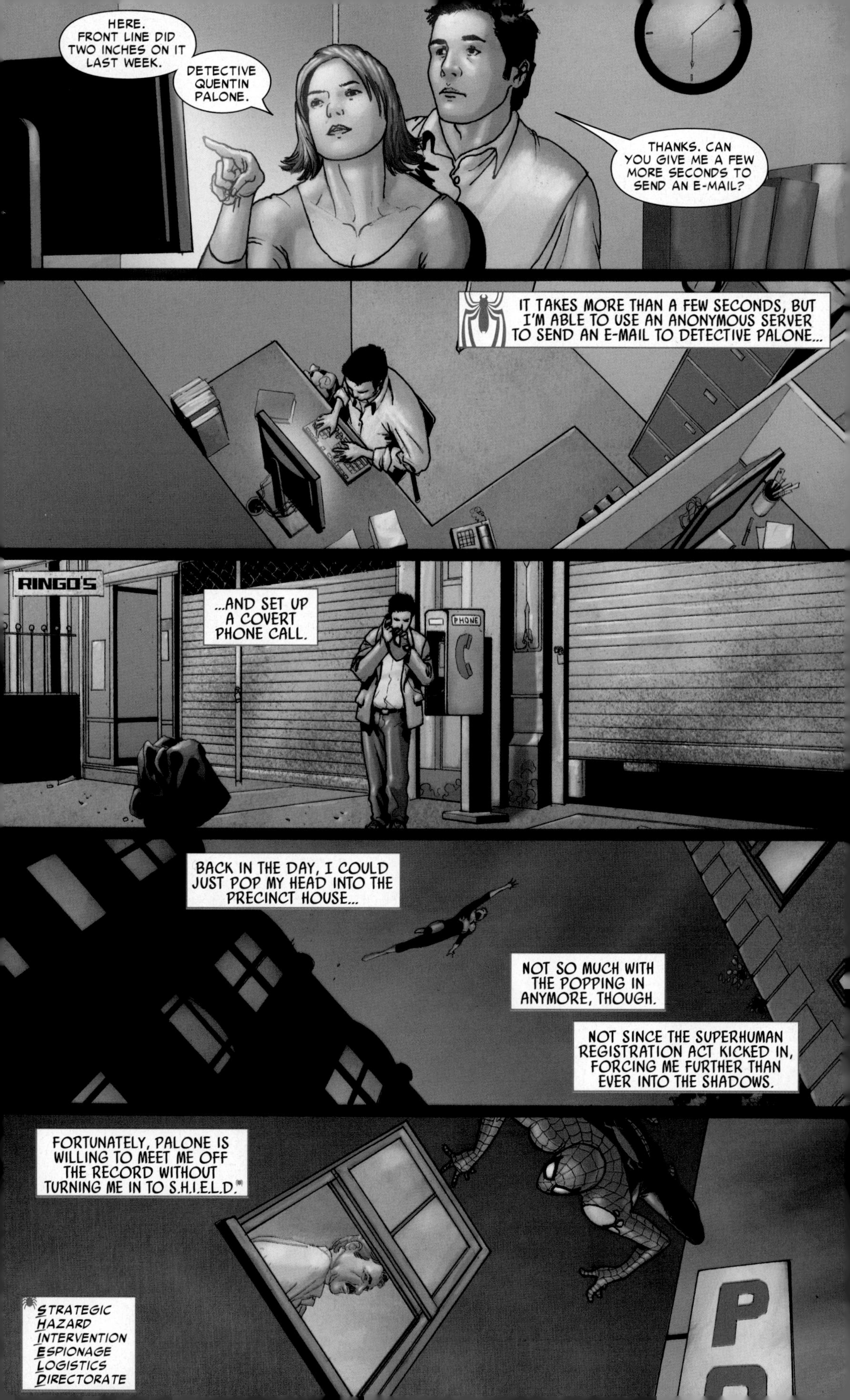
HERE. FRONT LINE DID TWO INCHES ON IT LAST WEEK.
DETECTIVE QUENTIN PALONE.
THANKS. CAN YOU GIVE ME A FEW MORE SECONDS TO SEND AN E-MAIL?
IT TAKES MORE THAN A FEW SECONDS, BUT I'M ABLE TO USE AN ANONYMOUS SERVER TO SEND AN E-MAIL TO DETECTIVE PALONE...
RINGO'S
...AND SET UP A COVERT PHONE CALL.
PHONE
BACK IN THE DAY, I COULD JUST POP MY HEAD INTO THE PRECINCT HOUSE...
NOT SO MUCH WITH THE POPPING IN ANYMORE, THOUGH.
NOT SINCE THE SUPERHUMAN REGISTRATION ACT KICKED IN, FORCING ME FURTHER THAN EVER INTO THE SHADOWS.
FORTUNATELY, PALONE IS WILLING TO MEET ME OFF THE RECORD WITHOUT TURNING ME IN TO S.H.I.E.L.D.*
*STRATEGIC HAZARD INTERVENTION ESPIONAGE LOGISTICS DIRECTORATE

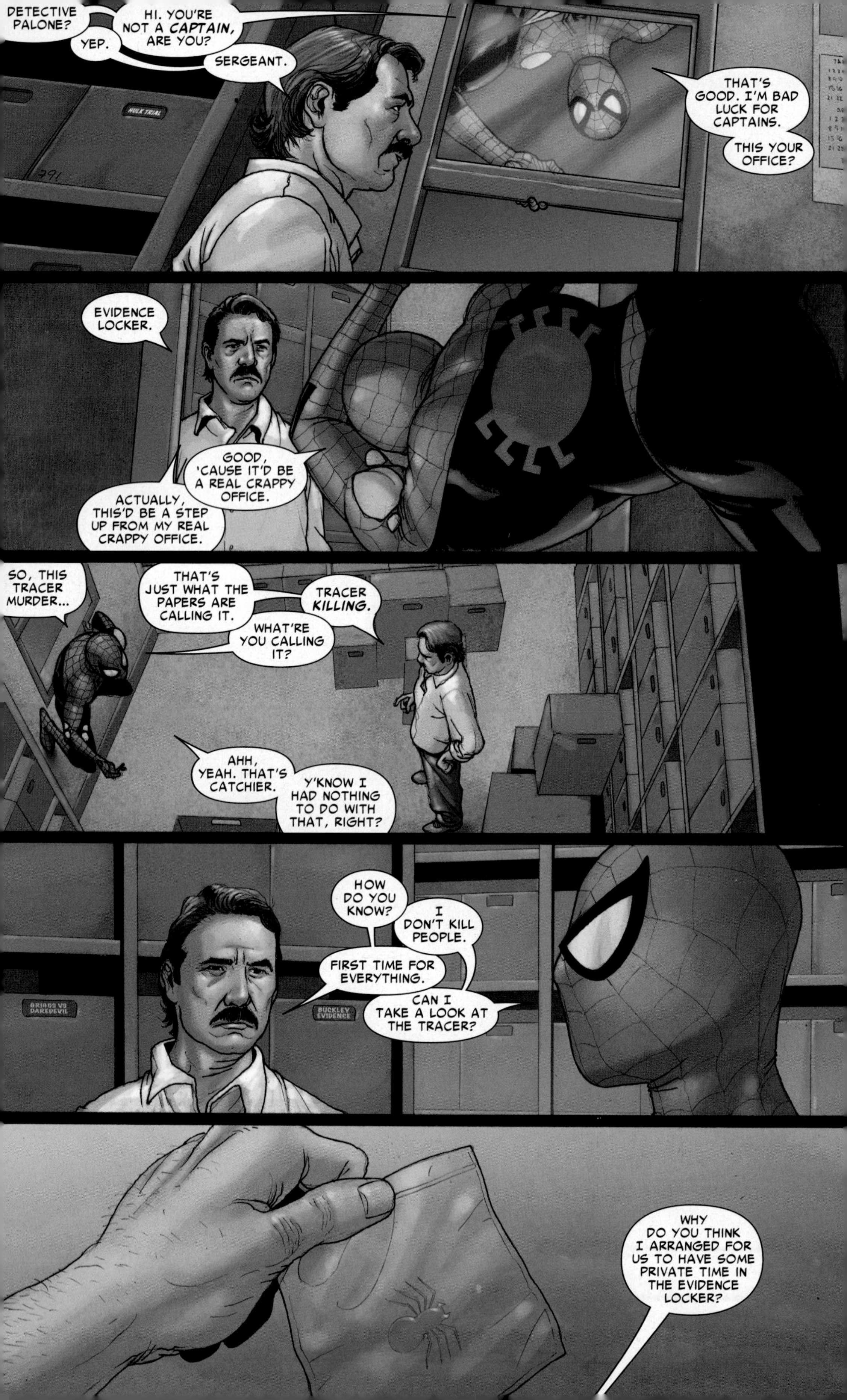
DETECTIVE PALONE?
HI. YOU'RE NOT A *CAPTAIN,* ARE YOU?
YEP.
SERGEANT.
THAT'S GOOD. I'M BAD LUCK FOR CAPTAINS.
THIS YOUR OFFICE?
HULK TRIAL
EVIDENCE LOCKER.
GOOD, 'CAUSE IT'D BE A REAL CRAPPY OFFICE.
ACTUALLY, THIS'D BE A STEP UP FROM MY REAL CRAPPY OFFICE.
SO, THIS TRACER MURDER...
THAT'S JUST WHAT THE PAPERS ARE CALLING IT.
TRACER *KILLING.*
WHAT'RE YOU CALLING IT?
AHH, YEAH. THAT'S CATCHIER.
Y'KNOW I HAD NOTHING TO DO WITH THAT, RIGHT?
HOW DO YOU KNOW?
I DON'T KILL PEOPLE.
FIRST TIME FOR EVERYTHING.
CAN I TAKE A LOOK AT THE TRACER?
GRIGGS VS DAREDEVIL
BUCKLEY EVIDENCE
WHY DO YOU THINK I ARRANGED FOR US TO HAVE SOME PRIVATE TIME IN THE EVIDENCE LOCKER?

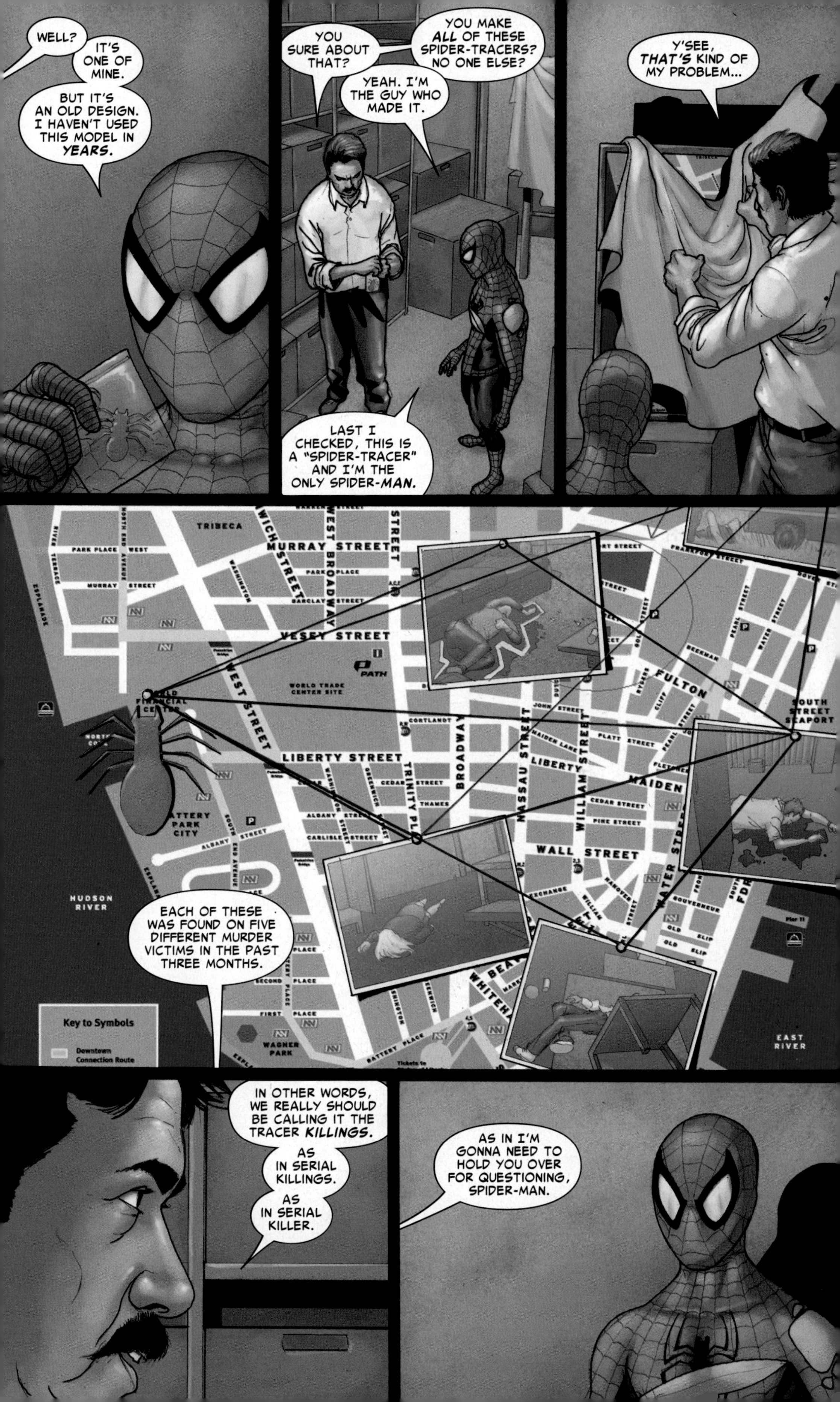
WELL?
IT'S ONE OF MINE.
BUT IT'S AN OLD DESIGN. I HAVEN'T USED THIS MODEL IN YEARS.
YOU SURE ABOUT THAT?
YOU MAKE ALL OF THESE SPIDER-TRACERS? NO ONE ELSE?
YEAH. I'M THE GUY WHO MADE IT.
LAST I CHECKED, THIS IS A "SPIDER-TRACER" AND I'M THE ONLY SPIDER-MAN.
Y'SEE, THAT'S KIND OF MY PROBLEM...
EACH OF THESE WAS FOUND ON FIVE DIFFERENT MURDER VICTIMS IN THE PAST THREE MONTHS.
IN OTHER WORDS, WE REALLY SHOULD BE CALLING IT THE TRACER KILLINGS.
AS IN SERIAL KILLINGS.
AS IN SERIAL KILLER.
AS IN I'M GONNA NEED TO HOLD YOU OVER FOR QUESTIONING, SPIDER-MAN.

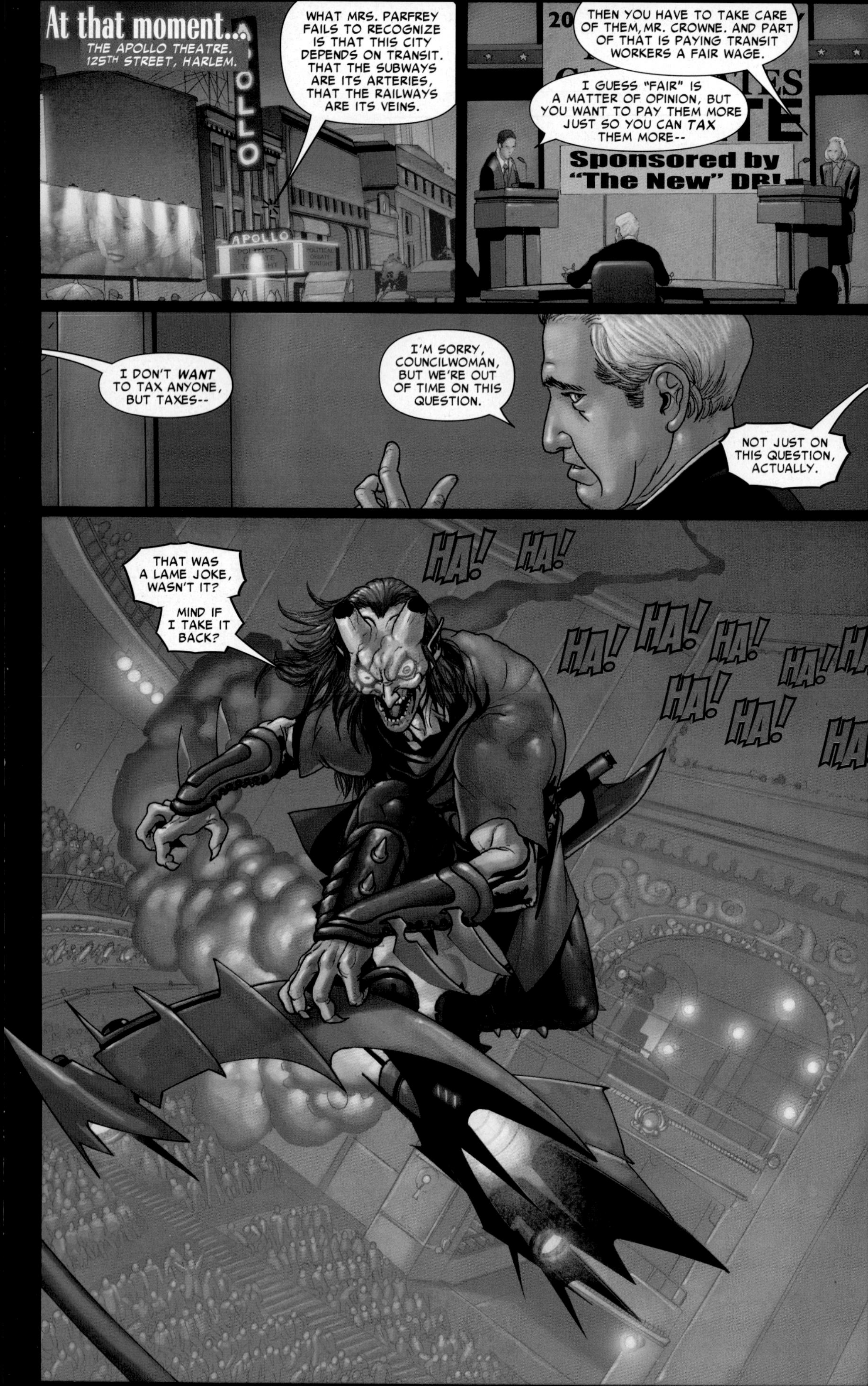
At that moment...
THE APOLLO THEATRE. 125TH STREET, HARLEM.
APOLLO
WHAT MRS. PARFREY FAILS TO RECOGNIZE IS THAT THIS CITY DEPENDS ON TRANSIT. THAT THE SUBWAYS ARE ITS ARTERIES, THAT THE RAILWAYS ARE ITS VEINS.
THEN YOU HAVE TO TAKE CARE OF THEM, MR. CROWNE. AND PART OF THAT IS PAYING TRANSIT WORKERS A FAIR WAGE.
I GUESS "FAIR" IS A MATTER OF OPINION, BUT YOU WANT TO PAY THEM MORE JUST SO YOU CAN TAX THEM MORE--
Sponsored by "The New" DB!
I DON'T WANT TO TAX ANYONE, BUT TAXES--
I'M SORRY, COUNCILWOMAN, BUT WE'RE OUT OF TIME ON THIS QUESTION.
NOT JUST ON THIS QUESTION, ACTUALLY.
HA! HA!
THAT WAS A LAME JOKE, WASN'T IT?
MIND IF I TAKE IT BACK?
HA! HA! HA! HA! HA! HA! HA!

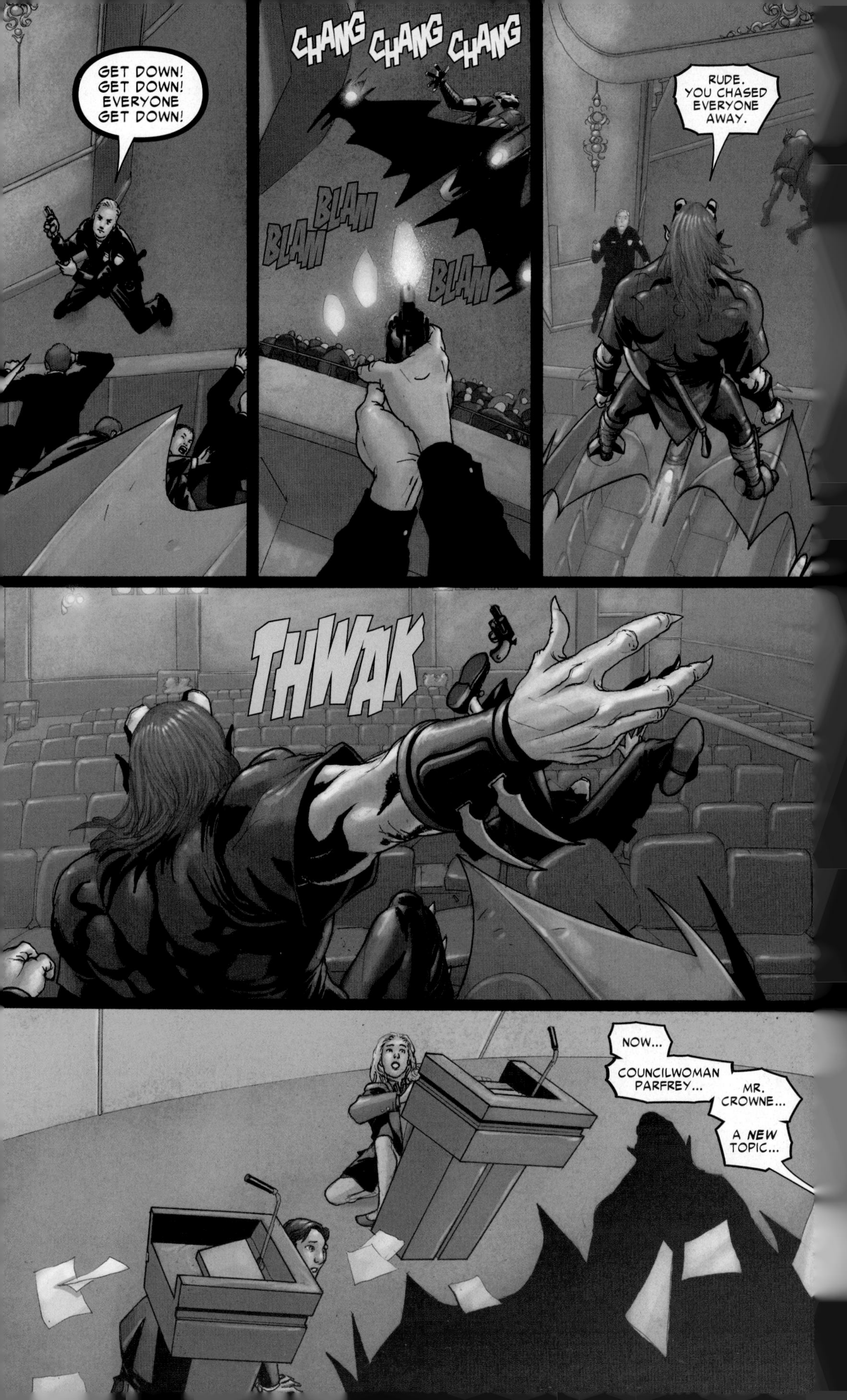
GET DOWN! GET DOWN! EVERYONE GET DOWN!
CHANG CHANG CHANG
BLAM BLAM
BLAM
RUDE. YOU CHASED EVERYONE AWAY.
THWAK
NOW...
COUNCILWOMAN PARFREY...
MR. CROWNE...
A *NEW* TOPIC...

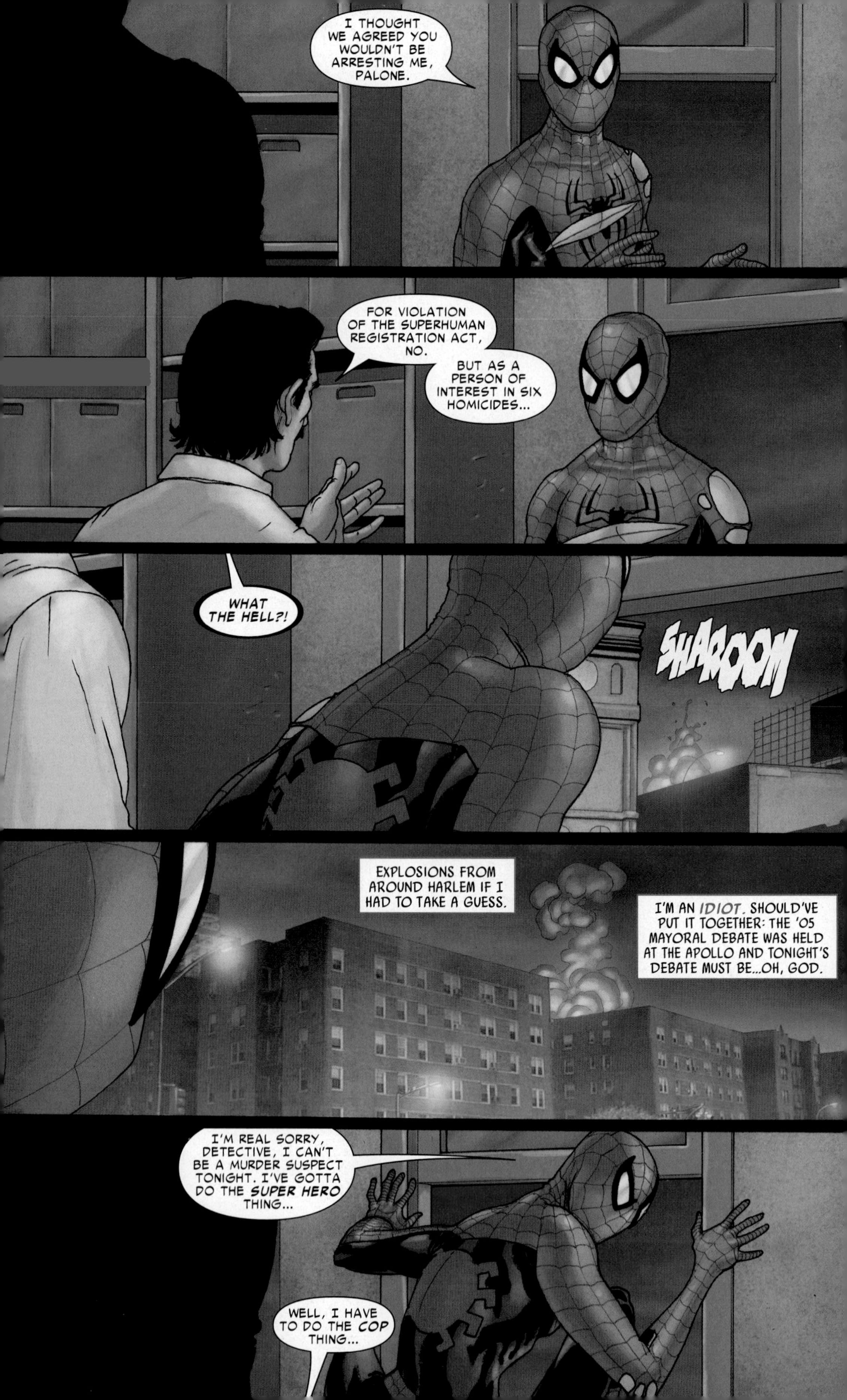
I THOUGHT WE AGREED YOU WOULDN'T BE ARRESTING ME, PALONE.
FOR VIOLATION OF THE SUPERHUMAN REGISTRATION ACT, NO.
BUT AS A PERSON OF INTEREST IN SIX HOMICIDES...
WHAT THE HELL?!
SHAROOM
EXPLOSIONS FROM AROUND HARLEM IF I HAD TO TAKE A GUESS.
I'M AN IDIOT. SHOULD'VE PUT IT TOGETHER: THE '05 MAYORAL DEBATE WAS HELD AT THE APOLLO AND TONIGHT'S DEBATE MUST BE...OH, GOD.
I'M REAL SORRY, DETECTIVE, I CAN'T BE A MURDER SUSPECT TONIGHT. I'VE GOTTA DO THE SUPER HERO THING...
WELL, I HAVE TO DO THE COP THING...

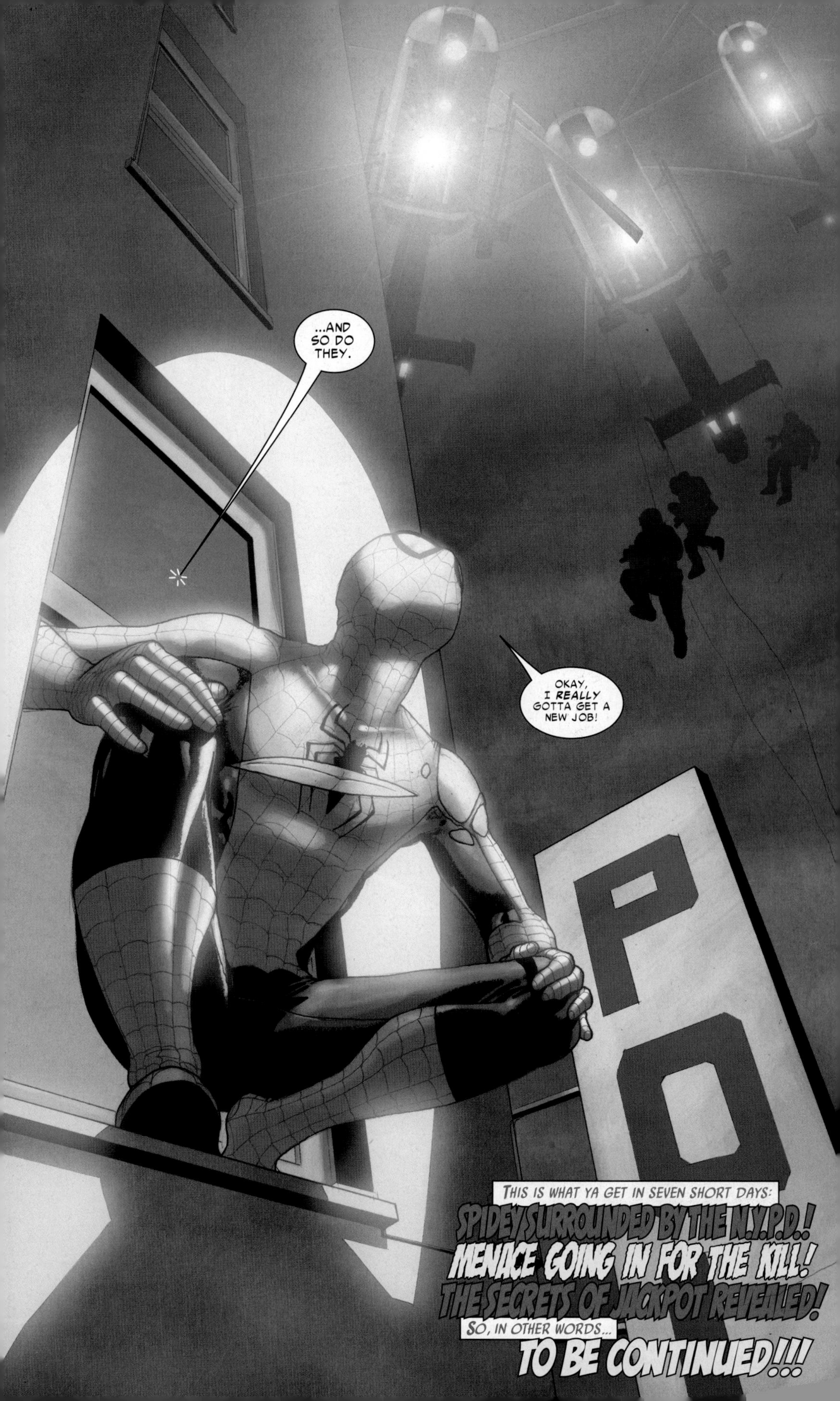
...AND SO DO THEY.
OKAY, I REALLY GOTTA GET A NEW JOB!
THIS IS WHAT YA GET IN SEVEN SHORT DAYS:
SPIDEY SURROUNDED BY THE N.Y.P.D.!
MENACE GOING IN FOR THE KILL!
THE SECRETS OF JACKPOT REVEALED!
SO, IN OTHER WORDS...
TO BE CONTINUED!!!

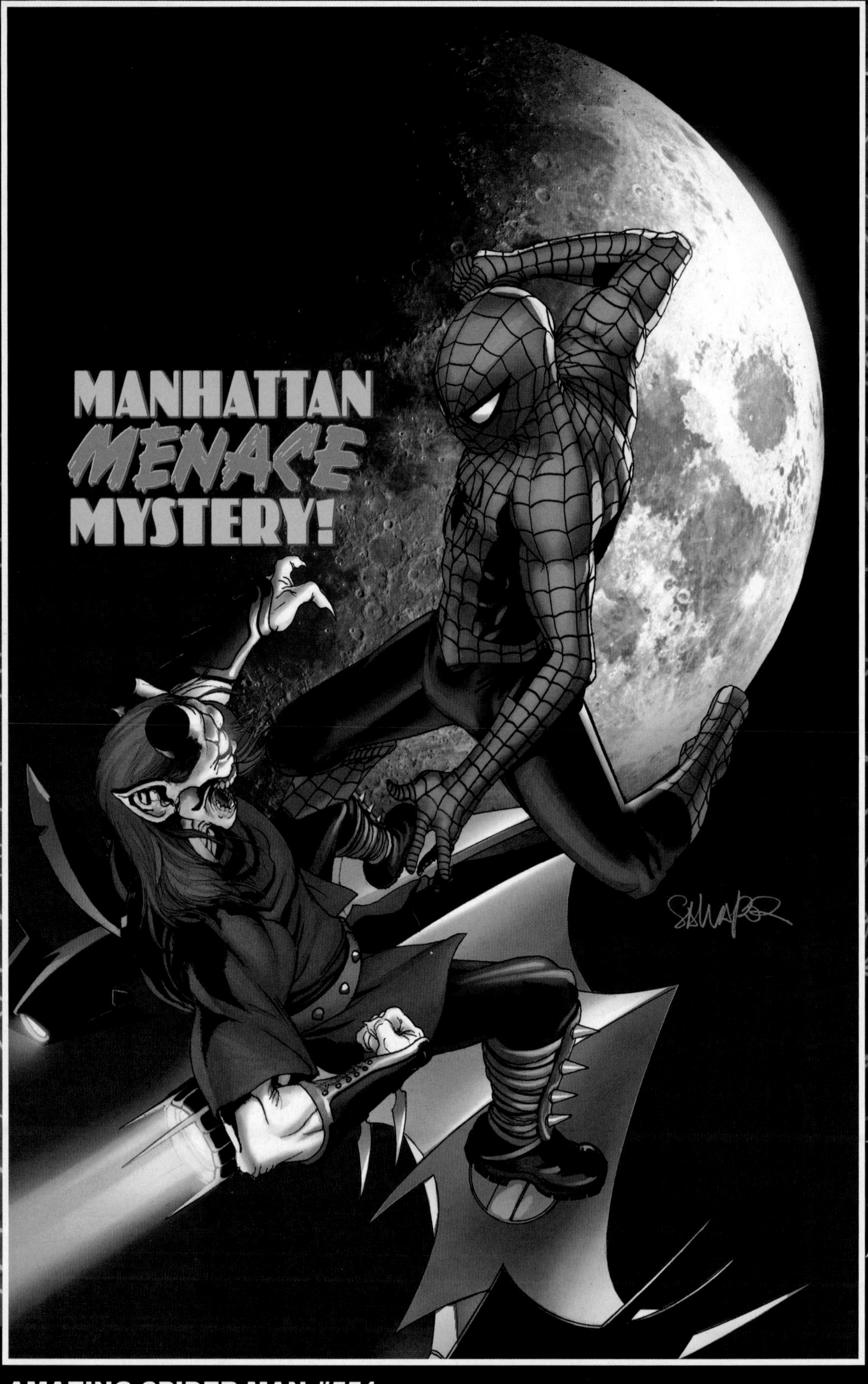
MANHATTAN
MENACE
MYSTERY!

AMAZING SPIDER-MAN #551
COVER BY **SALVADOR LARROCA & JASON KEITH**

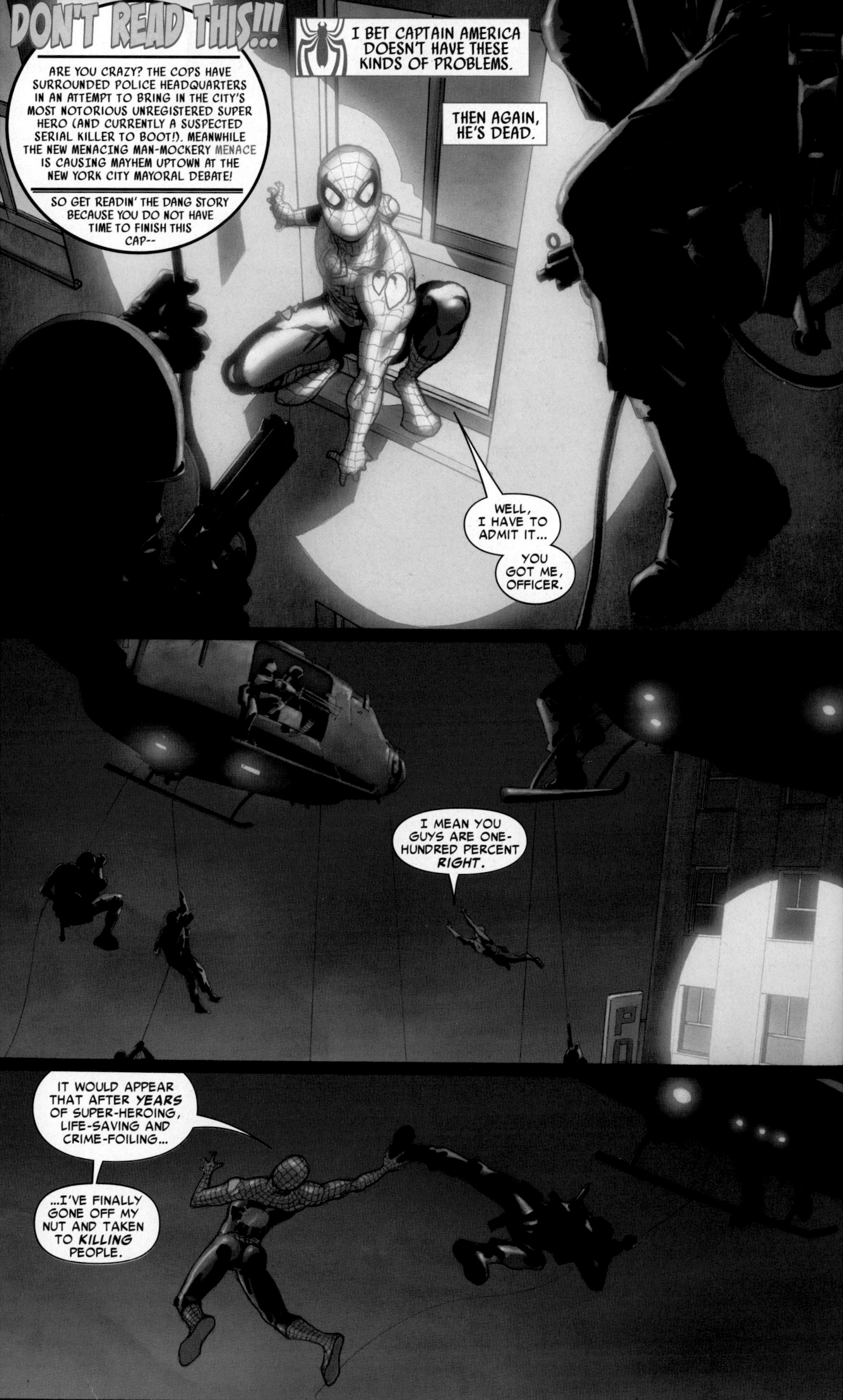
DON'T READ THIS!!!
ARE YOU CRAZY? THE COPS HAVE SURROUNDED POLICE HEADQUARTERS IN AN ATTEMPT TO BRING IN THE CITY'S MOST NOTORIOUS UNREGISTERED SUPER HERO (AND CURRENTLY A SUSPECTED SERIAL KILLER TO BOOT!). MEANWHILE THE NEW MENACING MAN-MOCKERY MENACE IS CAUSING MAYHEM UPTOWN AT THE NEW YORK CITY MAYORAL DEBATE!
SO GET READIN' THE DANG STORY BECAUSE YOU DO NOT HAVE TIME TO FINISH THIS CAP--
I BET CAPTAIN AMERICA DOESN'T HAVE THESE KINDS OF PROBLEMS.
THEN AGAIN, HE'S DEAD.
WELL, I HAVE TO ADMIT IT...
YOU GOT ME, OFFICER.
I MEAN YOU GUYS ARE ONE-HUNDRED PERCENT RIGHT.
IT WOULD APPEAR THAT AFTER YEARS OF SUPER-HEROING, LIFE-SAVING AND CRIME-FOILING...
...I'VE FINALLY GONE OFF MY NUT AND TAKEN TO KILLING PEOPLE.

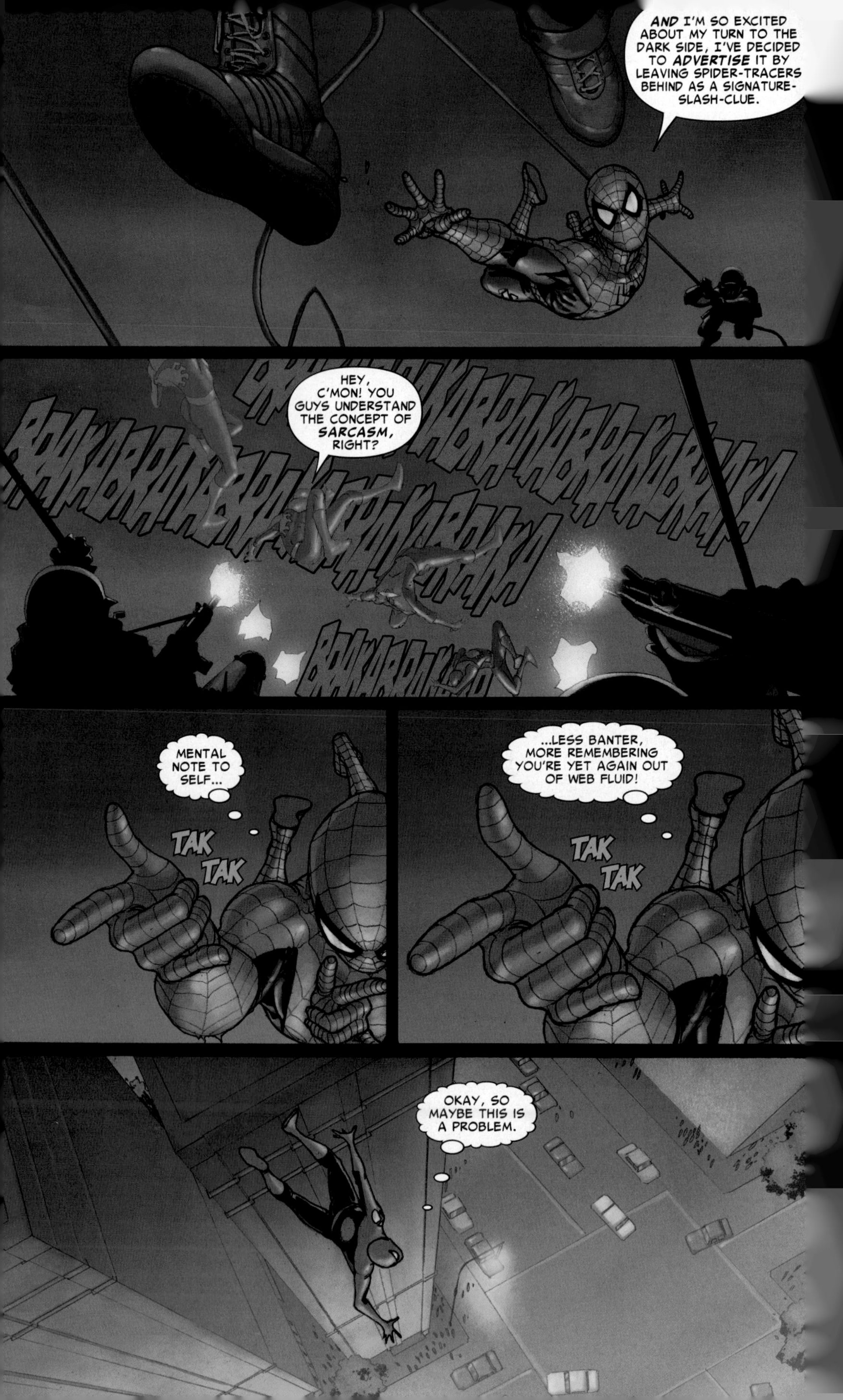

AND I'M SO EXCITED ABOUT MY TURN TO THE DARK SIDE, I'VE DECIDED TO ADVERTISE IT BY LEAVING SPIDER-TRACERS BEHIND AS A SIGNATURE-SLASH-CLUE.
HEY, C'MON! YOU GUYS UNDERSTAND THE CONCEPT OF SARCASM, RIGHT?
MENTAL NOTE TO SELF...
TAK TAK
...LESS BANTER, MORE REMEMBERING YOU'RE YET AGAIN OUT OF WEB FLUID!
TAK TAK
OKAY, SO MAYBE THIS IS A PROBLEM.

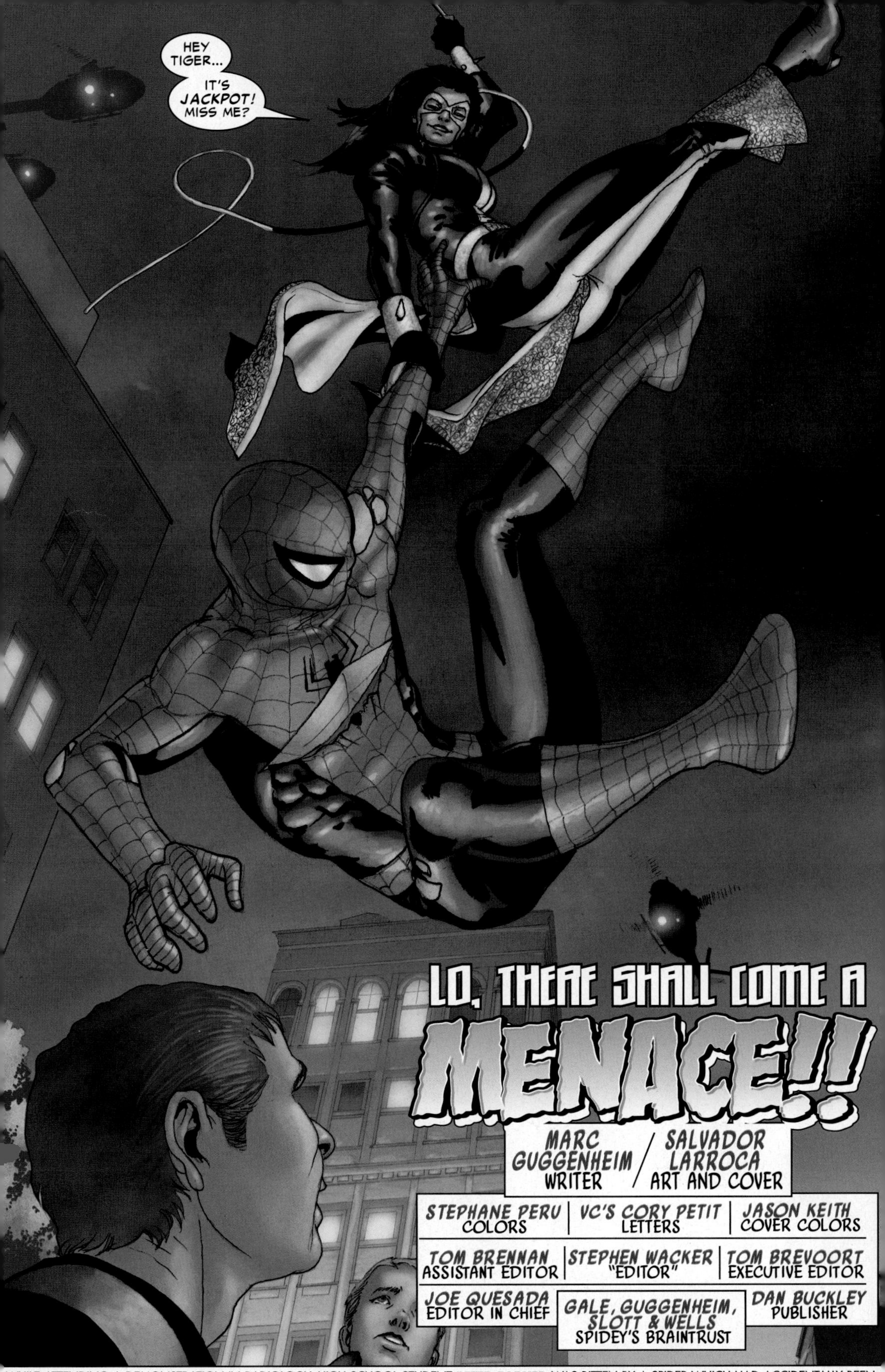
HEY TIGER... IT'S JACKPOT! MISS ME?
LO, THERE SHALL COME A MENACE!!
MARC GUGGENHEIM WRITER / SALVADOR LARROCA ART AND COVER
STEPHANE PERU COLORS
VC'S CORY PETIT LETTERS
JASON KEITH COVER COLORS
TOM BRENNAN ASSISTANT EDITOR
STEPHEN WACKER "EDITOR"
TOM BREVOORT EXECUTIVE EDITOR
JOE QUESADA EDITOR IN CHIEF
GALE, GUGGENHEIM, SLOTT & WELLS SPIDEY'S BRAINTRUST
DAN BUCKLEY PUBLISHER

WHILE ATTENDING A DEMONSTRATION IN RADIOLOGY, HIGH SCHOOL STUDENT **PETER PARKER** WAS BITTEN BY A SPIDER WHICH HAD ACCIDENTALLY BEEN EXPOSED TO **RADIOACTIVE RAYS.** THROUGH A MIRACLE OF SCIENCE, PETER SOON FOUND THAT HE HAD **GAINED** THE SPIDER'S POWERS...AND HAD, IN EFFECT, BECOME A HUMAN SPIDER! FROM THAT DAY ON HE WAS...

THE AMAZING SPIDER-MAN™

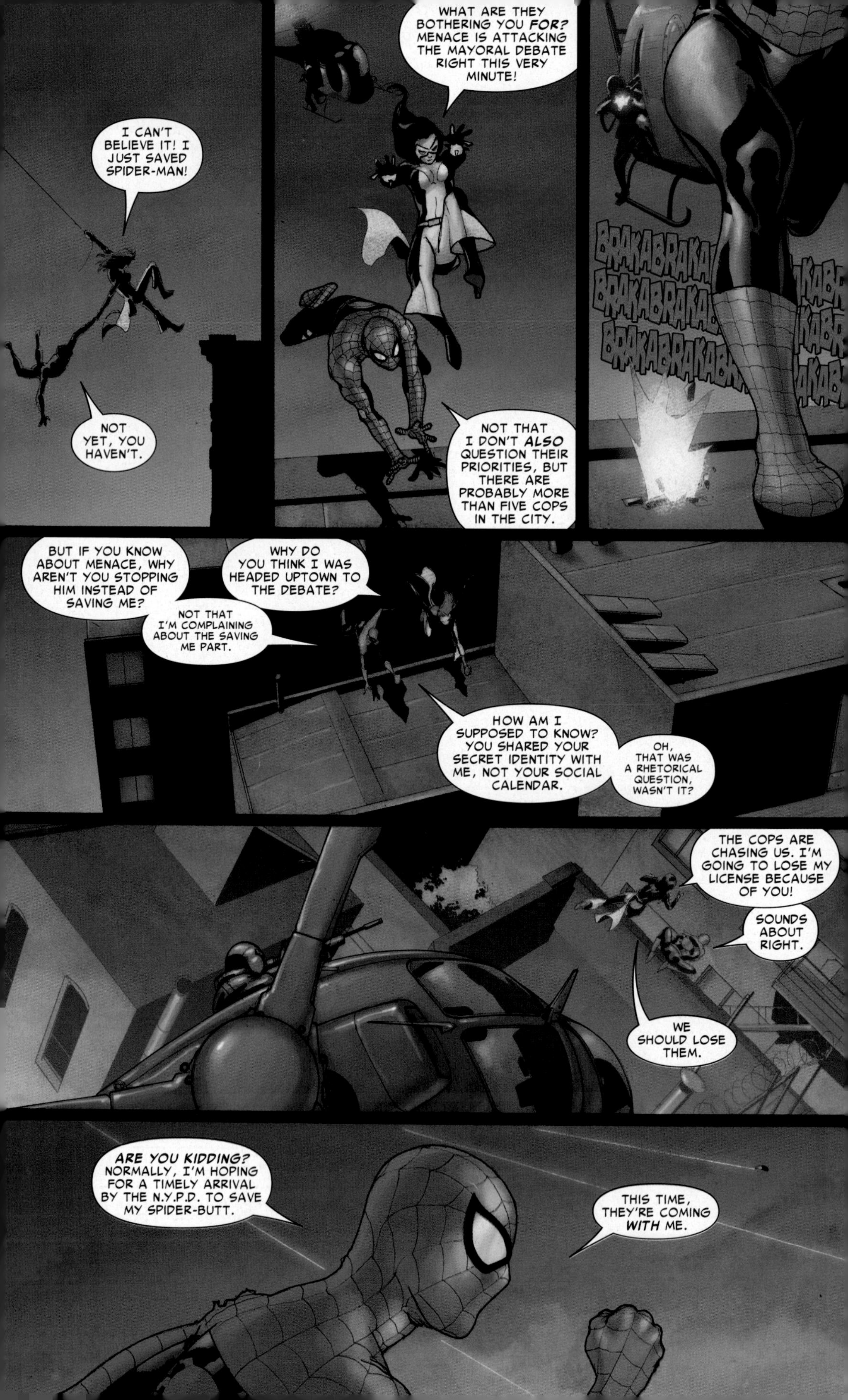
I CAN'T BELIEVE IT! I JUST SAVED SPIDER-MAN!
NOT YET, YOU HAVEN'T.
WHAT ARE THEY BOTHERING YOU *FOR?* MENACE IS ATTACKING THE MAYORAL DEBATE RIGHT THIS VERY MINUTE!
NOT THAT I DON'T *ALSO* QUESTION THEIR PRIORITIES, BUT THERE ARE PROBABLY MORE THAN FIVE COPS IN THE CITY.
BRAKABRAKA BRAKABRAKA BRAKABRAKABR
BUT IF YOU KNOW ABOUT MENACE, WHY AREN'T YOU STOPPING HIM INSTEAD OF SAVING ME?
NOT THAT I'M COMPLAINING ABOUT THE SAVING ME PART.
WHY DO YOU THINK I WAS HEADED UPTOWN TO THE DEBATE?
HOW AM I SUPPOSED TO KNOW? YOU SHARED YOUR SECRET IDENTITY WITH ME, NOT YOUR SOCIAL CALENDAR.
OH, THAT WAS A RHETORICAL QUESTION, WASN'T IT?
THE COPS ARE CHASING US. I'M GOING TO LOSE MY LICENSE BECAUSE OF YOU!
SOUNDS ABOUT RIGHT.
WE SHOULD LOSE THEM.
ARE YOU KIDDING? NORMALLY, I'M HOPING FOR A TIMELY ARRIVAL BY THE N.Y.P.D. TO SAVE MY SPIDER-BUTT.
THIS TIME, THEY'RE COMING *WITH* ME.

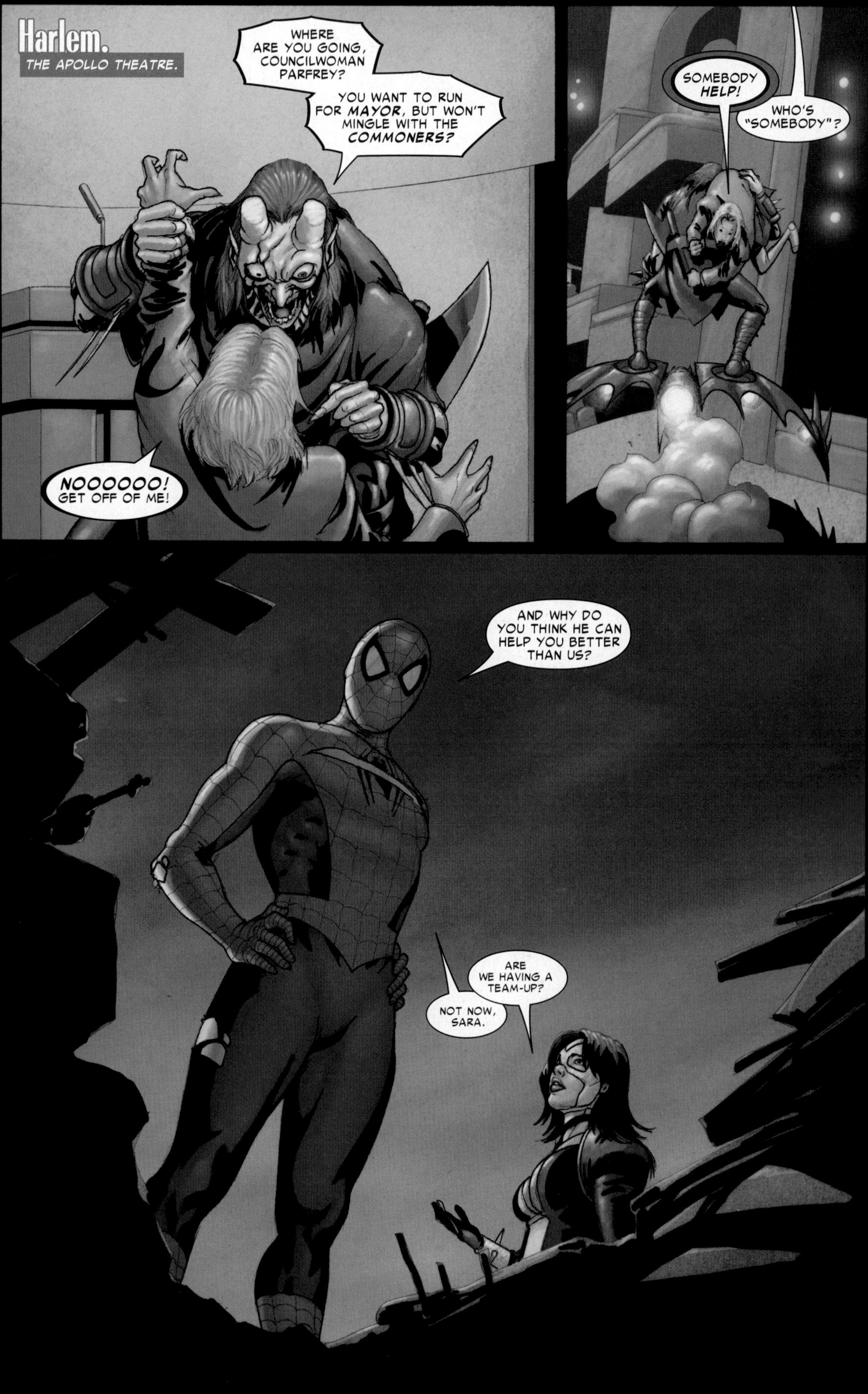

Harlem.
THE APOLLO THEATRE.
WHERE ARE YOU GOING, COUNCILWOMAN PARFREY?
YOU WANT TO RUN FOR MAYOR, BUT WON'T MINGLE WITH THE COMMONERS?
NOOOOOO! GET OFF OF ME!
SOMEBODY HELP!
WHO'S "SOMEBODY"?
AND WHY DO YOU THINK HE CAN HELP YOU BETTER THAN US?
ARE WE HAVING A TEAM-UP?
NOT NOW, SARA.

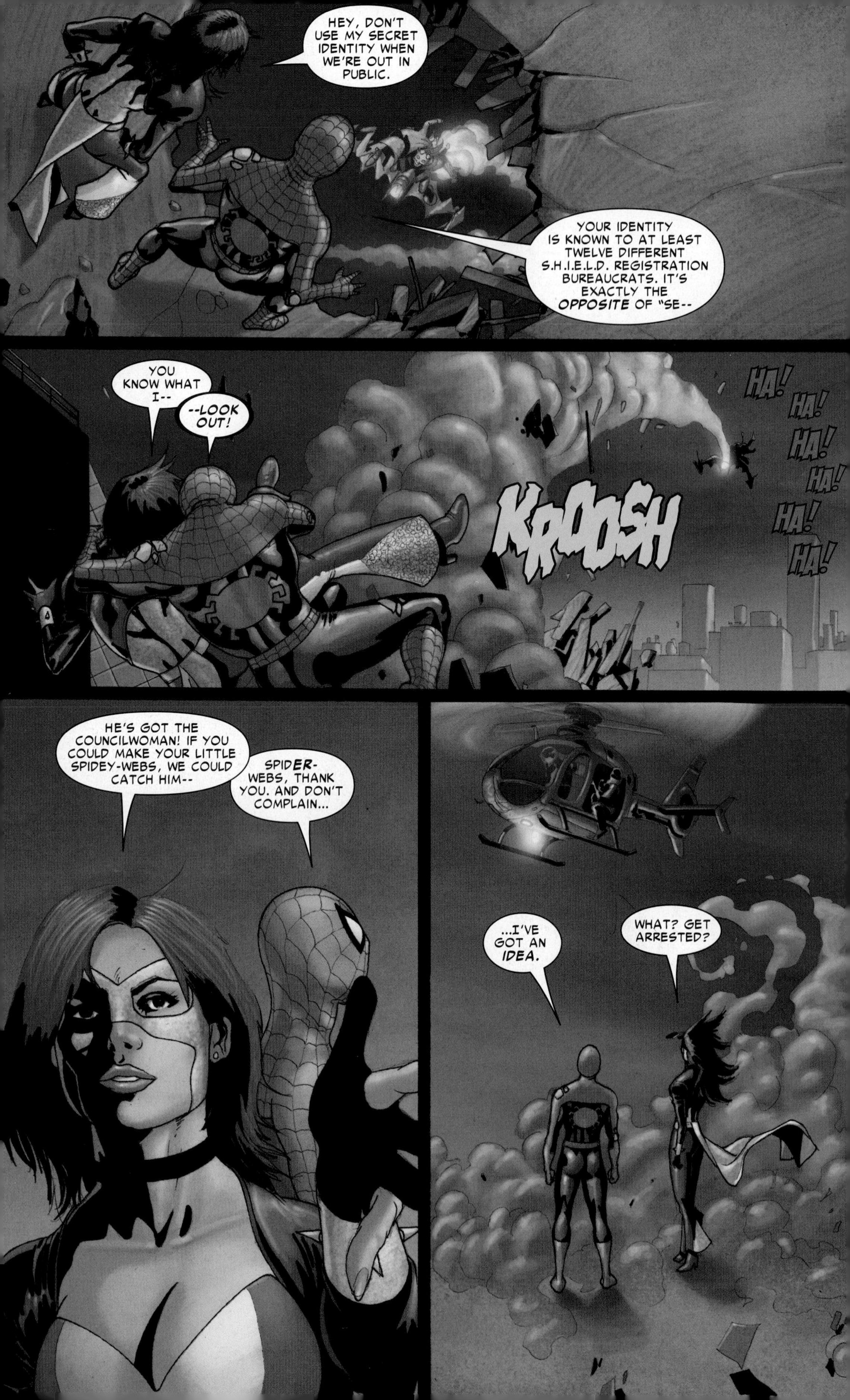
HEY, DON'T USE MY SECRET IDENTITY WHEN WE'RE OUT IN PUBLIC.
YOUR IDENTITY IS KNOWN TO AT LEAST TWELVE DIFFERENT S.H.I.E.L.D. REGISTRATION BUREAUCRATS. IT'S EXACTLY THE OPPOSITE OF "SE--
YOU KNOW WHAT I--
--LOOK OUT!
KROOSH
HA! HA! HA! HA! HA! HA!
HE'S GOT THE COUNCILWOMAN! IF YOU COULD MAKE YOUR LITTLE SPIDEY-WEBS, WE COULD CATCH HIM--
SPIDER-WEBS, THANK YOU. AND DON'T COMPLAIN...
...I'VE GOT AN IDEA.
WHAT? GET ARRESTED?

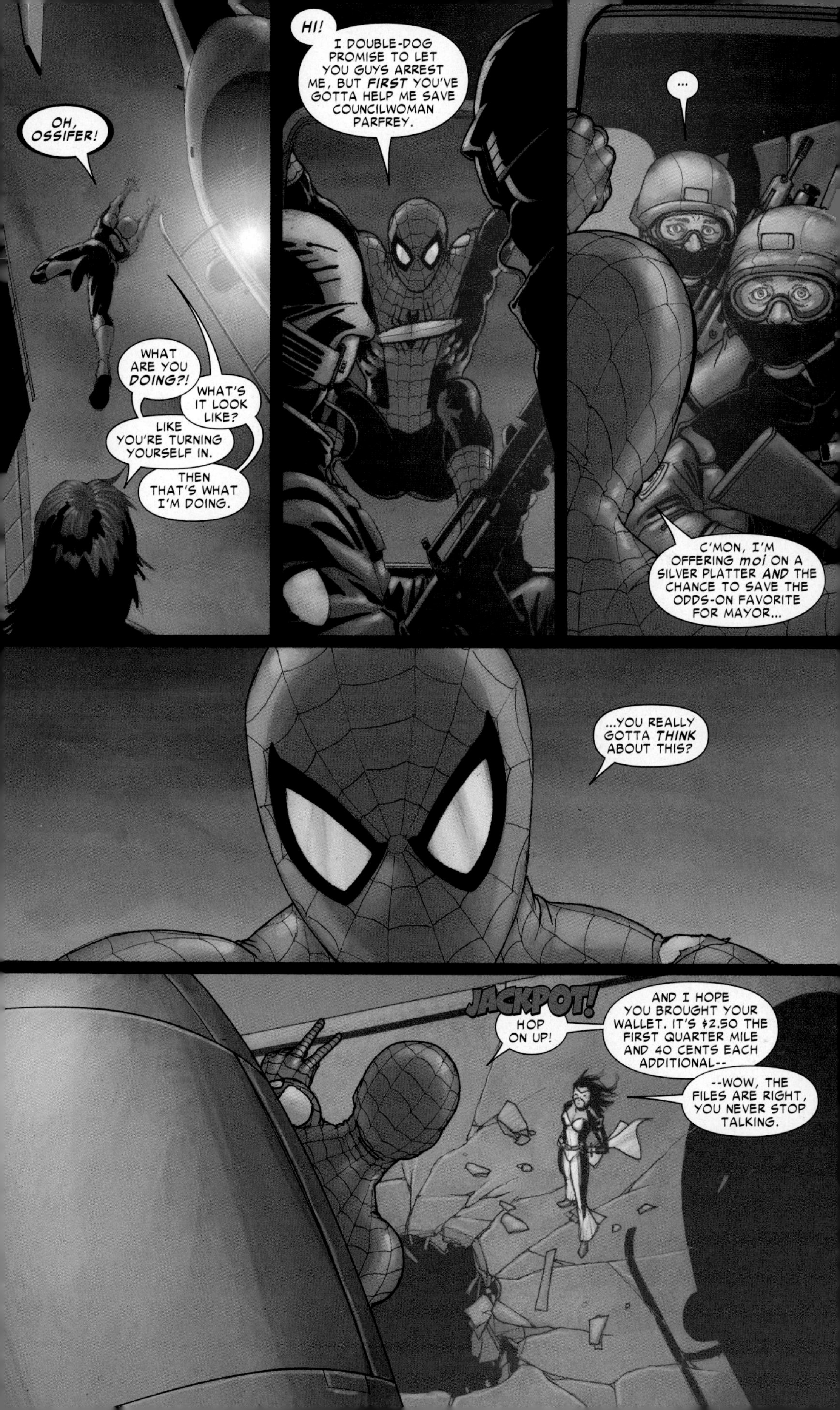

OH, OSSIFER!
WHAT ARE YOU DOING?!
WHAT'S IT LOOK LIKE?
LIKE YOU'RE TURNING YOURSELF IN.
THEN THAT'S WHAT I'M DOING.
HI!
I DOUBLE-DOG PROMISE TO LET YOU GUYS ARREST ME, BUT FIRST YOU'VE GOTTA HELP ME SAVE COUNCILWOMAN PARFREY.
...
C'MON, I'M OFFERING moi ON A SILVER PLATTER AND THE CHANCE TO SAVE THE ODDS-ON FAVORITE FOR MAYOR...
...YOU REALLY GOTTA THINK ABOUT THIS?
JACKPOT!
HOP ON UP!
AND I HOPE YOU BROUGHT YOUR WALLET. IT'S $2.50 THE FIRST QUARTER MILE AND 40 CENTS EACH ADDITIONAL--
--WOW, THE FILES ARE RIGHT, YOU NEVER STOP TALKING.

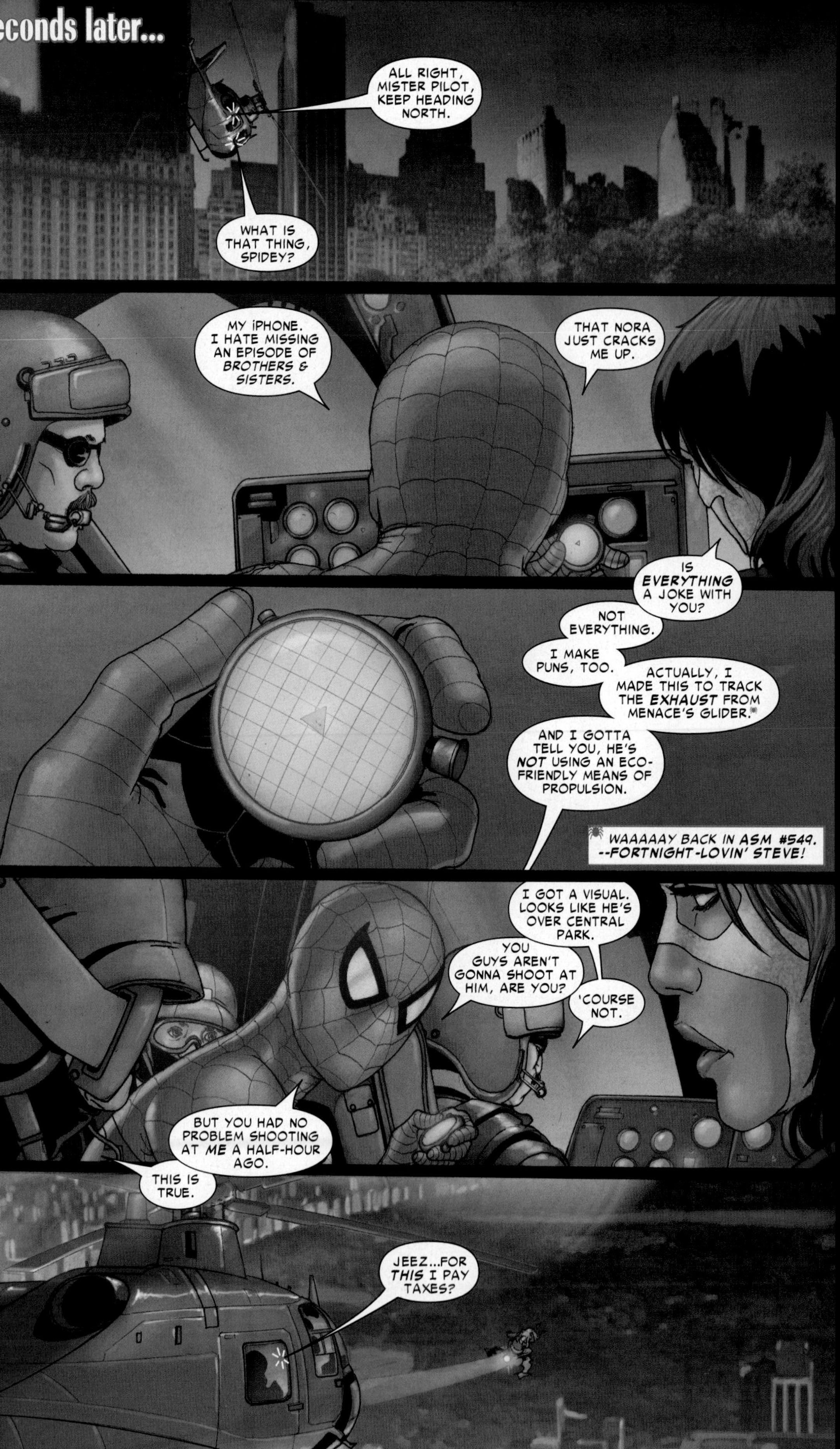

econds later...
ALL RIGHT, MISTER PILOT, KEEP HEADING NORTH.
WHAT IS THAT THING, SPIDEY?
MY iPHONE. I HATE MISSING AN EPISODE OF BROTHERS & SISTERS.
THAT NORA JUST CRACKS ME UP.
IS EVERYTHING A JOKE WITH YOU?
NOT EVERYTHING.
I MAKE PUNS, TOO.
ACTUALLY, I MADE THIS TO TRACK THE EXHAUST FROM MENACE'S GLIDER.*
AND I GOTTA TELL YOU, HE'S NOT USING AN ECO-FRIENDLY MEANS OF PROPULSION.
WAAAAAY BACK IN ASM #549. --FORTNIGHT-LOVIN' STEVE!
I GOT A VISUAL. LOOKS LIKE HE'S OVER CENTRAL PARK.
YOU GUYS AREN'T GONNA SHOOT AT HIM, ARE YOU?
'COURSE NOT.
BUT YOU HAD NO PROBLEM SHOOTING AT ME A HALF-HOUR AGO.
THIS IS TRUE.
JEEZ...FOR THIS I PAY TAXES?

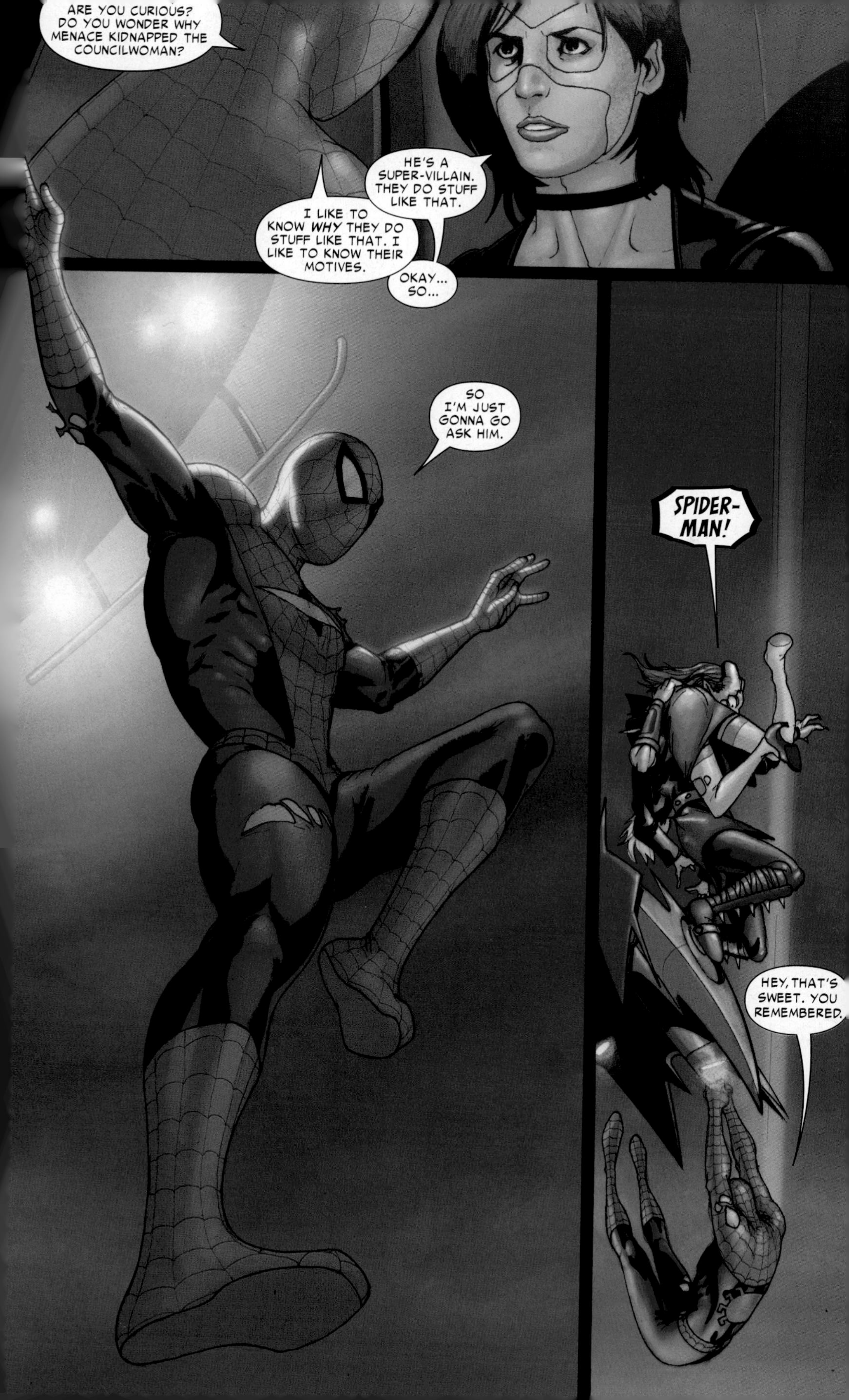
ARE YOU CURIOUS? DO YOU WONDER WHY MENACE KIDNAPPED THE COUNCILWOMAN?
HE'S A SUPER-VILLAIN. THEY DO STUFF LIKE THAT.
I LIKE TO KNOW WHY THEY DO STUFF LIKE THAT. I LIKE TO KNOW THEIR MOTIVES.
OKAY... SO...
SO I'M JUST GONNA GO ASK HIM.
SPIDER-MAN!
HEY, THAT'S SWEET. YOU REMEMBERED.

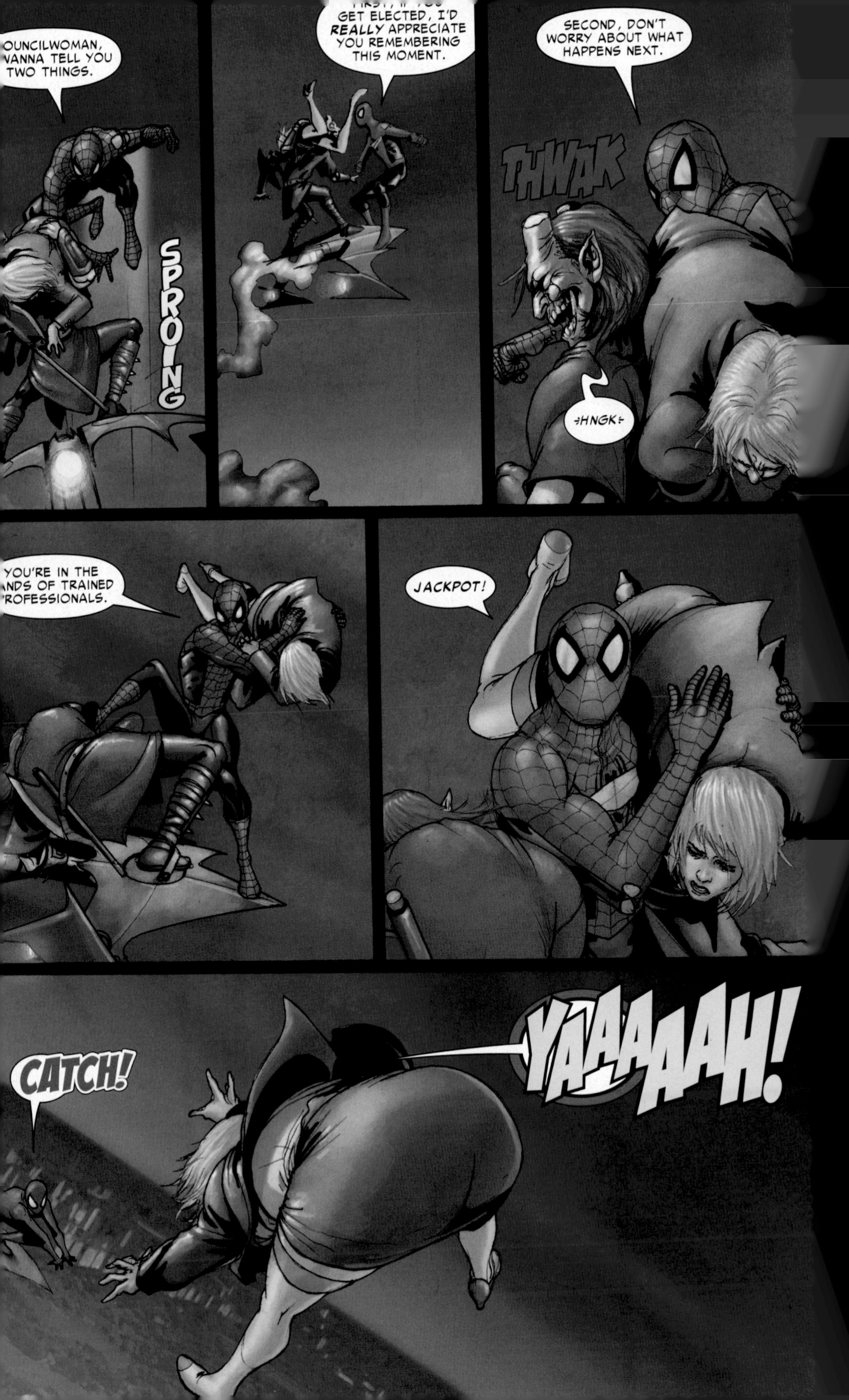

OUNCILWOMAN, VANNA TELL YOU TWO THINGS.
SPROING
GET ELECTED, I'D REALLY APPRECIATE YOU REMEMBERING THIS MOMENT.
SECOND, DON'T WORRY ABOUT WHAT HAPPENS NEXT.
THWAK
HNGK
YOU'RE IN THE ANDS OF TRAINED ROFESSIONALS.
JACKPOT!
CATCH!
YAAAAAH!

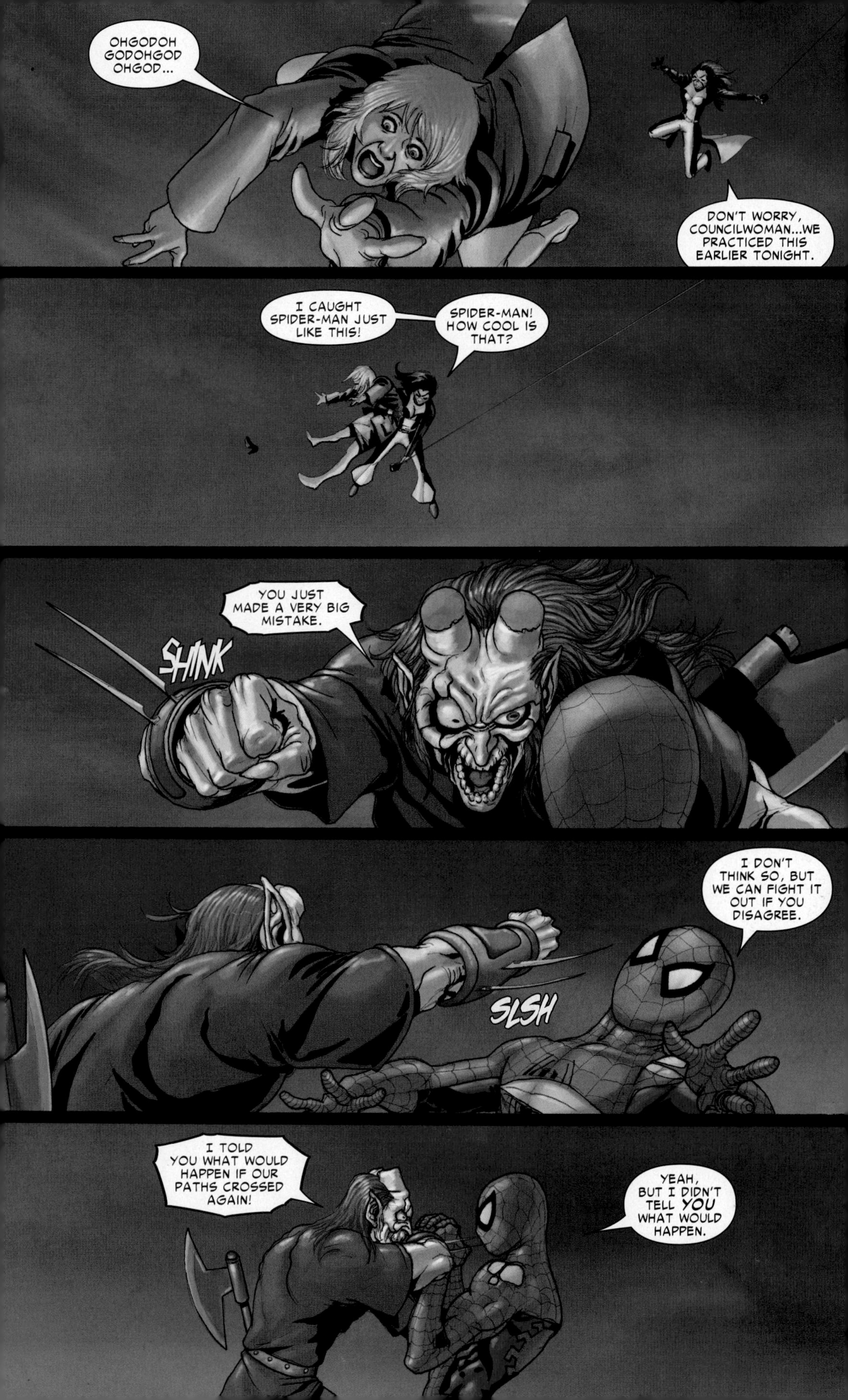
OHGODOH GODOHGOD OHGOD...
DON'T WORRY, COUNCILWOMAN...WE PRACTICED THIS EARLIER TONIGHT.
I CAUGHT SPIDER-MAN JUST LIKE THIS!
SPIDER-MAN! HOW COOL IS THAT?
YOU JUST MADE A VERY BIG MISTAKE.
SHINK
I DON'T THINK SO, BUT WE CAN FIGHT IT OUT IF YOU DISAGREE.
SLSH
I TOLD YOU WHAT WOULD HAPPEN IF OUR PATHS CROSSED AGAIN!
YEAH, BUT I DIDN'T TELL YOU WHAT WOULD HAPPEN.

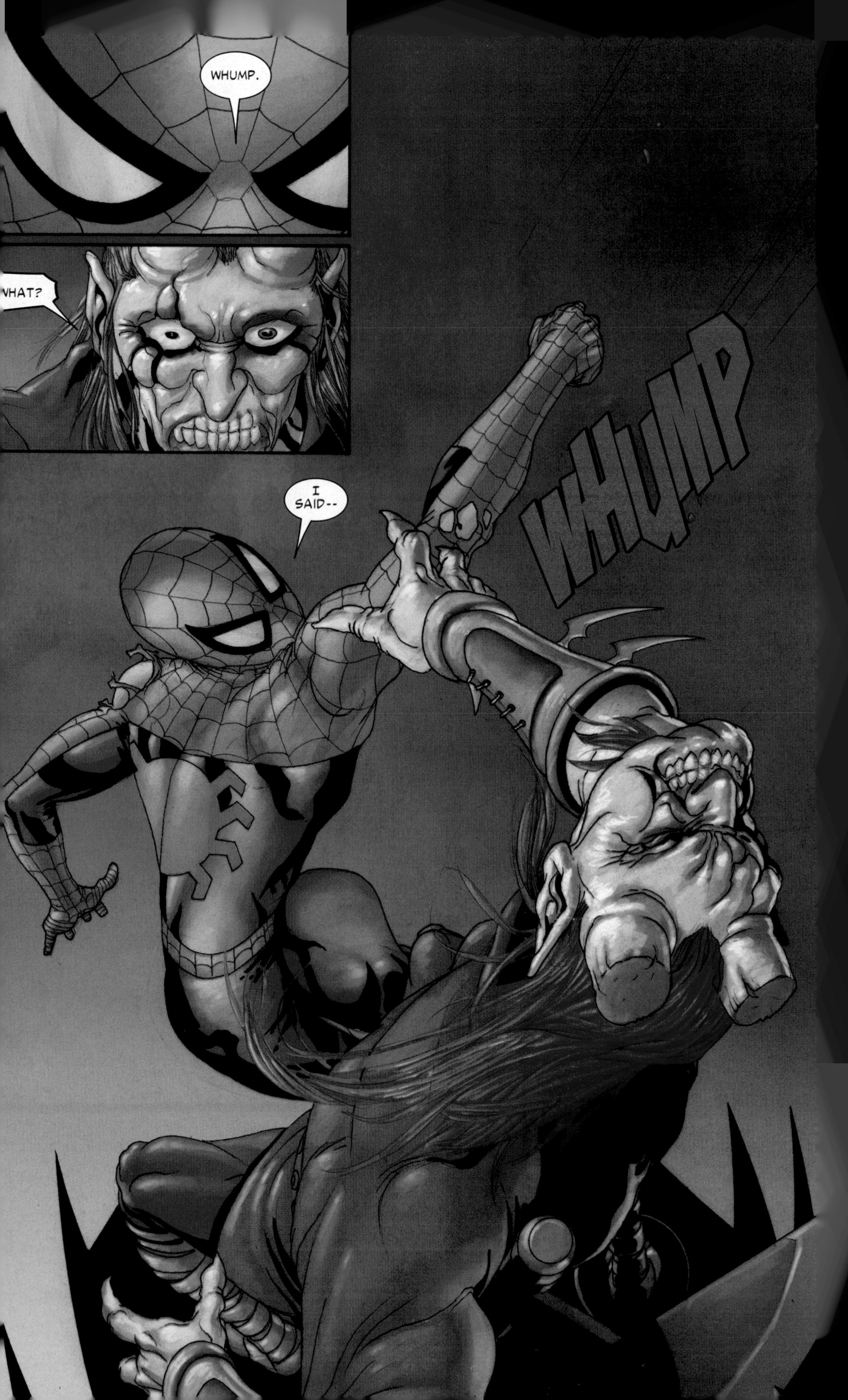
WHUMP.
WHAT?
I SAID--
WHUMP

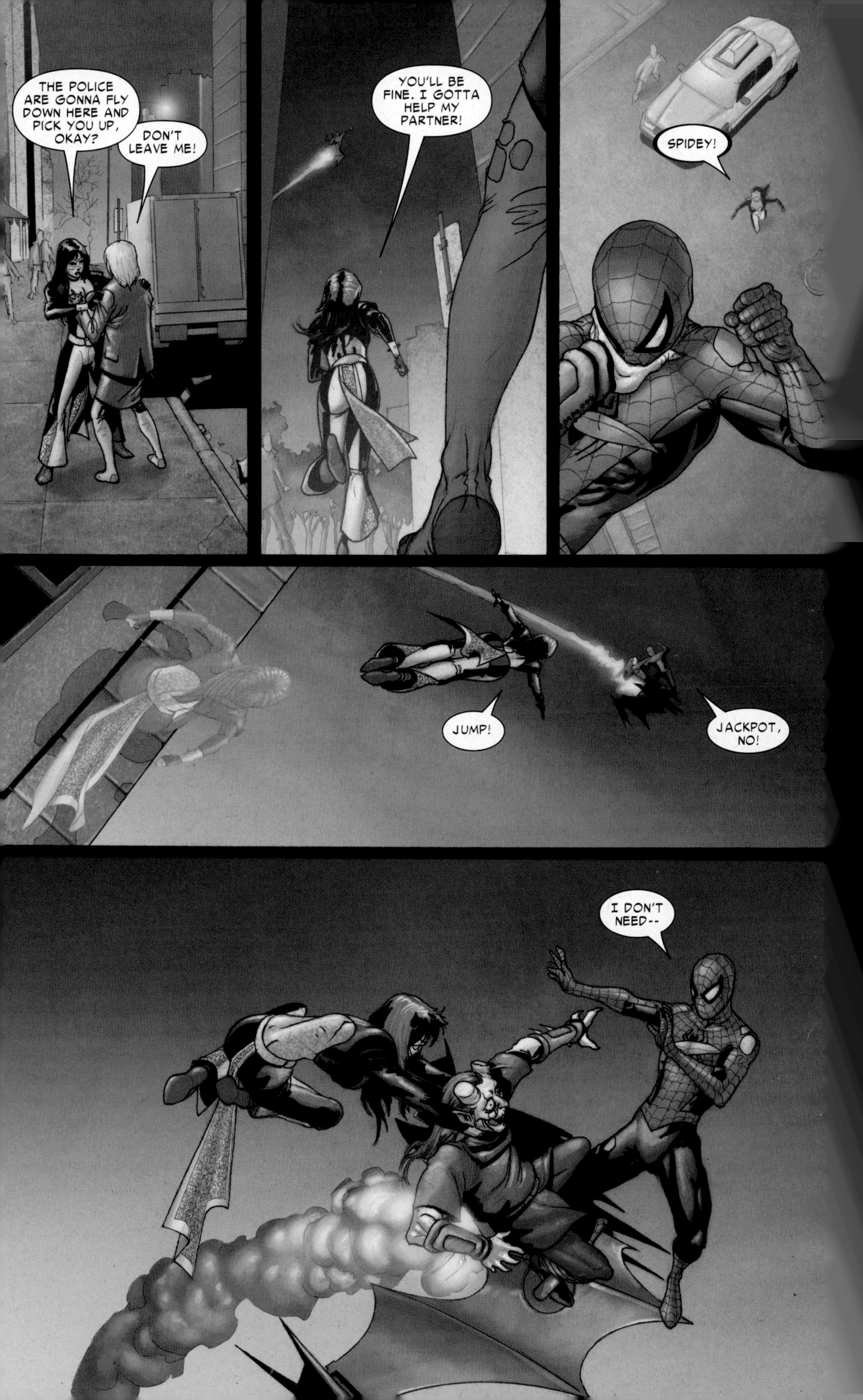
THE POLICE ARE GONNA FLY DOWN HERE AND PICK YOU UP, OKAY?
DON'T LEAVE ME!
YOU'LL BE FINE. I GOTTA HELP MY PARTNER!
SPIDEY!
JUMP!
JACKPOT, NO!
I DON'T NEED--

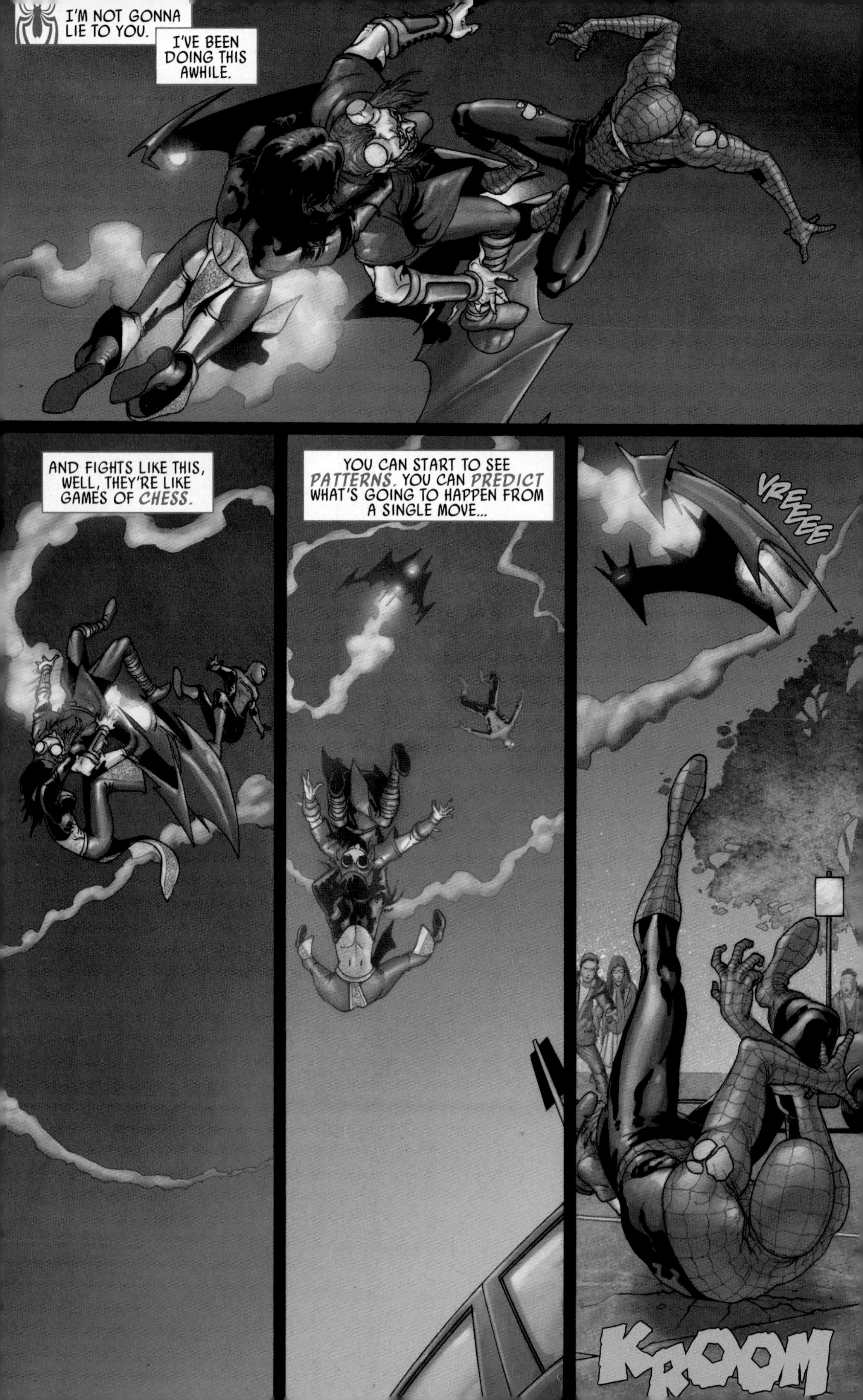
I'M NOT GONNA LIE TO YOU.
I'VE BEEN DOING THIS AWHILE.
AND FIGHTS LIKE THIS, WELL, THEY'RE LIKE GAMES OF CHESS.
YOU CAN START TO SEE PATTERNS. YOU CAN PREDICT WHAT'S GOING TO HAPPEN FROM A SINGLE MOVE...
VREEEE
KROOM

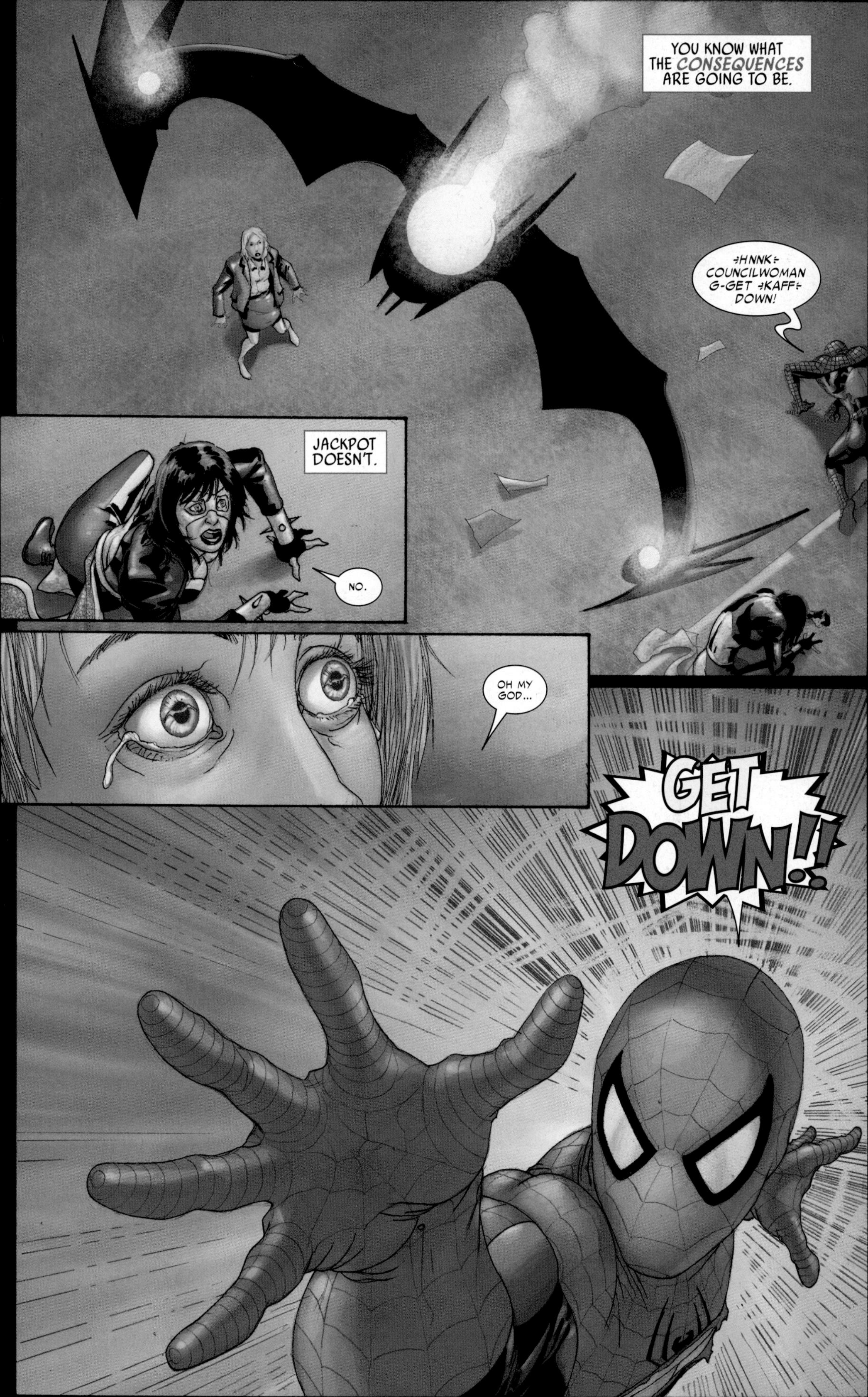
YOU KNOW WHAT THE CONSEQUENCES ARE GOING TO BE.
=HNNK= COUNCILWOMAN G-GET =KAFF= DOWN!
JACKPOT DOESN'T.
NO.
OH MY GOD...
GET DOWN!!

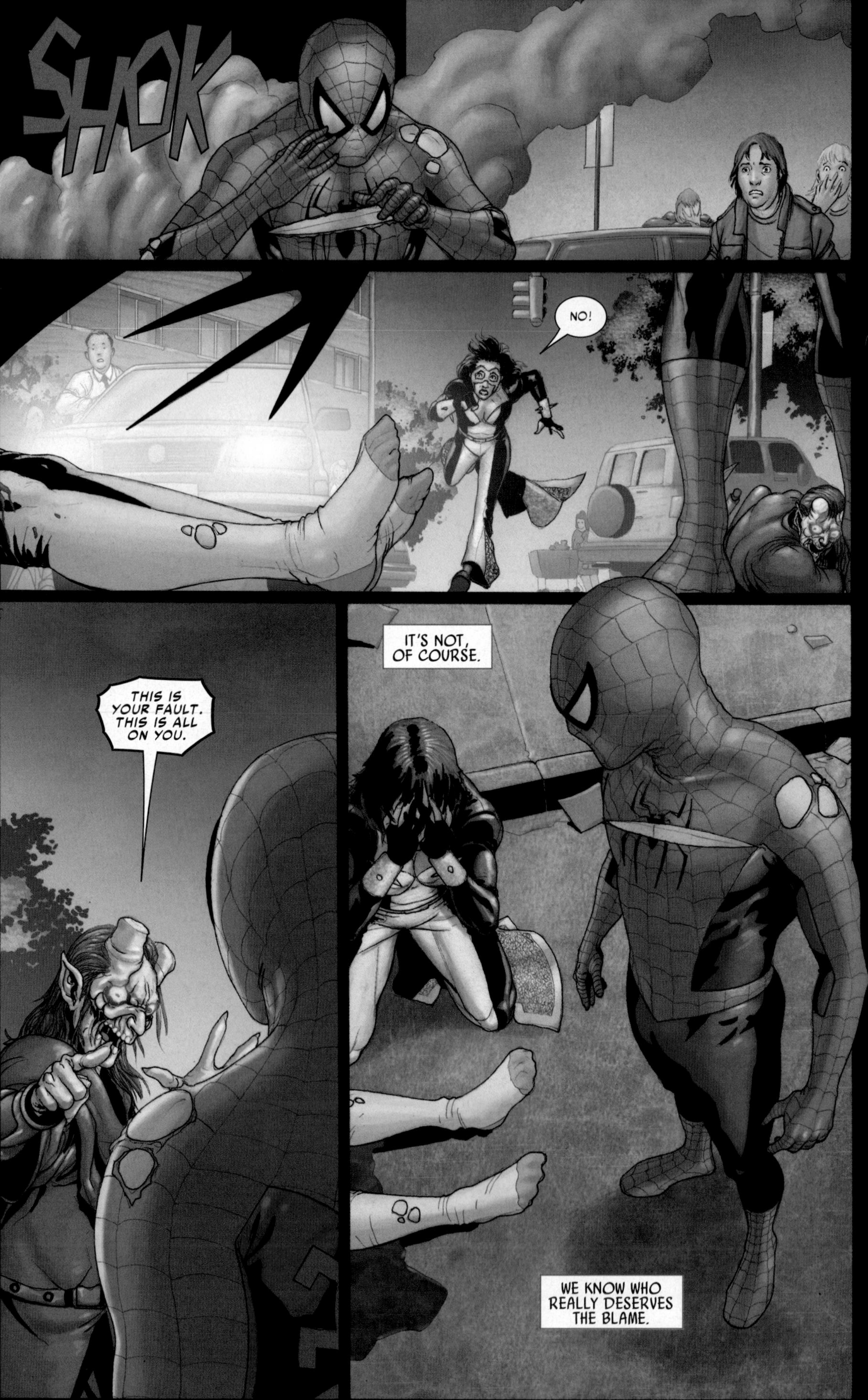
SHOK
NO!
THIS IS YOUR FAULT. THIS IS ALL ON YOU.
IT'S NOT, OF COURSE.
WE KNOW WHO REALLY DESERVES THE BLAME.

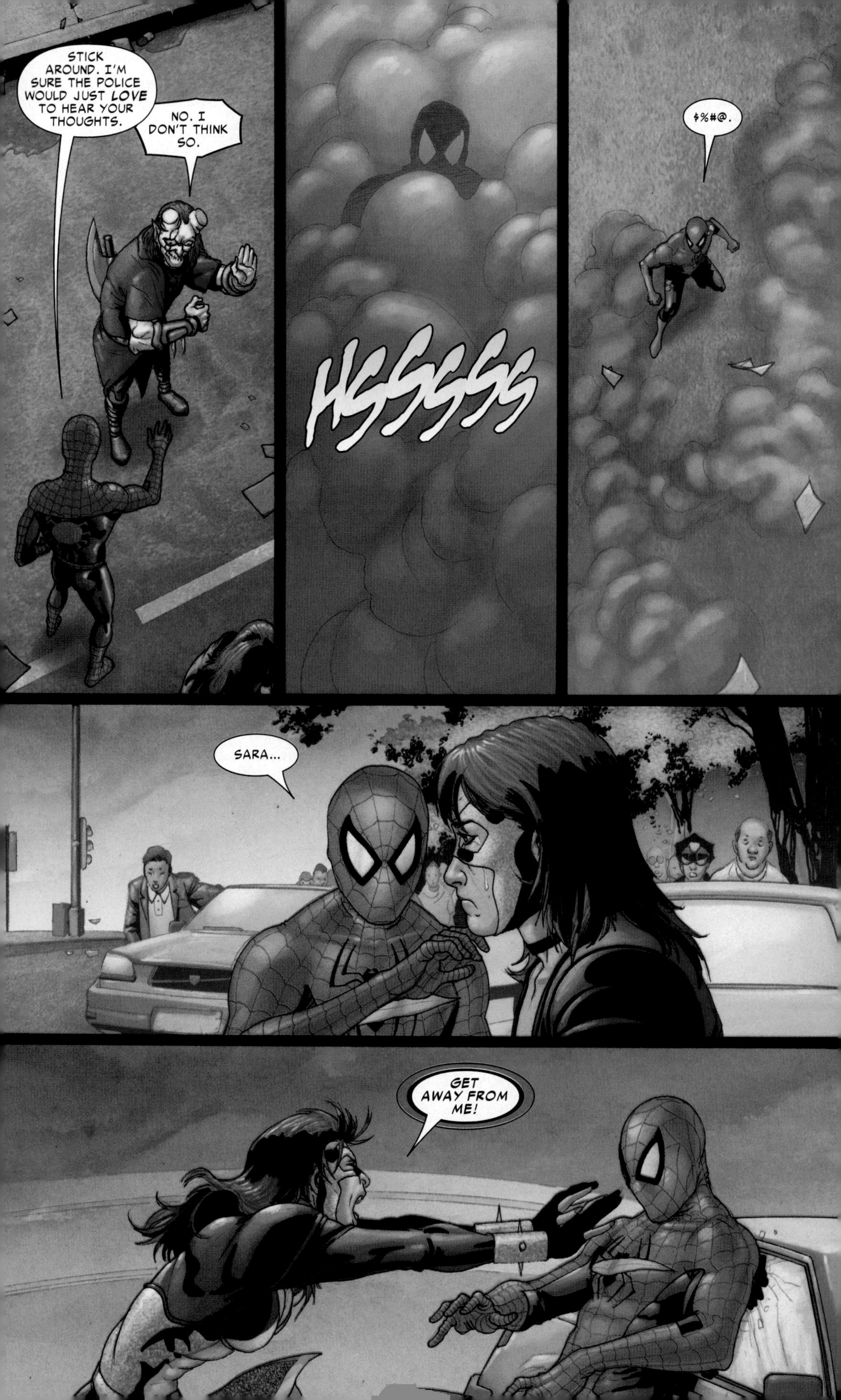

STICK AROUND. I'M SURE THE POLICE WOULD JUST LOVE TO HEAR YOUR THOUGHTS.
NO. I DON'T THINK SO.
HSSSSS
$%#@.
SARA...
GET AWAY FROM ME!

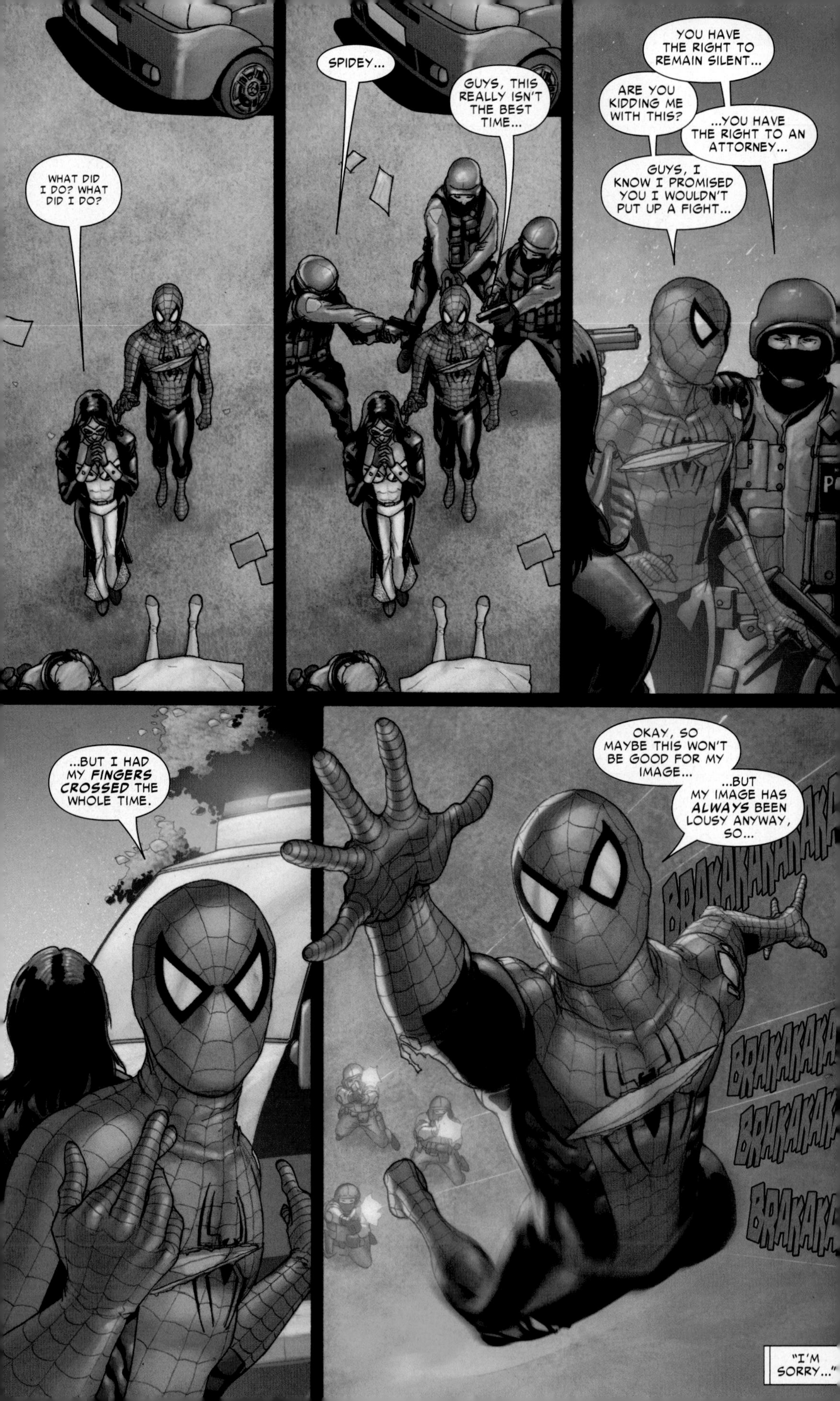

WHAT DID I DO? WHAT DID I DO?
SPIDEY...
GUYS, THIS REALLY ISN'T THE BEST TIME...
YOU HAVE THE RIGHT TO REMAIN SILENT...
ARE YOU KIDDING ME WITH THIS?
...YOU HAVE THE RIGHT TO AN ATTORNEY...
GUYS, I KNOW I PROMISED YOU I WOULDN'T PUT UP A FIGHT...
...BUT I HAD MY FINGERS CROSSED THE WHOLE TIME.
OKAY, SO MAYBE THIS WON'T BE GOOD FOR MY IMAGE...
...BUT MY IMAGE HAS ALWAYS BEEN LOUSY ANYWAY, SO...
BRAKAKAKAKAKAKA
BRAKAKAKA
BRAKAKAK
BRAKAKA
"I'M SORRY..."

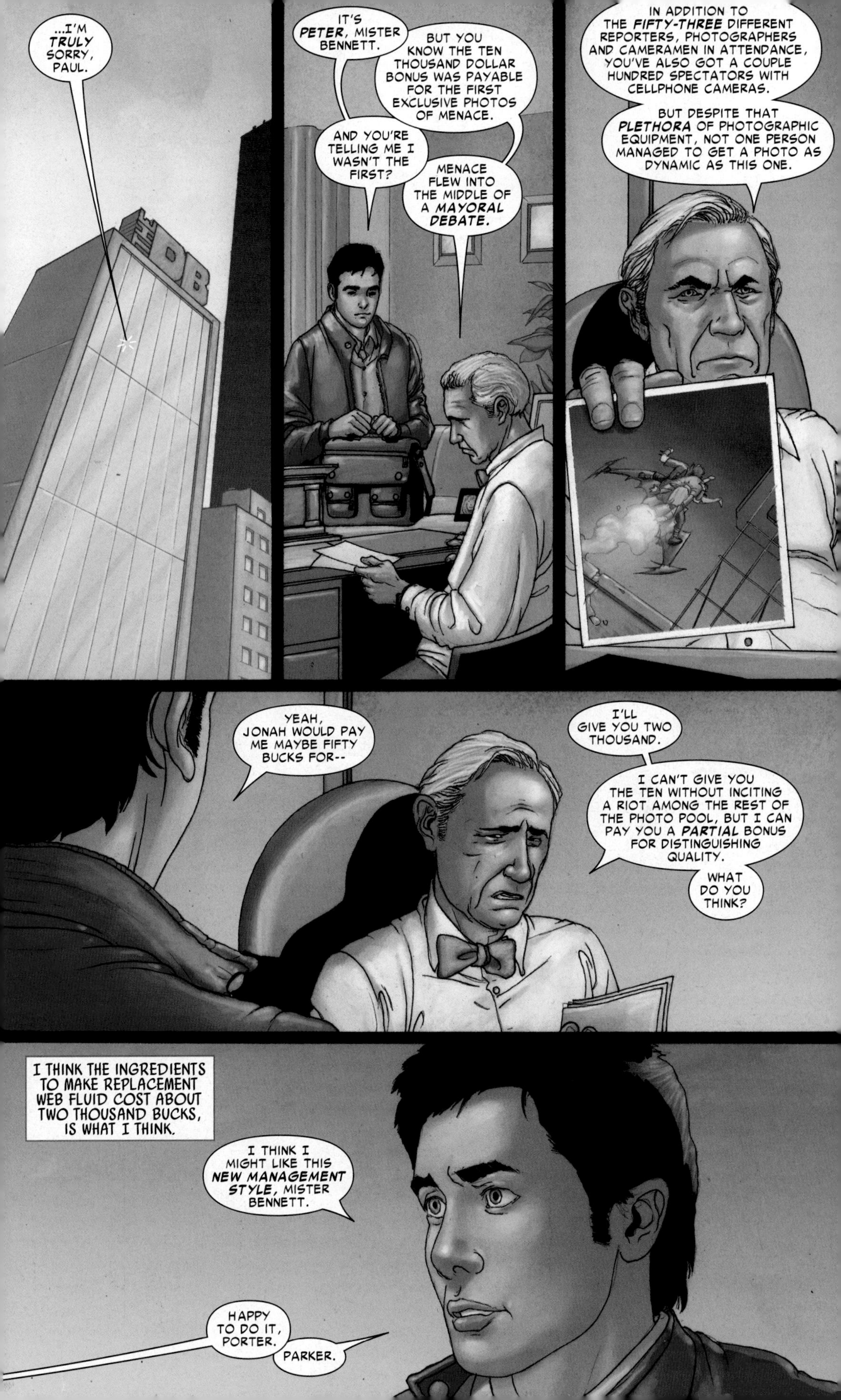
...I'M TRULY SORRY, PAUL.
DB
IT'S PETER, MISTER BENNETT.
BUT YOU KNOW THE TEN THOUSAND DOLLAR BONUS WAS PAYABLE FOR THE FIRST EXCLUSIVE PHOTOS OF MENACE.
AND YOU'RE TELLING ME I WASN'T THE FIRST?
MENACE FLEW INTO THE MIDDLE OF A MAYORAL DEBATE.
IN ADDITION TO THE FIFTY-THREE DIFFERENT REPORTERS, PHOTOGRAPHERS AND CAMERAMEN IN ATTENDANCE, YOU'VE ALSO GOT A COUPLE HUNDRED SPECTATORS WITH CELLPHONE CAMERAS.
BUT DESPITE THAT PLETHORA OF PHOTOGRAPHIC EQUIPMENT, NOT ONE PERSON MANAGED TO GET A PHOTO AS DYNAMIC AS THIS ONE.
YEAH, JONAH WOULD PAY ME MAYBE FIFTY BUCKS FOR--
I'LL GIVE YOU TWO THOUSAND.
I CAN'T GIVE YOU THE TEN WITHOUT INCITING A RIOT AMONG THE REST OF THE PHOTO POOL, BUT I CAN PAY YOU A PARTIAL BONUS FOR DISTINGUISHING QUALITY.
WHAT DO YOU THINK?
I THINK THE INGREDIENTS TO MAKE REPLACEMENT WEB FLUID COST ABOUT TWO THOUSAND BUCKS, IS WHAT I THINK.
I THINK I MIGHT LIKE THIS NEW MANAGEMENT STYLE, MISTER BENNETT.
HAPPY TO DO IT, PORTER.
PARKER.

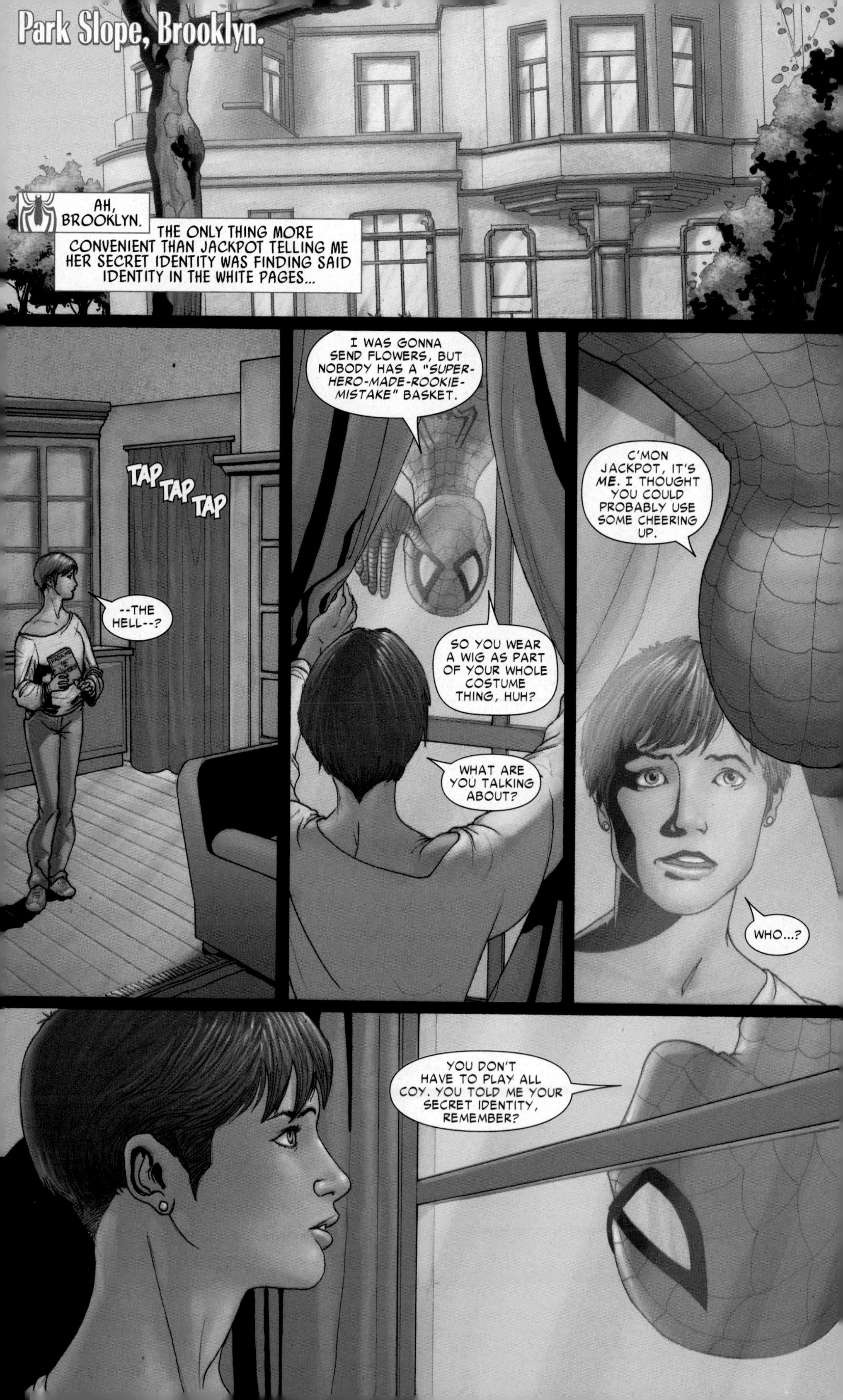

Park Slope, Brooklyn.
AH, BROOKLYN.
THE ONLY THING MORE CONVENIENT THAN JACKPOT TELLING ME HER SECRET IDENTITY WAS FINDING SAID IDENTITY IN THE WHITE PAGES...
TAP TAP TAP
--THE HELL--?
I WAS GONNA SEND FLOWERS, BUT NOBODY HAS A "SUPER-HERO-MADE-ROOKIE-MISTAKE" BASKET.
SO YOU WEAR A WIG AS PART OF YOUR WHOLE COSTUME THING, HUH?
WHAT ARE YOU TALKING ABOUT?
C'MON JACKPOT, IT'S ME. I THOUGHT YOU COULD PROBABLY USE SOME CHEERING UP.
WHO...?
YOU DON'T HAVE TO PLAY ALL COY. YOU TOLD ME YOUR SECRET IDENTITY, REMEMBER?

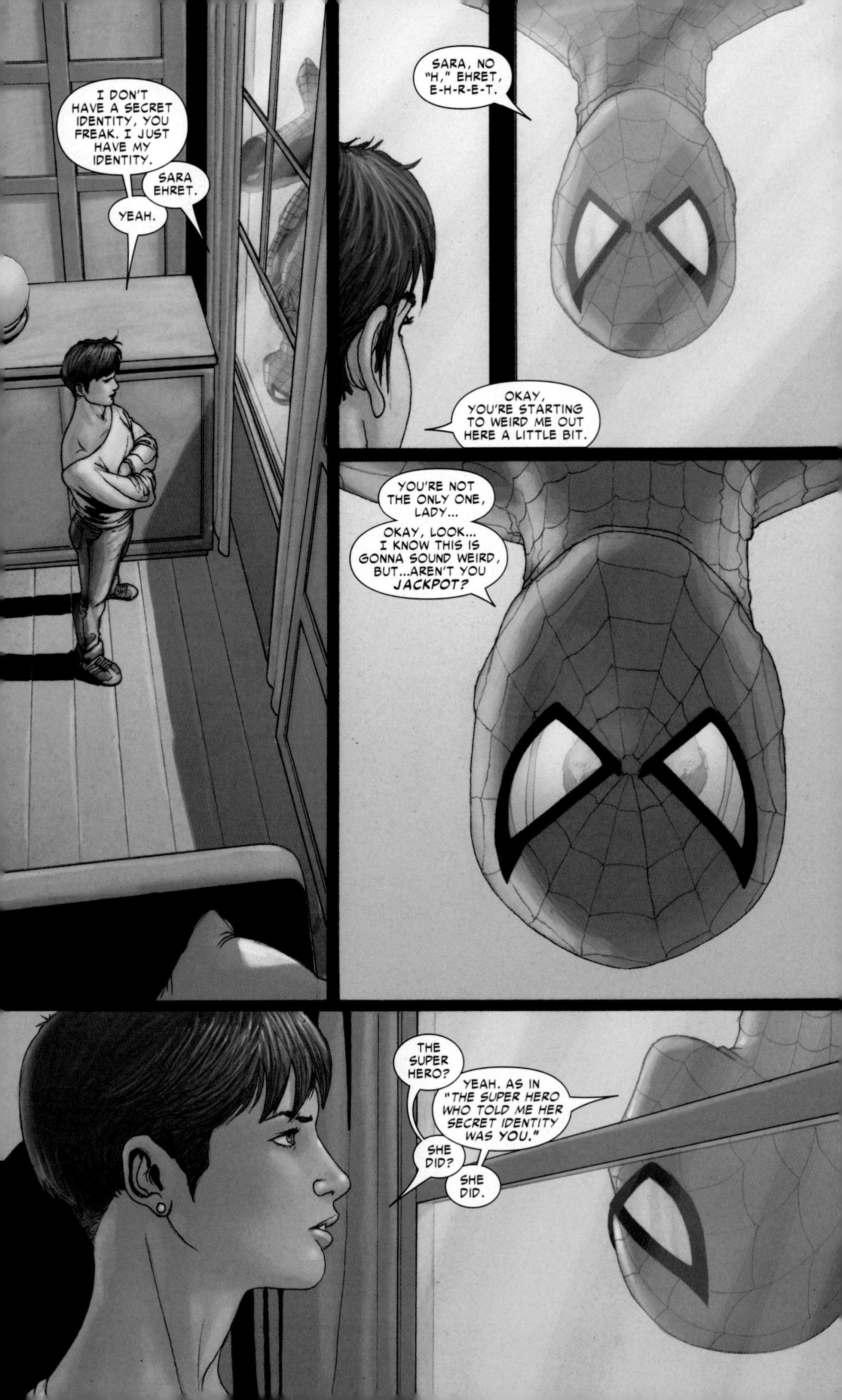
I DON'T HAVE A SECRET IDENTITY, YOU FREAK. I JUST HAVE MY IDENTITY.
SARA EHRET.
YEAH.
SARA, NO "H," EHRET, E-H-R-E-T.
OKAY, YOU'RE STARTING TO WEIRD ME OUT HERE A LITTLE BIT.
YOU'RE NOT THE ONLY ONE, LADY...
OKAY, LOOK... I KNOW THIS IS GONNA SOUND WEIRD, BUT...AREN'T YOU JACKPOT?
THE SUPER HERO?
YEAH. AS IN "THE SUPER HERO WHO TOLD ME HER SECRET IDENTITY WAS YOU."
SHE DID?
SHE DID.

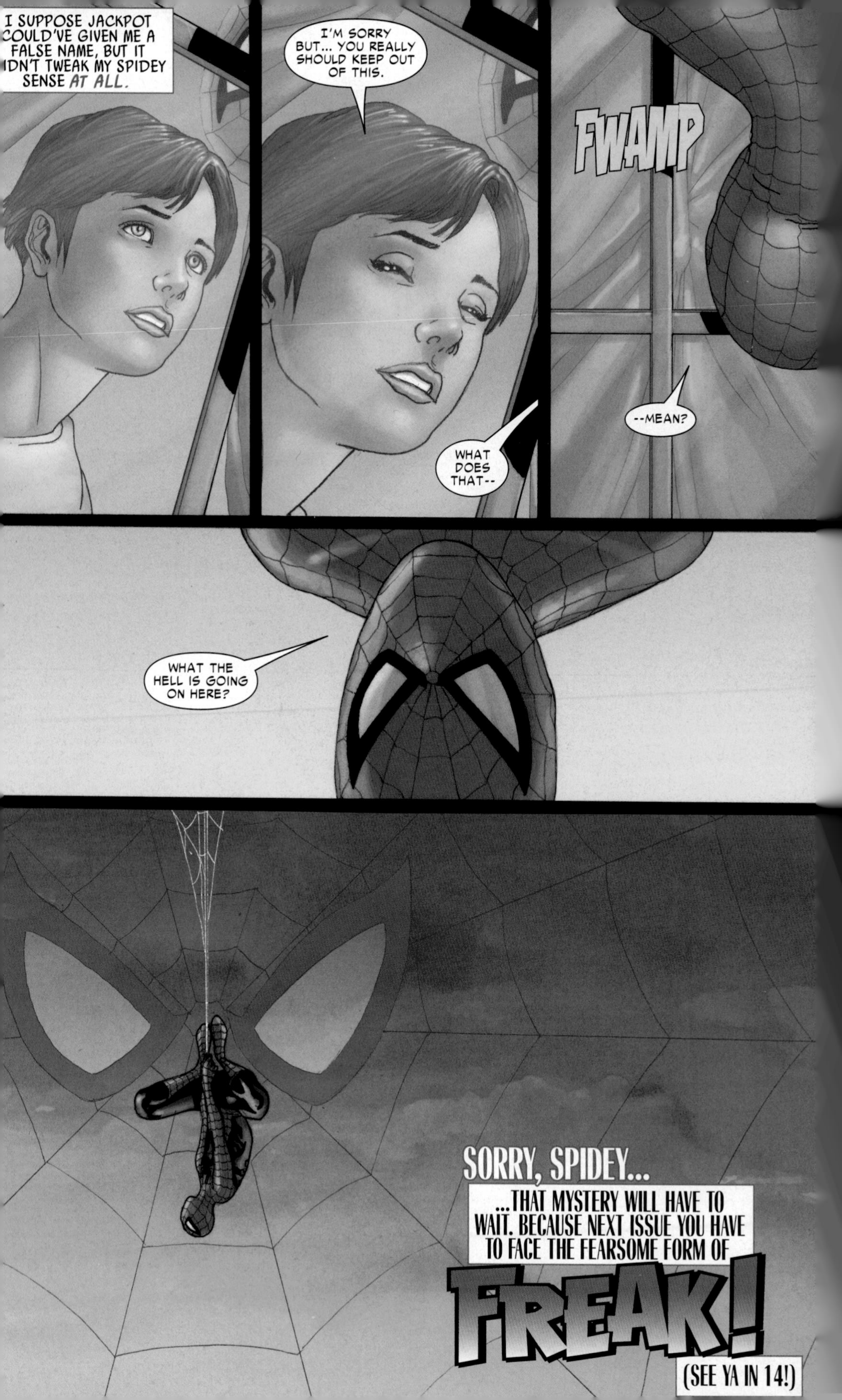
I SUPPOSE JACKPOT COULD'VE GIVEN ME A FALSE NAME, BUT IT DIDN'T TWEAK MY SPIDEY SENSE AT ALL.
I'M SORRY BUT... YOU REALLY SHOULD KEEP OUT OF THIS.
WHAT DOES THAT--
FWAMP
--MEAN?
WHAT THE HELL IS GOING ON HERE?
SORRY, SPIDEY...
...THAT MYSTERY WILL HAVE TO WAIT. BECAUSE NEXT ISSUE YOU HAVE TO FACE THE FEARSOME FORM OF
FREAK!
(SEE YA IN 14!)

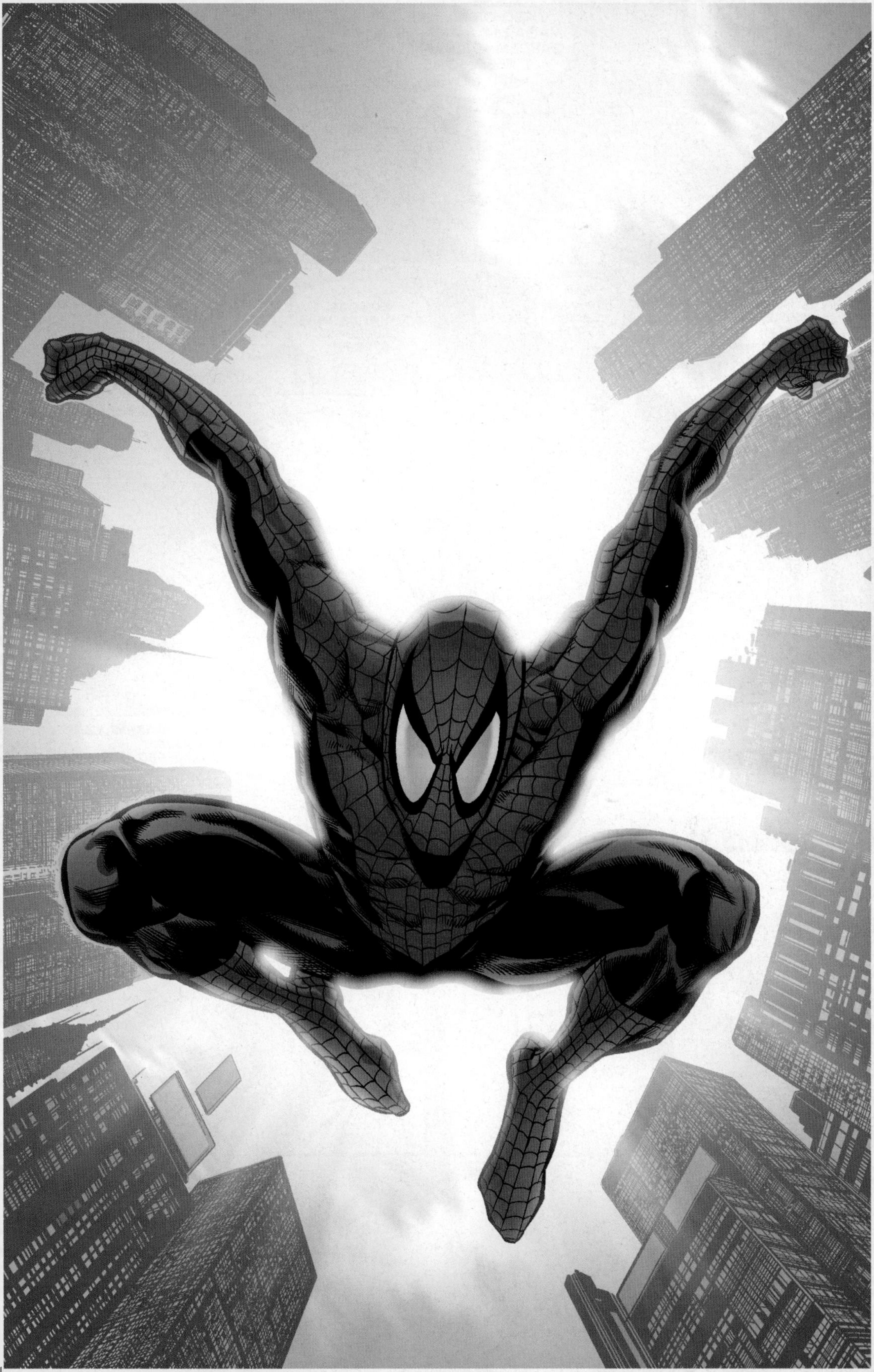

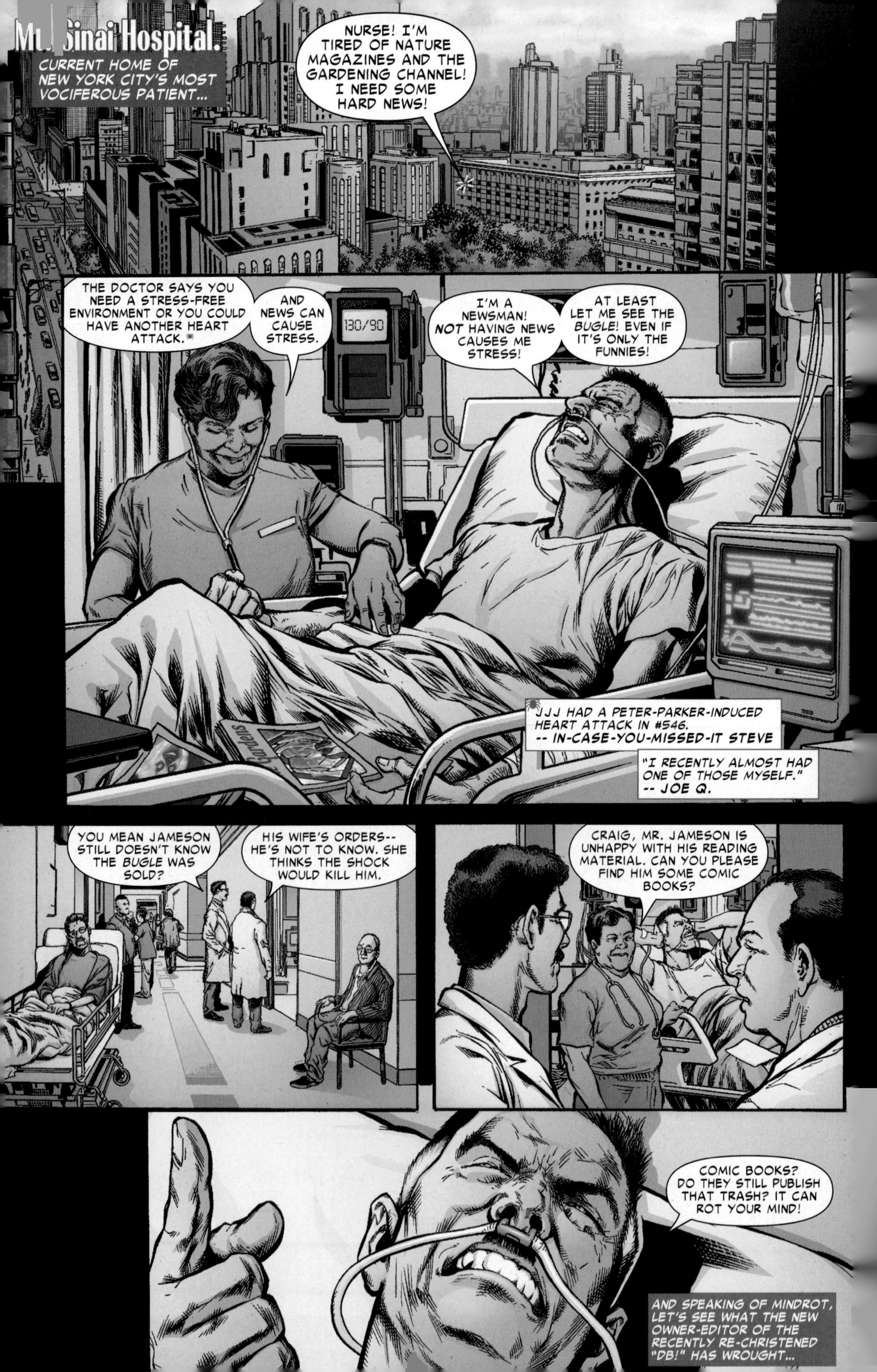
Mt. Sinai Hospital.
CURRENT HOME OF NEW YORK CITY'S MOST VOCIFEROUS PATIENT...
NURSE! I'M TIRED OF NATURE MAGAZINES AND THE GARDENING CHANNEL! I NEED SOME HARD NEWS!
THE DOCTOR SAYS YOU NEED A STRESS-FREE ENVIRONMENT OR YOU COULD HAVE ANOTHER HEART ATTACK.*
AND NEWS CAN CAUSE STRESS.
130/90
I'M A NEWSMAN! NOT HAVING NEWS CAUSES ME STRESS!
AT LEAST LET ME SEE THE BUGLE! EVEN IF IT'S ONLY THE FUNNIES!
Gardens
*JJJ HAD A PETER-PARKER-INDUCED HEART ATTACK IN #546. -- IN-CASE-YOU-MISSED-IT STEVE
"I RECENTLY ALMOST HAD ONE OF THOSE MYSELF." -- JOE Q.
YOU MEAN JAMESON STILL DOESN'T KNOW THE BUGLE WAS SOLD?
HIS WIFE'S ORDERS-- HE'S NOT TO KNOW. SHE THINKS THE SHOCK WOULD KILL HIM.
CRAIG, MR. JAMESON IS UNHAPPY WITH HIS READING MATERIAL. CAN YOU PLEASE FIND HIM SOME COMIC BOOKS?
COMIC BOOKS? DO THEY STILL PUBLISH THAT TRASH? IT CAN ROT YOUR MIND!
AND SPEAKING OF MINDROT, LET'S SEE WHAT THE NEW OWNER-EDITOR OF THE RECENTLY RE-CHRISTENED "DB!" HAS WROUGHT...

THE OFFICIAL NEWSPAPER OF SPIDER-MAN

THE DB

50 CENTS • THURSDAY

WEIRD WEATHER AHEAD: CHANCE OF SNOW BY THE END OF THE WEEK! TIPS ON HOW TO SURVIVE!

SPIDER-MAN: SERIAL KILLER!

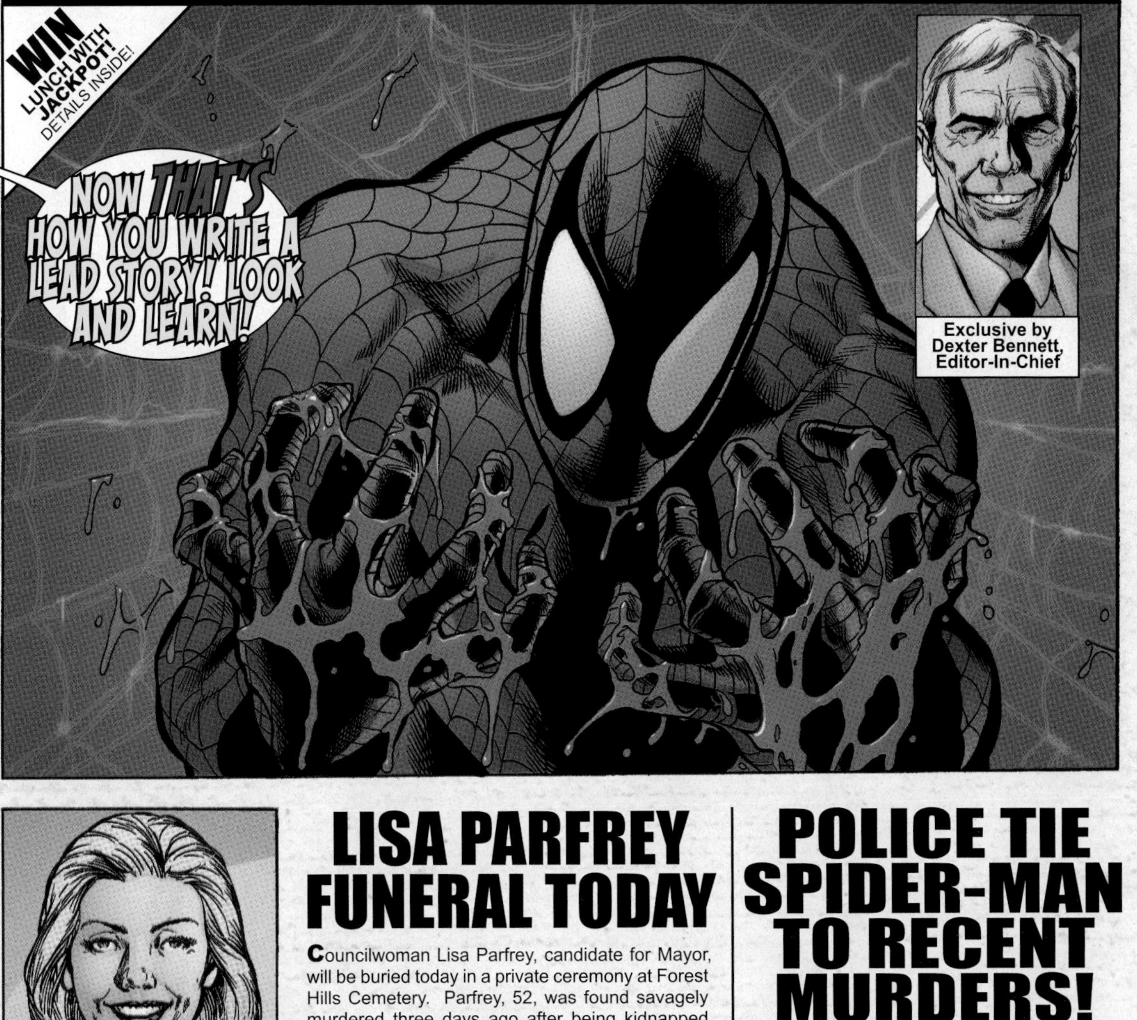
WIN LUNCH WITH JACKPOT!
DETAILS INSIDE!
NOW THAT'S HOW YOU WRITE A LEAD STORY! LOOK AND LEARN!

Exclusive by Dexter Bennett, Editor-In-Chief

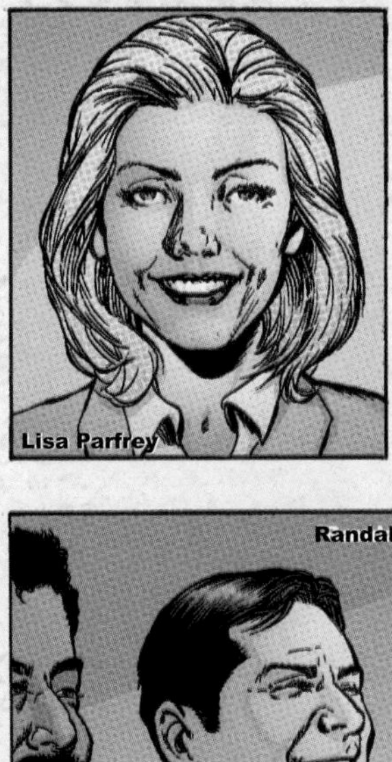

Lisa Parfrey

LISA PARFREY FUNERAL TODAY

Councilwoman Lisa Parfrey, candidate for Mayor, will be buried today in a private ceremony at Forest Hills Cemetery. Parfrey, 52, was found savagely murdered three days ago after being kidnapped from a political debate at the Apollo Theatre by a mysterious super human known as Menace. Menace is the only suspect in the brutal killing. Parfrey's tragic demise shocked the…

CONTINUED ON A-3

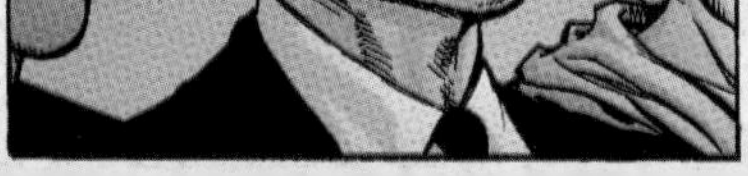

Randall Crowne

WILL CROWNE RUN UNOPPOSED?

With no serious prospect stepping up to take the place of the late Mayoral candidate Lisa Parfrey, it is possible that Randall Crowne may become New York's next mayor by default. If so, it will be the first time in the history of the city that…

CONTINUED ON A-6

POLICE TIE SPIDER-MAN TO RECENT MURDERS!

EXCLUSIVE TO THE DB!

In off the record conversations with DB Staffers, police have confirmed that Spider-Man is the key suspect in the string of recent murders that has shocked this city. Although Police have been reticent to discuss the specifics of the murders, so-called "Spider Tracers" have definitely been found on each victim, leaving no doubt as to the involvement of Spider-Man. Spider-Man is already wanted for violations of…

CONTINUED ON A-2

JUST BLAME SPIDER-MAN

Bob Gale-writer **Phil Jimenez-**pencils **Andy Lanning-**inks **Jeromy Cox-**colors **VC's Cory Petit-**letters
Thomas Brennan-assistant editor **Stephen Whack Her-**editor **Tom Brevoort-**executive editor
Joe Quesada-editor-in-chief **Dan Buckley-**publisher **Gale, Guggenheim, Slott, Wells-**Spidey Braintrust

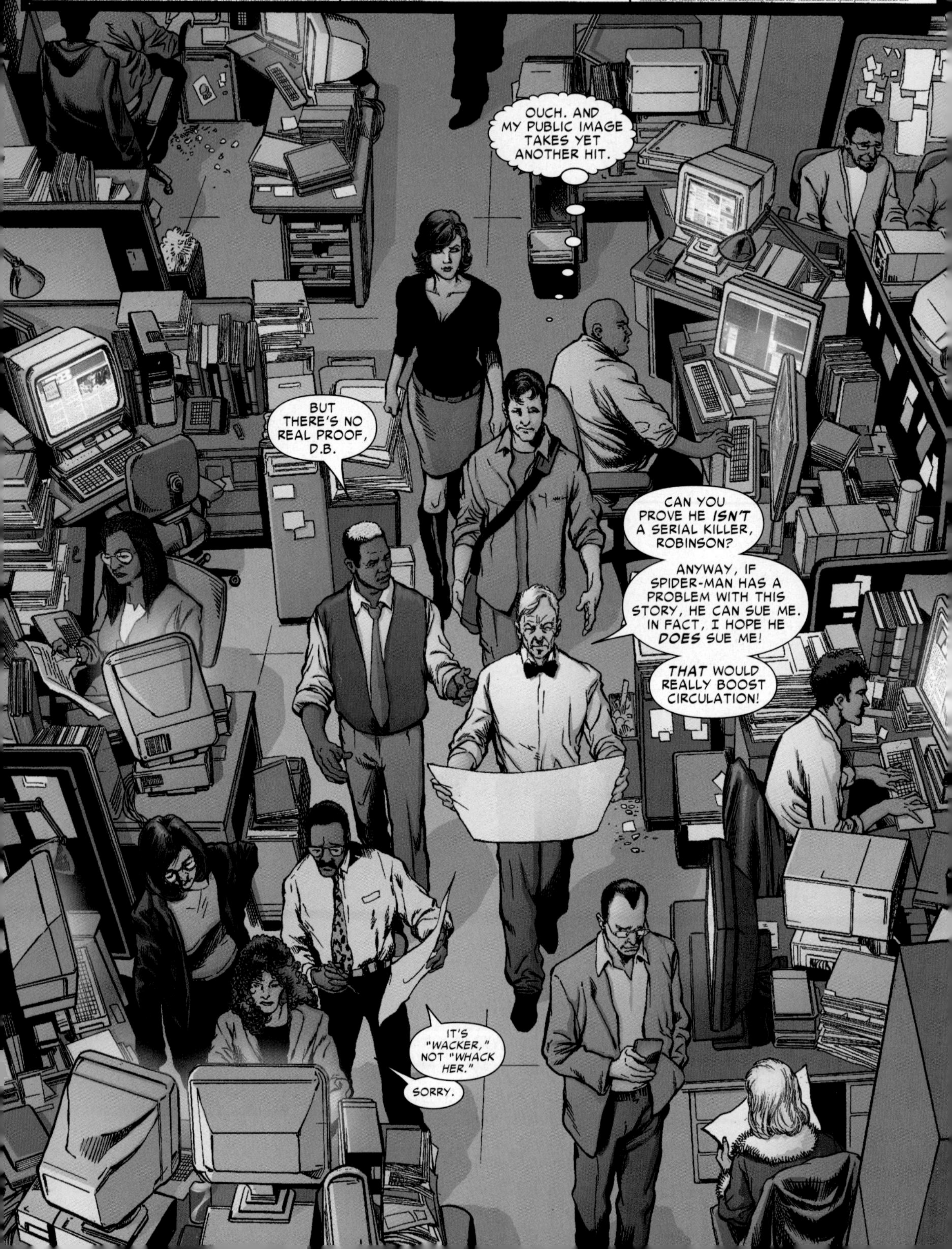
OUCH. AND MY PUBLIC IMAGE TAKES YET ANOTHER HIT.
BUT THERE'S NO REAL PROOF, D.B.
CAN YOU PROVE HE ISN'T A SERIAL KILLER, ROBINSON?
ANYWAY, IF SPIDER-MAN HAS A PROBLEM WITH THIS STORY, HE CAN SUE ME. IN FACT, I HOPE HE DOES SUE ME!
THAT WOULD REALLY BOOST CIRCULATION!
IT'S "WACKER," NOT "WHACK HER."
SORRY.

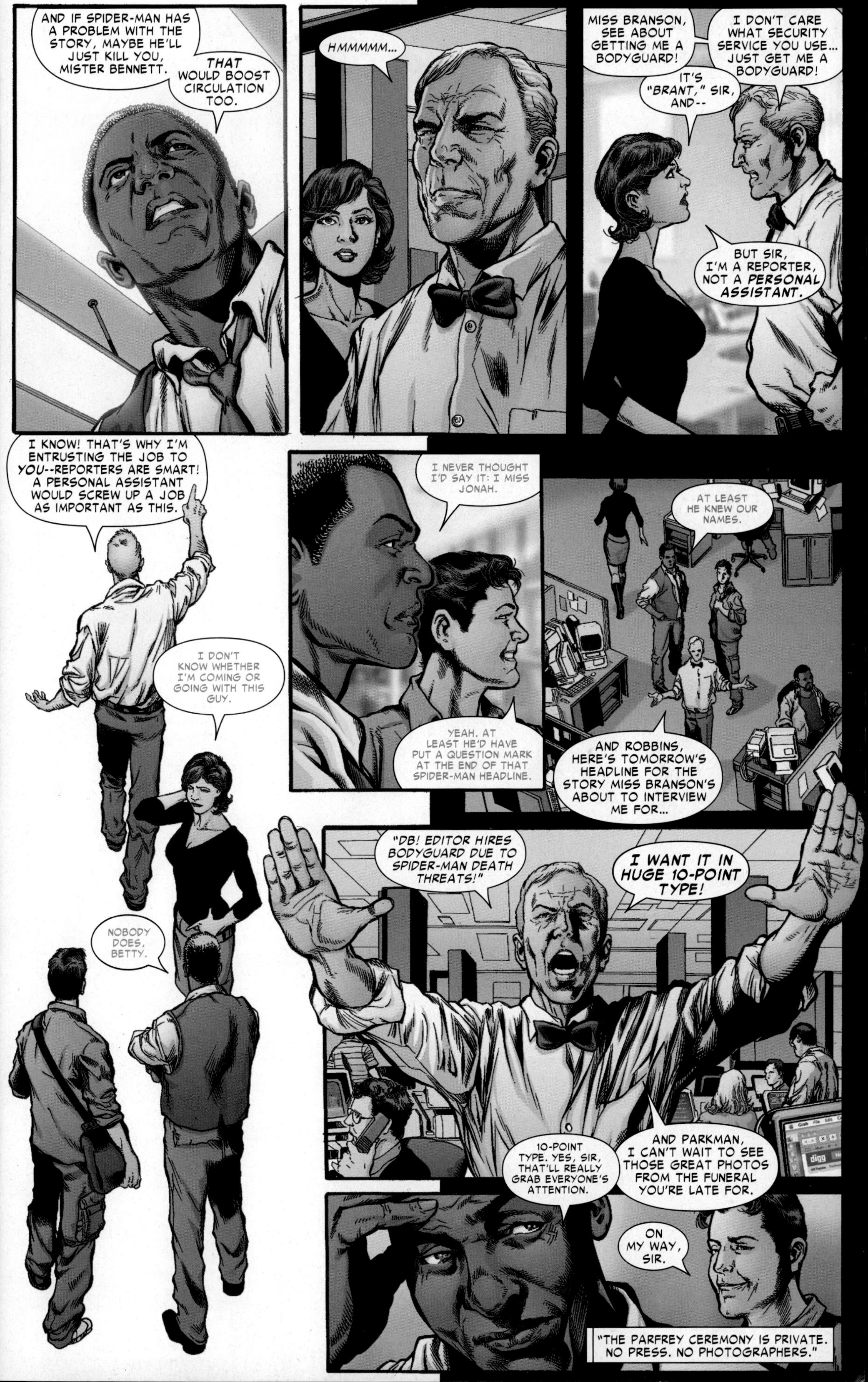
AND IF SPIDER-MAN HAS A PROBLEM WITH THE STORY, MAYBE HE'LL JUST KILL YOU, MISTER BENNETT.
THAT WOULD BOOST CIRCULATION TOO.
HMMMMM...
MISS BRANSON, SEE ABOUT GETTING ME A BODYGUARD!
IT'S "BRANT," SIR, AND--
I DON'T CARE WHAT SECURITY SERVICE YOU USE... JUST GET ME A BODYGUARD!
BUT SIR, I'M A REPORTER, NOT A PERSONAL ASSISTANT.
I KNOW! THAT'S WHY I'M ENTRUSTING THE JOB TO YOU--REPORTERS ARE SMART! A PERSONAL ASSISTANT WOULD SCREW UP A JOB AS IMPORTANT AS THIS.
I DON'T KNOW WHETHER I'M COMING OR GOING WITH THIS GUY.
NOBODY DOES, BETTY.
I NEVER THOUGHT I'D SAY IT: I MISS JONAH.
YEAH. AT LEAST HE'D HAVE PUT A QUESTION MARK AT THE END OF THAT SPIDER-MAN HEADLINE.
AT LEAST HE KNEW OUR NAMES.
AND ROBBINS, HERE'S TOMORROW'S HEADLINE FOR THE STORY MISS BRANSON'S ABOUT TO INTERVIEW ME FOR...
"DB! EDITOR HIRES BODYGUARD DUE TO SPIDER-MAN DEATH THREATS!"
I WANT IT IN HUGE 10-POINT TYPE!
10-POINT TYPE. YES, SIR, THAT'LL REALLY GRAB EVERYONE'S ATTENTION.
AND PARKMAN, I CAN'T WAIT TO SEE THOSE GREAT PHOTOS FROM THE FUNERAL YOU'RE LATE FOR.
ON MY WAY, SIR.
"THE PARFREY CEREMONY IS PRIVATE. NO PRESS. NO PHOTOGRAPHERS."

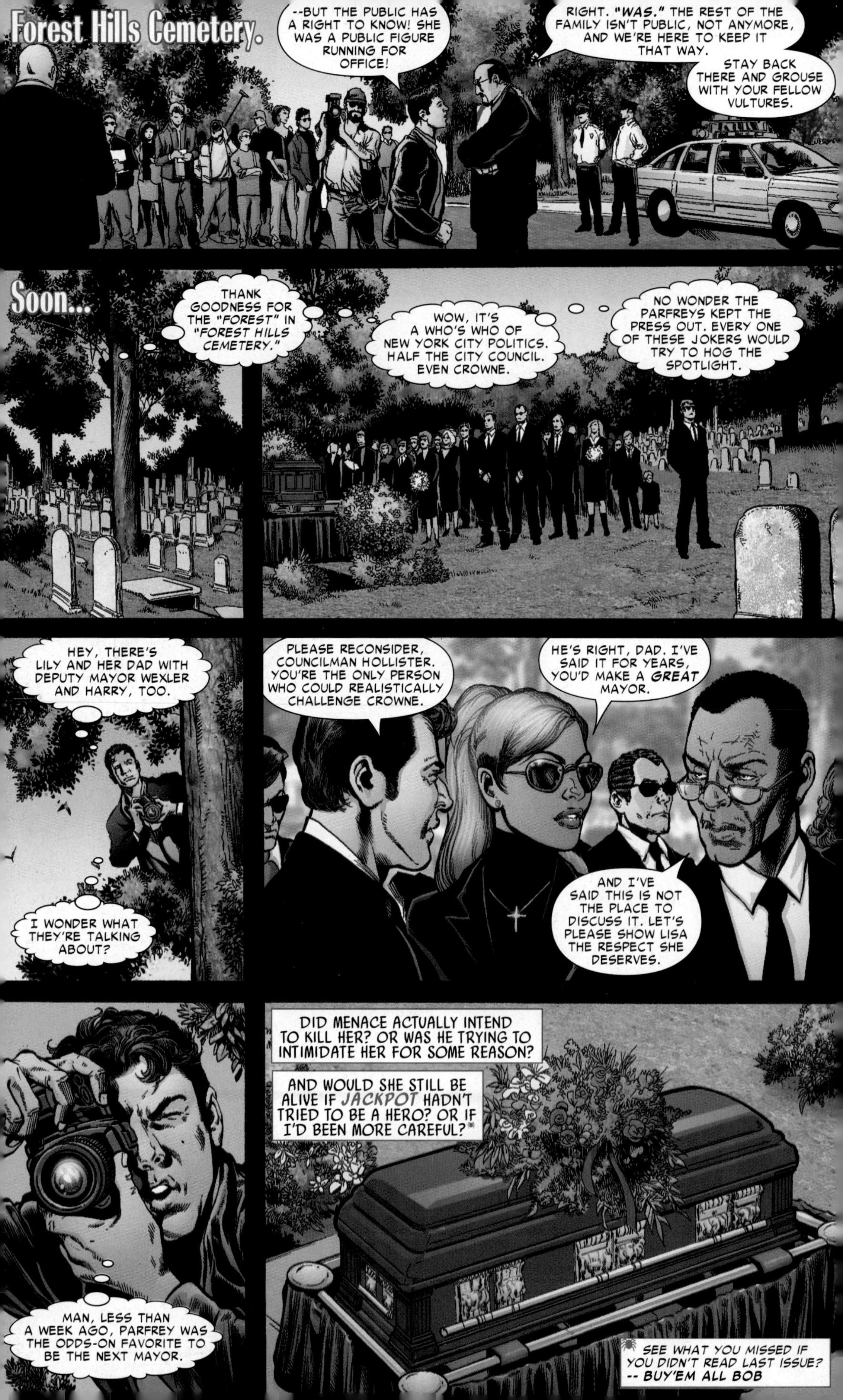
Forest Hills Cemetery.
--BUT THE PUBLIC HAS A RIGHT TO KNOW! SHE WAS A PUBLIC FIGURE RUNNING FOR OFFICE!
RIGHT. "WAS." THE REST OF THE FAMILY ISN'T PUBLIC, NOT ANYMORE, AND WE'RE HERE TO KEEP IT THAT WAY.
STAY BACK THERE AND GROUSE WITH YOUR FELLOW VULTURES.
Soon...
THANK GOODNESS FOR THE "FOREST" IN "FOREST HILLS CEMETERY."
WOW, IT'S A WHO'S WHO OF NEW YORK CITY POLITICS. HALF THE CITY COUNCIL. EVEN CROWNE.
NO WONDER THE PARFREYS KEPT THE PRESS OUT. EVERY ONE OF THESE JOKERS WOULD TRY TO HOG THE SPOTLIGHT.
HEY, THERE'S LILY AND HER DAD WITH DEPUTY MAYOR WEXLER AND HARRY, TOO.
I WONDER WHAT THEY'RE TALKING ABOUT?
PLEASE RECONSIDER, COUNCILMAN HOLLISTER. YOU'RE THE ONLY PERSON WHO COULD REALISTICALLY CHALLENGE CROWNE.
HE'S RIGHT, DAD. I'VE SAID IT FOR YEARS, YOU'D MAKE A GREAT MAYOR.
AND I'VE SAID THIS IS NOT THE PLACE TO DISCUSS IT. LET'S PLEASE SHOW LISA THE RESPECT SHE DESERVES.
MAN, LESS THAN A WEEK AGO, PARFREY WAS THE ODDS-ON FAVORITE TO BE THE NEXT MAYOR.
DID MENACE ACTUALLY INTEND TO KILL HER? OR WAS HE TRYING TO INTIMIDATE HER FOR SOME REASON?
AND WOULD SHE STILL BE ALIVE IF JACKPOT HADN'T TRIED TO BE A HERO? OR IF I'D BEEN MORE CAREFUL?*
*SEE WHAT YOU MISSED IF YOU DIDN'T READ LAST ISSUE? -- BUY'EM ALL BOB

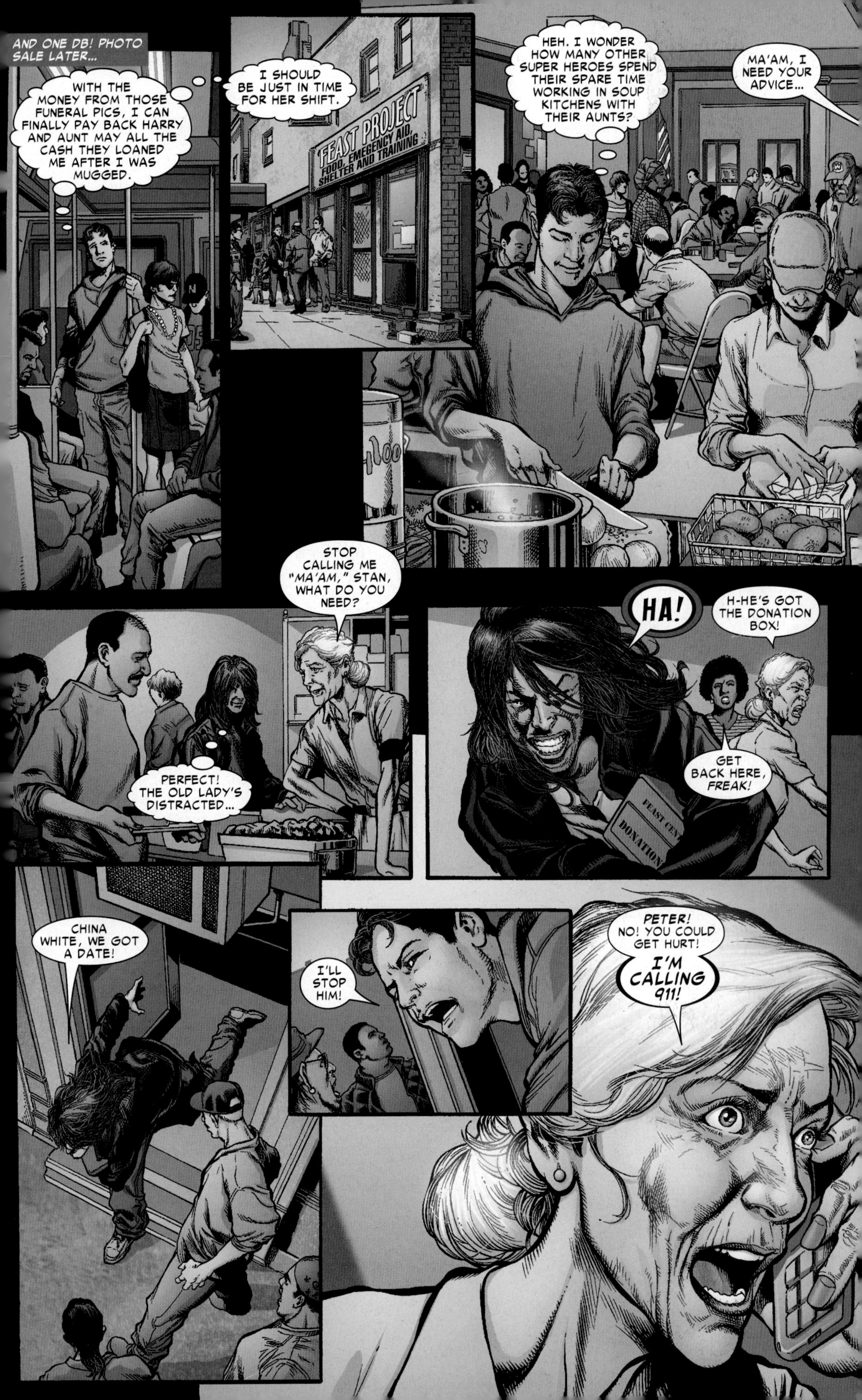
AND ONE DB! PHOTO SALE LATER...
WITH THE MONEY FROM THOSE FUNERAL PICS, I CAN FINALLY PAY BACK HARRY AND AUNT MAY ALL THE CASH THEY LOANED ME AFTER I WAS MUGGED.
I SHOULD BE JUST IN TIME FOR HER SHIFT.
FEAST PROJECT
FOOD, EMERGENCY AID, SHELTER AND TRAINING
HEH. I WONDER HOW MANY OTHER SUPER HEROES SPEND THEIR SPARE TIME WORKING IN SOUP KITCHENS WITH THEIR AUNTS?
MA'AM, I NEED YOUR ADVICE...
STOP CALLING ME "MA'AM," STAN, WHAT DO YOU NEED?
PERFECT! THE OLD LADY'S DISTRACTED...
HA!
H-HE'S GOT THE DONATION BOX!
GET BACK HERE, FREAK!
DONATION
CHINA WHITE, WE GOT A DATE!
I'LL STOP HIM!
PETER! NO! YOU COULD GET HURT!
I'M CALLING 911!

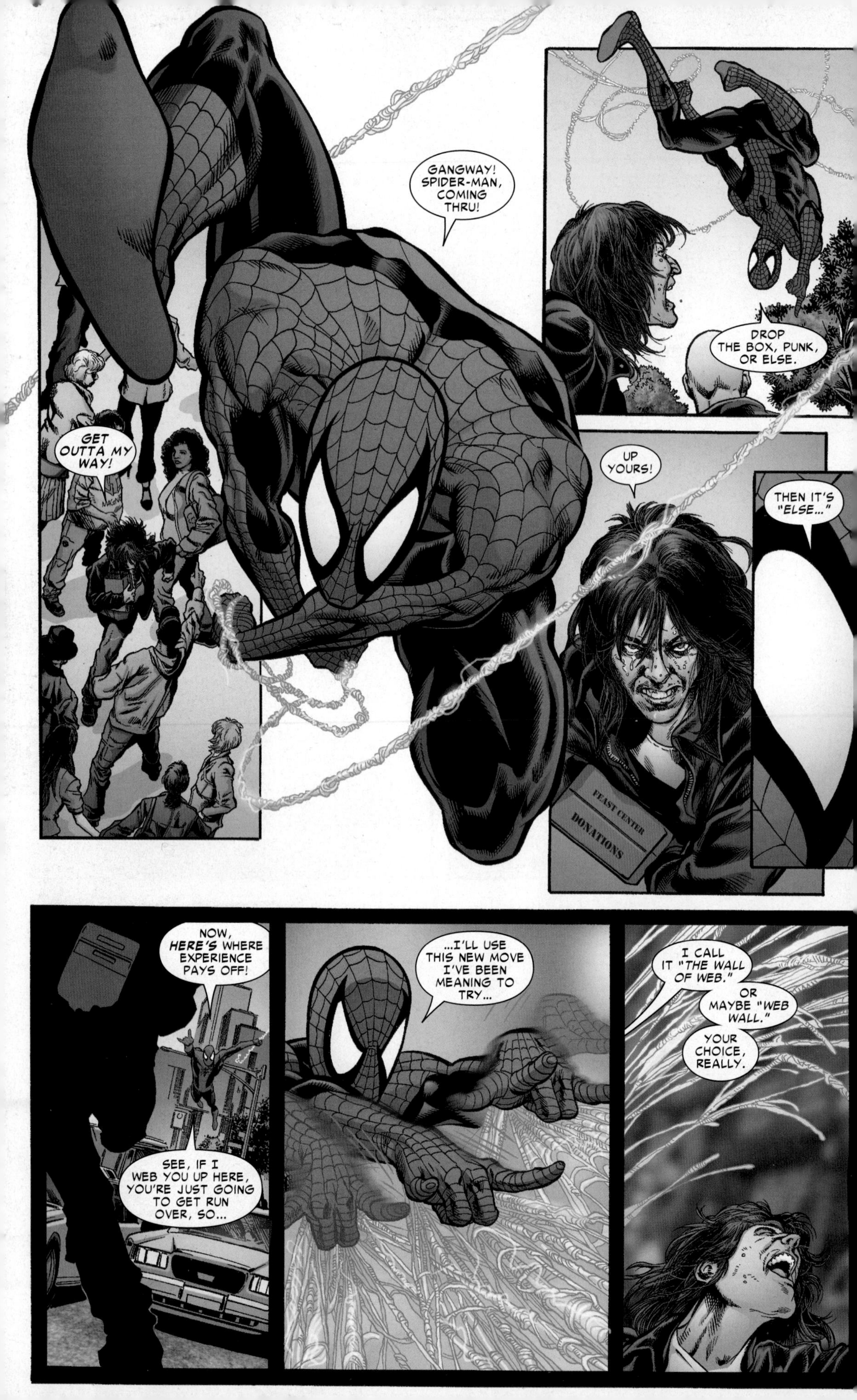
GANGWAY! SPIDER-MAN, COMING THRU!
GET OUTTA MY WAY!
DROP THE BOX, PUNK, OR ELSE.
UP YOURS!
THEN IT'S "ELSE..."
FEAST CENTER DONATIONS
NOW, HERE'S WHERE EXPERIENCE PAYS OFF!
SEE, IF I WEB YOU UP HERE, YOU'RE JUST GOING TO GET RUN OVER, SO...
...I'LL USE THIS NEW MOVE I'VE BEEN MEANING TO TRY...
I CALL IT "THE WALL OF WEB."
OR MAYBE "WEB WALL."
YOUR CHOICE, REALLY.

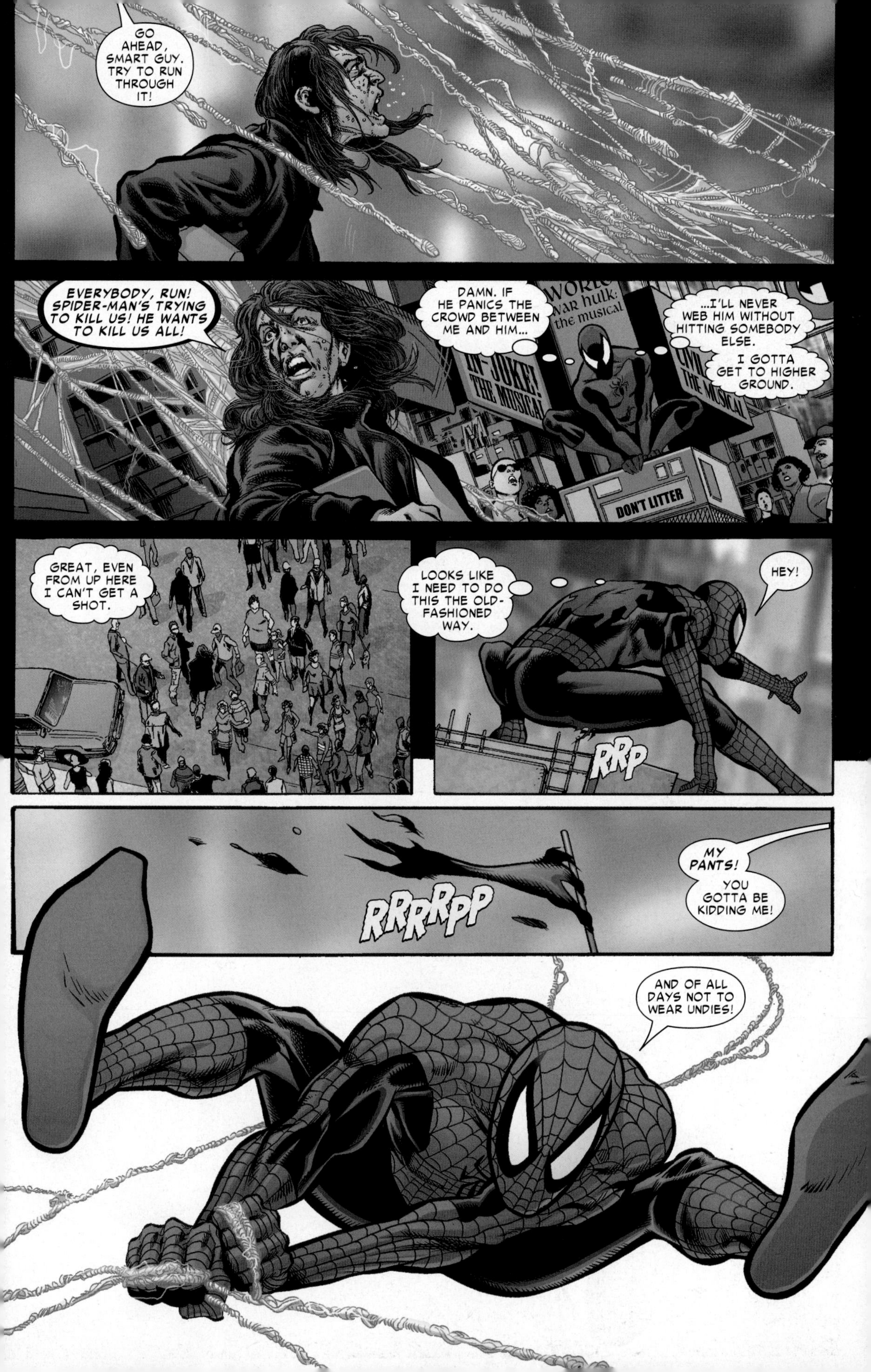
GO AHEAD, SMART GUY. TRY TO RUN THROUGH IT!
EVERYBODY, RUN! SPIDER-MAN'S TRYING TO KILL US! HE WANTS TO KILL US ALL!
DAMN. IF HE PANICS THE CROWD BETWEEN ME AND HIM...
...I'LL NEVER WEB HIM WITHOUT HITTING SOMEBODY ELSE.
I GOTTA GET TO HIGHER GROUND.
IN-JUKE! THE MUSICAL
war hulk: the musical
DON'T LITTER
GREAT, EVEN FROM UP HERE I CAN'T GET A SHOT.
LOOKS LIKE I NEED TO DO THIS THE OLD-FASHIONED WAY.
HEY!
RRP
RRRRPP
MY PANTS!
YOU GOTTA BE KIDDING ME!
AND OF ALL DAYS NOT TO WEAR UNDIES!

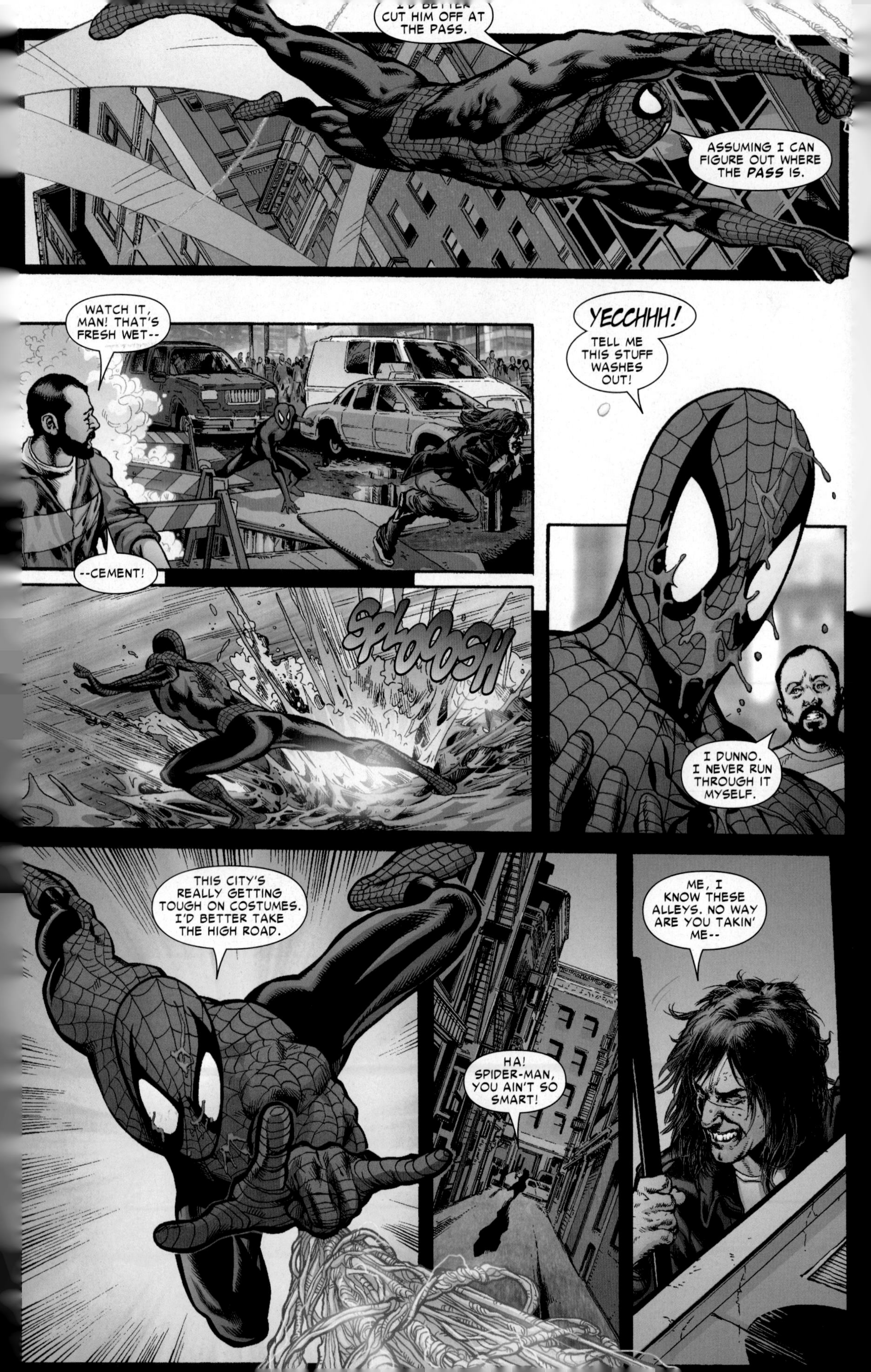
CUT HIM OFF AT THE PASS.
ASSUMING I CAN FIGURE OUT WHERE THE PASS IS.
WATCH IT, MAN! THAT'S FRESH WET--
--CEMENT!
SPLOOOSH
YECCHHH! TELL ME THIS STUFF WASHES OUT!
I DUNNO. I NEVER RUN THROUGH IT MYSELF.
THIS CITY'S REALLY GETTING TOUGH ON COSTUMES. I'D BETTER TAKE THE HIGH ROAD.
HA! SPIDER-MAN, YOU AIN'T SO SMART!
ME, I KNOW THESE ALLEYS. NO WAY ARE YOU TAKIN' ME--

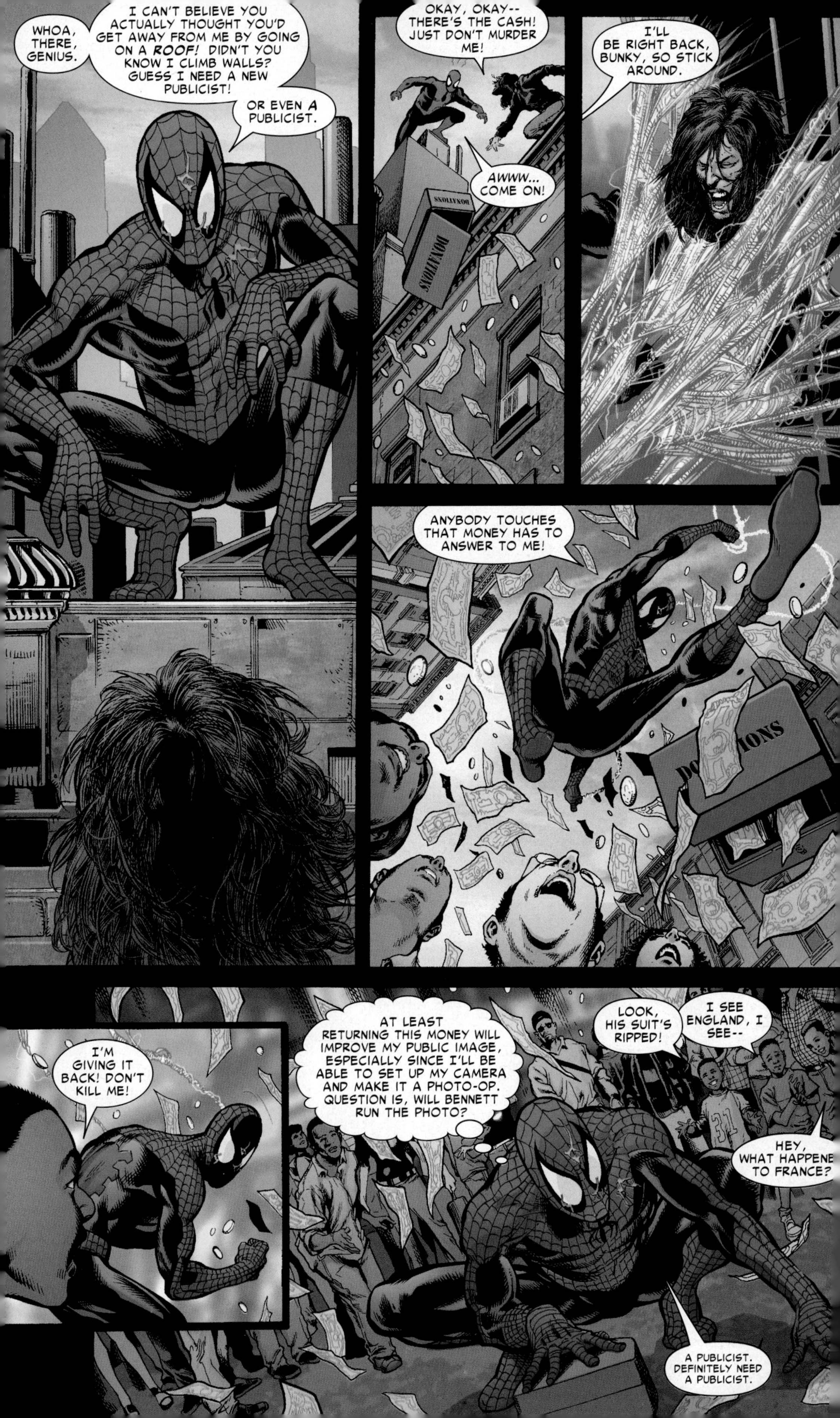
WHOA, THERE, GENIUS.
I CAN'T BELIEVE YOU ACTUALLY THOUGHT YOU'D GET AWAY FROM ME BY GOING ON A *ROOF!* DIDN'T YOU KNOW I CLIMB WALLS? GUESS I NEED A NEW PUBLICIST!
OR EVEN *A* PUBLICIST.
OKAY, OKAY-- THERE'S THE CASH! JUST DON'T MURDER ME!
AWWW... COME ON!
DONATIONS
I'LL BE RIGHT BACK, BUNKY, SO STICK AROUND.
ANYBODY TOUCHES THAT MONEY HAS TO ANSWER TO ME!
I'M GIVING IT BACK! DON'T KILL ME!
AT LEAST RETURNING THIS MONEY WILL IMPROVE MY PUBLIC IMAGE, ESPECIALLY SINCE I'LL BE ABLE TO SET UP MY CAMERA AND MAKE IT A PHOTO-OP. QUESTION IS, WILL BENNETT RUN THE PHOTO?
LOOK, HIS SUIT'S RIPPED!
I SEE ENGLAND, I SEE--
HEY, WHAT HAPPENE TO FRANCE?
A PUBLICIST. DEFINITELY NEED A PUBLICIST.

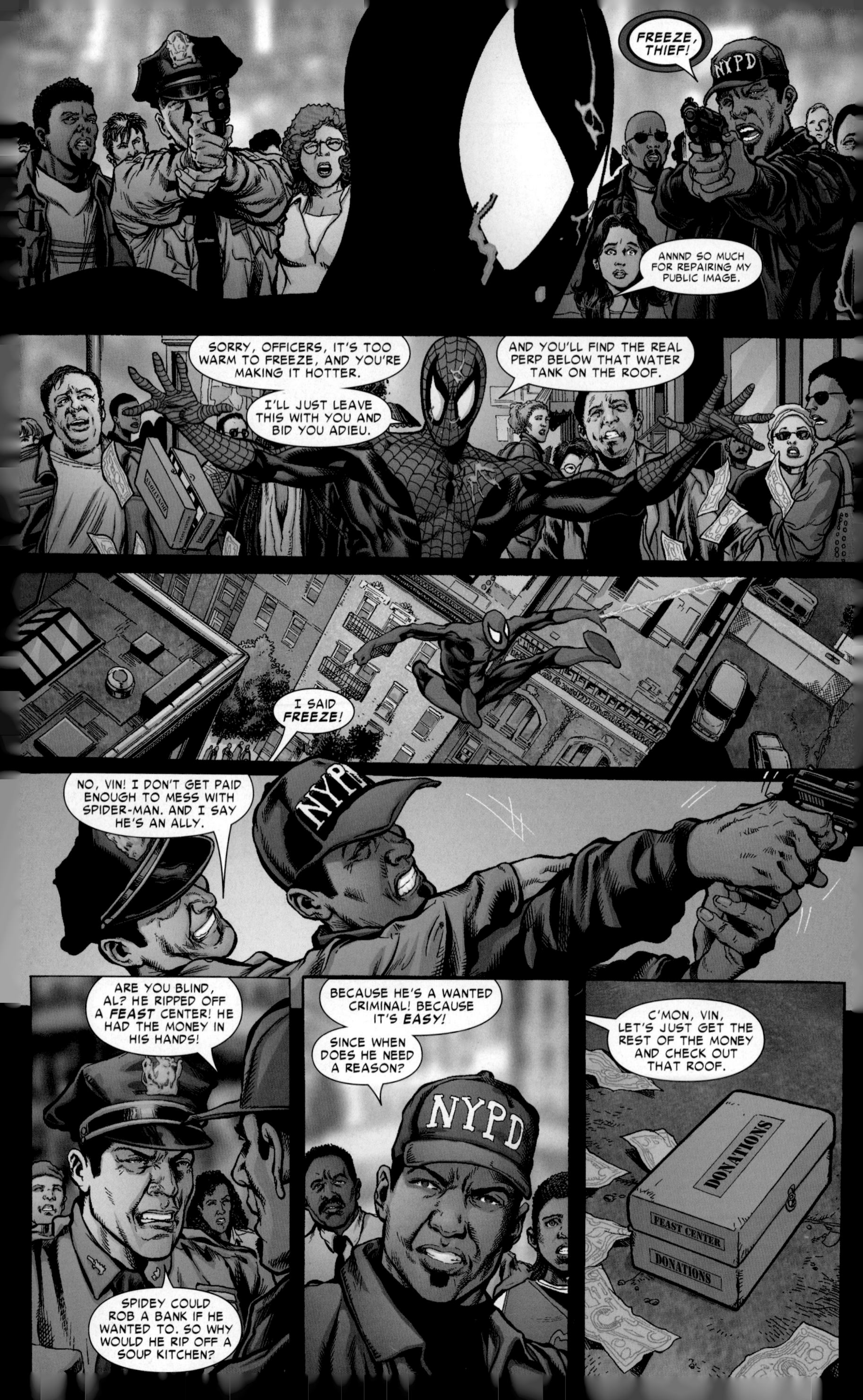
FREEZE, THIEF!
ANNND SO MUCH FOR REPAIRING MY PUBLIC IMAGE.
SORRY, OFFICERS, IT'S TOO WARM TO FREEZE, AND YOU'RE MAKING IT HOTTER.
I'LL JUST LEAVE THIS WITH YOU AND BID YOU ADIEU.
AND YOU'LL FIND THE REAL PERP BELOW THAT WATER TANK ON THE ROOF.
I SAID FREEZE!
NO, VIN! I DON'T GET PAID ENOUGH TO MESS WITH SPIDER-MAN. AND I SAY HE'S AN ALLY.
NYPD
ARE YOU BLIND, AL? HE RIPPED OFF A FEAST CENTER! HE HAD THE MONEY IN HIS HANDS!
SPIDEY COULD ROB A BANK IF HE WANTED TO. SO WHY WOULD HE RIP OFF A SOUP KITCHEN?
BECAUSE HE'S A WANTED CRIMINAL! BECAUSE IT'S EASY!
SINCE WHEN DOES HE NEED A REASON?
NYPD
C'MON, VIN, LET'S JUST GET THE REST OF THE MONEY AND CHECK OUT THAT ROOF.
DONATIONS
FEAST CENTER
DONATIONS

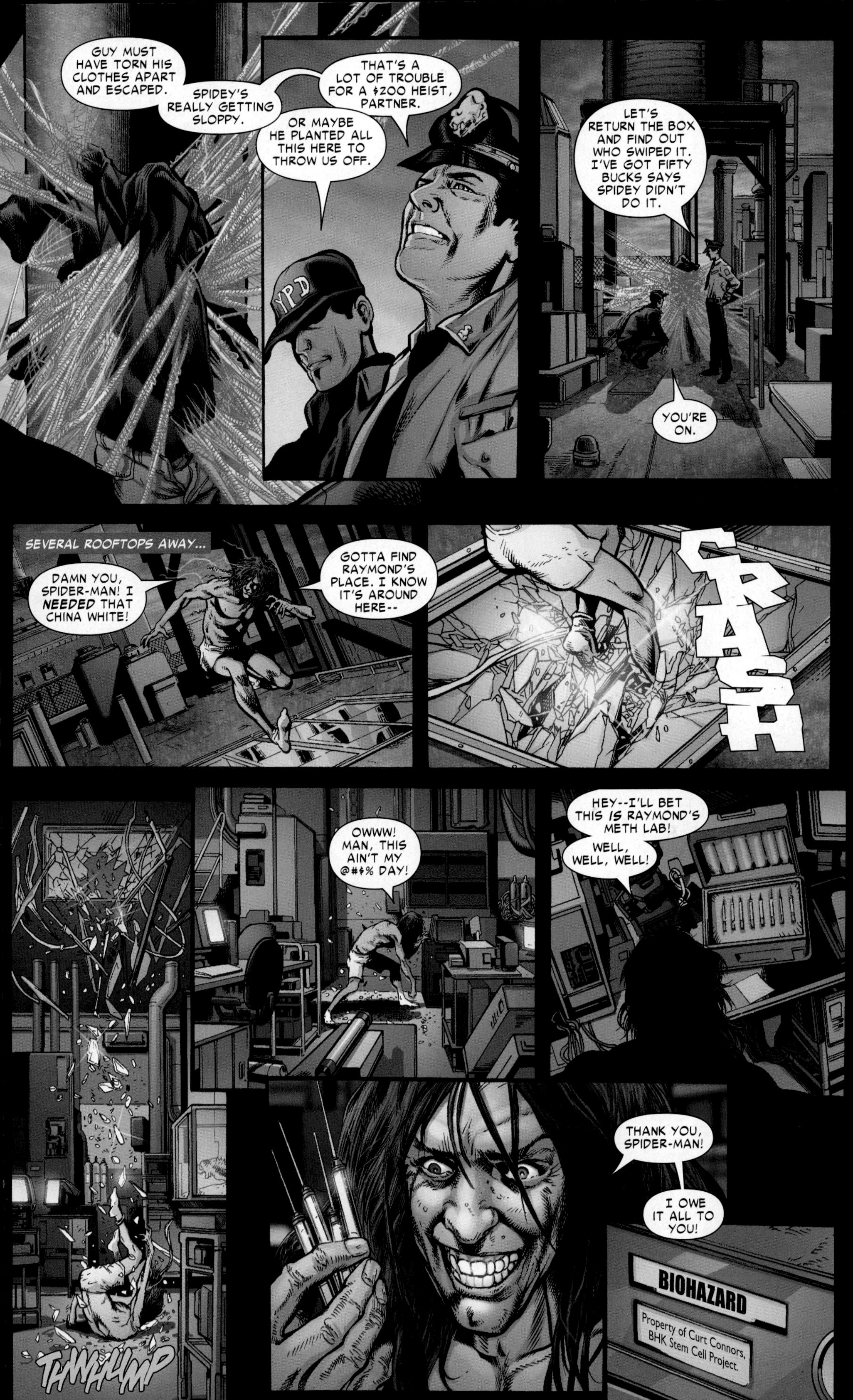
GUY MUST HAVE TORN HIS CLOTHES APART AND ESCAPED.
SPIDEY'S REALLY GETTING SLOPPY.
THAT'S A LOT OF TROUBLE FOR A $200 HEIST, PARTNER.
OR MAYBE HE PLANTED ALL THIS HERE TO THROW US OFF.
YPD
LET'S RETURN THE BOX AND FIND OUT WHO SWIPED IT. I'VE GOT FIFTY BUCKS SAYS SPIDEY DIDN'T DO IT.
YOU'RE ON.
SEVERAL ROOFTOPS AWAY...
DAMN YOU, SPIDER-MAN! I NEEDED THAT CHINA WHITE!
GOTTA FIND RAYMOND'S PLACE. I KNOW IT'S AROUND HERE--
CRASH
THWHUMP
OWWW! MAN, THIS AIN'T MY @#$% DAY!
HEY--I'LL BET THIS IS RAYMOND'S METH LAB!
WELL, WELL, WELL!
THANK YOU, SPIDER-MAN!
I OWE IT ALL TO YOU!
BIOHAZARD
Property of Curt Connors, BHK Stem Cell Project.

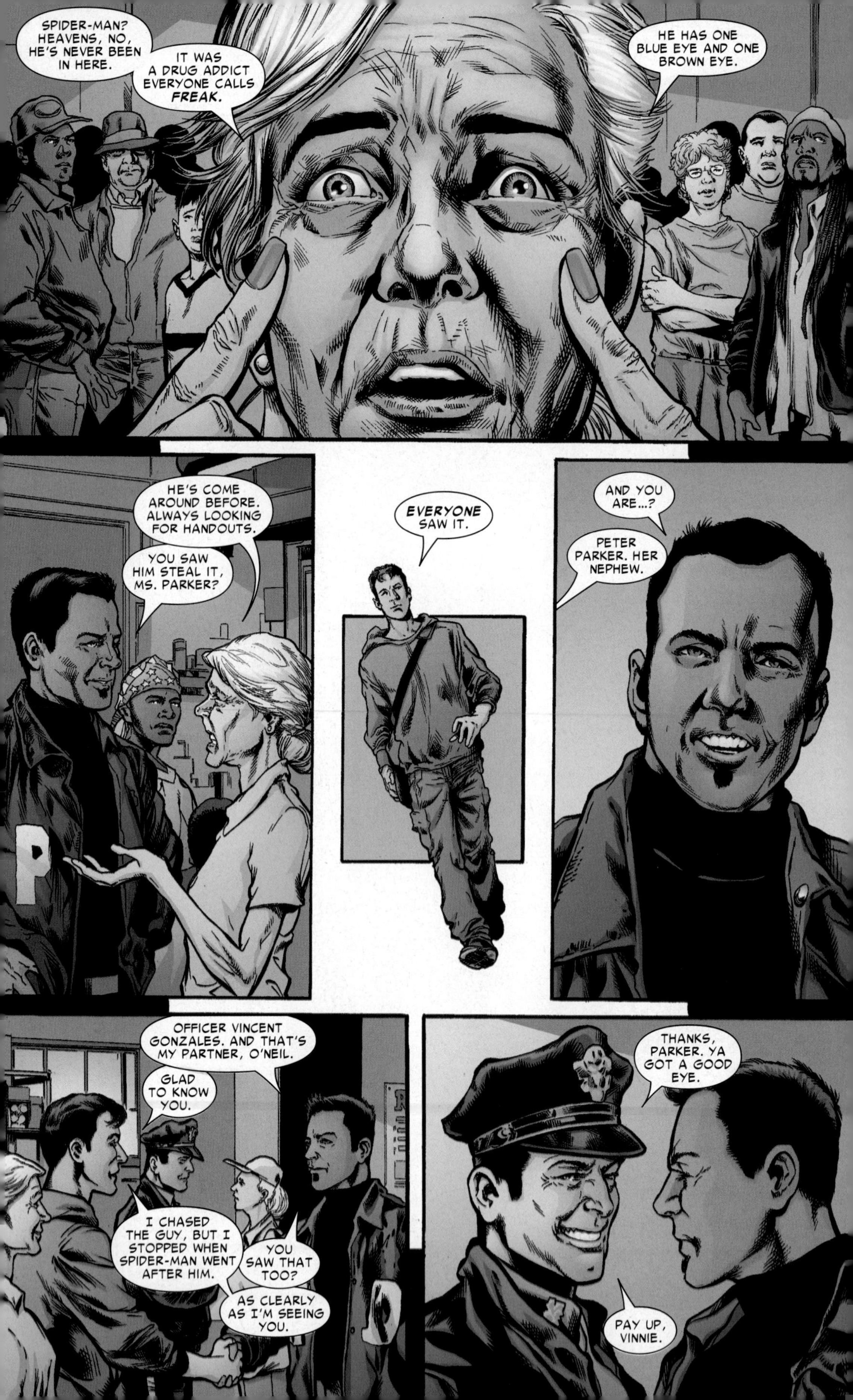
SPIDER-MAN? HEAVENS, NO, HE'S NEVER BEEN IN HERE.
IT WAS A DRUG ADDICT EVERYONE CALLS *FREAK.*
HE HAS ONE BLUE EYE AND ONE BROWN EYE.
HE'S COME AROUND BEFORE. ALWAYS LOOKING FOR HANDOUTS.
YOU SAW HIM STEAL IT, MS. PARKER?
EVERYONE SAW IT.
AND YOU ARE...?
PETER PARKER. HER NEPHEW.
OFFICER VINCENT GONZALES. AND THAT'S MY PARTNER, O'NEIL.
GLAD TO KNOW YOU.
I CHASED THE GUY, BUT I STOPPED WHEN SPIDER-MAN WENT AFTER HIM.
YOU SAW THAT TOO?
AS CLEARLY AS I'M SEEING YOU.
THANKS, PARKER. YA GOT A GOOD EYE.
PAY UP, VINNIE.

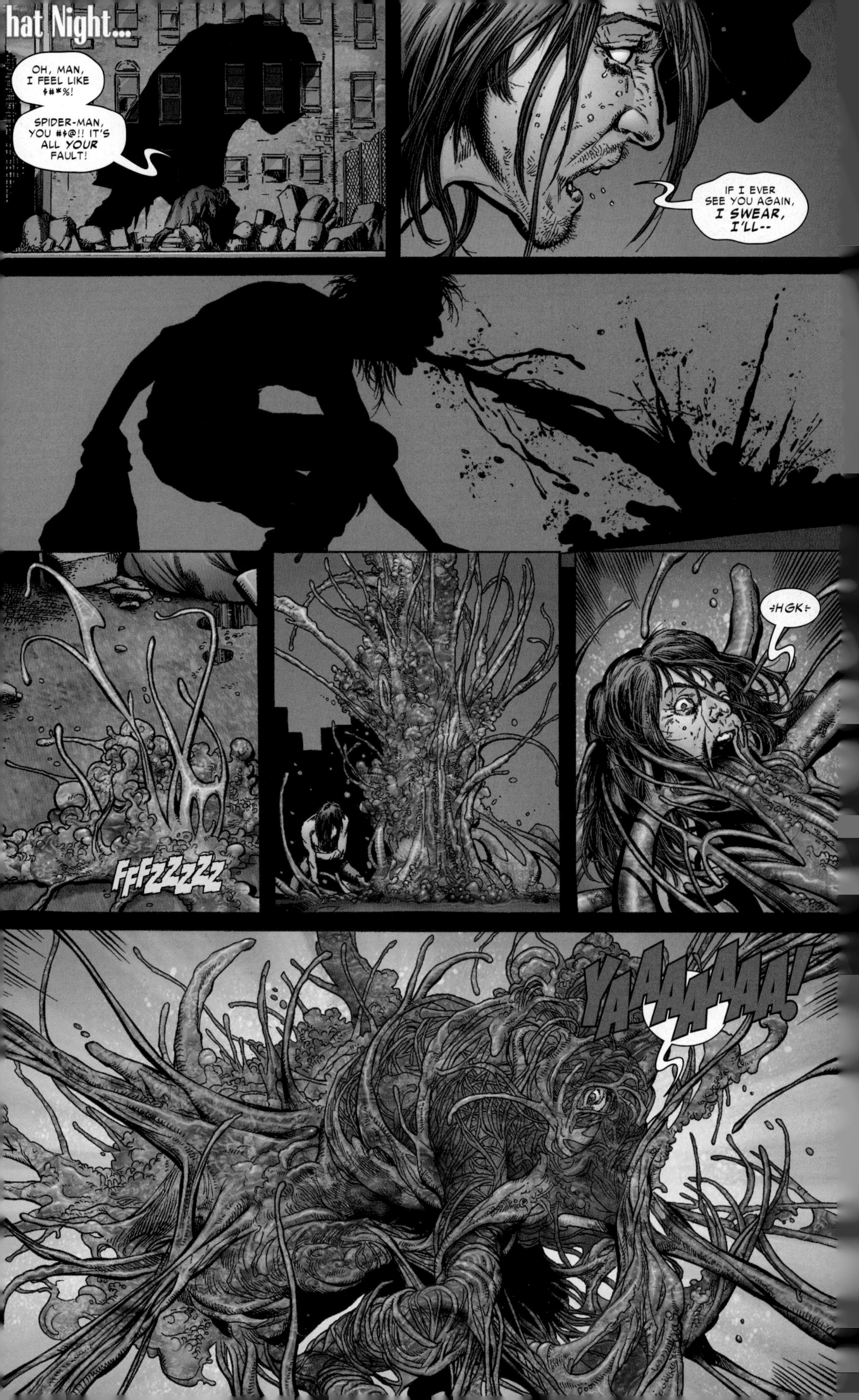
hat Night...
OH, MAN, I FEEL LIKE $#*%!
SPIDER-MAN, YOU #$@!! IT'S ALL YOUR FAULT!
IF I EVER SEE YOU AGAIN, I SWEAR, I'LL--
FFFZZZZZ
HGK
YAAAAAA!

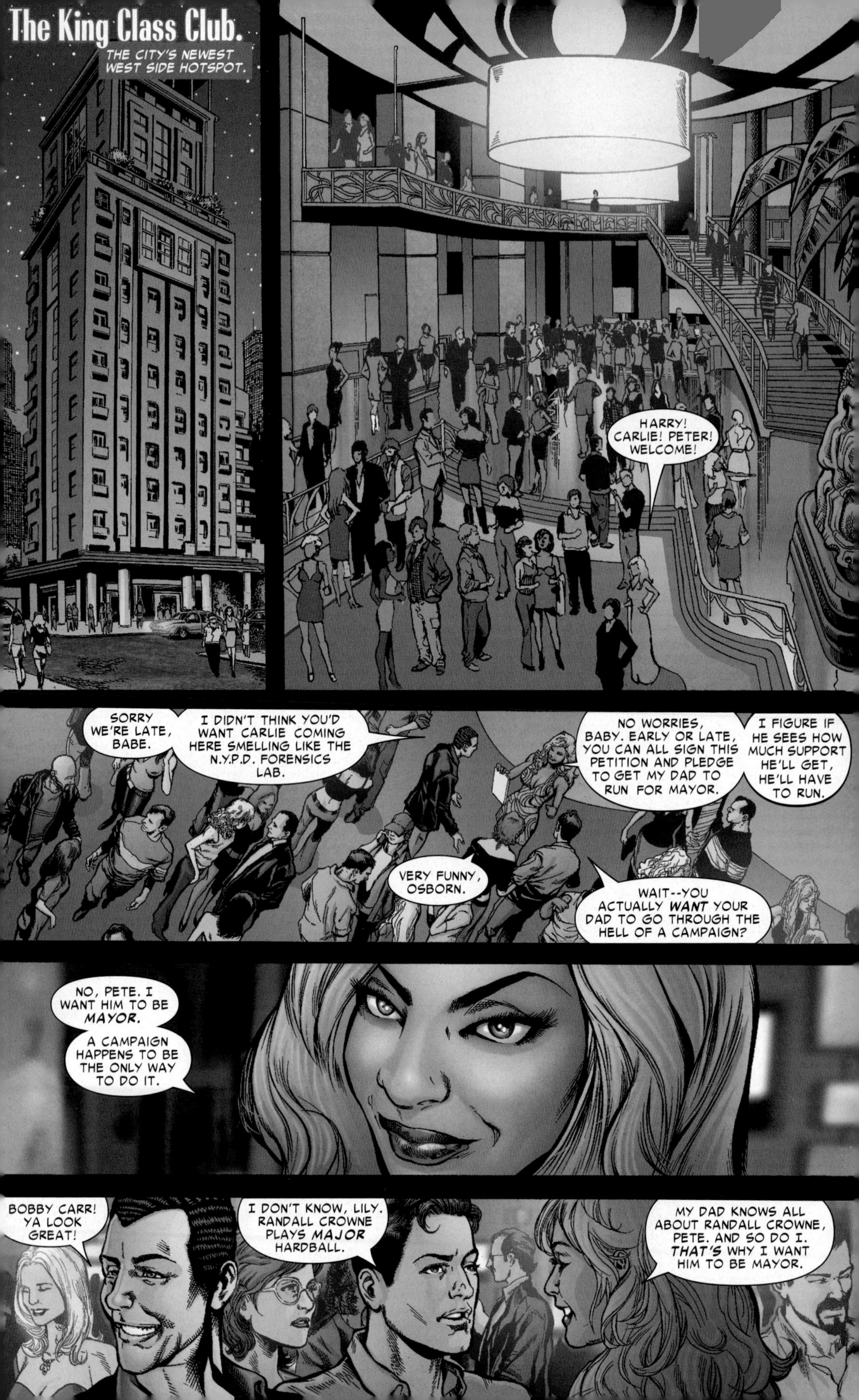

The King Class Club.
THE CITY'S NEWEST WEST SIDE HOTSPOT.
HARRY! CARLIE! PETER! WELCOME!
SORRY WE'RE LATE, BABE.
I DIDN'T THINK YOU'D WANT CARLIE COMING HERE SMELLING LIKE THE N.Y.P.D. FORENSICS LAB.
NO WORRIES, BABY. EARLY OR LATE, YOU CAN ALL SIGN THIS PETITION AND PLEDGE TO GET MY DAD TO RUN FOR MAYOR.
I FIGURE IF HE SEES HOW MUCH SUPPORT HE'LL GET, HE'LL HAVE TO RUN.
VERY FUNNY, OSBORN.
WAIT--YOU ACTUALLY WANT YOUR DAD TO GO THROUGH THE HELL OF A CAMPAIGN?
NO, PETE. I WANT HIM TO BE MAYOR.
A CAMPAIGN HAPPENS TO BE THE ONLY WAY TO DO IT.
BOBBY CARR! YA LOOK GREAT!
I DON'T KNOW, LILY. RANDALL CROWNE PLAYS MAJOR HARDBALL.
MY DAD KNOWS ALL ABOUT RANDALL CROWNE, PETE. AND SO DO I. THAT'S WHY I WANT HIM TO BE MAYOR.

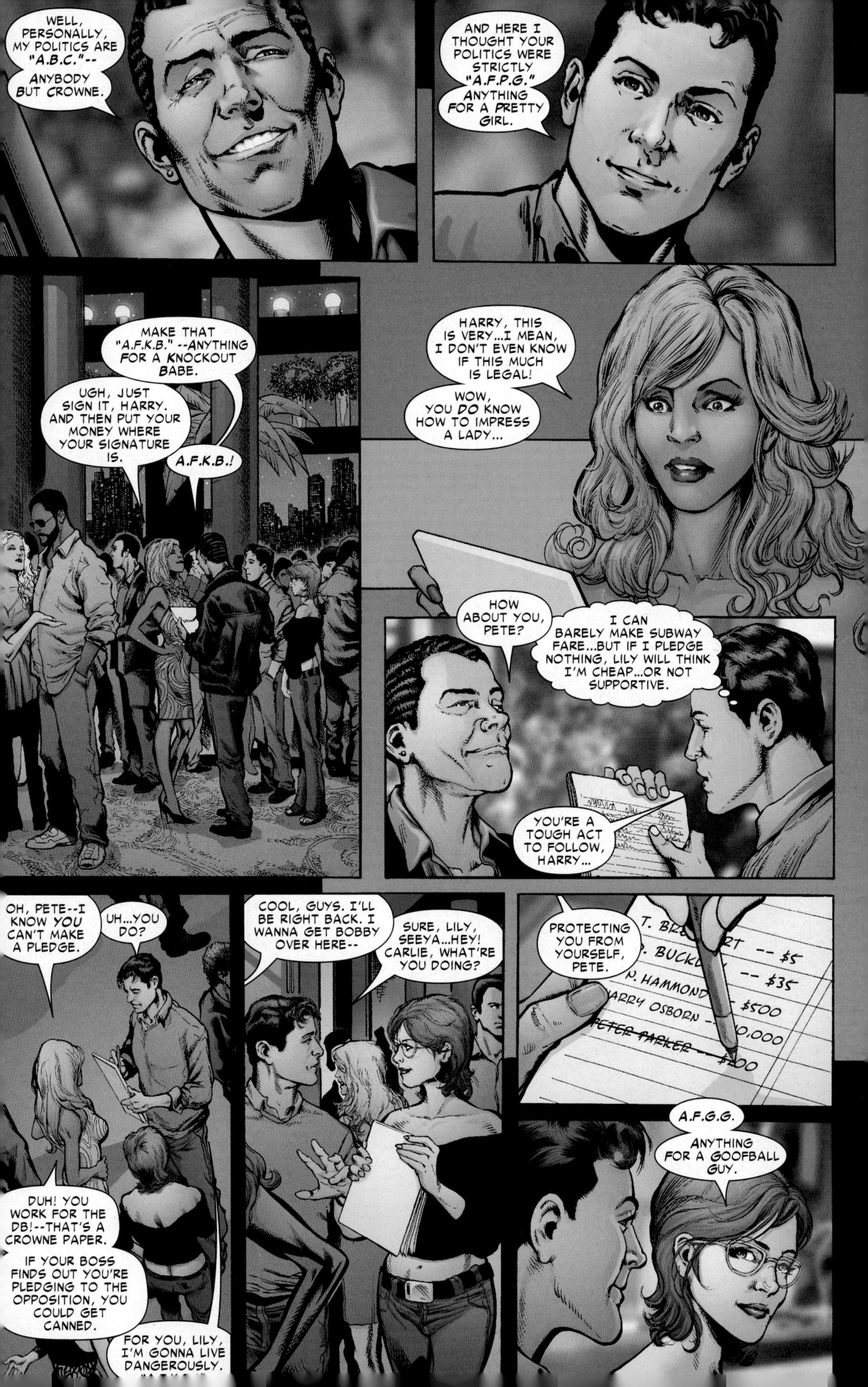
WELL, PERSONALLY, MY POLITICS ARE "A.B.C."-- ANYBODY BUT CROWNE.
AND HERE I THOUGHT YOUR POLITICS WERE STRICTLY "A.F.P.G." ANYTHING FOR A PRETTY GIRL.
MAKE THAT "A.F.K.B." --ANYTHING FOR A KNOCKOUT BABE.
UGH, JUST SIGN IT, HARRY. AND THEN PUT YOUR MONEY WHERE YOUR SIGNATURE IS.
A.F.K.B.!
HARRY, THIS IS VERY...I MEAN, I DON'T EVEN KNOW IF THIS MUCH IS LEGAL!
WOW, YOU DO KNOW HOW TO IMPRESS A LADY...
HOW ABOUT YOU, PETE?
I CAN BARELY MAKE SUBWAY FARE...BUT IF I PLEDGE NOTHING, LILY WILL THINK I'M CHEAP...OR NOT SUPPORTIVE.
YOU'RE A TOUGH ACT TO FOLLOW, HARRY...
OH, PETE--I KNOW YOU CAN'T MAKE A PLEDGE.
UH...YOU DO?
DUH! YOU WORK FOR THE DB!--THAT'S A CROWNE PAPER.
IF YOUR BOSS FINDS OUT YOU'RE PLEDGING TO THE OPPOSITION, YOU COULD GET CANNED.
FOR YOU, LILY, I'M GONNA LIVE DANGEROUSLY.
COOL, GUYS. I'LL BE RIGHT BACK. I WANNA GET BOBBY OVER HERE--
SURE, LILY, SEEYA...HEY! CARLIE, WHAT'RE YOU DOING?
PROTECTING YOU FROM YOURSELF, PETE.
HARRY OSBORN -- $500
PETER PARKER
A.F.G.G.
ANYTHING FOR A GOOFBALL GUY.

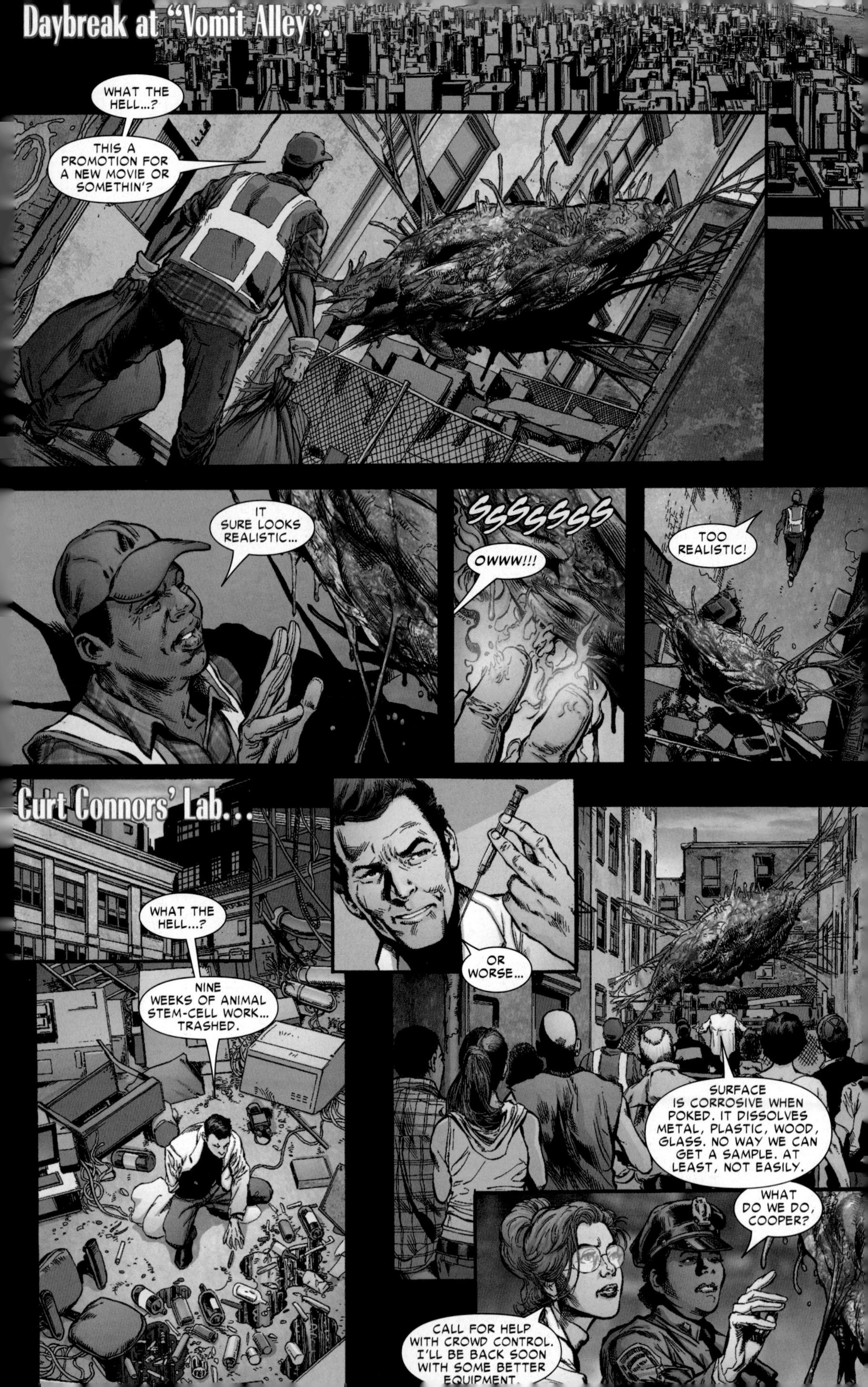
Daybreak at "Vomit Alley".
WHAT THE HELL...?
THIS A PROMOTION FOR A NEW MOVIE OR SOMETHIN'?
IT SURE LOOKS REALISTIC...
SSSSSSS
OWWW!!!
TOO REALISTIC!
Curt Connors' Lab...
WHAT THE HELL...?
NINE WEEKS OF ANIMAL STEM-CELL WORK... TRASHED.
OR WORSE...
SURFACE IS CORROSIVE WHEN POKED. IT DISSOLVES METAL, PLASTIC, WOOD, GLASS. NO WAY WE CAN GET A SAMPLE. AT LEAST, NOT EASILY.
WHAT DO WE DO, COOPER?
CALL FOR HELP WITH CROWD CONTROL. I'LL BE BACK SOON WITH SOME BETTER EQUIPMENT.

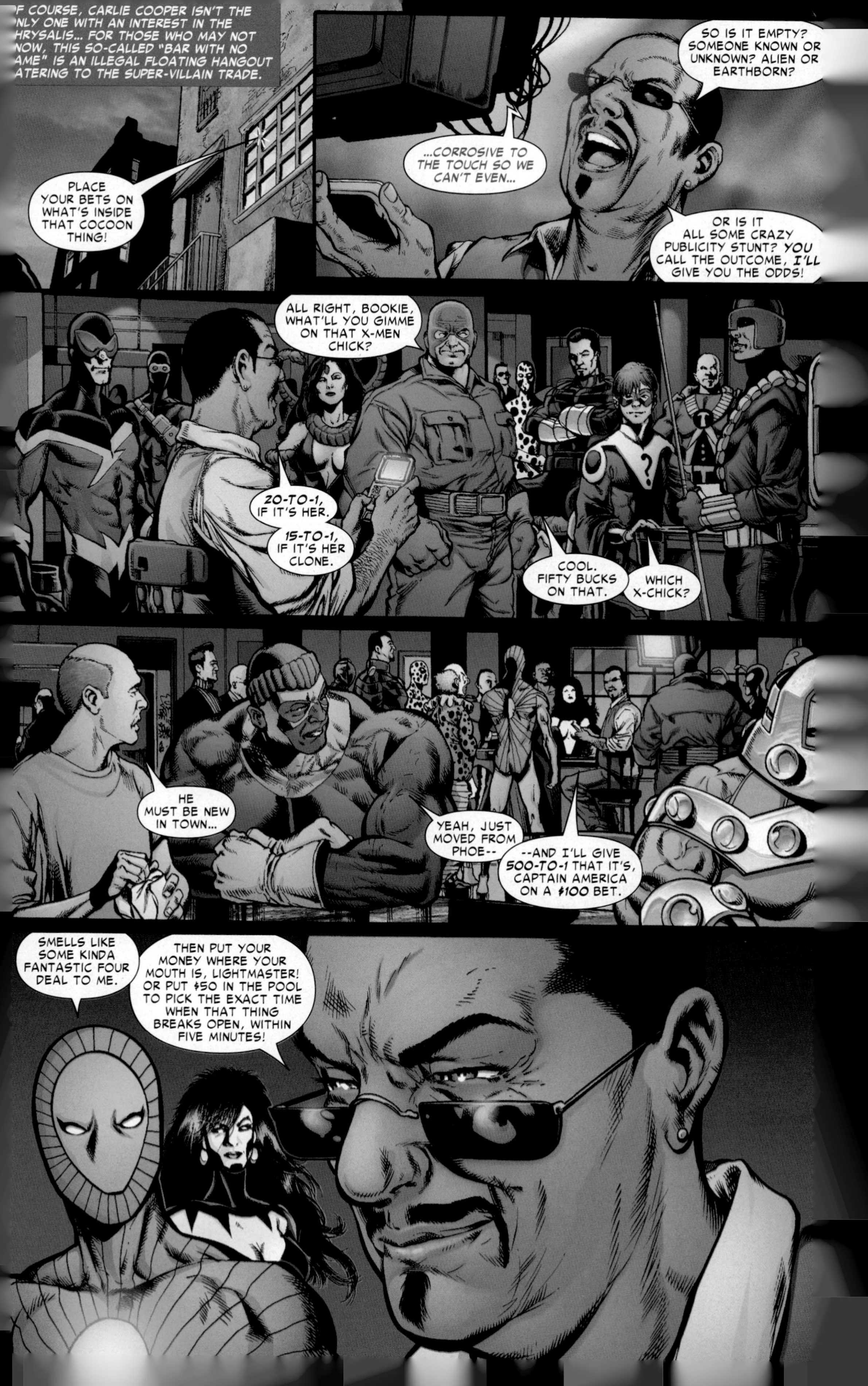
F COURSE, CARLIE COOPER ISN'T THE NLY ONE WITH AN INTEREST IN THE HRYSALIS... FOR THOSE WHO MAY NOT NOW, THIS SO-CALLED "BAR WITH NO AME" IS AN ILLEGAL FLOATING HANGOUT ATERING TO THE SUPER-VILLAIN TRADE.
PLACE YOUR BETS ON WHAT'S INSIDE THAT COCOON THING!
...CORROSIVE TO THE TOUCH SO WE CAN'T EVEN...
SO IS IT EMPTY? SOMEONE KNOWN OR UNKNOWN? ALIEN OR EARTHBORN?
OR IS IT ALL SOME CRAZY PUBLICITY STUNT? YOU CALL THE OUTCOME, I'LL GIVE YOU THE ODDS!
ALL RIGHT, BOOKIE, WHAT'LL YOU GIMME ON THAT X-MEN CHICK?
20-TO-1, IF IT'S HER.
15-TO-1, IF IT'S HER CLONE.
COOL. FIFTY BUCKS ON THAT.
WHICH X-CHICK?
HE MUST BE NEW IN TOWN...
YEAH, JUST MOVED FROM PHOE--
--AND I'LL GIVE 500-TO-1 THAT IT'S, CAPTAIN AMERICA ON A $100 BET.
SMELLS LIKE SOME KINDA FANTASTIC FOUR DEAL TO ME.
THEN PUT YOUR MONEY WHERE YOUR MOUTH IS, LIGHTMASTER! OR PUT $50 IN THE POOL TO PICK THE EXACT TIME WHEN THAT THING BREAKS OPEN, WITHIN FIVE MINUTES!

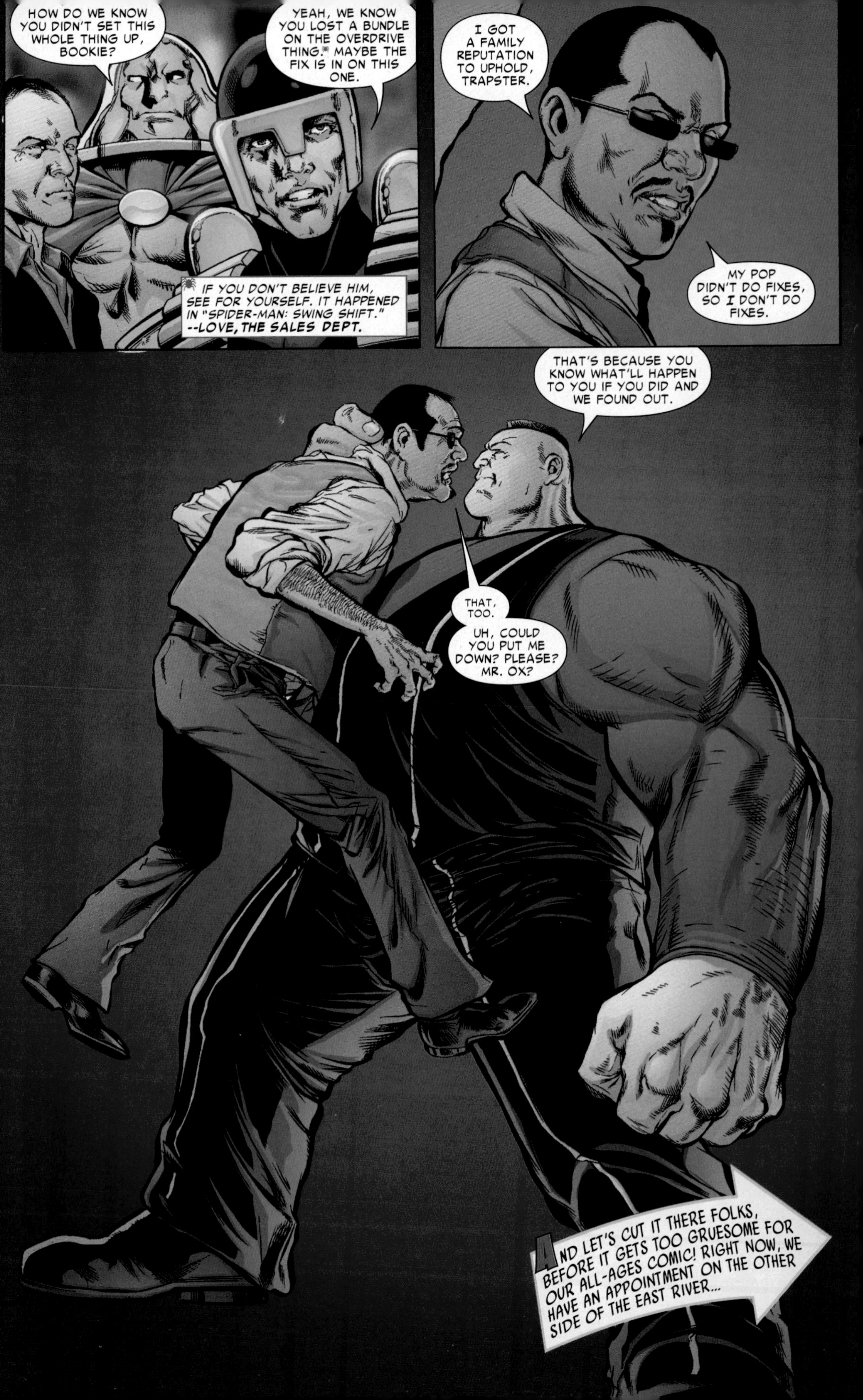
HOW DO WE KNOW YOU DIDN'T SET THIS WHOLE THING UP, BOOKIE?
YEAH, WE KNOW YOU LOST A BUNDLE ON THE OVERDRIVE THING.* MAYBE THE FIX IS IN ON THIS ONE.
*IF YOU DON'T BELIEVE HIM, SEE FOR YOURSELF. IT HAPPENED IN "SPIDER-MAN: SWING SHIFT." --LOVE, THE SALES DEPT.
I GOT A FAMILY REPUTATION TO UPHOLD, TRAPSTER.
MY POP DIDN'T DO FIXES, SO I DON'T DO FIXES.
THAT'S BECAUSE YOU KNOW WHAT'LL HAPPEN TO YOU IF YOU DID AND WE FOUND OUT.
THAT, TOO.
UH, COULD YOU PUT ME DOWN? PLEASE? MR. OX?
AND LET'S CUT IT THERE FOLKS, BEFORE IT GETS TOO GRUESOME FOR OUR ALL-AGES COMIC! RIGHT NOW, WE HAVE AN APPOINTMENT ON THE OTHER SIDE OF THE EAST RIVER...

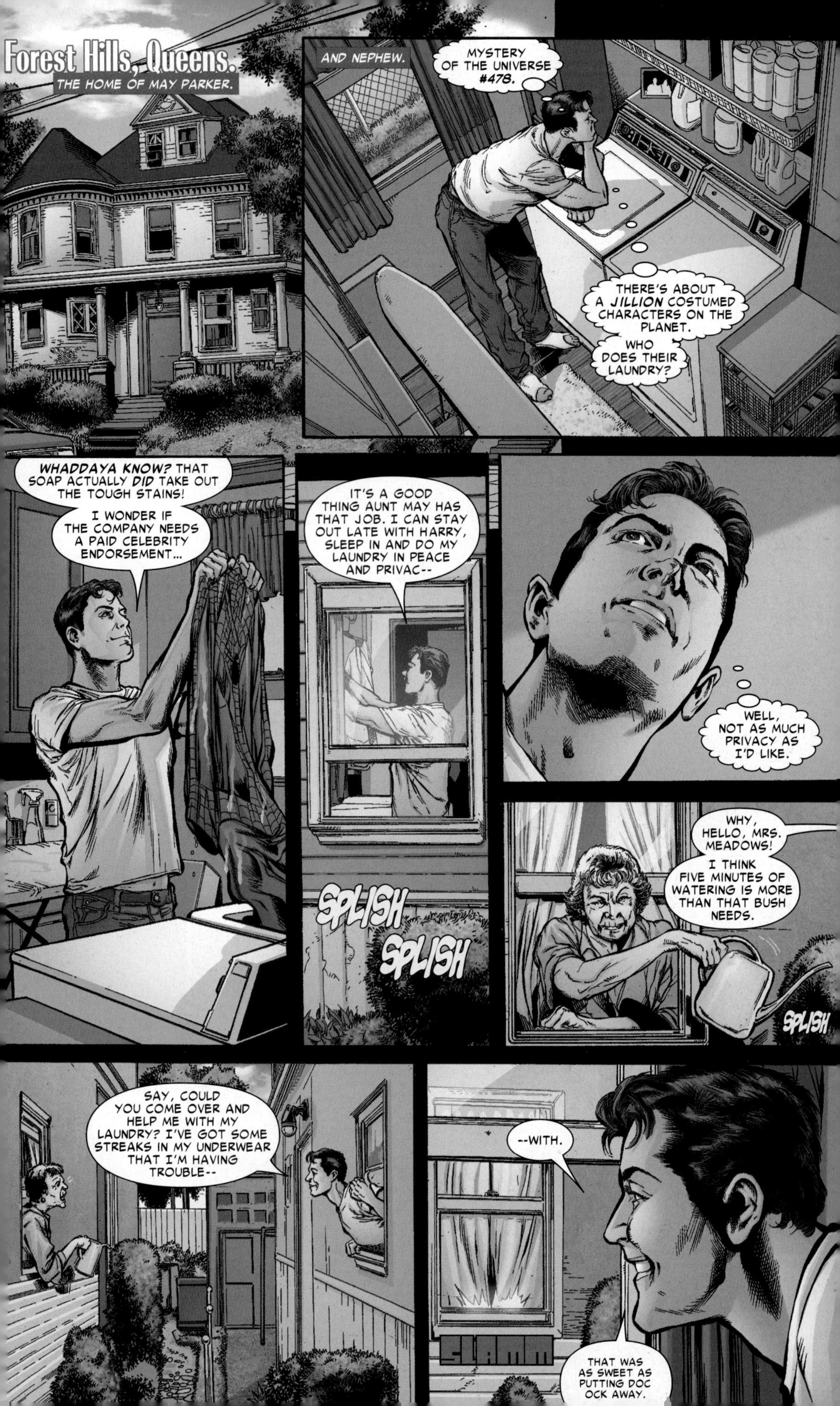

Forest Hills, Queens.
THE HOME OF MAY PARKER.
AND NEPHEW.
MYSTERY OF THE UNIVERSE #478.
THERE'S ABOUT A JILLION COSTUMED CHARACTERS ON THE PLANET.
WHO DOES THEIR LAUNDRY?
WHADDAYA KNOW? THAT SOAP ACTUALLY DID TAKE OUT THE TOUGH STAINS!
I WONDER IF THE COMPANY NEEDS A PAID CELEBRITY ENDORSEMENT...
IT'S A GOOD THING AUNT MAY HAS THAT JOB. I CAN STAY OUT LATE WITH HARRY, SLEEP IN AND DO MY LAUNDRY IN PEACE AND PRIVAC--
SPLISH
SPLISH
WELL, NOT AS MUCH PRIVACY AS I'D LIKE.
WHY, HELLO, MRS. MEADOWS!
I THINK FIVE MINUTES OF WATERING IS MORE THAN THAT BUSH NEEDS.
SPLISH
SAY, COULD YOU COME OVER AND HELP ME WITH MY LAUNDRY? I'VE GOT SOME STREAKS IN MY UNDERWEAR THAT I'M HAVING TROUBLE--
--WITH.
SLAMM
THAT WAS AS SWEET AS PUTTING DOC OCK AWAY.

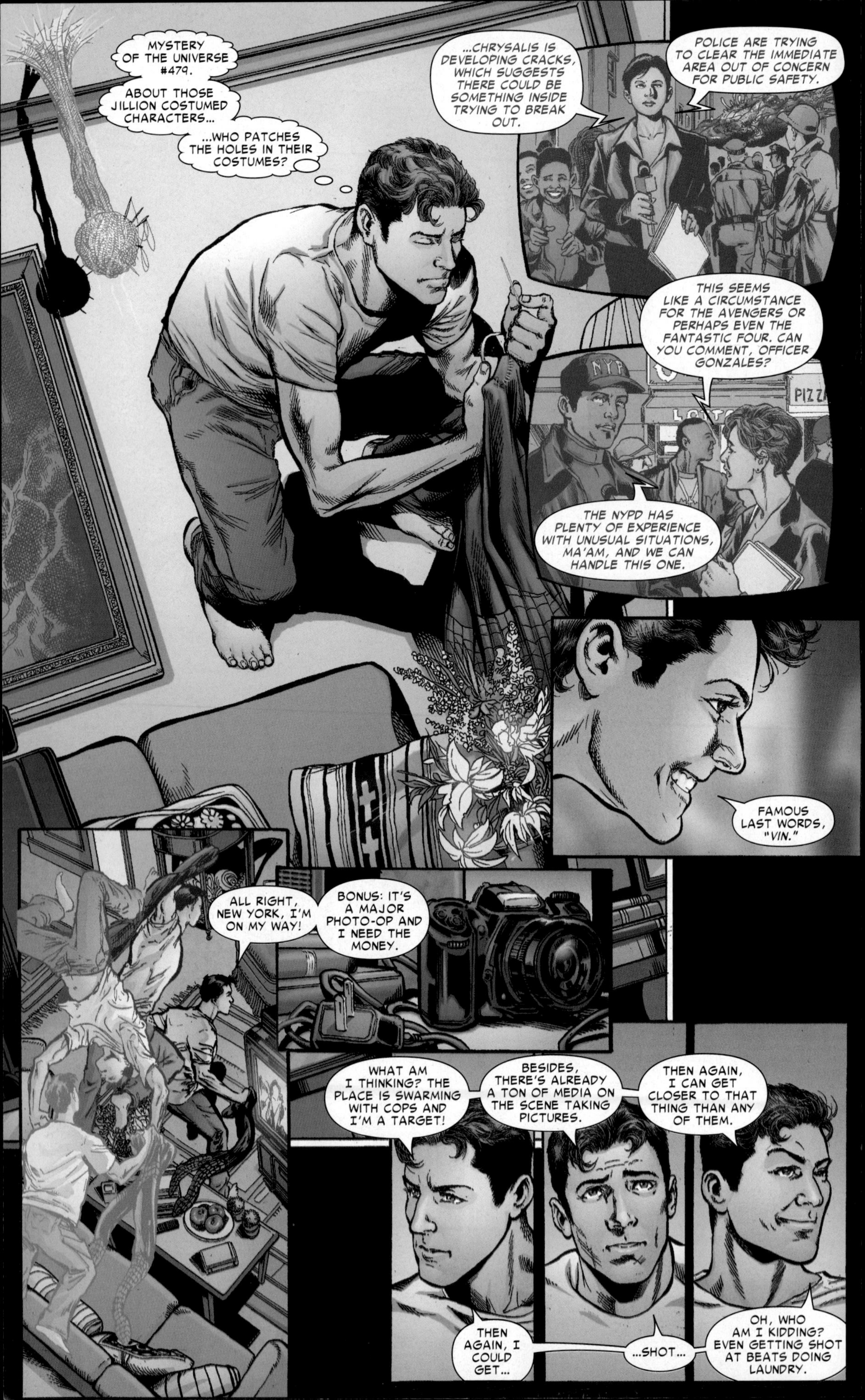
MYSTERY OF THE UNIVERSE #479.
ABOUT THOSE JILLION COSTUMED CHARACTERS...
...WHO PATCHES THE HOLES IN THEIR COSTUMES?
...CHRYSALIS IS DEVELOPING CRACKS, WHICH SUGGESTS THERE COULD BE SOMETHING INSIDE TRYING TO BREAK OUT.
POLICE ARE TRYING TO CLEAR THE IMMEDIATE AREA OUT OF CONCERN FOR PUBLIC SAFETY.
THIS SEEMS LIKE A CIRCUMSTANCE FOR THE AVENGERS OR PERHAPS EVEN THE FANTASTIC FOUR. CAN YOU COMMENT, OFFICER GONZALES?
NYPD
PIZZA
THE NYPD HAS PLENTY OF EXPERIENCE WITH UNUSUAL SITUATIONS, MA'AM, AND WE CAN HANDLE THIS ONE.
FAMOUS LAST WORDS, "VIN."
ALL RIGHT, NEW YORK, I'M ON MY WAY!
BONUS: IT'S A MAJOR PHOTO-OP AND I NEED THE MONEY.
WHAT AM I THINKING? THE PLACE IS SWARMING WITH COPS AND I'M A TARGET!
BESIDES, THERE'S ALREADY A TON OF MEDIA ON THE SCENE TAKING PICTURES.
THEN AGAIN, I CAN GET CLOSER TO THAT THING THAN ANY OF THEM.
THEN AGAIN, I COULD GET...
...SHOT...
OH, WHO AM I KIDDING? EVEN GETTING SHOT AT BEATS DOING LAUNDRY.

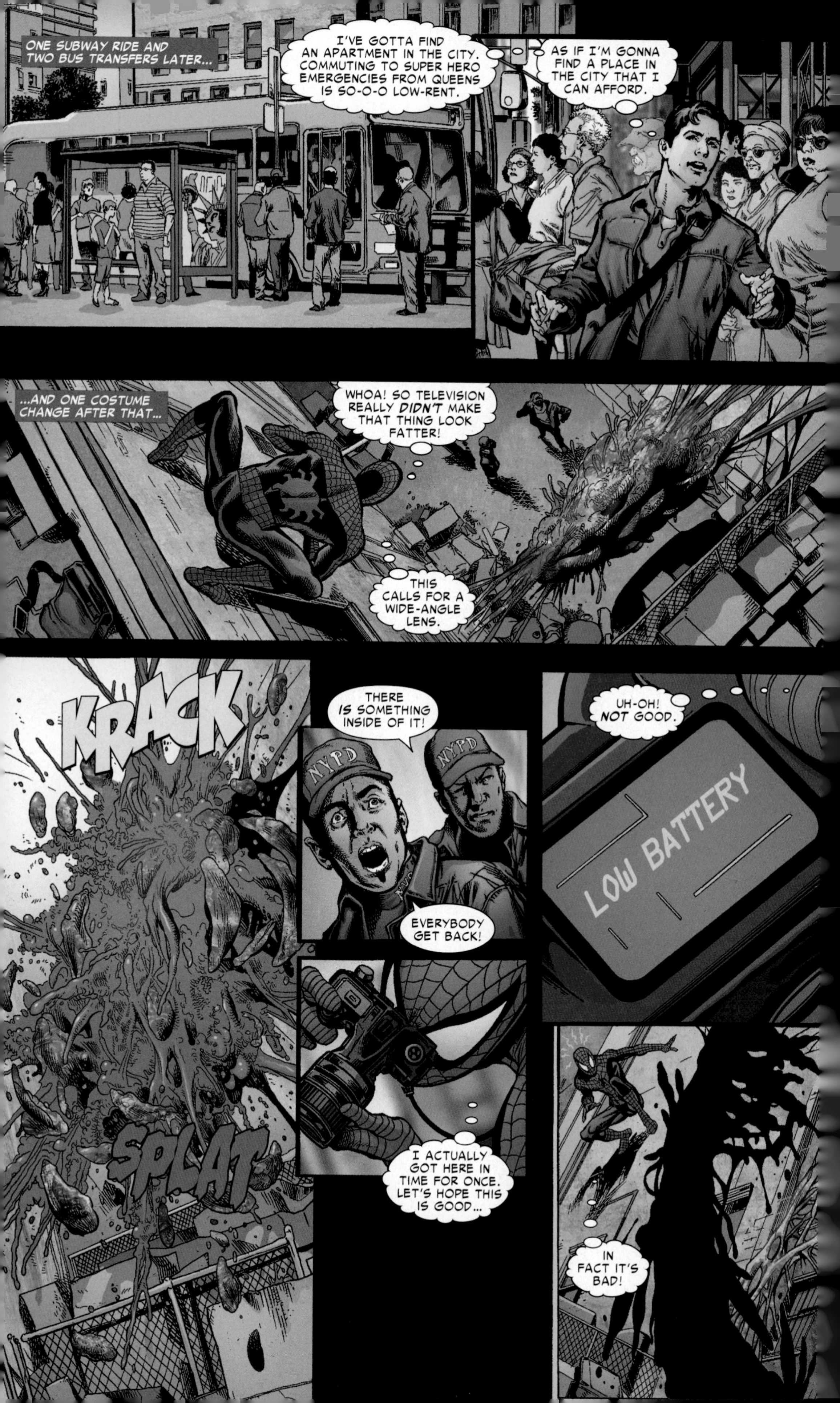
ONE SUBWAY RIDE AND TWO BUS TRANSFERS LATER...
I'VE GOTTA FIND AN APARTMENT IN THE CITY. COMMUTING TO SUPER HERO EMERGENCIES FROM QUEENS IS SO-O-O LOW-RENT.
AS IF I'M GONNA FIND A PLACE IN THE CITY THAT I CAN AFFORD.
...AND ONE COSTUME CHANGE AFTER THAT...
WHOA! SO TELEVISION REALLY *DIDN'T* MAKE THAT THING LOOK FATTER!
THIS CALLS FOR A WIDE-ANGLE LENS.
KRACK
SPLAT
THERE *IS* SOMETHING INSIDE OF IT!
EVERYBODY GET BACK!
I ACTUALLY GOT HERE IN TIME FOR ONCE. LET'S HOPE THIS IS GOOD...
UH-OH! *NOT* GOOD.
LOW BATTERY
IN FACT IT'S BAD!

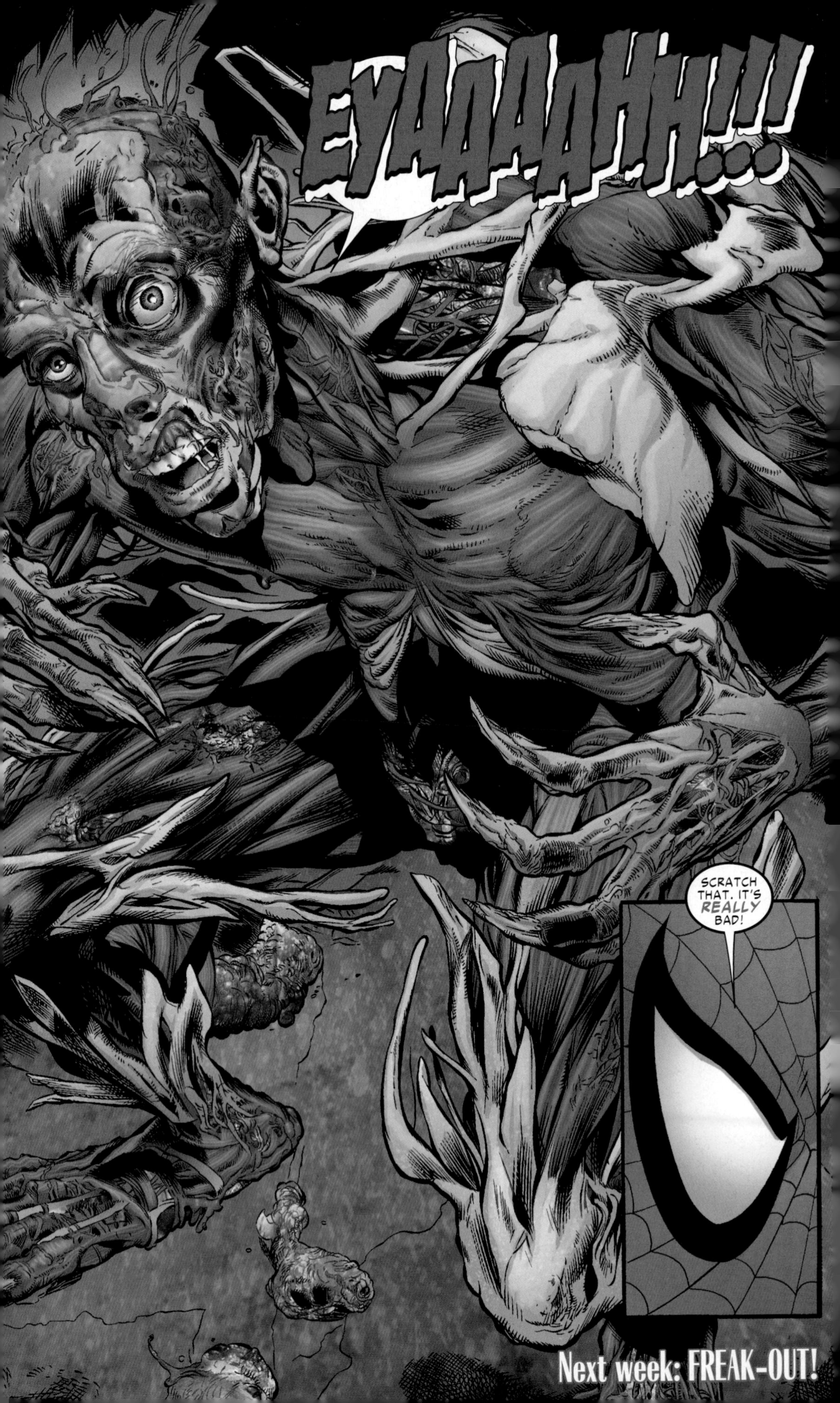
EYAAAAHH!!!
SCRATCH THAT. IT'S *REALLY* BAD!
Next week: FREAK-OUT!

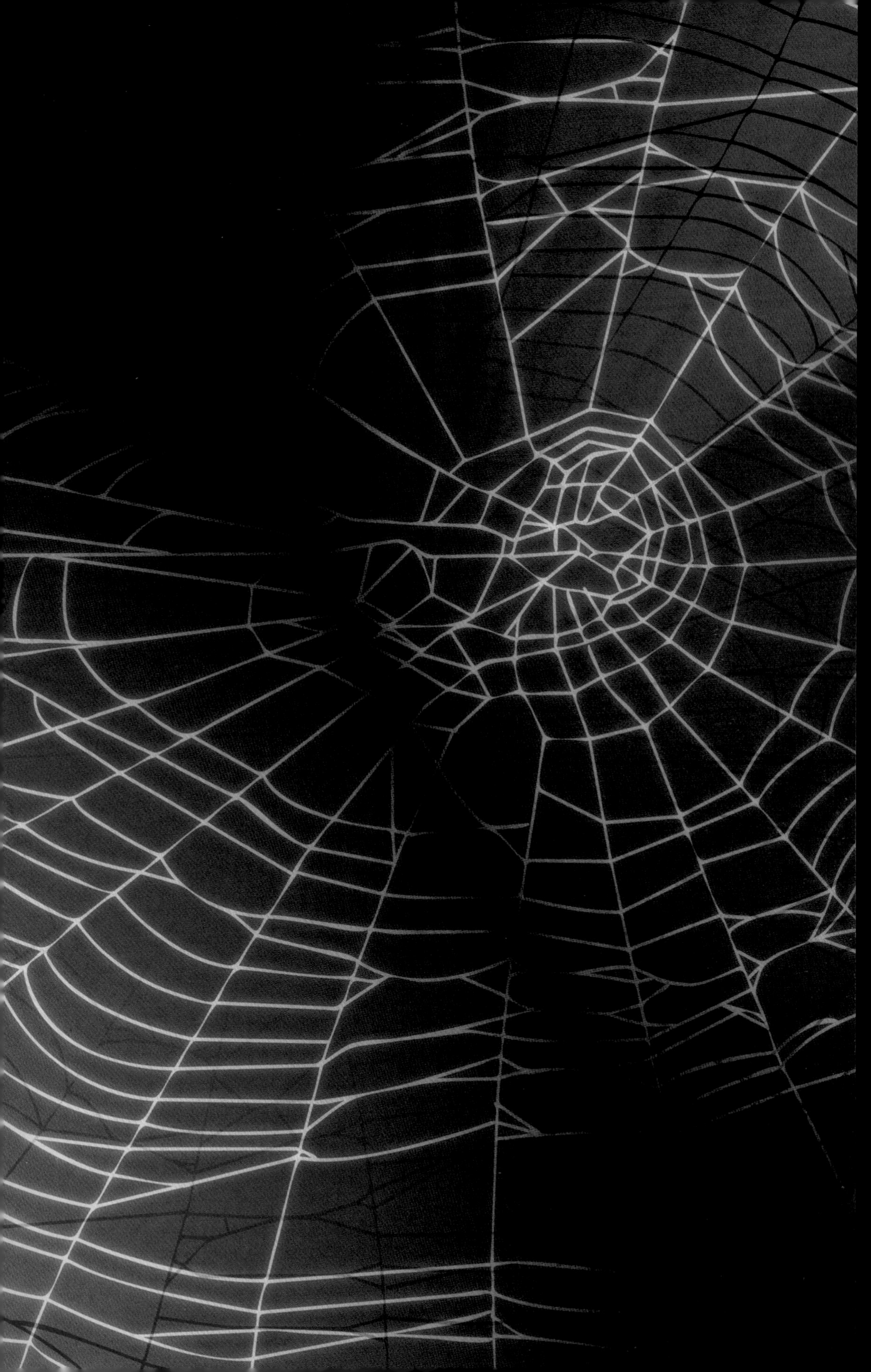

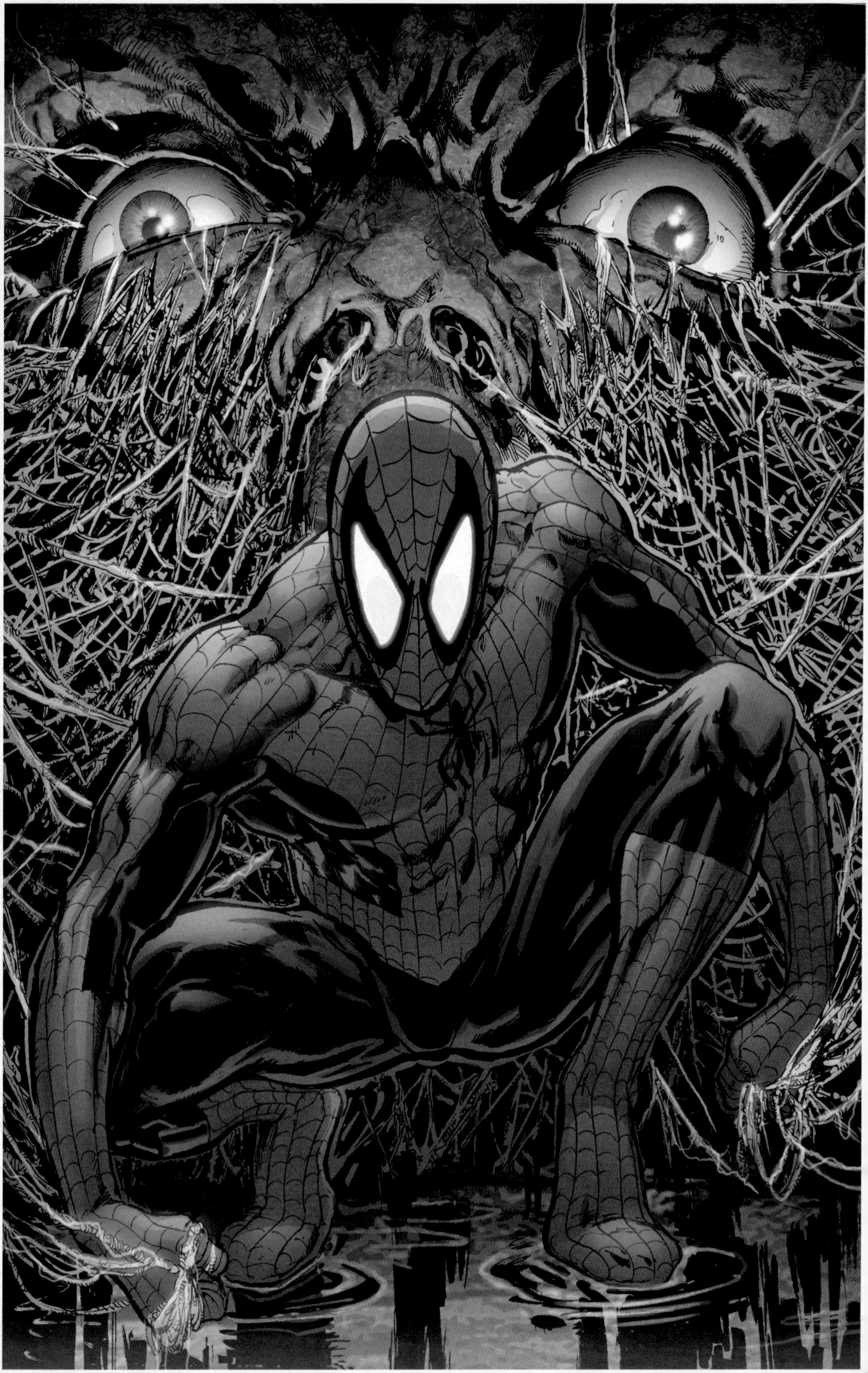

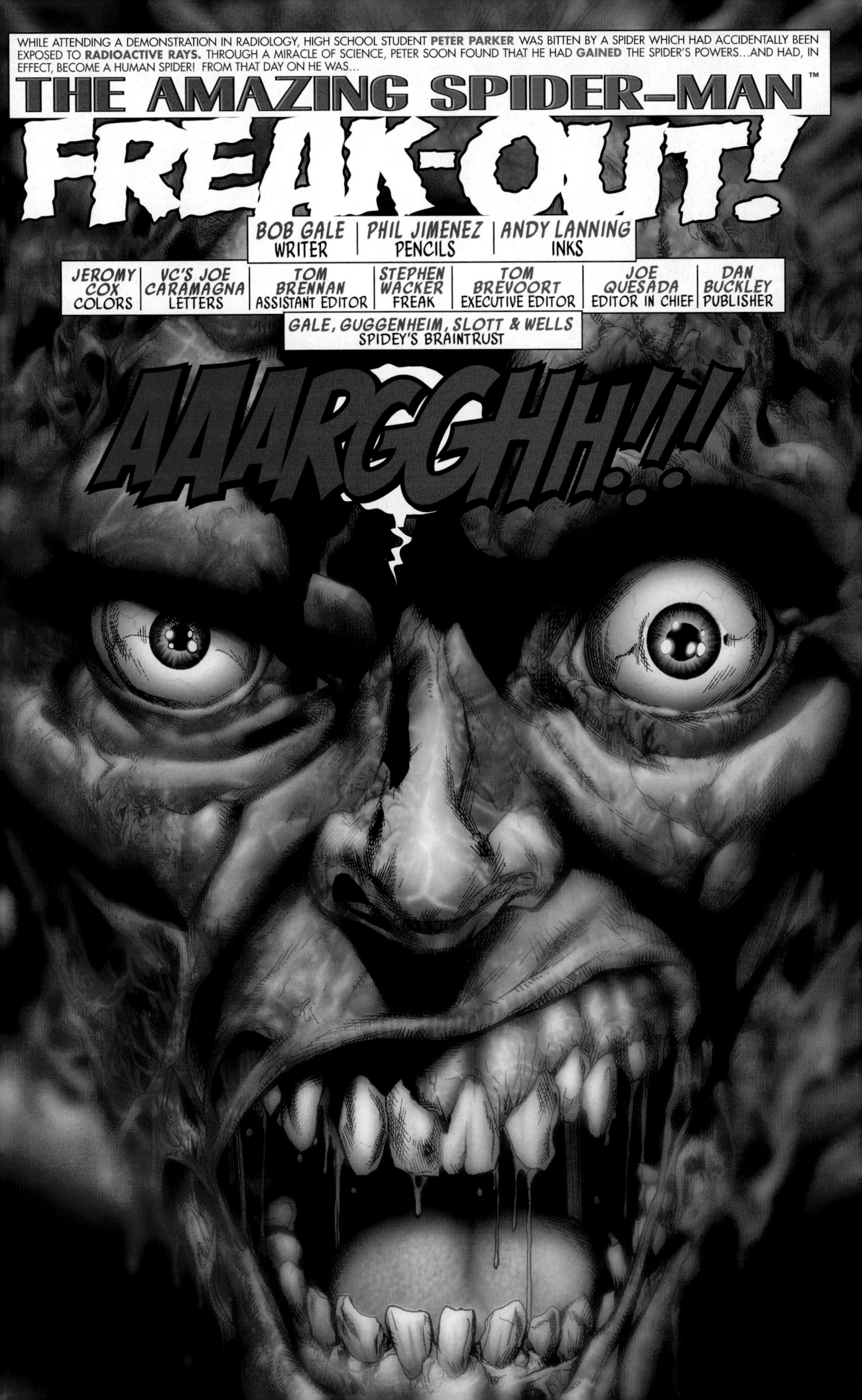
WHILE ATTENDING A DEMONSTRATION IN RADIOLOGY, HIGH SCHOOL STUDENT PETER PARKER WAS BITTEN BY A SPIDER WHICH HAD ACCIDENTALLY BEEN EXPOSED TO RADIOACTIVE RAYS. THROUGH A MIRACLE OF SCIENCE, PETER SOON FOUND THAT HE HAD GAINED THE SPIDER'S POWERS…AND HAD, IN EFFECT, BECOME A HUMAN SPIDER! FROM THAT DAY ON HE WAS…
THE AMAZING SPIDER-MAN™
FREAK-OUT!
BOB GALE WRITER | PHIL JIMENEZ PENCILS | ANDY LANNING INKS
JEROMY COX COLORS | VC'S JOE CARAMAGNA LETTERS | TOM BRENNAN ASSISTANT EDITOR | STEPHEN WACKER FREAK | TOM BREVOORT EXECUTIVE EDITOR | JOE QUESADA EDITOR IN CHIEF | DAN BUCKLEY PUBLISHER
GALE, GUGGENHEIM, SLOTT & WELLS SPIDEY'S BRAINTRUST
AAARGGHH!!!

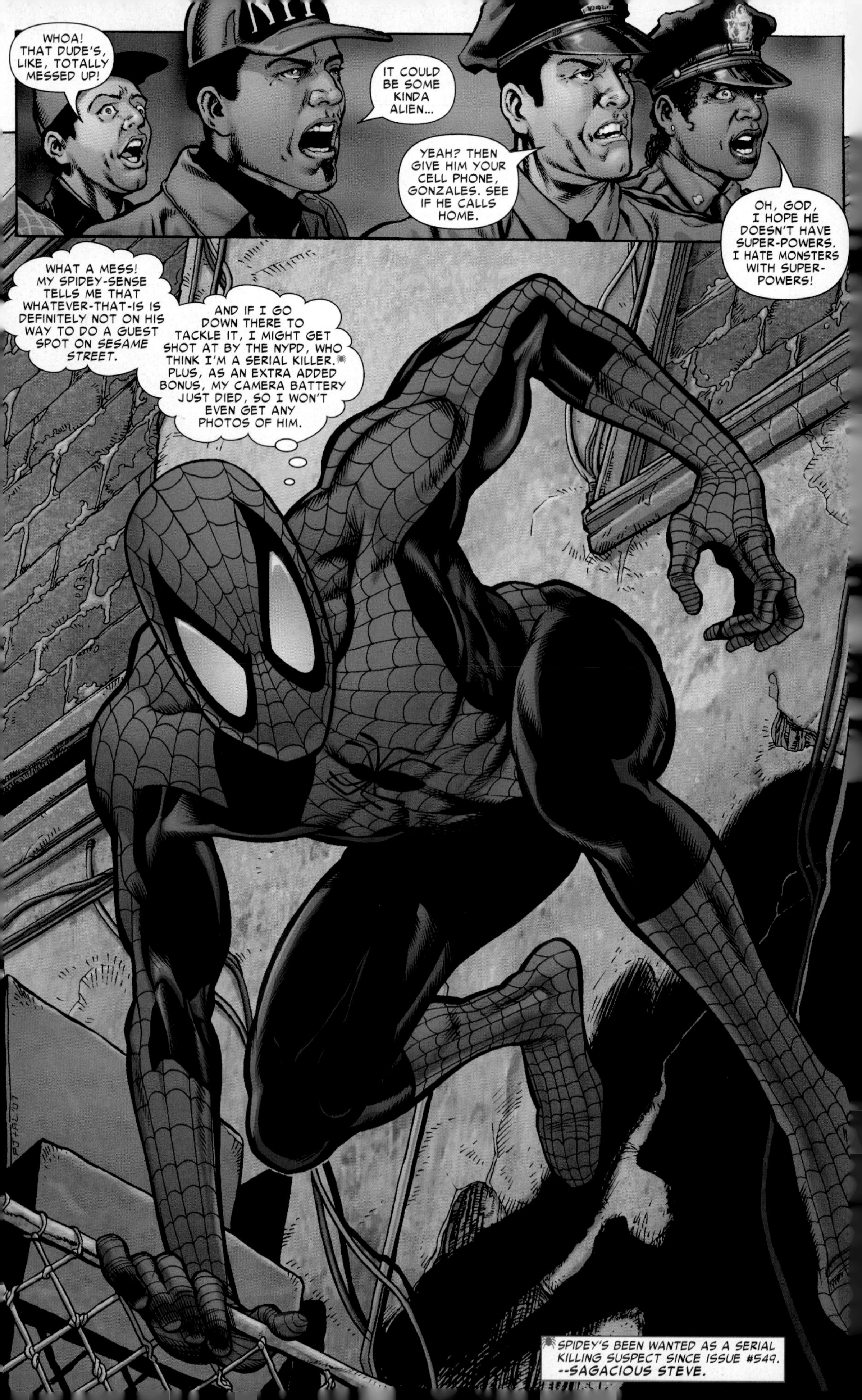

WHOA! THAT DUDE'S, LIKE, TOTALLY MESSED UP!
IT COULD BE SOME KINDA ALIEN...
YEAH? THEN GIVE HIM YOUR CELL PHONE, GONZALES. SEE IF HE CALLS HOME.
OH, GOD, I HOPE HE DOESN'T HAVE SUPER-POWERS. I HATE MONSTERS WITH SUPER-POWERS!
WHAT A MESS! MY SPIDEY-SENSE TELLS ME THAT WHATEVER-THAT-IS IS DEFINITELY NOT ON HIS WAY TO DO A GUEST SPOT ON SESAME STREET.
AND IF I GO DOWN THERE TO TACKLE IT, I MIGHT GET SHOT AT BY THE NYPD, WHO THINK I'M A SERIAL KILLER. PLUS, AS AN EXTRA ADDED BONUS, MY CAMERA BATTERY JUST DIED, SO I WON'T EVEN GET ANY PHOTOS OF HIM.
SPIDEY'S BEEN WANTED AS A SERIAL KILLING SUSPECT SINCE ISSUE #549. --SAGACIOUS STEVE.

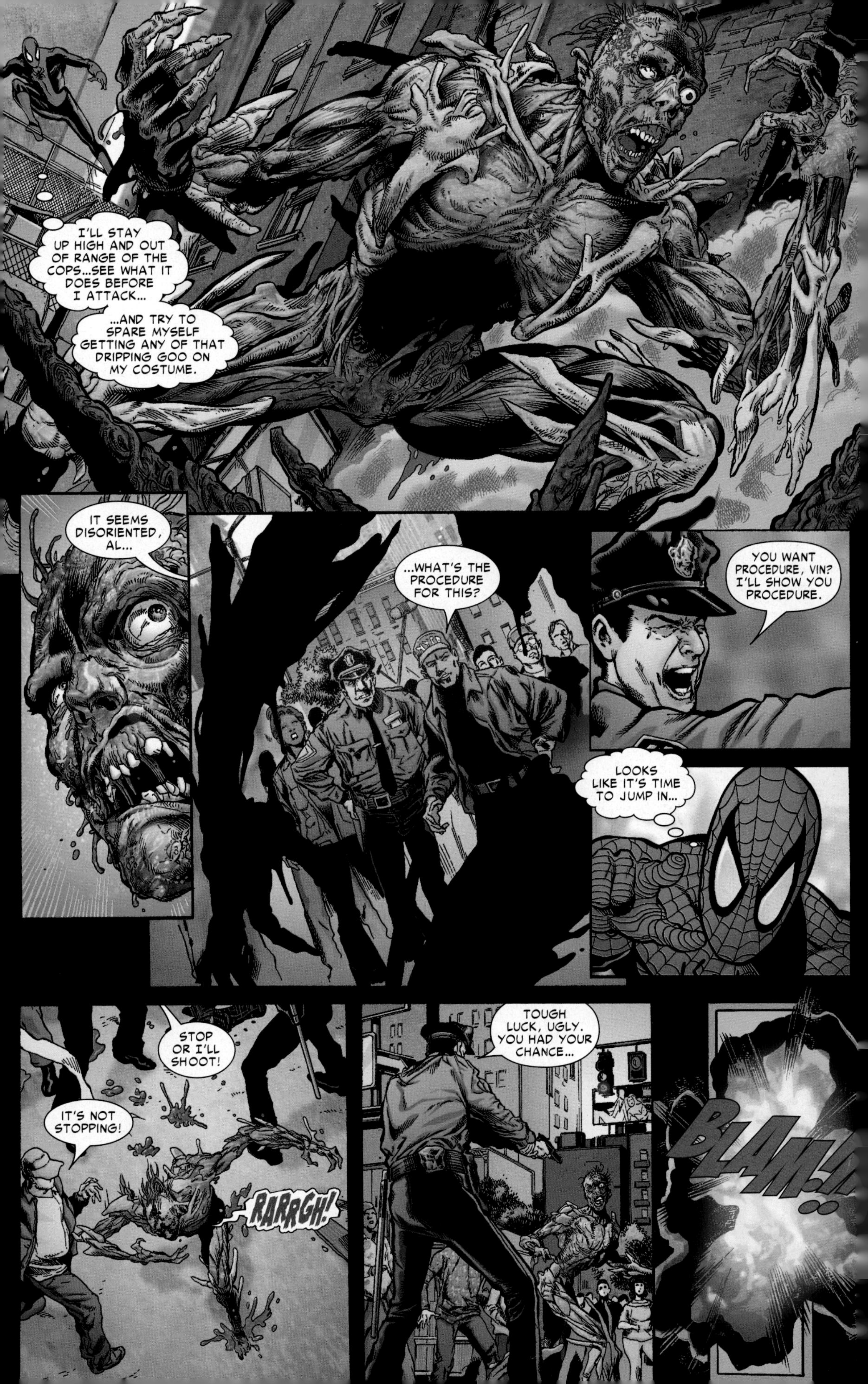

I'LL STAY UP HIGH AND OUT OF RANGE OF THE COPS...SEE WHAT IT DOES BEFORE I ATTACK...
...AND TRY TO SPARE MYSELF GETTING ANY OF THAT DRIPPING GOO ON MY COSTUME.
IT SEEMS DISORIENTED, AL...
...WHAT'S THE PROCEDURE FOR THIS?
YOU WANT PROCEDURE, VIN? I'LL SHOW YOU PROCEDURE.
LOOKS LIKE IT'S TIME TO JUMP IN...
STOP OR I'LL SHOOT!
IT'S NOT STOPPING!
RARRGH!
TOUGH LUCK, UGLY. YOU HAD YOUR CHANCE...
BLAM!!

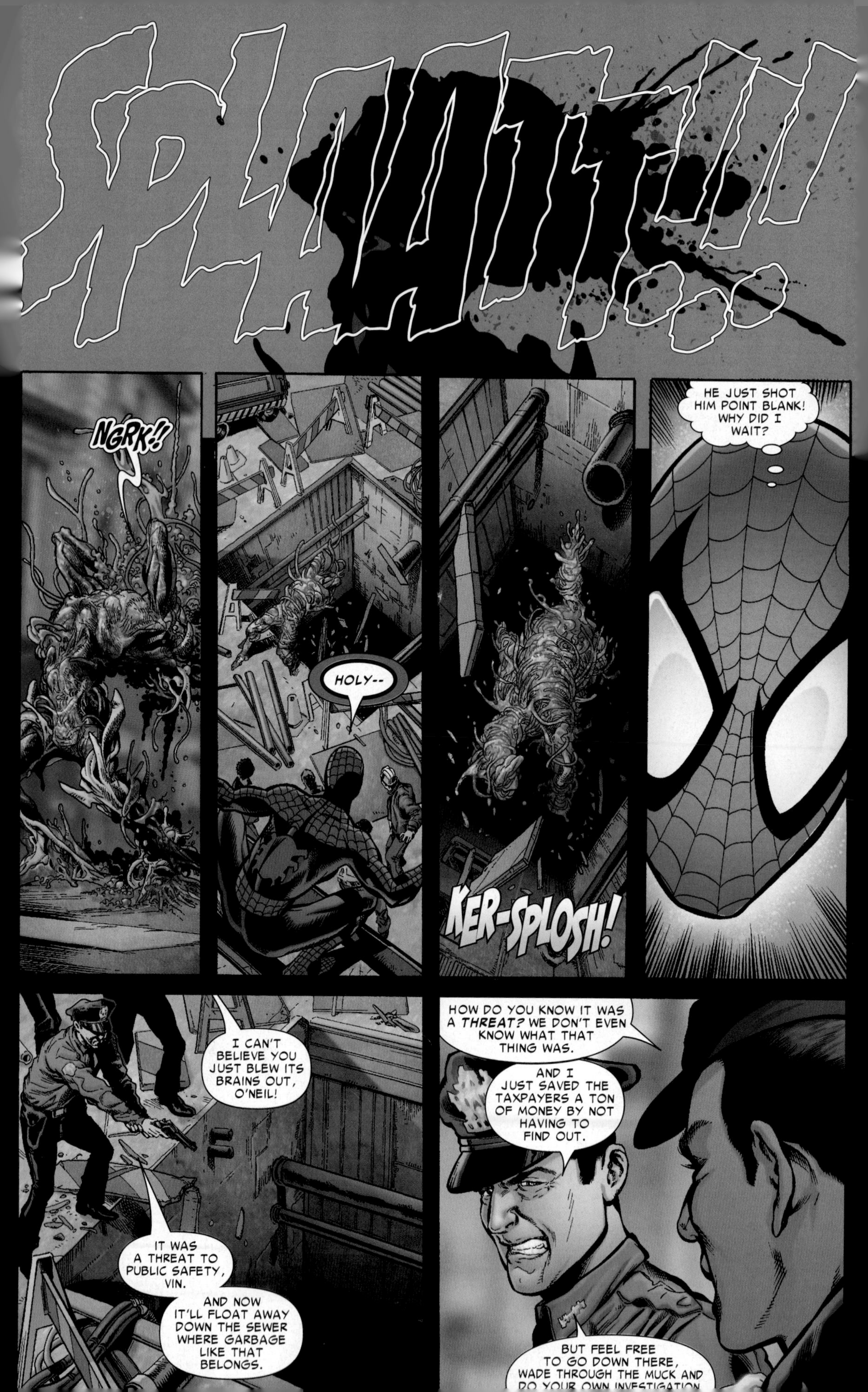
SPLAAATT!!
NGRK!!
HOLY--
KER-SPLOSH!
HE JUST SHOT HIM POINT BLANK! WHY DID I WAIT?
I CAN'T BELIEVE YOU JUST BLEW ITS BRAINS OUT, O'NEIL!
IT WAS A THREAT TO PUBLIC SAFETY, VIN.
AND NOW IT'LL FLOAT AWAY DOWN THE SEWER WHERE GARBAGE LIKE THAT BELONGS.
HOW DO YOU KNOW IT WAS A *THREAT?* WE DON'T EVEN KNOW WHAT THAT THING WAS.
AND I JUST SAVED THE TAXPAYERS A TON OF MONEY BY NOT HAVING TO FIND OUT.
BUT FEEL FREE TO GO DOWN THERE, WADE THROUGH THE MUCK AND DO YOUR OWN INVESTIGATION

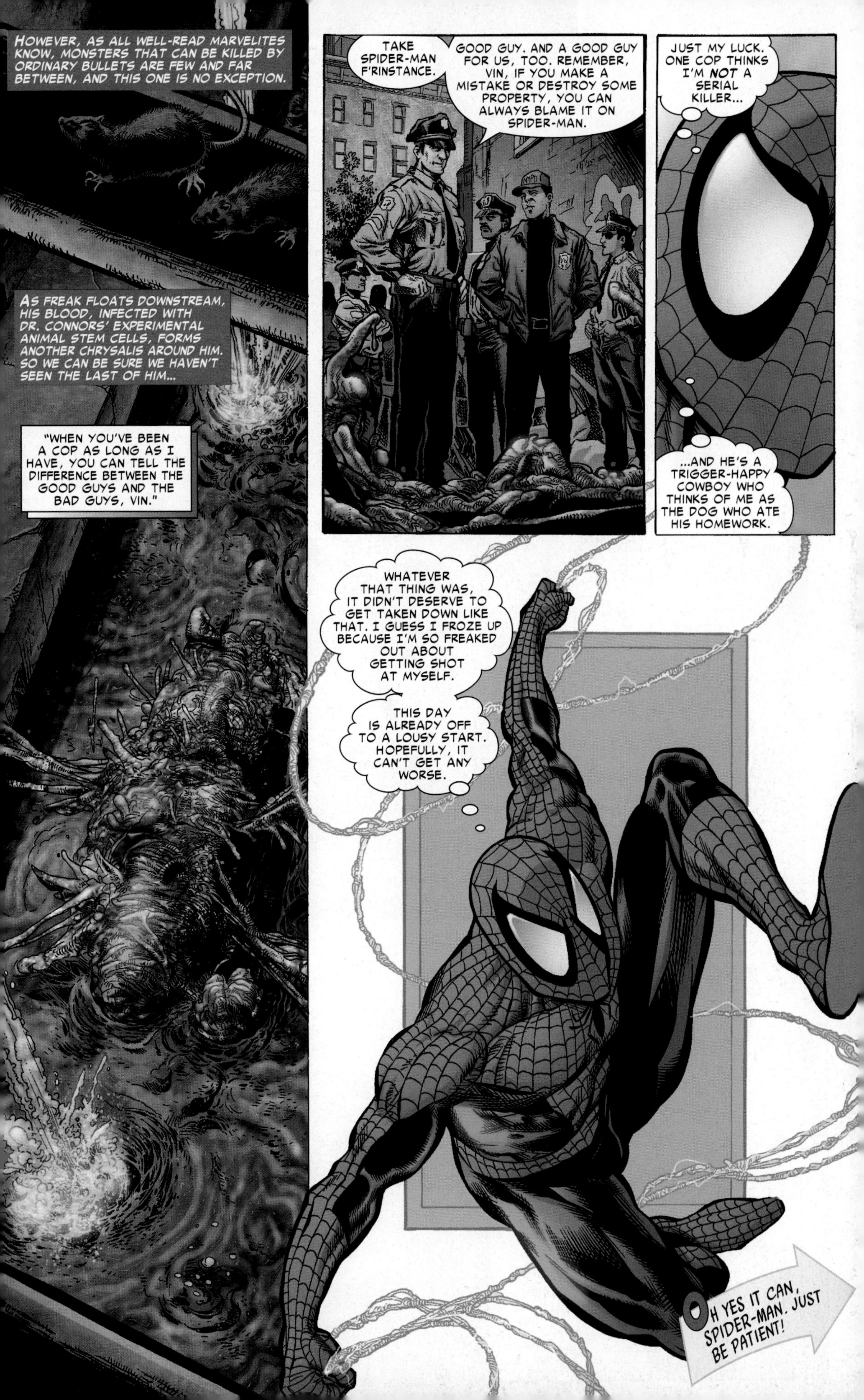
HOWEVER, AS ALL WELL-READ MARVELITES KNOW, MONSTERS THAT CAN BE KILLED BY ORDINARY BULLETS ARE FEW AND FAR BETWEEN, AND THIS ONE IS NO EXCEPTION.
AS FREAK FLOATS DOWNSTREAM, HIS BLOOD, INFECTED WITH DR. CONNORS' EXPERIMENTAL ANIMAL STEM CELLS, FORMS ANOTHER CHRYSALIS AROUND HIM. SO WE CAN BE SURE WE HAVEN'T SEEN THE LAST OF HIM...
"WHEN YOU'VE BEEN A COP AS LONG AS I HAVE, YOU CAN TELL THE DIFFERENCE BETWEEN THE GOOD GUYS AND THE BAD GUYS, VIN."
TAKE SPIDER-MAN F'RINSTANCE.
GOOD GUY. AND A GOOD GUY FOR US, TOO. REMEMBER, VIN, IF YOU MAKE A MISTAKE OR DESTROY SOME PROPERTY, YOU CAN ALWAYS BLAME IT ON SPIDER-MAN.
JUST MY LUCK. ONE COP THINKS I'M **NOT** A SERIAL KILLER...
...AND HE'S A TRIGGER-HAPPY COWBOY WHO THINKS OF ME AS THE DOG WHO ATE HIS HOMEWORK.
WHATEVER THAT THING WAS, IT DIDN'T DESERVE TO GET TAKEN DOWN LIKE THAT. I GUESS I FROZE UP BECAUSE I'M SO FREAKED OUT ABOUT GETTING SHOT AT MYSELF.
THIS DAY IS ALREADY OFF TO A LOUSY START. HOPEFULLY, IT CAN'T GET ANY WORSE.
OH YES IT CAN, SPIDER-MAN. JUST BE PATIENT!

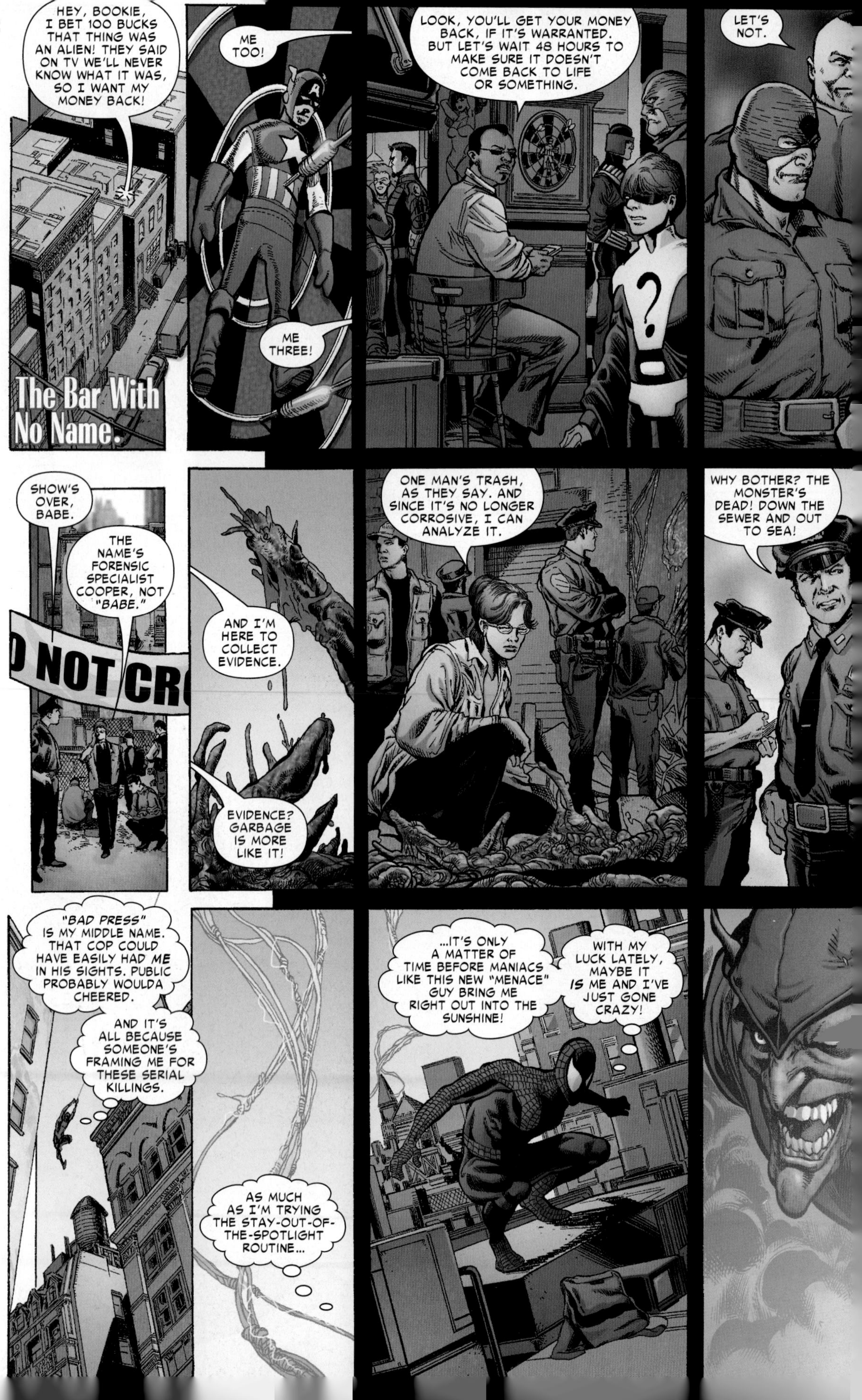
HEY, BOOKIE, I BET 100 BUCKS THAT THING WAS AN ALIEN! THEY SAID ON TV WE'LL NEVER KNOW WHAT IT WAS, SO I WANT MY MONEY BACK!
The Bar With No Name.
ME TOO!
ME THREE!
LOOK, YOU'LL GET YOUR MONEY BACK, IF IT'S WARRANTED. BUT LET'S WAIT 48 HOURS TO MAKE SURE IT DOESN'T COME BACK TO LIFE OR SOMETHING.
LET'S NOT.
SHOW'S OVER, BABE.
THE NAME'S FORENSIC SPECIALIST COOPER, NOT "BABE."
O NOT CRO
AND I'M HERE TO COLLECT EVIDENCE.
EVIDENCE? GARBAGE IS MORE LIKE IT!
ONE MAN'S TRASH, AS THEY SAY. AND SINCE IT'S NO LONGER CORROSIVE, I CAN ANALYZE IT.
WHY BOTHER? THE MONSTER'S DEAD! DOWN THE SEWER AND OUT TO SEA!
"BAD PRESS" IS MY MIDDLE NAME. THAT COP COULD HAVE EASILY HAD ME IN HIS SIGHTS. PUBLIC PROBABLY WOULDA CHEERED.
AND IT'S ALL BECAUSE SOMEONE'S FRAMING ME FOR THESE SERIAL KILLINGS.
AS MUCH AS I'M TRYING THE STAY-OUT-OF-THE-SPOTLIGHT ROUTINE...
...IT'S ONLY A MATTER OF TIME BEFORE MANIACS LIKE THIS NEW "MENACE" GUY BRING ME RIGHT OUT INTO THE SUNSHINE!
WITH MY LUCK LATELY, MAYBE IT IS ME AND I'VE JUST GONE CRAZY!

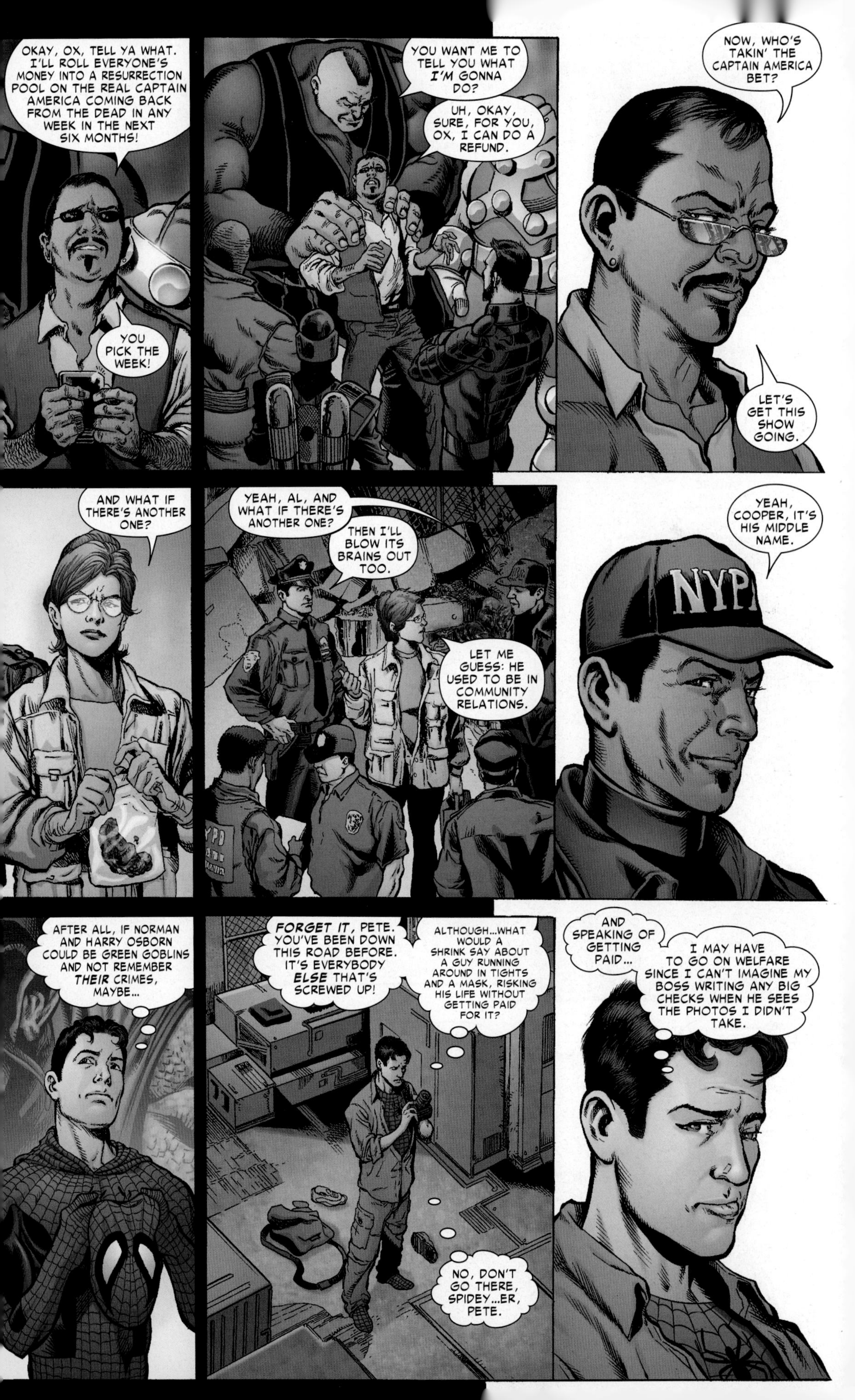

OKAY, OX, TELL YA WHAT. I'LL ROLL EVERYONE'S MONEY INTO A RESURRECTION POOL ON THE REAL CAPTAIN AMERICA COMING BACK FROM THE DEAD IN ANY WEEK IN THE NEXT SIX MONTHS!
YOU PICK THE WEEK!
YOU WANT ME TO TELL YOU WHAT I'M GONNA DO?
UH, OKAY, SURE, FOR YOU, OX, I CAN DO A REFUND.
NOW, WHO'S TAKIN' THE CAPTAIN AMERICA BET?
LET'S GET THIS SHOW GOING.
AND WHAT IF THERE'S ANOTHER ONE?
YEAH, AL, AND WHAT IF THERE'S ANOTHER ONE?
THEN I'LL BLOW ITS BRAINS OUT TOO.
LET ME GUESS: HE USED TO BE IN COMMUNITY RELATIONS.
YEAH, COOPER, IT'S HIS MIDDLE NAME.
NYPD
AFTER ALL, IF NORMAN AND HARRY OSBORN COULD BE GREEN GOBLINS AND NOT REMEMBER THEIR CRIMES, MAYBE...
FORGET IT, PETE. YOU'VE BEEN DOWN THIS ROAD BEFORE. IT'S EVERYBODY ELSE THAT'S SCREWED UP!
ALTHOUGH...WHAT WOULD A SHRINK SAY ABOUT A GUY RUNNING AROUND IN TIGHTS AND A MASK, RISKING HIS LIFE WITHOUT GETTING PAID FOR IT?
NO, DON'T GO THERE, SPIDEY...ER, PETE.
AND SPEAKING OF GETTING PAID...
I MAY HAVE TO GO ON WELFARE SINCE I CAN'T IMAGINE MY BOSS WRITING ANY BIG CHECKS WHEN HE SEES THE PHOTOS I DIDN'T TAKE.

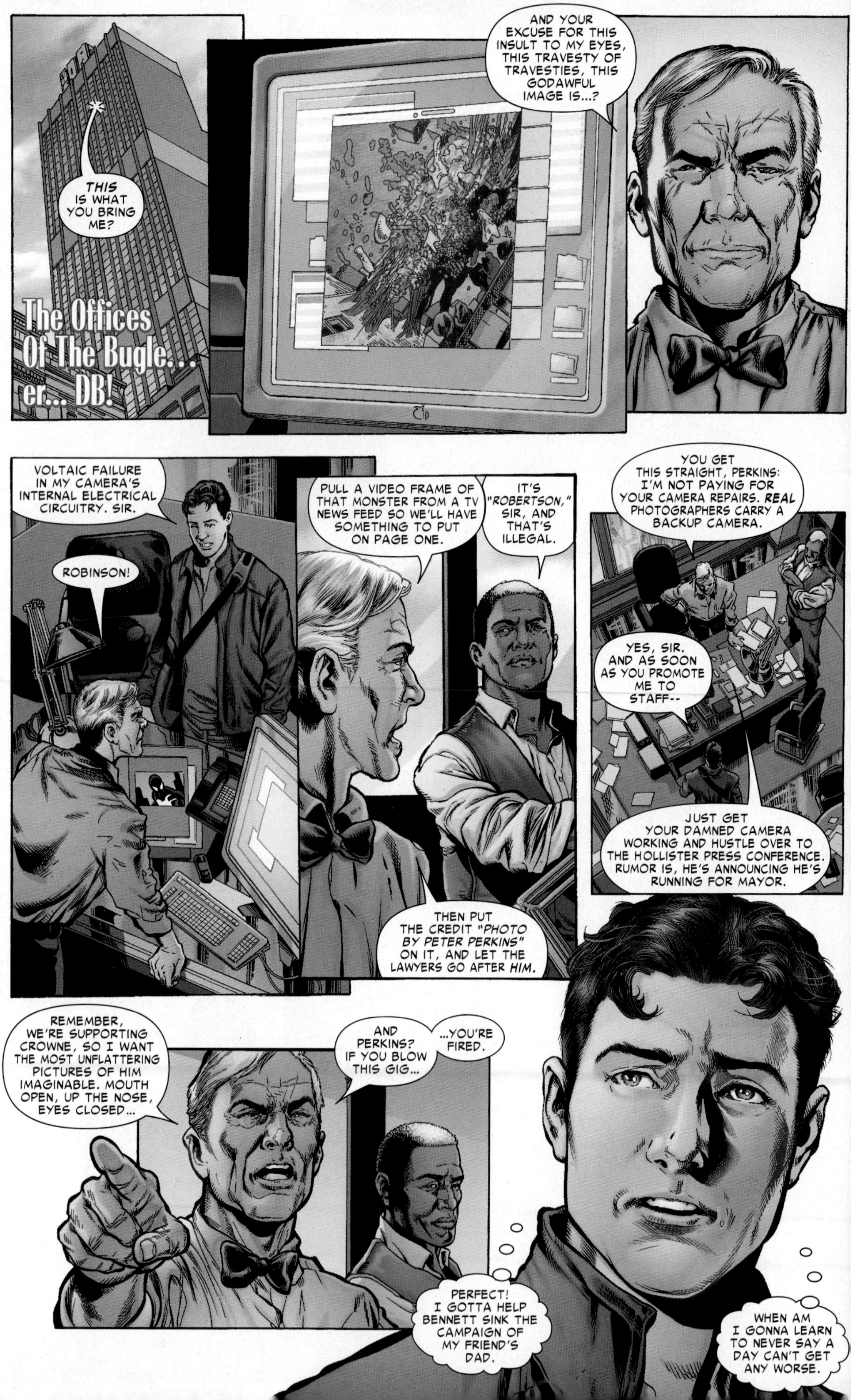

THIS IS WHAT YOU BRING ME?
The Offices Of The Bugle... er... DB!
AND YOUR EXCUSE FOR THIS INSULT TO MY EYES, THIS TRAVESTY OF TRAVESTIES, THIS GODAWFUL IMAGE IS...?
VOLTAIC FAILURE IN MY CAMERA'S INTERNAL ELECTRICAL CIRCUITRY. SIR.
ROBINSON!
PULL A VIDEO FRAME OF THAT MONSTER FROM A TV NEWS FEED SO WE'LL HAVE SOMETHING TO PUT ON PAGE ONE.
IT'S "ROBERTSON," SIR, AND THAT'S ILLEGAL.
THEN PUT THE CREDIT "PHOTO BY PETER PERKINS" ON IT, AND LET THE LAWYERS GO AFTER HIM.
YOU GET THIS STRAIGHT, PERKINS: I'M NOT PAYING FOR YOUR CAMERA REPAIRS. REAL PHOTOGRAPHERS CARRY A BACKUP CAMERA.
YES, SIR. AND AS SOON AS YOU PROMOTE ME TO STAFF--
JUST GET YOUR DAMNED CAMERA WORKING AND HUSTLE OVER TO THE HOLLISTER PRESS CONFERENCE. RUMOR IS, HE'S ANNOUNCING HE'S RUNNING FOR MAYOR.
REMEMBER, WE'RE SUPPORTING CROWNE, SO I WANT THE MOST UNFLATTERING PICTURES OF HIM IMAGINABLE. MOUTH OPEN, UP THE NOSE, EYES CLOSED...
AND PERKINS? IF YOU BLOW THIS GIG...
...YOU'RE FIRED.
PERFECT! I GOTTA HELP BENNETT SINK THE CAMPAIGN OF MY FRIEND'S DAD.
WHEN AM I GONNA LEARN TO NEVER SAY A DAY CAN'T GET ANY WORSE.

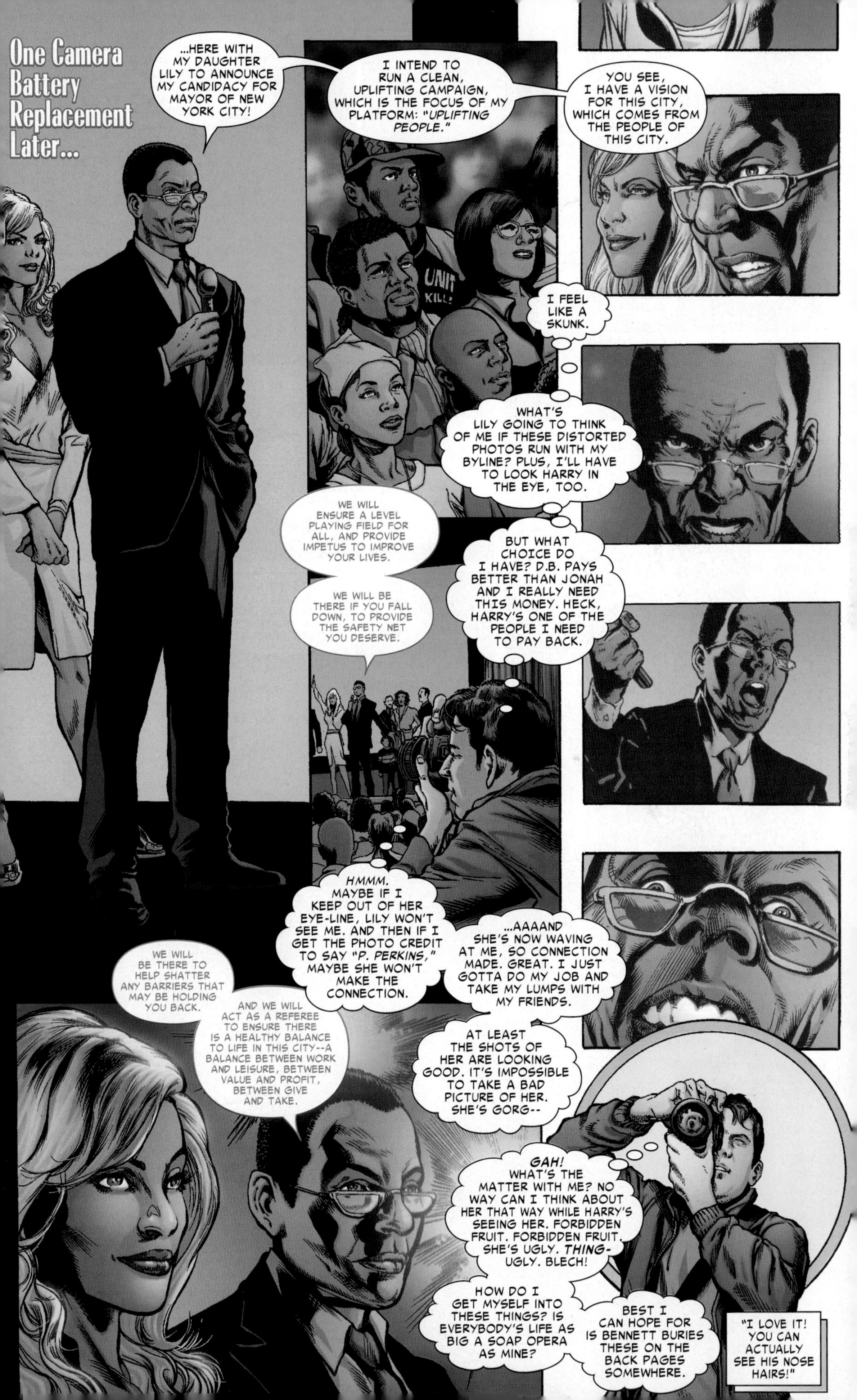
One Camera Battery Replacement Later...
...HERE WITH MY DAUGHTER LILY TO ANNOUNCE MY CANDIDACY FOR MAYOR OF NEW YORK CITY!
I INTEND TO RUN A CLEAN, UPLIFTING CAMPAIGN, WHICH IS THE FOCUS OF MY PLATFORM: "UPLIFTING PEOPLE."
YOU SEE, I HAVE A VISION FOR THIS CITY, WHICH COMES FROM THE PEOPLE OF THIS CITY.
I FEEL LIKE A SKUNK.
WHAT'S LILY GOING TO THINK OF ME IF THESE DISTORTED PHOTOS RUN WITH MY BYLINE? PLUS, I'LL HAVE TO LOOK HARRY IN THE EYE, TOO.
WE WILL ENSURE A LEVEL PLAYING FIELD FOR ALL, AND PROVIDE IMPETUS TO IMPROVE YOUR LIVES.
BUT WHAT CHOICE DO I HAVE? D.B. PAYS BETTER THAN JONAH AND I REALLY NEED THIS MONEY. HECK, HARRY'S ONE OF THE PEOPLE I NEED TO PAY BACK.
WE WILL BE THERE IF YOU FALL DOWN, TO PROVIDE THE SAFETY NET YOU DESERVE.
HMMM. MAYBE IF I KEEP OUT OF HER EYE-LINE, LILY WON'T SEE ME. AND THEN IF I GET THE PHOTO CREDIT TO SAY "P. PERKINS," MAYBE SHE WON'T MAKE THE CONNECTION.
...AAAAND SHE'S NOW WAVING AT ME, SO CONNECTION MADE. GREAT. I JUST GOTTA DO MY JOB AND TAKE MY LUMPS WITH MY FRIENDS.
WE WILL BE THERE TO HELP SHATTER ANY BARRIERS THAT MAY BE HOLDING YOU BACK.
AND WE WILL ACT AS A REFEREE TO ENSURE THERE IS A HEALTHY BALANCE TO LIFE IN THIS CITY--A BALANCE BETWEEN WORK AND LEISURE, BETWEEN VALUE AND PROFIT, BETWEEN GIVE AND TAKE.
AT LEAST THE SHOTS OF HER ARE LOOKING GOOD. IT'S IMPOSSIBLE TO TAKE A BAD PICTURE OF HER. SHE'S GORG--
GAH! WHAT'S THE MATTER WITH ME? NO WAY CAN I THINK ABOUT HER THAT WAY WHILE HARRY'S SEEING HER. FORBIDDEN FRUIT. FORBIDDEN FRUIT. SHE'S UGLY. THING-UGLY. BLECH!
HOW DO I GET MYSELF INTO THESE THINGS? IS EVERYBODY'S LIFE AS BIG A SOAP OPERA AS MINE?
BEST I CAN HOPE FOR IS BENNETT BURIES THESE ON THE BACK PAGES SOMEWHERE.
"I LOVE IT! YOU CAN ACTUALLY SEE HIS NOSE HAIRS!"

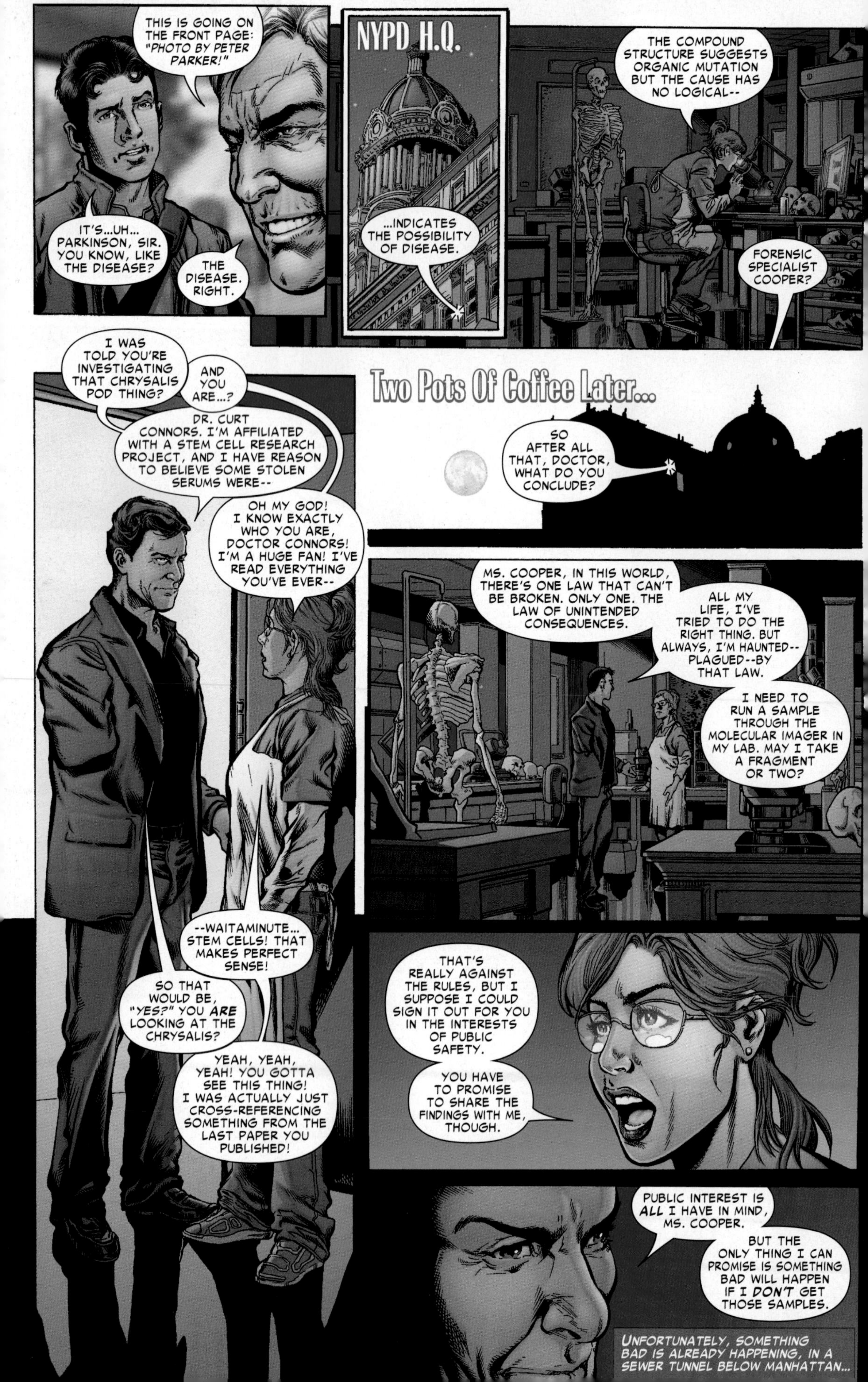
THIS IS GOING ON THE FRONT PAGE: "PHOTO BY PETER PARKER!"
IT'S...UH... PARKINSON, SIR. YOU KNOW, LIKE THE DISEASE?
THE DISEASE. RIGHT.
NYPD H.Q.
THE COMPOUND STRUCTURE SUGGESTS ORGANIC MUTATION BUT THE CAUSE HAS NO LOGICAL--
...INDICATES THE POSSIBILITY OF DISEASE.
FORENSIC SPECIALIST COOPER?
I WAS TOLD YOU'RE INVESTIGATING THAT CHRYSALIS POD THING?
AND YOU ARE...?
DR. CURT CONNORS. I'M AFFILIATED WITH A STEM CELL RESEARCH PROJECT, AND I HAVE REASON TO BELIEVE SOME STOLEN SERUMS WERE--
OH MY GOD! I KNOW EXACTLY WHO YOU ARE, DOCTOR CONNORS! I'M A HUGE FAN! I'VE READ EVERYTHING YOU'VE EVER--
--WAITAMINUTE... STEM CELLS! THAT MAKES PERFECT SENSE!
SO THAT WOULD BE, "YES?" YOU ARE LOOKING AT THE CHRYSALIS?
YEAH, YEAH, YEAH! YOU GOTTA SEE THIS THING! I WAS ACTUALLY JUST CROSS-REFERENCING SOMETHING FROM THE LAST PAPER YOU PUBLISHED!
Two Pots Of Coffee Later...
SO AFTER ALL THAT, DOCTOR, WHAT DO YOU CONCLUDE?
MS. COOPER, IN THIS WORLD, THERE'S ONE LAW THAT CAN'T BE BROKEN. ONLY ONE. THE LAW OF UNINTENDED CONSEQUENCES.
ALL MY LIFE, I'VE TRIED TO DO THE RIGHT THING. BUT ALWAYS, I'M HAUNTED--PLAGUED--BY THAT LAW.
I NEED TO RUN A SAMPLE THROUGH THE MOLECULAR IMAGER IN MY LAB. MAY I TAKE A FRAGMENT OR TWO?
THAT'S REALLY AGAINST THE RULES, BUT I SUPPOSE I COULD SIGN IT OUT FOR YOU IN THE INTERESTS OF PUBLIC SAFETY.
YOU HAVE TO PROMISE TO SHARE THE FINDINGS WITH ME, THOUGH.
PUBLIC INTEREST IS ALL I HAVE IN MIND, MS. COOPER.
BUT THE ONLY THING I CAN PROMISE IS SOMETHING BAD WILL HAPPEN IF I DON'T GET THOSE SAMPLES.
UNFORTUNATELY, SOMETHING BAD IS ALREADY HAPPENING, IN A SEWER TUNNEL BELOW MANHATTAN...

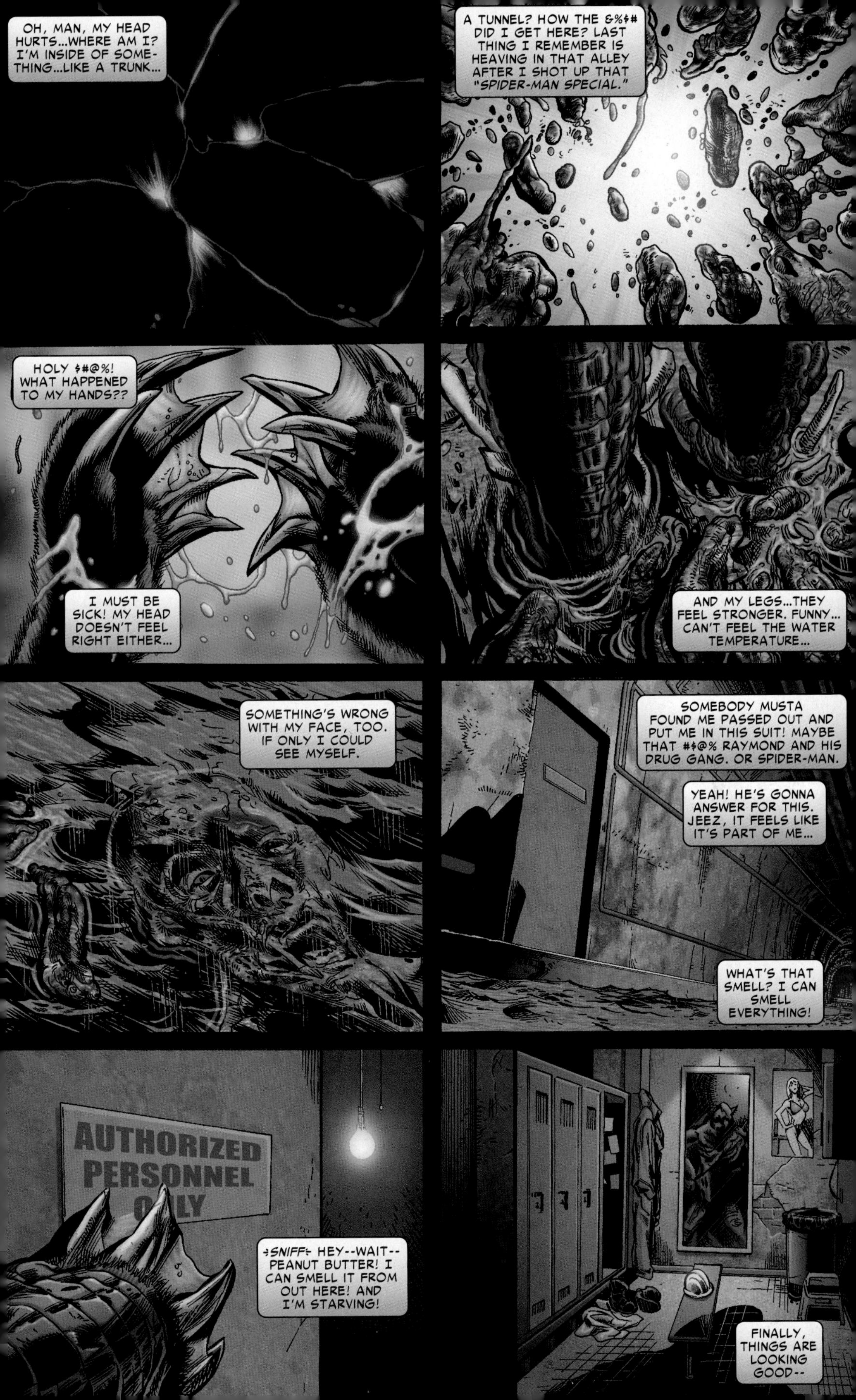
OH, MAN, MY HEAD HURTS...WHERE AM I? I'M INSIDE OF SOME-THING...LIKE A TRUNK...
A TUNNEL? HOW THE &%$# DID I GET HERE? LAST THING I REMEMBER IS HEAVING IN THAT ALLEY AFTER I SHOT UP THAT "SPIDER-MAN SPECIAL."
HOLY $#@%! WHAT HAPPENED TO MY HANDS??
I MUST BE SICK! MY HEAD DOESN'T FEEL RIGHT EITHER...
AND MY LEGS...THEY FEEL STRONGER. FUNNY... CAN'T FEEL THE WATER TEMPERATURE...
SOMETHING'S WRONG WITH MY FACE, TOO. IF ONLY I COULD SEE MYSELF.
SOMEBODY MUSTA FOUND ME PASSED OUT AND PUT ME IN THIS SUIT! MAYBE THAT #$@% RAYMOND AND HIS DRUG GANG. OR SPIDER-MAN.
YEAH! HE'S GONNA ANSWER FOR THIS. JEEZ, IT FEELS LIKE IT'S PART OF ME...
WHAT'S THAT SMELL? I CAN SMELL EVERYTHING!
AUTHORIZED PERSONNEL ONLY
SNIFF HEY--WAIT-- PEANUT BUTTER! I CAN SMELL IT FROM OUT HERE! AND I'M STARVING!
FINALLY, THINGS ARE LOOKING GOOD--

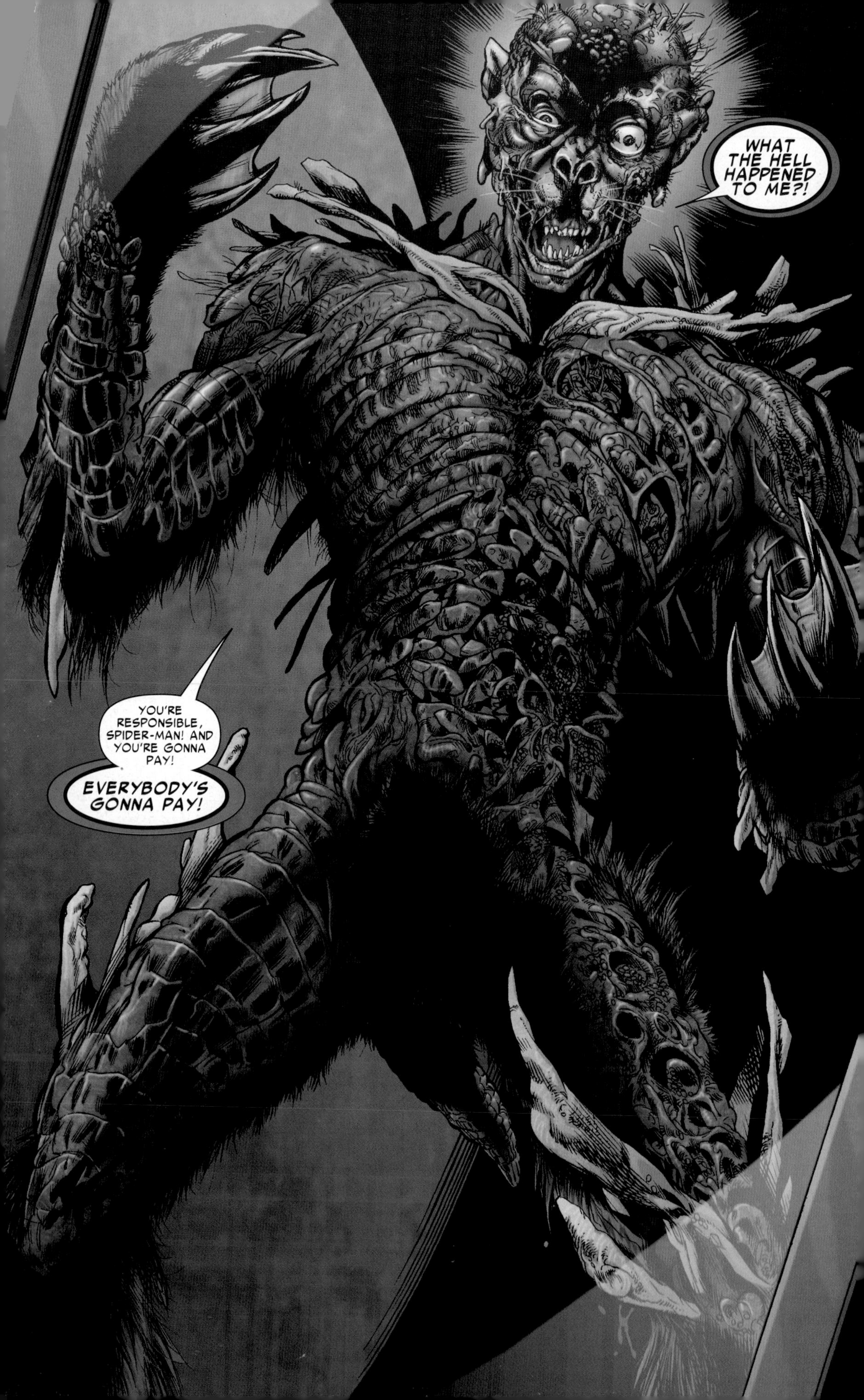
WHAT THE HELL HAPPENED TO ME?!
YOU'RE RESPONSIBLE, SPIDER-MAN! AND YOU'RE GONNA PAY!
EVERYBODY'S GONNA PAY!

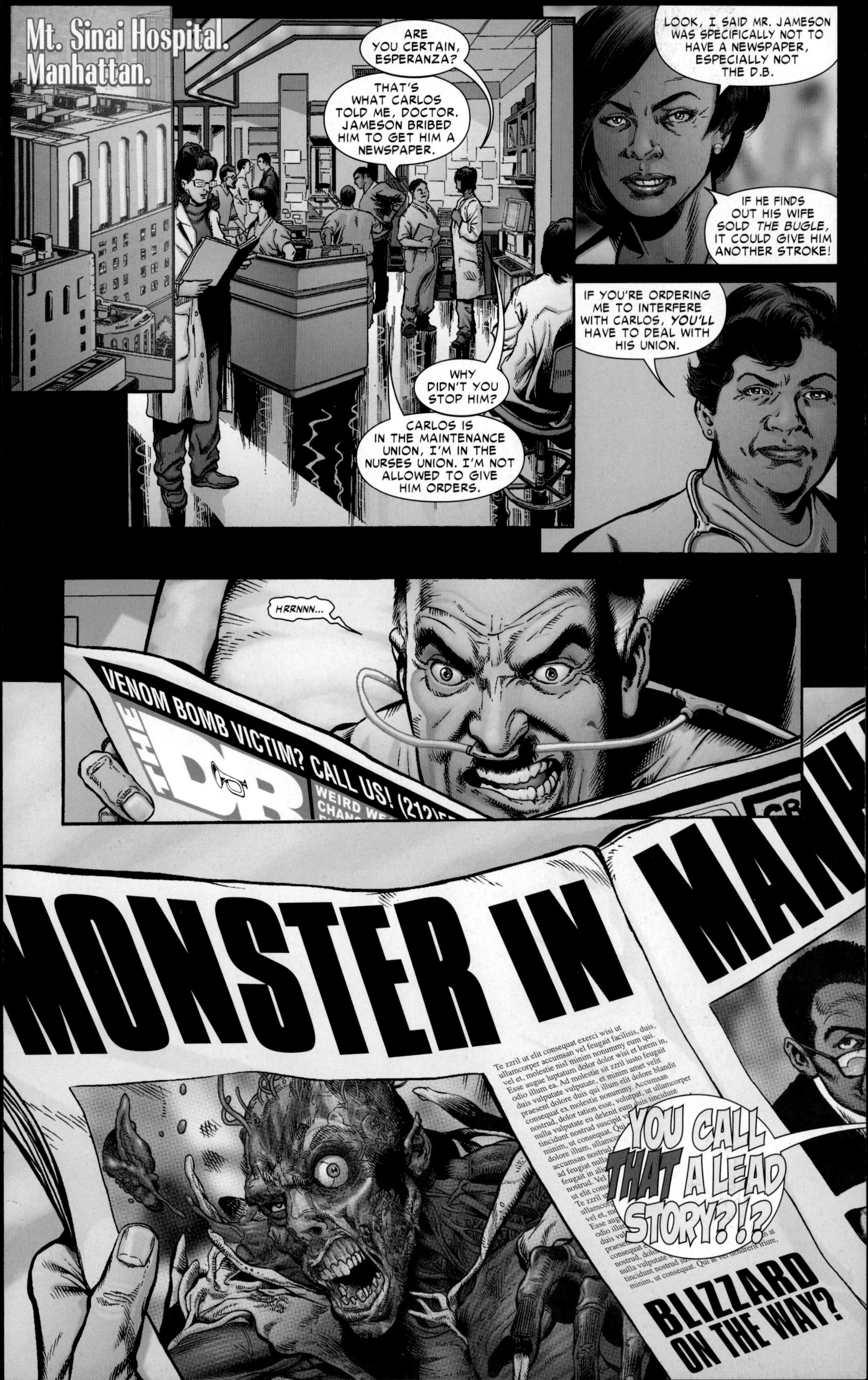

Mt. Sinai Hospital. Manhattan.
ARE YOU CERTAIN, ESPERANZA?
THAT'S WHAT CARLOS TOLD ME, DOCTOR. JAMESON BRIBED HIM TO GET HIM A NEWSPAPER.
WHY DIDN'T YOU STOP HIM?
CARLOS IS IN THE MAINTENANCE UNION, I'M IN THE NURSES UNION. I'M NOT ALLOWED TO GIVE HIM ORDERS.
LOOK, I SAID MR. JAMESON WAS SPECIFICALLY NOT TO HAVE A NEWSPAPER, ESPECIALLY NOT THE D.B.
IF HE FINDS OUT HIS WIFE SOLD *THE BUGLE*, IT COULD GIVE HIM ANOTHER STROKE!
IF YOU'RE ORDERING ME TO INTERFERE WITH CARLOS, *YOU'LL* HAVE TO DEAL WITH HIS UNION.
HRRNNN...
VENOM BOMB VICTIM? CALL US! (212)
THE DB
MONSTER IN MAN
Te zzril ut elit consequat exerci wisi ut ullamcorper accumsan vel feugait facilisis, duis, vel et, molestie nisl minim nonummy eum qui.
YOU CALL *THAT* A LEAD STORY?!?
BLIZZARD ON THE WAY?

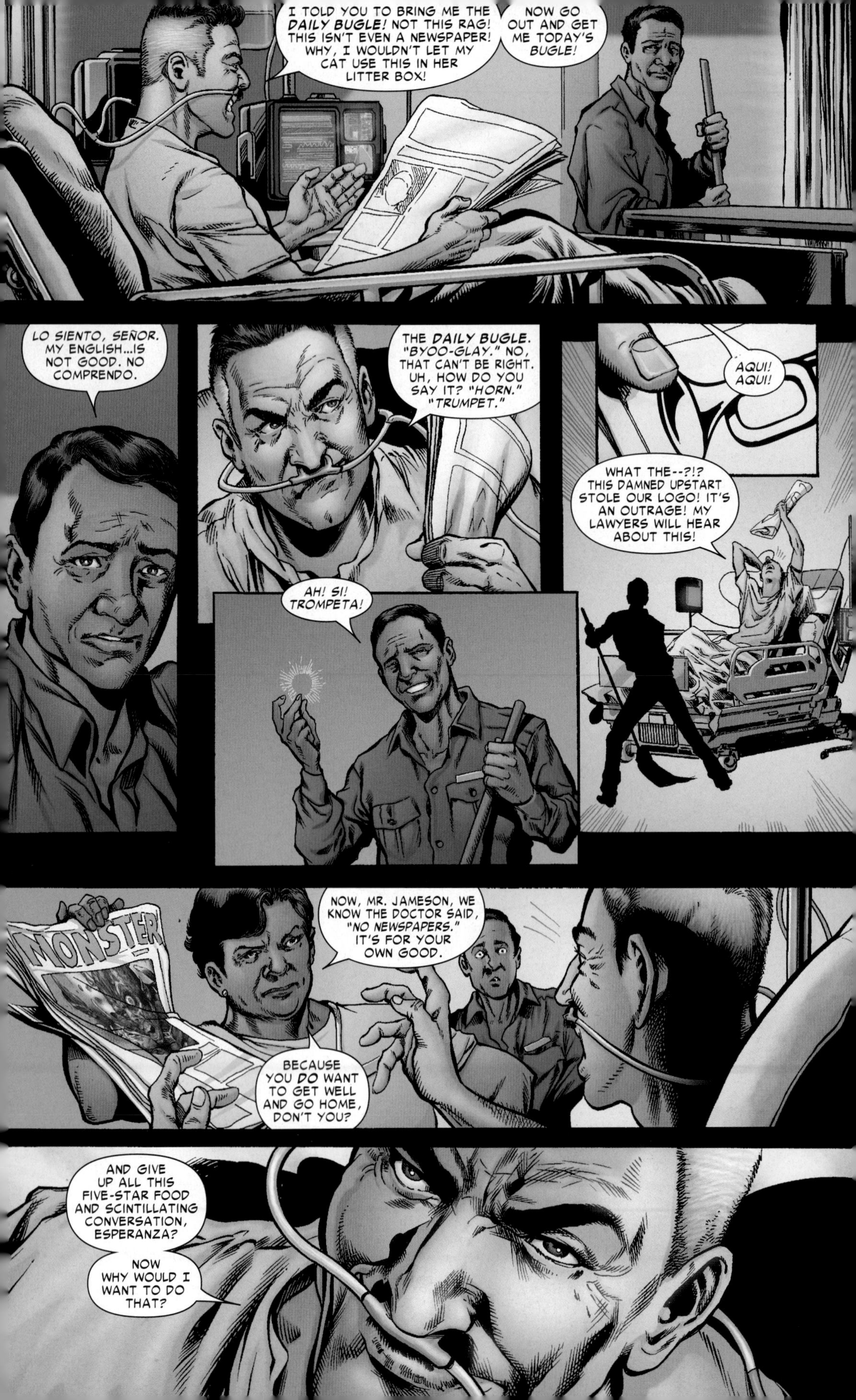
I TOLD YOU TO BRING ME THE DAILY BUGLE! NOT THIS RAG! THIS ISN'T EVEN A NEWSPAPER! WHY, I WOULDN'T LET MY CAT USE THIS IN HER LITTER BOX!
NOW GO OUT AND GET ME TODAY'S BUGLE!
LO SIENTO, SEÑOR. MY ENGLISH...IS NOT GOOD. NO COMPRENDO.
THE DAILY BUGLE. "BYOO-GLAY." NO, THAT CAN'T BE RIGHT. UH, HOW DO YOU SAY IT? "HORN." "TRUMPET."
AH! SI! TROMPETA!
AQUI! AQUI!
WHAT THE--?!? THIS DAMNED UPSTART STOLE OUR LOGO! IT'S AN OUTRAGE! MY LAWYERS WILL HEAR ABOUT THIS!
MONSTER
NOW, MR. JAMESON, WE KNOW THE DOCTOR SAID, "NO NEWSPAPERS." IT'S FOR YOUR OWN GOOD.
BECAUSE YOU DO WANT TO GET WELL AND GO HOME, DON'T YOU?
AND GIVE UP ALL THIS FIVE-STAR FOOD AND SCINTILLATING CONVERSATION, ESPERANZA?
NOW WHY WOULD I WANT TO DO THAT?

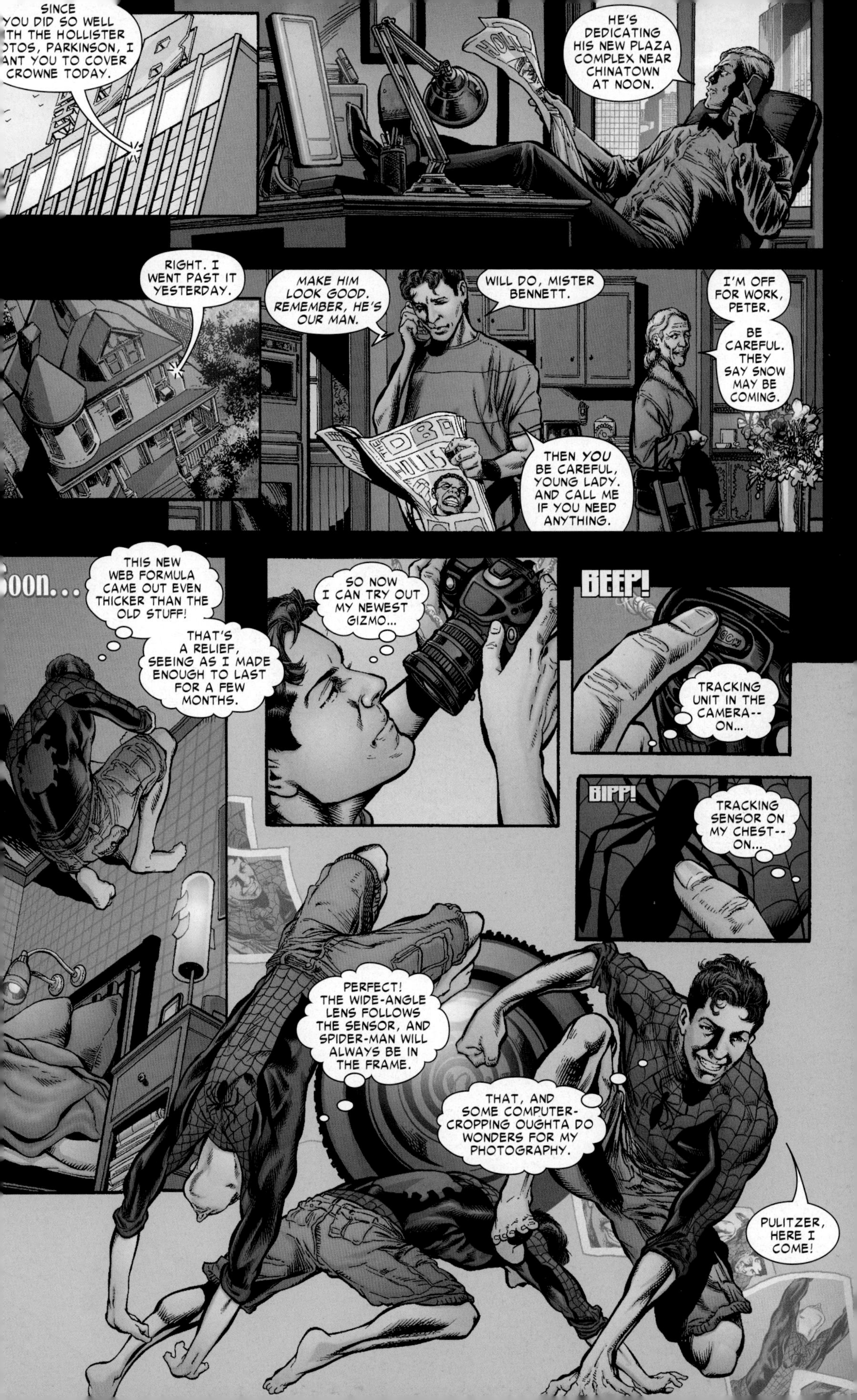
SINCE YOU DID SO WELL TH THE HOLLISTER OTOS, PARKINSON, I ANT YOU TO COVER CROWNE TODAY.
HE'S DEDICATING HIS NEW PLAZA COMPLEX NEAR CHINATOWN AT NOON.
RIGHT. I WENT PAST IT YESTERDAY.
MAKE HIM LOOK GOOD. REMEMBER, HE'S OUR MAN.
WILL DO, MISTER BENNETT.
I'M OFF FOR WORK, PETER.
BE CAREFUL. THEY SAY SNOW MAY BE COMING.
THEN YOU BE CAREFUL, YOUNG LADY. AND CALL ME IF YOU NEED ANYTHING.
oon. . .
THIS NEW WEB FORMULA CAME OUT EVEN THICKER THAN THE OLD STUFF!
THAT'S A RELIEF, SEEING AS I MADE ENOUGH TO LAST FOR A FEW MONTHS.
SO NOW I CAN TRY OUT MY NEWEST GIZMO...
BEEP!
TRACKING UNIT IN THE CAMERA-- ON...
BIPP!
TRACKING SENSOR ON MY CHEST-- ON...
PERFECT! THE WIDE-ANGLE LENS FOLLOWS THE SENSOR, AND SPIDER-MAN WILL ALWAYS BE IN THE FRAME.
THAT, AND SOME COMPUTER-CROPPING OUGHTA DO WONDERS FOR MY PHOTOGRAPHY.
PULITZER, HERE I COME!

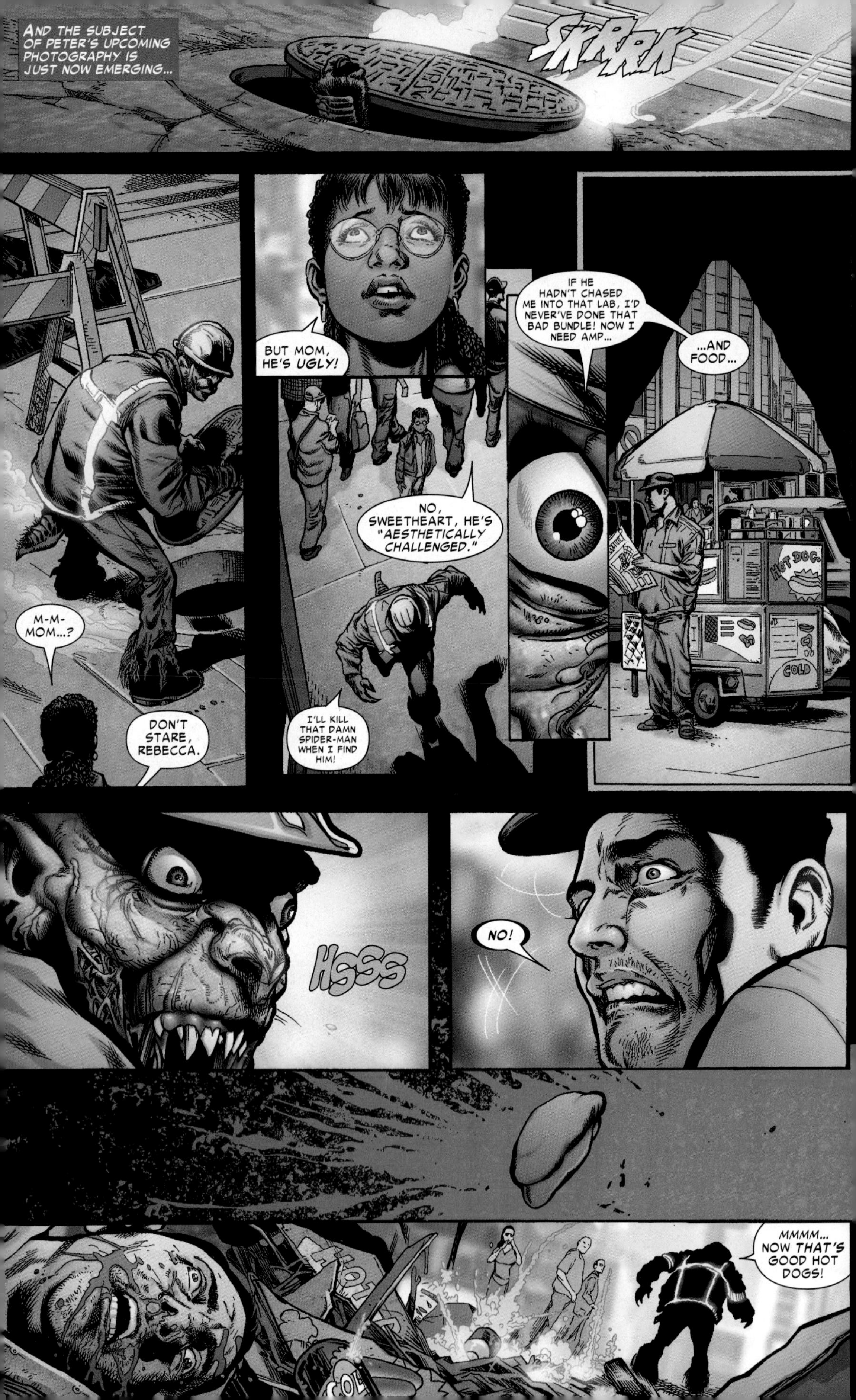
AND THE SUBJECT OF PETER'S UPCOMING PHOTOGRAPHY IS JUST NOW EMERGING...
SKRRK
BUT MOM, HE'S UGLY!
IF HE HADN'T CHASED ME INTO THAT LAB, I'D NEVER'VE DONE THAT BAD BUNDLE! NOW I NEED AMP...
...AND FOOD...
M-M-MOM...?
DON'T STARE, REBECCA.
NO, SWEETHEART, HE'S "AESTHETICALLY CHALLENGED."
I'LL KILL THAT DAMN SPIDER-MAN WHEN I FIND HIM!
HOT DOGS
COLD
HSSS
NO!
MMMM... NOW THAT'S GOOD HOT DOGS!

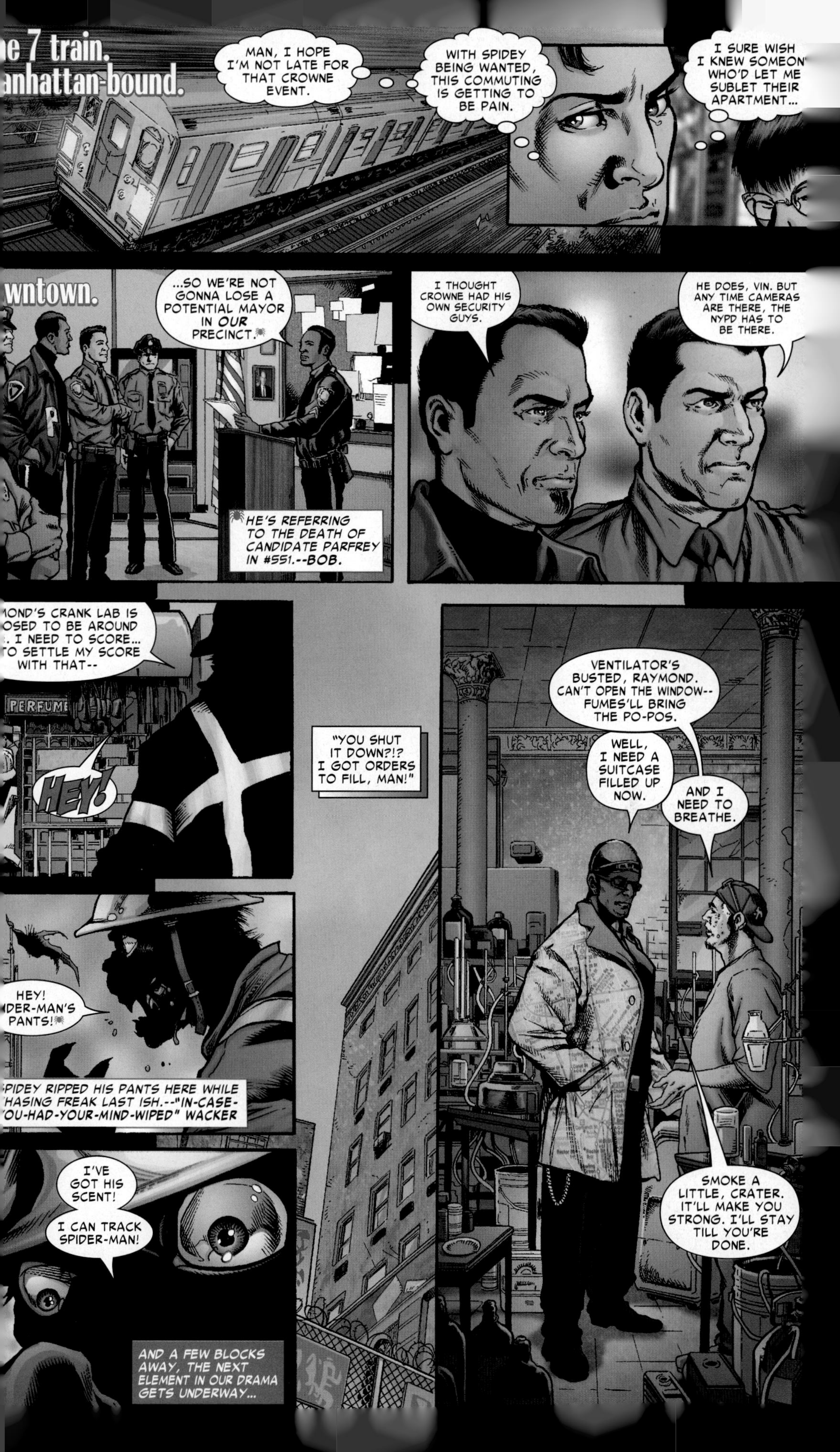

he 7 train.
anhattan-bound.
MAN, I HOPE I'M NOT LATE FOR THAT CROWNE EVENT.
WITH SPIDEY BEING WANTED, THIS COMMUTING IS GETTING TO BE PAIN.
I SURE WISH I KNEW SOMEON WHO'D LET ME SUBLET THEIR APARTMENT...
wntown.
...SO WE'RE NOT GONNA LOSE A POTENTIAL MAYOR IN OUR PRECINCT.
HE'S REFERRING TO THE DEATH OF CANDIDATE PARFREY IN #551.--BOB.
I THOUGHT CROWNE HAD HIS OWN SECURITY GUYS.
HE DOES, VIN. BUT ANY TIME CAMERAS ARE THERE, THE NYPD HAS TO BE THERE.
MOND'S CRANK LAB IS OSED TO BE AROUND . I NEED TO SCORE... TO SETTLE MY SCORE WITH THAT--
PERFUME
HEY!
HEY! DER-MAN'S PANTS!
PIDEY RIPPED HIS PANTS HERE WHILE HASING FREAK LAST ISH.--"IN-CASE-OU-HAD-YOUR-MIND-WIPED" WACKER
I'VE GOT HIS SCENT!
I CAN TRACK SPIDER-MAN!
AND A FEW BLOCKS AWAY, THE NEXT ELEMENT IN OUR DRAMA GETS UNDERWAY...
"YOU SHUT IT DOWN?!? I GOT ORDERS TO FILL, MAN!"
VENTILATOR'S BUSTED, RAYMOND. CAN'T OPEN THE WINDOW-- FUMES'LL BRING THE PO-POS.
WELL, I NEED A SUITCASE FILLED UP NOW.
AND I NEED TO BREATHE.
SMOKE A LITTLE, CRATER. IT'LL MAKE YOU STRONG. I'LL STAY TILL YOU'RE DONE.

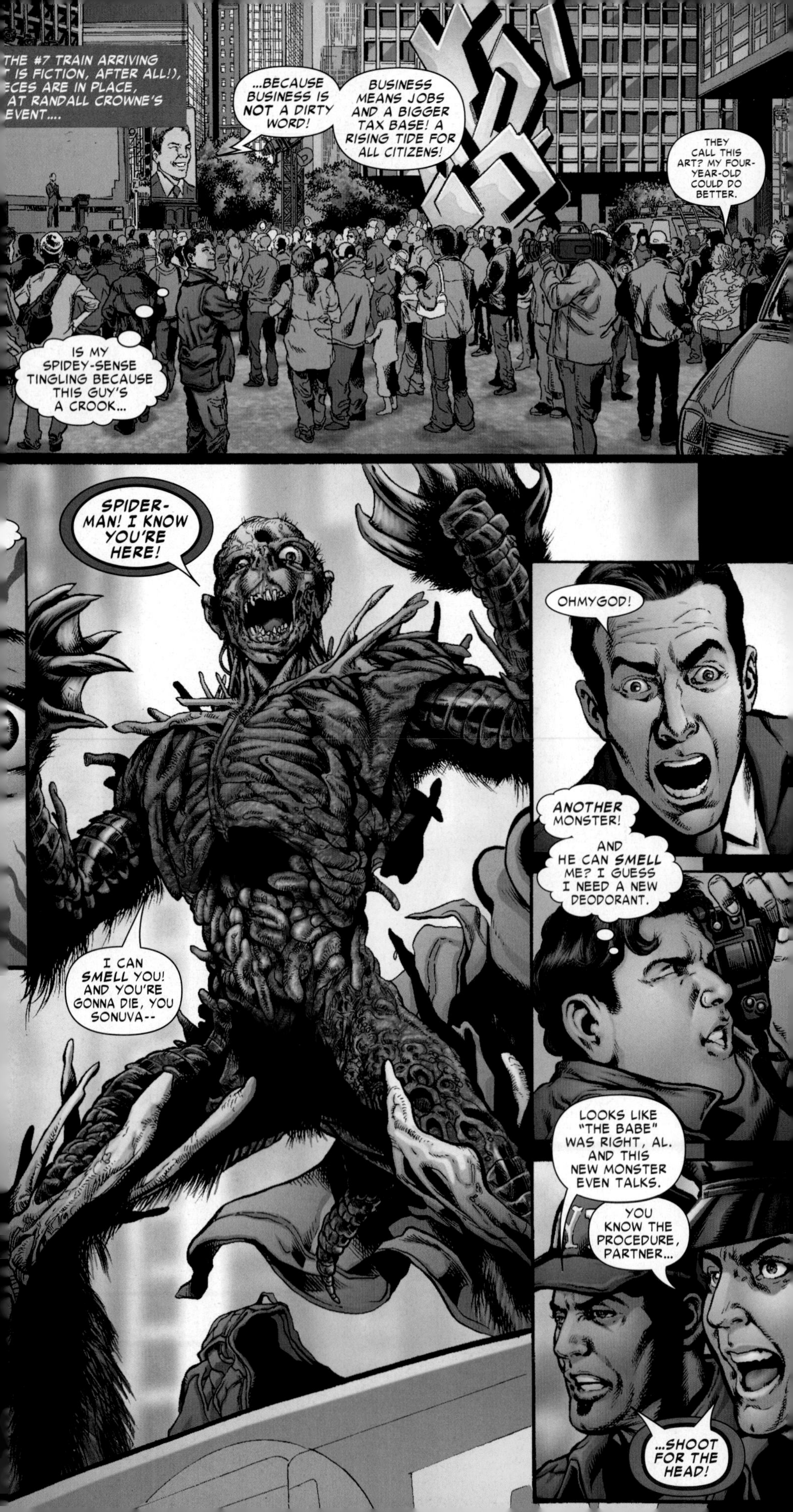

THE #7 TRAIN ARRIVING
T IS FICTION, AFTER ALL!),
ECES ARE IN PLACE,
AT RANDALL CROWNE'S
EVENT....
...BECAUSE BUSINESS IS NOT A DIRTY WORD!
BUSINESS MEANS JOBS AND A BIGGER TAX BASE! A RISING TIDE FOR ALL CITIZENS!
THEY CALL THIS ART? MY FOUR-YEAR-OLD COULD DO BETTER.
IS MY SPIDEY-SENSE TINGLING BECAUSE THIS GUY'S A CROOK...
SPIDER-MAN! I KNOW YOU'RE HERE!
I CAN SMELL YOU! AND YOU'RE GONNA DIE, YOU SONUVA--
OHMYGOD!
ANOTHER MONSTER!
AND HE CAN SMELL ME? I GUESS I NEED A NEW DEODORANT.
LOOKS LIKE "THE BABE" WAS RIGHT, AL. AND THIS NEW MONSTER EVEN TALKS.
YOU KNOW THE PROCEDURE, PARTNER...
...SHOOT FOR THE HEAD!

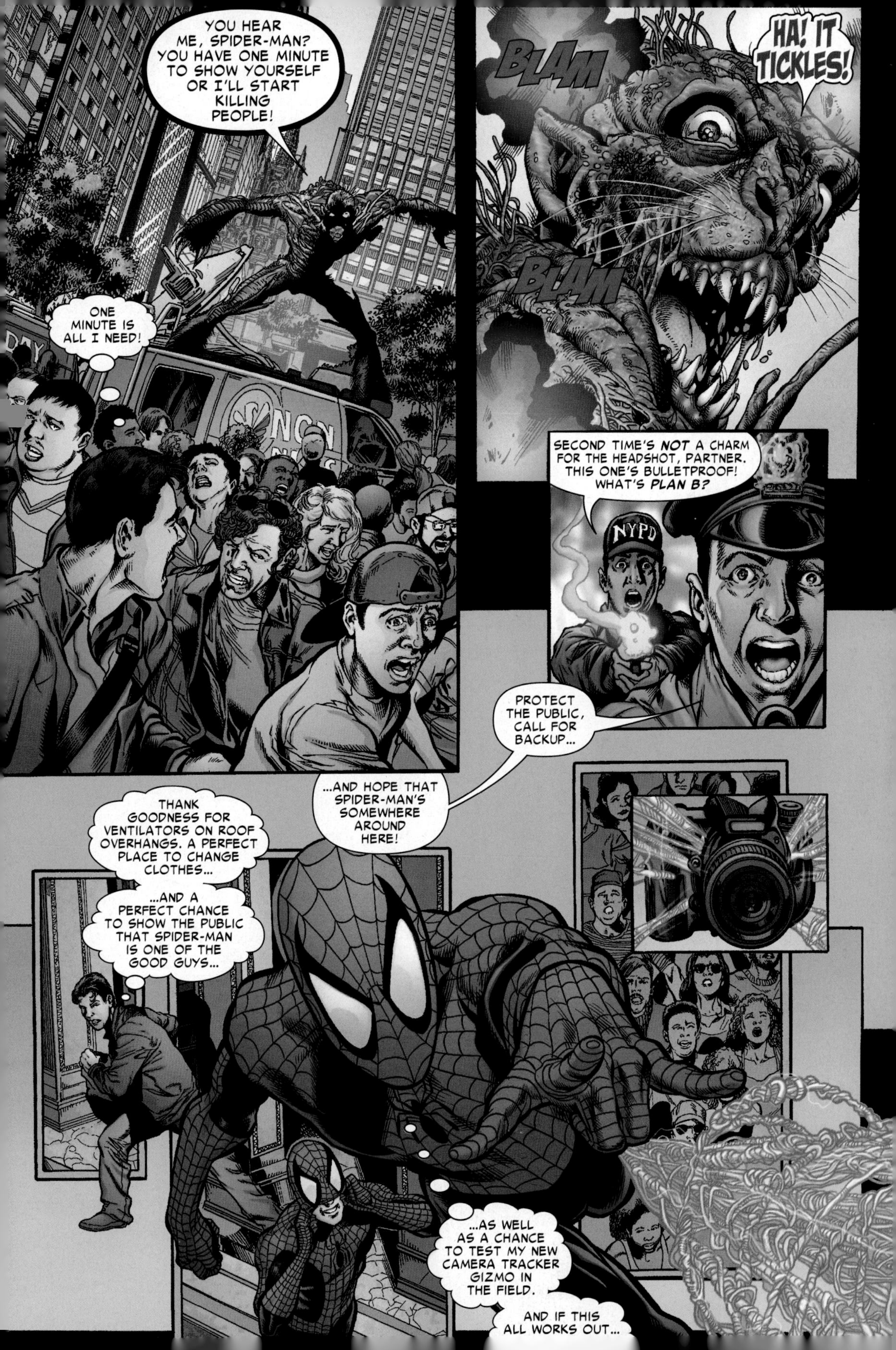
YOU HEAR ME, SPIDER-MAN? YOU HAVE ONE MINUTE TO SHOW YOURSELF OR I'LL START KILLING PEOPLE!
ONE MINUTE IS ALL I NEED!
BLAM
BLAM
HA! IT TICKLES!
SECOND TIME'S NOT A CHARM FOR THE HEADSHOT, PARTNER. THIS ONE'S BULLETPROOF! WHAT'S PLAN B?
NYPD
PROTECT THE PUBLIC, CALL FOR BACKUP...
...AND HOPE THAT SPIDER-MAN'S SOMEWHERE AROUND HERE!
THANK GOODNESS FOR VENTILATORS ON ROOF OVERHANGS. A PERFECT PLACE TO CHANGE CLOTHES...
...AND A PERFECT CHANCE TO SHOW THE PUBLIC THAT SPIDER-MAN IS ONE OF THE GOOD GUYS...
...AS WELL AS A CHANCE TO TEST MY NEW CAMERA TRACKER GIZMO IN THE FIELD.
AND IF THIS ALL WORKS OUT...

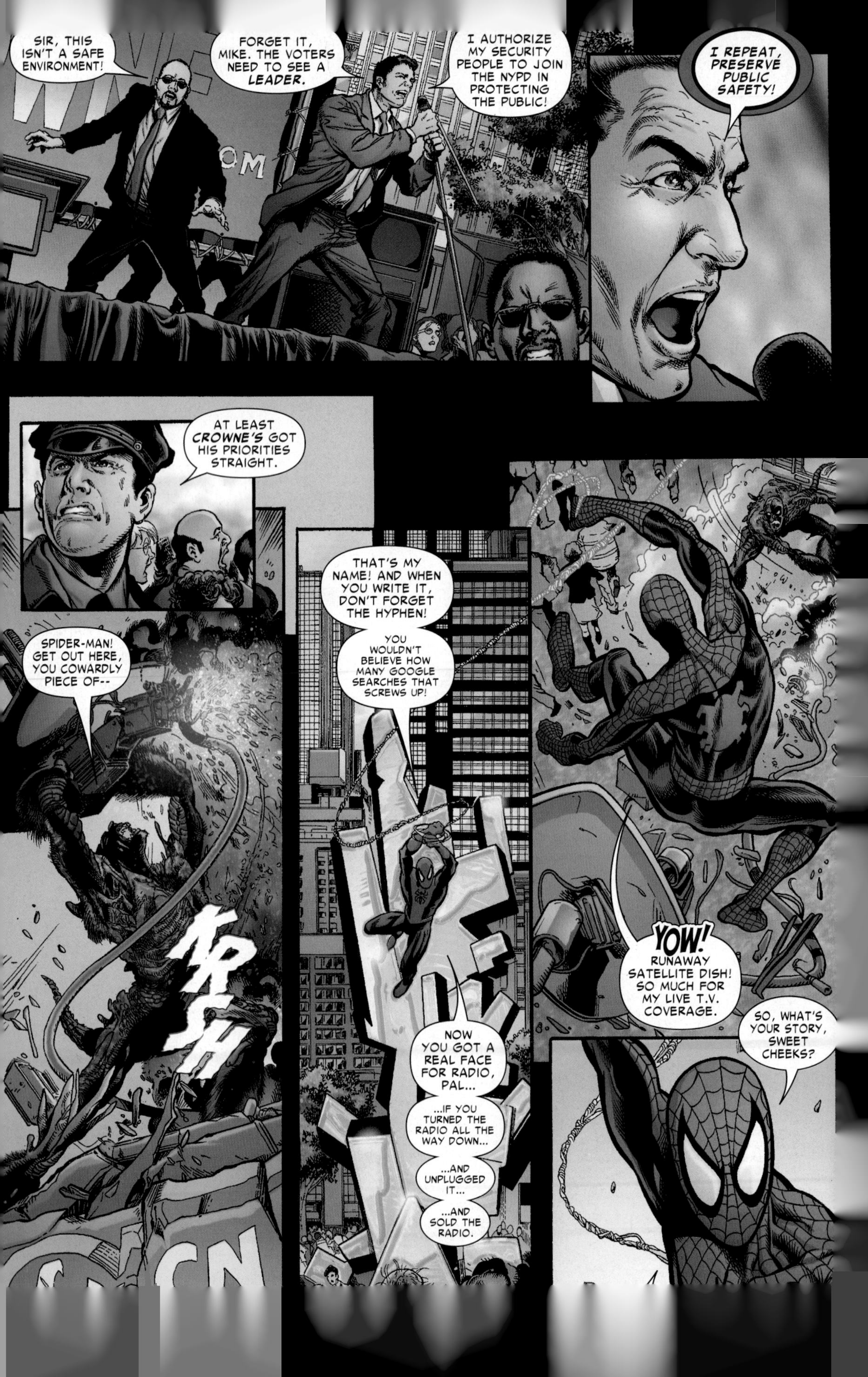
SIR, THIS ISN'T A SAFE ENVIRONMENT!
FORGET IT, MIKE. THE VOTERS NEED TO SEE A LEADER.
I AUTHORIZE MY SECURITY PEOPLE TO JOIN THE NYPD IN PROTECTING THE PUBLIC!
I REPEAT, PRESERVE PUBLIC SAFETY!
AT LEAST CROWNE'S GOT HIS PRIORITIES STRAIGHT.
SPIDER-MAN! GET OUT HERE, YOU COWARDLY PIECE OF--
KRSH
THAT'S MY NAME! AND WHEN YOU WRITE IT, DON'T FORGET THE HYPHEN!
YOU WOULDN'T BELIEVE HOW MANY GOOGLE SEARCHES THAT SCREWS UP!
YOW!
RUNAWAY SATELLITE DISH! SO MUCH FOR MY LIVE T.V. COVERAGE.
NOW YOU GOT A REAL FACE FOR RADIO, PAL...
...IF YOU TURNED THE RADIO ALL THE WAY DOWN...
...AND UNPLUGGED IT...
...AND SOLD THE RADIO.
SO, WHAT'S YOUR STORY, SWEET CHEEKS?

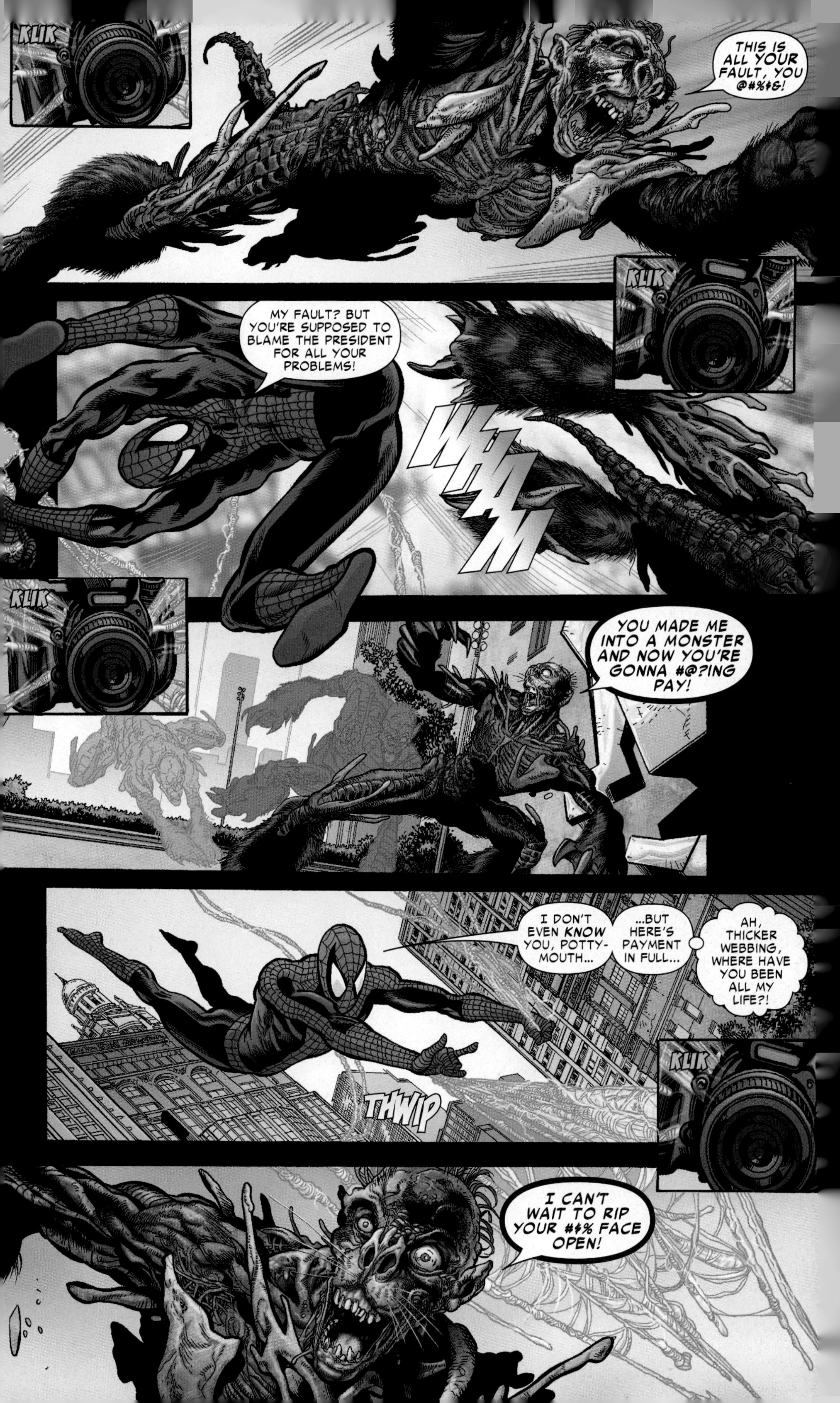
KLIK
THIS IS ALL YOUR FAULT, YOU @#%¢&!
KLIK
MY FAULT? BUT YOU'RE SUPPOSED TO BLAME THE PRESIDENT FOR ALL YOUR PROBLEMS!
WHAM
KLIK
YOU MADE ME INTO A MONSTER AND NOW YOU'RE GONNA #@?ING PAY!
I DON'T EVEN KNOW YOU, POTTY-MOUTH...
...BUT HERE'S PAYMENT IN FULL...
AH, THICKER WEBBING, WHERE HAVE YOU BEEN ALL MY LIFE?!
THWIP
KLIK
I CAN'T WAIT TO RIP YOUR #¢% FACE OPEN!

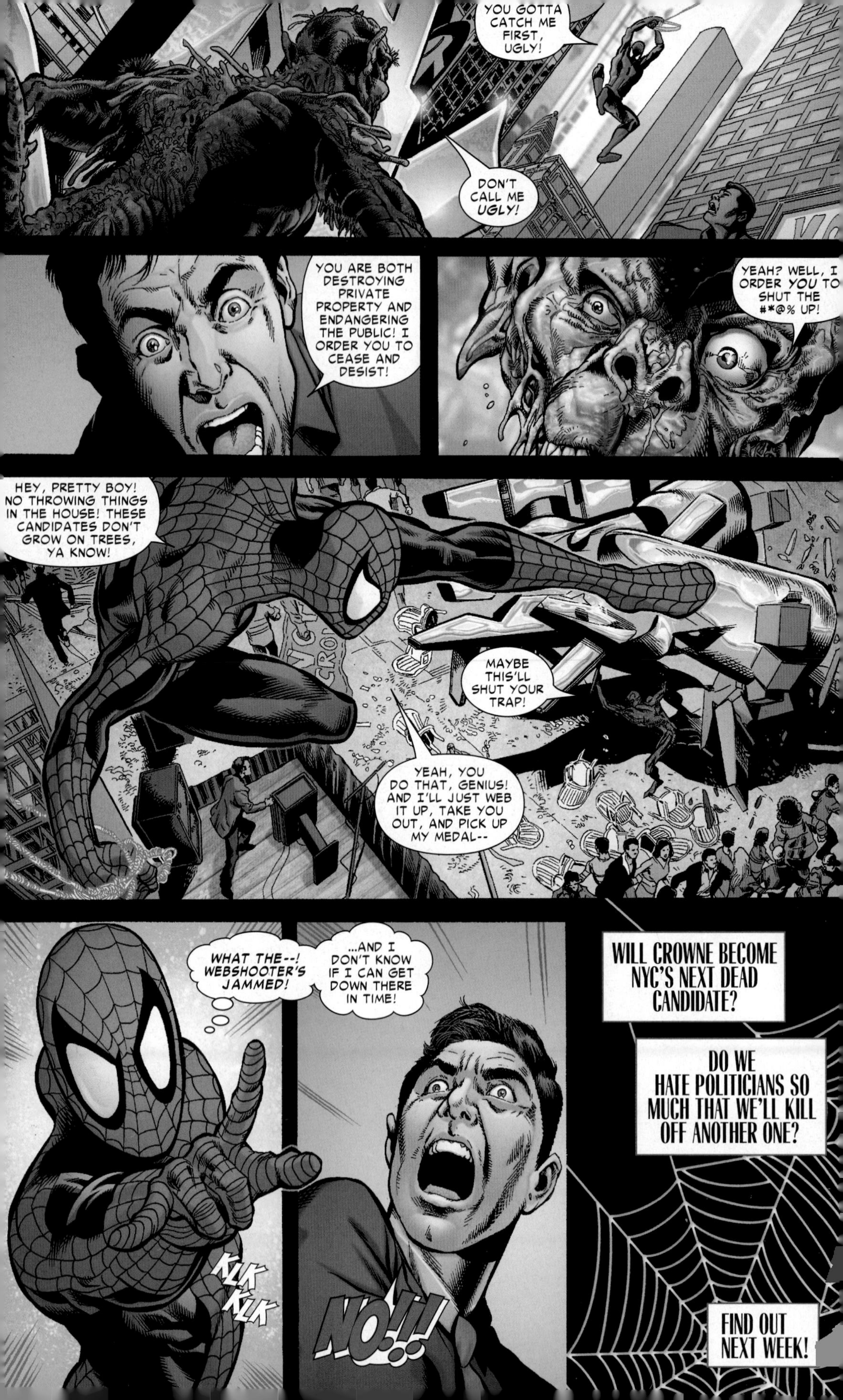
YOU GOTTA CATCH ME FIRST, UGLY!
DON'T CALL ME UGLY!
YOU ARE BOTH DESTROYING PRIVATE PROPERTY AND ENDANGERING THE PUBLIC! I ORDER YOU TO CEASE AND DESIST!
YEAH? WELL, I ORDER YOU TO SHUT THE #*@% UP!
HEY, PRETTY BOY! NO THROWING THINGS IN THE HOUSE! THESE CANDIDATES DON'T GROW ON TREES, YA KNOW!
MAYBE THIS'LL SHUT YOUR TRAP!
YEAH, YOU DO THAT, GENIUS! AND I'LL JUST WEB IT UP, TAKE YOU OUT, AND PICK UP MY MEDAL--
WHAT THE--! WEBSHOOTER'S JAMMED!
...AND I DON'T KNOW IF I CAN GET DOWN THERE IN TIME!
KLIK KLIK
NO!!!
WILL CROWNE BECOME NYC'S NEXT DEAD CANDIDATE?
DO WE HATE POLITICIANS SO MUCH THAT WE'LL KILL OFF ANOTHER ONE?
FIND OUT NEXT WEEK!

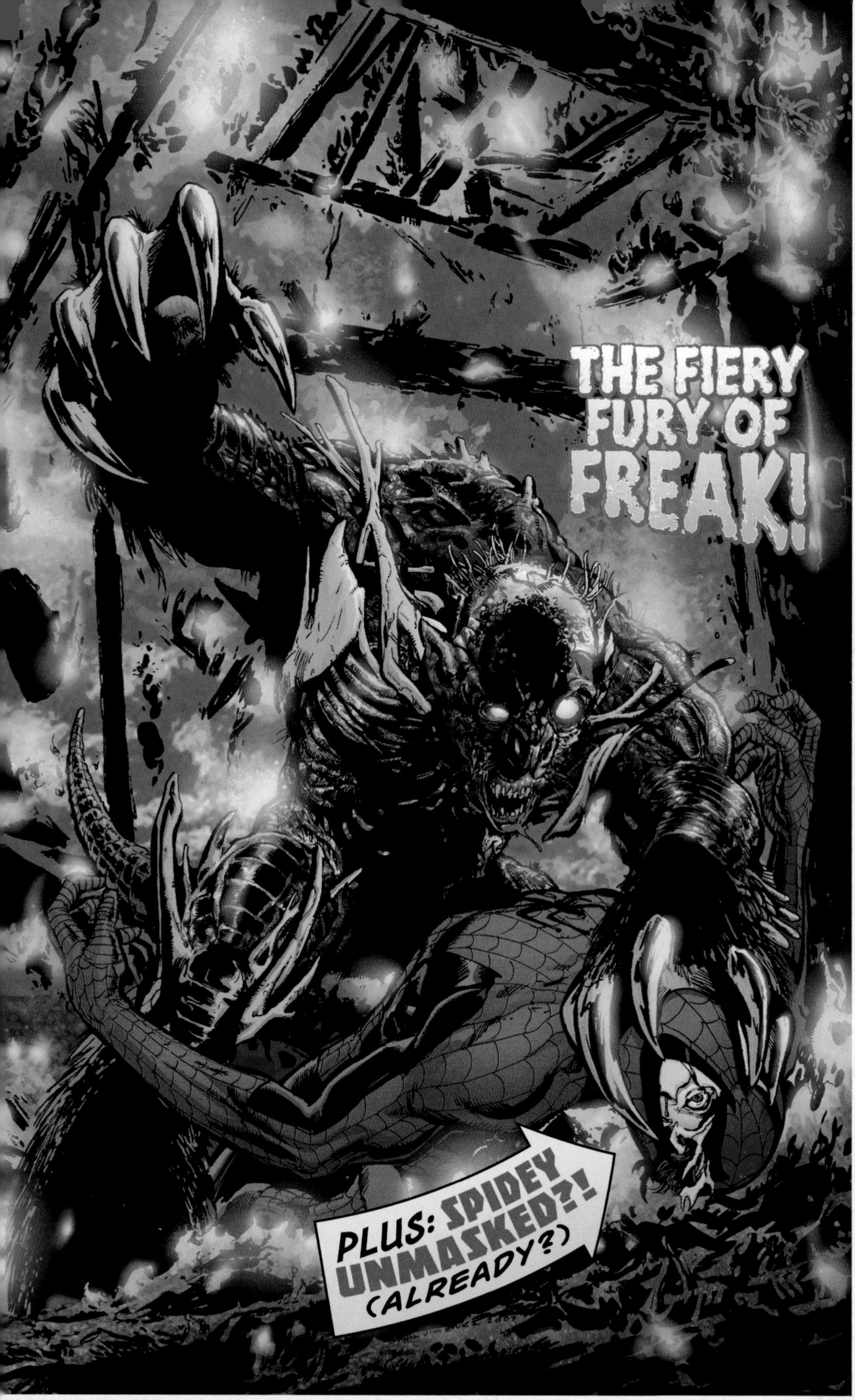
THE FIERY FURY OF FREAK!
PLUS: SPIDEY UNMASKED?! (ALREADY?)

AMAZING SPIDER-MAN #554

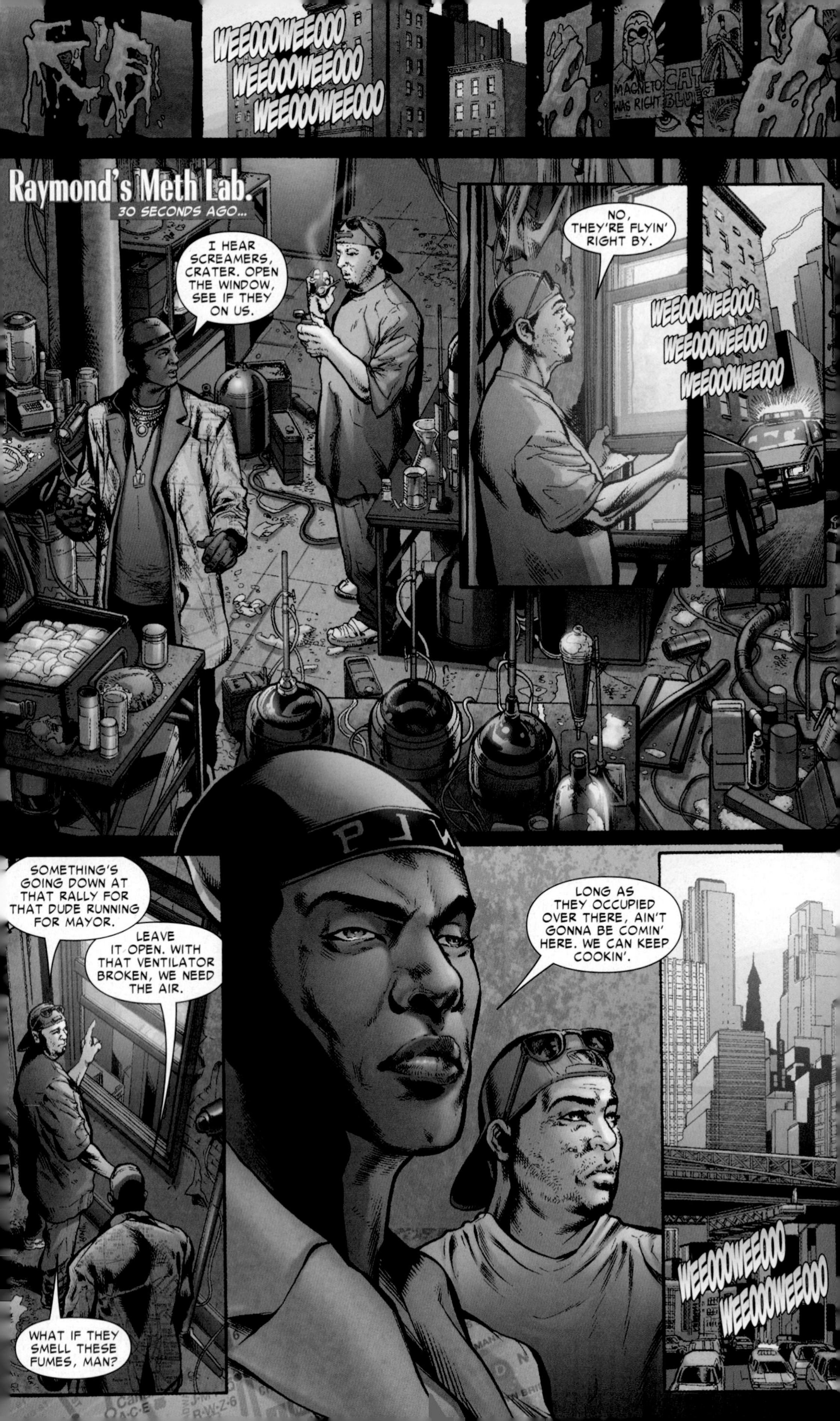
WEEOOOWEEOOO
WEEOOOWEEOOO
WEEOOOWEEOOO
MAGNETO WAS RIGHT
CAT BLUES
Raymond's Meth Lab.
30 SECONDS AGO...
I HEAR SCREAMERS, CRATER. OPEN THE WINDOW, SEE IF THEY ON US.
NO, THEY'RE FLYIN' RIGHT BY.
WEEOOOWEEOOO
WEEOOOWEEOOO
WEEOOOWEEOOO
SOMETHING'S GOING DOWN AT THAT RALLY FOR THAT DUDE RUNNING FOR MAYOR.
LEAVE IT OPEN. WITH THAT VENTILATOR BROKEN, WE NEED THE AIR.
WHAT IF THEY SMELL THESE FUMES, MAN?
LONG AS THEY OCCUPIED OVER THERE, AIN'T GONNA BE COMIN' HERE. WE CAN KEEP COOKIN'.
WEEOOOWEEOOO
WEEOOOWEEOOO

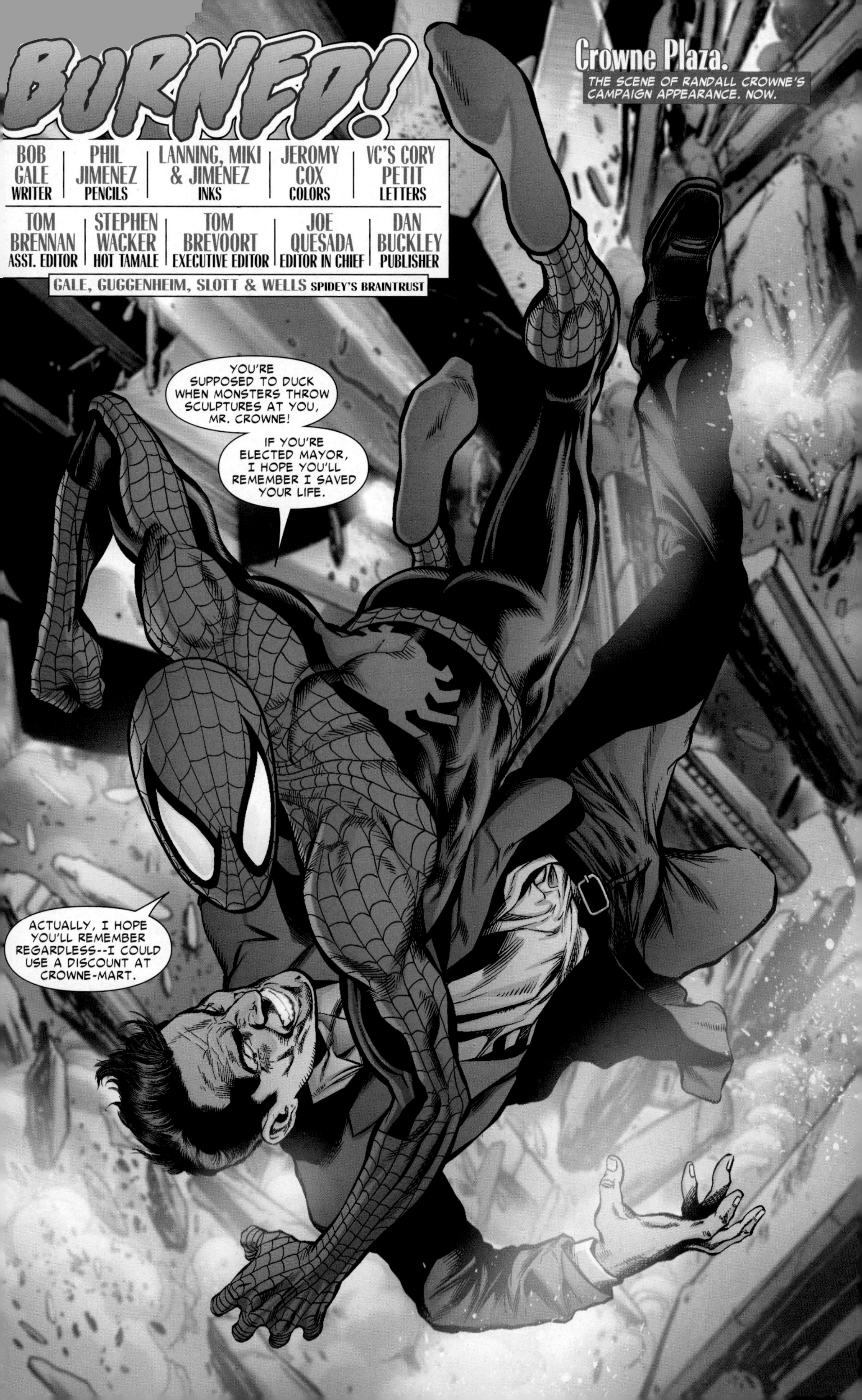
BURNED!
BOB GALE WRITER
PHIL JIMENEZ PENCILS
LANNING, MIKI & JIMENEZ INKS
JEROMY COX COLORS
VC'S CORY PETIT LETTERS
TOM BRENNAN ASST. EDITOR
STEPHEN WACKER HOT TAMALE
TOM BREVOORT EXECUTIVE EDITOR
JOE QUESADA EDITOR IN CHIEF
DAN BUCKLEY PUBLISHER
GALE, GUGGENHEIM, SLOTT & WELLS SPIDEY'S BRAINTRUST
Crowne Plaza.
THE SCENE OF RANDALL CROWNE'S CAMPAIGN APPEARANCE. NOW.
YOU'RE SUPPOSED TO DUCK WHEN MONSTERS THROW SCULPTURES AT YOU, MR. CROWNE!
IF YOU'RE ELECTED MAYOR, I HOPE YOU'LL REMEMBER I SAVED YOUR LIFE.
ACTUALLY, I HOPE YOU'LL REMEMBER REGARDLESS--I COULD USE A DISCOUNT AT CROWNE-MART.

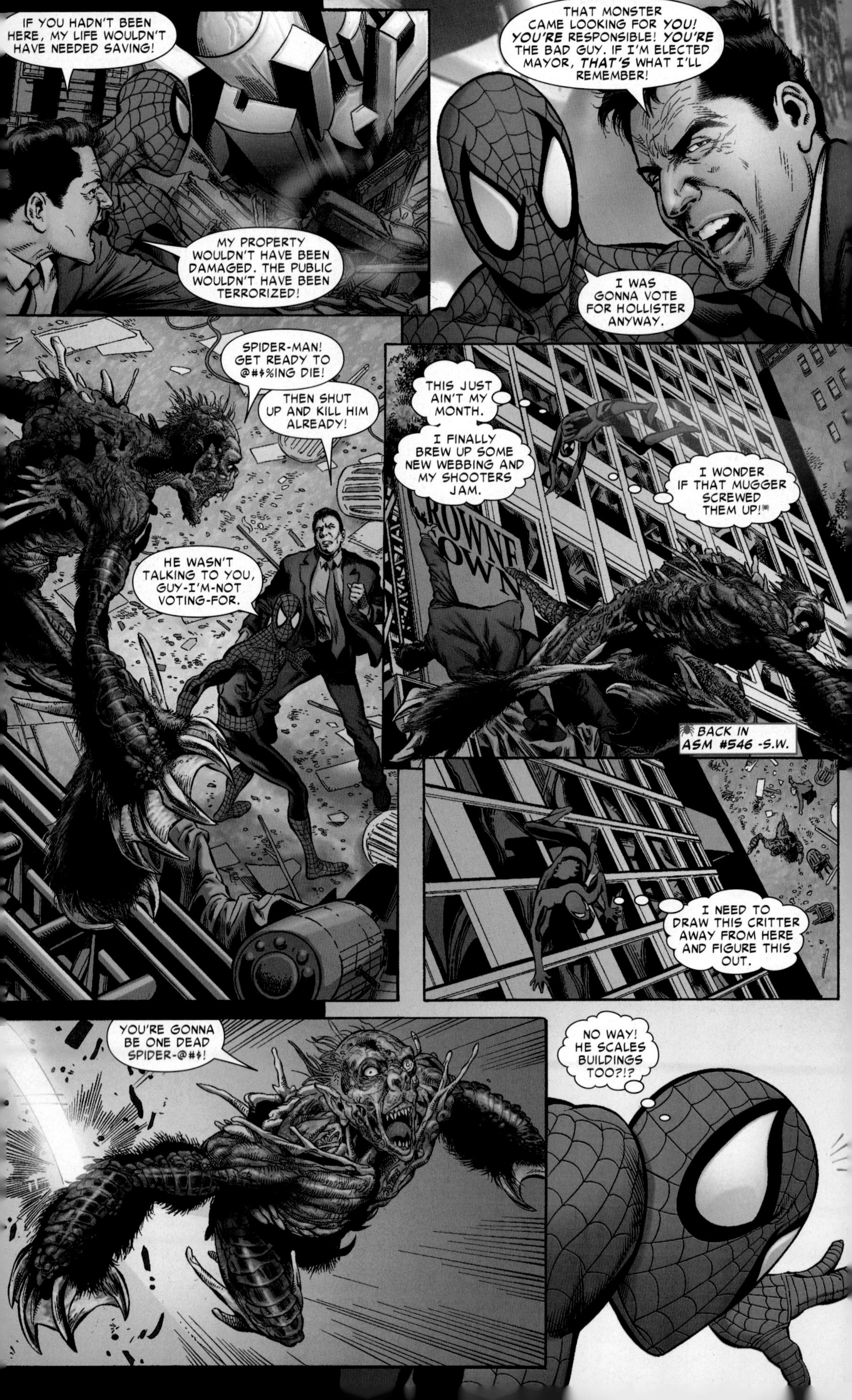

IF YOU HADN'T BEEN HERE, MY LIFE WOULDN'T HAVE NEEDED SAVING!
MY PROPERTY WOULDN'T HAVE BEEN DAMAGED. THE PUBLIC WOULDN'T HAVE BEEN TERRORIZED!
THAT MONSTER CAME LOOKING FOR YOU! YOU'RE RESPONSIBLE! YOU'RE THE BAD GUY. IF I'M ELECTED MAYOR, THAT'S WHAT I'LL REMEMBER!
I WAS GONNA VOTE FOR HOLLISTER ANYWAY.
SPIDER-MAN! GET READY TO @#$%ING DIE!
THEN SHUT UP AND KILL HIM ALREADY!
HE WASN'T TALKING TO YOU, GUY-I'M-NOT VOTING-FOR.
THIS JUST AIN'T MY MONTH.
I FINALLY BREW UP SOME NEW WEBBING AND MY SHOOTERS JAM.
I WONDER IF THAT MUGGER SCREWED THEM UP!*
*BACK IN ASM #546 -S.W.
I NEED TO DRAW THIS CRITTER AWAY FROM HERE AND FIGURE THIS OUT.
YOU'RE GONNA BE ONE DEAD SPIDER-@#$!
NO WAY! HE SCALES BUILDINGS TOO?!?

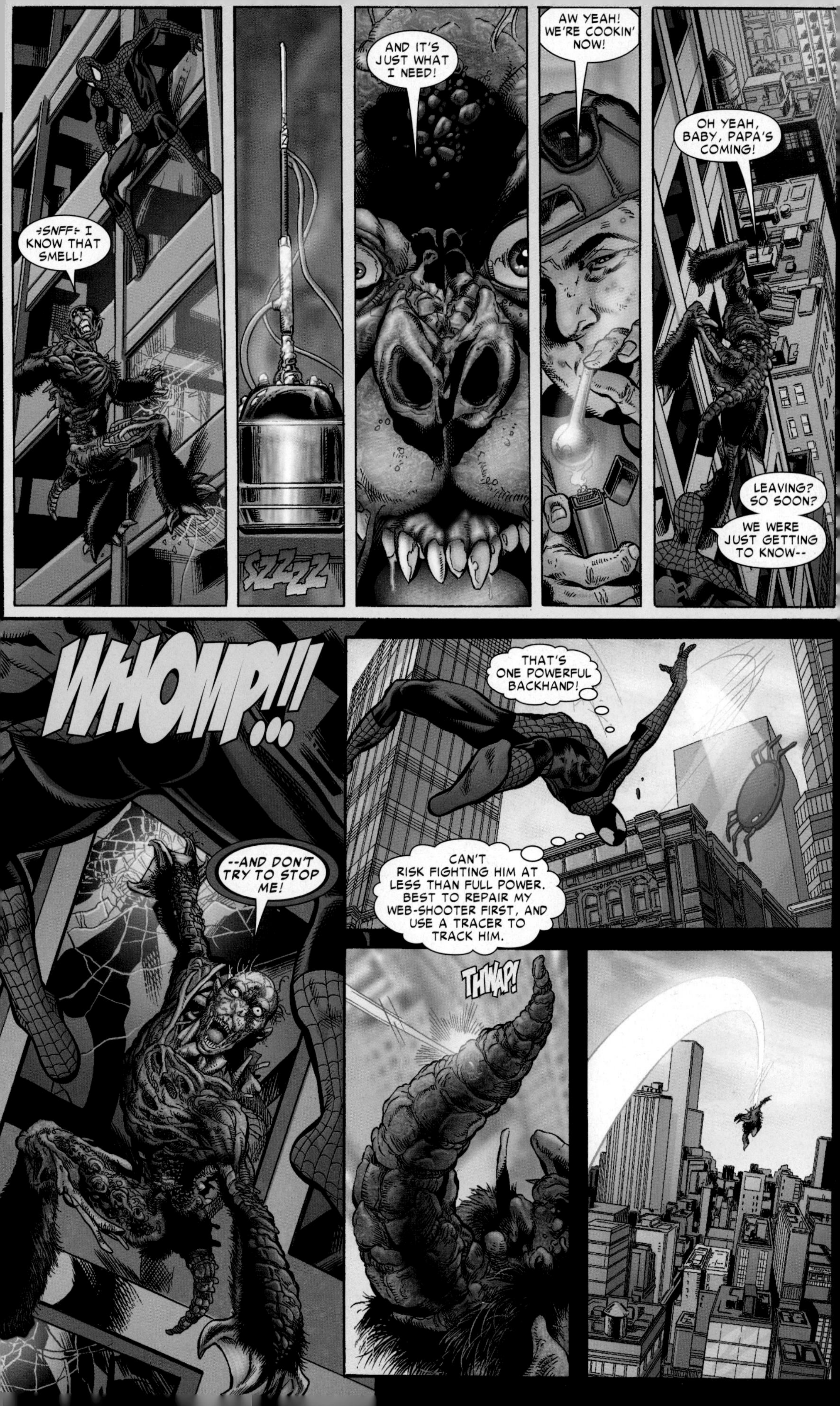

÷SNFF÷ I KNOW THAT SMELL!
SZZZZ
AND IT'S JUST WHAT I NEED!
AW YEAH! WE'RE COOKIN' NOW!
OH YEAH, BABY, PAPA'S COMING!
LEAVING? SO SOON?
WE WERE JUST GETTING TO KNOW--
WHOMP!!!...
--AND DON'T TRY TO STOP ME!
THAT'S ONE POWERFUL BACKHAND!
CAN'T RISK FIGHTING HIM AT LESS THAN FULL POWER. BEST TO REPAIR MY WEB-SHOOTER FIRST, AND USE A TRACER TO TRACK HIM.
THWAP!

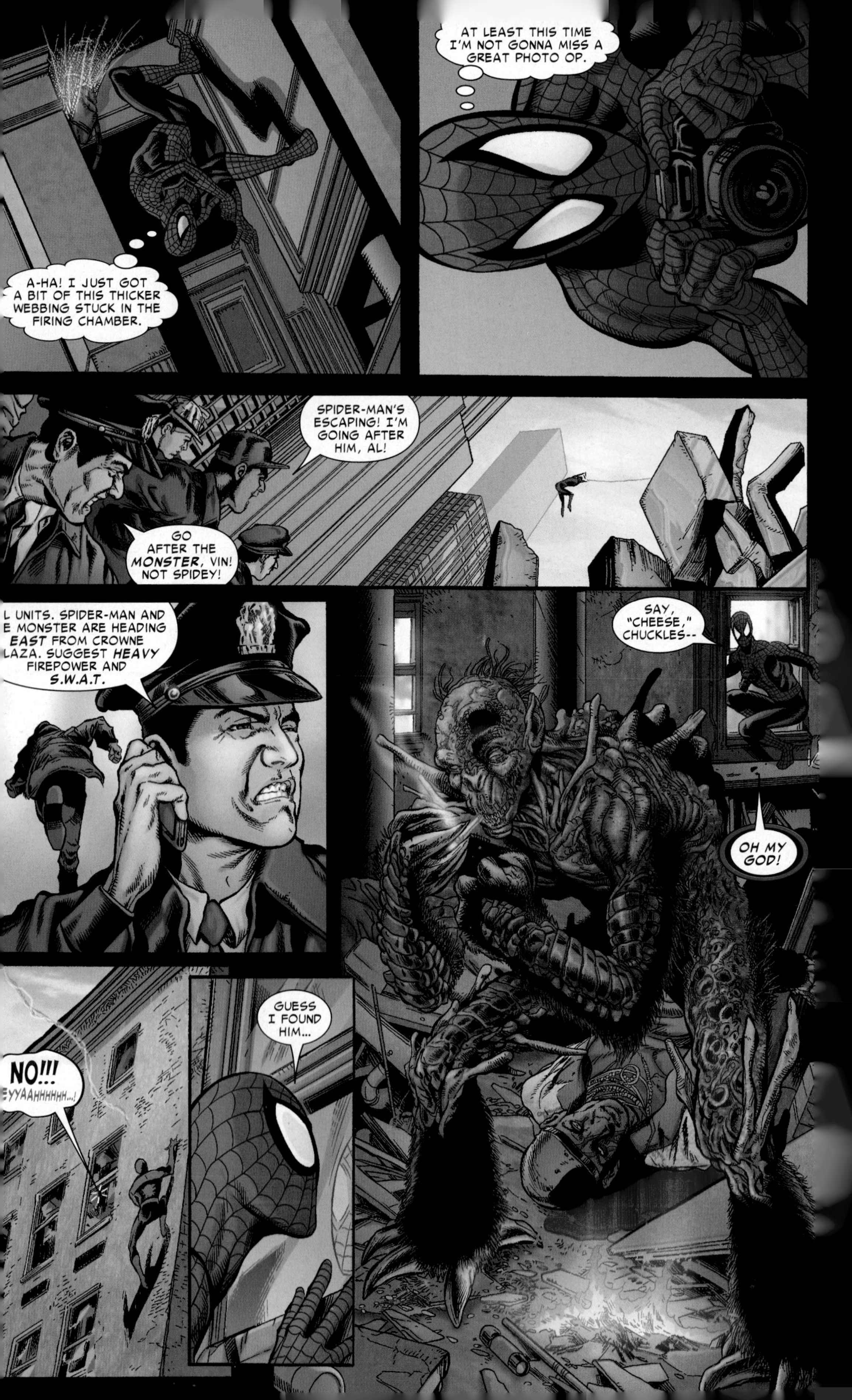
A-HA! I JUST GOT A BIT OF THIS THICKER WEBBING STUCK IN THE FIRING CHAMBER.
AT LEAST THIS TIME I'M NOT GONNA MISS A GREAT PHOTO OP.
SPIDER-MAN'S ESCAPING! I'M GOING AFTER HIM, AL!
GO AFTER THE MONSTER, VIN! NOT SPIDEY!
L UNITS. SPIDER-MAN AND E MONSTER ARE HEADING EAST FROM CROWNE LAZA. SUGGEST HEAVY FIREPOWER AND S.W.A.T.
NO!!!
YYAAHHHHHH...!
GUESS I FOUND HIM...
SAY, "CHEESE," CHUCKLES--
OH MY GOD!

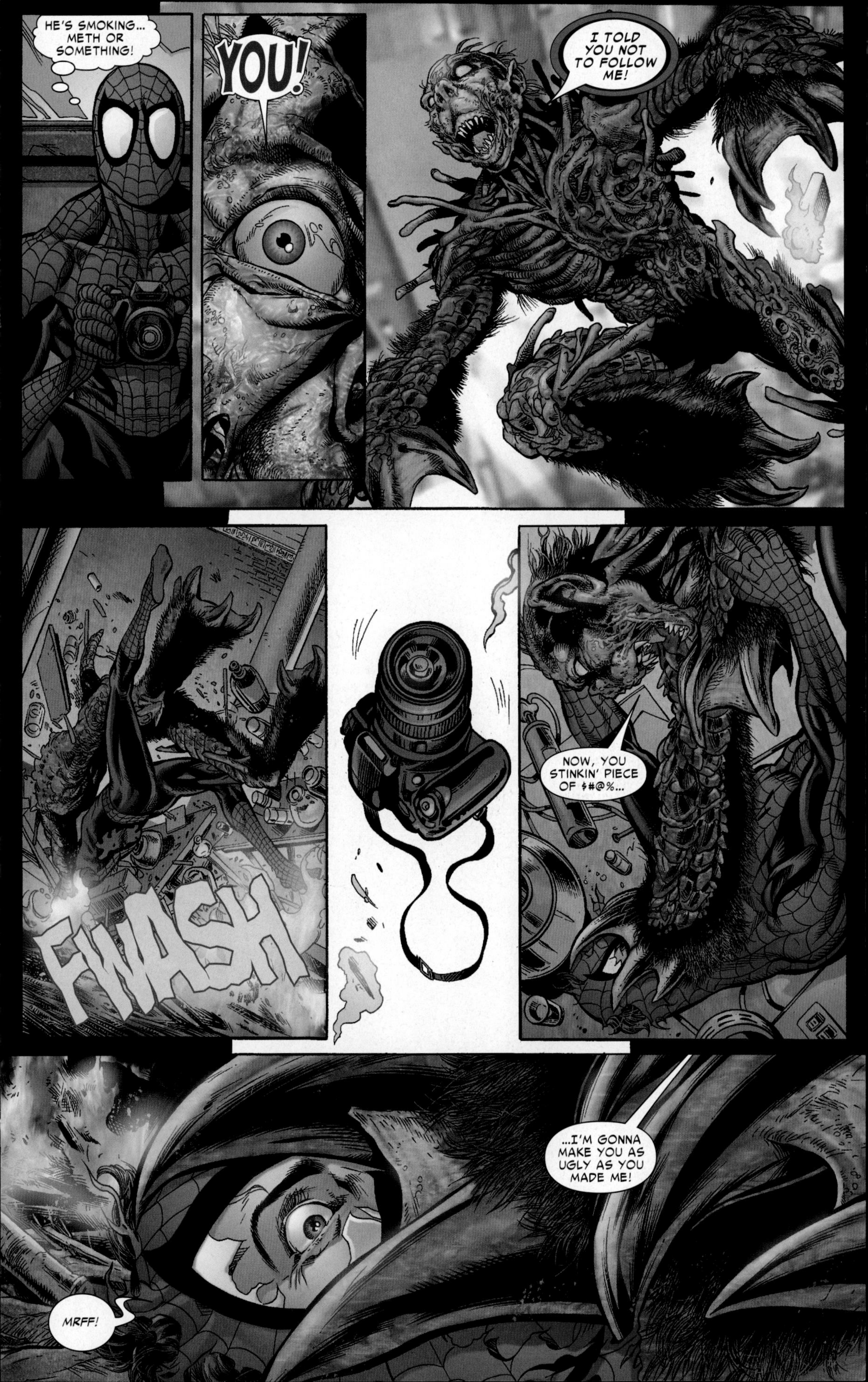
HE'S SMOKING... METH OR SOMETHING!
YOU!
I TOLD YOU NOT TO FOLLOW ME!
FWASH
NOW, YOU STINKIN' PIECE OF $#@%...
...I'M GONNA MAKE YOU AS UGLY AS YOU MADE ME!
MRFF!

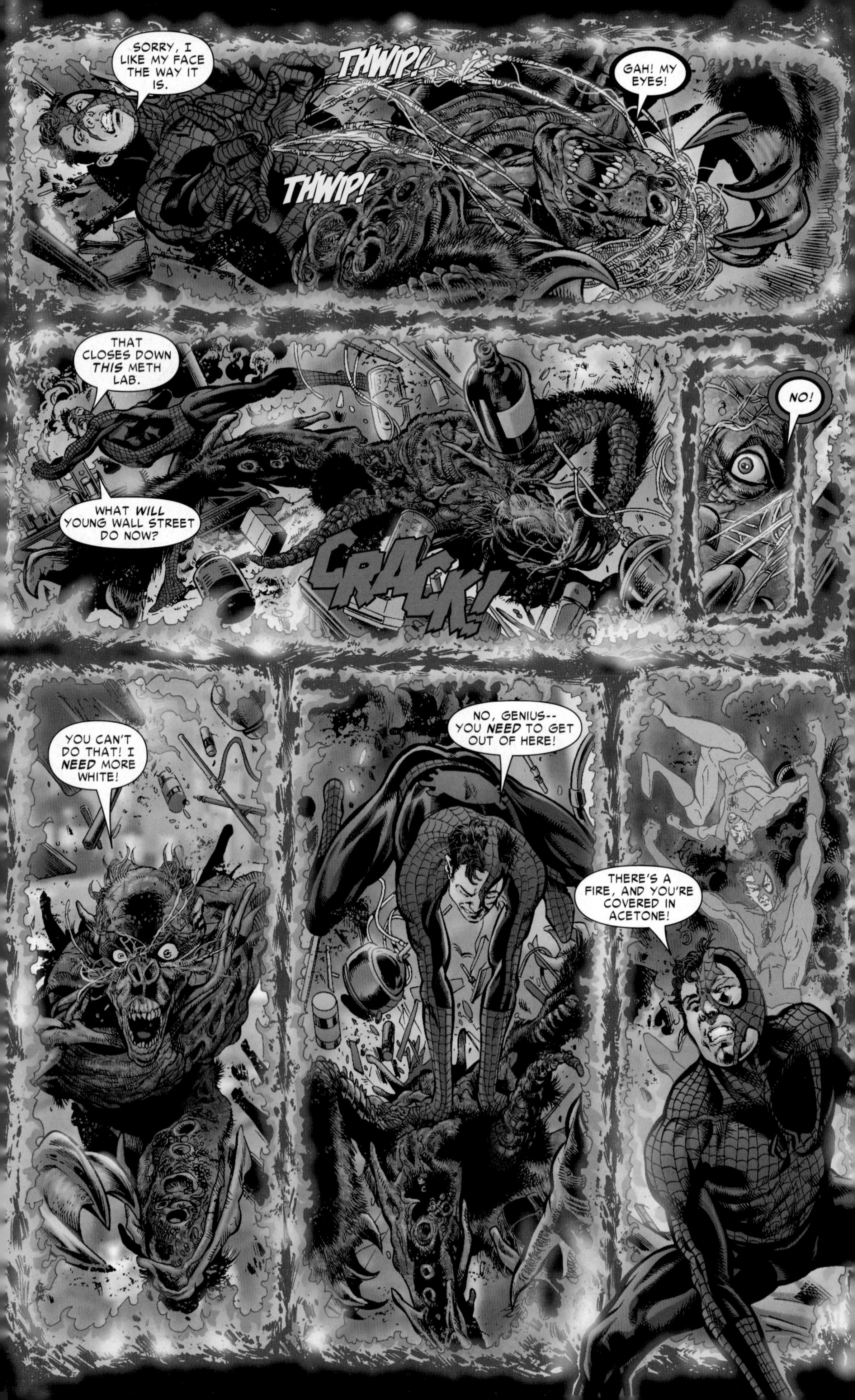
SORRY, I LIKE MY FACE THE WAY IT IS.
THWIP!
GAH! MY EYES!
THWIP!
THAT CLOSES DOWN THIS METH LAB.
WHAT WILL YOUNG WALL STREET DO NOW?
CRACK!
NO!
YOU CAN'T DO THAT! I NEED MORE WHITE!
NO, GENIUS-- YOU NEED TO GET OUT OF HERE!
THERE'S A FIRE, AND YOU'RE COVERED IN ACETONE!

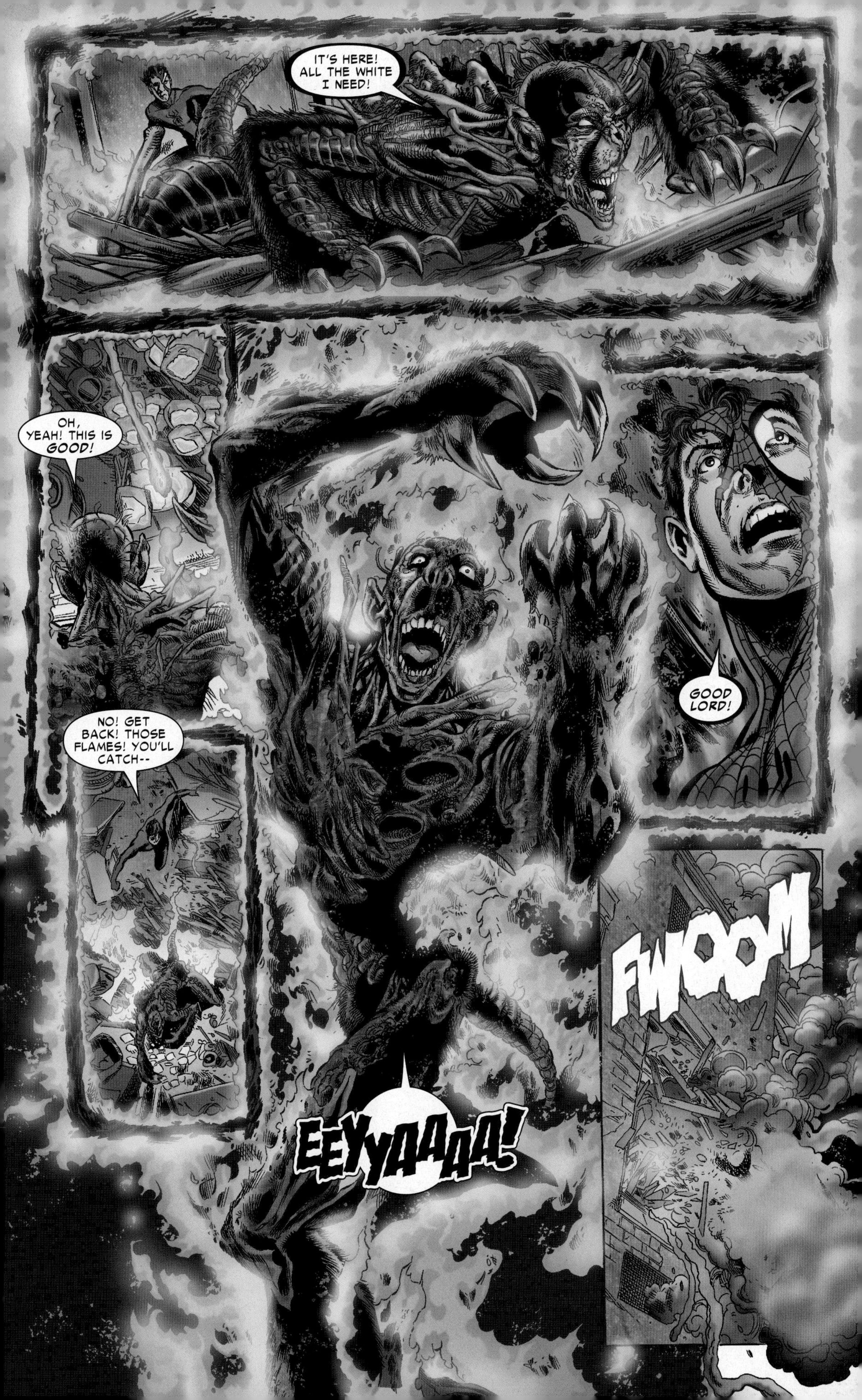
IT'S HERE! ALL THE WHITE I NEED!
OH, YEAH! THIS IS GOOD!
NO! GET BACK! THOSE FLAMES! YOU'LL CATCH--
GOOD LORD!
EEYYAAAA!
FWOOM

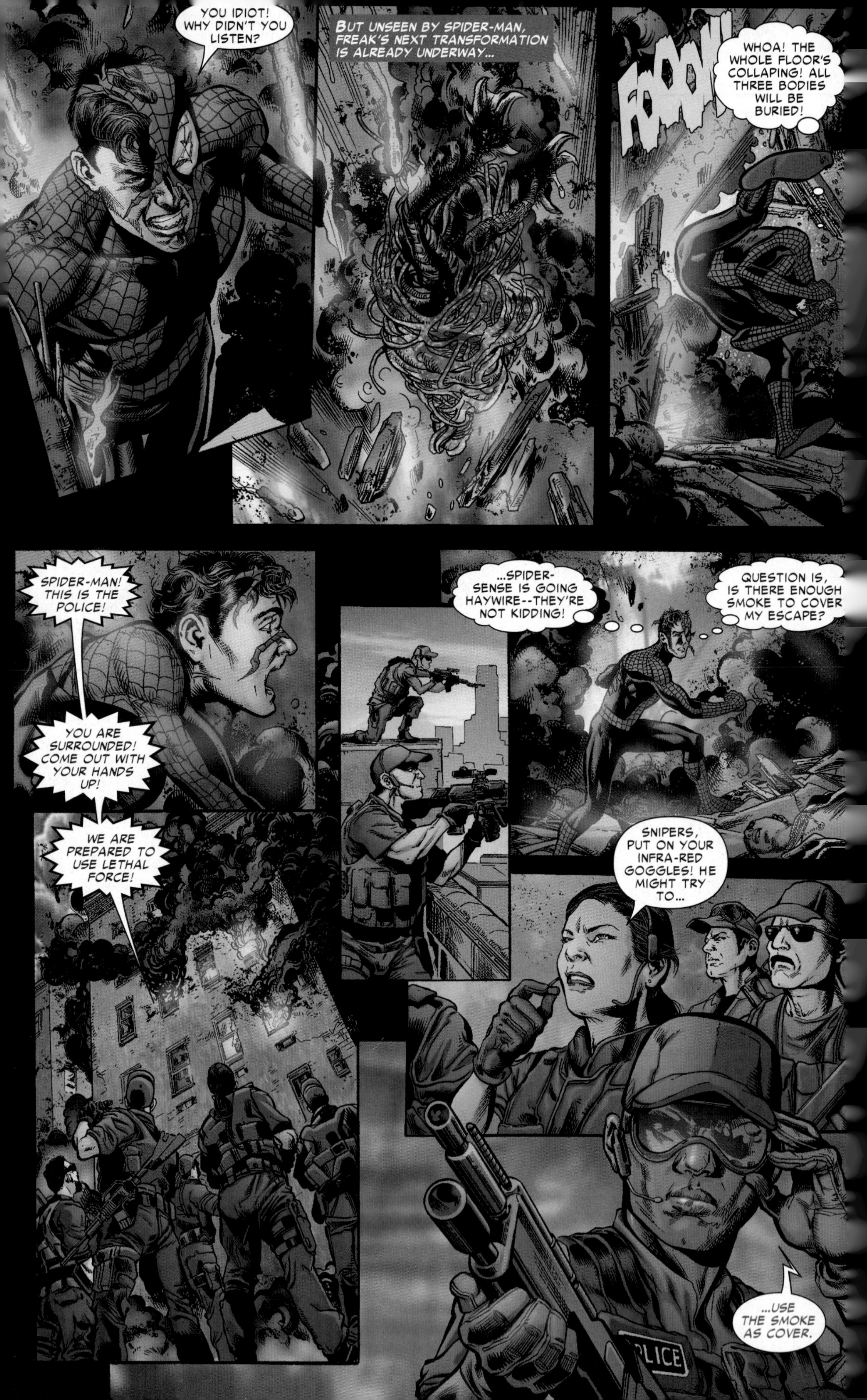
YOU IDIOT! WHY DIDN'T YOU LISTEN?
BUT UNSEEN BY SPIDER-MAN, FREAK'S NEXT TRANSFORMATION IS ALREADY UNDERWAY...
FOOOM!
WHOA! THE WHOLE FLOOR'S COLLAPING! ALL THREE BODIES WILL BE BURIED!
SPIDER-MAN! THIS IS THE POLICE!
YOU ARE SURROUNDED! COME OUT WITH YOUR HANDS UP!
WE ARE PREPARED TO USE LETHAL FORCE!
...SPIDER-SENSE IS GOING HAYWIRE--THEY'RE NOT KIDDING!
QUESTION IS, IS THERE ENOUGH SMOKE TO COVER MY ESCAPE?
SNIPERS, PUT ON YOUR INFRA-RED GOGGLES! HE MIGHT TRY TO...
...USE THE SMOKE AS COVER.

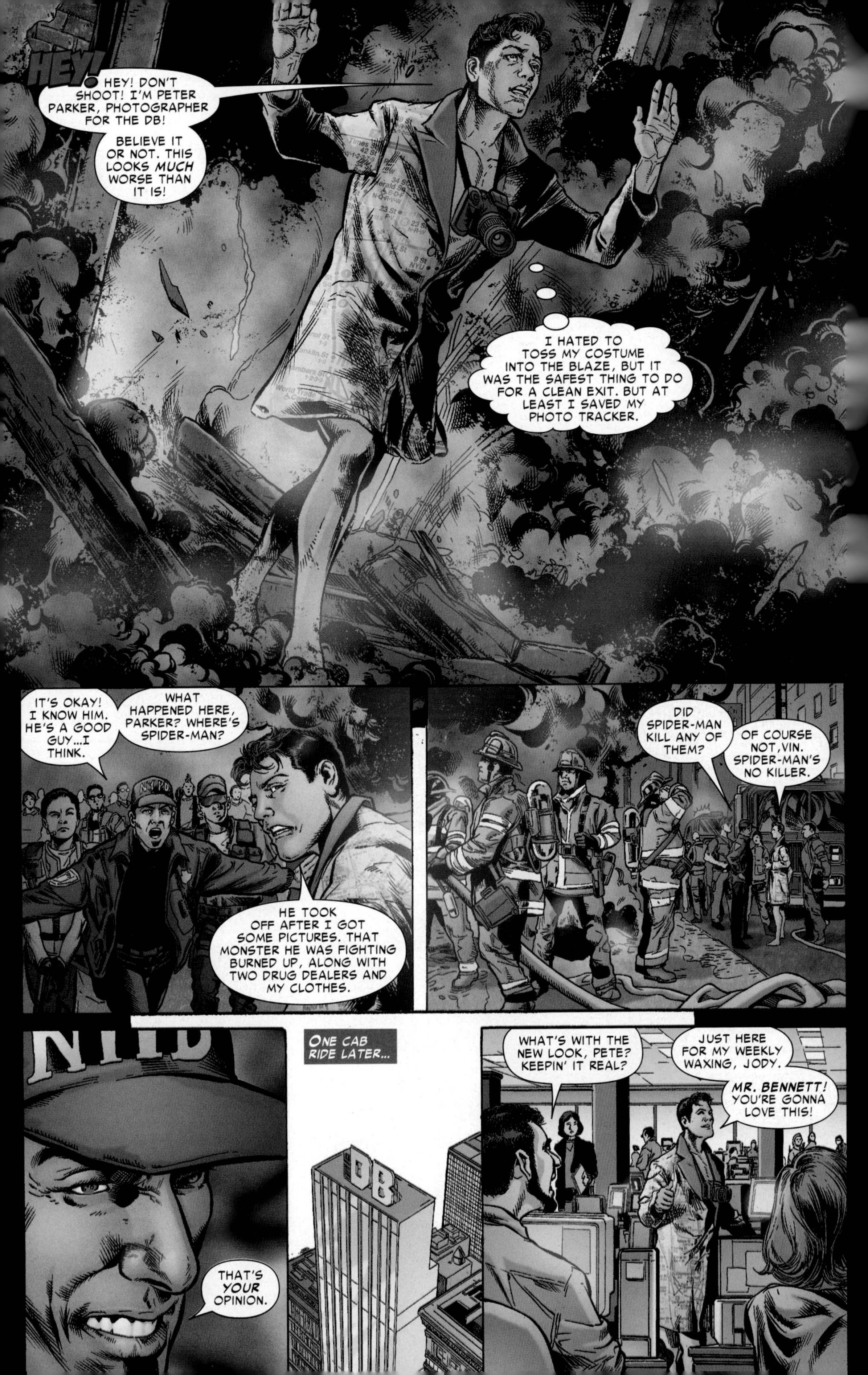
HEY!
HEY! DON'T SHOOT! I'M PETER PARKER, PHOTOGRAPHER FOR THE DB!
BELIEVE IT OR NOT. THIS LOOKS *MUCH* WORSE THAN IT IS!
I HATED TO TOSS MY COSTUME INTO THE BLAZE, BUT IT WAS THE SAFEST THING TO DO FOR A CLEAN EXIT. BUT AT LEAST I SAVED MY PHOTO TRACKER.
IT'S OKAY! I KNOW HIM. HE'S A GOOD GUY...I THINK.
WHAT HAPPENED HERE, PARKER? WHERE'S SPIDER-MAN?
HE TOOK OFF AFTER I GOT SOME PICTURES. THAT MONSTER HE WAS FIGHTING BURNED UP, ALONG WITH TWO DRUG DEALERS AND MY CLOTHES.
DID SPIDER-MAN KILL ANY OF THEM?
OF COURSE NOT, VIN. SPIDER-MAN'S NO KILLER.
THAT'S *YOUR* OPINION.
ONE CAB RIDE LATER...
WHAT'S WITH THE NEW LOOK, PETE? KEEPIN' IT REAL?
JUST HERE FOR MY WEEKLY WAXING, JODY.
MR. BENNETT! YOU'RE GONNA LOVE THIS!

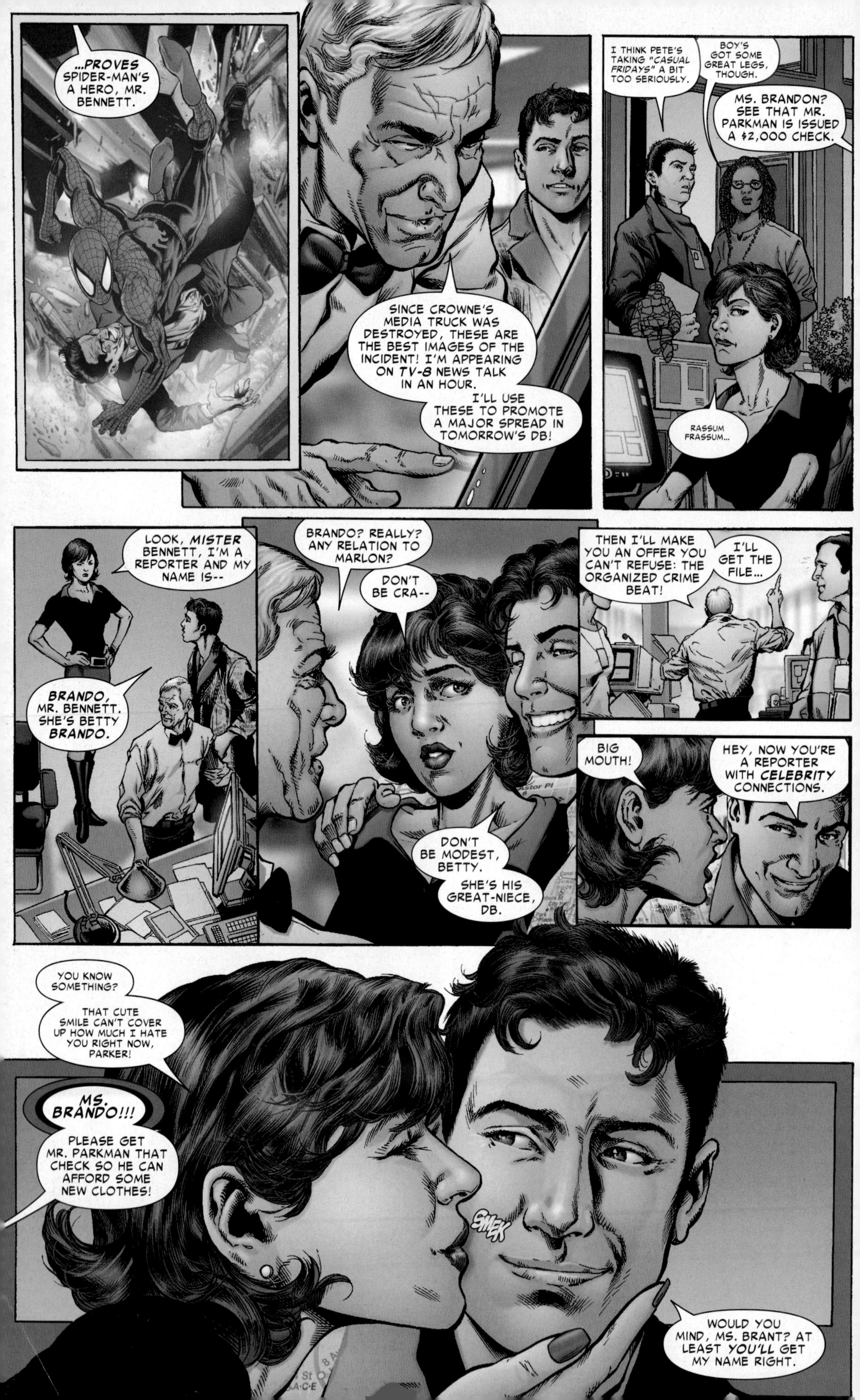
...PROVES SPIDER-MAN'S A HERO, MR. BENNETT.
SINCE CROWNE'S MEDIA TRUCK WAS DESTROYED, THESE ARE THE BEST IMAGES OF THE INCIDENT! I'M APPEARING ON TV-8 NEWS TALK IN AN HOUR.
I'LL USE THESE TO PROMOTE A MAJOR SPREAD IN TOMORROW'S DB!
I THINK PETE'S TAKING "CASUAL FRIDAYS" A BIT TOO SERIOUSLY.
BOY'S GOT SOME GREAT LEGS, THOUGH.
MS. BRANDON? SEE THAT MR. PARKMAN IS ISSUED A $2,000 CHECK.
RASSUM FRASSUM...
LOOK, MISTER BENNETT, I'M A REPORTER AND MY NAME IS--
BRANDO, MR. BENNETT. SHE'S BETTY BRANDO.
BRANDO? REALLY? ANY RELATION TO MARLON?
DON'T BE CRA--
DON'T BE MODEST, BETTY.
SHE'S HIS GREAT-NIECE, DB.
THEN I'LL MAKE YOU AN OFFER YOU CAN'T REFUSE: THE ORGANIZED CRIME BEAT!
I'LL GET THE FILE...
BIG MOUTH!
HEY, NOW YOU'RE A REPORTER WITH CELEBRITY CONNECTIONS.
YOU KNOW SOMETHING?
THAT CUTE SMILE CAN'T COVER UP HOW MUCH I HATE YOU RIGHT NOW, PARKER!
MS. BRANDO!!!
PLEASE GET MR. PARKMAN THAT CHECK SO HE CAN AFFORD SOME NEW CLOTHES!
SMEK
WOULD YOU MIND, MS. BRANT? AT LEAST YOU'LL GET MY NAME RIGHT.

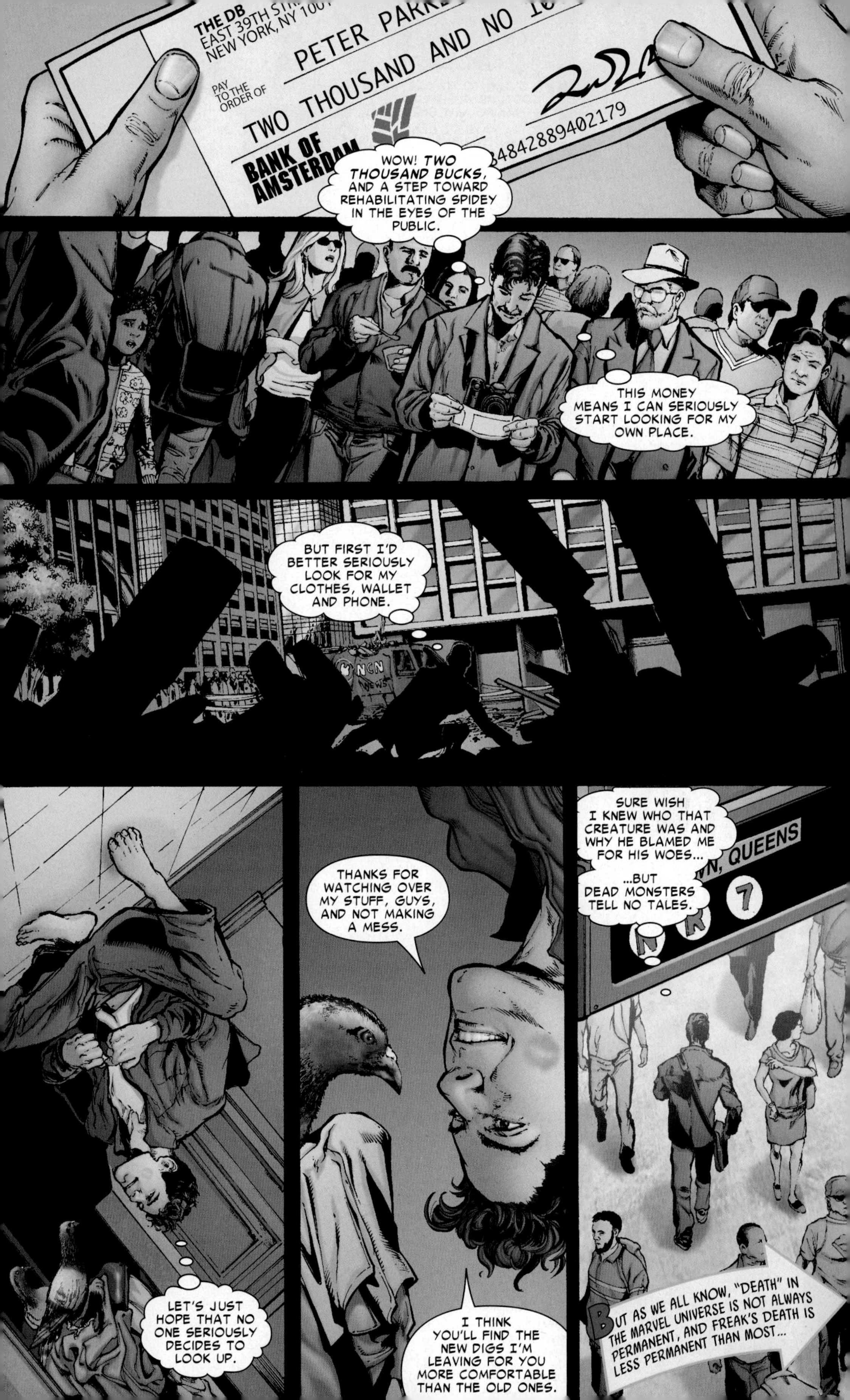
THE DB
EAST 39TH STR
NEW YORK, NY 100
PAY TO THE ORDER OF
PETER PARK
TWO THOUSAND AND NO 10
BANK OF AMSTERDAM
8484288940217 9
WOW! TWO THOUSAND BUCKS, AND A STEP TOWARD REHABILITATING SPIDEY IN THE EYES OF THE PUBLIC.
THIS MONEY MEANS I CAN SERIOUSLY START LOOKING FOR MY OWN PLACE.
BUT FIRST I'D BETTER SERIOUSLY LOOK FOR MY CLOTHES, WALLET AND PHONE.
NCN NEWS
LET'S JUST HOPE THAT NO ONE SERIOUSLY DECIDES TO LOOK UP.
THANKS FOR WATCHING OVER MY STUFF, GUYS, AND NOT MAKING A MESS.
I THINK YOU'LL FIND THE NEW DIGS I'M LEAVING FOR YOU MORE COMFORTABLE THAN THE OLD ONES.
SURE WISH I KNEW WHO THAT CREATURE WAS AND WHY HE BLAMED ME FOR HIS WOES...
...BUT DEAD MONSTERS TELL NO TALES.
N, QUEENS
N R 7
BUT AS WE ALL KNOW, "DEATH" IN THE MARVEL UNIVERSE IS NOT ALWAYS PERMANENT, AND FREAK'S DEATH IS LESS PERMANENT THAN MOST...

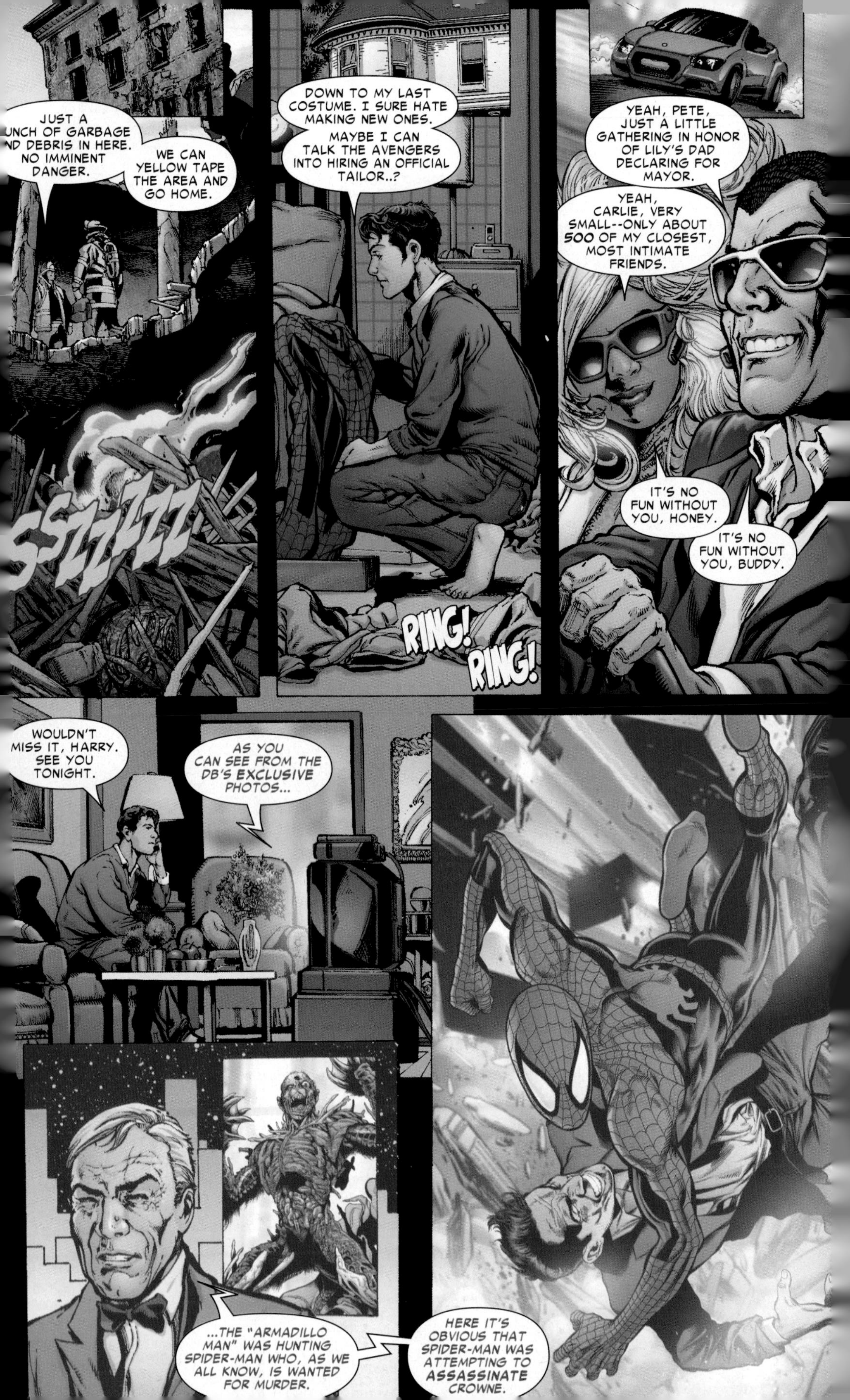
UNCH OF GARBAGE ND DEBRIS IN HERE. NO IMMINENT DANGER.
WE CAN YELLOW TAPE THE AREA AND GO HOME.
SSZZZZZ
DOWN TO MY LAST COSTUME. I SURE HATE MAKING NEW ONES.
MAYBE I CAN TALK THE AVENGERS INTO HIRING AN OFFICIAL TAILOR..?
RING! RING!
YEAH, PETE, JUST A LITTLE GATHERING IN HONOR OF LILY'S DAD DECLARING FOR MAYOR.
YEAH, CARLIE, VERY SMALL--ONLY ABOUT 500 OF MY CLOSEST, MOST INTIMATE FRIENDS.
IT'S NO FUN WITHOUT YOU, HONEY.
IT'S NO FUN WITHOUT YOU, BUDDY.
WOULDN'T MISS IT, HARRY. SEE YOU TONIGHT.
AS YOU CAN SEE FROM THE DB'S EXCLUSIVE PHOTOS...
...THE "ARMADILLO MAN" WAS HUNTING SPIDER-MAN WHO, AS WE ALL KNOW, IS WANTED FOR MURDER.
HERE IT'S OBVIOUS THAT SPIDER-MAN WAS ATTEMPTING TO ASSASSINATE CROWNE.

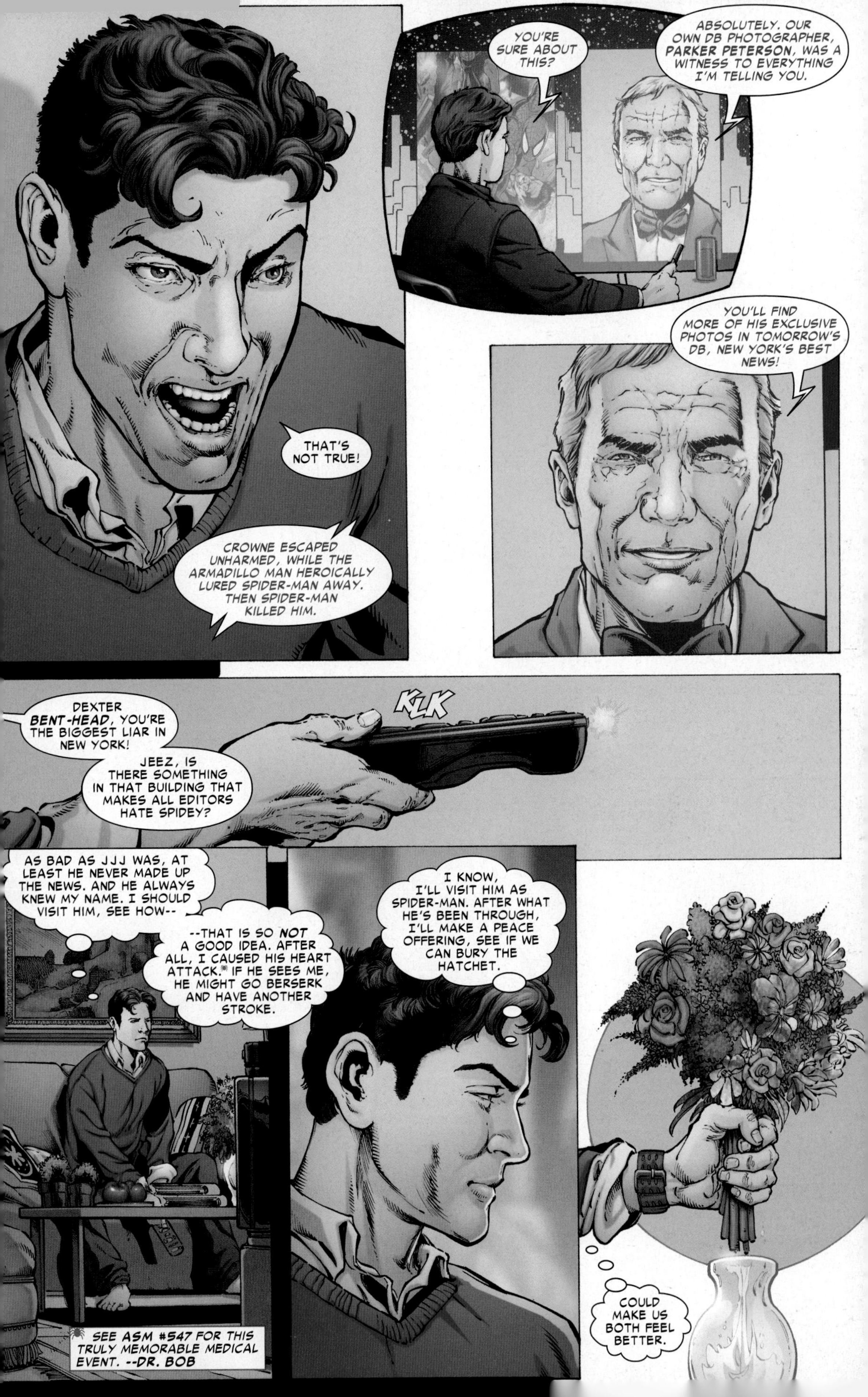
YOU'RE SURE ABOUT THIS?
ABSOLUTELY. OUR OWN DB PHOTOGRAPHER, PARKER PETERSON, WAS A WITNESS TO EVERYTHING I'M TELLING YOU.
THAT'S NOT TRUE!
CROWNE ESCAPED UNHARMED, WHILE THE ARMADILLO MAN HEROICALLY LURED SPIDER-MAN AWAY. THEN SPIDER-MAN KILLED HIM.
YOU'LL FIND MORE OF HIS EXCLUSIVE PHOTOS IN TOMORROW'S DB, NEW YORK'S BEST NEWS!
KLIK
DEXTER BENT-HEAD, YOU'RE THE BIGGEST LIAR IN NEW YORK!
JEEZ, IS THERE SOMETHING IN THAT BUILDING THAT MAKES ALL EDITORS HATE SPIDEY?
AS BAD AS JJJ WAS, AT LEAST HE NEVER MADE UP THE NEWS. AND HE ALWAYS KNEW MY NAME. I SHOULD VISIT HIM, SEE HOW--
--THAT IS SO NOT A GOOD IDEA. AFTER ALL, I CAUSED HIS HEART ATTACK.* IF HE SEES ME, HE MIGHT GO BERSERK AND HAVE ANOTHER STROKE.
* SEE ASM #547 FOR THIS TRULY MEMORABLE MEDICAL EVENT. --DR. BOB
I KNOW, I'LL VISIT HIM AS SPIDER-MAN. AFTER WHAT HE'S BEEN THROUGH, I'LL MAKE A PEACE OFFERING, SEE IF WE CAN BURY THE HATCHET.
COULD MAKE US BOTH FEEL BETTER.

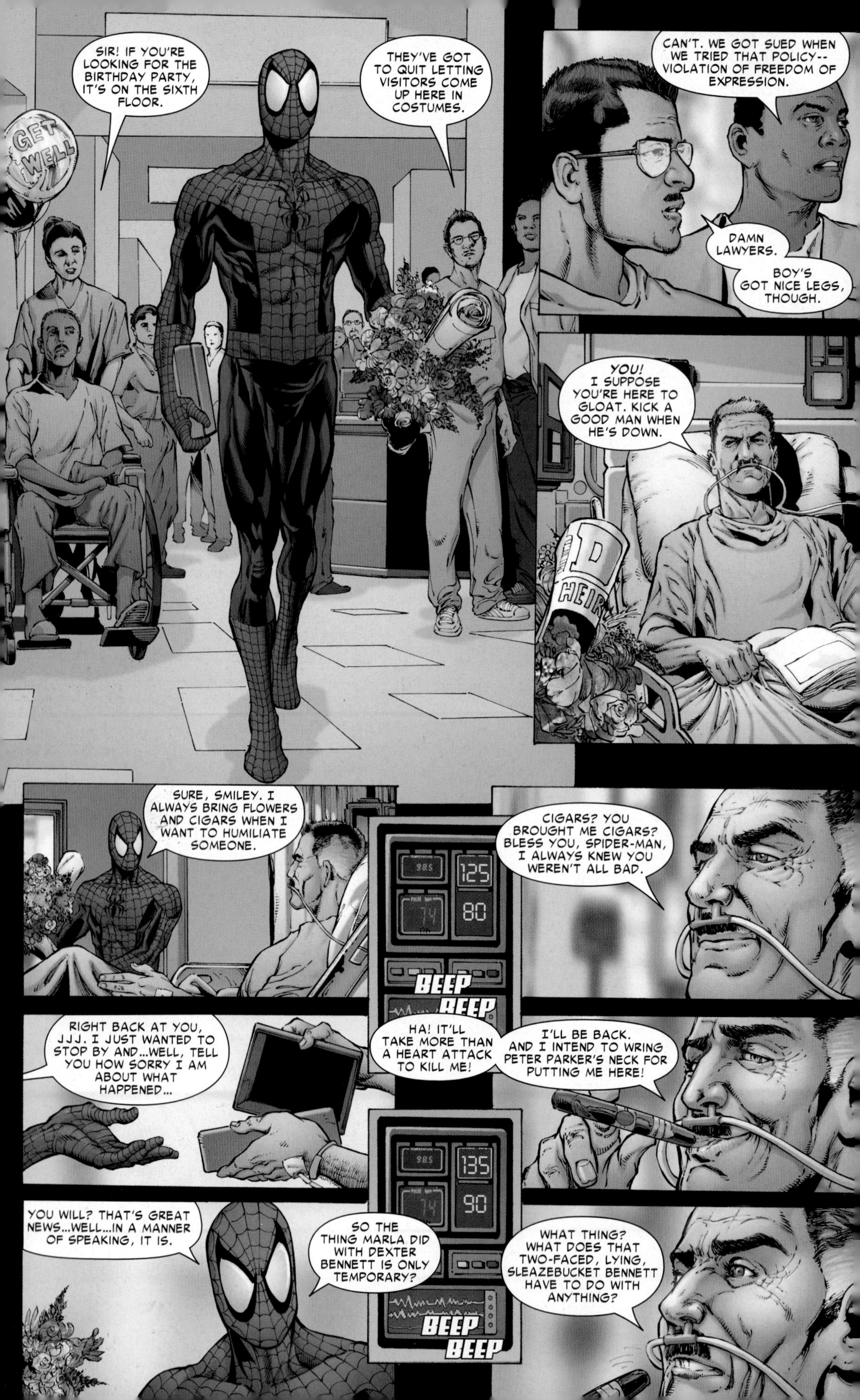
GET WELL
SIR! IF YOU'RE LOOKING FOR THE BIRTHDAY PARTY, IT'S ON THE SIXTH FLOOR.
THEY'VE GOT TO QUIT LETTING VISITORS COME UP HERE IN COSTUMES.
CAN'T. WE GOT SUED WHEN WE TRIED THAT POLICY-- VIOLATION OF FREEDOM OF EXPRESSION.
DAMN LAWYERS.
BOY'S GOT NICE LEGS, THOUGH.
YOU! I SUPPOSE YOU'RE HERE TO GLOAT. KICK A GOOD MAN WHEN HE'S DOWN.
SURE, SMILEY. I ALWAYS BRING FLOWERS AND CIGARS WHEN I WANT TO HUMILIATE SOMEONE.
CIGARS? YOU BROUGHT ME CIGARS? BLESS YOU, SPIDER-MAN, I ALWAYS KNEW YOU WEREN'T ALL BAD.
BEEP
BEEP
RIGHT BACK AT YOU, JJJ. I JUST WANTED TO STOP BY AND...WELL, TELL YOU HOW SORRY I AM ABOUT WHAT HAPPENED...
HA! IT'LL TAKE MORE THAN A HEART ATTACK TO KILL ME!
I'LL BE BACK. AND I INTEND TO WRING PETER PARKER'S NECK FOR PUTTING ME HERE!
YOU WILL? THAT'S GREAT NEWS...WELL...IN A MANNER OF SPEAKING, IT IS.
SO THE THING MARLA DID WITH DEXTER BENNETT IS ONLY TEMPORARY?
WHAT THING? WHAT DOES THAT TWO-FACED, LYING, SLEAZEBUCKET BENNETT HAVE TO DO WITH ANYTHING?
BEEP
BEEP

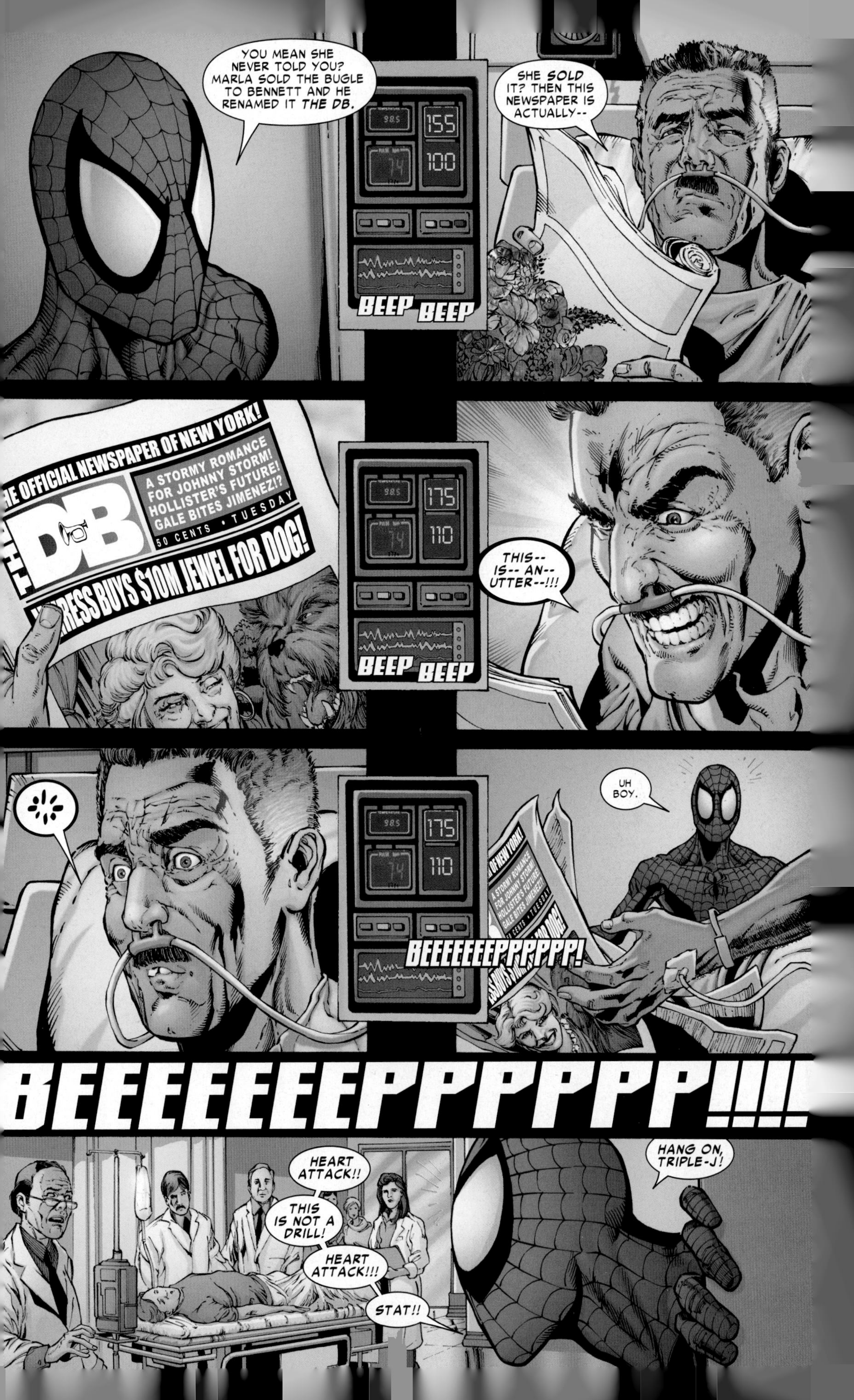
YOU MEAN SHE NEVER TOLD YOU? MARLA SOLD THE BUGLE TO BENNETT AND HE RENAMED IT THE DB.
SHE SOLD IT? THEN THIS NEWSPAPER IS ACTUALLY--
BEEP BEEP
THE OFFICIAL NEWSPAPER OF NEW YORK!
THE DB
A STORMY ROMANCE FOR JOHNNY STORM! HOLLISTER'S FUTURE! GALE BITES JIMENEZ!?
50 CENTS • TUESDAY
HEIRESS BUYS $10M JEWEL FOR DOG!
THIS-- IS-- AN-- UTTER--!!!
BEEP BEEP
UH BOY.
BEEEEEEEPPPPPP!
BEEEEEEEEPPPPPPP!!!!
HEART ATTACK!!
THIS IS NOT A DRILL!
HEART ATTACK!!!
STAT!!
HANG ON, TRIPLE-J!

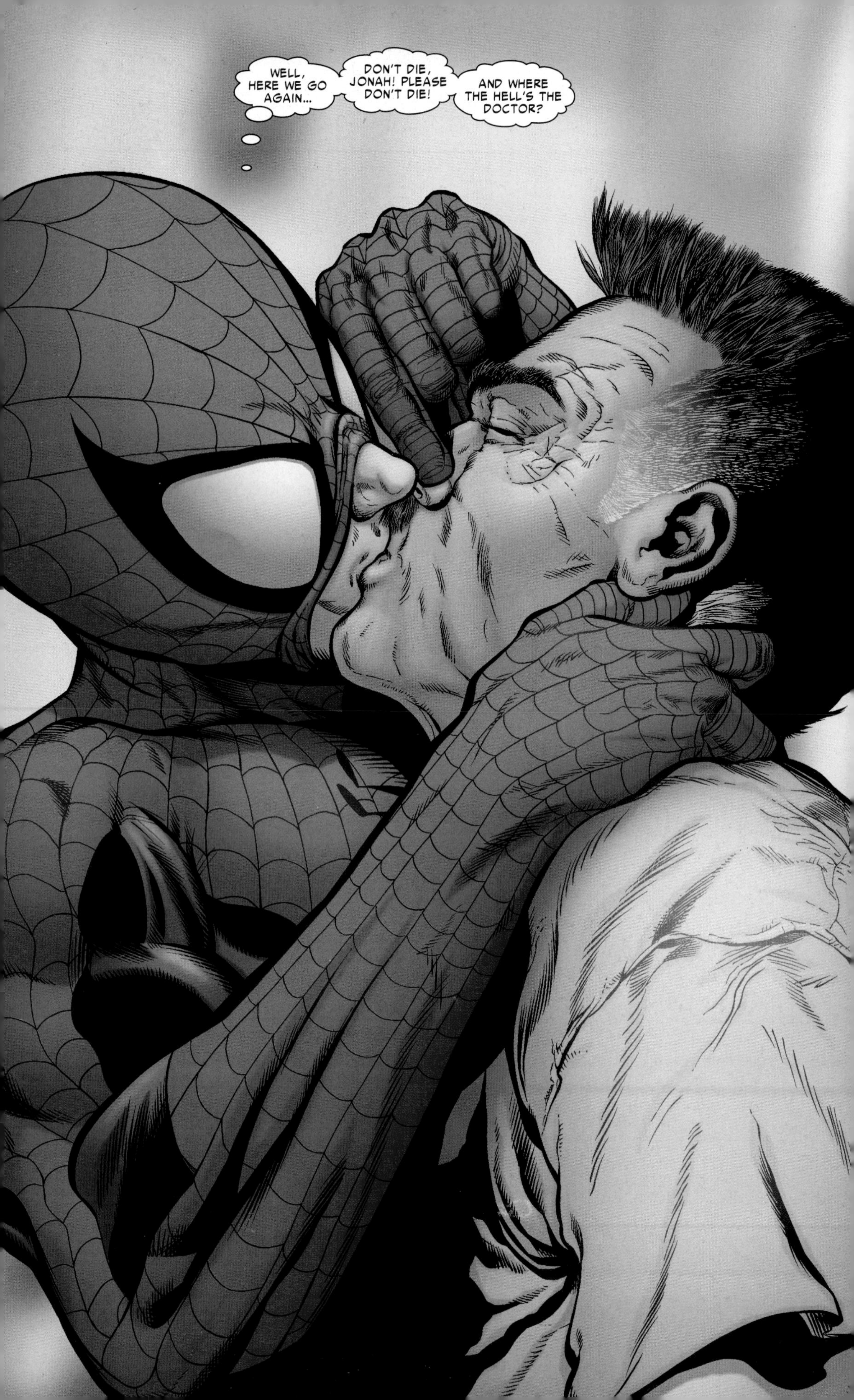
WELL, HERE WE GO AGAIN...
DON'T DIE, JONAH! PLEASE DON'T DIE!
AND WHERE THE HELL'S THE DOCTOR?

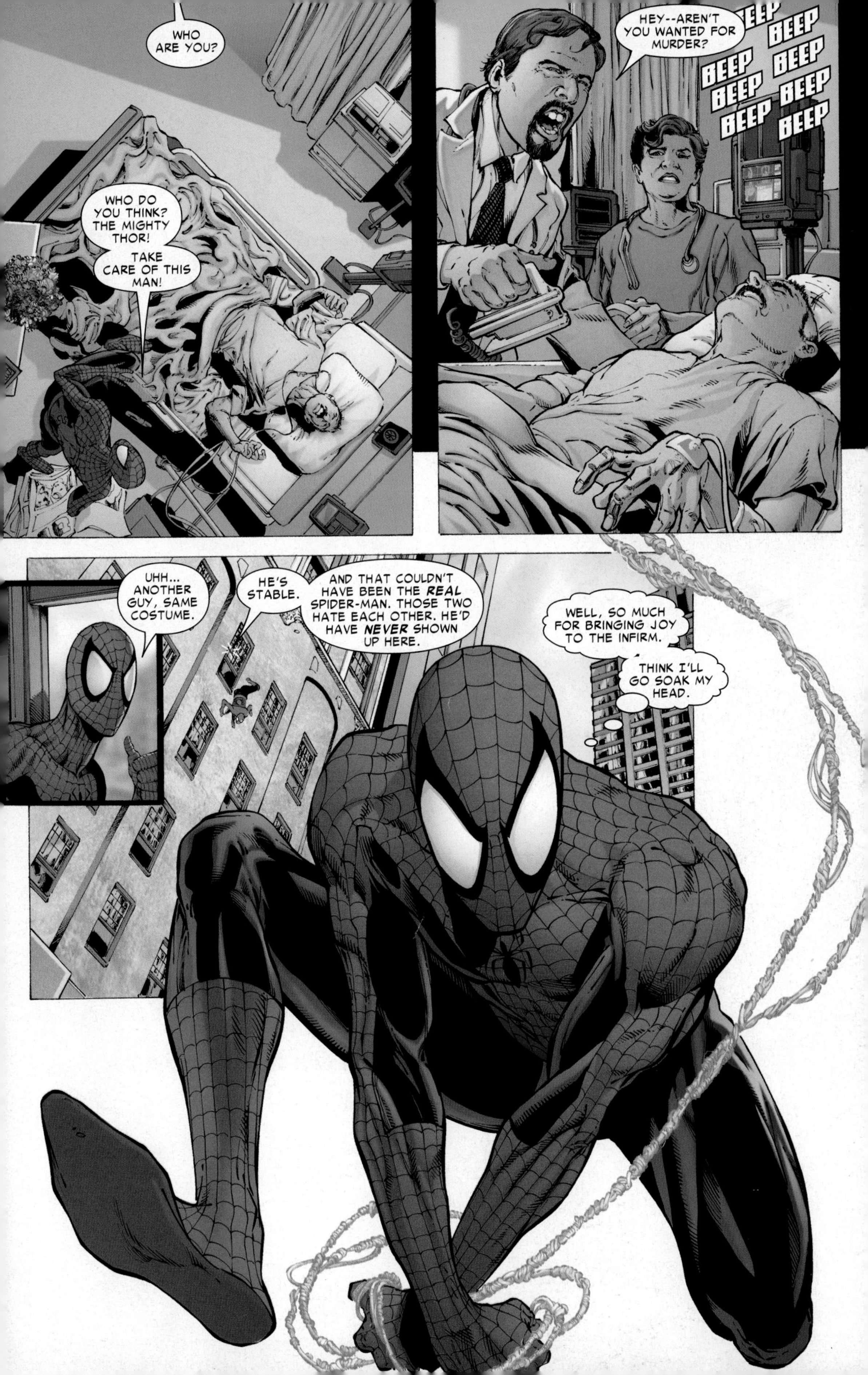
WHO ARE YOU?
WHO DO YOU THINK? THE MIGHTY THOR!
TAKE CARE OF THIS MAN!
HEY--AREN'T YOU WANTED FOR MURDER?
BEEP BEEP BEEP BEEP BEEP BEEP BEEP BEEP BEEP
UHH... ANOTHER GUY, SAME COSTUME.
HE'S STABLE.
AND THAT COULDN'T HAVE BEEN THE **REAL** SPIDER-MAN. THOSE TWO HATE EACH OTHER. HE'D HAVE **NEVER** SHOWN UP HERE.
WELL, SO MUCH FOR BRINGING JOY TO THE INFIRM.
THINK I'LL GO SOAK MY HEAD.

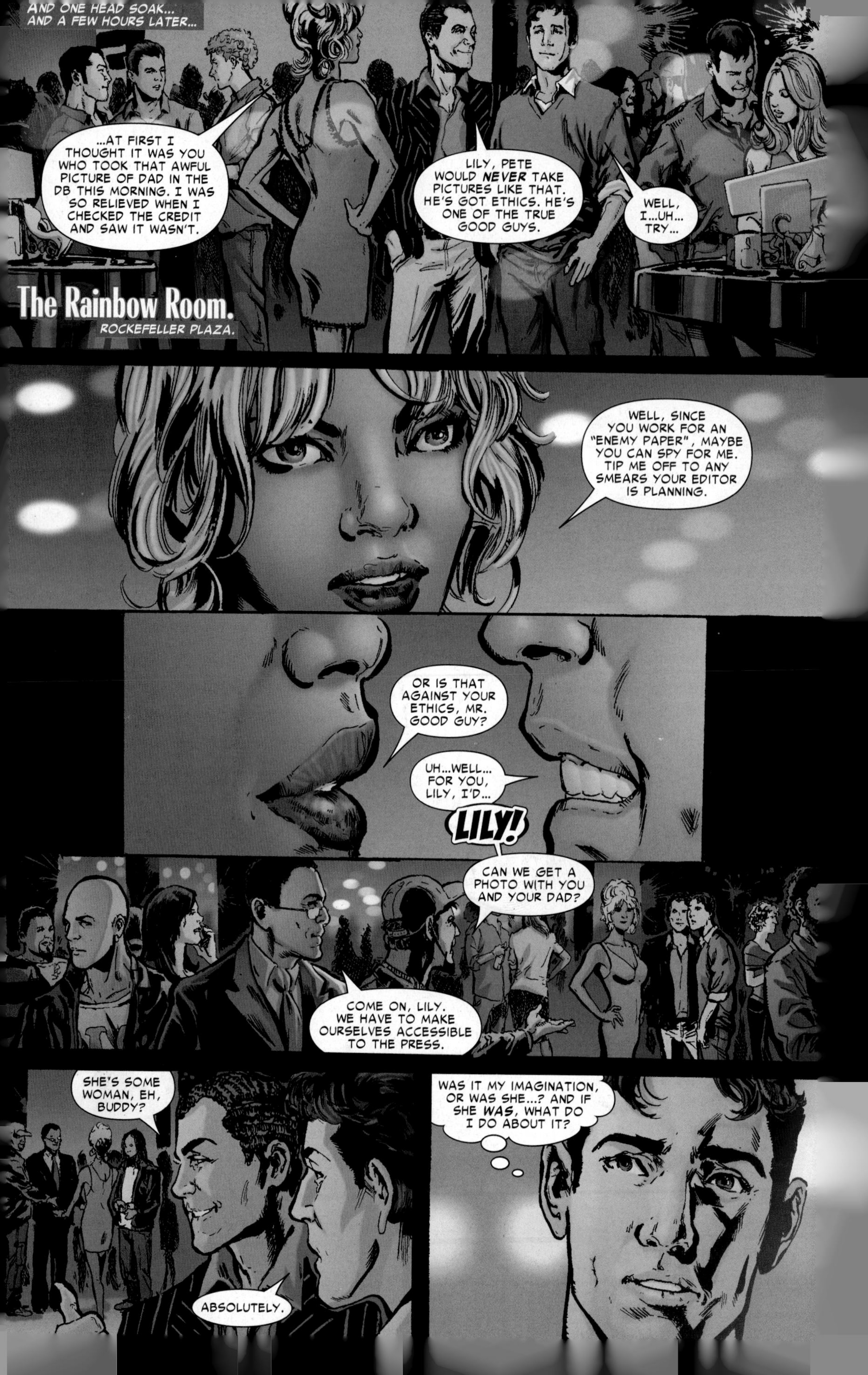
AND ONE HEAD SOAK... AND A FEW HOURS LATER...
...AT FIRST I THOUGHT IT WAS YOU WHO TOOK THAT AWFUL PICTURE OF DAD IN THE DB THIS MORNING. I WAS SO RELIEVED WHEN I CHECKED THE CREDIT AND SAW IT WASN'T.
LILY, PETE WOULD NEVER TAKE PICTURES LIKE THAT. HE'S GOT ETHICS. HE'S ONE OF THE TRUE GOOD GUYS.
WELL, I...UH... TRY...
The Rainbow Room.
ROCKEFELLER PLAZA.
WELL, SINCE YOU WORK FOR AN "ENEMY PAPER", MAYBE YOU CAN SPY FOR ME. TIP ME OFF TO ANY SMEARS YOUR EDITOR IS PLANNING.
OR IS THAT AGAINST YOUR ETHICS, MR. GOOD GUY?
UH...WELL... FOR YOU, LILY, I'D...
LILY!
CAN WE GET A PHOTO WITH YOU AND YOUR DAD?
COME ON, LILY. WE HAVE TO MAKE OURSELVES ACCESSIBLE TO THE PRESS.
SHE'S SOME WOMAN, EH, BUDDY?
ABSOLUTELY.
WAS IT MY IMAGINATION, OR WAS SHE...? AND IF SHE WAS, WHAT DO I DO ABOUT IT?

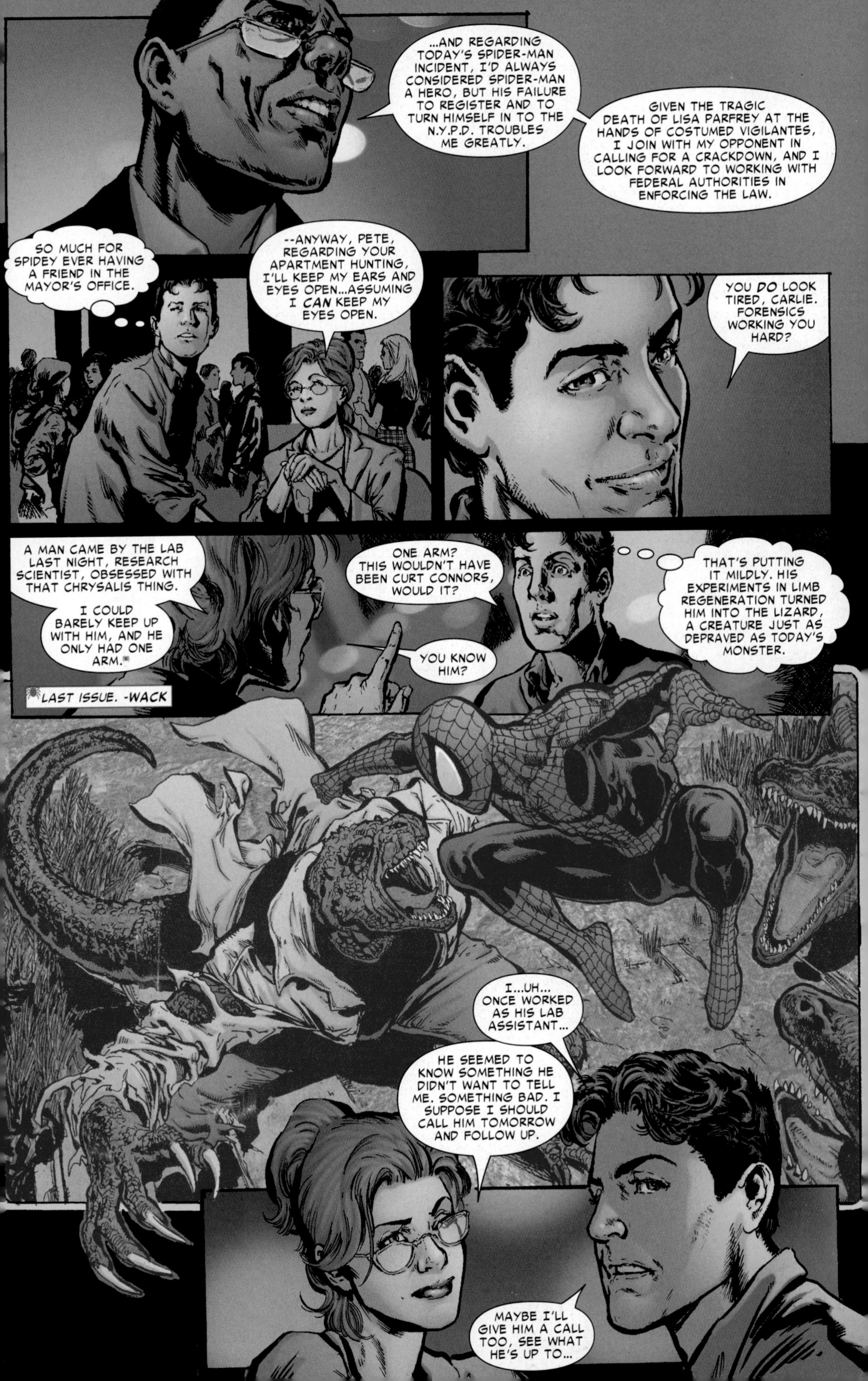
...AND REGARDING TODAY'S SPIDER-MAN INCIDENT, I'D ALWAYS CONSIDERED SPIDER-MAN A HERO, BUT HIS FAILURE TO REGISTER AND TO TURN HIMSELF IN TO THE N.Y.P.D. TROUBLES ME GREATLY.
GIVEN THE TRAGIC DEATH OF LISA PARFREY AT THE HANDS OF COSTUMED VIGILANTES, I JOIN WITH MY OPPONENT IN CALLING FOR A CRACKDOWN, AND I LOOK FORWARD TO WORKING WITH FEDERAL AUTHORITIES IN ENFORCING THE LAW.
SO MUCH FOR SPIDEY EVER HAVING A FRIEND IN THE MAYOR'S OFFICE.
--ANYWAY, PETE, REGARDING YOUR APARTMENT HUNTING, I'LL KEEP MY EARS AND EYES OPEN...ASSUMING I CAN KEEP MY EYES OPEN.
YOU DO LOOK TIRED, CARLIE. FORENSICS WORKING YOU HARD?
A MAN CAME BY THE LAB LAST NIGHT, RESEARCH SCIENTIST, OBSESSED WITH THAT CHRYSALIS THING.
I COULD BARELY KEEP UP WITH HIM, AND HE ONLY HAD ONE ARM.*
ONE ARM? THIS WOULDN'T HAVE BEEN CURT CONNORS, WOULD IT?
YOU KNOW HIM?
THAT'S PUTTING IT MILDLY. HIS EXPERIMENTS IN LIMB REGENERATION TURNED HIM INTO THE LIZARD, A CREATURE JUST AS DEPRAVED AS TODAY'S MONSTER.
*LAST ISSUE. -WACK
I...UH... ONCE WORKED AS HIS LAB ASSISTANT...
HE SEEMED TO KNOW SOMETHING HE DIDN'T WANT TO TELL ME. SOMETHING BAD. I SUPPOSE I SHOULD CALL HIM TOMORROW AND FOLLOW UP.
MAYBE I'LL GIVE HIM A CALL TOO, SEE WHAT HE'S UP TO...

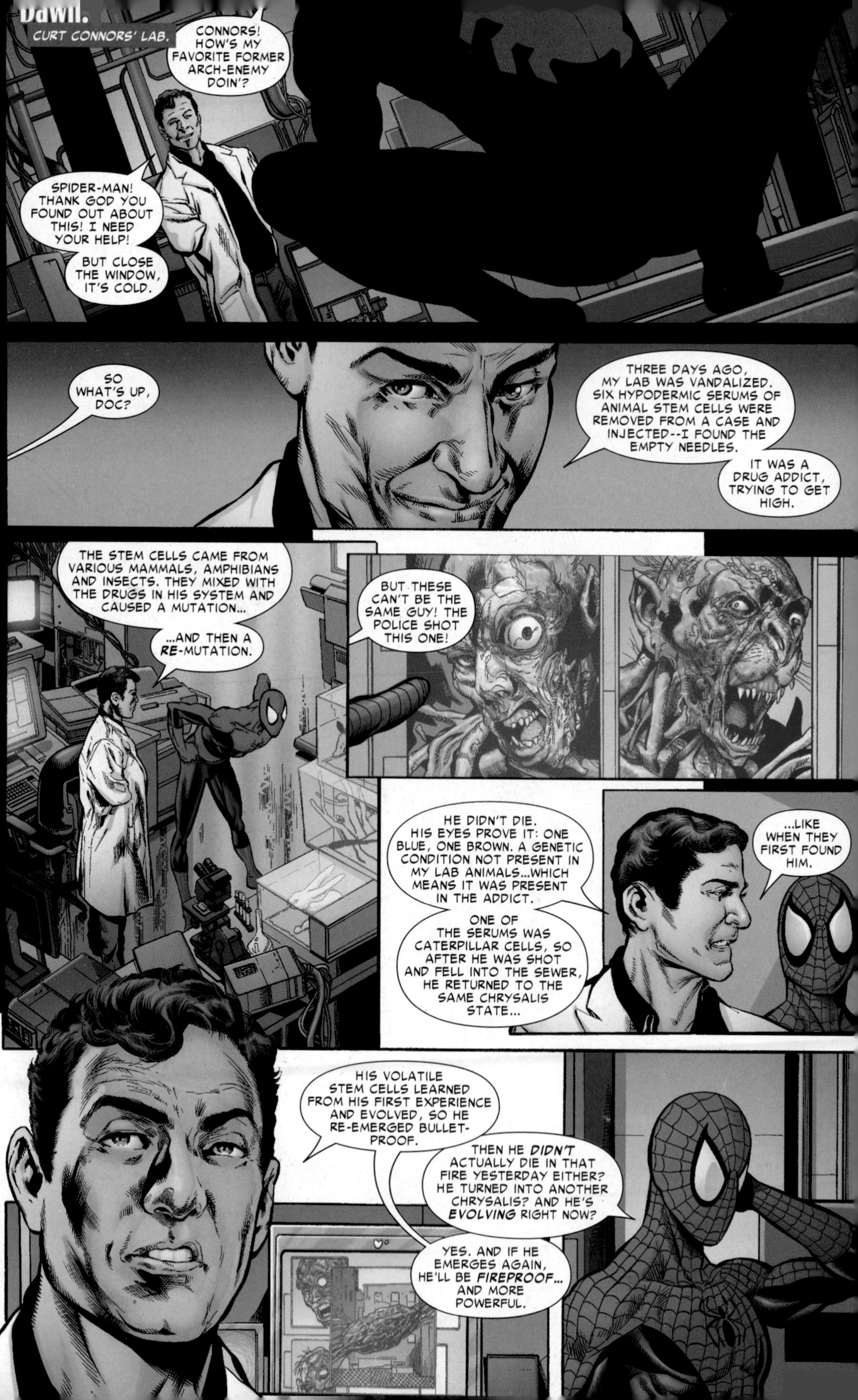

CURT CONNORS' LAB.
CONNORS! HOW'S MY FAVORITE FORMER ARCH-ENEMY DOIN'?
SPIDER-MAN! THANK GOD YOU FOUND OUT ABOUT THIS! I NEED YOUR HELP!
BUT CLOSE THE WINDOW, IT'S COLD.
SO WHAT'S UP, DOC?
THREE DAYS AGO, MY LAB WAS VANDALIZED. SIX HYPODERMIC SERUMS OF ANIMAL STEM CELLS WERE REMOVED FROM A CASE AND INJECTED--I FOUND THE EMPTY NEEDLES.
IT WAS A DRUG ADDICT, TRYING TO GET HIGH.
THE STEM CELLS CAME FROM VARIOUS MAMMALS, AMPHIBIANS AND INSECTS. THEY MIXED WITH THE DRUGS IN HIS SYSTEM AND CAUSED A MUTATION...
...AND THEN A *RE*-MUTATION.
BUT THESE CAN'T BE THE SAME GUY! THE POLICE SHOT THIS ONE!
HE DIDN'T DIE. HIS EYES PROVE IT: ONE BLUE, ONE BROWN. A GENETIC CONDITION NOT PRESENT IN MY LAB ANIMALS...WHICH MEANS IT WAS PRESENT IN THE ADDICT.
ONE OF THE SERUMS WAS CATERPILLAR CELLS, SO AFTER HE WAS SHOT AND FELL INTO THE SEWER, HE RETURNED TO THE SAME CHRYSALIS STATE...
...LIKE WHEN THEY FIRST FOUND HIM.
HIS VOLATILE STEM CELLS LEARNED FROM HIS FIRST EXPERIENCE AND EVOLVED, SO HE RE-EMERGED BULLET-PROOF.
THEN HE *DIDN'T* ACTUALLY DIE IN THAT FIRE YESTERDAY EITHER? HE TURNED INTO ANOTHER CHRYSALIS? AND HE'S *EVOLVING* RIGHT NOW?
YES. AND IF HE EMERGES AGAIN, HE'LL BE *FIREPROOF*... AND MORE POWERFUL.

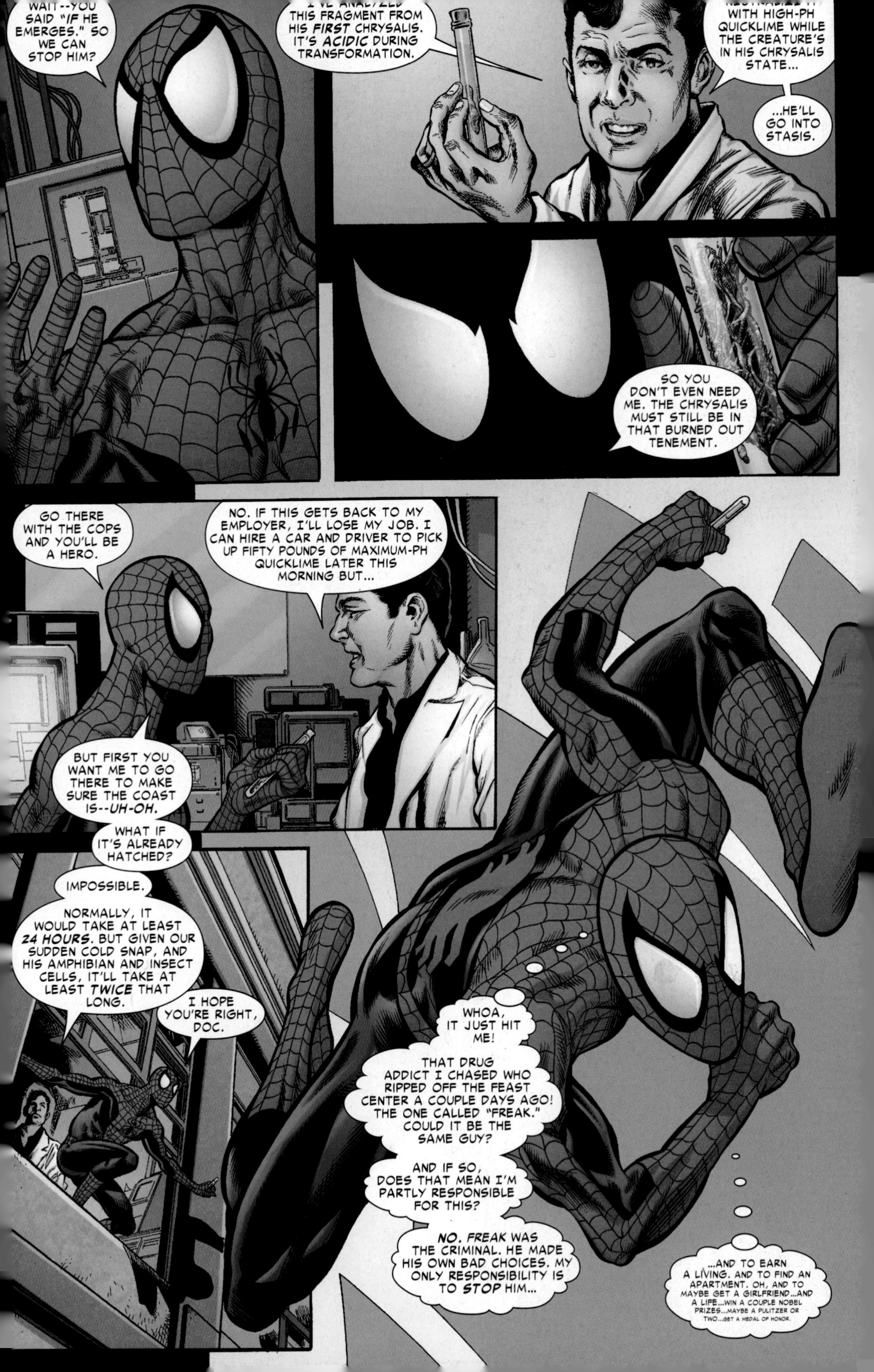
WAIT--YOU SAID "IF HE EMERGES." SO WE CAN STOP HIM?
THIS FRAGMENT FROM HIS FIRST CHRYSALIS. IT'S ACIDIC DURING TRANSFORMATION.
WITH HIGH-PH QUICKLIME WHILE THE CREATURE'S IN HIS CHRYSALIS STATE...
...HE'LL GO INTO STASIS.
SO YOU DON'T EVEN NEED ME. THE CHRYSALIS MUST STILL BE IN THAT BURNED OUT TENEMENT.
GO THERE WITH THE COPS AND YOU'LL BE A HERO.
NO. IF THIS GETS BACK TO MY EMPLOYER, I'LL LOSE MY JOB. I CAN HIRE A CAR AND DRIVER TO PICK UP FIFTY POUNDS OF MAXIMUM-PH QUICKLIME LATER THIS MORNING BUT...
BUT FIRST YOU WANT ME TO GO THERE TO MAKE SURE THE COAST IS--UH-OH.
WHAT IF IT'S ALREADY HATCHED?
IMPOSSIBLE.
NORMALLY, IT WOULD TAKE AT LEAST 24 HOURS. BUT GIVEN OUR SUDDEN COLD SNAP, AND HIS AMPHIBIAN AND INSECT CELLS, IT'LL TAKE AT LEAST TWICE THAT LONG.
I HOPE YOU'RE RIGHT, DOC.
WHOA, IT JUST HIT ME!
THAT DRUG ADDICT I CHASED WHO RIPPED OFF THE FEAST CENTER A COUPLE DAYS AGO! THE ONE CALLED "FREAK." COULD IT BE THE SAME GUY?
AND IF SO, DOES THAT MEAN I'M PARTLY RESPONSIBLE FOR THIS?
NO. FREAK WAS THE CRIMINAL. HE MADE HIS OWN BAD CHOICES. MY ONLY RESPONSIBILITY IS TO STOP HIM...
...AND TO EARN A LIVING. AND TO FIND AN APARTMENT. OH, AND TO MAYBE GET A GIRLFRIEND...AND A LIFE...WIN A COUPLE NOBEL PRIZES...MAYBE A PULITZER OR TWO...GET A MEDAL OF HONOR.

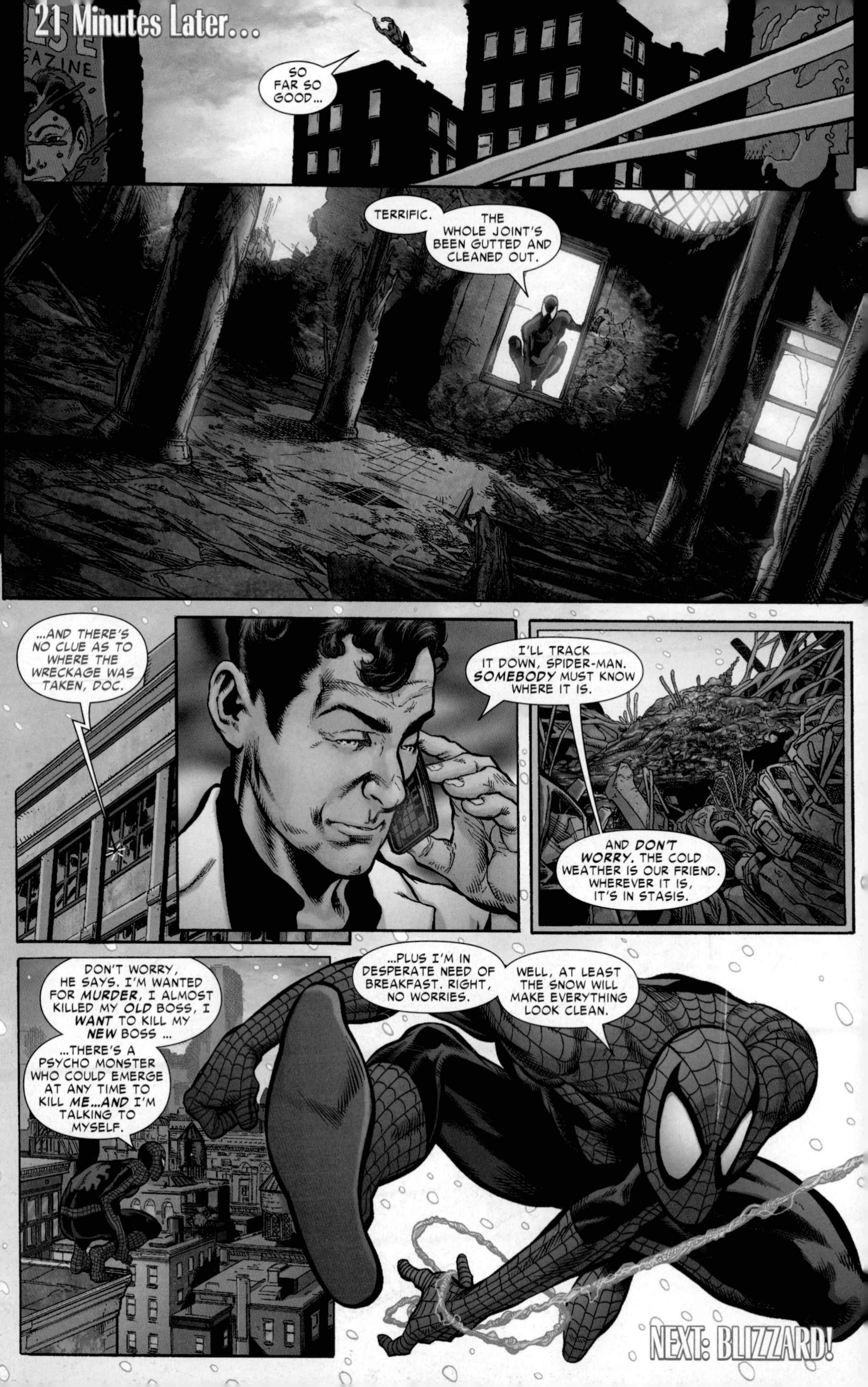
21 Minutes Later...
SO FAR SO GOOD...
TERRIFIC.
THE WHOLE JOINT'S BEEN GUTTED AND CLEANED OUT.
...AND THERE'S NO CLUE AS TO WHERE THE WRECKAGE WAS TAKEN, DOC.
I'LL TRACK IT DOWN, SPIDER-MAN. SOMEBODY MUST KNOW WHERE IT IS.
AND DON'T WORRY. THE COLD WEATHER IS OUR FRIEND. WHEREVER IT IS, IT'S IN STASIS.
DON'T WORRY, HE SAYS. I'M WANTED FOR MURDER, I ALMOST KILLED MY OLD BOSS, I WANT TO KILL MY NEW BOSS ...
...THERE'S A PSYCHO MONSTER WHO COULD EMERGE AT ANY TIME TO KILL ME...AND I'M TALKING TO MYSELF.
...PLUS I'M IN DESPERATE NEED OF BREAKFAST. RIGHT, NO WORRIES.
WELL, AT LEAST THE SNOW WILL MAKE EVERYTHING LOOK CLEAN.
NEXT: BLIZZARD!

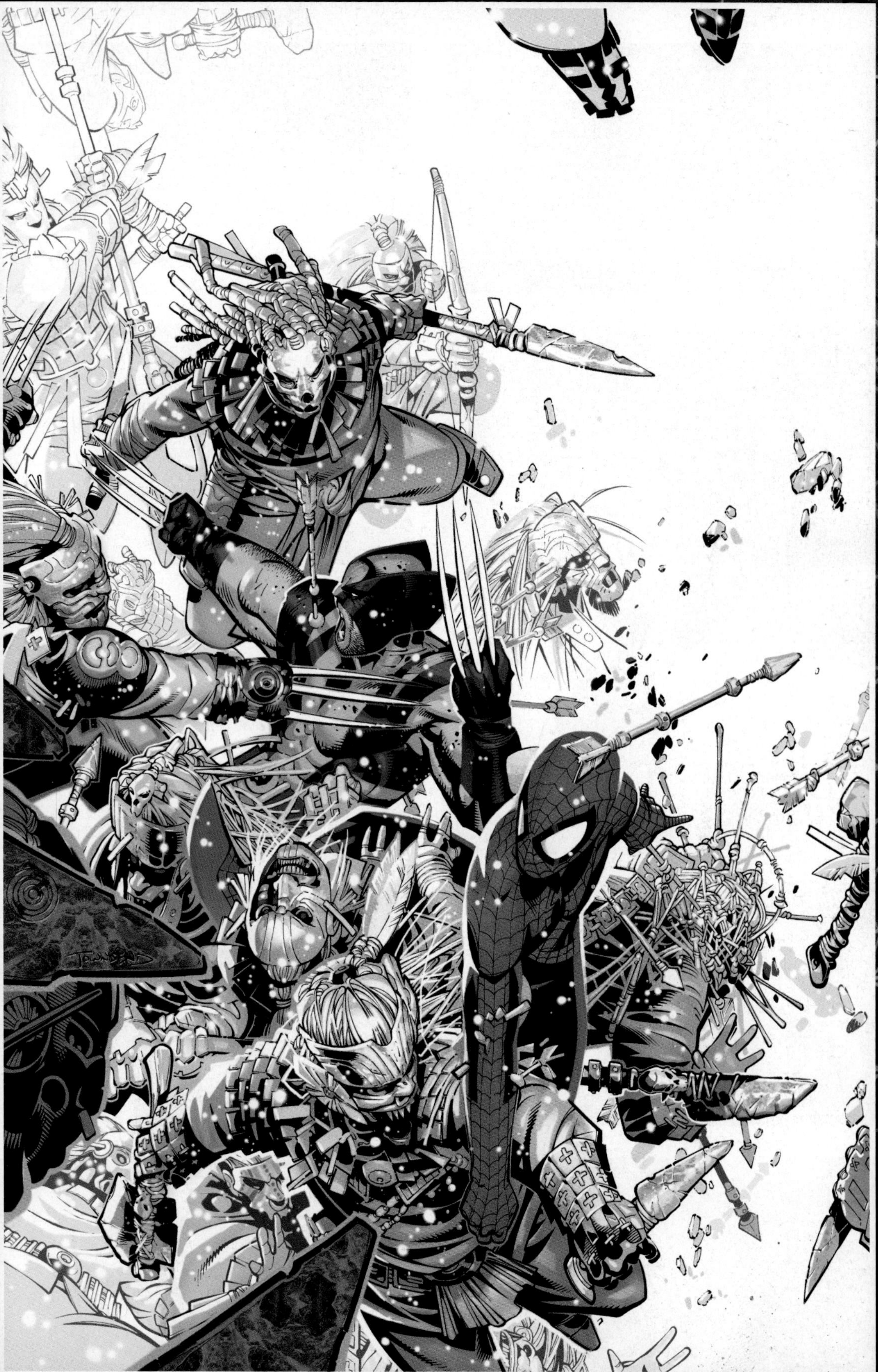
TOWNSEND

AMAZING SPIDER-MAN #555
COVER BY **CHRIS BACHALO & TIM TOWNSEND**

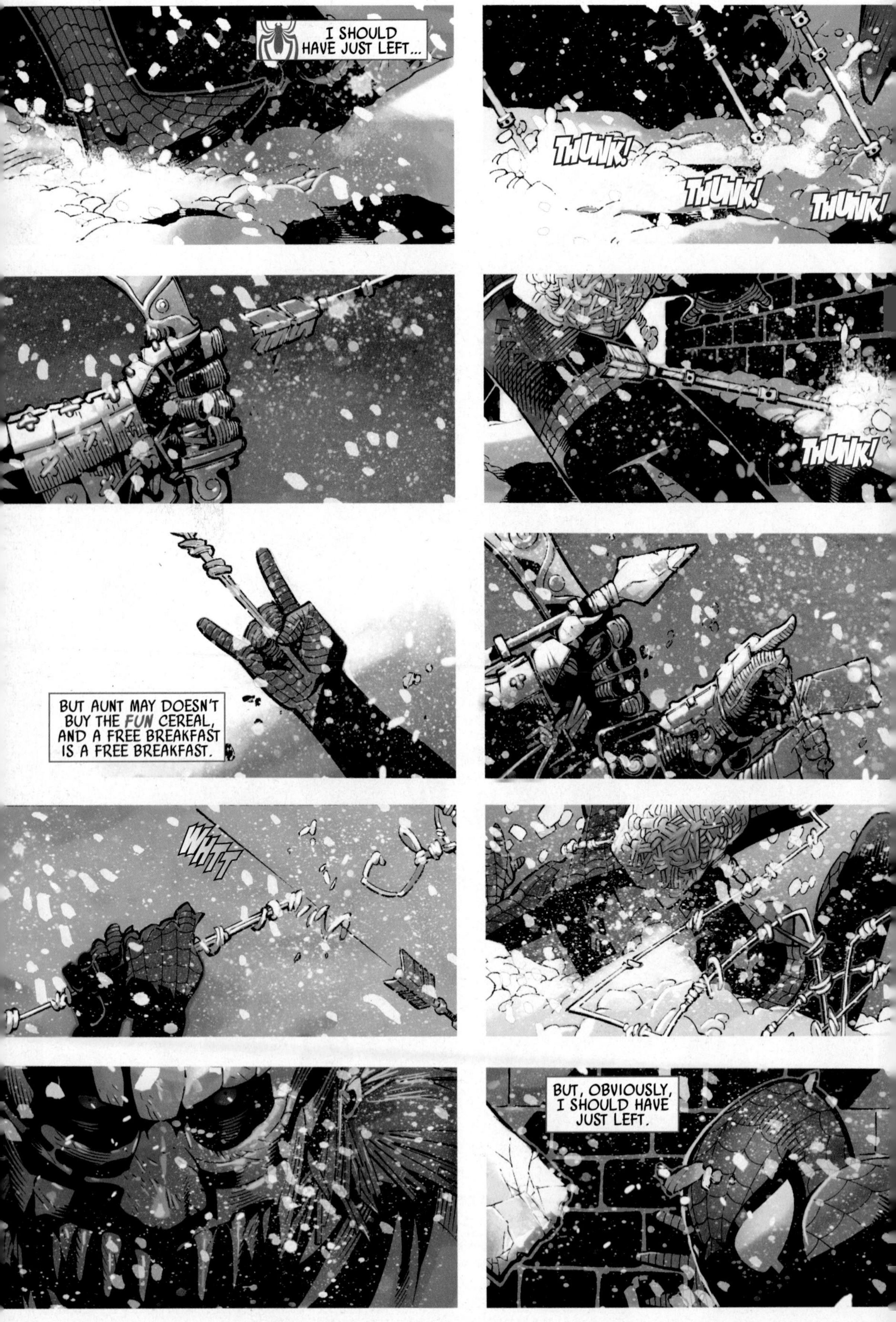
I SHOULD HAVE JUST LEFT...
THUNK!
THUNK!
THUNK!
THUNK!
BUT AUNT MAY DOESN'T BUY THE FUN CEREAL, AND A FREE BREAKFAST IS A FREE BREAKFAST.
WHTT
BUT, OBVIOUSLY, I SHOULD HAVE JUST LEFT.

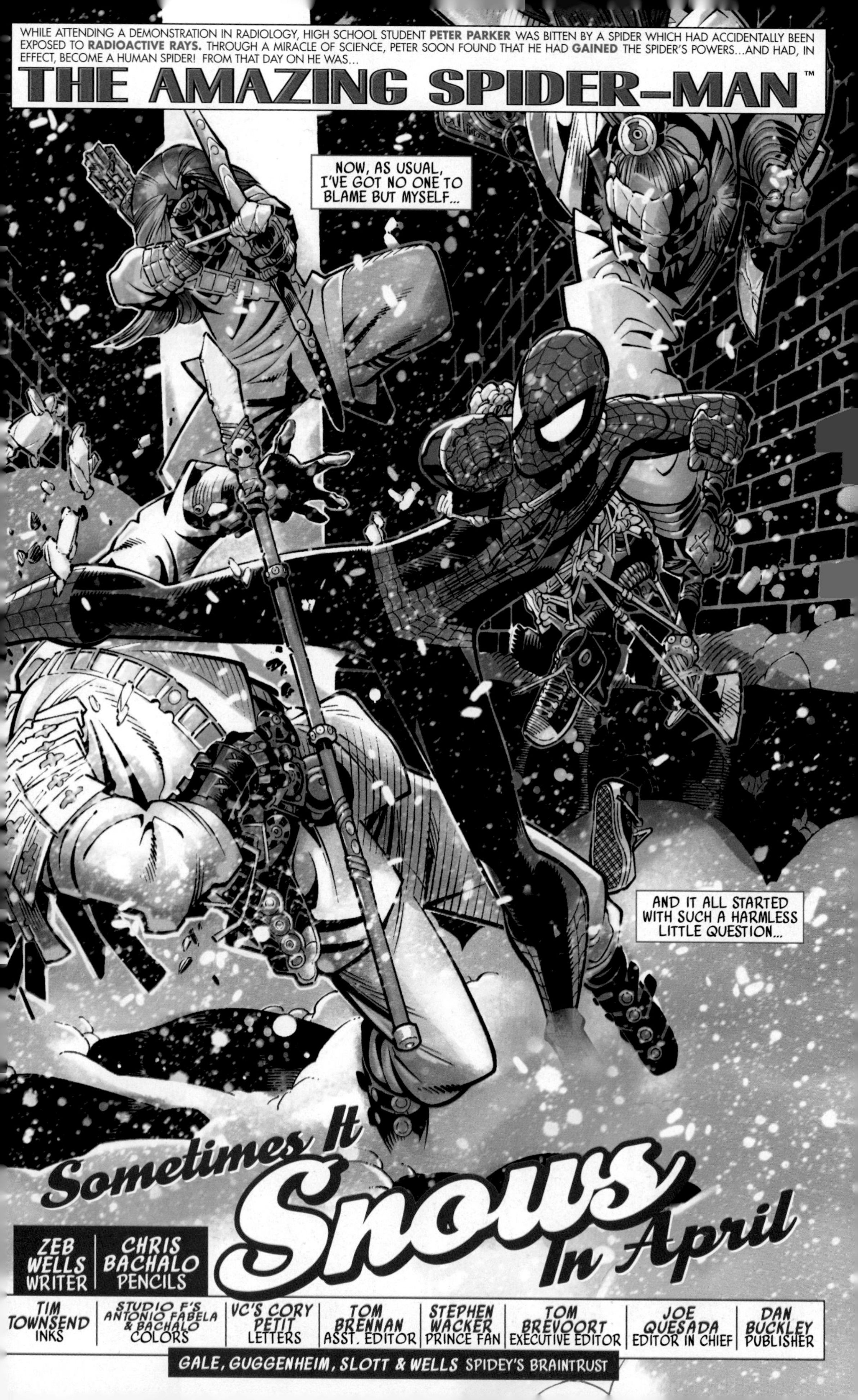
WHILE ATTENDING A DEMONSTRATION IN RADIOLOGY, HIGH SCHOOL STUDENT PETER PARKER WAS BITTEN BY A SPIDER WHICH HAD ACCIDENTALLY BEEN EXPOSED TO RADIOACTIVE RAYS. THROUGH A MIRACLE OF SCIENCE, PETER SOON FOUND THAT HE HAD GAINED THE SPIDER'S POWERS...AND HAD, IN EFFECT, BECOME A HUMAN SPIDER! FROM THAT DAY ON HE WAS...
THE AMAZING SPIDER-MAN™
NOW, AS USUAL, I'VE GOT NO ONE TO BLAME BUT MYSELF...
AND IT ALL STARTED WITH SUCH A HARMLESS LITTLE QUESTION...
Sometimes It Snows In April
ZEB WELLS WRITER
CHRIS BACHALO PENCILS
TIM TOWNSEND INKS
STUDIO F'S ANTONIO FABELA & BACHALO COLORS
VC'S CORY PETIT LETTERS
TOM BRENNAN ASST. EDITOR
STEPHEN WACKER PRINCE FAN
TOM BREVOORT EXECUTIVE EDITOR
JOE QUESADA EDITOR IN CHIEF
DAN BUCKLEY PUBLISHER
GALE, GUGGENHEIM, SLOTT & WELLS SPIDEY'S BRAINTRUST

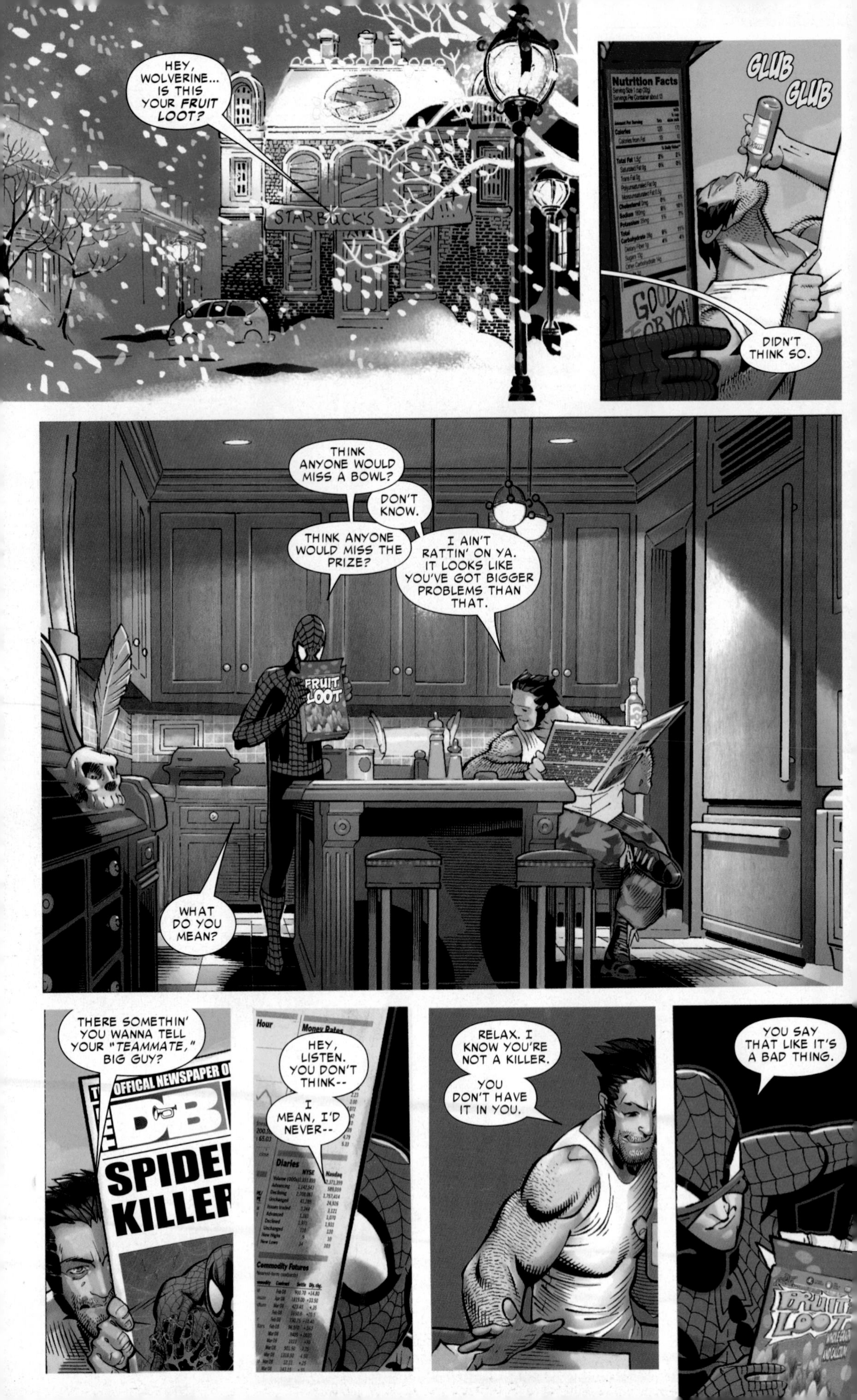
HEY, WOLVERINE... IS THIS YOUR FRUIT LOOT?
STARBUCK'S S...N!!!
GLUB GLUB
Nutrition Facts
GOOD FOR YOU
DIDN'T THINK SO.
THINK ANYONE WOULD MISS A BOWL?
DON'T KNOW.
THINK ANYONE WOULD MISS THE PRIZE?
I AIN'T RATTIN' ON YA. IT LOOKS LIKE YOU'VE GOT BIGGER PROBLEMS THAN THAT.
FRUIT LOOT
WHAT DO YOU MEAN?
THERE SOMETHIN' YOU WANNA TELL YOUR "TEAMMATE," BIG GUY?
OFFICAL NEWSPAPER O
DB
SPIDE
KILLER
HEY, LISTEN. YOU DON'T THINK--
I MEAN, I'D NEVER--
Money Rates
Diaries
Commodity Futures
RELAX. I KNOW YOU'RE NOT A KILLER.
YOU DON'T HAVE IT IN YOU.
YOU SAY THAT LIKE IT'S A BAD THING.
FRUIT LOOT

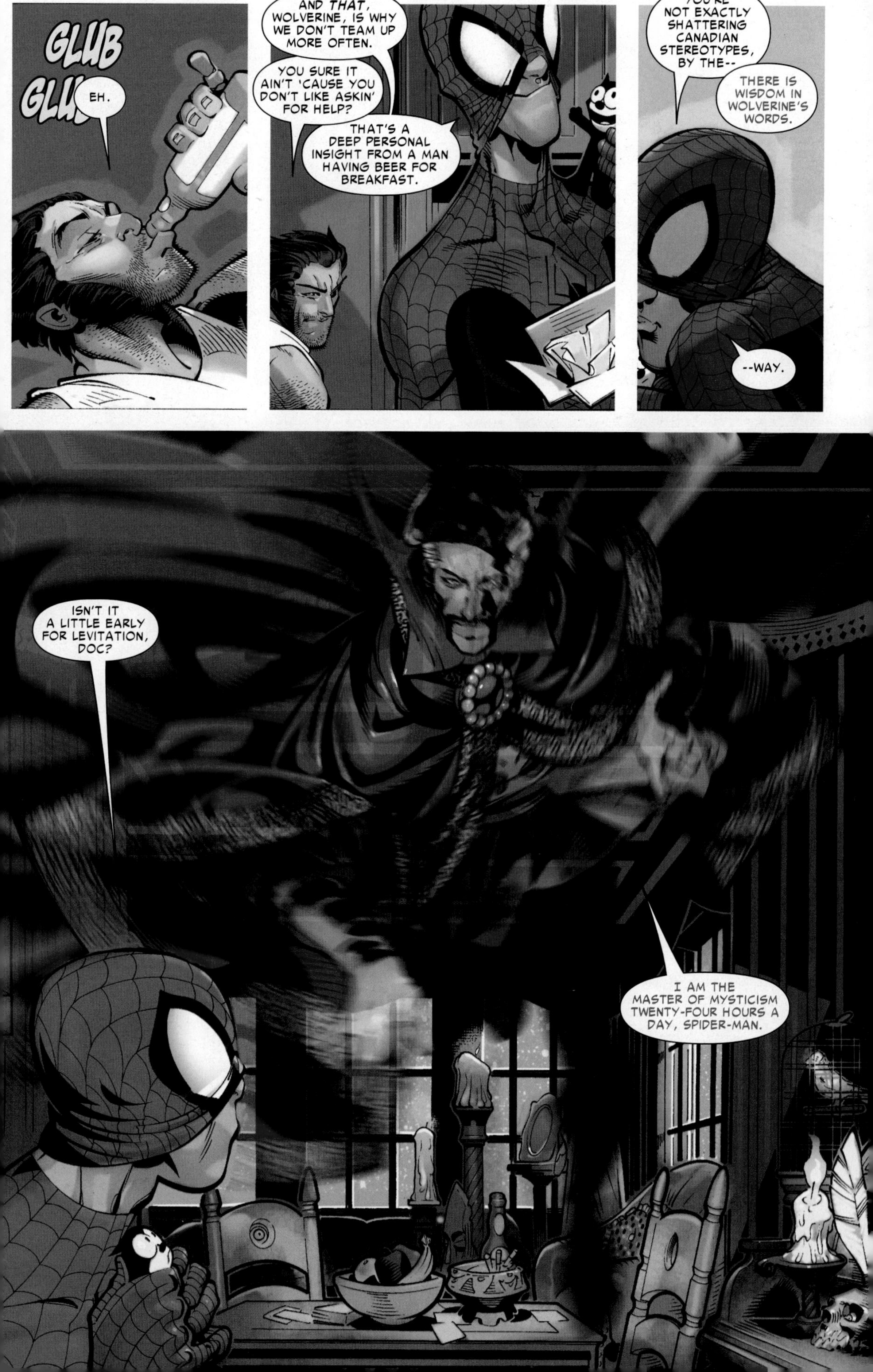
GLUB GLUB
EH.
AND THAT, WOLVERINE, IS WHY WE DON'T TEAM UP MORE OFTEN.
YOU SURE IT AIN'T 'CAUSE YOU DON'T LIKE ASKIN' FOR HELP?
THAT'S A DEEP PERSONAL INSIGHT FROM A MAN HAVING BEER FOR BREAKFAST.
YOU'RE NOT EXACTLY SHATTERING CANADIAN STEREOTYPES, BY THE--
THERE IS WISDOM IN WOLVERINE'S WORDS.
--WAY.
ISN'T IT A LITTLE EARLY FOR LEVITATION, DOC?
I AM THE MASTER OF MYSTICISM TWENTY-FOUR HOURS A DAY, SPIDER-MAN.

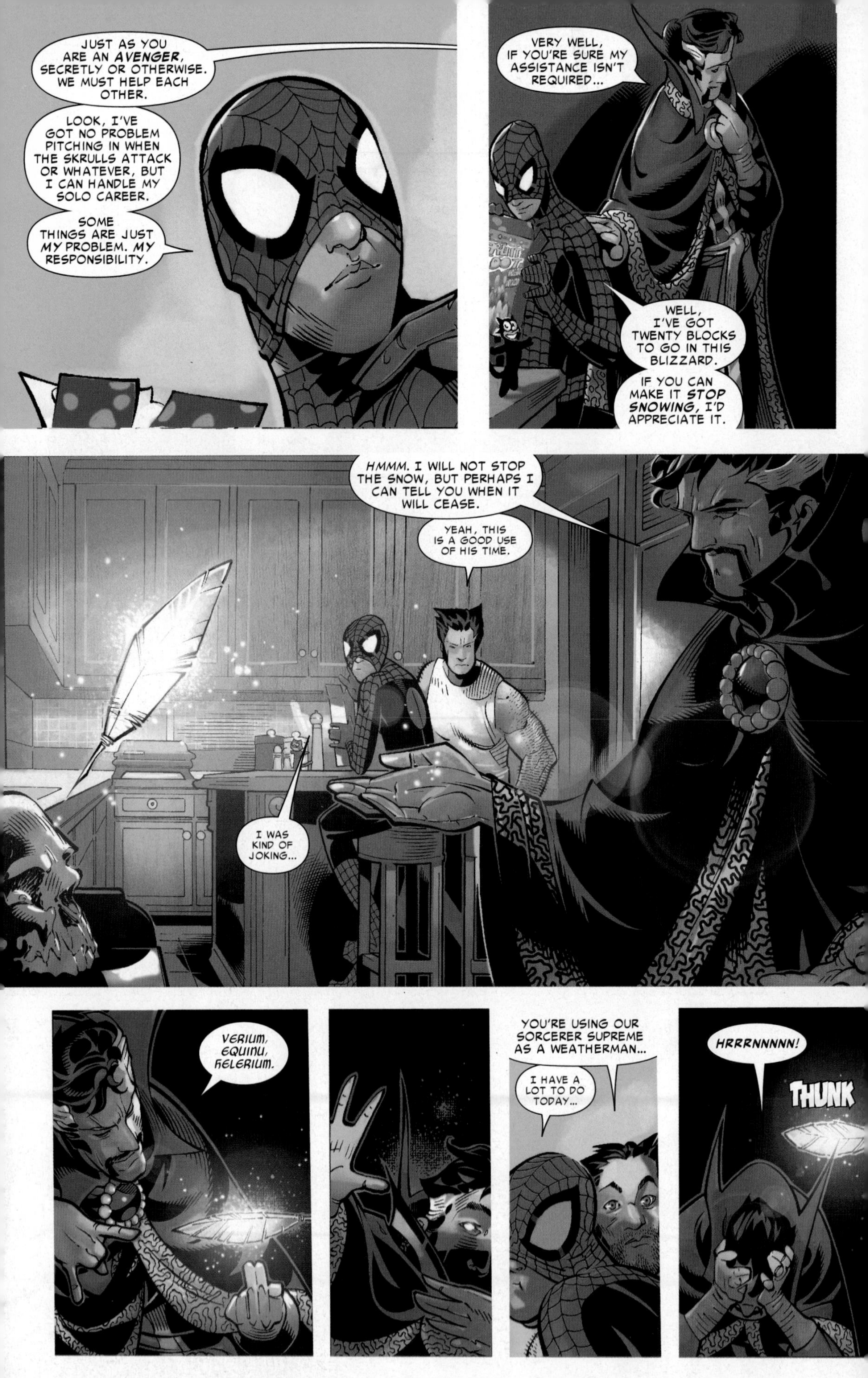

JUST AS YOU ARE AN AVENGER, SECRETLY OR OTHERWISE. WE MUST HELP EACH OTHER.
LOOK, I'VE GOT NO PROBLEM PITCHING IN WHEN THE SKRULLS ATTACK OR WHATEVER, BUT I CAN HANDLE MY SOLO CAREER.
SOME THINGS ARE JUST MY PROBLEM. MY RESPONSIBILITY.
VERY WELL, IF YOU'RE SURE MY ASSISTANCE ISN'T REQUIRED...
WELL, I'VE GOT TWENTY BLOCKS TO GO IN THIS BLIZZARD.
IF YOU CAN MAKE IT STOP SNOWING, I'D APPRECIATE IT.
HMMM. I WILL NOT STOP THE SNOW, BUT PERHAPS I CAN TELL YOU WHEN IT WILL CEASE.
YEAH, THIS IS A GOOD USE OF HIS TIME.
I WAS KIND OF JOKING...
VERIUM, EQUINU, FELERIUM.
YOU'RE USING OUR SORCERER SUPREME AS A WEATHERMAN...
I HAVE A LOT TO DO TODAY...
HRRRNNNNN!
THUNK

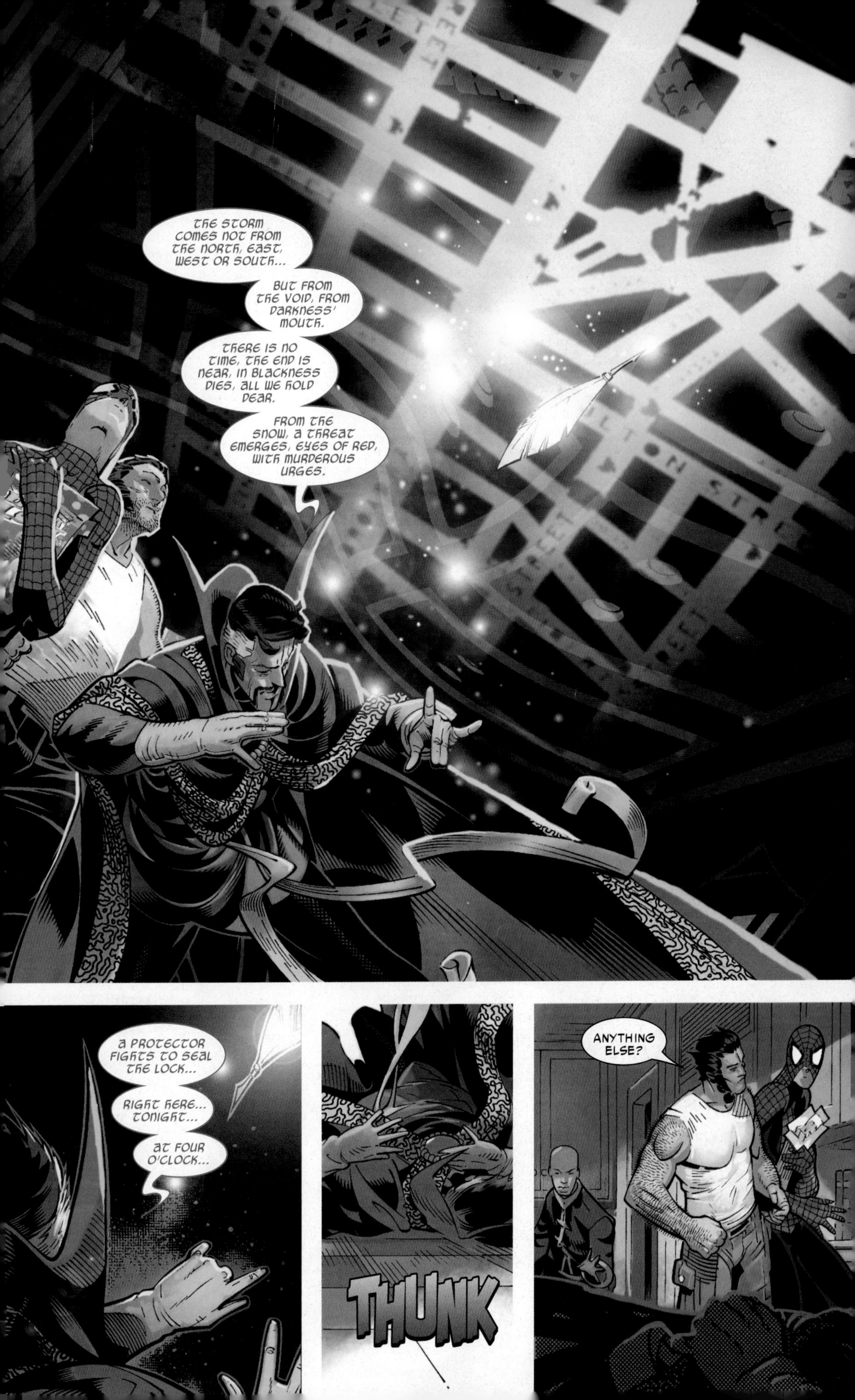
THE STORM COMES NOT FROM THE NORTH, EAST, WEST OR SOUTH...
BUT FROM THE VOID, FROM DARKNESS' MOUTH.
THERE IS NO TIME, THE END IS NEAR, IN BLACKNESS DIES, ALL WE HOLD DEAR.
FROM THE SNOW, A THREAT EMERGES, EYES OF RED, WITH MURDEROUS URGES.
A PROTECTOR FIGHTS TO SEAL THE LOCK...
RIGHT HERE... TONIGHT...
AT FOUR O'CLOCK...
THUNK
ANYTHING ELSE?

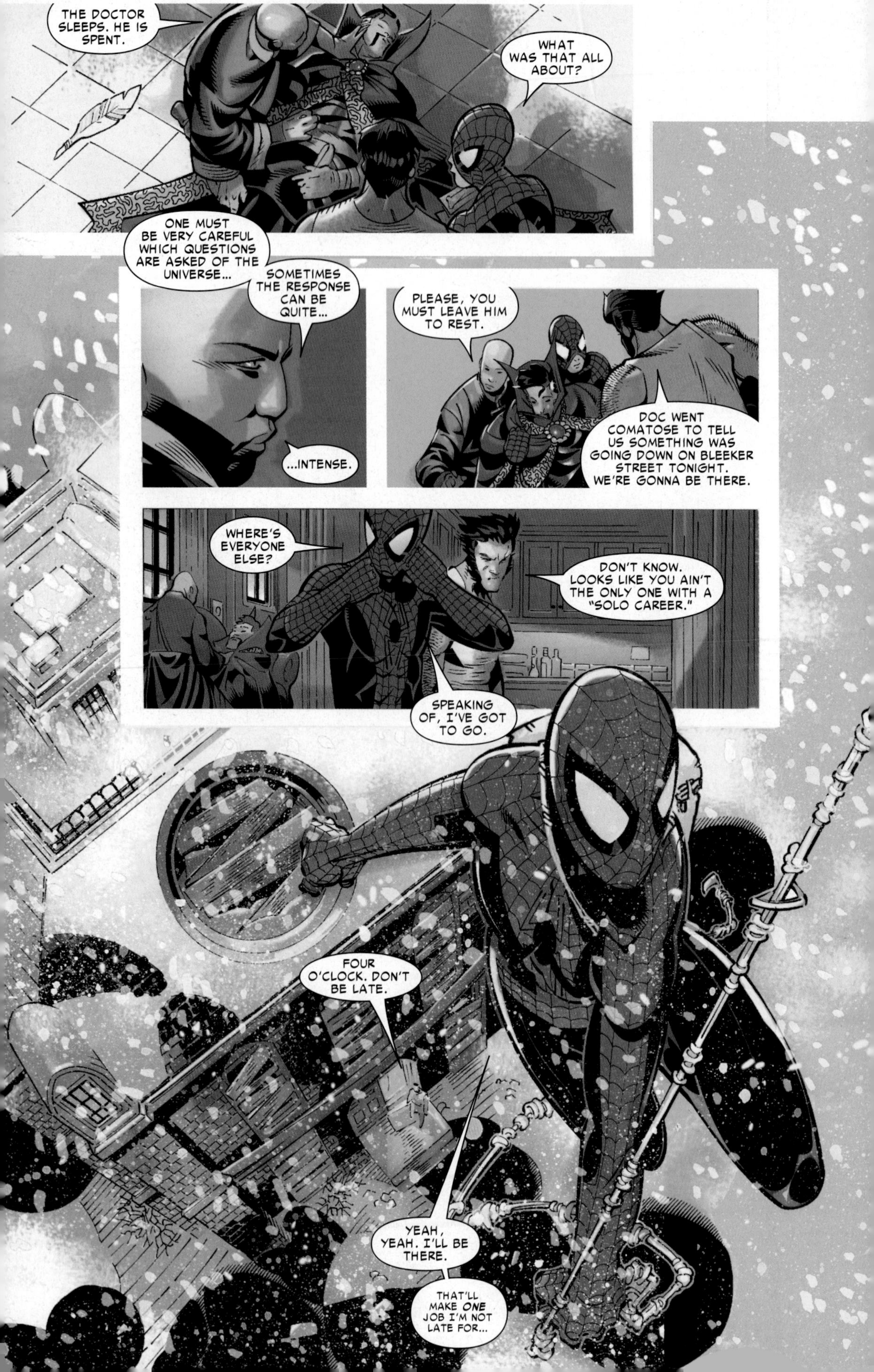
THE DOCTOR SLEEPS. HE IS SPENT.
WHAT WAS THAT ALL ABOUT?
ONE MUST BE VERY CAREFUL WHICH QUESTIONS ARE ASKED OF THE UNIVERSE...
SOMETIMES THE RESPONSE CAN BE QUITE...
...INTENSE.
PLEASE, YOU MUST LEAVE HIM TO REST.
DOC WENT COMATOSE TO TELL US SOMETHING WAS GOING DOWN ON BLEEKER STREET TONIGHT. WE'RE GONNA BE THERE.
WHERE'S EVERYONE ELSE?
DON'T KNOW. LOOKS LIKE YOU AIN'T THE ONLY ONE WITH A "SOLO CAREER."
SPEAKING OF, I'VE GOT TO GO.
FOUR O'CLOCK. DON'T BE LATE.
YEAH, YEAH. I'LL BE THERE.
THAT'LL MAKE ONE JOB I'M NOT LATE FOR...

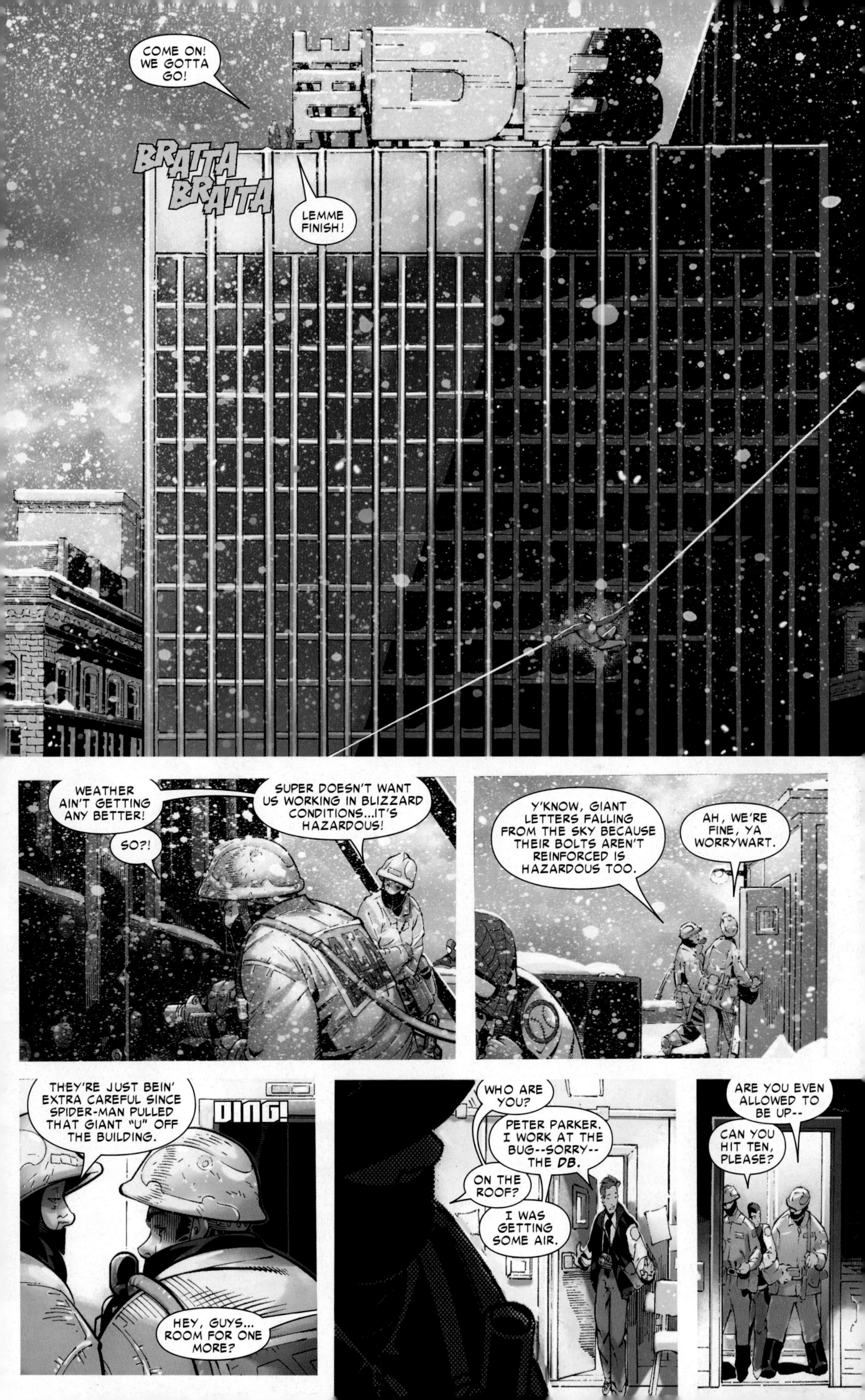
COME ON! WE GOTTA GO!
THE DB
BRATTA BRATTA
LEMME FINISH!
WEATHER AIN'T GETTING ANY BETTER!
SUPER DOESN'T WANT US WORKING IN BLIZZARD CONDITIONS...IT'S HAZARDOUS!
SO?!
Y'KNOW, GIANT LETTERS FALLING FROM THE SKY BECAUSE THEIR BOLTS AREN'T REINFORCED IS HAZARDOUS TOO.
AH, WE'RE FINE, YA WORRYWART.
THEY'RE JUST BEIN' EXTRA CAREFUL SINCE SPIDER-MAN PULLED THAT GIANT "U" OFF THE BUILDING.
DING!
HEY, GUYS... ROOM FOR ONE MORE?
WHO ARE YOU?
PETER PARKER. I WORK AT THE BUG--SORRY--THE DB.
ON THE ROOF?
I WAS GETTING SOME AIR.
ARE YOU EVEN ALLOWED TO BE UP--
CAN YOU HIT TEN, PLEASE?

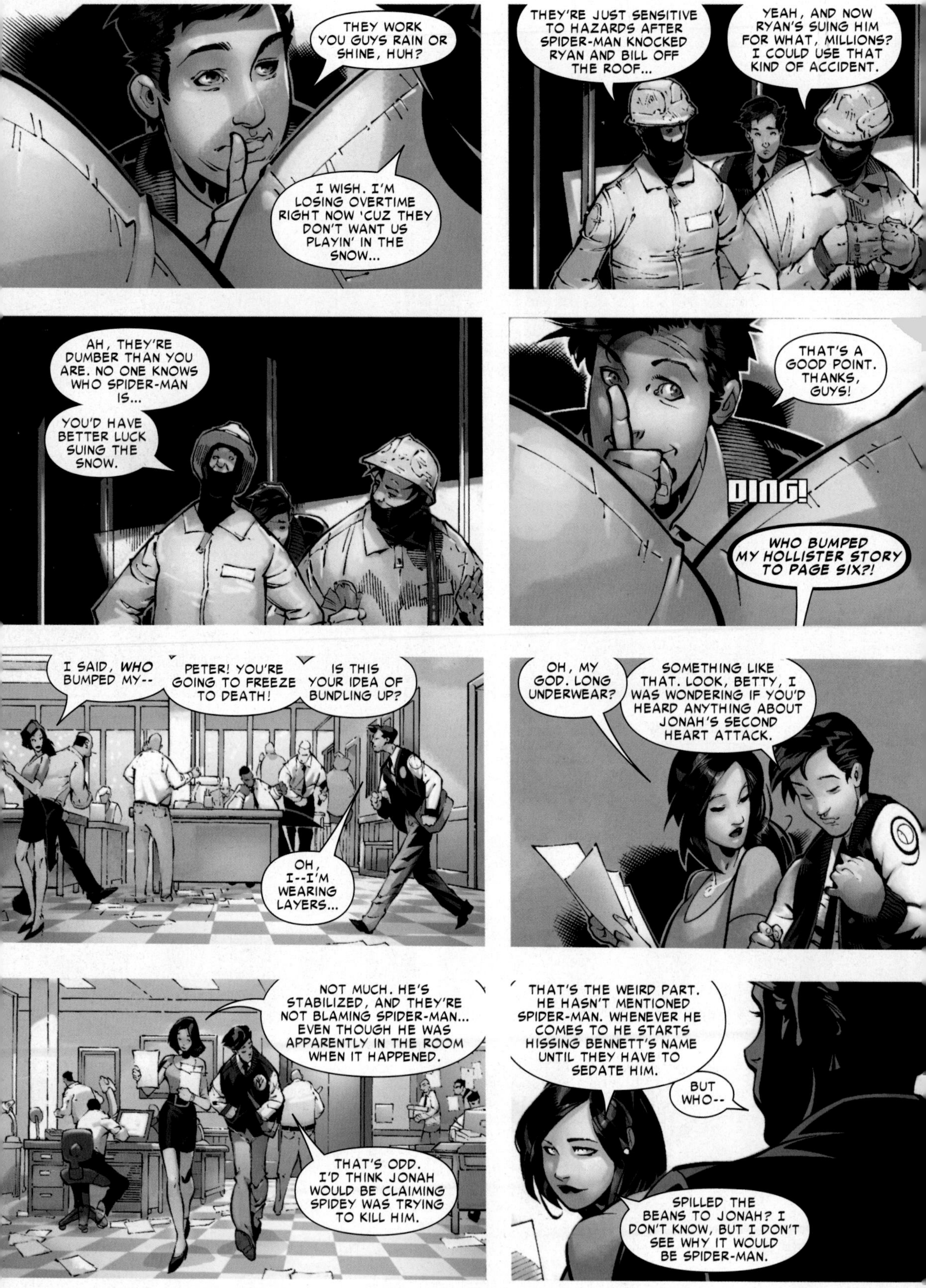
THEY WORK YOU GUYS RAIN OR SHINE, HUH?
I WISH. I'M LOSING OVERTIME RIGHT NOW 'CUZ THEY DON'T WANT US PLAYIN' IN THE SNOW...
THEY'RE JUST SENSITIVE TO HAZARDS AFTER SPIDER-MAN KNOCKED RYAN AND BILL OFF THE ROOF...
YEAH, AND NOW RYAN'S SUING HIM FOR WHAT, MILLIONS? I COULD USE THAT KIND OF ACCIDENT.
AH, THEY'RE DUMBER THAN YOU ARE. NO ONE KNOWS WHO SPIDER-MAN IS...
YOU'D HAVE BETTER LUCK SUING THE SNOW.
THAT'S A GOOD POINT. THANKS, GUYS!
DING!
WHO BUMPED MY HOLLISTER STORY TO PAGE SIX?!
I SAID, WHO BUMPED MY--
PETER! YOU'RE GOING TO FREEZE TO DEATH!
IS THIS YOUR IDEA OF BUNDLING UP?
OH, I--I'M WEARING LAYERS...
OH, MY GOD. LONG UNDERWEAR?
SOMETHING LIKE THAT. LOOK, BETTY, I WAS WONDERING IF YOU'D HEARD ANYTHING ABOUT JONAH'S SECOND HEART ATTACK.
NOT MUCH. HE'S STABILIZED, AND THEY'RE NOT BLAMING SPIDER-MAN... EVEN THOUGH HE WAS APPARENTLY IN THE ROOM WHEN IT HAPPENED.
THAT'S ODD. I'D THINK JONAH WOULD BE CLAIMING SPIDEY WAS TRYING TO KILL HIM.
THAT'S THE WEIRD PART. HE HASN'T MENTIONED SPIDER-MAN. WHENEVER HE COMES TO HE STARTS HISSING BENNETT'S NAME UNTIL THEY HAVE TO SEDATE HIM.
BUT WHO--
SPILLED THE BEANS TO JONAH? I DON'T KNOW, BUT I DON'T SEE WHY IT WOULD BE SPIDER-MAN.

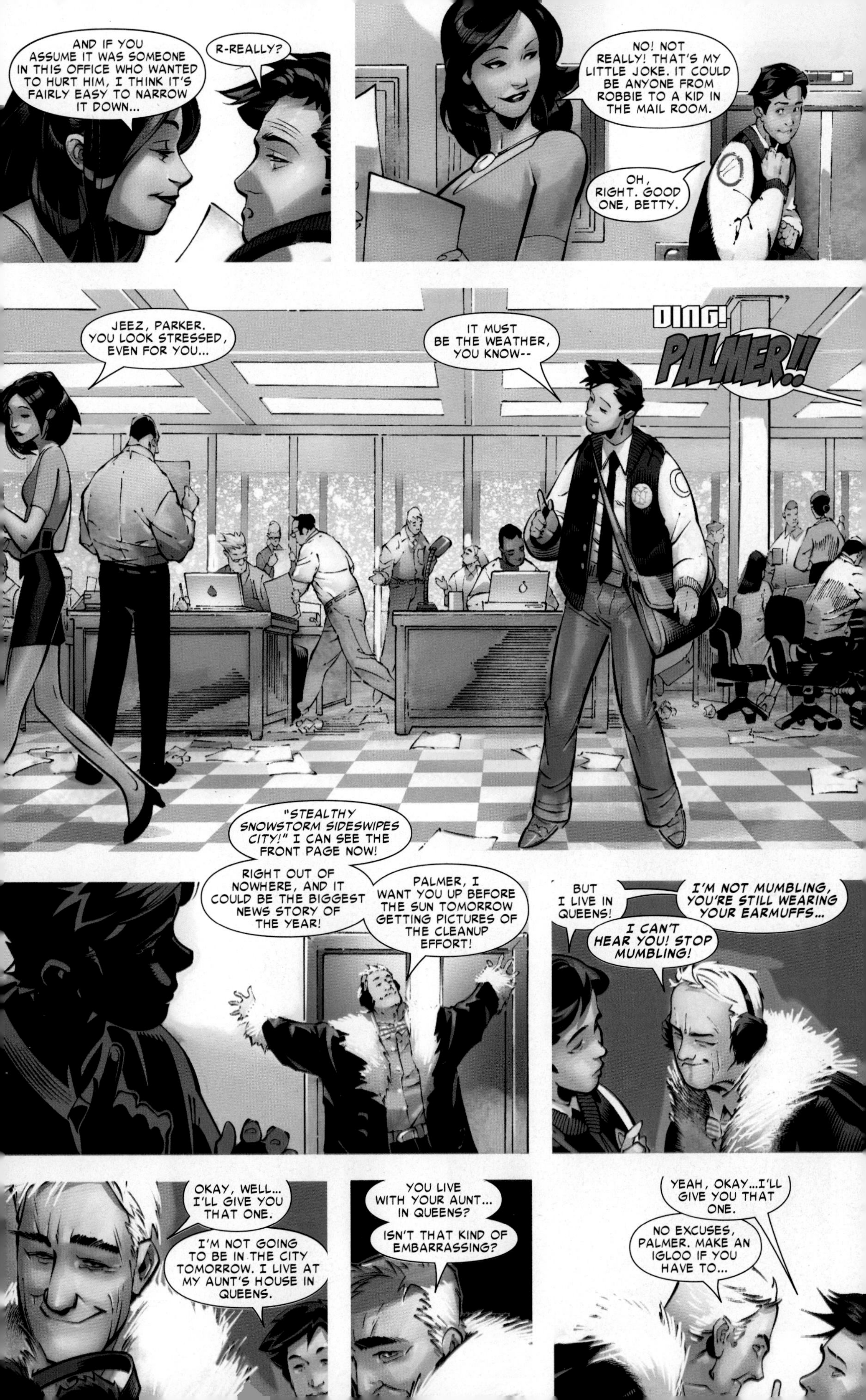
AND IF YOU ASSUME IT WAS SOMEONE IN THIS OFFICE WHO WANTED TO HURT HIM, I THINK IT'S FAIRLY EASY TO NARROW IT DOWN...
R-REALLY?
NO! NOT REALLY! THAT'S MY LITTLE JOKE. IT COULD BE ANYONE FROM ROBBIE TO A KID IN THE MAIL ROOM.
OH, RIGHT. GOOD ONE, BETTY.
JEEZ, PARKER. YOU LOOK STRESSED, EVEN FOR YOU...
IT MUST BE THE WEATHER, YOU KNOW--
DING!
PALMER!!
"STEALTHY SNOWSTORM SIDESWIPES CITY!" I CAN SEE THE FRONT PAGE NOW!
RIGHT OUT OF NOWHERE, AND IT COULD BE THE BIGGEST NEWS STORY OF THE YEAR!
PALMER, I WANT YOU UP BEFORE THE SUN TOMORROW GETTING PICTURES OF THE CLEANUP EFFORT!
BUT I LIVE IN QUEENS!
I'M NOT MUMBLING, YOU'RE STILL WEARING YOUR EARMUFFS...
I CAN'T HEAR YOU! STOP MUMBLING!
OKAY, WELL... I'LL GIVE YOU THAT ONE.
I'M NOT GOING TO BE IN THE CITY TOMORROW. I LIVE AT MY AUNT'S HOUSE IN QUEENS.
YOU LIVE WITH YOUR AUNT... IN QUEENS?
ISN'T THAT KIND OF EMBARRASSING?
YEAH, OKAY...I'LL GIVE YOU THAT ONE.
NO EXCUSES, PALMER. MAKE AN IGLOO IF YOU HAVE TO...

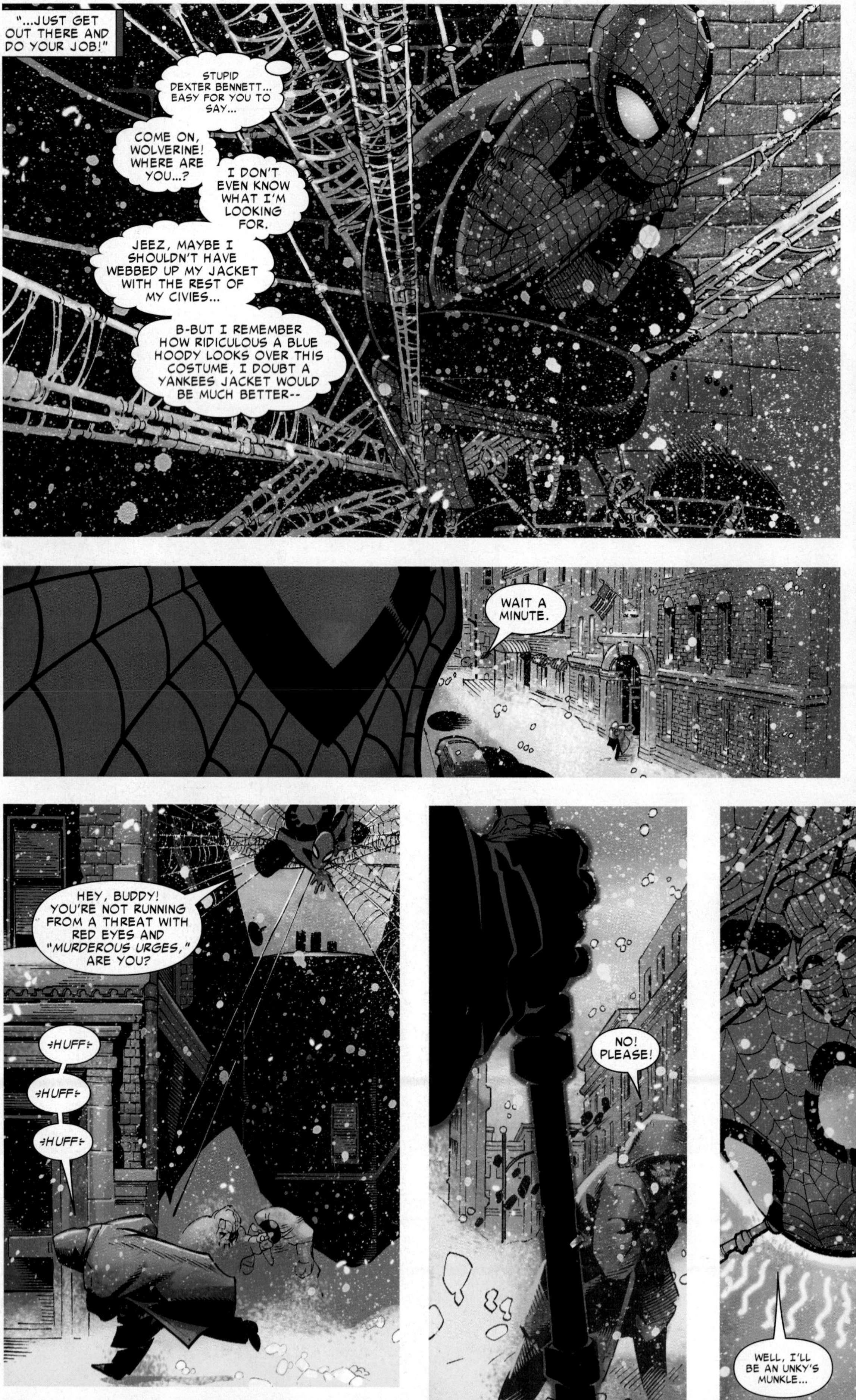

"...JUST GET OUT THERE AND DO YOUR JOB!"
STUPID DEXTER BENNETT... EASY FOR YOU TO SAY...
COME ON, WOLVERINE! WHERE ARE YOU...?
I DON'T EVEN KNOW WHAT I'M LOOKING FOR.
JEEZ, MAYBE I SHOULDN'T HAVE WEBBED UP MY JACKET WITH THE REST OF MY CIVIES...
B-BUT I REMEMBER HOW RIDICULOUS A BLUE HOODY LOOKS OVER THIS COSTUME, I DOUBT A YANKEES JACKET WOULD BE MUCH BETTER--
WAIT A MINUTE.
HEY, BUDDY! YOU'RE NOT RUNNING FROM A THREAT WITH RED EYES AND "MURDEROUS URGES," ARE YOU?
HUFF
HUFF
HUFF
NO! PLEASE!
WELL, I'LL BE AN UNKY'S MUNKLE...

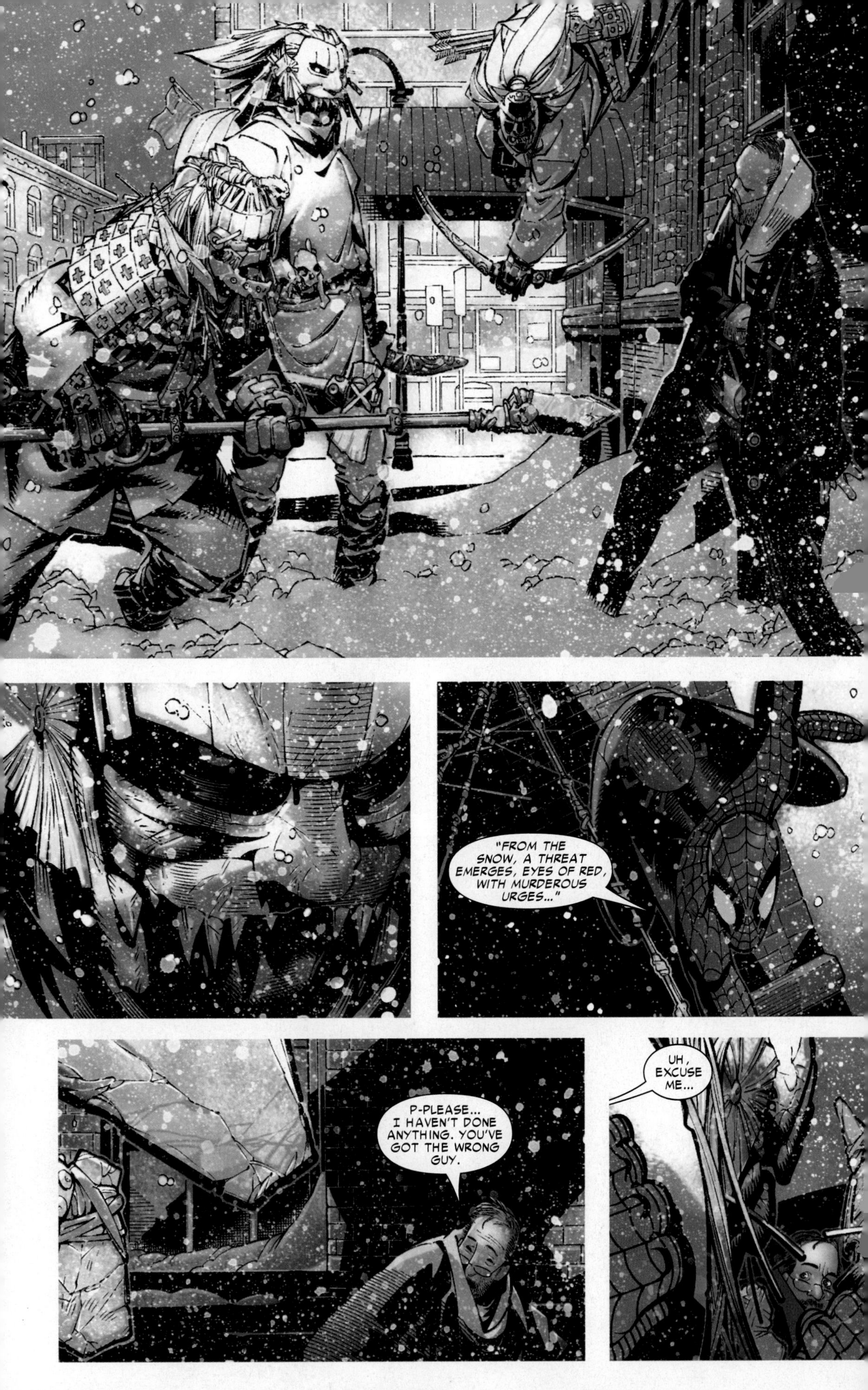
"FROM THE SNOW, A THREAT EMERGES, EYES OF RED, WITH MURDEROUS URGES..."
P-PLEASE... I HAVEN'T DONE ANYTHING. YOU'VE GOT THE WRONG GUY.
UH, EXCUSE ME...

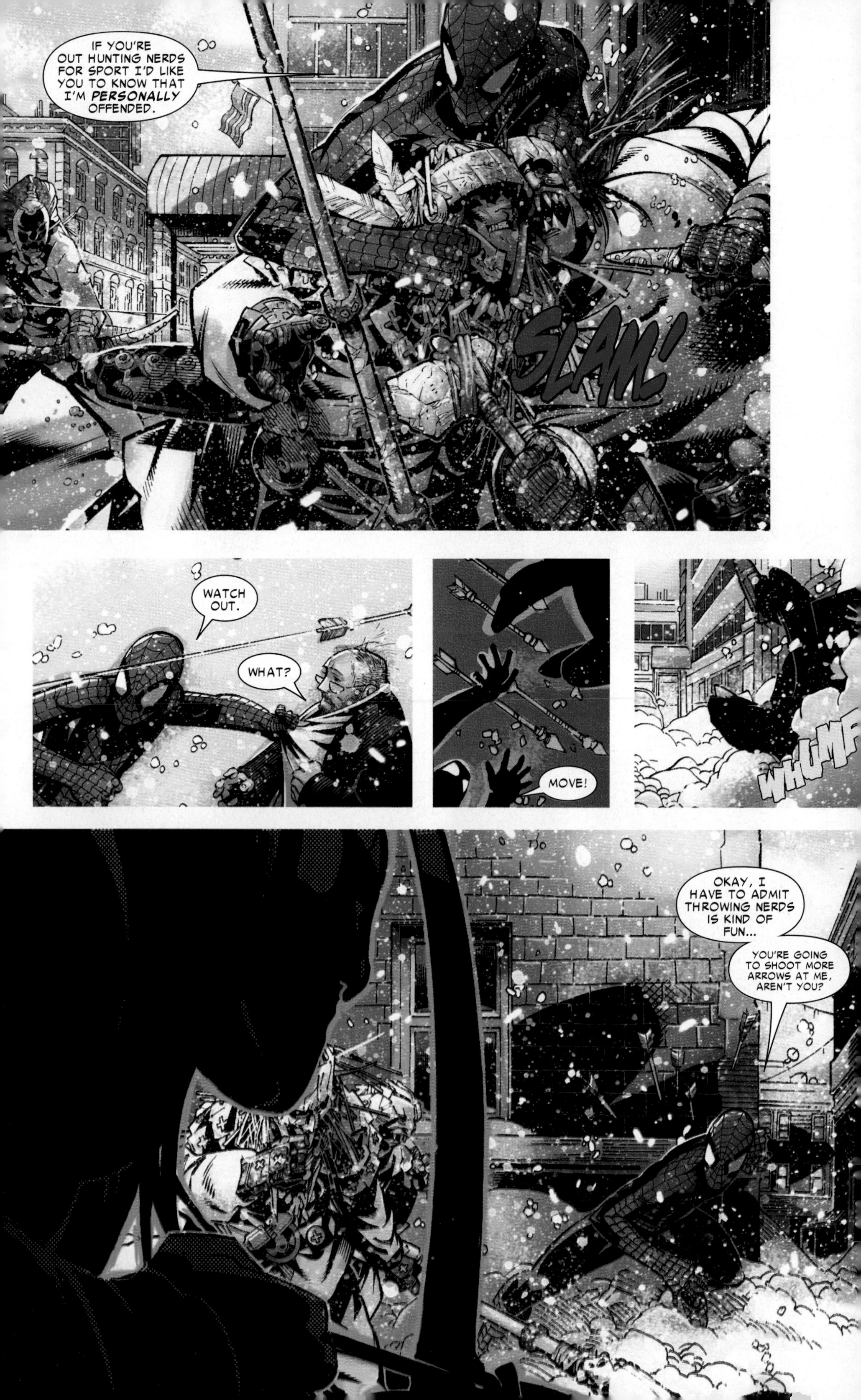
IF YOU'RE OUT HUNTING NERDS FOR SPORT I'D LIKE YOU TO KNOW THAT I'M *PERSONALLY* OFFENDED.
SLAM!
WATCH OUT.
WHAT?
MOVE!
WHUMF
OKAY, I HAVE TO ADMIT THROWING NERDS IS KIND OF FUN...
YOU'RE GOING TO SHOOT MORE ARROWS AT ME, AREN'T YOU?

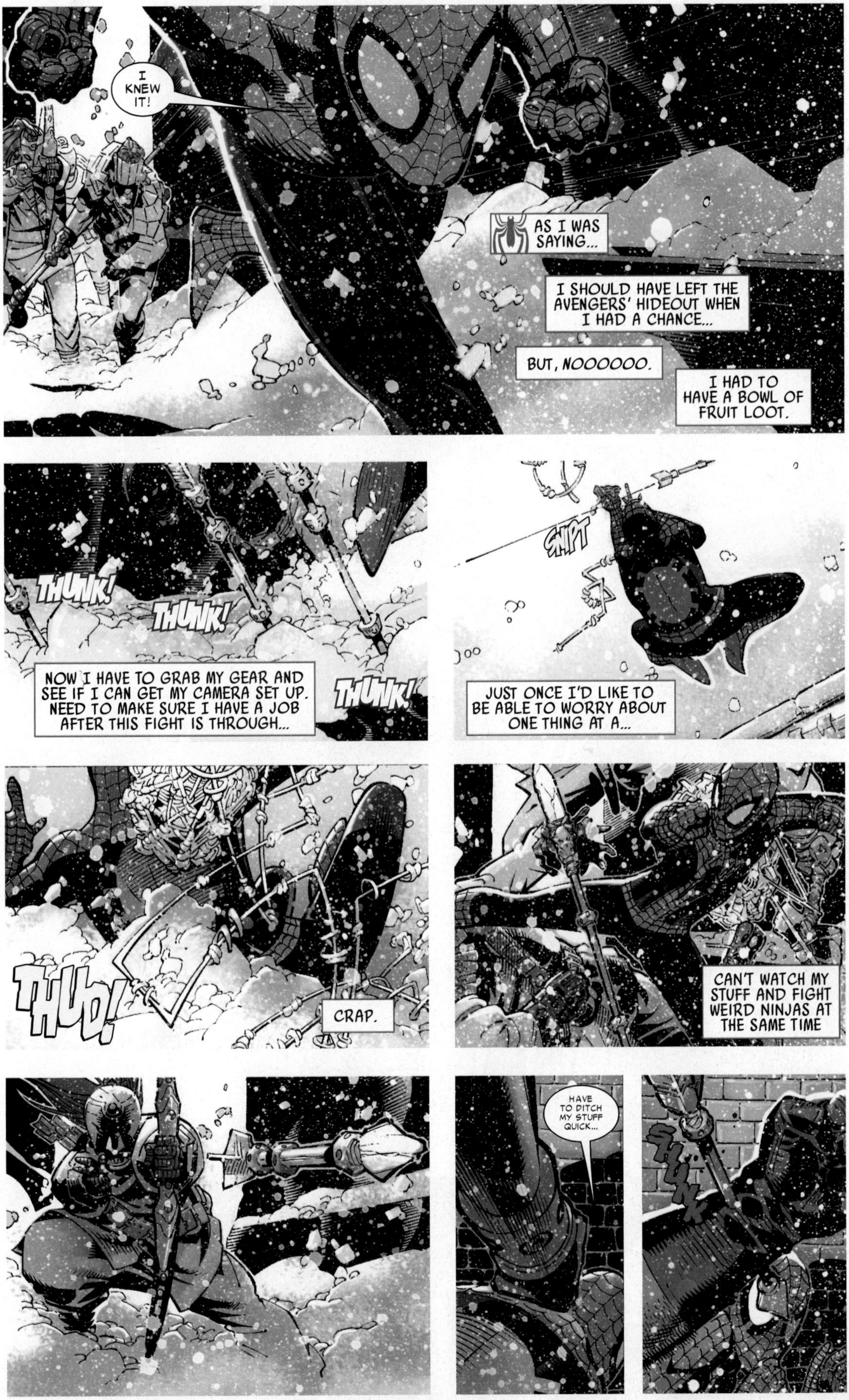

I KNEW IT!
AS I WAS SAYING...
I SHOULD HAVE LEFT THE AVENGERS' HIDEOUT WHEN I HAD A CHANCE...
BUT, NOOOOOO.
I HAD TO HAVE A BOWL OF FRUIT LOOT.
THUNK!
THUNK!
NOW I HAVE TO GRAB MY GEAR AND SEE IF I CAN GET MY CAMERA SET UP. NEED TO MAKE SURE I HAVE A JOB AFTER THIS FIGHT IS THROUGH...
THUNK!
SNIPT
JUST ONCE I'D LIKE TO BE ABLE TO WORRY ABOUT ONE THING AT A...
THUD!
CRAP.
CAN'T WATCH MY STUFF AND FIGHT WEIRD NINJAS AT THE SAME TIME
HAVE TO DITCH MY STUFF QUICK...
SHUNK

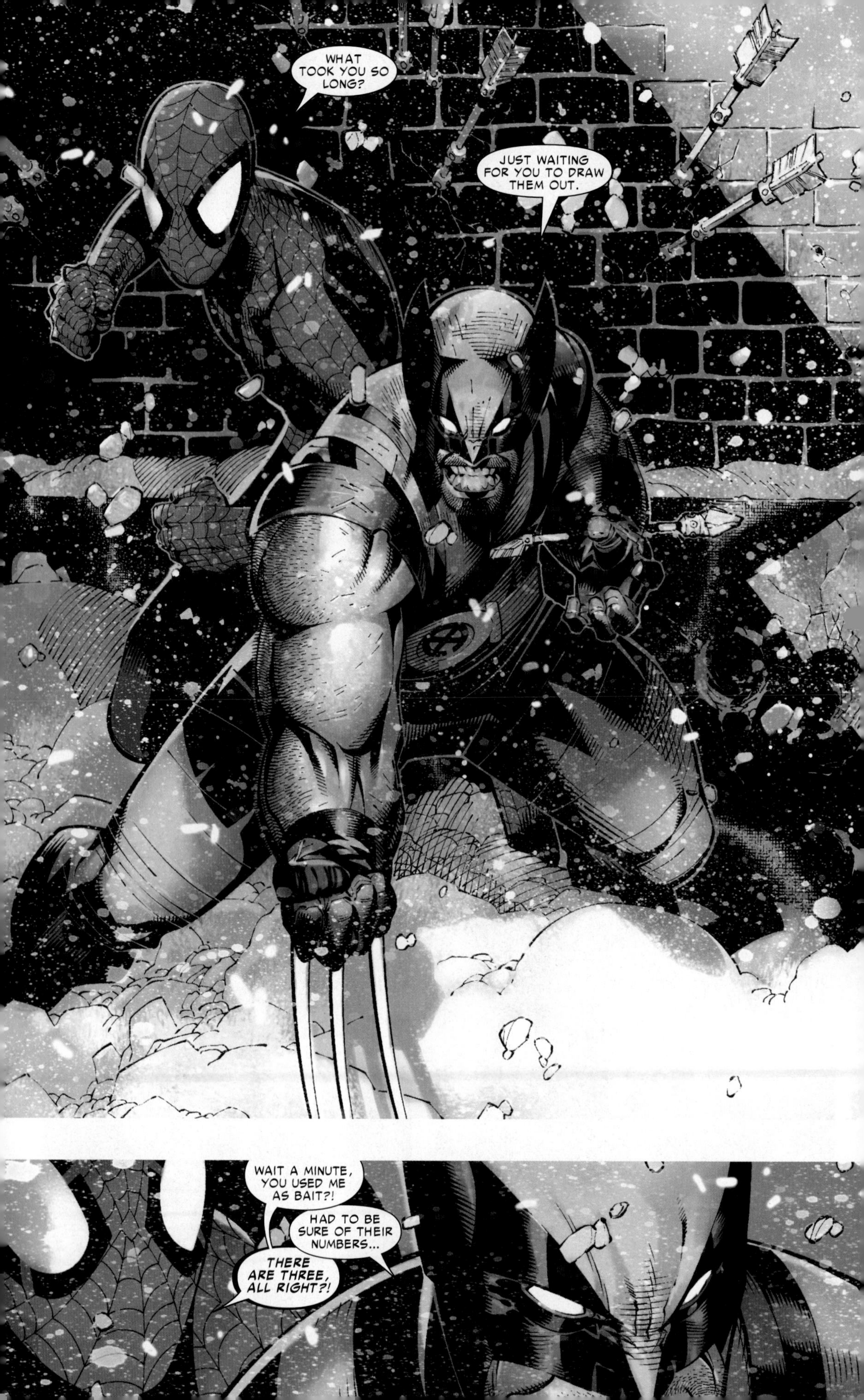
WHAT TOOK YOU SO LONG?
JUST WAITING FOR YOU TO DRAW THEM OUT.
WAIT A MINUTE, YOU USED ME AS BAIT?!
HAD TO BE SURE OF THEIR NUMBERS...
THERE ARE THREE, ALL RIGHT?!

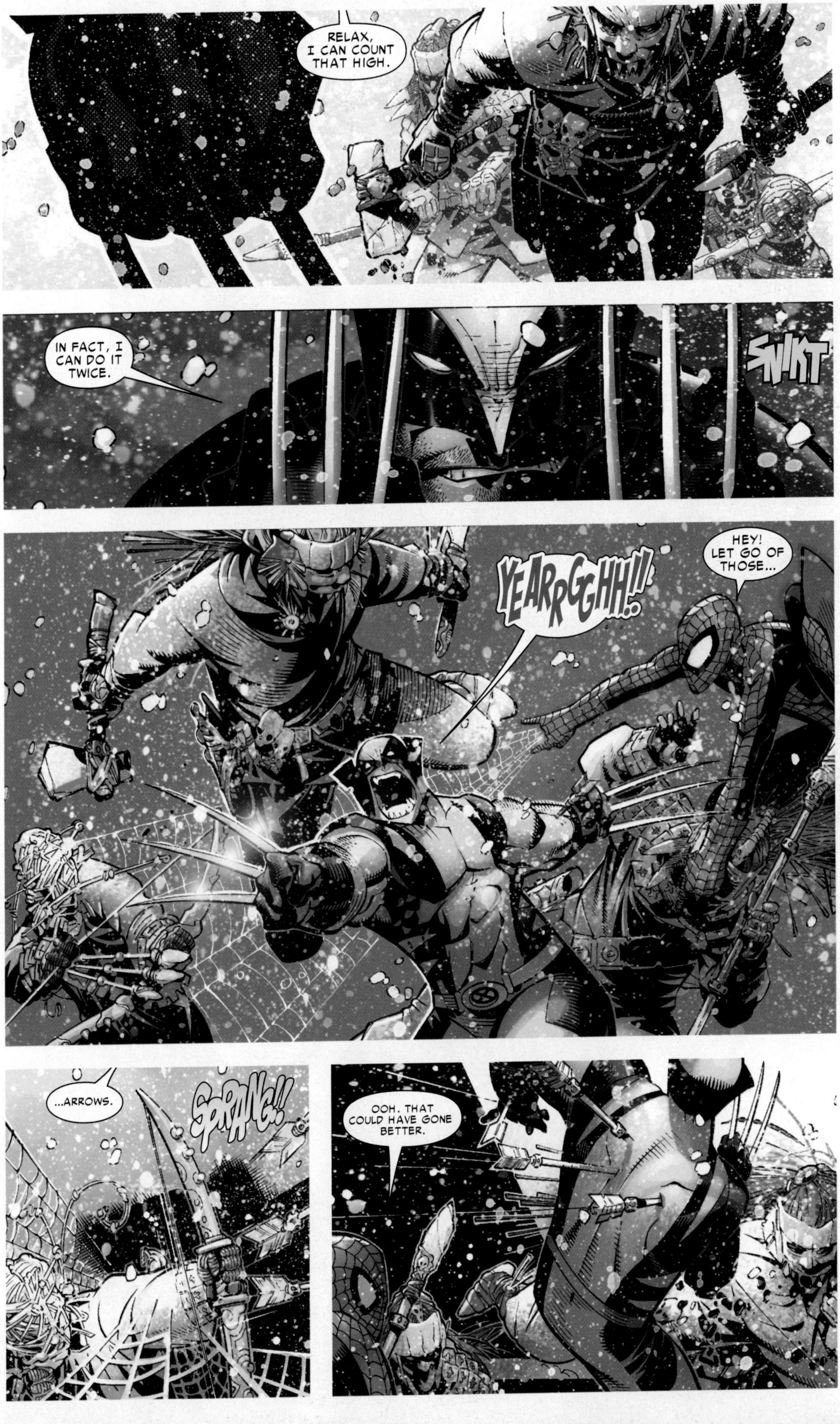
RELAX, I CAN COUNT THAT HIGH.
IN FACT, I CAN DO IT TWICE.
SNIKT
YEARRGGHH!!!
HEY! LET GO OF THOSE...
...ARROWS.
SPRANG!!
OOH. THAT COULD HAVE GONE BETTER.

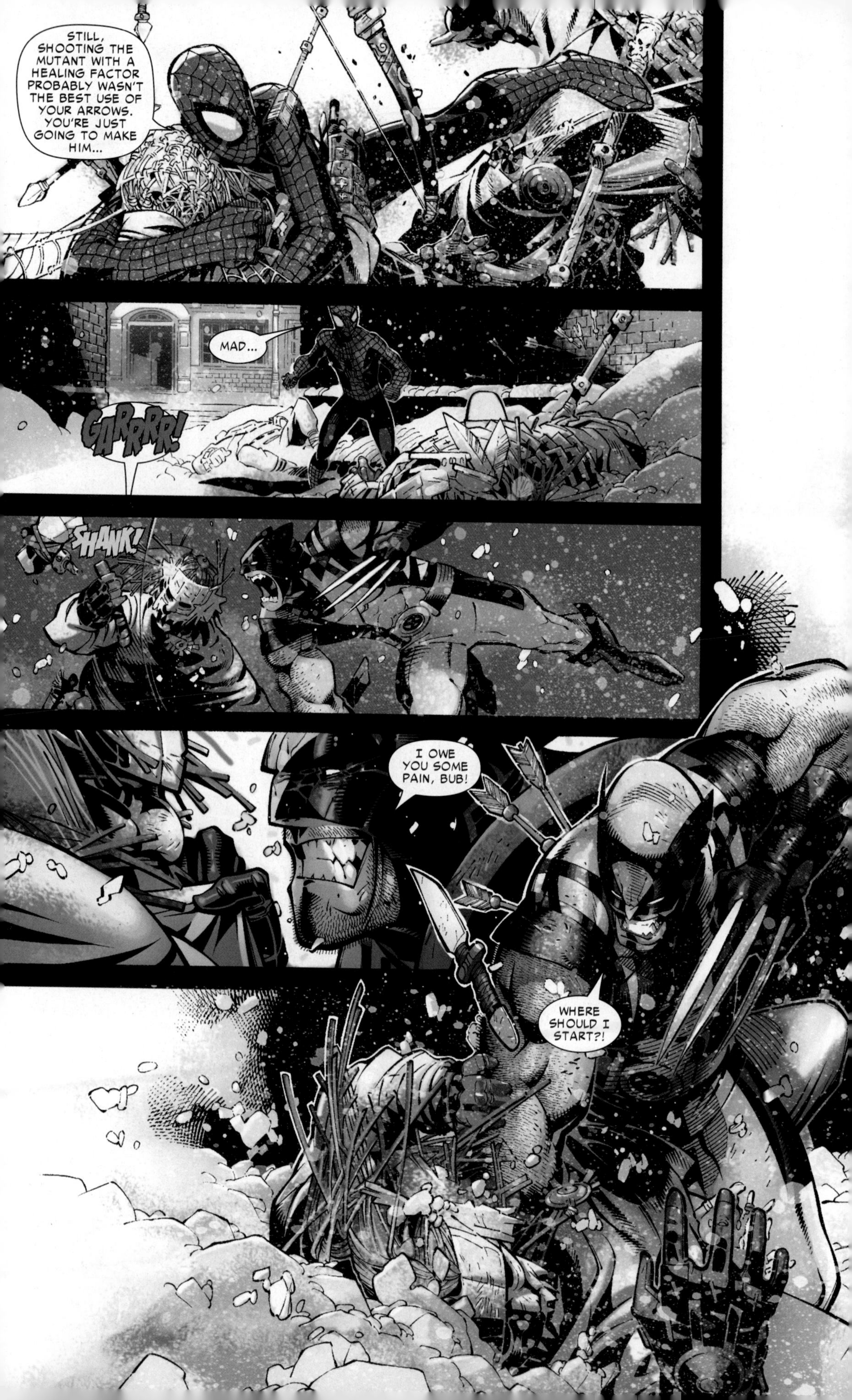
STILL, SHOOTING THE MUTANT WITH A HEALING FACTOR PROBABLY WASN'T THE BEST USE OF YOUR ARROWS. YOU'RE JUST GOING TO MAKE HIM...
MAD...
GARRRR!
SHANK!
I OWE YOU SOME PAIN, BUB!
WHERE SHOULD I START?!

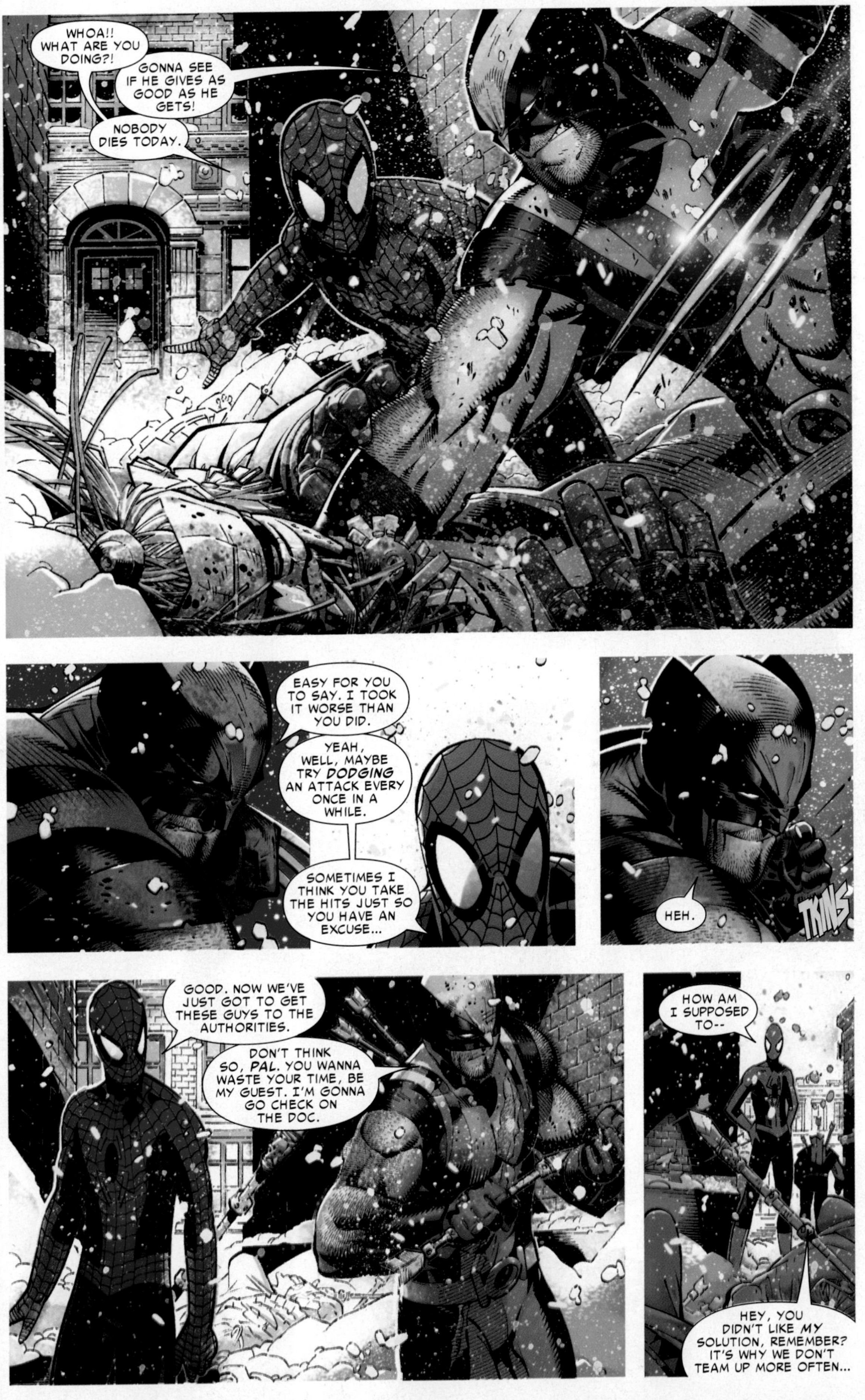
WHOA!! WHAT ARE YOU DOING?!
GONNA SEE IF HE GIVES AS GOOD AS HE GETS!
NOBODY DIES TODAY.
EASY FOR YOU TO SAY. I TOOK IT WORSE THAN YOU DID.
YEAH, WELL, MAYBE TRY DODGING AN ATTACK EVERY ONCE IN A WHILE.
SOMETIMES I THINK YOU TAKE THE HITS JUST SO YOU HAVE AN EXCUSE...
HEH.
TKINS
GOOD. NOW WE'VE JUST GOT TO GET THESE GUYS TO THE AUTHORITIES.
DON'T THINK SO, PAL. YOU WANNA WASTE YOUR TIME, BE MY GUEST. I'M GONNA GO CHECK ON THE DOC.
HOW AM I SUPPOSED TO--
HEY, YOU DIDN'T LIKE MY SOLUTION, REMEMBER? IT'S WHY WE DON'T TEAM UP MORE OFTEN...

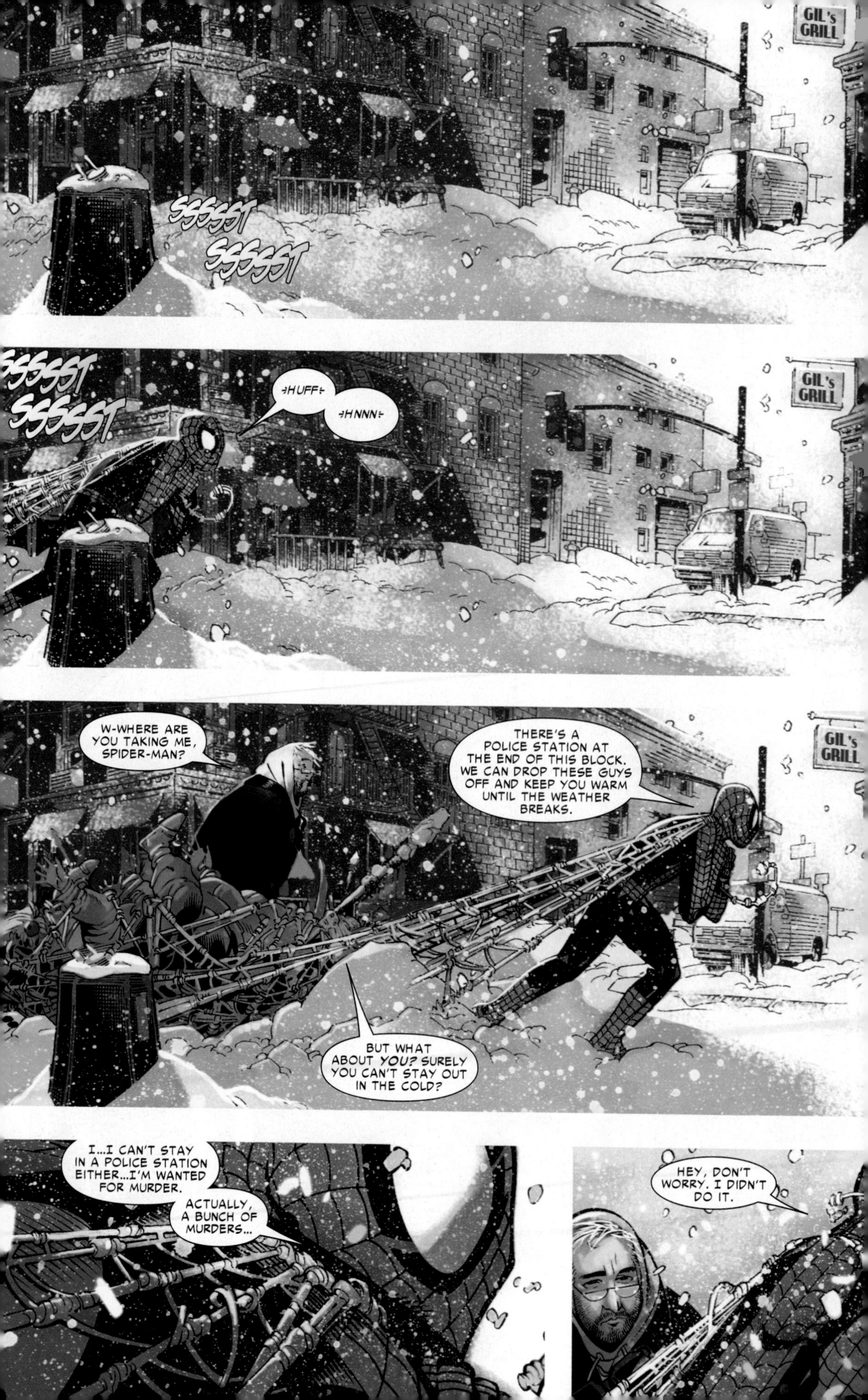

GIL's GRILL
SSSSST
SSSSST
SSSSST
SSSSST
HUFF
HNNN
GIL's GRILL
W-WHERE ARE YOU TAKING ME, SPIDER-MAN?
THERE'S A POLICE STATION AT THE END OF THIS BLOCK. WE CAN DROP THESE GUYS OFF AND KEEP YOU WARM UNTIL THE WEATHER BREAKS.
GIL's GRILL
BUT WHAT ABOUT YOU? SURELY YOU CAN'T STAY OUT IN THE COLD?
I...I CAN'T STAY IN A POLICE STATION EITHER...I'M WANTED FOR MURDER.
ACTUALLY, A BUNCH OF MURDERS...
HEY, DON'T WORRY. I DIDN'T DO IT.

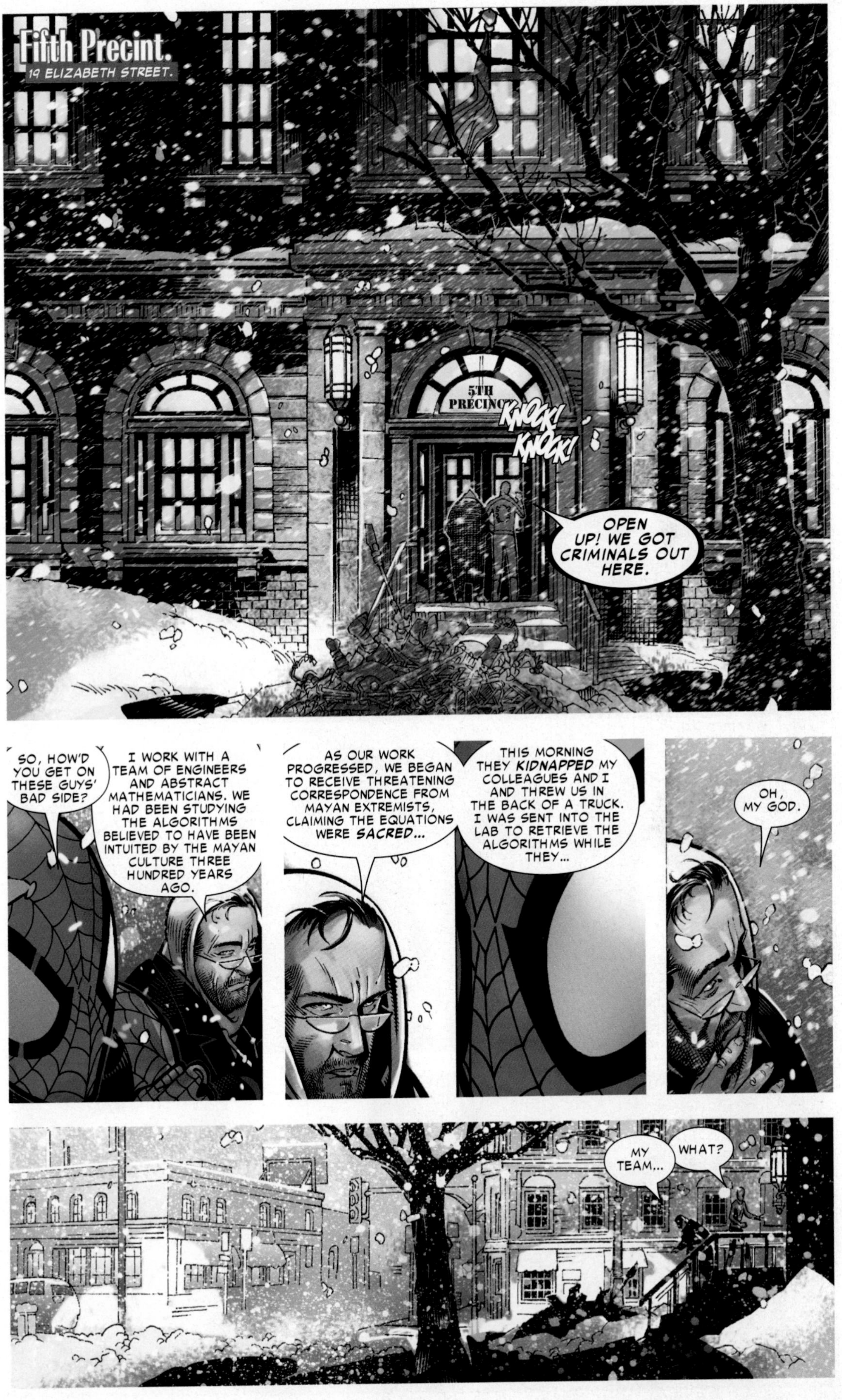
Fifth Precint.
19 ELIZABETH STREET.
5TH PRECINCT
KNOCK! KNOCK!
OPEN UP! WE GOT CRIMINALS OUT HERE.
SO, HOW'D YOU GET ON THESE GUYS' BAD SIDE?
I WORK WITH A TEAM OF ENGINEERS AND ABSTRACT MATHEMATICIANS. WE HAD BEEN STUDYING THE ALGORITHMS BELIEVED TO HAVE BEEN INTUITED BY THE MAYAN CULTURE THREE HUNDRED YEARS AGO.
AS OUR WORK PROGRESSED, WE BEGAN TO RECEIVE THREATENING CORRESPONDENCE FROM MAYAN EXTREMISTS, CLAIMING THE EQUATIONS WERE SACRED...
THIS MORNING THEY KIDNAPPED MY COLLEAGUES AND I AND THREW US IN THE BACK OF A TRUCK. I WAS SENT INTO THE LAB TO RETRIEVE THE ALGORITHMS WHILE THEY...
OH, MY GOD.
MY TEAM...
WHAT?

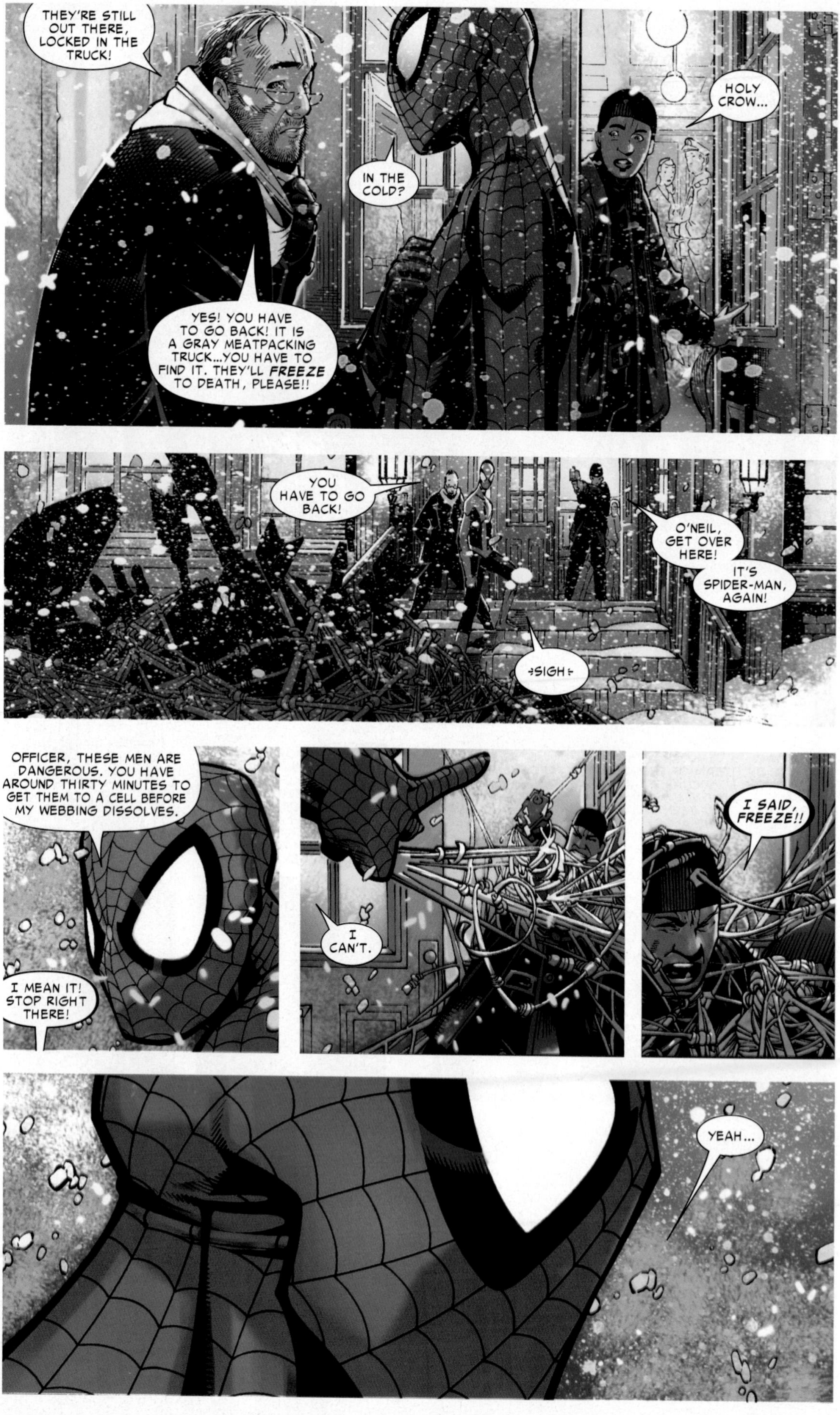
THEY'RE STILL OUT THERE, LOCKED IN THE TRUCK!
IN THE COLD?
HOLY CROW...
YES! YOU HAVE TO GO BACK! IT IS A GRAY MEATPACKING TRUCK...YOU HAVE TO FIND IT. THEY'LL FREEZE TO DEATH, PLEASE!!
YOU HAVE TO GO BACK!
O'NEIL, GET OVER HERE!
IT'S SPIDER-MAN, AGAIN!
SIGH
OFFICER, THESE MEN ARE DANGEROUS. YOU HAVE AROUND THIRTY MINUTES TO GET THEM TO A CELL BEFORE MY WEBBING DISSOLVES.
I MEAN IT! STOP RIGHT THERE!
I CAN'T.
I SAID, FREEZE!!
YEAH...

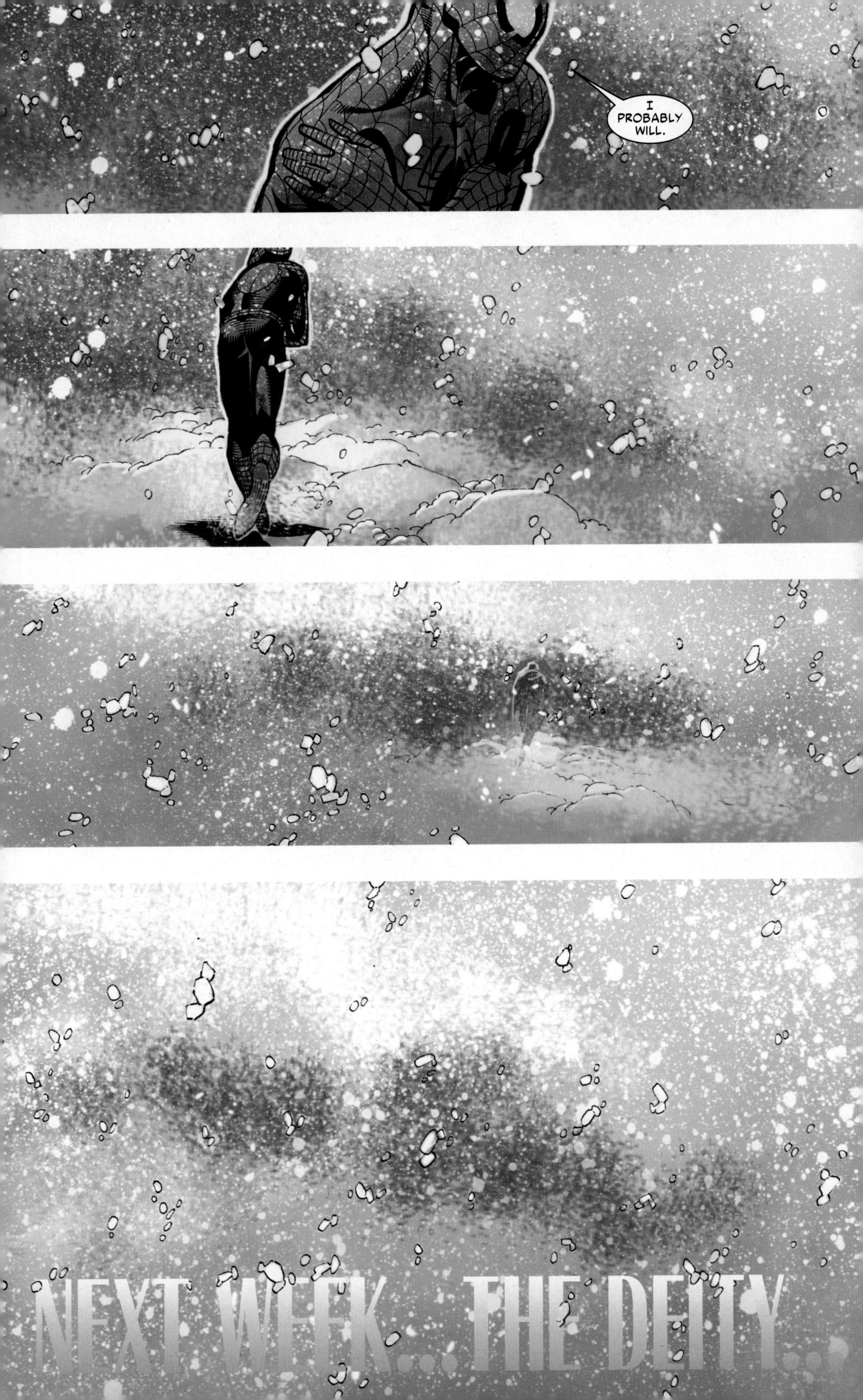
I PROBABLY WILL.
NEXT WEEK... THE DEITY...?

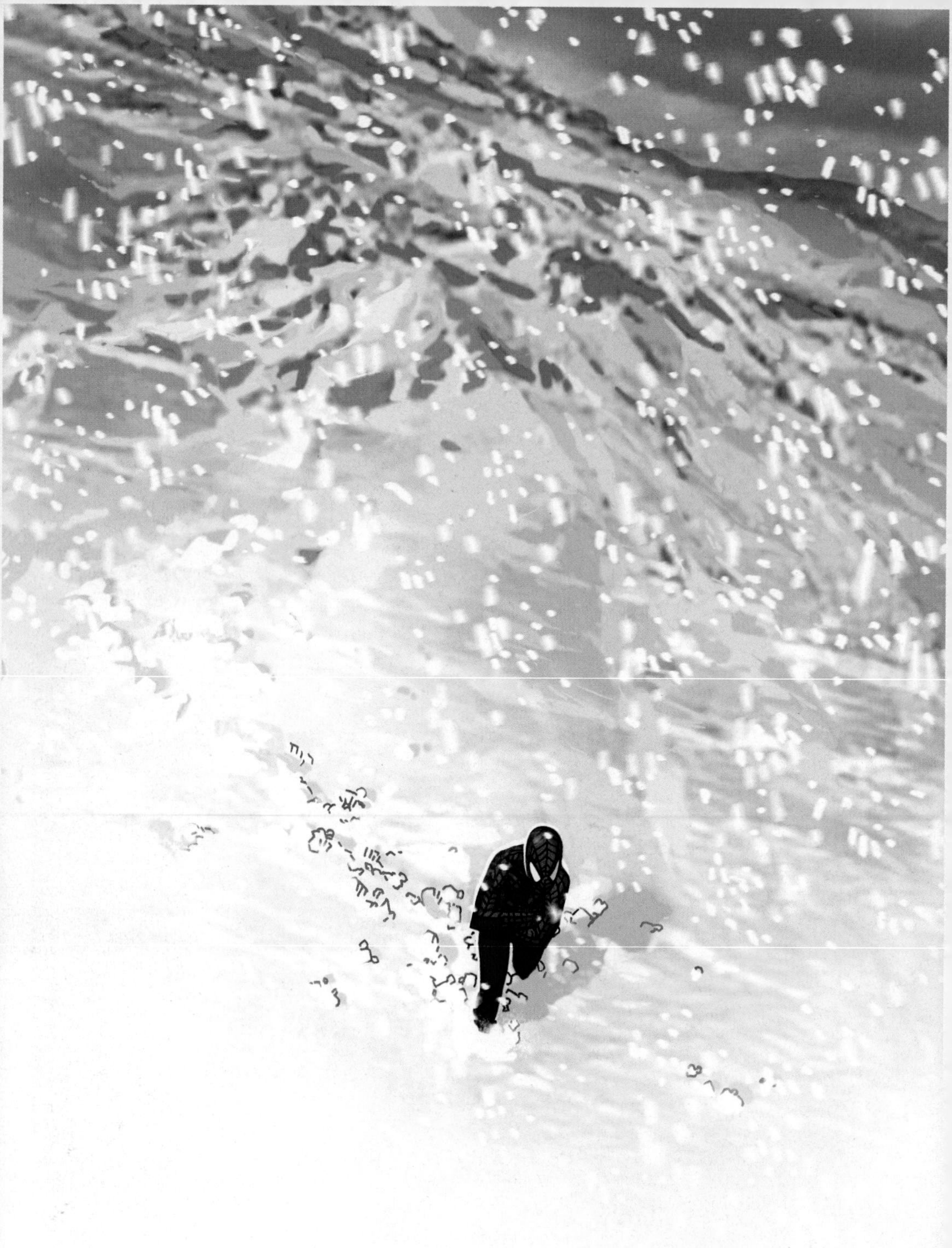

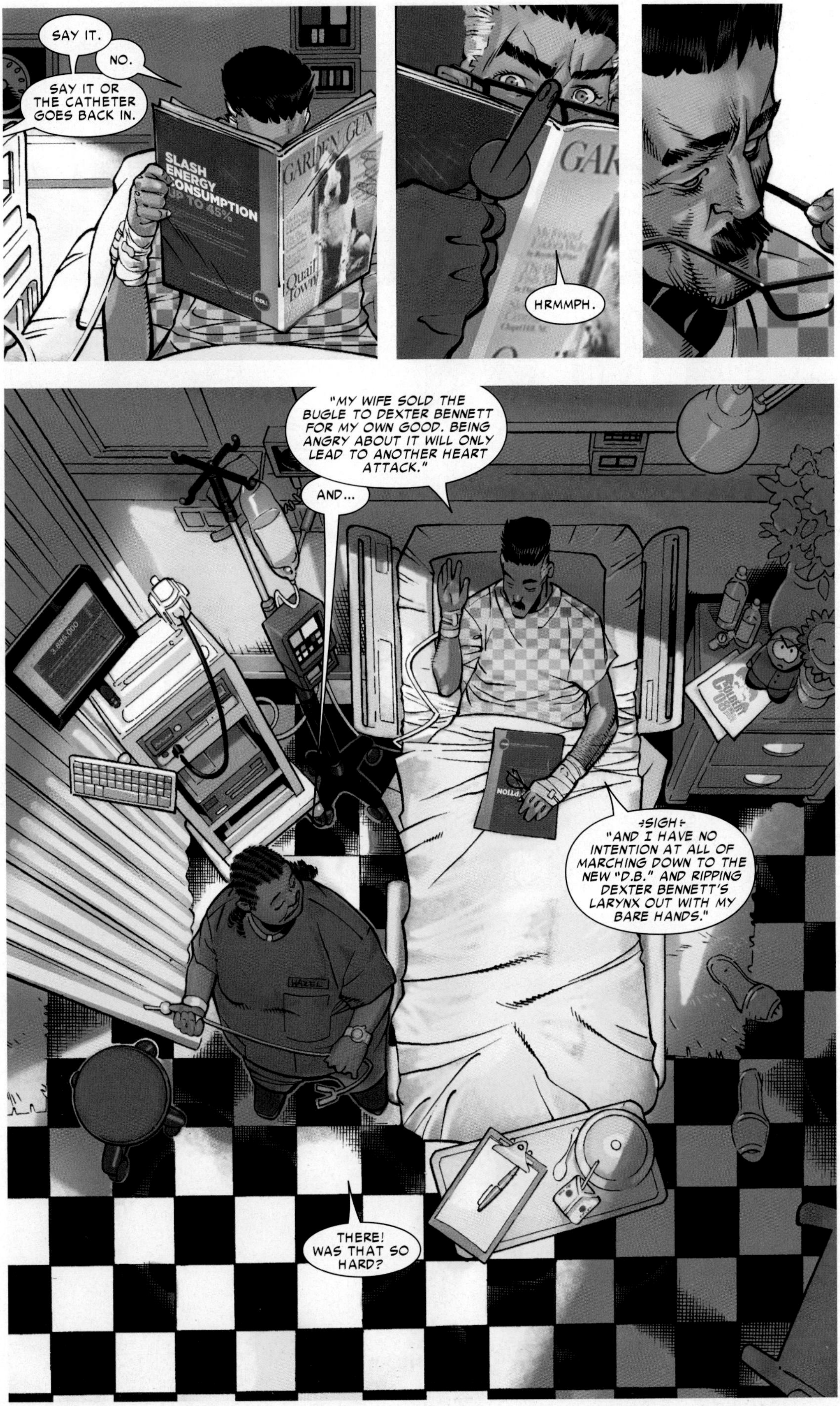
SAY IT.
NO.
SAY IT OR THE CATHETER GOES BACK IN.
HRMMPH.
"MY WIFE SOLD THE BUGLE TO DEXTER BENNETT FOR MY OWN GOOD. BEING ANGRY ABOUT IT WILL ONLY LEAD TO ANOTHER HEART ATTACK."
AND...
SIGH "AND I HAVE NO INTENTION AT ALL OF MARCHING DOWN TO THE NEW "D.B." AND RIPPING DEXTER BENNETT'S LARYNX OUT WITH MY BARE HANDS."
THERE! WAS THAT SO HARD?

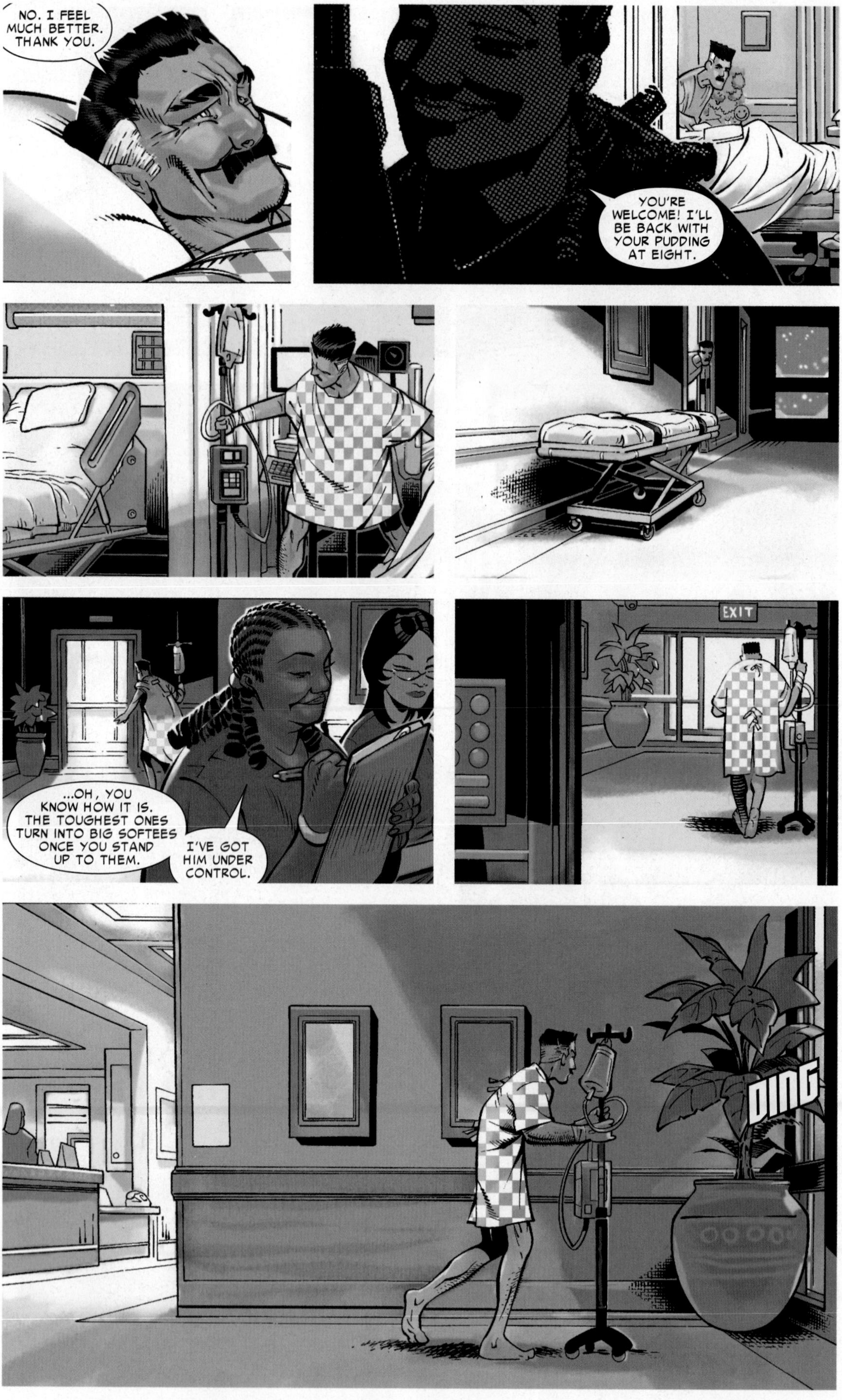
NO. I FEEL MUCH BETTER. THANK YOU.
YOU'RE WELCOME! I'LL BE BACK WITH YOUR PUDDING AT EIGHT.
...OH, YOU KNOW HOW IT IS. THE TOUGHEST ONES TURN INTO BIG SOFTEES ONCE YOU STAND UP TO THEM.
I'VE GOT HIM UNDER CONTROL.
EXIT
DING

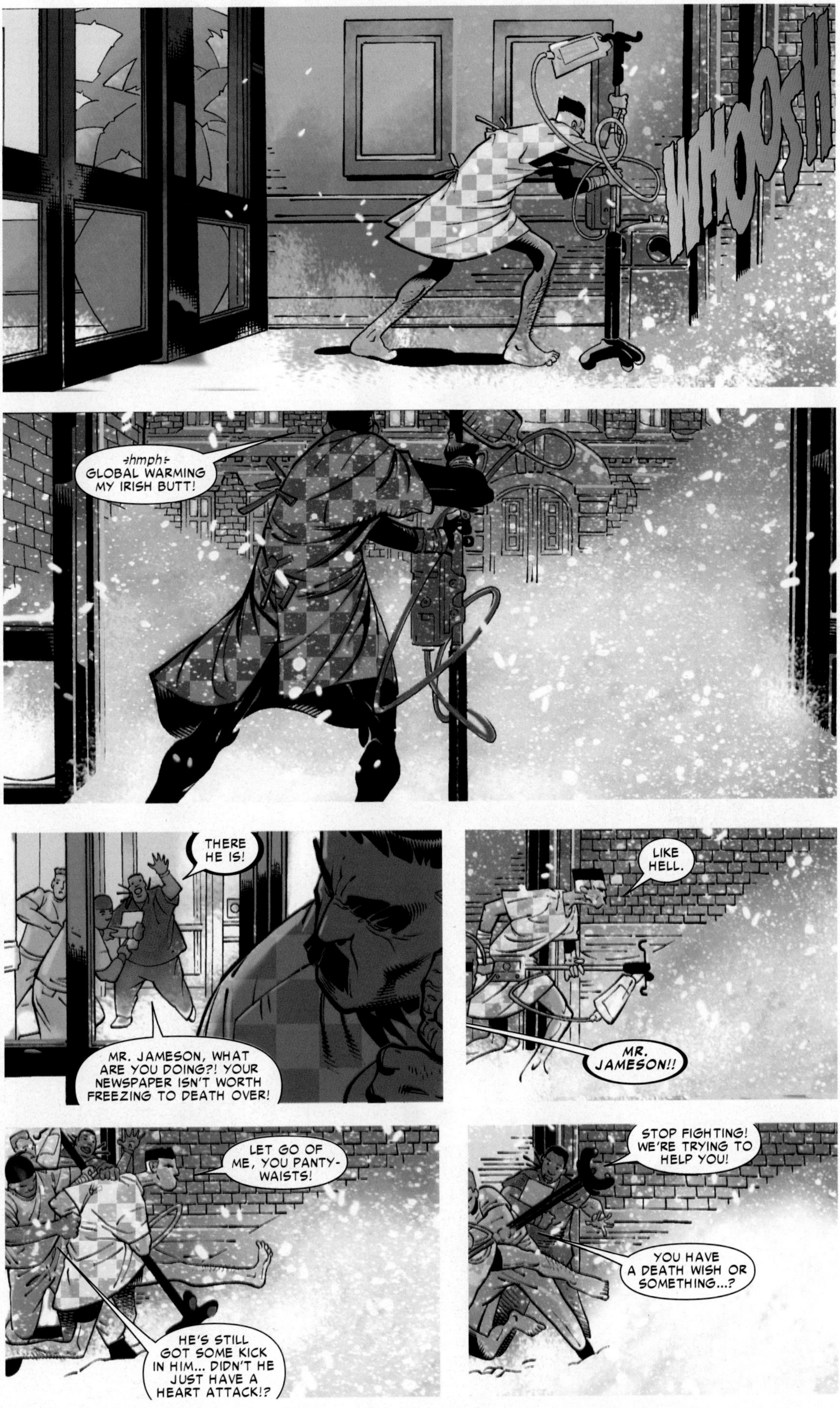
WHOOSH
-hmph-
GLOBAL WARMING MY IRISH BUTT!
THERE HE IS!
MR. JAMESON, WHAT ARE YOU DOING?! YOUR NEWSPAPER ISN'T WORTH FREEZING TO DEATH OVER!
LIKE HELL.
MR. JAMESON!!
LET GO OF ME, YOU PANTY-WAISTS!
HE'S STILL GOT SOME KICK IN HIM... DIDN'T HE JUST HAVE A HEART ATTACK!?
STOP FIGHTING! WE'RE TRYING TO HELP YOU!
YOU HAVE A DEATH WISH OR SOMETHING...?

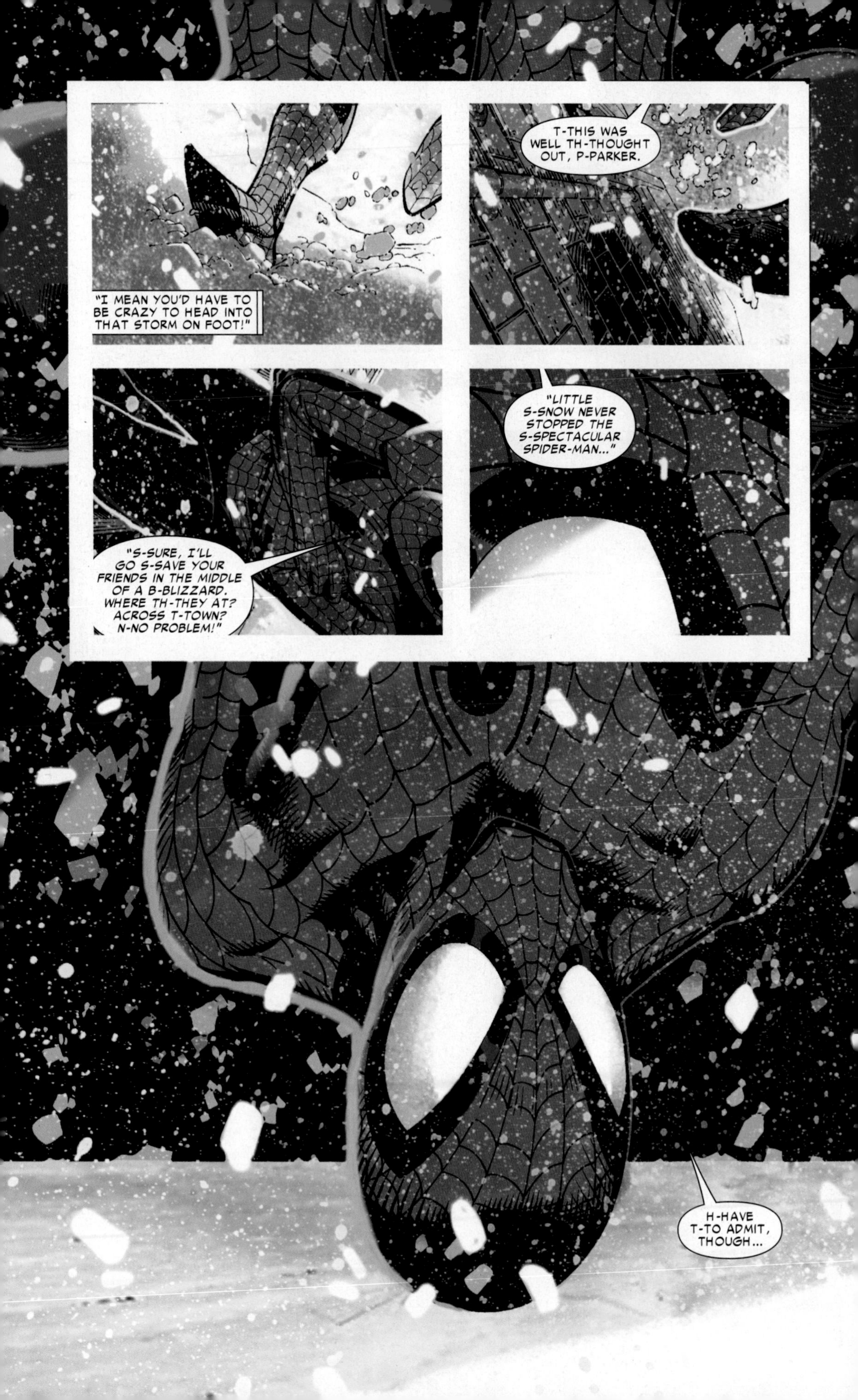
"I MEAN YOU'D HAVE TO BE CRAZY TO HEAD INTO THAT STORM ON FOOT!"
T-THIS WAS WELL TH-THOUGHT OUT, P-PARKER.
"S-SURE, I'LL GO S-SAVE YOUR FRIENDS IN THE MIDDLE OF A B-BLIZZARD. WHERE TH-THEY AT? ACROSS T-TOWN? N-NO PROBLEM!"
"LITTLE S-SNOW NEVER STOPPED THE S-SPECTACULAR SPIDER-MAN..."
H-HAVE T-TO ADMIT, THOUGH...

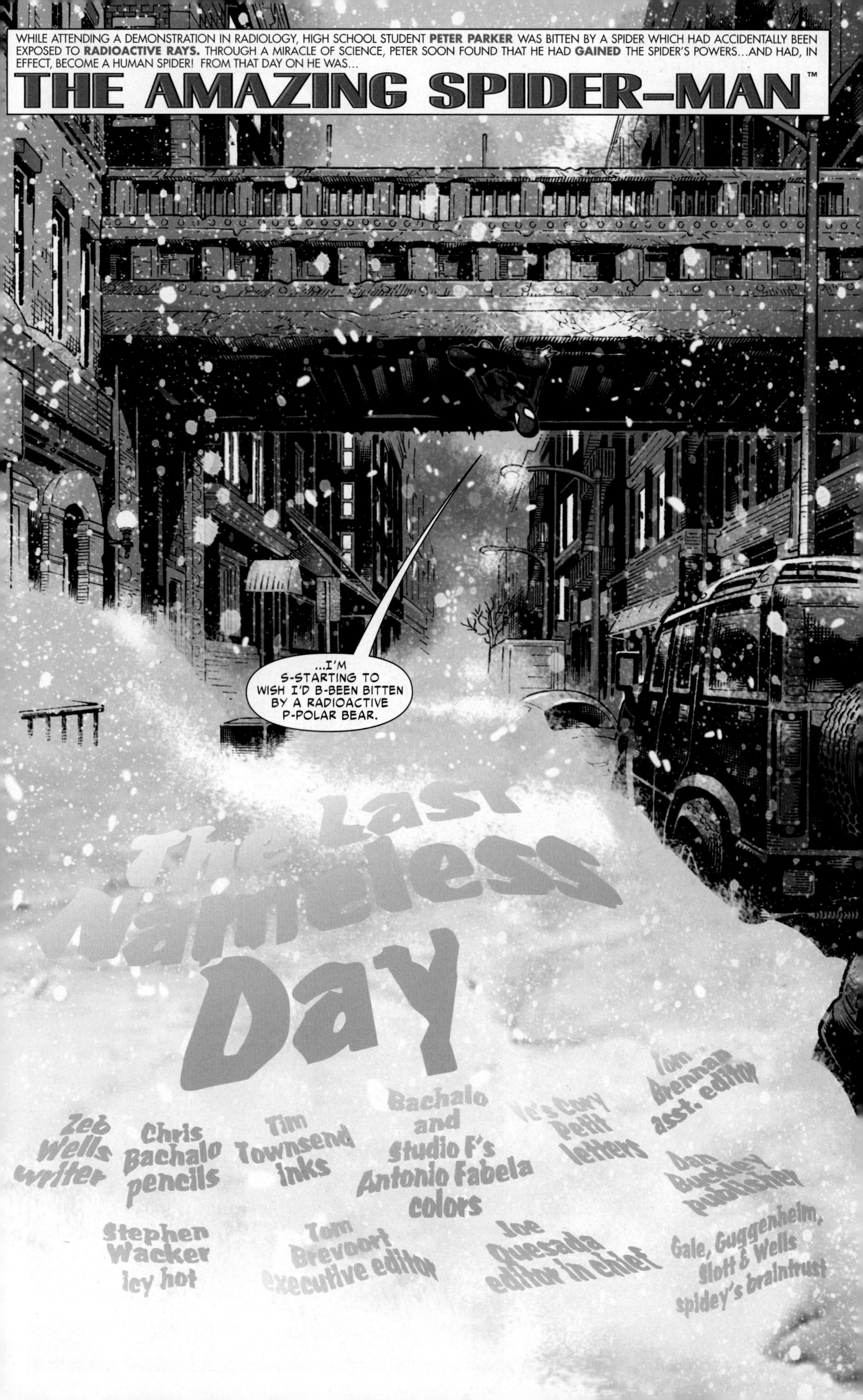
WHILE ATTENDING A DEMONSTRATION IN RADIOLOGY, HIGH SCHOOL STUDENT **PETER PARKER** WAS BITTEN BY A SPIDER WHICH HAD ACCIDENTALLY BEEN EXPOSED TO **RADIOACTIVE RAYS.** THROUGH A MIRACLE OF SCIENCE, PETER SOON FOUND THAT HE HAD **GAINED** THE SPIDER'S POWERS...AND HAD, IN EFFECT, BECOME A HUMAN SPIDER! FROM THAT DAY ON HE WAS...
THE AMAZING SPIDER-MAN™
...I'M S-STARTING TO WISH I'D B-BEEN BITTEN BY A RADIOACTIVE P-POLAR BEAR.
The Last Nameless Day
Zeb Wells writer
Chris Bachalo pencils
Tim Townsend inks
Bachalo and Studio F's Antonio Fabela colors
VC's Cory Petit letters
Tom Brennan asst. editor
Dan Buckley publisher
Stephen Wacker icy hot
Tom Brevoort executive editor
Joe Quesada editor in chief
Gale, Guggenheim, Slott & Wells spidey's braintrust

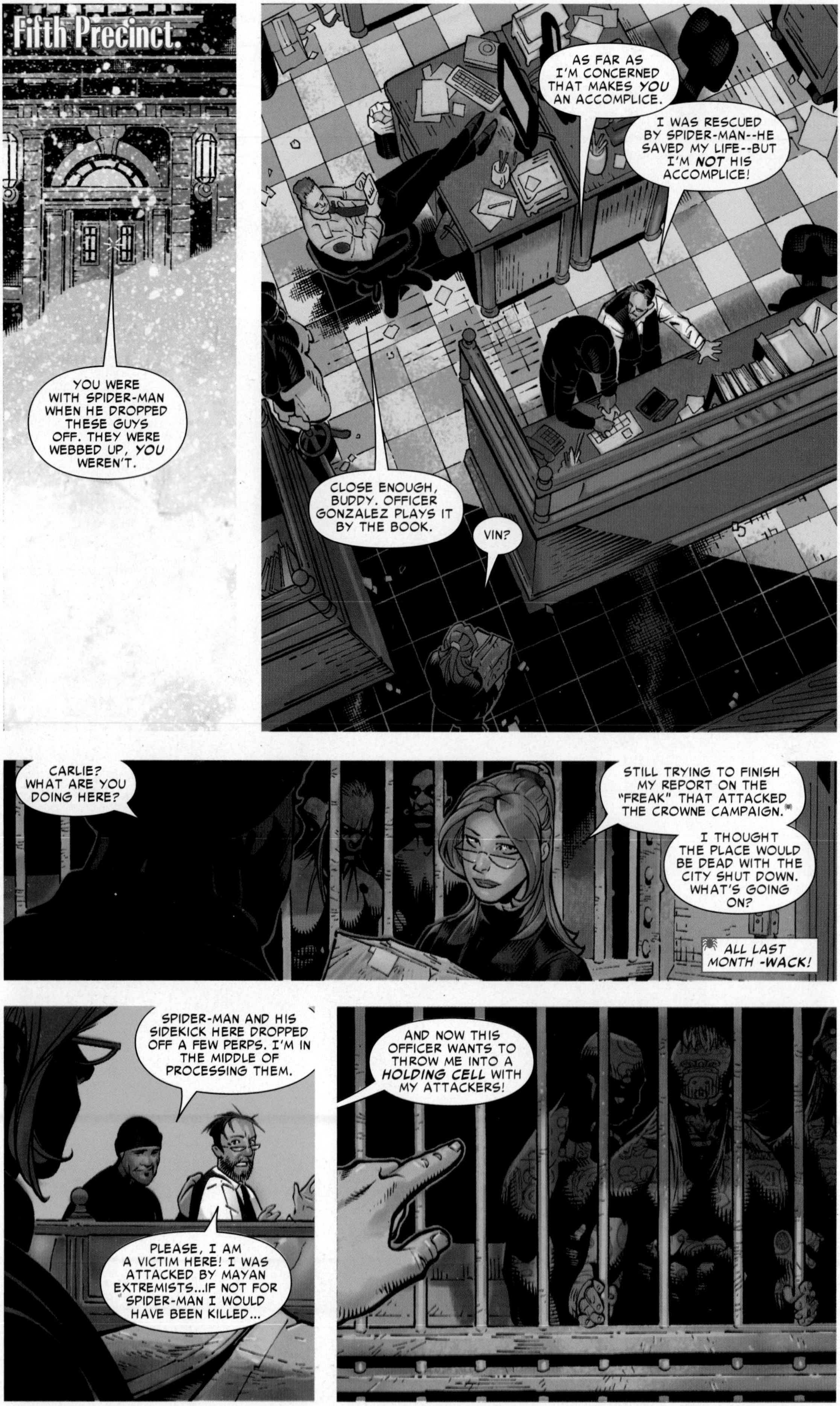
Fifth Precinct.
YOU WERE WITH SPIDER-MAN WHEN HE DROPPED THESE GUYS OFF. THEY WERE WEBBED UP, YOU WEREN'T.
AS FAR AS I'M CONCERNED THAT MAKES YOU AN ACCOMPLICE.
I WAS RESCUED BY SPIDER-MAN--HE SAVED MY LIFE--BUT I'M NOT HIS ACCOMPLICE!
CLOSE ENOUGH, BUDDY. OFFICER GONZALEZ PLAYS IT BY THE BOOK.
VIN?
CARLIE? WHAT ARE YOU DOING HERE?
STILL TRYING TO FINISH MY REPORT ON THE "FREAK" THAT ATTACKED THE CROWNE CAMPAIGN.
I THOUGHT THE PLACE WOULD BE DEAD WITH THE CITY SHUT DOWN. WHAT'S GOING ON?
ALL LAST MONTH -WACK!
SPIDER-MAN AND HIS SIDEKICK HERE DROPPED OFF A FEW PERPS. I'M IN THE MIDDLE OF PROCESSING THEM.
PLEASE, I AM A VICTIM HERE! I WAS ATTACKED BY MAYAN EXTREMISTS...IF NOT FOR SPIDER-MAN I WOULD HAVE BEEN KILLED...
AND NOW THIS OFFICER WANTS TO THROW ME INTO A HOLDING CELL WITH MY ATTACKERS!

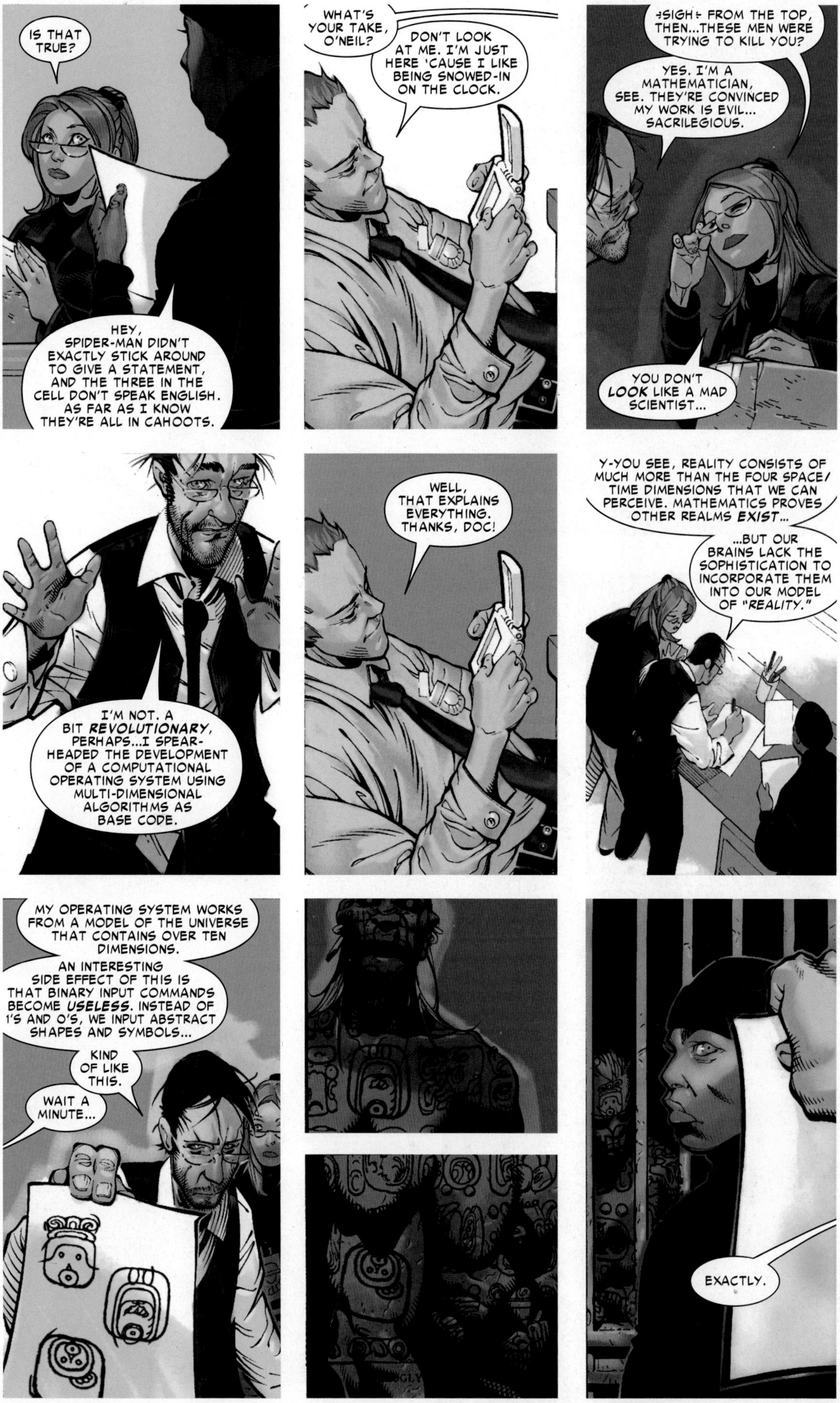
IS THAT TRUE?
HEY, SPIDER-MAN DIDN'T EXACTLY STICK AROUND TO GIVE A STATEMENT, AND THE THREE IN THE CELL DON'T SPEAK ENGLISH. AS FAR AS I KNOW THEY'RE ALL IN CAHOOTS.
WHAT'S YOUR TAKE, O'NEIL?
DON'T LOOK AT ME. I'M JUST HERE 'CAUSE I LIKE BEING SNOWED-IN ON THE CLOCK.
÷SIGH÷ FROM THE TOP, THEN...THESE MEN WERE TRYING TO KILL YOU?
YES. I'M A MATHEMATICIAN, SEE. THEY'RE CONVINCED MY WORK IS EVIL... SACRILEGIOUS.
YOU DON'T LOOK LIKE A MAD SCIENTIST...
I'M NOT. A BIT REVOLUTIONARY, PERHAPS...I SPEAR-HEADED THE DEVELOPMENT OF A COMPUTATIONAL OPERATING SYSTEM USING MULTI-DIMENSIONAL ALGORITHMS AS BASE CODE.
WELL, THAT EXPLAINS EVERYTHING. THANKS, DOC!
Y-YOU SEE, REALITY CONSISTS OF MUCH MORE THAN THE FOUR SPACE/TIME DIMENSIONS THAT WE CAN PERCEIVE. MATHEMATICS PROVES OTHER REALMS EXIST...
...BUT OUR BRAINS LACK THE SOPHISTICATION TO INCORPORATE THEM INTO OUR MODEL OF "REALITY."
MY OPERATING SYSTEM WORKS FROM A MODEL OF THE UNIVERSE THAT CONTAINS OVER TEN DIMENSIONS.
AN INTERESTING SIDE EFFECT OF THIS IS THAT BINARY INPUT COMMANDS BECOME USELESS. INSTEAD OF 1'S AND 0'S, WE INPUT ABSTRACT SHAPES AND SYMBOLS...
KIND OF LIKE THIS.
WAIT A MINUTE...
EXACTLY.

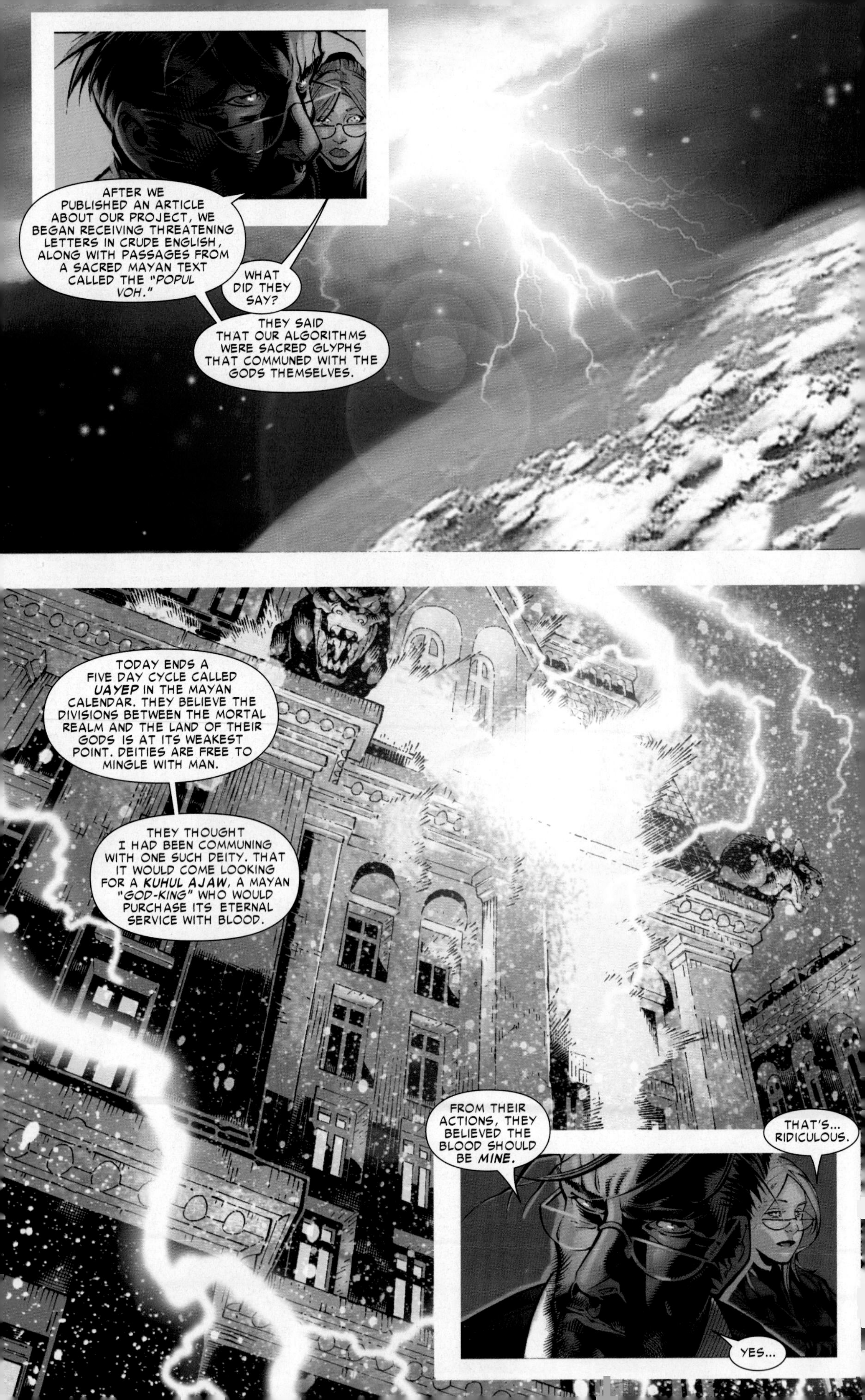
AFTER WE PUBLISHED AN ARTICLE ABOUT OUR PROJECT, WE BEGAN RECEIVING THREATENING LETTERS IN CRUDE ENGLISH, ALONG WITH PASSAGES FROM A SACRED MAYAN TEXT CALLED THE "POPUL VOH."
WHAT DID THEY SAY?
THEY SAID THAT OUR ALGORITHMS WERE SACRED GLYPHS THAT COMMUNED WITH THE GODS THEMSELVES.
TODAY ENDS A FIVE DAY CYCLE CALLED UAYEP IN THE MAYAN CALENDAR. THEY BELIEVE THE DIVISIONS BETWEEN THE MORTAL REALM AND THE LAND OF THEIR GODS IS AT ITS WEAKEST POINT. DEITIES ARE FREE TO MINGLE WITH MAN.
THEY THOUGHT I HAD BEEN COMMUNING WITH ONE SUCH DEITY. THAT IT WOULD COME LOOKING FOR A KUHUL AJAW, A MAYAN "GOD-KING" WHO WOULD PURCHASE ITS ETERNAL SERVICE WITH BLOOD.
FROM THEIR ACTIONS, THEY BELIEVED THE BLOOD SHOULD BE MINE.
THAT'S... RIDICULOUS.
YES...

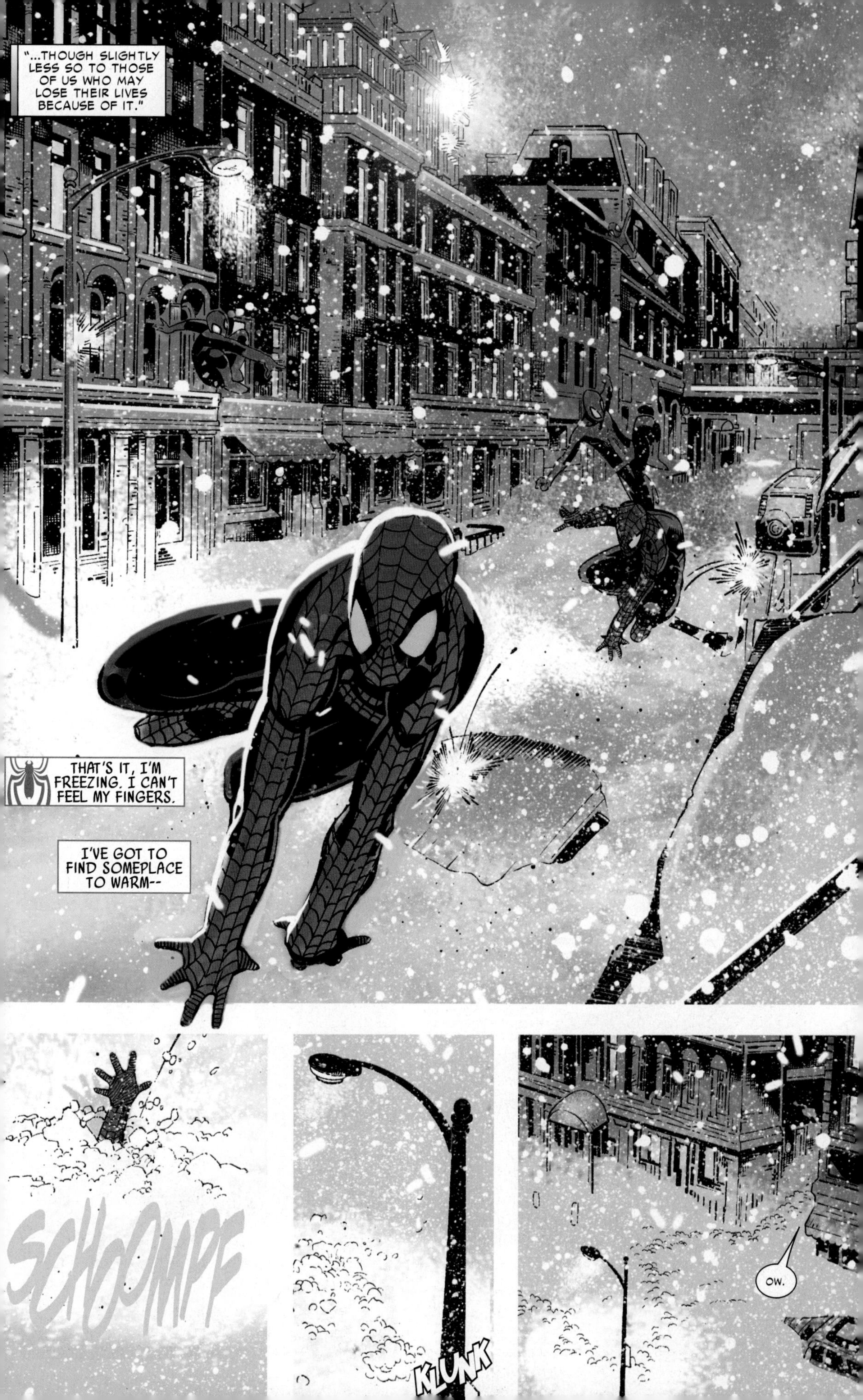
"...THOUGH SLIGHTLY LESS SO TO THOSE OF US WHO MAY LOSE THEIR LIVES BECAUSE OF IT."
THAT'S IT, I'M FREEZING. I CAN'T FEEL MY FINGERS.
I'VE GOT TO FIND SOMEPLACE TO WARM--
SCHOOMPF
KLUNK
OW.

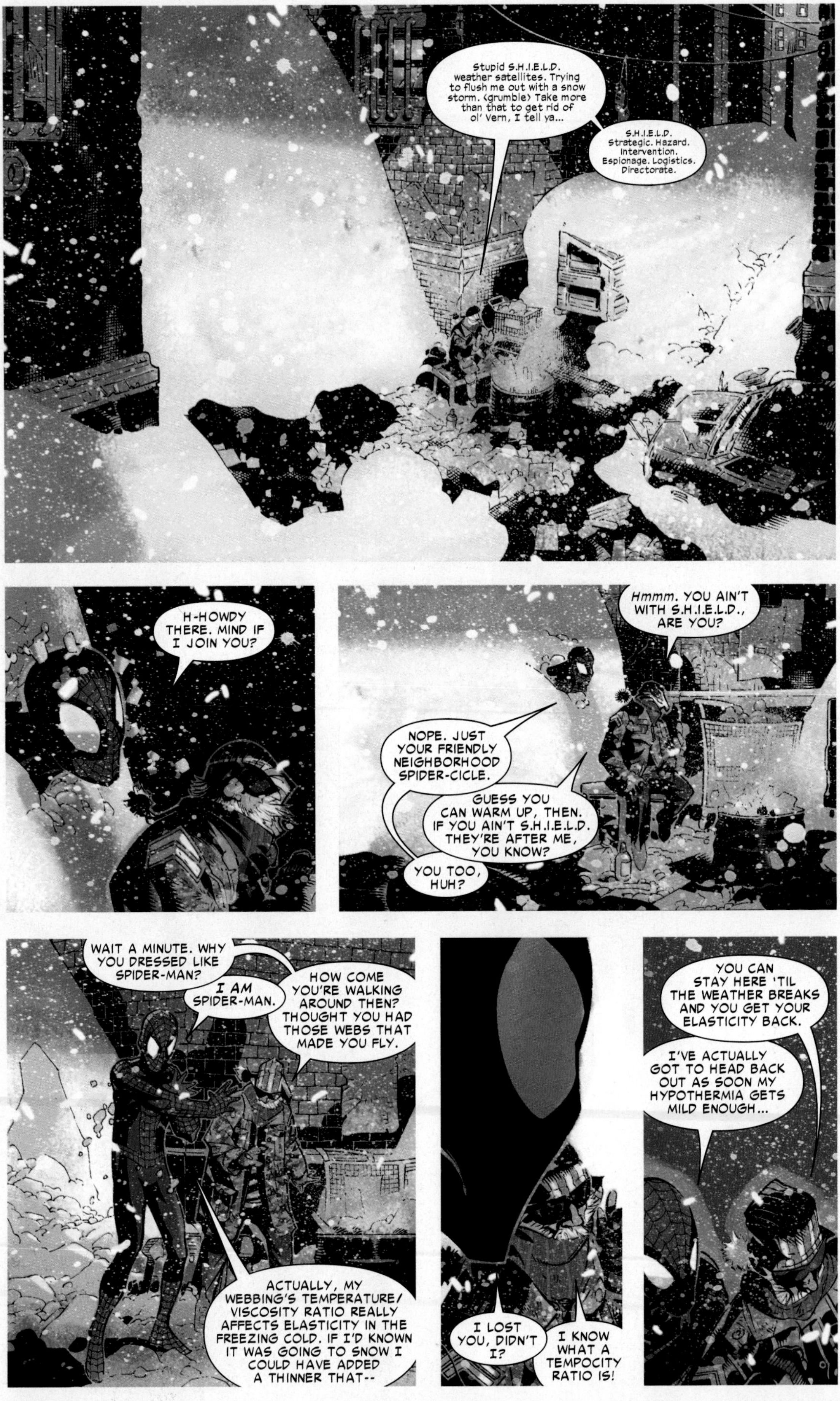
Stupid S.H.I.E.L.D. weather satellites. Trying to flush me out with a snow storm. <grumble> Take more than that to get rid of ol' Vern, I tell ya...
S.H.I.E.L.D. Strategic. Hazard. Intervention. Espionage. Logistics. Directorate.
H-HOWDY THERE. MIND IF I JOIN YOU?
Hmmm. YOU AIN'T WITH S.H.I.E.L.D., ARE YOU?
NOPE. JUST YOUR FRIENDLY NEIGHBORHOOD SPIDER-CICLE.
GUESS YOU CAN WARM UP, THEN. IF YOU AIN'T S.H.I.E.L.D. THEY'RE AFTER ME, YOU KNOW?
YOU TOO, HUH?
WAIT A MINUTE. WHY YOU DRESSED LIKE SPIDER-MAN?
I AM SPIDER-MAN.
HOW COME YOU'RE WALKING AROUND THEN? THOUGHT YOU HAD THOSE WEBS THAT MADE YOU FLY.
ACTUALLY, MY WEBBING'S TEMPERATURE/ VISCOSITY RATIO REALLY AFFECTS ELASTICITY IN THE FREEZING COLD. IF I'D KNOWN IT WAS GOING TO SNOW I COULD HAVE ADDED A THINNER THAT--
I LOST YOU, DIDN'T I?
I KNOW WHAT A TEMPOCITY RATIO IS!
YOU CAN STAY HERE 'TIL THE WEATHER BREAKS AND YOU GET YOUR ELASTICITY BACK.
I'VE ACTUALLY GOT TO HEAD BACK OUT AS SOON MY HYPOTHERMIA GETS MILD ENOUGH...

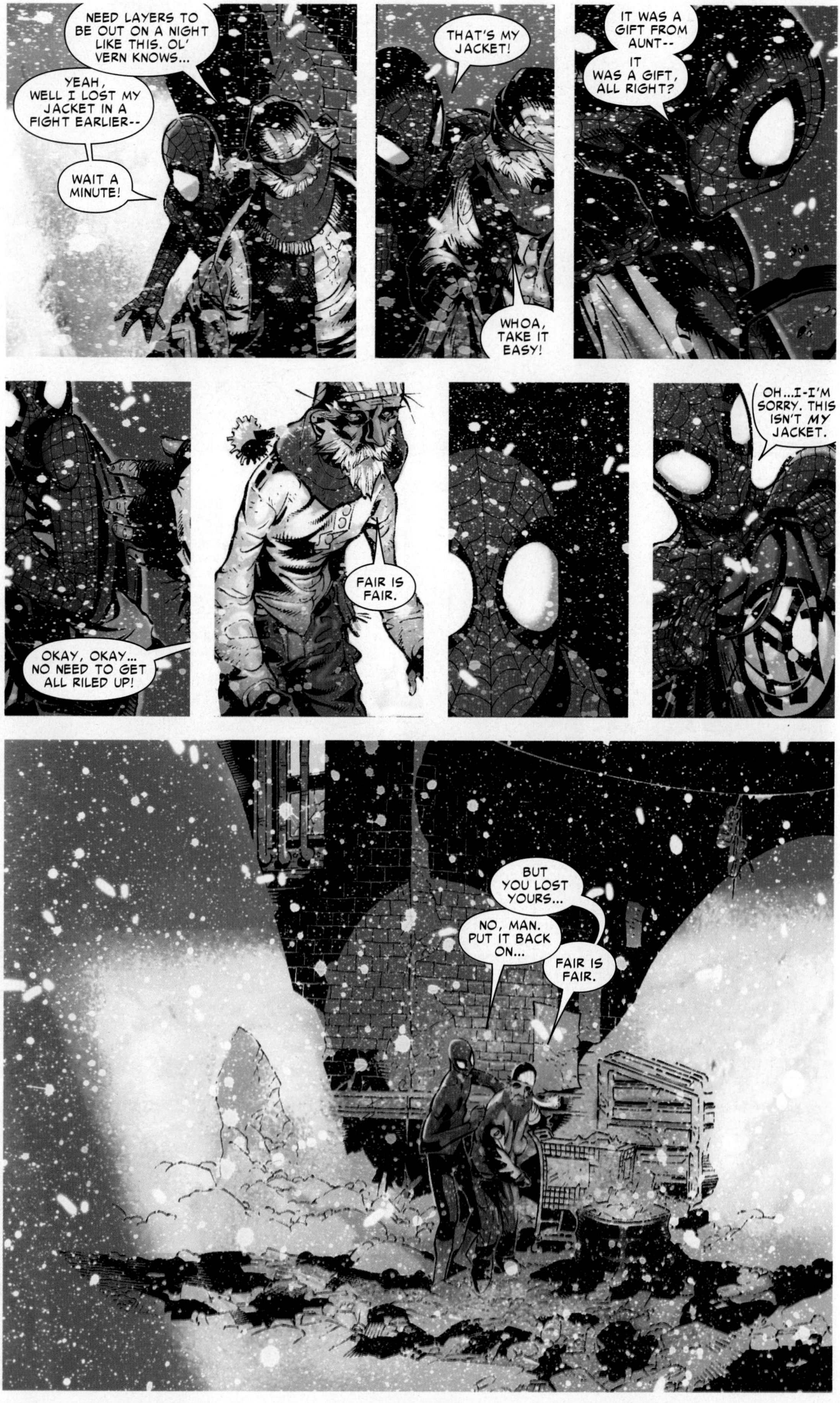
NEED LAYERS TO BE OUT ON A NIGHT LIKE THIS. OL' VERN KNOWS...
YEAH, WELL I LOST MY JACKET IN A FIGHT EARLIER--
WAIT A MINUTE!
THAT'S MY JACKET!
WHOA, TAKE IT EASY!
IT WAS A GIFT FROM AUNT--
IT WAS A GIFT, ALL RIGHT?
OKAY, OKAY... NO NEED TO GET ALL RILED UP!
FAIR IS FAIR.
OH...I-I'M SORRY. THIS ISN'T MY JACKET.
BUT YOU LOST YOURS...
NO, MAN. PUT IT BACK ON...
FAIR IS FAIR.

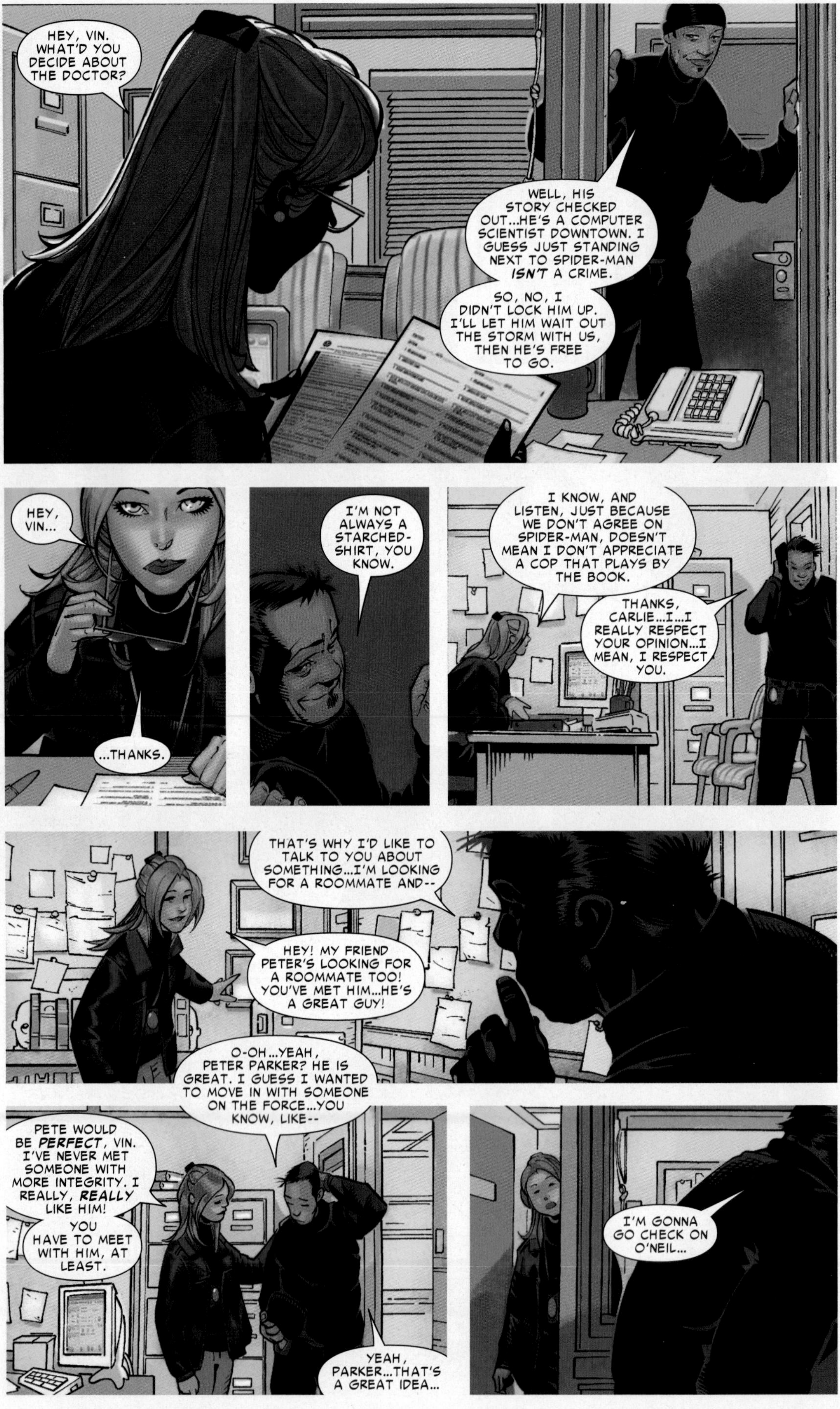
HEY, VIN. WHAT'D YOU DECIDE ABOUT THE DOCTOR?
WELL, HIS STORY CHECKED OUT...HE'S A COMPUTER SCIENTIST DOWNTOWN. I GUESS JUST STANDING NEXT TO SPIDER-MAN ISN'T A CRIME.
SO, NO, I DIDN'T LOCK HIM UP. I'LL LET HIM WAIT OUT THE STORM WITH US, THEN HE'S FREE TO GO.
HEY, VIN...
...THANKS.
I'M NOT ALWAYS A STARCHED-SHIRT, YOU KNOW.
I KNOW, AND LISTEN, JUST BECAUSE WE DON'T AGREE ON SPIDER-MAN, DOESN'T MEAN I DON'T APPRECIATE A COP THAT PLAYS BY THE BOOK.
THANKS, CARLIE...I...I REALLY RESPECT YOUR OPINION...I MEAN, I RESPECT YOU.
THAT'S WHY I'D LIKE TO TALK TO YOU ABOUT SOMETHING...I'M LOOKING FOR A ROOMMATE AND--
HEY! MY FRIEND PETER'S LOOKING FOR A ROOMMATE TOO! YOU'VE MET HIM...HE'S A GREAT GUY!
O-OH...YEAH, PETER PARKER? HE IS GREAT. I GUESS I WANTED TO MOVE IN WITH SOMEONE ON THE FORCE...YOU KNOW, LIKE--
PETE WOULD BE PERFECT, VIN. I'VE NEVER MET SOMEONE WITH MORE INTEGRITY. I REALLY, REALLY LIKE HIM!
YOU HAVE TO MEET WITH HIM, AT LEAST.
YEAH, PARKER...THAT'S A GREAT IDEA...
I'M GONNA GO CHECK ON O'NEIL...

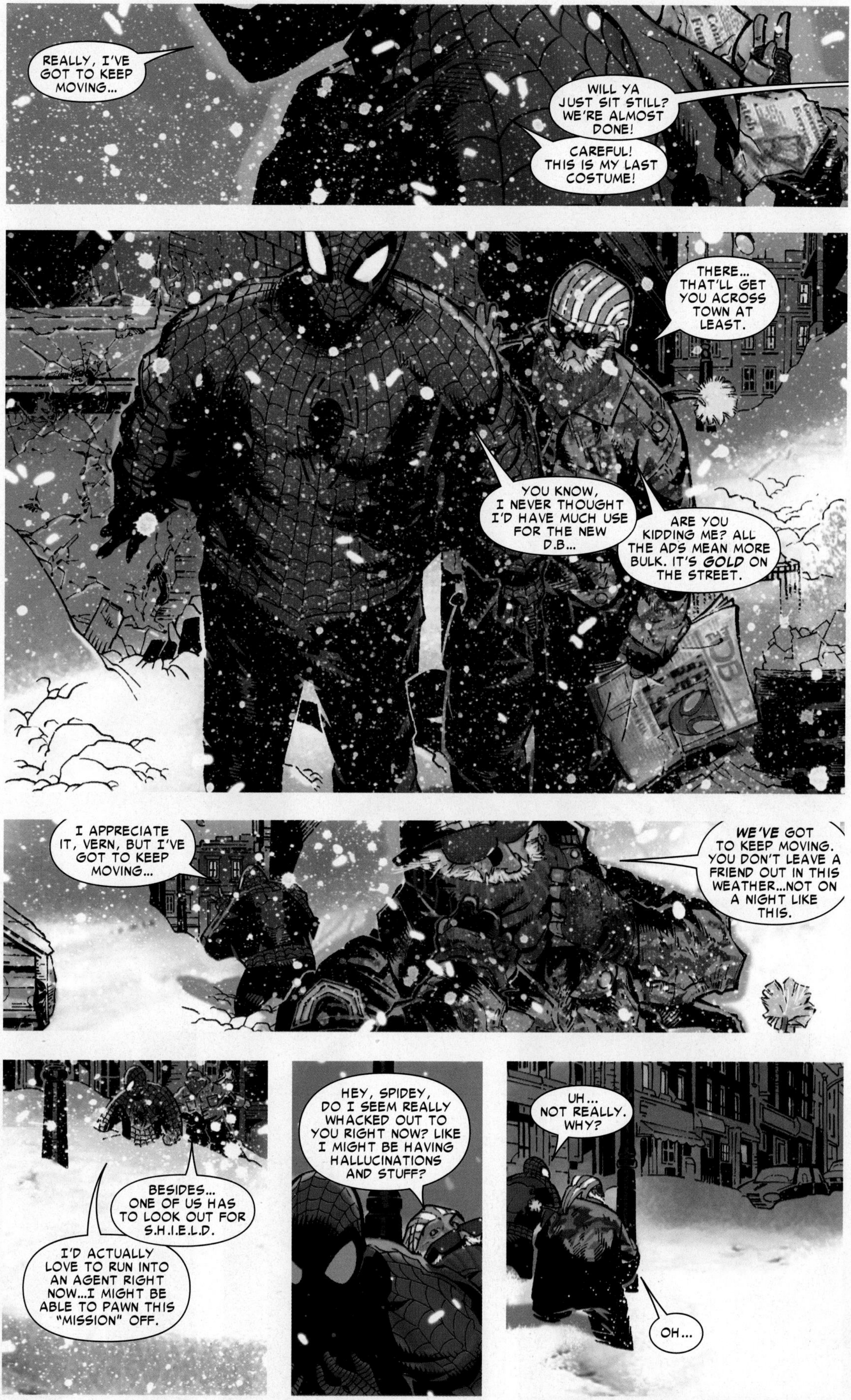

REALLY, I'VE GOT TO KEEP MOVING...
WILL YA JUST SIT STILL? WE'RE ALMOST DONE!
CAREFUL! THIS IS MY LAST COSTUME!
THERE... THAT'LL GET YOU ACROSS TOWN AT LEAST.
YOU KNOW, I NEVER THOUGHT I'D HAVE MUCH USE FOR THE NEW D.B...
ARE YOU KIDDING ME? ALL THE ADS MEAN MORE BULK. IT'S GOLD ON THE STREET.
I APPRECIATE IT, VERN, BUT I'VE GOT TO KEEP MOVING...
WE'VE GOT TO KEEP MOVING. YOU DON'T LEAVE A FRIEND OUT IN THIS WEATHER...NOT ON A NIGHT LIKE THIS.
BESIDES... ONE OF US HAS TO LOOK OUT FOR S.H.I.E.L.D.
I'D ACTUALLY LOVE TO RUN INTO AN AGENT RIGHT NOW...I MIGHT BE ABLE TO PAWN THIS "MISSION" OFF.
HEY, SPIDEY, DO I SEEM REALLY WHACKED OUT TO YOU RIGHT NOW? LIKE I MIGHT BE HAVING HALLUCINATIONS AND STUFF?
UH... NOT REALLY. WHY?
OH...

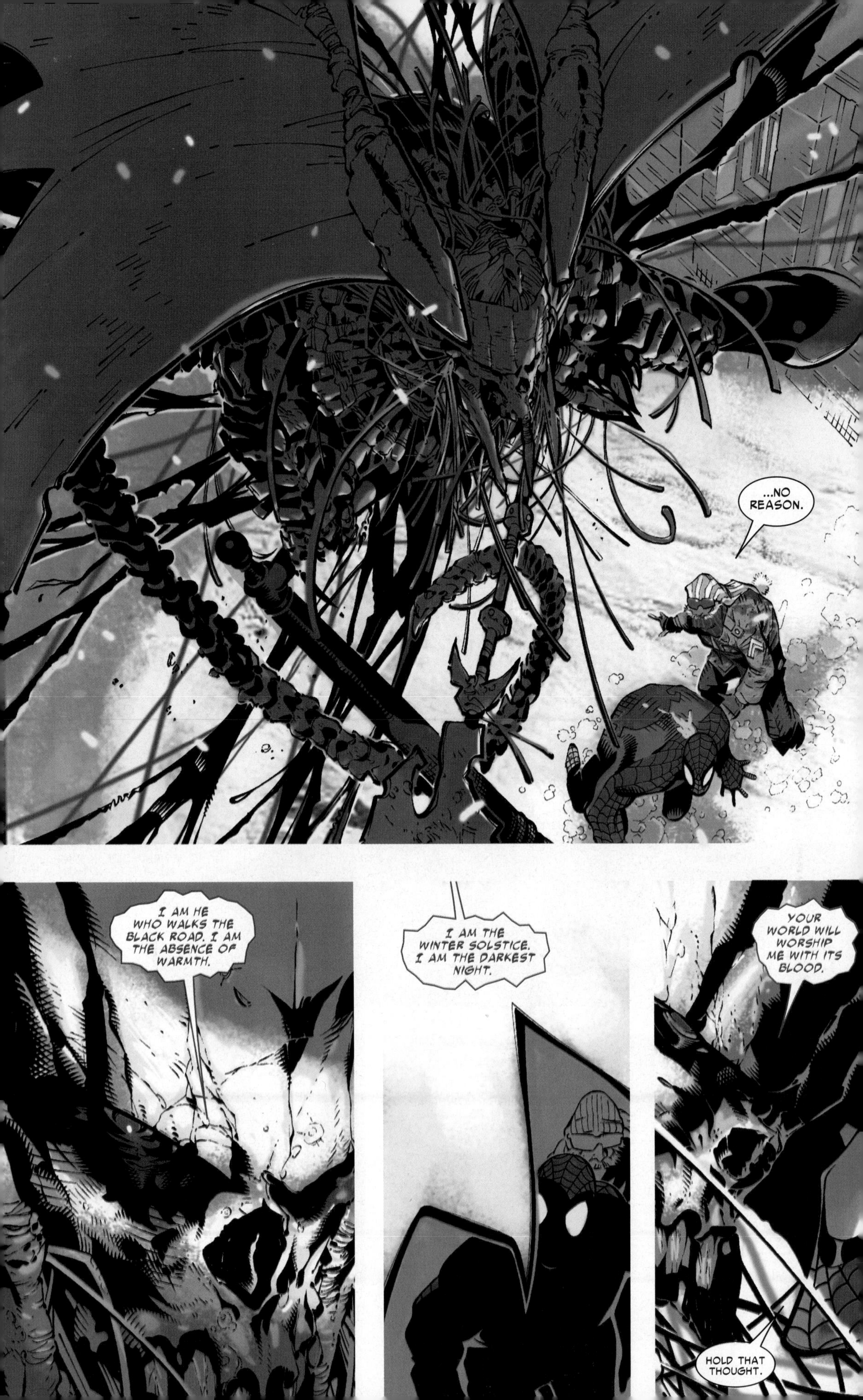
...NO REASON.
I AM HE WHO WALKS THE BLACK ROAD. I AM THE ABSENCE OF WARMTH.
I AM THE WINTER SOLSTICE. I AM THE DARKEST NIGHT.
YOUR WORLD WILL WORSHIP ME WITH ITS BLOOD.
HOLD THAT THOUGHT.

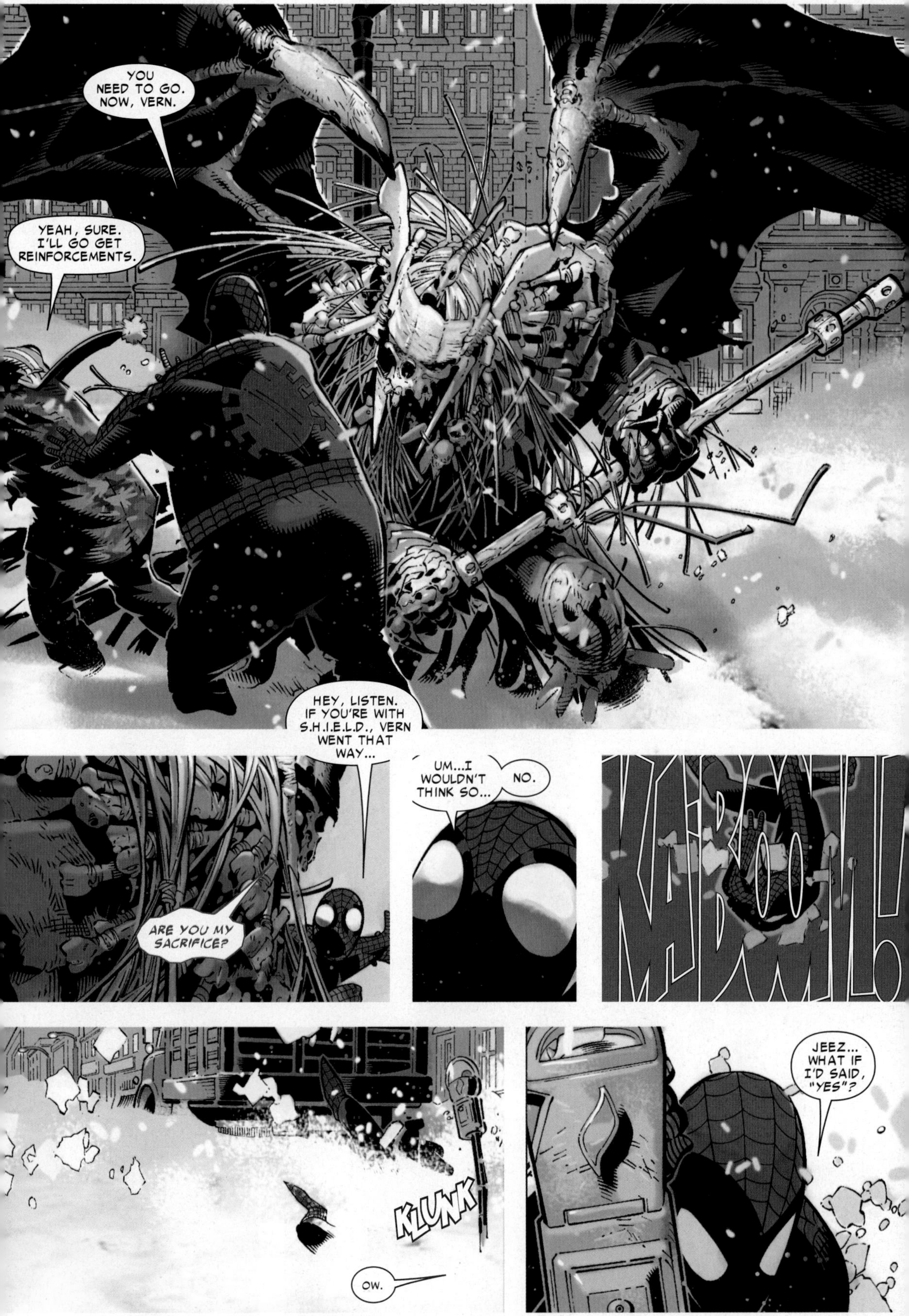
YOU NEED TO GO. NOW, VERN.
YEAH, SURE. I'LL GO GET REINFORCEMENTS.
HEY, LISTEN. IF YOU'RE WITH S.H.I.E.L.D., VERN WENT THAT WAY...
ARE YOU MY SACRIFICE?
UM...I WOULDN'T THINK SO...
NO.
KLUNK
OW.
JEEZ... WHAT IF I'D SAID, "YES"?

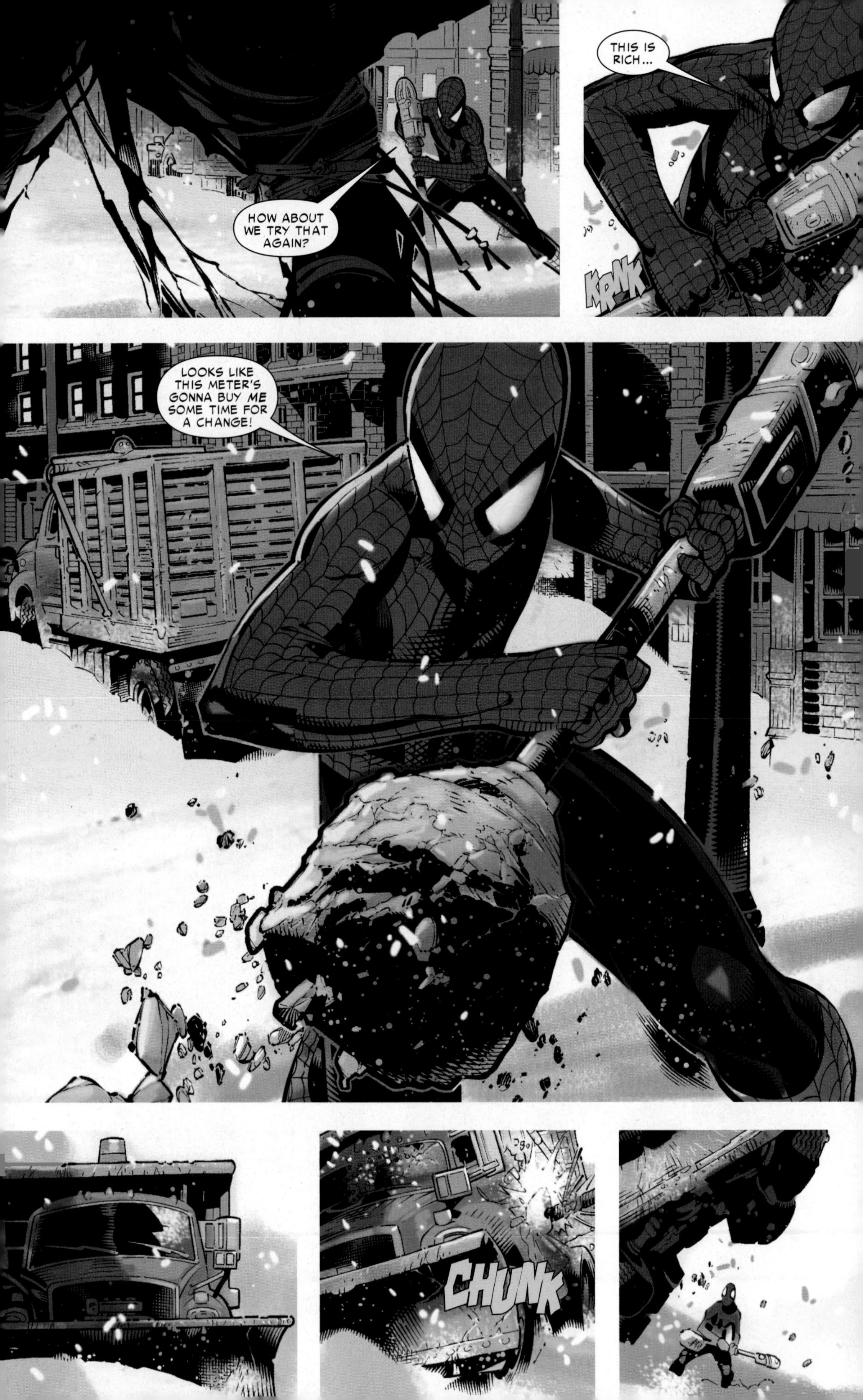
HOW ABOUT WE TRY THAT AGAIN?
THIS IS RICH...
KRNK
LOOKS LIKE THIS METER'S GONNA BUY *ME* SOME TIME FOR A CHANGE!
CHUNK

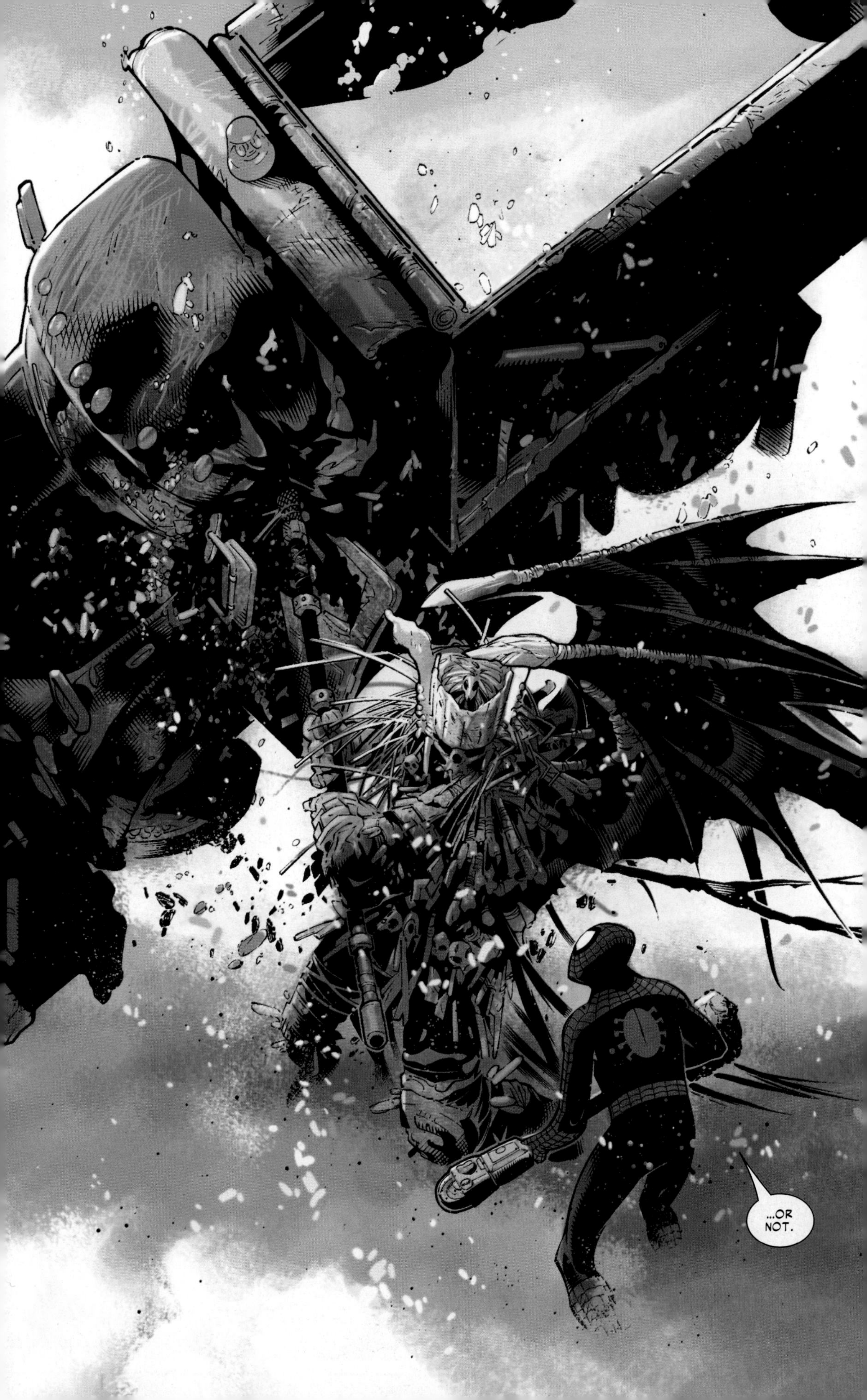
...OR NOT.

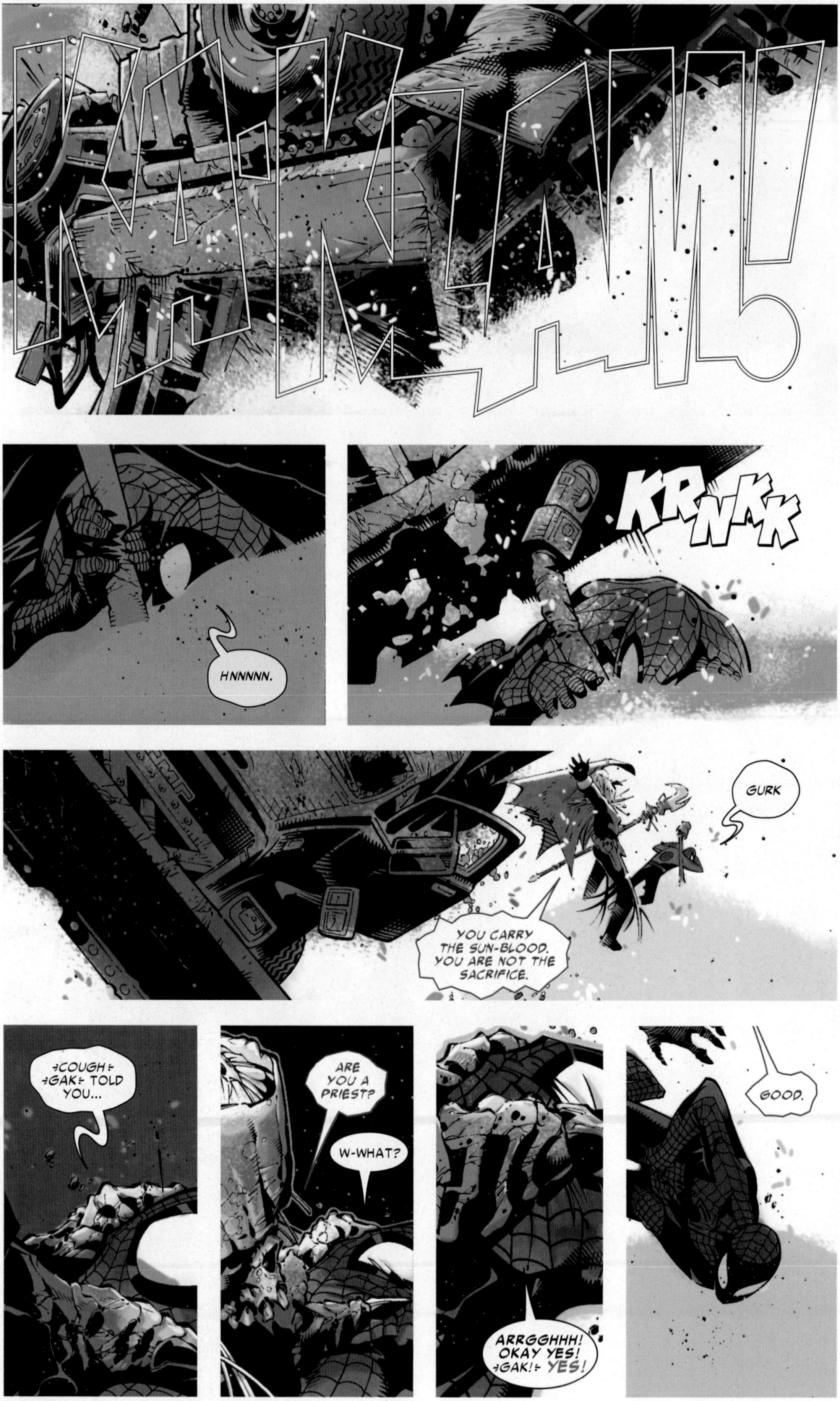
HNNNNN.
KRNKK
GURK
YOU CARRY THE SUN-BLOOD. YOU ARE NOT THE SACRIFICE.
⸗COUGH⸗ ⸗GAK⸗ TOLD YOU...
ARE YOU A PRIEST?
W-WHAT?
ARRGGHHH! OKAY YES! ⸗GAK!⸗ YES!
GOOD.

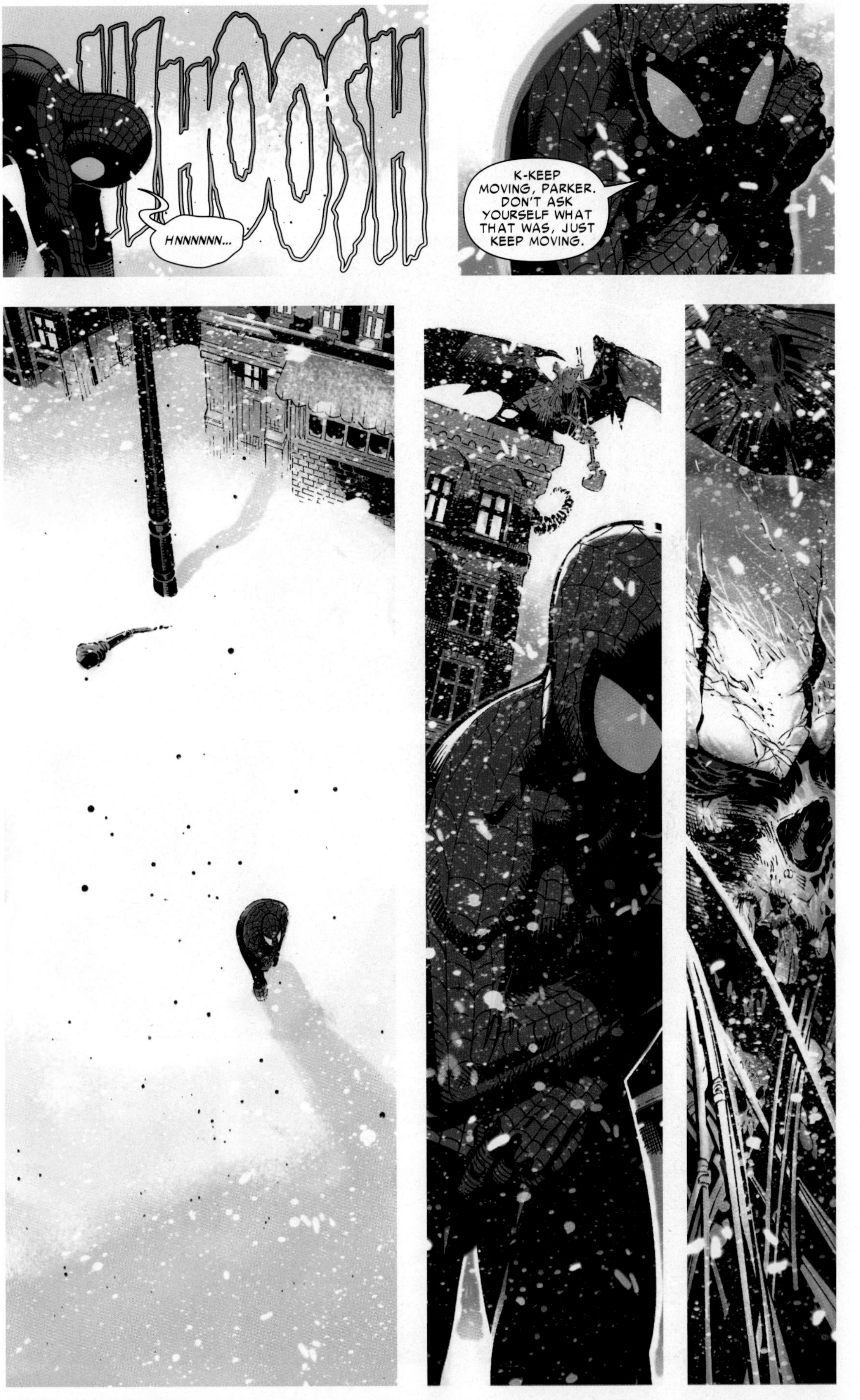
WHOOOSH
HNNNNNN...
K-KEEP MOVING, PARKER. DON'T ASK YOURSELF WHAT THAT WAS, JUST KEEP MOVING.

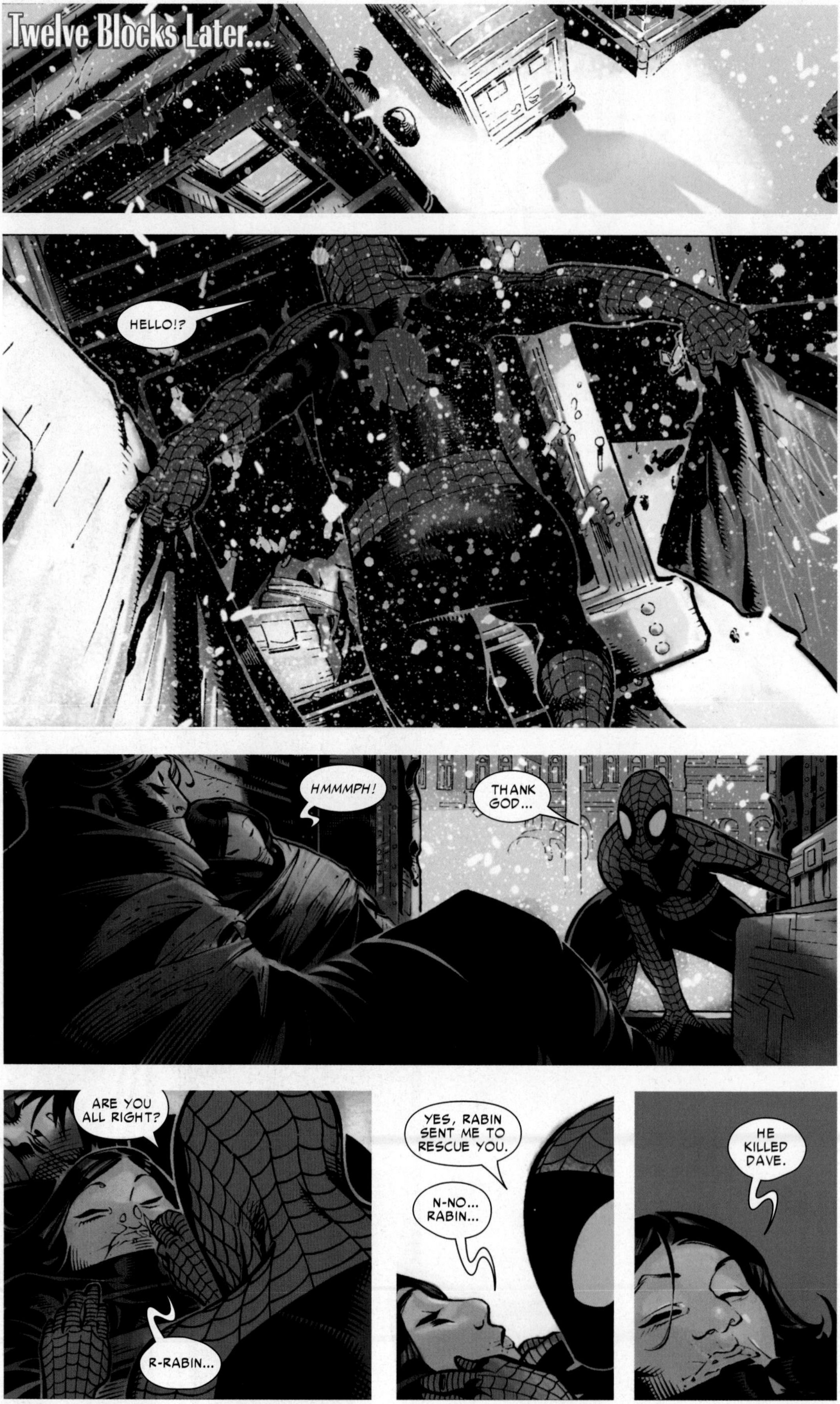
Twelve Blocks Later...
HELLO!?
HMMMPH!
THANK GOD...
ARE YOU ALL RIGHT?
R-RABIN...
YES, RABIN SENT ME TO RESCUE YOU.
N-NO... RABIN...
HE KILLED DAVE.

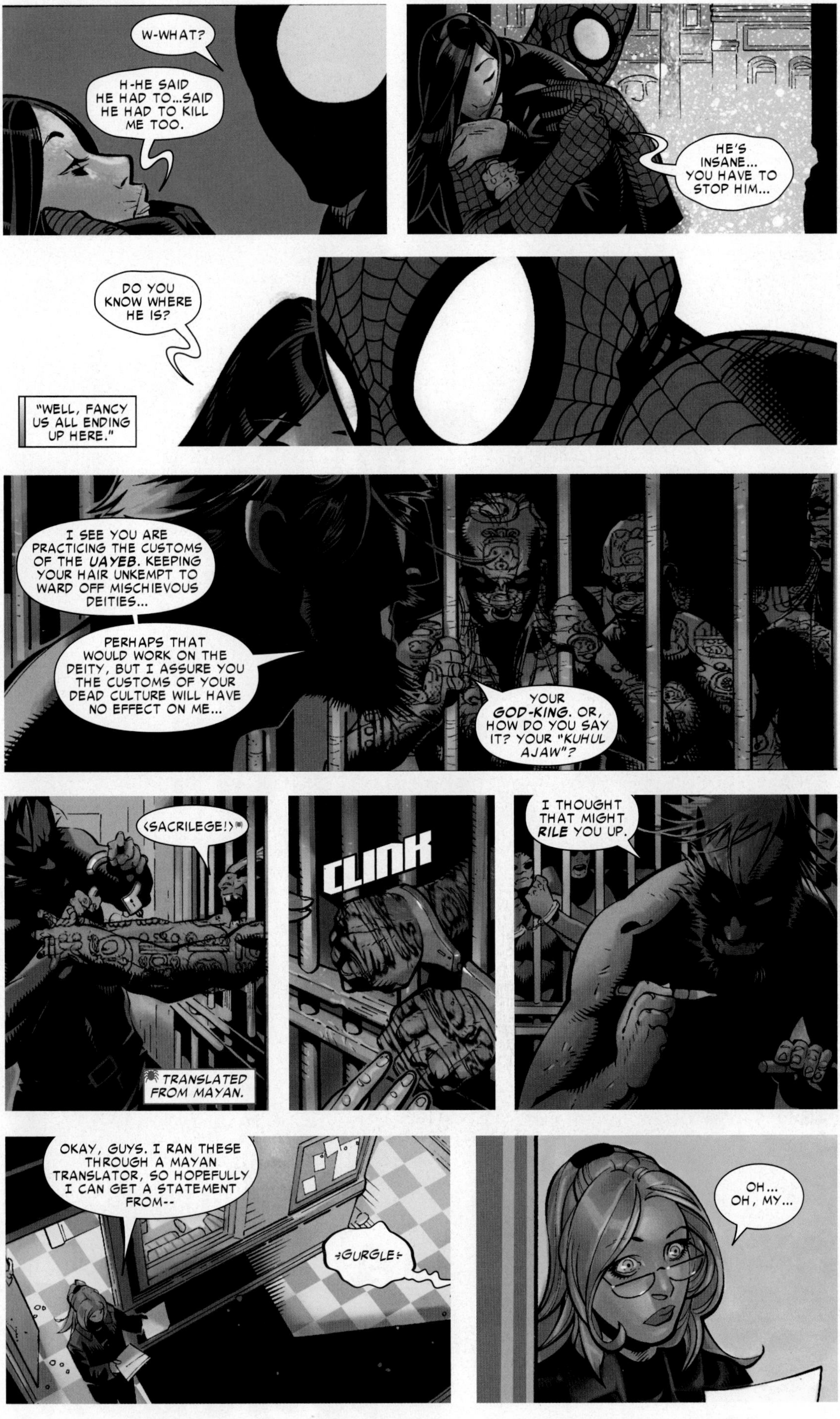
W-WHAT?
H-HE SAID HE HAD TO...SAID HE HAD TO KILL ME TOO.
HE'S INSANE... YOU HAVE TO STOP HIM...
DO YOU KNOW WHERE HE IS?
"WELL, FANCY US ALL ENDING UP HERE."
I SEE YOU ARE PRACTICING THE CUSTOMS OF THE UAYEB. KEEPING YOUR HAIR UNKEMPT TO WARD OFF MISCHIEVOUS DEITIES...
PERHAPS THAT WOULD WORK ON THE DEITY, BUT I ASSURE YOU THE CUSTOMS OF YOUR DEAD CULTURE WILL HAVE NO EFFECT ON ME...
YOUR GOD-KING. OR, HOW DO YOU SAY IT? YOUR "KUHUL AJAW"?
<SACRILEGE!>
TRANSLATED FROM MAYAN.
CLINK
I THOUGHT THAT MIGHT RILE YOU UP.
OKAY, GUYS. I RAN THESE THROUGH A MAYAN TRANSLATOR, SO HOPEFULLY I CAN GET A STATEMENT FROM--
GURGLE
OH... OH, MY...

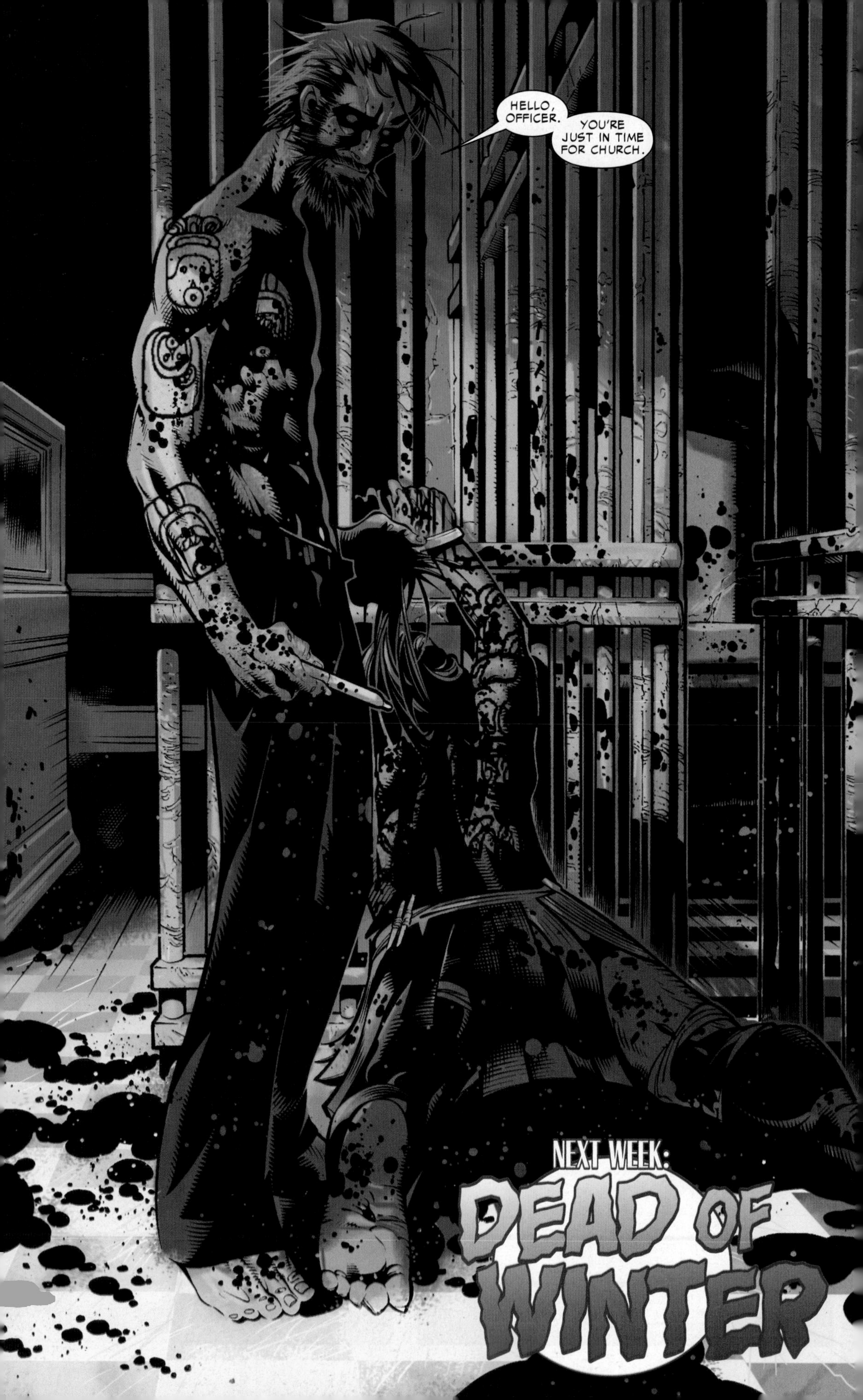
HELLO, OFFICER.
YOU'RE JUST IN TIME FOR CHURCH.
NEXT WEEK:
DEAD OF WINTER

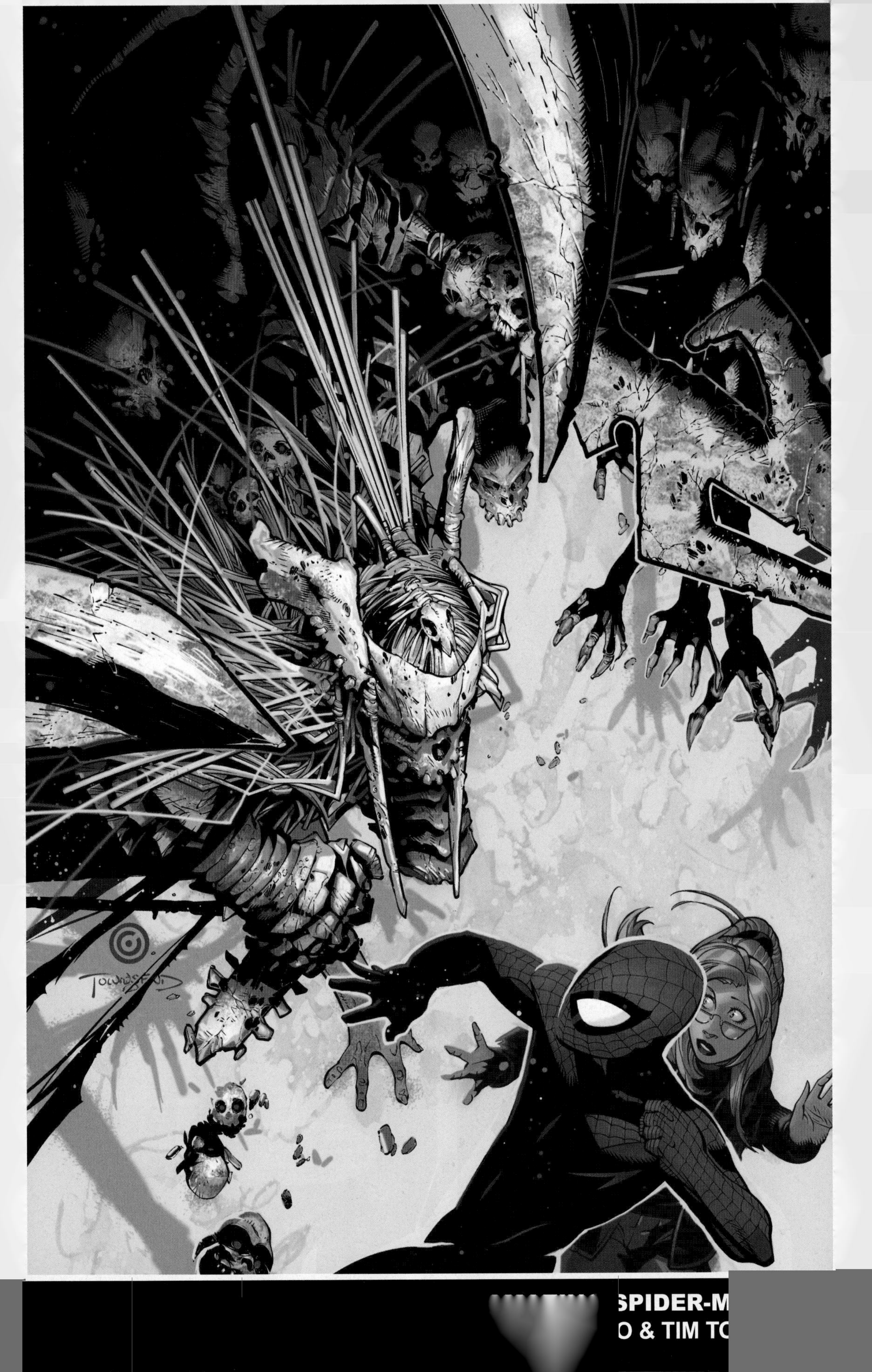

SPIDER-M
O & TIM TO

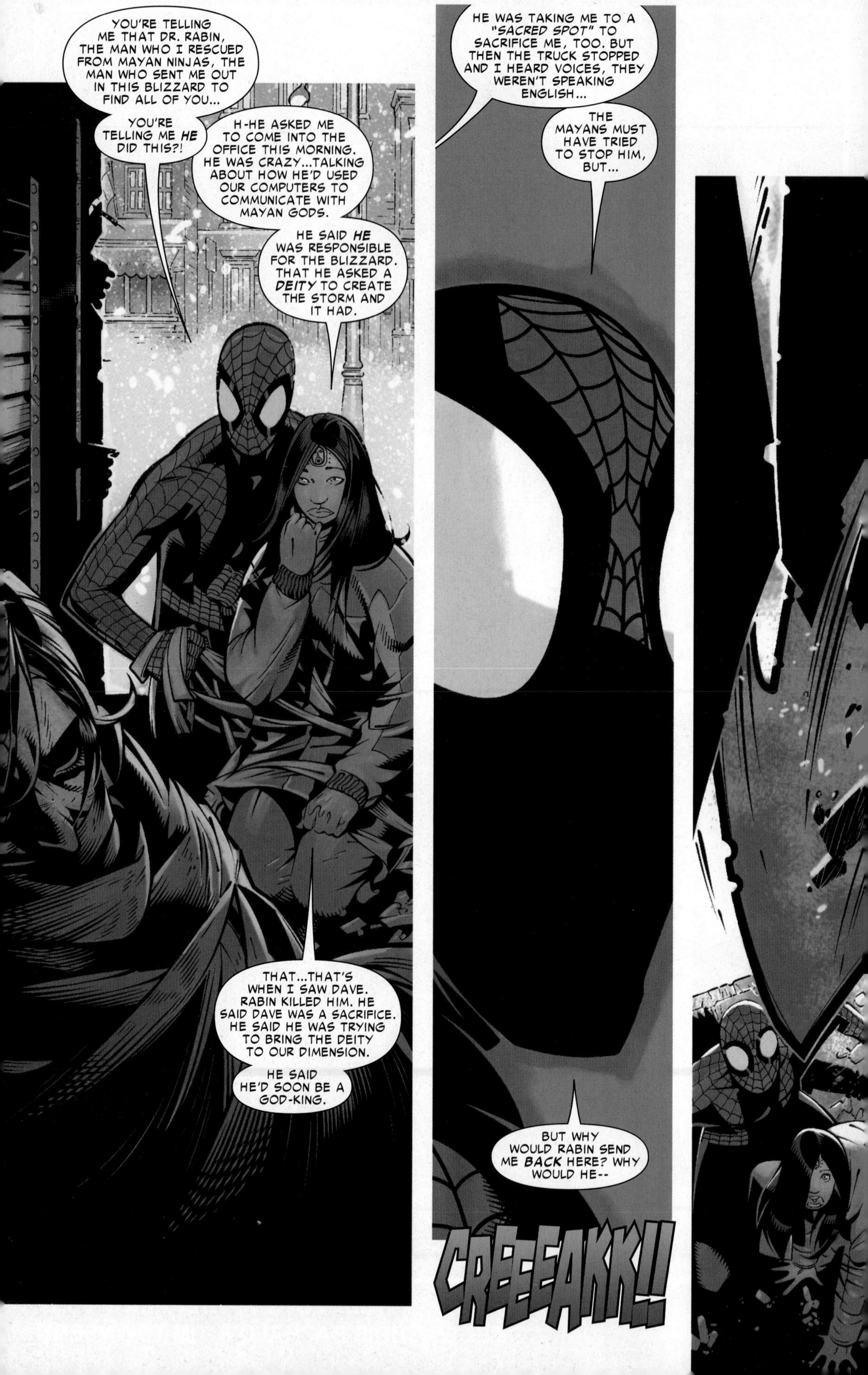

YOU'RE TELLING ME THAT DR. RABIN, THE MAN WHO I RESCUED FROM MAYAN NINJAS, THE MAN WHO SENT ME OUT IN THIS BLIZZARD TO FIND ALL OF YOU...
YOU'RE TELLING ME *HE* DID THIS?!
H-HE ASKED ME TO COME INTO THE OFFICE THIS MORNING. HE WAS CRAZY...TALKING ABOUT HOW HE'D USED OUR COMPUTERS TO COMMUNICATE WITH MAYAN GODS.
HE SAID *HE* WAS RESPONSIBLE FOR THE BLIZZARD. THAT HE ASKED A *DEITY* TO CREATE THE STORM AND IT HAD.
THAT...THAT'S WHEN I SAW DAVE. RABIN KILLED HIM. HE SAID DAVE WAS A SACRIFICE. HE SAID HE WAS TRYING TO BRING THE DEITY TO OUR DIMENSION.
HE SAID HE'D SOON BE A GOD-KING.
HE WAS TAKING ME TO A *"SACRED SPOT"* TO SACRIFICE ME, TOO. BUT THEN THE TRUCK STOPPED AND I HEARD VOICES, THEY WEREN'T SPEAKING ENGLISH...
THE MAYANS MUST HAVE TRIED TO STOP HIM, BUT...
BUT WHY WOULD RABIN SEND ME *BACK* HERE? WHY WOULD HE--
CREEEAKK!!

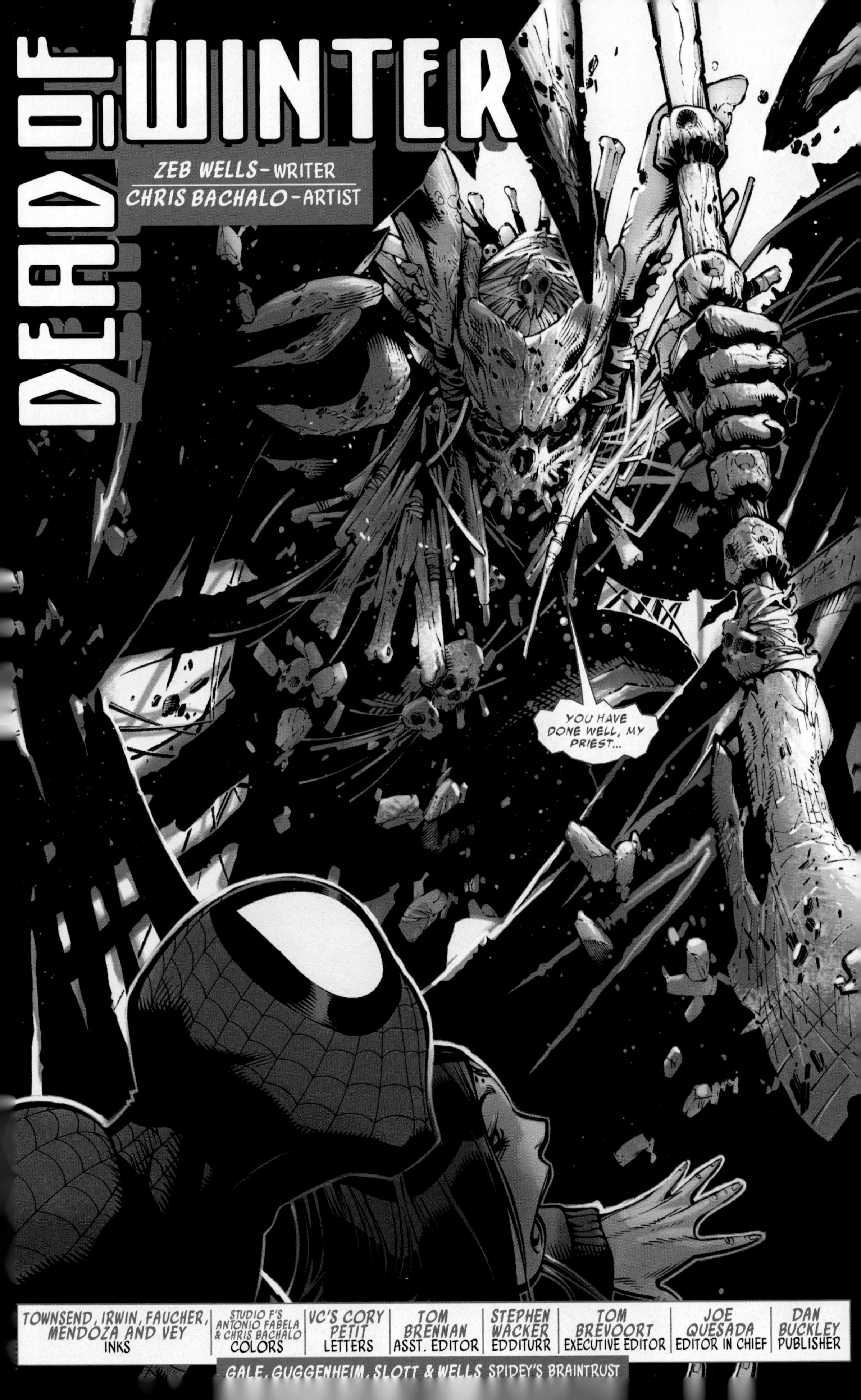
DEAD OF WINTER
ZEB WELLS-WRITER
CHRIS BACHALO-ARTIST
YOU HAVE DONE WELL, MY PRIEST...
TOWNSEND, IRWIN, FAUCHER, MENDOZA AND VEY INKS
STUDIO F'S ANTONIO FABELA & CHRIS BACHALO COLORS
VC'S CORY PETIT LETTERS
TOM BRENNAN ASST. EDITOR
STEPHEN WACKER EDDITURR
TOM BREVOORT EXECUTIVE EDITOR
JOE QUESADA EDITOR IN CHIEF
DAN BUCKLEY PUBLISHER
GALE, GUGGENHEIM, SLOTT & WELLS SPIDEY'S BRAINTRUST

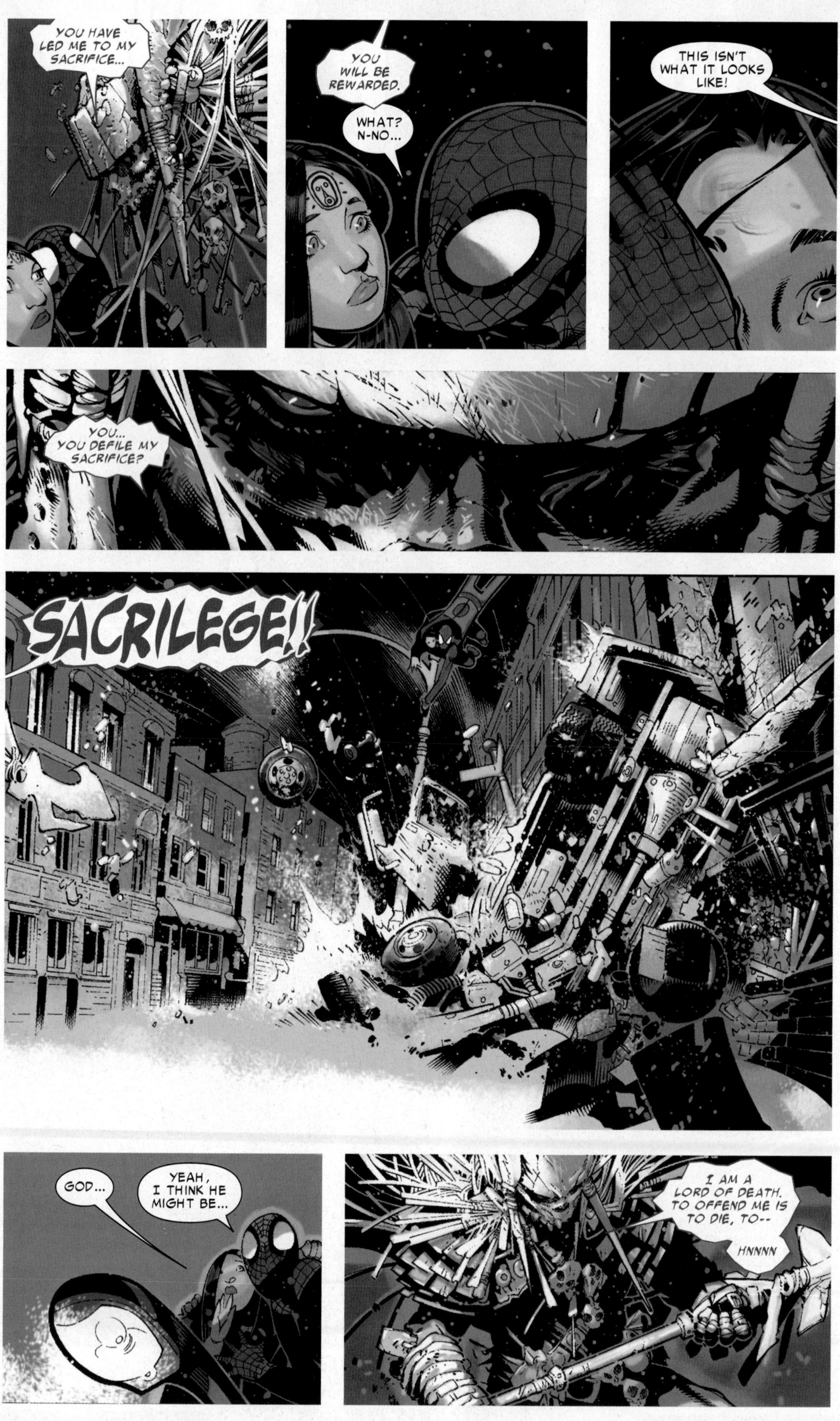

YOU HAVE LED ME TO MY SACRIFICE...
YOU WILL BE REWARDED.
WHAT? N-NO...
THIS ISN'T WHAT IT LOOKS LIKE!
YOU... YOU DEFILE MY SACRIFICE?
SACRILEGE!!
GOD...
YEAH, I THINK HE MIGHT BE...
I AM A LORD OF DEATH. TO OFFEND ME IS TO DIE, TO--
HNNNN

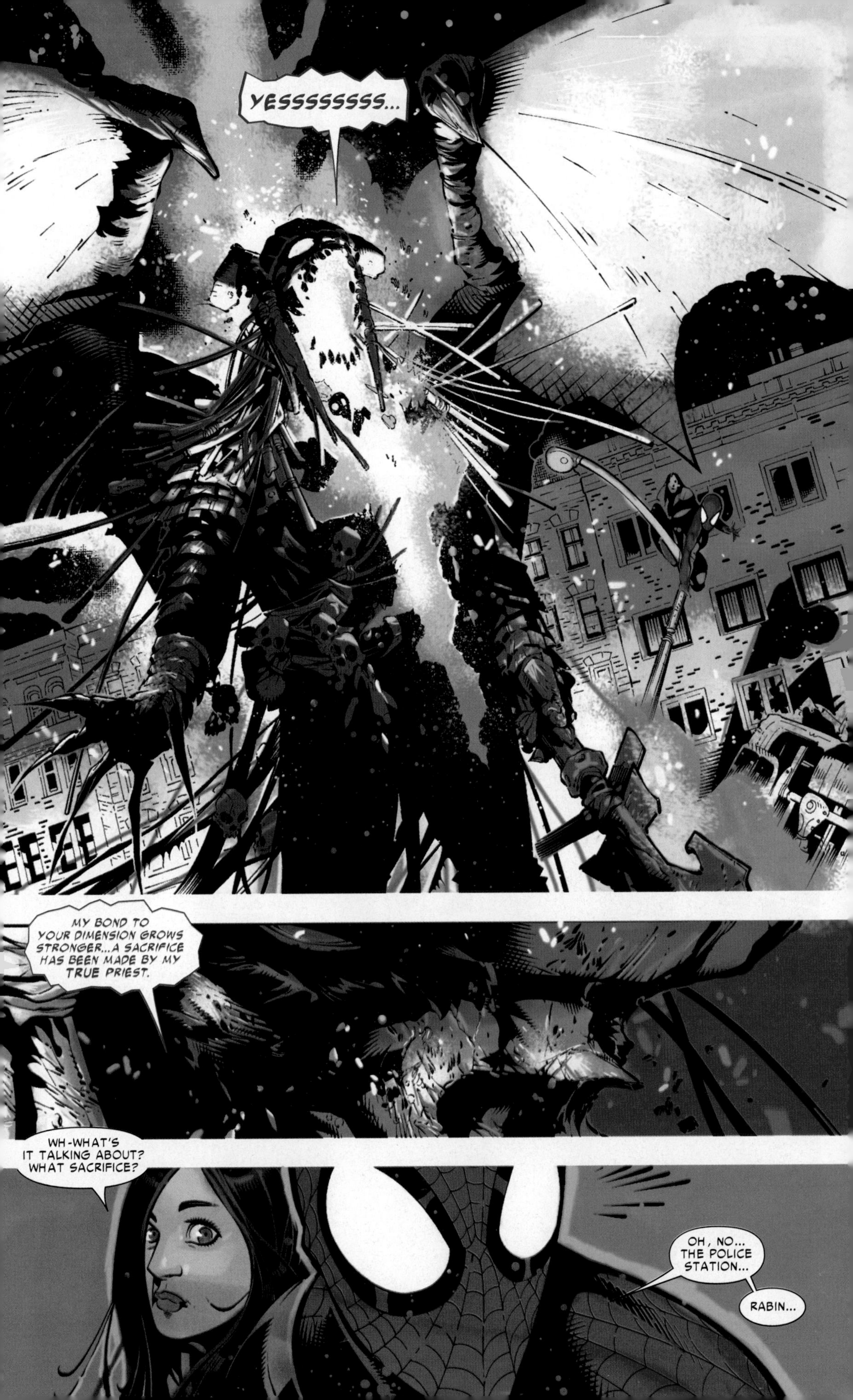
YESSSSSSSS...
MY BOND TO YOUR DIMENSION GROWS STRONGER...A SACRIFICE HAS BEEN MADE BY MY TRUE PRIEST.
WH-WHAT'S IT TALKING ABOUT? WHAT SACRIFICE?
OH, NO... THE POLICE STATION...
RABIN...

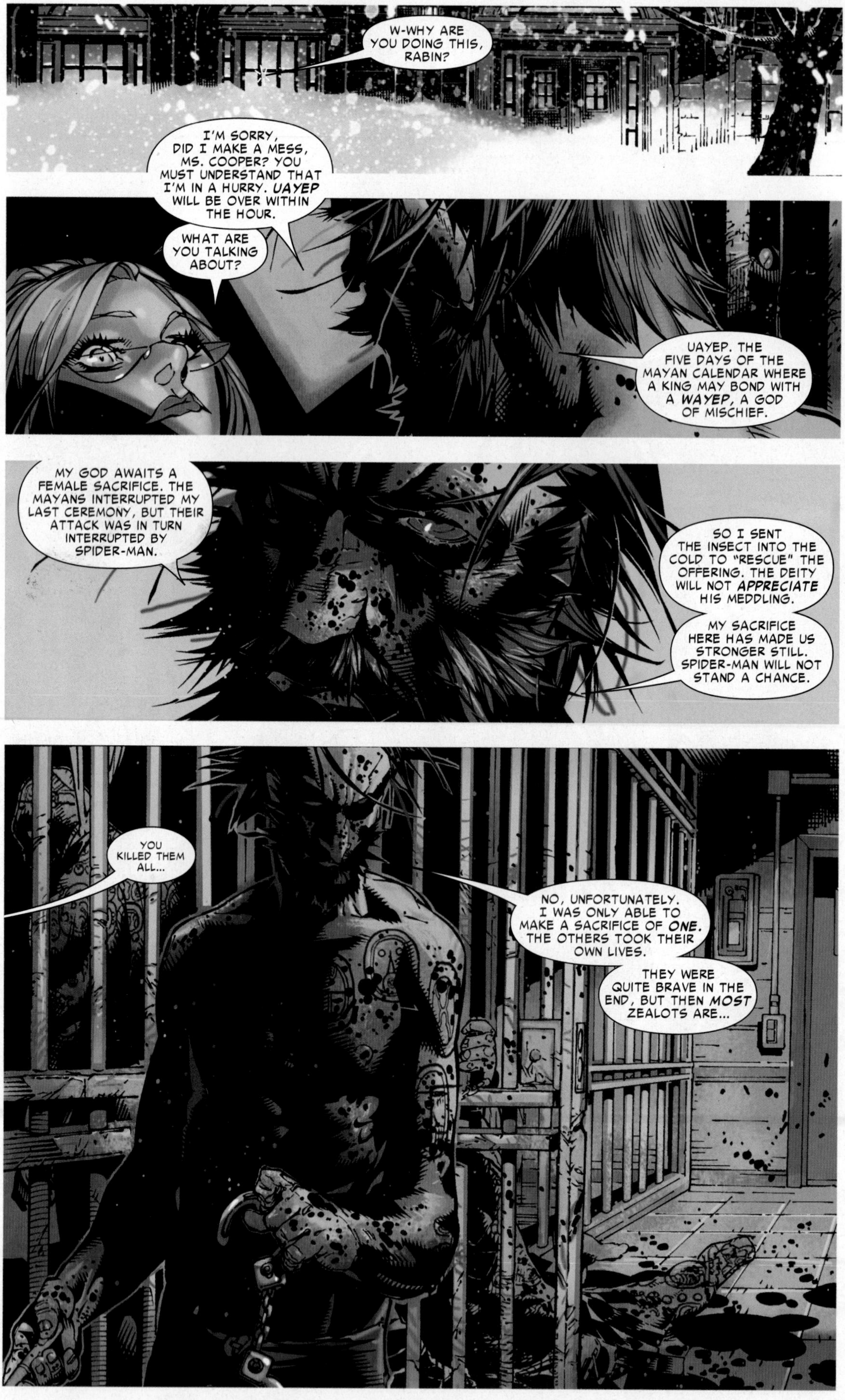
W-WHY ARE YOU DOING THIS, RABIN?
I'M SORRY, DID I MAKE A MESS, MS. COOPER? YOU MUST UNDERSTAND THAT I'M IN A HURRY. UAYEP WILL BE OVER WITHIN THE HOUR.
WHAT ARE YOU TALKING ABOUT?
UAYEP. THE FIVE DAYS OF THE MAYAN CALENDAR WHERE A KING MAY BOND WITH A WAYEP, A GOD OF MISCHIEF.
MY GOD AWAITS A FEMALE SACRIFICE. THE MAYANS INTERRUPTED MY LAST CEREMONY, BUT THEIR ATTACK WAS IN TURN INTERRUPTED BY SPIDER-MAN.
SO I SENT THE INSECT INTO THE COLD TO "RESCUE" THE OFFERING. THE DEITY WILL NOT APPRECIATE HIS MEDDLING.
MY SACRIFICE HERE HAS MADE US STRONGER STILL. SPIDER-MAN WILL NOT STAND A CHANCE.
YOU KILLED THEM ALL...
NO, UNFORTUNATELY. I WAS ONLY ABLE TO MAKE A SACRIFICE OF ONE. THE OTHERS TOOK THEIR OWN LIVES.
THEY WERE QUITE BRAVE IN THE END, BUT THEN MOST ZEALOTS ARE...

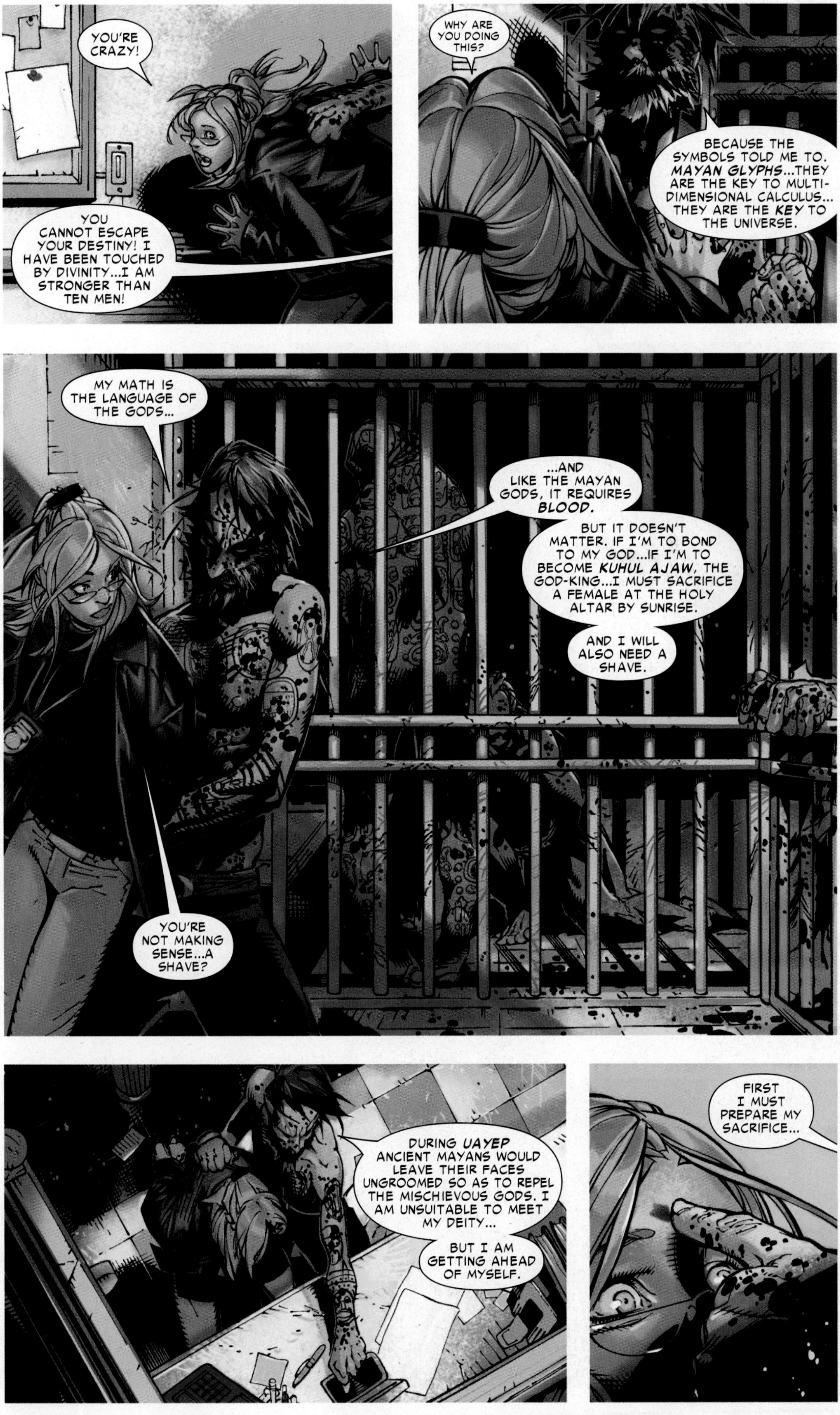
YOU'RE CRAZY!
YOU CANNOT ESCAPE YOUR DESTINY! I HAVE BEEN TOUCHED BY DIVINITY...I AM STRONGER THAN TEN MEN!
WHY ARE YOU DOING THIS?
BECAUSE THE SYMBOLS TOLD ME TO. MAYAN GLYPHS...THEY ARE THE KEY TO MULTI-DIMENSIONAL CALCULUS... THEY ARE THE KEY TO THE UNIVERSE.
MY MATH IS THE LANGUAGE OF THE GODS...
...AND LIKE THE MAYAN GODS, IT REQUIRES BLOOD.
BUT IT DOESN'T MATTER. IF I'M TO BOND TO MY GOD...IF I'M TO BECOME KUHUL AJAW, THE GOD-KING...I MUST SACRIFICE A FEMALE AT THE HOLY ALTAR BY SUNRISE.
AND I WILL ALSO NEED A SHAVE.
YOU'RE NOT MAKING SENSE...A SHAVE?
DURING UAYEP ANCIENT MAYANS WOULD LEAVE THEIR FACES UNGROOMED SO AS TO REPEL THE MISCHIEVOUS GODS. I AM UNSUITABLE TO MEET MY DEITY...
BUT I AM GETTING AHEAD OF MYSELF.
FIRST I MUST PREPARE MY SACRIFICE...

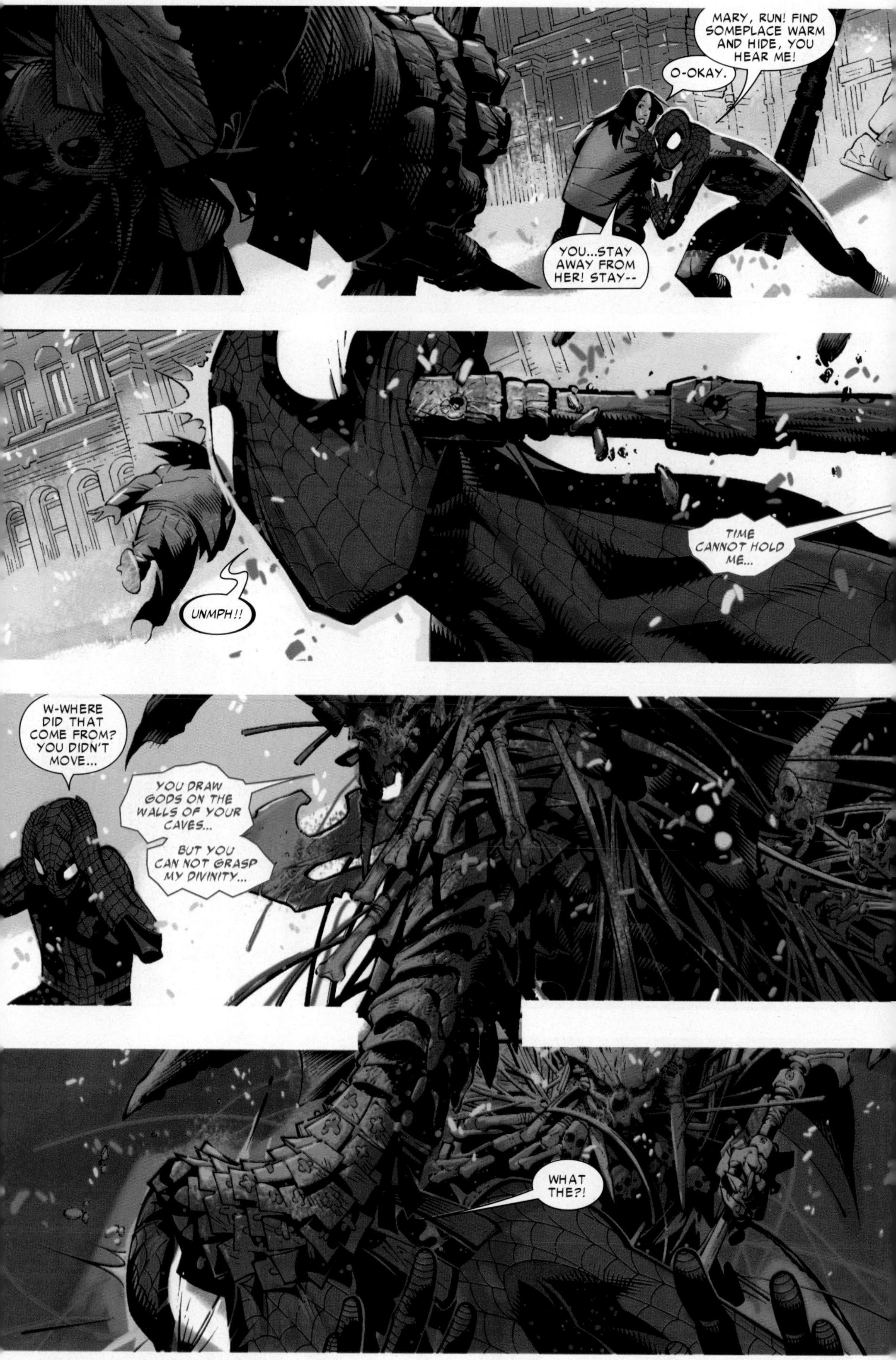
MARY, RUN! FIND SOMEPLACE WARM AND HIDE, YOU HEAR ME!
O-OKAY.
YOU...STAY AWAY FROM HER! STAY--
TIME CANNOT HOLD ME...
UNMPH!!
W-WHERE DID THAT COME FROM? YOU DIDN'T MOVE...
YOU DRAW GODS ON THE WALLS OF YOUR CAVES...
BUT YOU CAN NOT GRASP MY DIVINITY...
WHAT THE?!

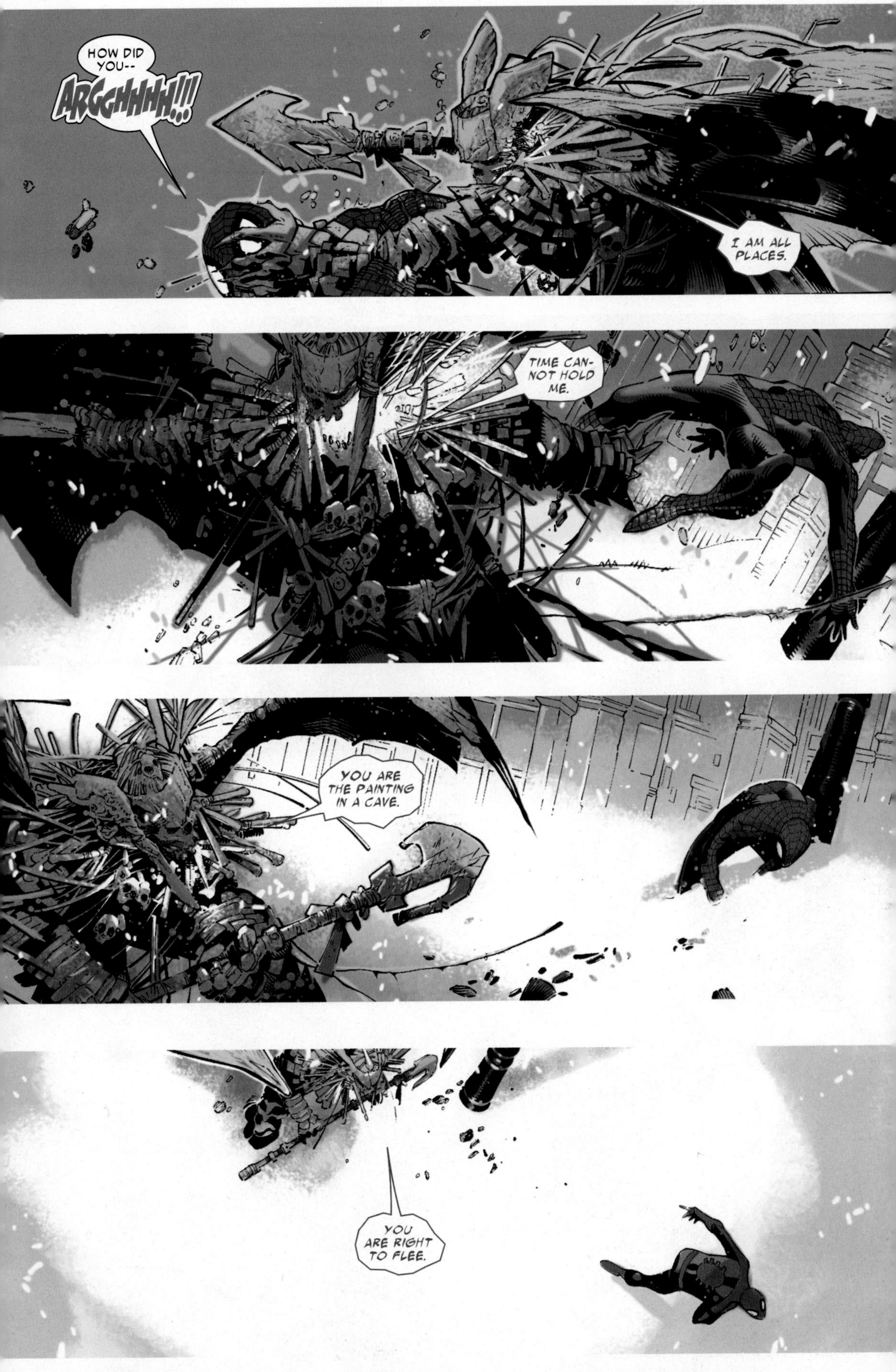
HOW DID YOU--
ARGGHHHH!!!
I AM ALL PLACES.
TIME CAN-NOT HOLD ME.
YOU ARE THE PAINTING IN A CAVE.
YOU ARE RIGHT TO FLEE.

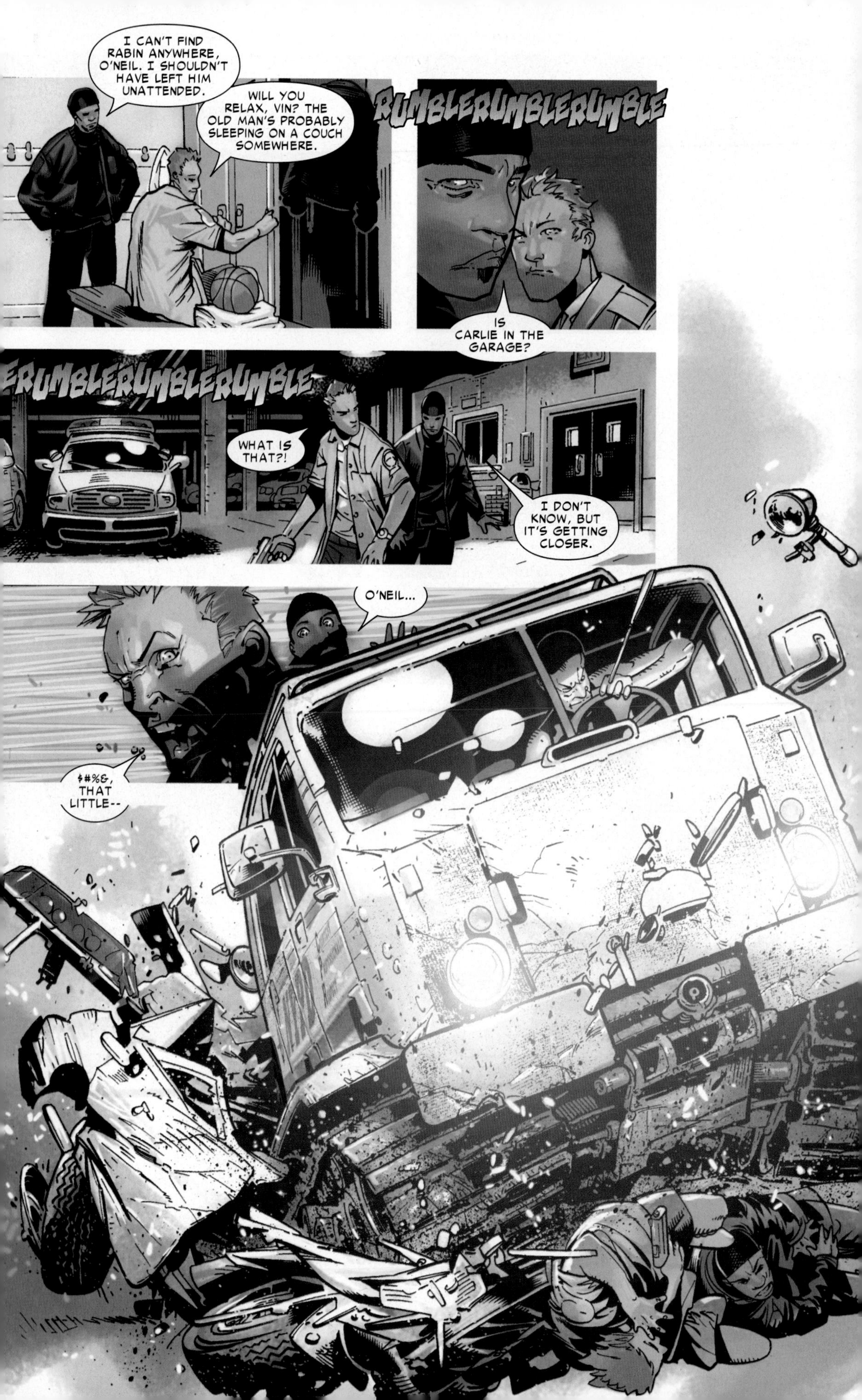
I CAN'T FIND RABIN ANYWHERE, O'NEIL. I SHOULDN'T HAVE LEFT HIM UNATTENDED.
WILL YOU RELAX, VIN? THE OLD MAN'S PROBABLY SLEEPING ON A COUCH SOMEWHERE.
RUMBLERUMBLERUMBLE
IS CARLIE IN THE GARAGE?
ERUMBLERUMBLERUMBLE
WHAT IS THAT?!
I DON'T KNOW, BUT IT'S GETTING CLOSER.
O'NEIL...
$#%&, THAT LITTLE--

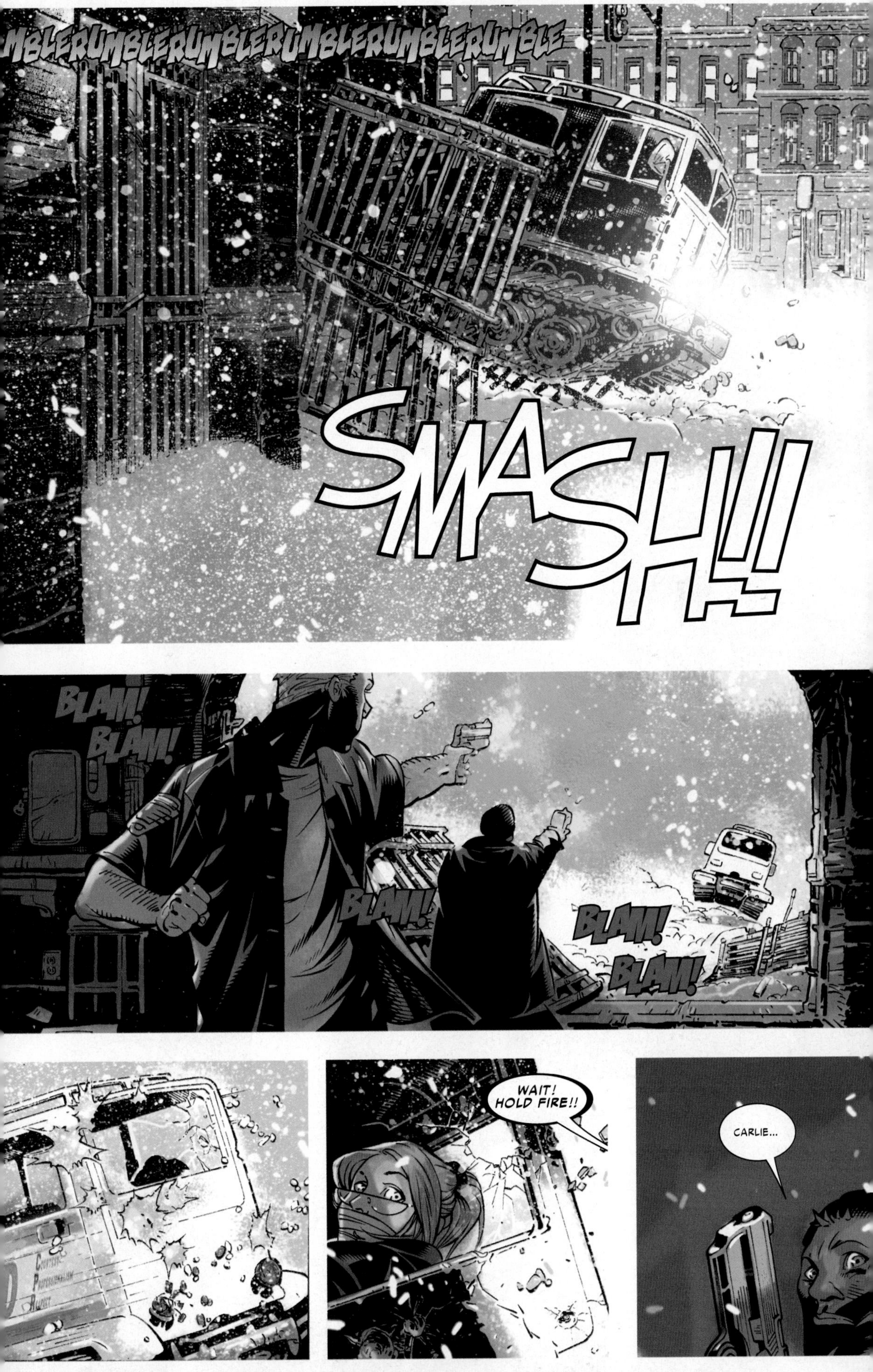
MBLERUMBLERUMBLERUMBLERUMBLERUMBLE
SMASH!!!
BLAM! BLAM!
BLAM!
BLAM!
BLAM!
WAIT! HOLD FIRE!!
CARLIE...

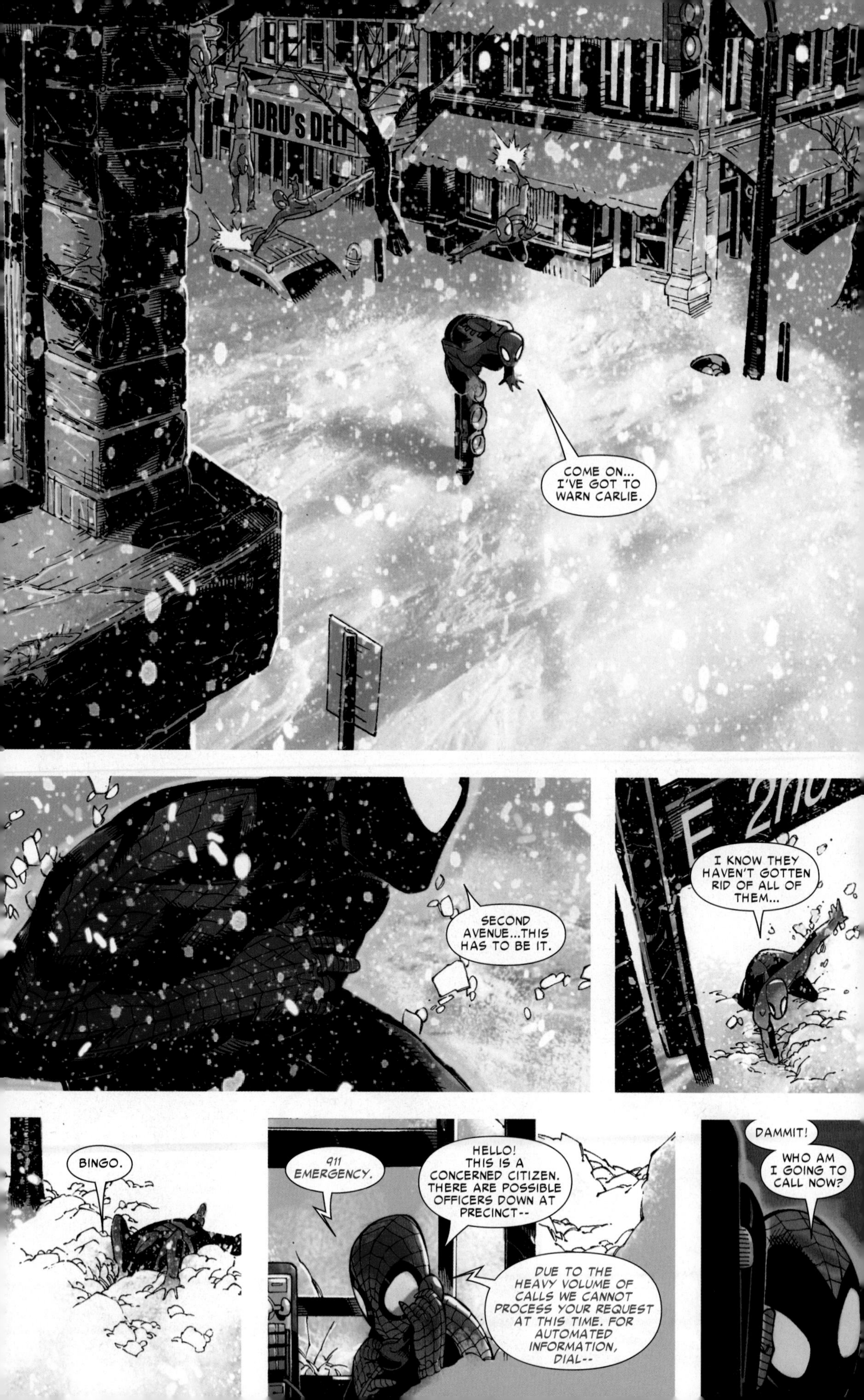
MADRU's DELI
COME ON... I'VE GOT TO WARN CARLIE.
SECOND AVENUE...THIS HAS TO BE IT.
E 2nd
I KNOW THEY HAVEN'T GOTTEN RID OF ALL OF THEM...
BINGO.
911 EMERGENCY.
HELLO! THIS IS A CONCERNED CITIZEN. THERE ARE POSSIBLE OFFICERS DOWN AT PRECINCT--
DUE TO THE HEAVY VOLUME OF CALLS WE CANNOT PROCESS YOUR REQUEST AT THIS TIME. FOR AUTOMATED INFORMATION, DIAL--
DAMMIT!
WHO AM I GOING TO CALL NOW?

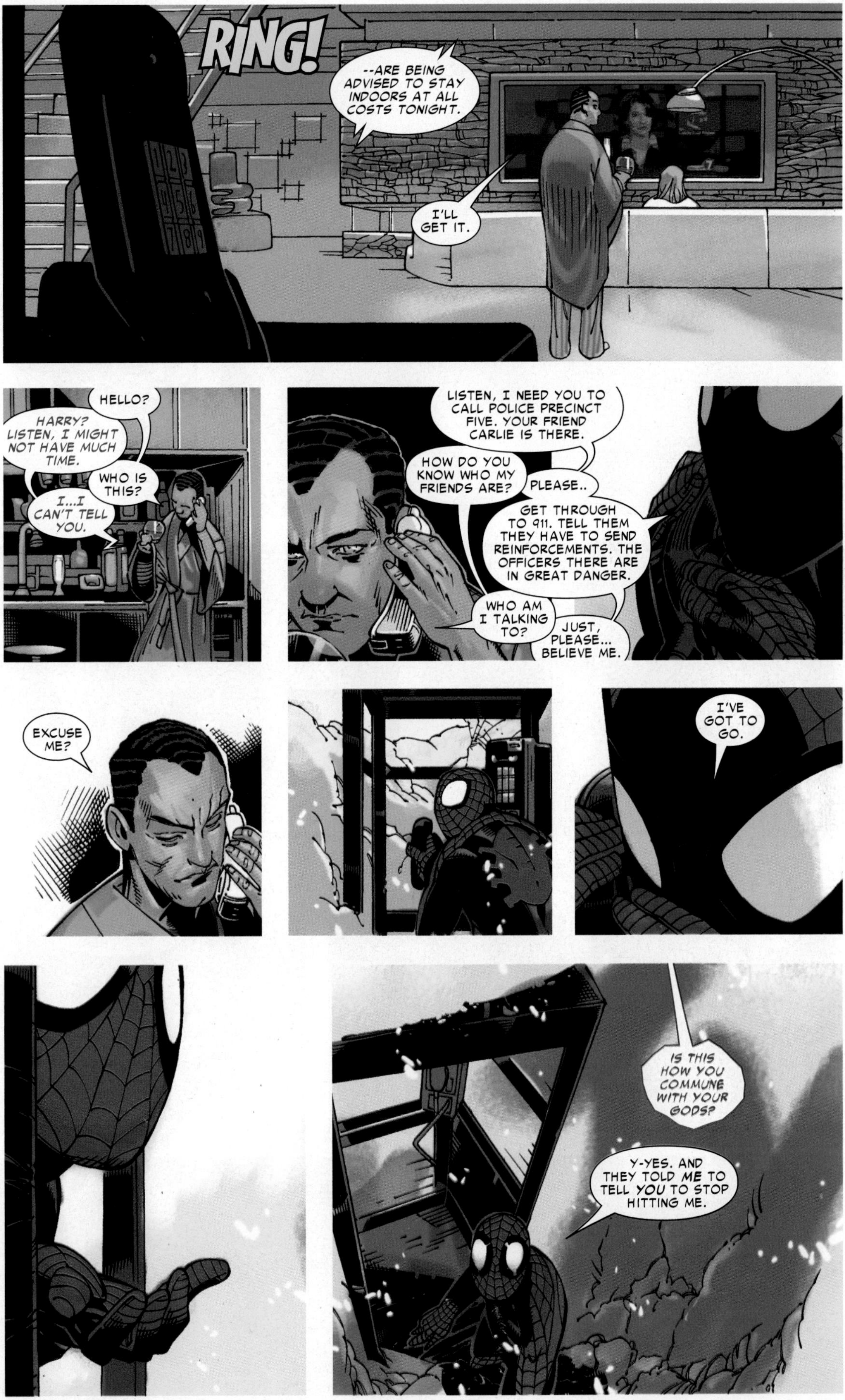
RING!
--ARE BEING ADVISED TO STAY INDOORS AT ALL COSTS TONIGHT.
I'LL GET IT.
HELLO?
HARRY? LISTEN, I MIGHT NOT HAVE MUCH TIME.
WHO IS THIS?
I...I CAN'T TELL YOU.
LISTEN, I NEED YOU TO CALL POLICE PRECINCT FIVE. YOUR FRIEND CARLIE IS THERE.
HOW DO YOU KNOW WHO MY FRIENDS ARE?
PLEASE..
GET THROUGH TO 911. TELL THEM THEY HAVE TO SEND REINFORCEMENTS. THE OFFICERS THERE ARE IN GREAT DANGER.
WHO AM I TALKING TO?
JUST, PLEASE... BELIEVE ME.
EXCUSE ME?
I'VE GOT TO GO.
IS THIS HOW YOU COMMUNE WITH YOUR GODS?
Y-YES. AND THEY TOLD ME TO TELL YOU TO STOP HITTING ME.

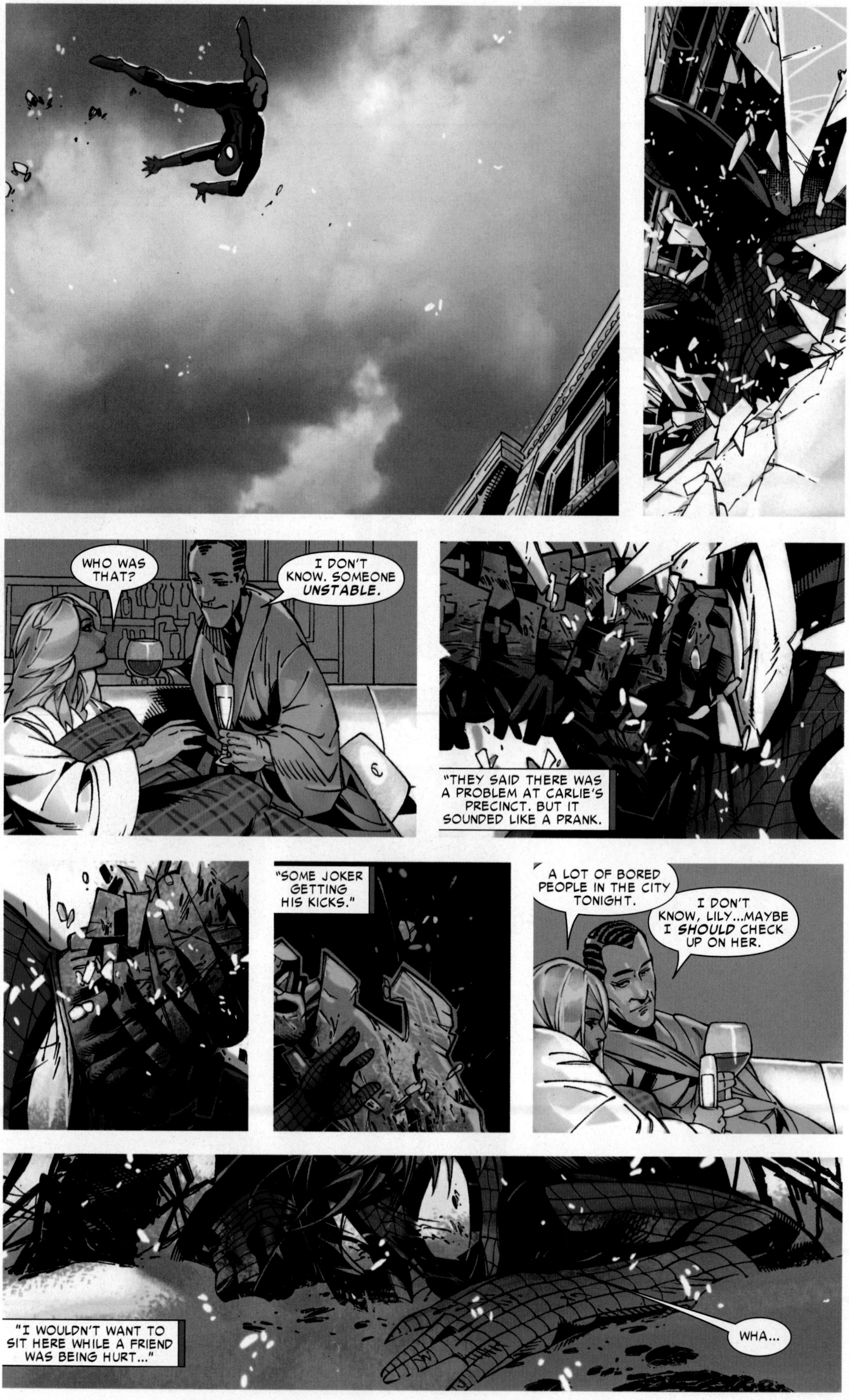
WHO WAS THAT?
I DON'T KNOW. SOMEONE UNSTABLE.
"THEY SAID THERE WAS A PROBLEM AT CARLIE'S PRECINCT. BUT IT SOUNDED LIKE A PRANK.
"SOME JOKER GETTING HIS KICKS."
A LOT OF BORED PEOPLE IN THE CITY TONIGHT.
I DON'T KNOW, LILY...MAYBE I SHOULD CHECK UP ON HER.
"I WOULDN'T WANT TO SIT HERE WHILE A FRIEND WAS BEING HURT..."
WHA...

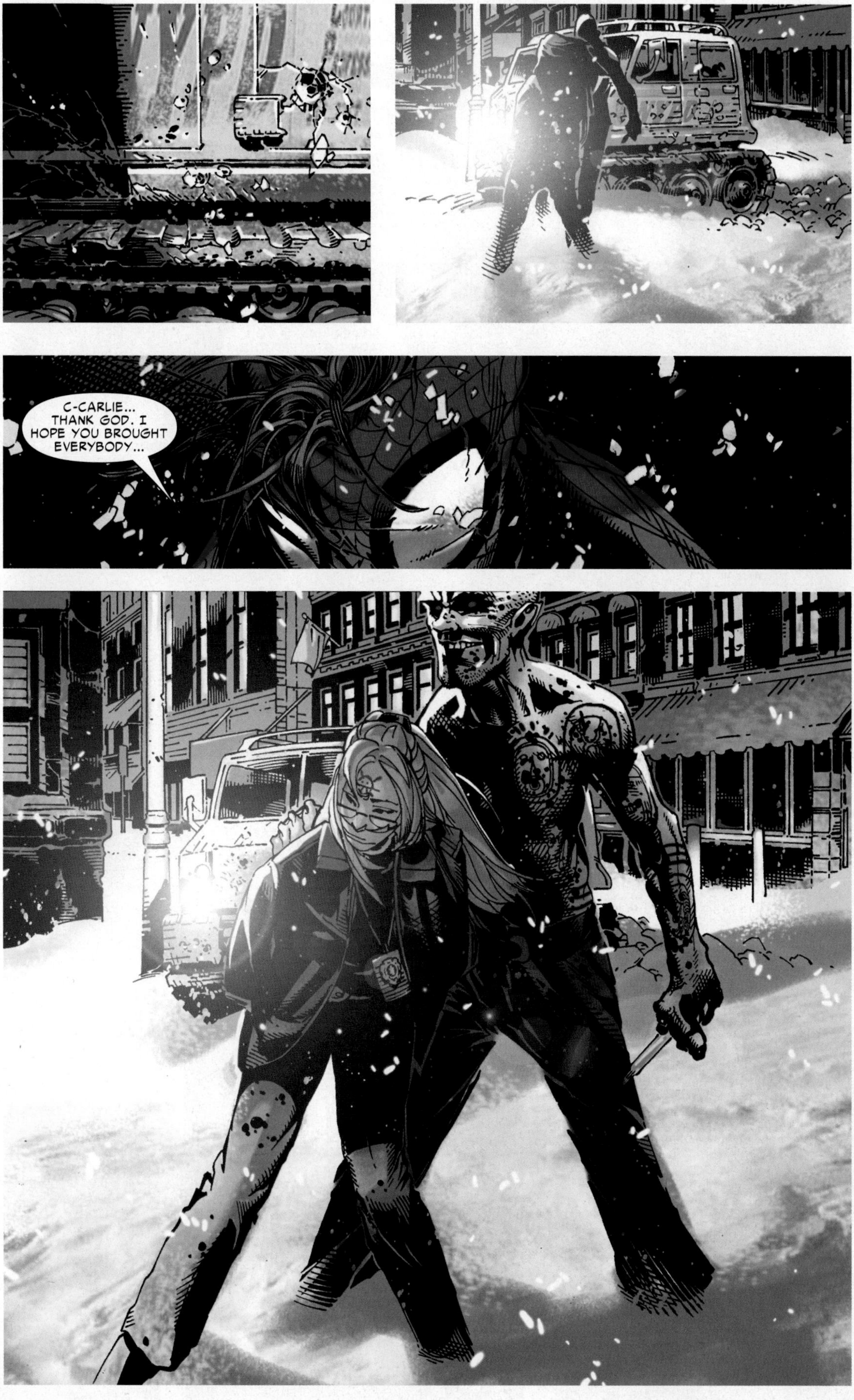
C-CARLIE... THANK GOD. I HOPE YOU BROUGHT EVERYBODY...

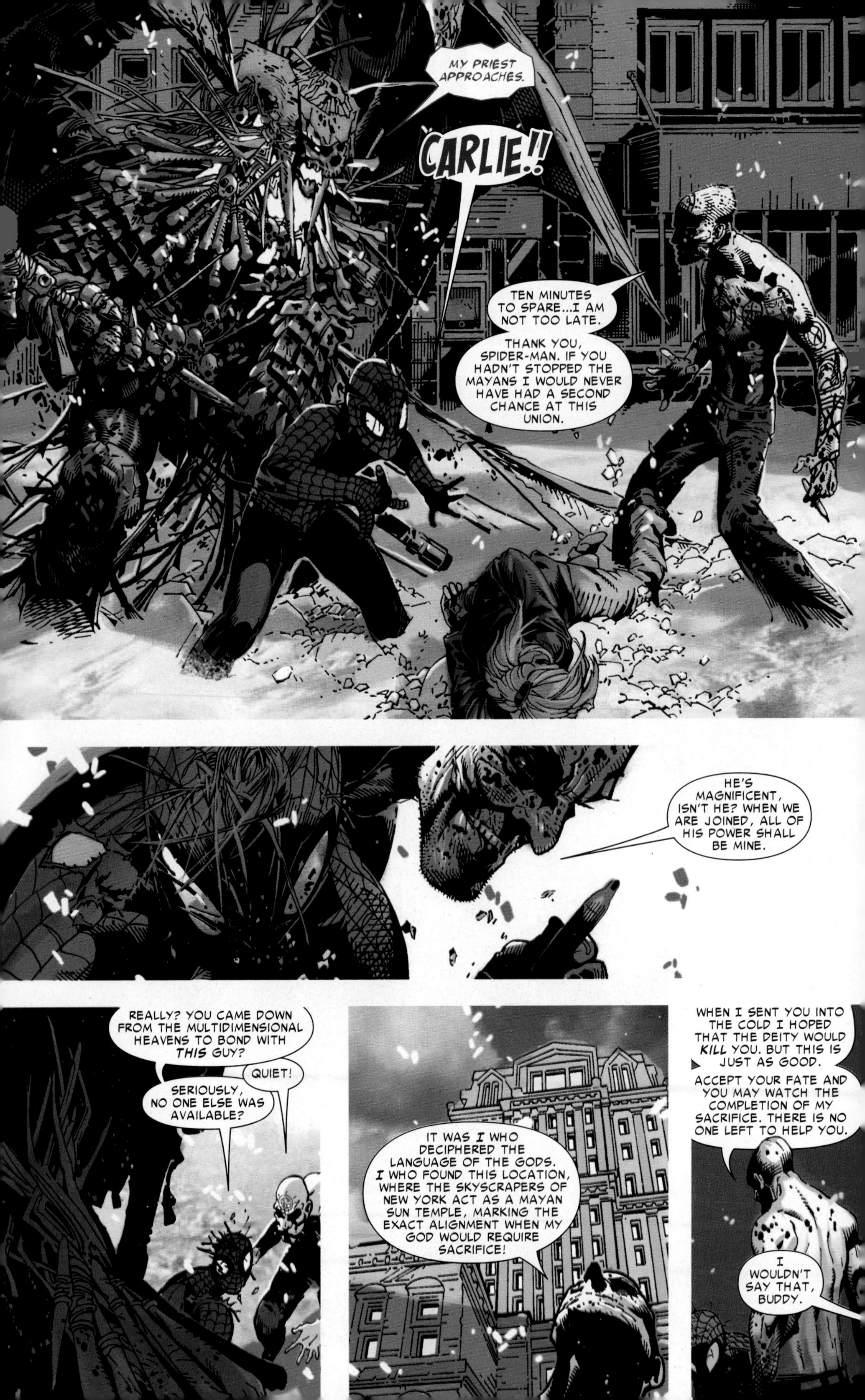
MY PRIEST APPROACHES.
CARLIE!!
TEN MINUTES TO SPARE...I AM NOT TOO LATE.
THANK YOU, SPIDER-MAN. IF YOU HADN'T STOPPED THE MAYANS I WOULD NEVER HAVE HAD A SECOND CHANCE AT THIS UNION.
HE'S MAGNIFICENT, ISN'T HE? WHEN WE ARE JOINED, ALL OF HIS POWER SHALL BE MINE.
REALLY? YOU CAME DOWN FROM THE MULTIDIMENSIONAL HEAVENS TO BOND WITH *THIS* GUY?
QUIET!
SERIOUSLY, NO ONE ELSE WAS AVAILABLE?
IT WAS *I* WHO DECIPHERED THE LANGUAGE OF THE GODS. *I* WHO FOUND THIS LOCATION, WHERE THE SKYSCRAPERS OF NEW YORK ACT AS A MAYAN SUN TEMPLE, MARKING THE EXACT ALIGNMENT WHEN MY GOD WOULD REQUIRE SACRIFICE!
WHEN I SENT YOU INTO THE COLD I HOPED THAT THE DEITY WOULD *KILL* YOU. BUT THIS IS JUST AS GOOD.
ACCEPT YOUR FATE AND YOU MAY WATCH THE COMPLETION OF MY SACRIFICE. THERE IS NO ONE LEFT TO HELP YOU.
I WOULDN'T SAY THAT, BUDDY.

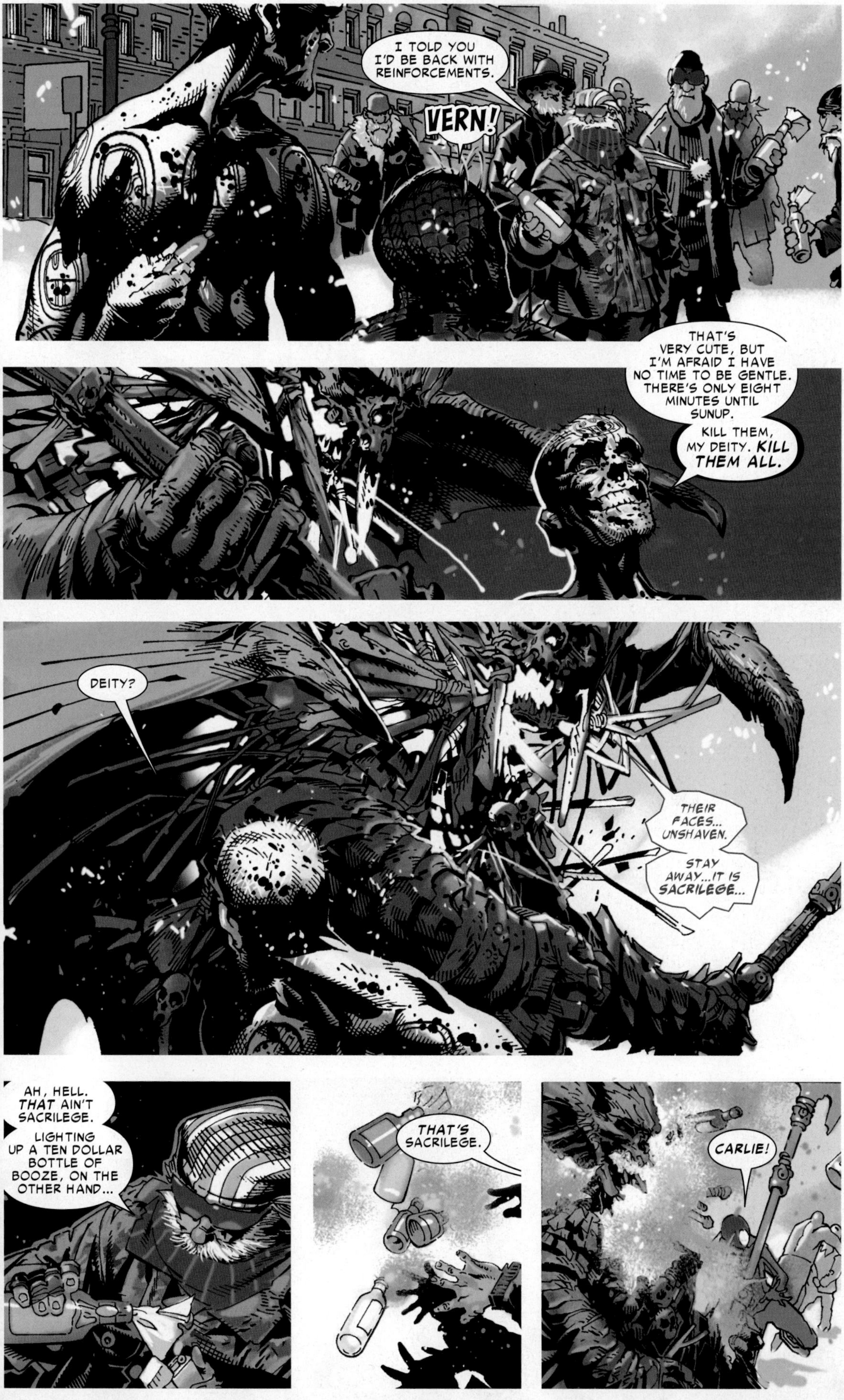
I TOLD YOU I'D BE BACK WITH REINFORCEMENTS.
VERN!
THAT'S VERY CUTE, BUT I'M AFRAID I HAVE NO TIME TO BE GENTLE. THERE'S ONLY EIGHT MINUTES UNTIL SUNUP.
KILL THEM, MY DEITY. KILL THEM ALL.
DEITY?
THEIR FACES... UNSHAVEN.
STAY AWAY...IT IS SACRILEGE...
AH, HELL. THAT AIN'T SACRILEGE.
LIGHTING UP A TEN DOLLAR BOTTLE OF BOOZE, ON THE OTHER HAND...
THAT'S SACRILEGE.
CARLIE!

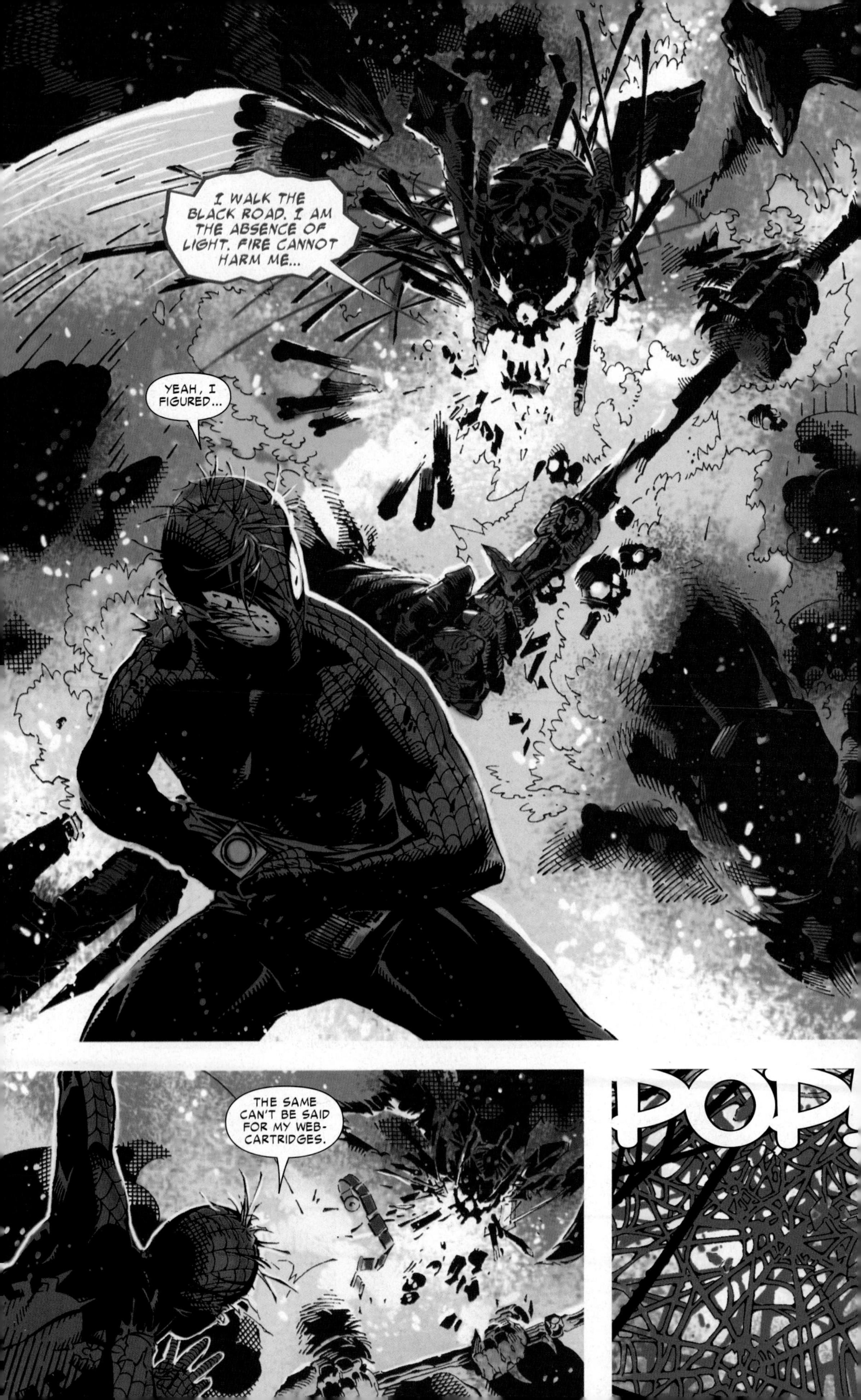

I WALK THE BLACK ROAD. I AM THE ABSENCE OF LIGHT. FIRE CANNOT HARM ME...
YEAH, I FIGURED...
THE SAME CAN'T BE SAID FOR MY WEB-CARTRIDGES.
POP!

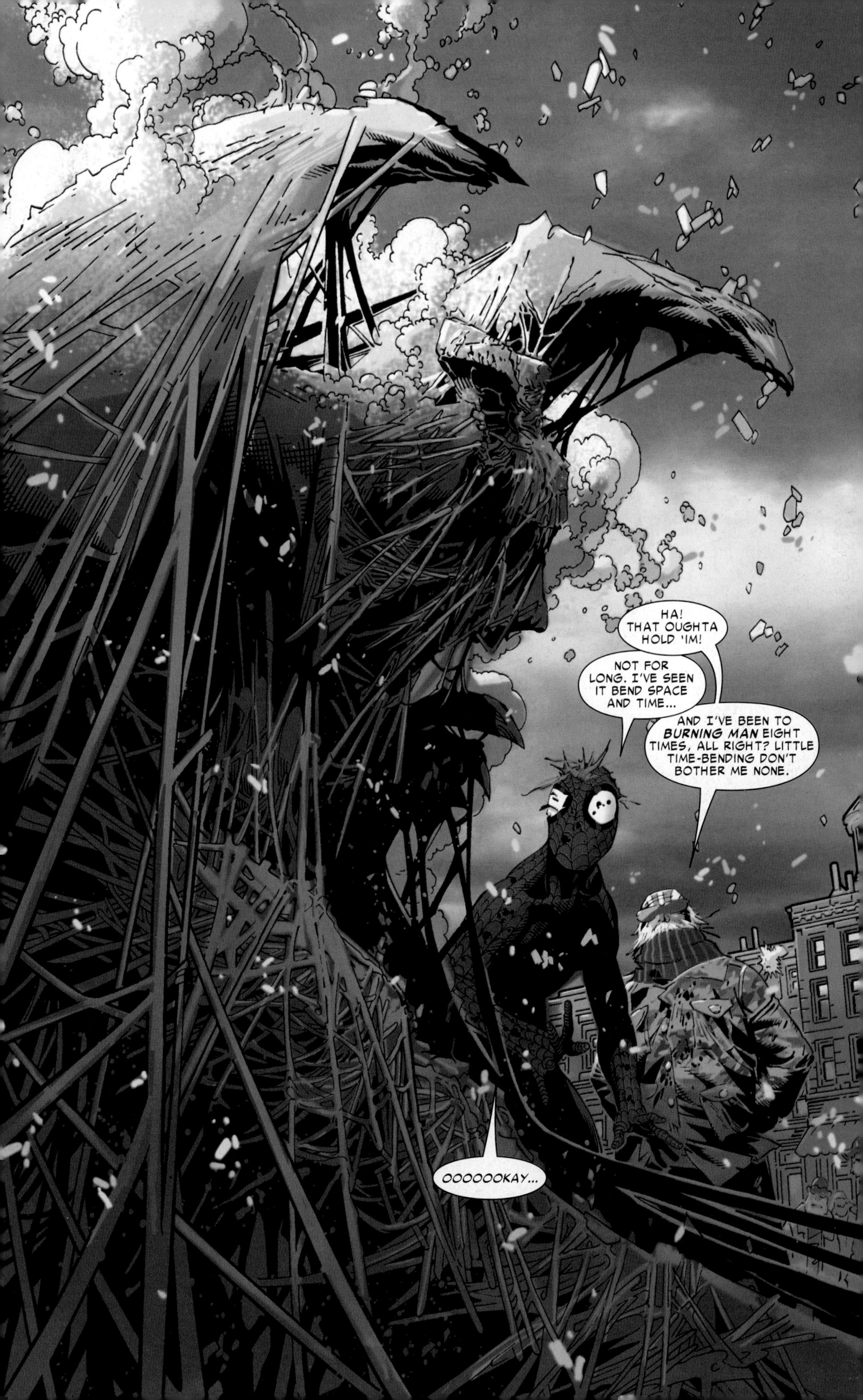
HA! THAT OUGHTA HOLD 'IM!
NOT FOR LONG. I'VE SEEN IT BEND SPACE AND TIME...
AND I'VE BEEN TO BURNING MAN EIGHT TIMES, ALL RIGHT? LITTLE TIME-BENDING DON'T BOTHER ME NONE.
OOOOOOKAY...

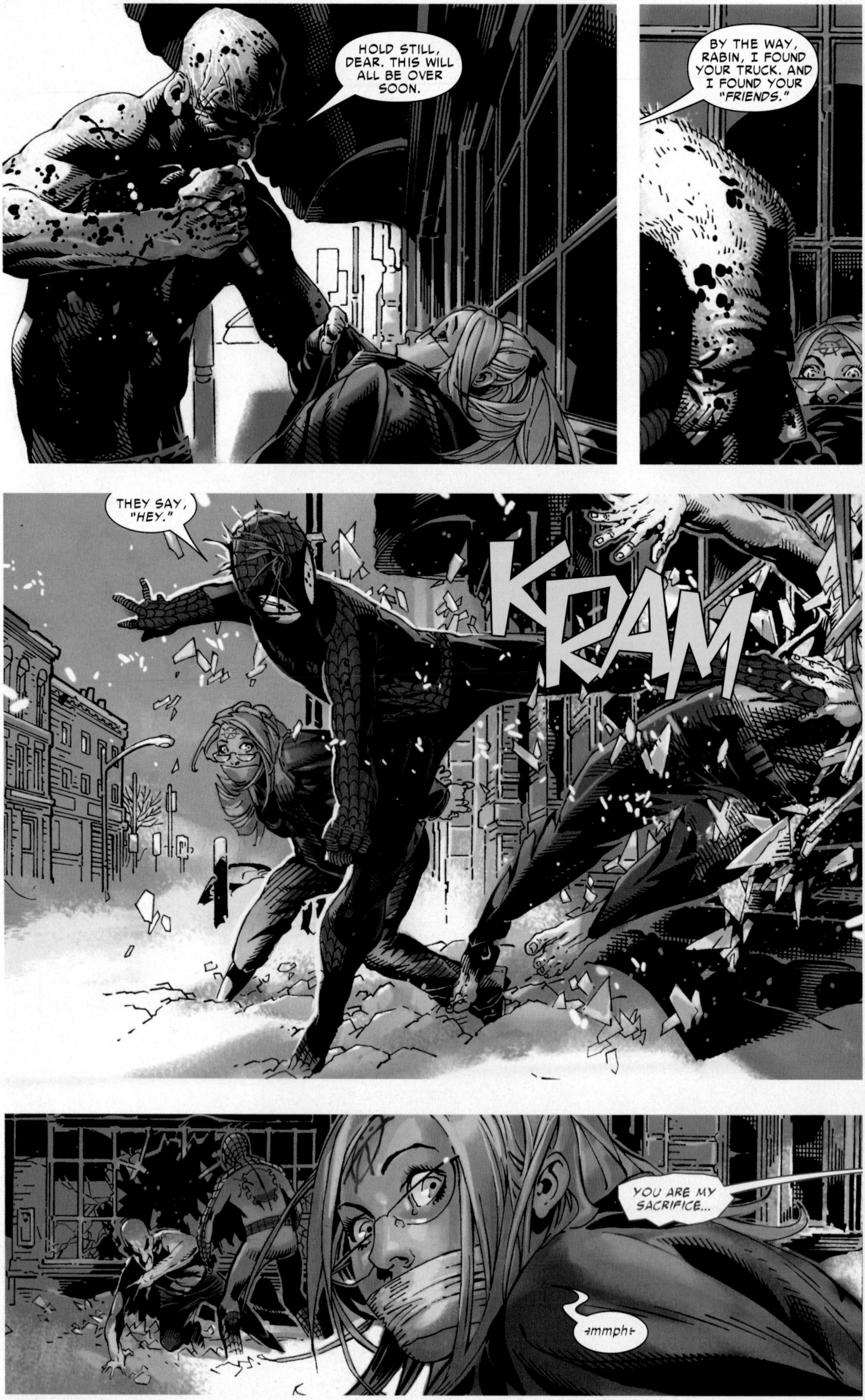
HOLD STILL, DEAR. THIS WILL ALL BE OVER SOON.
BY THE WAY, RABIN, I FOUND YOUR TRUCK. AND I FOUND YOUR "FRIENDS."
THEY SAY, "HEY."
KRAM
YOU ARE MY SACRIFICE...
mmph

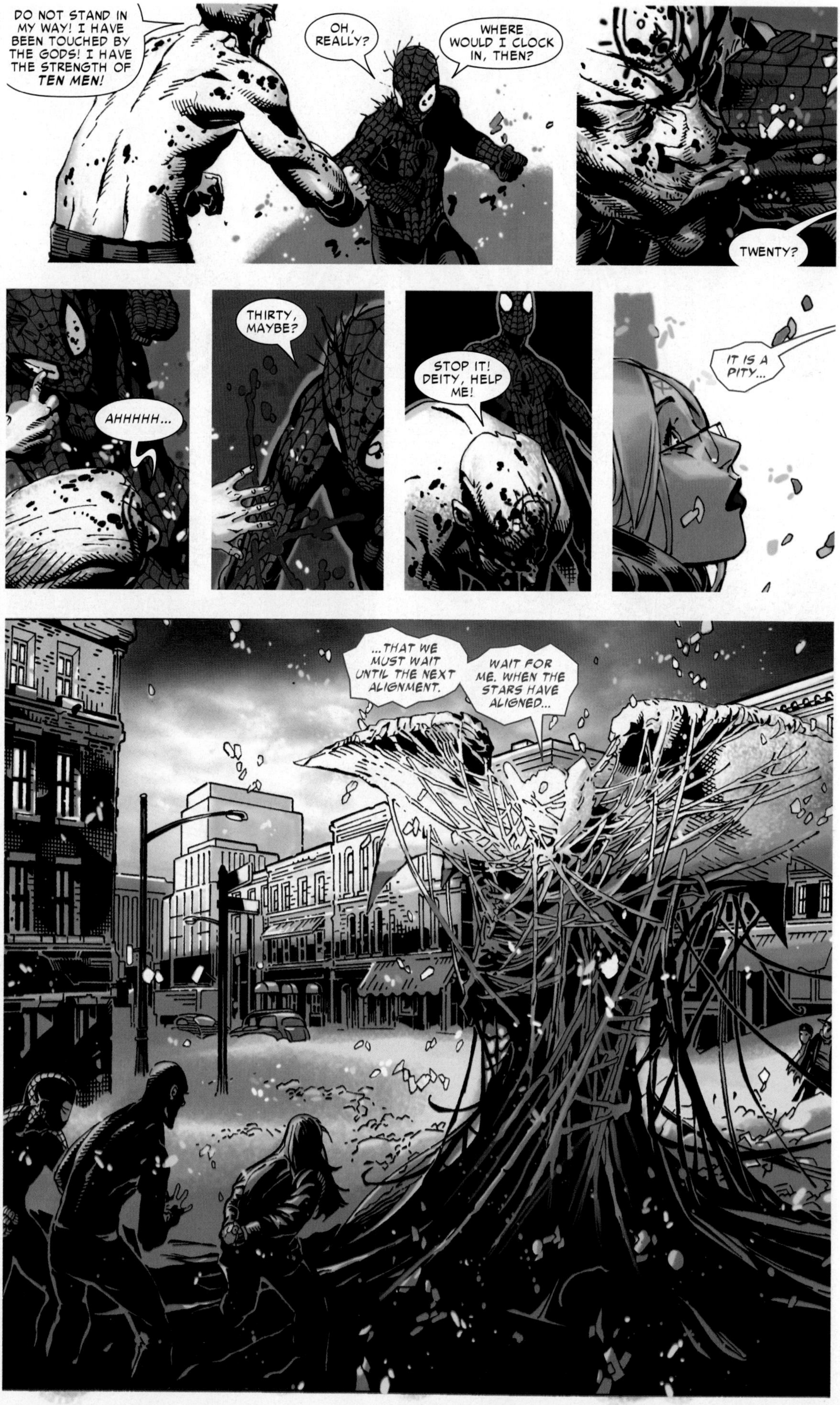
DO NOT STAND IN MY WAY! I HAVE BEEN TOUCHED BY THE GODS! I HAVE THE STRENGTH OF TEN MEN!
OH, REALLY?
WHERE WOULD I CLOCK IN, THEN?
TWENTY?
AHHHHH...
THIRTY, MAYBE?
STOP IT! DEITY, HELP ME!
IT IS A PITY...
...THAT WE MUST WAIT UNTIL THE NEXT ALIGNMENT.
WAIT FOR ME. WHEN THE STARS HAVE ALIGNED...

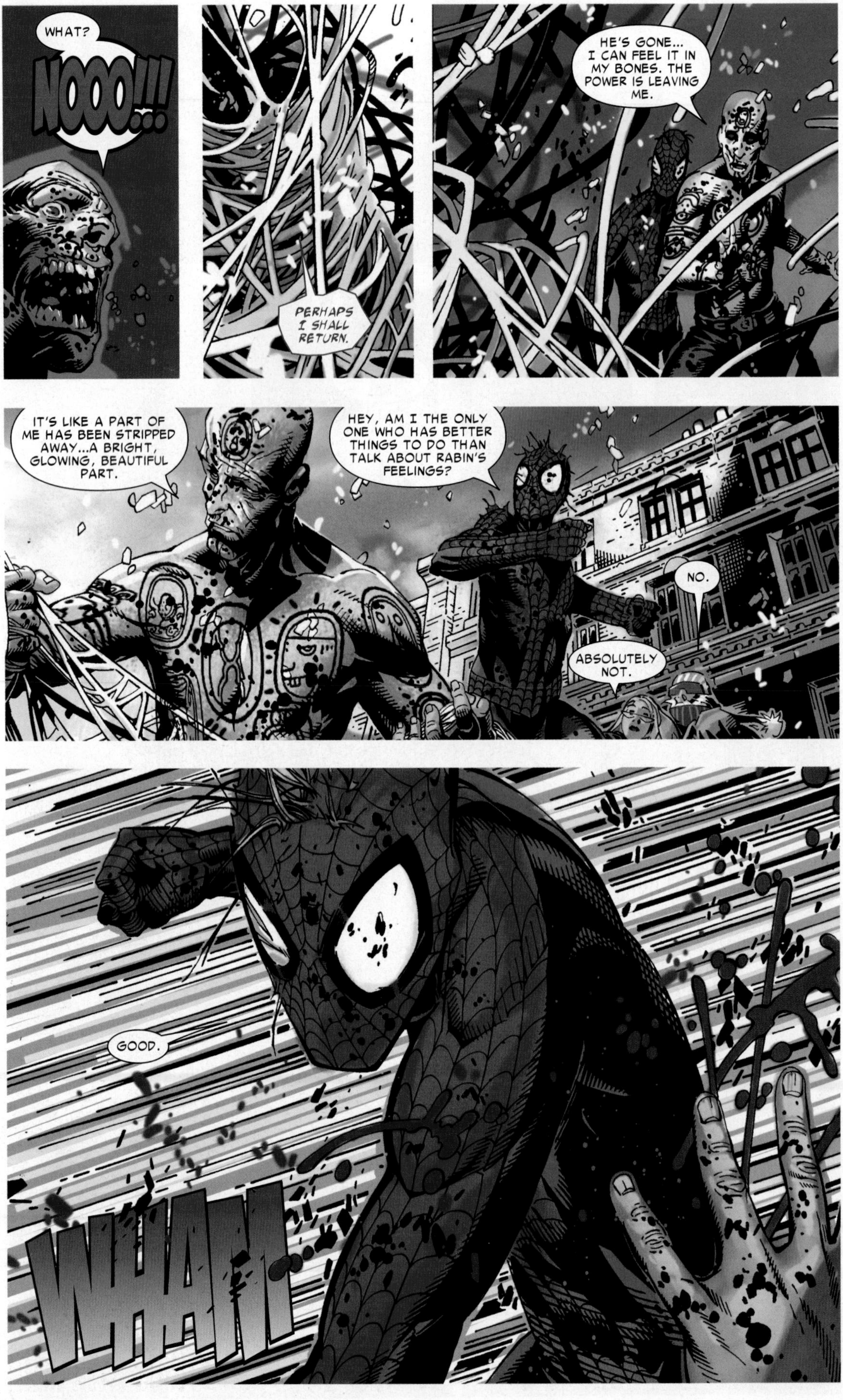
WHAT?
NOOO...!!!
PERHAPS I SHALL RETURN.
HE'S GONE... I CAN FEEL IT IN MY BONES. THE POWER IS LEAVING ME.
IT'S LIKE A PART OF ME HAS BEEN STRIPPED AWAY...A BRIGHT, GLOWING, BEAUTIFUL PART.
HEY, AM I THE ONLY ONE WHO HAS BETTER THINGS TO DO THAN TALK ABOUT RABIN'S FEELINGS?
NO.
ABSOLUTELY NOT.
GOOD.
WHAM

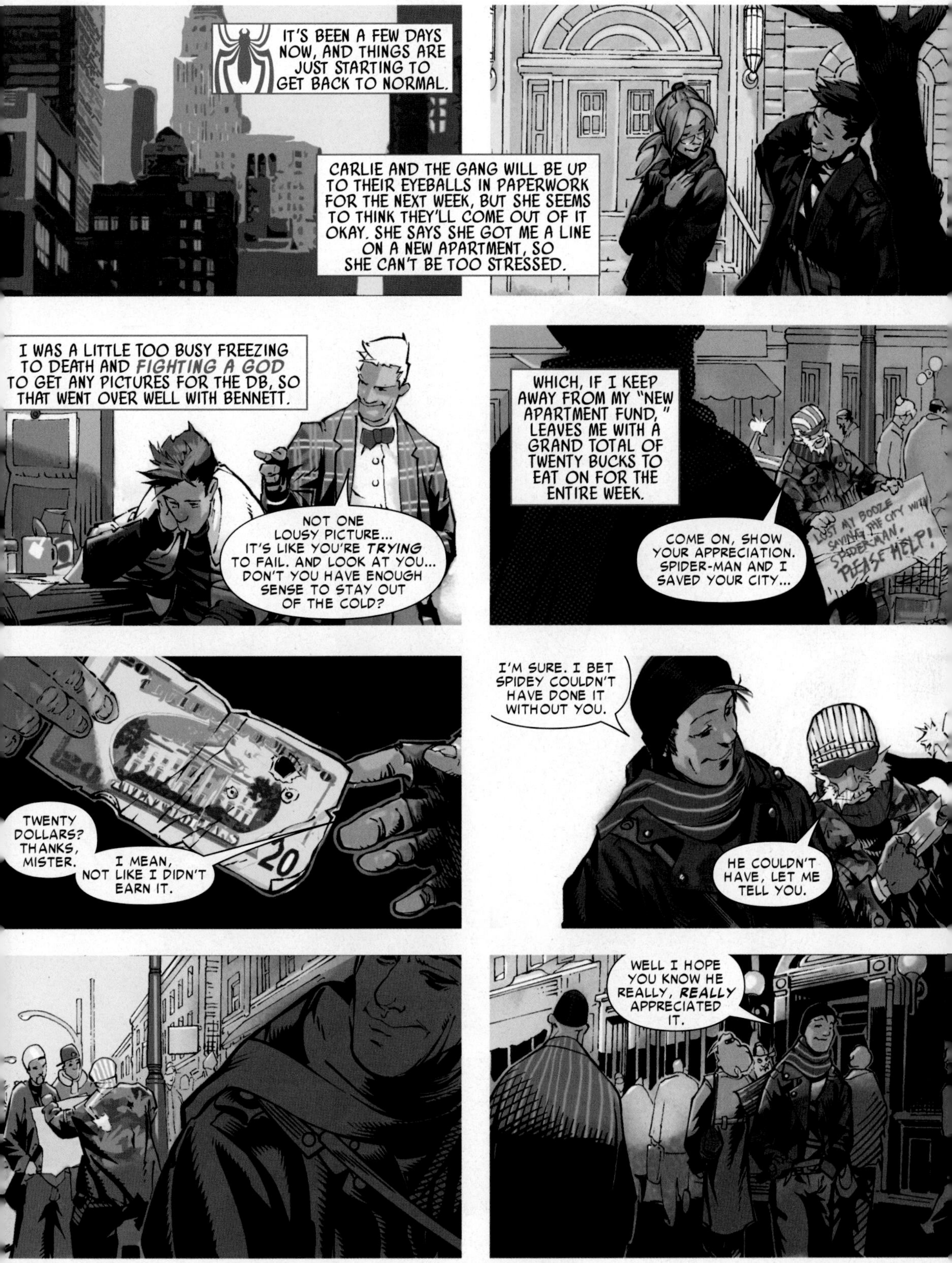
IT'S BEEN A FEW DAYS NOW, AND THINGS ARE JUST STARTING TO GET BACK TO NORMAL.
CARLIE AND THE GANG WILL BE UP TO THEIR EYEBALLS IN PAPERWORK FOR THE NEXT WEEK, BUT SHE SEEMS TO THINK THEY'LL COME OUT OF IT OKAY. SHE SAYS SHE GOT ME A LINE ON A NEW APARTMENT, SO SHE CAN'T BE TOO STRESSED.
I WAS A LITTLE TOO BUSY FREEZING TO DEATH AND FIGHTING A GOD TO GET ANY PICTURES FOR THE DB, SO THAT WENT OVER WELL WITH BENNETT.
NOT ONE LOUSY PICTURE... IT'S LIKE YOU'RE TRYING TO FAIL. AND LOOK AT YOU... DON'T YOU HAVE ENOUGH SENSE TO STAY OUT OF THE COLD?
WHICH, IF I KEEP AWAY FROM MY "NEW APARTMENT FUND," LEAVES ME WITH A GRAND TOTAL OF TWENTY BUCKS TO EAT ON FOR THE ENTIRE WEEK.
COME ON, SHOW YOUR APPRECIATION. SPIDER-MAN AND I SAVED YOUR CITY...
LOST MY BOOZE SAVING THE CITY WITH SPIDER-MAN. PLEASE HELP!
TWENTY DOLLARS? THANKS, MISTER.
I MEAN, NOT LIKE I DIDN'T EARN IT.
I'M SURE. I BET SPIDEY COULDN'T HAVE DONE IT WITHOUT YOU.
HE COULDN'T HAVE, LET ME TELL YOU.
WELL I HOPE YOU KNOW HE REALLY, REALLY APPRECIATED IT.

NEXT: FREAK'S BACK (AND HE'S BRINGING BARRY KITSON WITH HIM!)

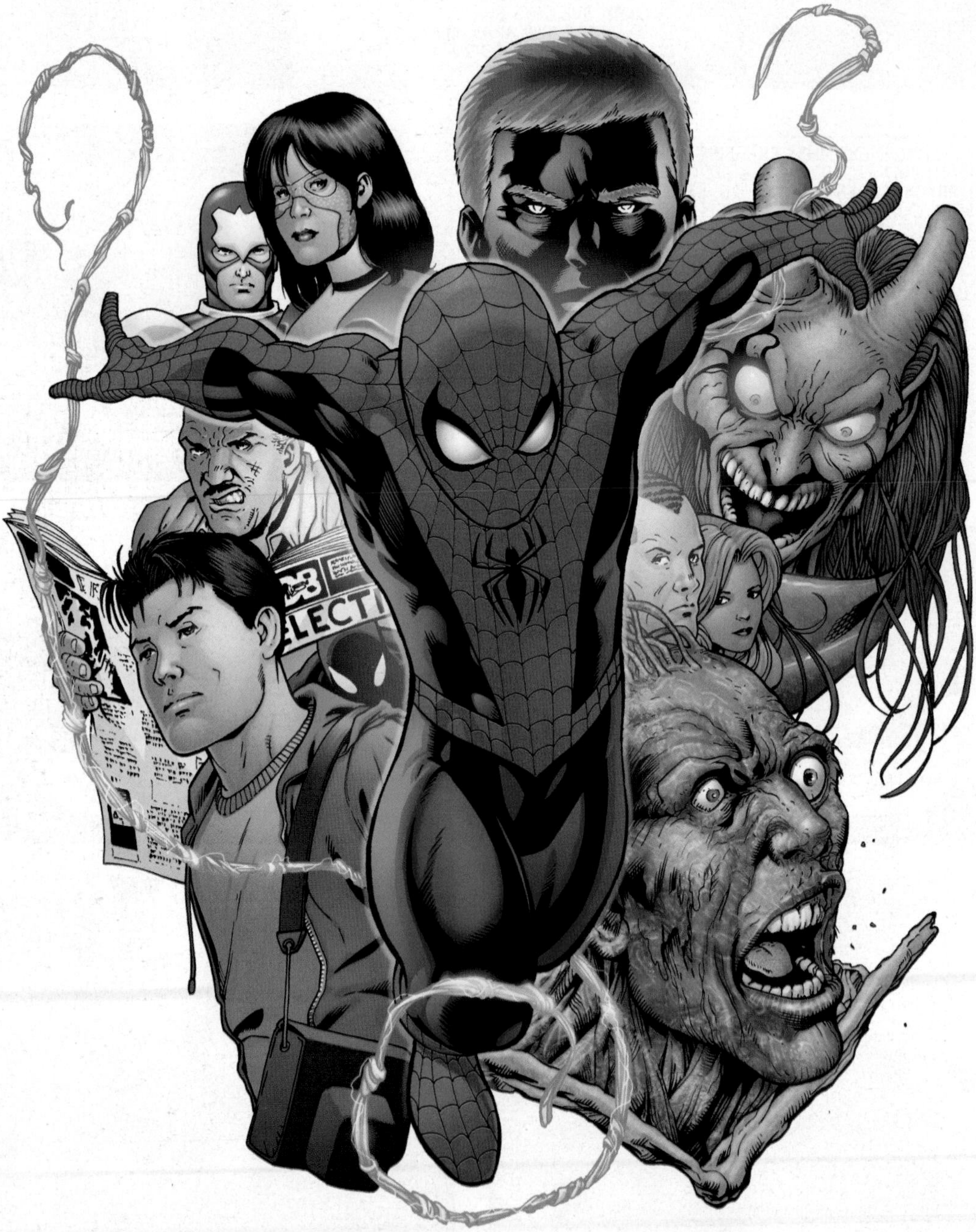

ELECTI

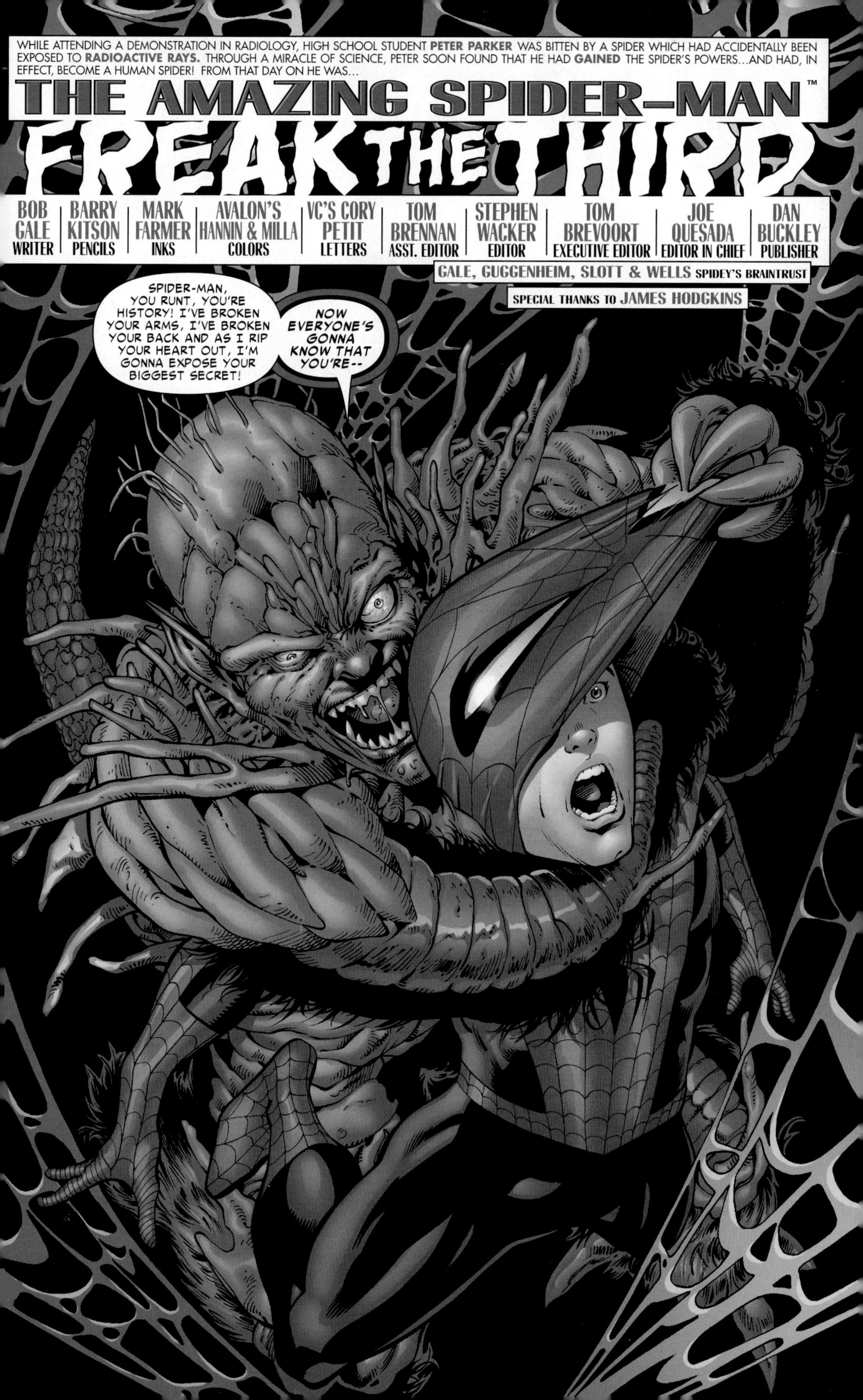
WHILE ATTENDING A DEMONSTRATION IN RADIOLOGY, HIGH SCHOOL STUDENT PETER PARKER WAS BITTEN BY A SPIDER WHICH HAD ACCIDENTALLY BEEN EXPOSED TO RADIOACTIVE RAYS. THROUGH A MIRACLE OF SCIENCE, PETER SOON FOUND THAT HE HAD GAINED THE SPIDER'S POWERS…AND HAD, IN EFFECT, BECOME A HUMAN SPIDER! FROM THAT DAY ON HE WAS…
THE AMAZING SPIDER-MAN™
FREAK THE THIRD
BOB GALE WRITER | BARRY KITSON PENCILS | MARK FARMER INKS | AVALON'S HANNIN & MILLA COLORS | VC'S CORY PETIT LETTERS | TOM BRENNAN ASST. EDITOR | STEPHEN WACKER EDITOR | TOM BREVOORT EXECUTIVE EDITOR | JOE QUESADA EDITOR IN CHIEF | DAN BUCKLEY PUBLISHER
GALE, GUGGENHEIM, SLOTT & WELLS SPIDEY'S BRAINTRUST
SPECIAL THANKS TO JAMES HODGKINS
SPIDER-MAN, YOU RUNT, YOU'RE HISTORY! I'VE BROKEN YOUR ARMS, I'VE BROKEN YOUR BACK AND AS I RIP YOUR HEART OUT, I'M GONNA EXPOSE YOUR BIGGEST SECRET!
NOW EVERYONE'S GONNA KNOW THAT YOU'RE--

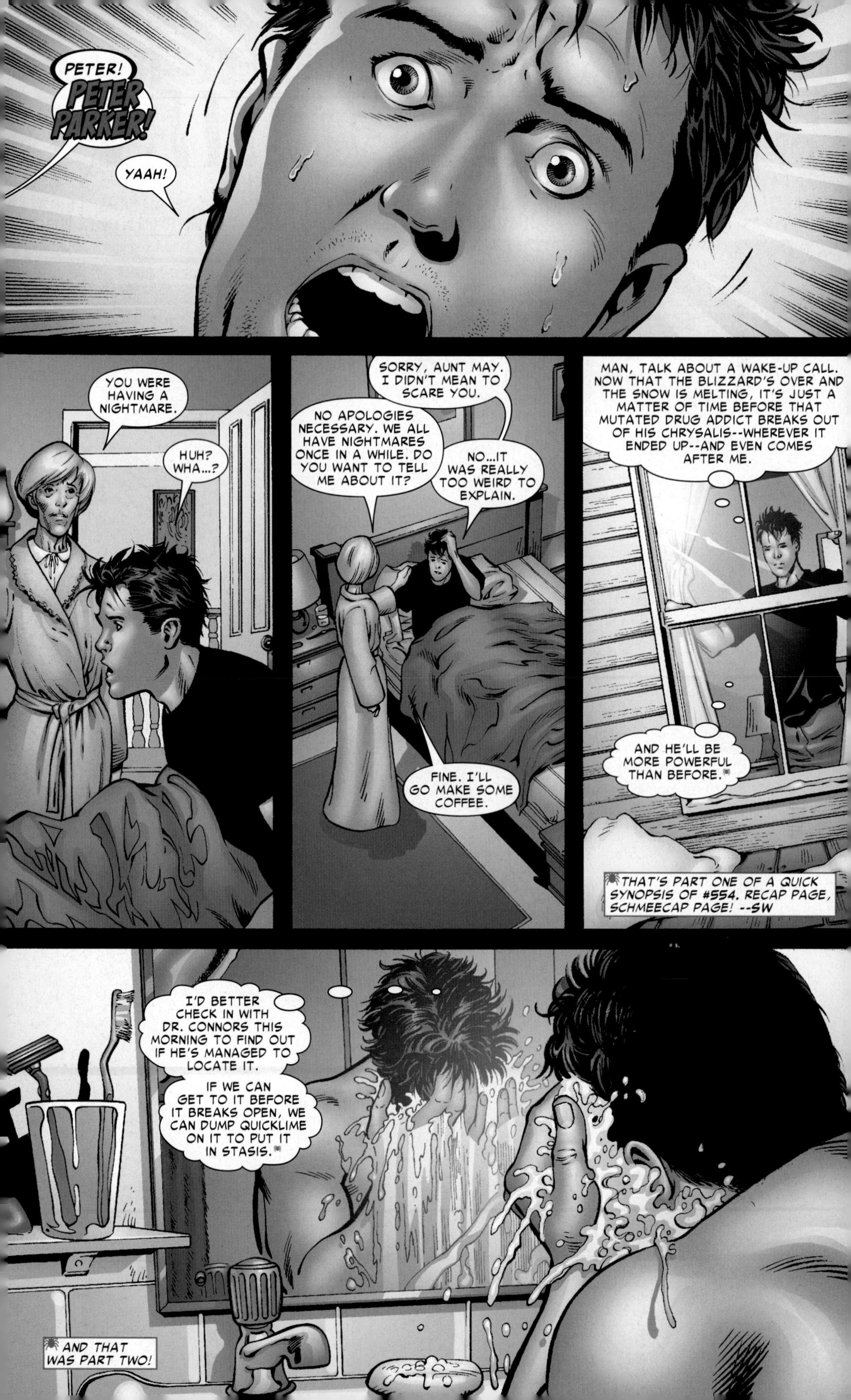
PETER! PETER PARKER!
YAAH!
YOU WERE HAVING A NIGHTMARE.
HUH? WHA...?
SORRY, AUNT MAY. I DIDN'T MEAN TO SCARE YOU.
NO APOLOGIES NECESSARY. WE ALL HAVE NIGHTMARES ONCE IN A WHILE. DO YOU WANT TO TELL ME ABOUT IT?
NO...IT WAS REALLY TOO WEIRD TO EXPLAIN.
FINE. I'LL GO MAKE SOME COFFEE.
MAN, TALK ABOUT A WAKE-UP CALL. NOW THAT THE BLIZZARD'S OVER AND THE SNOW IS MELTING, IT'S JUST A MATTER OF TIME BEFORE THAT MUTATED DRUG ADDICT BREAKS OUT OF HIS CHRYSALIS--WHEREVER IT ENDED UP--AND EVEN COMES AFTER ME.
AND HE'LL BE MORE POWERFUL THAN BEFORE.
THAT'S PART ONE OF A QUICK SYNOPSIS OF #554. RECAP PAGE, SCHMEECAP PAGE! --SW
I'D BETTER CHECK IN WITH DR. CONNORS THIS MORNING TO FIND OUT IF HE'S MANAGED TO LOCATE IT.
IF WE CAN GET TO IT BEFORE IT BREAKS OPEN, WE CAN DUMP QUICKLIME ON IT TO PUT IT IN STASIS.
AND THAT WAS PART TWO!

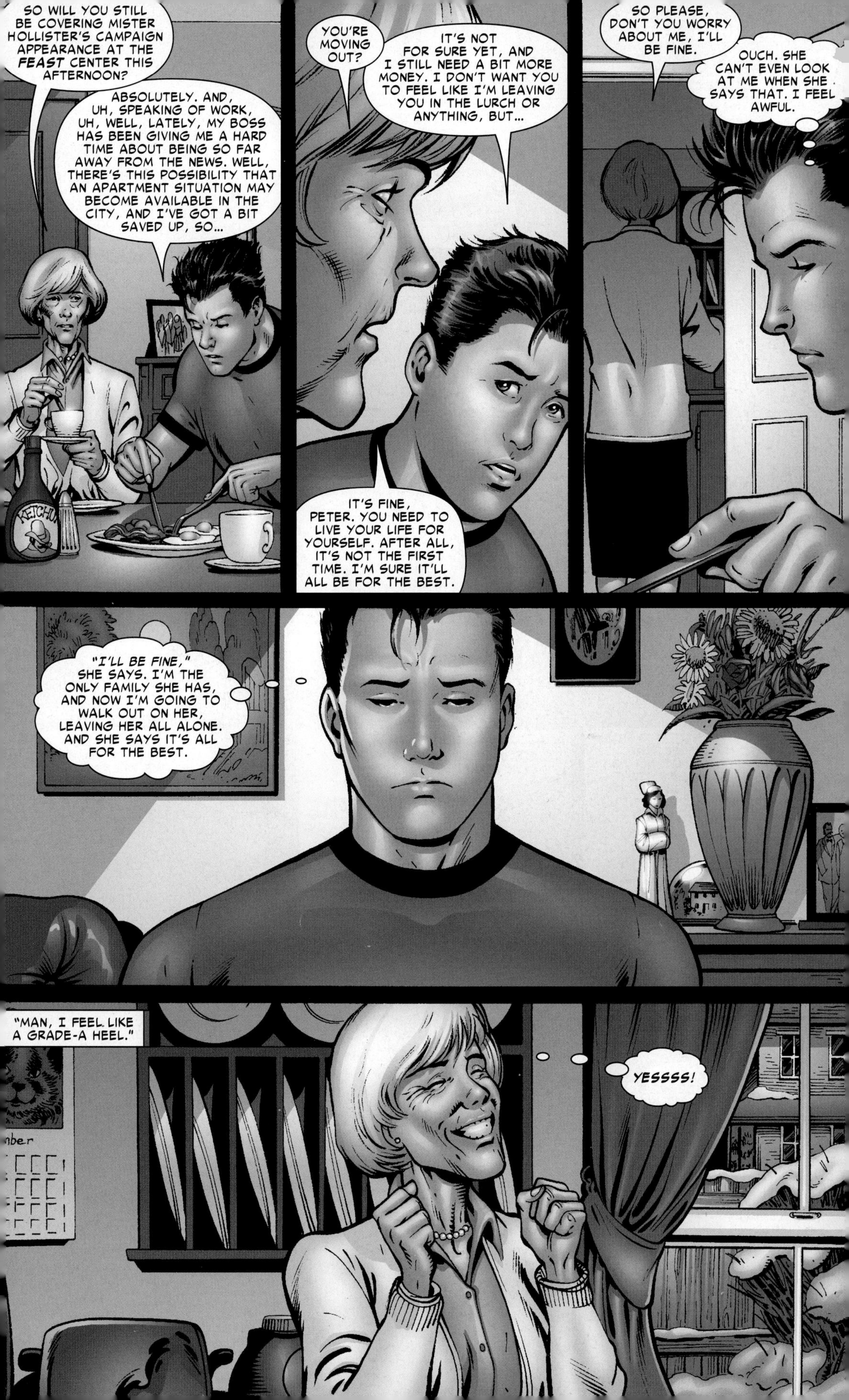
SO WILL YOU STILL BE COVERING MISTER HOLLISTER'S CAMPAIGN APPEARANCE AT THE FEAST CENTER THIS AFTERNOON?
ABSOLUTELY. AND, UH, SPEAKING OF WORK, UH, WELL, LATELY, MY BOSS HAS BEEN GIVING ME A HARD TIME ABOUT BEING SO FAR AWAY FROM THE NEWS. WELL, THERE'S THIS POSSIBILITY THAT AN APARTMENT SITUATION MAY BECOME AVAILABLE IN THE CITY, AND I'VE GOT A BIT SAVED UP, SO...
YOU'RE MOVING OUT?
IT'S NOT FOR SURE YET, AND I STILL NEED A BIT MORE MONEY. I DON'T WANT YOU TO FEEL LIKE I'M LEAVING YOU IN THE LURCH OR ANYTHING, BUT...
IT'S FINE, PETER. YOU NEED TO LIVE YOUR LIFE FOR YOURSELF. AFTER ALL, IT'S NOT THE FIRST TIME. I'M SURE IT'LL ALL BE FOR THE BEST.
SO PLEASE, DON'T YOU WORRY ABOUT ME, I'LL BE FINE.
OUCH. SHE CAN'T EVEN LOOK AT ME WHEN SHE SAYS THAT. I FEEL AWFUL.
"I'LL BE FINE," SHE SAYS. I'M THE ONLY FAMILY SHE HAS, AND NOW I'M GOING TO WALK OUT ON HER, LEAVING HER ALL ALONE. AND SHE SAYS IT'S ALL FOR THE BEST.
"MAN, I FEEL LIKE A GRADE-A HEEL."
YESSSS!

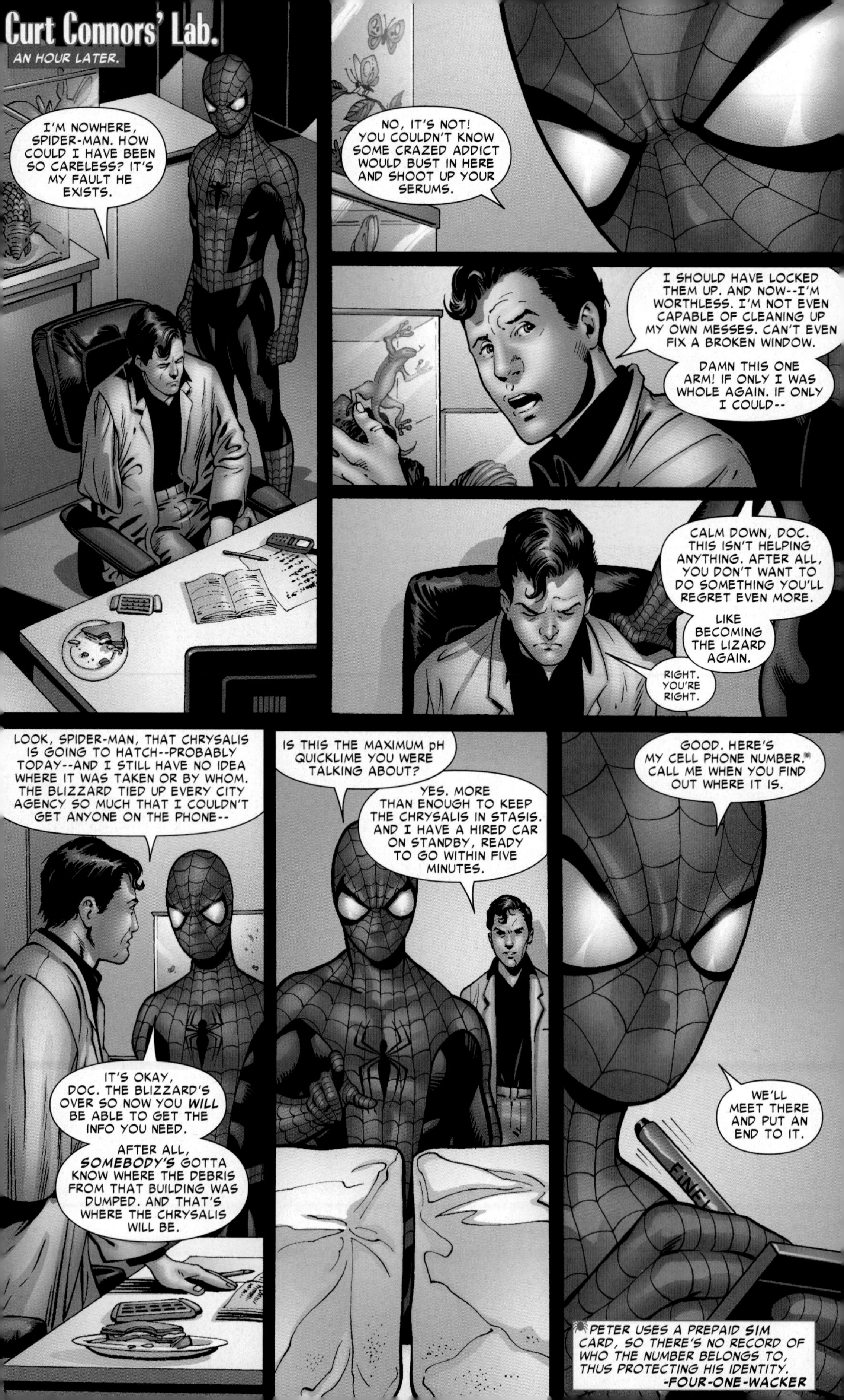
Curt Connors' Lab.
AN HOUR LATER.
I'M NOWHERE, SPIDER-MAN. HOW COULD I HAVE BEEN SO CARELESS? IT'S MY FAULT HE EXISTS.
NO, IT'S NOT! YOU COULDN'T KNOW SOME CRAZED ADDICT WOULD BUST IN HERE AND SHOOT UP YOUR SERUMS.
I SHOULD HAVE LOCKED THEM UP. AND NOW--I'M WORTHLESS. I'M NOT EVEN CAPABLE OF CLEANING UP MY OWN MESSES. CAN'T EVEN FIX A BROKEN WINDOW.
DAMN THIS ONE ARM! IF ONLY I WAS WHOLE AGAIN. IF ONLY I COULD--
CALM DOWN, DOC. THIS ISN'T HELPING ANYTHING. AFTER ALL, YOU DON'T WANT TO DO SOMETHING YOU'LL REGRET EVEN MORE.
LIKE BECOMING THE LIZARD AGAIN.
RIGHT. YOU'RE RIGHT.
LOOK, SPIDER-MAN, THAT CHRYSALIS IS GOING TO HATCH--PROBABLY TODAY--AND I STILL HAVE NO IDEA WHERE IT WAS TAKEN OR BY WHOM. THE BLIZZARD TIED UP EVERY CITY AGENCY SO MUCH THAT I COULDN'T GET ANYONE ON THE PHONE--
IT'S OKAY, DOC. THE BLIZZARD'S OVER SO NOW YOU *WILL* BE ABLE TO GET THE INFO YOU NEED.
AFTER ALL, *SOMEBODY'S* GOTTA KNOW WHERE THE DEBRIS FROM THAT BUILDING WAS DUMPED. AND THAT'S WHERE THE CHRYSALIS WILL BE.
IS THIS THE MAXIMUM pH QUICKLIME YOU WERE TALKING ABOUT?
YES. MORE THAN ENOUGH TO KEEP THE CHRYSALIS IN STASIS. AND I HAVE A HIRED CAR ON STANDBY, READY TO GO WITHIN FIVE MINUTES.
GOOD. HERE'S MY CELL PHONE NUMBER.* CALL ME WHEN YOU FIND OUT WHERE IT IS.
WE'LL MEET THERE AND PUT AN END TO IT.
FINE
*PETER USES A PREPAID SIM CARD, SO THERE'S NO RECORD OF WHO THE NUMBER BELONGS TO, THUS PROTECTING HIS IDENTITY. -FOUR-ONE-WACKER

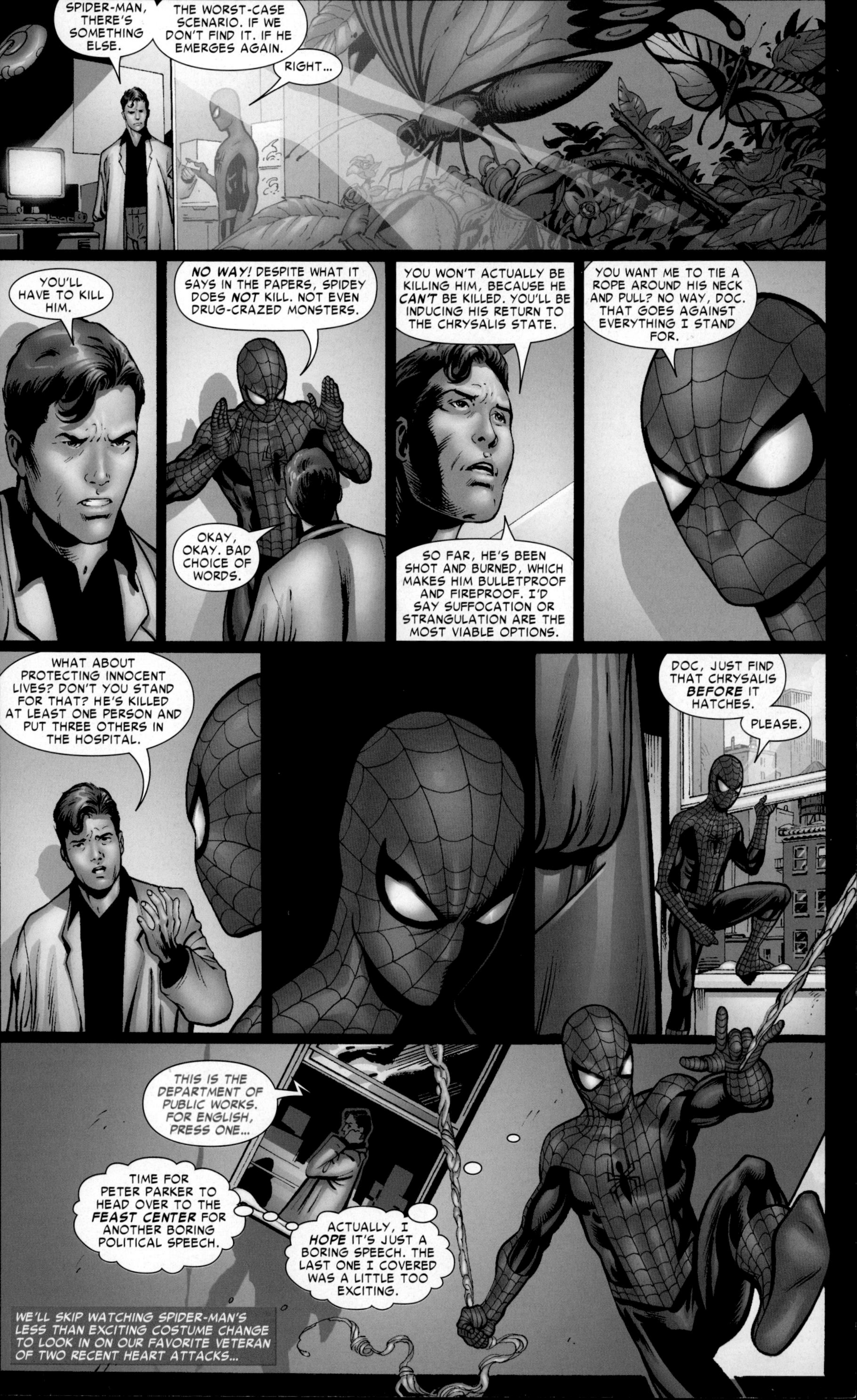
SPIDER-MAN, THERE'S SOMETHING ELSE.
THE WORST-CASE SCENARIO. IF WE DON'T FIND IT. IF HE EMERGES AGAIN.
RIGHT...
YOU'LL HAVE TO KILL HIM.
NO WAY! DESPITE WHAT IT SAYS IN THE PAPERS, SPIDEY DOES NOT KILL. NOT EVEN DRUG-CRAZED MONSTERS.
OKAY, OKAY. BAD CHOICE OF WORDS.
YOU WON'T ACTUALLY BE KILLING HIM, BECAUSE HE CAN'T BE KILLED. YOU'LL BE INDUCING HIS RETURN TO THE CHRYSALIS STATE.
SO FAR, HE'S BEEN SHOT AND BURNED, WHICH MAKES HIM BULLETPROOF AND FIREPROOF. I'D SAY SUFFOCATION OR STRANGULATION ARE THE MOST VIABLE OPTIONS.
YOU WANT ME TO TIE A ROPE AROUND HIS NECK AND PULL? NO WAY, DOC. THAT GOES AGAINST EVERYTHING I STAND FOR.
WHAT ABOUT PROTECTING INNOCENT LIVES? DON'T YOU STAND FOR THAT? HE'S KILLED AT LEAST ONE PERSON AND PUT THREE OTHERS IN THE HOSPITAL.
DOC, JUST FIND THAT CHRYSALIS BEFORE IT HATCHES.
PLEASE.
THIS IS THE DEPARTMENT OF PUBLIC WORKS. FOR ENGLISH, PRESS ONE...
TIME FOR PETER PARKER TO HEAD OVER TO THE FEAST CENTER FOR ANOTHER BORING POLITICAL SPEECH.
ACTUALLY, I HOPE IT'S JUST A BORING SPEECH. THE LAST ONE I COVERED WAS A LITTLE TOO EXCITING.
WE'LL SKIP WATCHING SPIDER-MAN'S LESS THAN EXCITING COSTUME CHANGE TO LOOK IN ON OUR FAVORITE VETERAN OF TWO RECENT HEART ATTACKS...

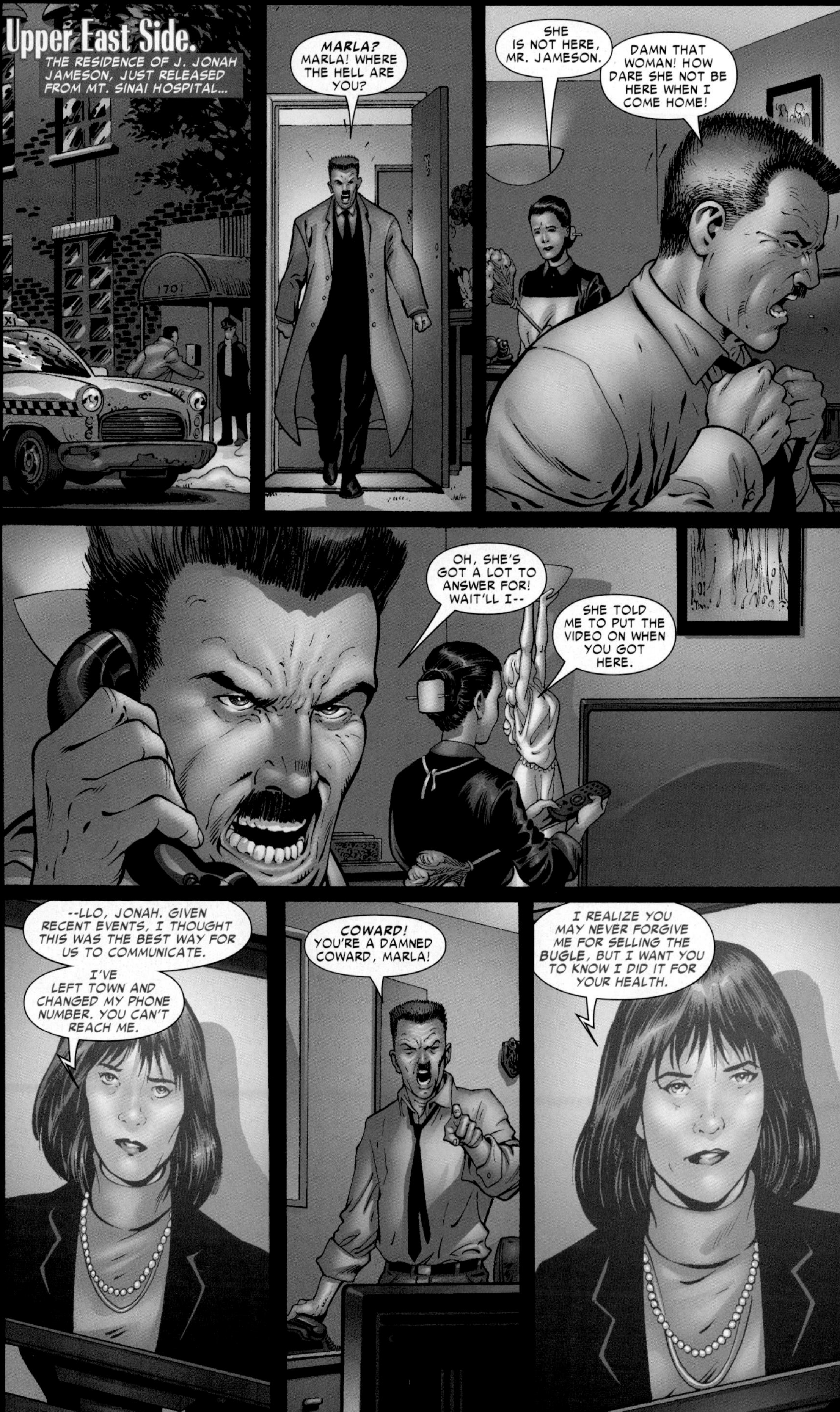
Upper East Side.
THE RESIDENCE OF J. JONAH JAMESON, JUST RELEASED FROM MT. SINAI HOSPITAL...
1701
MARLA? MARLA! WHERE THE HELL ARE YOU?
SHE IS NOT HERE, MR. JAMESON.
DAMN THAT WOMAN! HOW DARE SHE NOT BE HERE WHEN I COME HOME!
OH, SHE'S GOT A LOT TO ANSWER FOR! WAIT'LL I--
SHE TOLD ME TO PUT THE VIDEO ON WHEN YOU GOT HERE.
--LLO, JONAH. GIVEN RECENT EVENTS, I THOUGHT THIS WAS THE BEST WAY FOR US TO COMMUNICATE.
I'VE LEFT TOWN AND CHANGED MY PHONE NUMBER. YOU CAN'T REACH ME.
COWARD! YOU'RE A DAMNED COWARD, MARLA!
I REALIZE YOU MAY NEVER FORGIVE ME FOR SELLING THE BUGLE, BUT I WANT YOU TO KNOW I DID IT FOR YOUR HEALTH.

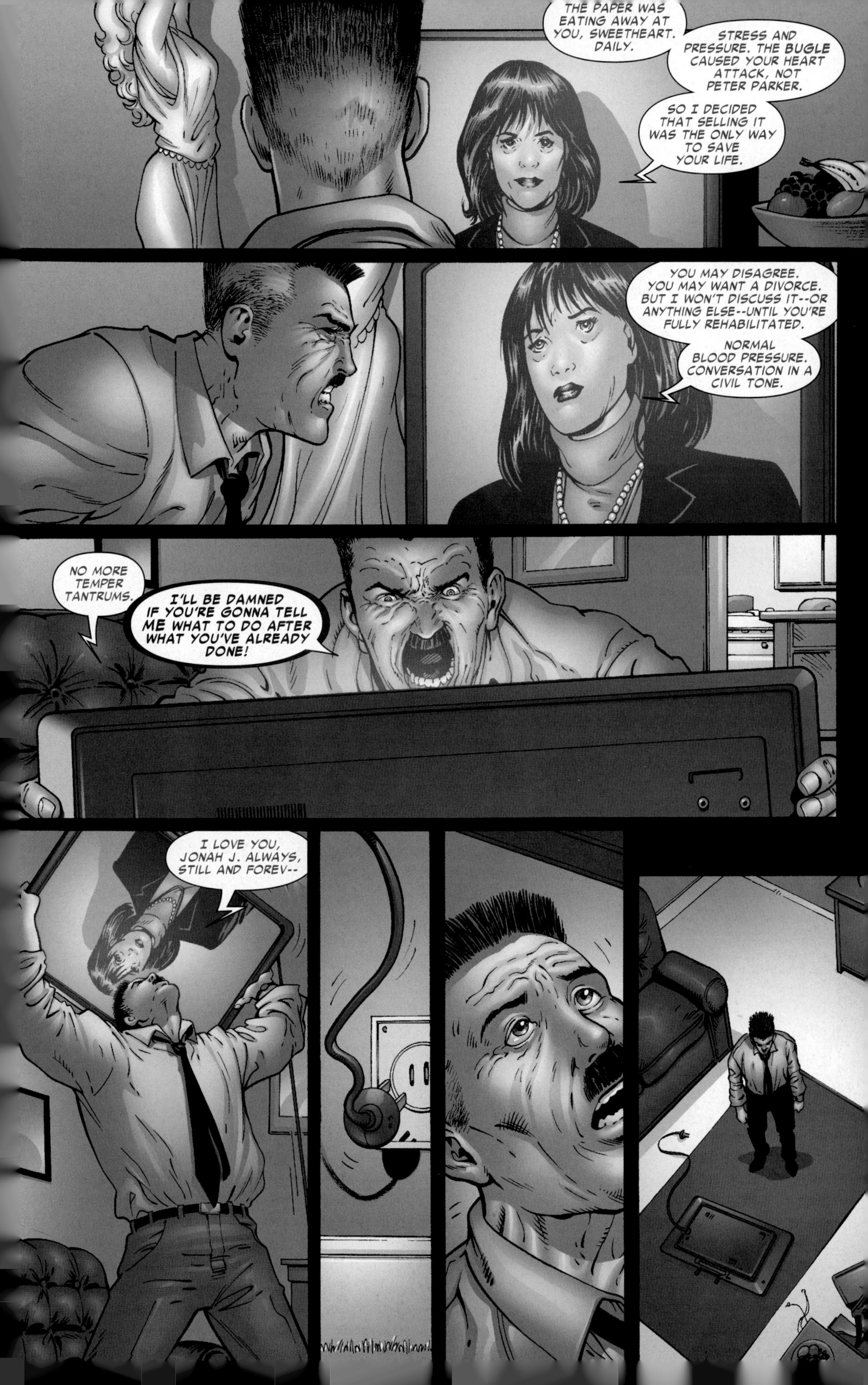
THE PAPER WAS EATING AWAY AT YOU, SWEETHEART. DAILY.
STRESS AND PRESSURE. THE BUGLE CAUSED YOUR HEART ATTACK, NOT PETER PARKER.
SO I DECIDED THAT SELLING IT WAS THE ONLY WAY TO SAVE YOUR LIFE.
YOU MAY DISAGREE. YOU MAY WANT A DIVORCE. BUT I WON'T DISCUSS IT--OR ANYTHING ELSE--UNTIL YOU'RE FULLY REHABILITATED.
NORMAL BLOOD PRESSURE. CONVERSATION IN A CIVIL TONE.
NO MORE TEMPER TANTRUMS.
I'LL BE DAMNED IF YOU'RE GONNA TELL ME WHAT TO DO AFTER WHAT YOU'VE ALREADY DONE!
I LOVE YOU, JONAH J. ALWAYS, STILL AND FOREV--

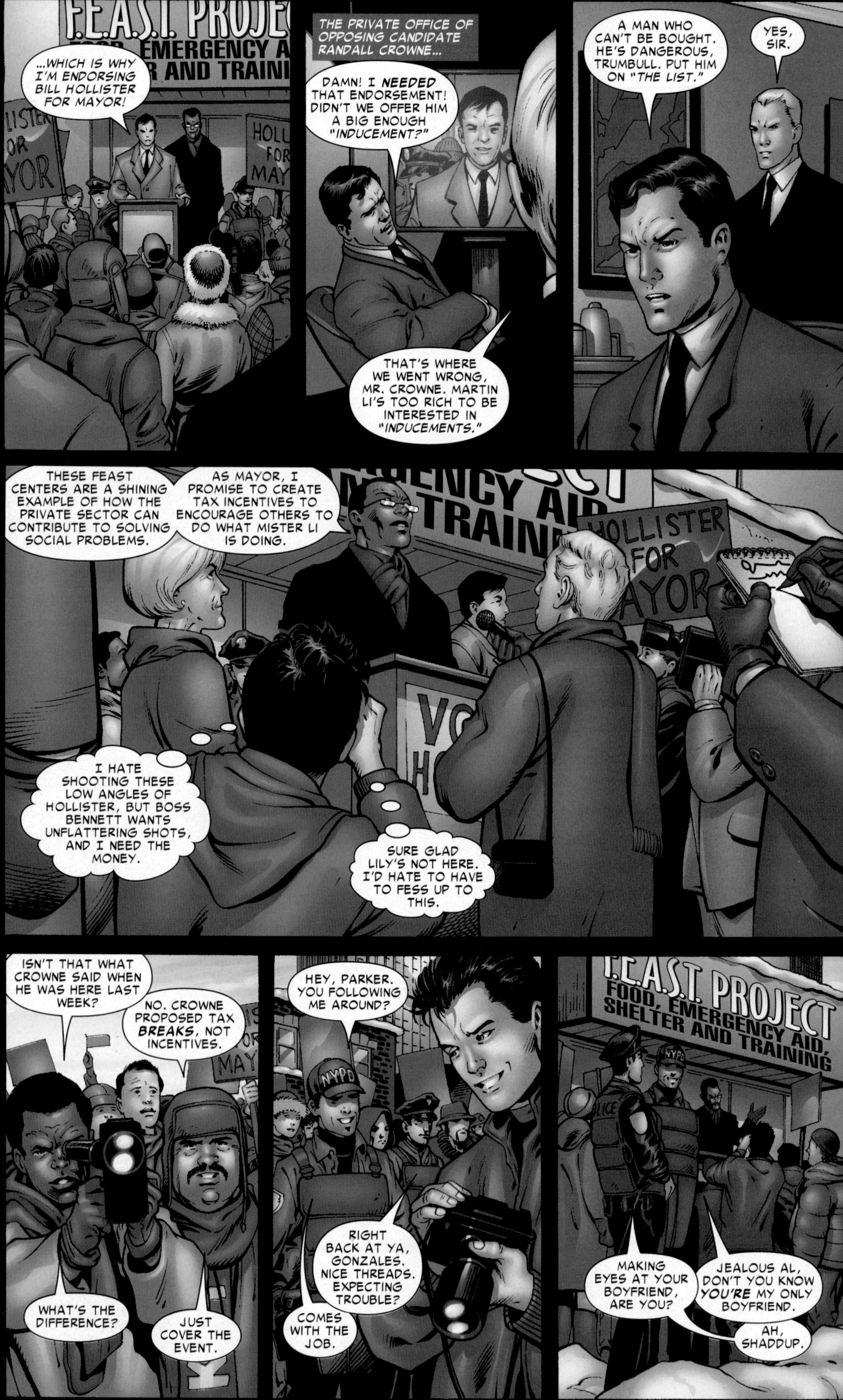
F.E.A.S.T. PROJEC
FOOD, EMERGENCY A
R AND TRAINI
...WHICH IS WHY I'M ENDORSING BILL HOLLISTER FOR MAYOR!
THE PRIVATE OFFICE OF OPPOSING CANDIDATE RANDALL CROWNE...
DAMN! I NEEDED THAT ENDORSEMENT! DIDN'T WE OFFER HIM A BIG ENOUGH "INDUCEMENT?"
THAT'S WHERE WE WENT WRONG, MR. CROWNE. MARTIN LI'S TOO RICH TO BE INTERESTED IN "INDUCEMENTS."
A MAN WHO CAN'T BE BOUGHT. HE'S DANGEROUS, TRUMBULL. PUT HIM ON "THE LIST."
YES, SIR.
THESE FEAST CENTERS ARE A SHINING EXAMPLE OF HOW THE PRIVATE SECTOR CAN CONTRIBUTE TO SOLVING SOCIAL PROBLEMS.
AS MAYOR, I PROMISE TO CREATE TAX INCENTIVES TO ENCOURAGE OTHERS TO DO WHAT MISTER LI IS DOING.
HOLLISTER FOR MAYOR
I HATE SHOOTING THESE LOW ANGLES OF HOLLISTER, BUT BOSS BENNETT WANTS UNFLATTERING SHOTS, AND I NEED THE MONEY.
SURE GLAD LILY'S NOT HERE. I'D HATE TO HAVE TO FESS UP TO THIS.
ISN'T THAT WHAT CROWNE SAID WHEN HE WAS HERE LAST WEEK?
NO. CROWNE PROPOSED TAX BREAKS, NOT INCENTIVES.
WHAT'S THE DIFFERENCE?
JUST COVER THE EVENT.
HEY, PARKER. YOU FOLLOWING ME AROUND?
RIGHT BACK AT YA, GONZALES. NICE THREADS. EXPECTING TROUBLE?
COMES WITH THE JOB.
NYPD
F.E.A.S.T. PROJECT
FOOD, EMERGENCY AID, SHELTER AND TRAINING
MAKING EYES AT YOUR BOYFRIEND, ARE YOU?
JEALOUS AL, DON'T YOU KNOW YOU'RE MY ONLY BOYFRIEND.
AH, SHADDUP.

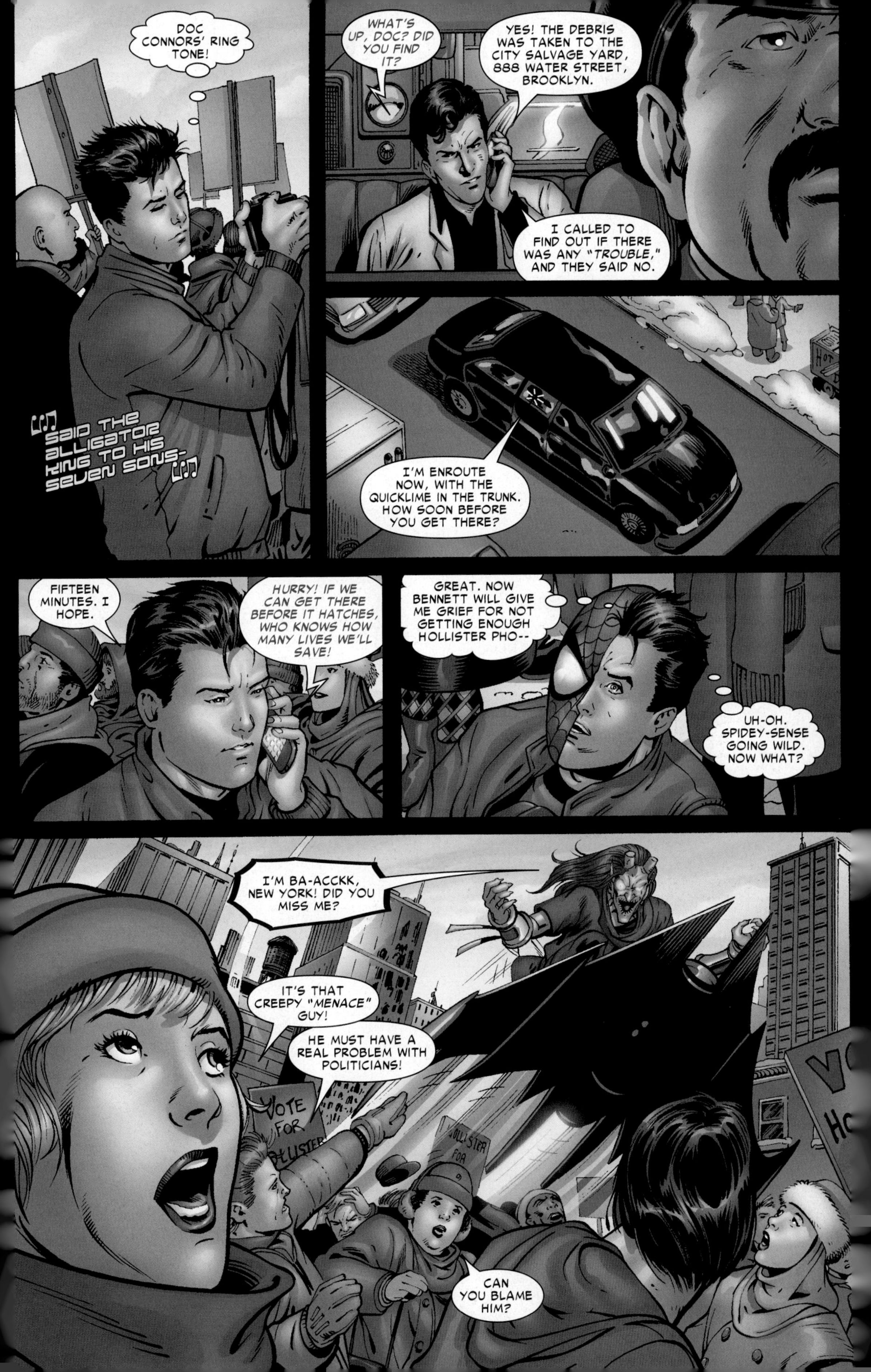

DOC CONNORS' RING TONE!
SAID THE ALLIGATOR KING TO HIS SEVEN SONS-
WHAT'S UP, DOC? DID YOU FIND IT?
YES! THE DEBRIS WAS TAKEN TO THE CITY SALVAGE YARD, 888 WATER STREET, BROOKLYN.
I CALLED TO FIND OUT IF THERE WAS ANY "TROUBLE," AND THEY SAID NO.
I'M ENROUTE NOW, WITH THE QUICKLIME IN THE TRUNK. HOW SOON BEFORE YOU GET THERE?
FIFTEEN MINUTES. I HOPE.
HURRY! IF WE CAN GET THERE BEFORE IT HATCHES, WHO KNOWS HOW MANY LIVES WE'LL SAVE!
GREAT. NOW BENNETT WILL GIVE ME GRIEF FOR NOT GETTING ENOUGH HOLLISTER PHO--
UH-OH. SPIDEY-SENSE GOING WILD. NOW WHAT?
I'M BA-ACCKK, NEW YORK! DID YOU MISS ME?
IT'S THAT CREEPY "MENACE" GUY!
HE MUST HAVE A REAL PROBLEM WITH POLITICIANS!
VOTE FOR
CAN YOU BLAME HIM?

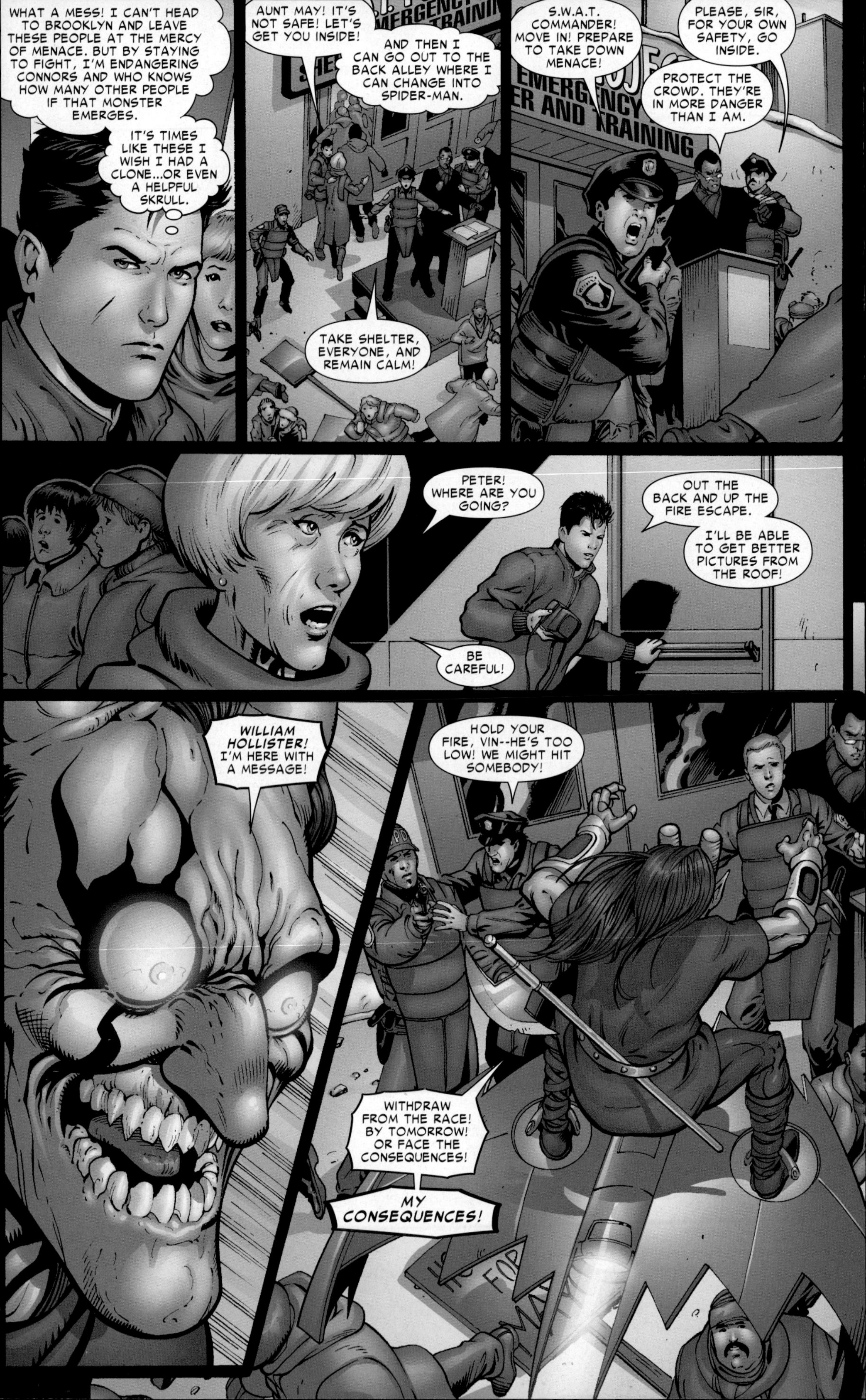
WHAT A MESS! I CAN'T HEAD TO BROOKLYN AND LEAVE THESE PEOPLE AT THE MERCY OF MENACE. BUT BY STAYING TO FIGHT, I'M ENDANGERING CONNORS AND WHO KNOWS HOW MANY OTHER PEOPLE IF THAT MONSTER EMERGES.
IT'S TIMES LIKE THESE I WISH I HAD A CLONE...OR EVEN A HELPFUL SKRULL.
AUNT MAY! IT'S NOT SAFE! LET'S GET YOU INSIDE!
AND THEN I CAN GO OUT TO THE BACK ALLEY WHERE I CAN CHANGE INTO SPIDER-MAN.
TAKE SHELTER, EVERYONE, AND REMAIN CALM!
S.W.A.T. COMMANDER! MOVE IN! PREPARE TO TAKE DOWN MENACE!
PLEASE, SIR, FOR YOUR OWN SAFETY, GO INSIDE.
PROTECT THE CROWD. THEY'RE IN MORE DANGER THAN I AM.
EMERGENCY ER AND TRAINING
PETER! WHERE ARE YOU GOING?
OUT THE BACK AND UP THE FIRE ESCAPE.
I'LL BE ABLE TO GET BETTER PICTURES FROM THE ROOF!
BE CAREFUL!
WILLIAM HOLLISTER! I'M HERE WITH A MESSAGE!
HOLD YOUR FIRE, VIN--HE'S TOO LOW! WE MIGHT HIT SOMEBODY!
WITHDRAW FROM THE RACE! BY TOMORROW! OR FACE THE CONSEQUENCES!
MY CONSEQUENCES!

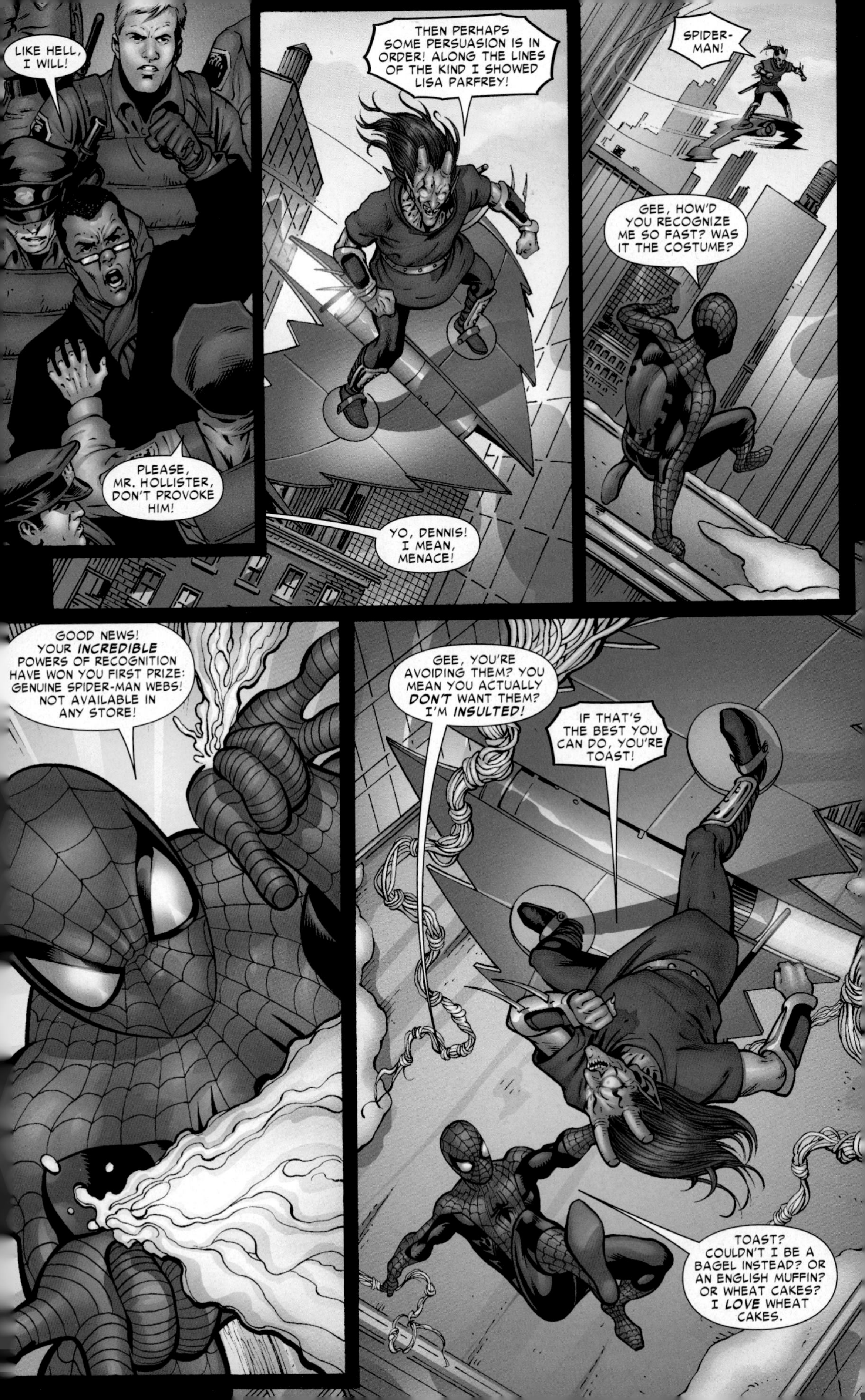
LIKE HELL, I WILL!
PLEASE, MR. HOLLISTER, DON'T PROVOKE HIM!
THEN PERHAPS SOME PERSUASION IS IN ORDER! ALONG THE LINES OF THE KIND I SHOWED LISA PARFREY!
YO, DENNIS! I MEAN, MENACE!
SPIDER-MAN!
GEE, HOW'D YOU RECOGNIZE ME SO FAST? WAS IT THE COSTUME?
GOOD NEWS! YOUR INCREDIBLE POWERS OF RECOGNITION HAVE WON YOU FIRST PRIZE: GENUINE SPIDER-MAN WEBS! NOT AVAILABLE IN ANY STORE!
GEE, YOU'RE AVOIDING THEM? YOU MEAN YOU ACTUALLY DON'T WANT THEM? I'M INSULTED!
IF THAT'S THE BEST YOU CAN DO, YOU'RE TOAST!
TOAST? COULDN'T I BE A BAGEL INSTEAD? OR AN ENGLISH MUFFIN? OR WHEAT CAKES? I LOVE WHEAT CAKES.

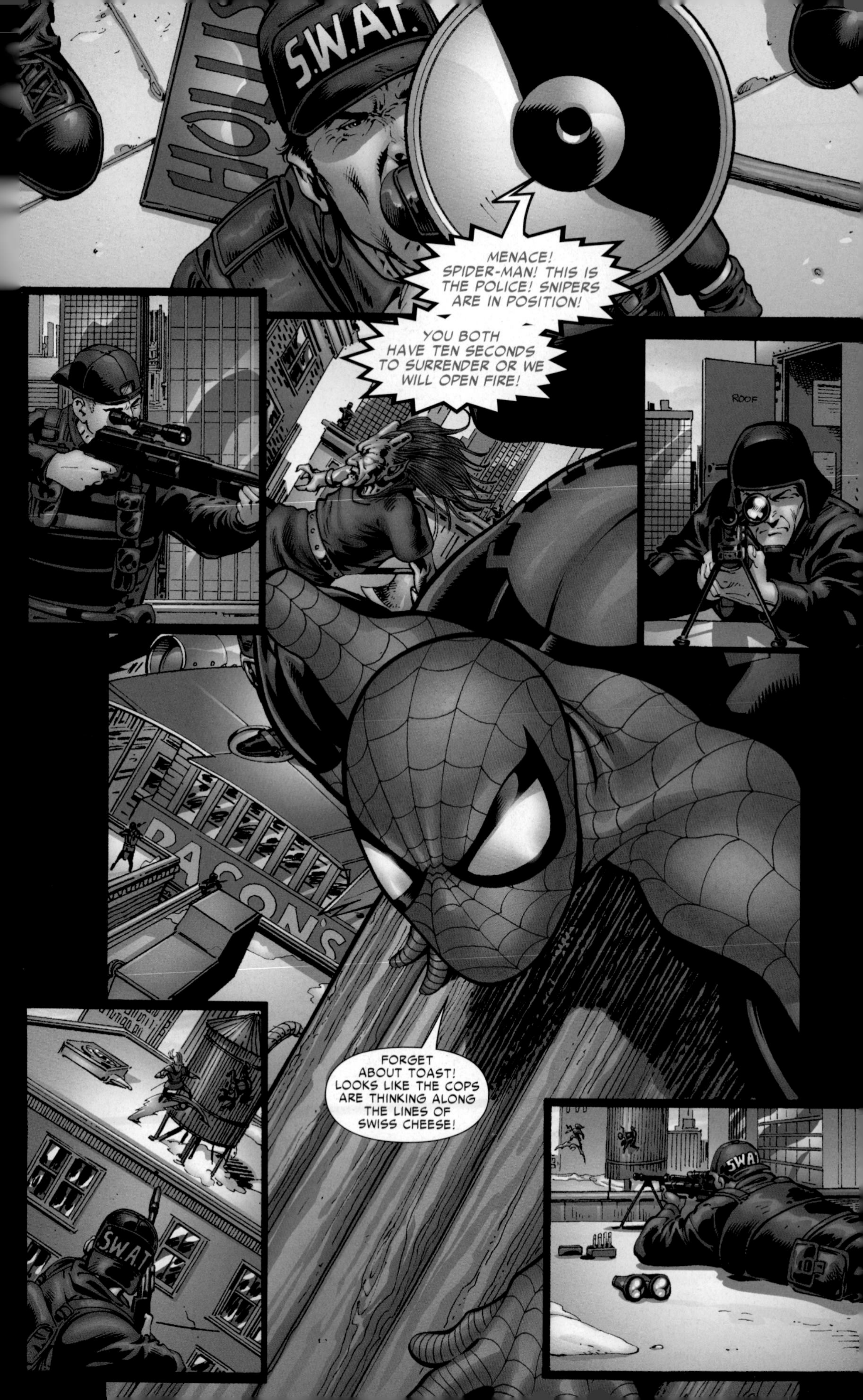
MENACE! SPIDER-MAN! THIS IS THE POLICE! SNIPERS ARE IN POSITION!
YOU BOTH HAVE TEN SECONDS TO SURRENDER OR WE WILL OPEN FIRE!
ROOF
FORGET ABOUT TOAST! LOOKS LIKE THE COPS ARE THINKING ALONG THE LINES OF SWISS CHEESE!

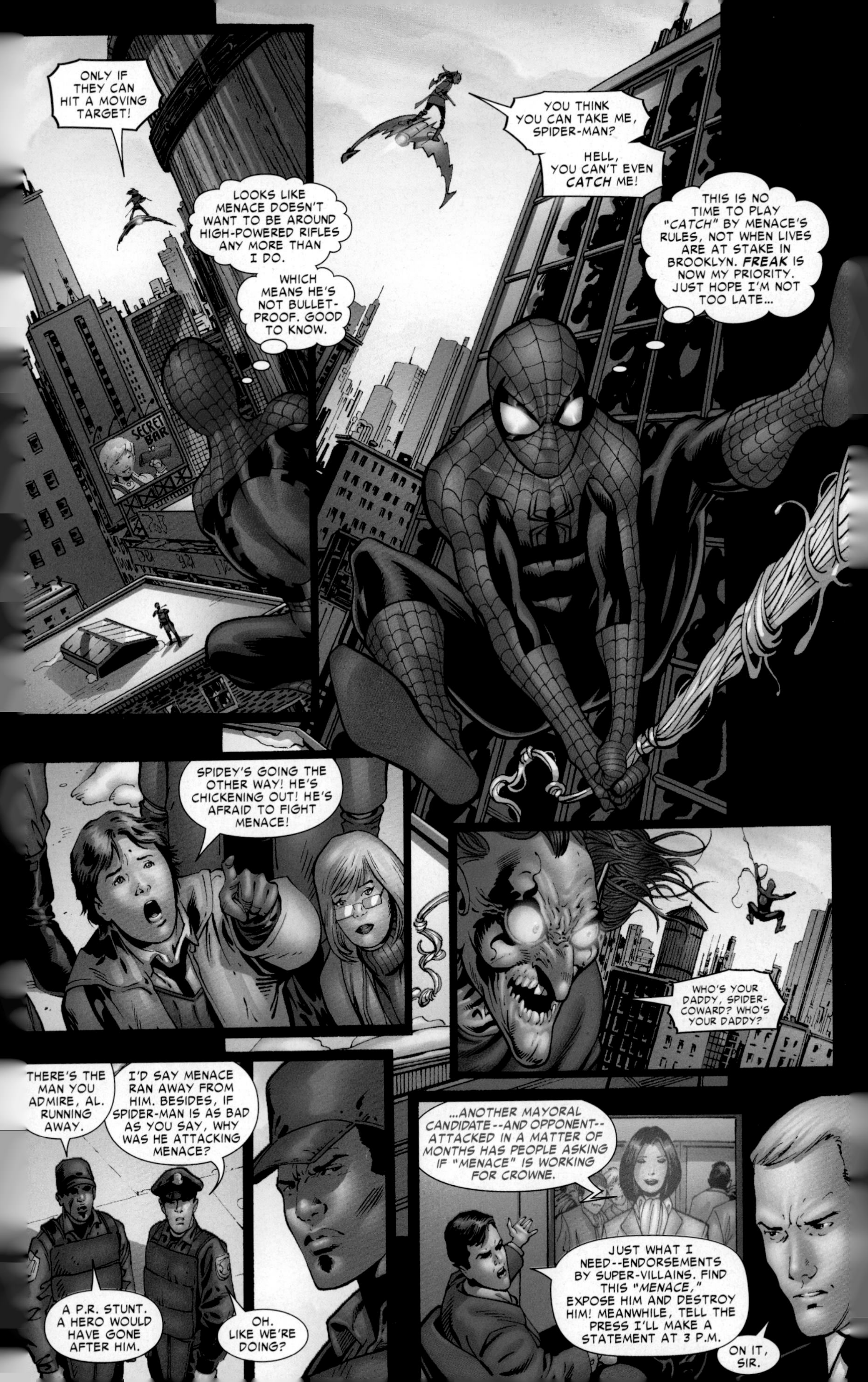
ONLY IF THEY CAN HIT A MOVING TARGET!
LOOKS LIKE MENACE DOESN'T WANT TO BE AROUND HIGH-POWERED RIFLES ANY MORE THAN I DO.
WHICH MEANS HE'S NOT BULLET-PROOF. GOOD TO KNOW.
SECRET BAR
YOU THINK YOU CAN TAKE ME, SPIDER-MAN?
HELL, YOU CAN'T EVEN *CATCH* ME!
THIS IS NO TIME TO PLAY "*CATCH*" BY MENACE'S RULES, NOT WHEN LIVES ARE AT STAKE IN BROOKLYN. ***FREAK*** IS NOW MY PRIORITY. JUST HOPE I'M NOT TOO LATE...
SPIDEY'S GOING THE OTHER WAY! HE'S CHICKENING OUT! HE'S AFRAID TO FIGHT MENACE!
WHO'S YOUR DADDY, SPIDER-COWARD? WHO'S YOUR DADDY?
THERE'S THE MAN YOU ADMIRE, AL. RUNNING AWAY.
I'D SAY MENACE RAN AWAY FROM HIM. BESIDES, IF SPIDER-MAN IS AS BAD AS YOU SAY, WHY WAS HE ATTACKING MENACE?
A P.R. STUNT. A HERO WOULD HAVE GONE AFTER HIM.
OH. LIKE WE'RE DOING?
...ANOTHER MAYORAL CANDIDATE--AND OPPONENT--ATTACKED IN A MATTER OF MONTHS HAS PEOPLE ASKING IF "MENACE" IS WORKING FOR CROWNE.
JUST WHAT I NEED--ENDORSEMENTS BY SUPER-VILLAINS. FIND THIS "*MENACE*," EXPOSE HIM AND DESTROY HIM! MEANWHILE, TELL THE PRESS I'LL MAKE A STATEMENT AT 3 P.M.
ON IT, SIR.

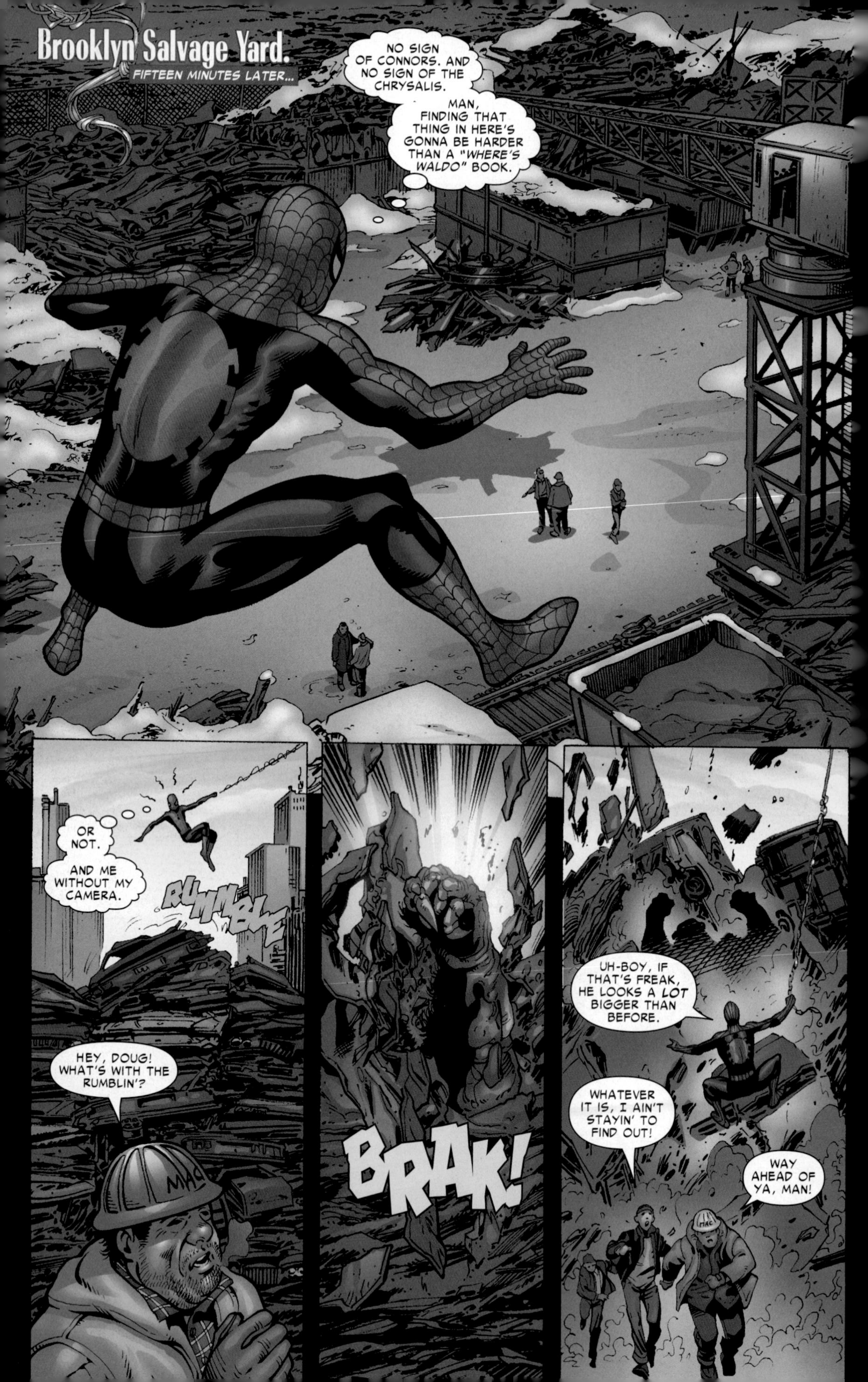
Brooklyn Salvage Yard.
FIFTEEN MINUTES LATER...
NO SIGN OF CONNORS. AND NO SIGN OF THE CHRYSALIS.
MAN, FINDING THAT THING IN HERE'S GONNA BE HARDER THAN A "WHERE'S WALDO" BOOK.
OR NOT.
AND ME WITHOUT MY CAMERA.
RUMMBLE
HEY, DOUG! WHAT'S WITH THE RUMBLIN'?
MAC
BRAK!
UH-BOY, IF THAT'S FREAK, HE LOOKS A LOT BIGGER THAN BEFORE.
WHATEVER IT IS, I AIN'T STAYIN' TO FIND OUT!
WAY AHEAD OF YA, MAN!

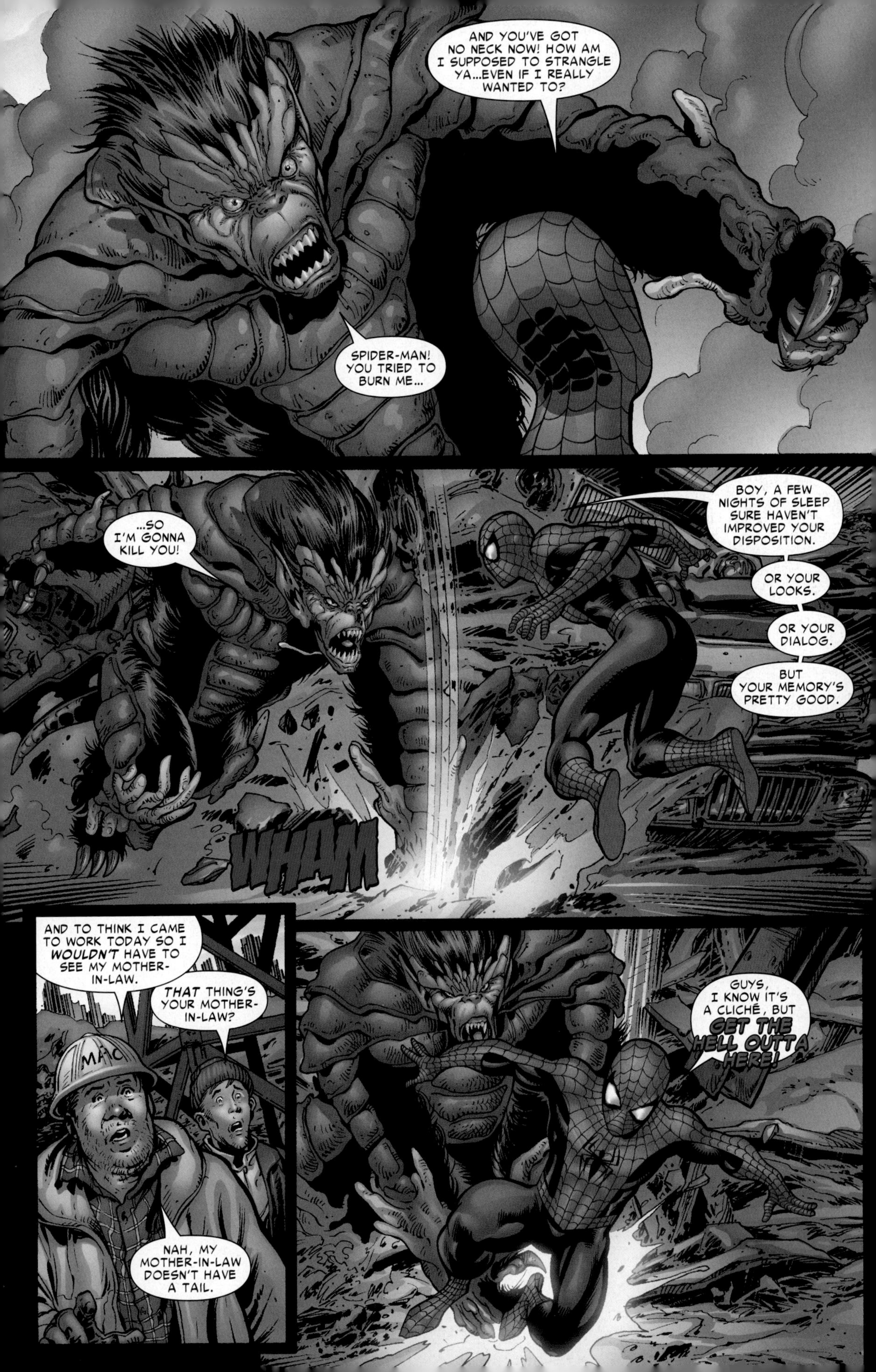
SPIDER-MAN! YOU TRIED TO BURN ME...
AND YOU'VE GOT NO NECK NOW! HOW AM I SUPPOSED TO STRANGLE YA...EVEN IF I REALLY WANTED TO?
...SO I'M GONNA KILL YOU!
BOY, A FEW NIGHTS OF SLEEP SURE HAVEN'T IMPROVED YOUR DISPOSITION.
OR YOUR LOOKS.
OR YOUR DIALOG.
BUT YOUR MEMORY'S PRETTY GOOD.
WHAM
AND TO THINK I CAME TO WORK TODAY SO I WOULDN'T HAVE TO SEE MY MOTHER-IN-LAW.
THAT THING'S YOUR MOTHER-IN-LAW?
NAH, MY MOTHER-IN-LAW DOESN'T HAVE A TAIL.
MAC
GUYS, I KNOW IT'S A CLICHÉ, BUT GET THE HELL OUTTA HERE!

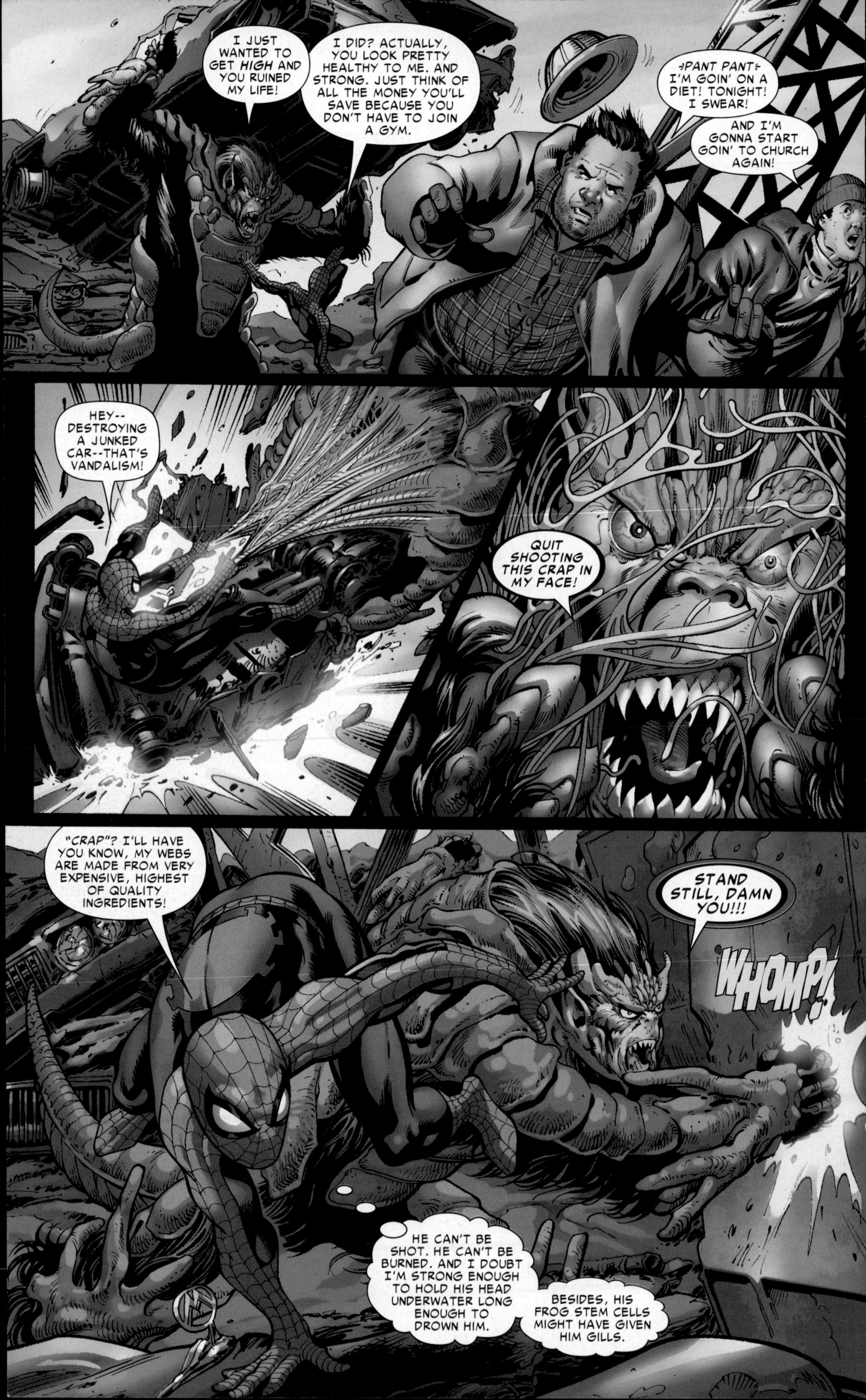

I JUST WANTED TO GET HIGH AND YOU RUINED MY LIFE!
I DID? ACTUALLY, YOU LOOK PRETTY HEALTHY TO ME. AND STRONG. JUST THINK OF ALL THE MONEY YOU'LL SAVE BECAUSE YOU DON'T HAVE TO JOIN A GYM.
≠PANT PANT≠ I'M GOIN' ON A DIET! TONIGHT! I SWEAR!
AND I'M GONNA START GOIN' TO CHURCH AGAIN!
HEY--DESTROYING A JUNKED CAR--THAT'S VANDALISM!
QUIT SHOOTING THIS CRAP IN MY FACE!
"CRAP"? I'LL HAVE YOU KNOW, MY WEBS ARE MADE FROM VERY EXPENSIVE, HIGHEST OF QUALITY INGREDIENTS!
STAND STILL, DAMN YOU!!!
WHOMP!
HE CAN'T BE SHOT. HE CAN'T BE BURNED. AND I DOUBT I'M STRONG ENOUGH TO HOLD HIS HEAD UNDERWATER LONG ENOUGH TO DROWN HIM.
BESIDES, HIS FROG STEM CELLS MIGHT HAVE GIVEN HIM GILLS.

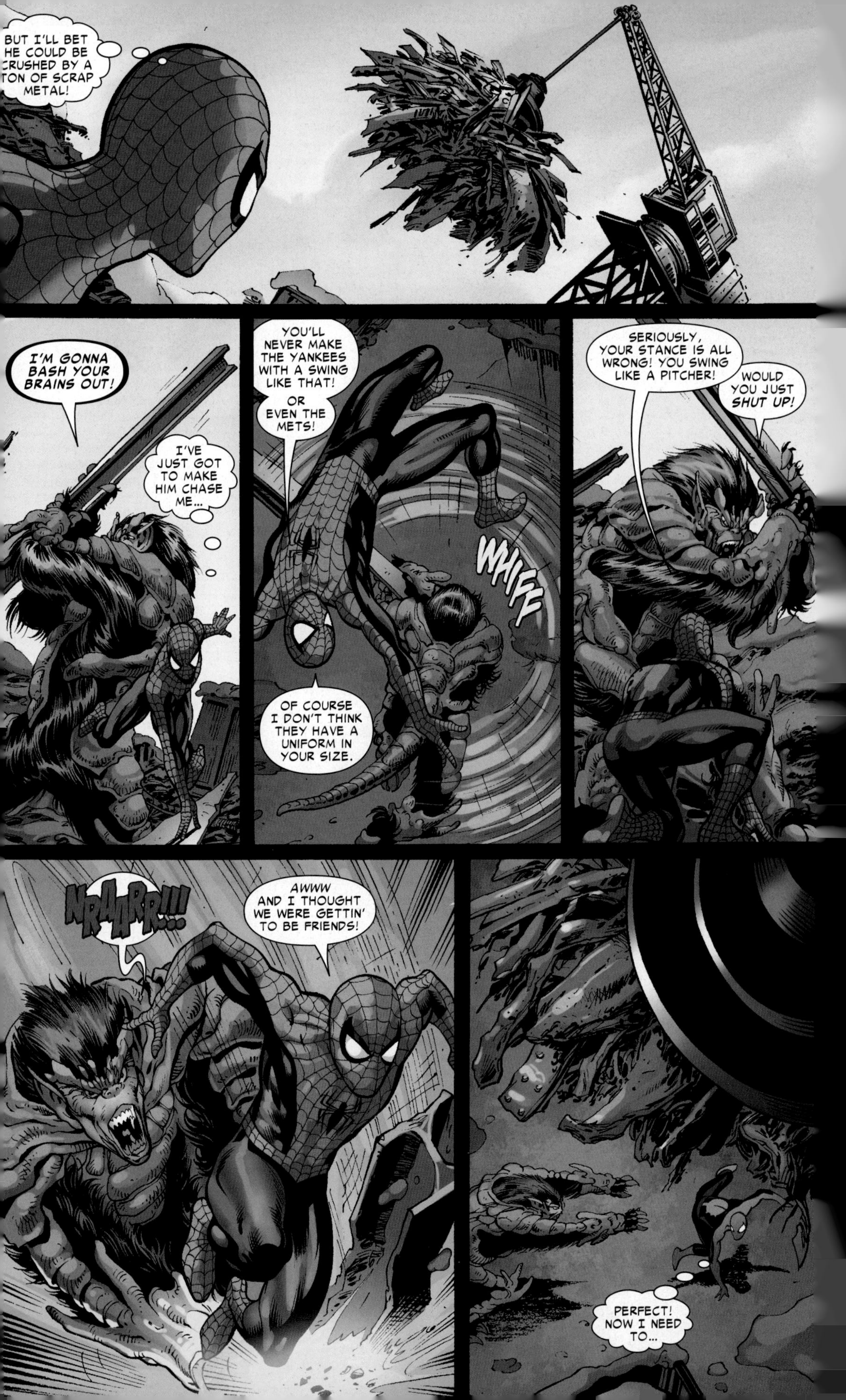

BUT I'LL BET HE COULD BE CRUSHED BY A TON OF SCRAP METAL!
I'M GONNA BASH YOUR BRAINS OUT!
I'VE JUST GOT TO MAKE HIM CHASE ME...
YOU'LL NEVER MAKE THE YANKEES WITH A SWING LIKE THAT!
OR EVEN THE METS!
WHIFF
OF COURSE I DON'T THINK THEY HAVE A UNIFORM IN YOUR SIZE.
SERIOUSLY, YOUR STANCE IS ALL WRONG! YOU SWING LIKE A PITCHER!
WOULD YOU JUST SHUT UP!
NRAARR!!!...
AWWW AND I THOUGHT WE WERE GETTIN' TO BE FRIENDS!
PERFECT! NOW I NEED TO...

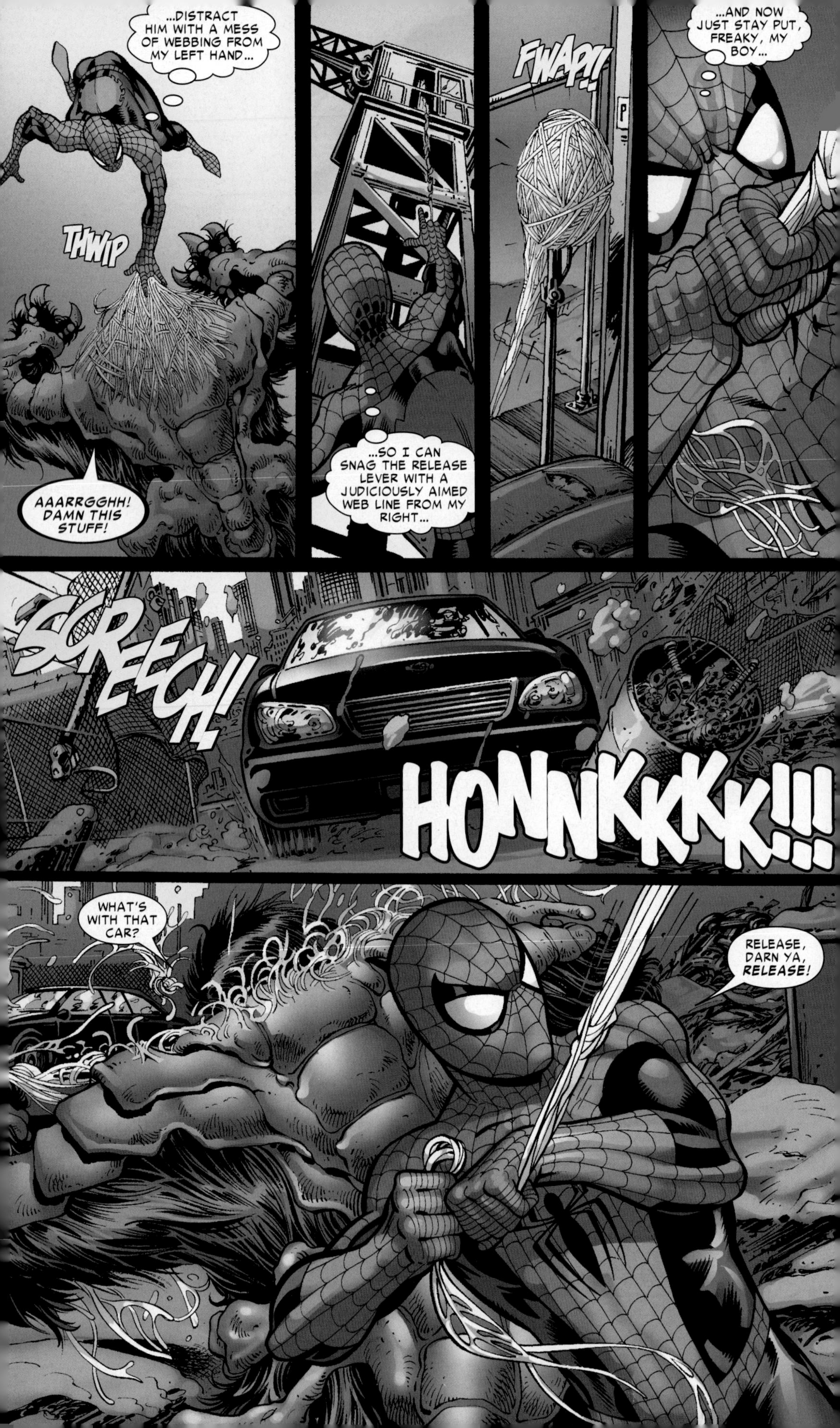
...DISTRACT HIM WITH A MESS OF WEBBING FROM MY LEFT HAND...
THWIP
AAARRGGHH! DAMN THIS STUFF!
...SO I CAN SNAG THE RELEASE LEVER WITH A JUDICIOUSLY AIMED WEB LINE FROM MY RIGHT...
FWAP!!
...AND NOW JUST STAY PUT, FREAKY, MY BOY...
SCREECH!
HONNKKKK!!!
WHAT'S WITH THAT CAR?
RELEASE, DARN YA, RELEASE!

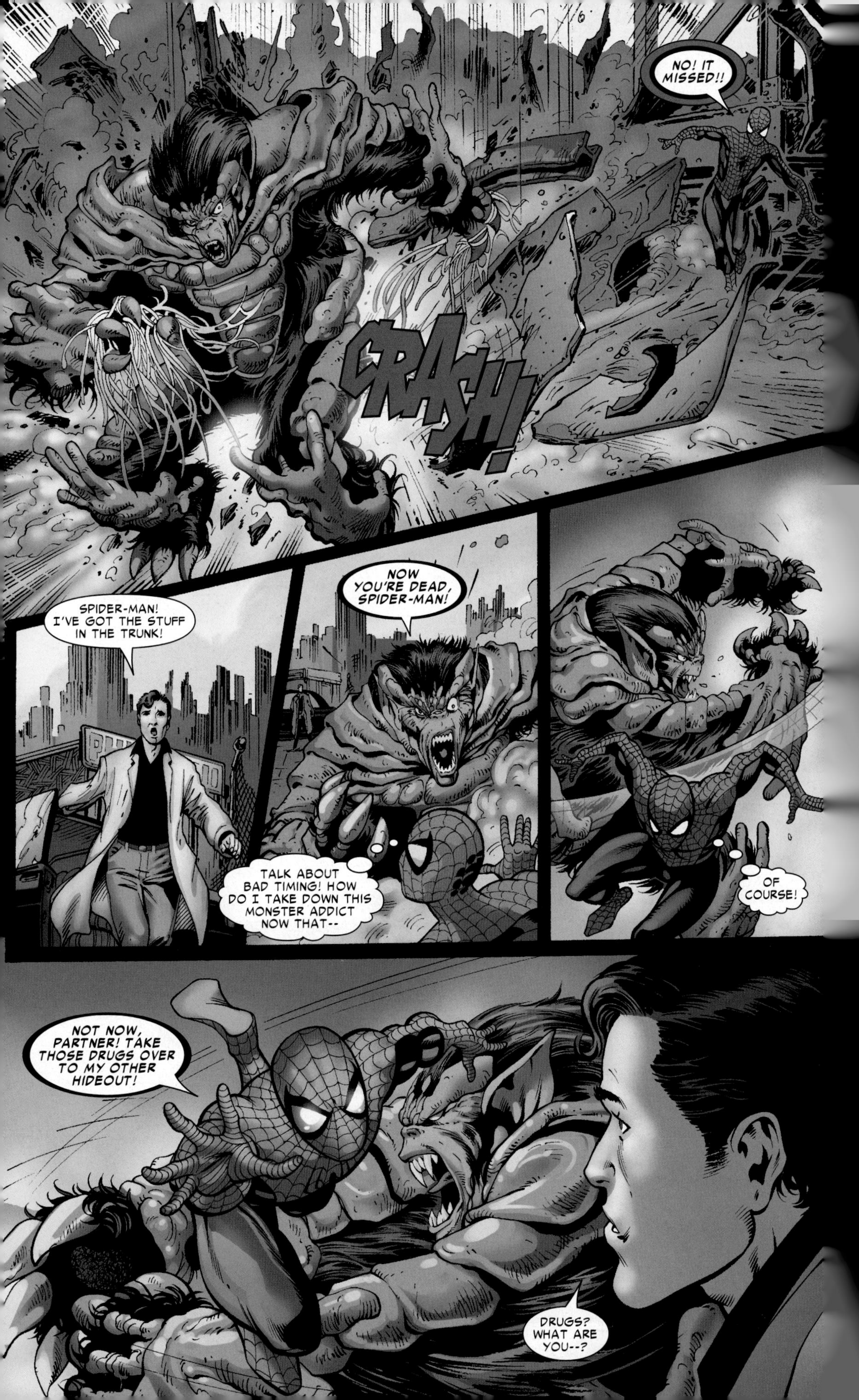
NO! IT MISSED!!
CRASH!
SPIDER-MAN! I'VE GOT THE STUFF IN THE TRUNK!
NOW YOU'RE DEAD, SPIDER-MAN!
TALK ABOUT BAD TIMING! HOW DO I TAKE DOWN THIS MONSTER ADDICT NOW THAT--
OF COURSE!
NOT NOW, PARTNER! TAKE THOSE DRUGS OVER TO MY OTHER HIDEOUT!
DRUGS? WHAT ARE YOU--?

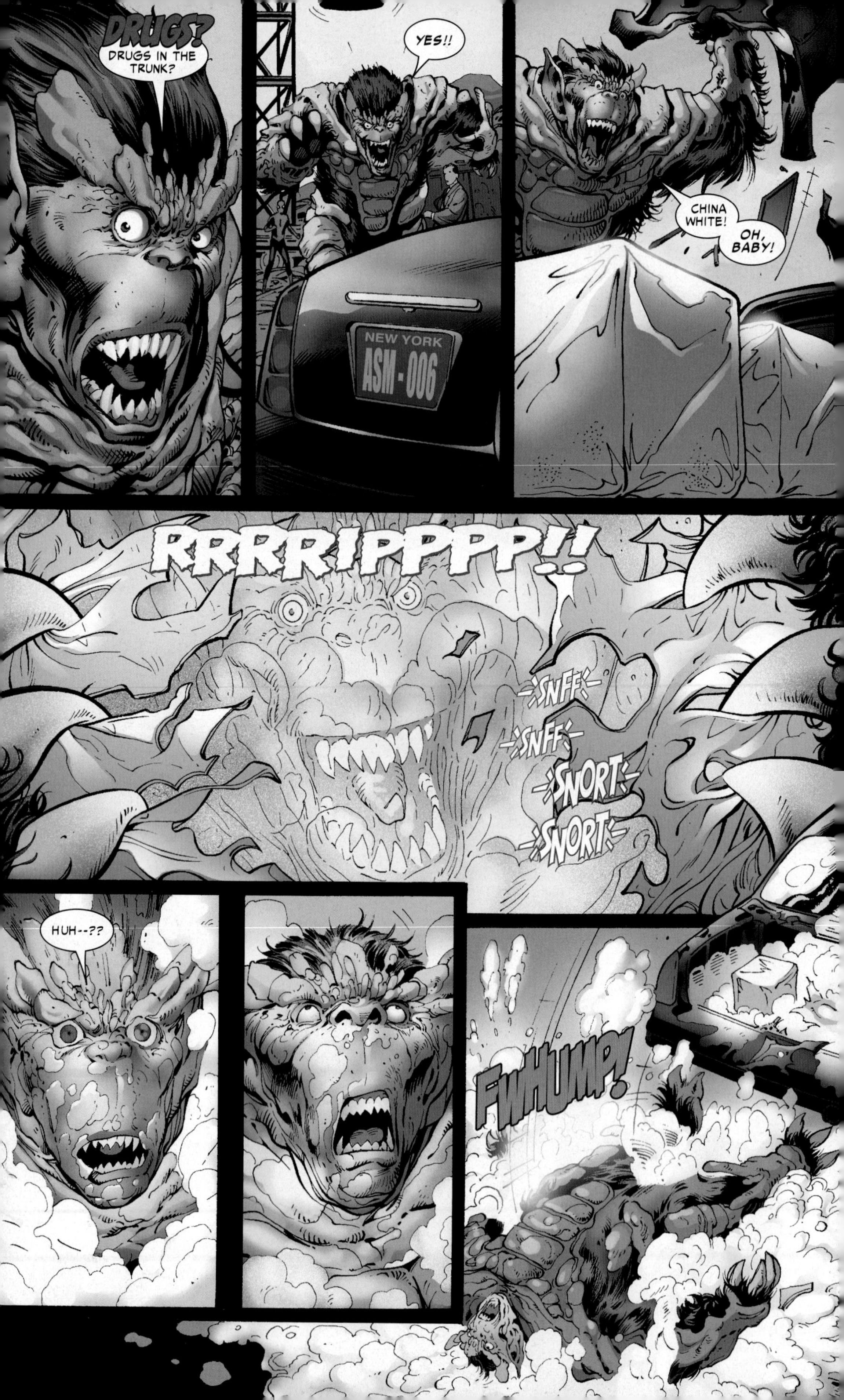
DRUGS?
DRUGS IN THE TRUNK?
YES!!
NEW YORK
ASM-006
CHINA WHITE!
OH, BABY!
RRRRIPPPPP!!
SNFF
SNFF
SNORT
SNORT
HUH--??
FWHUMP!

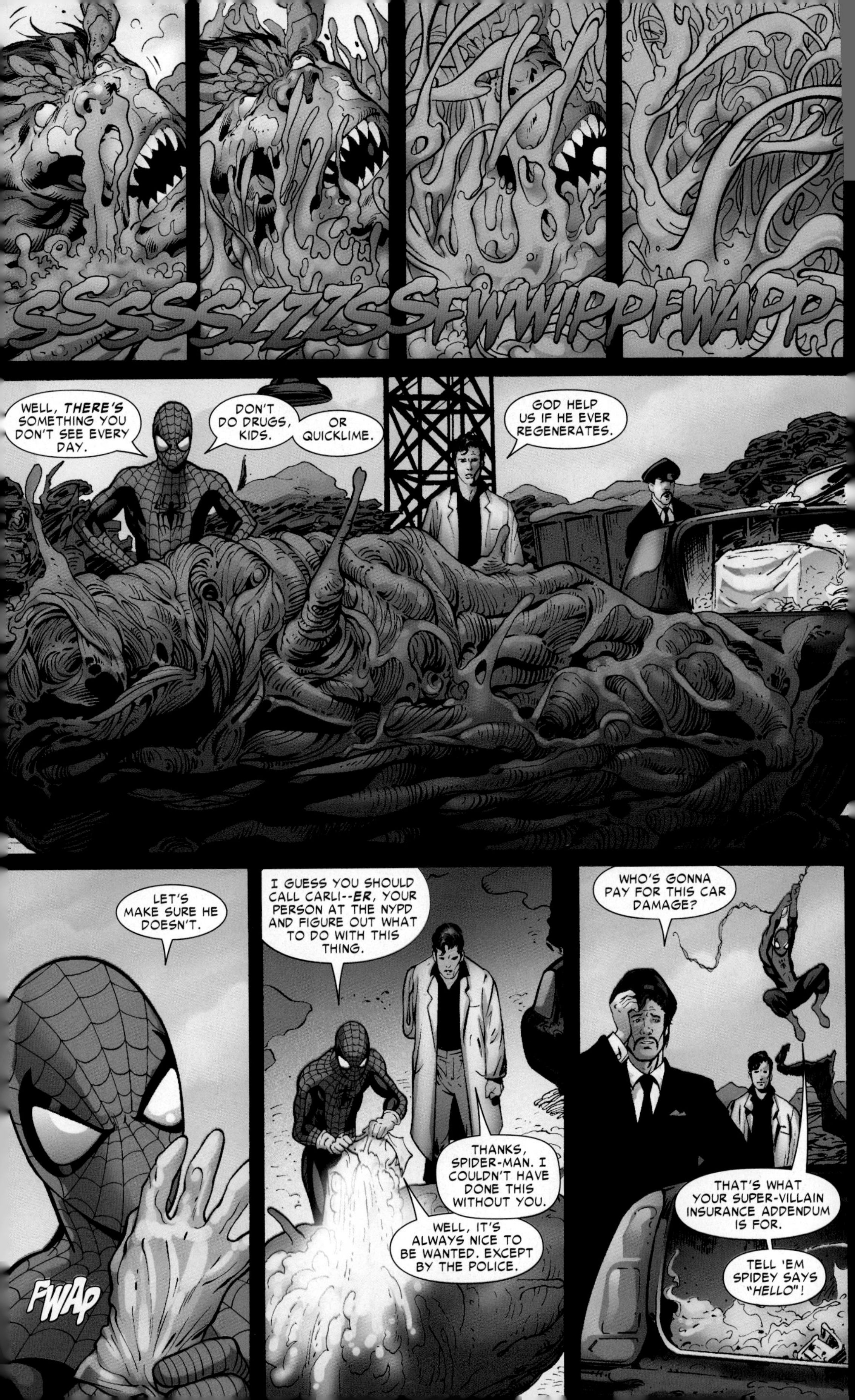

SSSSSSZZZZSSFWWIPPFWAPP
WELL, THERE'S SOMETHING YOU DON'T SEE EVERY DAY.
DON'T DO DRUGS, KIDS.
OR QUICKLIME.
GOD HELP US IF HE EVER REGENERATES.
LET'S MAKE SURE HE DOESN'T.
FWAP
I GUESS YOU SHOULD CALL CARLI--ER, YOUR PERSON AT THE NYPD AND FIGURE OUT WHAT TO DO WITH THIS THING.
THANKS, SPIDER-MAN. I COULDN'T HAVE DONE THIS WITHOUT YOU.
WELL, IT'S ALWAYS NICE TO BE WANTED. EXCEPT BY THE POLICE.
WHO'S GONNA PAY FOR THIS CAR DAMAGE?
THAT'S WHAT YOUR SUPER-VILLAIN INSURANCE ADDENDUM IS FOR.
TELL 'EM SPIDEY SAYS "HELLO"!

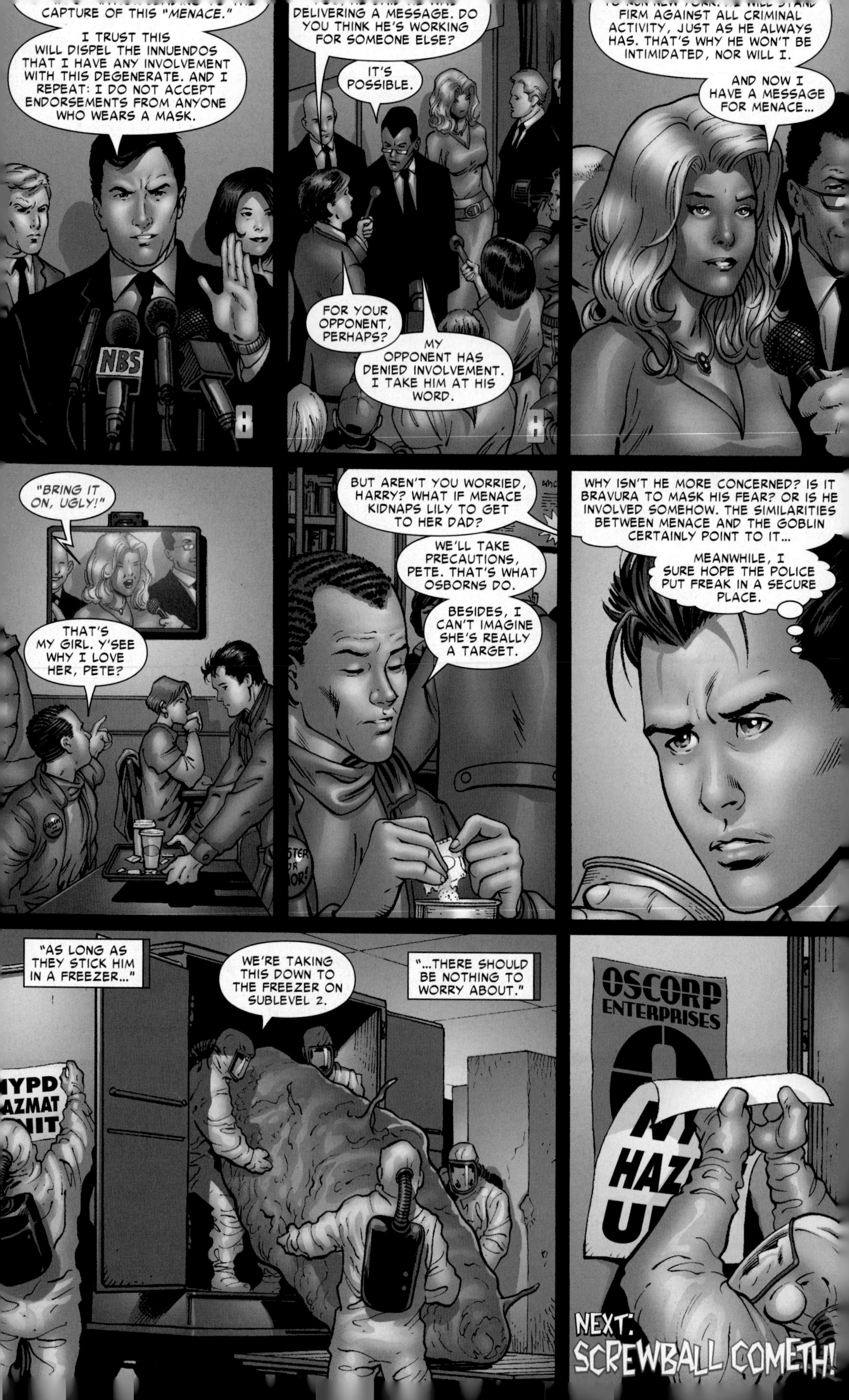

CAPTURE OF THIS "MENACE."
I TRUST THIS WILL DISPEL THE INNUENDOS THAT I HAVE ANY INVOLVEMENT WITH THIS DEGENERATE. AND I REPEAT: I DO NOT ACCEPT ENDORSEMENTS FROM ANYONE WHO WEARS A MASK.
NBS
DELIVERING A MESSAGE. DO YOU THINK HE'S WORKING FOR SOMEONE ELSE?
IT'S POSSIBLE.
FOR YOUR OPPONENT, PERHAPS?
MY OPPONENT HAS DENIED INVOLVEMENT. I TAKE HIM AT HIS WORD.
FIRM AGAINST ALL CRIMINAL ACTIVITY, JUST AS HE ALWAYS HAS. THAT'S WHY HE WON'T BE INTIMIDATED, NOR WILL I.
AND NOW I HAVE A MESSAGE FOR MENACE...
"BRING IT ON, UGLY!"
THAT'S MY GIRL. Y'SEE WHY I LOVE HER, PETE?
BUT AREN'T YOU WORRIED, HARRY? WHAT IF MENACE KIDNAPS LILY TO GET TO HER DAD?
WE'LL TAKE PRECAUTIONS, PETE. THAT'S WHAT OSBORNS DO.
BESIDES, I CAN'T IMAGINE SHE'S REALLY A TARGET.
WHY ISN'T HE MORE CONCERNED? IS IT BRAVURA TO MASK HIS FEAR? OR IS HE INVOLVED SOMEHOW. THE SIMILARITIES BETWEEN MENACE AND THE GOBLIN CERTAINLY POINT TO IT...
MEANWHILE, I SURE HOPE THE POLICE PUT FREAK IN A SECURE PLACE.
"AS LONG AS THEY STICK HIM IN A FREEZER..."
WE'RE TAKING THIS DOWN TO THE FREEZER ON SUBLEVEL 2.
"...THERE SHOULD BE NOTHING TO WORRY ABOUT."
NYPD HAZMAT UNIT
OSCORP ENTERPRISES
NEXT:
SCREWBALL COMETH!

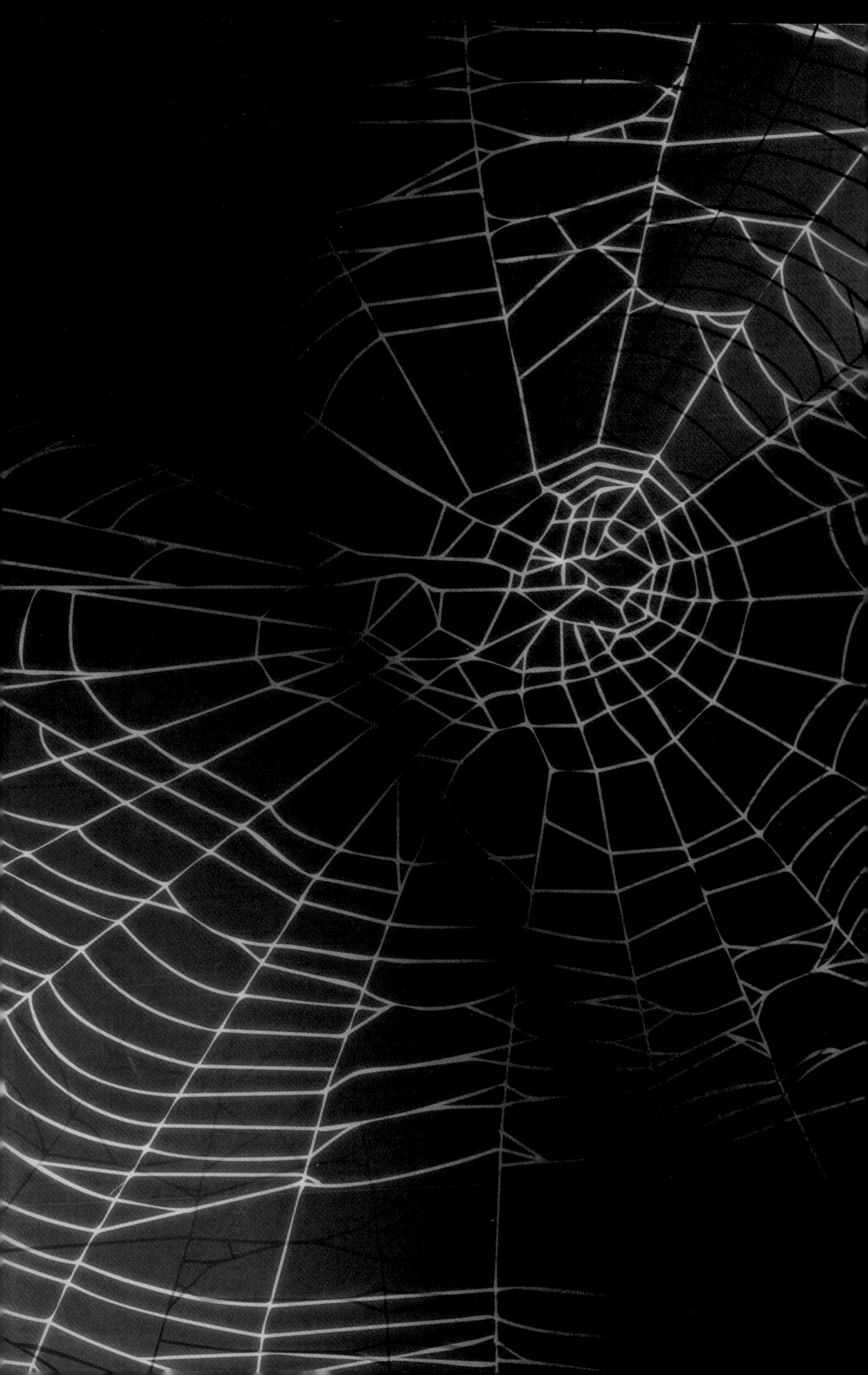

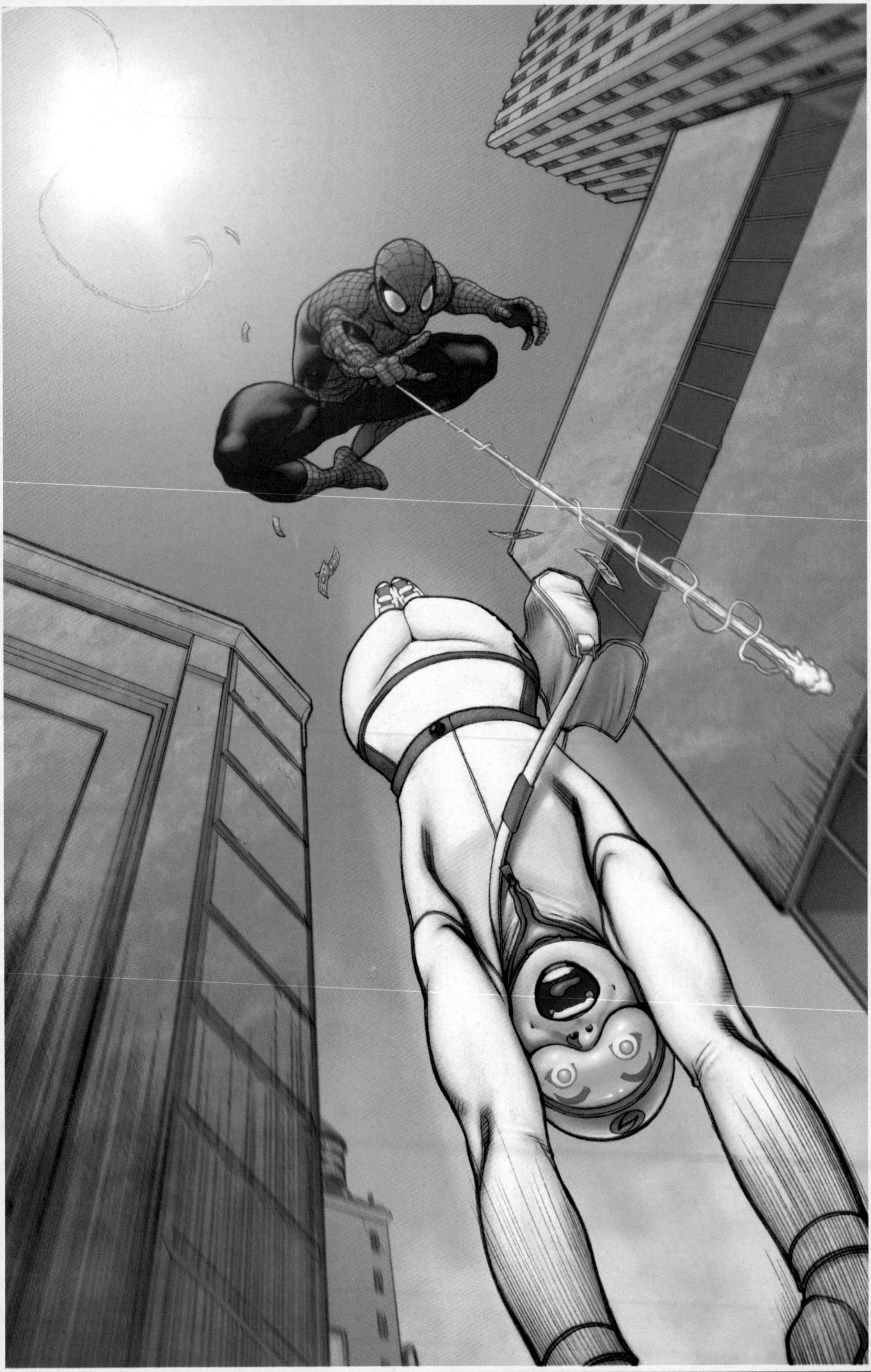

AMAZING SPIDER-MAN #559

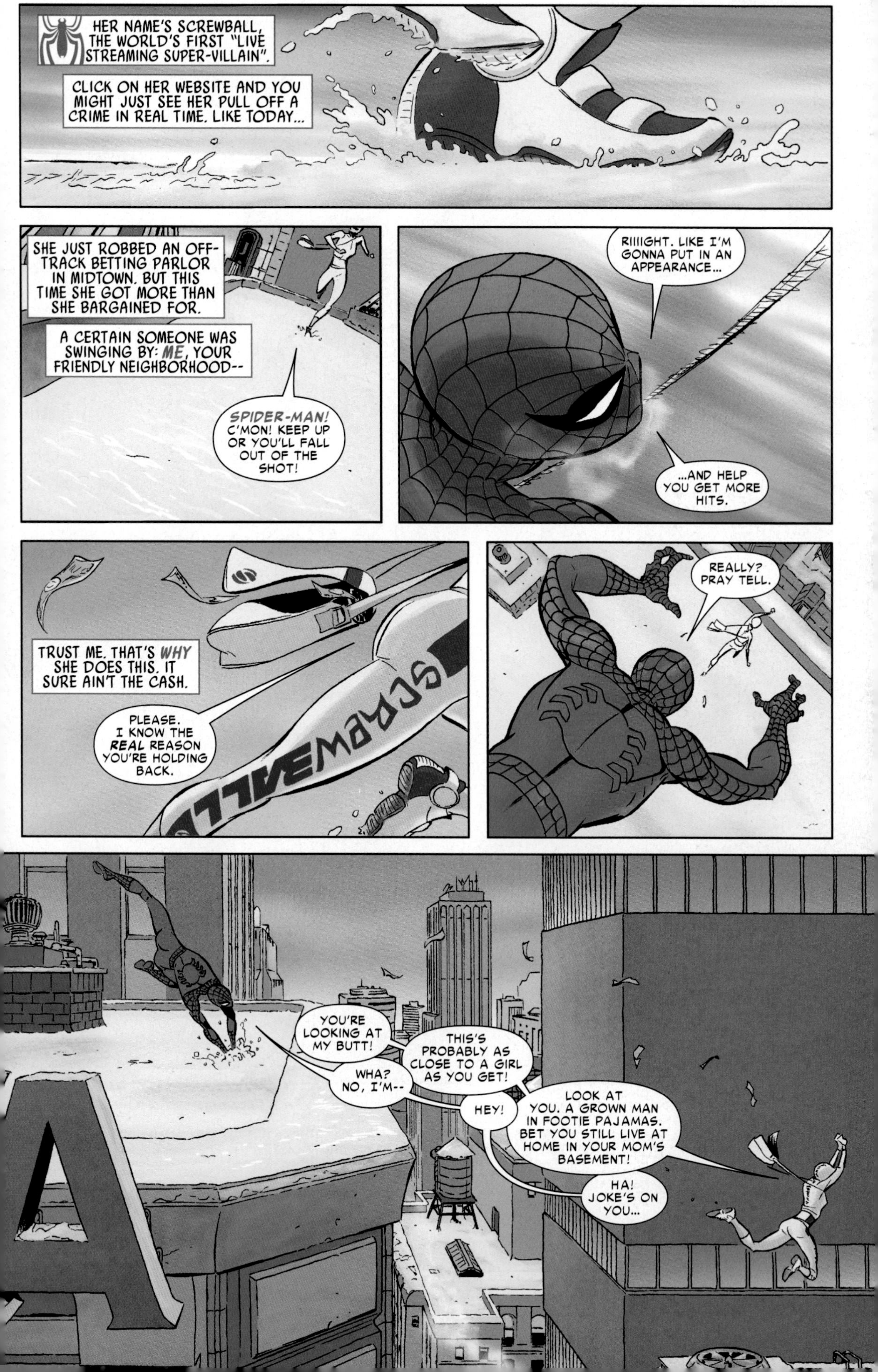
HER NAME'S SCREWBALL, THE WORLD'S FIRST "LIVE STREAMING SUPER-VILLAIN".
CLICK ON HER WEBSITE AND YOU MIGHT JUST SEE HER PULL OFF A CRIME IN REAL TIME. LIKE TODAY...
SHE JUST ROBBED AN OFF-TRACK BETTING PARLOR IN MIDTOWN. BUT THIS TIME SHE GOT MORE THAN SHE BARGAINED FOR.
A CERTAIN SOMEONE WAS SWINGING BY: ME, YOUR FRIENDLY NEIGHBORHOOD--
SPIDER-MAN! C'MON! KEEP UP OR YOU'LL FALL OUT OF THE SHOT!
RIIIGHT. LIKE I'M GONNA PUT IN AN APPEARANCE...
...AND HELP YOU GET MORE HITS.
TRUST ME. THAT'S WHY SHE DOES THIS. IT SURE AIN'T THE CASH.
PLEASE. I KNOW THE REAL REASON YOU'RE HOLDING BACK.
REALLY? PRAY TELL.
YOU'RE LOOKING AT MY BUTT!
THIS'S PROBABLY AS CLOSE TO A GIRL AS YOU GET!
WHA? NO, I'M--
HEY!
LOOK AT YOU. A GROWN MAN IN FOOTIE PAJAMAS. BET YOU STILL LIVE AT HOME IN YOUR MOM'S BASEMENT!
HA! JOKE'S ON YOU...

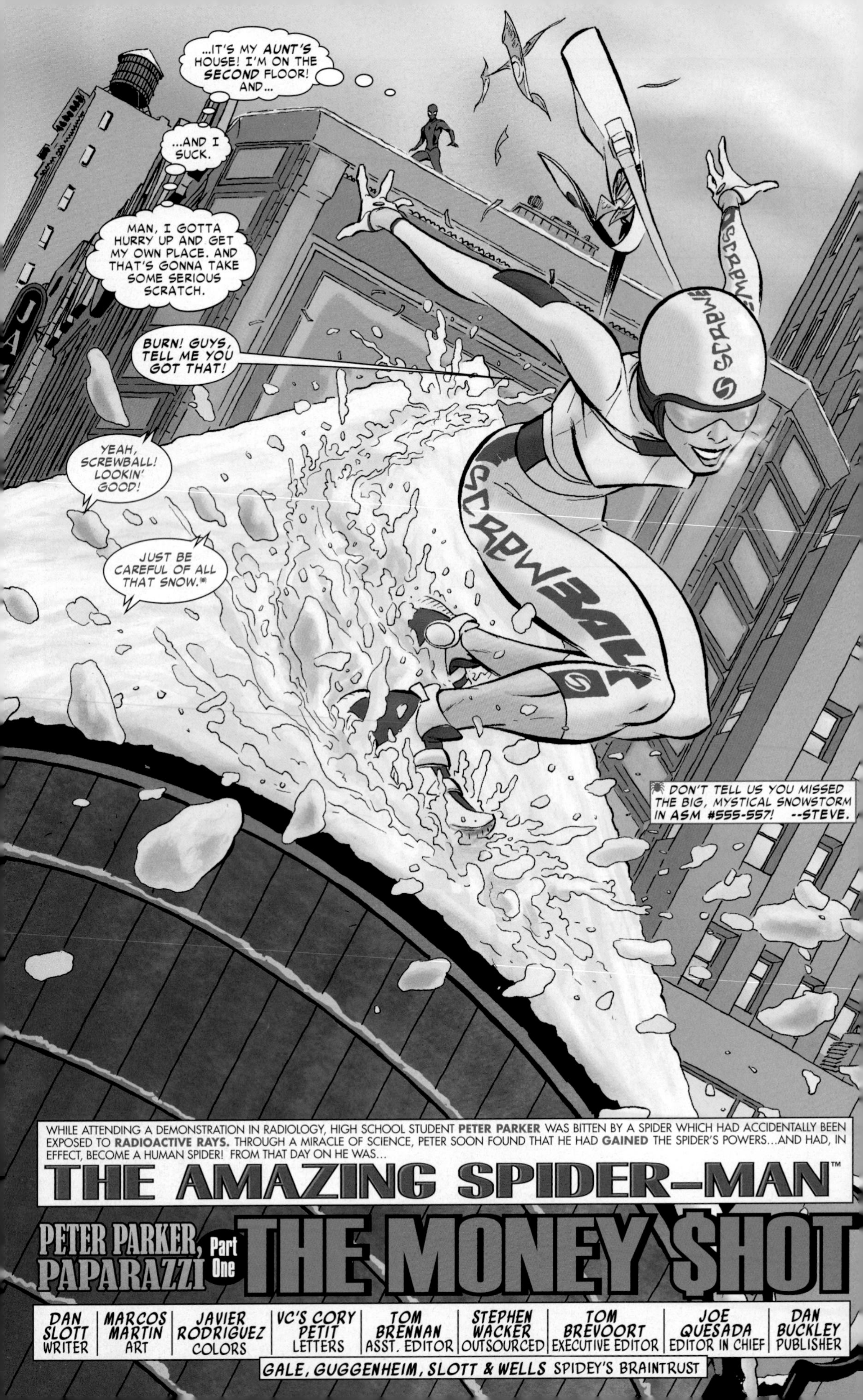
...IT'S MY AUNT'S HOUSE! I'M ON THE SECOND FLOOR! AND...
...AND I SUCK.
MAN, I GOTTA HURRY UP AND GET MY OWN PLACE. AND THAT'S GONNA TAKE SOME SERIOUS SCRATCH.
BURN! GUYS, TELL ME YOU GOT THAT!
YEAH, SCREWBALL! LOOKIN' GOOD!
JUST BE CAREFUL OF ALL THAT SNOW.*
SCREWBALL
*DON'T TELL US YOU MISSED THE BIG, MYSTICAL SNOWSTORM IN ASM #555-557! --STEVE.
WHILE ATTENDING A DEMONSTRATION IN RADIOLOGY, HIGH SCHOOL STUDENT PETER PARKER WAS BITTEN BY A SPIDER WHICH HAD ACCIDENTALLY BEEN EXPOSED TO RADIOACTIVE RAYS. THROUGH A MIRACLE OF SCIENCE, PETER SOON FOUND THAT HE HAD GAINED THE SPIDER'S POWERS...AND HAD, IN EFFECT, BECOME A HUMAN SPIDER! FROM THAT DAY ON HE WAS...
THE AMAZING SPIDER-MAN™
PETER PARKER, PAPARAZZI Part One THE MONEY $HOT
DAN SLOTT WRITER
MARCOS MARTIN ART
JAVIER RODRIGUEZ COLORS
VC'S CORY PETIT LETTERS
TOM BRENNAN ASST. EDITOR
STEPHEN WACKER OUTSOURCED
TOM BREVOORT EXECUTIVE EDITOR
JOE QUESADA EDITOR IN CHIEF
DAN BUCKLEY PUBLISHER
GALE, GUGGENHEIM, SLOTT & WELLS SPIDEY'S BRAINTRUST

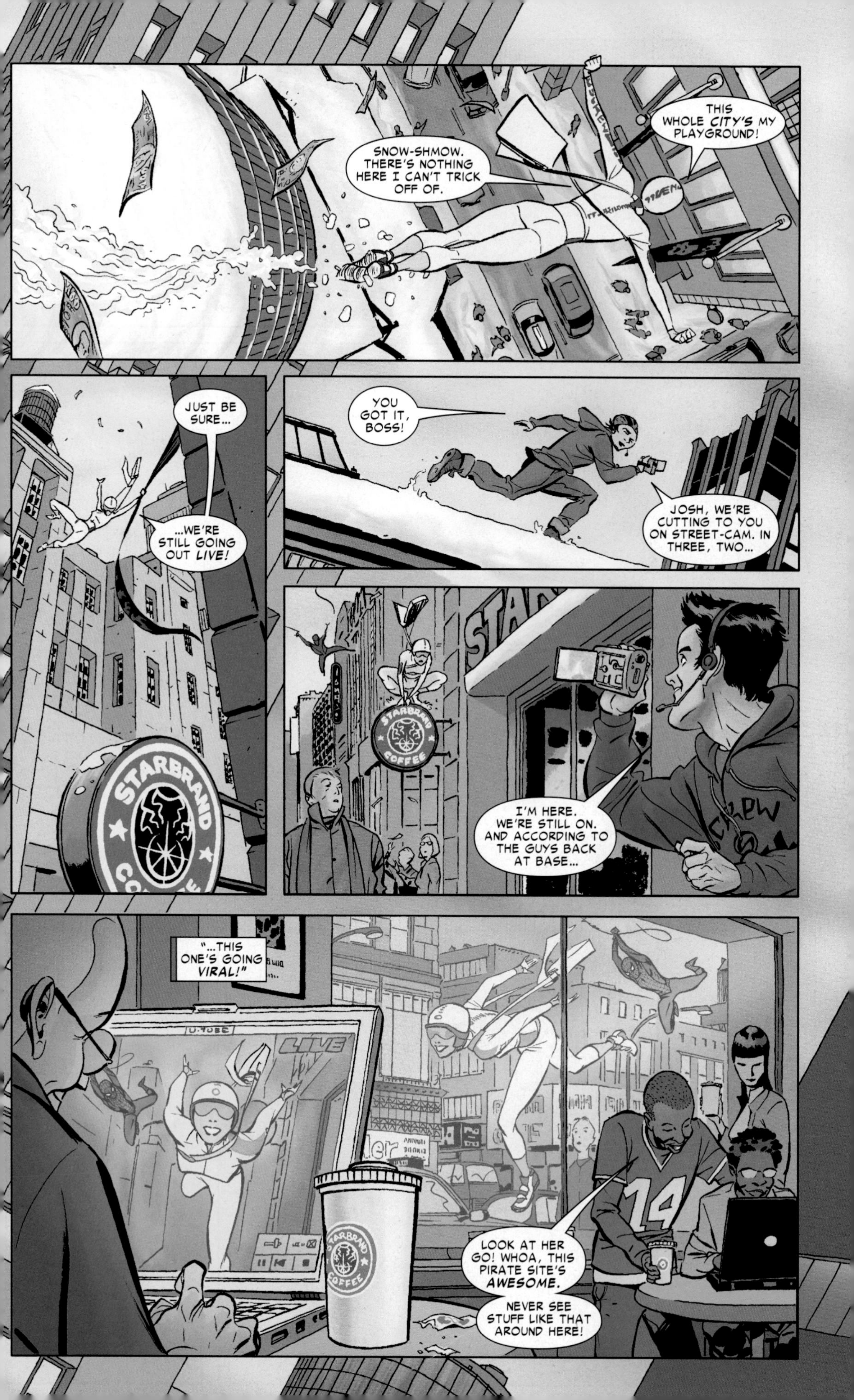
SNOW-SHMOW. THERE'S NOTHING HERE I CAN'T TRICK OFF OF.
THIS WHOLE *CITY'S* MY PLAYGROUND!
JUST BE SURE...
...WE'RE STILL GOING OUT *LIVE!*
YOU GOT IT, BOSS!
JOSH, WE'RE CUTTING TO YOU ON STREET-CAM. IN THREE, TWO...
I'M HERE. WE'RE STILL ON. AND ACCORDING TO THE GUYS BACK AT BASE...
"...THIS ONE'S GOING *VIRAL!*"
LIVE
LOOK AT HER GO! WHOA, THIS PIRATE SITE'S **AWESOME.**
NEVER SEE STUFF LIKE THAT AROUND HERE!

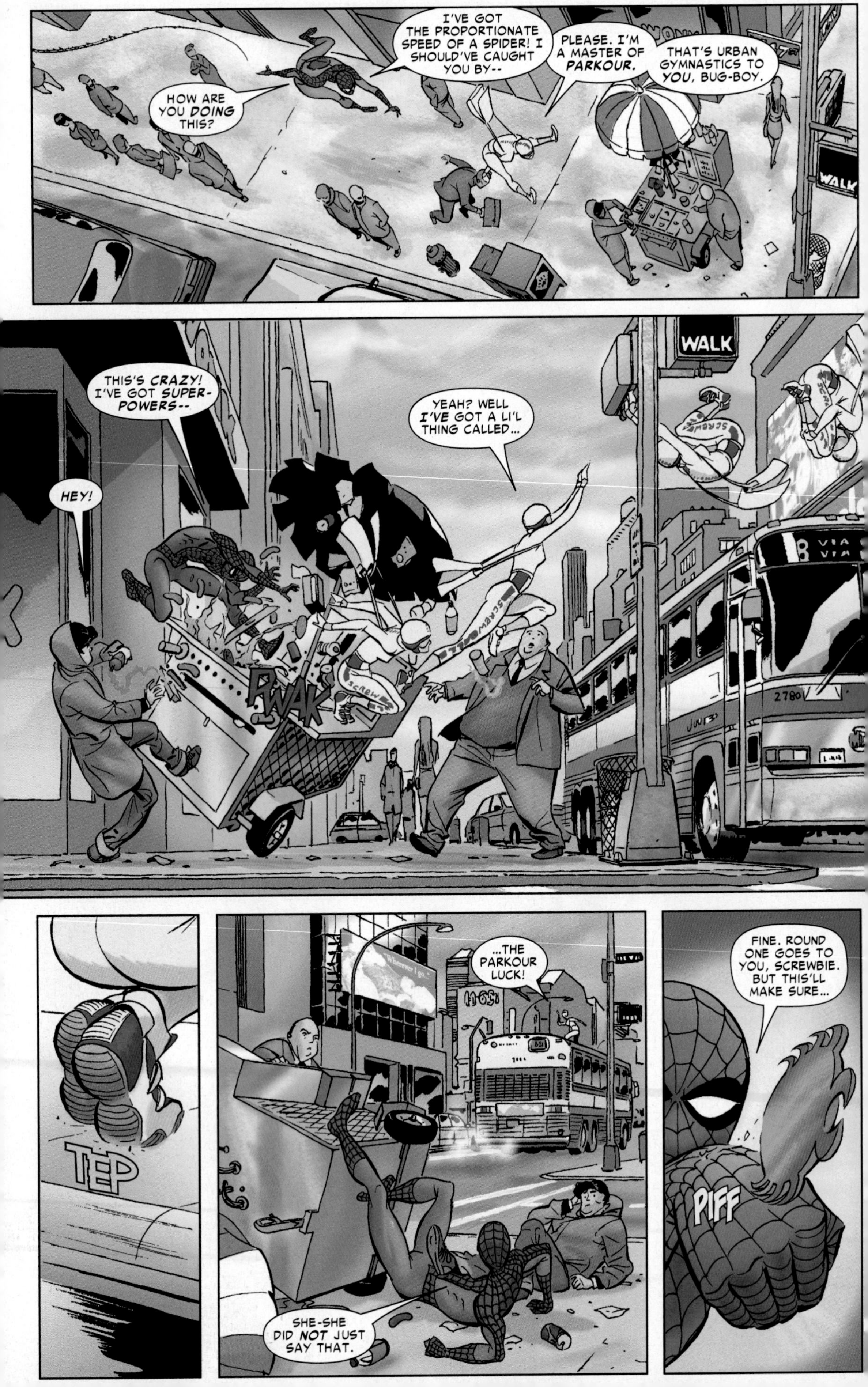
HOW ARE YOU DOING THIS?
I'VE GOT THE PROPORTIONATE SPEED OF A SPIDER! I SHOULD'VE CAUGHT YOU BY--
PLEASE. I'M A MASTER OF PARKOUR.
THAT'S URBAN GYMNASTICS TO YOU, BUG-BOY.
WALK
THIS'S CRAZY! I'VE GOT SUPER-POWERS--
YEAH? WELL I'VE GOT A LI'L THING CALLED...
WALK
HEY!
PWAK
2780
TEP
...THE PARKOUR LUCK!
SHE-SHE DID NOT JUST SAY THAT.
FINE. ROUND ONE GOES TO YOU, SCREWBIE. BUT THIS'LL MAKE SURE...
PIFF

"...I FIND YOU FOR ROUND TWO!"

AAHHHH!

NO TRESPASSING

SIXTIES

NOW.

POLICE!

OFFICERS! HELP!!! SPIDER-MAN! HE'S AFTER ME! I DIDN'T BELIEVE IT WAS TRUE...

...BUT IT'S JUST LIKE THE PAPERS SAID! HE'S THE SPIDER-TRACER KILLER!

HERE, I HELD UP THE O.T.B.* ON 3RD AVE. I'M TURNING MYSELF IN, OKAY?

ARREST ME! DO WHATEVER YOU HAVE TO! JUST KEEP HIM AWAY FROM ME!

* OFF TRACK BETTING -SW

HURRY! THAT PSYCHO PUT A SPIDER-TRACER ON ME!

HE MARKED ME FOR DEATH! GET IT OFF A' ME!

EASY, MA'AM. WE'LL GET TO THE BOTTOM OF THIS.

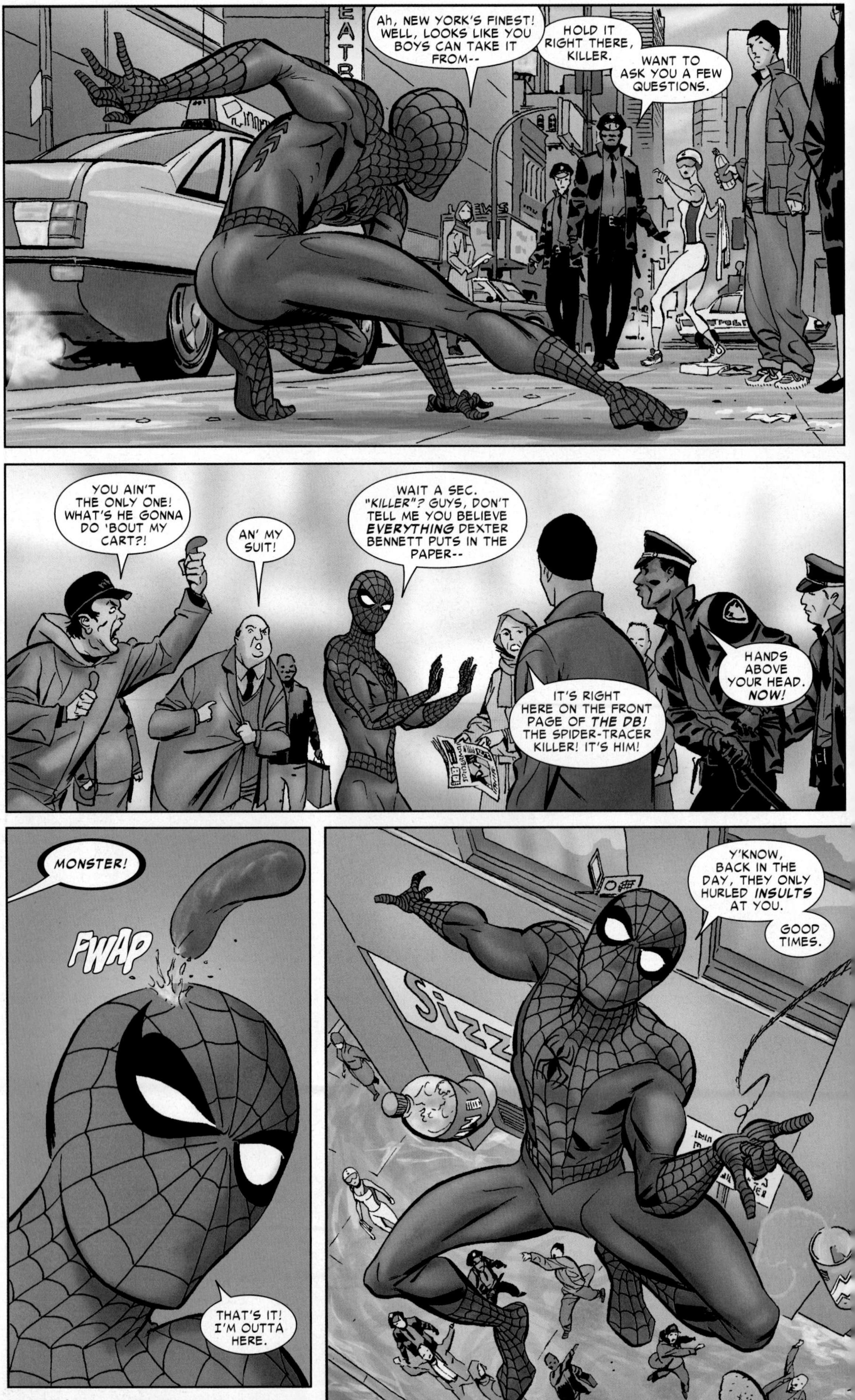
Ah, NEW YORK'S FINEST! WELL, LOOKS LIKE YOU BOYS CAN TAKE IT FROM--
HOLD IT RIGHT THERE, KILLER.
WANT TO ASK YOU A FEW QUESTIONS.
YOU AIN'T THE ONLY ONE! WHAT'S HE GONNA DO 'BOUT MY CART?!
AN' MY SUIT!
WAIT A SEC. *"KILLER"?* GUYS, DON'T TELL ME YOU BELIEVE ***EVERYTHING*** DEXTER BENNETT PUTS IN THE PAPER--
IT'S RIGHT HERE ON THE FRONT PAGE OF *THE DB!* THE SPIDER-TRACER KILLER! IT'S HIM!
HANDS ABOVE YOUR HEAD. ***NOW!***
MONSTER!
FWAP
THAT'S IT! I'M OUTTA HERE.
Y'KNOW, BACK IN THE DAY, THEY ONLY HURLED ***INSULTS*** AT YOU.
GOOD TIMES.

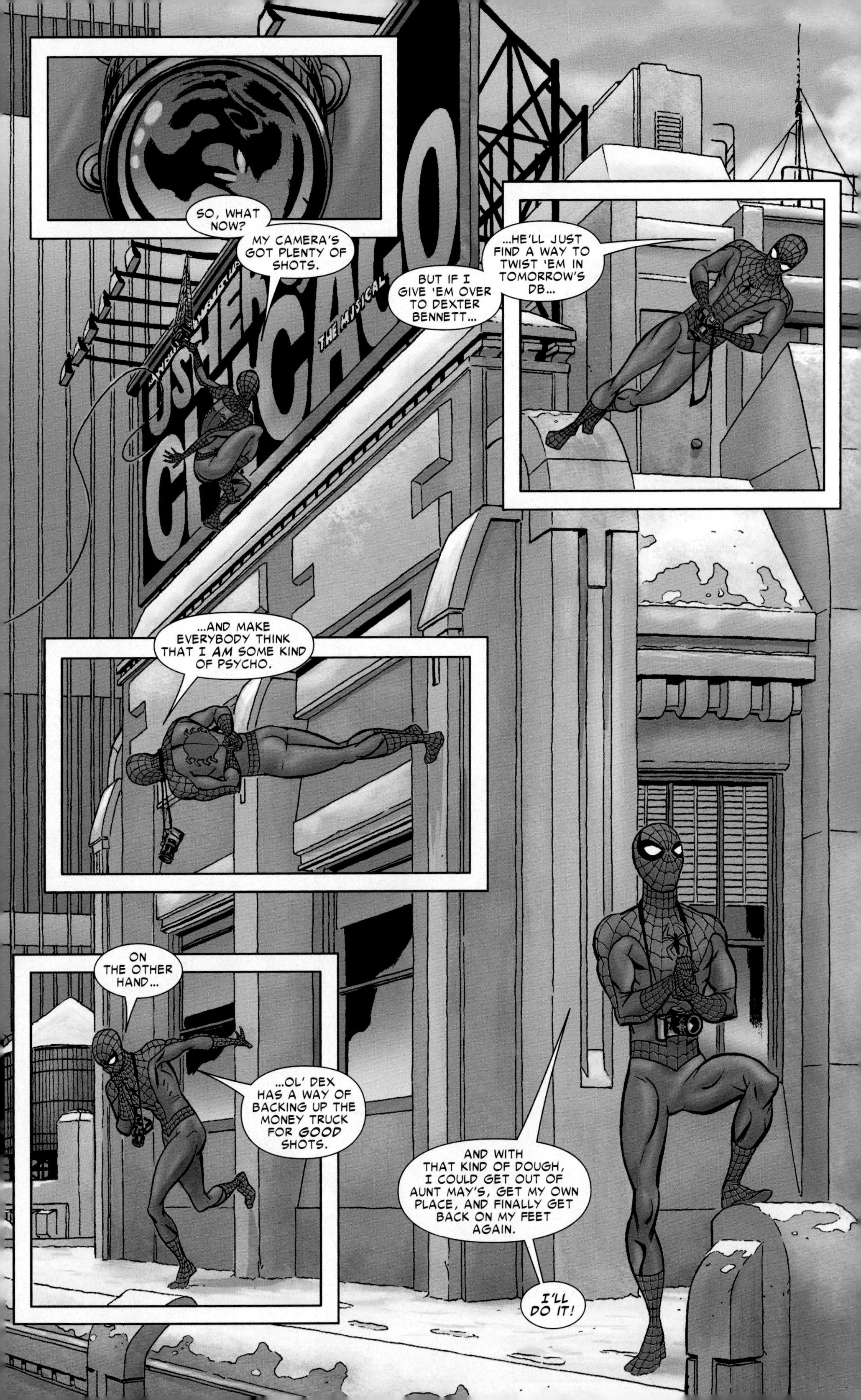

SO, WHAT NOW?
MY CAMERA'S GOT PLENTY OF SHOTS.
BUT IF I GIVE 'EM OVER TO DEXTER BENNETT...
...HE'LL JUST FIND A WAY TO TWIST 'EM IN TOMORROW'S DB...
...AND MAKE EVERYBODY THINK THAT I AM SOME KIND OF PSYCHO.
ON THE OTHER HAND...
...OL' DEX HAS A WAY OF BACKING UP THE MONEY TRUCK FOR GOOD SHOTS.
AND WITH THAT KIND OF DOUGH, I COULD GET OUT OF AUNT MAY'S, GET MY OWN PLACE, AND FINALLY GET BACK ON MY FEET AGAIN.
I'LL DO IT!

THE DB

YOU'RE TOO LATE, KID.

WHAT?! BUT MR. BENNETT, I JUST *CAME* FROM THE WHOLE SPIDEY/SCREWBALL DUST-UP...

DEXTER BENNETT
EDITOR-IN-CHIEF

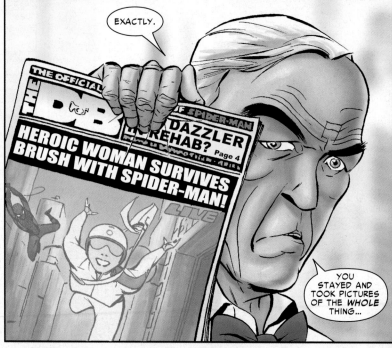

EXACTLY.

THE OFFICIAL DB

THE OFFICIAL ...OF SPIDER-MAN!

DAZZLER IN REHAB? Page 4

HEROIC WOMAN SURVIVES BRUSH WITH SPIDER-MAN!

LIVE

YOU STAYED AND TOOK PICTURES OF THE *WHOLE* THING...

...WHILE EVERYONE *ELSE* WITH A DIGITAL CAMERA OR A CHEAP CELL PHONE TOOK THE *SAME* SHOTS...

...AND *E-MAILED* THEM IN. GET WITH THE TIMES, PEKAR.

PARKER.

WHATEVER. YOU KEEP BRINGING US THIS STUFF *AFTER* THE FACT. THE DB IS ALL ABOUT THE *NOW*, SON. I WANNA SEE THE NEWS *AS* IT HAPPENS! CAN YOU DO *THAT?*

THAT'D BE...KINDA TRICKY.

THESE *ARE* GOOD, PETE. SORRY WE CAN'T USE 'EM.

DON'T LET JOE BRING YOU DOWN, BOY. 'CAUSE I THINK I'VE GOT A *USE* FOR YOU.

SOMETHING THAT'S THE *PERFECT* MATCH FOR YOUR SKILL SET.

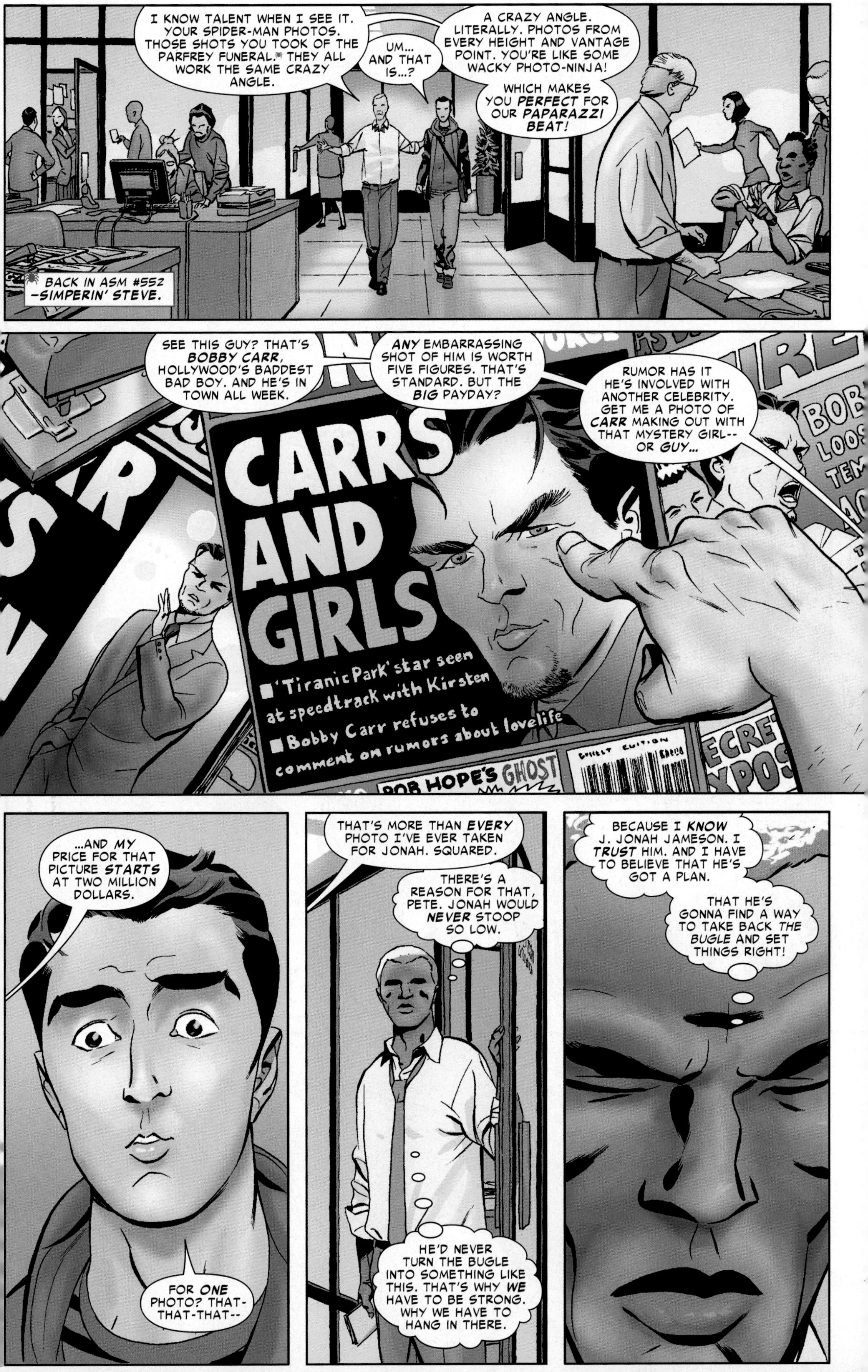
I KNOW TALENT WHEN I SEE IT. YOUR SPIDER-MAN PHOTOS. THOSE SHOTS YOU TOOK OF THE PARFREY FUNERAL.* THEY ALL WORK THE SAME CRAZY ANGLE.
UM... AND THAT IS...?
A CRAZY ANGLE. LITERALLY. PHOTOS FROM EVERY HEIGHT AND VANTAGE POINT. YOU'RE LIKE SOME WACKY PHOTO-NINJA!
WHICH MAKES YOU PERFECT FOR OUR PAPARAZZI BEAT!
*BACK IN ASM #552 —SIMPERIN' STEVE.
SEE THIS GUY? THAT'S BOBBY CARR, HOLLYWOOD'S BADDEST BAD BOY. AND HE'S IN TOWN ALL WEEK.
ANY EMBARRASSING SHOT OF HIM IS WORTH FIVE FIGURES. THAT'S STANDARD. BUT THE BIG PAYDAY?
RUMOR HAS IT HE'S INVOLVED WITH ANOTHER CELEBRITY. GET ME A PHOTO OF CARR MAKING OUT WITH THAT MYSTERY GIRL-- OR GUY...
CARRS AND GIRLS
'Tiranic Park' star seen at speedtrack with Kirsten
Bobby Carr refuses to comment on rumors about lovelife
BOB HOPE'S GHOST
SECRET EXPOS
...AND MY PRICE FOR THAT PICTURE STARTS AT TWO MILLION DOLLARS.
FOR ONE PHOTO? THAT-THAT-THAT--
THAT'S MORE THAN EVERY PHOTO I'VE EVER TAKEN FOR JONAH. SQUARED.
THERE'S A REASON FOR THAT, PETE. JONAH WOULD NEVER STOOP SO LOW.
HE'D NEVER TURN THE BUGLE INTO SOMETHING LIKE THIS. THAT'S WHY WE HAVE TO BE STRONG. WHY WE HAVE TO HANG IN THERE.
BECAUSE I KNOW J. JONAH JAMESON. I TRUST HIM. AND I HAVE TO BELIEVE THAT HE'S GOT A PLAN.
THAT HE'S GONNA FIND A WAY TO TAKE BACK THE BUGLE AND SET THINGS RIGHT!

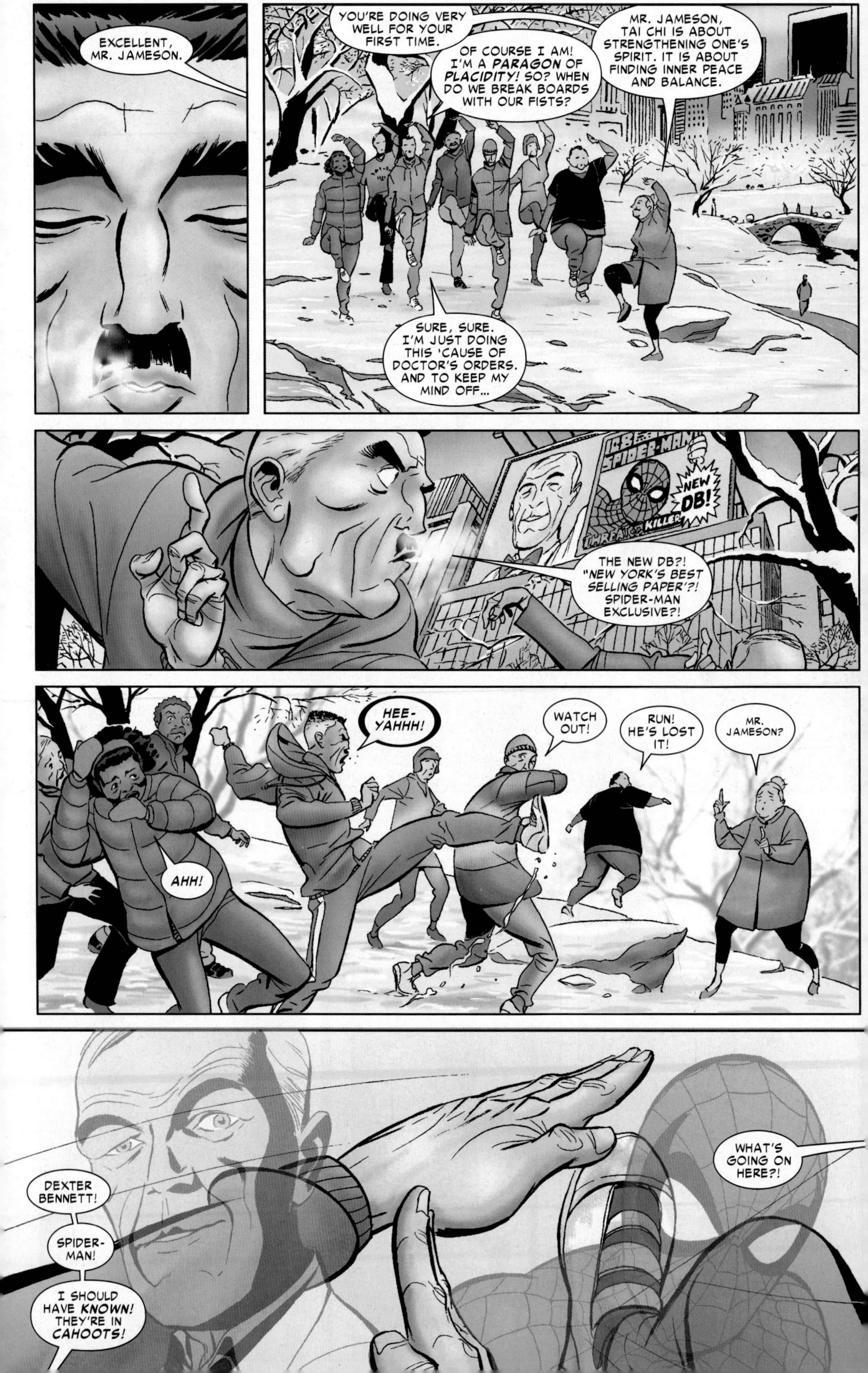
EXCELLENT, MR. JAMESON.
YOU'RE DOING VERY WELL FOR YOUR FIRST TIME.
OF COURSE I AM! I'M A *PARAGON* OF *PLACIDITY!* SO? WHEN DO WE BREAK BOARDS WITH OUR FISTS?
MR. JAMESON, TAI CHI IS ABOUT STRENGTHENING ONE'S SPIRIT. IT IS ABOUT FINDING INNER PEACE AND BALANCE.
SURE, SURE. I'M JUST DOING THIS 'CAUSE OF DOCTOR'S ORDERS. AND TO KEEP MY MIND OFF...
SPIDER-MAN
NEW DB!
THREAT
KILLER
THE NEW DB?! "NEW YORK'S BEST SELLING PAPER"?! SPIDER-MAN EXCLUSIVE?!
HEE-YAHHH!
AHH!
WATCH OUT!
RUN! HE'S LOST IT!
MR. JAMESON?
DEXTER BENNETT!
SPIDER-MAN!
I SHOULD HAVE *KNOWN!* THEY'RE IN *CAHOOTS!*
WHAT'S GOING ON HERE?!

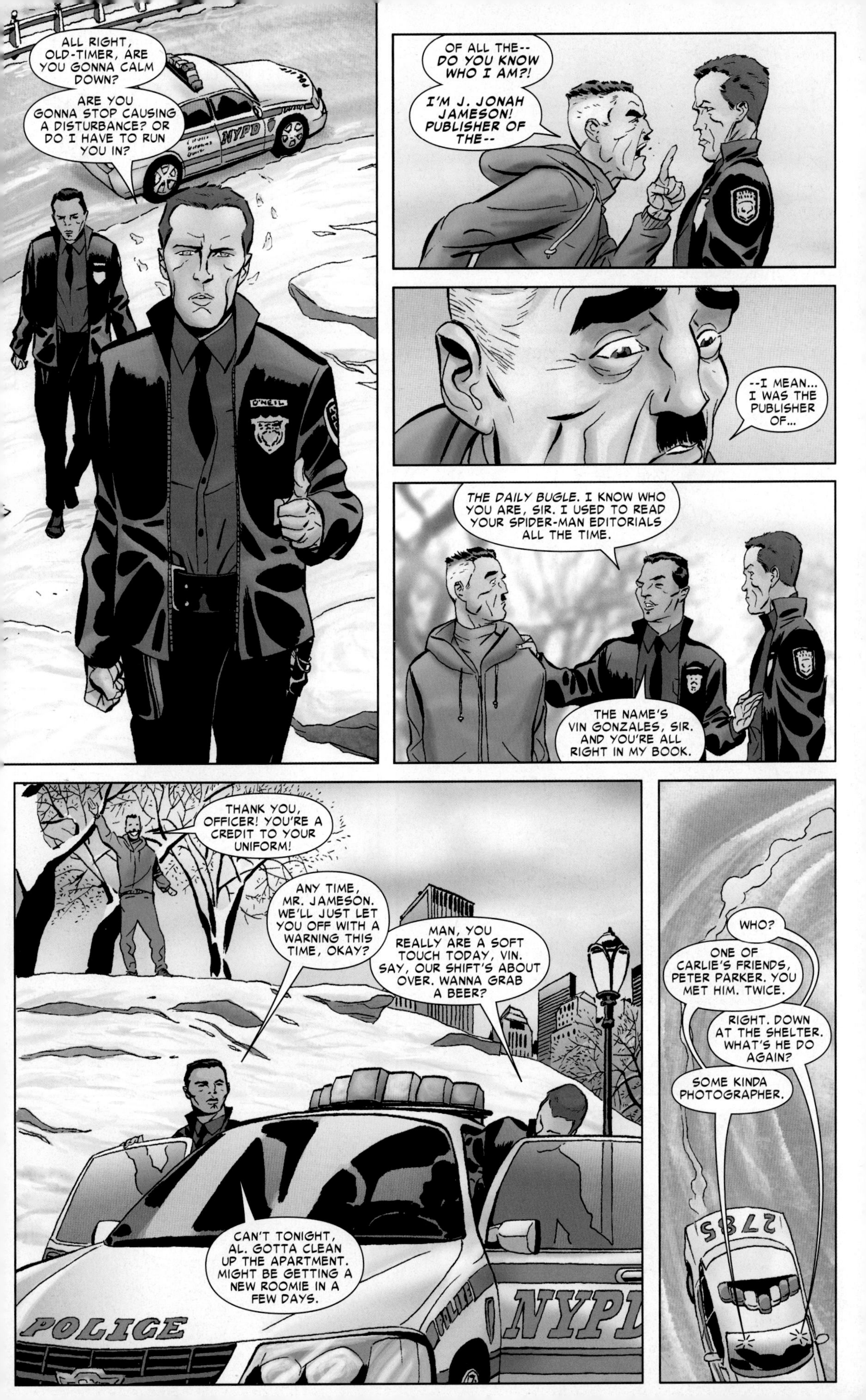
ALL RIGHT, OLD-TIMER, ARE YOU GONNA CALM DOWN?
ARE YOU GONNA STOP CAUSING A DISTURBANCE? OR DO I HAVE TO RUN YOU IN?
NYPD
O'NEIL
OF ALL THE-- DO YOU KNOW WHO I AM?!
I'M J. JONAH JAMESON! PUBLISHER OF THE--
--I MEAN... I WAS THE PUBLISHER OF...
THE DAILY BUGLE. I KNOW WHO YOU ARE, SIR. I USED TO READ YOUR SPIDER-MAN EDITORIALS ALL THE TIME.
THE NAME'S VIN GONZALES, SIR. AND YOU'RE ALL RIGHT IN MY BOOK.
THANK YOU, OFFICER! YOU'RE A CREDIT TO YOUR UNIFORM!
ANY TIME, MR. JAMESON. WE'LL JUST LET YOU OFF WITH A WARNING THIS TIME, OKAY?
MAN, YOU REALLY ARE A SOFT TOUCH TODAY, VIN. SAY, OUR SHIFT'S ABOUT OVER. WANNA GRAB A BEER?
CAN'T TONIGHT, AL. GOTTA CLEAN UP THE APARTMENT. MIGHT BE GETTING A NEW ROOMIE IN A FEW DAYS.
POLICE
NYPD
WHO?
ONE OF CARLIE'S FRIENDS, PETER PARKER. YOU MET HIM. TWICE.
RIGHT. DOWN AT THE SHELTER. WHAT'S HE DO AGAIN?
SOME KINDA PHOTOGRAPHER.
2785

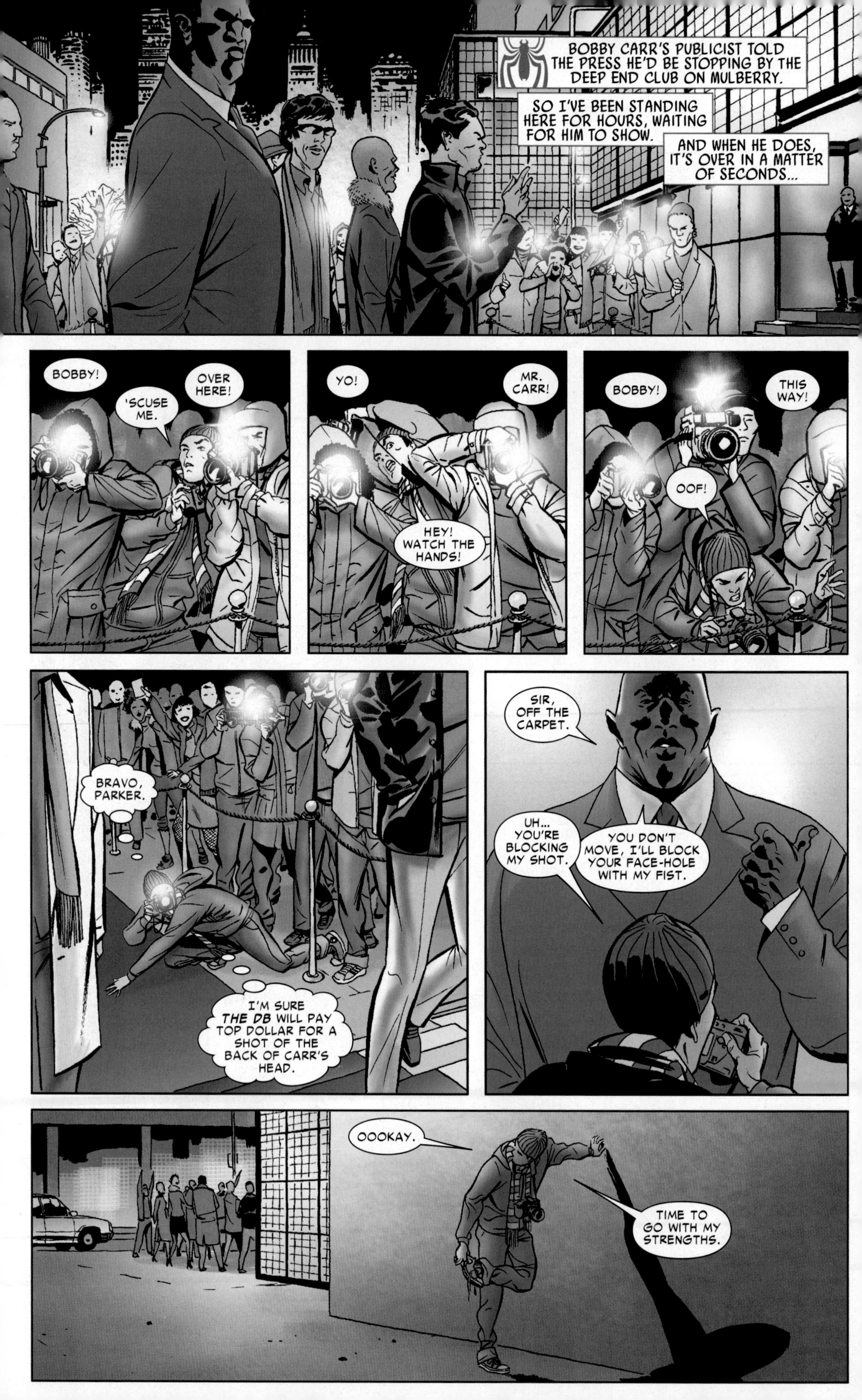
BOBBY CARR'S PUBLICIST TOLD THE PRESS HE'D BE STOPPING BY THE DEEP END CLUB ON MULBERRY.
SO I'VE BEEN STANDING HERE FOR HOURS, WAITING FOR HIM TO SHOW.
AND WHEN HE DOES, IT'S OVER IN A MATTER OF SECONDS...
BOBBY!
'SCUSE ME.
OVER HERE!
YO!
MR. CARR!
HEY! WATCH THE HANDS!
BOBBY!
THIS WAY!
OOF!
BRAVO, PARKER.
I'M SURE THE DB WILL PAY TOP DOLLAR FOR A SHOT OF THE BACK OF CARR'S HEAD.
SIR, OFF THE CARPET.
UH... YOU'RE BLOCKING MY SHOT.
YOU DON'T MOVE, I'LL BLOCK YOUR FACE-HOLE WITH MY FIST.
OOOKAY.
TIME TO GO WITH MY STRENGTHS.

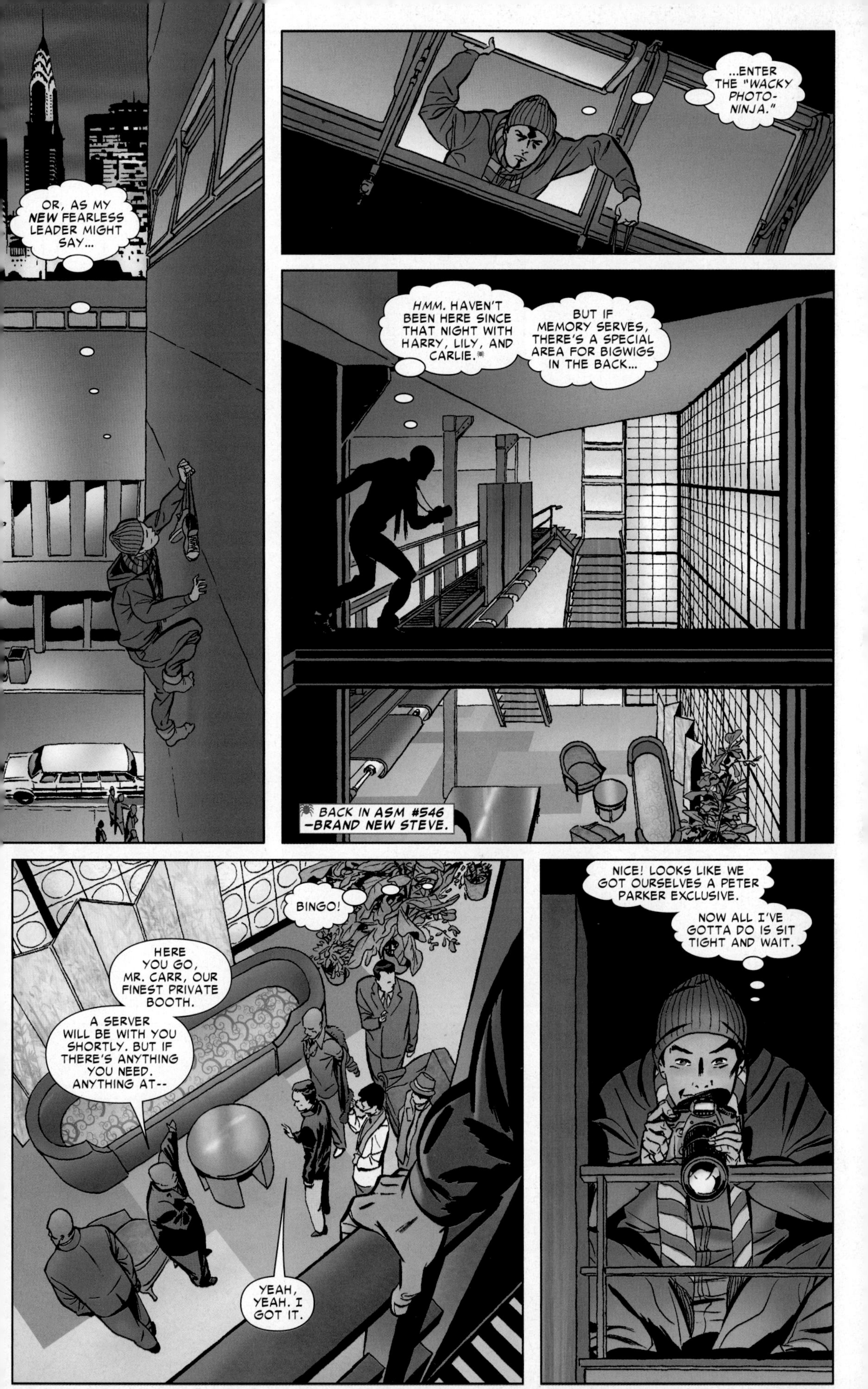
OR, AS MY NEW FEARLESS LEADER MIGHT SAY...
...ENTER THE "WACKY PHOTO-NINJA."
HMM. HAVEN'T BEEN HERE SINCE THAT NIGHT WITH HARRY, LILY, AND CARLIE.*
BUT IF MEMORY SERVES, THERE'S A SPECIAL AREA FOR BIGWIGS IN THE BACK...
*BACK IN ASM #546 —BRAND NEW STEVE.
BINGO!
HERE YOU GO, MR. CARR, OUR FINEST PRIVATE BOOTH.
A SERVER WILL BE WITH YOU SHORTLY. BUT IF THERE'S ANYTHING YOU NEED. ANYTHING AT--
YEAH, YEAH. I GOT IT.
NICE! LOOKS LIKE WE GOT OURSELVES A PETER PARKER EXCLUSIVE.
NOW ALL I'VE GOTTA DO IS SIT TIGHT AND WAIT.

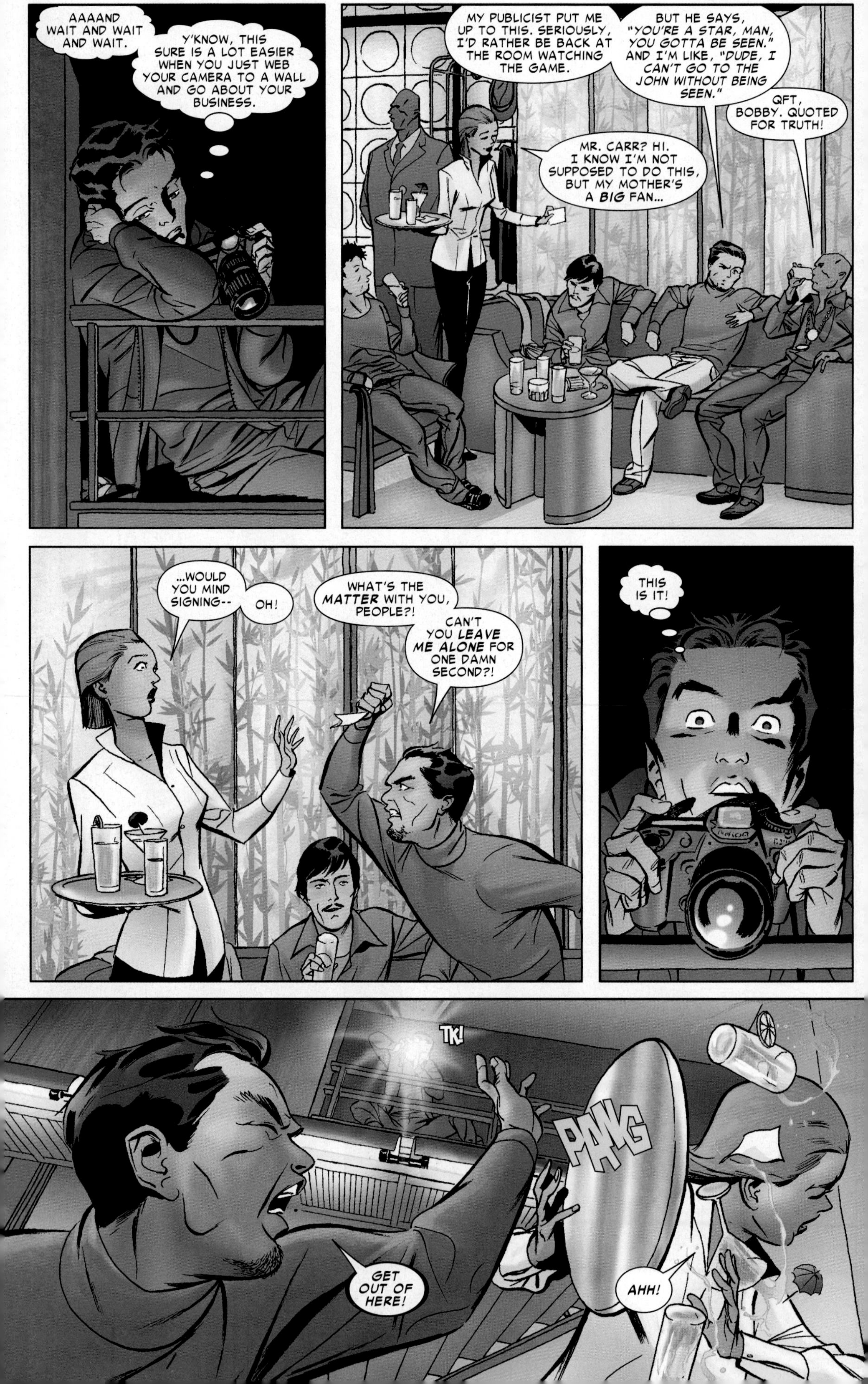

AAAAND WAIT AND WAIT AND WAIT.
Y'KNOW, THIS SURE IS A LOT EASIER WHEN YOU JUST WEB YOUR CAMERA TO A WALL AND GO ABOUT YOUR BUSINESS.
MY PUBLICIST PUT ME UP TO THIS. SERIOUSLY, I'D RATHER BE BACK AT THE ROOM WATCHING THE GAME.
BUT HE SAYS, "YOU'RE A STAR, MAN, YOU GOTTA BE SEEN." AND I'M LIKE, "DUDE, I CAN'T GO TO THE JOHN WITHOUT BEING SEEN."
QFT, BOBBY. QUOTED FOR TRUTH!
MR. CARR? HI. I KNOW I'M NOT SUPPOSED TO DO THIS, BUT MY MOTHER'S A BIG FAN...
...WOULD YOU MIND SIGNING--
OH!
WHAT'S THE MATTER WITH YOU, PEOPLE?!
CAN'T YOU LEAVE ME ALONE FOR ONE DAMN SECOND?!
THIS IS IT!
TK!
PANG
GET OUT OF HERE!
AHH!

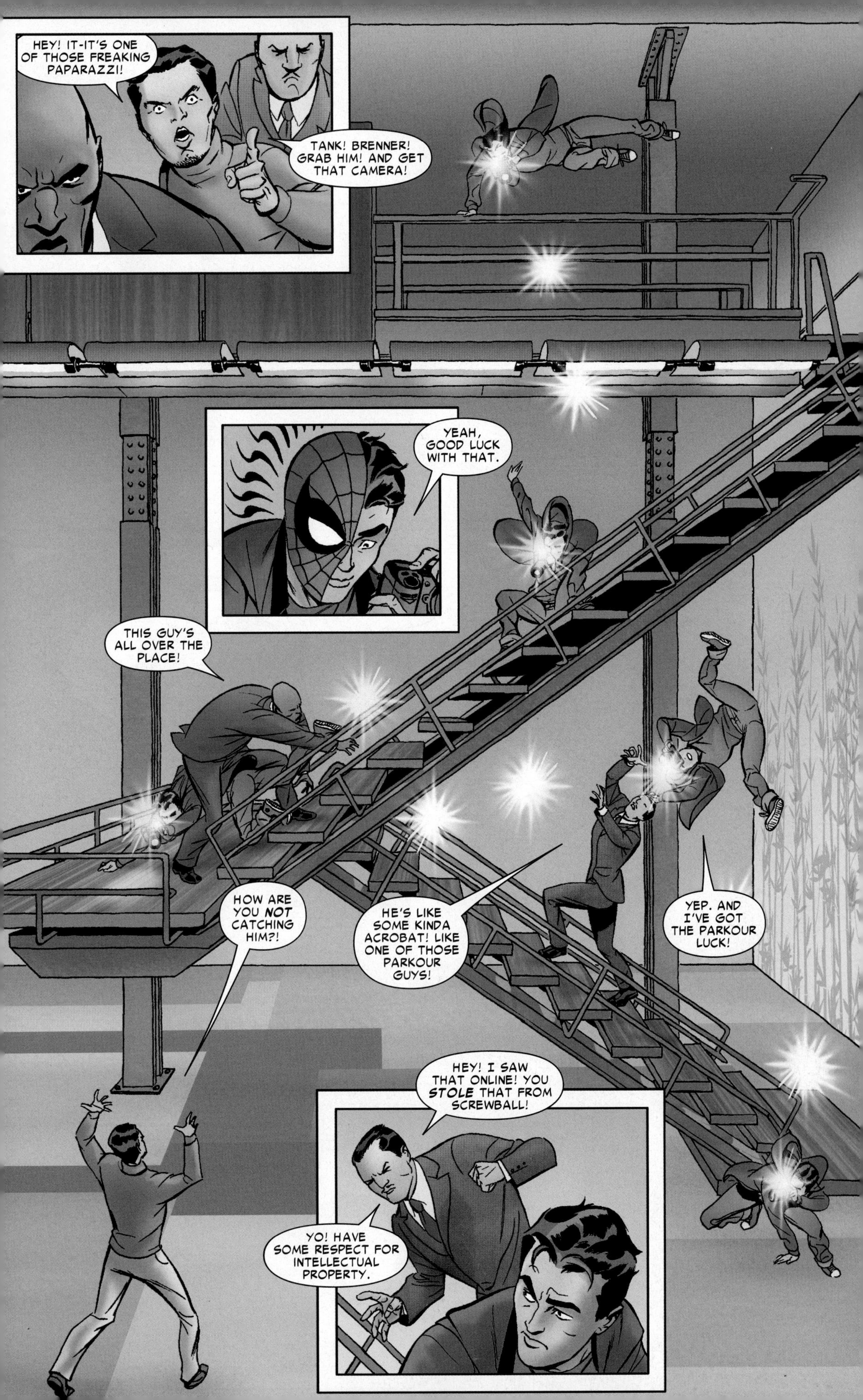
HEY! IT-IT'S ONE OF THOSE FREAKING PAPARAZZI!
TANK! BRENNER! GRAB HIM! AND GET THAT CAMERA!
YEAH, GOOD LUCK WITH THAT.
THIS GUY'S ALL OVER THE PLACE!
HOW ARE YOU NOT CATCHING HIM?!
HE'S LIKE SOME KINDA ACROBAT! LIKE ONE OF THOSE PARKOUR GUYS!
YEP. AND I'VE GOT THE PARKOUR LUCK!
HEY! I SAW THAT ONLINE! YOU STOLE THAT FROM SCREWBALL!
YO! HAVE SOME RESPECT FOR INTELLECTUAL PROPERTY.

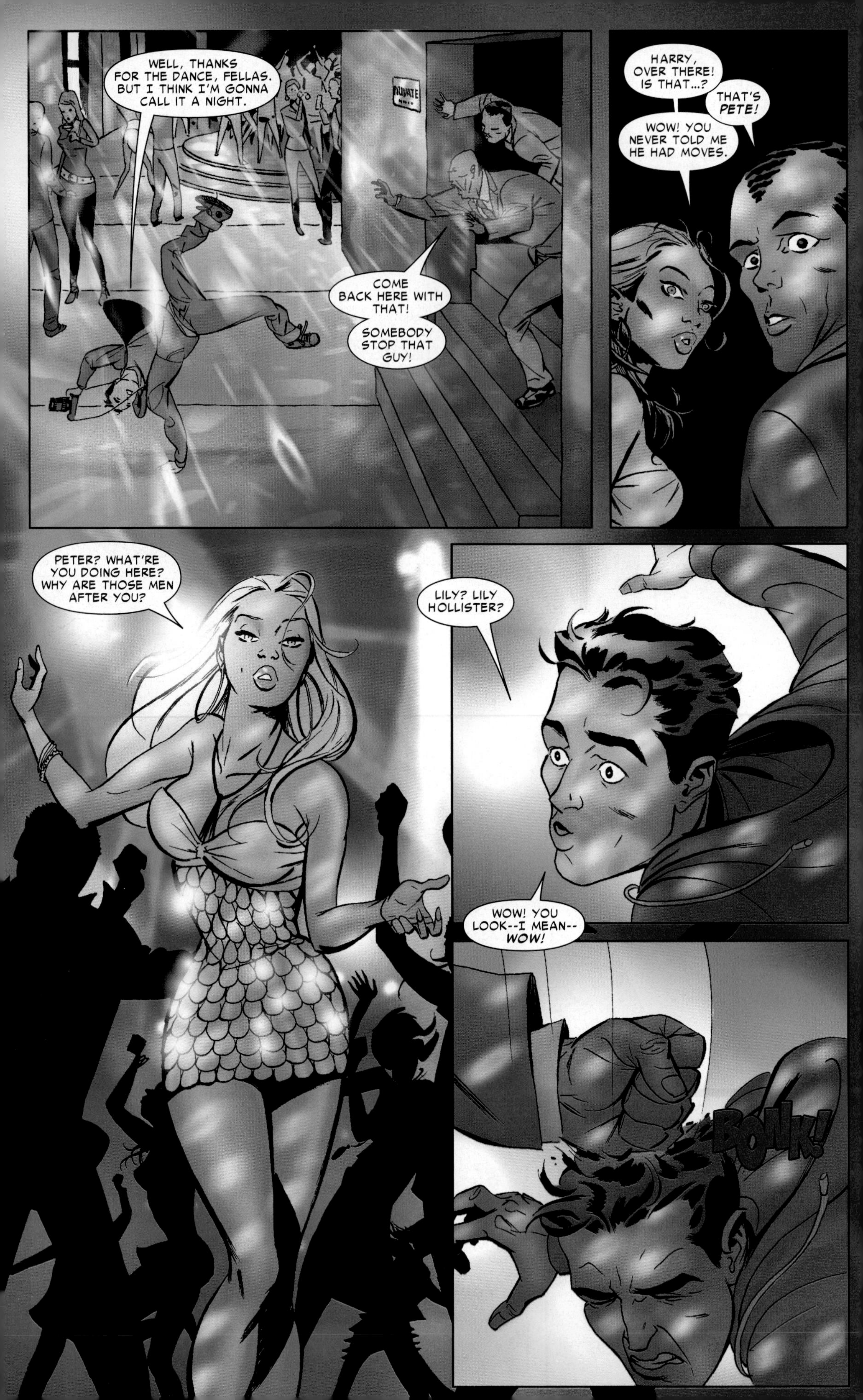

WELL, THANKS FOR THE DANCE, FELLAS. BUT I THINK I'M GONNA CALL IT A NIGHT.
PRIVATE
COME BACK HERE WITH THAT!
SOMEBODY STOP THAT GUY!
HARRY, OVER THERE! IS THAT...?
THAT'S *PETE!*
WOW! YOU NEVER TOLD ME HE HAD MOVES.
PETER? WHAT'RE YOU DOING HERE? WHY ARE THOSE MEN AFTER YOU?
LILY? LILY HOLLISTER?
WOW! YOU LOOK--I MEAN-- *WOW!*
BONK!

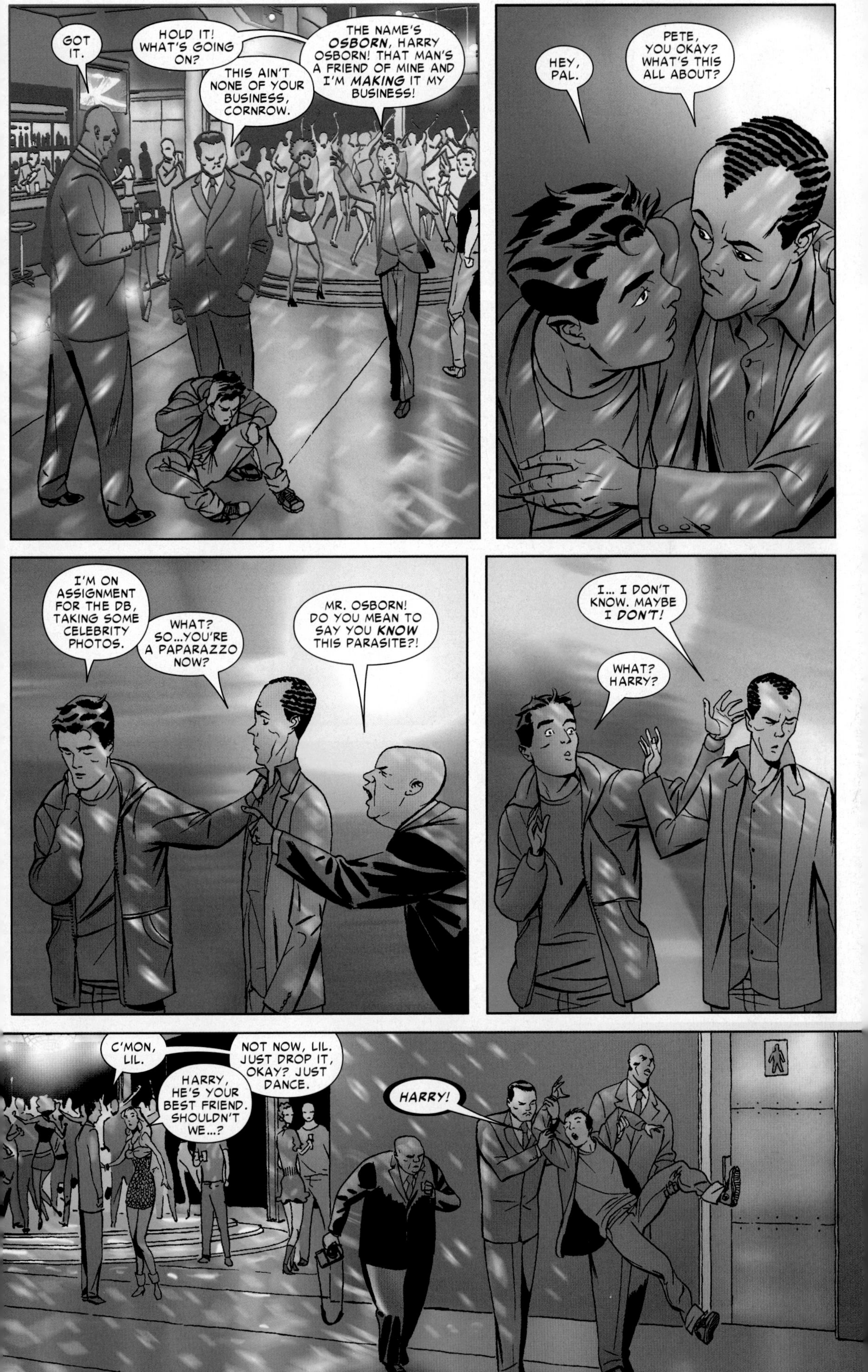
GOT IT.
HOLD IT! WHAT'S GOING ON?
THIS AIN'T NONE OF YOUR BUSINESS, CORNROW.
THE NAME'S OSBORN, HARRY OSBORN! THAT MAN'S A FRIEND OF MINE AND I'M MAKING IT MY BUSINESS!
HEY, PAL.
PETE, YOU OKAY? WHAT'S THIS ALL ABOUT?
I'M ON ASSIGNMENT FOR THE DB, TAKING SOME CELEBRITY PHOTOS.
WHAT? SO...YOU'RE A PAPARAZZO NOW?
MR. OSBORN! DO YOU MEAN TO SAY YOU KNOW THIS PARASITE?!
I... I DON'T KNOW. MAYBE I DON'T!
WHAT? HARRY?
C'MON, LIL.
NOT NOW, LIL. JUST DROP IT, OKAY? JUST DANCE.
HARRY, HE'S YOUR BEST FRIEND. SHOULDN'T WE...?
HARRY!

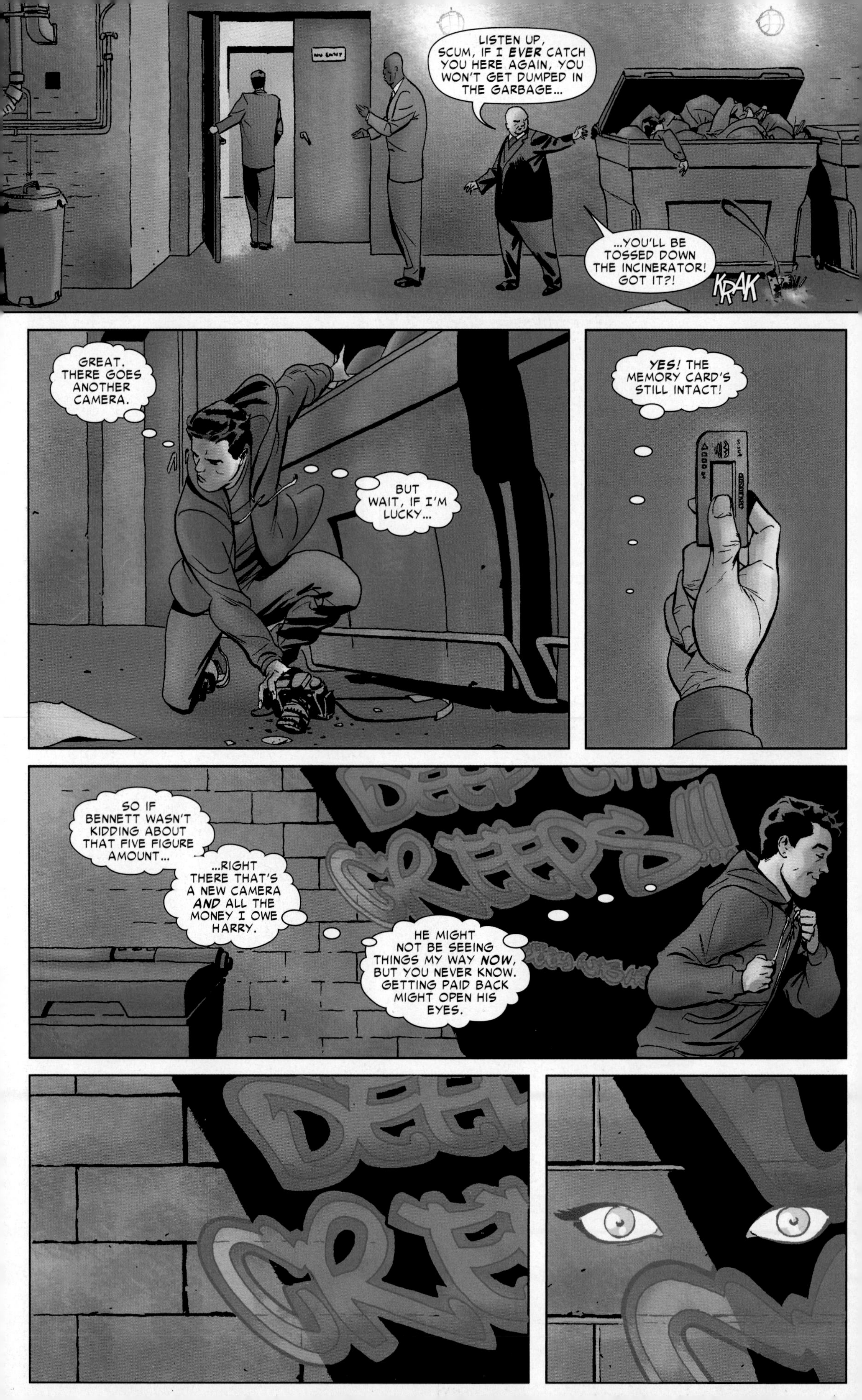
LISTEN UP, SCUM, IF I EVER CATCH YOU HERE AGAIN, YOU WON'T GET DUMPED IN THE GARBAGE...
...YOU'LL BE TOSSED DOWN THE INCINERATOR! GOT IT?!
KRAK
GREAT. THERE GOES ANOTHER CAMERA.
BUT WAIT, IF I'M LUCKY...
YES! THE MEMORY CARD'S STILL INTACT!
SO IF BENNETT WASN'T KIDDING ABOUT THAT FIVE FIGURE AMOUNT...
...RIGHT THERE THAT'S A NEW CAMERA AND ALL THE MONEY I OWE HARRY.
HE MIGHT NOT BE SEEING THINGS MY WAY NOW, BUT YOU NEVER KNOW. GETTING PAID BACK MIGHT OPEN HIS EYES.

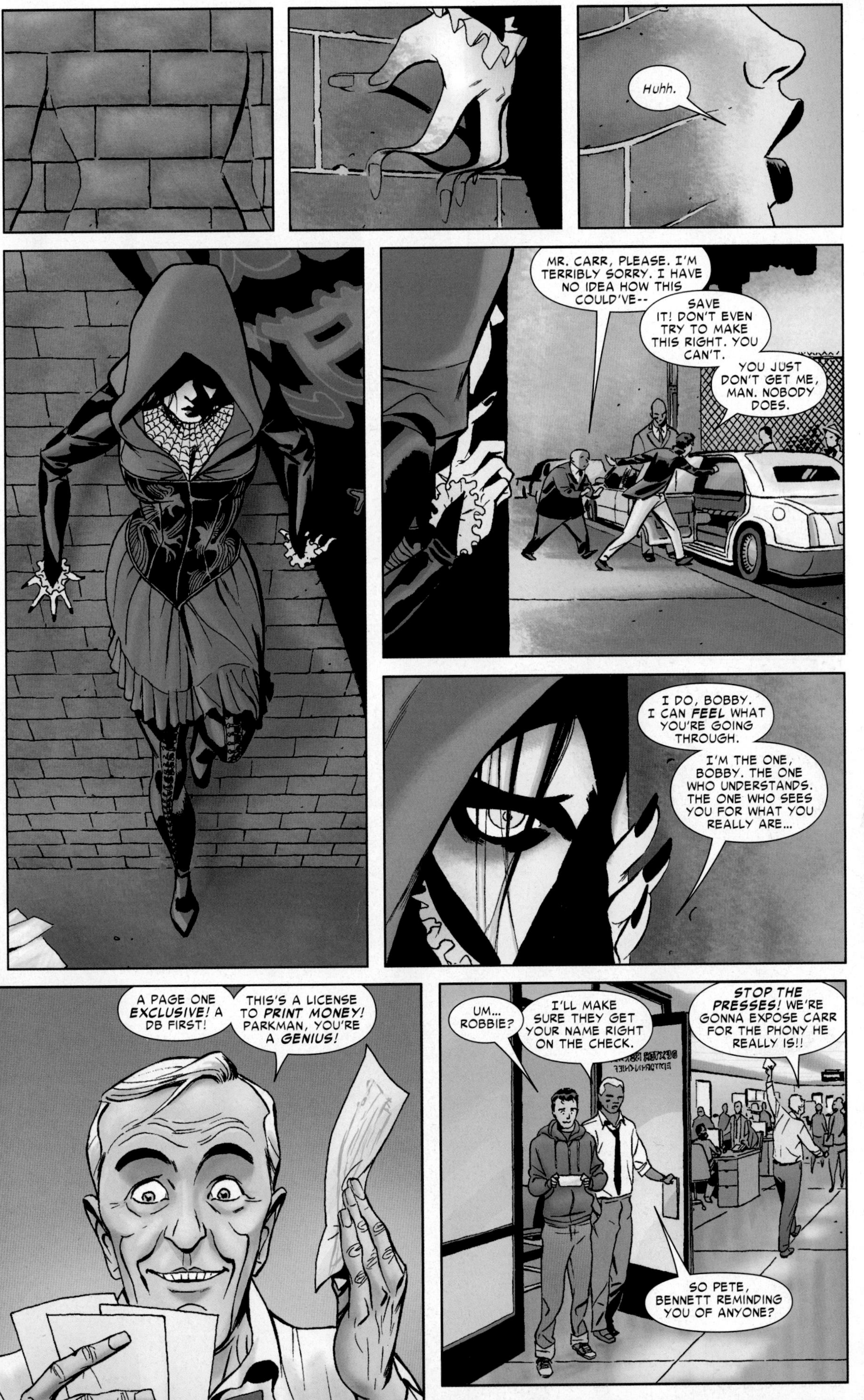
Huhh.
MR. CARR, PLEASE. I'M TERRIBLY SORRY. I HAVE NO IDEA HOW THIS COULD'VE--
SAVE IT! DON'T EVEN TRY TO MAKE THIS RIGHT. YOU CAN'T.
YOU JUST DON'T GET ME, MAN. NOBODY DOES.
I DO, BOBBY. I CAN *FEEL* WHAT YOU'RE GOING THROUGH.
I'M THE ONE, BOBBY. THE ONE WHO UNDERSTANDS. THE ONE WHO SEES YOU FOR WHAT YOU REALLY ARE...
A PAGE ONE *EXCLUSIVE!* A DB FIRST!
THIS'S A LICENSE TO *PRINT MONEY!* PARKMAN, YOU'RE A *GENIUS!*
UM... ROBBIE?
I'LL MAKE SURE THEY GET YOUR NAME RIGHT ON THE CHECK.
STOP THE PRESSES! WE'RE GONNA EXPOSE CARR FOR THE PHONY HE REALLY IS!!
SO PETE, BENNETT REMINDING YOU OF ANYONE?

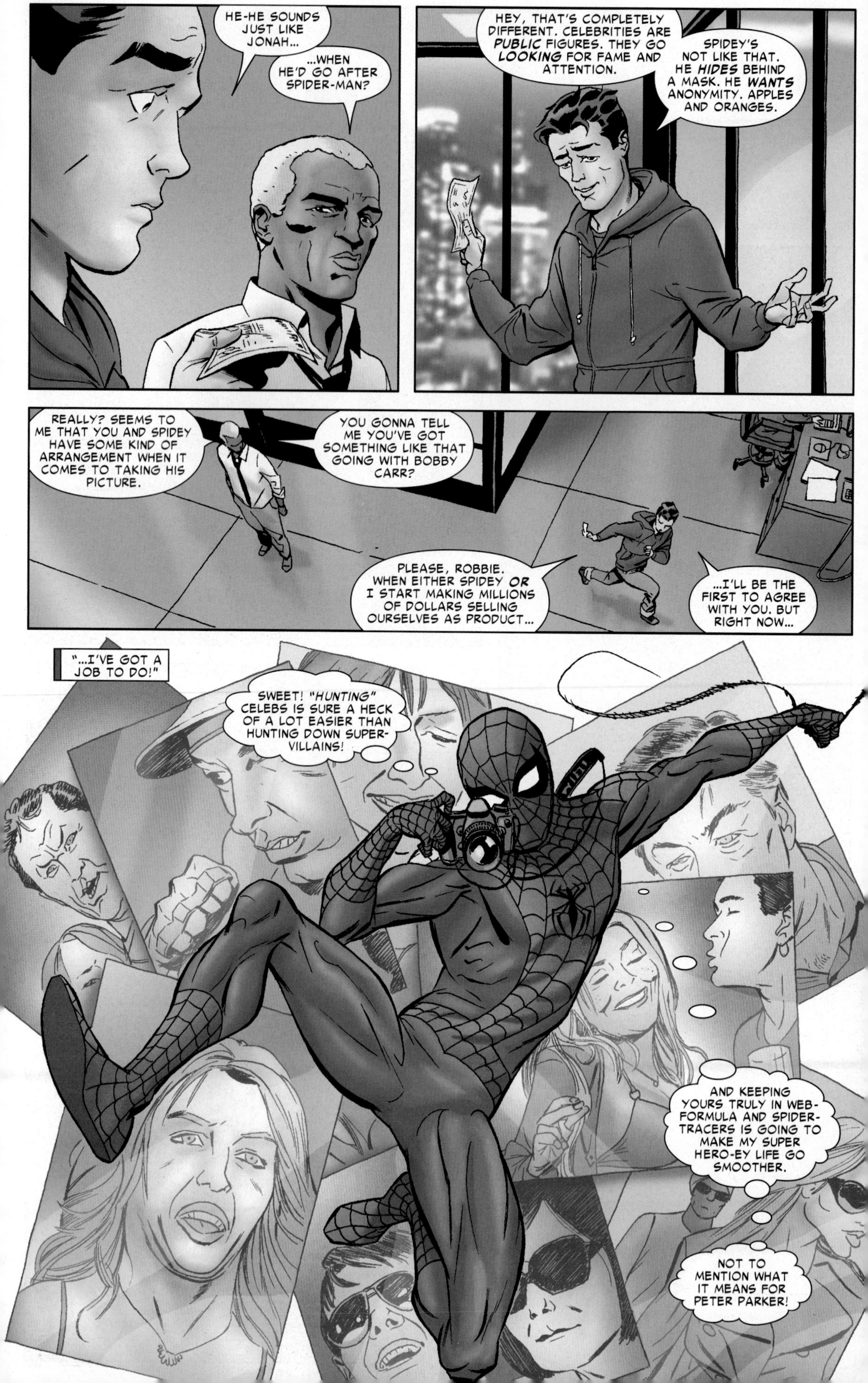
HE-HE SOUNDS JUST LIKE JONAH...
...WHEN HE'D GO AFTER SPIDER-MAN?
HEY, THAT'S COMPLETELY DIFFERENT. CELEBRITIES ARE PUBLIC FIGURES. THEY GO LOOKING FOR FAME AND ATTENTION.
SPIDEY'S NOT LIKE THAT. HE HIDES BEHIND A MASK. HE WANTS ANONYMITY. APPLES AND ORANGES.
REALLY? SEEMS TO ME THAT YOU AND SPIDEY HAVE SOME KIND OF ARRANGEMENT WHEN IT COMES TO TAKING HIS PICTURE.
YOU GONNA TELL ME YOU'VE GOT SOMETHING LIKE THAT GOING WITH BOBBY CARR?
PLEASE, ROBBIE. WHEN EITHER SPIDEY OR I START MAKING MILLIONS OF DOLLARS SELLING OURSELVES AS PRODUCT...
...I'LL BE THE FIRST TO AGREE WITH YOU. BUT RIGHT NOW...
"...I'VE GOT A JOB TO DO!"
SWEET! "HUNTING" CELEBS IS SURE A HECK OF A LOT EASIER THAN HUNTING DOWN SUPER-VILLAINS!
AND KEEPING YOURS TRULY IN WEB-FORMULA AND SPIDER-TRACERS IS GOING TO MAKE MY SUPER HERO-EY LIFE GO SMOOTHER.
NOT TO MENTION WHAT IT MEANS FOR PETER PARKER!

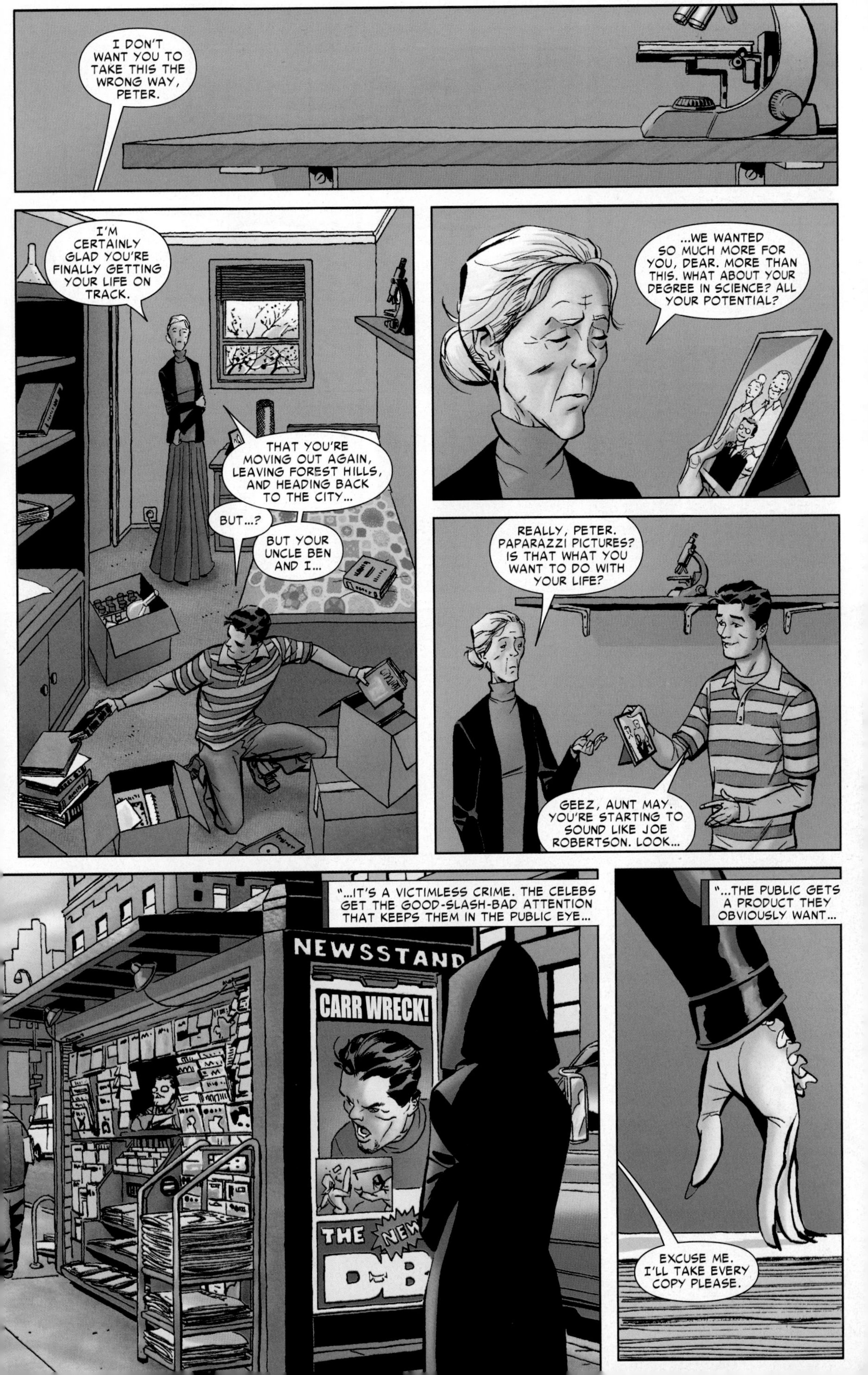
I DON'T WANT YOU TO TAKE THIS THE WRONG WAY, PETER.
I'M CERTAINLY GLAD YOU'RE FINALLY GETTING YOUR LIFE ON TRACK.
THAT YOU'RE MOVING OUT AGAIN, LEAVING FOREST HILLS, AND HEADING BACK TO THE CITY...
BUT...?
BUT YOUR UNCLE BEN AND I...
...WE WANTED SO MUCH MORE FOR YOU, DEAR. MORE THAN THIS. WHAT ABOUT YOUR DEGREE IN SCIENCE? ALL YOUR POTENTIAL?
REALLY, PETER. PAPARAZZI PICTURES? IS THAT WHAT YOU WANT TO DO WITH YOUR LIFE?
GEEZ, AUNT MAY. YOU'RE STARTING TO SOUND LIKE JOE ROBERTSON. LOOK...
"...IT'S A VICTIMLESS CRIME. THE CELEBS GET THE GOOD-SLASH-BAD ATTENTION THAT KEEPS THEM IN THE PUBLIC EYE...
NEWSSTAND
CARR WRECK!
THE NEW DB
"...THE PUBLIC GETS A PRODUCT THEY OBVIOUSLY WANT...
EXCUSE ME. I'LL TAKE EVERY COPY PLEASE.

"...EVERYBODY'S HAPPY. WHO DOES IT HURT?"

HOME AGAIN. WITH A NEW TREASURE.

AND THIS ONE'S PERFECT.

THE RIGHT SIZE. LIFE SIZE.

THE DB

DIVO WAN' SCAN

BOBBY

LIKE IT'S SUPPOSED TO BE. WITH THE TWO OF US. TOGETHER.

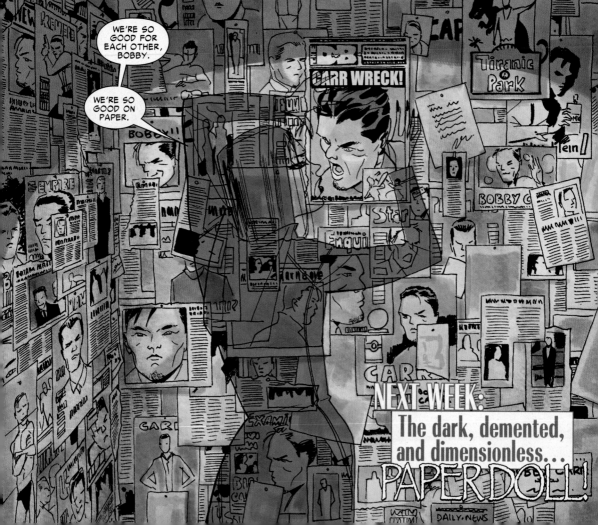

WE'RE SO GOOD FOR EACH OTHER, BOBBY.

WE'RE SO GOOD ON PAPER.

THE DB

CARR WRECK!

NEXT WEEK: The dark, demented, and dimensionless... PAPER DOLL!

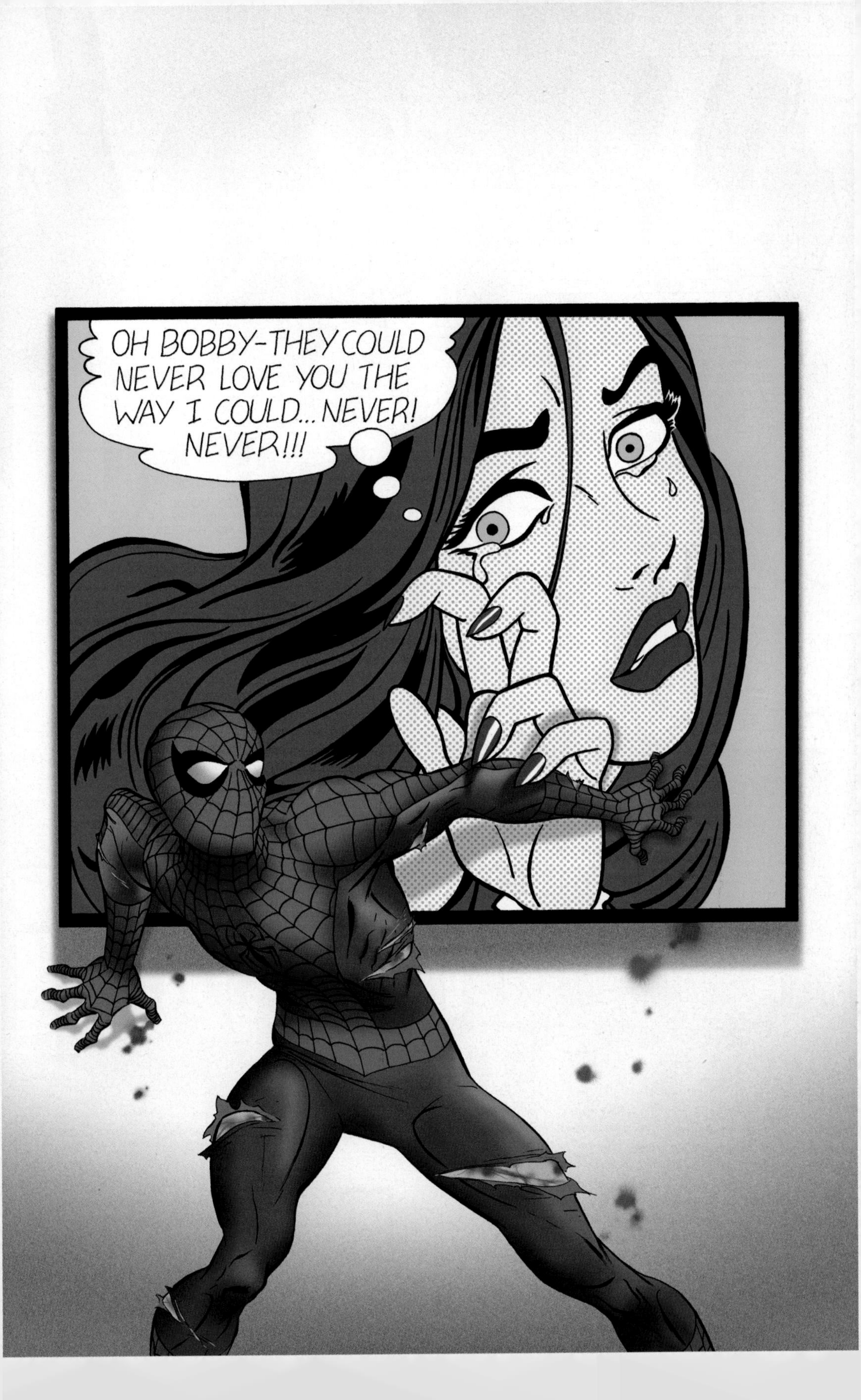
OH BOBBY-THEY COULD NEVER LOVE YOU THE WAY I COULD... NEVER! NEVER!!!

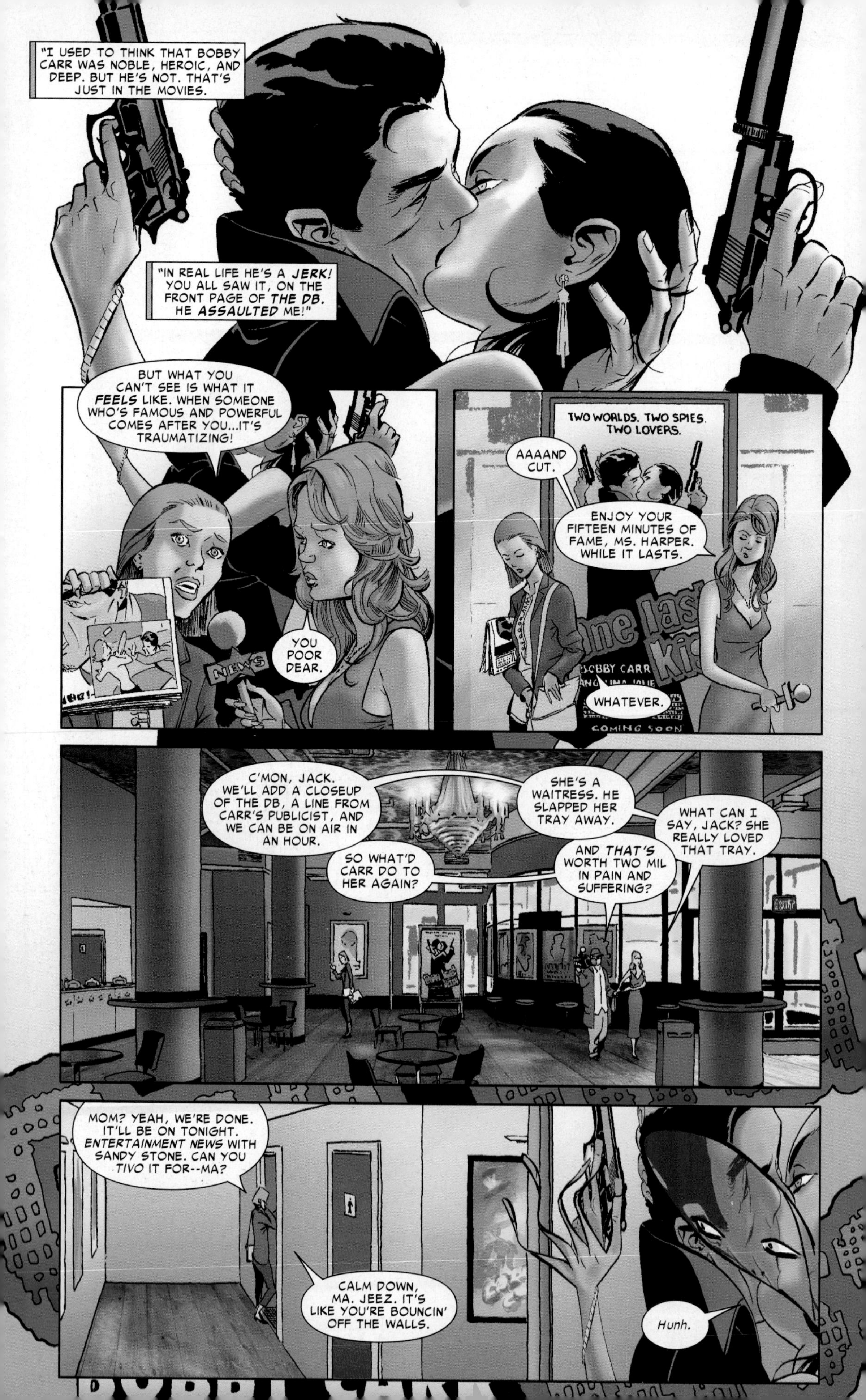
"I USED TO THINK THAT BOBBY CARR WAS NOBLE, HEROIC, AND DEEP. BUT HE'S NOT. THAT'S JUST IN THE MOVIES.
"IN REAL LIFE HE'S A JERK! YOU ALL SAW IT, ON THE FRONT PAGE OF THE DB. HE ASSAULTED ME!"
BUT WHAT YOU CAN'T SEE IS WHAT IT FEELS LIKE. WHEN SOMEONE WHO'S FAMOUS AND POWERFUL COMES AFTER YOU...IT'S TRAUMATIZING!
NEWS
YOU POOR DEAR.
TWO WORLDS. TWO SPIES. TWO LOVERS.
AAAAND CUT.
ENJOY YOUR FIFTEEN MINUTES OF FAME, MS. HARPER. WHILE IT LASTS.
BOBBY CARR
WHATEVER.
COMING SOON
C'MON, JACK. WE'LL ADD A CLOSEUP OF THE DB, A LINE FROM CARR'S PUBLICIST, AND WE CAN BE ON AIR IN AN HOUR.
SO WHAT'D CARR DO TO HER AGAIN?
SHE'S A WAITRESS. HE SLAPPED HER TRAY AWAY.
AND THAT'S WORTH TWO MIL IN PAIN AND SUFFERING?
WHAT CAN I SAY, JACK? SHE REALLY LOVED THAT TRAY.
MOM? YEAH, WE'RE DONE. IT'LL BE ON TONIGHT. ENTERTAINMENT NEWS WITH SANDY STONE. CAN YOU TIVO IT FOR--MA?
CALM DOWN, MA. JEEZ. IT'S LIKE YOU'RE BOUNCIN' OFF THE WALLS.
Hunh.

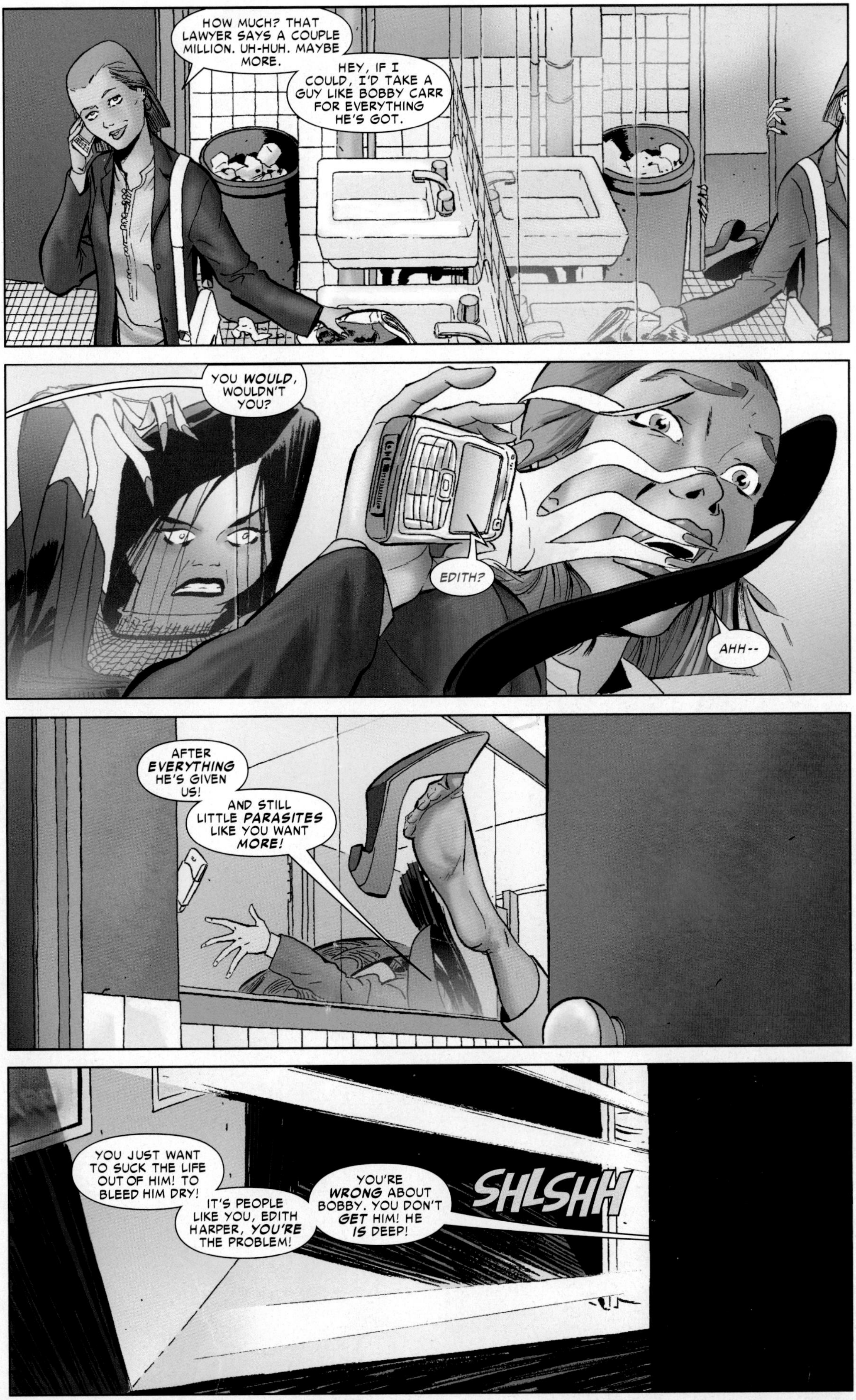
HOW MUCH? THAT LAWYER SAYS A COUPLE MILLION. UH-HUH. MAYBE MORE.
HEY, IF I COULD, I'D TAKE A GUY LIKE BOBBY CARR FOR EVERYTHING HE'S GOT.
YOU WOULD, WOULDN'T YOU?
EDITH?
AHH--
AFTER EVERYTHING HE'S GIVEN US!
AND STILL LITTLE PARASITES LIKE YOU WANT MORE!
YOU JUST WANT TO SUCK THE LIFE OUT OF HIM! TO BLEED HIM DRY!
IT'S PEOPLE LIKE YOU, EDITH HARPER, YOU'RE THE PROBLEM!
YOU'RE WRONG ABOUT BOBBY. YOU DON'T GET HIM! HE IS DEEP!
SHLSHH

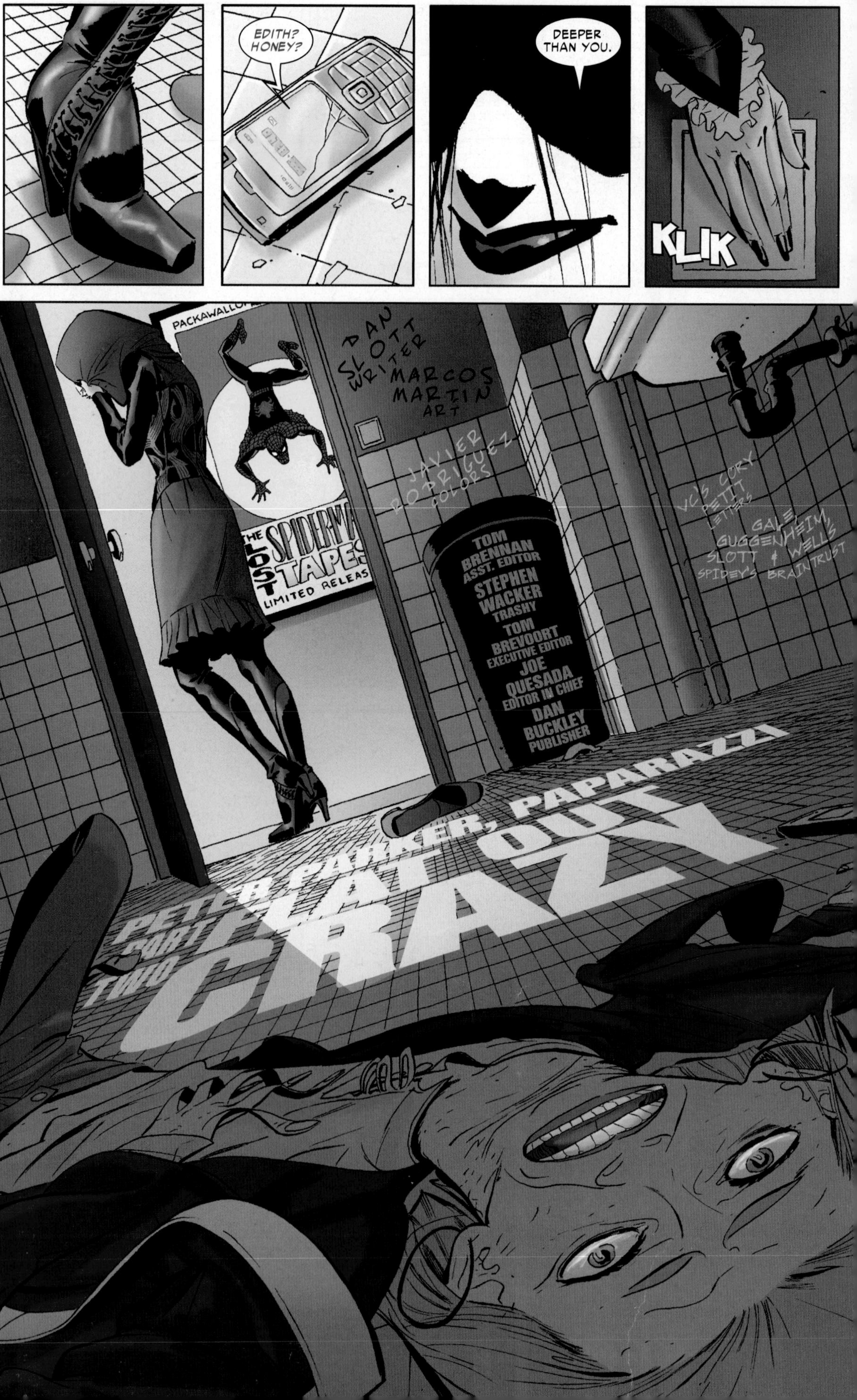
EDITH? HONEY?
DEEPER THAN YOU.
KLIK
PACKAWALLOP
THE LOST SPIDER-MAN TAPES
LIMITED RELEASE
DAN SLOTT WRITER
MARCOS MARTIN ART
JAVIER RODRIGUEZ COLORS
VC'S CORY PETIT LETTERS
GALE, GUGGENHEIM, SLOTT & WELLS SPIDEY'S BRAINTRUST
TOM BRENNAN ASST. EDITOR
STEPHEN WACKER TRASHY
TOM BREVOORT EXECUTIVE EDITOR
JOE QUESADA EDITOR IN CHIEF
DAN BUCKLEY PUBLISHER
PETER PARKER, PAPARAZZI
PART TWO
FLAT-OUT CRAZY

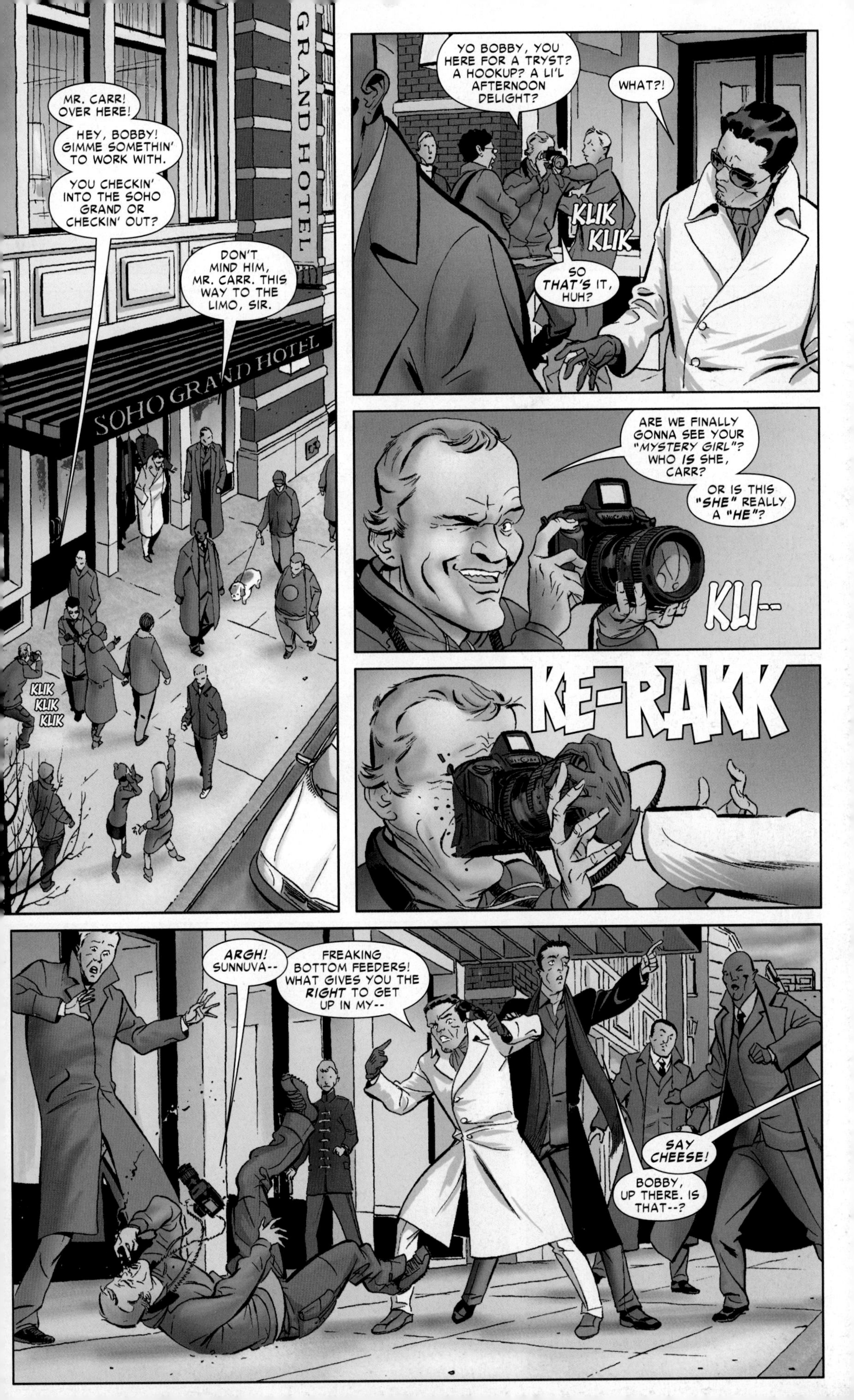

GRAND HOTEL
MR. CARR! OVER HERE!
HEY, BOBBY! GIMME SOMETHIN' TO WORK WITH.
YOU CHECKIN' INTO THE SOHO GRAND OR CHECKIN' OUT?
DON'T MIND HIM, MR. CARR. THIS WAY TO THE LIMO, SIR.
SOHO GRAND HOTEL
KLIK KLIK KLIK
YO BOBBY, YOU HERE FOR A TRYST? A HOOKUP? A LI'L AFTERNOON DELIGHT?
WHAT?!
KLIK KLIK
SO THAT'S IT, HUH?
ARE WE FINALLY GONNA SEE YOUR "MYSTERY GIRL"? WHO IS SHE, CARR?
OR IS THIS "SHE" REALLY A "HE"?
KLI--
KE-RAKK
ARGH! SUNNUVA--
FREAKING BOTTOM FEEDERS! WHAT GIVES YOU THE RIGHT TO GET UP IN MY--
SAY CHEESE!
BOBBY, UP THERE. IS THAT--?

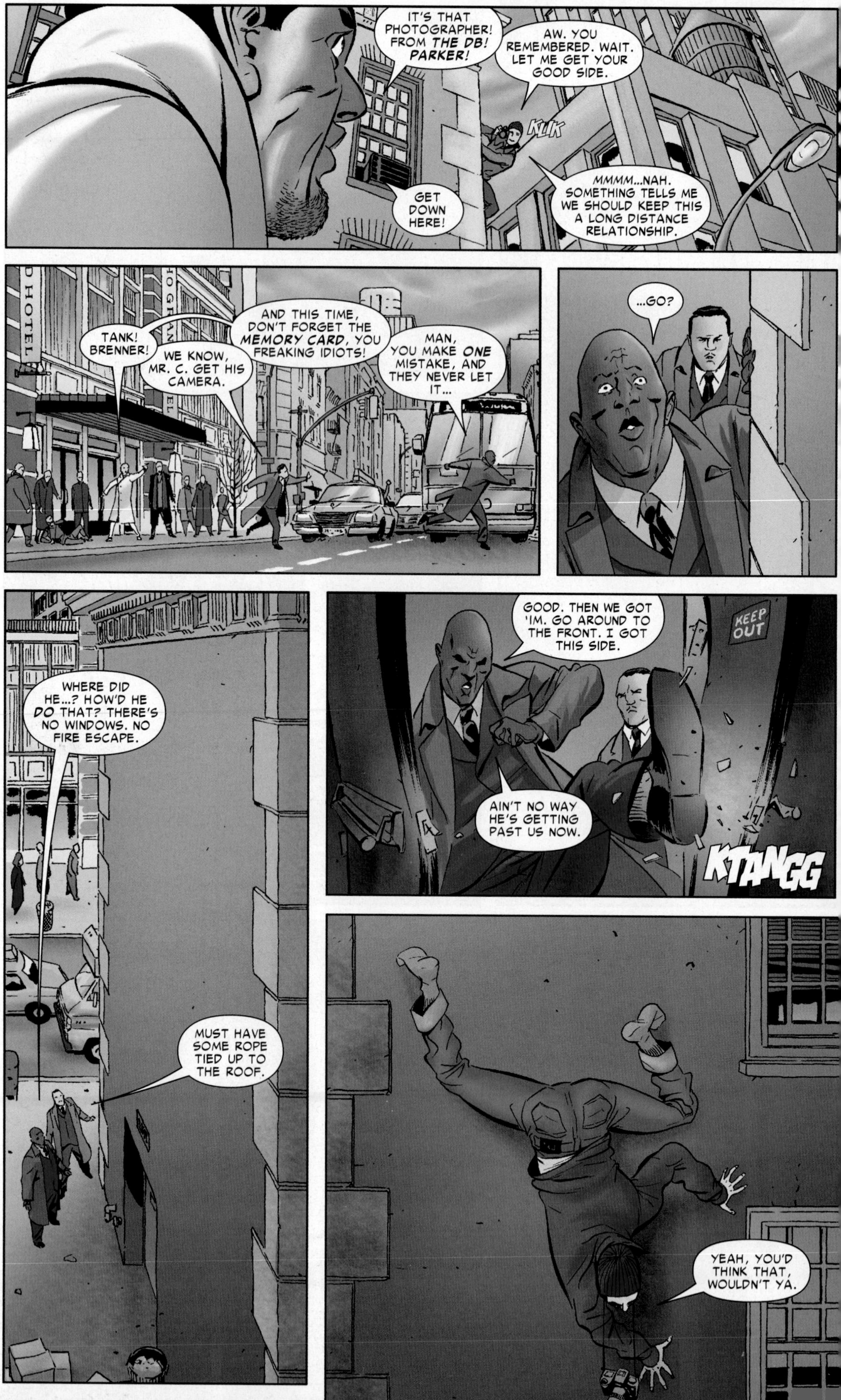
IT'S THAT PHOTOGRAPHER! FROM THE DB! PARKER!
AW. YOU REMEMBERED. WAIT. LET ME GET YOUR GOOD SIDE.
KLIK
GET DOWN HERE!
MMMM...NAH. SOMETHING TELLS ME WE SHOULD KEEP THIS A LONG DISTANCE RELATIONSHIP.
TANK! BRENNER!
AND THIS TIME, DON'T FORGET THE MEMORY CARD, YOU FREAKING IDIOTS!
WE KNOW, MR. C. GET HIS CAMERA.
MAN, YOU MAKE ONE MISTAKE, AND THEY NEVER LET IT...
HOTEL
...GO?
WHERE DID HE...? HOW'D HE DO THAT? THERE'S NO WINDOWS. NO FIRE ESCAPE.
MUST HAVE SOME ROPE TIED UP TO THE ROOF.
GOOD. THEN WE GOT 'IM. GO AROUND TO THE FRONT. I GOT THIS SIDE.
KEEP OUT
AIN'T NO WAY HE'S GETTING PAST US NOW.
KTANGG
YEAH, YOU'D THINK THAT, WOULDN'T YA.

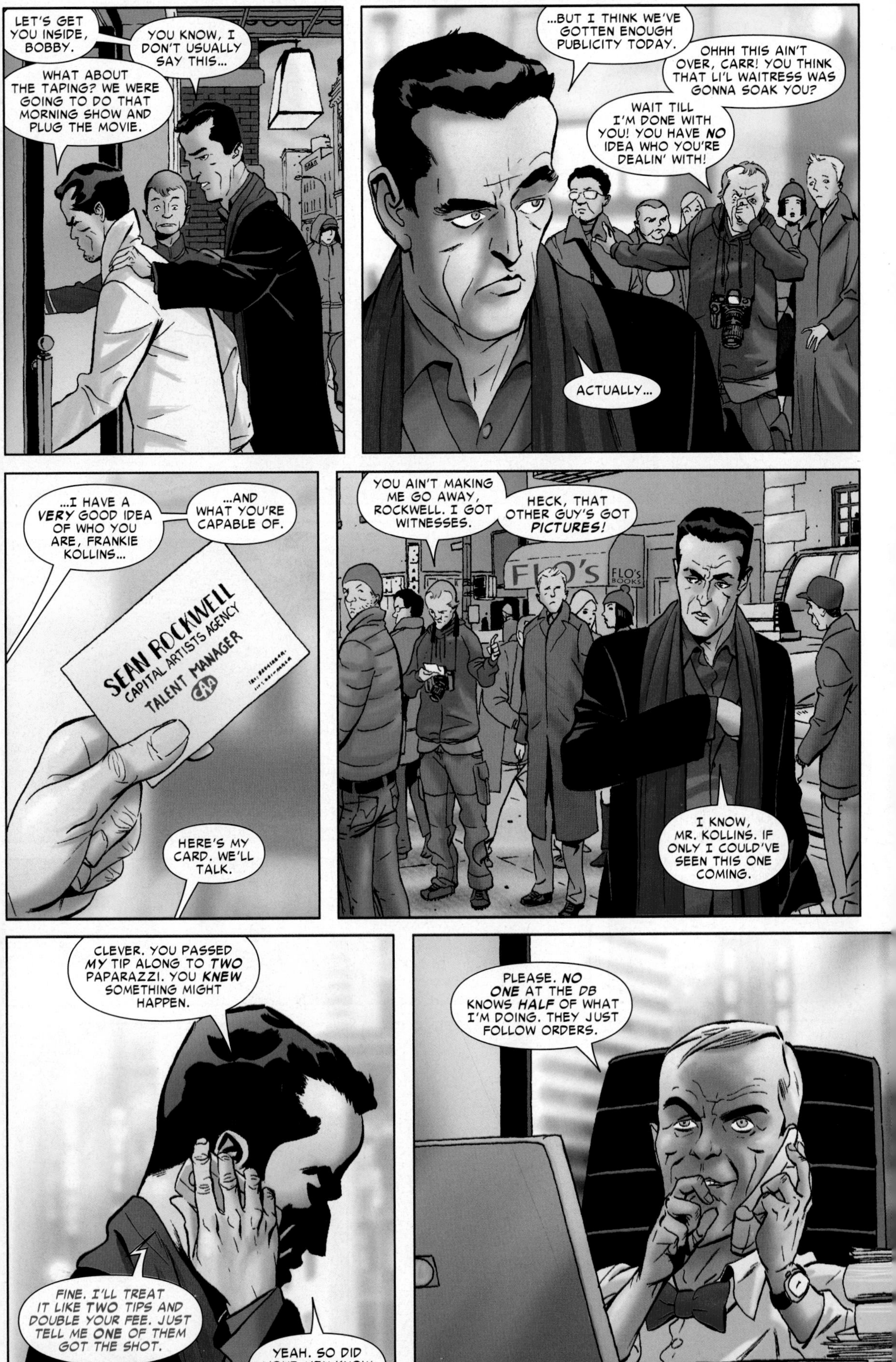
LET'S GET YOU INSIDE, BOBBY.
YOU KNOW, I DON'T USUALLY SAY THIS...
WHAT ABOUT THE TAPING? WE WERE GOING TO DO THAT MORNING SHOW AND PLUG THE MOVIE.
...BUT I THINK WE'VE GOTTEN ENOUGH PUBLICITY TODAY.
OHHH THIS AIN'T OVER, CARR! YOU THINK THAT LI'L WAITRESS WAS GONNA SOAK YOU?
WAIT TILL I'M DONE WITH YOU! YOU HAVE NO IDEA WHO YOU'RE DEALIN' WITH!
ACTUALLY...
...I HAVE A VERY GOOD IDEA OF WHO YOU ARE, FRANKIE KOLLINS...
...AND WHAT YOU'RE CAPABLE OF.
SEAN ROCKWELL
CAPITAL ARTISTS AGENCY
TALENT MANAGER
CAA
HERE'S MY CARD. WE'LL TALK.
YOU AIN'T MAKING ME GO AWAY, ROCKWELL. I GOT WITNESSES.
HECK, THAT OTHER GUY'S GOT PICTURES!
FLO'S
FLO'S BOOKS
I KNOW, MR. KOLLINS. IF ONLY I COULD'VE SEEN THIS ONE COMING.
CLEVER. YOU PASSED MY TIP ALONG TO TWO PAPARAZZI. YOU KNEW SOMETHING MIGHT HAPPEN.
FINE. I'LL TREAT IT LIKE TWO TIPS AND DOUBLE YOUR FEE. JUST TELL ME ONE OF THEM GOT THE SHOT.
YEAH. SO DID YOUR MEN KNOW THEY WERE BOTH COMING?
PLEASE. NO ONE AT THE DB KNOWS HALF OF WHAT I'M DOING. THEY JUST FOLLOW ORDERS.
DEXTER BENNETT

YOU *KNOW* WHAT I WANT!

GIVE ME *COFFEE,* YOU SLACK-JAWED SODA JERK! *REAL COFFEE!* NOT *DECAFFEINATED* DISHRAG JUICE!

I *DEMAND* TO SEE THE *MANAGER!*

OSSSBORN!

MR. JAMESON, PLEASE...

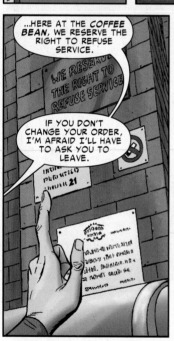

...HERE AT THE *COFFEE BEAN,* WE RESERVE THE RIGHT TO REFUSE SERVICE.

WE RESERVE THE RIGHT TO REFUSE SERVICE

IF YOU DON'T *CHANGE* YOUR ORDER, I'M AFRAID I'LL HAVE TO ASK YOU TO *LEAVE.*

WHAT?! HAROLD T. OSBORN, I AM *GOOD* FRIENDS WITH YOUR *FATHER!* HOW *DARE* YOU TREAT ME LIKE--

IT'S FOR *YOUR OWN GOOD,* MR. JAMESON. YOUR *WIFE* CAME IN LAST WEEK, AFTER YOUR... *EPISODE...*

...AND MADE ME *PROMISE* NOT TO SERVE YOU *ANYTHING* WITH CAFFEINE IN IT. IN FACT...

...I THINK SHE HIT *EVERY* COFFEE SHOP FOR *TWENTY* BLOCKS.

BLAST THAT WOMAN. SHE'LL BE THE *DEATH* OF ME.

QUITE THE OPPOSITE, MR. JAMESON. NOW LET ME GET YOU A CUP OF *CHAI TEA.* ON THE *HOUSE.*

HERE, WE'LL SET YOU UP WITH A NICE VIEW OF THE--

--WHAT IS *HE* DOING HERE?

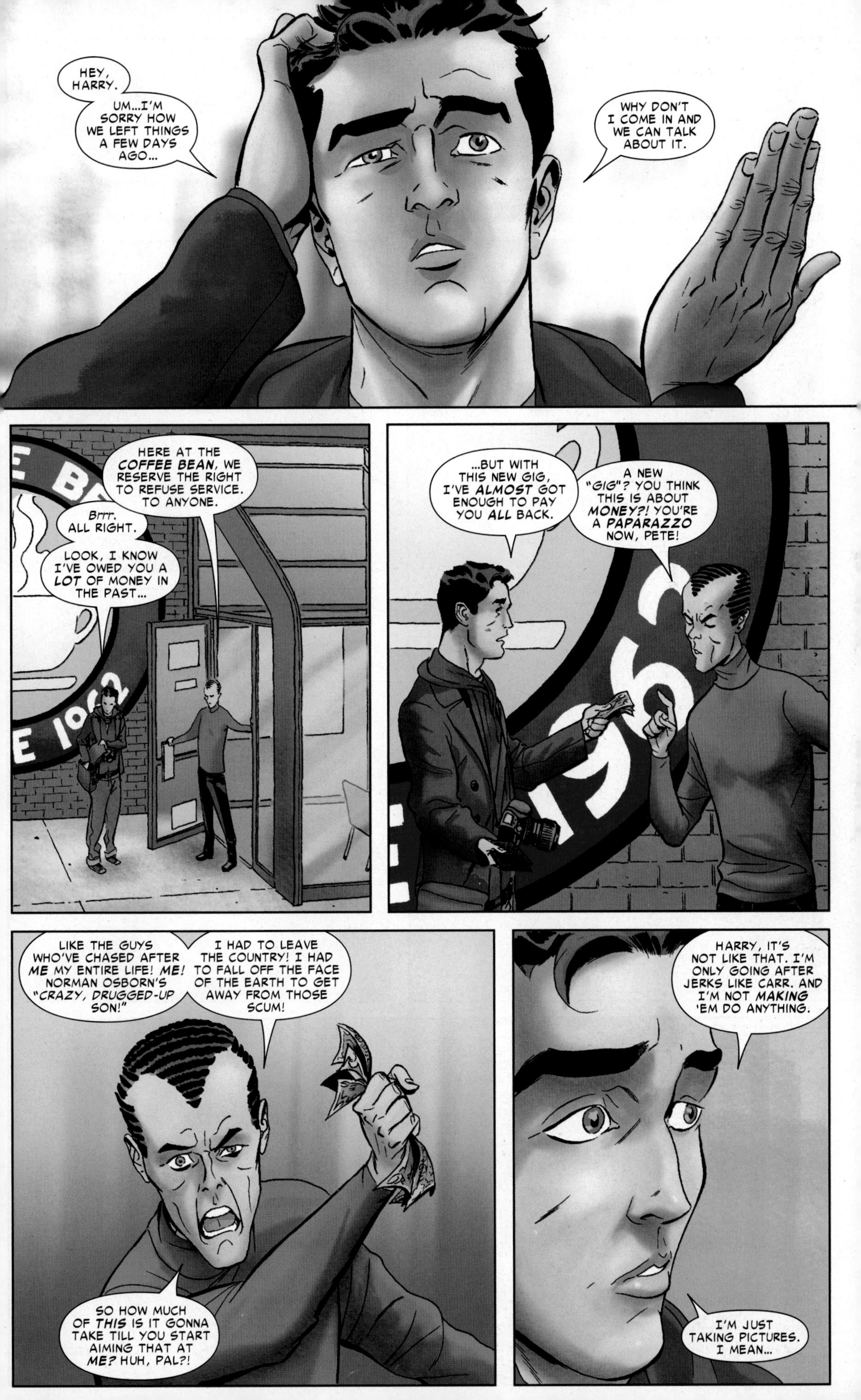
HEY, HARRY.
UM...I'M SORRY HOW WE LEFT THINGS A FEW DAYS AGO...
WHY DON'T I COME IN AND WE CAN TALK ABOUT IT.
HERE AT THE *COFFEE BEAN*, WE RESERVE THE RIGHT TO REFUSE SERVICE. TO ANYONE.
Brrr. ALL RIGHT.
LOOK, I KNOW I'VE OWED YOU A **LOT** OF MONEY IN THE PAST...
...BUT WITH THIS NEW GIG, I'VE **ALMOST** GOT ENOUGH TO PAY YOU **ALL** BACK.
A NEW "*GIG*"? YOU THINK THIS IS ABOUT ***MONEY?!*** YOU'RE A ***PAPARAZZO*** NOW, PETE!
LIKE THE GUYS WHO'VE CHASED AFTER ***ME*** MY ENTIRE LIFE! ***ME!*** NORMAN OSBORN'S *"CRAZY, DRUGGED-UP SON!"*
I HAD TO LEAVE THE COUNTRY! I HAD TO FALL OFF THE FACE OF THE EARTH TO GET AWAY FROM THOSE SCUM!
SO HOW MUCH OF ***THIS*** IS IT GONNA TAKE TILL YOU START AIMING THAT AT ***ME?*** HUH, PAL?!
HARRY, IT'S NOT LIKE THAT. I'M ONLY GOING AFTER JERKS LIKE CARR. AND I'M NOT ***MAKING*** 'EM DO ANYTHING.
I'M JUST TAKING PICTURES. I MEAN...

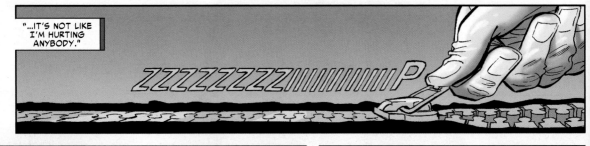

"...IT'S NOT LIKE I'M HURTING ANYBODY."

ZZZZZZZZZZIIIIIIIIIIIIIP

HI, O'NEIL.

HEY, BRANT. SO IT'S TRUE, THE DEEBS HAS YOU WORKING THE *CRIME BEAT*?

YEAH. SO WHAT'S THE STORY HERE? WHAT HAPPENED TO THE VIC?

SOMEONE FLATTENED HER.

SO ANYWAY, CARLIE, AFTER THIS I WAS WONDERIN'...IF YOU'D LIKE TO COME OVER TONIGHT AND HANG OUT?

WOW, VIN. I WAS WONDERING WHEN YOU GUYS WERE GOING TO INVITE ME OVER.

ACTUALLY, IT'S JUST ME. PARKER'S NOT MOVING IN FOR A FEW DAYS.

OH. SO PETE'S NOT GONNA BE THERE?

SAY, COOPER, YOU WANT A PIECE A' THIS ONE?

WHAT? ARE YOU SERIOUS, PALONE? YOU'RE GONNA LET ME WORK ON A PARANORMAL CASE?

IT'LL MEAN A LATE NIGHT. YOU UP FOR IT?

SURE!

...SO THEY'RE GETTING THE THEATER READY FOR THE BIG MOVIE PREMIERE, WHEN THE CLEANING STAFF FOUND THE-- *WAIT.* AREN'T YOU GUYS GONNA REMOVE THE BODY?

BETTY, THAT *IS* THE BODY. LIKE I TOLD YA, SOMEBODY *FLATTENED* HER.

WHOA...

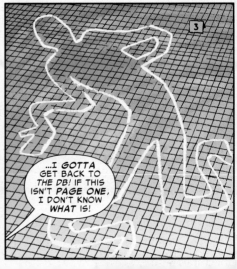

...*I GOTTA GET BACK TO THE DB!* IF THIS ISN'T *PAGE ONE*, I DON'T KNOW WHAT IS!

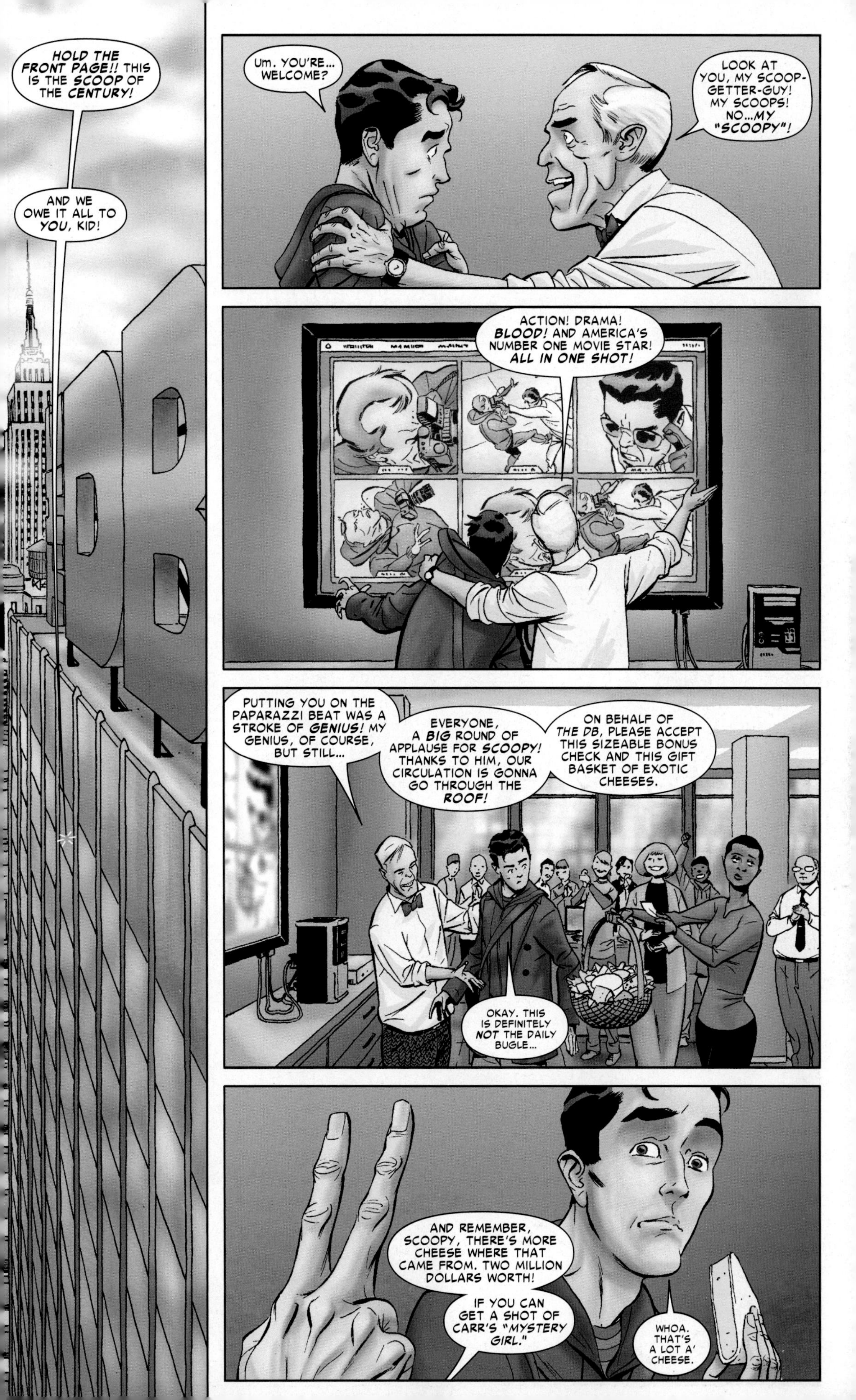

HOLD THE FRONT PAGE!! THIS IS THE SCOOP OF THE CENTURY!
AND WE OWE IT ALL TO YOU, KID!
Um. YOU'RE... WELCOME?
LOOK AT YOU, MY SCOOP-GETTER-GUY! MY SCOOPS! NO...MY "SCOOPY"!
ACTION! DRAMA! BLOOD! AND AMERICA'S NUMBER ONE MOVIE STAR! ALL IN ONE SHOT!
PUTTING YOU ON THE PAPARAZZI BEAT WAS A STROKE OF GENIUS! MY GENIUS, OF COURSE, BUT STILL...
EVERYONE, A BIG ROUND OF APPLAUSE FOR SCOOPY! THANKS TO HIM, OUR CIRCULATION IS GONNA GO THROUGH THE ROOF!
ON BEHALF OF THE DB, PLEASE ACCEPT THIS SIZEABLE BONUS CHECK AND THIS GIFT BASKET OF EXOTIC CHEESES.
OKAY. THIS IS DEFINITELY NOT THE DAILY BUGLE...
AND REMEMBER, SCOOPY, THERE'S MORE CHEESE WHERE THAT CAME FROM. TWO MILLION DOLLARS WORTH!
IF YOU CAN GET A SHOT OF CARR'S "MYSTERY GIRL."
WHOA. THAT'S A LOT A' CHEESE.

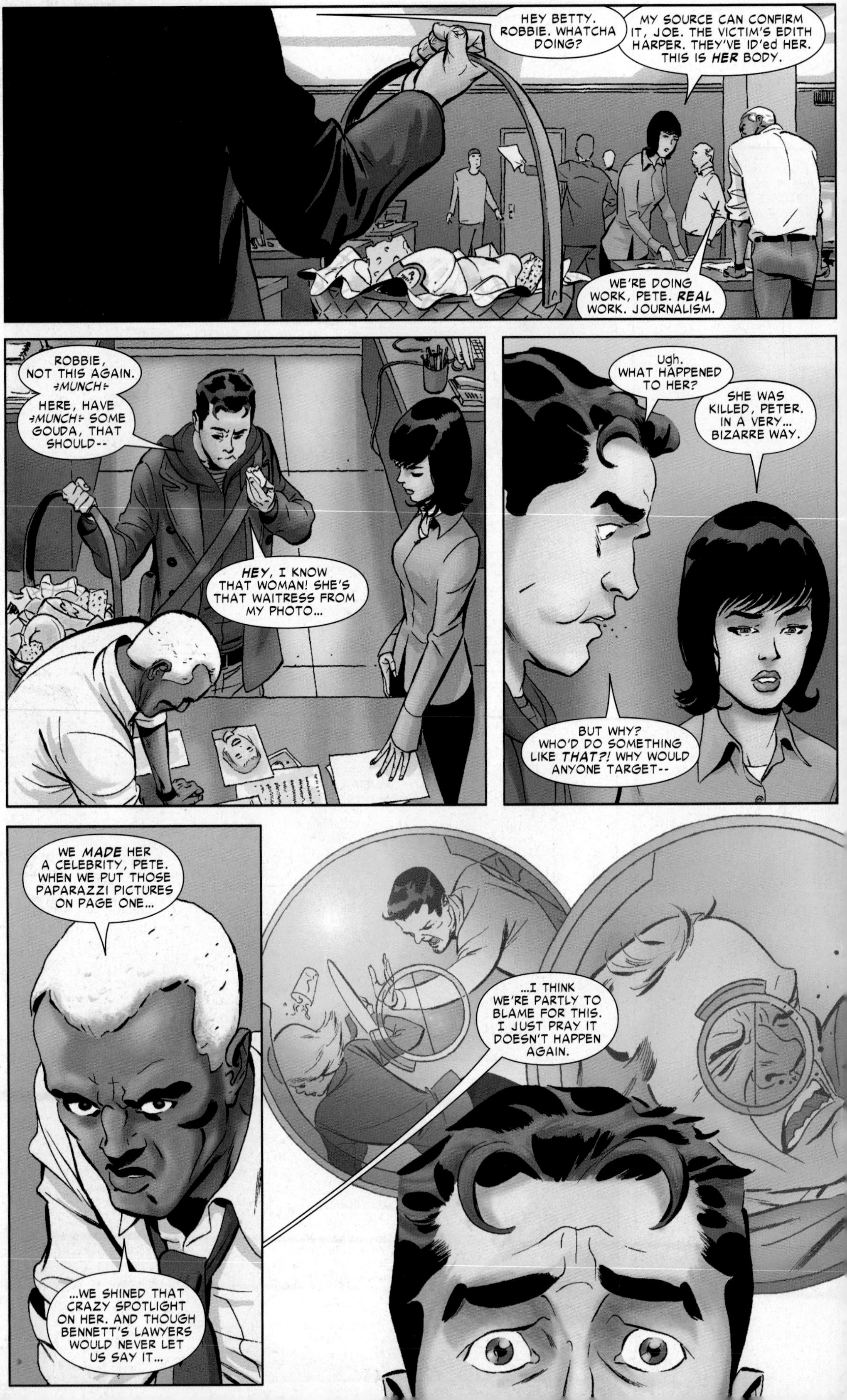
HEY BETTY. ROBBIE. WHATCHA DOING?
MY SOURCE CAN CONFIRM IT, JOE. THE VICTIM'S EDITH HARPER. THEY'VE ID'ed HER. THIS IS HER BODY.
WE'RE DOING WORK, PETE. REAL WORK. JOURNALISM.
ROBBIE, NOT THIS AGAIN. ⇇MUNCH⇉
HERE, HAVE ⇇MUNCH⇉ SOME GOUDA, THAT SHOULD--
HEY, I KNOW THAT WOMAN! SHE'S THAT WAITRESS FROM MY PHOTO...
Ugh. WHAT HAPPENED TO HER?
SHE WAS KILLED, PETER. IN A VERY... BIZARRE WAY.
BUT WHY? WHO'D DO SOMETHING LIKE THAT?! WHY WOULD ANYONE TARGET--
WE MADE HER A CELEBRITY, PETE. WHEN WE PUT THOSE PAPARAZZI PICTURES ON PAGE ONE...
...WE SHINED THAT CRAZY SPOTLIGHT ON HER. AND THOUGH BENNETT'S LAWYERS WOULD NEVER LET US SAY IT...
...I THINK WE'RE PARTLY TO BLAME FOR THIS. I JUST PRAY IT DOESN'T HAPPEN AGAIN.

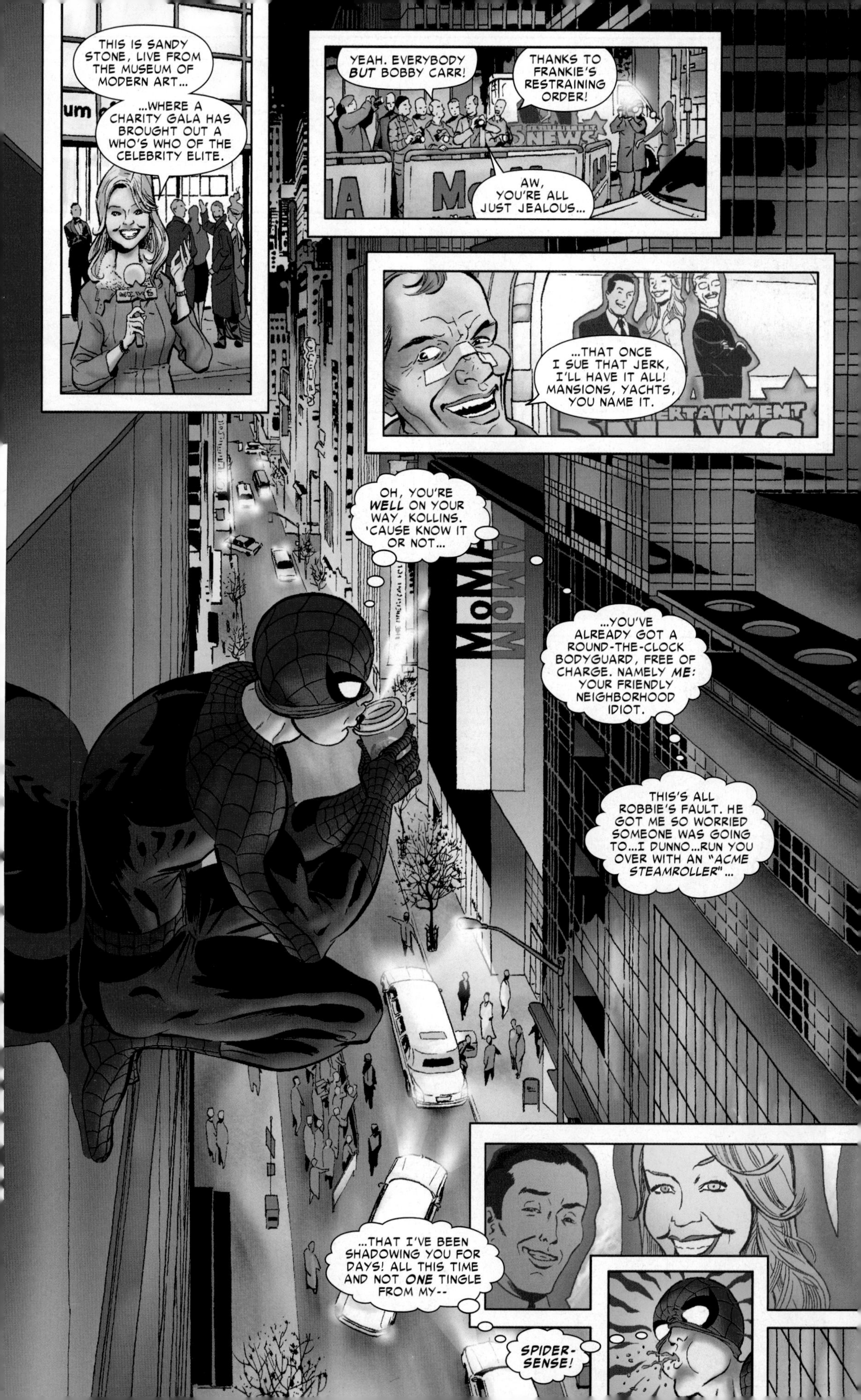
THIS IS SANDY STONE, LIVE FROM THE MUSEUM OF MODERN ART...
...WHERE A CHARITY GALA HAS BROUGHT OUT A WHO'S WHO OF THE CELEBRITY ELITE.
YEAH. EVERYBODY *BUT* BOBBY CARR!
THANKS TO FRANKIE'S RESTRAINING ORDER!
AW, YOU'RE ALL JUST JEALOUS...
...THAT ONCE I SUE THAT JERK, I'LL HAVE IT ALL! MANSIONS, YACHTS, YOU NAME IT.
OH, YOU'RE *WELL* ON YOUR WAY, KOLLINS. 'CAUSE KNOW IT OR NOT...
...YOU'VE ALREADY GOT A ROUND-THE-CLOCK BODYGUARD, FREE OF CHARGE. NAMELY *ME*: YOUR FRIENDLY NEIGHBORHOOD IDIOT.
THIS'S ALL ROBBIE'S FAULT. HE GOT ME SO WORRIED SOMEONE WAS GOING TO...I DUNNO...RUN YOU OVER WITH AN "*ACME STEAMROLLER*"...
...THAT I'VE BEEN SHADOWING YOU FOR DAYS! ALL THIS TIME AND NOT *ONE* TINGLE FROM MY--
SPIDER-SENSE!

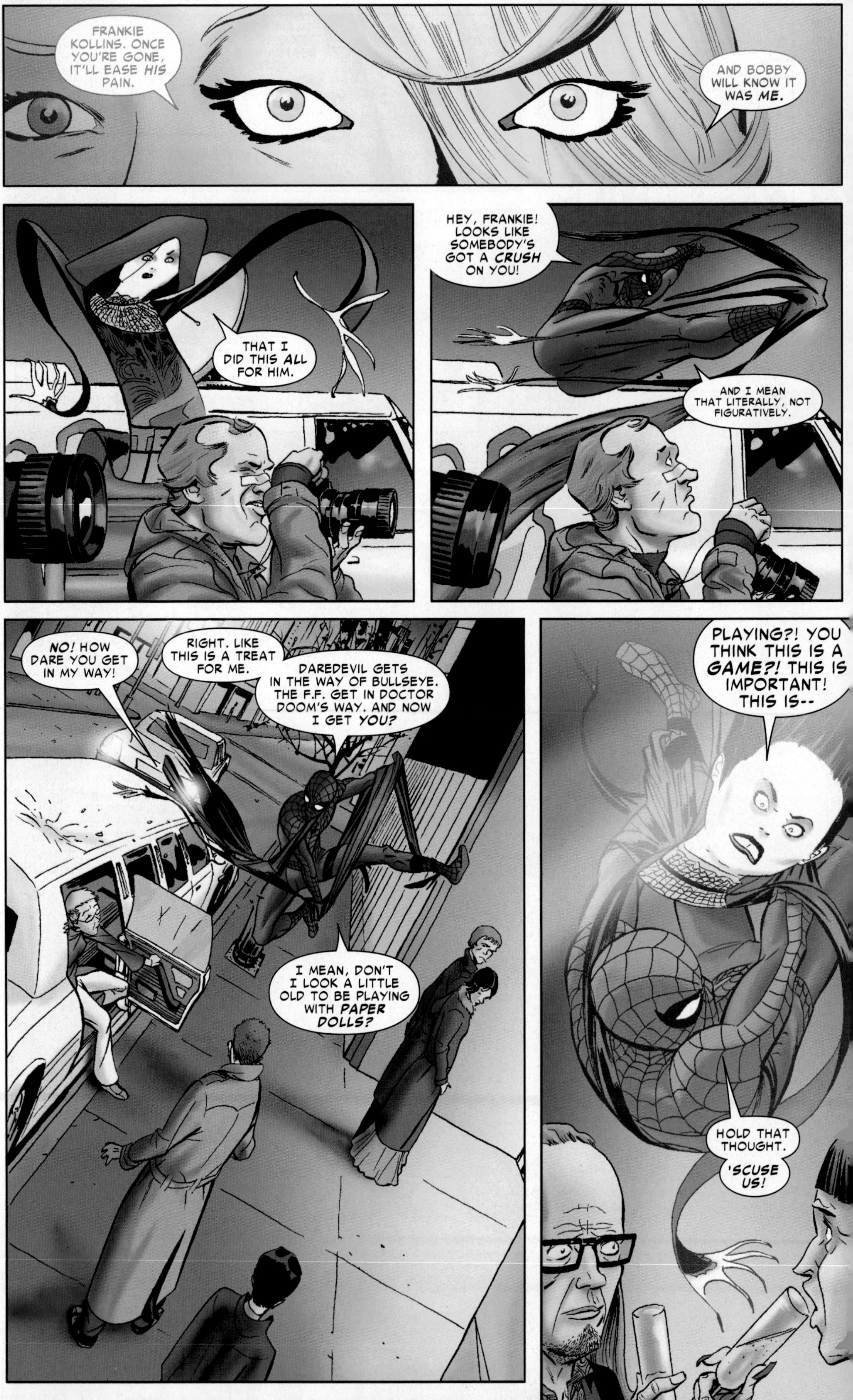
FRANKIE KOLLINS. ONCE YOU'RE GONE, IT'LL EASE HIS PAIN.
AND BOBBY WILL KNOW IT WAS ME.
THAT I DID THIS ALL FOR HIM.
HEY, FRANKIE! LOOKS LIKE SOMEBODY'S GOT A CRUSH ON YOU!
AND I MEAN THAT LITERALLY, NOT FIGURATIVELY.
NO! HOW DARE YOU GET IN MY WAY!
RIGHT. LIKE THIS IS A TREAT FOR ME.
DAREDEVIL GETS IN THE WAY OF BULLSEYE. THE F.F. GET IN DOCTOR DOOM'S WAY. AND NOW I GET YOU?
I MEAN, DON'T I LOOK A LITTLE OLD TO BE PLAYING WITH PAPER DOLLS?
PLAYING?! YOU THINK THIS IS A GAME?! THIS IS IMPORTANT! THIS IS--
HOLD THAT THOUGHT.
'SCUSE US!

KASHH SWEET SIXTIE
AN AMERICAN RETROSPECTI

COMIN' THROUGH!

SUPER-VILLAIN FIGHT IN PROGRESS! HAVE YOUR TAGS READY AT THE COAT CHECK LINE AND...

...OH YEAH, TRY *NOT* TO TRAMPLE THE SUPER HERO ON YOUR WAY OUT!

THANKS FOR SUPPORTING THE ARTS. COME AGAIN.

HELLO? CREEPY WAIF GIRL?

SORRY ABOUT THE *"PAPER DOLL"* CRACK. THAT SEEMED TO TOUCH A NERVE. YOU STILL HERE?

'CAUSE IF YOU ARE, WE HAVE TO TALK. ABOUT A WOMAN NAMED EDITH HARPER. AND WHAT I THINK YOU DID TO HER.

KLIK

Hunh?!

FRANKIE! WHAT'RE YOU DOING IN HERE?!

WHAT? I GOT A CAMERA AND THIS'S WHERE THE STORY IS.

SO EVERYONE RUNNING IN THE *OTHER* DIRECTION WASN'T A BIG CLUE?

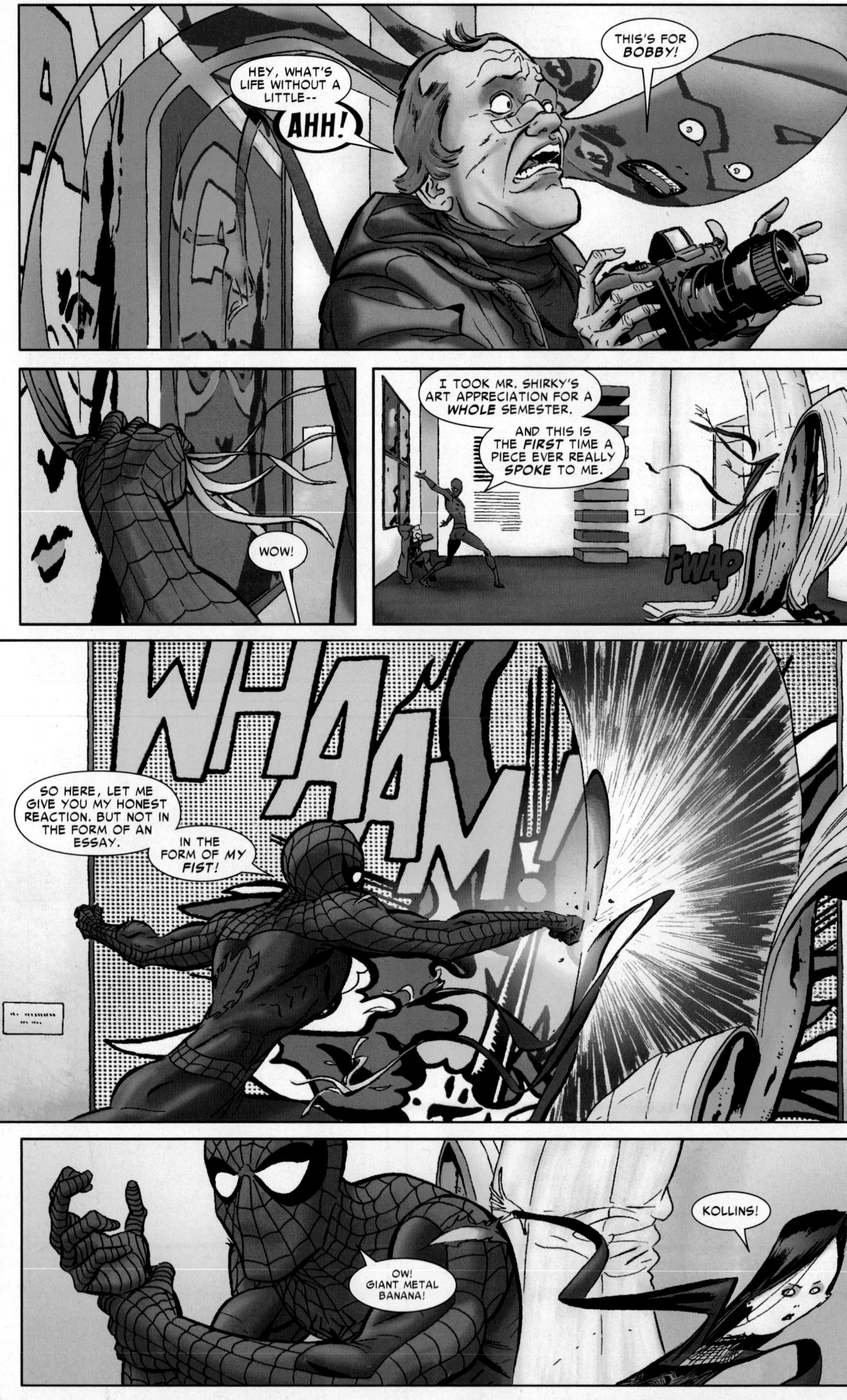

HEY, WHAT'S LIFE WITHOUT A LITTLE--
AHH!
THIS'S FOR BOBBY!
WOW!
I TOOK MR. SHIRKY'S ART APPRECIATION FOR A WHOLE SEMESTER.
AND THIS IS THE FIRST TIME A PIECE EVER REALLY SPOKE TO ME.
FWAP
WHAAM!
SO HERE, LET ME GIVE YOU MY HONEST REACTION. BUT NOT IN THE FORM OF AN ESSAY.
IN THE FORM OF MY FIST!
OW! GIANT METAL BANANA!
KOLLINS!

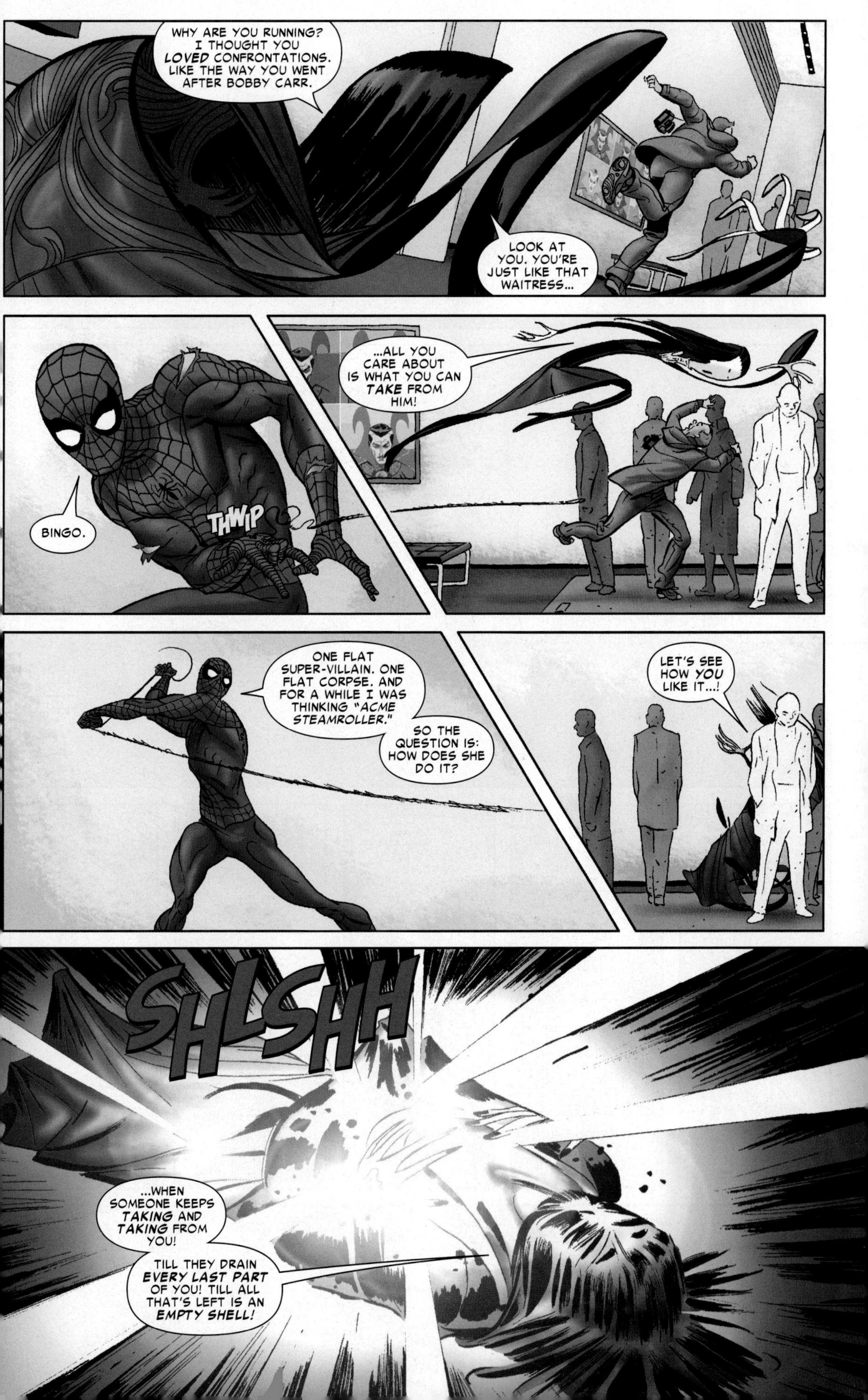
WHY ARE YOU RUNNING? I THOUGHT YOU *LOVED* CONFRONTATIONS. LIKE THE WAY YOU WENT AFTER BOBBY CARR.
LOOK AT YOU. YOU'RE JUST LIKE THAT WAITRESS...
BINGO.
THWIP
...ALL YOU CARE ABOUT IS WHAT YOU CAN *TAKE* FROM HIM!
ONE FLAT SUPER-VILLAIN. ONE FLAT CORPSE. AND FOR A WHILE I WAS THINKING *"ACME STEAMROLLER."*
SO THE QUESTION IS: HOW DOES SHE DO IT?
LET'S SEE HOW *YOU* LIKE IT...!
SHLSHH
...WHEN SOMEONE KEEPS *TAKING* AND *TAKING* FROM YOU!
TILL THEY DRAIN *EVERY LAST PART* OF YOU! TILL ALL THAT'S LEFT IS AN *EMPTY SHELL!*

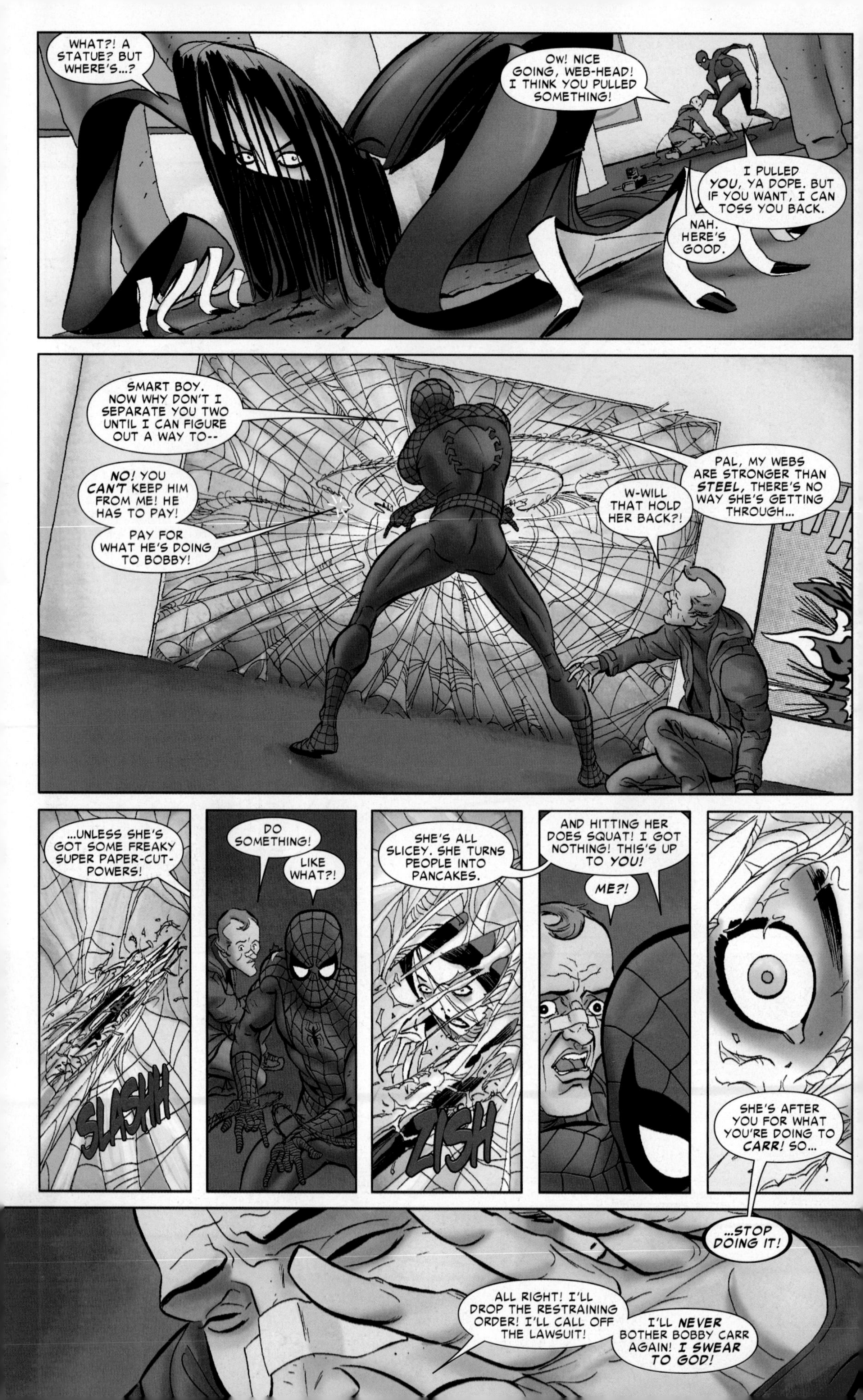

WHAT?! A STATUE? BUT WHERE'S...?
OW! NICE GOING, WEB-HEAD! I THINK YOU PULLED SOMETHING!
I PULLED YOU, YA DOPE. BUT IF YOU WANT, I CAN TOSS YOU BACK.
NAH. HERE'S GOOD.
SMART BOY. NOW WHY DON'T I SEPARATE YOU TWO UNTIL I CAN FIGURE OUT A WAY TO--
NO! YOU CAN'T KEEP HIM FROM ME! HE HAS TO PAY!
PAY FOR WHAT HE'S DOING TO BOBBY!
W-WILL THAT HOLD HER BACK?!
PAL, MY WEBS ARE STRONGER THAN STEEL, THERE'S NO WAY SHE'S GETTING THROUGH...
...UNLESS SHE'S GOT SOME FREAKY SUPER PAPER-CUT-POWERS!
SLASHH
DO SOMETHING!
LIKE WHAT?!
SHE'S ALL SLICEY. SHE TURNS PEOPLE INTO PANCAKES.
AND HITTING HER DOES SQUAT! I GOT NOTHING! THIS'S UP TO YOU!
ZISH
ME?!
SHE'S AFTER YOU FOR WHAT YOU'RE DOING TO CARR! SO...
...STOP DOING IT!
ALL RIGHT! I'LL DROP THE RESTRAINING ORDER! I'LL CALL OFF THE LAWSUIT!
I'LL NEVER BOTHER BOBBY CARR AGAIN! I SWEAR TO GOD!

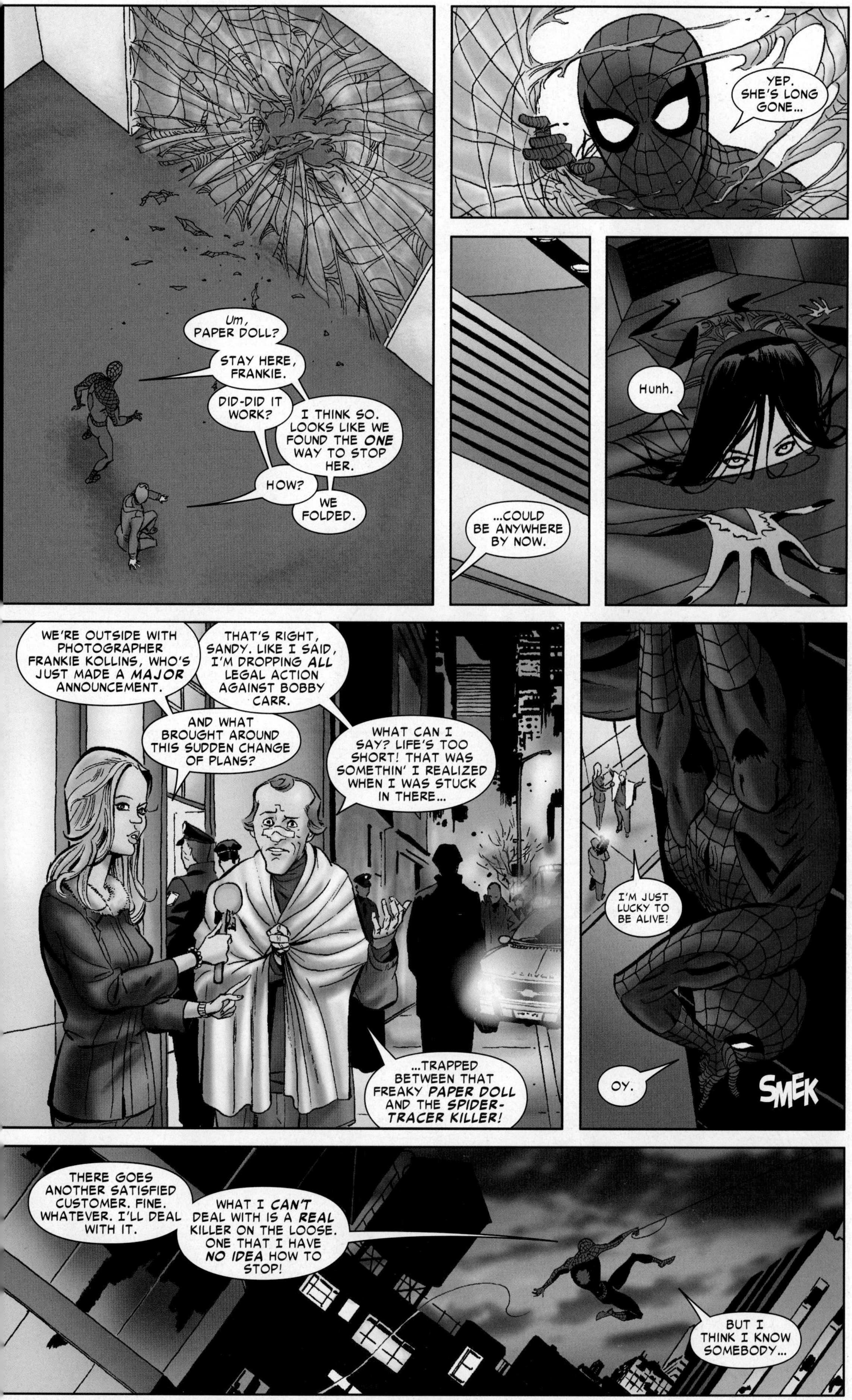
Um, PAPER DOLL?
STAY HERE, FRANKIE.
DID-DID IT WORK?
I THINK SO. LOOKS LIKE WE FOUND THE ONE WAY TO STOP HER.
HOW?
WE FOLDED.
YEP. SHE'S LONG GONE...
...COULD BE ANYWHERE BY NOW.
Hunh.
WE'RE OUTSIDE WITH PHOTOGRAPHER FRANKIE KOLLINS, WHO'S JUST MADE A MAJOR ANNOUNCEMENT.
THAT'S RIGHT, SANDY. LIKE I SAID, I'M DROPPING ALL LEGAL ACTION AGAINST BOBBY CARR.
AND WHAT BROUGHT AROUND THIS SUDDEN CHANGE OF PLANS?
WHAT CAN I SAY? LIFE'S TOO SHORT! THAT WAS SOMETHIN' I REALIZED WHEN I WAS STUCK IN THERE...
...TRAPPED BETWEEN THAT FREAKY PAPER DOLL AND THE SPIDER-TRACER KILLER!
I'M JUST LUCKY TO BE ALIVE!
OY.
SMEK
THERE GOES ANOTHER SATISFIED CUSTOMER. FINE. WHATEVER. I'LL DEAL WITH IT.
WHAT I CAN'T DEAL WITH IS A REAL KILLER ON THE LOOSE. ONE THAT I HAVE NO IDEA HOW TO STOP!
BUT I THINK I KNOW SOMEBODY...

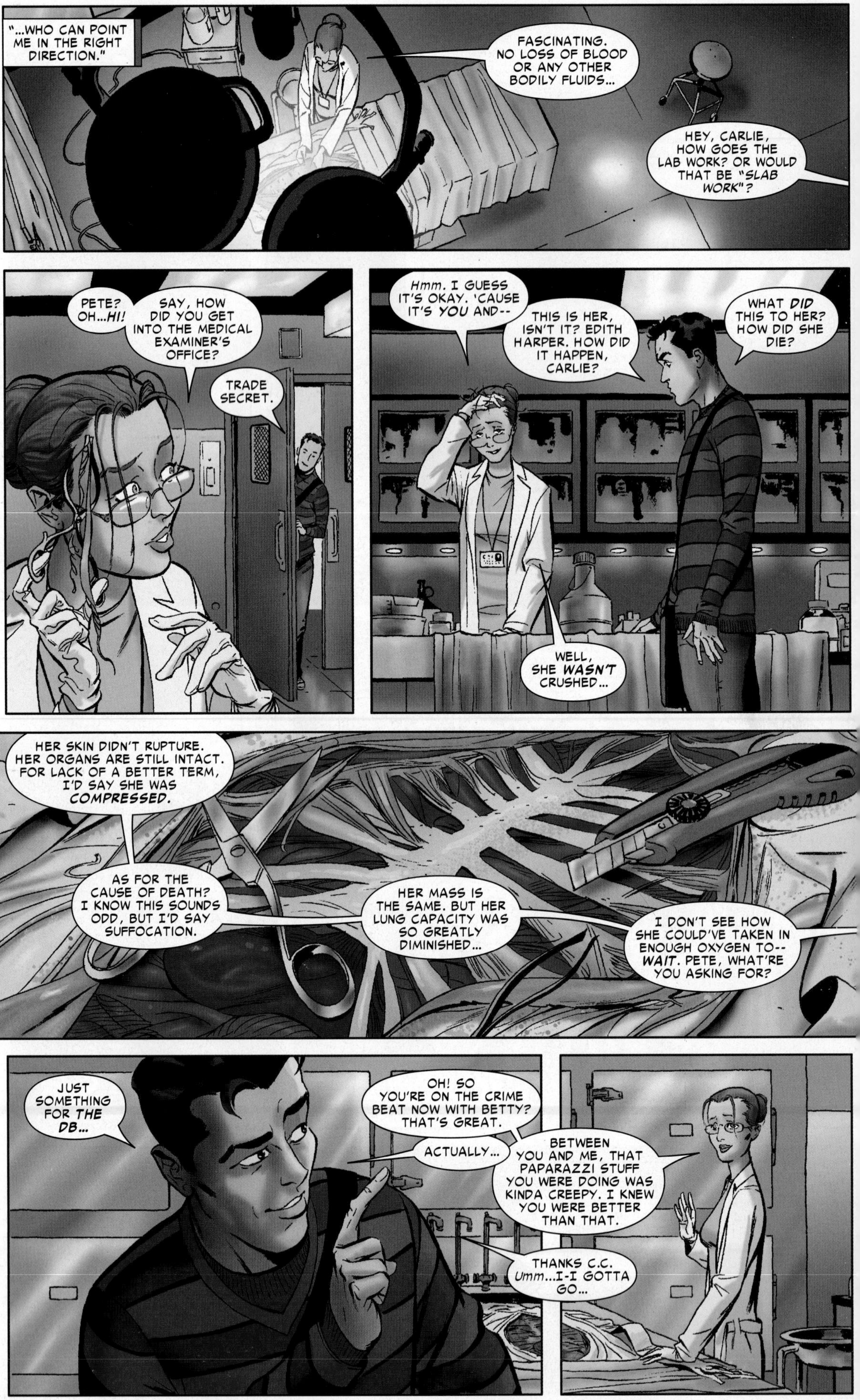
"...WHO CAN POINT ME IN THE RIGHT DIRECTION."
FASCINATING. NO LOSS OF BLOOD OR ANY OTHER BODILY FLUIDS...
HEY, CARLIE, HOW GOES THE LAB WORK? OR WOULD THAT BE "SLAB WORK"?
PETE? OH...HI!
SAY, HOW DID YOU GET INTO THE MEDICAL EXAMINER'S OFFICE?
TRADE SECRET.
Hmm. I GUESS IT'S OKAY. 'CAUSE IT'S YOU AND--
THIS IS HER, ISN'T IT? EDITH HARPER. HOW DID IT HAPPEN, CARLIE?
WHAT DID THIS TO HER? HOW DID SHE DIE?
WELL, SHE WASN'T CRUSHED...
HER SKIN DIDN'T RUPTURE. HER ORGANS ARE STILL INTACT. FOR LACK OF A BETTER TERM, I'D SAY SHE WAS COMPRESSED.
AS FOR THE CAUSE OF DEATH? I KNOW THIS SOUNDS ODD, BUT I'D SAY SUFFOCATION.
HER MASS IS THE SAME. BUT HER LUNG CAPACITY WAS SO GREATLY DIMINISHED...
I DON'T SEE HOW SHE COULD'VE TAKEN IN ENOUGH OXYGEN TO-- WAIT. PETE, WHAT'RE YOU ASKING FOR?
JUST SOMETHING FOR THE DB...
OH! SO YOU'RE ON THE CRIME BEAT NOW WITH BETTY? THAT'S GREAT.
ACTUALLY...
BETWEEN YOU AND ME, THAT PAPARAZZI STUFF YOU WERE DOING WAS KINDA CREEPY. I KNEW YOU WERE BETTER THAN THAT.
THANKS C.C. Umm...I-I GOTTA GO...

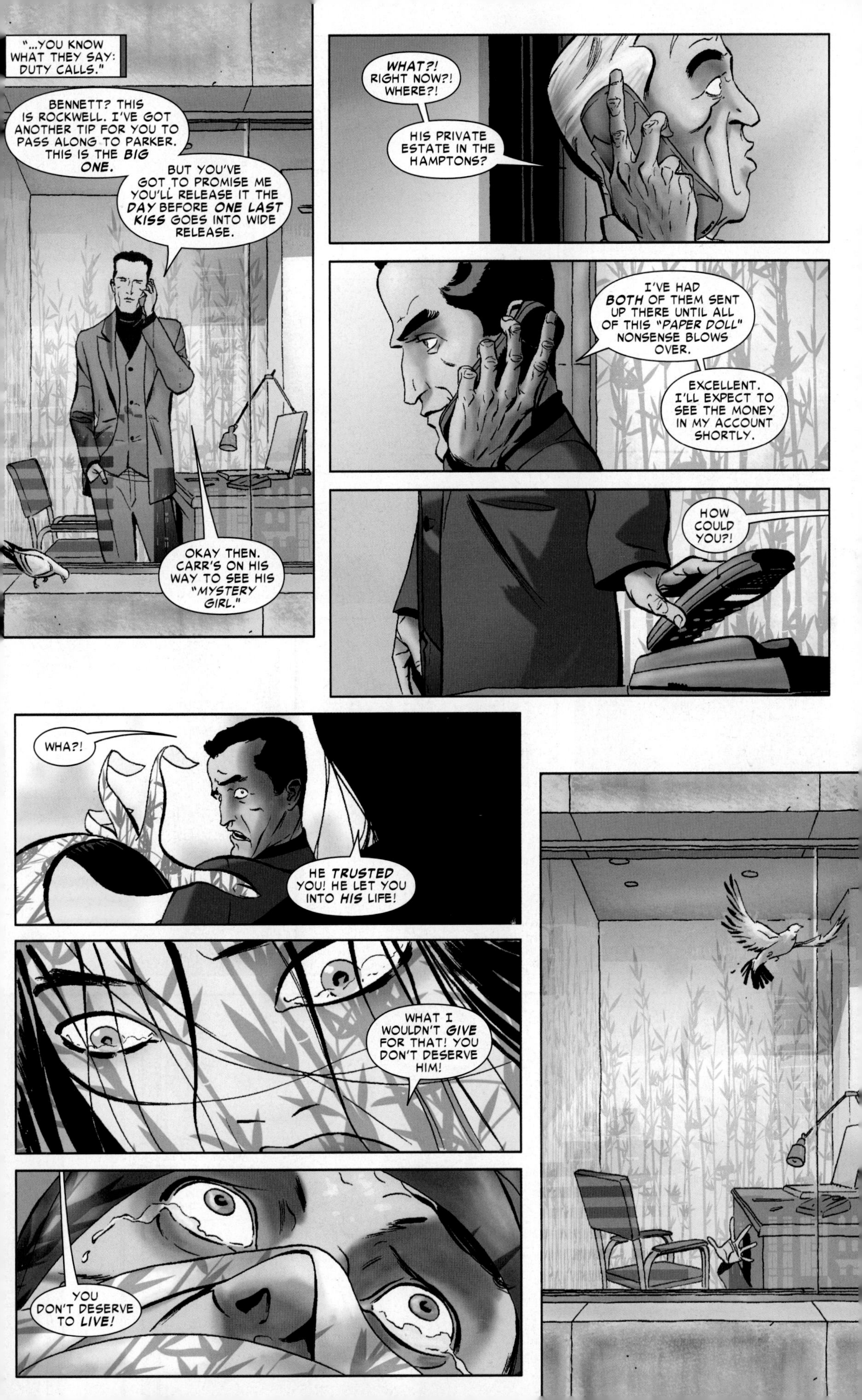
"...YOU KNOW WHAT THEY SAY: DUTY CALLS."
BENNETT? THIS IS ROCKWELL. I'VE GOT ANOTHER TIP FOR YOU TO PASS ALONG TO PARKER. THIS IS THE BIG ONE.
BUT YOU'VE GOT TO PROMISE ME YOU'LL RELEASE IT THE DAY BEFORE ONE LAST KISS GOES INTO WIDE RELEASE.
OKAY THEN. CARR'S ON HIS WAY TO SEE HIS "MYSTERY GIRL."
WHAT?! RIGHT NOW?! WHERE?!
HIS PRIVATE ESTATE IN THE HAMPTONS?
I'VE HAD BOTH OF THEM SENT UP THERE UNTIL ALL OF THIS "PAPER DOLL" NONSENSE BLOWS OVER.
EXCELLENT. I'LL EXPECT TO SEE THE MONEY IN MY ACCOUNT SHORTLY.
HOW COULD YOU?!
WHA?!
HE TRUSTED YOU! HE LET YOU INTO HIS LIFE!
WHAT I WOULDN'T GIVE FOR THAT! YOU DON'T DESERVE HIM!
YOU DON'T DESERVE TO LIVE!

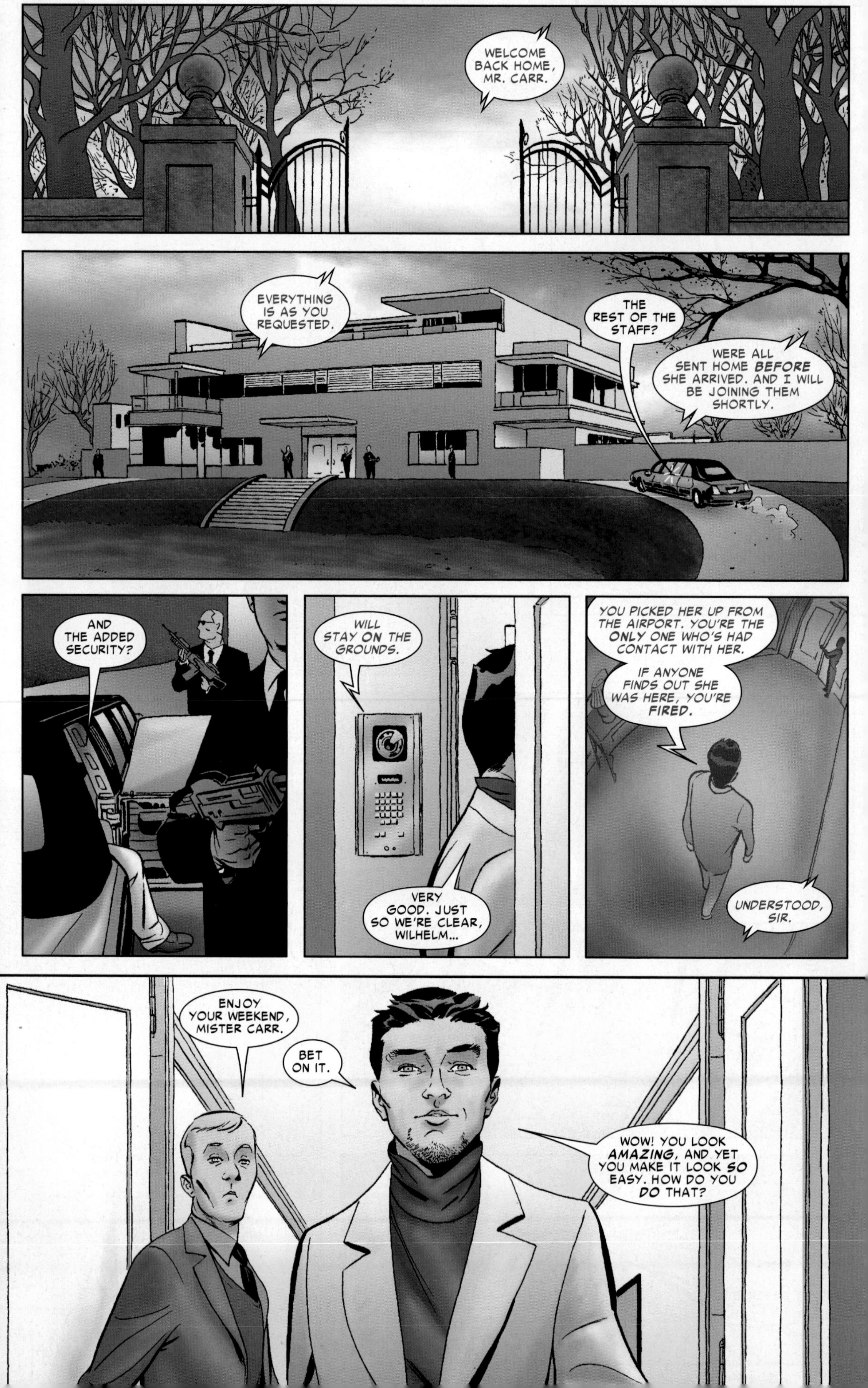
WELCOME BACK HOME, MR. CARR.
EVERYTHING IS AS YOU REQUESTED.
THE REST OF THE STAFF?
WERE ALL SENT HOME BEFORE SHE ARRIVED. AND I WILL BE JOINING THEM SHORTLY.
AND THE ADDED SECURITY?
WILL STAY ON THE GROUNDS.
VERY GOOD. JUST SO WE'RE CLEAR, WILHELM...
YOU PICKED HER UP FROM THE AIRPORT. YOU'RE THE ONLY ONE WHO'S HAD CONTACT WITH HER.
IF ANYONE FINDS OUT SHE WAS HERE, YOU'RE FIRED.
UNDERSTOOD, SIR.
ENJOY YOUR WEEKEND, MISTER CARR.
BET ON IT.
WOW! YOU LOOK AMAZING, AND YET YOU MAKE IT LOOK SO EASY. HOW DO YOU DO THAT?

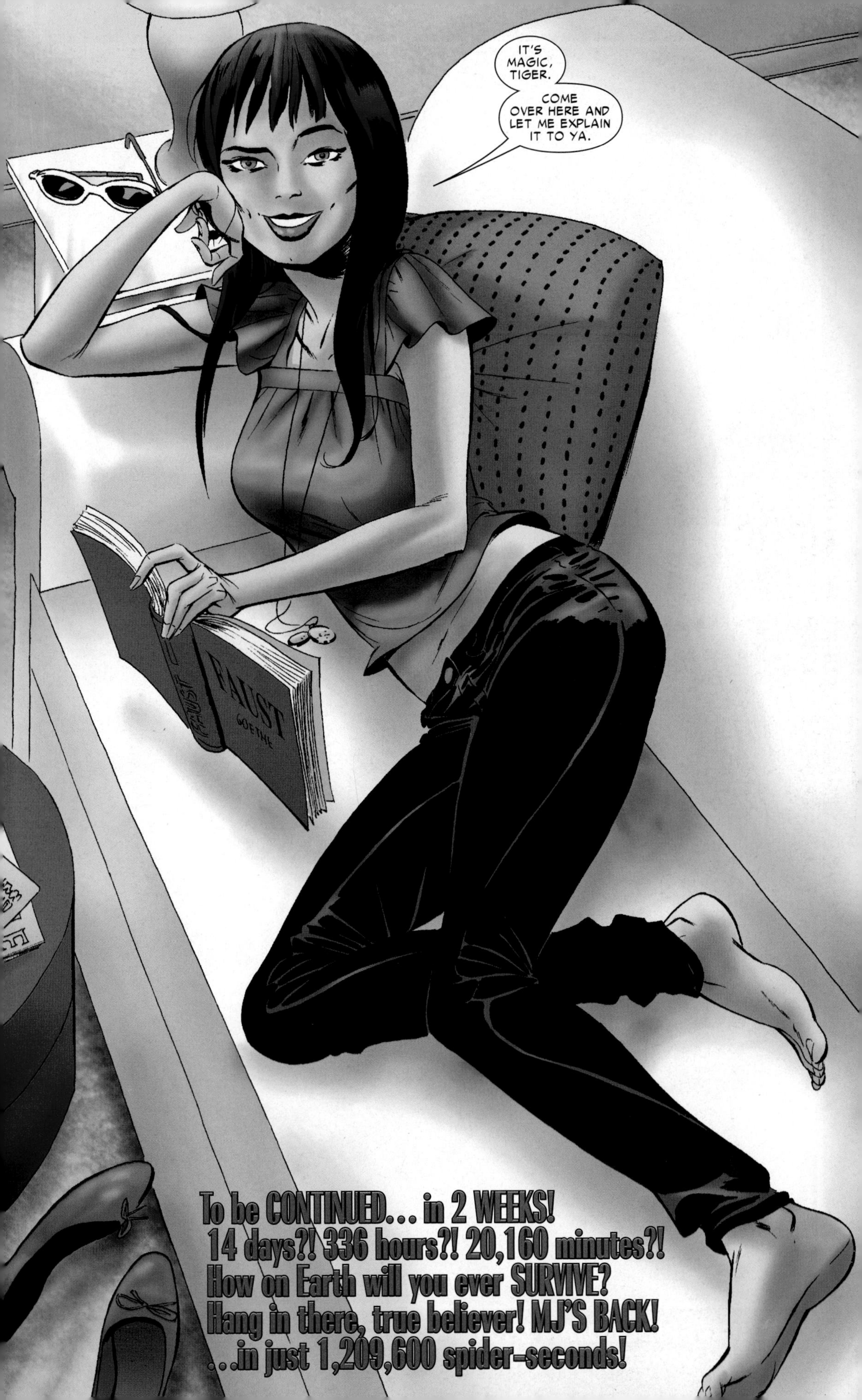
IT'S MAGIC, TIGER.
COME OVER HERE AND LET ME EXPLAIN IT TO YA.
FAUST
GOETHE
To be CONTINUED... in 2 WEEKS!
14 days?! 336 hours?! 20,160 minutes?!
How on Earth will you ever SURVIVE?
Hang in there, true believer! MJ'S BACK!
...in just 1,209,600 spider-seconds!

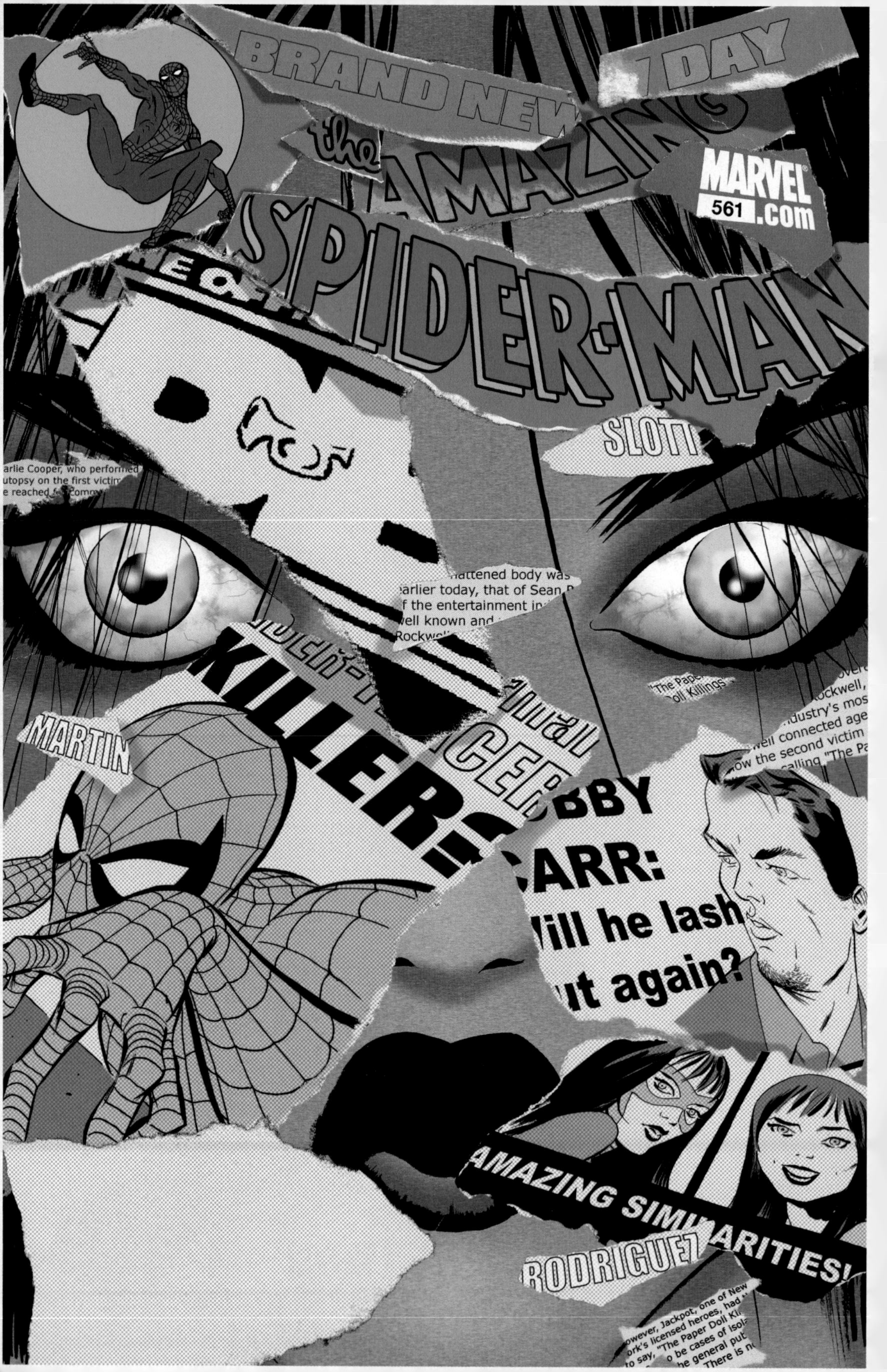

BRAND NEW DAY
the AMAZING SPIDER-MAN
MARVEL
561 .com
SLOTT
MARTIN
RODRIGUEZ
KILLER!
BBY
CARR:
Vill he lash
ut again?
AMAZING SIMILARITIES!

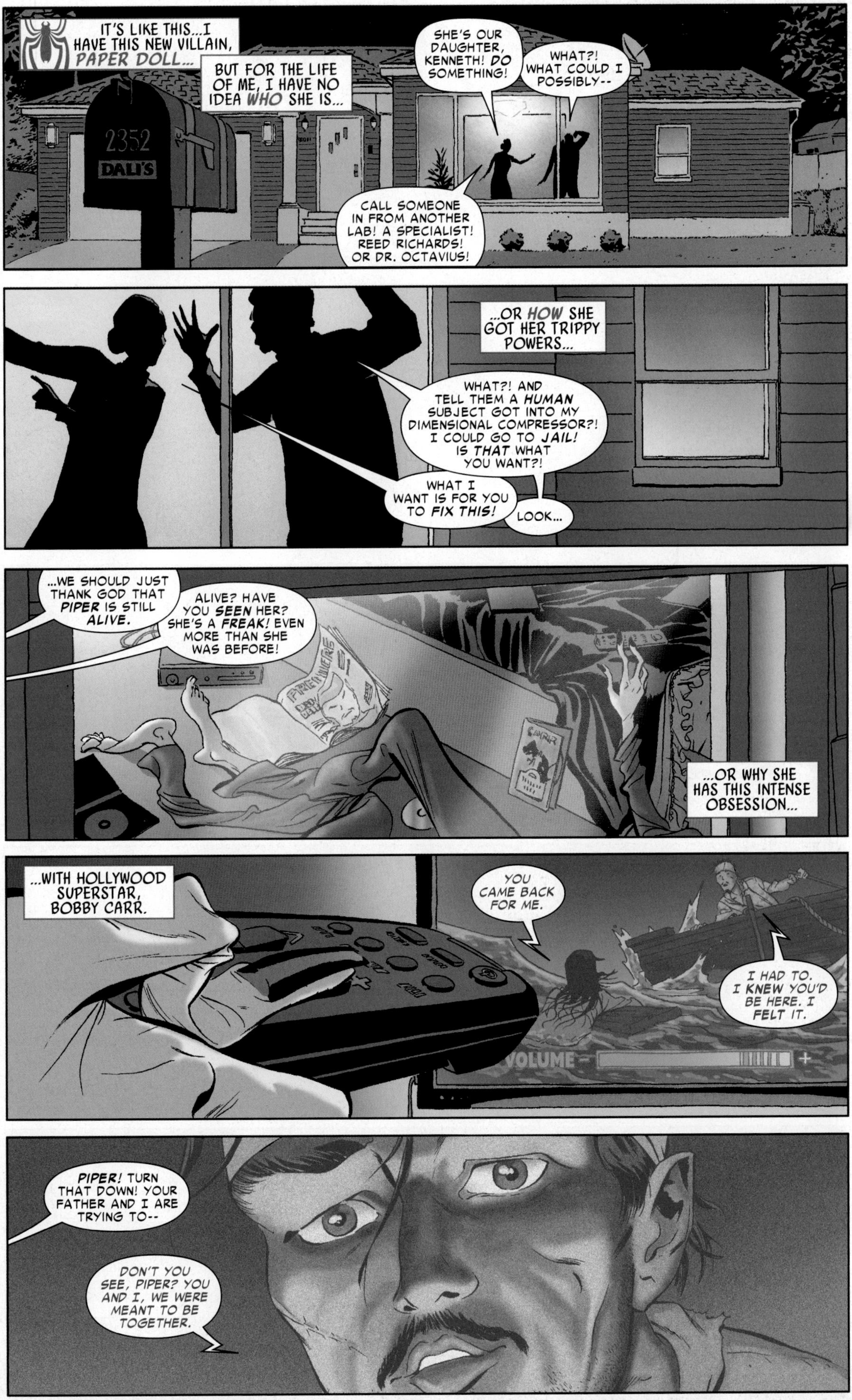
IT'S LIKE THIS...I HAVE THIS NEW VILLAIN, PAPER DOLL...
BUT FOR THE LIFE OF ME, I HAVE NO IDEA WHO SHE IS...
2352
DALI'S
SHE'S OUR DAUGHTER, KENNETH! DO SOMETHING!
WHAT?! WHAT COULD I POSSIBLY--
CALL SOMEONE IN FROM ANOTHER LAB! A SPECIALIST! REED RICHARDS! OR DR. OCTAVIUS!
...OR HOW SHE GOT HER TRIPPY POWERS...
WHAT?! AND TELL THEM A HUMAN SUBJECT GOT INTO MY DIMENSIONAL COMPRESSOR?! I COULD GO TO JAIL! IS THAT WHAT YOU WANT?!
WHAT I WANT IS FOR YOU TO FIX THIS!
LOOK...
...WE SHOULD JUST THANK GOD THAT PIPER IS STILL ALIVE.
ALIVE? HAVE YOU SEEN HER? SHE'S A FREAK! EVEN MORE THAN SHE WAS BEFORE!
CARR
...OR WHY SHE HAS THIS INTENSE OBSESSION...
...WITH HOLLYWOOD SUPERSTAR, BOBBY CARR.
YOU CAME BACK FOR ME.
I HAD TO. I KNEW YOU'D BE HERE. I FELT IT.
VOLUME
PIPER! TURN THAT DOWN! YOUR FATHER AND I ARE TRYING TO--
DON'T YOU SEE, PIPER? YOU AND I, WE WERE MEANT TO BE TOGETHER.

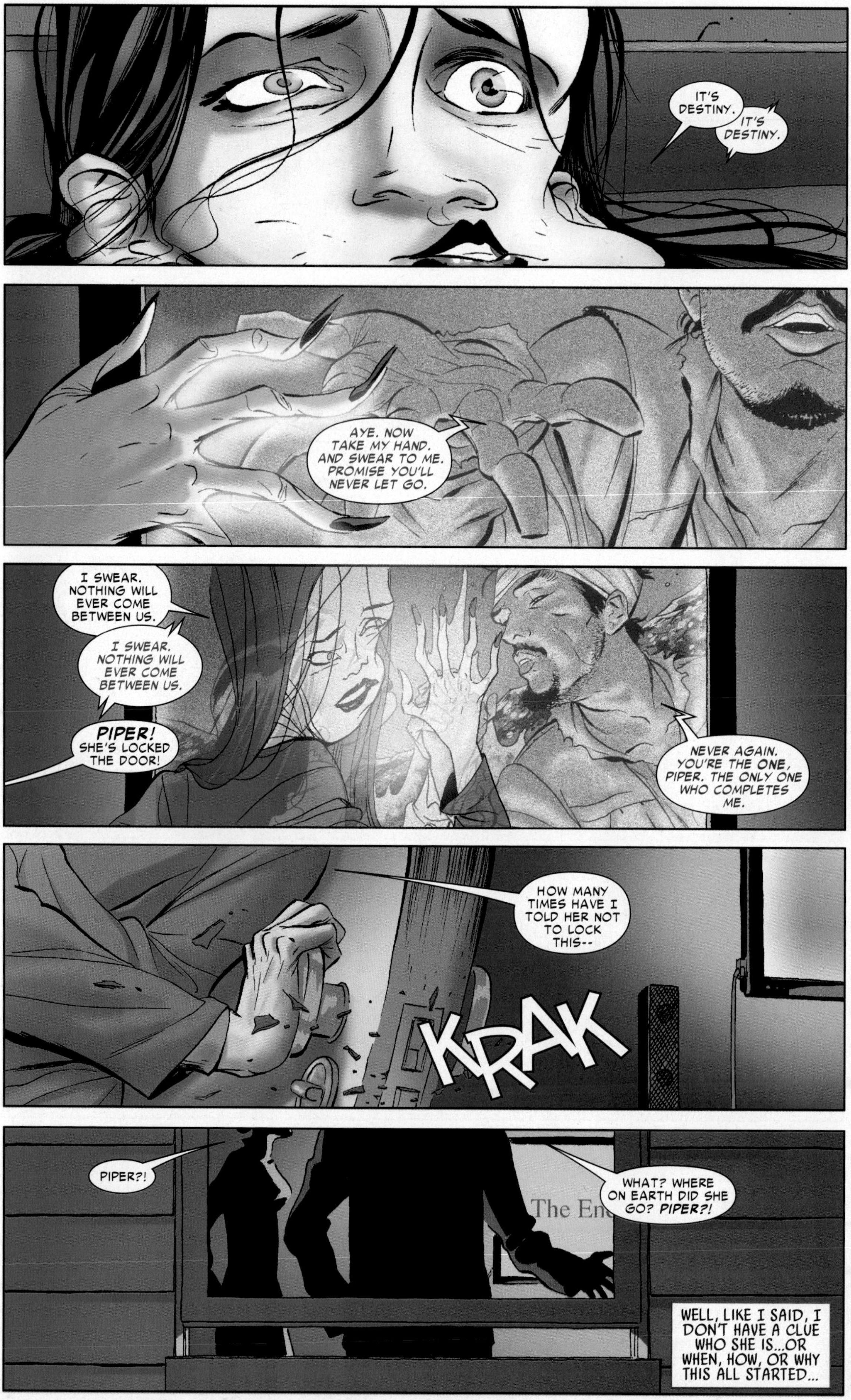

IT'S DESTINY.
IT'S DESTINY.
AYE. NOW TAKE MY HAND. AND SWEAR TO ME. PROMISE YOU'LL NEVER LET GO.
I SWEAR. NOTHING WILL EVER COME BETWEEN US.
I SWEAR. NOTHING WILL EVER COME BETWEEN US.
NEVER AGAIN. YOU'RE THE ONE, PIPER. THE ONLY ONE WHO COMPLETES ME.
PIPER! SHE'S LOCKED THE DOOR!
HOW MANY TIMES HAVE I TOLD HER NOT TO LOCK THIS--
KRAK
PIPER?!
WHAT? WHERE ON EARTH DID SHE GO? PIPER?!
The En
WELL, LIKE I SAID, I DON'T HAVE A CLUE WHO SHE IS...OR WHEN, HOW, OR WHY THIS ALL STARTED...

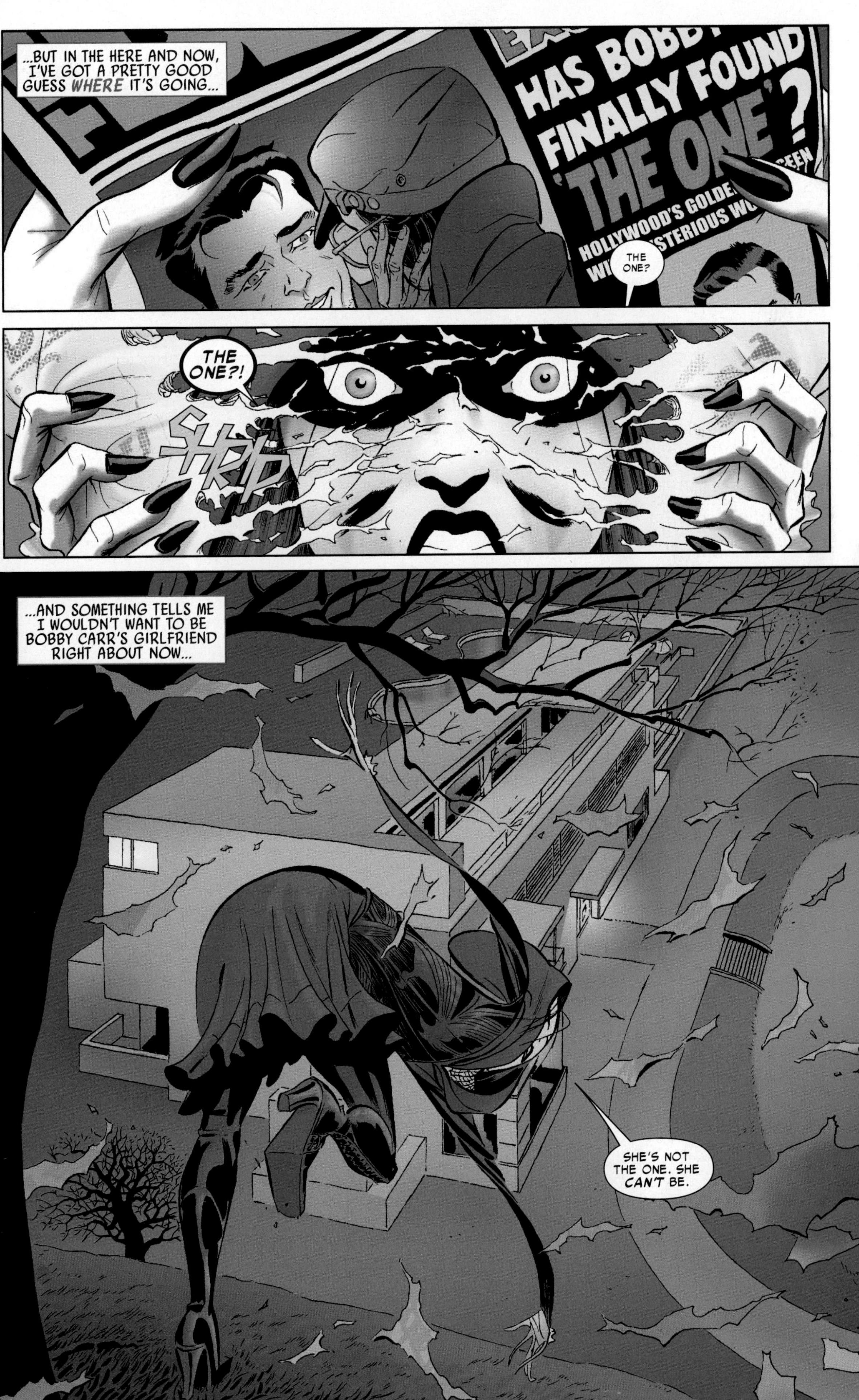

...BUT IN THE HERE AND NOW, I'VE GOT A PRETTY GOOD GUESS *WHERE* IT'S GOING...
HAS BOBB
FINALLY FOUND
'THE ONE'?
HOLLYWOOD'S GOLDE
STERIOUS WO
THE ONE?
THE ONE?!
SHRIP
...AND SOMETHING TELLS ME I WOULDN'T WANT TO BE BOBBY CARR'S GIRLFRIEND RIGHT ABOUT NOW...
SHE'S NOT THE ONE. SHE *CAN'T* BE.

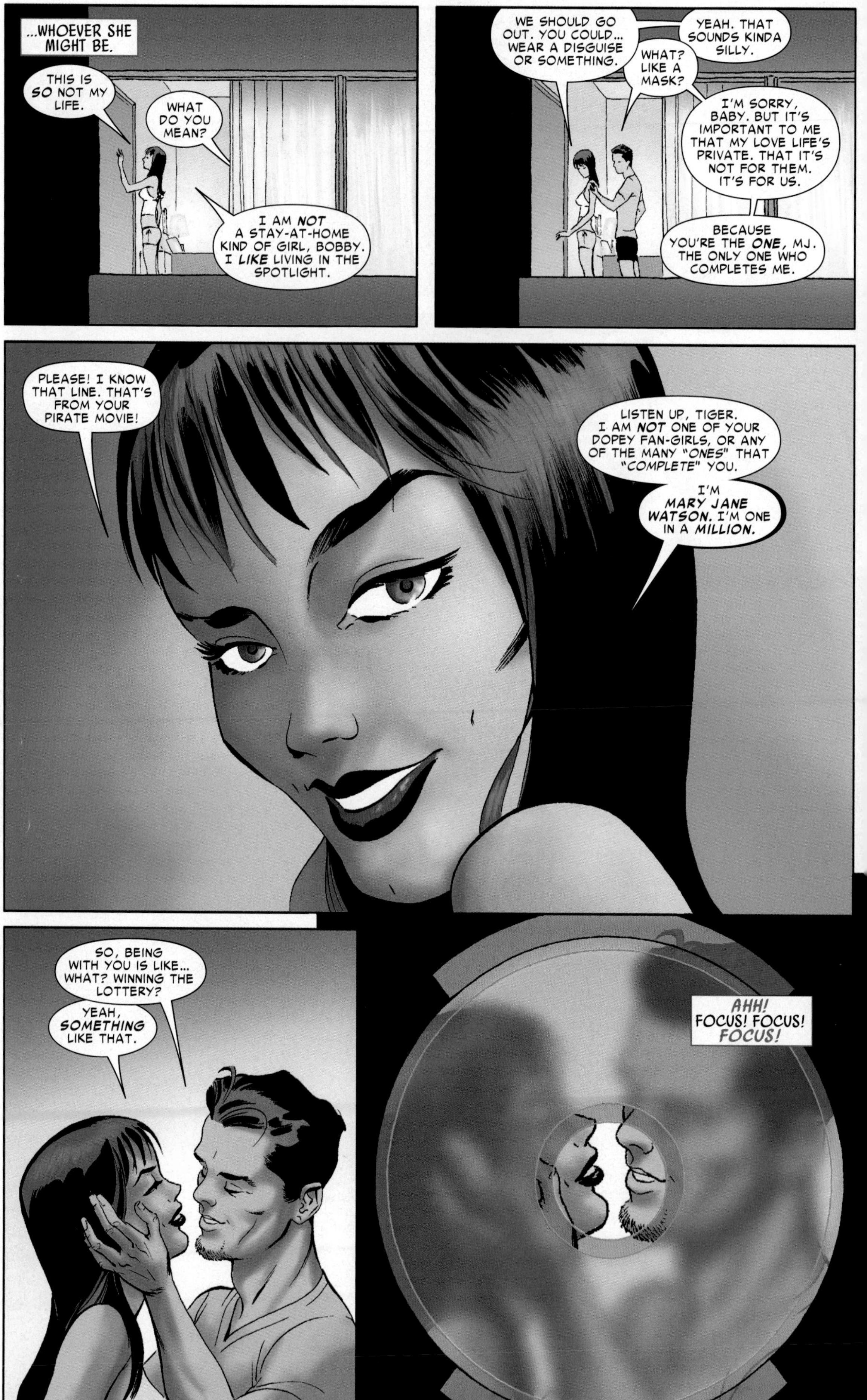
...WHOEVER SHE MIGHT BE.
THIS IS SO NOT MY LIFE.
WHAT DO YOU MEAN?
I AM NOT A STAY-AT-HOME KIND OF GIRL, BOBBY. I LIKE LIVING IN THE SPOTLIGHT.
WE SHOULD GO OUT. YOU COULD... WEAR A DISGUISE OR SOMETHING.
YEAH. THAT SOUNDS KINDA SILLY.
WHAT? LIKE A MASK?
I'M SORRY, BABY. BUT IT'S IMPORTANT TO ME THAT MY LOVE LIFE'S PRIVATE. THAT IT'S NOT FOR THEM. IT'S FOR US.
BECAUSE YOU'RE THE ONE, MJ. THE ONLY ONE WHO COMPLETES ME.
PLEASE! I KNOW THAT LINE. THAT'S FROM YOUR PIRATE MOVIE!
LISTEN UP, TIGER. I AM NOT ONE OF YOUR DOPEY FAN-GIRLS, OR ANY OF THE MANY "ONES" THAT "COMPLETE" YOU.
I'M MARY JANE WATSON. I'M ONE IN A MILLION.
SO, BEING WITH YOU IS LIKE... WHAT? WINNING THE LOTTERY?
YEAH, SOMETHING LIKE THAT.
AHH! FOCUS! FOCUS! FOCUS!

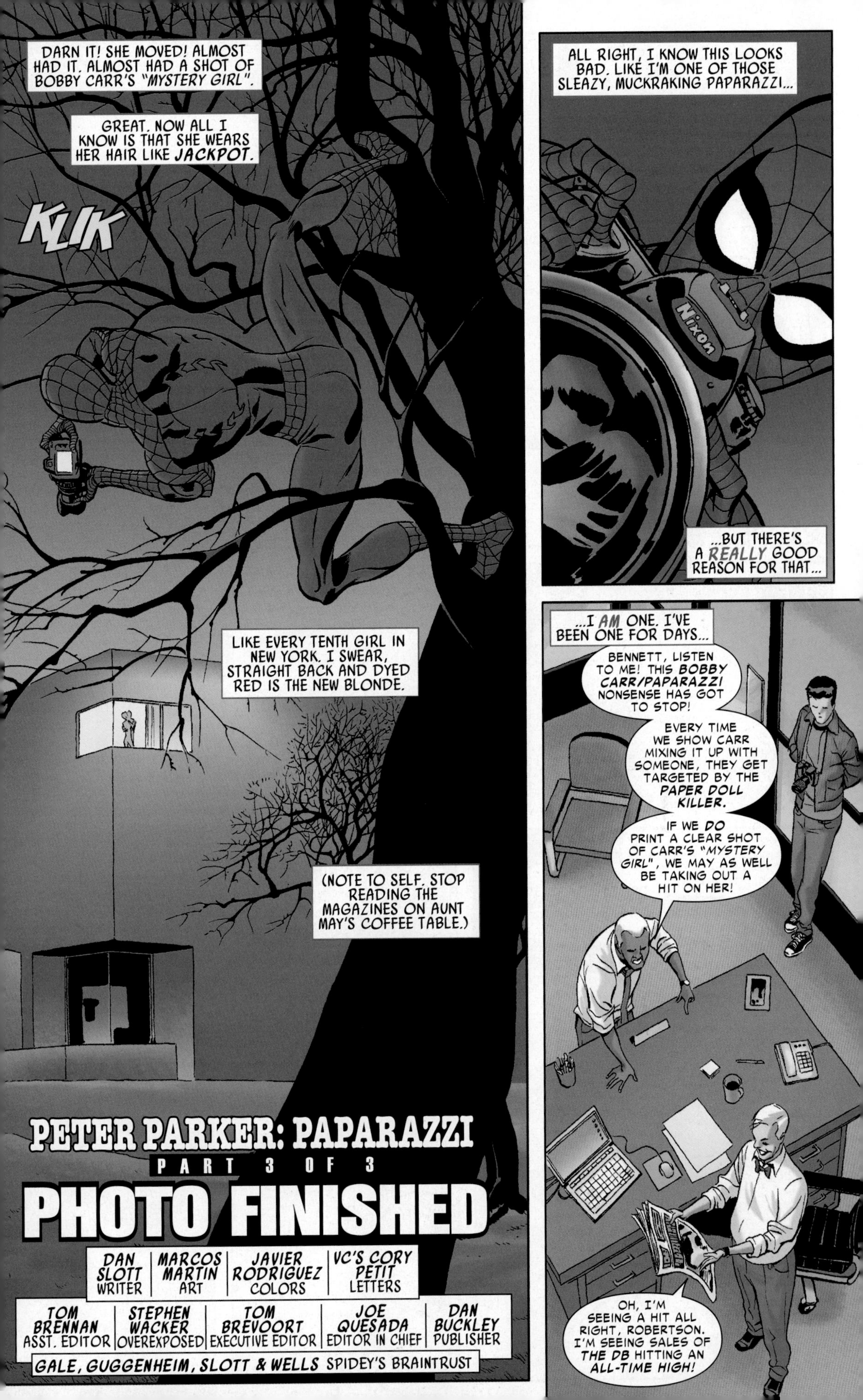
DARN IT! SHE MOVED! ALMOST HAD IT. ALMOST HAD A SHOT OF BOBBY CARR'S "MYSTERY GIRL".
GREAT. NOW ALL I KNOW IS THAT SHE WEARS HER HAIR LIKE JACKPOT.
KLIK
LIKE EVERY TENTH GIRL IN NEW YORK. I SWEAR, STRAIGHT BACK AND DYED RED IS THE NEW BLONDE.
(NOTE TO SELF. STOP READING THE MAGAZINES ON AUNT MAY'S COFFEE TABLE.)
PETER PARKER: PAPARAZZI
PART 3 OF 3
PHOTO FINISHED
DAN SLOTT WRITER
MARCOS MARTIN ART
JAVIER RODRIGUEZ COLORS
VC'S CORY PETIT LETTERS
TOM BRENNAN ASST. EDITOR
STEPHEN WACKER OVEREXPOSED
TOM BREVOORT EXECUTIVE EDITOR
JOE QUESADA EDITOR IN CHIEF
DAN BUCKLEY PUBLISHER
GALE, GUGGENHEIM, SLOTT & WELLS SPIDEY'S BRAINTRUST
ALL RIGHT, I KNOW THIS LOOKS BAD. LIKE I'M ONE OF THOSE SLEAZY, MUCKRAKING PAPARAZZI...
Nixon
...BUT THERE'S A REALLY GOOD REASON FOR THAT...
...I AM ONE. I'VE BEEN ONE FOR DAYS...
BENNETT, LISTEN TO ME! THIS BOBBY CARR/PAPARAZZI NONSENSE HAS GOT TO STOP!
EVERY TIME WE SHOW CARR MIXING IT UP WITH SOMEONE, THEY GET TARGETED BY THE PAPER DOLL KILLER.
IF WE DO PRINT A CLEAR SHOT OF CARR'S "MYSTERY GIRL", WE MAY AS WELL BE TAKING OUT A HIT ON HER!
OH, I'M SEEING A HIT ALL RIGHT, ROBERTSON. I'M SEEING SALES OF THE DB HITTING AN ALL-TIME HIGH!

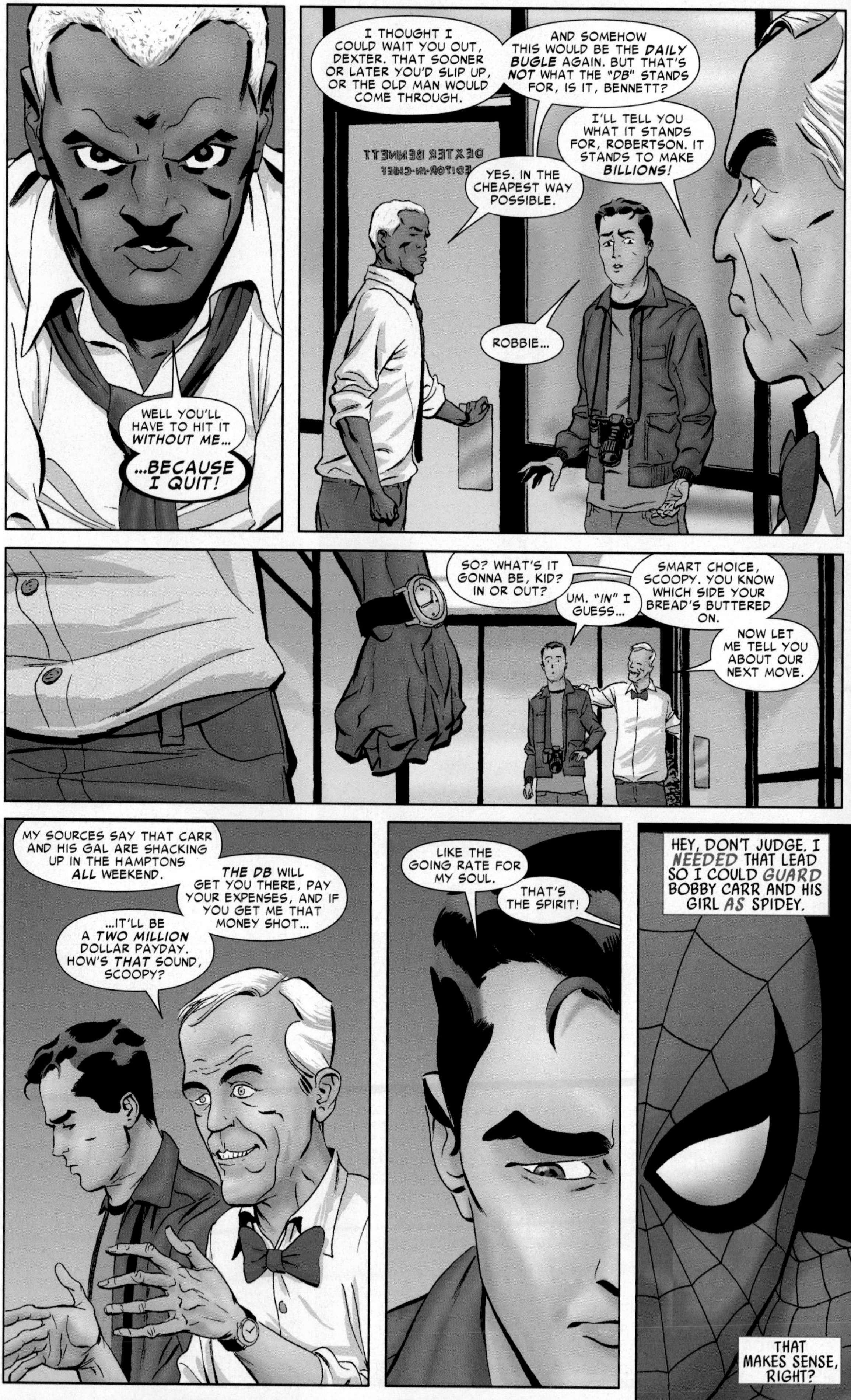
WELL YOU'LL HAVE TO HIT IT WITHOUT ME...
...BECAUSE I QUIT!
I THOUGHT I COULD WAIT YOU OUT, DEXTER. THAT SOONER OR LATER YOU'D SLIP UP, OR THE OLD MAN WOULD COME THROUGH.
AND SOMEHOW THIS WOULD BE THE DAILY BUGLE AGAIN. BUT THAT'S NOT WHAT THE "DB" STANDS FOR, IS IT, BENNETT?
DEXTER BENNETT
EDITOR-IN-CHIEF
YES. IN THE CHEAPEST WAY POSSIBLE.
I'LL TELL YOU WHAT IT STANDS FOR, ROBERTSON. IT STANDS TO MAKE BILLIONS!
ROBBIE...
SO? WHAT'S IT GONNA BE, KID? IN OR OUT?
UM. "IN" I GUESS...
SMART CHOICE, SCOOPY. YOU KNOW WHICH SIDE YOUR BREAD'S BUTTERED ON.
NOW LET ME TELL YOU ABOUT OUR NEXT MOVE.
MY SOURCES SAY THAT CARR AND HIS GAL ARE SHACKING UP IN THE HAMPTONS ALL WEEKEND.
THE DB WILL GET YOU THERE, PAY YOUR EXPENSES, AND IF YOU GET ME THAT MONEY SHOT...
...IT'LL BE A TWO MILLION DOLLAR PAYDAY. HOW'S THAT SOUND, SCOOPY?
LIKE THE GOING RATE FOR MY SOUL.
THAT'S THE SPIRIT!
HEY, DON'T JUDGE. I NEEDED THAT LEAD SO I COULD GUARD BOBBY CARR AND HIS GIRL AS SPIDEY.
THAT MAKES SENSE, RIGHT?

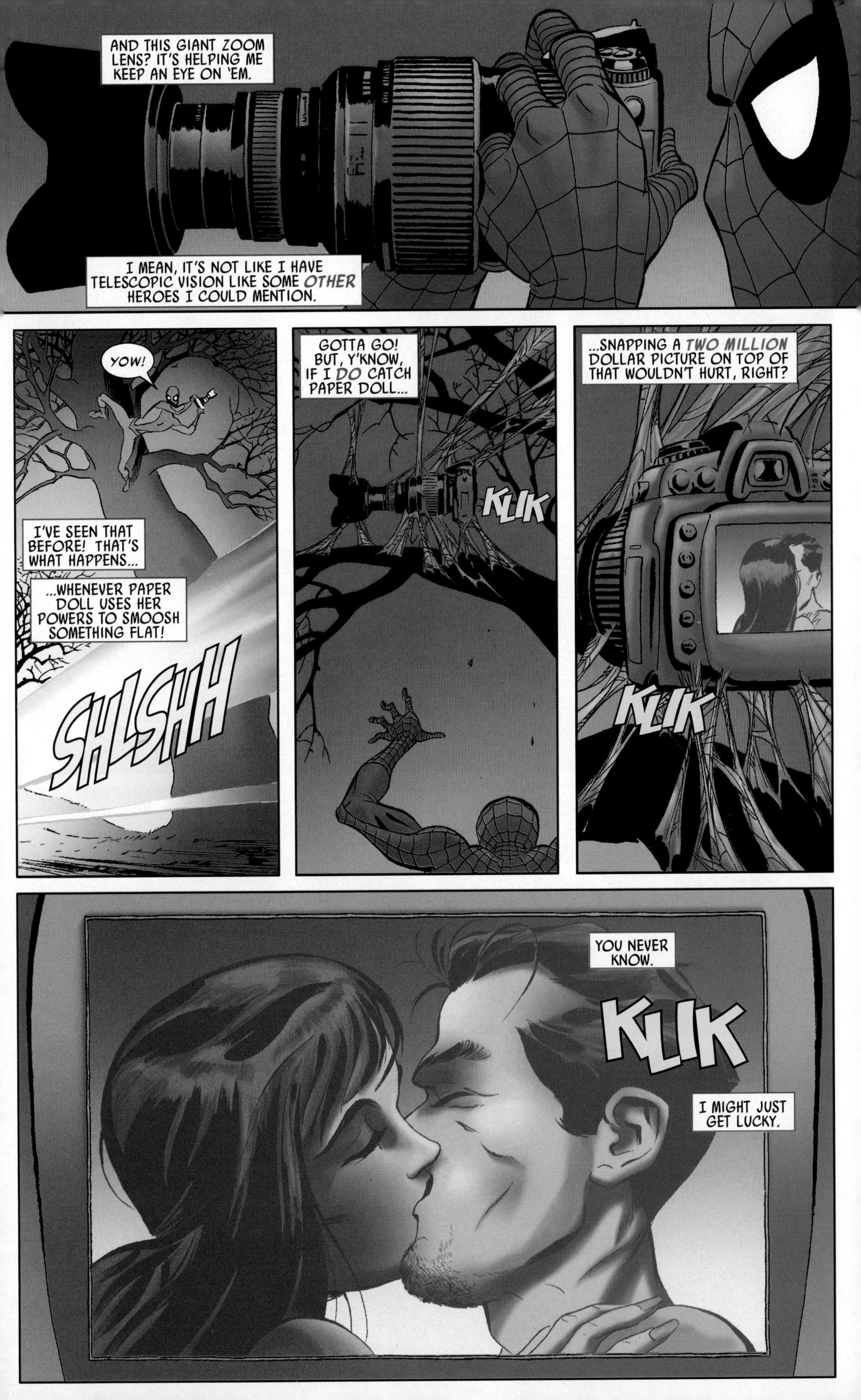

AND THIS GIANT ZOOM LENS? IT'S HELPING ME KEEP AN EYE ON 'EM.
I MEAN, IT'S NOT LIKE I HAVE TELESCOPIC VISION LIKE SOME OTHER HEROES I COULD MENTION.
YOW!
I'VE SEEN THAT BEFORE! THAT'S WHAT HAPPENS...
...WHENEVER PAPER DOLL USES HER POWERS TO SMOOSH SOMETHING FLAT!
SHLSHH
GOTTA GO! BUT, Y'KNOW, IF I DO CATCH PAPER DOLL...
KLIK
...SNAPPING A TWO MILLION DOLLAR PICTURE ON TOP OF THAT WOULDN'T HURT, RIGHT?
KLIK
YOU NEVER KNOW.
KLIK
I MIGHT JUST GET LUCKY.

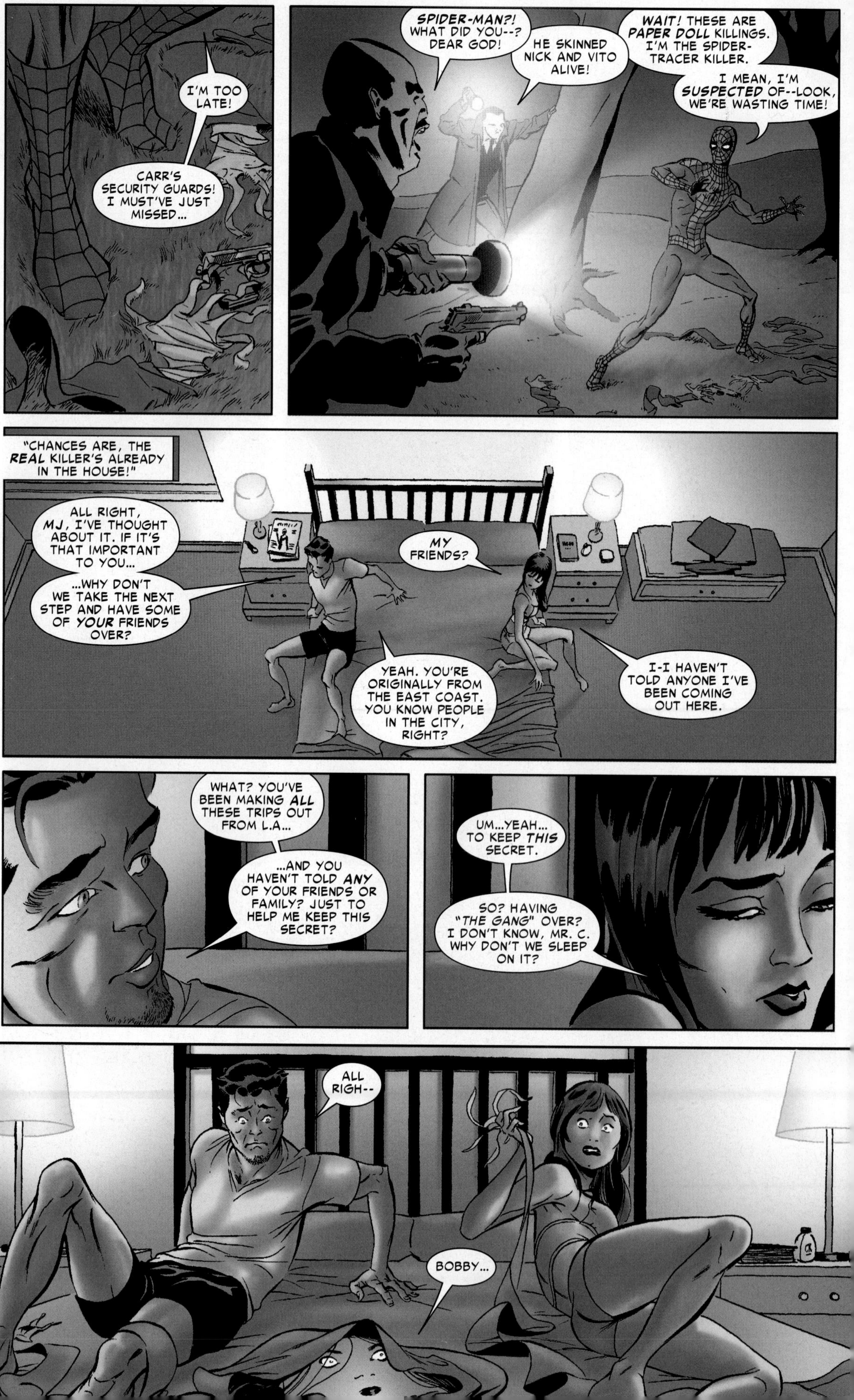
I'M TOO LATE!
CARR'S SECURITY GUARDS! I MUST'VE JUST MISSED...
SPIDER-MAN?! WHAT DID YOU--? DEAR GOD!
HE SKINNED NICK AND VITO ALIVE!
WAIT! THESE ARE PAPER DOLL KILLINGS. I'M THE SPIDER-TRACER KILLER.
I MEAN, I'M SUSPECTED OF--LOOK, WE'RE WASTING TIME!
"CHANCES ARE, THE REAL KILLER'S ALREADY IN THE HOUSE!"
ALL RIGHT, MJ, I'VE THOUGHT ABOUT IT. IF IT'S THAT IMPORTANT TO YOU...
...WHY DON'T WE TAKE THE NEXT STEP AND HAVE SOME OF YOUR FRIENDS OVER?
MY FRIENDS?
YEAH. YOU'RE ORIGINALLY FROM THE EAST COAST. YOU KNOW PEOPLE IN THE CITY, RIGHT?
I-I HAVEN'T TOLD ANYONE I'VE BEEN COMING OUT HERE.
WHAT? YOU'VE BEEN MAKING ALL THESE TRIPS OUT FROM L.A...
...AND YOU HAVEN'T TOLD ANY OF YOUR FRIENDS OR FAMILY? JUST TO HELP ME KEEP THIS SECRET?
UM...YEAH... TO KEEP THIS SECRET.
SO? HAVING "THE GANG" OVER? I DON'T KNOW, MR. C. WHY DON'T WE SLEEP ON IT?
ALL RIGH--
BOBBY...

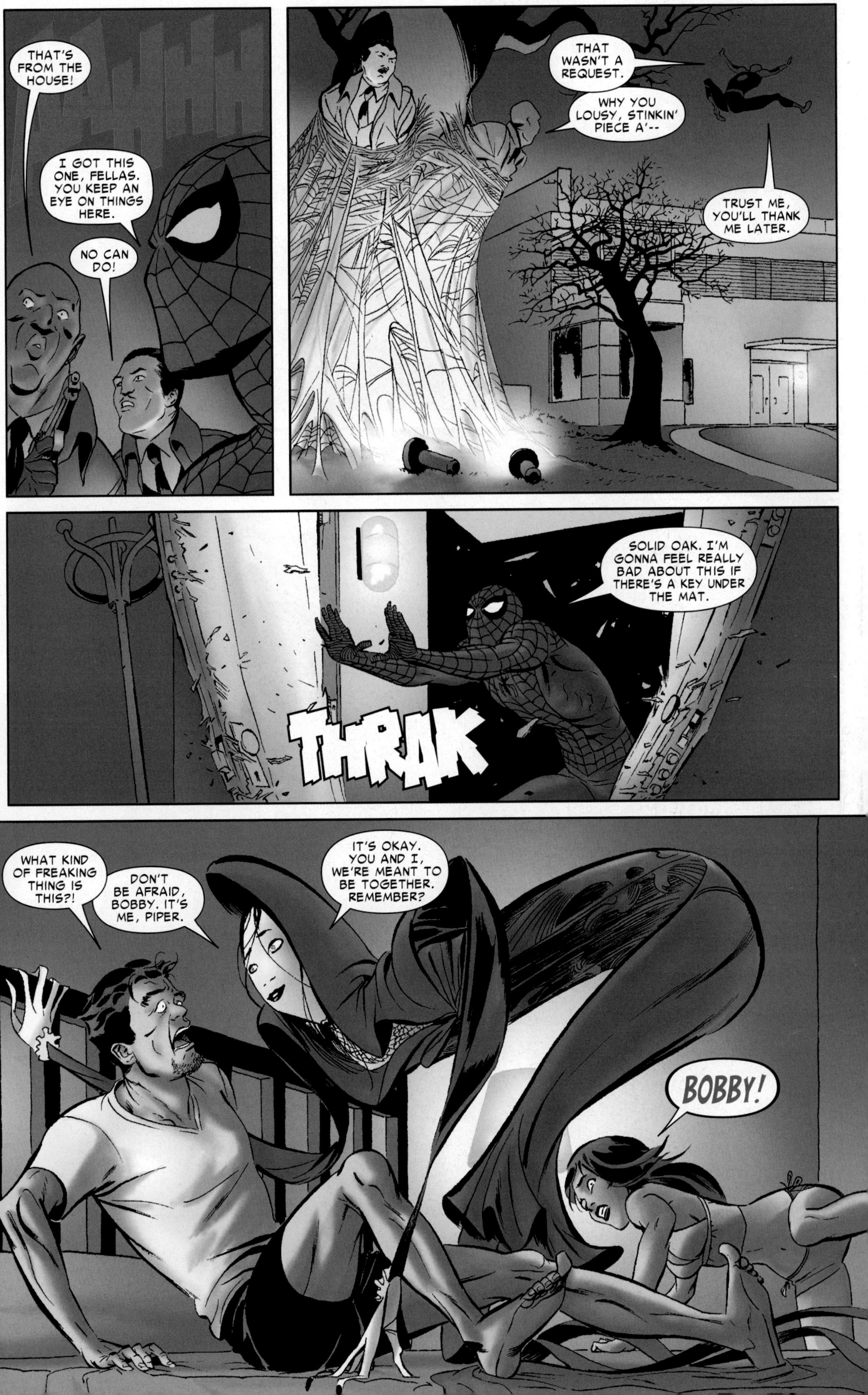
THAT'S FROM THE HOUSE!
I GOT THIS ONE, FELLAS. YOU KEEP AN EYE ON THINGS HERE.
NO CAN DO!
THAT WASN'T A REQUEST.
WHY YOU LOUSY, STINKIN' PIECE A'--
TRUST ME, YOU'LL THANK ME LATER.
SOLID OAK. I'M GONNA FEEL REALLY BAD ABOUT THIS IF THERE'S A KEY UNDER THE MAT.
THRAK
WHAT KIND OF FREAKING THING IS THIS?!
DON'T BE AFRAID, BOBBY. IT'S ME, PIPER.
IT'S OKAY. YOU AND I, WE'RE MEANT TO BE TOGETHER. REMEMBER?
BOBBY!

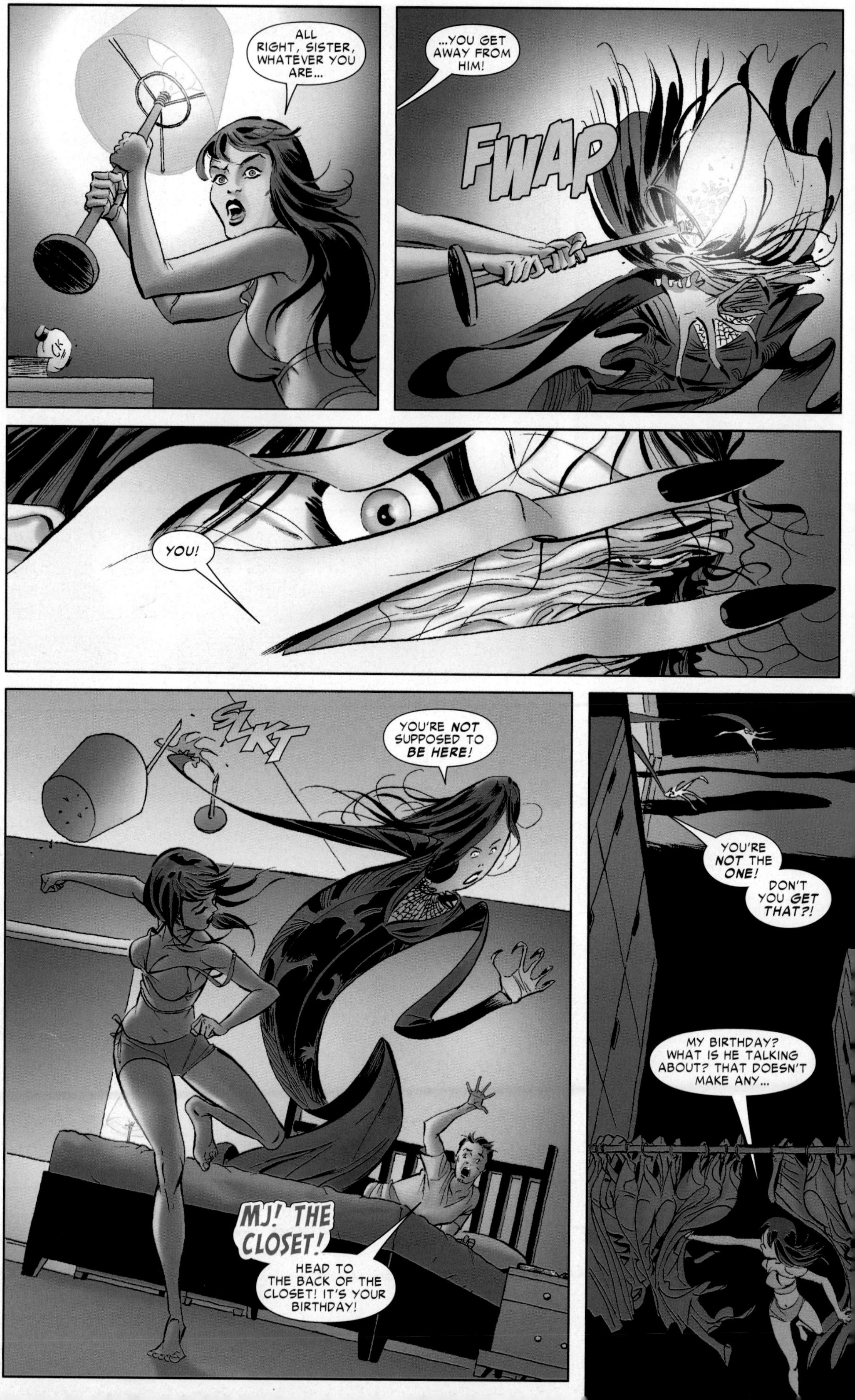
ALL RIGHT, SISTER, WHATEVER YOU ARE...
...YOU GET AWAY FROM HIM!
FWAP
YOU!
SLKT
YOU'RE NOT SUPPOSED TO BE HERE!
MJ! THE CLOSET!
HEAD TO THE BACK OF THE CLOSET! IT'S YOUR BIRTHDAY!
YOU'RE NOT THE ONE!
DON'T YOU GET THAT?!
MY BIRTHDAY? WHAT IS HE TALKING ABOUT? THAT DOESN'T MAKE ANY...

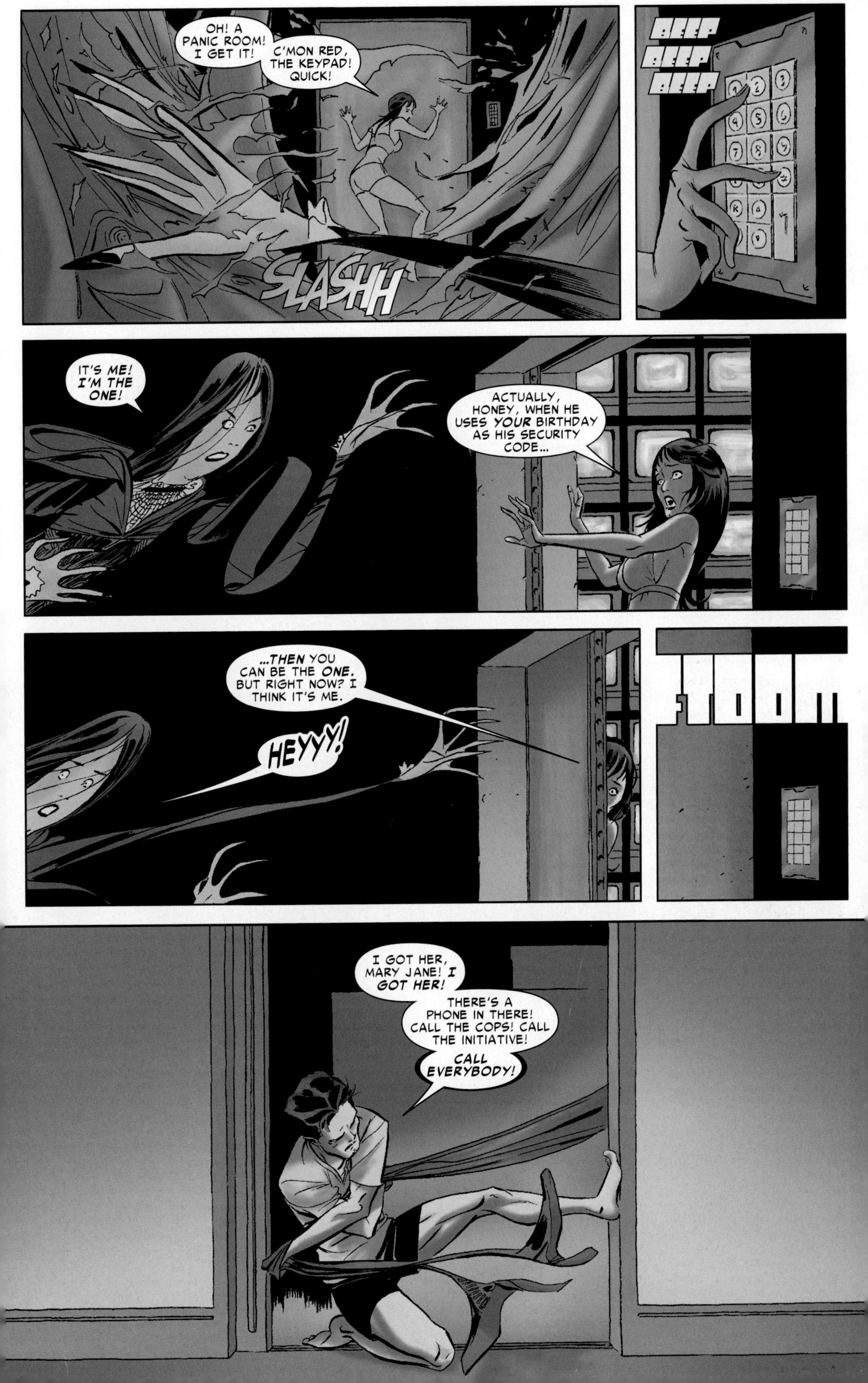
OH! A PANIC ROOM! I GET IT!
C'MON RED, THE KEYPAD! QUICK!
SLASHH
BEEP
BEEP
BEEP
IT'S ME! I'M THE ONE!
ACTUALLY, HONEY, WHEN HE USES YOUR BIRTHDAY AS HIS SECURITY CODE...
...THEN YOU CAN BE THE ONE. BUT RIGHT NOW? I THINK IT'S ME.
HEYYY!
FTOOM
I GOT HER, MARY JANE! I GOT HER!
THERE'S A PHONE IN THERE! CALL THE COPS! CALL THE INITIATIVE!
CALL EVERYBODY!

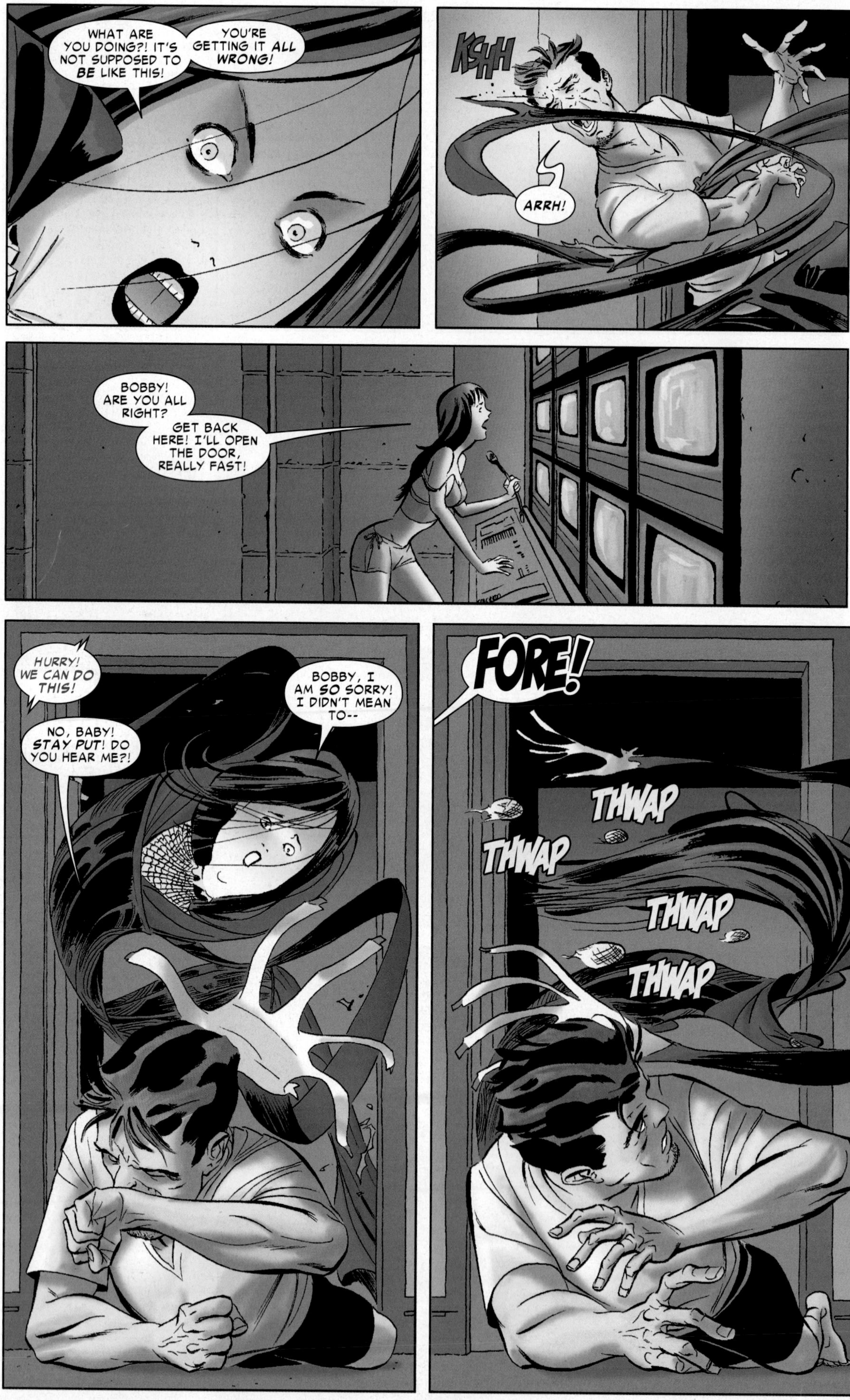
WHAT ARE YOU DOING?! IT'S NOT SUPPOSED TO BE LIKE THIS!
YOU'RE GETTING IT ALL WRONG!
KSHH
ARRH!
BOBBY! ARE YOU ALL RIGHT?
GET BACK HERE! I'LL OPEN THE DOOR, REALLY FAST!
HURRY! WE CAN DO THIS!
NO, BABY! STAY PUT! DO YOU HEAR ME?!
BOBBY, I AM SO SORRY! I DIDN'T MEAN TO--
FORE!
THWAP
THWAP
THWAP
THWAP

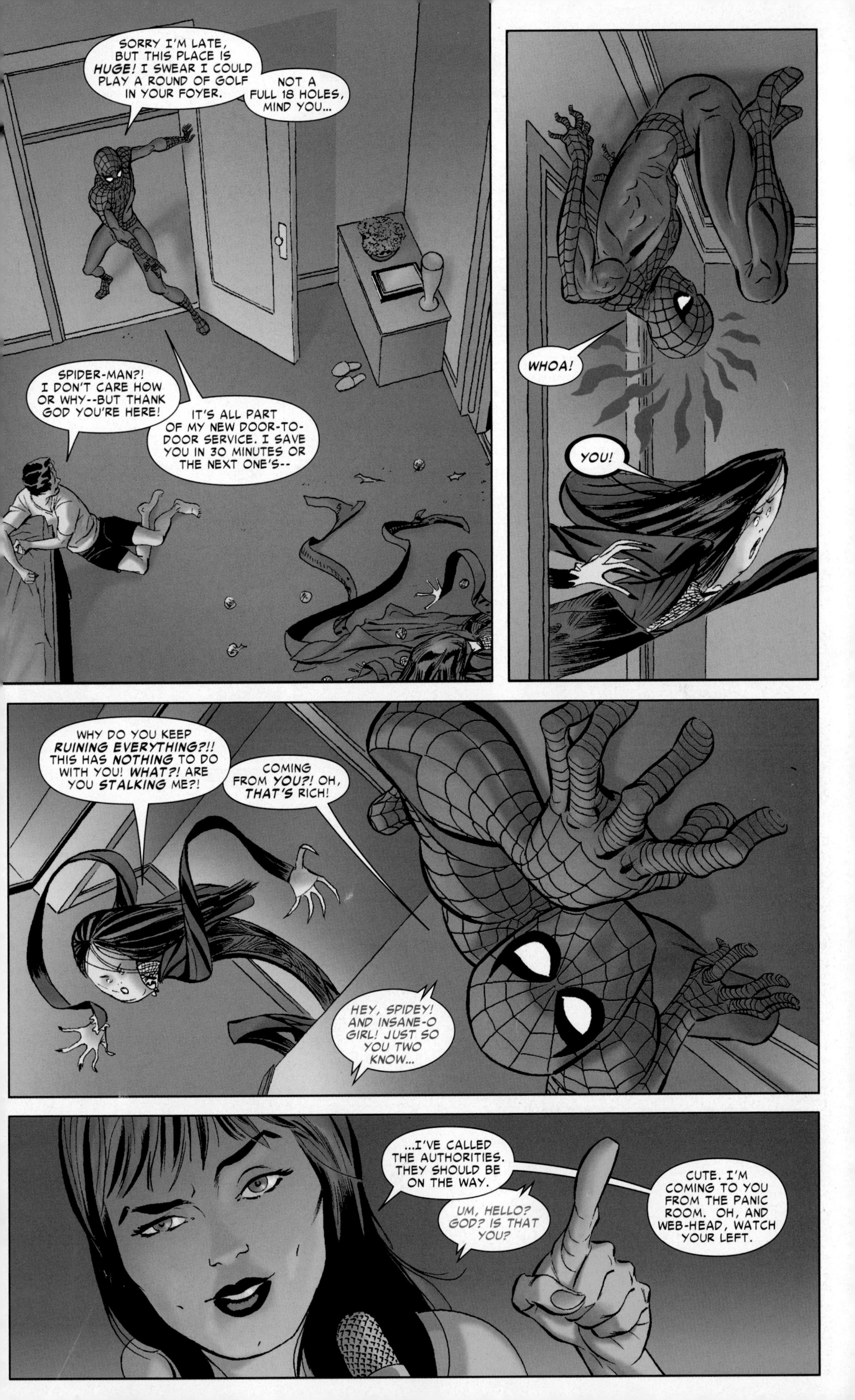
SORRY I'M LATE, BUT THIS PLACE IS HUGE! I SWEAR I COULD PLAY A ROUND OF GOLF IN YOUR FOYER.
NOT A FULL 18 HOLES, MIND YOU...
SPIDER-MAN?! I DON'T CARE HOW OR WHY--BUT THANK GOD YOU'RE HERE!
IT'S ALL PART OF MY NEW DOOR-TO-DOOR SERVICE. I SAVE YOU IN 30 MINUTES OR THE NEXT ONE'S--
WHOA!
YOU!
WHY DO YOU KEEP RUINING EVERYTHING?!! THIS HAS NOTHING TO DO WITH YOU! WHAT?! ARE YOU STALKING ME?!
COMING FROM YOU?! OH, THAT'S RICH!
HEY, SPIDEY! AND INSANE-O GIRL! JUST SO YOU TWO KNOW...
...I'VE CALLED THE AUTHORITIES. THEY SHOULD BE ON THE WAY.
UM, HELLO? GOD? IS THAT YOU?
CUTE. I'M COMING TO YOU FROM THE PANIC ROOM. OH, AND WEB-HEAD, WATCH YOUR LEFT.

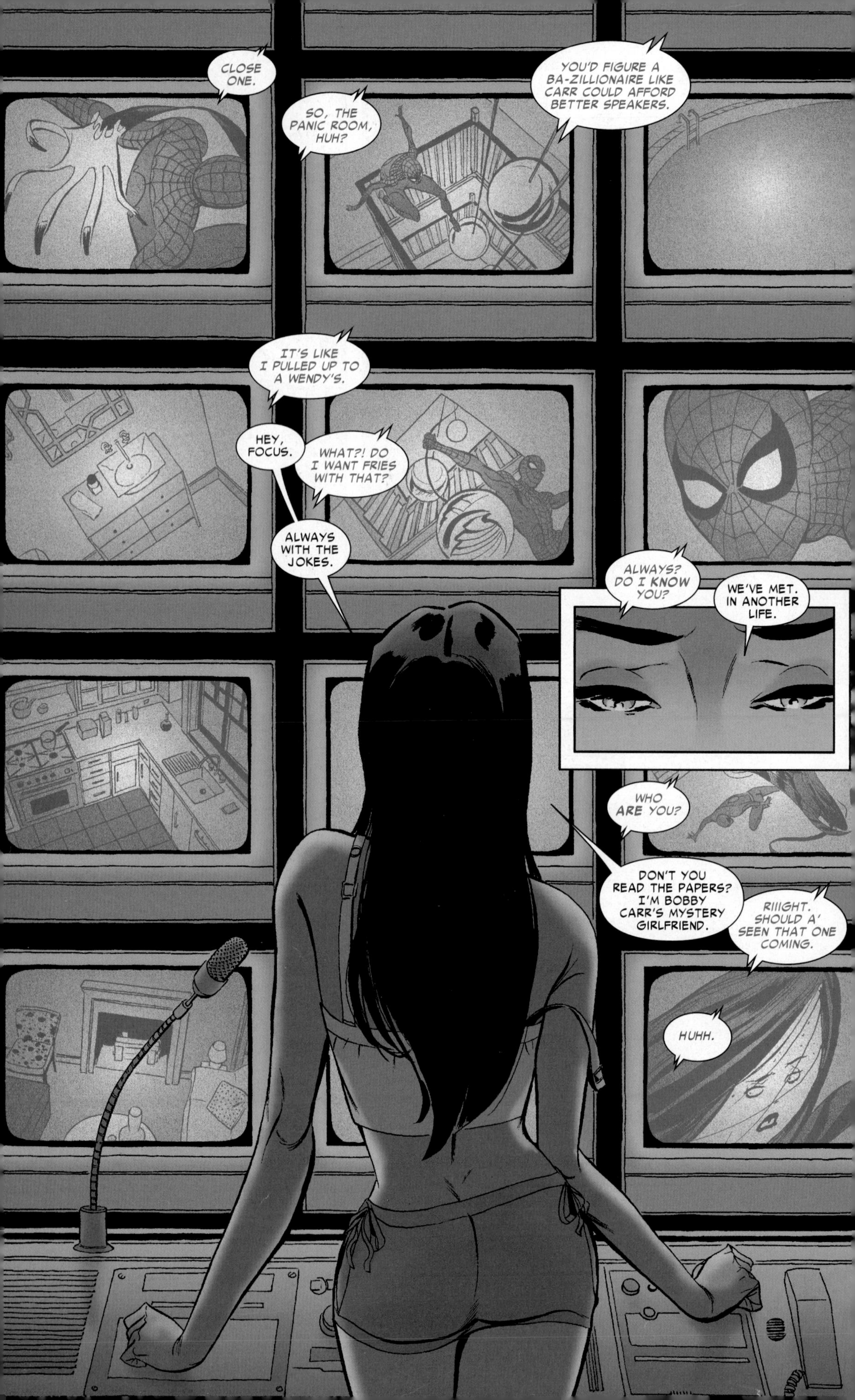
CLOSE ONE.
SO, THE PANIC ROOM, HUH?
YOU'D FIGURE A BA-ZILLIONAIRE LIKE CARR COULD AFFORD BETTER SPEAKERS.
IT'S LIKE I PULLED UP TO A WENDY'S.
HEY, FOCUS.
WHAT?! DO I WANT FRIES WITH THAT?
ALWAYS WITH THE JOKES.
ALWAYS? DO I KNOW YOU?
WE'VE MET. IN ANOTHER LIFE.
WHO ARE YOU?
DON'T YOU READ THE PAPERS? I'M BOBBY CARR'S MYSTERY GIRLFRIEND.
RIIIGHT. SHOULD A' SEEN THAT ONE COMING.
HUHH.

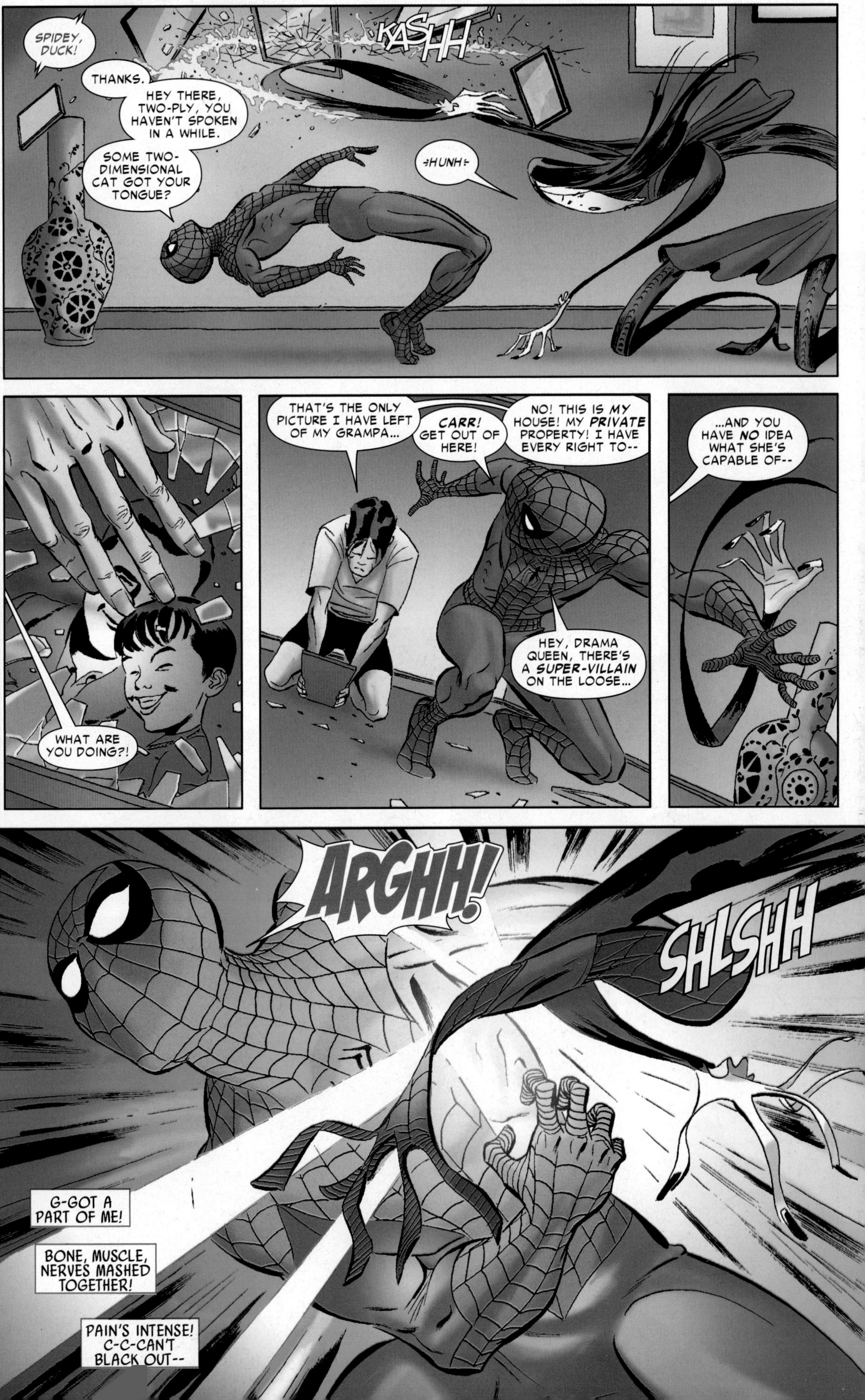
SPIDEY, DUCK!
KASHH
THANKS.
HEY THERE, TWO-PLY, YOU HAVEN'T SPOKEN IN A WHILE.
SOME TWO-DIMENSIONAL CAT GOT YOUR TONGUE?
HUNH
WHAT ARE YOU DOING?!
THAT'S THE ONLY PICTURE I HAVE LEFT OF MY GRAMPA...
CARR! GET OUT OF HERE!
NO! THIS IS MY HOUSE! MY PRIVATE PROPERTY! I HAVE EVERY RIGHT TO--
HEY, DRAMA QUEEN, THERE'S A SUPER-VILLAIN ON THE LOOSE...
...AND YOU HAVE NO IDEA WHAT SHE'S CAPABLE OF--
ARGHH!
SHLSHH
G-GOT A PART OF ME!
BONE, MUSCLE, NERVES MASHED TOGETHER!
PAIN'S INTENSE! C-C-CAN'T BLACK OUT--

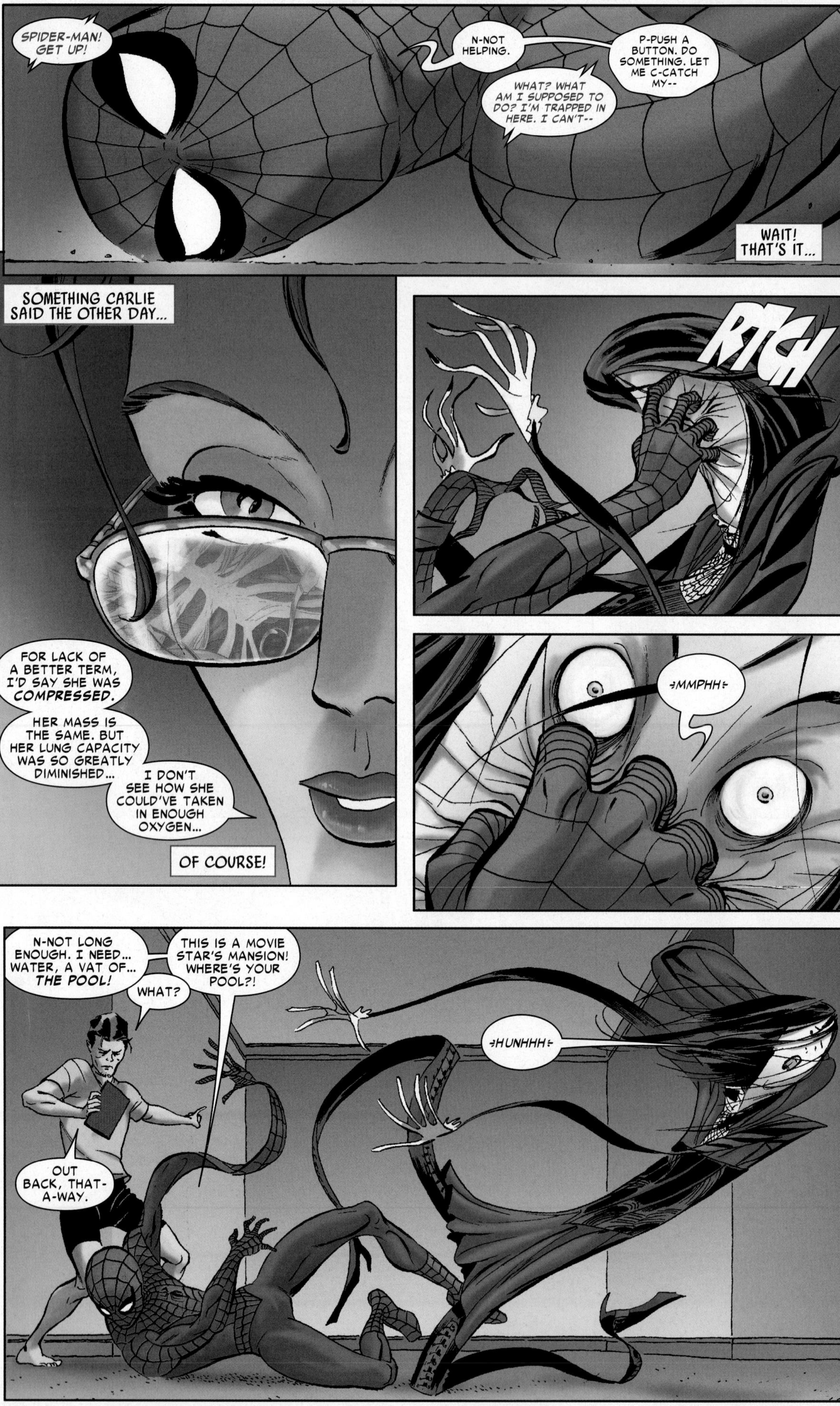
SPIDER-MAN! GET UP!
N-NOT HELPING.
P-PUSH A BUTTON. DO SOMETHING. LET ME C-CATCH MY--
WHAT? WHAT AM I SUPPOSED TO DO? I'M TRAPPED IN HERE. I CAN'T--
WAIT! THAT'S IT...
SOMETHING CARLIE SAID THE OTHER DAY...
FOR LACK OF A BETTER TERM, I'D SAY SHE WAS COMPRESSED.
HER MASS IS THE SAME. BUT HER LUNG CAPACITY WAS SO GREATLY DIMINISHED...
I DON'T SEE HOW SHE COULD'VE TAKEN IN ENOUGH OXYGEN...
OF COURSE!
RTCH
MMPHH
N-NOT LONG ENOUGH. I NEED... WATER, A VAT OF... THE POOL!
WHAT?
THIS IS A MOVIE STAR'S MANSION! WHERE'S YOUR POOL?!
OUT BACK, THAT-A-WAY.
HUNHHH

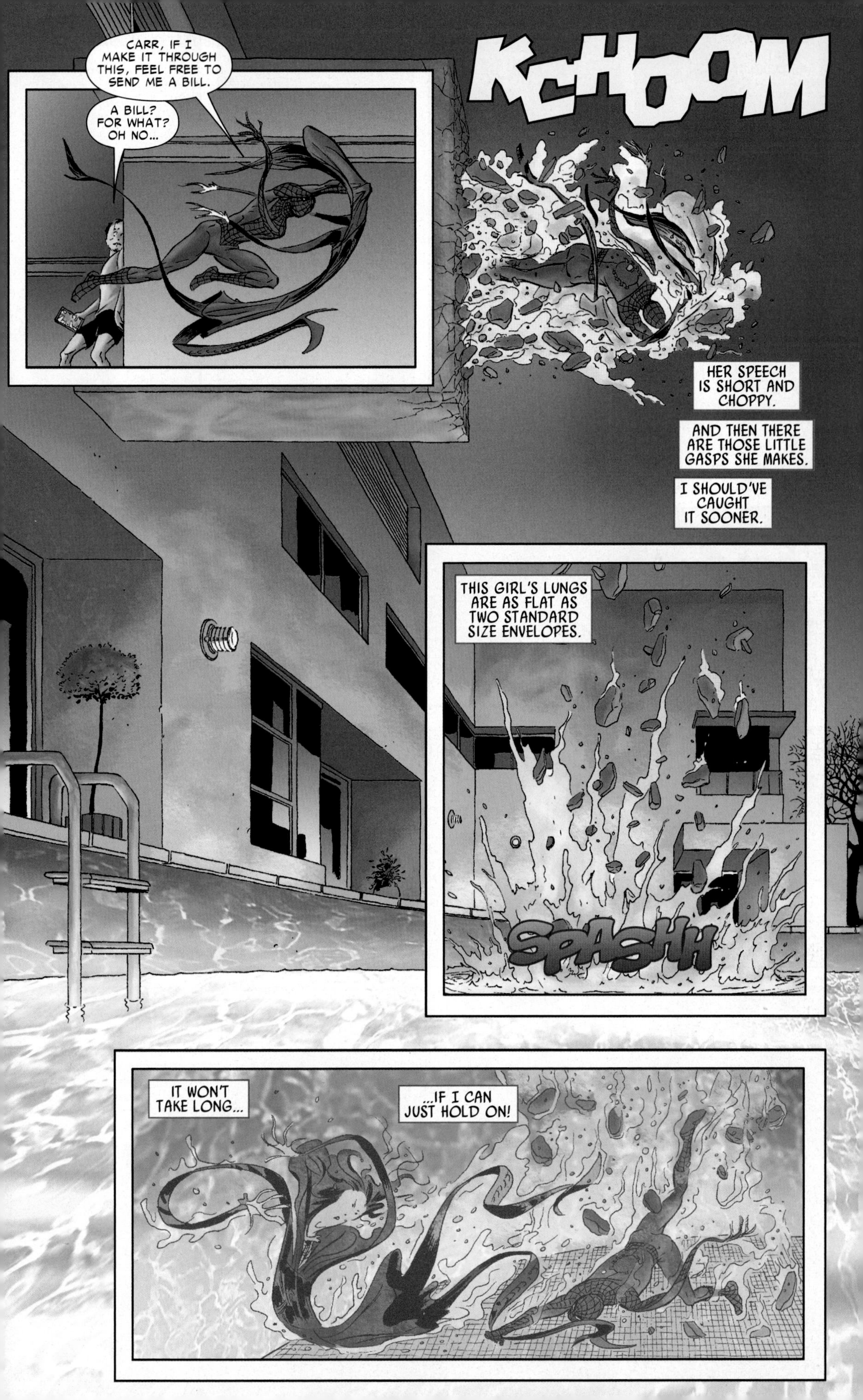
CARR, IF I MAKE IT THROUGH THIS, FEEL FREE TO SEND ME A BILL.
A BILL? FOR WHAT? OH NO...
KCHOOM
HER SPEECH IS SHORT AND CHOPPY.
AND THEN THERE ARE THOSE LITTLE GASPS SHE MAKES.
I SHOULD'VE CAUGHT IT SOONER.
THIS GIRL'S LUNGS ARE AS FLAT AS TWO STANDARD SIZE ENVELOPES.
SPASHH
IT WON'T TAKE LONG...
...IF I CAN JUST HOLD ON!

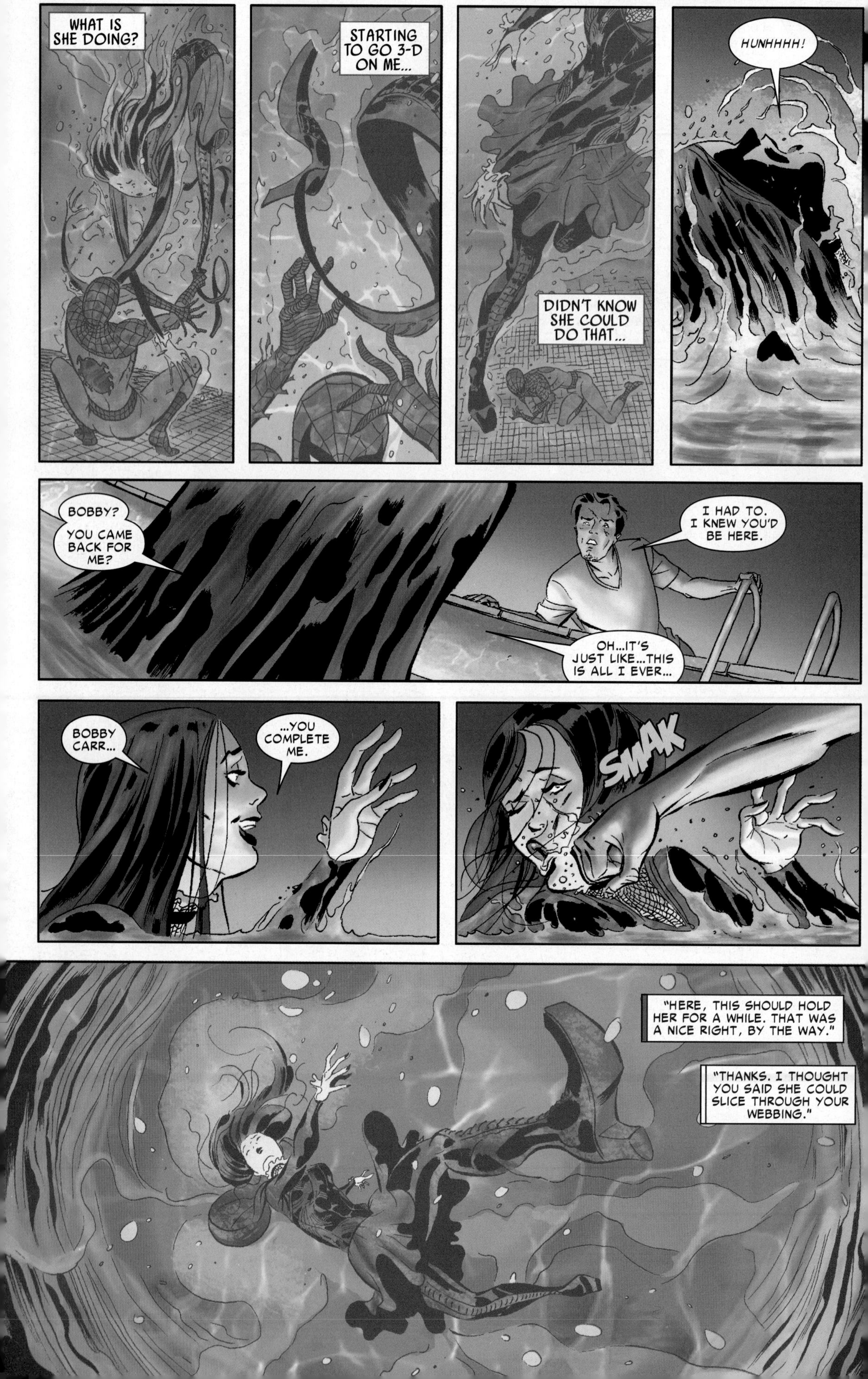
WHAT IS SHE DOING?
STARTING TO GO 3-D ON ME...
DIDN'T KNOW SHE COULD DO THAT...
HUNHHHH!
BOBBY? YOU CAME BACK FOR ME?
I HAD TO. I KNEW YOU'D BE HERE.
OH...IT'S JUST LIKE...THIS IS ALL I EVER...
BOBBY CARR...
...YOU COMPLETE ME.
SMAK
"HERE, THIS SHOULD HOLD HER FOR A WHILE. THAT WAS A NICE RIGHT, BY THE WAY."
"THANKS. I THOUGHT YOU SAID SHE COULD SLICE THROUGH YOUR WEBBING."

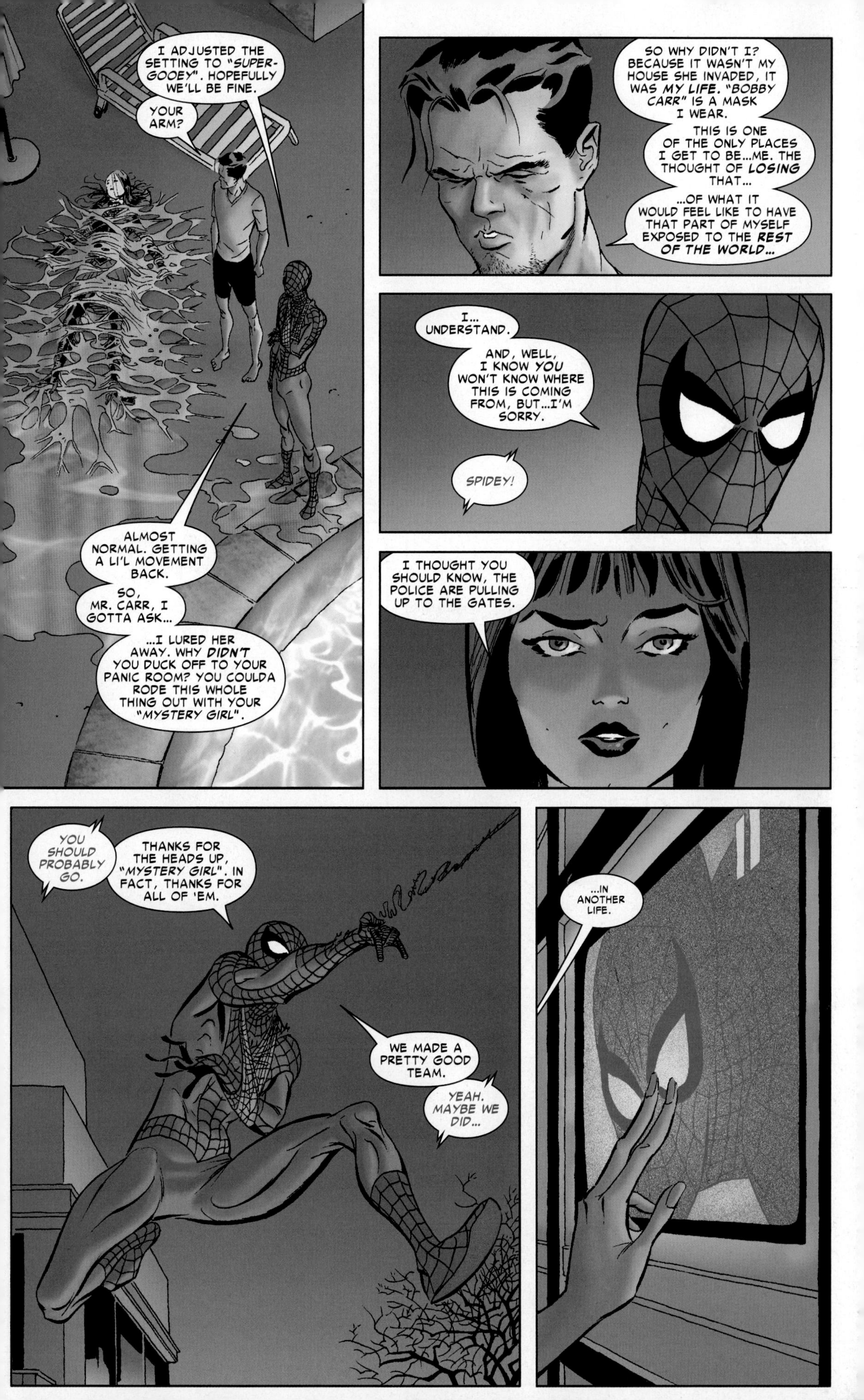
I ADJUSTED THE SETTING TO "SUPER-GOOEY". HOPEFULLY WE'LL BE FINE.
YOUR ARM?
ALMOST NORMAL. GETTING A LI'L MOVEMENT BACK.
SO, MR. CARR, I GOTTA ASK...
...I LURED HER AWAY. WHY DIDN'T YOU DUCK OFF TO YOUR PANIC ROOM? YOU COULDA RODE THIS WHOLE THING OUT WITH YOUR "MYSTERY GIRL".
SO WHY DIDN'T I? BECAUSE IT WASN'T MY HOUSE SHE INVADED, IT WAS MY LIFE. "BOBBY CARR" IS A MASK I WEAR.
THIS IS ONE OF THE ONLY PLACES I GET TO BE...ME. THE THOUGHT OF LOSING THAT...
...OF WHAT IT WOULD FEEL LIKE TO HAVE THAT PART OF MYSELF EXPOSED TO THE REST OF THE WORLD...
I... UNDERSTAND.
AND, WELL, I KNOW YOU WON'T KNOW WHERE THIS IS COMING FROM, BUT...I'M SORRY.
SPIDEY!
I THOUGHT YOU SHOULD KNOW, THE POLICE ARE PULLING UP TO THE GATES.
YOU SHOULD PROBABLY GO.
THANKS FOR THE HEADS UP, "MYSTERY GIRL". IN FACT, THANKS FOR ALL OF 'EM.
WE MADE A PRETTY GOOD TEAM.
YEAH. MAYBE WE DID...
...IN ANOTHER LIFE.

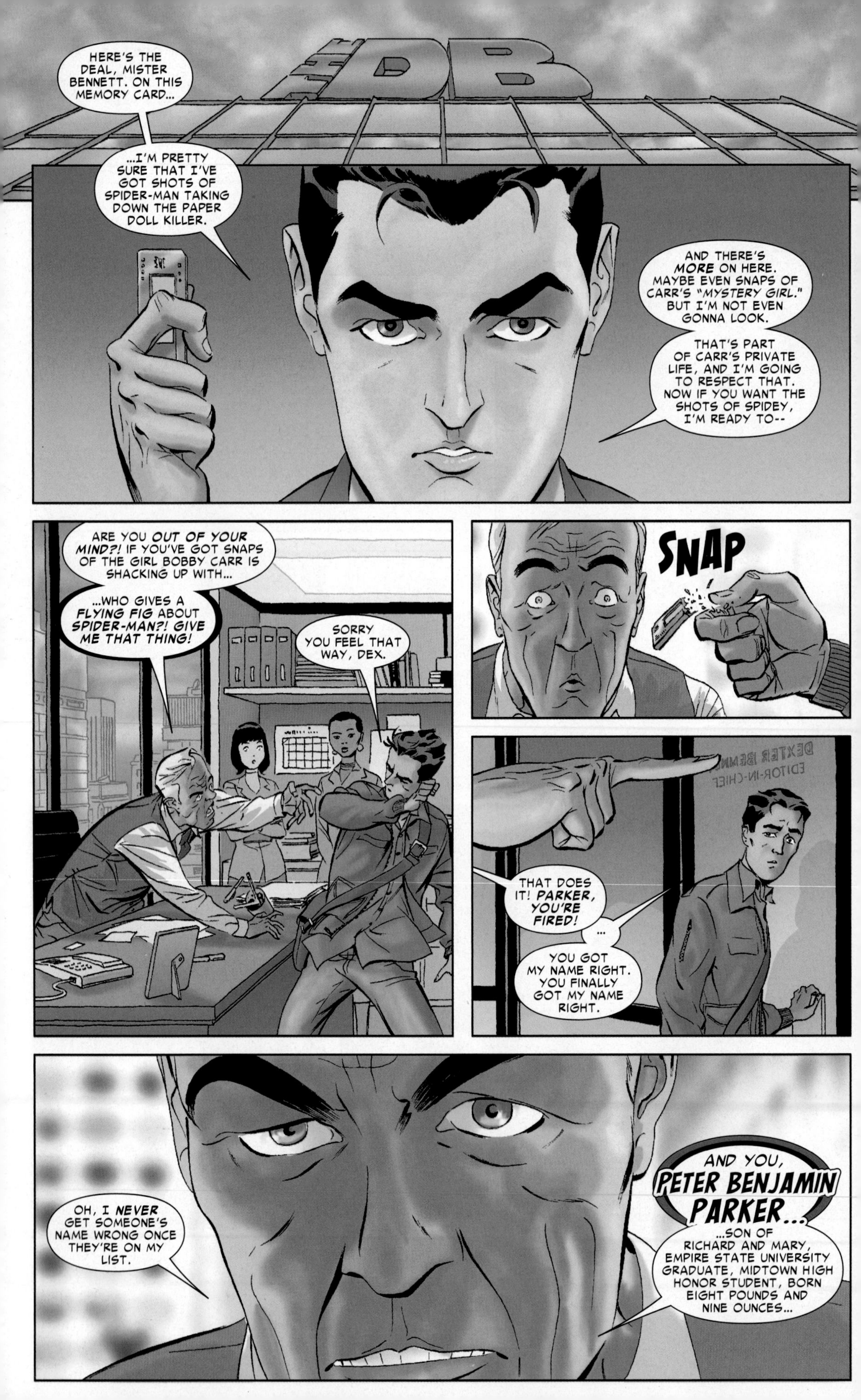

THE DB
HERE'S THE DEAL, MISTER BENNETT. ON THIS MEMORY CARD...
...I'M PRETTY SURE THAT I'VE GOT SHOTS OF SPIDER-MAN TAKING DOWN THE PAPER DOLL KILLER.
AND THERE'S MORE ON HERE. MAYBE EVEN SNAPS OF CARR'S "MYSTERY GIRL." BUT I'M NOT EVEN GONNA LOOK.
THAT'S PART OF CARR'S PRIVATE LIFE, AND I'M GOING TO RESPECT THAT. NOW IF YOU WANT THE SHOTS OF SPIDEY, I'M READY TO--
ARE YOU OUT OF YOUR MIND?! IF YOU'VE GOT SNAPS OF THE GIRL BOBBY CARR IS SHACKING UP WITH...
...WHO GIVES A FLYING FIG ABOUT SPIDER-MAN?! GIVE ME THAT THING!
SORRY YOU FEEL THAT WAY, DEX.
SNAP
DEXTER BENNETT EDITOR-IN-CHIEF
THAT DOES IT! PARKER, YOU'RE FIRED!
...
YOU GOT MY NAME RIGHT. YOU FINALLY GOT MY NAME RIGHT.
OH, I NEVER GET SOMEONE'S NAME WRONG ONCE THEY'RE ON MY LIST.
AND YOU, PETER BENJAMIN PARKER...
...SON OF RICHARD AND MARY, EMPIRE STATE UNIVERSITY GRADUATE, MIDTOWN HIGH HONOR STUDENT, BORN EIGHT POUNDS AND NINE OUNCES...

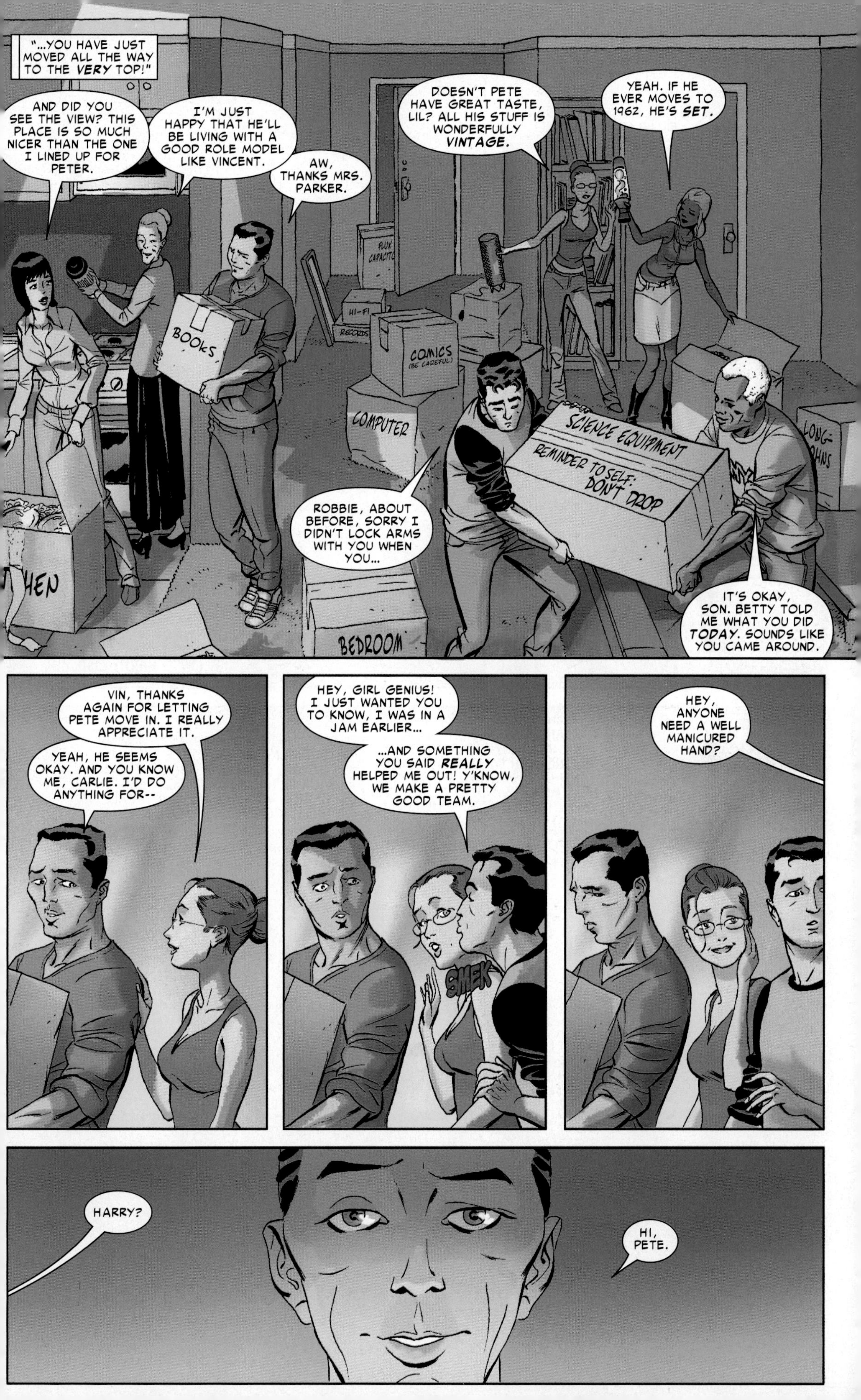

"...YOU HAVE JUST MOVED ALL THE WAY TO THE *VERY* TOP!"
AND DID YOU SEE THE VIEW? THIS PLACE IS SO MUCH NICER THAN THE ONE I LINED UP FOR PETER.
I'M JUST HAPPY THAT HE'LL BE LIVING WITH A GOOD ROLE MODEL LIKE VINCENT.
AW, THANKS MRS. PARKER.
DOESN'T PETE HAVE GREAT TASTE, LIL? ALL HIS STUFF IS WONDERFULLY ***VINTAGE.***
YEAH. IF HE EVER MOVES TO 1962, HE'S ***SET.***
BOOKS
HI-FI
RECORDS
COMICS (BE CAREFUL)
COMPUTER
SCIENCE EQUIPMENT
REMINDER TO SELF: DON'T DROP
BEDROOM
ROBBIE, ABOUT BEFORE, SORRY I DIDN'T LOCK ARMS WITH YOU WHEN YOU...
IT'S OKAY, SON. BETTY TOLD ME WHAT YOU DID *TODAY*. SOUNDS LIKE YOU CAME AROUND.
VIN, THANKS AGAIN FOR LETTING PETE MOVE IN. I REALLY APPRECIATE IT.
YEAH, HE SEEMS OKAY. AND YOU KNOW ME, CARLIE. I'D DO ANYTHING FOR--
HEY, GIRL GENIUS! I JUST WANTED YOU TO KNOW, I WAS IN A JAM EARLIER...
...AND SOMETHING YOU SAID ***REALLY*** HELPED ME OUT! Y'KNOW, WE MAKE A PRETTY GOOD TEAM.
SMEK
HEY, ANYONE NEED A WELL MANICURED HAND?
HARRY?
HI, PETE.

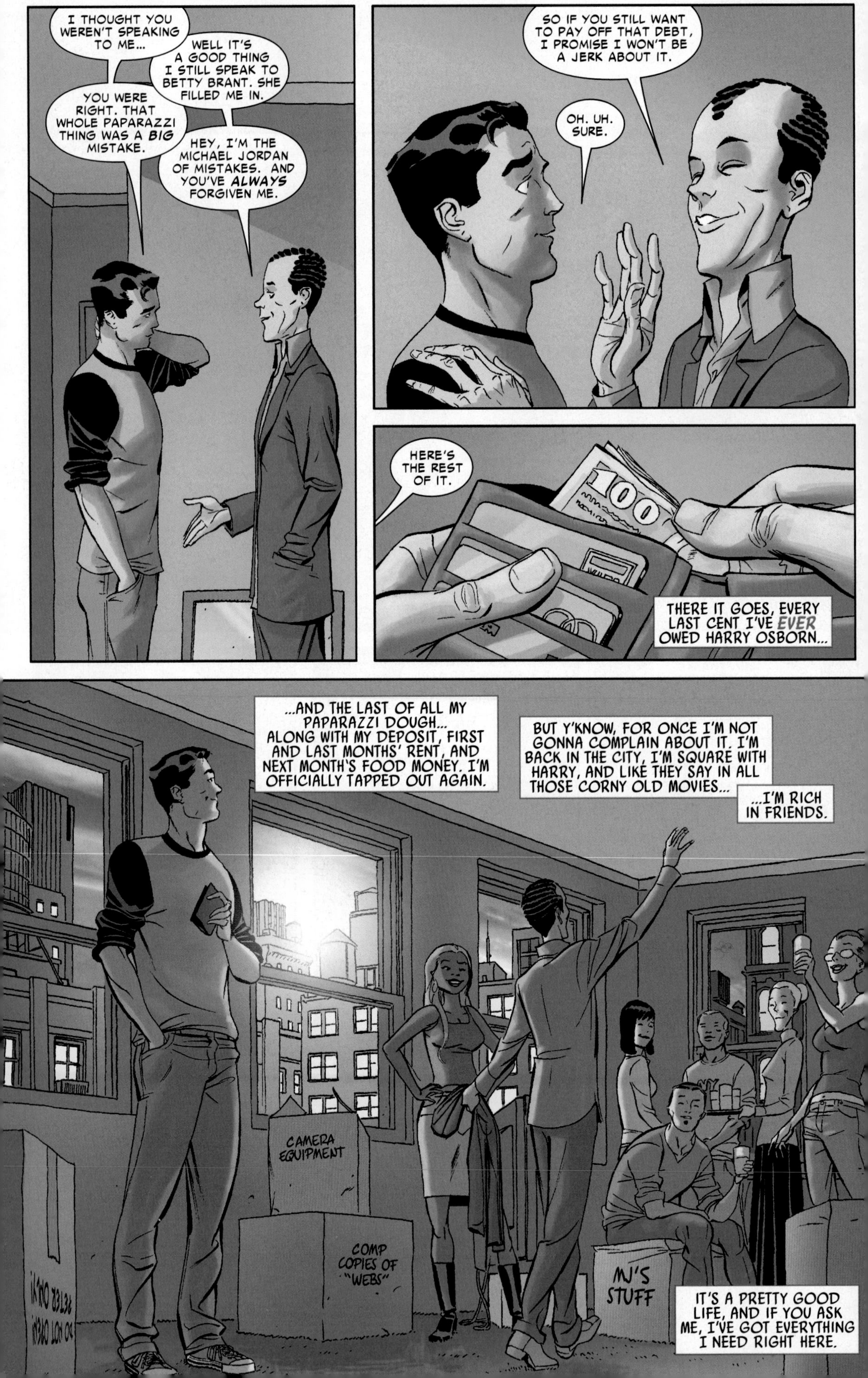
I THOUGHT YOU WEREN'T SPEAKING TO ME...
WELL IT'S A GOOD THING I STILL SPEAK TO BETTY BRANT. SHE FILLED ME IN.
YOU WERE RIGHT. THAT WHOLE PAPARAZZI THING WAS A **BIG** MISTAKE.
HEY, I'M THE MICHAEL JORDAN OF MISTAKES. AND YOU'VE **ALWAYS** FORGIVEN ME.
SO IF YOU STILL WANT TO PAY OFF THAT DEBT, I PROMISE I WON'T BE A JERK ABOUT IT.
OH. UH. SURE.
HERE'S THE REST OF IT.
100
THERE IT GOES, EVERY LAST CENT I'VE *EVER* OWED HARRY OSBORN...
...AND THE LAST OF ALL MY PAPARAZZI DOUGH... ALONG WITH MY DEPOSIT, FIRST AND LAST MONTHS' RENT, AND NEXT MONTH'S FOOD MONEY. I'M OFFICIALLY TAPPED OUT AGAIN.
BUT Y'KNOW, FOR ONCE I'M NOT GONNA COMPLAIN ABOUT IT. I'M BACK IN THE CITY, I'M SQUARE WITH HARRY, AND LIKE THEY SAY IN ALL THOSE CORNY OLD MOVIES...
...I'M RICH IN FRIENDS.
CAMERA EQUIPMENT
COMP COPIES OF "WEBS"
MJ'S STUFF
IT'S A PRETTY GOOD LIFE, AND IF YOU ASK ME, I'VE GOT EVERYTHING I NEED RIGHT HERE.

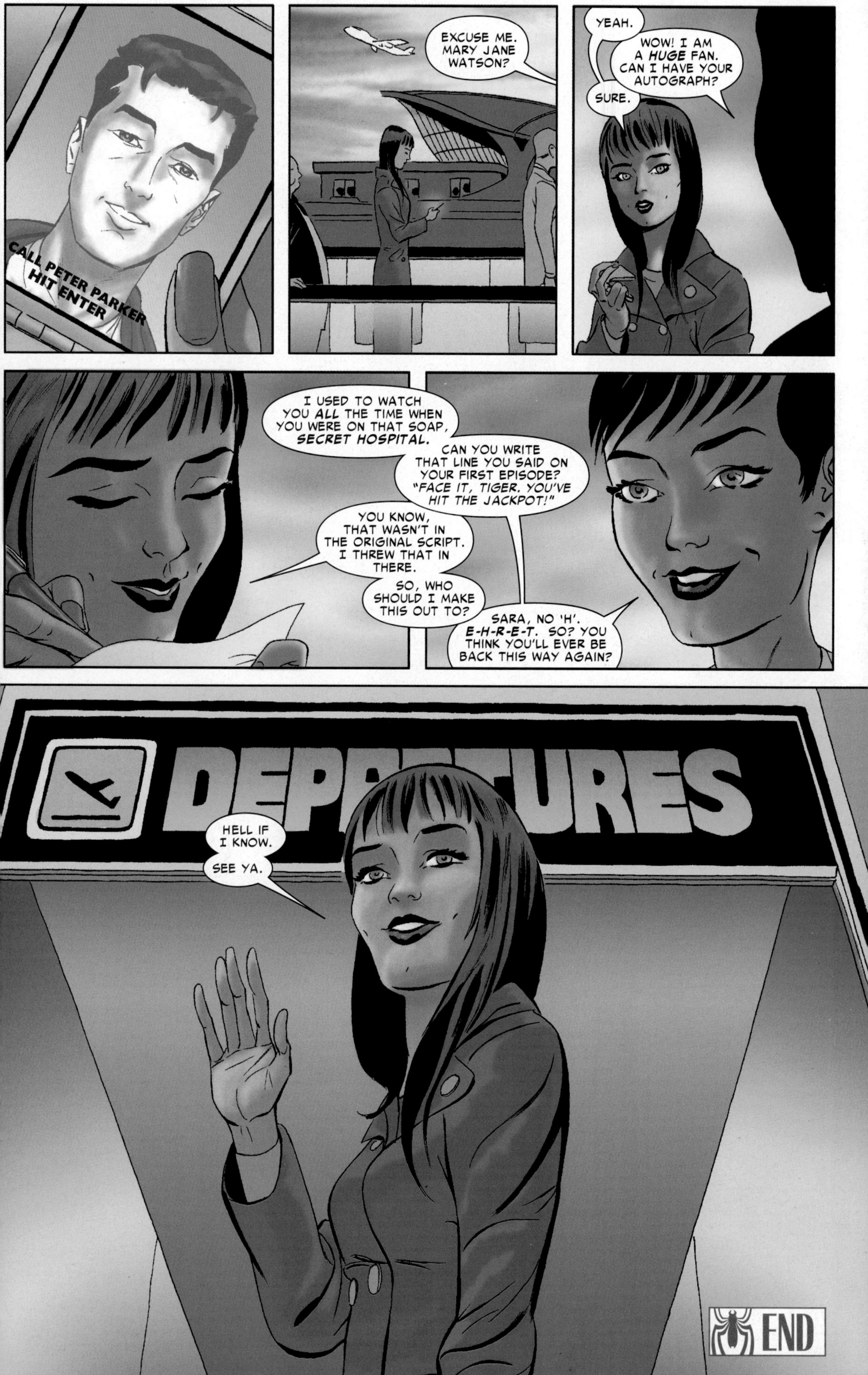
CALL PETER PARKER
HIT ENTER
EXCUSE ME. MARY JANE WATSON?
YEAH.
WOW! I AM A HUGE FAN. CAN I HAVE YOUR AUTOGRAPH?
SURE.
I USED TO WATCH YOU ALL THE TIME WHEN YOU WERE ON THAT SOAP, SECRET HOSPITAL.
CAN YOU WRITE THAT LINE YOU SAID ON YOUR FIRST EPISODE? "FACE IT, TIGER. YOU'VE HIT THE JACKPOT!"
YOU KNOW, THAT WASN'T IN THE ORIGINAL SCRIPT. I THREW THAT IN THERE.
SO, WHO SHOULD I MAKE THIS OUT TO?
SARA, NO 'H'. E-H-R-E-T. SO? YOU THINK YOU'LL EVER BE BACK THIS WAY AGAIN?
DEPARTURES
HELL IF I KNOW.
SEE YA.
END

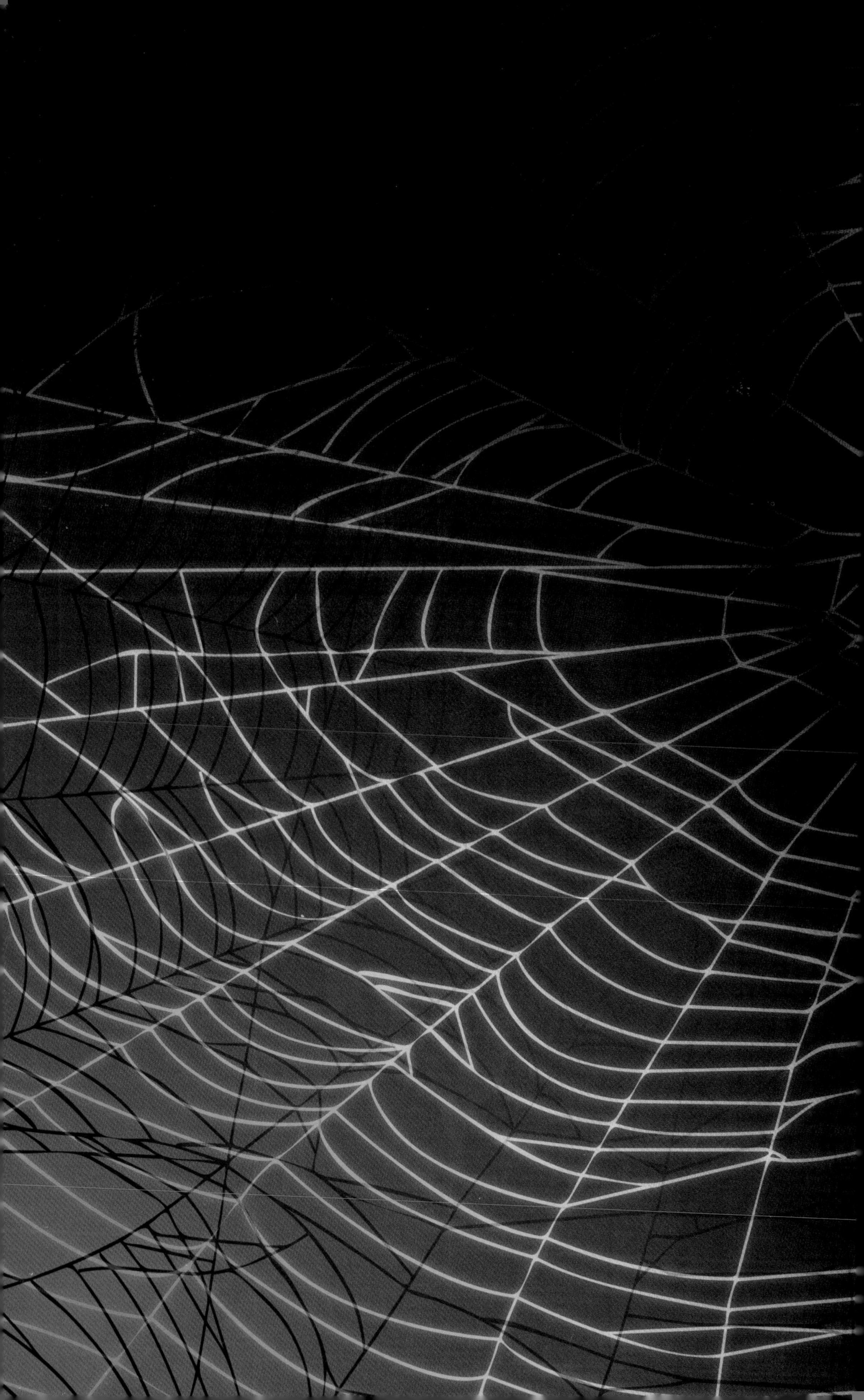

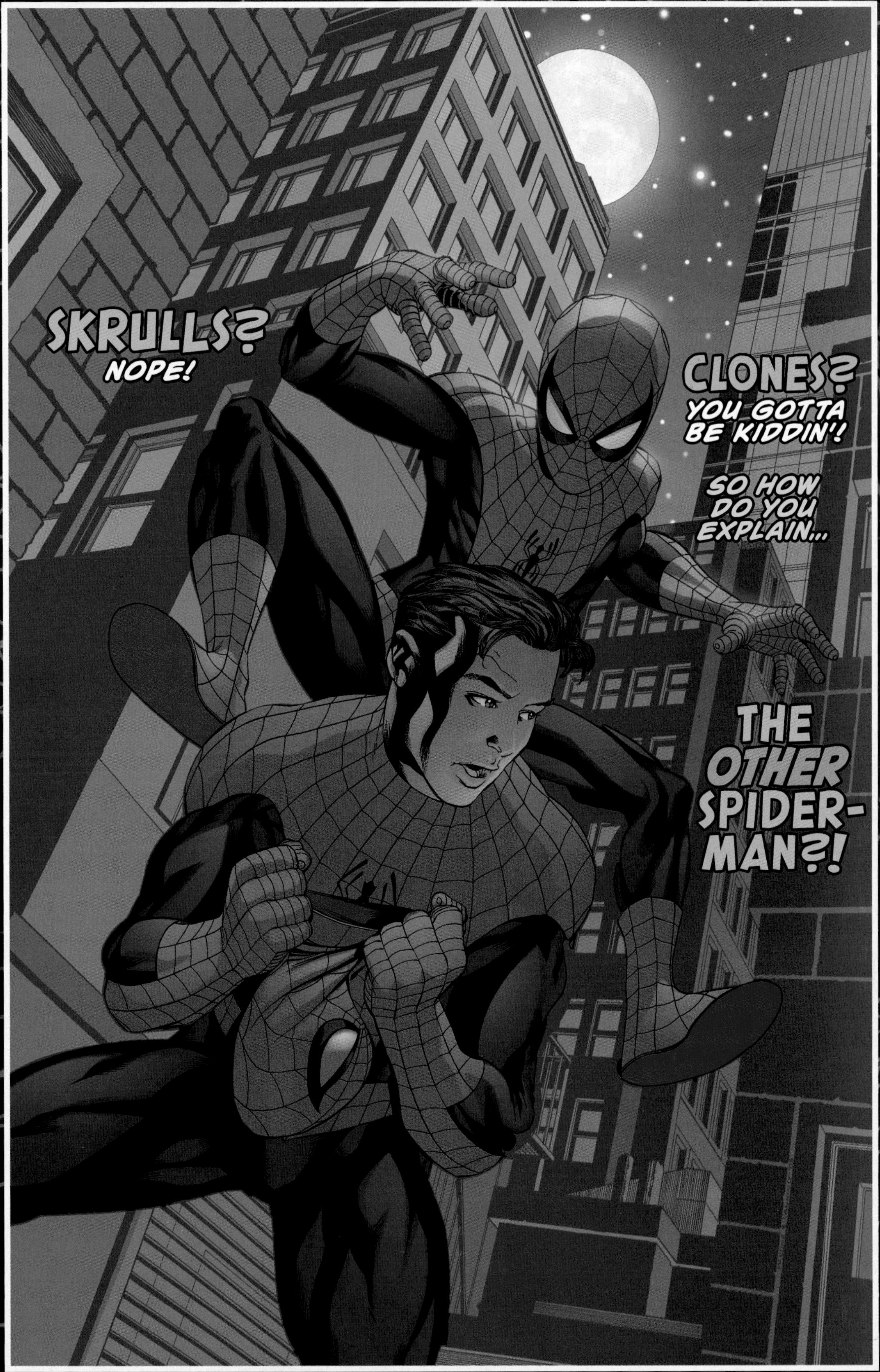
SKRULLS?
NOPE!
CLONES?
YOU GOTTA BE KIDDIN'!
SO HOW DO YOU EXPLAIN...
THE OTHER SPIDER-MAN?!

AMAZING SPIDER-MAN #562
COVER BY **MIKE MCKONE, ANDY LANNING & MORRY HOLLOWELL**

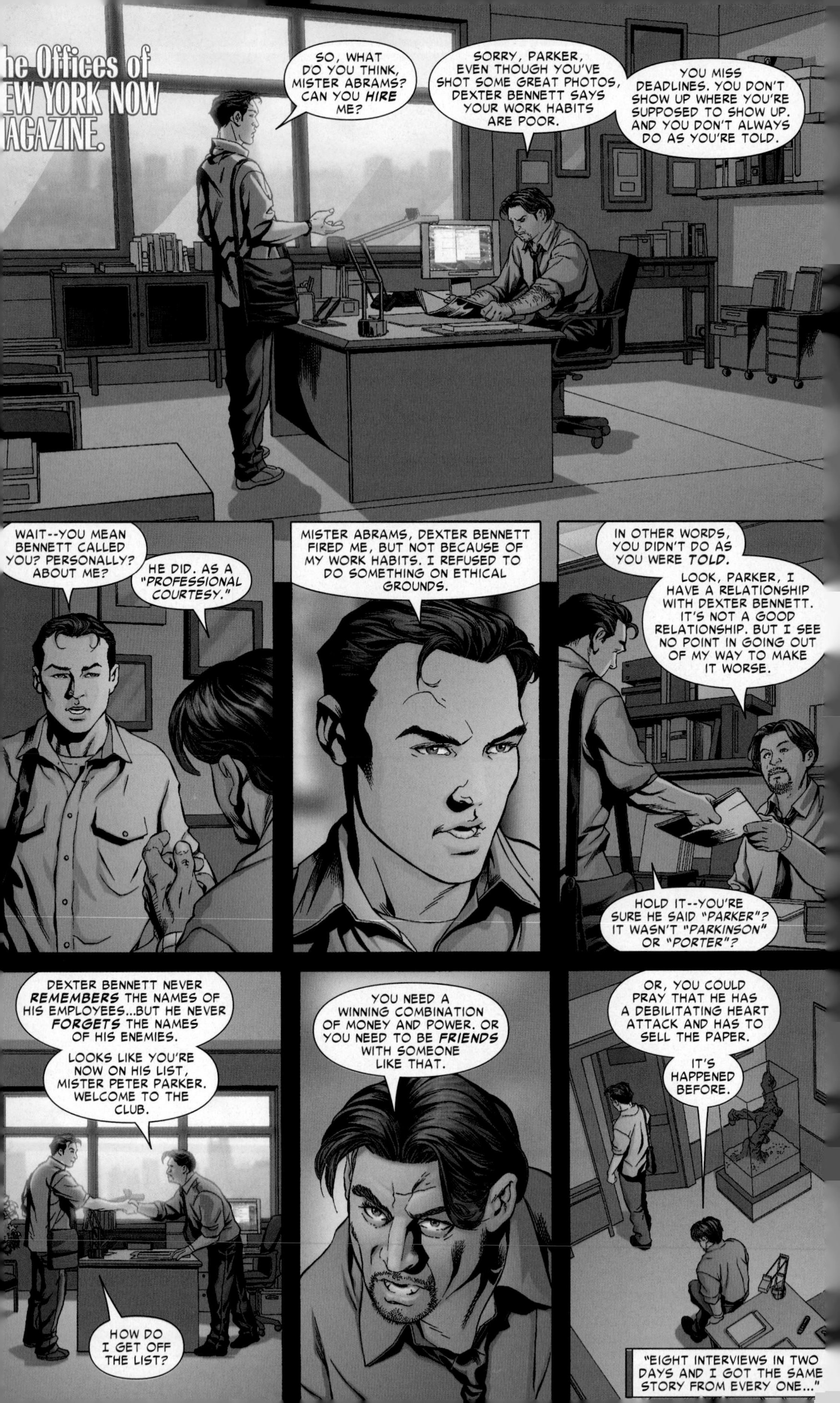

he Offices of EW YORK NOW AGAZINE.
SO, WHAT DO YOU THINK, MISTER ABRAMS? CAN YOU *HIRE* ME?
SORRY, PARKER, EVEN THOUGH YOU'VE SHOT SOME GREAT PHOTOS, DEXTER BENNETT SAYS YOUR WORK HABITS ARE POOR.
YOU MISS DEADLINES. YOU DON'T SHOW UP WHERE YOU'RE SUPPOSED TO SHOW UP. AND YOU DON'T ALWAYS DO AS YOU'RE TOLD.
WAIT--YOU MEAN BENNETT CALLED YOU? PERSONALLY? ABOUT ME?
HE DID. AS A "*PROFESSIONAL COURTESY.*"
MISTER ABRAMS, DEXTER BENNETT FIRED ME, BUT NOT BECAUSE OF MY WORK HABITS. I REFUSED TO DO SOMETHING ON ETHICAL GROUNDS.
IN OTHER WORDS, YOU DIDN'T DO AS YOU WERE *TOLD*.
LOOK, PARKER, I HAVE A RELATIONSHIP WITH DEXTER BENNETT. IT'S NOT A GOOD RELATIONSHIP. BUT I SEE NO POINT IN GOING OUT OF MY WAY TO MAKE IT WORSE.
HOLD IT--YOU'RE SURE HE SAID "*PARKER*"? IT WASN'T "*PARKINSON*" OR "*PORTER*"?
DEXTER BENNETT NEVER ***REMEMBERS*** THE NAMES OF HIS EMPLOYEES...BUT HE NEVER ***FORGETS*** THE NAMES OF HIS ENEMIES.
LOOKS LIKE YOU'RE NOW ON HIS LIST, MISTER PETER PARKER. WELCOME TO THE CLUB.
HOW DO I GET OFF THE LIST?
YOU NEED A WINNING COMBINATION OF MONEY AND POWER. OR YOU NEED TO BE *FRIENDS* WITH SOMEONE LIKE THAT.
OR, YOU COULD PRAY THAT HE HAS A DEBILITATING HEART ATTACK AND HAS TO SELL THE PAPER.
IT'S HAPPENED BEFORE.
"EIGHT INTERVIEWS IN TWO DAYS AND I GOT THE SAME STORY FROM EVERY ONE..."

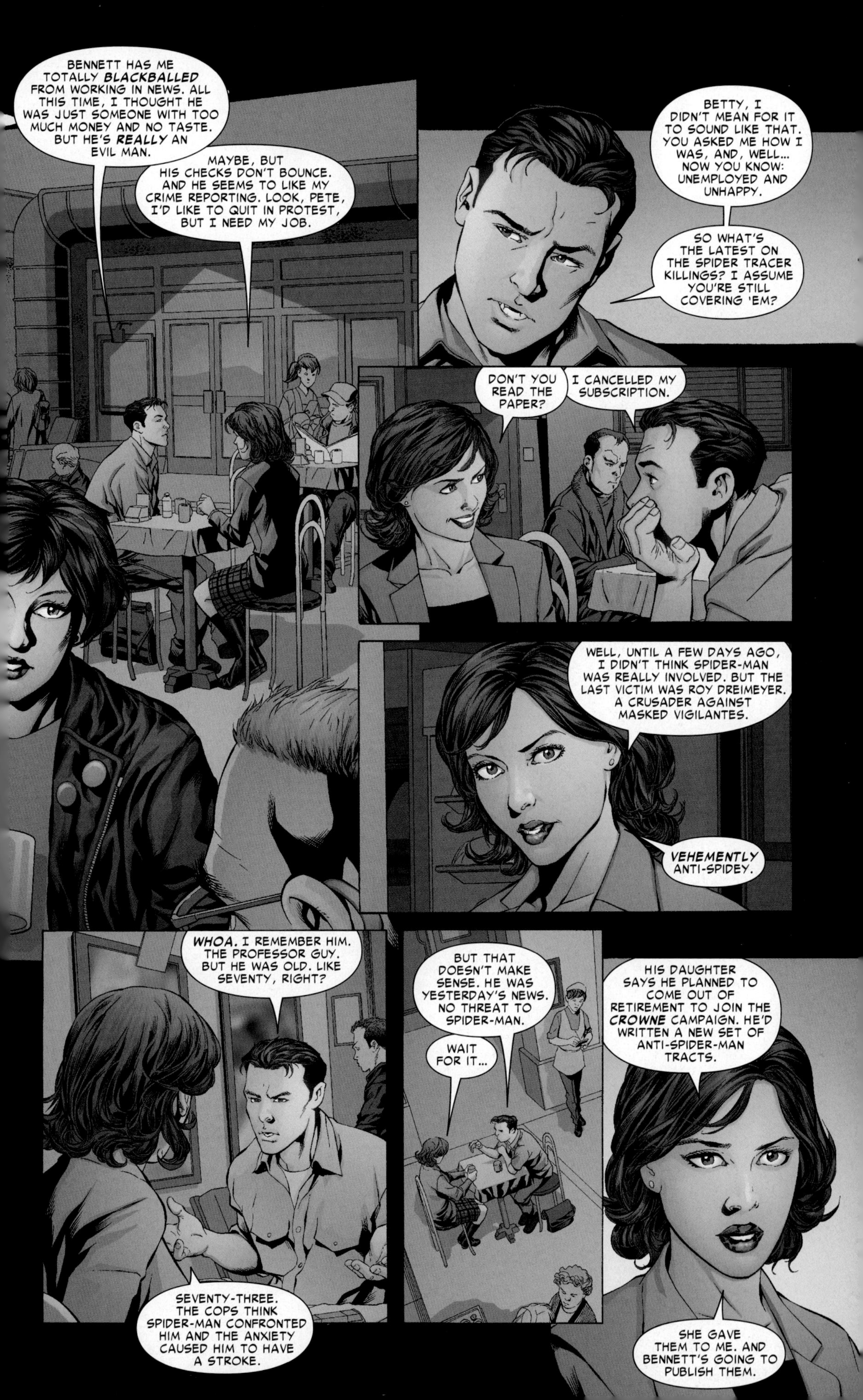
BENNETT HAS ME TOTALLY *BLACKBALLED* FROM WORKING IN NEWS. ALL THIS TIME, I THOUGHT HE WAS JUST SOMEONE WITH TOO MUCH MONEY AND NO TASTE. BUT HE'S *REALLY* AN EVIL MAN.
MAYBE, BUT HIS CHECKS DON'T BOUNCE. AND HE SEEMS TO LIKE MY CRIME REPORTING. LOOK, PETE, I'D LIKE TO QUIT IN PROTEST, BUT I NEED MY JOB.
BETTY, I DIDN'T MEAN FOR IT TO SOUND LIKE THAT. YOU ASKED ME HOW I WAS, AND, WELL... NOW YOU KNOW: UNEMPLOYED AND UNHAPPY.
SO WHAT'S THE LATEST ON THE SPIDER TRACER KILLINGS? I ASSUME YOU'RE STILL COVERING 'EM?
DON'T YOU READ THE PAPER?
I CANCELLED MY SUBSCRIPTION.
WELL, UNTIL A FEW DAYS AGO, I DIDN'T THINK SPIDER-MAN WAS REALLY INVOLVED. BUT THE LAST VICTIM WAS ROY DREIMEYER. A CRUSADER AGAINST MASKED VIGILANTES.
VEHEMENTLY ANTI-SPIDEY.
WHOA. I REMEMBER HIM. THE PROFESSOR GUY. BUT HE WAS OLD. LIKE SEVENTY, RIGHT?
SEVENTY-THREE. THE COPS THINK SPIDER-MAN CONFRONTED HIM AND THE ANXIETY CAUSED HIM TO HAVE A STROKE.
BUT THAT DOESN'T MAKE SENSE. HE WAS YESTERDAY'S NEWS. NO THREAT TO SPIDER-MAN.
WAIT FOR IT...
HIS DAUGHTER SAYS HE PLANNED TO COME OUT OF RETIREMENT TO JOIN THE *CROWNE* CAMPAIGN. HE'D WRITTEN A NEW SET OF ANTI-SPIDER-MAN TRACTS.
SHE GAVE THEM TO ME. AND BENNETT'S GOING TO PUBLISH THEM.

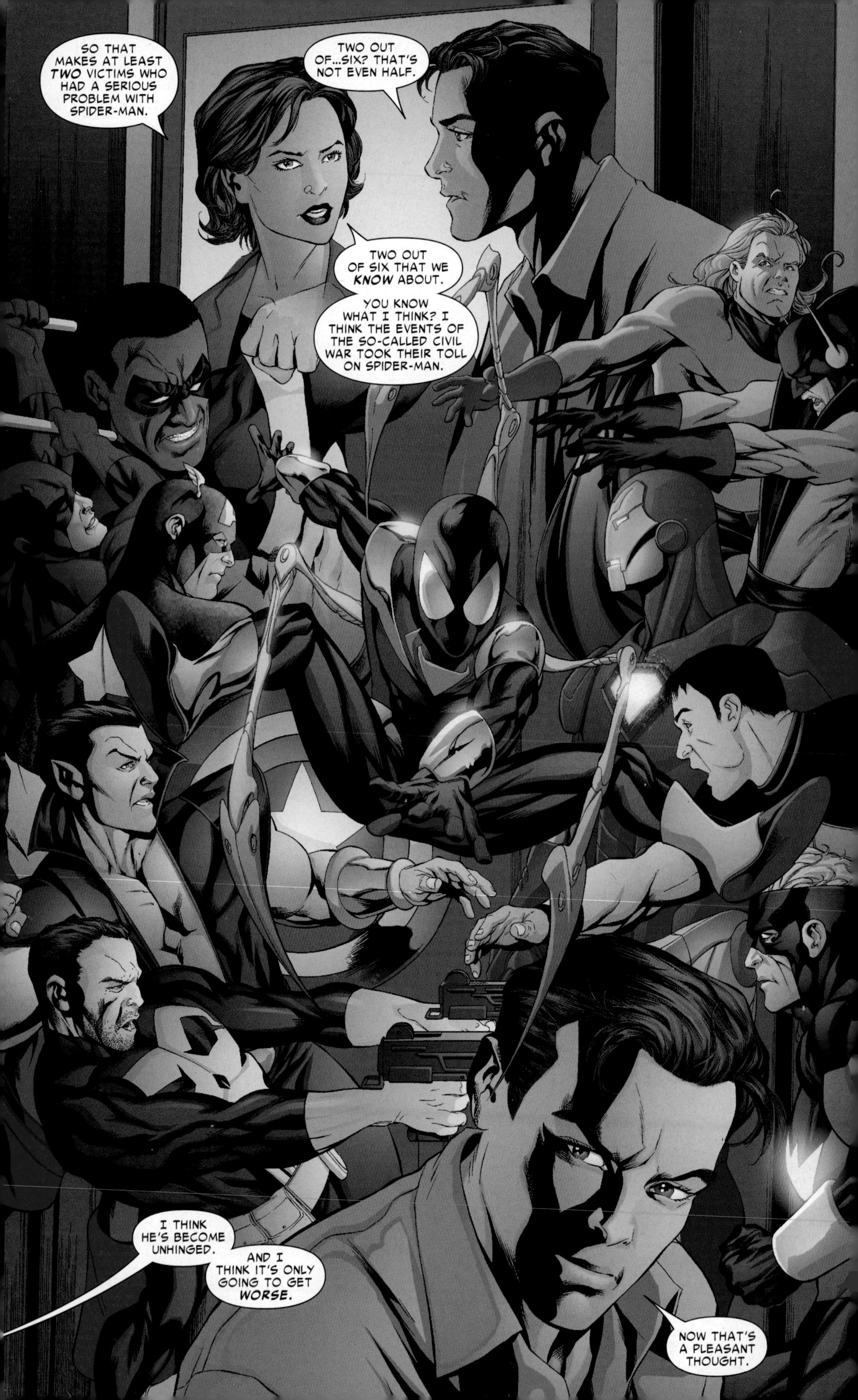
SO THAT MAKES AT LEAST TWO VICTIMS WHO HAD A SERIOUS PROBLEM WITH SPIDER-MAN.
TWO OUT OF...SIX? THAT'S NOT EVEN HALF.
TWO OUT OF SIX THAT WE KNOW ABOUT.
YOU KNOW WHAT I THINK? I THINK THE EVENTS OF THE SO-CALLED CIVIL WAR TOOK THEIR TOLL ON SPIDER-MAN.
I THINK HE'S BECOME UNHINGED.
AND I THINK IT'S ONLY GOING TO GET WORSE.
NOW THAT'S A PLEASANT THOUGHT.

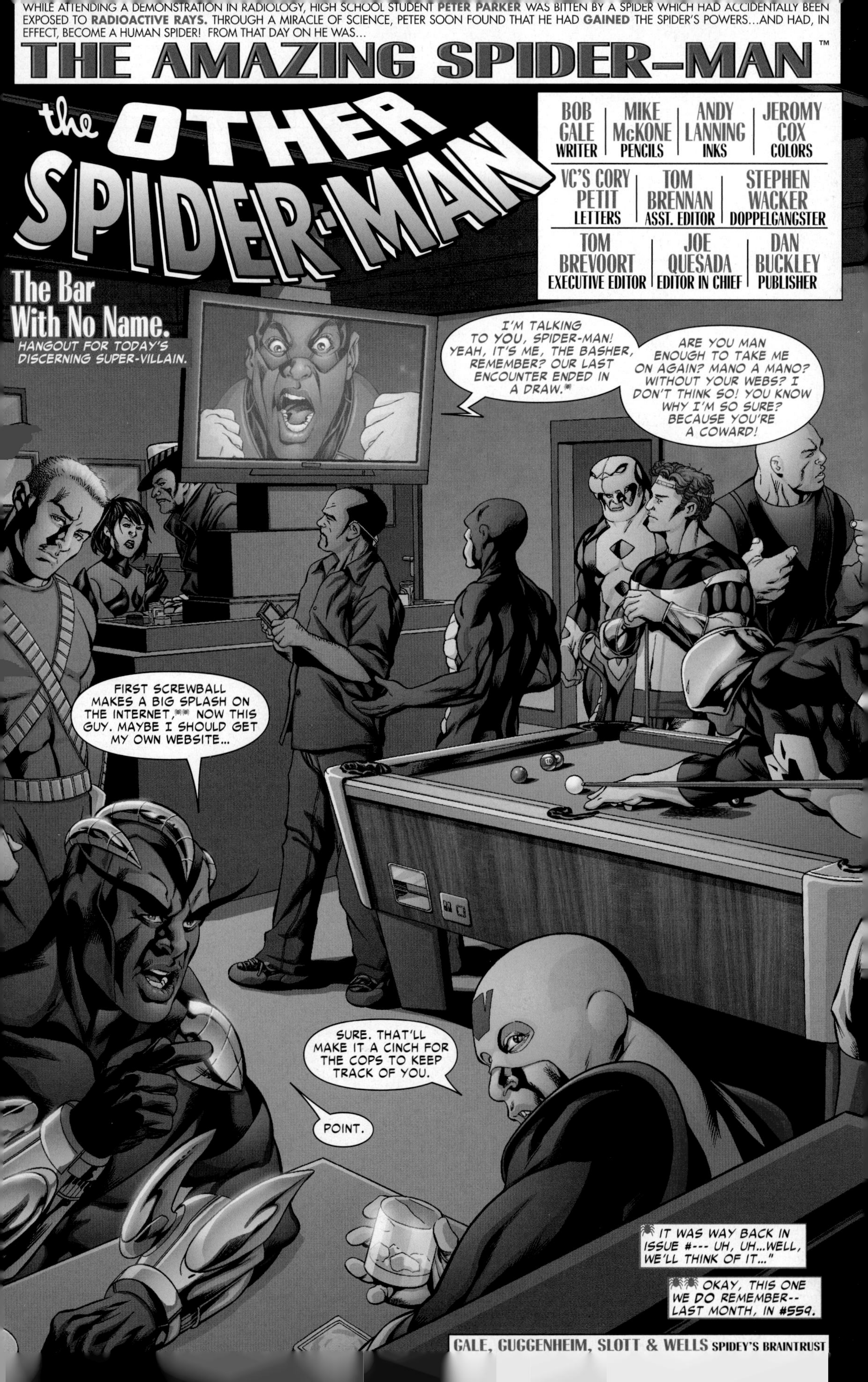
WHILE ATTENDING A DEMONSTRATION IN RADIOLOGY, HIGH SCHOOL STUDENT PETER PARKER WAS BITTEN BY A SPIDER WHICH HAD ACCIDENTALLY BEEN EXPOSED TO RADIOACTIVE RAYS. THROUGH A MIRACLE OF SCIENCE, PETER SOON FOUND THAT HE HAD GAINED THE SPIDER'S POWERS...AND HAD, IN EFFECT, BECOME A HUMAN SPIDER! FROM THAT DAY ON HE WAS...
THE AMAZING SPIDER-MAN™
the OTHER SPIDER-MAN
BOB GALE WRITER
MIKE McKONE PENCILS
ANDY LANNING INKS
JEROMY COX COLORS
VC'S CORY PETIT LETTERS
TOM BRENNAN ASST. EDITOR
STEPHEN WACKER DOPPELGANGSTER
TOM BREVOORT EXECUTIVE EDITOR
JOE QUESADA EDITOR IN CHIEF
DAN BUCKLEY PUBLISHER
The Bar With No Name.
HANGOUT FOR TODAY'S DISCERNING SUPER-VILLAIN.
I'M TALKING TO YOU, SPIDER-MAN! YEAH, IT'S ME, THE BASHER, REMEMBER? OUR LAST ENCOUNTER ENDED IN A DRAW.*
ARE YOU MAN ENOUGH TO TAKE ME ON AGAIN? MANO A MANO? WITHOUT YOUR WEBS? I DON'T THINK SO! YOU KNOW WHY I'M SO SURE? BECAUSE YOU'RE A COWARD!
FIRST SCREWBALL MAKES A BIG SPLASH ON THE INTERNET,** NOW THIS GUY. MAYBE I SHOULD GET MY OWN WEBSITE...
SURE. THAT'LL MAKE IT A CINCH FOR THE COPS TO KEEP TRACK OF YOU.
POINT.
* IT WAS WAY BACK IN ISSUE #--- UH, UH...WELL, WE'LL THINK OF IT..."
** OKAY, THIS ONE WE DO REMEMBER-- LAST MONTH, IN #559.
GALE, GUGGENHEIM, SLOTT & WELLS SPIDEY'S BRAINTRUST

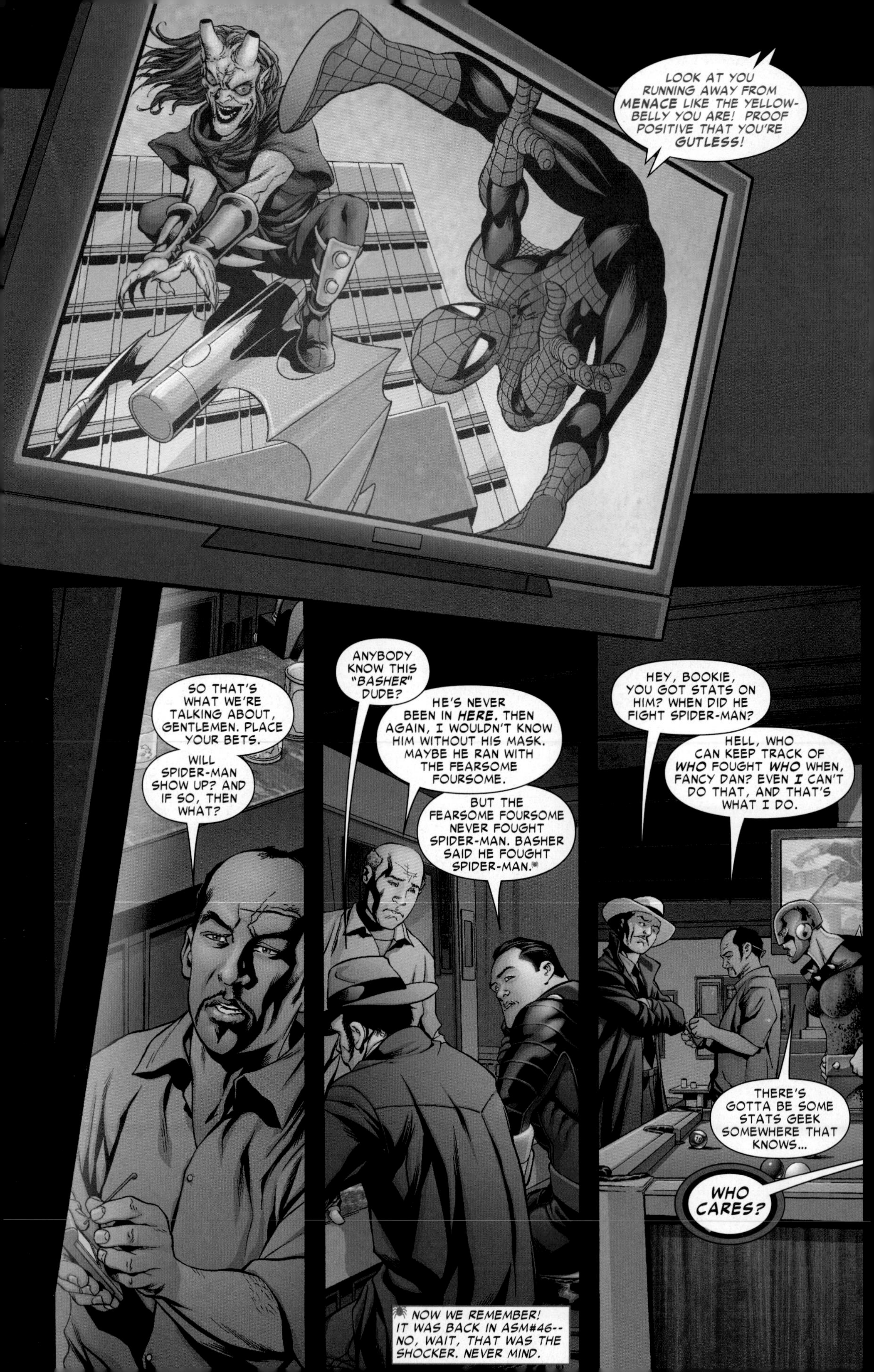
LOOK AT YOU RUNNING AWAY FROM MENACE LIKE THE YELLOW-BELLY YOU ARE! PROOF POSITIVE THAT YOU'RE GUTLESS!
SO THAT'S WHAT WE'RE TALKING ABOUT, GENTLEMEN. PLACE YOUR BETS.
WILL SPIDER-MAN SHOW UP? AND IF SO, THEN WHAT?
ANYBODY KNOW THIS "BASHER" DUDE?
HE'S NEVER BEEN IN HERE. THEN AGAIN, I WOULDN'T KNOW HIM WITHOUT HIS MASK. MAYBE HE RAN WITH THE FEARSOME FOURSOME.
BUT THE FEARSOME FOURSOME NEVER FOUGHT SPIDER-MAN. BASHER SAID HE FOUGHT SPIDER-MAN.*
NOW WE REMEMBER! IT WAS BACK IN ASM#46--NO, WAIT, THAT WAS THE SHOCKER. NEVER MIND.
HEY, BOOKIE, YOU GOT STATS ON HIM? WHEN DID HE FIGHT SPIDER-MAN?
HELL, WHO CAN KEEP TRACK OF WHO FOUGHT WHO WHEN, FANCY DAN? EVEN I CAN'T DO THAT, AND THAT'S WHAT I DO.
THERE'S GOTTA BE SOME STATS GEEK SOMEWHERE THAT KNOWS...
WHO CARES?

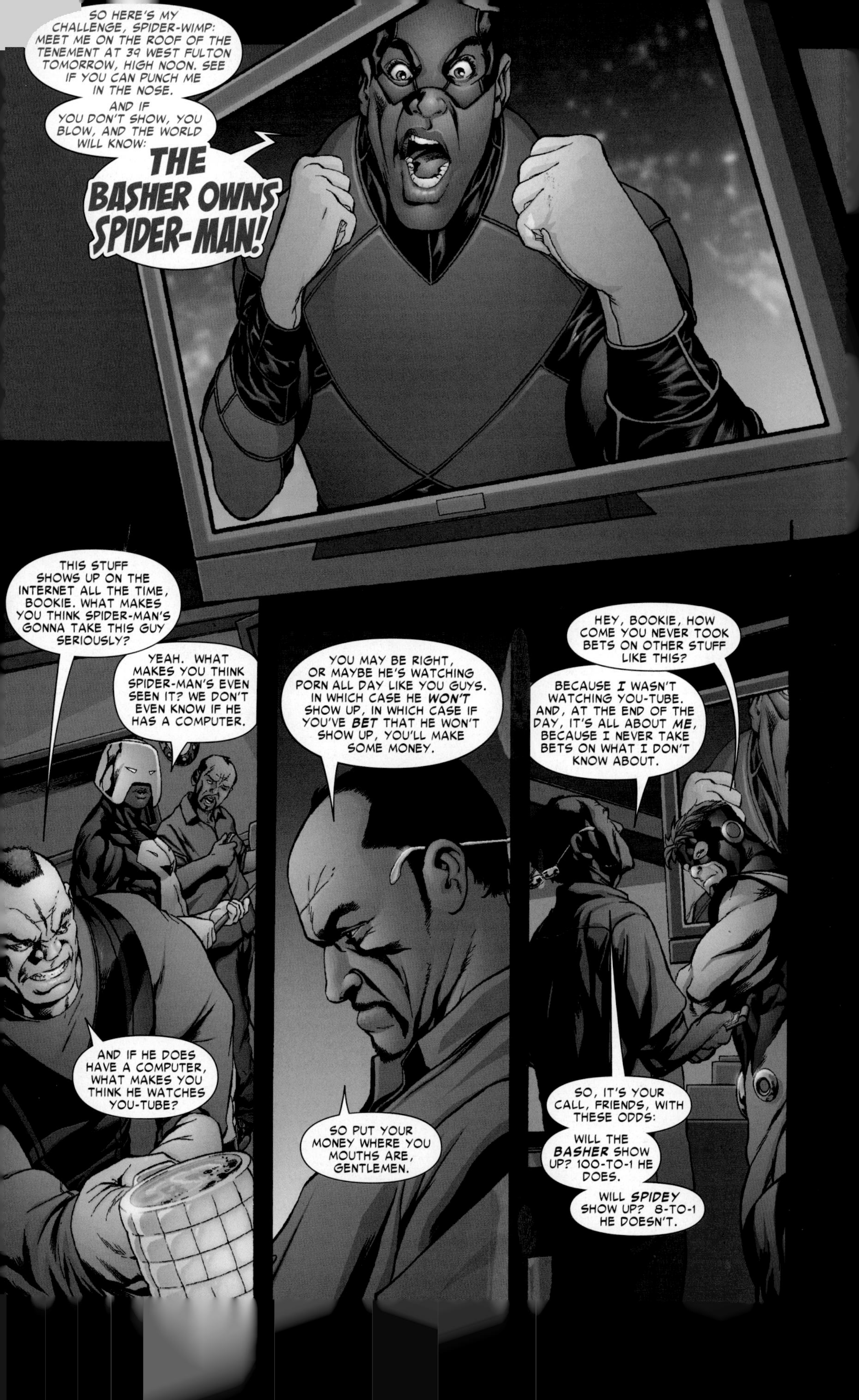
SO HERE'S MY CHALLENGE, SPIDER-WIMP: MEET ME ON THE ROOF OF THE TENEMENT AT 39 WEST FULTON TOMORROW, HIGH NOON. SEE IF YOU CAN PUNCH ME IN THE NOSE.
AND IF YOU DON'T SHOW, YOU BLOW, AND THE WORLD WILL KNOW:
THE BASHER OWNS SPIDER-MAN!
THIS STUFF SHOWS UP ON THE INTERNET ALL THE TIME, BOOKIE. WHAT MAKES YOU THINK SPIDER-MAN'S GONNA TAKE THIS GUY SERIOUSLY?
YEAH. WHAT MAKES YOU THINK SPIDER-MAN'S EVEN SEEN IT? WE DON'T EVEN KNOW IF HE HAS A COMPUTER.
AND IF HE DOES HAVE A COMPUTER, WHAT MAKES YOU THINK HE WATCHES YOU-TUBE?
YOU MAY BE RIGHT, OR MAYBE HE'S WATCHING PORN ALL DAY LIKE YOU GUYS. IN WHICH CASE HE WON'T SHOW UP, IN WHICH CASE IF YOU'VE BET THAT HE WON'T SHOW UP, YOU'LL MAKE SOME MONEY.
SO PUT YOUR MONEY WHERE YOU MOUTHS ARE, GENTLEMEN.
HEY, BOOKIE, HOW COME YOU NEVER TOOK BETS ON OTHER STUFF LIKE THIS?
BECAUSE I WASN'T WATCHING YOU-TUBE. AND, AT THE END OF THE DAY, IT'S ALL ABOUT ME, BECAUSE I NEVER TAKE BETS ON WHAT I DON'T KNOW ABOUT.
SO, IT'S YOUR CALL, FRIENDS, WITH THESE ODDS:
WILL THE BASHER SHOW UP? 100-TO-1 HE DOES.
WILL SPIDEY SHOW UP? 8-TO-1 HE DOESN'T.

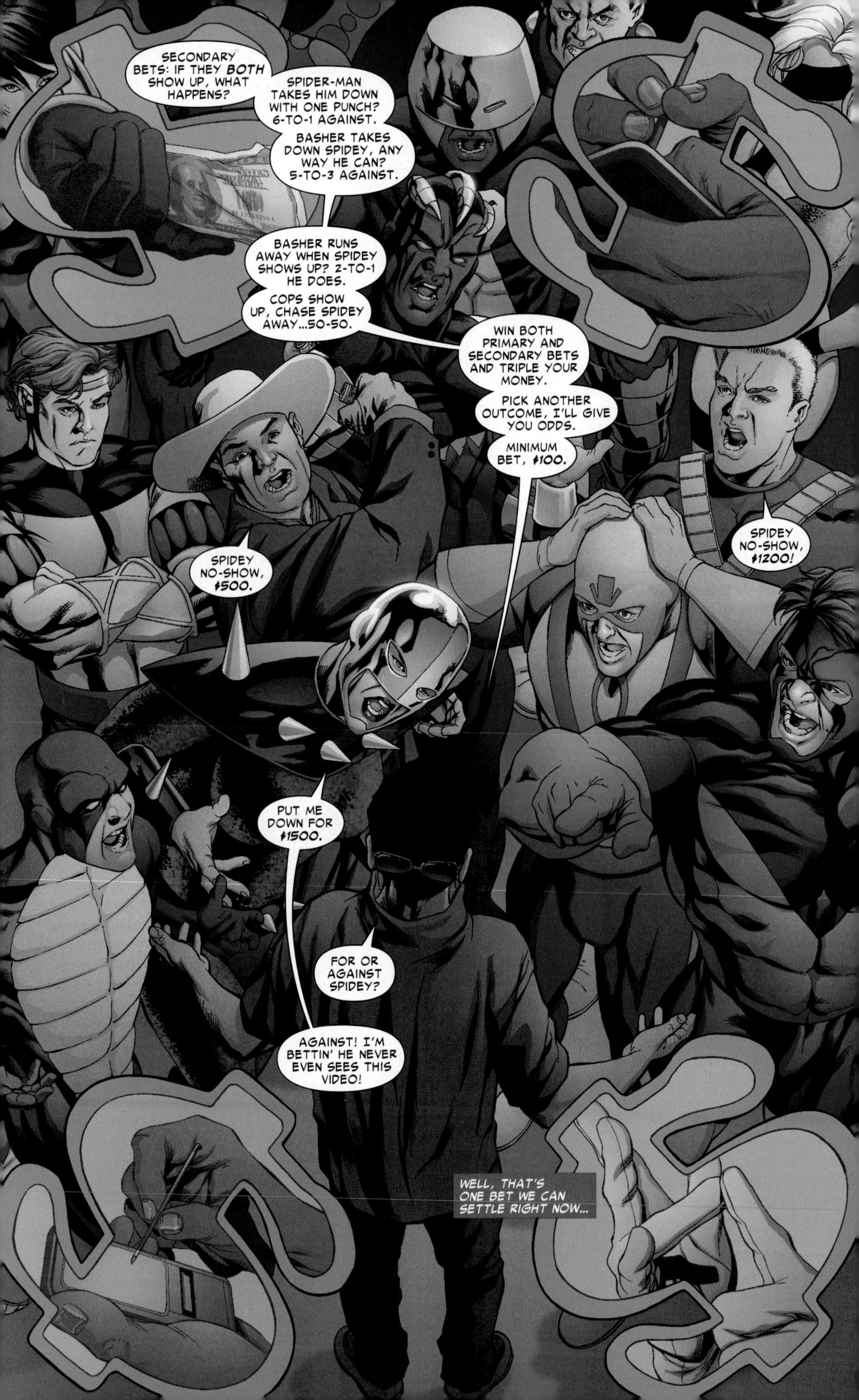

SECONDARY BETS: IF THEY *BOTH* SHOW UP, WHAT HAPPENS?
SPIDER-MAN TAKES HIM DOWN WITH ONE PUNCH? 6-TO-1 AGAINST.
BASHER TAKES DOWN SPIDEY, ANY WAY HE CAN? 5-TO-3 AGAINST.
BASHER RUNS AWAY WHEN SPIDEY SHOWS UP? 2-TO-1 HE DOES.
COPS SHOW UP, CHASE SPIDEY AWAY...50-50.
WIN BOTH PRIMARY AND SECONDARY BETS AND TRIPLE YOUR MONEY.
PICK ANOTHER OUTCOME, I'LL GIVE YOU ODDS.
MINIMUM BET, *$100.*
SPIDEY NO-SHOW, *$500.*
SPIDEY NO-SHOW, *$1200!*
PUT ME DOWN FOR *$1500.*
FOR OR AGAINST SPIDEY?
AGAINST! I'M BETTIN' HE NEVER EVEN SEES THIS VIDEO!
WELL, THAT'S ONE BET WE CAN SETTLE RIGHT NOW...

...BASHER OWNS SPIDER-MAN!

SO HE'S CALLING OUT SPIDER-MAN AND THE NYPD ISN'T GOING TO ARREST HIM?

WE CAN'T. THERE'S NO FILE ON HIM AND HE'S NOT WANTED FOR ANYTHING. AND THERE'S NO LAW AGAINST GOING OUT IN PUBLIC AND MAKING A *FOOL* OF YOURSELF-- OTHERWISE HALF THE CITY WOULD BE IN JAIL.

BUT I THOUGHT THERE MIGHT BE A NEWS STORY IN IT FOR YOU.

FUNNY, I DON'T REMEMBER EVER FIGHTING THIS GUY. WELL, THAT'S WHAT I GET FOR NOT KEEPING A JOURNAL. OR MAYBE BETTY'S RIGHT. MAYBE I *AM* LOSING IT...

AFTER ALL, I'VE GOTTA MAKE SURE MY ROOMIE IS FINANCIALLY SOLVENT, SINCE I HAVEN'T NOTICED ANY OF YOUR PIX IN THE DB LATELY...

I REALLY SHOULD TELL VIN I WAS FIRED, BUT THE LAST THING I NEED IS FOR HIM TO THINK HE'S ROOMING WITH A FLAKE.

LUCKILY, I STILL HAVE *THIS* MONTH'S RENT COVERED. HERE'S HOPING I FIND SOMETHING SOON.

WELL, IT'S ALL ABOUT BEING AT THE RIGHT PLACE AT THE RIGHT TIME, AND I...UH... HAVEN'T BEEN AT EITHER ONE LATELY.

SMOOTH, PARKER. NOW HE'LL THINK YOU'RE JUST A LOSER WITH BAD TIMING.

I HEAR YOU. SAME DRILL WHEN YOU'RE TRYING TO CATCH THE BAD GUYS.

SO THE NYPD WON'T BE STAKING THIS AREA OUT TOMORROW IN HOPES OF CATCHING SPIDER-MAN?

GET REAL. IF *YOU* WERE SPIDER-MAN, WOULD YOU BOTHER SHOWING UP TO VALIDATE THIS BLOWHARD?

NO, I GUESS NOT.

BUT IT WOULDN'T HURT TO SHOW UP AS PETER PARKER, JUST TO SCOPE IT OUT AND MAKE SURE NO ONE GETS HURT.

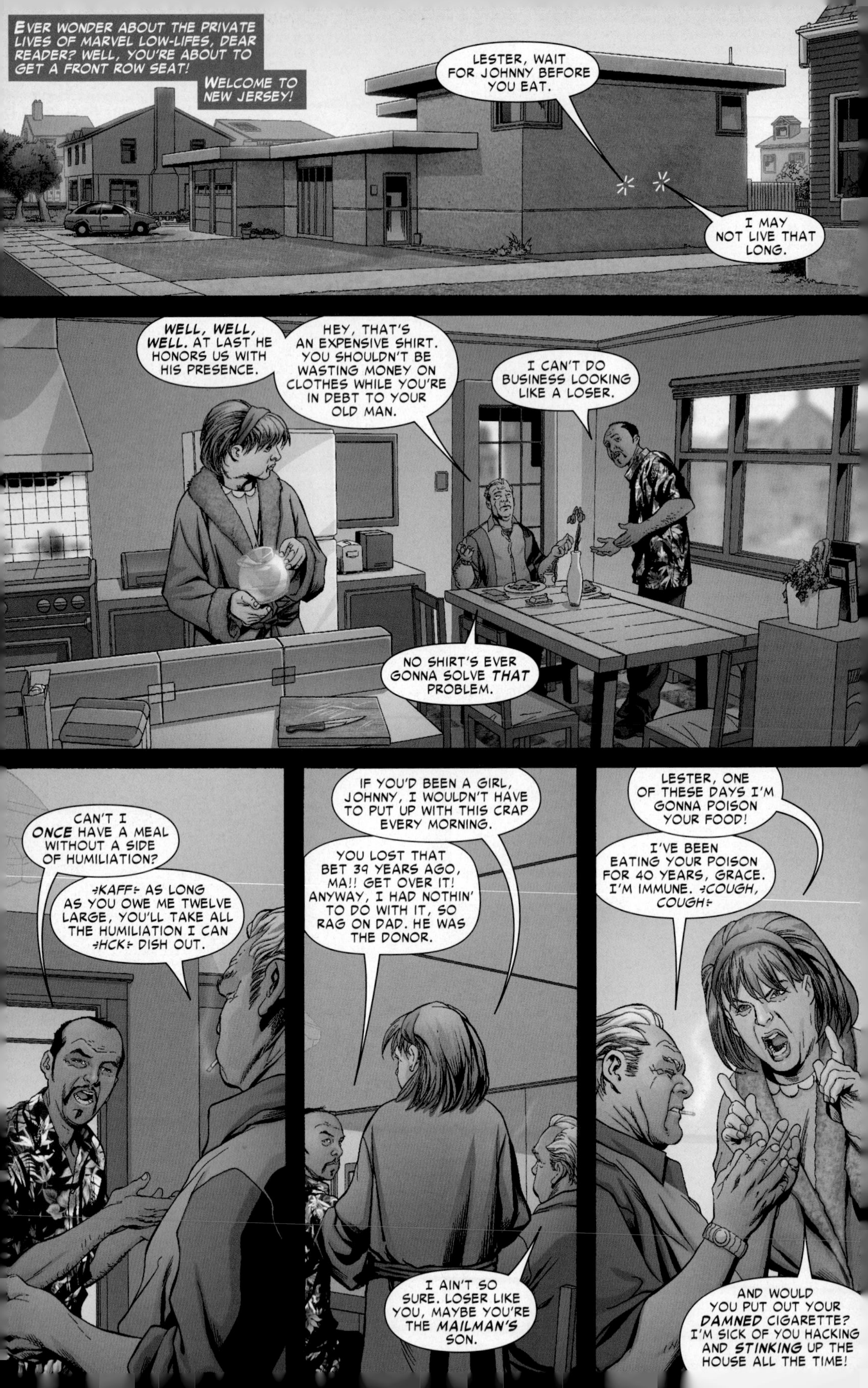
EVER WONDER ABOUT THE PRIVATE LIVES OF MARVEL LOW-LIFES, DEAR READER? WELL, YOU'RE ABOUT TO GET A FRONT ROW SEAT!
WELCOME TO NEW JERSEY!
LESTER, WAIT FOR JOHNNY BEFORE YOU EAT.
I MAY NOT LIVE THAT LONG.
WELL, WELL, WELL. AT LAST HE HONORS US WITH HIS PRESENCE.
HEY, THAT'S AN EXPENSIVE SHIRT. YOU SHOULDN'T BE WASTING MONEY ON CLOTHES WHILE YOU'RE IN DEBT TO YOUR OLD MAN.
I CAN'T DO BUSINESS LOOKING LIKE A LOSER.
NO SHIRT'S EVER GONNA SOLVE THAT PROBLEM.
CAN'T I ONCE HAVE A MEAL WITHOUT A SIDE OF HUMILIATION?
KAFF AS LONG AS YOU OWE ME TWELVE LARGE, YOU'LL TAKE ALL THE HUMILIATION I CAN *HCK* DISH OUT.
IF YOU'D BEEN A GIRL, JOHNNY, I WOULDN'T HAVE TO PUT UP WITH THIS CRAP EVERY MORNING.
YOU LOST THAT BET 39 YEARS AGO, MA!! GET OVER IT! ANYWAY, I HAD NOTHIN' TO DO WITH IT, SO RAG ON DAD. HE WAS THE DONOR.
I AIN'T SO SURE. LOSER LIKE YOU, MAYBE YOU'RE THE MAILMAN'S SON.
LESTER, ONE OF THESE DAYS I'M GONNA POISON YOUR FOOD!
I'VE BEEN EATING YOUR POISON FOR 40 YEARS, GRACE. I'M IMMUNE. *COUGH, COUGH*
AND WOULD YOU PUT OUT YOUR DAMNED CIGARETTE? I'M SICK OF YOU HACKING AND STINKING UP THE HOUSE ALL THE TIME!

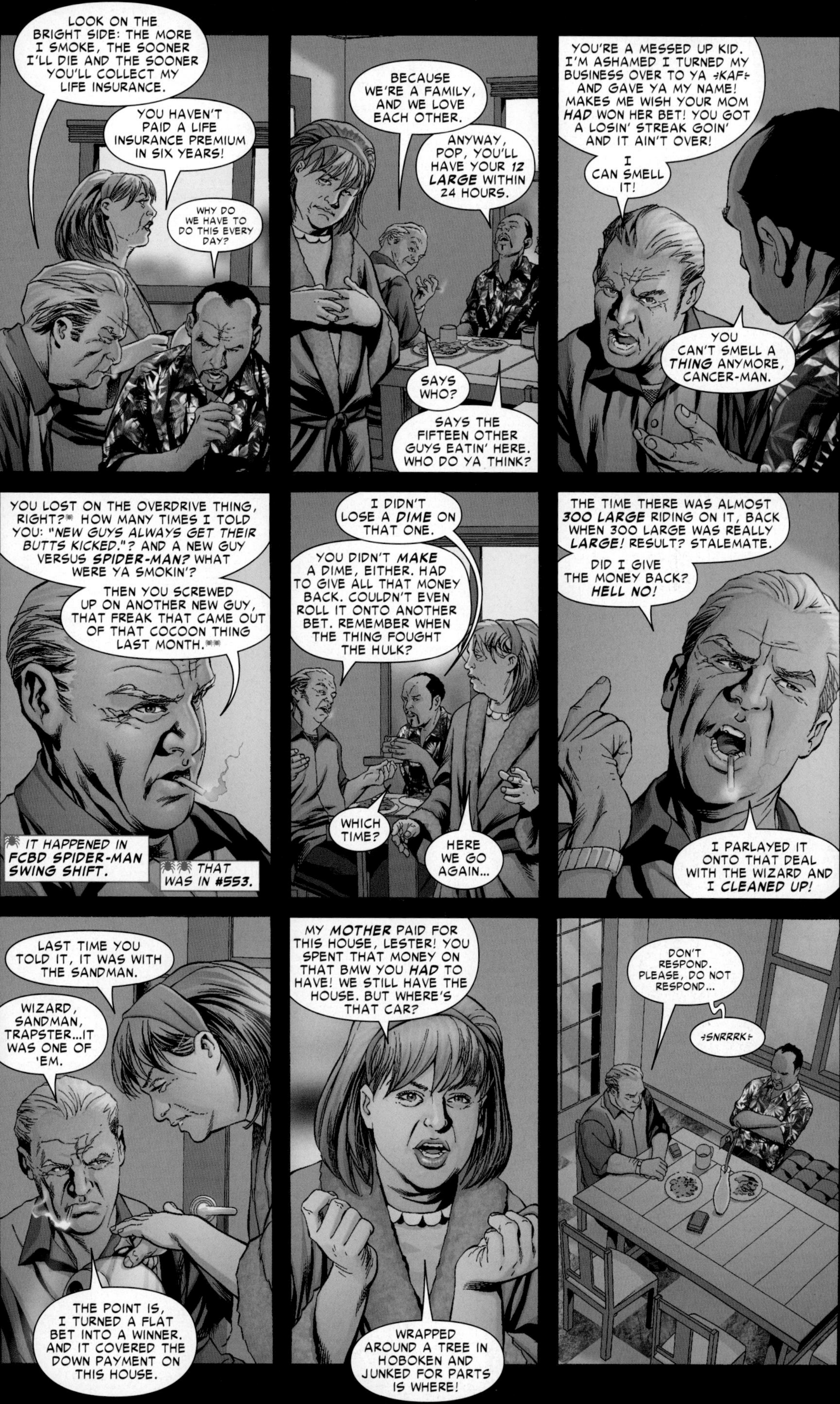

LOOK ON THE BRIGHT SIDE: THE MORE I SMOKE, THE SOONER I'LL DIE AND THE SOONER YOU'LL COLLECT MY LIFE INSURANCE.
YOU HAVEN'T PAID A LIFE INSURANCE PREMIUM IN SIX YEARS!
WHY DO WE HAVE TO DO THIS EVERY DAY?
BECAUSE WE'RE A FAMILY, AND WE LOVE EACH OTHER.
ANYWAY, POP, YOU'LL HAVE YOUR 12 LARGE WITHIN 24 HOURS.
SAYS WHO?
SAYS THE FIFTEEN OTHER GUYS EATIN' HERE. WHO DO YA THINK?
YOU'RE A MESSED UP KID. I'M ASHAMED I TURNED MY BUSINESS OVER TO YA ≑KAF≑ AND GAVE YA MY NAME! MAKES ME WISH YOUR MOM HAD WON HER BET! YOU GOT A LOSIN' STREAK GOIN' AND IT AIN'T OVER!
I CAN SMELL IT!
YOU CAN'T SMELL A THING ANYMORE, CANCER-MAN.
YOU LOST ON THE OVERDRIVE THING, RIGHT?* HOW MANY TIMES I TOLD YOU: "NEW GUYS ALWAYS GET THEIR BUTTS KICKED."? AND A NEW GUY VERSUS SPIDER-MAN? WHAT WERE YA SMOKIN'?
THEN YOU SCREWED UP ON ANOTHER NEW GUY, THAT FREAK THAT CAME OUT OF THAT COCOON THING LAST MONTH.**
*IT HAPPENED IN FCBD SPIDER-MAN SWING SHIFT.
**THAT WAS IN #553.
I DIDN'T LOSE A DIME ON THAT ONE.
YOU DIDN'T MAKE A DIME, EITHER. HAD TO GIVE ALL THAT MONEY BACK. COULDN'T EVEN ROLL IT ONTO ANOTHER BET. REMEMBER WHEN THE THING FOUGHT THE HULK?
WHICH TIME?
HERE WE GO AGAIN...
THE TIME THERE WAS ALMOST 300 LARGE RIDING ON IT, BACK WHEN 300 LARGE WAS REALLY LARGE! RESULT? STALEMATE.
DID I GIVE THE MONEY BACK? HELL NO!
I PARLAYED IT ONTO THAT DEAL WITH THE WIZARD AND I CLEANED UP!
LAST TIME YOU TOLD IT, IT WAS WITH THE SANDMAN.
WIZARD, SANDMAN, TRAPSTER...IT WAS ONE OF 'EM.
THE POINT IS, I TURNED A FLAT BET INTO A WINNER. AND IT COVERED THE DOWN PAYMENT ON THIS HOUSE.
MY MOTHER PAID FOR THIS HOUSE, LESTER! YOU SPENT THAT MONEY ON THAT BMW YOU HAD TO HAVE! WE STILL HAVE THE HOUSE. BUT WHERE'S THAT CAR?
WRAPPED AROUND A TREE IN HOBOKEN AND JUNKED FOR PARTS IS WHERE!
DON'T RESPOND. PLEASE, DO NOT RESPOND...
≑SNRRRK≑

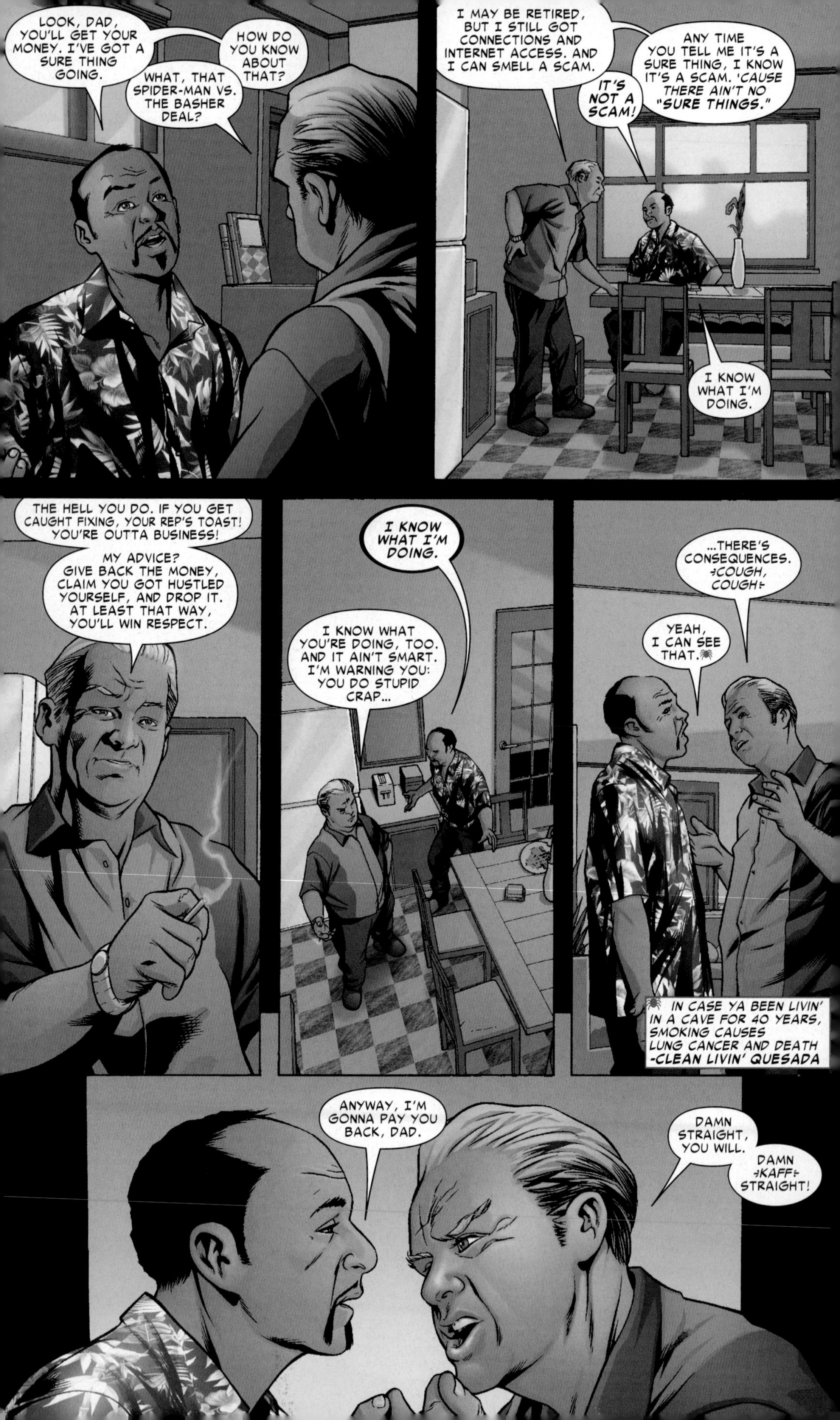
LOOK, DAD, YOU'LL GET YOUR MONEY. I'VE GOT A SURE THING GOING.
HOW DO YOU KNOW ABOUT THAT?
WHAT, THAT SPIDER-MAN VS. THE BASHER DEAL?
I MAY BE RETIRED, BUT I STILL GOT CONNECTIONS AND INTERNET ACCESS. AND I CAN SMELL A SCAM.
ANY TIME YOU TELL ME IT'S A SURE THING, I KNOW IT'S A SCAM. 'CAUSE THERE AIN'T NO "SURE THINGS."
IT'S NOT A SCAM!
I KNOW WHAT I'M DOING.
THE HELL YOU DO. IF YOU GET CAUGHT FIXING, YOUR REP'S TOAST! YOU'RE OUTTA BUSINESS!
MY ADVICE? GIVE BACK THE MONEY, CLAIM YOU GOT HUSTLED YOURSELF, AND DROP IT. AT LEAST THAT WAY, YOU'LL WIN RESPECT.
I KNOW WHAT I'M DOING.
I KNOW WHAT YOU'RE DOING, TOO. AND IT AIN'T SMART. I'M WARNING YOU: YOU DO STUPID CRAP...
...THERE'S CONSEQUENCES. COUGH, COUGH
YEAH, I CAN SEE THAT.
IN CASE YA BEEN LIVIN' IN A CAVE FOR 40 YEARS, SMOKING CAUSES LUNG CANCER AND DEATH -CLEAN LIVIN' QUESADA
ANYWAY, I'M GONNA PAY YOU BACK, DAD.
DAMN STRAIGHT, YOU WILL.
DAMN KAFF STRAIGHT!

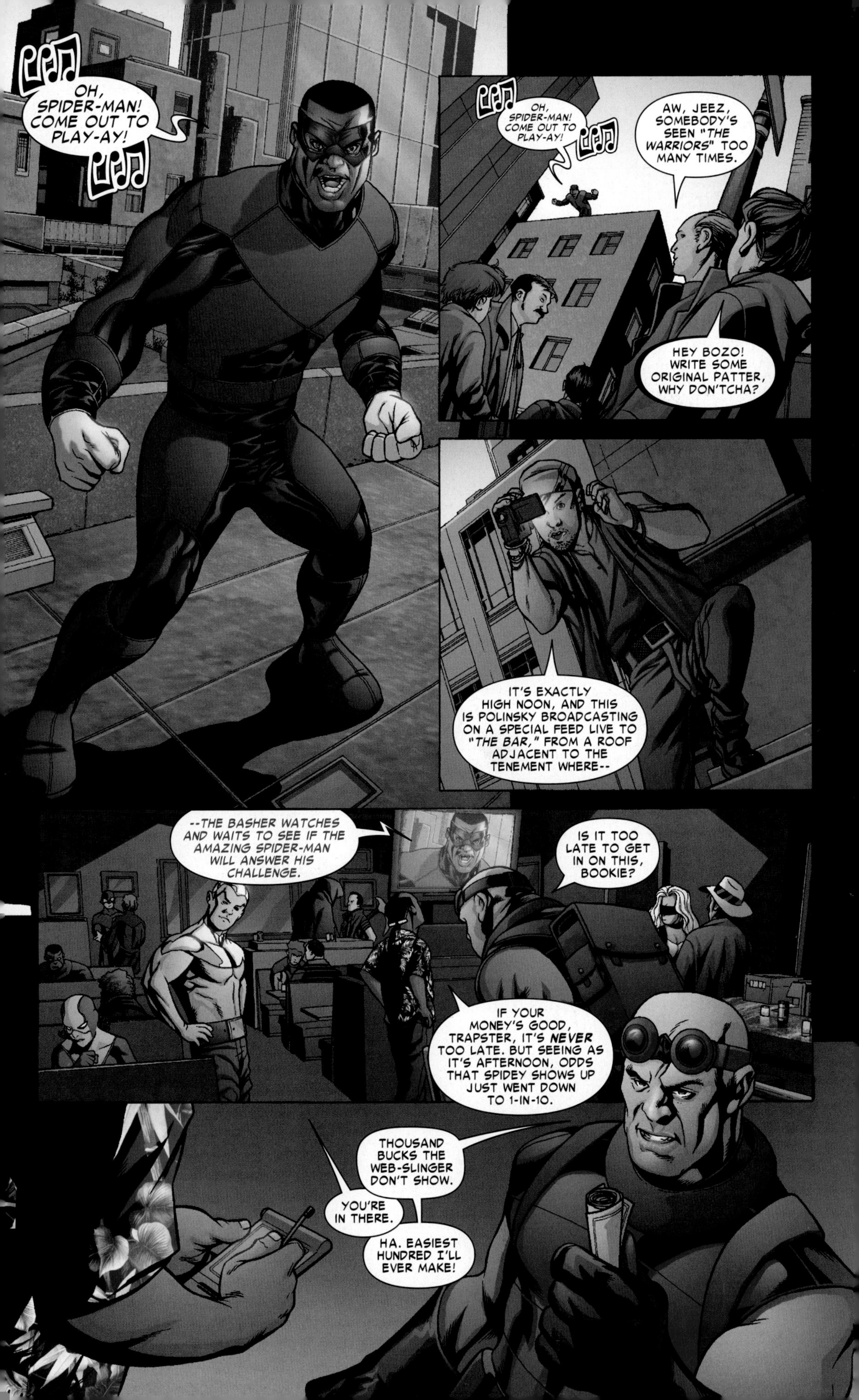
OH, SPIDER-MAN! COME OUT TO PLAY-AY!
OH, SPIDER-MAN! COME OUT TO PLAY-AY!
AW, JEEZ, SOMEBODY'S SEEN "THE WARRIORS" TOO MANY TIMES.
HEY BOZO! WRITE SOME ORIGINAL PATTER, WHY DON'TCHA?
IT'S EXACTLY HIGH NOON, AND THIS IS POLINSKY BROADCASTING ON A SPECIAL FEED LIVE TO "THE BAR," FROM A ROOF ADJACENT TO THE TENEMENT WHERE--
--THE BASHER WATCHES AND WAITS TO SEE IF THE AMAZING SPIDER-MAN WILL ANSWER HIS CHALLENGE.
IS IT TOO LATE TO GET IN ON THIS, BOOKIE?
IF YOUR MONEY'S GOOD, TRAPSTER, IT'S NEVER TOO LATE. BUT SEEING AS IT'S AFTERNOON, ODDS THAT SPIDEY SHOWS UP JUST WENT DOWN TO 1-IN-10.
THOUSAND BUCKS THE WEB-SLINGER DON'T SHOW.
YOU'RE IN THERE.
HA. EASIEST HUNDRED I'LL EVER MAKE!

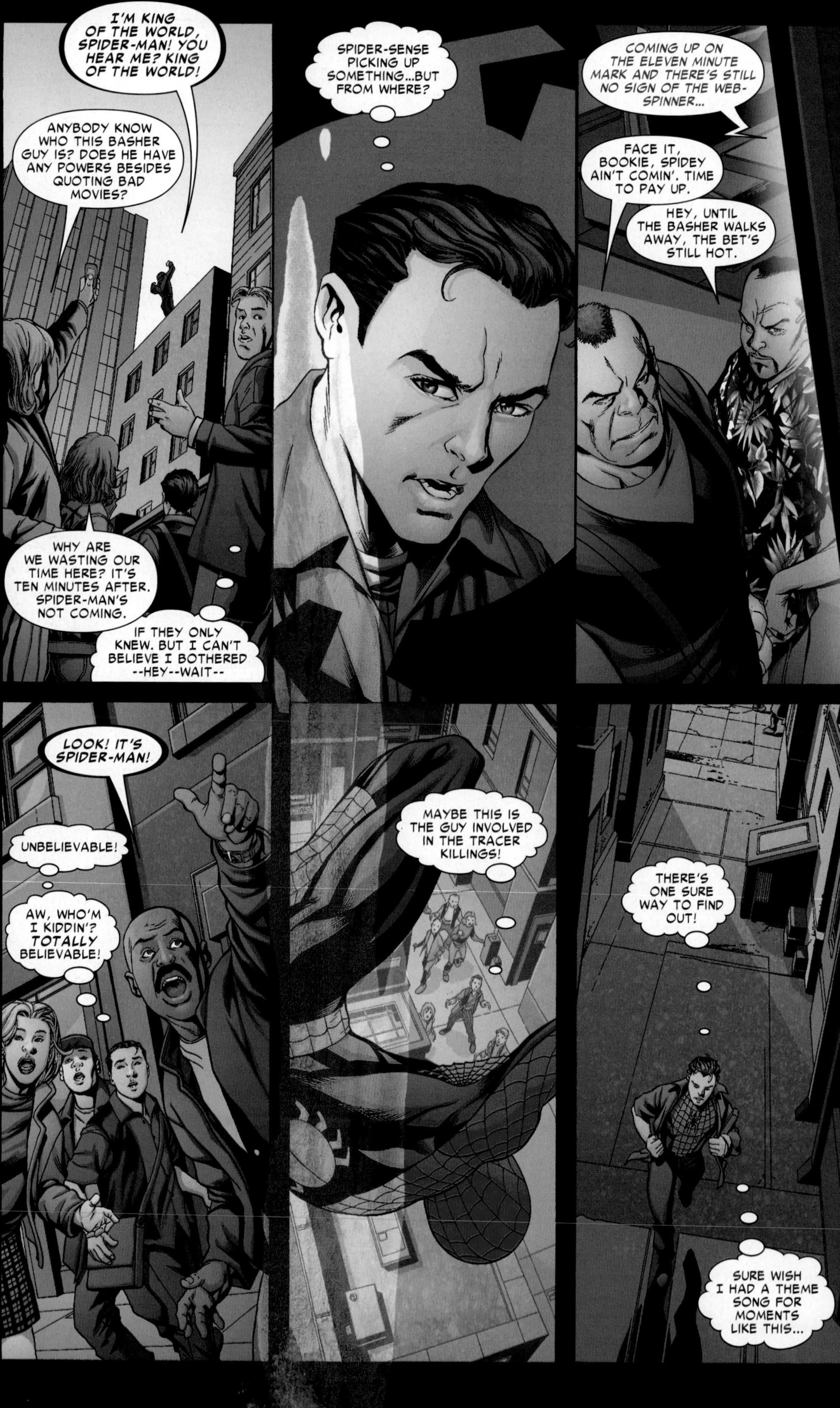

I'M KING OF THE WORLD, SPIDER-MAN! YOU HEAR ME? KING OF THE WORLD!
ANYBODY KNOW WHO THIS BASHER GUY IS? DOES HE HAVE ANY POWERS BESIDES QUOTING BAD MOVIES?
WHY ARE WE WASTING OUR TIME HERE? IT'S TEN MINUTES AFTER. SPIDER-MAN'S NOT COMING.
IF THEY ONLY KNEW. BUT I CAN'T BELIEVE I BOTHERED --HEY--WAIT--
SPIDER-SENSE PICKING UP SOMETHING...BUT FROM WHERE?
COMING UP ON THE ELEVEN MINUTE MARK AND THERE'S STILL NO SIGN OF THE WEB-SPINNER...
FACE IT, BOOKIE, SPIDEY AIN'T COMIN'. TIME TO PAY UP.
HEY, UNTIL THE BASHER WALKS AWAY, THE BET'S STILL HOT.
LOOK! IT'S SPIDER-MAN!
UNBELIEVABLE!
AW, WHO'M I KIDDIN'? TOTALLY BELIEVABLE!
MAYBE THIS IS THE GUY INVOLVED IN THE TRACER KILLINGS!
THERE'S ONE SURE WAY TO FIND OUT!
SURE WISH I HAD A THEME SONG FOR MOMENTS LIKE THIS...

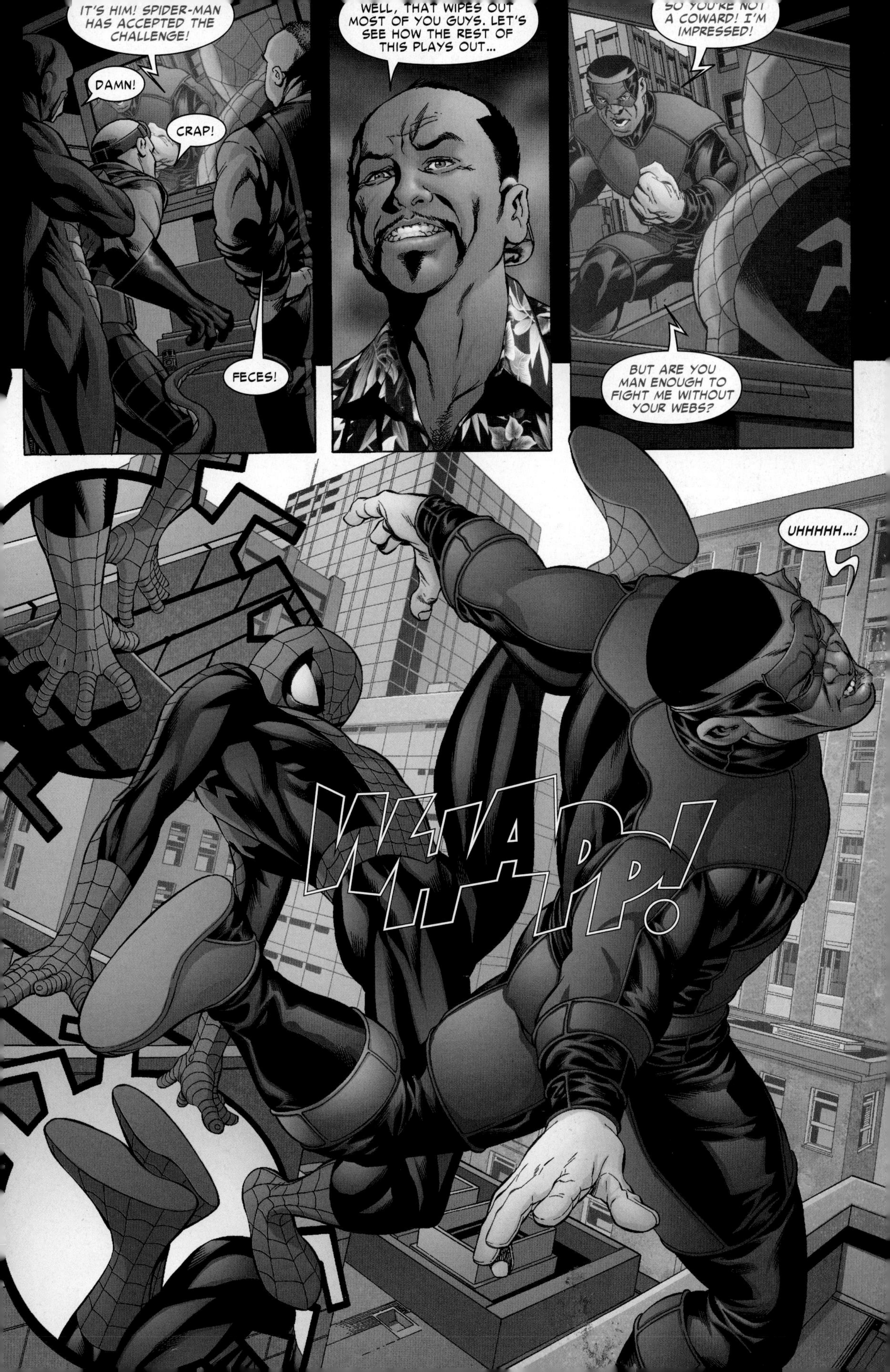
IT'S HIM! SPIDER-MAN HAS ACCEPTED THE CHALLENGE!
DAMN!
CRAP!
FECES!
WELL, THAT WIPES OUT MOST OF YOU GUYS. LET'S SEE HOW THE REST OF THIS PLAYS OUT...
SO YOU'RE NOT A COWARD! I'M IMPRESSED!
BUT ARE YOU MAN ENOUGH TO FIGHT ME WITHOUT YOUR WEBS?
UHHHHH...!
WHAP!

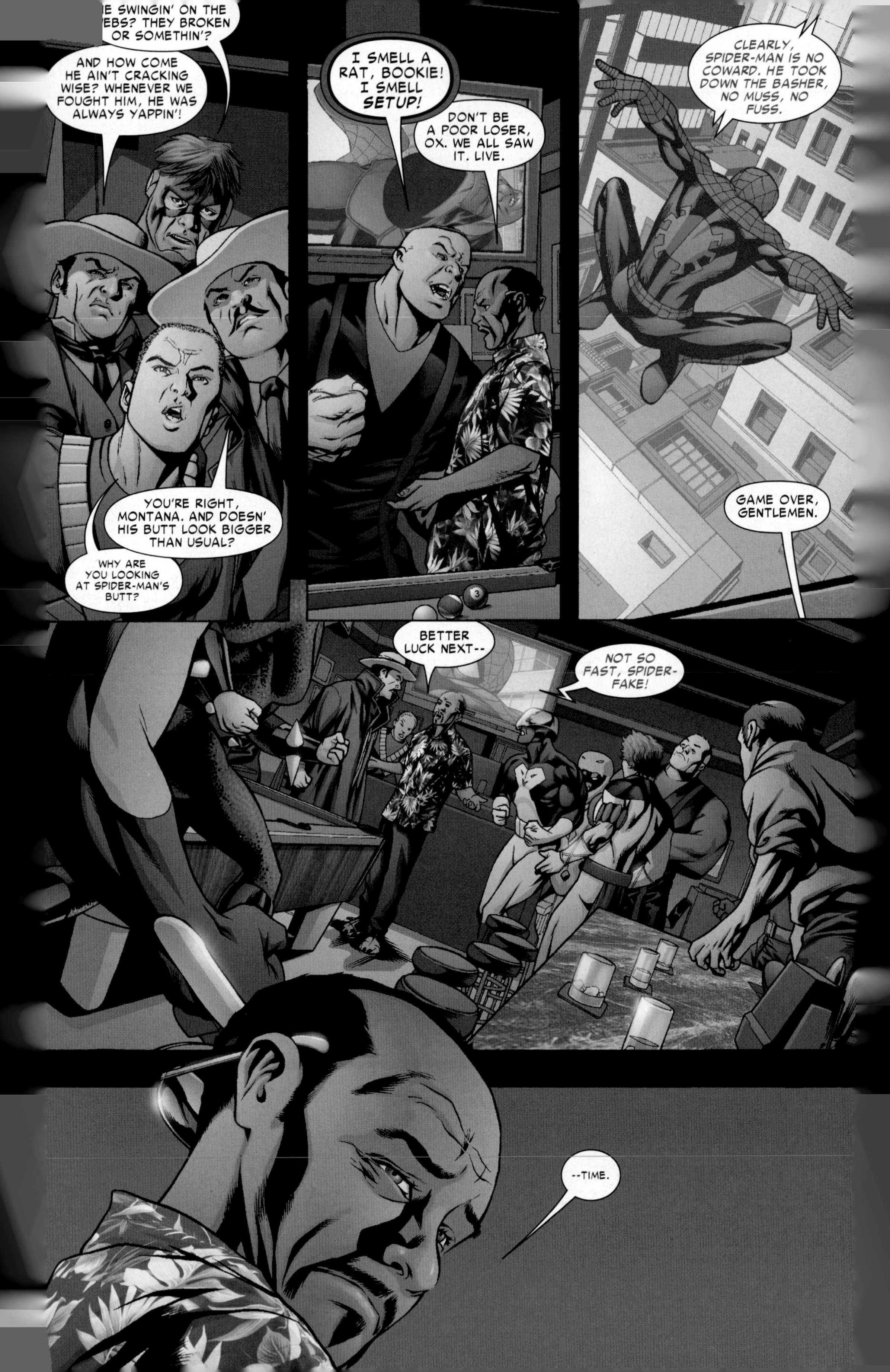

...E SWINGIN' ON THE WEBS? THEY BROKEN OR SOMETHIN'?
AND HOW COME HE AIN'T CRACKING WISE? WHENEVER WE FOUGHT HIM, HE WAS ALWAYS YAPPIN'!
YOU'RE RIGHT, MONTANA. AND DOESN' HIS BUTT LOOK BIGGER THAN USUAL?
WHY ARE YOU LOOKING AT SPIDER-MAN'S BUTT?
I SMELL A RAT, BOOKIE! I SMELL SETUP!
DON'T BE A POOR LOSER, OX. WE ALL SAW IT. LIVE.
CLEARLY, SPIDER-MAN IS NO COWARD. HE TOOK DOWN THE BASHER, NO MUSS, NO FUSS.
GAME OVER, GENTLEMEN.
BETTER LUCK NEXT--
NOT SO FAST, SPIDER-FAKE!
--TIME.

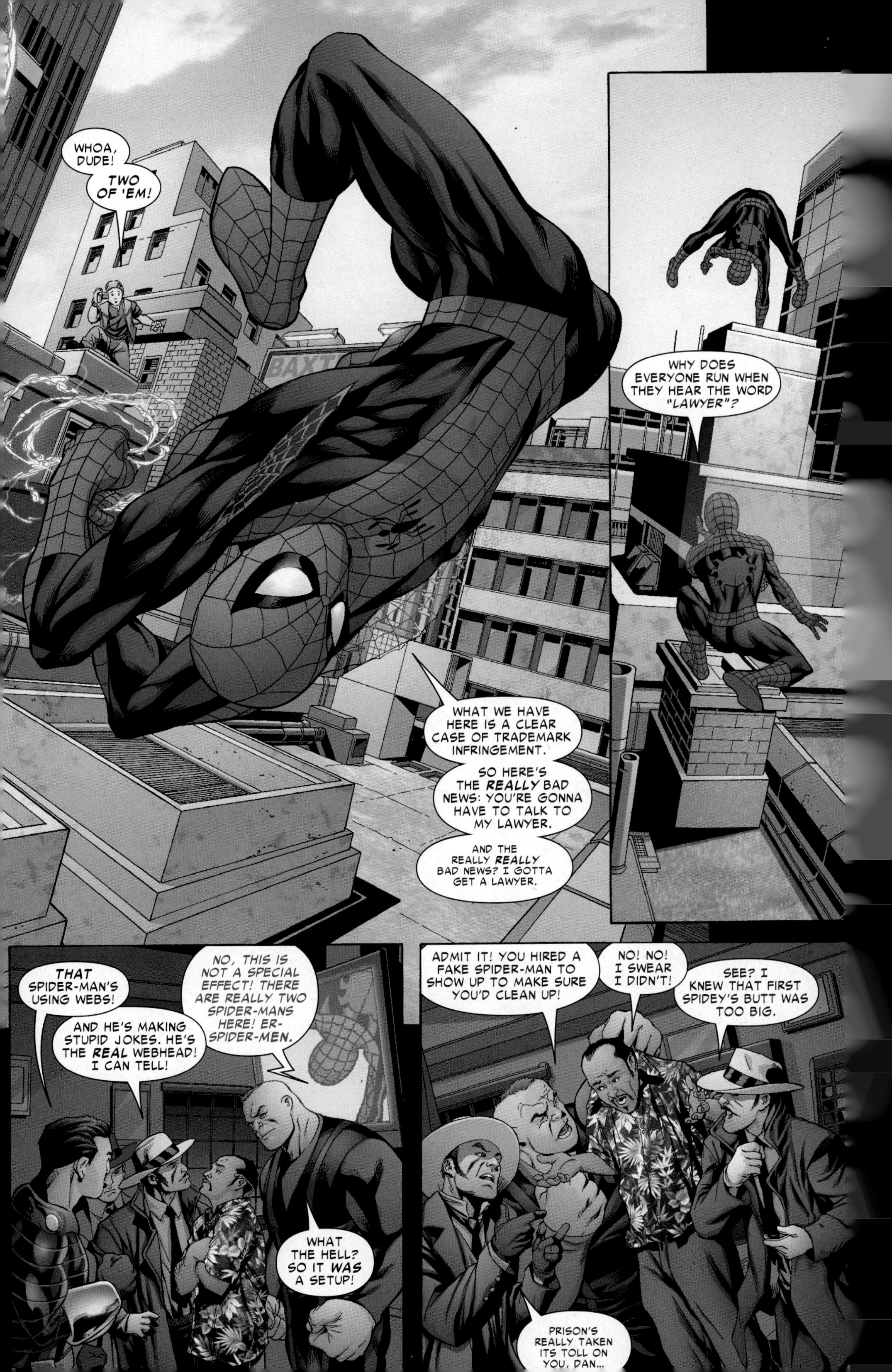
WHOA, DUDE! TWO OF 'EM!
WHY DOES EVERYONE RUN WHEN THEY HEAR THE WORD "LAWYER"?
WHAT WE HAVE HERE IS A CLEAR CASE OF TRADEMARK INFRINGEMENT.
SO HERE'S THE REALLY BAD NEWS: YOU'RE GONNA HAVE TO TALK TO MY LAWYER.
AND THE REALLY REALLY BAD NEWS? I GOTTA GET A LAWYER.
THAT SPIDER-MAN'S USING WEBS!
AND HE'S MAKING STUPID JOKES. HE'S THE REAL WEBHEAD! I CAN TELL!
NO, THIS IS NOT A SPECIAL EFFECT! THERE ARE REALLY TWO SPIDER-MANS HERE! ER-SPIDER-MEN.
WHAT THE HELL? SO IT WAS A SETUP!
ADMIT IT! YOU HIRED A FAKE SPIDER-MAN TO SHOW UP TO MAKE SURE YOU'D CLEAN UP!
NO! NO! I SWEAR I DIDN'T!
SEE? I KNEW THAT FIRST SPIDEY'S BUTT WAS TOO BIG.
PRISON'S REALLY TAKEN ITS TOLL ON YOU, DAN...

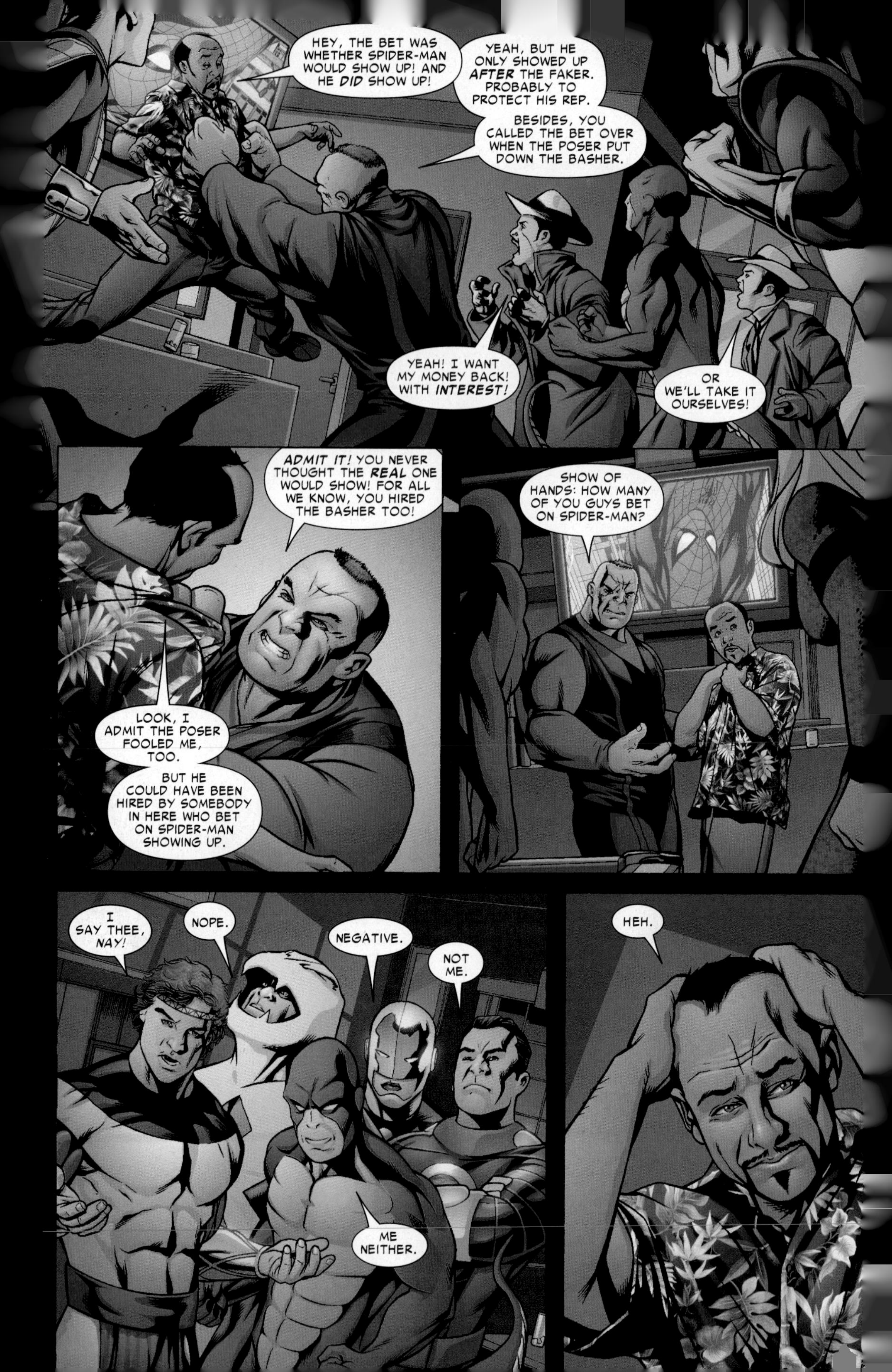
HEY, THE BET WAS WHETHER SPIDER-MAN WOULD SHOW UP! AND HE *DID* SHOW UP!
YEAH, BUT HE ONLY SHOWED UP ***AFTER*** THE FAKER. PROBABLY TO PROTECT HIS REP.
BESIDES, YOU CALLED THE BET OVER WHEN THE POSER PUT DOWN THE BASHER.
YEAH! I WANT MY MONEY BACK! WITH ***INTEREST***!
OR WE'LL TAKE IT OURSELVES!
ADMIT IT! YOU NEVER THOUGHT THE ***REAL*** ONE WOULD SHOW! FOR ALL WE KNOW, YOU HIRED THE BASHER TOO!
LOOK, I ADMIT THE POSER FOOLED ME, TOO.
BUT HE COULD HAVE BEEN HIRED BY SOMEBODY IN HERE WHO BET ON SPIDER-MAN SHOWING UP.
SHOW OF HANDS: HOW MANY OF YOU GUYS BET ON SPIDER-MAN?
I SAY THEE, *NAY!*
NOPE.
NEGATIVE.
NOT ME.
ME NEITHER.
HEH.

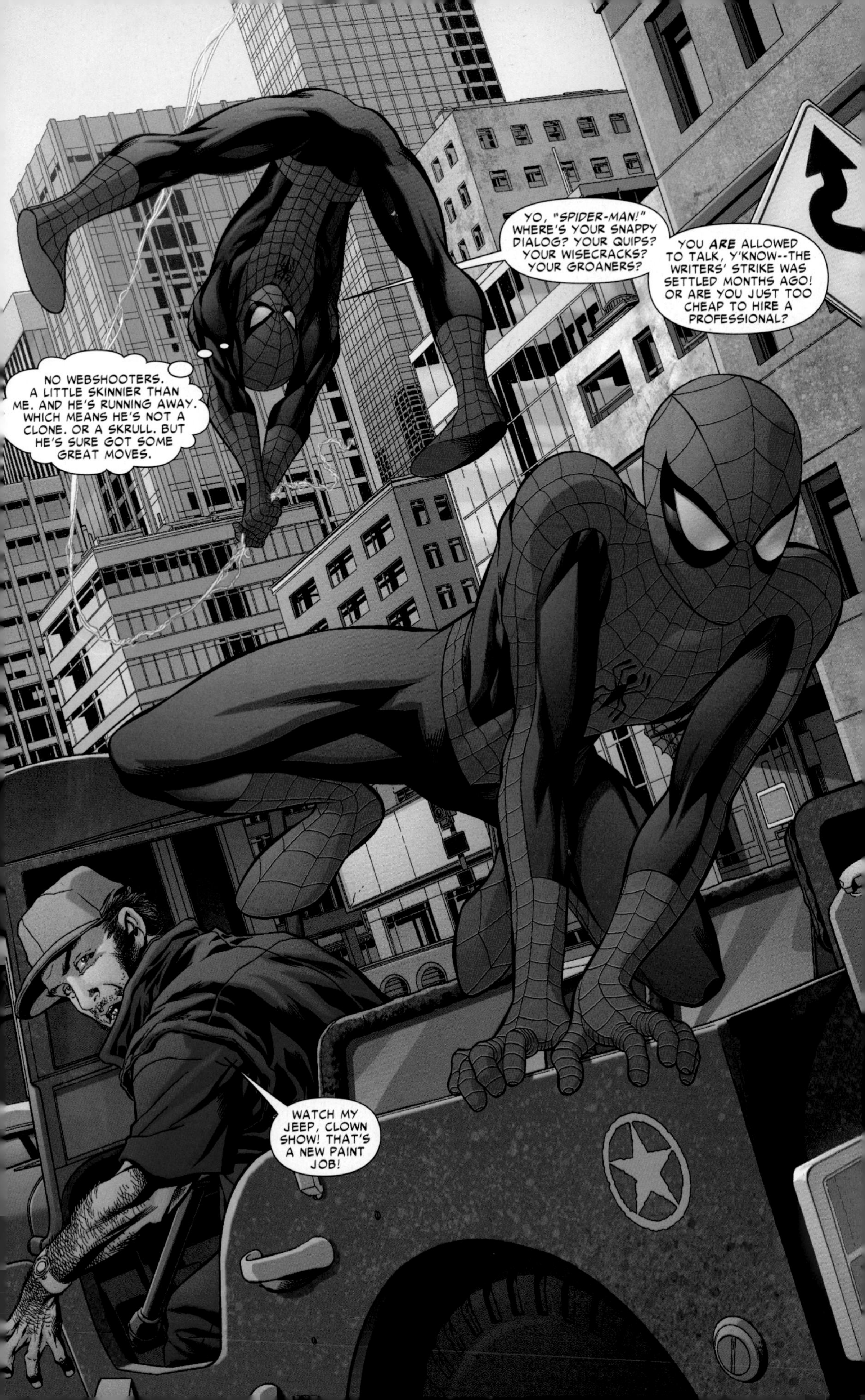
NO WEBSHOOTERS. A LITTLE SKINNIER THAN ME. AND HE'S RUNNING AWAY. WHICH MEANS HE'S NOT A CLONE. OR A SKRULL. BUT HE'S SURE GOT SOME GREAT MOVES.
YO, "SPIDER-MAN!" WHERE'S YOUR SNAPPY DIALOG? YOUR QUIPS? YOUR WISECRACKS? YOUR GROANERS?
YOU ARE ALLOWED TO TALK, Y'KNOW--THE WRITERS' STRIKE WAS SETTLED MONTHS AGO! OR ARE YOU JUST TOO CHEAP TO HIRE A PROFESSIONAL?
WATCH MY JEEP, CLOWN SHOW! THAT'S A NEW PAINT JOB!

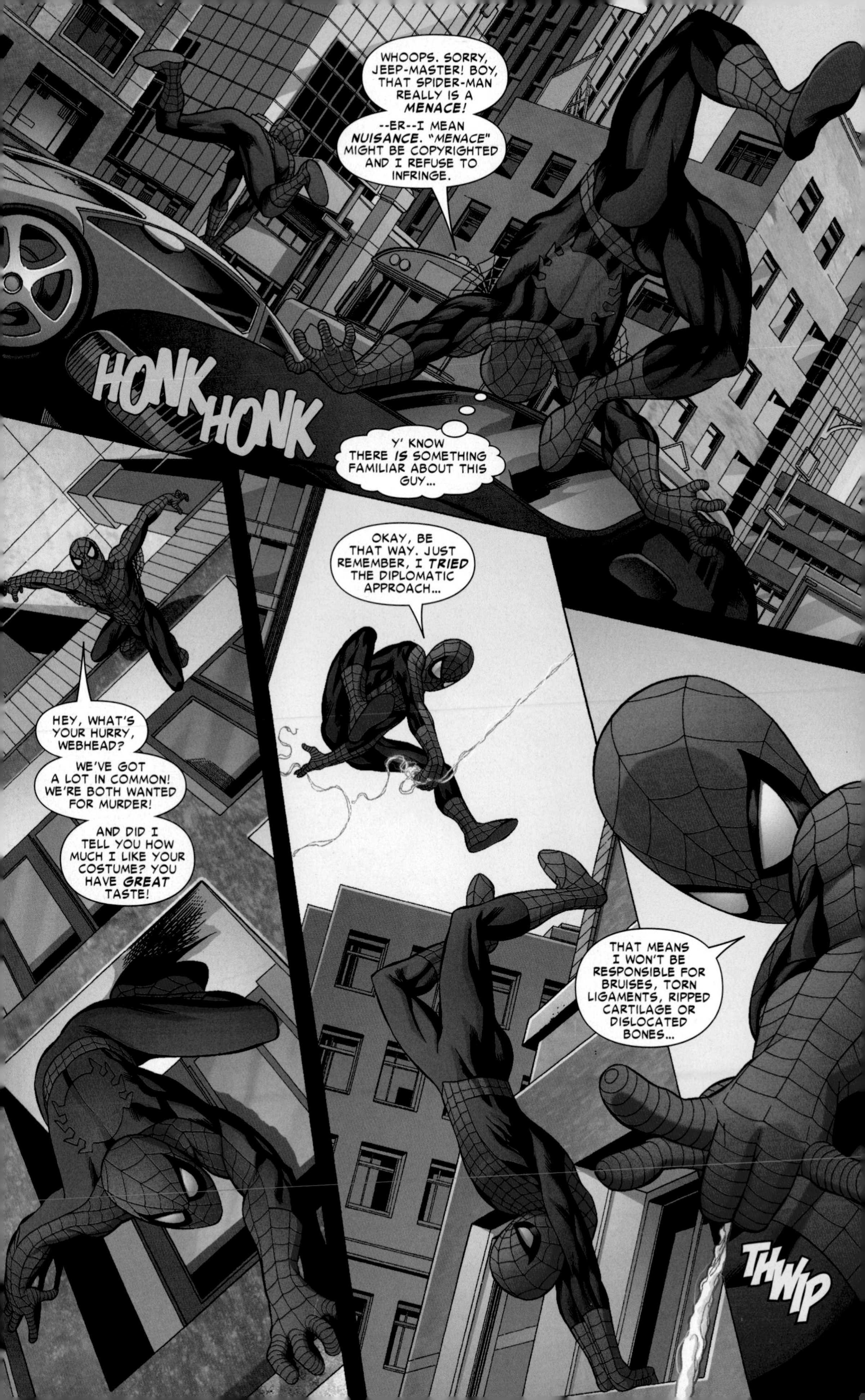
WHOOPS. SORRY, JEEP-MASTER! BOY, THAT SPIDER-MAN REALLY IS A MENACE!
--ER--I MEAN NUISANCE. "MENACE" MIGHT BE COPYRIGHTED AND I REFUSE TO INFRINGE.
HONK HONK
Y' KNOW THERE IS SOMETHING FAMILIAR ABOUT THIS GUY...
HEY, WHAT'S YOUR HURRY, WEBHEAD?
WE'VE GOT A LOT IN COMMON! WE'RE BOTH WANTED FOR MURDER!
AND DID I TELL YOU HOW MUCH I LIKE YOUR COSTUME? YOU HAVE GREAT TASTE!
OKAY, BE THAT WAY. JUST REMEMBER, I TRIED THE DIPLOMATIC APPROACH...
THAT MEANS I WON'T BE RESPONSIBLE FOR BRUISES, TORN LIGAMENTS, RIPPED CARTILAGE OR DISLOCATED BONES...
THWIP

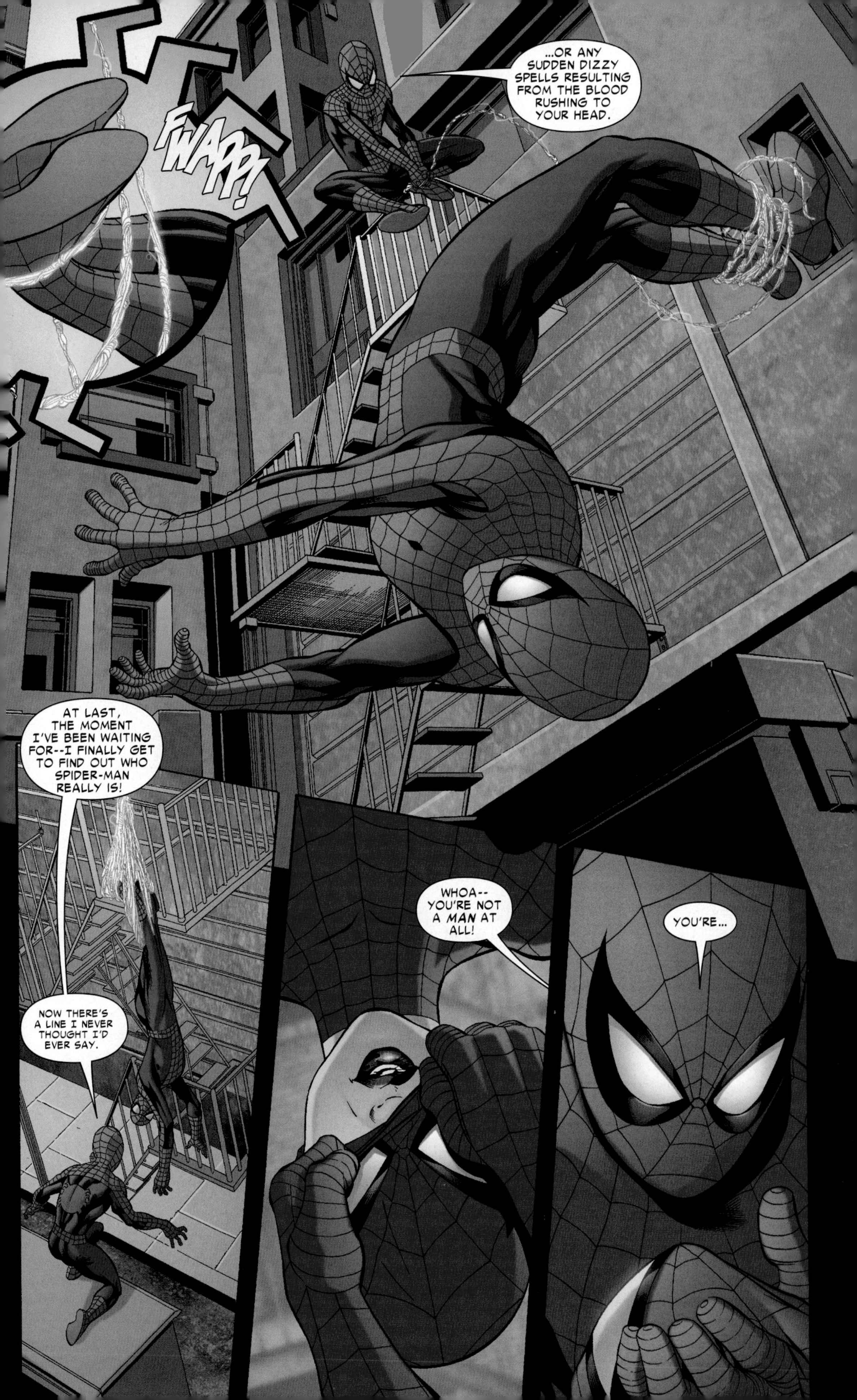
FWAPP!
...OR ANY SUDDEN DIZZY SPELLS RESULTING FROM THE BLOOD RUSHING TO YOUR HEAD.
AT LAST, THE MOMENT I'VE BEEN WAITING FOR--I FINALLY GET TO FIND OUT WHO SPIDER-MAN REALLY IS!
NOW THERE'S A LINE I NEVER THOUGHT I'D EVER SAY.
WHOA-- YOU'RE NOT A MAN AT ALL!
YOU'RE...

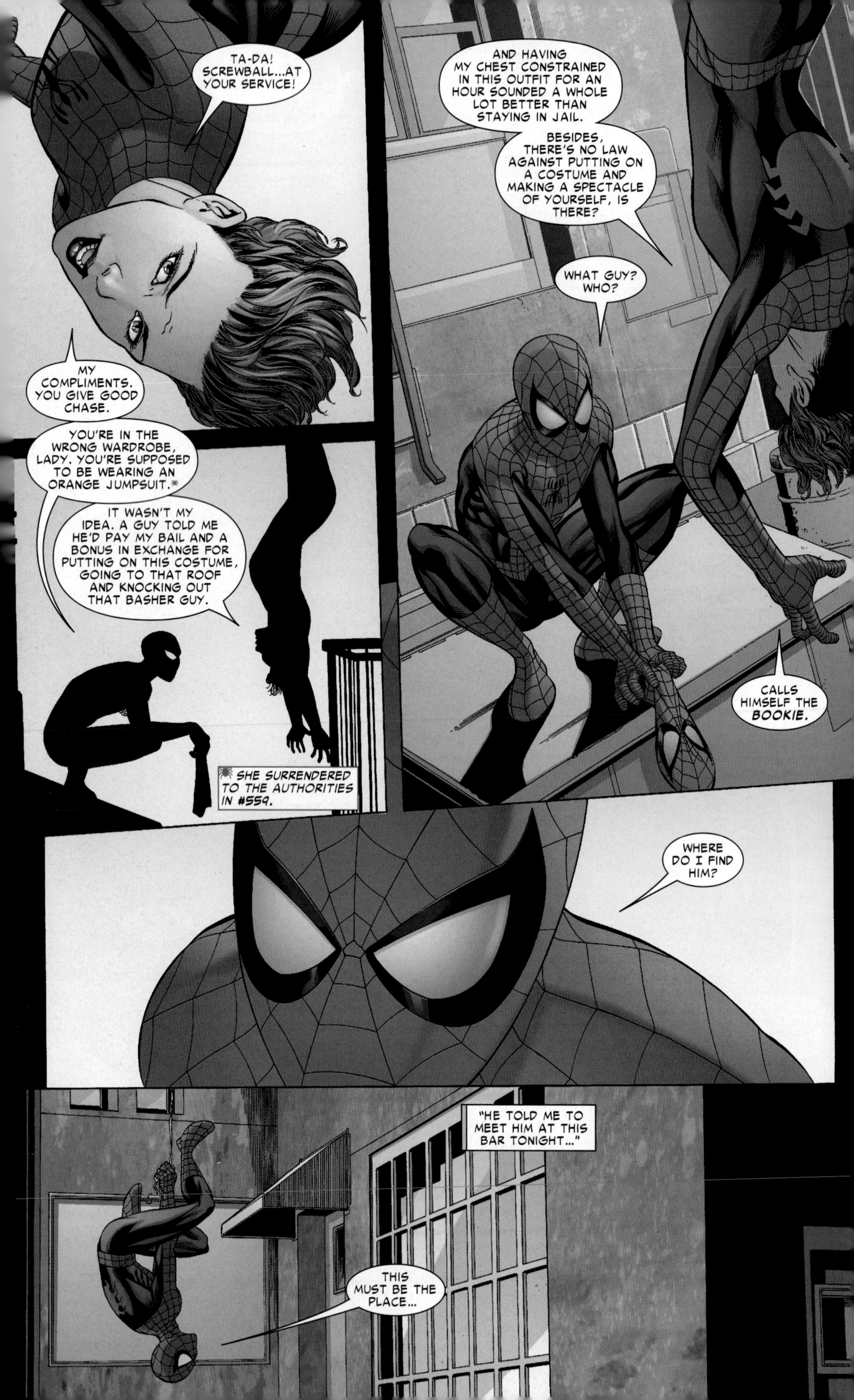
TA-DA! SCREWBALL...AT YOUR SERVICE!
MY COMPLIMENTS. YOU GIVE GOOD CHASE.
YOU'RE IN THE WRONG WARDROBE, LADY. YOU'RE SUPPOSED TO BE WEARING AN ORANGE JUMPSUIT.*
IT WASN'T MY IDEA. A GUY TOLD ME HE'D PAY MY BAIL AND A BONUS IN EXCHANGE FOR PUTTING ON THIS COSTUME, GOING TO THAT ROOF AND KNOCKING OUT THAT BASHER GUY.
*SHE SURRENDERED TO THE AUTHORITIES IN #559.
AND HAVING MY CHEST CONSTRAINED IN THIS OUTFIT FOR AN HOUR SOUNDED A WHOLE LOT BETTER THAN STAYING IN JAIL.
BESIDES, THERE'S NO LAW AGAINST PUTTING ON A COSTUME AND MAKING A SPECTACLE OF YOURSELF, IS THERE?
WHAT GUY? WHO?
CALLS HIMSELF THE BOOKIE.
WHERE DO I FIND HIM?
"HE TOLD ME TO MEET HIM AT THIS BAR TONIGHT..."
THIS MUST BE THE PLACE...

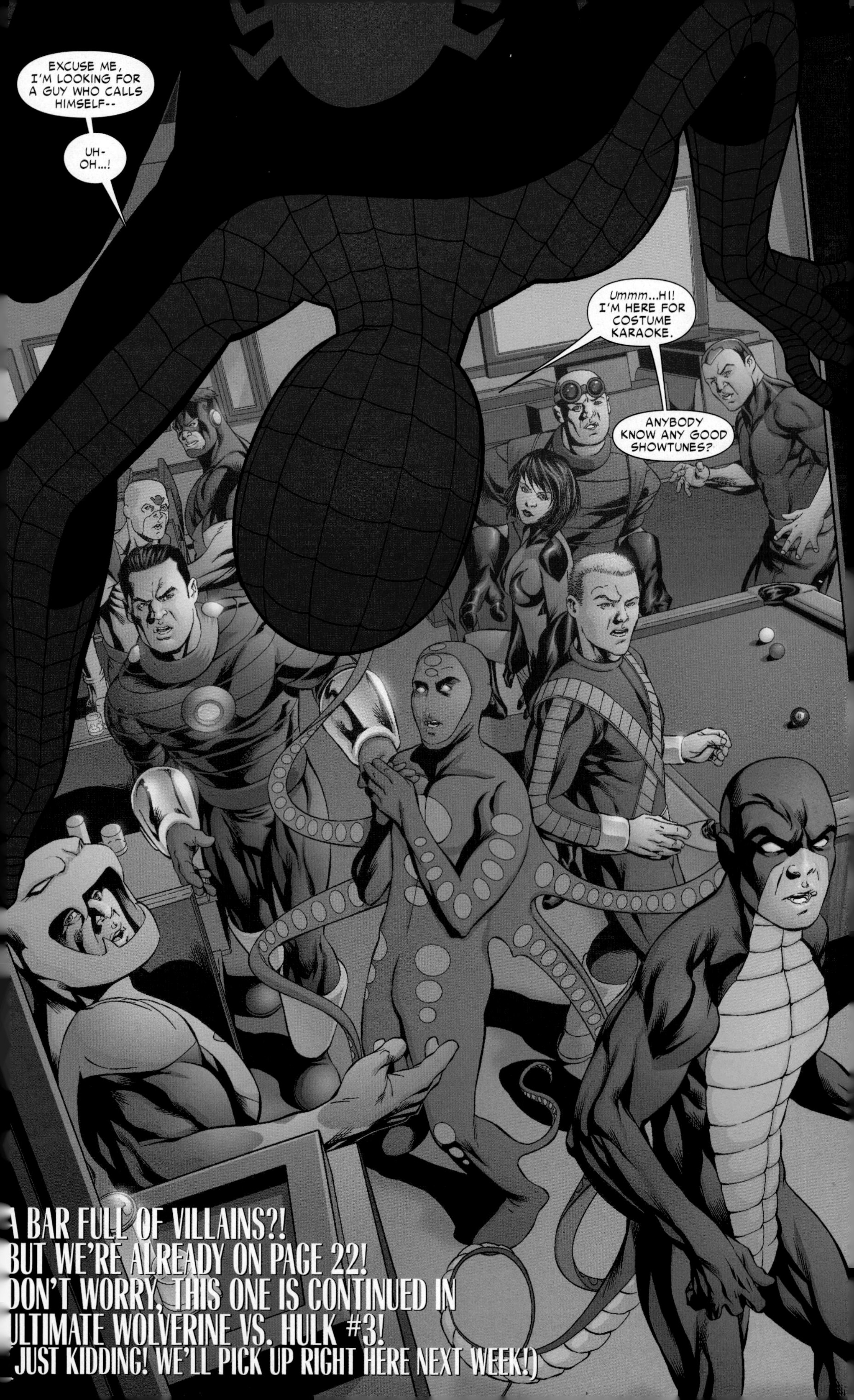
EXCUSE ME, I'M LOOKING FOR A GUY WHO CALLS HIMSELF--
UH-OH...!
Ummm...HI! I'M HERE FOR COSTUME KARAOKE.
ANYBODY KNOW ANY GOOD SHOWTUNES?
A BAR FULL OF VILLAINS?!
BUT WE'RE ALREADY ON PAGE 22!
DON'T WORRY, THIS ONE IS CONTINUED IN
ULTIMATE WOLVERINE VS. HULK #3!
(JUST KIDDING! WE'LL PICK UP RIGHT HERE NEXT WEEK!)

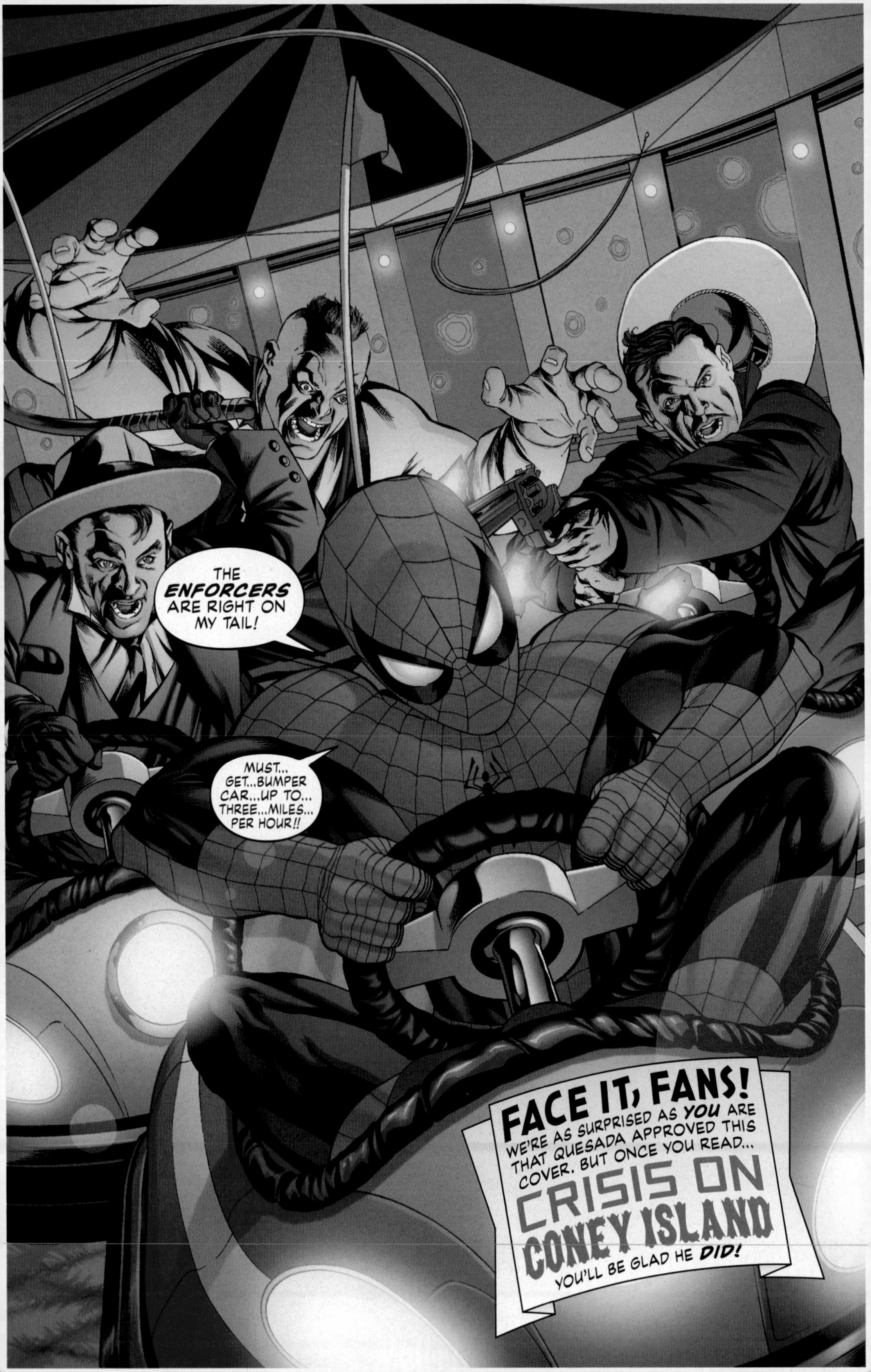
THE ENFORCERS ARE RIGHT ON MY TAIL!
MUST... GET...BUMPER CAR...UP TO... THREE...MILES... PER HOUR!!
FACE IT, FANS!
WE'RE AS SURPRISED AS YOU ARE THAT QUESADA APPROVED THIS COVER. BUT ONCE YOU READ...
CRISIS ON CONEY ISLAND
YOU'LL BE GLAD HE DID!

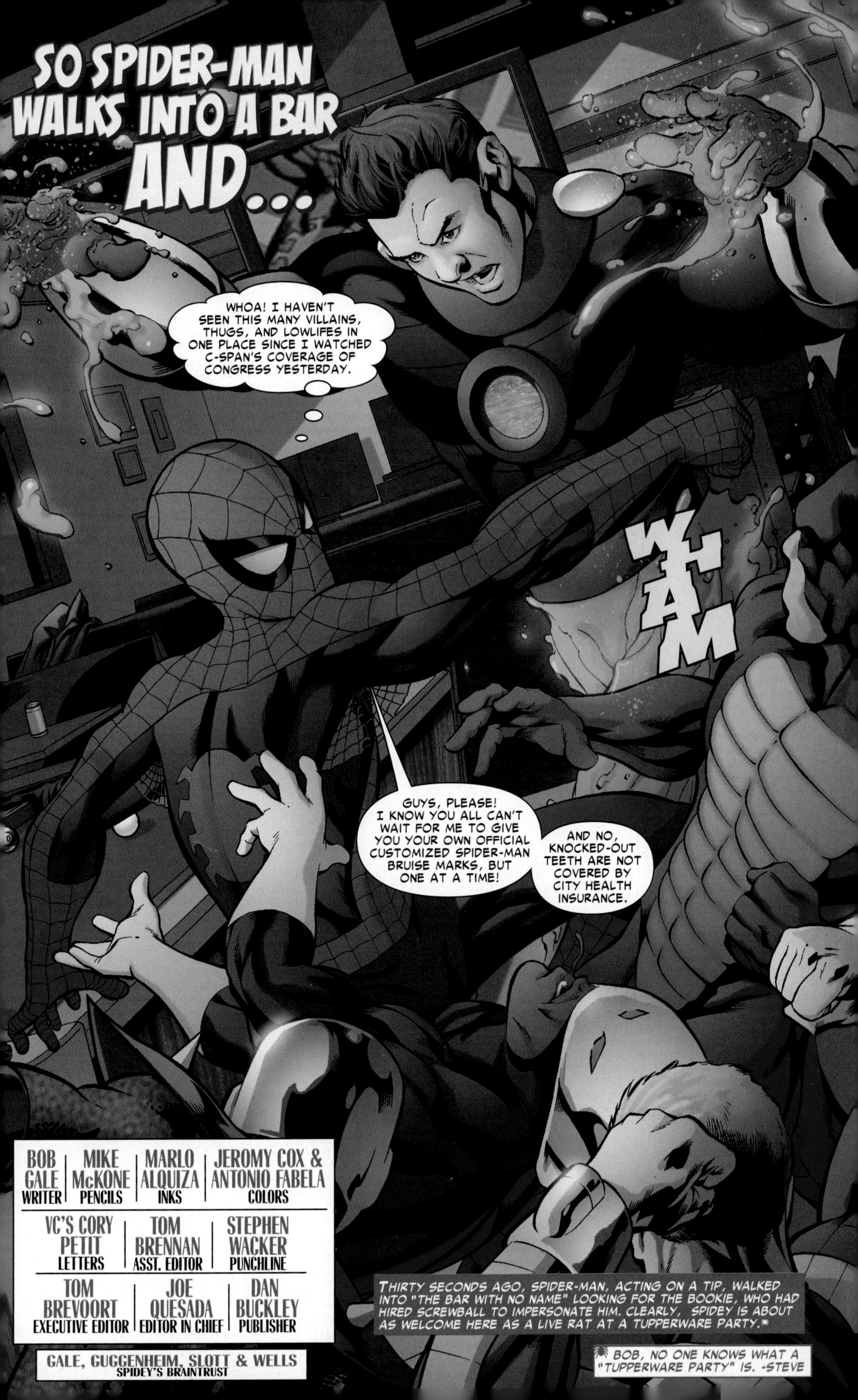
SO SPIDER-MAN WALKS INTO A BAR AND...
WHOA! I HAVEN'T SEEN THIS MANY VILLAINS, THUGS, AND LOWLIFES IN ONE PLACE SINCE I WATCHED C-SPAN'S COVERAGE OF CONGRESS YESTERDAY.
WHAM
GUYS, PLEASE! I KNOW YOU ALL CAN'T WAIT FOR ME TO GIVE YOU YOUR OWN OFFICIAL CUSTOMIZED SPIDER-MAN BRUISE MARKS, BUT ONE AT A TIME!
AND NO, KNOCKED-OUT TEETH ARE NOT COVERED BY CITY HEALTH INSURANCE.
BOB GALE WRITER | MIKE McKONE PENCILS | MARLO ALQUIZA INKS | JEROMY COX & ANTONIO FABELA COLORS
VC'S CORY PETIT LETTERS | TOM BRENNAN ASST. EDITOR | STEPHEN WACKER PUNCHLINE
TOM BREVOORT EXECUTIVE EDITOR | JOE QUESADA EDITOR IN CHIEF | DAN BUCKLEY PUBLISHER
GALE, GUGGENHEIM, SLOTT & WELLS SPIDEY'S BRAINTRUST
THIRTY SECONDS AGO, SPIDER-MAN, ACTING ON A TIP, WALKED INTO "THE BAR WITH NO NAME" LOOKING FOR THE BOOKIE, WHO HAD HIRED SCREWBALL TO IMPERSONATE HIM. CLEARLY, SPIDEY IS ABOUT AS WELCOME HERE AS A LIVE RAT AT A TUPPERWARE PARTY.*
*BOB, NO ONE KNOWS WHAT A "TUPPERWARE PARTY" IS. -STEVE

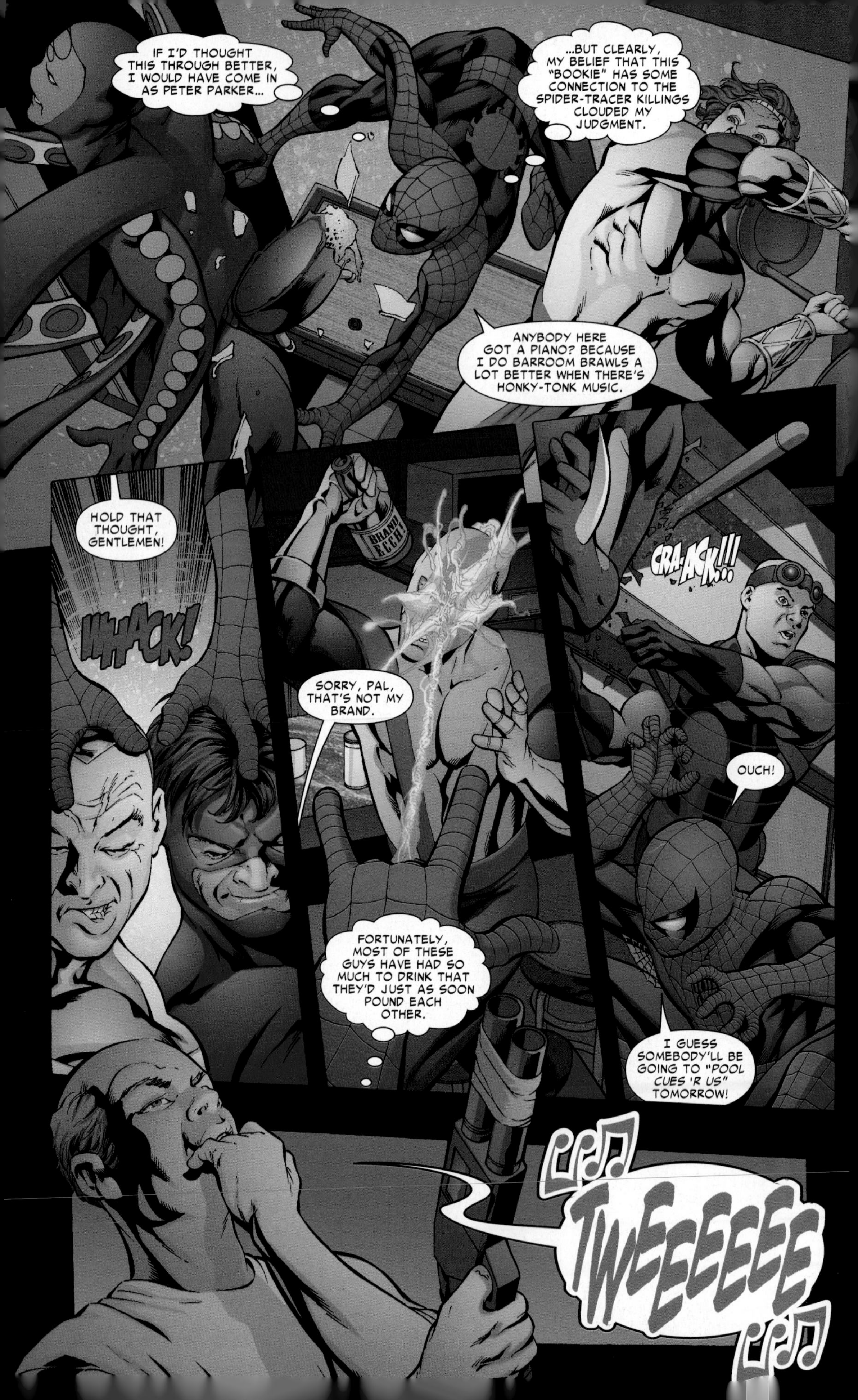
IF I'D THOUGHT THIS THROUGH BETTER, I WOULD HAVE COME IN AS PETER PARKER...
...BUT CLEARLY, MY BELIEF THAT THIS "BOOKIE" HAS SOME CONNECTION TO THE SPIDER-TRACER KILLINGS CLOUDED MY JUDGMENT.
ANYBODY HERE GOT A PIANO? BECAUSE I DO BARROOM BRAWLS A LOT BETTER WHEN THERE'S HONKY-TONK MUSIC.
HOLD THAT THOUGHT, GENTLEMEN!
WHACK!
BRAND ECCH!
SORRY, PAL, THAT'S NOT MY BRAND.
FORTUNATELY, MOST OF THESE GUYS HAVE HAD SO MUCH TO DRINK THAT THEY'D JUST AS SOON POUND EACH OTHER.
CRA-ACK!!!
OUCH!
I GUESS SOMEBODY'LL BE GOING TO "POOL CUES 'R US" TOMORROW!
TWEEEEEE

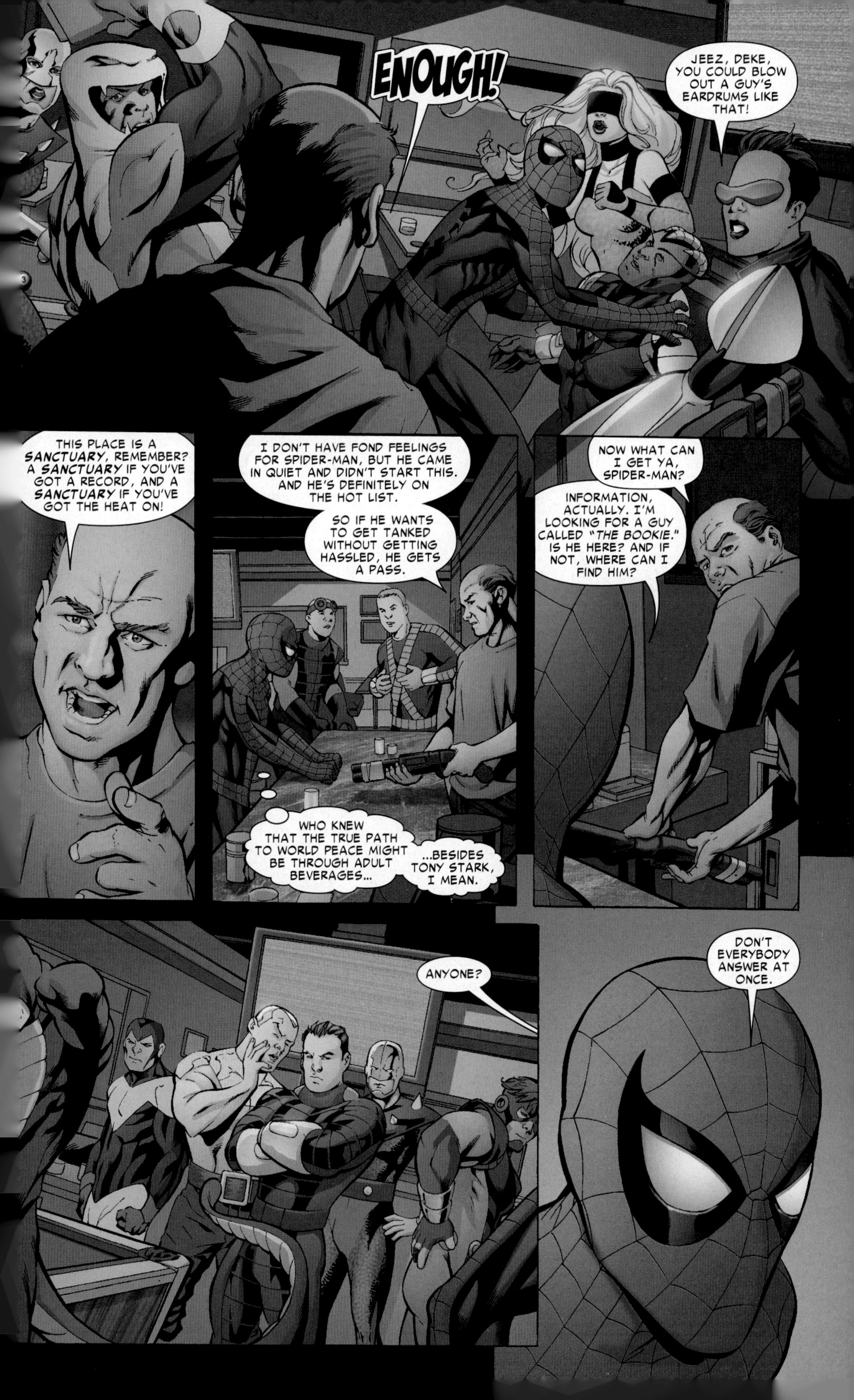
ENOUGH!
JEEZ, DEKE, YOU COULD BLOW OUT A GUY'S EARDRUMS LIKE THAT!
THIS PLACE IS A SANCTUARY, REMEMBER? A SANCTUARY IF YOU'VE GOT A RECORD, AND A SANCTUARY IF YOU'VE GOT THE HEAT ON!
I DON'T HAVE FOND FEELINGS FOR SPIDER-MAN, BUT HE CAME IN QUIET AND DIDN'T START THIS. AND HE'S DEFINITELY ON THE HOT LIST.
SO IF HE WANTS TO GET TANKED WITHOUT GETTING HASSLED, HE GETS A PASS.
WHO KNEW THAT THE TRUE PATH TO WORLD PEACE MIGHT BE THROUGH ADULT BEVERAGES...
...BESIDES TONY STARK, I MEAN.
NOW WHAT CAN I GET YA, SPIDER-MAN?
INFORMATION, ACTUALLY. I'M LOOKING FOR A GUY CALLED "THE BOOKIE." IS HE HERE? AND IF NOT, WHERE CAN I FIND HIM?
ANYONE?
DON'T EVERYBODY ANSWER AT ONCE.

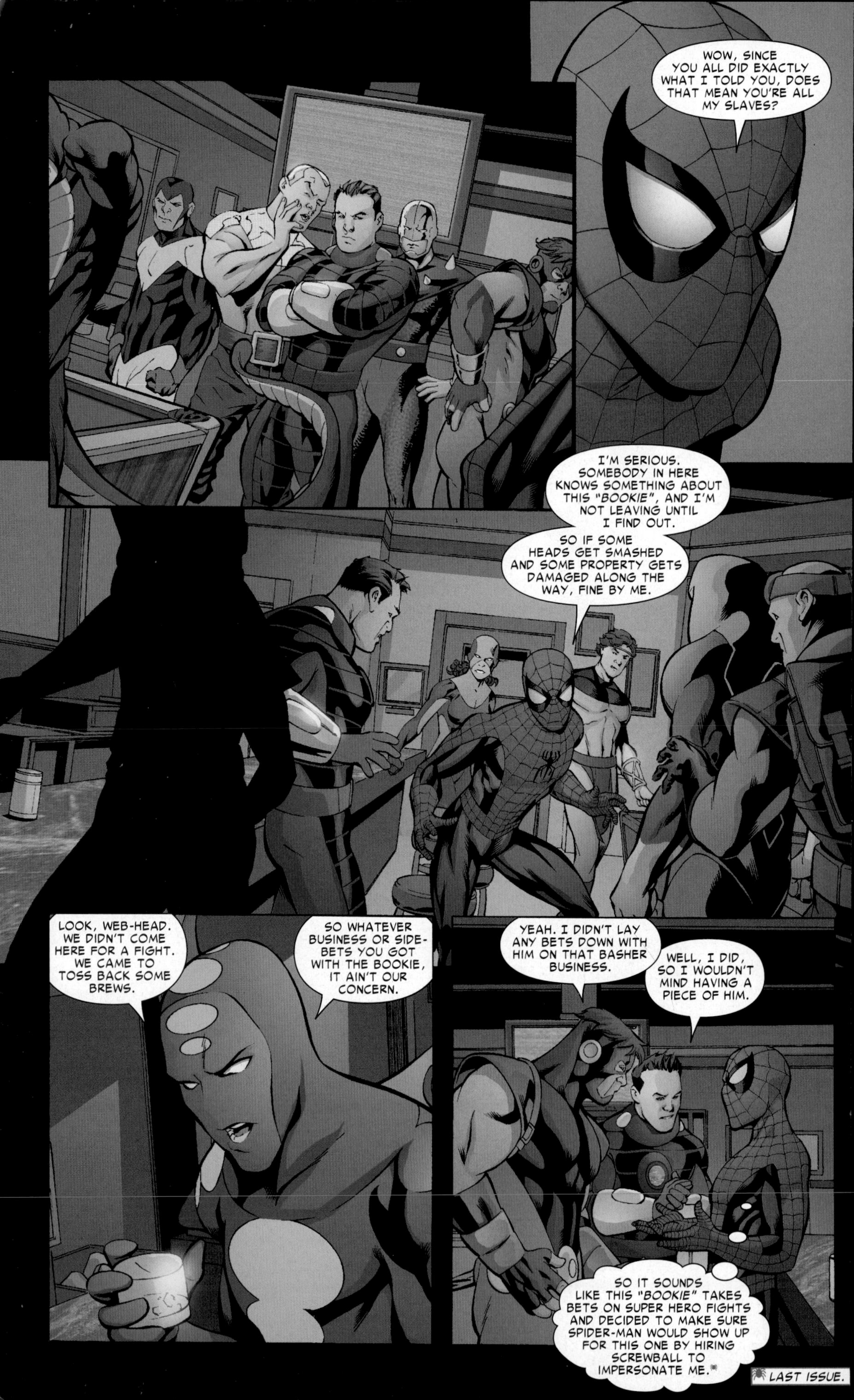
WOW, SINCE YOU ALL DID EXACTLY WHAT I TOLD YOU, DOES THAT MEAN YOU'RE ALL MY SLAVES?
I'M SERIOUS. SOMEBODY IN HERE KNOWS SOMETHING ABOUT THIS "BOOKIE", AND I'M NOT LEAVING UNTIL I FIND OUT.
SO IF SOME HEADS GET SMASHED AND SOME PROPERTY GETS DAMAGED ALONG THE WAY, FINE BY ME.
LOOK, WEB-HEAD. WE DIDN'T COME HERE FOR A FIGHT. WE CAME TO TOSS BACK SOME BREWS.
SO WHATEVER BUSINESS OR SIDE-BETS YOU GOT WITH THE BOOKIE, IT AIN'T OUR CONCERN.
YEAH. I DIDN'T LAY ANY BETS DOWN WITH HIM ON THAT BASHER BUSINESS.
WELL, I DID, SO I WOULDN'T MIND HAVING A PIECE OF HIM.
SO IT SOUNDS LIKE THIS "BOOKIE" TAKES BETS ON SUPER HERO FIGHTS AND DECIDED TO MAKE SURE SPIDER-MAN WOULD SHOW UP FOR THIS ONE BY HIRING SCREWBALL TO IMPERSONATE ME.*
*LAST ISSUE.

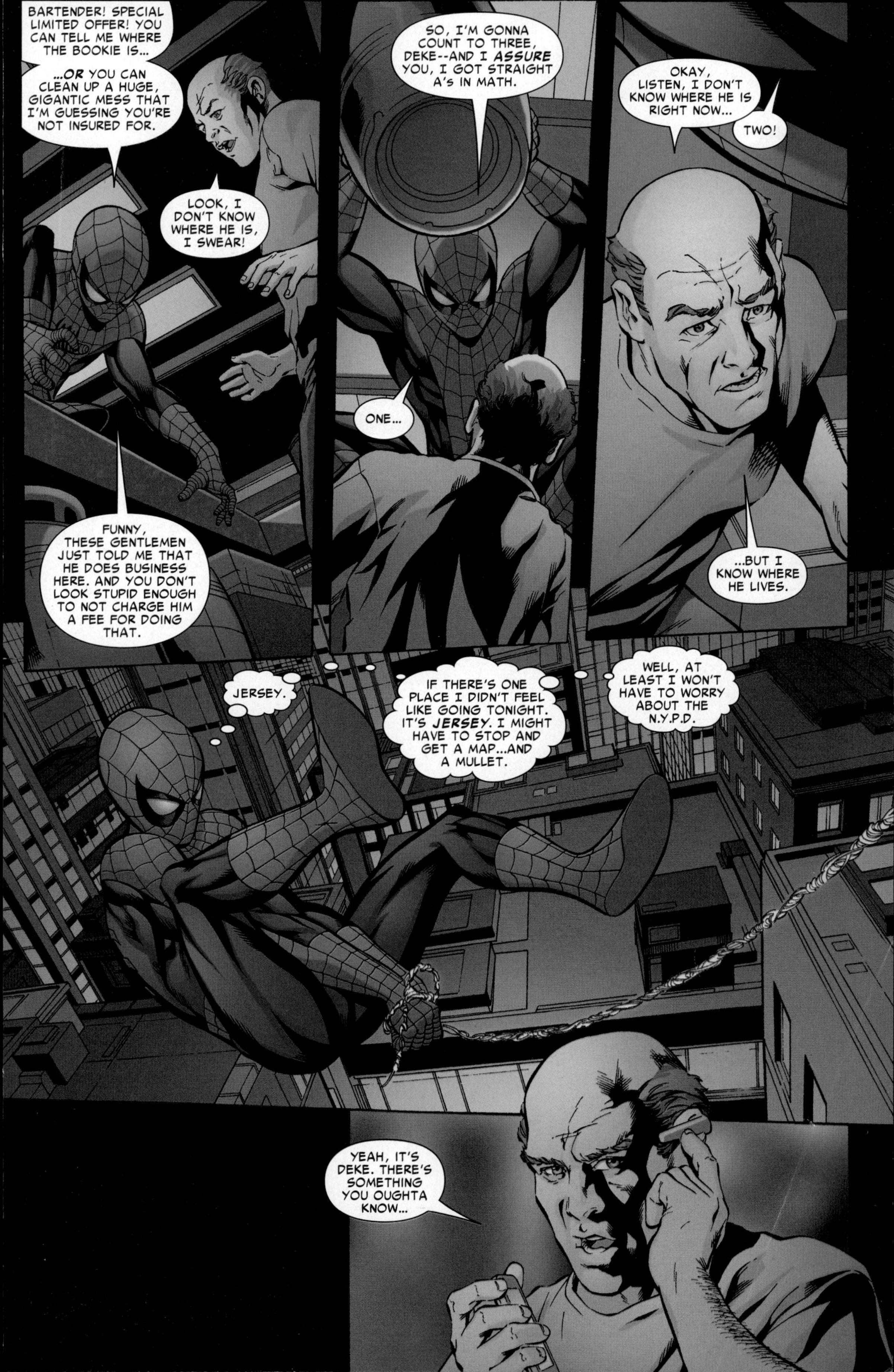
BARTENDER! SPECIAL LIMITED OFFER! YOU CAN TELL ME WHERE THE BOOKIE IS...
...OR YOU CAN CLEAN UP A HUGE, GIGANTIC MESS THAT I'M GUESSING YOU'RE NOT INSURED FOR.
LOOK, I DON'T KNOW WHERE HE IS, I SWEAR!
FUNNY, THESE GENTLEMEN JUST TOLD ME THAT HE DOES BUSINESS HERE. AND YOU DON'T LOOK STUPID ENOUGH TO NOT CHARGE HIM A FEE FOR DOING THAT.
SO, I'M GONNA COUNT TO THREE, DEKE--AND I ASSURE YOU, I GOT STRAIGHT A'S IN MATH.
ONE...
OKAY, LISTEN, I DON'T KNOW WHERE HE IS RIGHT NOW...
TWO!
...BUT I KNOW WHERE HE LIVES.
JERSEY.
IF THERE'S ONE PLACE I DIDN'T FEEL LIKE GOING TONIGHT. IT'S JERSEY. I MIGHT HAVE TO STOP AND GET A MAP...AND A MULLET.
WELL, AT LEAST I WON'T HAVE TO WORRY ABOUT THE N.Y.P.D.
YEAH, IT'S DEKE. THERE'S SOMETHING YOU OUGHTA KNOW...

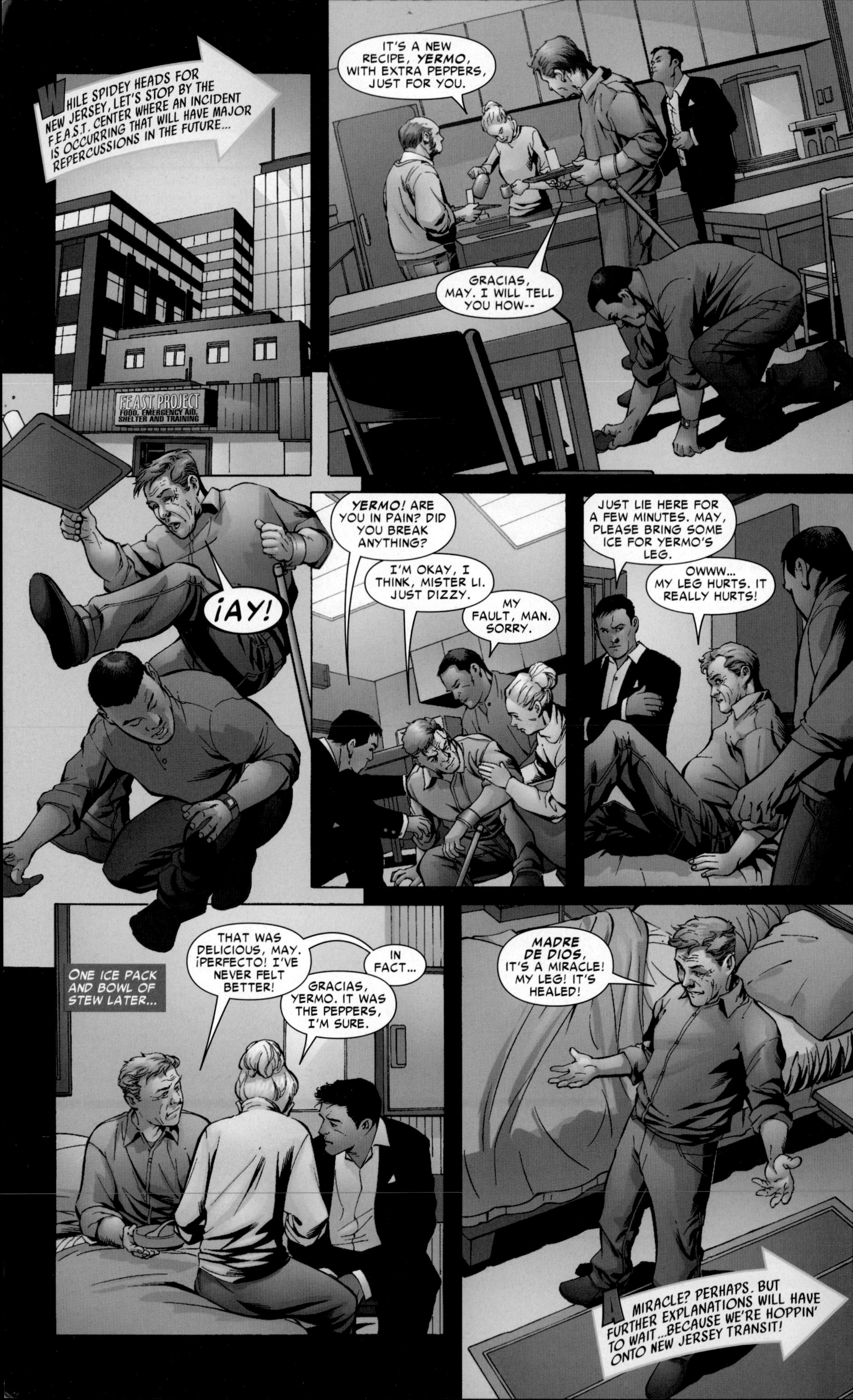

WHILE SPIDEY HEADS FOR NEW JERSEY, LET'S STOP BY THE F.E.A.S.T. CENTER WHERE AN INCIDENT IS OCCURRING THAT WILL HAVE MAJOR REPERCUSSIONS IN THE FUTURE...
F.E.A.S.T. PROJECT FOOD, EMERGENCY AID, SHELTER AND TRAINING
IT'S A NEW RECIPE, YERMO, WITH EXTRA PEPPERS, JUST FOR YOU.
GRACIAS, MAY. I WILL TELL YOU HOW--
¡AY!
YERMO! ARE YOU IN PAIN? DID YOU BREAK ANYTHING?
I'M OKAY, I THINK, MISTER LI. JUST DIZZY.
MY FAULT, MAN. SORRY.
JUST LIE HERE FOR A FEW MINUTES. MAY, PLEASE BRING SOME ICE FOR YERMO'S LEG.
OWWW... MY LEG HURTS. IT REALLY HURTS!
ONE ICE PACK AND BOWL OF STEW LATER...
THAT WAS DELICIOUS, MAY. ¡PERFECTO! I'VE NEVER FELT BETTER!
IN FACT...
GRACIAS, YERMO. IT WAS THE PEPPERS, I'M SURE.
MADRE DE DIOS, IT'S A MIRACLE! MY LEG! IT'S HEALED!
A MIRACLE? PERHAPS. BUT FURTHER EXPLANATIONS WILL HAVE TO WAIT...BECAUSE WE'RE HOPPIN' ONTO NEW JERSEY TRANSIT!

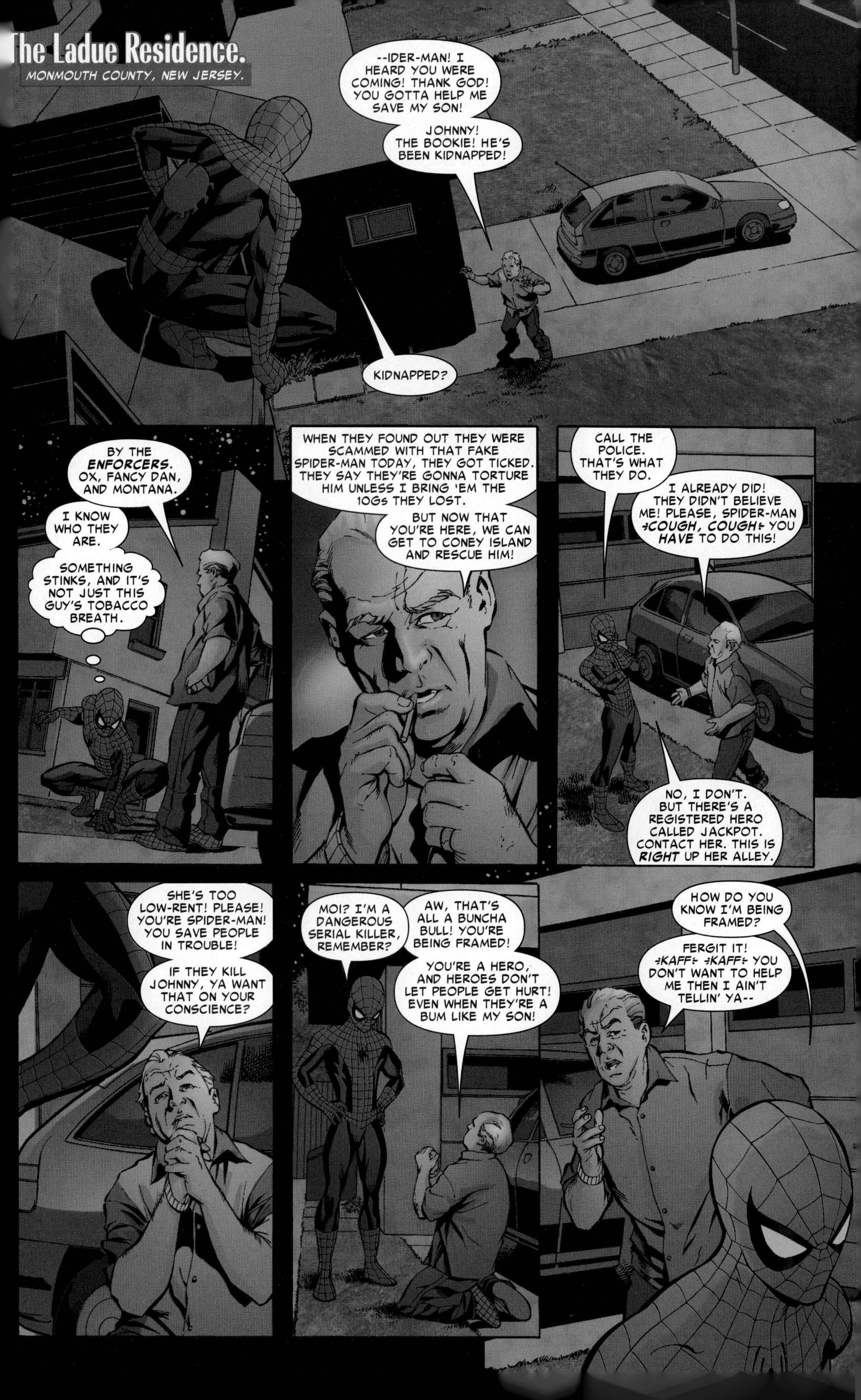
The Ladue Residence.
MONMOUTH COUNTY, NEW JERSEY.
--IDER-MAN! I HEARD YOU WERE COMING! THANK GOD! YOU GOTTA HELP ME SAVE MY SON!
JOHNNY! THE BOOKIE! HE'S BEEN KIDNAPPED!
KIDNAPPED?
BY THE ENFORCERS. OX, FANCY DAN, AND MONTANA.
I KNOW WHO THEY ARE.
SOMETHING STINKS, AND IT'S NOT JUST THIS GUY'S TOBACCO BREATH.
WHEN THEY FOUND OUT THEY WERE SCAMMED WITH THAT FAKE SPIDER-MAN TODAY, THEY GOT TICKED. THEY SAY THEY'RE GONNA TORTURE HIM UNLESS I BRING 'EM THE 10Gs THEY LOST.
BUT NOW THAT YOU'RE HERE, WE CAN GET TO CONEY ISLAND AND RESCUE HIM!
CALL THE POLICE. THAT'S WHAT THEY DO.
I ALREADY DID! THEY DIDN'T BELIEVE ME! PLEASE, SPIDER-MAN *COUGH, COUGH* YOU HAVE TO DO THIS!
NO, I DON'T. BUT THERE'S A REGISTERED HERO CALLED JACKPOT. CONTACT HER. THIS IS RIGHT UP HER ALLEY.
SHE'S TOO LOW-RENT! PLEASE! YOU'RE SPIDER-MAN! YOU SAVE PEOPLE IN TROUBLE!
IF THEY KILL JOHNNY, YA WANT THAT ON YOUR CONSCIENCE?
MOI? I'M A DANGEROUS SERIAL KILLER, REMEMBER?
AW, THAT'S ALL A BUNCHA BULL! YOU'RE BEING FRAMED!
YOU'RE A HERO, AND HEROES DON'T LET PEOPLE GET HURT! EVEN WHEN THEY'RE A BUM LIKE MY SON!
HOW DO YOU KNOW I'M BEING FRAMED?
FERGIT IT! *KAFF* *KAFF* YOU DON'T WANT TO HELP ME THEN I AIN'T TELLIN' YA--

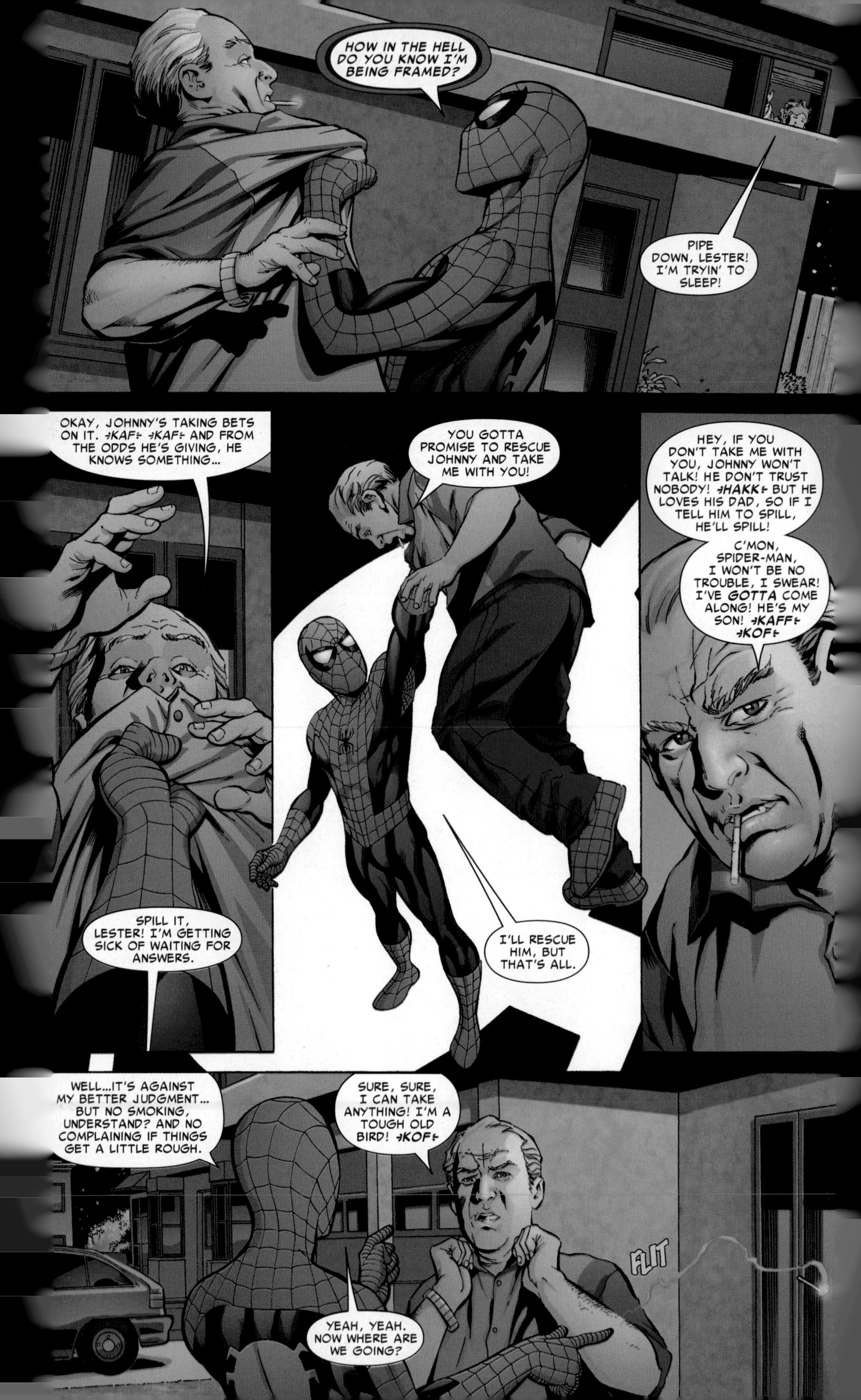
HOW IN THE HELL DO YOU KNOW I'M BEING FRAMED?
PIPE DOWN, LESTER! I'M TRYIN' TO SLEEP!
OKAY, JOHNNY'S TAKING BETS ON IT. *KAF* *KAF* AND FROM THE ODDS HE'S GIVING, HE KNOWS SOMETHING...
SPILL IT, LESTER! I'M GETTING SICK OF WAITING FOR ANSWERS.
YOU GOTTA PROMISE TO RESCUE JOHNNY AND TAKE ME WITH YOU!
I'LL RESCUE HIM, BUT THAT'S ALL.
HEY, IF YOU DON'T TAKE ME WITH YOU, JOHNNY WON'T TALK! HE DON'T TRUST NOBODY! *HAKK* BUT HE LOVES HIS DAD, SO IF I TELL HIM TO SPILL, HE'LL SPILL!
C'MON, SPIDER-MAN, I WON'T BE NO TROUBLE, I SWEAR! I'VE GOTTA COME ALONG! HE'S MY SON! *KAFF* *KOF*
WELL...IT'S AGAINST MY BETTER JUDGMENT... BUT NO SMOKING, UNDERSTAND? AND NO COMPLAINING IF THINGS GET A LITTLE ROUGH.
SURE, SURE, I CAN TAKE ANYTHING! I'M A TOUGH OLD BIRD! *KOF*
FLIT
YEAH, YEAH. NOW WHERE ARE WE GOING?

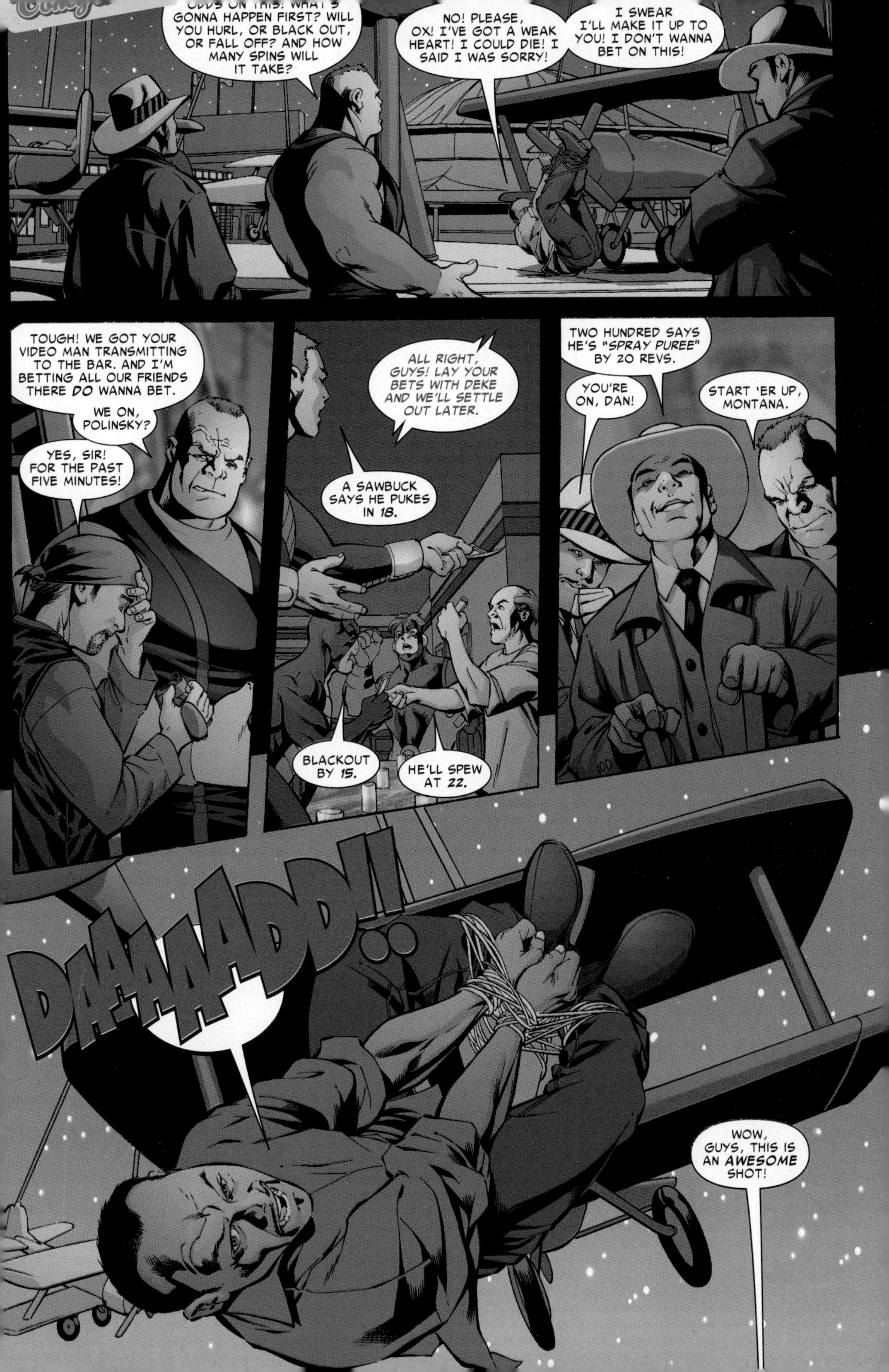
GONNA HAPPEN FIRST? WILL YOU HURL, OR BLACK OUT, OR FALL OFF? AND HOW MANY SPINS WILL IT TAKE?
NO! PLEASE, OX! I'VE GOT A WEAK HEART! I COULD DIE! I SAID I WAS SORRY!
I SWEAR I'LL MAKE IT UP TO YOU! I DON'T WANNA BET ON THIS!
TOUGH! WE GOT YOUR VIDEO MAN TRANSMITTING TO THE BAR. AND I'M BETTING ALL OUR FRIENDS THERE DO WANNA BET.
WE ON, POLINSKY?
YES, SIR! FOR THE PAST FIVE MINUTES!
ALL RIGHT, GUYS! LAY YOUR BETS WITH DEKE AND WE'LL SETTLE OUT LATER.
A SAWBUCK SAYS HE PUKES IN 18.
BLACKOUT BY 15.
HE'LL SPEW AT 22.
TWO HUNDRED SAYS HE'S "SPRAY PUREE" BY 20 REVS.
YOU'RE ON, DAN!
START 'ER UP, MONTANA.
DAAAAADD!!
WOW, GUYS, THIS IS AN AWESOME SHOT!

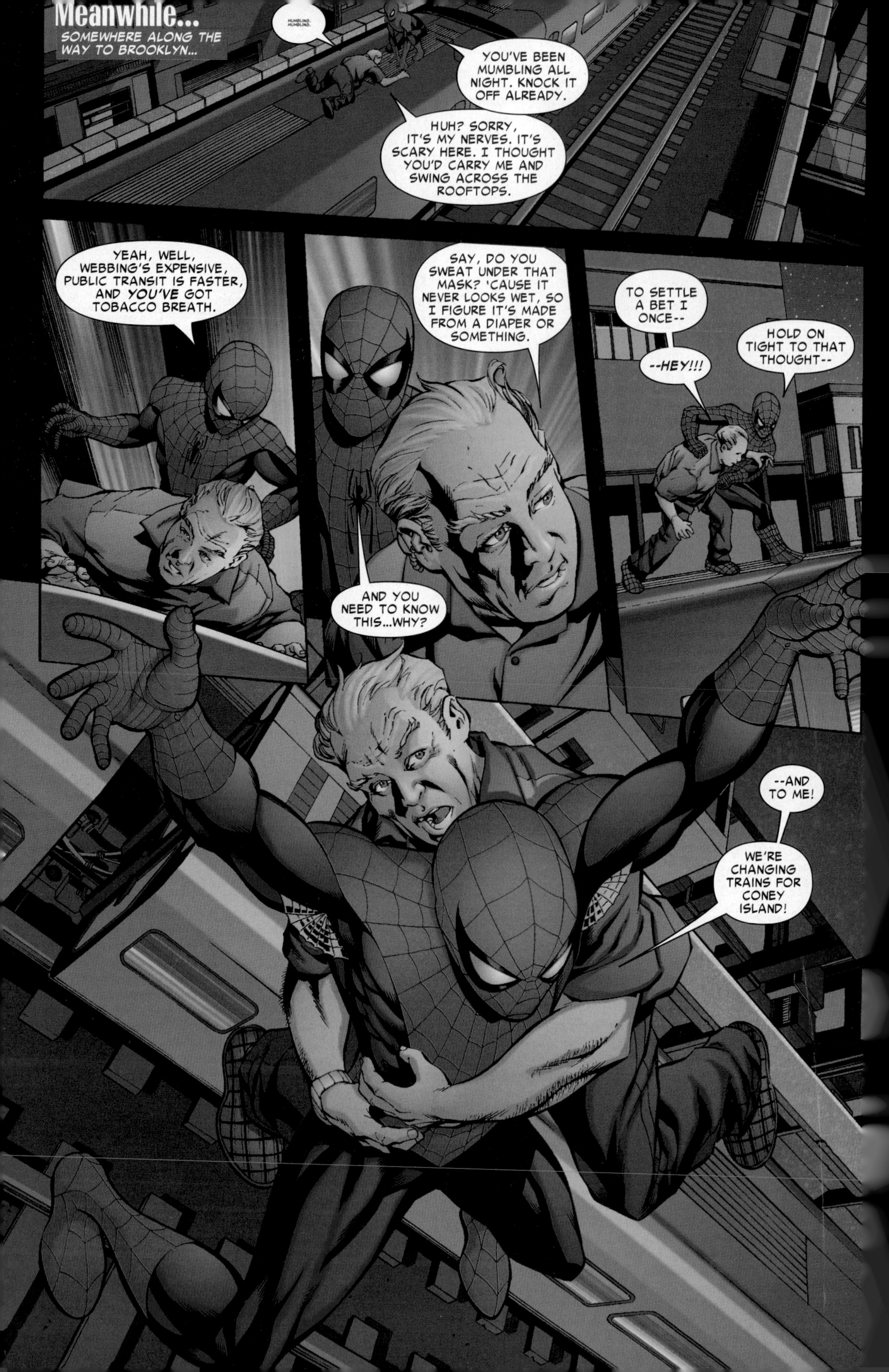
Meanwhile...
SOMEWHERE ALONG THE WAY TO BROOKLYN...
MUMBLING. MUMBLING.
YOU'VE BEEN MUMBLING ALL NIGHT. KNOCK IT OFF ALREADY.
HUH? SORRY, IT'S MY NERVES. IT'S SCARY HERE. I THOUGHT YOU'D CARRY ME AND SWING ACROSS THE ROOFTOPS.
YEAH, WELL, WEBBING'S EXPENSIVE, PUBLIC TRANSIT IS FASTER, AND *YOU'VE* GOT TOBACCO BREATH.
SAY, DO YOU SWEAT UNDER THAT MASK? 'CAUSE IT NEVER LOOKS WET, SO I FIGURE IT'S MADE FROM A DIAPER OR SOMETHING.
AND YOU NEED TO KNOW THIS...WHY?
TO SETTLE A BET I ONCE--
HOLD ON TIGHT TO THAT THOUGHT--
--HEY!!!
--AND TO ME!
WE'RE CHANGING TRAINS FOR CONEY ISLAND!

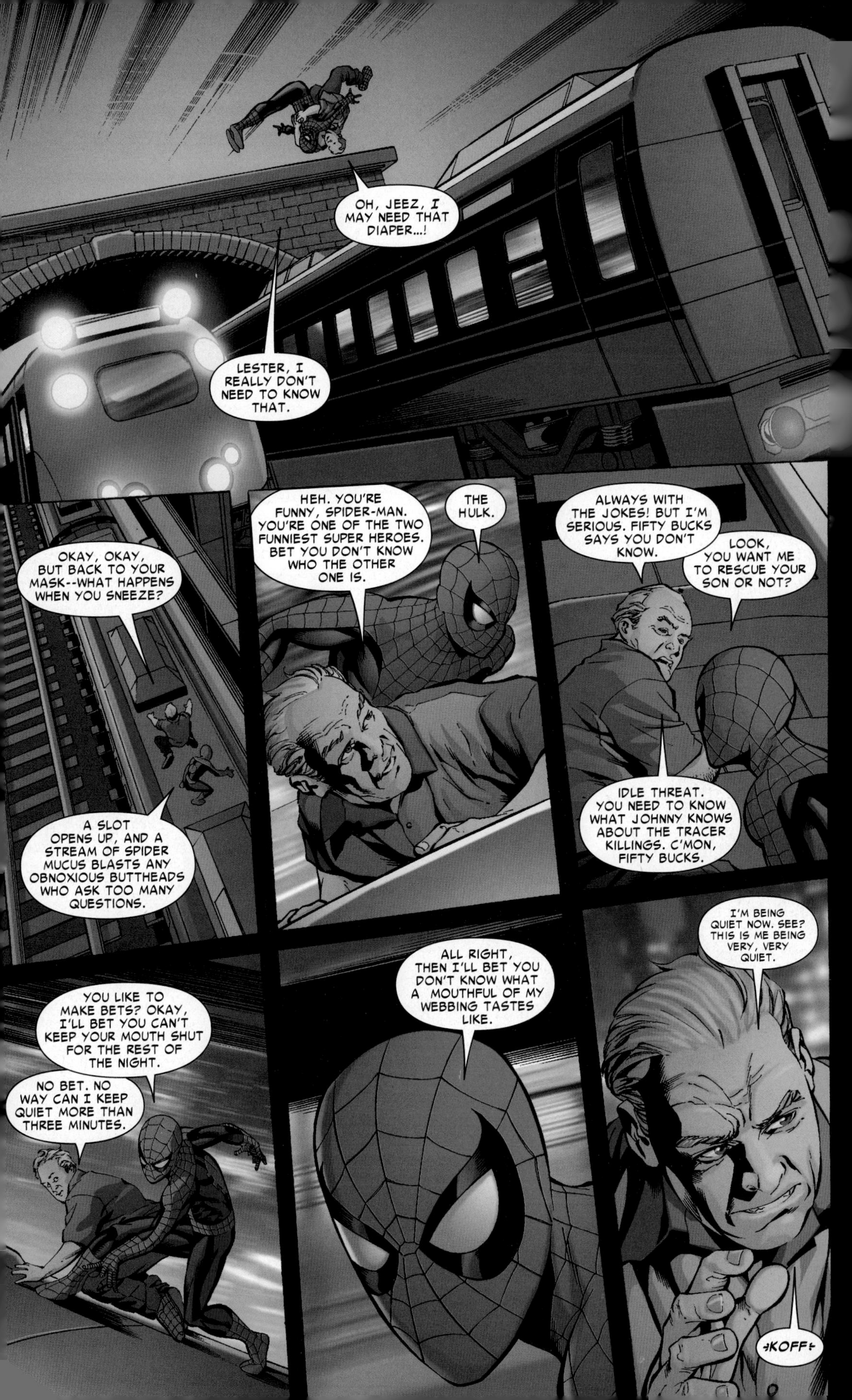
OH, JEEZ, I MAY NEED THAT DIAPER...!
LESTER, I REALLY DON'T NEED TO KNOW THAT.
OKAY, OKAY, BUT BACK TO YOUR MASK--WHAT HAPPENS WHEN YOU SNEEZE?
A SLOT OPENS UP, AND A STREAM OF SPIDER MUCUS BLASTS ANY OBNOXIOUS BUTTHEADS WHO ASK TOO MANY QUESTIONS.
HEH. YOU'RE FUNNY, SPIDER-MAN. YOU'RE ONE OF THE TWO FUNNIEST SUPER HEROES. BET YOU DON'T KNOW WHO THE OTHER ONE IS.
THE HULK.
ALWAYS WITH THE JOKES! BUT I'M SERIOUS. FIFTY BUCKS SAYS YOU DON'T KNOW.
LOOK, YOU WANT ME TO RESCUE YOUR SON OR NOT?
IDLE THREAT. YOU NEED TO KNOW WHAT JOHNNY KNOWS ABOUT THE TRACER KILLINGS. C'MON, FIFTY BUCKS.
YOU LIKE TO MAKE BETS? OKAY, I'LL BET YOU CAN'T KEEP YOUR MOUTH SHUT FOR THE REST OF THE NIGHT.
NO BET. NO WAY CAN I KEEP QUIET MORE THAN THREE MINUTES.
ALL RIGHT, THEN I'LL BET YOU DON'T KNOW WHAT A MOUTHFUL OF MY WEBBING TASTES LIKE.
I'M BEING QUIET NOW. SEE? THIS IS ME BEING VERY, VERY QUIET.
KOFF

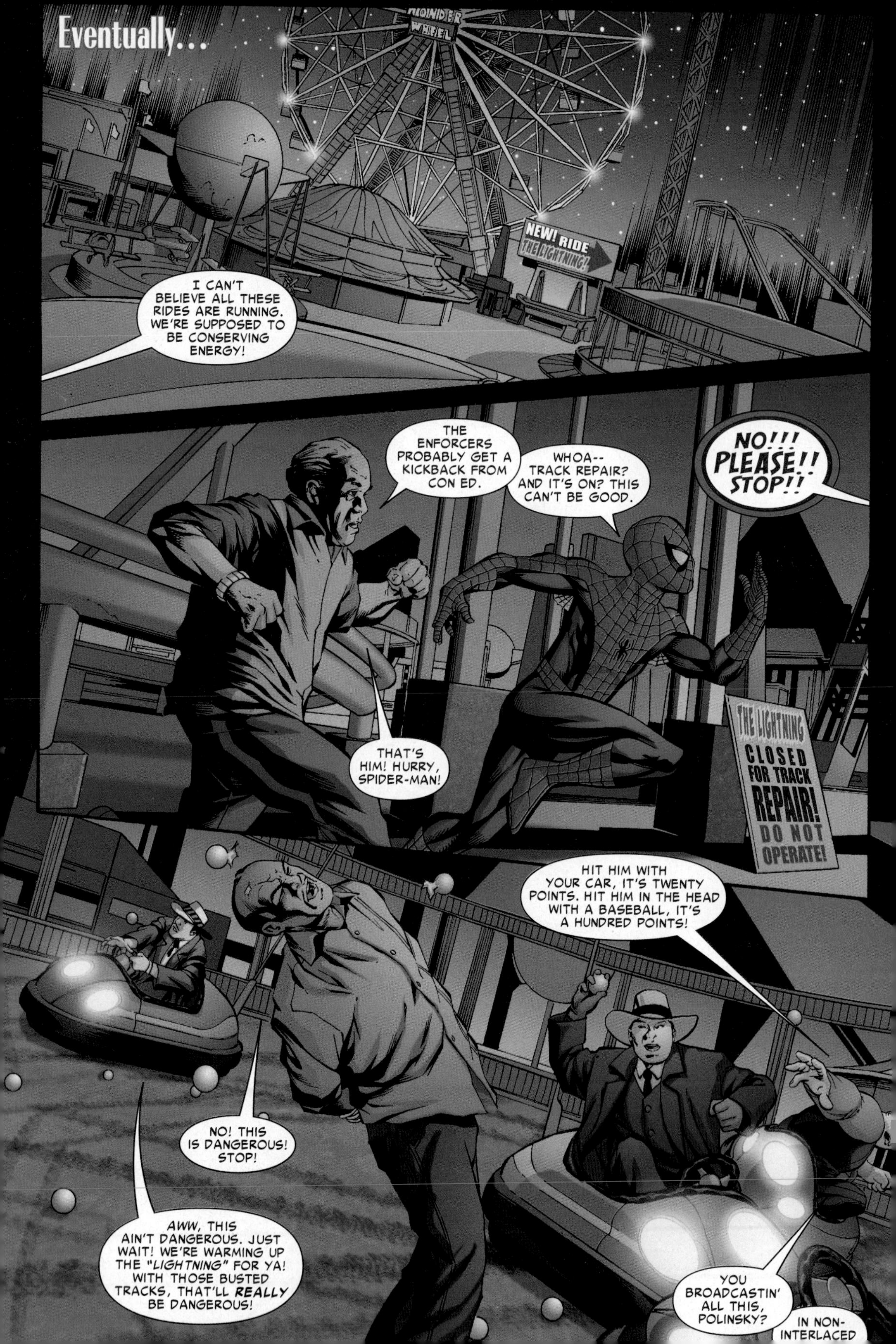
Eventually...
WONDER WHEEL
NEW! RIDE THE LIGHTNING!
I CAN'T BELIEVE ALL THESE RIDES ARE RUNNING. WE'RE SUPPOSED TO BE CONSERVING ENERGY!
THE ENFORCERS PROBABLY GET A KICKBACK FROM CON ED.
WHOA-- TRACK REPAIR? AND IT'S ON? THIS CAN'T BE GOOD.
NO!!! PLEASE!! STOP!!
THAT'S HIM! HURRY, SPIDER-MAN!
THE LIGHTNING CLOSED FOR TRACK REPAIR! DO NOT OPERATE!
HIT HIM WITH YOUR CAR, IT'S TWENTY POINTS. HIT HIM IN THE HEAD WITH A BASEBALL, IT'S A HUNDRED POINTS!
NO! THIS IS DANGEROUS! STOP!
AWW, THIS AIN'T DANGEROUS. JUST WAIT! WE'RE WARMING UP THE "LIGHTNING" FOR YA! WITH THOSE BUSTED TRACKS, THAT'LL REALLY BE DANGEROUS!
YOU BROADCASTIN' ALL THIS, POLINSKY?
IN NON-INTERLACED

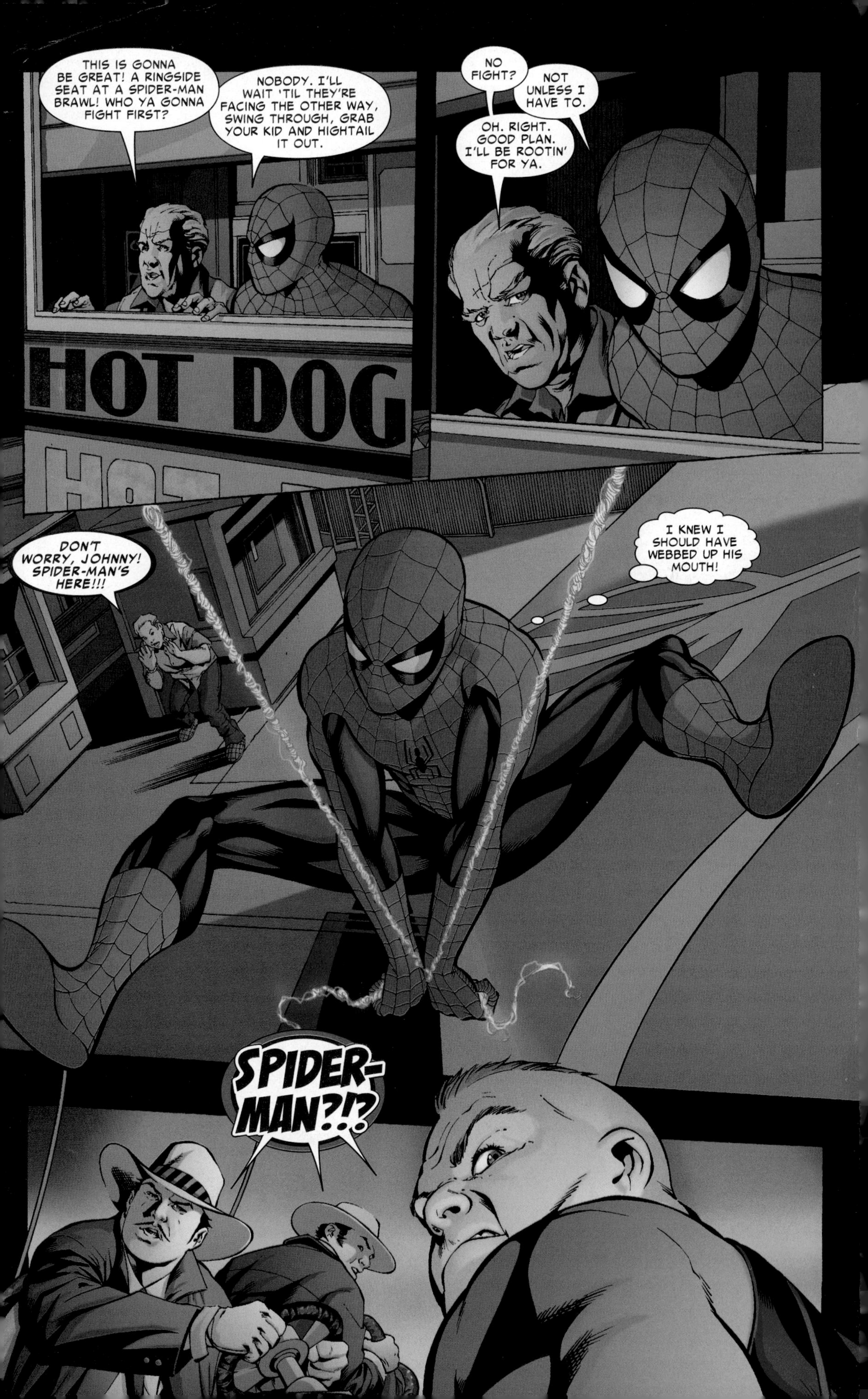
THIS IS GONNA BE GREAT! A RINGSIDE SEAT AT A SPIDER-MAN BRAWL! WHO YA GONNA FIGHT FIRST?
NOBODY. I'LL WAIT 'TIL THEY'RE FACING THE OTHER WAY, SWING THROUGH, GRAB YOUR KID AND HIGHTAIL IT OUT.
HOT DOG
NO FIGHT?
NOT UNLESS I HAVE TO.
OH. RIGHT. GOOD PLAN. I'LL BE ROOTIN' FOR YA.
DON'T WORRY, JOHNNY! SPIDER-MAN'S HERE!!!
I KNEW I SHOULD HAVE WEBBED UP HIS MOUTH!
SPIDER-MAN?!?

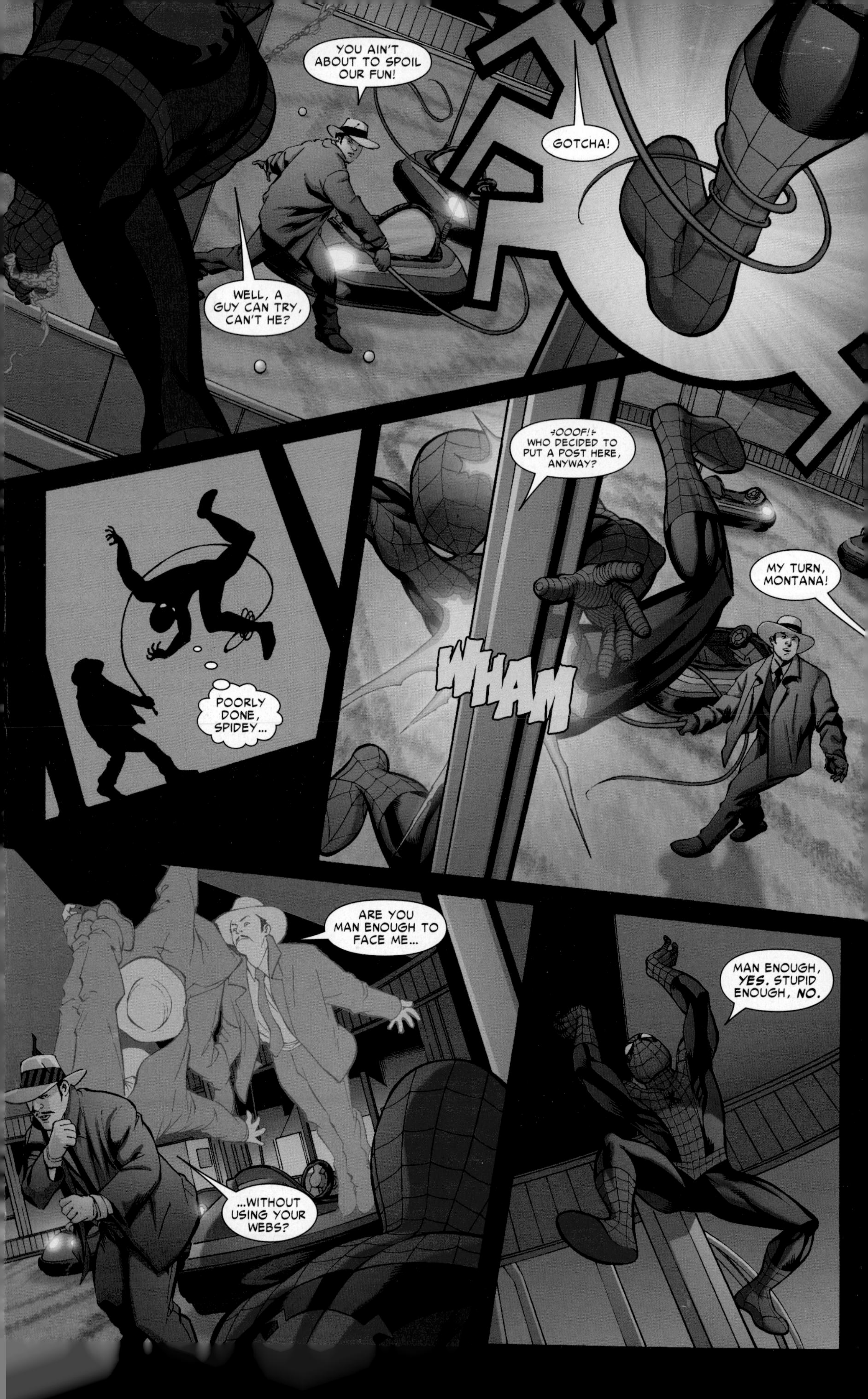
YOU AIN'T ABOUT TO SPOIL OUR FUN!
WELL, A GUY CAN TRY, CAN'T HE?
GOTCHA!
POORLY DONE, SPIDEY...
÷OOOF!÷ WHO DECIDED TO PUT A POST HERE, ANYWAY?
WHAM
MY TURN, MONTANA!
ARE YOU MAN ENOUGH TO FACE ME...
...WITHOUT USING YOUR WEBS?
MAN ENOUGH, YES. STUPID ENOUGH, NO.

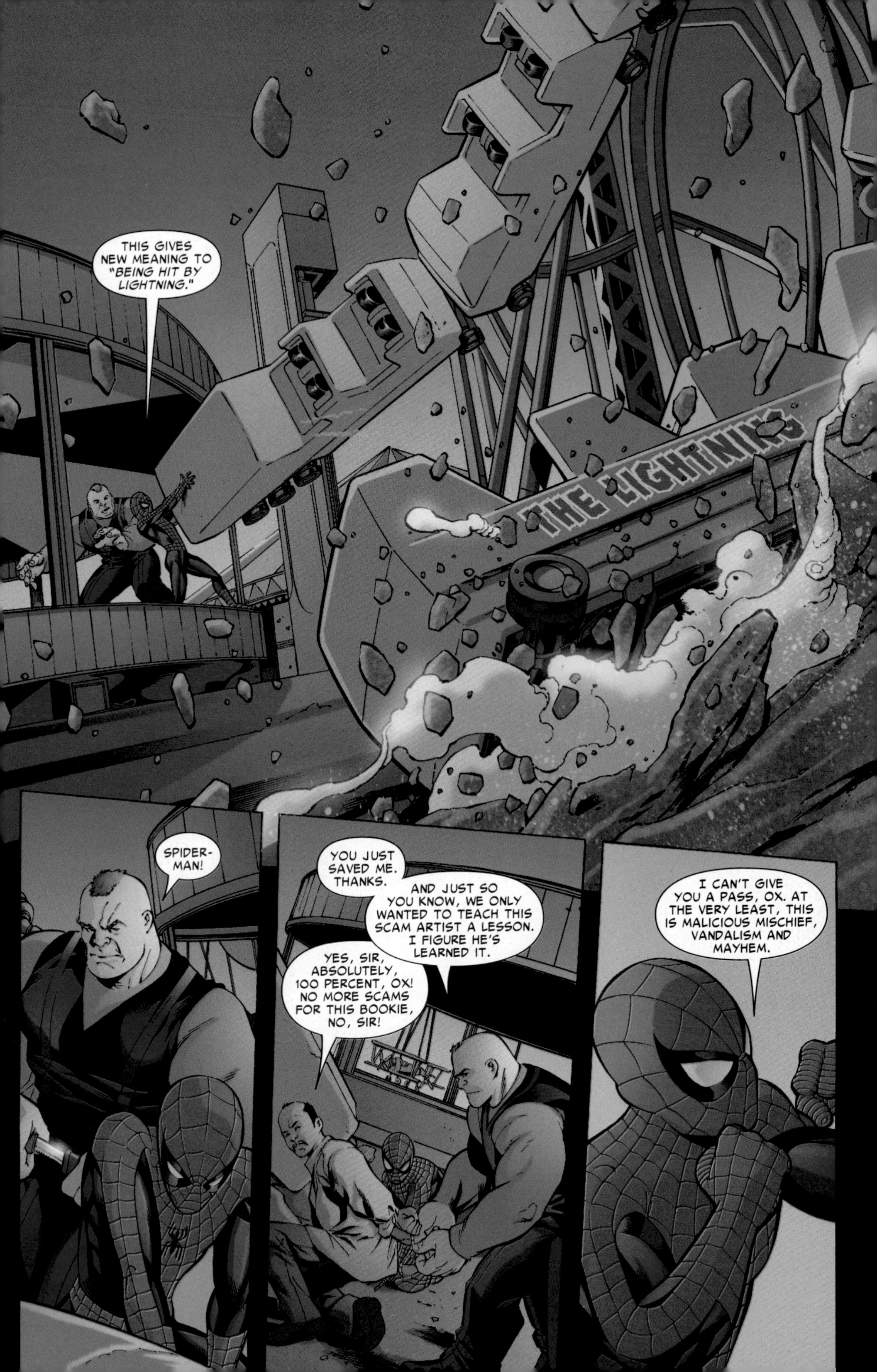
THIS GIVES NEW MEANING TO "BEING HIT BY LIGHTNING."
THE LIGHTNING
SPIDER-MAN!
YOU JUST SAVED ME. THANKS.
AND JUST SO YOU KNOW, WE ONLY WANTED TO TEACH THIS SCAM ARTIST A LESSON. I FIGURE HE'S LEARNED IT.
YES, SIR, ABSOLUTELY, 100 PERCENT, OX! NO MORE SCAMS FOR THIS BOOKIE, NO, SIR!
I CAN'T GIVE YOU A PASS, OX. AT THE VERY LEAST, THIS IS MALICIOUS MISCHIEF, VANDALISM AND MAYHEM.

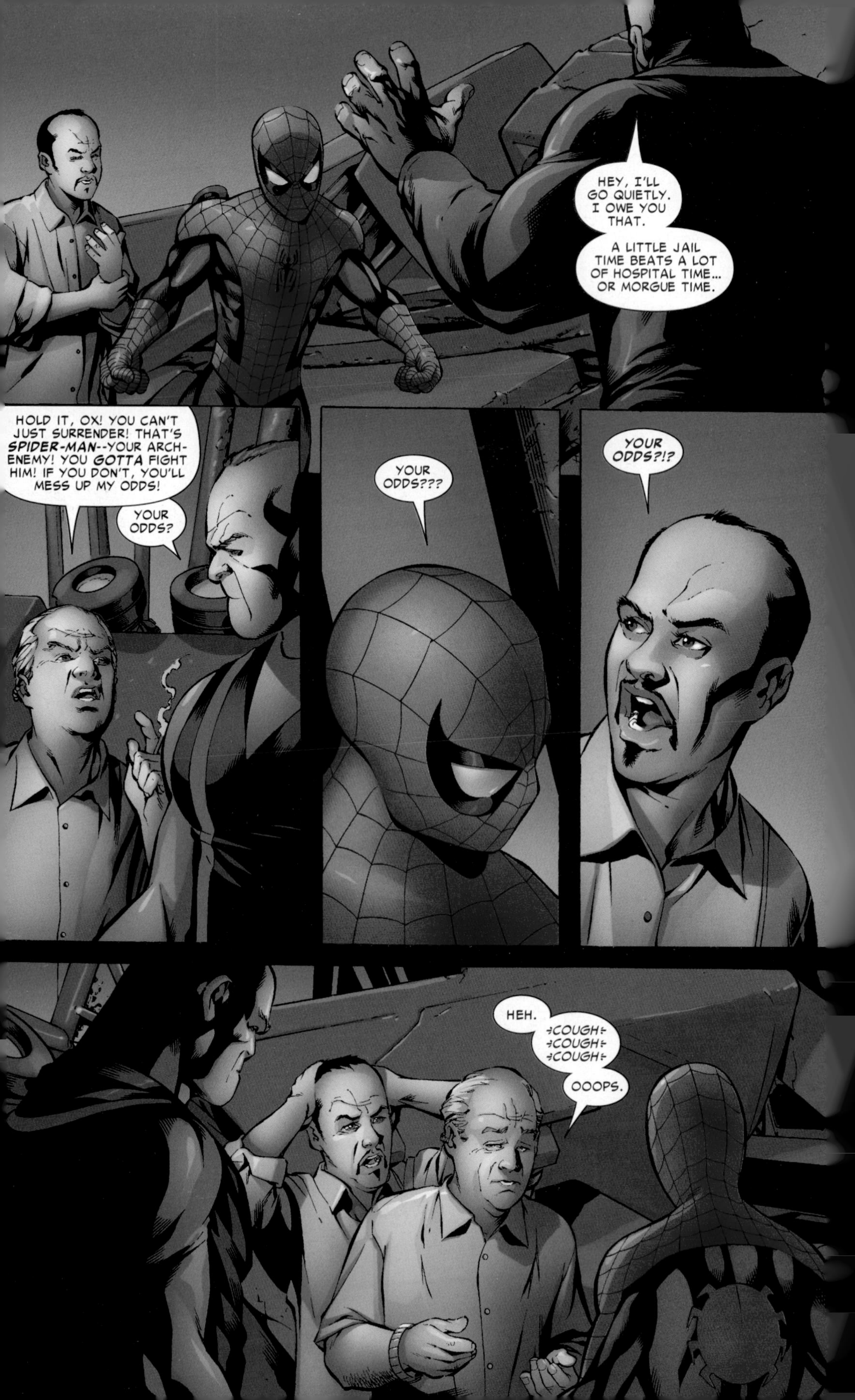
HEY, I'LL GO QUIETLY. I OWE YOU THAT.
A LITTLE JAIL TIME BEATS A LOT OF HOSPITAL TIME... OR MORGUE TIME.
HOLD IT, OX! YOU CAN'T JUST SURRENDER! THAT'S SPIDER-MAN--YOUR ARCH-ENEMY! YOU GOTTA FIGHT HIM! IF YOU DON'T, YOU'LL MESS UP MY ODDS!
YOUR ODDS?
YOUR ODDS???
YOUR ODDS?!?
HEH.
COUGH COUGH COUGH
OOOPS.

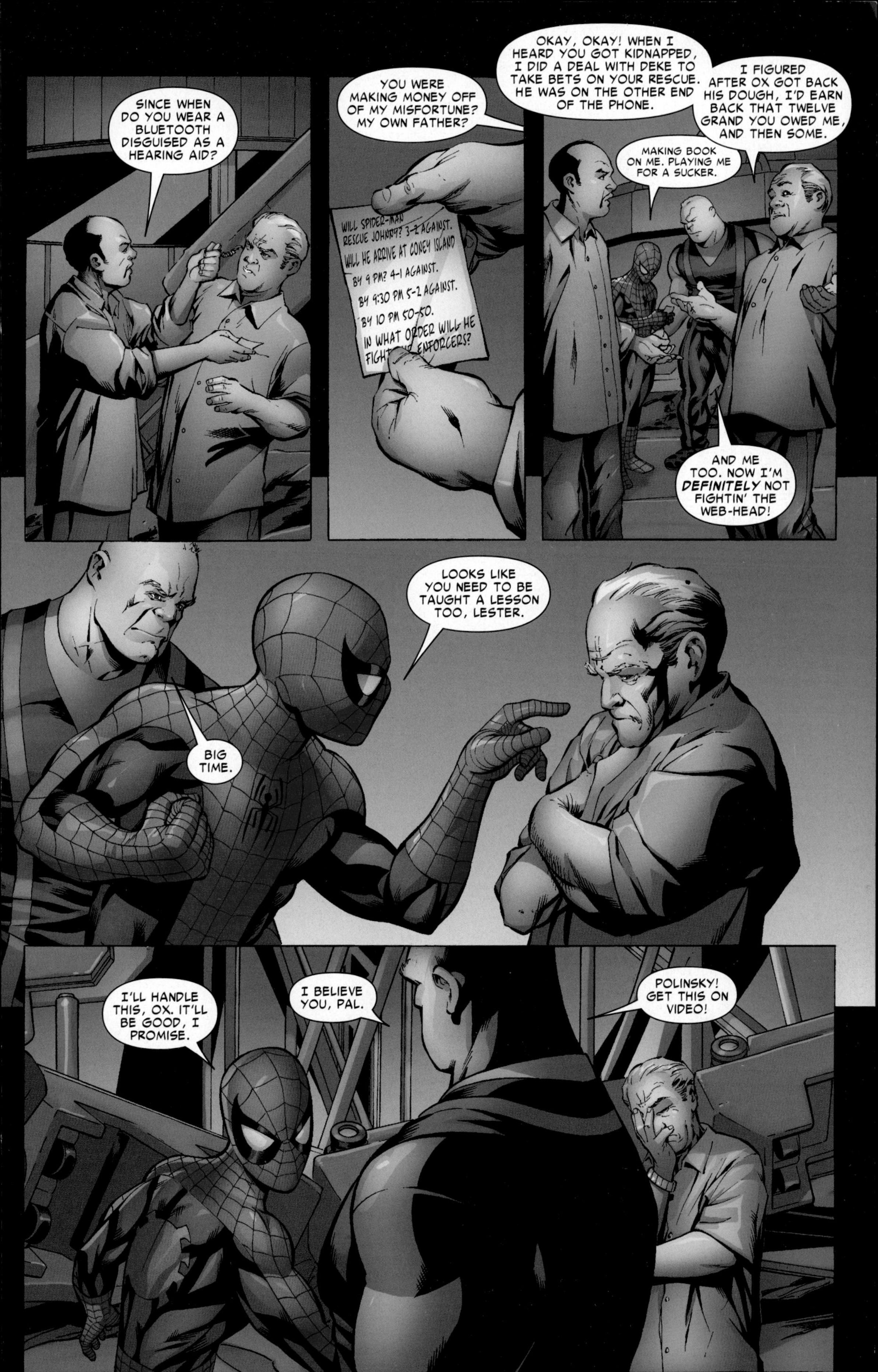
SINCE WHEN DO YOU WEAR A BLUETOOTH DISGUISED AS A HEARING AID?
YOU WERE MAKING MONEY OFF OF MY MISFORTUNE? MY OWN FATHER?
WILL SPIDER-MAN RESCUE JOHNNY? 3-2 AGAINST.
WILL HE ARRIVE AT CONEY ISLAND BY 9 PM? 4-1 AGAINST.
BY 9:30 PM 5-2 AGAINST.
BY 10 PM 50-50.
IN WHAT ORDER WILL HE FIGHT ENFORCERS?
OKAY, OKAY! WHEN I HEARD YOU GOT KIDNAPPED, I DID A DEAL WITH DEKE TO TAKE BETS ON YOUR RESCUE. HE WAS ON THE OTHER END OF THE PHONE.
I FIGURED AFTER OX GOT BACK HIS DOUGH, I'D EARN BACK THAT TWELVE GRAND YOU OWED ME, AND THEN SOME.
MAKING BOOK ON ME. PLAYING ME FOR A SUCKER.
AND ME TOO. NOW I'M *DEFINITELY* NOT FIGHTIN' THE WEB-HEAD!
LOOKS LIKE YOU NEED TO BE TAUGHT A LESSON TOO, LESTER.
BIG TIME.
I'LL HANDLE THIS, OX. IT'LL BE GOOD, I PROMISE.
I BELIEVE YOU, PAL.
POLINSKY! GET THIS ON VIDEO!

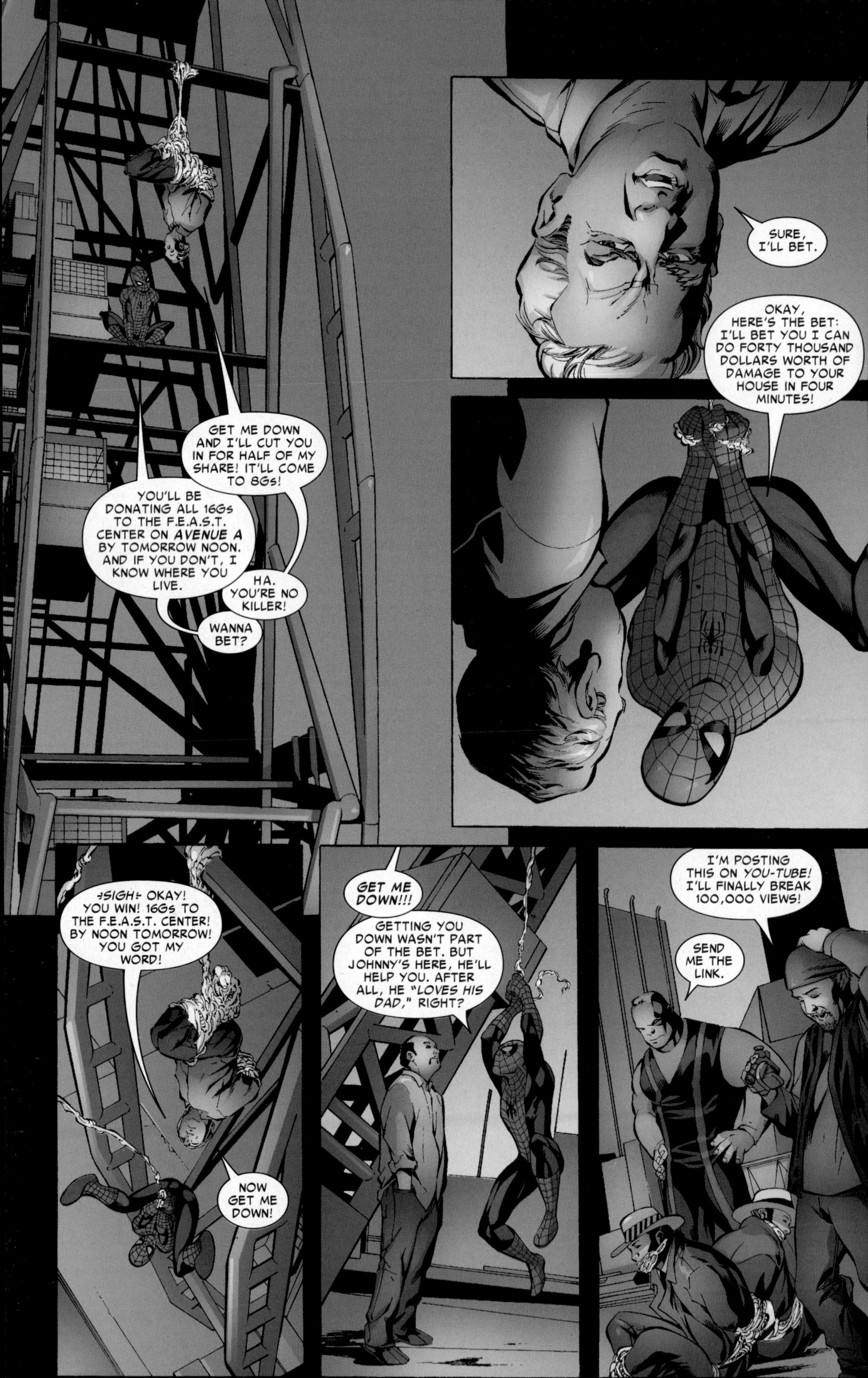
GET ME DOWN AND I'LL CUT YOU IN FOR HALF OF MY SHARE! IT'LL COME TO 8Gs!
YOU'LL BE DONATING ALL 16Gs TO THE F.E.A.S.T. CENTER ON *AVENUE A* BY TOMORROW NOON. AND IF YOU DON'T, I KNOW WHERE YOU LIVE.
HA. YOU'RE NO KILLER!
WANNA BET?
SURE, I'LL BET.
OKAY, HERE'S THE BET: I'LL BET YOU I CAN DO FORTY THOUSAND DOLLARS WORTH OF DAMAGE TO YOUR HOUSE IN FOUR MINUTES!
SIGH OKAY! YOU WIN! 16Gs TO THE F.E.A.S.T. CENTER! BY NOON TOMORROW! YOU GOT MY WORD!
NOW GET ME DOWN!
GET ME DOWN!!!
GETTING YOU DOWN WASN'T PART OF THE BET. BUT JOHNNY'S HERE, HE'LL HELP YOU. AFTER ALL, HE *"LOVES HIS DAD,"* RIGHT?
I'M POSTING THIS ON *YOU-TUBE!* I'LL FINALLY BREAK 100,000 VIEWS!
SEND ME THE LINK.

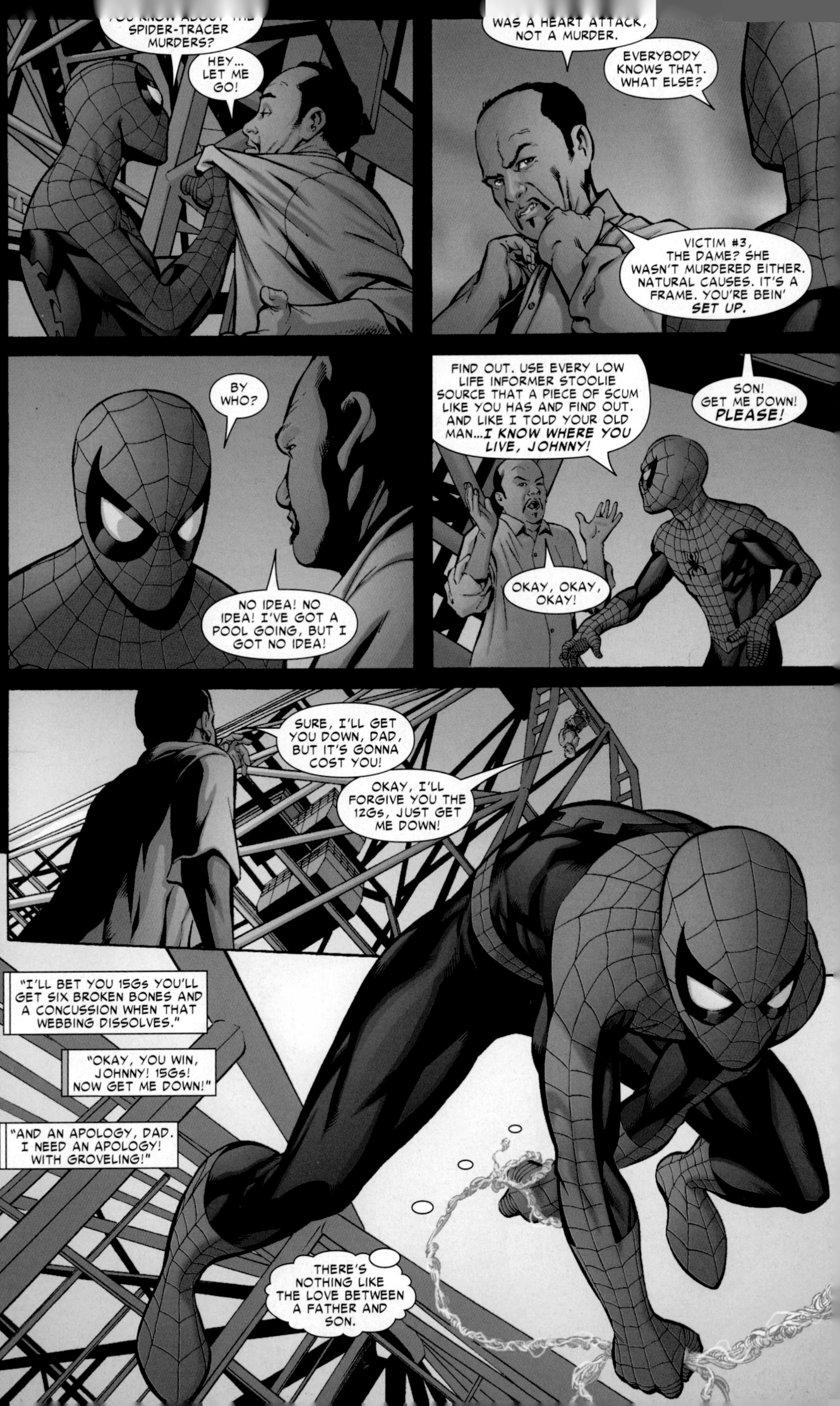

SPIDER-TRACER MURDERS?
HEY... LET ME GO!
WAS A HEART ATTACK, NOT A MURDER.
EVERYBODY KNOWS THAT. WHAT ELSE?
VICTIM #3, THE DAME? SHE WASN'T MURDERED EITHER. NATURAL CAUSES. IT'S A FRAME. YOU'RE BEIN' SET UP.
BY WHO?
NO IDEA! NO IDEA! I'VE GOT A POOL GOING, BUT I GOT NO IDEA!
FIND OUT. USE EVERY LOW LIFE INFORMER STOOLIE SOURCE THAT A PIECE OF SCUM LIKE YOU HAS AND FIND OUT. AND LIKE I TOLD YOUR OLD MAN...I KNOW WHERE YOU LIVE, JOHNNY!
SON! GET ME DOWN! PLEASE!
OKAY, OKAY, OKAY!
SURE, I'LL GET YOU DOWN, DAD, BUT IT'S GONNA COST YOU!
OKAY, I'LL FORGIVE YOU THE 12Gs, JUST GET ME DOWN!
"I'LL BET YOU 15Gs YOU'LL GET SIX BROKEN BONES AND A CONCUSSION WHEN THAT WEBBING DISSOLVES."
"OKAY, YOU WIN, JOHNNY! 15Gs! NOW GET ME DOWN!"
"AND AN APOLOGY, DAD. I NEED AN APOLOGY! WITH GROVELING!"
THERE'S NOTHING LIKE THE LOVE BETWEEN A FATHER AND SON.

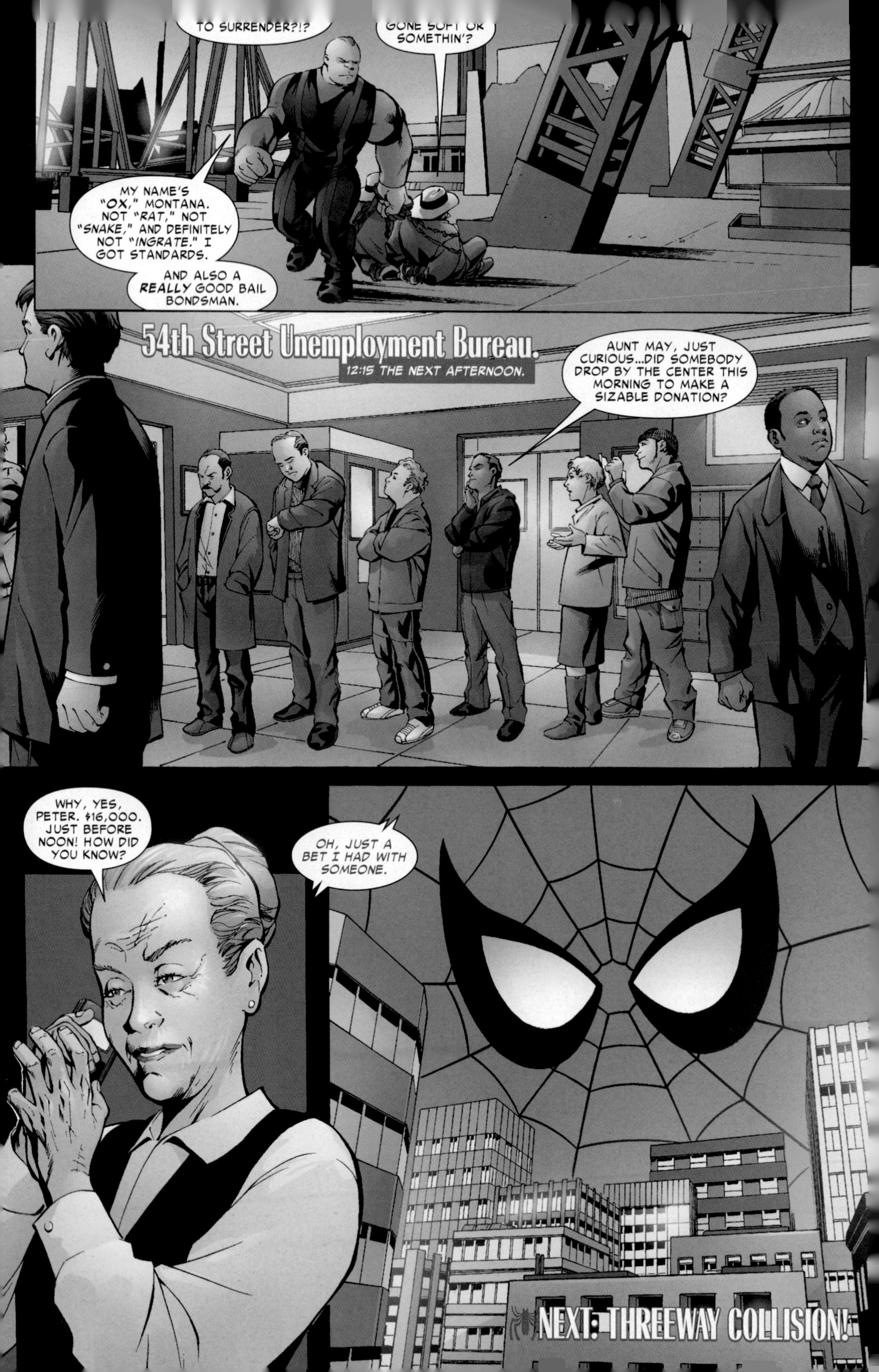
TO SURRENDER?!?
GONE SOFT OR SOMETHIN'?
MY NAME'S "OX," MONTANA. NOT "RAT," NOT "SNAKE," AND DEFINITELY NOT "INGRATE." I GOT STANDARDS.
AND ALSO A REALLY GOOD BAIL BONDSMAN.
54th Street Unemployment Bureau.
12:15 THE NEXT AFTERNOON.
AUNT MAY, JUST CURIOUS...DID SOMEBODY DROP BY THE CENTER THIS MORNING TO MAKE A SIZABLE DONATION?
WHY, YES, PETER. $16,000. JUST BEFORE NOON! HOW DID YOU KNOW?
OH, JUST A BET I HAD WITH SOMEONE.
NEXT: THREEWAY COLLISION!

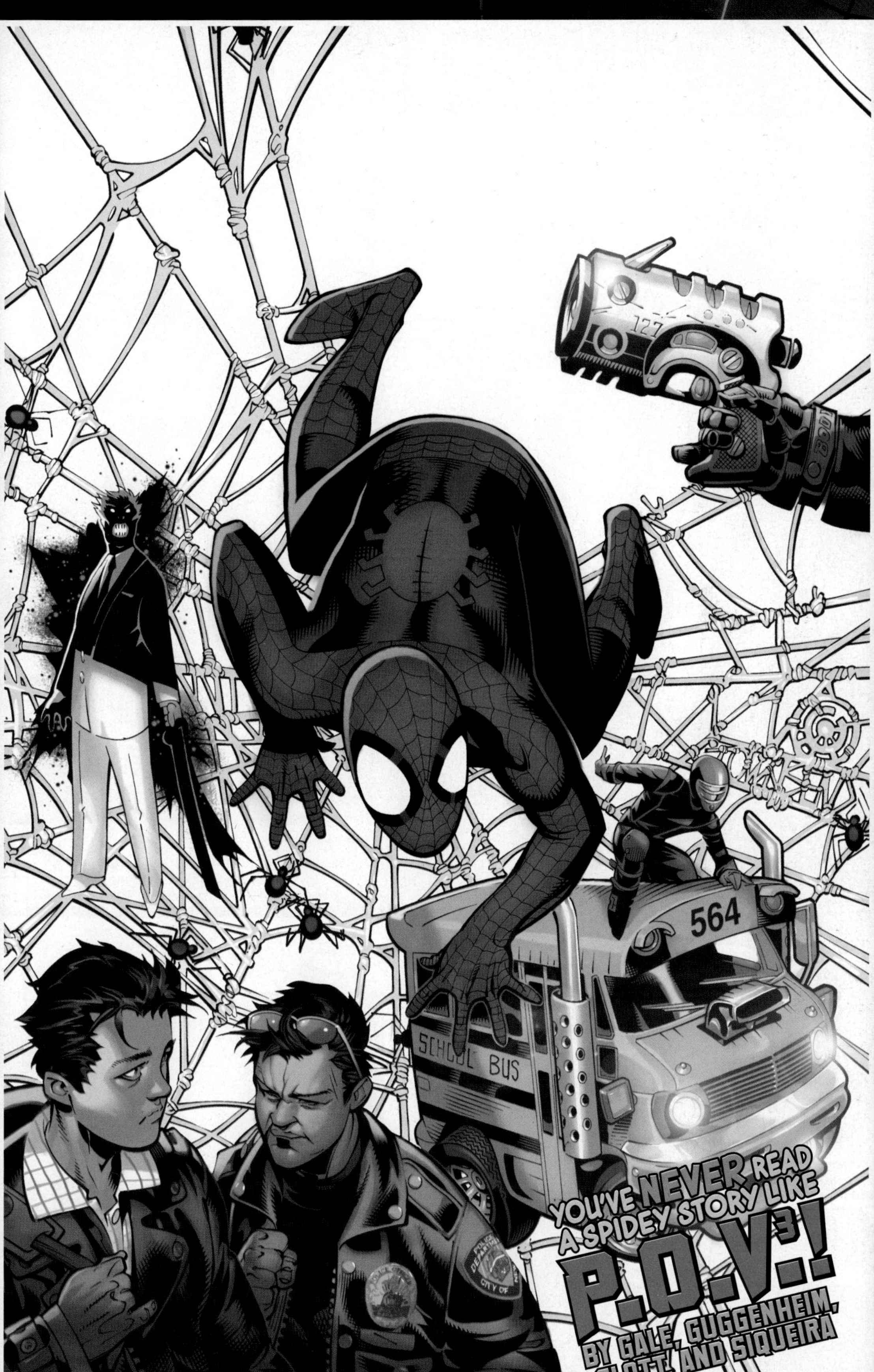
127
564
SCHOOL BUS
YOU'VE NEVER READ A SPIDEY STORY LIKE
P.O.V.[3]!
BY GALE, GUGGENHEIM, SLOTT, AND SIQUEIRA

AMAZING SPIDER-MAN #564
COVER BY **CHRIS BACHALO & TIM TOWNSEND**

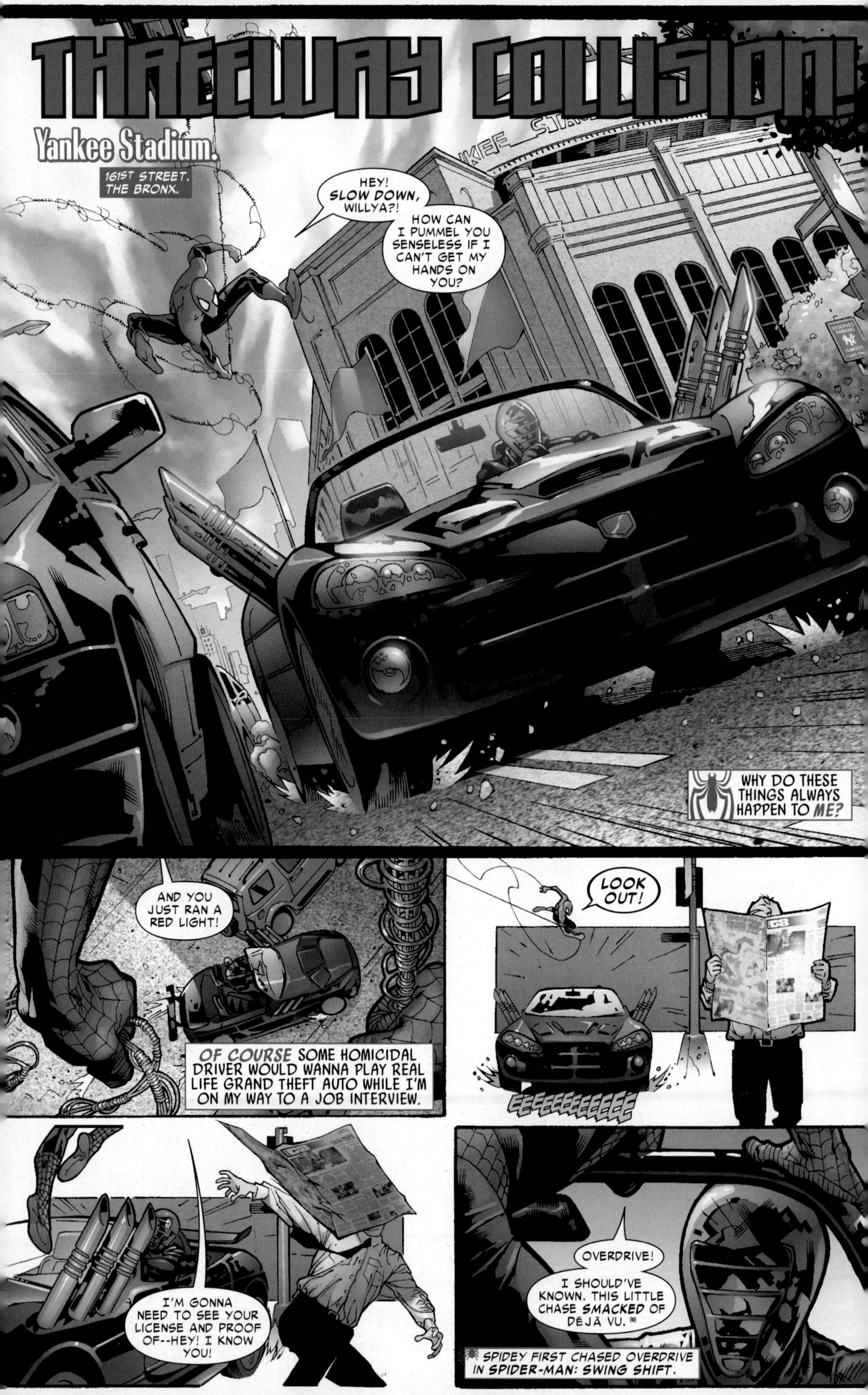
THREEWAY COLLISION!
Yankee Stadium.
161ST STREET. THE BRONX.
HEY! SLOW DOWN, WILLYA?!
HOW CAN I PUMMEL YOU SENSELESS IF I CAN'T GET MY HANDS ON YOU?
WHY DO THESE THINGS ALWAYS HAPPEN TO ME?
AND YOU JUST RAN A RED LIGHT!
OF COURSE SOME HOMICIDAL DRIVER WOULD WANNA PLAY REAL LIFE GRAND THEFT AUTO WHILE I'M ON MY WAY TO A JOB INTERVIEW.
LOOK OUT!
EEEEEEEEEEEE
I'M GONNA NEED TO SEE YOUR LICENSE AND PROOF OF--HEY! I KNOW YOU!
OVERDRIVE!
I SHOULD'VE KNOWN. THIS LITTLE CHASE SMACKED OF DÉJÀ VU.
SPIDEY FIRST CHASED OVERDRIVE IN SPIDER-MAN: SWING SHIFT.

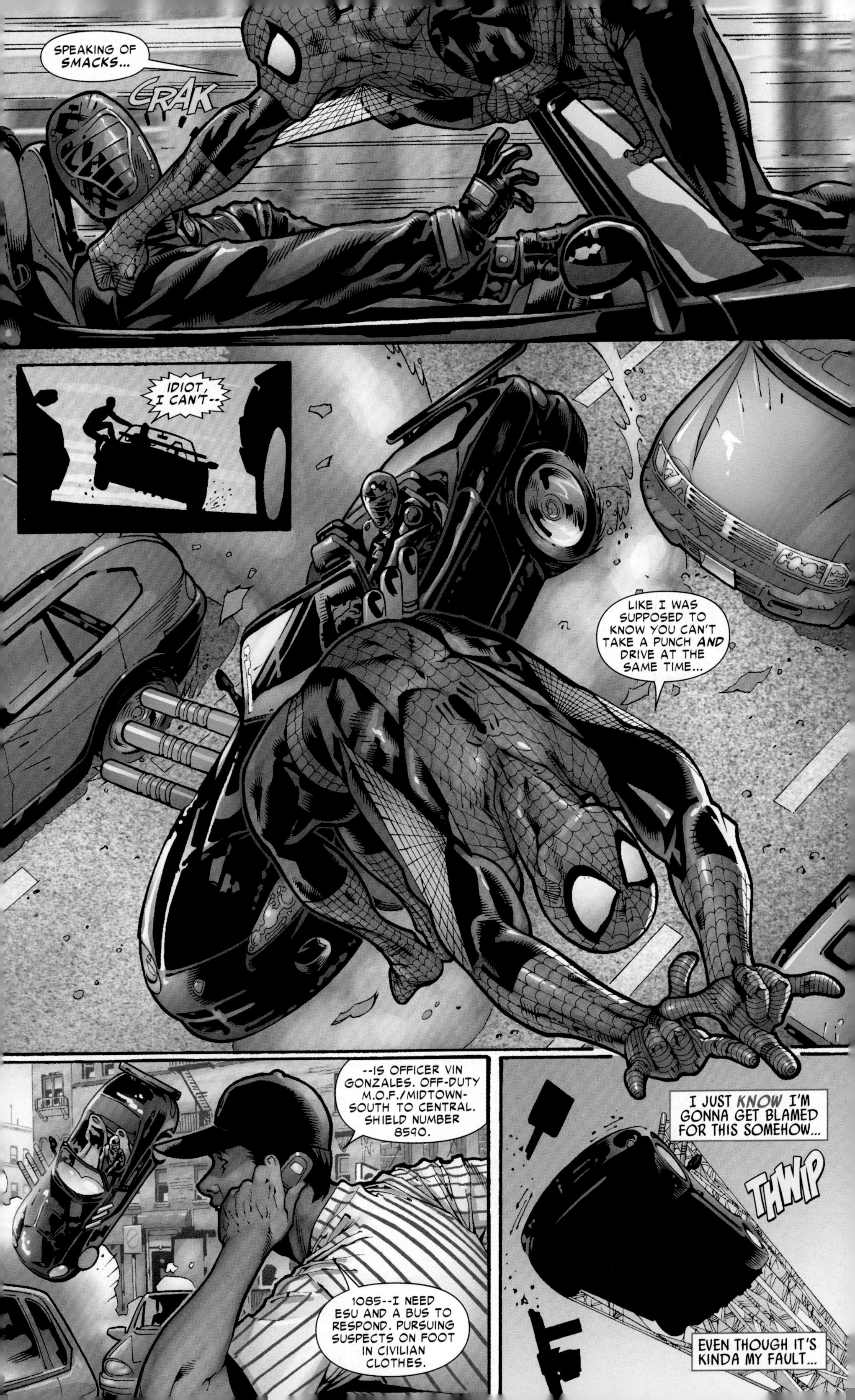

SPEAKING OF SMACKS...
CRAK
IDIOT, I CAN'T--
LIKE I WAS SUPPOSED TO KNOW YOU CAN'T TAKE A PUNCH AND DRIVE AT THE SAME TIME...
--IS OFFICER VIN GONZALES. OFF-DUTY M.O.F./MIDTOWN-SOUTH TO CENTRAL. SHIELD NUMBER 8590.
1085--I NEED ESU AND A BUS TO RESPOND. PURSUING SUSPECTS ON FOOT IN CIVILIAN CLOTHES.
I JUST KNOW I'M GONNA GET BLAMED FOR THIS SOMEHOW...
THWIP
EVEN THOUGH IT'S KINDA MY FAULT...

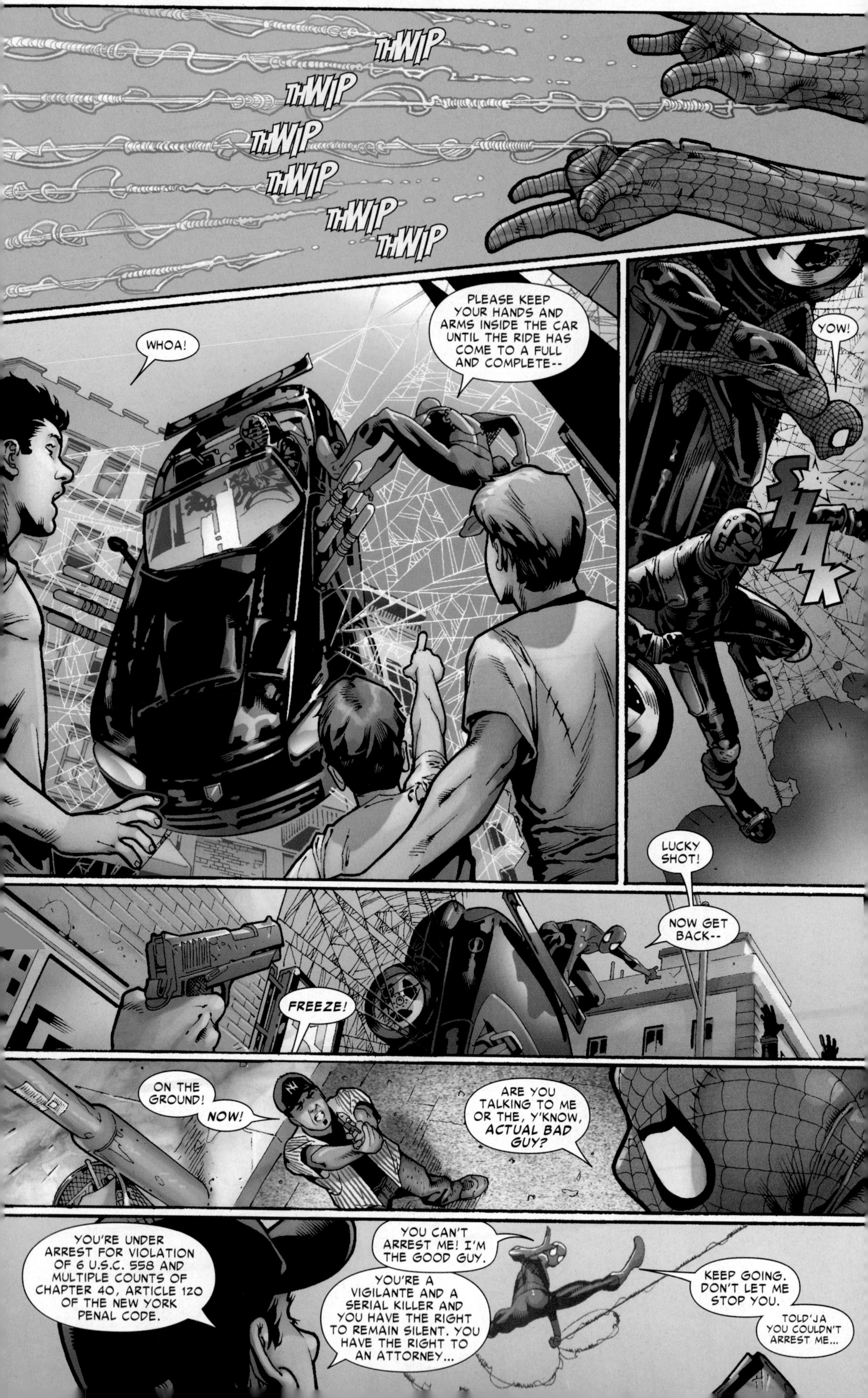
THWIP
THWIP
THWIP
THWIP
THWIP
THWIP
WHOA!
PLEASE KEEP YOUR HANDS AND ARMS INSIDE THE CAR UNTIL THE RIDE HAS COME TO A FULL AND COMPLETE--
YOW!
THAK
LUCKY SHOT!
NOW GET BACK--
FREEZE!
ON THE GROUND!
NOW!
ARE YOU TALKING TO ME OR THE, Y'KNOW, ACTUAL BAD GUY?
YOU'RE UNDER ARREST FOR VIOLATION OF 6 U.S.C. 558 AND MULTIPLE COUNTS OF CHAPTER 40, ARTICLE 120 OF THE NEW YORK PENAL CODE.
YOU CAN'T ARREST ME! I'M THE GOOD GUY.
YOU'RE A VIGILANTE AND A SERIAL KILLER AND YOU HAVE THE RIGHT TO REMAIN SILENT. YOU HAVE THE RIGHT TO AN ATTORNEY...
KEEP GOING. DON'T LET ME STOP YOU.
TOLD'JA YOU COULDN'T ARREST ME...

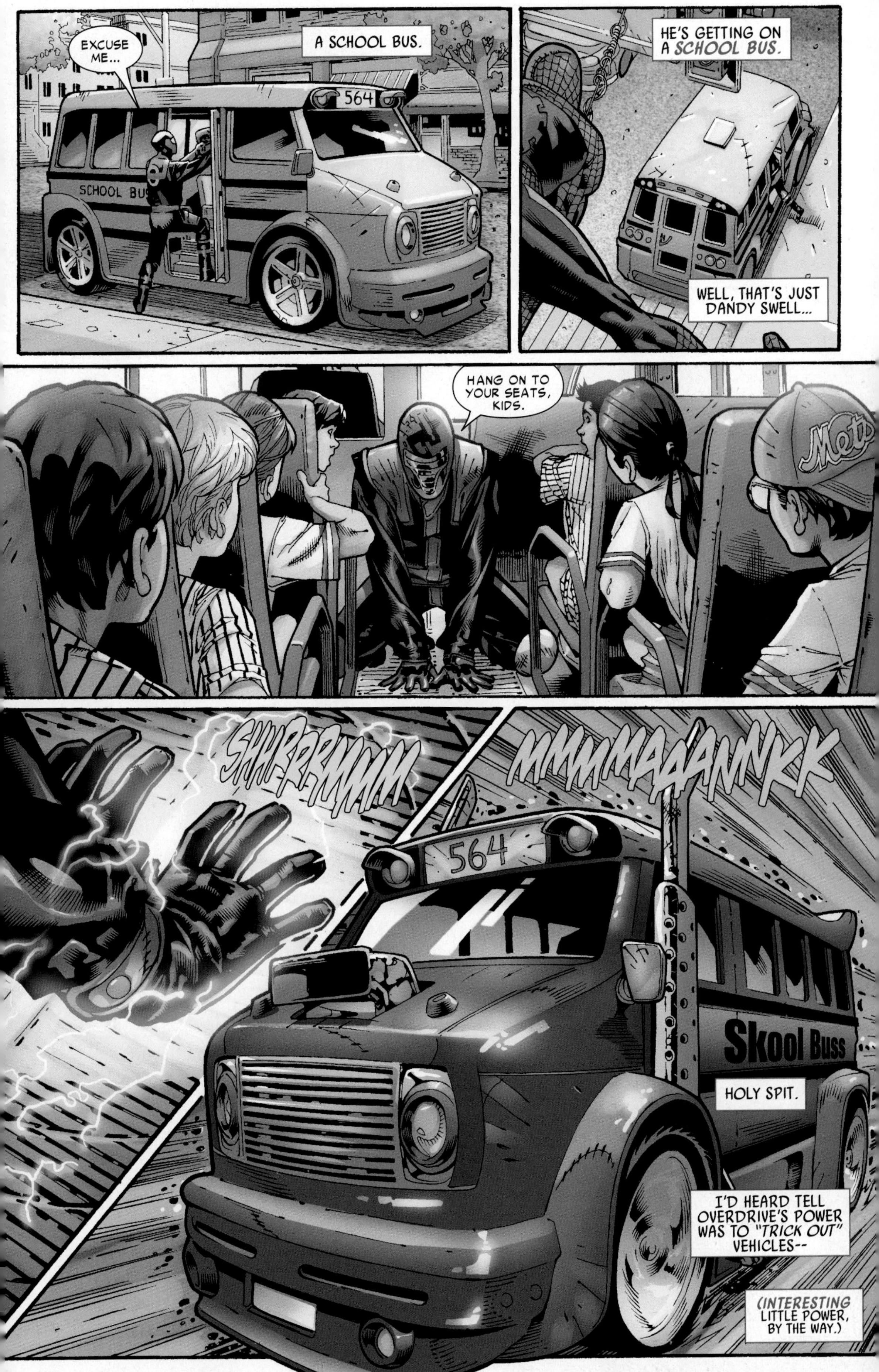
EXCUSE ME...
A SCHOOL BUS.
564
SCHOOL BUS
HE'S GETTING ON A SCHOOL BUS.
WELL, THAT'S JUST DANDY SWELL...
HANG ON TO YOUR SEATS, KIDS.
Mets
SHHRRRMMMM
MMMMAAAANNKK
564
Skool Buss
HOLY SPIT.
I'D HEARD TELL OVERDRIVE'S POWER WAS TO "TRICK OUT" VEHICLES--
(INTERESTING LITTLE POWER, BY THE WAY.)

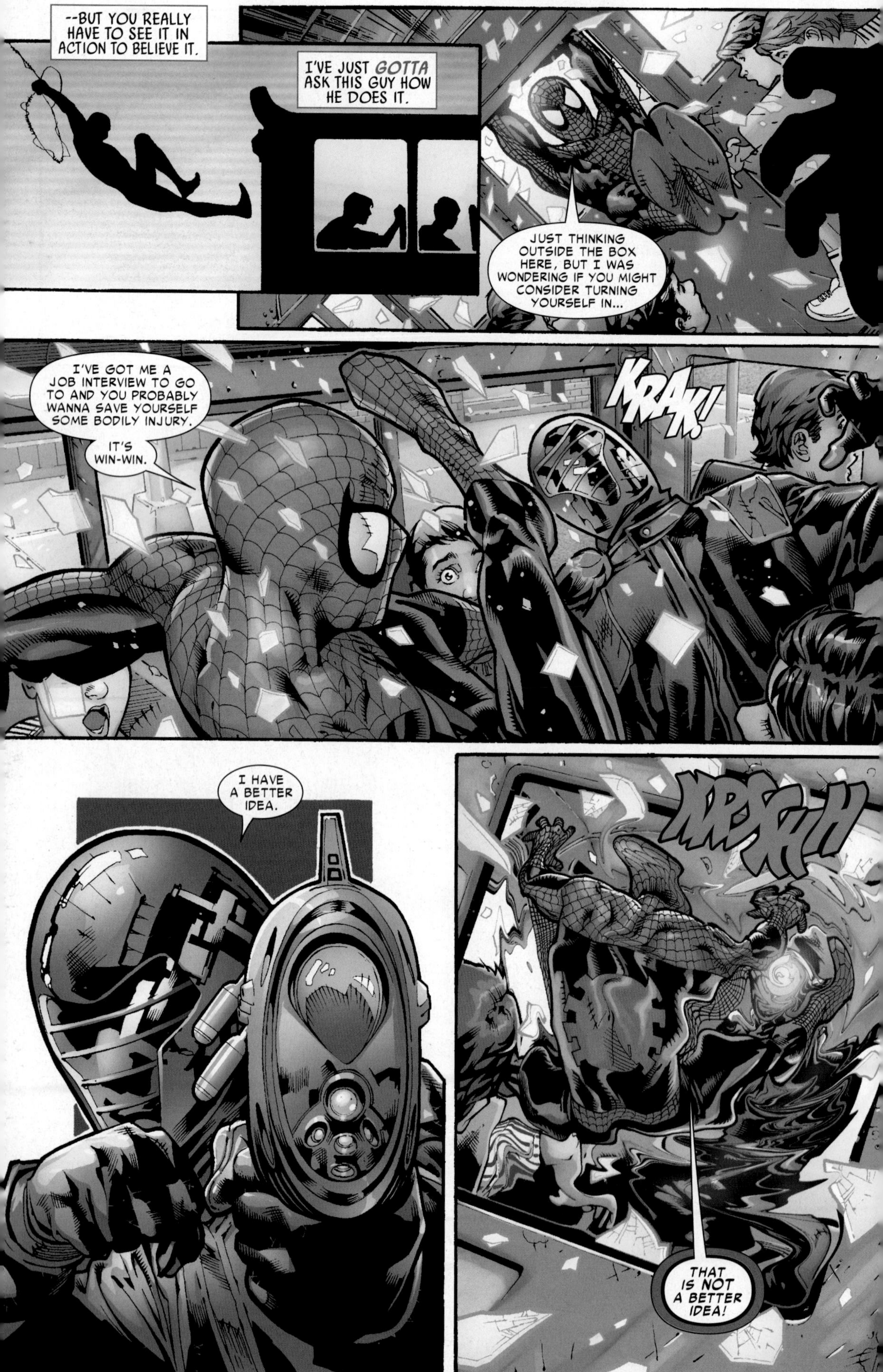
--BUT YOU REALLY HAVE TO SEE IT IN ACTION TO BELIEVE IT.
I'VE JUST GOTTA ASK THIS GUY HOW HE DOES IT.
JUST THINKING OUTSIDE THE BOX HERE, BUT I WAS WONDERING IF YOU MIGHT CONSIDER TURNING YOURSELF IN...
I'VE GOT ME A JOB INTERVIEW TO GO TO AND YOU PROBABLY WANNA SAVE YOURSELF SOME BODILY INJURY.
IT'S WIN-WIN.
KRAK!
I HAVE A BETTER IDEA.
THAT IS NOT A BETTER IDEA!

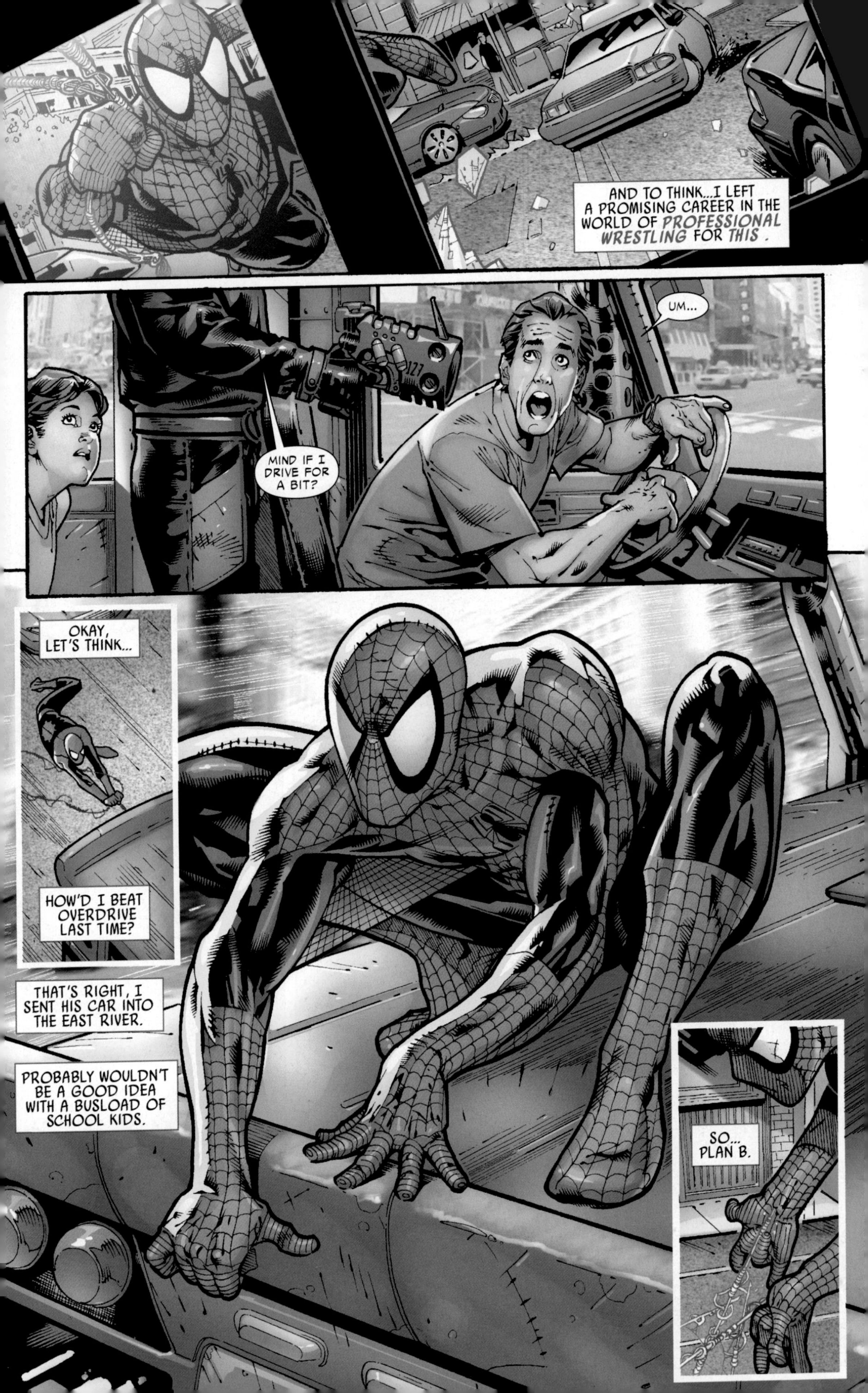
AND TO THINK...I LEFT A PROMISING CAREER IN THE WORLD OF PROFESSIONAL WRESTLING FOR THIS.
UM...
MIND IF I DRIVE FOR A BIT?
OKAY, LET'S THINK...
HOW'D I BEAT OVERDRIVE LAST TIME?
THAT'S RIGHT, I SENT HIS CAR INTO THE EAST RIVER.
PROBABLY WOULDN'T BE A GOOD IDEA WITH A BUSLOAD OF SCHOOL KIDS.
SO... PLAN B.

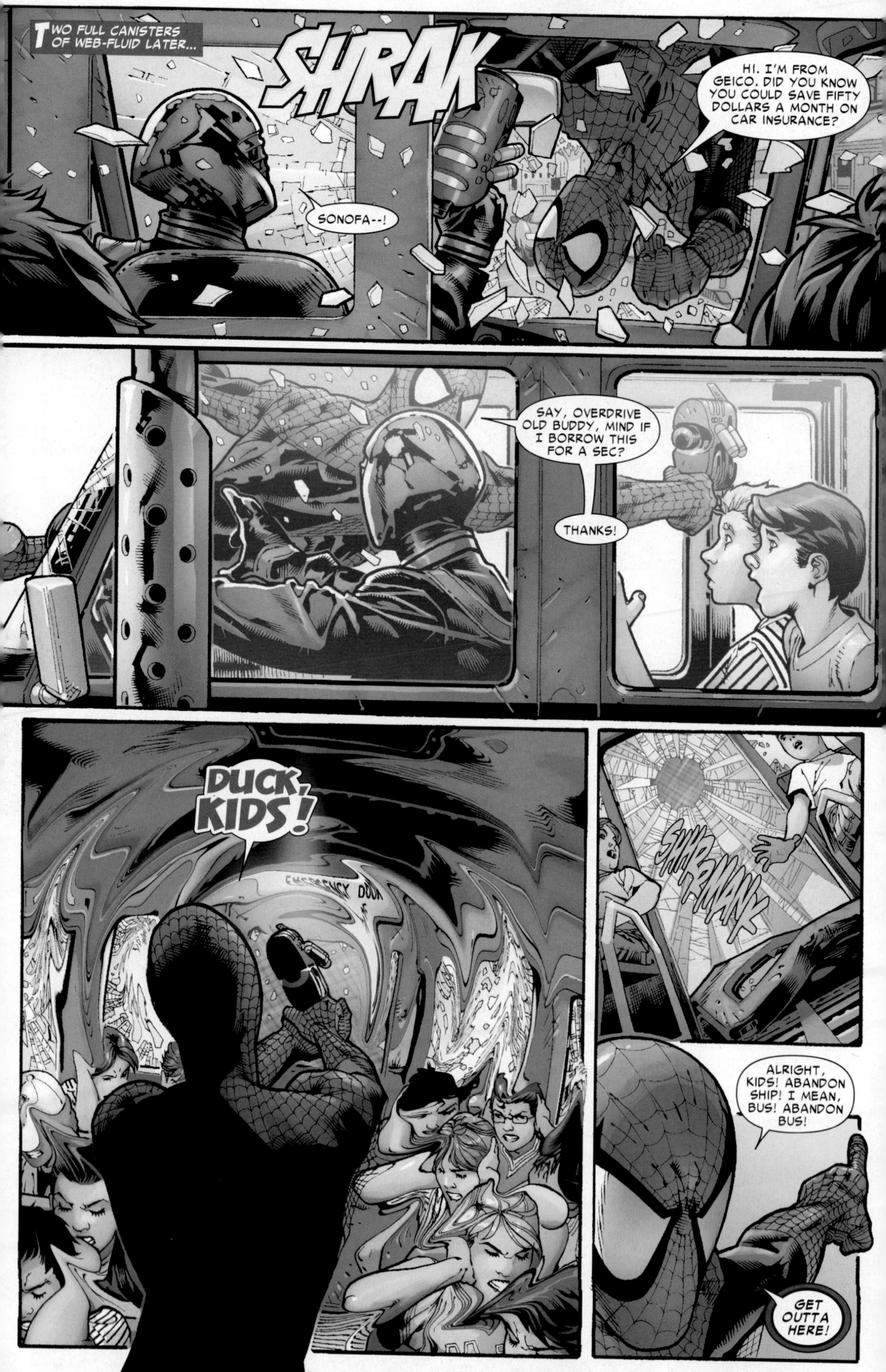
TWO FULL CANISTERS OF WEB-FLUID LATER...
SHRAK
HI. I'M FROM GEICO. DID YOU KNOW YOU COULD SAVE FIFTY DOLLARS A MONTH ON CAR INSURANCE?
SONOFA--!
SAY, OVERDRIVE OLD BUDDY, MIND IF I BORROW THIS FOR A SEC?
THANKS!
DUCK, KIDS!
ALRIGHT, KIDS! ABANDON SHIP! I MEAN, BUS! ABANDON BUS!
GET OUTTA HERE!

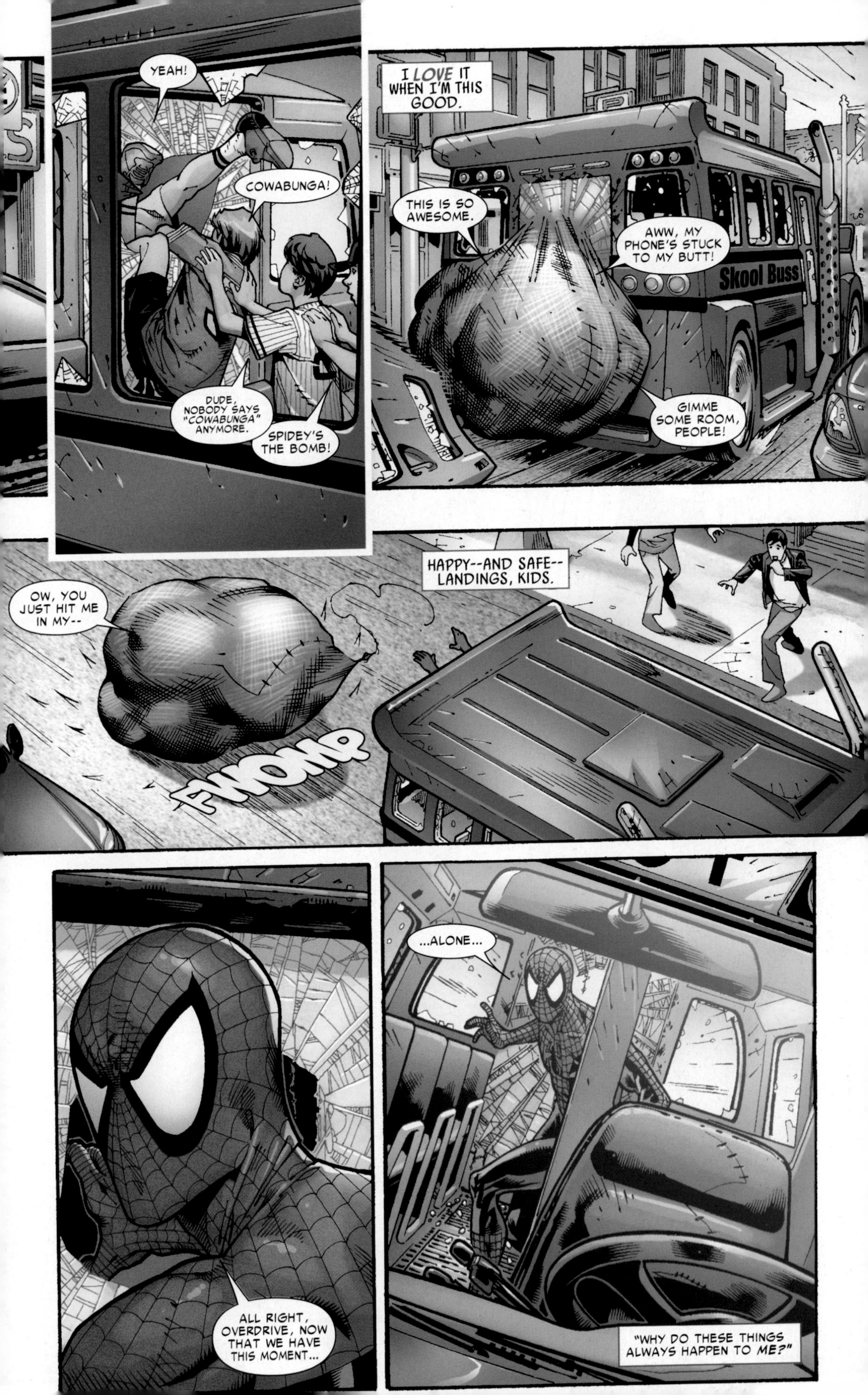
YEAH!
COWABUNGA!
DUDE, NOBODY SAYS "COWABUNGA" ANYMORE.
SPIDEY'S THE BOMB!
I LOVE IT WHEN I'M THIS GOOD.
THIS IS SO AWESOME.
AWW, MY PHONE'S STUCK TO MY BUTT!
Skool Buss
GIMME SOME ROOM, PEOPLE!
HAPPY--AND SAFE--LANDINGS, KIDS.
OW, YOU JUST HIT ME IN MY--
FWOMP
ALL RIGHT, OVERDRIVE, NOW THAT WE HAVE THIS MOMENT...
...ALONE...
"WHY DO THESE THINGS ALWAYS HAPPEN TO ME?"

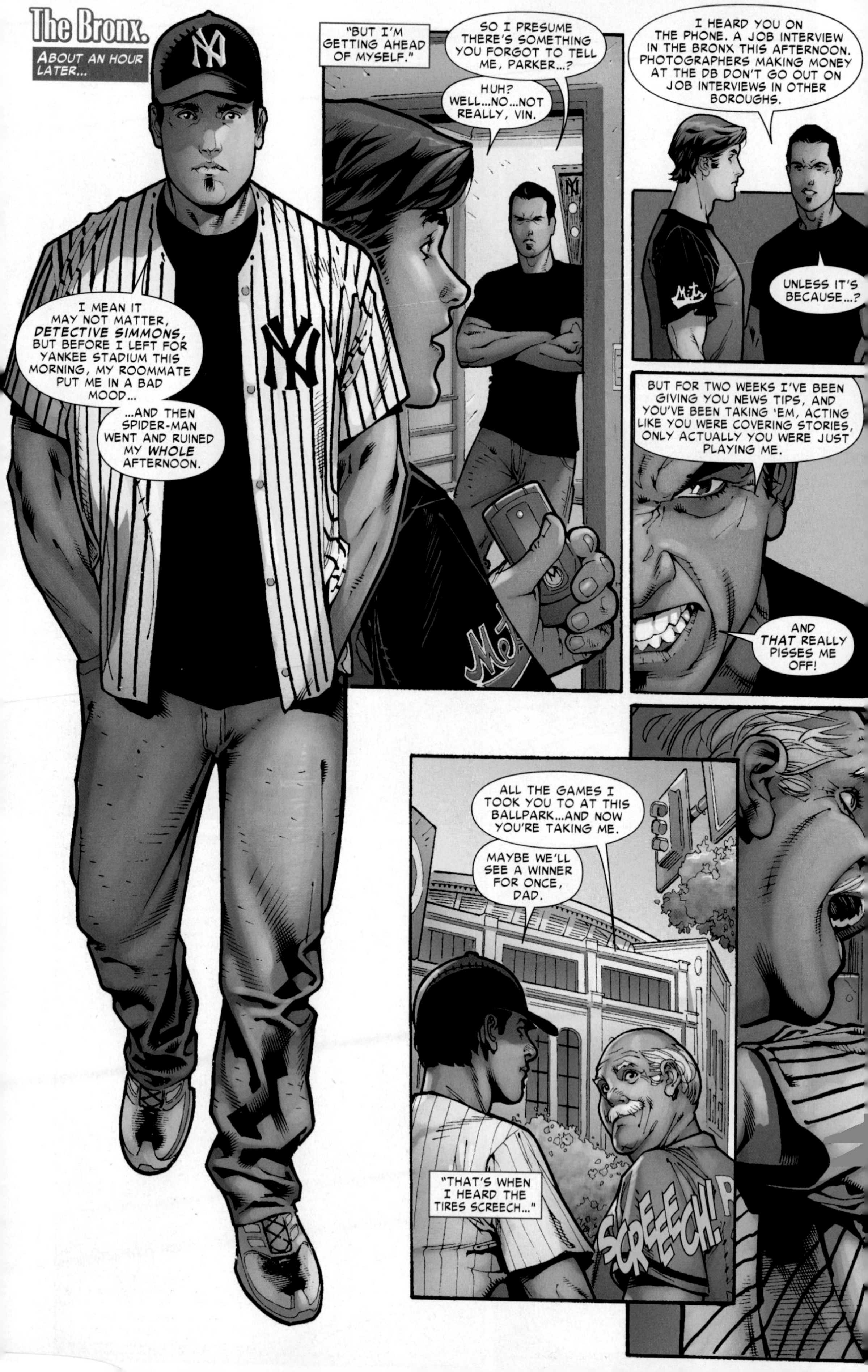
The Bronx.
ABOUT AN HOUR LATER...
I MEAN IT MAY NOT MATTER, DETECTIVE SIMMONS, BUT BEFORE I LEFT FOR YANKEE STADIUM THIS MORNING, MY ROOMMATE PUT ME IN A BAD MOOD...
...AND THEN SPIDER-MAN WENT AND RUINED MY WHOLE AFTERNOON.
"BUT I'M GETTING AHEAD OF MYSELF."
SO I PRESUME THERE'S SOMETHING YOU FORGOT TO TELL ME, PARKER...?
HUH? WELL...NO...NOT REALLY, VIN.
I HEARD YOU ON THE PHONE. A JOB INTERVIEW IN THE BRONX THIS AFTERNOON. PHOTOGRAPHERS MAKING MONEY AT THE DB DON'T GO OUT ON JOB INTERVIEWS IN OTHER BOROUGHS.
UNLESS IT'S BECAUSE...?
BUT FOR TWO WEEKS I'VE BEEN GIVING YOU NEWS TIPS, AND YOU'VE BEEN TAKING 'EM, ACTING LIKE YOU WERE COVERING STORIES, ONLY ACTUALLY YOU WERE JUST PLAYING ME.
AND THAT REALLY PISSES ME OFF!
ALL THE GAMES I TOOK YOU TO AT THIS BALLPARK...AND NOW YOU'RE TAKING ME.
MAYBE WE'LL SEE A WINNER FOR ONCE, DAD.
"THAT'S WHEN I HEARD THE TIRES SCREECH..."
SCREEECH!

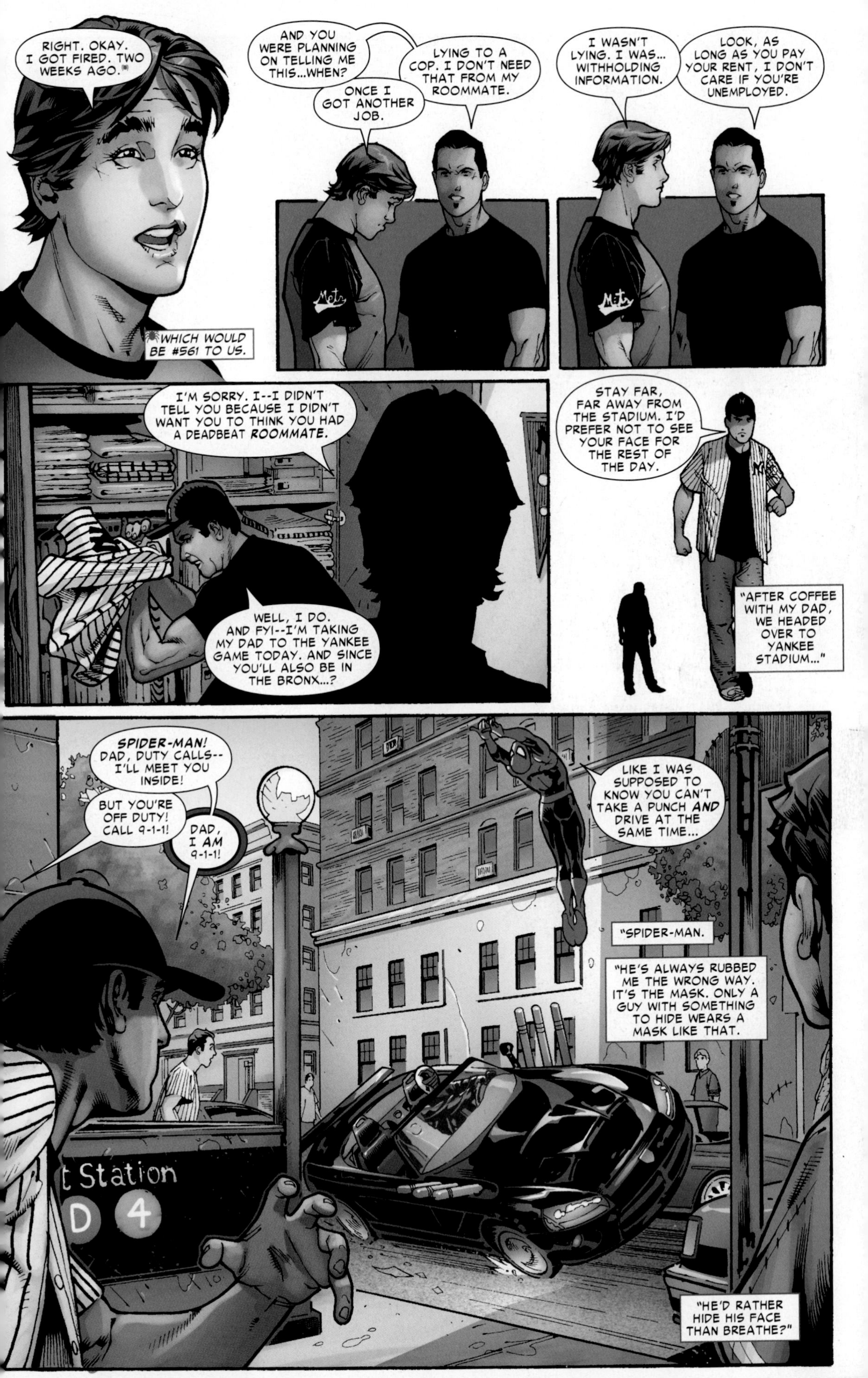
RIGHT. OKAY. I GOT FIRED. TWO WEEKS AGO.*
*WHICH WOULD BE #561 TO US.
AND YOU WERE PLANNING ON TELLING ME THIS...WHEN?
ONCE I GOT ANOTHER JOB.
LYING TO A COP. I DON'T NEED THAT FROM MY ROOMMATE.
I WASN'T LYING. I WAS... WITHHOLDING INFORMATION.
LOOK, AS LONG AS YOU PAY YOUR RENT, I DON'T CARE IF YOU'RE UNEMPLOYED.
I'M SORRY. I--I DIDN'T TELL YOU BECAUSE I DIDN'T WANT YOU TO THINK YOU HAD A DEADBEAT ROOMMATE.
WELL, I DO. AND FYI--I'M TAKING MY DAD TO THE YANKEE GAME TODAY. AND SINCE YOU'LL ALSO BE IN THE BRONX...?
STAY FAR, FAR AWAY FROM THE STADIUM. I'D PREFER NOT TO SEE YOUR FACE FOR THE REST OF THE DAY.
"AFTER COFFEE WITH MY DAD, WE HEADED OVER TO YANKEE STADIUM..."
SPIDER-MAN! DAD, DUTY CALLS-- I'LL MEET YOU INSIDE!
BUT YOU'RE OFF DUTY! CALL 9-1-1!
DAD, I AM 9-1-1!
LIKE I WAS SUPPOSED TO KNOW YOU CAN'T TAKE A PUNCH AND DRIVE AT THE SAME TIME...
"SPIDER-MAN.
"HE'S ALWAYS RUBBED ME THE WRONG WAY. IT'S THE MASK. ONLY A GUY WITH SOMETHING TO HIDE WEARS A MASK LIKE THAT.
"HE'D RATHER HIDE HIS FACE THAN BREATHE?"
t Station
D
4

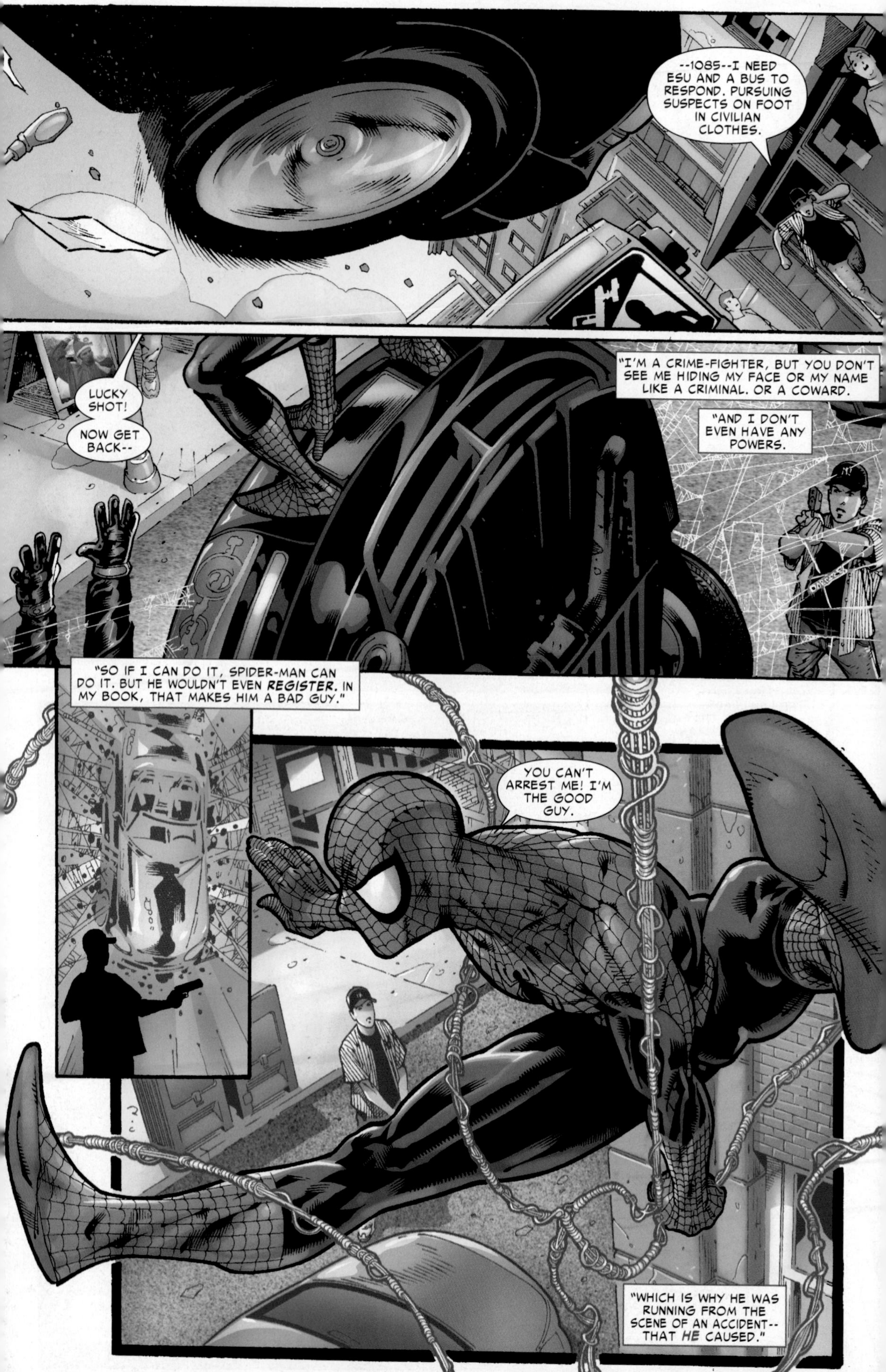
--1085--I NEED ESU AND A BUS TO RESPOND. PURSUING SUSPECTS ON FOOT IN CIVILIAN CLOTHES.
LUCKY SHOT!
NOW GET BACK--
"I'M A CRIME-FIGHTER, BUT YOU DON'T SEE ME HIDING MY FACE OR MY NAME LIKE A CRIMINAL. OR A COWARD.
"AND I DON'T EVEN HAVE ANY POWERS.
"SO IF I CAN DO IT, SPIDER-MAN CAN DO IT. BUT HE WOULDN'T EVEN REGISTER. IN MY BOOK, THAT MAKES HIM A BAD GUY."
YOU CAN'T ARREST ME! I'M THE GOOD GUY.
"WHICH IS WHY HE WAS RUNNING FROM THE SCENE OF AN ACCIDENT--THAT HE CAUSED."

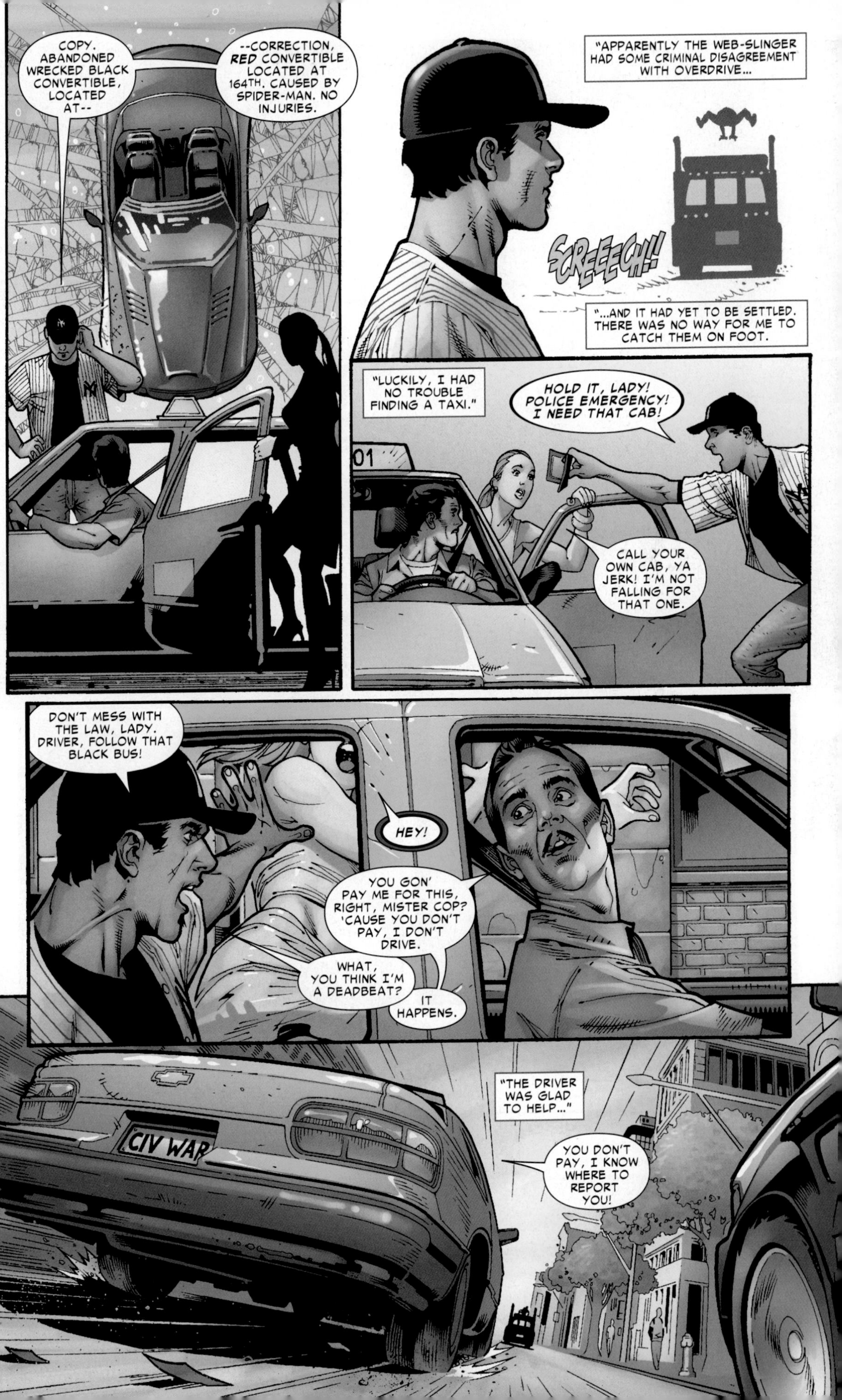
COPY. ABANDONED WRECKED BLACK CONVERTIBLE, LOCATED AT--
--CORRECTION, RED CONVERTIBLE LOCATED AT 164TH. CAUSED BY SPIDER-MAN. NO INJURIES.
"APPARENTLY THE WEB-SLINGER HAD SOME CRIMINAL DISAGREEMENT WITH OVERDRIVE...
SCREEECH!!
"...AND IT HAD YET TO BE SETTLED. THERE WAS NO WAY FOR ME TO CATCH THEM ON FOOT.
"LUCKILY, I HAD NO TROUBLE FINDING A TAXI."
HOLD IT, LADY! POLICE EMERGENCY! I NEED THAT CAB!
CALL YOUR OWN CAB, YA JERK! I'M NOT FALLING FOR THAT ONE.
DON'T MESS WITH THE LAW, LADY. DRIVER, FOLLOW THAT BLACK BUS!
HEY!
YOU GON' PAY ME FOR THIS, RIGHT, MISTER COP? 'CAUSE YOU DON'T PAY, I DON'T DRIVE.
WHAT, YOU THINK I'M A DEADBEAT?
IT HAPPENS.
"THE DRIVER WAS GLAD TO HELP..."
YOU DON'T PAY, I KNOW WHERE TO REPORT YOU!
CIV WAR

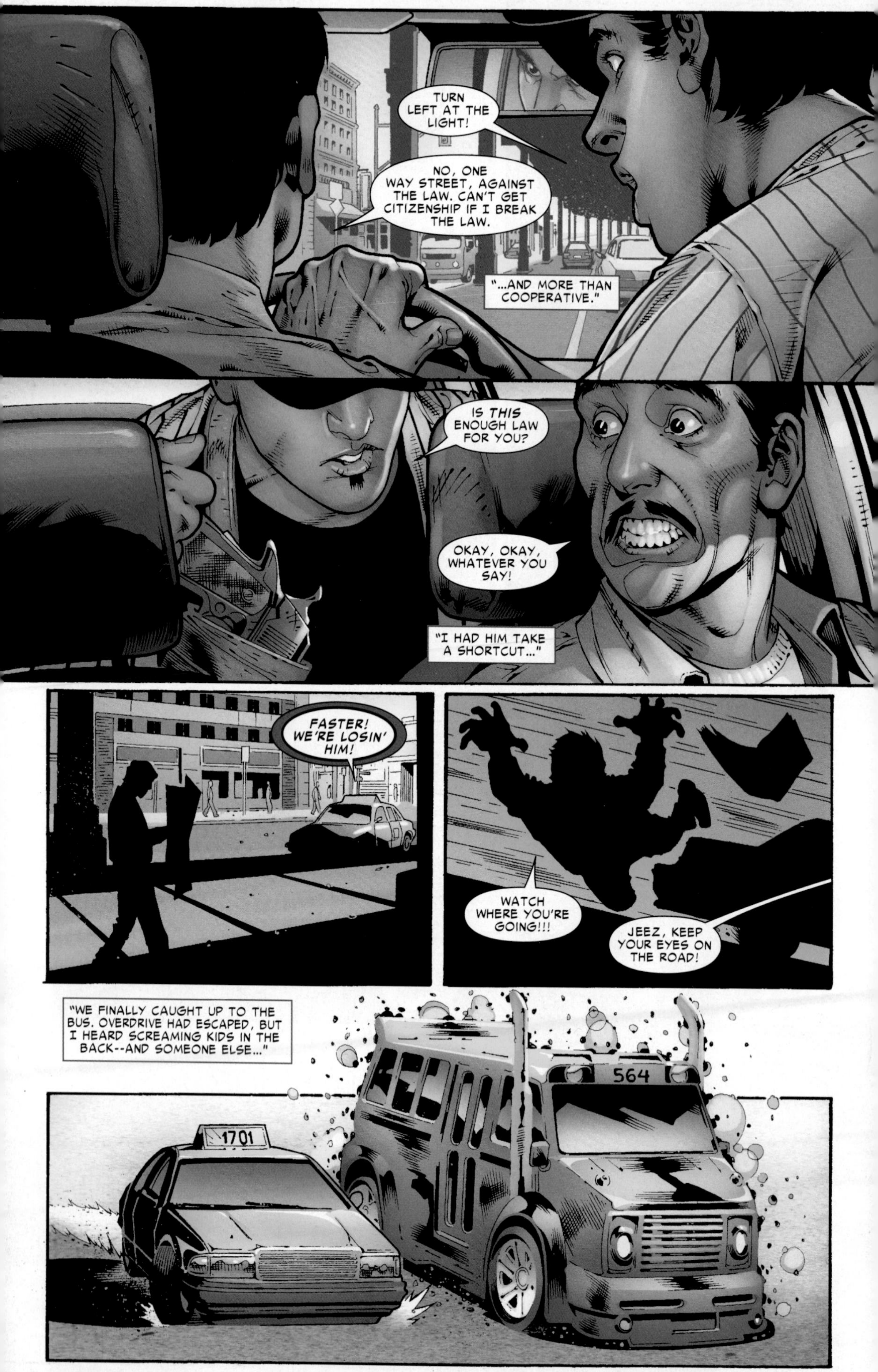
TURN LEFT AT THE LIGHT!
NO, ONE WAY STREET, AGAINST THE LAW. CAN'T GET CITIZENSHIP IF I BREAK THE LAW.
"...AND MORE THAN COOPERATIVE."
IS THIS ENOUGH LAW FOR YOU?
OKAY, OKAY, WHATEVER YOU SAY!
"I HAD HIM TAKE A SHORTCUT..."
FASTER! WE'RE LOSIN' HIM!
WATCH WHERE YOU'RE GOING!!!
JEEZ, KEEP YOUR EYES ON THE ROAD!
"WE FINALLY CAUGHT UP TO THE BUS. OVERDRIVE HAD ESCAPED, BUT I HEARD SCREAMING KIDS IN THE BACK--AND SOMEONE ELSE..."
564
1701

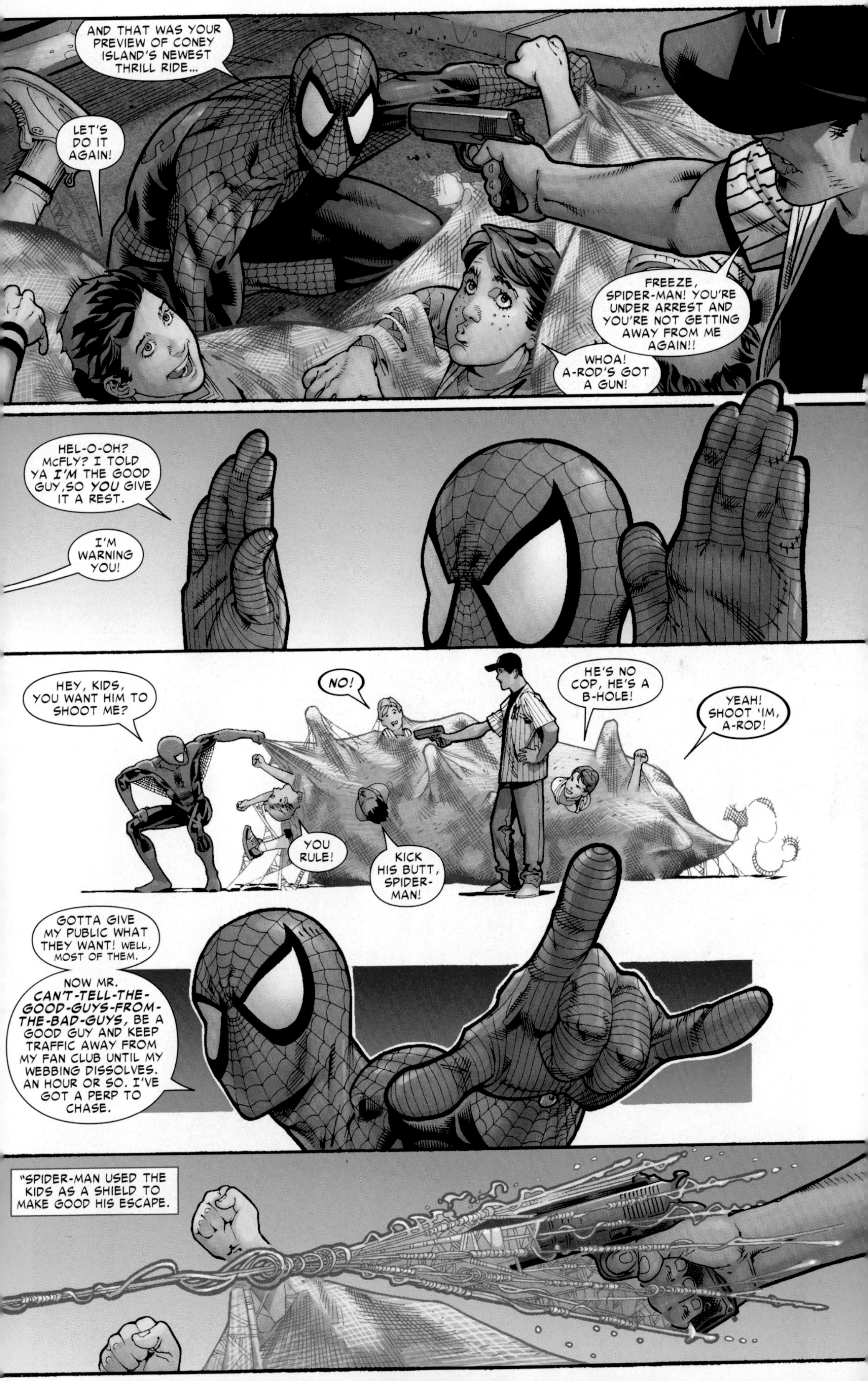
AND THAT WAS YOUR PREVIEW OF CONEY ISLAND'S NEWEST THRILL RIDE...
LET'S DO IT AGAIN!
FREEZE, SPIDER-MAN! YOU'RE UNDER ARREST AND YOU'RE NOT GETTING AWAY FROM ME AGAIN!!
WHOA! A-ROD'S GOT A GUN!
HEL-O-OH? McFLY? I TOLD YA I'M THE GOOD GUY, SO YOU GIVE IT A REST.
I'M WARNING YOU!
HEY, KIDS, YOU WANT HIM TO SHOOT ME?
NO!
HE'S NO COP, HE'S A B-HOLE!
YEAH! SHOOT 'IM, A-ROD!
YOU RULE!
KICK HIS BUTT, SPIDER-MAN!
GOTTA GIVE MY PUBLIC WHAT THEY WANT! WELL, MOST OF THEM.
NOW MR. CAN'T-TELL-THE-GOOD-GUYS-FROM-THE-BAD-GUYS, BE A GOOD GUY AND KEEP TRAFFIC AWAY FROM MY FAN CLUB UNTIL MY WEBBING DISSOLVES. AN HOUR OR SO. I'VE GOT A PERP TO CHASE.
"SPIDER-MAN USED THE KIDS AS A SHIELD TO MAKE GOOD HIS ESCAPE.

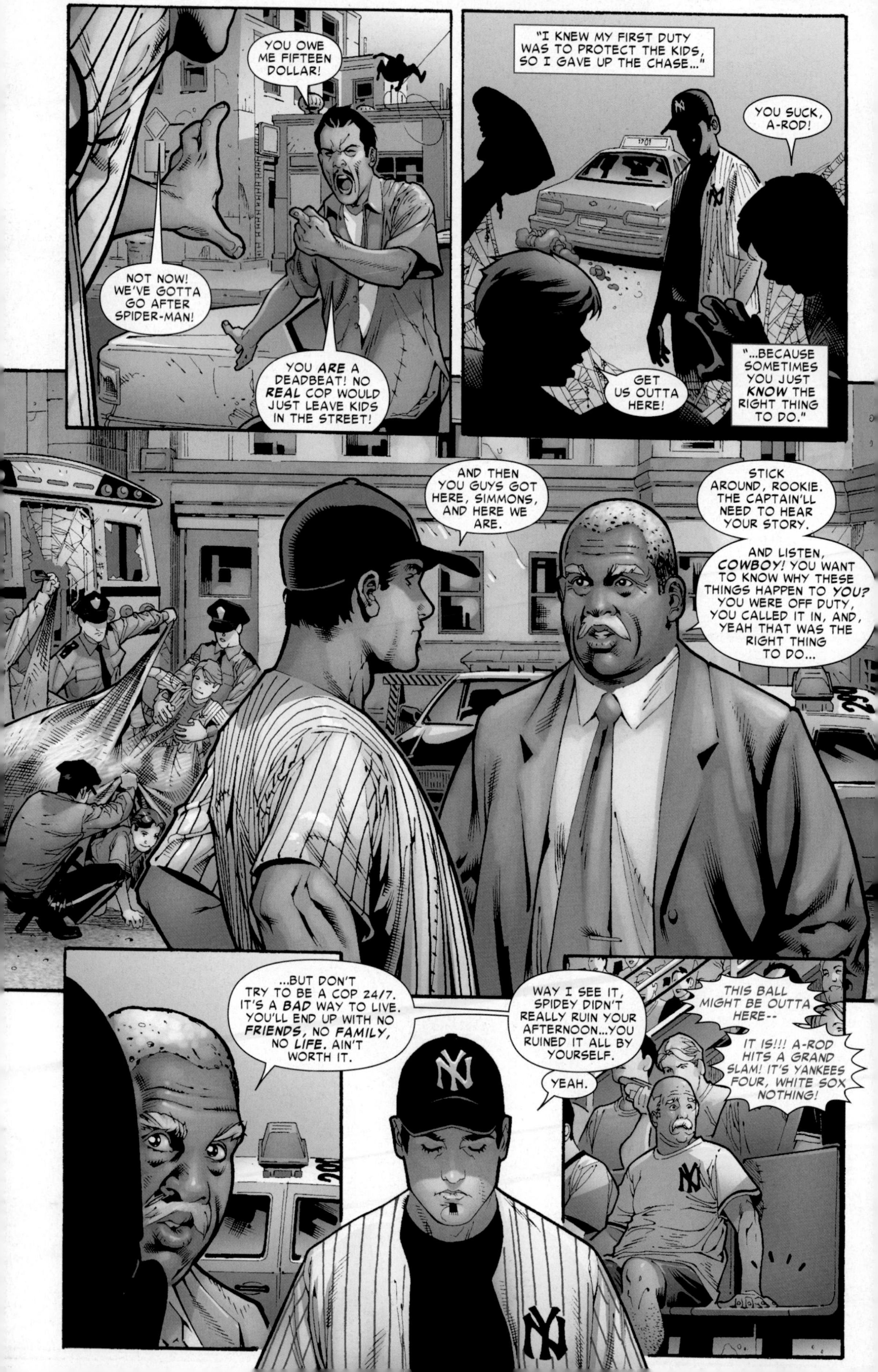
YOU OWE ME FIFTEEN DOLLAR!
NOT NOW! WE'VE GOTTA GO AFTER SPIDER-MAN!
YOU ARE A DEADBEAT! NO REAL COP WOULD JUST LEAVE KIDS IN THE STREET!
"I KNEW MY FIRST DUTY WAS TO PROTECT THE KIDS, SO I GAVE UP THE CHASE..."
YOU SUCK, A-ROD!
GET US OUTTA HERE!
"...BECAUSE SOMETIMES YOU JUST KNOW THE RIGHT THING TO DO."
AND THEN YOU GUYS GOT HERE, SIMMONS, AND HERE WE ARE.
STICK AROUND, ROOKIE. THE CAPTAIN'LL NEED TO HEAR YOUR STORY.
AND LISTEN, COWBOY! YOU WANT TO KNOW WHY THESE THINGS HAPPEN TO YOU? YOU WERE OFF DUTY, YOU CALLED IT IN, AND, YEAH THAT WAS THE RIGHT THING TO DO...
...BUT DON'T TRY TO BE A COP 24/7. IT'S A BAD WAY TO LIVE. YOU'LL END UP WITH NO FRIENDS, NO FAMILY, NO LIFE. AIN'T WORTH IT.
WAY I SEE IT, SPIDEY DIDN'T REALLY RUIN YOUR AFTERNOON...YOU RUINED IT ALL BY YOURSELF.
YEAH.
THIS BALL MIGHT BE OUTTA HERE--
IT IS!!! A-ROD HITS A GRAND SLAM! IT'S YANKEES FOUR, WHITE SOX NOTHING!

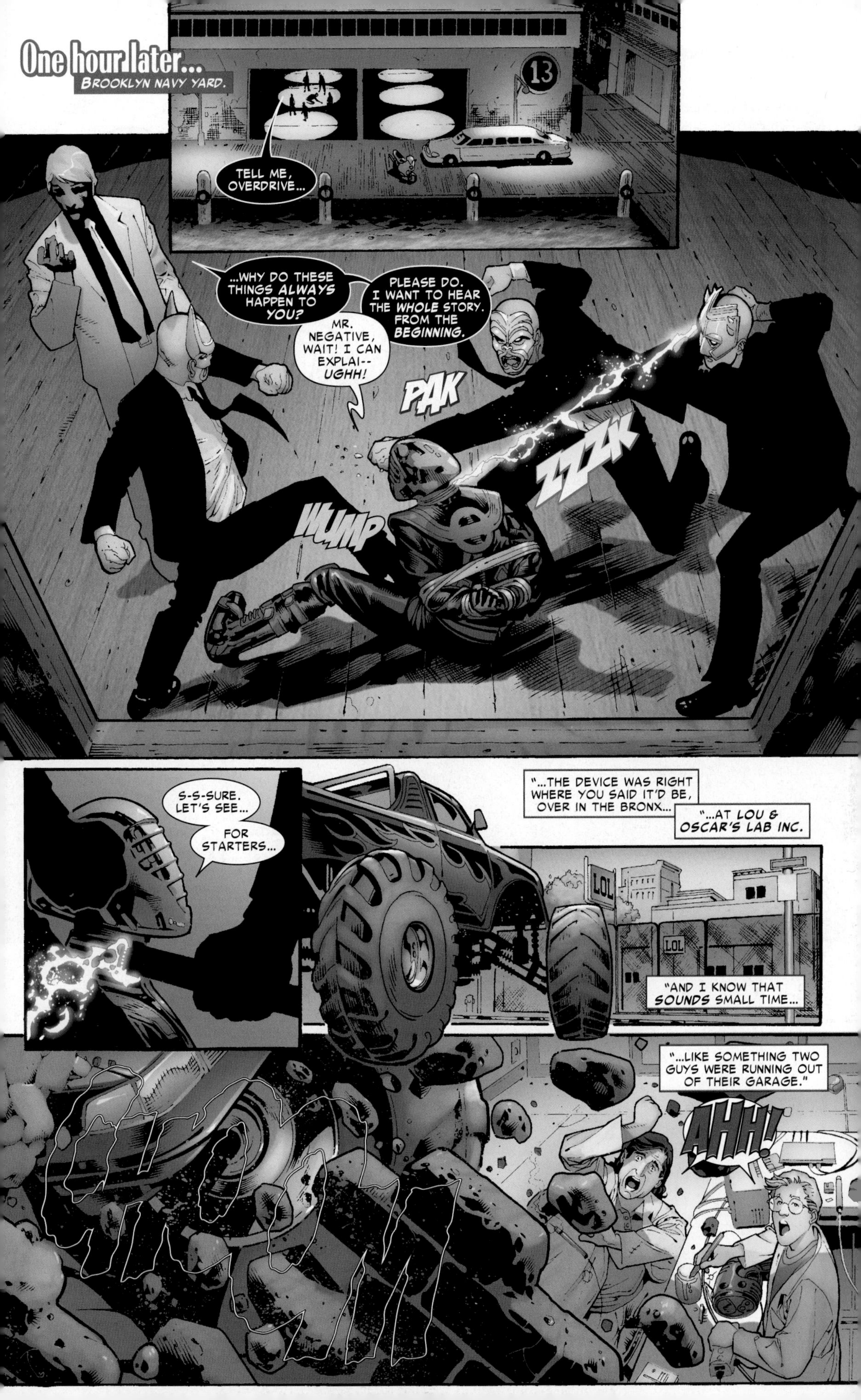
One hour later...
BROOKLYN NAVY YARD.
13
TELL ME, OVERDRIVE...
...WHY DO THESE THINGS ALWAYS HAPPEN TO YOU?
PLEASE DO. I WANT TO HEAR THE WHOLE STORY. FROM THE BEGINNING.
MR. NEGATIVE, WAIT! I CAN EXPLAI-- UGHH!
PAK
ZZZK
WUMP
S-S-SURE. LET'S SEE...
FOR STARTERS...
"...THE DEVICE WAS RIGHT WHERE YOU SAID IT'D BE, OVER IN THE BRONX...
"...AT LOU & OSCAR'S LAB INC.
LOL
LOL
"AND I KNOW THAT SOUNDS SMALL TIME...
"...LIKE SOMETHING TWO GUYS WERE RUNNING OUT OF THEIR GARAGE."
AHH!

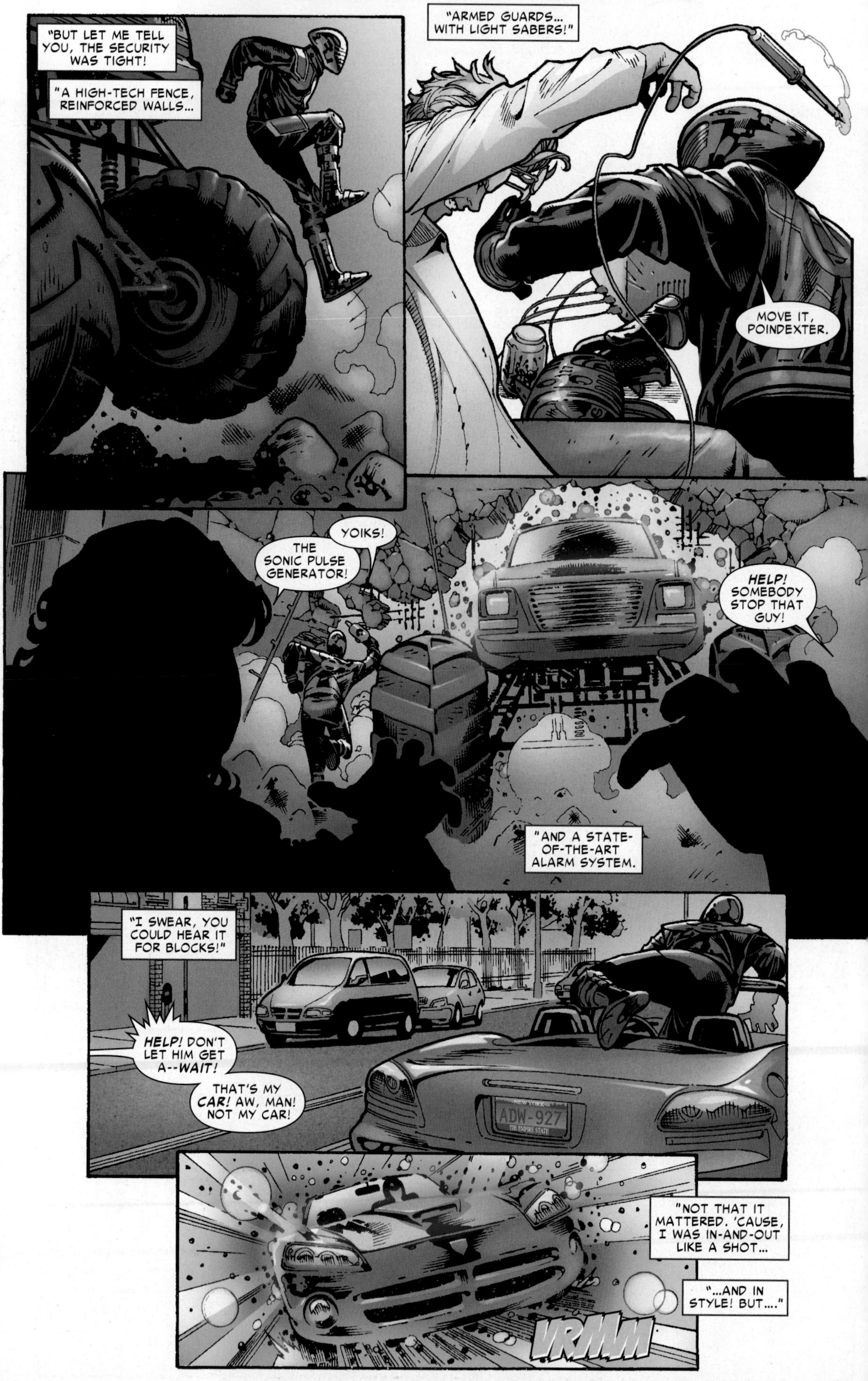
"BUT LET ME TELL YOU, THE SECURITY WAS TIGHT!
"A HIGH-TECH FENCE, REINFORCED WALLS...
"ARMED GUARDS... WITH LIGHT SABERS!"
MOVE IT, POINDEXTER.
THE SONIC PULSE GENERATOR!
YOIKS!
HELP! SOMEBODY STOP THAT GUY!
"AND A STATE-OF-THE-ART ALARM SYSTEM.
"I SWEAR, YOU COULD HEAR IT FOR BLOCKS!"
HELP! DON'T LET HIM GET A--WAIT!
THAT'S MY CAR! AW, MAN! NOT MY CAR!
NEW YORK
ADW-927
THE EMPIRE STATE
"NOT THAT IT MATTERED. 'CAUSE, I WAS IN-AND-OUT LIKE A SHOT...
"...AND IN STYLE! BUT...."
VRMM

BUT WHAT? PLEASE, GO ON. I'M HANGING ON YOUR *EVERY* WORD.

AS IF IT WERE A MATTER OF LIFE OR *DEATH.*

UM...THAT'S WHEN SPIDER-MAN SHOWED UP.

WHICH, I WON'T LIE TO YOU, WAS *AWESOME!* I MEAN, C'MON, THAT IS *SO COOL!*

"AH. I THINK I SEE WHERE THIS IS GOING."

POW

"NO. NO. NO. I GAVE AS GOOD AS I GOT. BETTER, IN FACT..."

"BUT THE PRIZE? WHAT OF THE *SONIC PULSE GENERATOR?!*"

"OH, THAT THING? LET'S JUST SAY...

"...I LET SPIDEY *HAVE* IT!"

BWOOM

"I MEAN, I *REALLY* LET SPIDEY HAVE IT!"

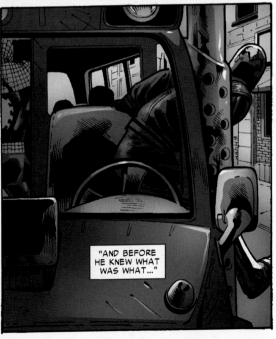

"AND BEFORE HE KNEW WHAT WAS WHAT..."

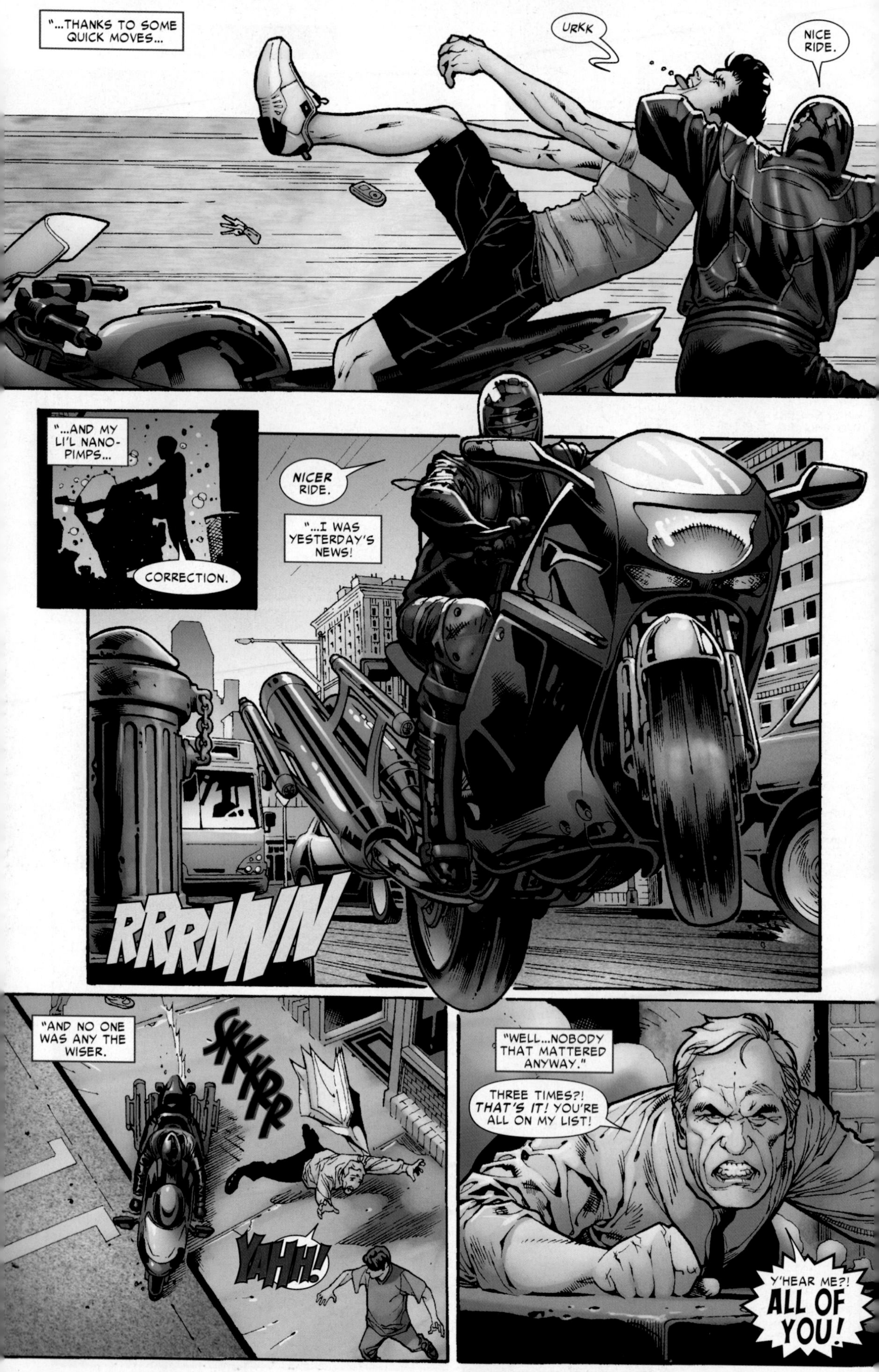
"...THANKS TO SOME QUICK MOVES...
URKK
NICE RIDE.
"...AND MY LI'L NANO-PIMPS...
CORRECTION.
NICER RIDE.
"...I WAS YESTERDAY'S NEWS!
RRRMNN
"AND NO ONE WAS ANY THE WISER.
SKKKRR
YAHH!
"WELL...NOBODY THAT MATTERED ANYWAY."
THREE TIMES?! THAT'S IT! YOU'RE ALL ON MY LIST!
Y'HEAR ME?! ALL OF YOU!

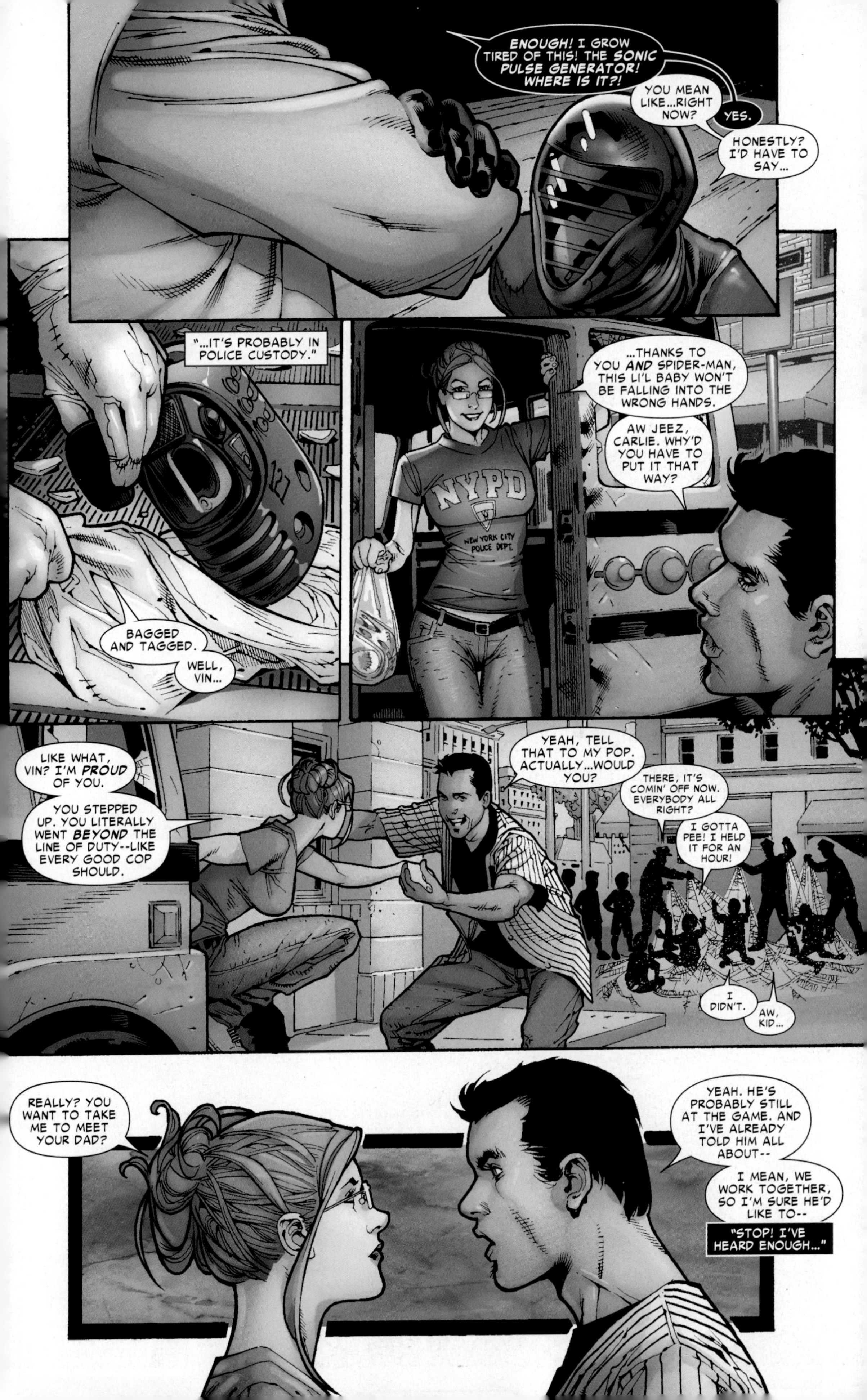
ENOUGH! I GROW TIRED OF THIS! THE SONIC PULSE GENERATOR! WHERE IS IT?!
YOU MEAN LIKE...RIGHT NOW?
YES.
HONESTLY? I'D HAVE TO SAY...
"...IT'S PROBABLY IN POLICE CUSTODY."
BAGGED AND TAGGED.
WELL, VIN...
...THANKS TO YOU AND SPIDER-MAN, THIS LI'L BABY WON'T BE FALLING INTO THE WRONG HANDS.
AW JEEZ, CARLIE. WHY'D YOU HAVE TO PUT IT THAT WAY?
NYPD
NEW YORK CITY POLICE DEPT.
LIKE WHAT, VIN? I'M PROUD OF YOU.
YOU STEPPED UP. YOU LITERALLY WENT BEYOND THE LINE OF DUTY--LIKE EVERY GOOD COP SHOULD.
YEAH, TELL THAT TO MY POP. ACTUALLY...WOULD YOU?
THERE, IT'S COMIN' OFF NOW. EVERYBODY ALL RIGHT?
I GOTTA PEE! I HELD IT FOR AN HOUR!
I DIDN'T.
AW, KID...
REALLY? YOU WANT TO TAKE ME TO MEET YOUR DAD?
YEAH. HE'S PROBABLY STILL AT THE GAME. AND I'VE ALREADY TOLD HIM ALL ABOUT--
I MEAN, WE WORK TOGETHER, SO I'M SURE HE'D LIKE TO--
"STOP! I'VE HEARD ENOUGH..."

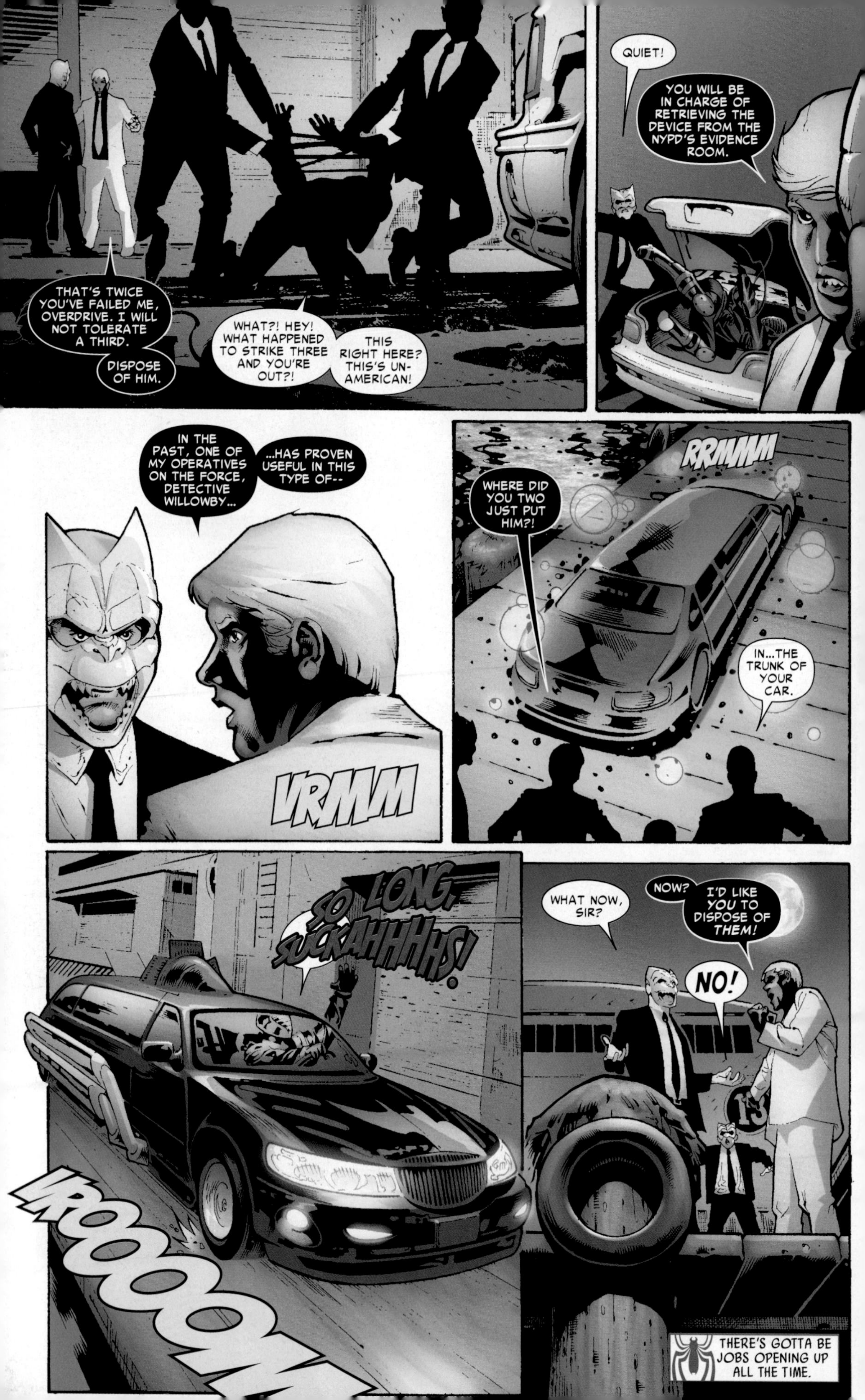
THAT'S TWICE YOU'VE FAILED ME, OVERDRIVE. I WILL NOT TOLERATE A THIRD.
DISPOSE OF HIM.
WHAT?! HEY! WHAT HAPPENED TO STRIKE THREE AND YOU'RE OUT?!
THIS RIGHT HERE? THIS'S UN-AMERICAN!
QUIET!
YOU WILL BE IN CHARGE OF RETRIEVING THE DEVICE FROM THE NYPD'S EVIDENCE ROOM.
IN THE PAST, ONE OF MY OPERATIVES ON THE FORCE, DETECTIVE WILLOWBY...
...HAS PROVEN USEFUL IN THIS TYPE OF--
VRMM
RRMMM
WHERE DID YOU TWO JUST PUT HIM?!
IN...THE TRUNK OF YOUR CAR.
SO LONG, SUCKAHHHHS!
VROOOOOM
WHAT NOW, SIR?
NOW?
I'D LIKE *YOU* TO DISPOSE OF *THEM!*
NO!
THERE'S GOTTA BE JOBS OPENING UP ALL THE TIME.

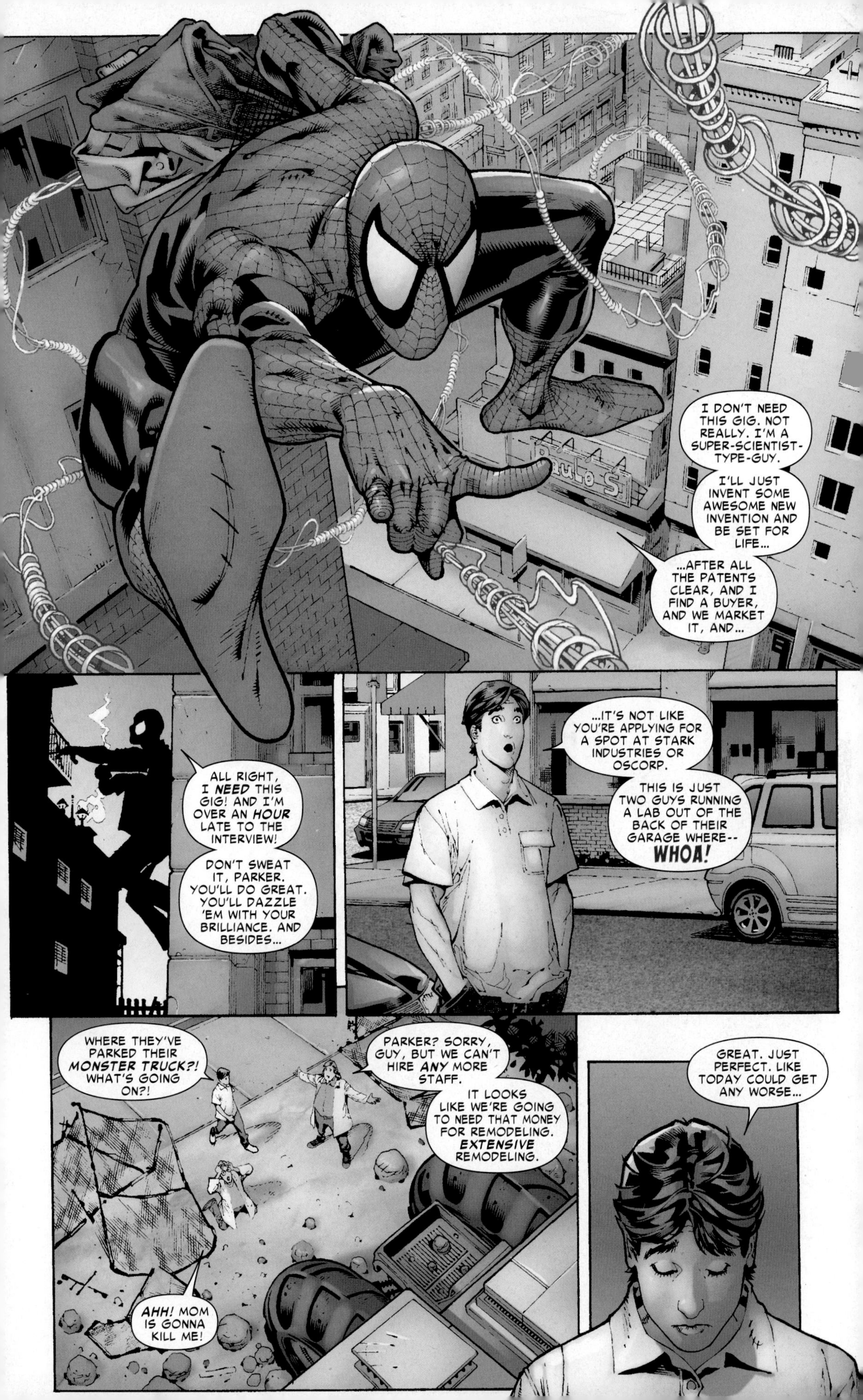
I DON'T NEED THIS GIG. NOT REALLY. I'M A SUPER-SCIENTIST-TYPE-GUY.
I'LL JUST INVENT SOME AWESOME NEW INVENTION AND BE SET FOR LIFE...
...AFTER ALL THE PATENTS CLEAR, AND I FIND A BUYER, AND WE MARKET IT, AND...
ALL RIGHT, I NEED THIS GIG! AND I'M OVER AN HOUR LATE TO THE INTERVIEW!
DON'T SWEAT IT, PARKER. YOU'LL DO GREAT. YOU'LL DAZZLE 'EM WITH YOUR BRILLIANCE. AND BESIDES...
...IT'S NOT LIKE YOU'RE APPLYING FOR A SPOT AT STARK INDUSTRIES OR OSCORP.
THIS IS JUST TWO GUYS RUNNING A LAB OUT OF THE BACK OF THEIR GARAGE WHERE-- WHOA!
WHERE THEY'VE PARKED THEIR MONSTER TRUCK?! WHAT'S GOING ON?!
PARKER? SORRY, GUY, BUT WE CAN'T HIRE ANY MORE STAFF.
IT LOOKS LIKE WE'RE GOING TO NEED THAT MONEY FOR REMODELING. EXTENSIVE REMODELING.
AHH! MOM IS GONNA KILL ME!
GREAT. JUST PERFECT. LIKE TODAY COULD GET ANY WORSE...

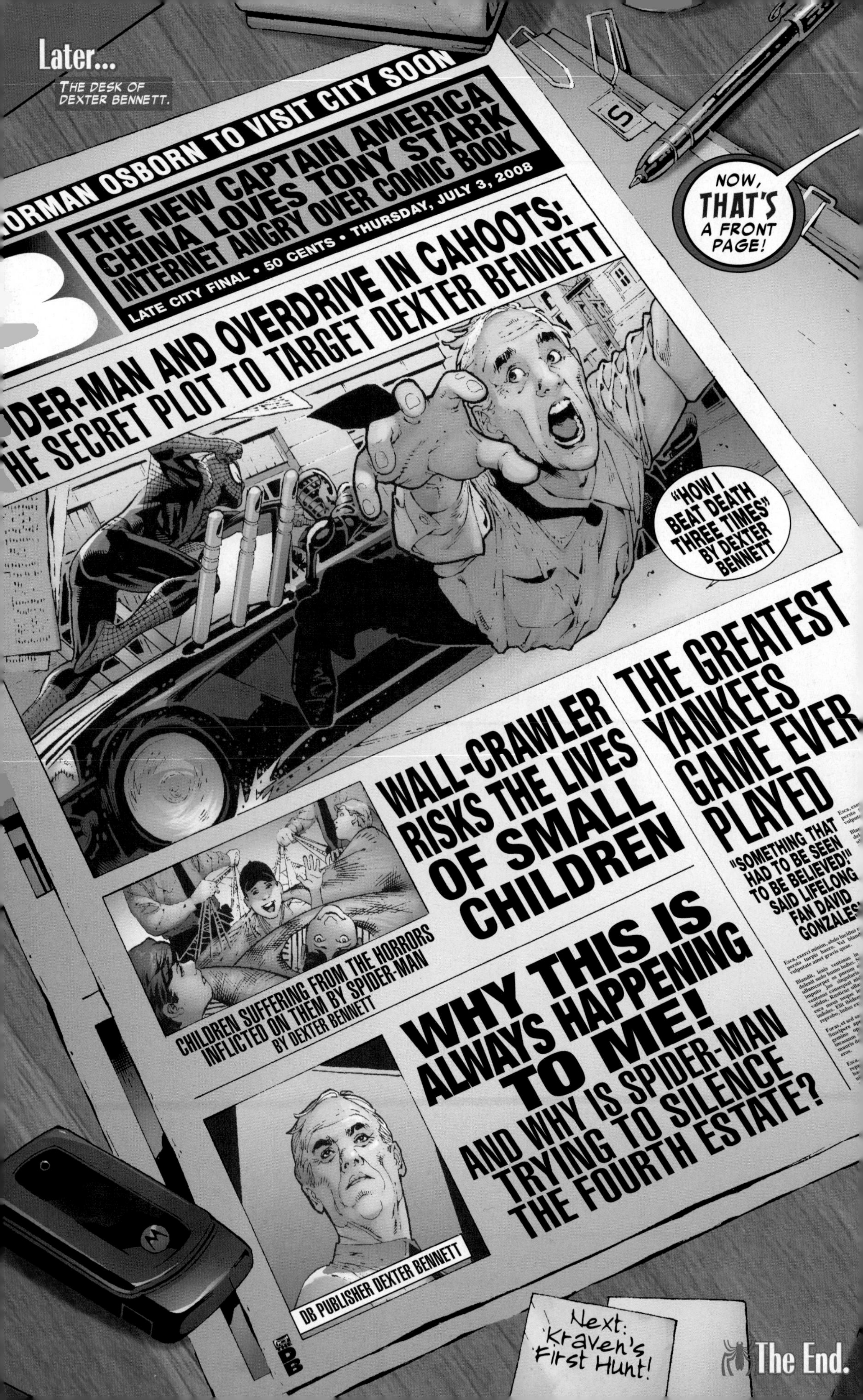
Later...
THE DESK OF DEXTER BENNETT.
NORMAN OSBORN TO VISIT CITY SOON
THE NEW CAPTAIN AMERICA
CHINA LOVES TONY STARK
INTERNET ANGRY OVER COMIC BOOK
LATE CITY FINAL • 50 CENTS • THURSDAY, JULY 3, 2008
SPIDER-MAN AND OVERDRIVE IN CAHOOTS:
THE SECRET PLOT TO TARGET DEXTER BENNETT
"HOW I BEAT DEATH THREE TIMES" BY DEXTER BENNETT
NOW, THAT'S A FRONT PAGE!
WALL-CRAWLER RISKS THE LIVES OF SMALL CHILDREN
THE GREATEST YANKEES GAME EVER PLAYED
"SOMETHING THAT HAD TO BE SEEN TO BE BELIEVED!" SAID LIFELONG FAN DAVID GONZALES
CHILDREN SUFFERING FROM THE HORRORS INFLICTED ON THEM BY SPIDER-MAN
BY DEXTER BENNETT
WHY THIS IS ALWAYS HAPPENING TO ME!
AND WHY IS SPIDER-MAN TRYING TO SILENCE THE FOURTH ESTATE?
DB PUBLISHER DEXTER BENNETT
DB
Next: Kraven's First Hunt!
The End.

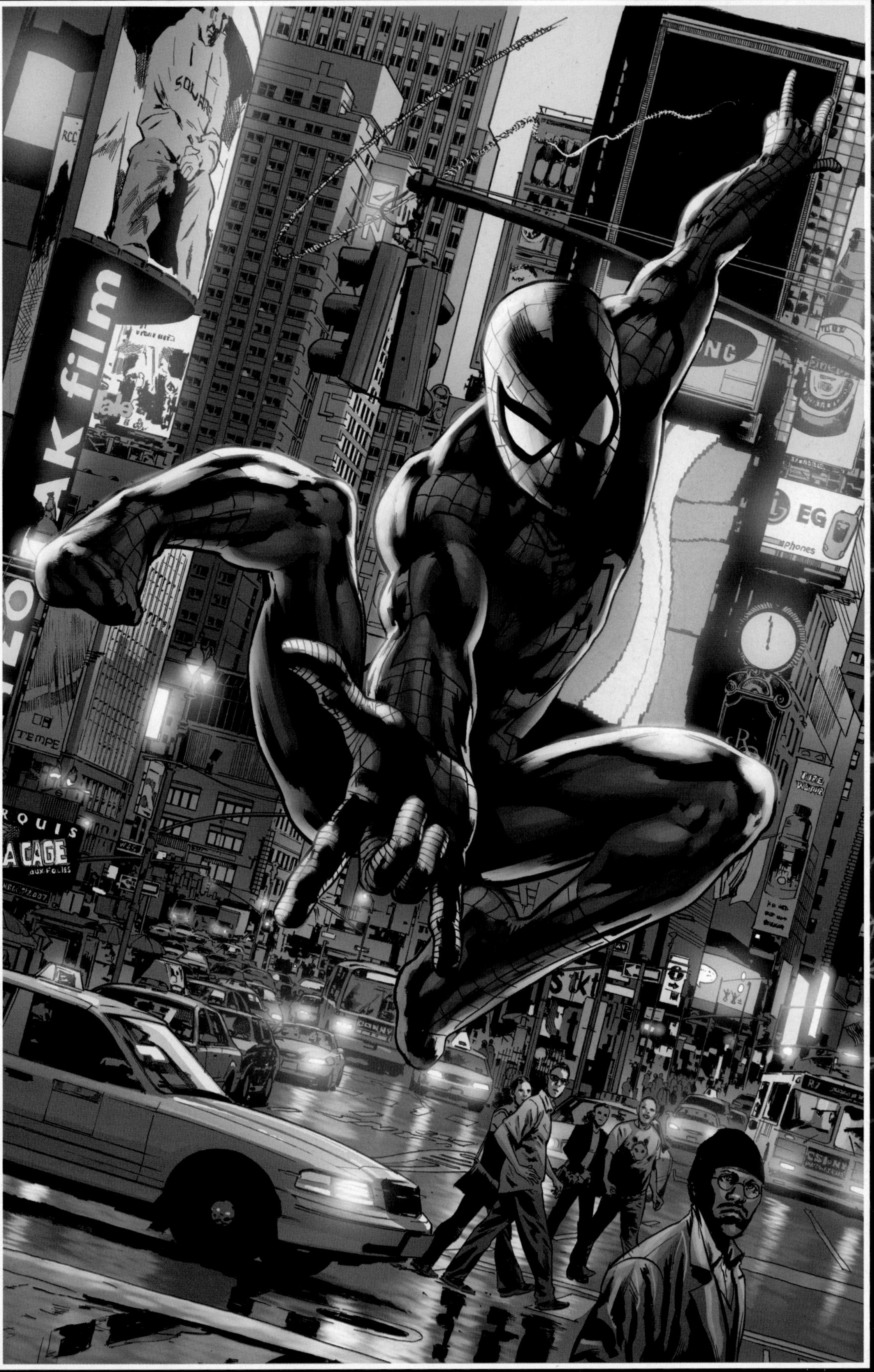
film
A CAGE
NG
EG
phones
TEMPE

AMAZING SPIDER-MAN #546 VARIANT

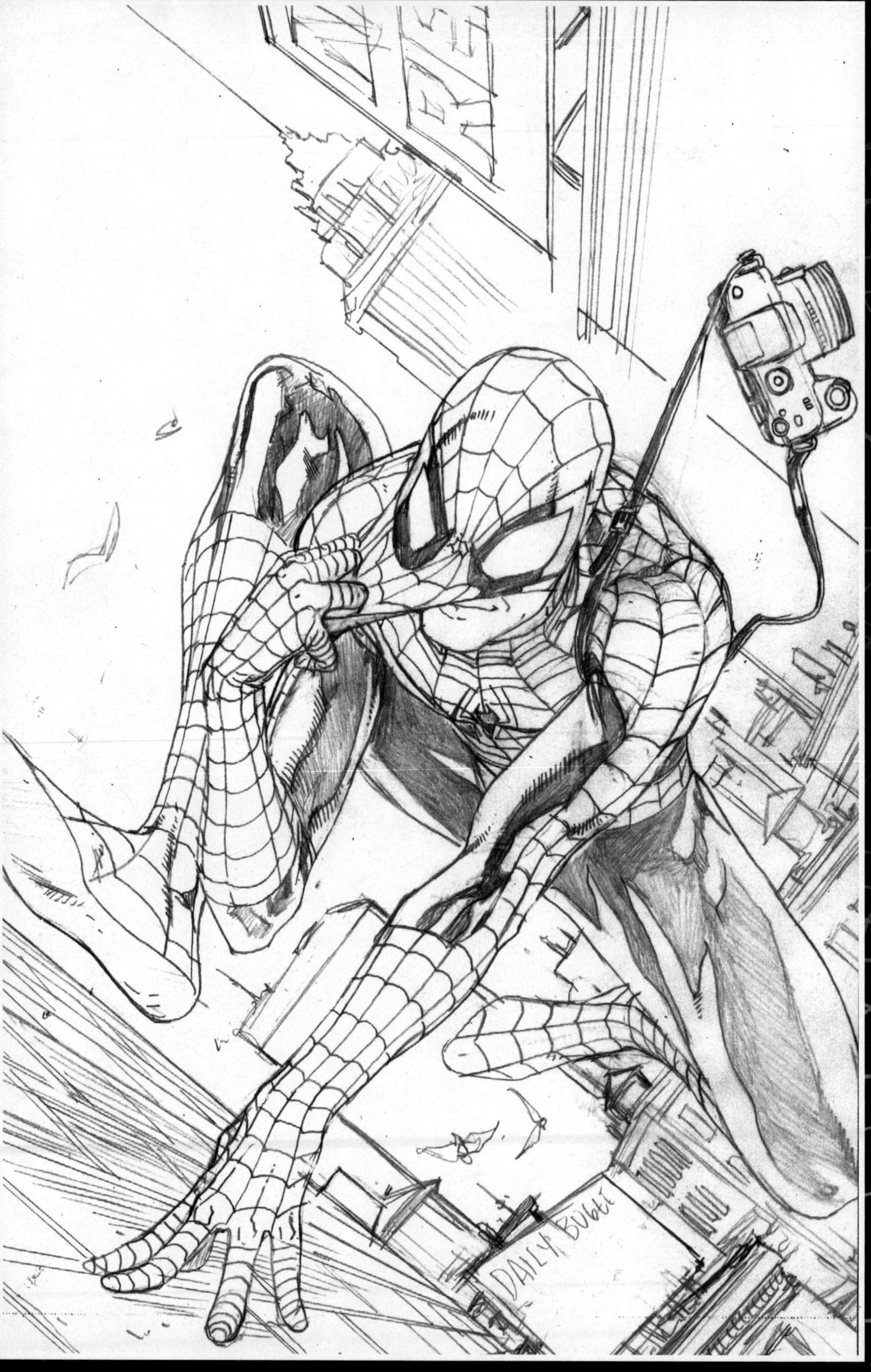

AMAZING SPIDER-MAN #546 SKETCH VARIANT
BY STEVE MCNIVEN

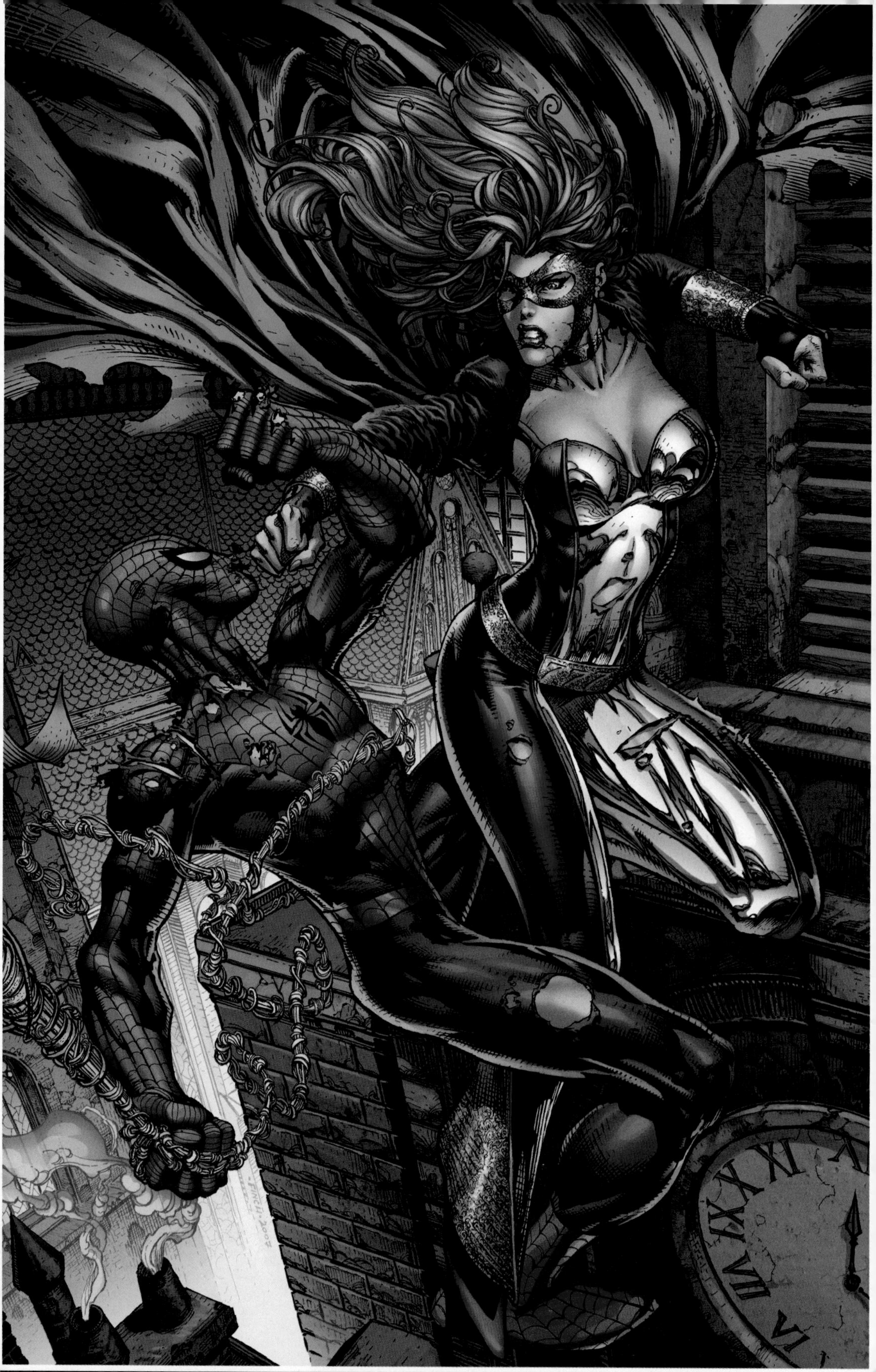

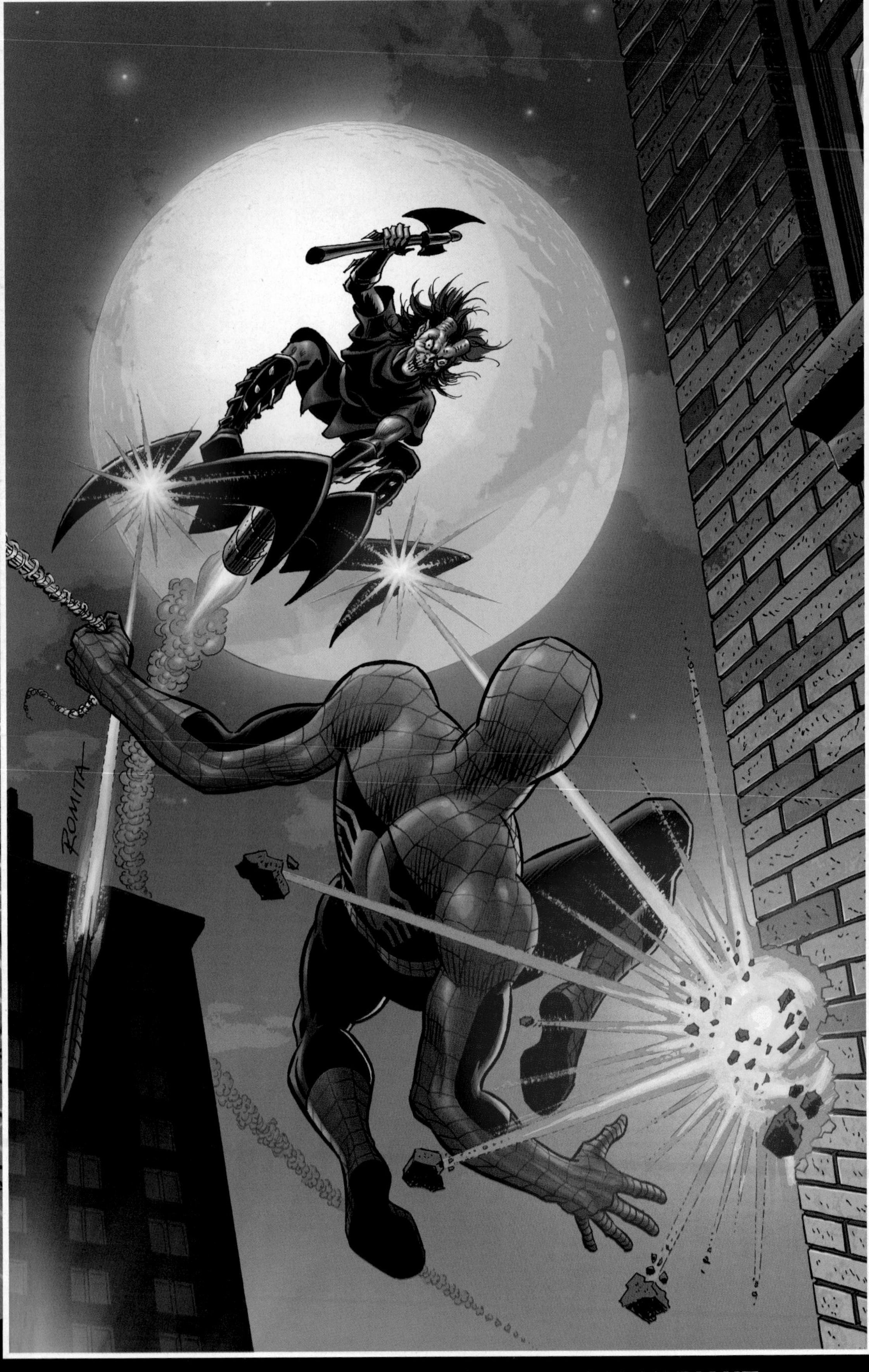
ROMITA

AMAZING SPIDER-MAN #549 DYNAMIC FORCES VARIANT

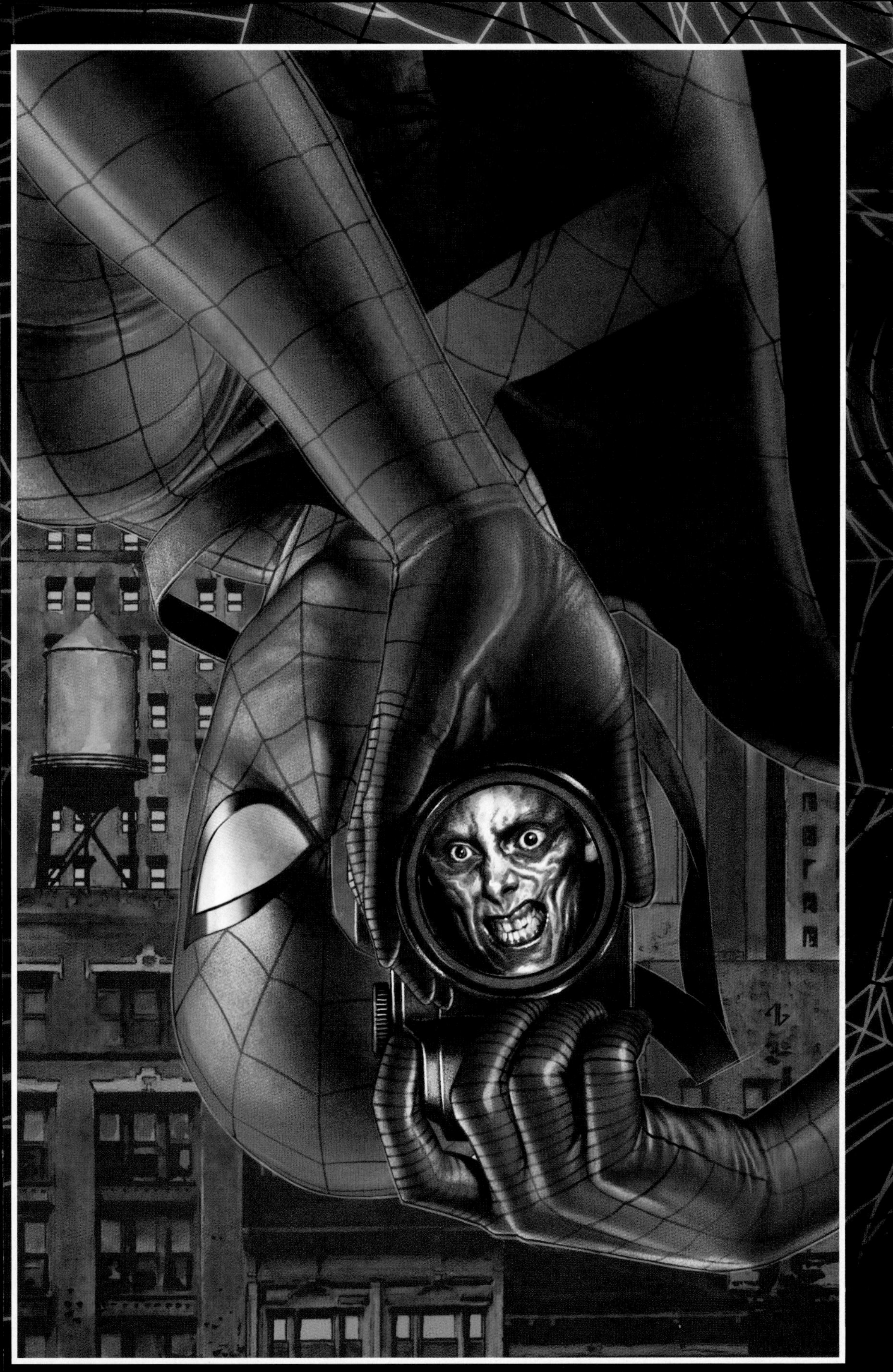

AMAZING SPIDER-MAN #552 VARIANT

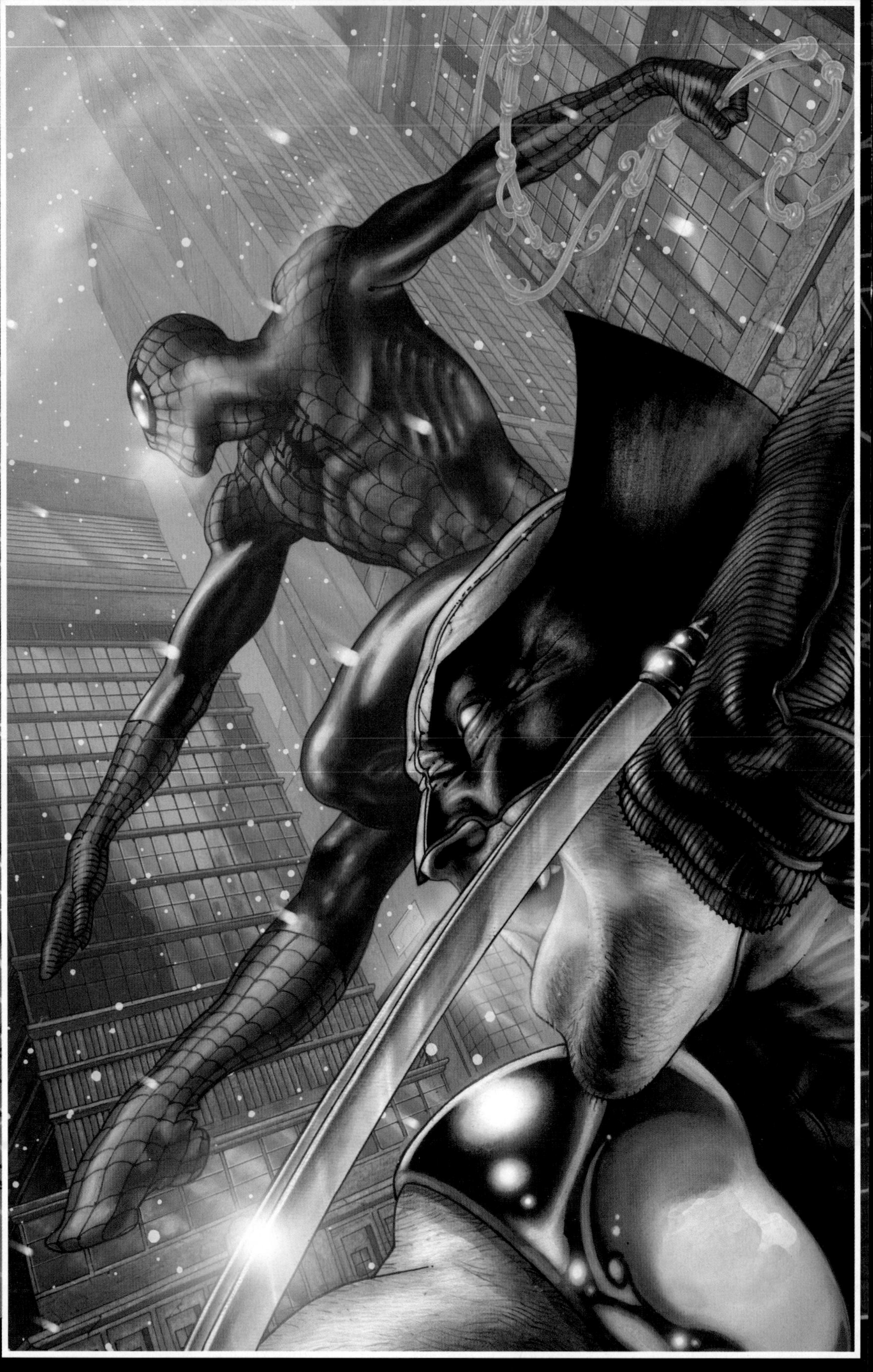

AMAZING SPIDER-MAN #555 VARIANT
BY **SIMONE BIANCHI & SIMONE PERUZZI**

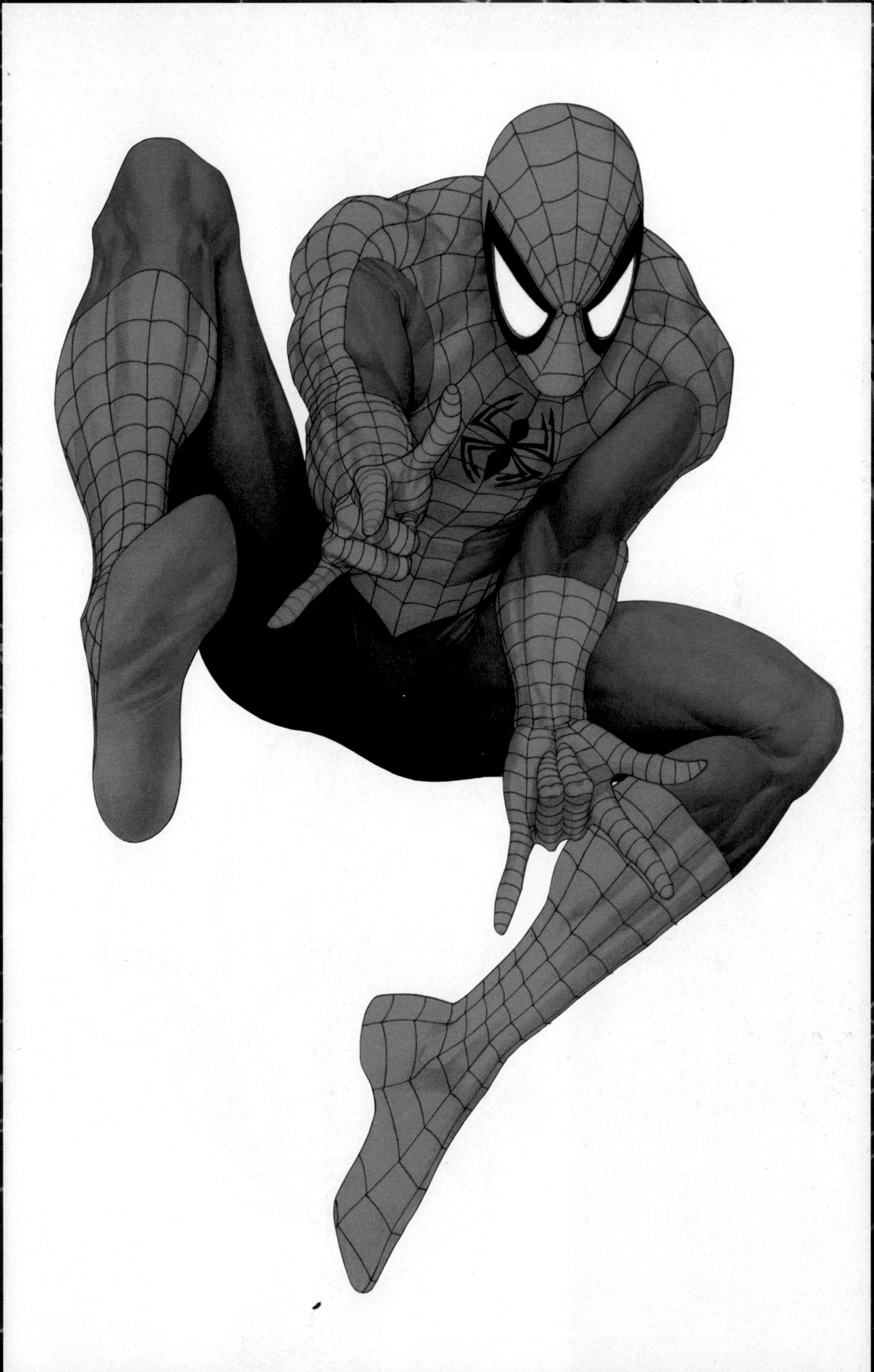

SPIDER-MAN: SWING SHIFT CORNER BOX ART

FREE COMIC BOOK DAY 2007 (SPIDER-MAN) COVER BY PHIL JIMENEZ & ANDY LANNING

FREE COMIC BOOK DAY 2007 (SPIDER-MAN) RECAP ART BY PHIL JIMENEZ & ANDY LANNIN

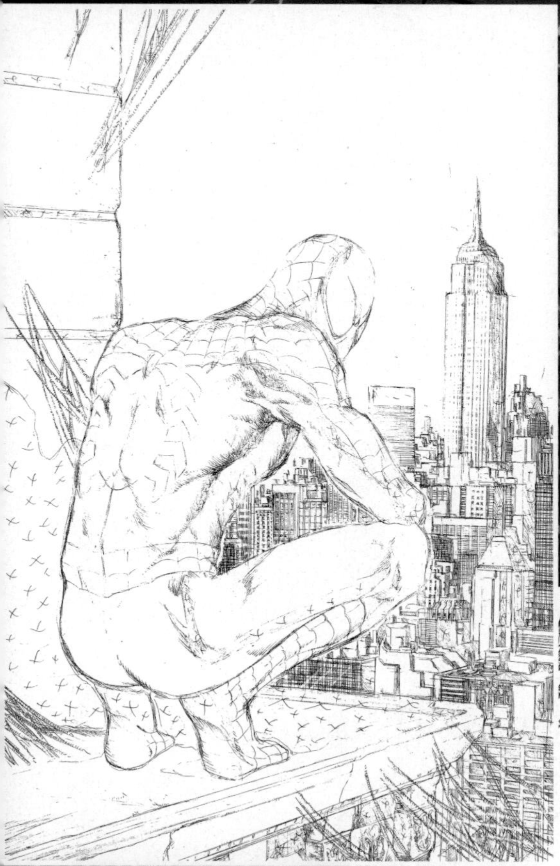

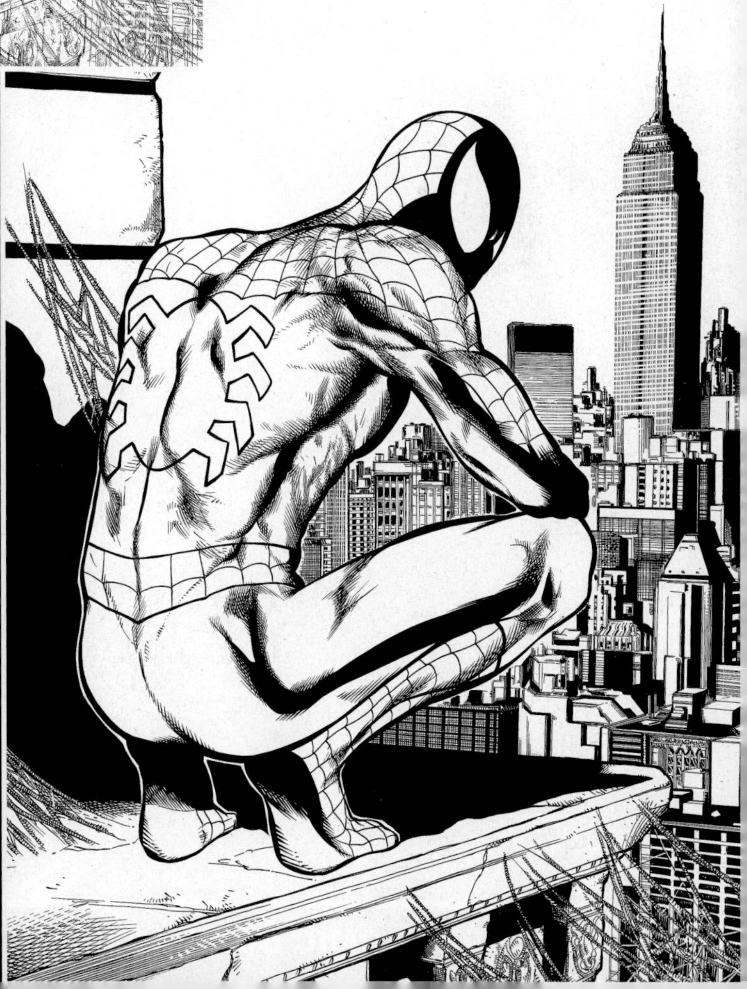

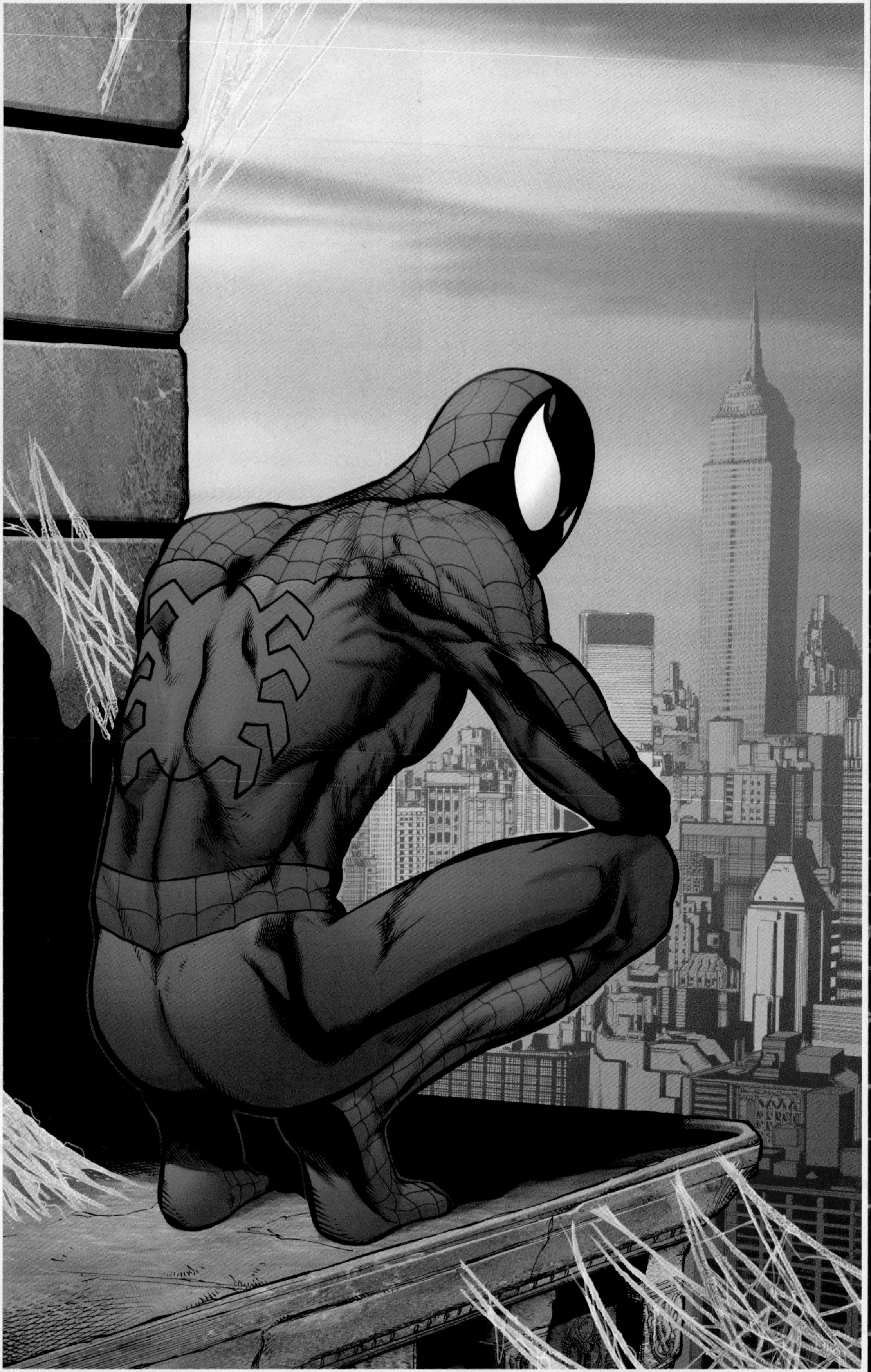

SPIDER-MAN: FREE COMIC BOOK DAY 2007 RECAP ART
BY **PHIL JIMENEZ**

As plans began to develop for the Spider-Man: Brand New Day relaunch, new Executive Editor of Amazing Spider-Man Tom Brevoort wrote the following document. It outlines for his creative and editorial teams his thoughts on what makes Spider-Man so appealing and enduring as a character along with the types of Spider-Man stories Marvel should be telling in a post-"One More Day" universe.

SPIDER-MAN MANIFESTO
by Tom Brevoort — 9/18/06

This'll be my vague attempt to sum up what I think we need to get the SPIDER-MAN books back to, what I think has been missing from the character and his world, and a general set of guidelines for how I'd like to proceed. None of this is intended to be looked upon as hard-and-fast rules, as there can always be exceptions. But this is where my mind is at right now.

SPIDER-MAN IS ABOUT PETER PARKER

This is the biggest and most basic concept that's kind of escaped us in the Spidey titles for the last decade or two. Peter Parker is Spider-Man, Spider-Man is not Peter Parker. By that I mean that it's Peter and his life and tribulations that's the through-line of the SPIDER-MAN titles, or should be, and Peter being Spider-Man is just one component part of the overall whole. But in the last few years, it's seemed like Pete is Spider-Man, first and foremost, and he kinda half-squeezes in a life around being Spidey — and that's wrong.

What made SPIDER-MAN the flagship of the Marvel line was the soap opera aspect of Peter's life, the fact that he was a young character, a character who could screw up, a character that life seemed to occasionally dump on in humorous ways, and yet would keep on striving to do right by everybody. An everyman, a schlemiel. Grounded in the real world. Grounded in Manhattan, Queens, Brooklyn.

One of the big advantages that ULTIMATE SPIDER-MAN has, beyond the fact of starting again at ground zero, is that there's only the one book, with the one writer. So the soap opera aspect of Peter's life is clearly the backbone of that series, and the engine that drives it. Even when a particular adventure isn't extraordinarily compelling, readers want to know what's going to happen with Peter and Mary and Gwen and Kitty and Flash and so forth and so on.

SPIDER-MAN 2 GETS IT RIGHT

The second SPIDER-MAN movie hits all of the right essential notes: Pete is a struggling young guy, has a tough time making ends meet, and his romantic life is complicated by the pull he feels to go out and take action as Spidey. Being Spider-Man is a release, but it's also a sacrifice. If you're not always putting Peter in a situation where he has to choose between his everyday responsibilities and those of being a super hero, then you're doing something wrong.

In my head, my ideal structure for the first issue of SPIDER-MAN that we do after the cosmic reset of the "One More Day" storyline spends the first 17 pages or so on Peter Parker: This is who he is, this is where his life is right now. This is his crummy apartment, he's 25 and trying to figure out what he wants from his life. This is his circle of friends, these are his personal conflicts, this is his Aunt May, etc. And in the background, some menace or threat is beginning to bubble up — so that, by page 18 or so, we bring Spidey on camera with a big, dramatic, Marvel-style splash and a quip, and then we rocket to a cliff-hanger or a story-twist at the end of the book. But you plant the stake in the ground right away: This is Peter Parker's comic book, not Spider-Man's.

SPIDER-MAN IS THE HARD-LUCK HERO

Somewhere along the line, we started to become afraid to humiliate our heroes for a laugh. But this sort of thing — life dumping on Peter — was such a hallmark in the Stan days. Nothing Spider-Man did ever turned out right. Even the simple things — he'd wash his costume, and it'd shrink, and he'd have to go out to fight the Green Goblin with it all bunching up. Or he'd hide his civilian clothes in a convenient smokestack, and when he'd get back to them, they'd smell like fish. And so forth. And the reverse was also true — Peter would spend issue after issue after issue ducking Aunt May's attempts to fix him up with Anna Watson's niece, figuring that she was a dog, and then he finally got to meet Mary Jane for the punchline.

Spider-Man was also always the hero who had to fight with a disadvantage. He'd sprain his arm, or have the flu, or develop an ulcer, and still have to go out and fight the villain of the day. This sort of thing tended to humanize him and make him relatable to the readers.

SPIDER-MAN MAKES MISTAKES AND BAD CHOICES

As a young guy, and a put-upon guy, Spidey was given the freedom by his writers to occasionally make the wrong move. One of my favorite classic panels is from an early Spidey story, in which Flash Thompson, masquerading in a Spider-Man costume, has been captured by Doctor Doom, who believes he's the real Spider-Man. Peter and Aunt May see a bulletin about this on the news, and there's this one evil-looking shot of Peter, with this big %&$*-eating grin on his face, as he thinks to himself that all he has to do is stay on the sidelines, and his nemesis Flash Thompson will never bother him again. A panel later, of course, he finds that he cannot bring himself to do this, but that one moment is so honest and so relatable. Similarly, Spidey would occasionally try to cash in on his powers, or think about using them to steal a present for Gwen's birthday or whatnot. Spider-Man isn't a square-jawed paragon of virtue. Spider-Man is heroic because he finds it within himself to be heroic.

Spider-Man also works best when he's an outsider hero. By and large, Spidey is distrusted by the authorities and the common man on the street. And no wonder — he's got an entire media outlet campaigning against him. And he's kind of creepy, and wears a mask, and so on. Spidey's intentions are often misunderstood, which is another way he's relatable to the audience — events tend to backfire on him, and trying to do the right thing often gets him in even more hot water.

SPIDER-MAN IS FUNNY
If you don't have at least one funny line or exchange or situation from Spidey in your issue (assuming he's in costume in the thing), then you've done something wrong. Spider-Man is the Groucho Marx and Bugs Bunny of super heroes.

WHERE WE START
Just to set the stage, so that everybody knows where we'll be after the JMS run on AMAZING wraps up in July, here are the Cliffs Notes: In order to save the life of Aunt May, who was struck down by a bullet intended for Mary Jane, Peter and Mary Jane make a deal with Mephisto. But the cost is their marriage. Using his demonic abilities, Mephisto "uncreates" the marriage, and all of the events associated with it — so all of those Spider-Man adventures of the last twenty years still happened, but they happened somewhat differently. So not only are Peter and MJ not married, they have never been married. Spider-Man's secret identity is a secret once again. And formerly dead characters such as Harry Osborn and possibly Gwen Stacy are alive again and back on the canvas. Some of the particulars are still open to change (and are discussed in more detail later), but this is the landscape when we set up shop.

GO FORWARD
Part of not looking backward is finding new wrinkles on the old, classic tropes. So if we've got Harry Osborn back in the picture, let's find something new to do with him, some way to put him into a new position in Peter's life, rather than just rehashing the past. The worst thing that can happen is for the aftermath of the "unmarrying" to feel like it's 1968 again. We want the familiar comfort food of the old characters, but we need to do something modern and interesting with them. We need to put them into new, interesting configurations.

For example, I think Betty Brant should be one of Peter's closest friends. They dated when Pete was in high school, and now they're friends, they hang out together in a non-involved way — she's the person who sets Peter up with dates, gives him the woman's perspective, and who ultimately "approves" of the women he gets involved with. This gives him a good touch-point at the Daily Bugle (where Betty is still working as a reporter), and gives Pete a non-involved female friend that goes back to the classic days. (And as a complication down the line, perhaps there could be a moment where they got involved for a second, in response to problems or difficulties in each of their lives at that moment. And then they'd spend the next few months trying to deal with it, and repair their friendship — or not.)

Mary Jane, on the other hand, should be off-the-canvas when we start our first issue. Some indeterminate amount of time will have passed since the end of "One More Day," and Mary Jane is simply not around. We probably don't even mention her at first. And then, we play with the notion of a reunion all through the year — maybe Aunt May gets a postcard from her at around the third month. Maybe she's in town in the sixth month, but because of bad timing, she and Peter never meet face-to-face. And then, in the ninth month, we get Peter and MJ together in the same place — and she introduces Peter to her fiancé. (Perhaps this is the point where Peter hooks up with Betty, if we go that route.)

Also, part of going forward is to cease the unending homages to the same three great Spidey stories of the past. So please, no girl-falling-from-the-bridge, and no lift-the-big-heavy-thing-off-his-back-to-save-Aunt-May. Let's stop repeating the story iconography of the past and come up with some new images to stick in the readers' minds.

CIRCLE OF FRIENDS
The biggest detriment to Peter Parker being at the core of the Spidey books right now is that he no longer has a circle of friends to function as a supporting cast. Time was, Spider-Man had the best supporting cast in comics, but one by one, over the years, they've either fallen away, been turned into villains, been killed off, or have become completely irrelevant. And most latter-day attempts to bring new people into Peter's circle have only lasted as long as the particular writer who invented them (much like most of the Spidey villains created in the last ten years). So, this is something we're going to need to fix.

I think we need to come at this from both directions at once. Even though we've more or less got all of the classic characters back and available, I want to be careful that the book doesn't feel retro. There's something creepy about a guy who's still hanging out with the same six guys he went to high school with. I'm not saying that we dump the classic cast members, though — only that we look at where they are on the canvas and what role they play, and make sure that it makes sense in 2006. Flash Thompson, for example, was traditionally the foil — yet he hasn't really had a structure in which to play that role since Peter left school. As a result, he's kind of been in Peter's orbit whenever there's been a need for Spidey to have a friend who's abducted by the villain or injured in a battle. But he hasn't really fulfilled a function that's made sense in a long time. At the same time, I do think we need to bring some new people into Peter's circle. I think the trick is to do this incrementally, rather than trying to shove half-a-dozen new characters down the readers' throats at once. But this should be easy enough to do organically, especially if all of the Spidey writers are working in a coordinated effort.

PETER LIVES & BEHAVES LIKE A 25-YEAR-OLD
Spider-Man doesn't grow up. He doesn't get a 9-to-5 job (and couldn't hold it if he did get one). The idea that JMS set up, with him teaching in his old school, had its merits, but they never really got fleshed out and explored enough — and making Peter a teacher definitely made him seem older.

The classic Stan Lee setup of Peter making his scratch by taking photos for the Daily Bugle is such a perfect structure that I'd like to get back to that. It also gave the book the Bugle regulars as another pool from which to draw the cast — J. Jonah Jameson and company have felt out of place since Peter stopped taking pictures for the newspaper regularly.

There's something lovely about the fact that, in order to support himself, Peter has to perpetuate the media machine that makes his life more difficult as a super hero. And at the same time, there's that secret satisfaction of knowing that he's putting one over on the guy who hates him the most. Additionally, the need to put food on the table always propelled Spider-Man into action, and gave writers a way to get him involved in stories that wouldn't otherwise immediately concern him — he'd hear about something going on, swing over to get some pictures, his spider-sense would go off, and he'd get embroiled in the conflict. With this structure taken away, we've been forced to have Spidey going "on patrol," which just seems wrong to me — being Spider-Man isn't a job, it's both a responsibility and a release. But Peter has an actual life to deal with, and so he's not really looking for excuses to be Spider-Man (unless he simply needs to blow off some steam by swinging around the rooftops — it is cool, after all).

Peter can try to do other things — one of the driving motivations for his character in the next year, I would think, is a general feeling that his life has gone off-track. Like so many young twentysomethings, he hasn't quite worked out what he wants to do with his life long-term, and he's been too busy trying to stay on the treadmill to really be able to ponder it. (Plus, he's subconsciously reeling from the loss of his marriage, not that we ever say this — it's simply a subtext.) But unless somebody comes up with something brilliant, these are probably all short-term solutions, and won't work out over the long haul (typically because Peter's life as Spider-Man will get in the way).

I also think there's something to the uncertainty of a freelancer's life that helps drive Peter onward to explore other options and possibilities in life — whether he makes any long-term progress or not.

WOULD PETE BE SHOOTING VIDEO FOOTAGE THESE DAYS?
It's worth examining the specifics of the classic setups, though, rather than simply defaulting to them, to make sure that they still hold water in 2006. For example, in the '60s it made sense for Peter to take still photos of himself in action and sell them in order to make his rent. But given the proliferation of technology today, and the needs of 24-hour news channels and the like, wouldn't it make more sense for him to have a small digital video camera and to shoot video of himself in action as Spider-Man? The payday would have to be better, especially if he could produce such footage on a regular basis. Is there some other drawback to doing this? And is this something that Peter should perhaps try, as an alternative to providing pictures to the Bugle, only to have it backfire in some way?

THE VILLAINS
Spider-Man has probably got just about the best rogues' gallery in comics. However, these classic villains have become somewhat tarnished due to years of overuse or misuse. And there really hasn't been a new Spidey villain created in the last ten years who's really stuck beyond his originator's tenure on the series. So this, too, is something we need to address.

NEW VILLAINS
We can't continue to coast on the laurels of the past, so we need to get some new blood into the Spider-Man universe when it comes to exciting new foes for the web-slinger to face. Again, much like with the supporting cast, this needs to be done selectively and deliberately, in that the readers aren't going to care if we just throw a bunch of costumes at them randomly.

The best Spider-Man foes tend to be "ground-level" villains — criminals, street thugs, crimelords, mercenaries and the like. As Spidey is more grounded in the real world, so too should be the opponents he goes up against. It's not a hard and fast rule, but in general Spider-Man should probably not often be dealing with aliens from space or magical creatures from another dimension.

One of the (probably unconscious) common traits of most of the classic Spidey villains when they were introduced is the fact that they're more or less all older men, which gave Spidey's battles a subtext of generational conflict. This doesn't mean that any new creations need to follow the same pattern — but it's helpful to be aware of these subtexts, as they can add another almost unconscious layer to the surface action conflicts between Spidey and his foes.

REVAMP OLD VILLAINS AND STICK TO THE REVAMPS

Everybody loves the classic Spider-Man villains, but they've become so overused in the past couple of years (and not just in the Spider-Man titles) that their impact has been largely blunted. Characters who once had very specific motives and M.O.'s have been ground down to generic criminals. So as we consider each character in turn, I think we need to delve into finding the defining characteristics of each, and then making those the centerpiece of whatever story we use them in, so that a Vulture story doesn't have the same tone or style as an Electro story. And, once we redefine these characters, we need to stick to that redefinition, at least for awhile. On some of these villains, they were turning up every two months with a completely different outlook, depending on the needs of that writer and series. That weakens the characters tremendously, and it's got to stop. So for any classic villain that we choose to use again, we need to give careful consideration as to how we use them to maximize their impact and longevity, and then we need to hold to it.

These villains need to be defined sharply, their personas and actions made dangerous and interesting again.

MYSTERY

One of the hallmarks of the Spider-Man books has always been the "mystery villain" — the crimelord whose true identity and motives are unknown to the readers, and whose true face, when it is finally revealed, comes as a shock. This worked with the Green Goblin, it worked with the Hobgoblin years later, and it can work again. Doing this sort of a mystery character in the Internet age creates a whole new level of problem, however, in that, in the pre-computer days, if one guy in Idaho tumbled to your reveal, the information didn't really travel much farther than that. Whereas now, it only takes one perceptive reader anywhere in the world to undercut the payoff for everybody.

Still, this is a very effective element, especially within the sort of yearlong uber-arc storytelling we're talking about, so it's worth giving some thought to. (And no, Uncle Ben cannot be the man behind the mystery villain's mask.)

ISSUES TO RESOLVE:

With the structure of the end of "One More Day" and the undoing of the Spider-Man marriage, there are a number of elements in play whose resolution we're going to want to lock down so that we can go forward smoothly. These include:

1) WHO WILL KNOW PETER'S SECRET NOW?

The world at large will have forgotten that Peter Parker is Spider-Man — but how far does this extend? Does Aunt May know any longer? Does Mary Jane know? (In continuity, she discovered that Peter was Spider-Man on the night he gained his powers — a retcon that did more damage than good.) What about folks like Norman Osborn or Eddie Brock?

This is crucial information to know, in that the conflict in Peter's life should always in some way be between his responsibilities as Spidey and his responsibilities as Peter. But if his closest friends and family know his true identity, and accept his mission, then there's no conflict — heck, they'll aid him in covering his exit and making excuses for his sudden departures.

There was always a nice paranoid edge to Peter's desperation towards keeping his costumed life a secret — one that any reader with a secret of his own could relate to: "My friends and family wouldn't accept me, wouldn't love me, if they knew what I really was." Whether this took the form of fearing that Aunt May would drop dead of a heart attack, or that the Green Goblin would throw another girlfriend off another bridge, this was always a powerful subtext, and a powerful motivator for the character.

2) DO WE WANT THE WEB-SHOOTERS BACK?

This restart gives us the opportunity to revert to the traditional mechanical web-shooters, as opposed to the latter-day movie-inspired organic ones. I think there's something to the added complications the mechanical ones allow (running out of webbing, breaking down, needing to purchase the chemicals necessary to mix up new batches of webbing — not to mention finding the time to do so, etc.).

3) GWEN?

For a while now, there's been talk about resurrecting Gwen as a component of the end of "One More Day." I think the problem with doing this is twofold: A) it robs the character of one of the essential tragedies that defines his character, and B) it locks you onto the treadmill of 1968 — if Peter's not going to go back to dating Gwen, then what's the point of bringing her back? And if he is going to go back to dating Gwen, doesn't that bring us back to 1968 again?

The only thing I can think of to do with Gwen that's different and yet makes sense with the setup (since it's the deal with Mephisto that's bringing her back to life) would be to have her be a spoiler—have her be a character whose sole purpose in life was to screw Peter's life up. She'd be his personal demon, in a sense. The problem is that this only really works if you understand that she's been resurrected by Mephisto, and supernatural elements like this are an awkward fit in the Spidey milieu, at least on a consistent basis.

Speaking for myself, I think it's probably a mistake to bring her back; good for the shock of the moment, but detrimental in the long run.

THE NEW METHODOLOGY

One of the factors that's sidelined the soap opera aspect of the SPIDER-MAN series from a logistical standpoint has been the fact that he's headlined in more than one ongoing title since the mid-'70s. The way this tended to play out, especially as more and more books were added, is that the core book, AMAZING, would be perceived as the "real deal," and the other titles would be looked upon as lesser adjuncts — and would sell at a lower level, to boot. And with different creative teams on each title, it's become harder and harder to coordinate the message, and to provide a consistent vision of the character. The line's identity became fractured because of the diverse hands and diverse directions across the different books. While there are some advantages to this approach, the one thing it really kiboshed, in an almost subliminal way, is the feeling that SPIDER-MAN is the linear story of Peter Parker's life.

So what I propose to do is not only to take us back down to only a single title, but to have that title come out as frequently as the many books do now. In essence, we'd bring SENSATIONAL SPIDER-MAN and FRIENDLY NEIGHBORHOOD SPIDER-MAN to an end, and instead we'd release AMAZING SPIDER-MAN three times a month.

HOW TO RUN THE THRICE-AMAZING:
The logistical difficulties with making all of the Spidey titles one series are pretty obvious: If one thing goes wrong, you potentially have books falling like dominos. But I think this is just a matter of clever planning, and of taking a cue from creator-driven television shows that practice arc-storytelling. In other words, you'd need to "block out" the major character beats, reversals, developing conflicts and story concepts for pretty much an entire year of the thrice-AMAZING at one time. This would also take the form of making the entire year one large 36-part Spider-Man novel.

From a manpower standpoint, you'd also need to adopt a system similar to that of a television series. I think you'd need a team of about five writers, with one functioning as the Head Writer. The Head Writer would take point in blocking out the overall year-beats (in consultation with everybody else on the team, of course), would probably write perhaps a quarter of the overall output if possible, and would function as a script doctor and overseer on everybody else's stories, making sure that the voice and the style was somewhat consistent.

Then, within the structure, the remaining writers would come on to the book to do stories ranging between one and six parts in length, largely devised by themselves within the larger structure (so that they would have an appropriate emotional investment in the material, and we'd avoid the problem the connected SUPERMAN titles faced years ago, in which a given writer would wind up writing only Part Two of another writer's idea). We'd need to get all of these writers working simultaneously, and we'd need to have them all supported by a similar team of artists, working as far ahead as possible to avoid deadline problems. This way, you could keep a consistent artist on each individual story as well, and

these artists would rotate in and out, much as the writers do.

As a safeguard, we'd also want to commission three or four single-issue evergreen-style stories, which could be folded into the run at whatever point the schedule started to slip.

Also, each main story would probably be produced as 20-page installments, which would give us room to insert modular subplot pages in order to properly set up future developments. So, for example, if Writer A has a Doctor Octopus storyline coming up in a few months, and there's a need to seed Doc's status quo or to foreshadow him ahead of time, then Writer A would write the subplot pages that do this, and they'd be inserted into earlier issues as necessary — even if those earlier stories were otherwise written by Writer B. This is where the Head Writer would be of help, as a backup in making sure that these drop-ins felt somewhat seamless. (And, ideally, the artist who was drawing Writer B's story would also draw the subplot pages written by Writer A — though we could break this guideline if we had to.)

Additionally, the five-man Spidey squad would be a good resource to have at our disposal when it comes to producing separate side Spidey limited series, either to tie into larger events in the Marvel U, or because of a budgetary need. Because these writers would be so enmeshed in the world and the tone of the core Spidey books, this should enable us to make such ancillary Spidey product feel more connected to the larger super-story running throughout the year, and thus of greater import to the readers.

Of greatest import in this plan: We shouldn't allow the fact that we'll be working with a team of writers to make us timid about trying interesting things with the way that stories are told within the Spider-Man books. For example, some of the strongest issues of ULTIMATE SPIDER-MAN have been the ones that focused on Mary Jane or Aunt May, and told a complete story from their point of view. Multiple writers needn't mean generic styling: In the same way that a series like Buffy can find a way to do "special" episodes based around either a narrative technique (the silent episode, the musical episode) or an offbeat approach to the story (the Death of Buffy's Mom episode), so too should we find a way to have that same latitude. We need to be careful not to become so locked into the process of production that we stifle creativity — nobody's ever quite run a regular ongoing title like this befvore, so we need to be cautious not to throw the baby out with the bathwater.

The following pages are from the "TOP SECRET" Amazing Spider-Man series bible, produced by the Brand New Day editorial team in the summer of 2007. The idea was for the compilation to serve as a status quo update and reference file for freelancers coming onto the book as well as an in-house guide for other editorial offices. After a scarce number of redacted copies were distributed to retailers at a conference in late 2007, we decided to fill in the blanks for you to take a look at! Enjoy!

TOP SECRET
the AMAZING SPIDER-MAN

2008 Bible
compiled by Tom Brennan

The All-New, All-Different
Spider-Man Status Quo!

The Events of *One More Day* changed the life of Peter Parker dramatically, bringing about a *Brand New Day*. If you're not 100% up to speed, fear not -- this guidebook will be a relatively painless way to get on track with all things Peter Parker. But first, a few important points:

- Peter's secret identity is...SECRET! Again! Although he DID unmask during the Civil War, the general public's memory has been wiped – they know he unmasked. They don't know who he is. No one does. Not MJ and Aunt May. Not the New Avengers. NO. ONE.

- MJ has split for the coast! Although they were engaged, the wedding never happened, although they continued to date for years. MJ is now living California.

- Aunt May is alive and well– and living life to its fullest, taking a part time volunteer job in the city.

- Harry Osborn is also alive and well! Well, as "well" as a any recovering drug addict-son of a psychotic killer-amnesiac part time super villain can be.

Spider-Man/Peter Parker

- Back to basics, Peter is a single guy living back home, until he can find an apartment he can afford.

- Struggling for cash, Peter goes back to his job taking pictures for the Daily Bugle.

- With the Superhuman Registration Act in effect and old-school villains on the run, the days of Spider-Man appear to be over – until new villains bring a new wave of terror to New York City.

- The day may be new, but you can still count on Spider-Man to be the one saving it!

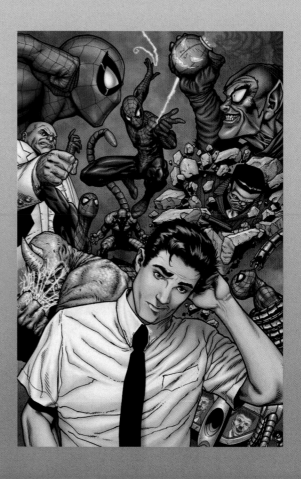

Aunt May

- May Parker currently volunteers at Martin Li's FEAST center, a soup kitchen in Manhattan....and anxiously awaiting the day her beloved nephew moves back out of her house.

Harry Osborn

- Peter's best friend is alive as can be, with no memory of his time as the Green Goblin – nor that his best friend is secretly his worst enemy.

- He still hates Spider-Man, but is now a little more focused on making something of himself as the new owner of *The Coffee Bean*.

- He's also dating Lily Hollister, the object of Peter's affections and daughter of District Attorney Bill Hollister.

Mary Jane

- Mary Jane and Peter Parker have broken up. The reasons why are unknown.
- Getting back to her acting career, MJ has split for the West Coast, leaving her life in New York behind and Peter Parker at the altar.

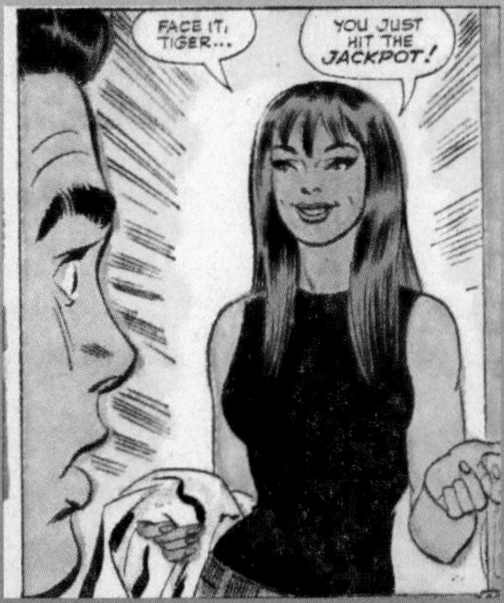

FACE IT, TIGER...
YOU JUST HIT THE JACKPOT!

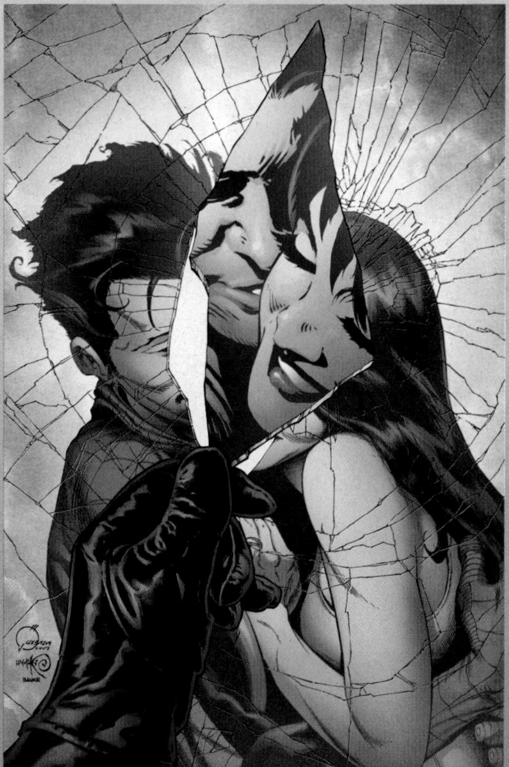

J. Jonah Jameson

- The day crusading newspaper man J. Jonah Jameson had worked for finally came – super-vigilantes were forced to unmask and be accountable to the government. But peace and order don't sell newspapers.
- When a heart attack sidelines him, his wife Marla sells the Bugle into the hands of his rival, Dexter Bennett.

Dexter Bennett

- Jonah Jameson's top rival is everything Jonah's not – slick, charming, generous to his photographers…and completely dishonest.
- When Jonah has a heart attack, Dexter takes over the Bugle…and renames it "The DB."
- Turning the paper into a celebrity-packed tabloid, "The DB" is a hit with the public.

Lily Hollister

- Daughter of the D.A.-turned-councilman Bill Hollister, Lilly is also his strongest supporter, campaigning for him at every turn..
- She's also the beautiful and charming new girlfriend of Harry Osborn.

Vin Gonzales

- Vin is a rookie police officer. He's proud of being a cop. Which means, of course, he doesn't like Spider-Man.
- Vin does come to trust Peter as a media informant…but he still doesn't like him.

Carlie Cooper

- Lily's best friend and a police forensic expert, Carlie Cooper is has eyes for Peter, but is too consumed with her work to do anything about it.
- She's hooks Pete up as a roommate for officer Vin Gonzales.

Jackpot

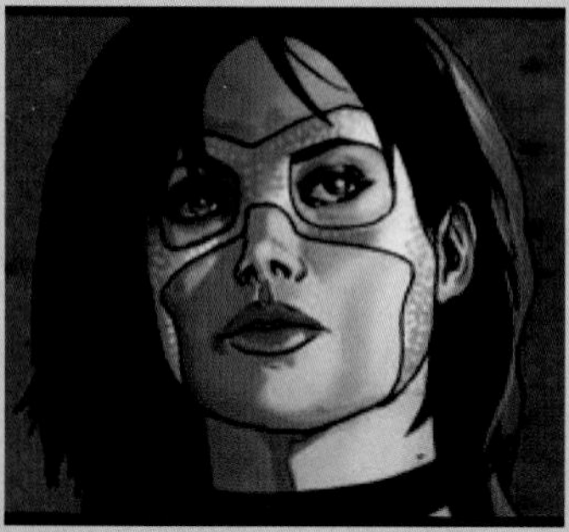

- An SHRA approved super-heroine whose red hair and free spirit seem all too familiar to Spidey.
- She baffles Spidey; Sometimes she behaves like a trained pro, but others it seems like she's a fan girl in a costume.

Joe Robertson

- J. Jonah Jameson's right hand man is still a steadying force at the Bugle, despite the ownership changes. He's also still doing his best to set an example for Peter Parker

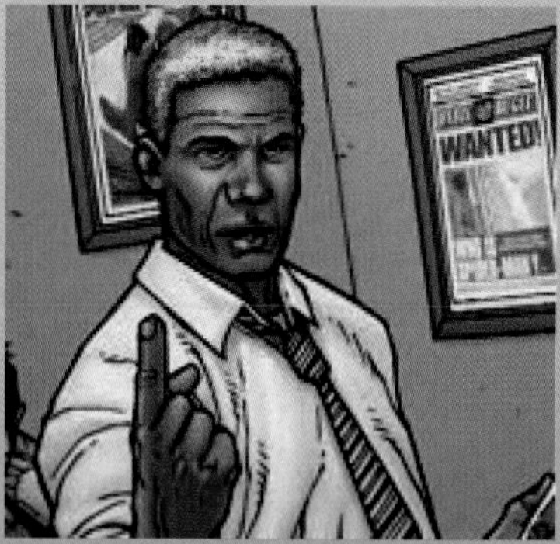
WANTED!

Betty Brant

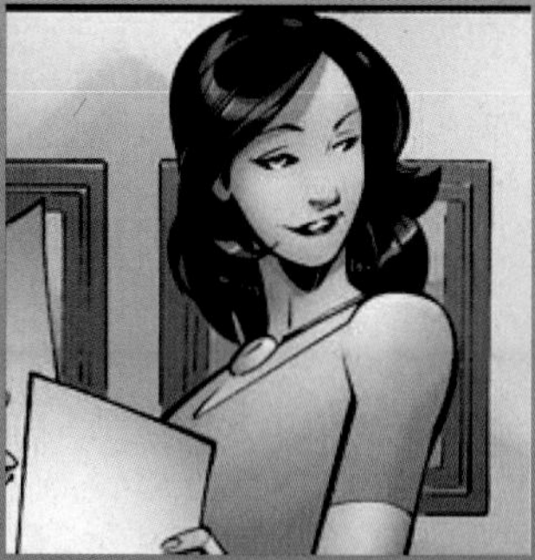

- Peter's best friend at the Bugle will be promoted to the crime beat.
- She's also trying to help Pete and Robbie weather the storm that is Dexter Bennett

Martin Li

A billionaire philanthropist, Li is Aunt May's boss at the FEAST center, a series of Homeless shelters across the city. He is secretly Mr. Negative.

Bill Hollister

Bill Hollister – Lily's father, this crusading D.A.-turned-councilman who becomes important to New York City politics after the actions of Menace

Alan O'Neil

- Vin's more experienced partner, O'Neil is a Spider-Man fan – not only does Spidey back cops up, but he's also a convenient scapegoat for police screw-ups.

Brand New Bad-Guys

Menace

Freak

The Parker Household

REAR DOOR
BATH
?
KITCHEN
SIDE DOOR
PANTRY
LIVING
DINING
ENTRY

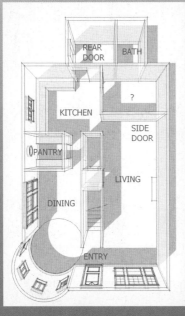

3D Modeling by Jason Christiansen

The Coffee Bean

Coffee Bean -
(lotsa bricks)

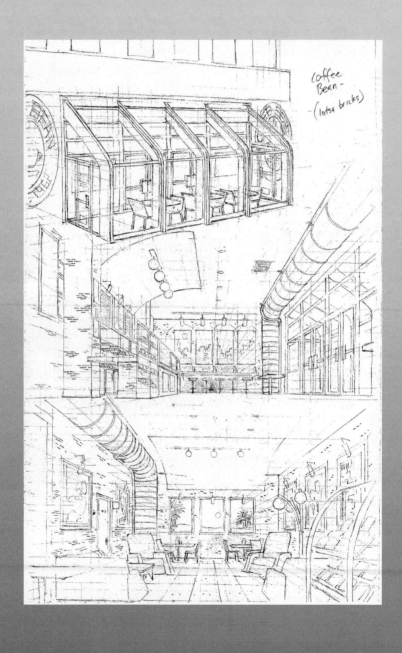

THE DB

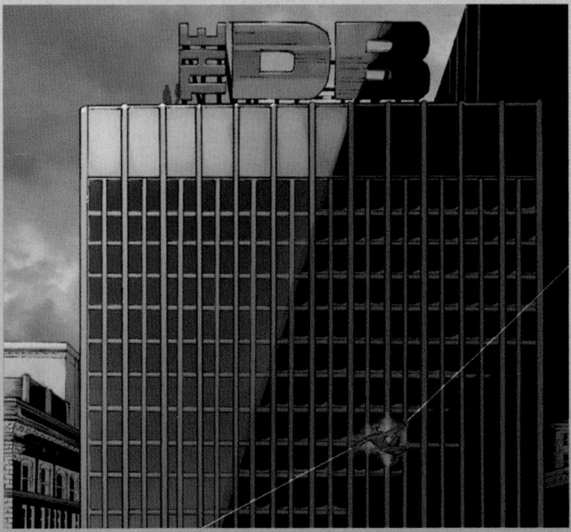
THE DB

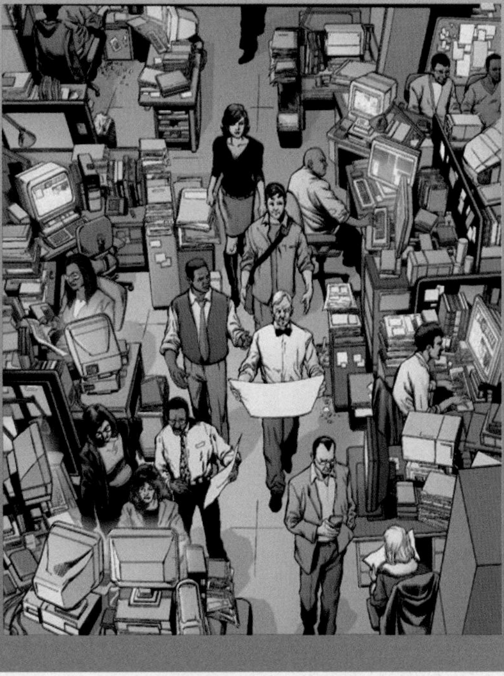

The "DB" Front Page Mock-Up

THE OFFICIAL NEWSPAPER OF SPIDER-MAN
THE DB
GREAT CAESAR'S GHOST! MAN BITES DOG! • SCANDAL ANOTHER STORY & MORE....
LATE CITY FINAL • 50 CENTS • WEDNESDAY, JULY 19, 2006
JUMPIN' JEHOSAPHAT!
THREAT OR MENACE?!

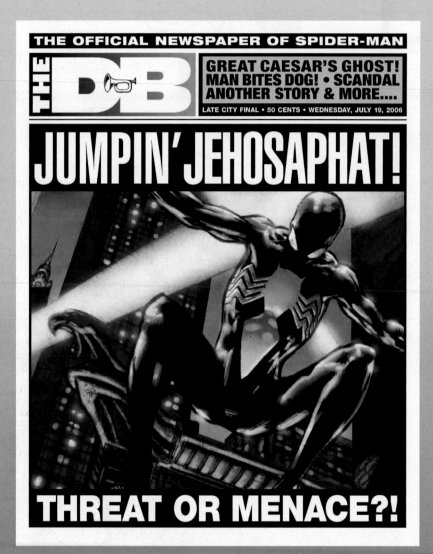

The Starting Lineups...

Month #1 (#546-#548)
Script by Dan Slott
Pencils by Steve McNiven
Inks by Dexter Vines
Color by Morry Hollowell &
Dave Stewart

Month #2 (#549-#551)
Script by Marc Guggenheim
Pencils & Inks by
Salvador Larocca
Color by Jason Keith &
Stephane Beru

Month #3 (#552-#554)
Script by Bob Gale
Pencils by Phil Jimenez
Inks by Andy Lanning
Color by Jeromy Cox

Month #4 (#555-#557)
Script by Zeb Wells
Pencils by Chris Bachalo
Inks by Tim Townsend
Color by Antonio Fabela

AMAZING SPIDER-MAN #564

Bob Gale, Marc Guggenheim & Dan Slott

PAGE 1 (5 PANELS)
PANEL 1 Big panel. Low angle. Street-level. We're in the Bronx, in the shadow of the NEW YANKEE STADIUM. Yeah, there's a new one, apparently.
A tricked-out (see below) CONVERTIBLE SPORTSCAR is racing towards "camera."
The driver of the sportscar is OVERDRIVE, the super-villain who first (and last) appeared in *Spider-Man: Swing Shift*.
The exterior of the sportscar itself actually mimics Overdrive's look -- i.e., shiny BLACK armor plating (think Night Rider, Street Hawk, Airwolf, etc.), CHROME grill & accessories, with NEON GREEN piping and lighting. The interior should be BLACK leather with NEON GREEN piping.
TITLE & CREDITS at the top of the page:

THREEWAY COLLISION!

Above the sportscar (but below our title), web-swinging in hot pursuit, is... SPIDER-MAN!
SPIDER-MAN: Hey! Slow down, willya?!
SPIDER-MAN CAPTION: Why do these things always happen to me?
SPIDER-MAN: How can I pummel you senseless if I can't get my hands on you?
PANEL 2 Behind Spidey now as he swings after the sportscar, which is weaving in and out of traffic.
SPIDER-MAN: And you just ran a red light!
SPIDER-MAN CAPTION: Of course some homicidal driver would wanna play real-life *Grand Theft Auto* while I'm on my way to a job interview.
PANEL 3 The sportscar SKIDS past a MAN walking on the sidewalk. His face OBSCURED by the copy of *THE DB* that he's got his nose buried in. **(SW-This is Dexter Bennett, though we don't realize that until chapter 3)**
SFX: SKREEEEEEEEEEEEEEEE
PANEL 4 Spidey is somersaulting down on to the hood of the convertible now as it brushes past the man, blowing the newspaper out of his hands (though in such a way that we still can't see his face).
SFX: FFFFFOOOOOOOOOMMMMMMMMMMMMMF
SPIDER-MAN: I'm gonna need to see your license and proof of-- Hey! I know you!
PANEL 5 New angle. Spidey's P.O.V.: Looking at Overdrive in the driver's seat.
SPIDER-MAN: Overdrive!
(CONT'D) I should've known. This little chase smacked of *déjà vu.**
CAPTION: *Spidey first chased Overdrive in *Spider-Man: Swing Shift*.
(CONT'D) What do you mean you didn't buy it? It was free.
(CONT'D) What do you mean "and you want your money back"? Go back on the Internet, fanboy.

PAGE 2 (5 PANELS)
PANEL 1 Spidey is leaning forward, over the windshield, and tagging Overdrive with a punch across the jaw.
SPIDER-MAN: Speaking of smacked...
SFX: CRAK
PANEL 2 Overdrive, reeling from Spidey's punch is losing control of the car...
OVERDRIVE: Idiot, I can't--
PANEL 3 Big panel. Spidey is LEAPING out of the way as the sportscar careens out of control.
SPIDER-MAN CAPTION: Like I was supposed to know the guy can't take a punch and drive at the same time...
PANEL 4 New angle. We're with VIN GONZALES, in civilian clothes, pursuing the action on foot, CELL PHONE pressed to his mouth, as the sportscar FLIPS OVER, SOMERSAULTING through the air.
VIN: Twenty-Adam-Twelve, Fifteen-Baker-Nine
<<COULD WE GET PROPER NYPD RADIO TAGS?>>.

(CONT'D) Need ESU and medics down here ay-sap. Continuing to pursue on foot. Officer in civilian clothes.
PANEL 5 Back with Spidey as he fires his webshooters at the still-flipping car.
SPIDER-MAN CAPTION: I just know I'm gonna get blamed for this somehow...
(CONT'D) Even though it's kind of my fault...
SFX: THWIP

PAGE 3 (6 PANELS)
PANEL 1 Spidey is tugging hard on his webstrands (both fists), trying to stop the car's momentum.
SPIDER-MAN: GNNNGG--
PANEL 2 Aftermath. The sportscar is webbed up and safely stopped now, upside down in the middle of the street. Spidey is leaping towards it.
SPIDER-MAN: Please keep your hands and arms inside the car until the ride has come to a full and complete--
PANEL 3 Overdrive is LEAPING out of the car, tagging Spidey with a PUNCH to the jaw.
SPIDER-MAN: OW.
SFX: SHAK
PANEL 4 Spidey is spinning around, reaching out to catch the fleeing Overdrive, but SOMEONE is edging into panel, holding a REVOLVER.
SPIDER-MAN (to Overdrive): Lucky shot!
OFF-PANEL SOMEONE: FREEZE!
PANEL 5 Spidey is wheeling back around to see that the person from the previous panel is Vin, holding his service revolver in a two-handed grip, pointed at Spider-Man.
VIN: On the ground!
SPIDER-MAN: Are you talking to me or the, y'know, ACTUAL BAD GUY?
PANEL 6 Spidey is leaping away, firing a web strand as he goes.
VIN: You're under arrest for violation of 6 U.S.C. § 558 and multiple counts of Chapter 40, Article 120 of the New York Penal Code.
SPIDER-MAN: You can't arrest me! I'm the good guy.
VIN: You're a vigilante and a serial killer and you have the right to remain silent. You have the right to an attorney...
SPIDER-MAN: Keep going. Don't let me stop you.
(CONT'D): Told'ja you couldn't arrest me...

PAGE 4 (6 PANELS)
PANEL 1 New angle. With Overdrive as he forces his way on to a YELLOW SCHOOL BUS. The short, van-like kind.
OVERDRIVE: Excuse me...
PANEL 2 Back with Spidey. Swinging in pursuit as Overdrive boards the bus.
SPIDER-MAN CAPTION: A school bus.
(CONT'D) He's getting on a school bus.
(CONT'D) Well, that's just dandy swell...
PANEL 3 In the bus. The BUS DRIVER stays at the wheel and Overdrive is kneeling down on the floor of the bus, pressing his palms to the floor. The SCHOOLKIDS are watching in amazement and awe. **(SW-Some kids should have NY Mets hats and jerseys and others should have NY Yankees)**
OVERDRIVE: Hang on to your seats, kids.
PANEL 4 Big energy effects are radiating from Overdrive's hands.
SFX: SHHHHHHRRRRRRRRRRRRRMMMMMMMMM
PANEL 5 Spidey is swinging into panel in the foreground, while in the background, the school bus is MORPHING into an "Overdrived" version of itself -- i.e., the same sleek black look described above for the convertible, but applied, incongruously, to a school bus.
SFX: MMMMMMMAAAAAAANNNNNNKKKKKKK
SPIDER-MAN CAPTION: Holy Spit.
(CONT'D) I'd heard tell Overdrive's power was to "trick out" vehicles --
(CONT'D) (Interesting little power, by the way.)

PAGE 5 (5 PANELS)
PANEL 1 High angle. Spidey is DIVING towards the bus' REAR WINDOW.
SPIDER-MAN CAPTION: -- but you really have to see it in action to believe it.
(CONT'D) I've just gotta ask this guy how he does it.
PANEL 2 Inside the bus. Spidey is CRASHING through the rear window.
SFX: SKRASH
SPIDER-MAN: Just thinking outside the box here, but I was wondering if you might consider turning yourself in...
PANEL 3 Maintaining his momentum from the previous panel, Spidey is landing a punch across Overdrive's face.
SFX: KRAK!
SPIDER-MAN: I've got me a job interview to go to and you probably wanna save yourself some bodily injury.
(CONT'D) It's win-win.
PANEL 4 Overdrive is pulling out a HI-TECH GUN from his costume.
OVERDRIVE: I have a better idea.
PANEL 5 The gun is creating a kind of SONIC WAVE, which is propelling Spidey towards the back of the bus.
SFX: BOOOOOOOOOFFFFFF
SPIDER-MAN: THAT IS NOT A BETTER IDEA!

PAGE 6 (5 PANELS)
PANEL 1 Outside now. Spidey is exploding out of the back of the bus. In the background, we can spot the TAXICAB that we'll see Vin in later in this issue.
SPIDER-MAN CAPTION: And to think... for this I left a promising career in the world of professional wrestling.
PANEL 2 Back in the bus. Overdrive is standing over the terrified bus driver, who's half-way out of his seat.
OVERDRIVE: Mind if I drive for a bit?
PANEL 3 With Spidey now. He's leaping back in pursuit of the bus.
SPIDER-MAN CAPTION: Okay, let's think...
(CONT'D) How'd I beat Overdrive last time?
PANEL 4 Spidey LANDS on the roof of the still-speeding bus.
SPIDER-MAN CAPTION: That's right, I sent his car into the East River.
(CONT'D) PROBABLY WOULDN'T BE A GOOD IDEA WITH A BUSLOAD OF SCHOOL KIDS.
PANEL 5 Spidey, facing the rear of the bus, is firing his webshooters at something off-panel.
SPIDER-MAN CAPTION: So... Plan B.

PAGE SEVEN (5 PANELS)
PANEL 1 Back in the bus. Overdrive, still at the wheel, is reacting to the sight of Spidey PUNCHING THROUGH the windshield.
LEGEND: Two full canisters of web-fluid later...
SPIDER-MAN: Hi. I'm from Geico. Did you know you could save fifty dollars a month on car insurance?
SFX: SHRAK
PANEL 2 Spidey is reaching forward and GRABBING the gun Overdrive had used on him earlier.
SPIDER-MAN: Mind if I borrow this for a sec? Thanks!
PANEL 3 Spidey is FIRING the gun towards the back of the bus.
SPIDER-MAN: DUCK KIDS!
PANEL 4 REVEAL that the REAR DOOR of the bus has been completely BLOWN OPEN. Through the open gap, instead of street, all we see is WEBBING.
SFX: SHHHHRRRRRMMMMAAANNNNNNKKKKK
PANEL 5 Spidey is pointing to the rear of the bus.
SPIDER-MAN: Alright, kids! Abandon ship! I mean, bus! Abandon bus! Get outta here!

PAGE 8 (5 PANELS)
PANEL 1 The kids are now JUMPING through the gap into the webbing.
KIDS: Yeah!
(CONT'D) Cowabunga!
(CONT'D) Dude, nobody says "cowabunga" anymore.
(CONT'D) Spidey's the bomb!

PANEL 2 Outside now. REVEAL that Spidey has webbed up a huge BUBBLE OF WEBBING to the back of the bus. It's CATCHING the kids as they jump out the back of the bus (which we don't need to see in this panel).
SPIDER-MAN CAPTION: I love it when I'm this good.
PANEL 3 The weight of the kids holds the webbing bubble down as the bus continues its forward momentum, causing the bubble to DETACH from the back of the bus. **(SW-Spidey needs to be seen detaching webbing)**
SPIDER-MAN CAPTION: Happy -- and safe -- landings, kids.
PANEL 4 Back in the bus. Spidey is turning back around, towards the front.
SPIDER-MAN: Now that we have this moment alone...
PANEL 5 REVEAL that Spidey is looking at... *an empty driver's seat.* Overdrive is nowhere to be found.
SPIDER-MAN CAPTION: Funny. I remember this from an *Indiana Jones* movie...

PAGES 9 AND 10 (11 PANELS ON 2 PAGES)
Paolo, I didn't call the page break because I don't want to impinge on your outstanding sense of layout. I'm guessing you'd want to put 6 or 7 panels on page 1, so that you'll have more space for bigger images on page 2, but you're the artist! (And a damned good one!)
PANEL 1 ON VIN, OUTDOORS SOMEWHERE - DAY
We start medium close on Vin – he's wearing a lightweight button down Yankees jersey, open so we can see a T-shirt underneath, and a Yankees baseball cap. We're not sure where we are, other than being outside in daylight.
VIN NARRATION: "Why do these things always happen to me? First Parker ruins my morning…and then Spider-Man ruins my afternoon."
PANEL 2 FLASHBACK BEGINS. VIN/PETE APARTMENT - DAY
The apartment of Pete and Vin. Living room or kitchen. Vin is in T-shirt and jeans. I'm thinking he's leaning against a doorway, arms crossed and not happy – he's just overheard his roommate, Peter Parker (also dressed very casually) **(Put Peter in a New York Mets jersey)** finishing up call on his cellphone in hand. So maybe this is the doorway that leads to Vin's bedroom – Vin just came out and overheard Pete on the phone. Pete has a sheepish expression.
VIN: So I presume there's something you forgot to tell me, Parker…?
PP: Huh? Well…no…not really.
PANEL 3 Vin steps closer to Pete.
VIN: I heard you on the phone. A job interview in the Bronx this afternoon, eh? Photographers who make good money at the DB don't go out on job interviews in other boroughs. Unless it's because…
PANEL 4 Favoring or single on Pete. Busted.
PP: Right. Okay. I got fired. Two weeks ago.*
FOOTNOTE: *Which would 561 to us.
PANEL 5 Vin and Pete. Pete's dropped his head.
VIN: And you were planning on telling me this…when?
PP: Once I got another job.
PANEL 6 VIN: Lying to a cop. I don't need that from my roommate.
P: I wasn't lying. I was…withholding information.
PANEL 7 On Vin
VIN: Look, as long as you pay your rent, I don't care if you're unemployed. But for two weeks I've been giving you news tips, and you've been taking 'em, acting like you were covering stories, only actually you were just playing me. And that really pisses me off!
PANEL 8 Vin pulls his Yankees jersey and cap out of the front closet. His body language shows he's pissed.
PP: I'm sorry. I -- I didn't tell you because I didn't want you to think you had a deadbeat roommate.
VIN: Well, I do. And FYI – I'm taking my Dad to the Yankee game today. And since you'll also be in the Bronx…?
PANEL 9 On Vin exiting – Vin should be in the foreground, Pete should be small in the background.
VIN: Stay far, far away from the stadium. I'd prefer not to see your face for the rest of the day.

VIN NARRATION: After coffee with my Dad, we headed over to Yankee Stadium…

PANEL 10 Across from Yankee Stadium. Vin (now with Jersey and cap) and his Dad (maybe dressed the same way) approach the stadium on foot.

DAD: All the games I took you to at this ballpark…and now you're taking me.

VIN: Maybe we'll see a winner for once.

VIN NARRATION: That's when I heard the tire screech…

SFX (small to denote distance): SCREEECH!!!

PANEL 11 Vin reacts to a tire screech -- and Spider-Man. This is Vin's viewpoint of Spidey on Overdrive's Sports Car. It shouldn't be too close because Vin is going to have to run to get there. (REF: Page 2, panel 3)

VIN: Spider-Man! Dad, duty calls -- I'll meet you inside!

DAD: But you're off duty! Call 9-1-1!

VIN: I am 9-1-1!

VIN NARRATION: Spider-Man. He's always rubbed me the wrong way. It's the mask. Only a guy with something to hide wears a mask like that. He'd rather hide his face than breathe?

PAGE 11 (4 PANELS)

PANEL 1 Vin runs after the flipping Sports car. He's talking into his cellphone as he runs. (This is a different view of the action we saw on page 2, panel 4)

VIN (into phone): Continuing to pursue black convertible on foot. Off-duty officer in civilian clothes.

VIN NARRATION: I mean, I'm a crime fighter. But I don't hide my face or my name like a criminal. Or a coward. And I don't even have any powers.

PANEL 2 This is a different p.o.v. of the action from Page 3. Vin has his pistol drawn on Spidey, near the webbed black car. Ideally, we should also see Overdrive escaping.

VIN NARRATION: So if I can do it, Spider-Man can do it. But he wouldn't even obey the law and register. In my book, that means he's a bad guy.

VIN: You have the right to remain silent…

SPIDEY: Hel-lo-oh? McFly? I'm the good guy and you're letting the bad guy get away!

PANEL 3 There's now a shimmering effect on the car as it begins to morph back to its original state – maybe we can do something along the lines of a Steranko op-art thing, but much cooler via computer assist.

Vin's head turns to see what it is – he's distracted -- Spidey prepares to take off…

VIN NARRATION: When I took a moment to check the car for injuries…

VIN: What the hell -- ??

SPIDEY: Thank goodness for special effects.

PANEL 4 Spidey bounds away, firing a webstrand – a different p.o.v. of page 4 panel 4. Vin has his gun pointing at Spidey but since this is a Bronx street, there are buildings and people around. Note: Let's try to not show the webbed transformed car here so we can save it for the next page.

VIN: Hey! Stop or I'll shoot!

SPIDEY: Told ya you couldn't arrest me…

VIN NARRATION: Spider-Man ran like hell, compounding his crime. Given the surroundings and proximity of civilians, I chose not to fire.

PAGE 12 (5 PANELS)

PANEL 1 Vin is on his cell phone again as he looks over the webbed car, which has changed back to a more ordinary looking red convertible, with dents and bondo. Any damage done to the car in the chase would still be evident. (In the background a WOMAN is coming out of a building toward a waiting TAXI.)

VIN (into phone): …caused by Spider-Man. Vehicle is now a red convertible and has no occupants.

VIN NARRATION: Apparently the web-slinger had some criminal disagreement with Overdrive…

DISTANT SFX: SCREEECH!!!

PANEL 2 Vin sees the souped up black bus way in the distance

(maybe it's a silhouette). Spider-Man is on the roof. (See page 7, panel 4)

VIN NARRATION: And it had yet to be settled.

There was no way for me to catch them on foot.

PANEL 3 Vin runs towards that taxi, holding out his badge. The woman is getting in. The taxi driver, when we finally see him, should be JAMAAL, from ASM 558. The style of cab should match 558 as well.

VIN: Hold it, Lady! Police emergency! I need that cab!

LADY: Call your own cab, jerk boy! I'm not falling for that one.

VIN NARRATION: Luckily, I had no trouble finding a taxi.

PANEL 4 Vin yanks her out.

VIN: Don't mess with the law, lady. Driver, follow that black bus!

PANEL 5 Ext. The street – the cab speeds along. (Note – this could also be done as a very high angle shot, giving a view of a lot of geography, showing the black bus is a distance away.)

JAMAAL: You gonna pay me for this, right, Mister Cop? 'Cause you don't pay, I don't drive.

VIN: What, you think I'm a deadbeat?

JAMAAL: It happens.

VIN NARRATION: The driver was glad to help…

PAGE 13 (5 PANELS)

PANEL 1 In the cab. Vin leans forward. Let's make this a street with elevated tracks, a la French Connection, to give us some cool shadows.

VIN: Turn left at the light! We can cut 'em off!

JAMAAL: Sorry, man -- one-way street, that's against the law. Can't get citizenship if I break the law.

VIN NARRATION: …and more than cooperative.

PANEL 2 Vin, now getting more irate, shows Jamal his holstered pistol – Vin's not pointing it, just showing it…a veiled threat. Ahead, through the windshield, a pedestrian is crossing the street.

VIN: Is this enough law for you?

JAMAAL: Okay, sir, whatever you say, sir.

VIN NARRATION: I had him take a shortcut…

PANELS 3 AND 4 EXT. STREET –

In turning the corner, the cab has a near miss with the pedestrian – it's the same guy who almost got hit in chapter 1, and will later be revealed as Dexter Bennett, but we don't see his face here – use the shadows from the elevated tracks to obscure his face, or compose so we only see the back of his head. (Maybe do motion blur or multiple image to show the close call.)

PEDESTRIAN: Watch it, it's a one-way street!!

VIN: Jeez, keep your eyes on the road!

PANEL 5 The taxi catches up to the stopped black bus – the shimmering effect tells us that it's about to change back into a yellow bus. (From this angle, we can't see the back of it, or the web bubble or Spider-Man.)

VIN NARRATION: We finally got to the bus. Overdrive had escaped, but I heard screaming kids in the back – and someone else…

WORD BALLOON FROM BEHIND THE BUS: And that, kids, was your preview of Coney Island's newest thrill ride…

WORD BALLOON 2: Let's do it again!

WORD BALLOON 3: Whoa, this stuff is sticky!

PAGE 14 (5 PANELS)

Paolo, these panel breaks and image descriptions are suggestions – please feel free to adjust things as you see fit to make the scene play. .

PANEL 1 Behind the now yellow, normal school bus. Vin draws on Spidey, who is making sure the kids are safe in the web net/bubble. (Note – the kids are stuck to it.)

VIN: Freeze, Spider-Man! You're under arrest and you're not getting away from me again!!

SPIDEY: Told you before, Sherlock, I'm the good guy, so YOU give it a rest.

VIN: I'm warning you!

PANEL 2 Spidey raises his hands up.

SPIDEY: Look, Einstein, since when do bad guys stop what they're doing to make sure children are safe?

VIN: Since when do good guys fail to register and become fugitives wanted for multiple murders?

PANEL 3 Favoring Spidey and the kids.

SPIDEY: Point. Tell you what, let's take a vote. Hey kids, you want him to shoot me?

KIDS: No way! Kick his butt, Spider-Man! He's no cop, he's a b-hole! You rule!

PANEL 4 Spidey aims his webshooter at Vin.

SPIDEY: Aw, you lose. Gotta give my public what they want!

PANEL 5 Spidey webs Vin's pistol, to the cheers and delight of the kids in the web net/bubble.

(Steve – your call if we should have Spidey web Vin's entire right hand.)

SPIDEY: Now Mr. Can't-Tell-The-Good-Guys-From-The-Bad-Guys, be a Good Guy and keep traffic away from my fan club until that web net dissolves. An hour or so. I've got a perp to chase.

VIN NARRATION: Spider-Man used the kids as a shield to make good his escape.

PAGE 15 (5 PANELS)

PANEL 1 As Spidey swings away, Vin frantically goes to Jamaal, standing next to his taxi, pointing an accusing finger at Vin.

JAMAAL: You owe me fifteen dollars, man.

VIN: Not now! We've gotta go after Spider-Man!

JAMAAL: You _are_ a deadbeat! No _real_ cop would just leave kids in the street!
And Spider-Man _is_ a good guy.*

*FOOTNOTE: Jamaal met Spidey back in 548. –Scorecard Steve

VIN NARRATION: I knew my first duty was to protect the kids, so I gave up the chase…

PANEL 2 The cab speeds off, leaving Vin with the kids in the web net/bubble. Vin is frustrated and ashamed.

KIDS: You suck, man! All Yankee fans suck! Get us outta here!

VIN NARRATION: …because sometimes you just _know_ the right thing to do.

PANEL 3 Flashback ends: this has all been Vin's tale to the VETERAN UNIFORMED COP at the scene. There are 2 squad cars, and other cops are trying to free the kids from the web bubble.

VIN: And then you guys got here, and here we are.

VETERAN COP: Stick around, Rookie. The Captain'll need to hear your story.

PANEL 4 Veteran Cop and Vin.

VETERAN COP: And listen, Cowboy: you were off duty, you called it in, and that was right. But don't try to be a cop 24/7. It's a bad way to live. You'll end up with no friends, no family, no life. Ain't worth it.

RADIO FROM NEARBY CAR: "This ball might be outta here---"

PANEL 5 Close on Vin – much like the very first panel of this chapter. Maybe he shouldn't have left his Dad at the ball park.

RADIO: "It is!!! A-Rod hits a Grand Slam! It's Yankees 4 to nothing!"

VIN: Yeah.

PANEL 6 Ending shot of Dad at the game. Dad looks sadly at the empty seat next to him while everyone else is having a great time.

FINAL VIN CAPTION BOX: "I guess Spider-Man didn't really ruin my afternoon. I ruined it all by myself."

PAGE 16 (5 PANELS)

PANEL 1 Establishing shot, a hangar/warehouse by the waterside. It's about an hour after the events from the previous page. The warehouse is open on one side, leading out towards the docks and the back street. We can see a white, luxury limo and a neon-green motorcycle nearby.

There are five small figures on the loading bay: MR. NEGATIVE, three of his INNER DEMONS, and OVERDRIVE.

OVERDRIVE is tied up on the ground. MR. NEGATIVE observes as his goons, the INNER DEMONS, go about beating the living hell out of OVERDRIVE.

The INNER DEMONS wear black suits and ties, white shirts, and dull, metallic Chinese demon masks (see ASM #547-548 for ref.). They are usually armed with hi-tech versions of Chinese martial arts weapons. This time, only one of them is armed. He is using an energy whip to beat on OVERDRIVE. The other INNER DEMONS join

in by kicking him—or they could just stand around looking tough.

PANEL 2 We go in closer so we can now see a good shot of MR. NEGATIVE interrogating OVERDRIVE while his INNER DEMONS continue to whip and kick him.

MR. NEGATIVE seems very controlled and nonplused. As OVERDRIVE yells out in pain, MR. NEGATIVE seems to be paying more attention as to how clean his own cuticles are.

MR. NEGATIVE asks OVERDRIVE to give him a full account of HOW he failed his mission today.

PANEL 3 Cut to OVERDRIVE, he swears he'll tell MR. NEGATIVE everything! In the foreground, the INNER DEMONS break into frame from about the chest down. We can see their clenched fists—and the dangling energy whip—primed and ready to start laying into OVERDRIVE again _if_ MR. NEGATIVE isn't satisfied with OVERDRIVE'S answers…

PANEL 4 Cut to EARLIER TODAY—as OVERDRIVE drives a pimped out, super MONSTER TRUCK towards the security gates of a small start up lab in the BRONX (something that is one step above a business that's run out of someone's garage—but with a little bit more security).

The MONSTER TRUCK has, of course, been tricked out FROM Overdrive's powers. Somewhere on the street, we should be able to see the NON-tricked-out version of the convertible that OVERDRIVE was driving on PAGE 1.

PANEL 5 Cut to INSIDE the LABORATORY. Two scientists (one's pudgy, the other's stringy—and both of them look like they're from the neighborhood) were working on their new invention, when suddenly…

…OVERDRIVE'S MONSTER TRUCK came bursting through their wall (and/or security gates from outside). The scientists yell and duck for cover as giant chunks of masonry go flying through the air.

PAGE 17 (5 PANELS)

PANEL 1 OVERDRIVE jumps out of the cab of the MONSTER TRUCK.

PANEL 2 CUT to a shot of OVERDRIVE'S hand as he steals the scientists' invention… It's THE SONIC GUN that OVERDRIVE used on SPIDER-MAN back on PAGE 6!

PANEL 3 As OVERDRIVE runs out the big gaping hole in the wall, he passes the MONSTER TRUCK. The truck is already returning back to normal—now that OVERDRIVE'S powers aren't keeping it "tricked out".

PANEL 4 Outside, OVERDRIVE jumps into that normal convertible…

PANEL 5 …and drives off in it—as his powers begin to convert it into the "tricked out" car we saw on PAGE 1.

PAGE 18 (6 PANELS)

PANEL 1 Back in the present—at the warehouse-- MR. NEGATIVE asks OVERDRIVE what happened next. OVERDRIVE tells him that everything was going great—until SPIDER-MAN interfered—AGAIN!

PANELS 2 THROUGH 6

These panels are highlights from the previous two stories, but drawn from different angles—favoring OVERDRIVE more.

PANEL 2 We see a new version of PAGE 3, PANEL THREE—where OVERDRIVE is leaping out of his webbed up convertible and punching SPIDEY in the jaw.

As he tells the story, OVERDRIVE makes it sound like he really let SPIDEY have it.

PANEL THREE We cut to a shot from OUTSIDE the TRICKED OUT SCHOOL BUS as SPIDER-MAN crashes in through the rear window (from PAGE 5, PANEL TWO).

In narration, OVERDRIVE mentions how he commandeered another vehicle—but SPIDEY wouldn't let up!

PANEL FOUR We see OVERDRIVE using the sonic gun on SPIDER-MAN from PAGE 5, PANEL FIVE.

PANEL 5 We see how SPIDEY later snatched the gun AWAY from OVERDRIVE…

PANEL 6 …and how, while SPIDEY was using the sonic gun himself, OVERDRIVE slipped out the driver side window and made good his escape!

PAGE 19 (5 PANELS)

PANEL 1 Out on the street, OVERDRIVE "clotheslined" a guy off of his neon-green motorcycle (the same motorcycle from PAGE 16, PANEL ONE)…

PANEL 2 We see a shot of OVERDRIVE getting on the motorcycle—while using his power to transform it into a new, tricked-out version.

PANEL 3 With the motorcycle completely transformed, OVERDRIVE tears through the streets—looking cool as all hell—and even popping a wheelie while he does it!

PANEL 4

As the tricked out motorcycle whhhhoooooosssssshes through the city streets, it avoids traffic by swerving up onto the sidewalk—almost hitting a poor old man who has to jump out of the way! It's the same person who almost got hit in both the first and second chapters .

PANEL 5

In a match shot, we stay on the street instead of the motorcycle. As the old man gets up, not only can we tell that he's REALLY PISSED OFF—but we can finally, CLEARLY see that he's DEXTER BENNETT—owner of THE DB, New York's best selling tabloid!

PAGE 20 (5 PANELS)

PANEL 1 Back in the present, MR. NEGATIVE asks ONE simple question. Where is the SONIC DEVICE that he asked OVERDRIVE to steal for him?! OVERDRIVE thinks hard…

"By now?" he says…

PANEL 2 "…probably in a precinct's evidence room."

Cut to crime scene investigator, CARLIE COOPER'S hand (in a surgical glove) picking up the SONIC DEVICE from the floor of the school bus.

PANEL 3 We pull back to see CARLIE coming out of the back of the school bus (which is back to normal and NOT tricked-out). CARLIE is telling VIN that thanks to him and Spider-Man, this weapon won't be falling into the wrong hands.

VIN rolls his eyes, he wants to know *why* CARLIE had to put it that way?

PANEL 4 CARLIE tells VIN that she's proud of him—that he stepped up and went BEYOND his duty—like every good cop should.

"Tell that to my dad," VIN sighs.

In the background police teams are pulling apart SPIDER-MAN'S web-ball and are helping all the kids out. It's been an hour and the webbing is starting to dissolve. (One of the kids could be complaining that he has to use the bathroom—he held it in for a full hour!).

PANEL 5 CLOSE UP on VIN and CARLIE in a kind of *possibly* romantic moment.

"Actually," says VIN, "would you? Tell that to my dad?"

"So?" CARLIE tells him, "You want to take me to meet your father?"

"Yeah. If that's okay. Um… He's probably still at the game."

"Oh. There was a game today? No one told me the Mets were playing."

PAGE 21 (6 PANELS)

PANEL 1 Cut back to the warehouse by the docks. As two of THE INNER DEMONS drag the tied-up OVERDRIVE away, MR. NEGATIVE addresses him.

"That's twice you've failed me Overdrive. I will not tolerate a third time. Dispose of him."

PANEL 2 As one of those two INNER DEMONS throws OVERDRIVE into the trunk of MR. NEGATIVE'S white limo in the background…

…in the foreground, MR. NEGATIVE talks to his third INNER DEMON. He says that for their next move they'll have to figure out a way of liberating the sonic device from one of the NYPD'S storage rooms….

PANEL 3 CLOSE UP on MR. NEGATIVE and the INNER DEMON that he was talking to… suddenly MR. NEGATIVE is distracted by a sound from off panel…

"In the past," says NEGATIVE, "one of my operatives on the force, Detective Willowby, has proven useful in this type of—"

VRROOMM!!!

PANEL 4 We pull back as MR. NEGATIVE and his INNER DEMONS

turn and watch as MR. NEGATIVE'S WHITE LIMO begins to morph and change into one of OVERDRIVE'S tricked-out vehicles.

"Where did you just put him?!" demands NEGATIVE.

"In—in the trunk of your… car," says the INNER DEMON who was last holding on to OVERDRIVE…

PANEL 5 Fully transformed into a super-black-tricked-out limo—with OVERDRIVE in the driver's seat, OVERDRIVE guns the car and takes off, while yelling, "So long, suckahhhs!"

PANEL 6 Standing on the docks, one of the INNER DEMONS asks MR. NEGATIVE, "What now, sir?"

"Now?" says NEGATIVE while pointing at the INNER DEMON who threw OVERDRIVE into the trunk, "Now I'd like you to dispose of HIM."

PAGE 22 (5 PANELS)

PANEL 1 Cut to SPIDEY swinging through the BRONX. He has all of his PETER PARKER clothes bundled up and crammed under one arm.

PANEL 2 Ducking behind some cover, he quickly changes back into PETER. Maybe there's still some time… to show up to a job interview an HOUR late.

PANEL 3 As PETER walks down the street towards his job interview… He pauses in shock as he sees…

PANEL 4 The lab from PAGE 16—with the huge hole in the wall and the monster truck sticking out of it. Outside, the two scientists are standing around looking quite upset.

PETER introduces himself as the potential new hire—and asks them what happened.

One of the scientists tells him that they're going to have to put that job on hold for a while. It looks like they're going to have to do some extensive remodeling first.

PANEL 5 CLOSE UP on PETE as he sighs and wonders how things could possibly get any worse.

PAGE 23

SW-Paulo if you need we can get you reference as to what the style of the "DB" newspaper is. It needs to be VERY sensationalistic)

CUT to the FRONT PAGE of TOMORROW'S DB. The headline proudly declares "DEXTER BENNETT TARGETED BY SPIDER-MAN"—with a big photo of an ACTION SHOT of the SPIDEY and OVERDRIVE in the school bus as it almost hits DEXTER BENNETT. A secondary photo on the page should be a HEROIC headshot of DEXTER BENNETT—with a sub-article of why SPIDER-MAN fears DEXTER BENNETT and is trying to silence this proud beacon of truth!

A third photo should be of the small children being helped out of the web ball, with a caption explaining that in order to pull off this mad scheme—SPIDER-MAN was willing to risk the lives of YOUNG CHILDREN!

And, in a small inset article, it's mentioned that the Yankees played one of the greatest games of all times! "Something that had to be seen to be believed!" said David Gonzalez.

THE END